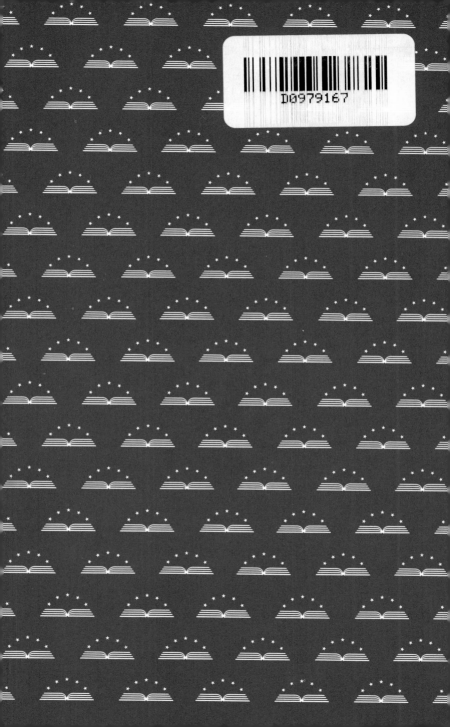

# MARK TWAIN

# Mark Twain

COLLECTED TALES, SKETCHES,
SPEECHES, & ESSAYS
1891–1910

THE LIBRARY OF AMERICA

Volume arrangement, notes, and chronology copyright © 1992 by
Literary Classics of the United States, Inc., New York, N.Y.
All rights reserved.
No part of this book may be reproduced commercially
by offset-lithographic or equivalent copying devices without
the permission of the publisher.

Copyright 1966, 1967, 1972, 1973, 1976
by The Mark Twain Foundation.
Published by arrangement with the University of California Press
and Robert H. Hirst, General Editor of the Mark Twain Project.
See Acknowledgments in the Note on the Texts.

"Concerning Tobacco" from *What Is Man? and Other Essays* by
Mark Twain. Copyright 1917 by the Mark Twain Company; copyright renewed 1945 by Clara Clemens Samassoud. Reprinted by
permission of HarperCollins Publishers Inc. "The Dervish and
the Offensive Stranger," "Dr. Loeb's Incredible Discovery," and
"Eve Speaks" from *Europe and Elsewhere* by Mark Twain. Copyright 1923 by the Mark Twain Company; copyright renewed 1951
by the Mark Twain Company. Reprinted by permission of Harper-
Collins Publishers Inc. "Cooper's Prose Style" from *Letters from
the Earth* by Mark Twain, edited by Bernard DeVoto. Copyright
1946, 1959, and 1962 by the Mark Twain Company; copyright renewed by the Mark Twain Company. Reprinted by permission of
HarperCollins Publishers Inc.

The paper used in this publication meets the
minimum requirements of the American National Standard for
Information Sciences—Permanence of Paper for Printed
Library Materials, ANSI Z39.48—1984.

Distributed to the trade in the United States
and Canada by the Viking Press.

Library of Congress Catalog Number: 92-52657
For cataloging information, see end of Index.
ISBN 0–940450–73–9

First Printing
The Library of America—61

Manufactured in the United States of America

LOUIS J. BUDD
SELECTED THE CONTENTS AND WROTE
THE NOTES FOR THIS VOLUME

*Grateful acknowledgment is made to the National Endowment for the Humanities, the Ford Foundation, and the Andrew W. Mellon Foundation for their generous support of this series.*

*The publishers express their appreciation to Robert H. Hirst and the Mark Twain Project for editorial assistance and the use of Mark Twain materials.*

# Contents

# Aix-les-Bains

Certainly Aix-les-Bains is an enchanting place. It is a strong word, but I think the facts justify it. True, there is a rabble of nobilities, big and little, here all the time, and often a king or two, but as these behave quite nicely and also keep mainly to themselves, they are little or no annoyance. And then a king makes the best advertisement there is, and the cheapest. All he costs is a reception at the station by the Mayor and the police in their Sunday uniforms, shop-front decorations along the route from station to hotel, brass band at the hotel, fireworks in the evening, free bath in the morning. This is the whole expense; and in return for it he goes away from here with the broad of his back metaphorically stenciled over with display ads, which shout to all the nations of the earth, assisted by the telegraph:

> Rheumatism routed at Aix-les-Bains!
> Gout admonished, Nerves braced up!
> All Diseases welcomed, and satisfaction
> given, or the money refunded at the door.

We leave nature's noble cliffs and crags undefiled and uninsulted by the advertiser's paint-brush. We use the back of a king, which is better and properer, and more effective, too, for the cliff stays still and few see it, but the king moves across the fields of the world, and is visible from all points like a constellation. We are out of kings this week, but one will be along soon—possibly his Satanic Majesty of Russia. There's a colossus for you! A mysterious and terrible form that towers up into unsearchable space and casts a shadow across the universe like a planet in eclipse. There will be but one absorbing spectacle in this world when we stencil him and start him out.

This is an old valley, this of Aix, both in the history of man and the geological records of its rocks. Its little Lake of Bourget carries the human history back to the lake dwellers, furnishing seven groups of their habitations, and Dr. William Wakefield says in his interesting local guide-book that the mountains round about furnish "geologically, a veritable epitome of the globe." The stratified chapters of the earth's history are clearly and permanently written on the sides of the roaring bulk of the Dent du Chat, but many of the layers of race, religion, and government, which in turn have flourished and perished here between the lake dweller of several thousand years ago and the French Republican of today, are ill-defined and uninforming by comparison. There were several varieties of pagans. They went their way, one after the other, down into night and oblivion, leaving no account of themselves, no memorials. The Romans arrived 2,300 years ago; other parts of France are rich with remembrances of their eight centuries of occupation, but not many are here. Other pagans followed the Romans. By and by Christianity arrived, some 400 years after the time of Christ. The long procession of races, languages, religions, and dynasties demolished each other's monuments and obliterated each other's records—it is man's way always.

As a result, nothing is left of the handiwork of the remoter inhabitants of the region except the constructions of the lake dwellers and some Roman odds and ends. There is part of a small Roman temple, there is part of a Roman bath, there is a graceful and battered Roman arch. It stands on a turfy level over the way from the present great bathhouse, is surrounded by magnolia trees, and is both a picturesque and suggestive object. It has stood there some 1,600 years. Its nearest neighbor, not twenty steps away, is a Catholic church. They are symbols of the two chief eras in the history of Aix. Yes, and of the European world. I judge that the venerable arch is held in reverent esteem by everybody, and that this esteem is its sufficient protection from insult, for it is the only public structure I have yet seen in France which lacks the sign, "It is forbidden to post bills here." Its neighbor, the church, has that sign on more than one of its sides, and other signs, too, forbidding certain other sorts of desecration.

The arch's next nearest neighbor—just at its elbow, like the church—is the telegraph office. So there you have the three great eras bunched together—the era of war, the era of theology, the era of business. You pass under the arch, and the buried Cæsars seem to rise from the dust of the centuries and flit before you; you pass by that old battered church, and are in touch with the middle ages, and with another step you can put down ten francs and shake hands with Oshkosh under the Atlantic.

It is curious to think what changes the last of the three symbols stands for; changes in men's ways and thoughts, changes in material civilization, changes in the Deity—or in men's conception of the Deity, if that is an exacter way of putting it. The second of the symbols arrived in the earth at a time when the Deity's possessions consisted of a small sky freckled with mustard seed stars, and under it a patch of landed estate not so big as the holdings of the Czar today, and all his time was taken up in trying to keep a handful of Jews in some sort of order—exactly the same number of them that the Czar has lately been dealing with in a more abrupt and far less loving and long-suffering way. At a later time—a time within all old men's memories—the Deity was otherwise engaged. He was dreaming his eternities away on his great white throne, steeped in the soft bliss of hymns of praise wafted aloft without ceasing from choirs of ransomed souls, Presbyterians and the rest. This was a Deity proper enough to the size and condition of things, no doubt a provincial Deity with provincial tastes. The change since has been inconceivably vast. His empire has been unimaginably enlarged. Today he is master of a universe made up of myriads upon myriads of gigantic suns, and among them, lost in that limitless sea of light, floats that atom, his earth, which once seemed so good and satisfactory and cost so many days of patient labor to build, a mere cork adrift in the waters of a shoreless Atlantic. This is the business era, and no doubt he is governing his huge empire now, not by dreaming the time away in the buzz of hymning choirs, with occasional explosions of arbitrary power disproportioned to the size of the annoyance, but, by applying laws of a sort proper and necessary to the sane and successful management of a complex and prodigious establishment, and by seeing to it that the exact and constant operation of these laws is not interfered with for the accommodation of any individual or political or religious faction or nation.

Mighty has been the advance of the nations and the liberal-

ization of thought. A result of it is a changed Deity, a Deity
of a dignity and sublimity proportioned to the majesty of his
office and the magnitude of his empire, a Deity who has been
freed from a hundred fretting chains and will in time be freed
from the rest by the several ecclesiastical bodies who have
these matters in charge. It was, without doubt, a mistake and
a step backward when the Presbyterian Synods of America
lately decided, by vote, to leave him still embarrassed with the
dogma of infant damnation. Situated as we are, we cannot at
present know with how much of anxiety he watched the
balloting, nor with how much of grieved disappointment he
observed the result.

Well, all these eras above spoken of are modern, they are of
last week, they are of yesterday, they are of this morning, so
to speak. The springs, the healing waters that gush up from
under this hillside village, indeed are ancient; they, indeed,
are a genuine antiquity; they antedate all those fresh human
matters by processions of centuries; they were born with the
fossils of the Dent du Chat, and they have been always limpid
and always abundant. They furnished a million gallons a day
to wash the lake dwellers with, the same to wash the Cæsars
with, no less to wash the Balzac with, and have not diminished on my account. A million gallons a day—for how many
days? Figures cannot set forth the number. The delivery, in
the aggregate, has amounted to an Atlantic. And there is still
an Atlantic down in there. By Dr. Wakefield's calculation that
Atlantic is three-quarters of a mile down in the earth. The
calculation is based upon the temperature of the water, which
is 114° to 117° Fahrenheit, the natural law being that below a
certain depth heat augments at the rate of one degree for
every sixty feet of descent.

Aix is handsome and handsomely situated, too, on its hill
slope, with its stately prospect of mountain range and plain
spread out before it and about it. The streets are mainly narrow, and steep, and crooked, and interesting, and offer considerable variety in the way of names; on the corner of one of
them you read this: Rue du Puits d'Enfer—pit of Hell street.
Some of the sidewalks are only eighteen inches wide; they are
for the cats probably. There is a pleasant park, and there are
spacious and beautiful grounds connected with the two great

pleasure resorts—the Cercle and the Villa des Fleurs. The town consists of big hotels, little hotels, and pensions. The season lasts about six months, beginning with May. When it is at its height there are thousands of visitors here, and in the course of the season as many as 20,000 in the aggregate come and go.

These are not all here for the baths; some come for the gambling facilities and some for the climate. It is a climate where the field strawberry flourishes through the spring, summer, and fall. It is hot in the summer, and hot in earnest; but this is only in the daytime; it is not hot at night. The English season is May and June; they get a good deal of rain then, and they like that. The Americans take July and the French take August. By the 1st of July the open air music and the evening concerts and operas and plays are fairly under way, and from that time onward the rush of pleasure has a steadily increasing boom. It is said that in August the great grounds and the gambling-rooms are crowded all the time and no end of ostensible fun going on.

It is a good place for rest and sleep and general recuperation of forces. The book of Dr. Wakefield says there is something about this atmosphere which is the deadly enemy of insomnia, and I think this must be true, for, if I am any judge, this town is at times the noisiest one in Europe, and yet a body gets more sleep here than he could at home, I don't care where his home is. Now we are living at a most comfortable and satisfactory pension, with a garden of shade trees and flowers and shrubs, and a convincing air of quiet and repose. But just across the little narrow street is the little market square, and at a corner of that is that church that is neighbor to the Roman arch, and that narrow street, and that billiard-table of a market place, and that church are able, on a bet, to turn out more noise to the cubic yard at the wrong time than any other similar combination in the earth or out of it. In the street you have the skull-bursting thunder of the passing hack, a volume of sound not producible by six hacks anywhere else; on the hack is a lunatic with a whip, which he cracks to notify the public to get out of his way. This crack is as keen and sharp and penetrating and ear-splitting as a pistol shot at close range, and the lunatic

delivers it in volleys, not single shots. You think you will not
be able to live till he gets by, and when he does get by he
only leaves a vacancy for the bandit who sells *Le Petit Journal*
to fill with his strange and awful yell. He arrives with the
early morning and the market people, and there is a dog that
arrives at about the same time and barks steadily at nothing
till he dies, and they fetch another dog just like him. The
bark of this breed is the twin of the whip volley, and stabs
like a knife. By and by, what is left of you the church-bell
gets. There are many bells, and apparently 6,000 or 7,000
town clocks, and as they are all five minutes apart—probably by law—there are no intervals. Some of them are striking all the time—at least, after you go to bed they are.
There is one clock that strikes the hour, and then strikes it
over again to see if it was right. Then for evenings and Sundays there is a chime—a chime that starts in pleasantly and
musically, then suddenly breaks into a frantic roar, and
boom, and crash of warring sounds that make you think
Paris is up and the revolution come again. And yet, as I have
said, one sleeps here—sleeps like the dead. Once he gets his
grip on his sleep neither hack, nor whip, nor news fiend, nor
dog, nor bell-cyclone, nor all of them together can wrench it
loose or mar its deep and tranquil continuity. Yes, there is
indeed something in this air that is death to insomnia.

The buildings of the Cercle and the Villa des Fleurs are
huge in size and each has a theater in it and a great restaurant,
also conveniences for gambling and general and variegated
entertainment. They stand in ornamental grounds of great
extent and beauty. The multitudes of fashionable folk sit at
refreshment tables in the open air afternoons and listen to
the music, and it is there that they mainly go to break the
Sabbath.

To get the privilege of entering these grounds and buildings
you buy a ticket for a few francs which is good for the whole
season. You are then free to go and come at all hours, attend
the plays and concerts free, except on special occasions,
gamble, buy refreshments, and make yourself symmetrically
comfortable.

Nothing could be handier than those two little theaters.
The curtain doesn't rise until 8:30. Then between the acts one

can idle for half an hour in the other departments of the building, damaging his appetite in the restaurants or his pocket in the baccarat room. The singers and actors are from Paris and their performance is beyond praise.

I was never in a fashionable gambling hell until I came here. I had read several millions of descriptions of such places, but the reality was new to me. I very much wanted to see this animal, especially the now historic game of baccarat, and this was a good place, for Aix ranks next to Monte Carlo for high play and plenty of it. But the result was what I might have expected—the interest of the looker-on perishes with the novelty of the spectacle—that is to say, in a few minutes. A permanent and intense interest is acquirable in baccarat or in any other game, but you have to buy it. You don't get it by standing around looking on.

The baccarat table is covered with green cloth and is marked off in divisions with chalk or something. The banker sits in the middle, the croupier opposite. The customers fill all the chairs at the table, and the rest of the crowd are massed at their backs and leaning over them to deposit chips or gold coins. Constantly money and chips are flung upon the table, and the game seems to consist in the croupier's reaching for those things with a flexible sculling oar and raking them home. It appeared to be a rational enough game for him, and if I could have borrowed his oar I would have staid, but I didn't see where the entertainment of the others came in. This was because I saw without perceiving and observed without understanding. For the widow and the orphan and the others do win money there. Once an old gray mother in Israel or elsewhere pulled out, and I heard her say to her daughter or her granddaughter as they passed me: "There, I've won six louis, and I'm going to quit while I'm ahead." Also there was this statistic. A friend pointed to a young man with the dead stub of a cigar in his mouth, which he kept munching nervously all the time and pitching hundred-dollar chips on the board while two sweet young girls reached down over his shoulders to deposit modest little gold pieces, and said: "He's only funning now; wasting a few hundred to pass the time— waiting for the 'gold room' to open, you know, which won't be till well after midnight—then you'll see him bet! He won

£14,000 there last night. They don't bet anything there but big money."

The thing I chiefly missed was the haggard people with the intense eye, the hunted look, the desperate mien, candidates for suicide and the pauper's grave. They are in the descriptions, as a rule, but they were off duty that night. All the gamblers, male and female, old and young, looked abnormally cheerful and prosperous.

However, all the nations were there, clothed richly, and speaking all the languages. Some of the women were painted and were evidently shaky as to character. These items tallied with the descriptions well enough.

The etiquette of the place was difficult to master. In the brilliant and populous halls and corridors you don't smoke, and you wear your hat, no matter how many ladies are in the thick throng of drifting humanity; but the moment you cross the sacred threshold and enter the gambling hell, off the hat must come, and everybody lights his cigar and goes to suffocating the ladies.

But what I came here for, five weeks ago, was the baths. My right arm was disabled with rheumatism. To sit at home in America and guess out the European bath best fitted for a particular ailment or combination of ailments, it is not possible, and it would not be a good idea to experiment in that way, anyhow. There are a great many curative baths on the continent, and some are good for one disease but bad for another. So it is necessary to let a physician name your bath for you. As a rule, Americans go to London to get this advice, and South Americans go to Paris for it. Now and then an economist chooses his bath himself and does a thousand miles of railroading to get to it, and then the local physicians tell him he has come to the wrong place. He sees that he has lost time and money and strength, and almost the minute that he realizes this he loses his temper. I had the rheumatism and was advised to go to Aix, not so much because I had that disease as because I had the promise of certain others. What they were was not explained to me, but they are either in the following menu or I have been sent to the wrong place. Dr. Wakefield's book says:

"We know that the class of maladies benefited by the water

and baths at Aix are those due to defect of nutrition, debility of the nervous system, or to a gouty, rheumatic, herpetic, or scrofulous diathesis—all diseases extremely debilitating and requiring a tonic, and not a depressing action of the remedy. This it seems to find here, as recorded experience and daily action can testify. . . . According to the line of treatment, followed particularly with due regard to the temperature, the action of the Aix waters can be made sedative, exciting, derivative, or alterative and tonic."

The "Establishment" is the property of France, and all the officers and servants are employés of the French Government. The bath-house is a huge and massive pile of white marble masonry, and looks more like a temple than anything else. It has several floors, and each is full of bath cabinets. There is every kind of bath—for the nose, the ears, the throat, vapor baths, tube baths, swimming baths, and all people's favorite, the douche. It is a good building to get lost in when you are not familiar with it. From early morning until nearly noon people are streaming in and streaming out without halt. The majority come afoot, but great numbers are brought in sedan chairs, a sufficiently ugly contrivance whose cover is a steep little tent made of striped canvas. You see nothing of the patient in this diving-bell as the bearers tramp along, except a glimpse of his ankles bound together and swathed around with blankets or towels to that generous degree that the result suggests a sore piano leg. By attention and practice the pall-bearers have got so that they can keep out of step all the time—and they do it. As a consequence their veiled churn goes rocking, tilting, swaying along like a bell-buoy in a ground swell. It makes the oldest sailor sea-sick to look at that spectacle.

The "course" is usually fifteen douche baths and five tub baths. You take the douche three days in succession, then knock off and take a tub. You keep up this distribution through the course. If one course does not cure you, you take another one after an interval. You seek a local physician and he examines your case and prescribes the kind of bath required for it, with various other particulars; then you buy your course tickets and pay for them in advance—$9. With the tickets you get a memorandum book with your dates and hours all set down in it. The doctor takes you into the bath the first morning and gives some instructions to the two doucheurs who are to handle you through the course. The pour boires are about 10 cents to each of the men for each bath, payable at the end of the course. Also, at the end of the course, you pay three or four francs to the superintendent of your department of the bath house. These are useful particulars to know, and are not to be found in the books. A servant of your hotel carries your towels and sheet to the bath daily and brings them away again. They are the property of the hotel; the French Government doesn't furnish these things.

You meet all kinds of people at a place like this, and if you give them a chance they will submerge you under their experiences, for they are either glad or sorry they came, and they want to spread their feelings out and enjoy them. One of these said to me:

"It's great, these baths. I didn't come here for my health—I only came to find out if there was anything the matter with me. The doctor told me if there was the symptoms would soon appear. After the first douche I had sharp pains in all my muscles. The doctor said it was different varieties of rheumatism, and the best varieties there were, too. After my second bath I had aches in my bones, and skull, and around. The doctor said it was different varieties of neuralgia, and the best in the market—anybody would tell me so. I got many new kinds of pains out of my third douche. These were in my joints. The doctor said it was gout, complicated with heart disease, and encouraged me to go on. Then we had the fourth douche, and I came out on a stretcher that time and fetched with me one vast, diversified, undulating, continental kind of pain, with horizons to it and zones and parallels of latitude and meridians of longitude and isothermal belts and variations of the compass—O, everything tidy and right up to the latest developments, you know. The doctor said it was inflammation of the soul, and just the very thing. Well, I went right on gathering them in—toothache, liver complaint, softening of the brain, nostalgia, bronchitis, osteology, fits, coleoptera, hydrangea, cyclopedia britannica, delirium tremens, and a lot of other things that I've got down in my list that I'll show you, and you can keep it if you like and tally off the bric-à-brac as you lay it in.

"The doctor said I was a grand proof of what these baths could do; said I had come here as innocent of disease as a grindstone, and inside of three weeks these baths had sluiced out of me every important ailment known to medical science, along with considerable more that were entirely new and patentable. Why he wanted to exhibit me in his bay window."

There seems to be a good many liars this year. I began to take the baths, and found them most enjoyable; so enjoyable that if I hadn't had a disease I would have borrowed one, just to have a pretext for going on. They took me into a stone-floored basin about fourteen feet square, which had enough strange-looking pipes and things in it to make it look like a torture chamber. The two half-naked men seated me on a pine stool, and kept a couple of warm-water jets as thick as one's wrist playing upon me while they kneaded me, stroked me, twisted me, and applied all the other details of the scientific massage to me for seven or eight minutes. Then they stood me up and played a powerful jet upon me all around for another minute. The cool shower bath came next, and the thing was over. I came out of the bath-house a few minutes later feeling younger and fresher and finer than I have felt since I was a boy. The spring and cheer and delight of this exaltation lasted three hours, and the same uplifting effect has followed the twenty douches which I have taken since.

After my first douche I went to the chemist's on the corner, as per instructions, and asked for half a glass of Challe water. It comes from a spring sixteen miles from here. It was furnished to me, but, perceiving that there was something the matter with it, I offered to wait till they could get some that was fresh, but they said it always smelt that way. They said that the reason that this was so much ranker than the sulphur water of the bath was that this contained thirty-two times as much sulphur as that. It may be true, but in my opinion that water comes from a cemetery, and not a fresh cemetery, either. History says that one of the early Roman Generals lost an army down there somewhere. If he could come back now I think this water would help him find it again. However, I

drank the Challe, and have drank it once or twice every day
since. I suppose it is all right, but I wish I knew what was the
matter with those Romans.

My first baths developed plenty of pain, but the subsequent
ones removed almost all of it. I have got back the use of my
arm these last few days, and I am going away now.

There are many beautiful drives about Aix, many interesting places to visit, and much pleasure to be found in paddling
around the little lake Bourget on the small steamers, but the
excursion which satisfied me best was a trip to Annecy and its
neighborhood. You go to Annecy in an hour by rail, through
a garden land that has not had its equal for beauty, perhaps,
since Eden; and certainly Eden was not cultivated as this garden is. The charm and loveliness of the whole region are bewildering. Picturesque rocks, forest-clothed hills, slopes richly
bright in the cleanest and greenest grass, fields of grain without fleck or flaw, dainty of color, and as shiny and shimmery
as silk, old gray mansions and towers half buried in foliage
and sunny eminences, deep chasms with precipitous walls,
and a swift stream of pale blue water between, with now and
then a tumbling cascade, and always noble mountains in view,
with vagrant white clouds curling about their summits.

Then at the end of an hour you come to Annecy and rattle
through its old crooked lanes, built solidly up with curious
old houses that are a dream of the middle ages, and presently
you come to the main object of your trip—Lake Annecy. It is
a revelation, it is a miracle. It brings the tears to a body's eyes
it is so enchanting. That is to say, it affects you just as all
things that you instantly recognize as perfect affect you—perfect music, perfect eloquence, perfect art, perfect joy, perfect
grief. It stretches itself out there in the caressing sunlight, and
away towards its border of majestic mountains, a crisped and
radiant plain of water of the divinest blue that can be imagined. All the blues are there, from the faintest shoal water
suggestion of the color, detectable only in the shadow of
some overhanging object, all the way through, a little blue
and a little bluer still, and again a shade bluer till you strike
the deep, rich Mediterranean splendor which breaks the heart
in your bosom, it is so beautiful.

And the mountains, as you skim along on the steamboat,

how stately their forms, how noble their proportions, how green their velvet slopes, how soft the mottlings of sun and shadow that play about the rocky ramparts that crown them, how opaline the vast upheavals of snow banked against the sky in the remotenesses beyond—Mont Blanc and the others—how shall anybody describe? Why, not even the painter can quite do it, and the most the pen can do is to suggest.

Up the lake there is an old abbey—Talloires—relic of the middle ages. We stopped there; stepped from the sparkling water and the rush and boom and fret and fever of the nineteenth century into the solemnity and the silence and the soft gloom and the brooding mystery of a remote antiquity. The stone step at the water's edge had the traces of a worn-out inscription on it; the wide flight of stone steps that led up to the front door was polished smooth by the passing feet of forgotten centuries, and there was not an unbroken stone among them all. Within the pile was the old square cloister with covered arcade all around it where the monks of the ancient times used to sit and meditate, and now and then welcome to their hospitalities the wandering knight with his tin breeches on, and in the middle of the square court (open to the sky) was a stone well curb, cracked and slick with age and use, and all about it were weeds, and among the weeds moldy brickbats that the Crusaders used to throw at each other. A passage at the further side of the cloister led to another weedy and roofless little inclosure beyond, where there was a ruined wall clothed to the top with masses of ivy and flanking it was a battered and picturesque arch. All over the building there were comfortable rooms and comfortable beds, and clean plank floors with no carpets on them. In one bedroom up-stairs were half a dozen portraits, dimming relics of the vanished centuries—portraits of abbots who used to be as grand as princes in their old day, and very rich and much worshiped and very holy; and in the next room there was a howling chromo and an electric bell. Down stairs there was an ancient wood carving with a Latin word commanding silence, and there was a spang new piano close by. Two elderly French women, with the kindest and honestest and sincerest faces, have the abbey now, and they board and lodge people who are tired of the roar of cities and want to be where the dead silence and serenity and peace of this old nest will heal their blistered spirits and patch up their ragged minds. They fed us well, they slept us well, and I wish I could have staid there a few years and got a solid rest.

*November 8, 1891*

# Playing Courier

A time would come when we must go from Aix-les-Bains to Geneva, and from thence, by a series of day-long and tangled journeys, to Bayreuth in Bavaria. I should have to have a courier, of course, to take care of so considerable a party as mine.

But I procrastinated. The time slipped along, and at last I woke up one day to the fact that we were ready to move and had no courier. I then resolved upon what I felt was a foolhardy thing, but I was in the humor of it. I said I would make the first stage without help—I did it.

I brought the party from Aix to Geneva by myself—four people. The distance was two hours and more, and there was one change of cars. There was not an accident of any kind, except leaving a valise and some other matters on the platform, a thing which can hardly be called an accident, it is so common. So I offered to conduct the party all the way to Bayreuth.

This was a blunder, though it did not seem so at the time. There was more detail than I thought there would be: 1. Two persons whom we had left in a Genevan pension some weeks before must be collected and brought to the hotel; 2. I must notify the people on the Grand Quay who store trunks to bring seven of our stored trunks to the hotel and carry back seven which they would find piled in the lobby; 3. I must find out what part of Europe Bayreuth was in, and buy seven railway tickets for that point; 4. I must send a telegram to a friend in the Netherlands; 5. It was now 2 o'clock in the afternoon and we must look sharp and be ready for the first night train, and make sure of sleeping-car tickets; 6. I must draw money at the bank.

It seemed to me that the sleeping-car tickets must be the most important thing, so I went to the station myself to make sure; hotel messengers are not always brisk people. It was a hot day, and I ought to have driven, but it seemed better economy to walk. It did not turn out so, because I lost my way and trebled the distance. I applied for the tickets, and they asked me which route I wanted to go by, and that em-

barrassed me and made me lose my head, there were so many
people standing around and I not knowing anything about
the routes and not supposing there were going to be two; so
I judged it best to go back and map out the road and come
again.

I took a cab this time, but on my way up-stairs at the hotel
I remembered that I was out of cigars, so I thought it would
be well to get some while the matter was in my mind. It was
only around the corner and I didn't need the cab. I asked the
cabman to wait where he was. Thinking of the telegram and
trying to word it in my head, I forgot the cigars and the cab,
and walked on indefinitely. I was going to have the hotel
people send the telegram, but as I could not be far from the
postoffice by this time, I thought I would do it myself. But it
was farther than I had supposed. I found the place at last and
wrote the telegram and handed it in. The clerk was a severe-
looking, fidgety man, and he began to fire French questions at
me in such a liquid form that I could not detect the joints
between his words, and this made me lose my head again. But
an Englishman stepped up and said the clerk wanted to know
where he was to send the telegram. I could not tell him, because it was not my telegram, and I explained that I was
merely sending it for a member of my party. But nothing
would pacify the clerk but the address, so I said that if he was
so particular I would go back and get it.

However, I thought I would go and collect those lacking
two persons first, for it would be best to do everything sys-
tematically and in order, and one detail at a time. Then I
remembered the cab was eating up my substance down at the
hotel yonder, so I called another cab and told the man to go
down and fetch it to the postoffice and wait till I came.

I had a long hot walk to collect those people, and when I
got there they couldn't come with me because they had heavy
satchels and must have a cab. I went away to find one, but
before I ran across any I noticed that I had reached the neighborhood of the Grand Quay—at least I thought I had—so I
judged I could save time by stepping around and arranging
about the trunks. I stepped around about a mile, and although I did not find the Grand Quay, I found a cigar shop
and remembered about the cigars. I said I was going to Bay-

reuth, and wanted enough for the journey. The man asked me which route I was going to take. I said I did not know. He said he would recommend me to go by Zurich and various other places which he named, and offered to sell me seven second-class through tickets for $22 apiece, which would be throwing off the discount which the railroads allowed him. I was already tired of riding second-class on first-class tickets, so I took him up.

By and by I found Natural & Co.'s storage office, and told them to send seven of our trunks to the hotel and pile them up in the lobby. It seemed to me that I was not delivering the whole of the message, still it was all that I could find in my head.

Next I found the bank and asked for some money, but I had left my letter of credit somewhere and was not able to draw. I remembered now that I must have left it lying on the table where I wrote my telegram; so I got a cab and drove to the postoffice and went upstairs, and they said that a letter of credit had indeed been left on the table, but that it was now in the hands of the police authorities, and it would be necessary for me to go there and prove property. They sent a boy with me, and we went out the back way and walked a couple of miles and found the place; and then I remembered about my cabs, and asked the boy to send them to me when he got back to the postoffice. It was nightfall now, and the Mayor had gone to dinner. I thought I would go to dinner myself, but the officer on duty thought differently, and I stayed. The Mayor dropped in at half-past 10, but said it was too late to do anything to-night—come at 9:30 in the morning. The officer wanted to keep me all night, and said I was a suspicious-looking person and probably did not own the letter of credit, and didn't know what a letter of credit was, but merely saw the real owner leave it lying on the table, and wanted to get it because I was probably a person that would want anything he could get, whether it was valuable or not. But the Mayor said he saw nothing suspicious about me and that I seemed a harmless person and nothing the matter with me but a wandering mind, and not much of that. So I thanked him and he set me free, and I went home in my three cabs.

As I was dog-tired and in no condition to answer questions with discretion, I thought I would not disturb the Expedition at that time of night, as there was a vacant room I knew of at the other end of the hall; but I did not quite arrive there, as a watch had been set, the expedition being anxious about me. I was placed in a galling situation. The Expedition sat stiff and forbidding on four chairs in a row, with shawls and things all on, satchels and guide-books in lap. They had been sitting like that for four hours, and the glass going down all the time. Yes, and they were waiting—waiting for me. It seemed to me that nothing but a sudden, happily contrived and brilliant tour de force could break this iron front and make a diversion in my favor; so I shied my hat into the arena, and followed it with a skip and a jump, shouting blithely:

"Ha, ha, here we all are, Mr. Merryman!"

Nothing could be deeper or stiller than the absence of applause which followed. But I kept on; there seemed no other way, though my confidence, poor enough before, had got a deadly check and was in effect gone.

I tried to be jocund out of a heavy heart, I tried to touch the other hearts there and soften the bitter resentment in those faces by throwing off bright and airy fun and making of the whole ghastly thing a joyously humorous incident, but this idea was not well conceived. It was not the right atmosphere for it. I got not one smile; not one line in those offended faces relaxed; I thawed nothing of the winter that looked out of those frosty eyes. I started one more breezy, poor effort, but the head of the Expedition cut into the center of it and said:

"Where have you been?"

I saw by the manner of this, that the idea was to get down to cold business, now. So I began my travels, but was cut short again.

"Where are the two others? We have been in frightful anxiety about them."

"Oh, they're all right. I was to fetch a cab. I will go straight off and——"

"Sit down! Don't you know it is 11 o'clock? Where did you leave them?"

"At the pension."

"Why didn't you bring them?"

"Because we couldn't carry the satchels. And so I thought——"

"Thought! You should not try to think. One cannot think without the proper machinery. It is two miles to that pension. Did you go there without a cab?"

"I—well, I didn't intend to; it only happened so."

"How did it happen so?"

"Because I was at the postoffice and I remembered that I had left a cab waiting here, and so, to stop that expense, I sent another cab to—to——"

"To what?"

"Well, I don't remember now, but I think the new cab was to have the hotel pay the old cab, and send it away."

"What good would that do?"

"What good would it do? It would stop the expense, wouldn't it?"

"By putting the new cab in its place to continue the expense?"

I didn't say anything.

"Why didn't you have the new cab come back for you?"

"Oh, that is what I did. I remember now. Yes, that is what I did. Because I recollect that when I——"

"Well, then, why didn't it come back for you?"

"To the Postoffice? Why, it did."

"Very well, then, how did you come to walk to the pension?"

"I—I don't quite remember how that happened. Oh, yes, I do remember, now. I wrote the dispatch to send to the Netherlands, and——"

"Oh, thank goodness, you did accomplish something! I wouldn't have had you fail to send—what makes you look like that! You are trying to avoid my eye. That dispatch is the most important thing that—You haven't sent that dispatch!"

"I haven't said I didn't send it."

"You don't need to. Oh, dear, I wouldn't have had that telegram fail for anything. Why didn't you send it?"

"Well, you see, with so many things to do and think of,

I—they're very particular there, and after I had written the telegram——"

"Oh, never mind, let it go; explanations can't help the matter now—what will he think of us?"

"Oh, that's all right, that's all right; he'll think we gave the telegram to the hotel people and that they——"

"Why, certainly! Why didn't you do that? There was no other rational way."

"Yes, I know; but then I had it on my mind that I must be sure and get to the bank and draw some money——"

"Well, you are entitled to some credit, after all, for thinking of that, and I don't wish to be too hard on you, though you must acknowledge yourself that you have cost us all a good deal of trouble, and some of it not necessary. How much did you draw?"

"Well, I—I had an idea that—that——"

"That what?"

"That—well, it seems to me that in the circumstances—so many of us, you know, and—and——"

"What are you mooning about? Do turn your face this way and let me—Why, you haven't drawn any money!"

"Well, the banker said——"

"Never mind what the banker said. You must have had a reason of your own. Not a reason, exactly, but something which——"

"Well, then, the simple fact was that I hadn't my letter of credit."

"Hadn't your letter of credit?"

"Hadn't my letter of credit."

"Don't repeat me like that. Where was it?"

"At the postoffice."

"What was it doing there?"

"Well, I forgot it and left it there."

"Upon my word, I've seen a good many couriers, but of all the couriers that ever I——"

"I've done the best I could."

"Well, so you have, poor thing, and I'm wrong to abuse you so when you've been working yourself to death while we've been sitting here only thinking of our vexations instead of feeling grateful for what you were trying to do for us. It will all come out right. We can take the 7:30 train in the morning just as well. You've bought the tickets?"

"I have—and it's a bargain, too. Second class."

"I'm glad of it. Everybody else travels second class, and we might just as well save that ruinous extra charge. What did you pay?"

"Twenty-two dollars apiece—through to Bayreuth."

"Why, I didn't know you could buy through tickets anywhere but in London and Paris."

"Some people can't, maybe; but some people can—of whom I am one of which, it appears."

"It seems a rather high price."

"On the contrary. The dealer knocked off his commission."

"Dealer?"

"Yes; I bought them at a cigar shop."

"That reminds me. We shall have to get up pretty early, and so there should be no packing to do. Your umbrella, your rubbers, your cigars—what is the matter?"

"Hang it! I've left the cigars at the bank."

"Just think of it! Well, your umbrella?"

"I'll have that all right. There's no hurry."

"What do you mean by that?"

"Oh, that's all right; I'll take care of——"

"Where is that umbrella?"

"It's just the merest step—it won't take me——"

"Where is it?"

"Well, I think I left it at the cigar shop; but anyway——"

"Take your feet out from under that thing. It's just as I expected! Where are your rubbers?"

"They—well——"

"Where are your rubbers?"

"It's got so dry now—well, everybody says there's not going to be another drop of——"

"Where—are—your—rubbers?"

"Well, you see—well, it was this way. First, the officer said——"

"What officer?"

"Police officer; but the Mayor, he——"

"What Mayor?"

"Mayor of Geneva; but I said——"

"Wait. What is the matter with you?"

"Who, me? Nothing. They both tried to persuade me to stay, and——"

"Stay where?"

"Well—the fact is——"

"Where have you been? What's kept you out till half-past 10 at night?"

"O, you see, after I lost my letter of credit, I——"

"You are beating around the bush a good deal. Now answer the question in just one straightforward word. Where are those rubbers?"

"They—well; they're in the county jail."

I started a placating smile, but it petrified. The climate was unsuitable. Spending three or four hours in jail did not seem to the expedition humorous. Neither did it to me, at bottom.

I had to explain the whole thing, and of course it came out then that we couldn't take the early train, because that would leave my letter of credit in hock still. It did look as if we had all got to go to bed estranged and unhappy, but by good luck that was prevented. There happened to be mention of the trunks, and I was able to say that I had attended to that feature.

"There you are just as good and thoughtful and painstaking and intelligent as you can be, and it's a shame to find so much fault with you, and there sha'n't be another word of it. You've done beautifully, admirably, and I'm sorry I ever said one ungrateful word to you."

This hit deeper than some of the other things, and made me uncomfortable, because I wasn't feeling as solid about that trunk errand as I wanted to. There seemed somehow to be a defect about it somewhere, though I couldn't put my finger on it, and didn't like to stir the matter just now, it being late and maybe well enough to let well enough alone.

Of course there was music in the morning, when it was found that we couldn't leave by the early train. But I had no time to wait; I got only the opening bars of the overture, and then started out to get my letter of credit.

It seemed a good time to look into the trunk business and rectify it if it needed it, and I had a suspicion that it did. I was too late. The concierge said he had shipped the trunks to Zurich the evening before. I asked him how he could do that without exhibiting passage tickets.

"Not necessary in Switzerland. You pay for your trunks and send them where you please. Nothing goes free but your hand baggage."

"How much did you pay on them?"

"A hundred and forty francs."

"Twenty-eight dollars. There's something wrong about that trunk business, sure."

Next I met the porter. He said:

"You have not slept well, is it not? You have the worn look. If you would like a courier, a good one has arrived last night, and is not engaged for five days already, by the name of Ludi. We recommend him; dass heiss, the Grande Hotel Beau Rivage recommends him."

I declined with coldness. My spirit was not broken yet. And I did not like having my condition taken notice of in this way. I was at the county jail by 9 o'clock, hoping that the mayor might chance to come before his regular hour, but he didn't. It was dull there. Every time I offered to touch anything, or look at anything, or do anything, or refrain from doing anything, the policeman said it was "defendu." I thought I would practice my French on him, but he wouldn't have that, either. It seemed to make him particularly bitter to hear his own tongue.

The Mayor came at last, and then there was no trouble; for the minute he had convened the Supreme Court—which they always do whenever there is valuable property in dispute—and got everything shipshape and sentries posted, and had prayer by the chaplain, my unsealed letter was brought and opened, and there wasn't anything in it but some photographs; because, as I remembered now, I had taken out the letter of credit so as to make room for the photographs and had put the letter in my other pocket, which I proved to everybody's satisfaction by fetching it out and showing it with a good deal of exultation. So then the Court looked at each other in a vacant kind of way, and then at me, and then at each other again, and finally let me go, but said it was imprudent for me to be at large, and asked me what my profession was. I said I was a courier. They lifted up their eyes in a kind of reverent way and said "Du lieber Gott!" and I said a word of courteous thanks for their apparent admiration and hurried off to the bank.

However, being a courier was already making me a great stickler for order and system and one thing at a time and each thing in its own proper turn; so I passed by the bank and branched off and started for the two lacking members of the Expedition. A cab lazied by, and I took it upon persuasion. I gained no speed by this, but it was a reposeful turnout, and I liked reposefulness. The week-long jubilations over the six hundredth anniversary of the birth of Swiss liberty and the Signing of the Compact was at flood tide, and all the streets were clothed in fluttering flags.

The horse and the driver had been drunk three days and nights, and had known no stall nor bed meantime. They looked as I felt—dreamy and seedy. But we arrived in the course of time. I went in and rang, and asked the housemaid to rush out the lacking members. She said something which I did not understand, and I returned to the chariot. The girl had probably told me that those people did not belong on her floor, and that it would be judicious for me to go higher and ring from floor to floor till I found them; for in those Swiss flats there does not seem to be any way to find the right family but to be patient and guess your way along up. I calculated that I must wait fifteen minutes, there being three details inseparable from an occasion of this sort: 1, put on hats, come down and climb in; 2, return of one to get "my other glove"; 3, presently, return of the other one to fetch "my French Verbs at a Glance." I would muse during the fifteen minutes and take it easy.

A very still and blank interval ensued, and then I felt a hand on my shoulder and started. The intruder was a policeman. I glanced up and perceived that there was new scenery. There was a good deal of a crowd, and they had that pleased and interested look which such a crowd wears when they see that somebody is out of luck. The horse was asleep, and so was the driver, and some boys had hung them and me full of gaudy decorations stolen from the innumerable banner poles. It was a scandalous spectacle. The officer said:

"I'm sorry, but we can't have you sleeping here all day."

I was wounded and said with dignity:

"I beg your pardon. I was not sleeping, I was thinking."

"Well, you can think if you want to, but you've got to think to yourself; you disturb the whole neighborhood."

It was a poor joke, but it made the crowd laugh. I snore at night, sometimes, but it is not likely that I would do such a thing in the daytime and in such a place. The officer undecorated us and seemed sorry for our friendlessness, and really tried to be humane; but he said we mustn't stop there any longer or he would have to charge us rent. It was the law, he said, and he went on to say in a sociable way that I was looking pretty moldy and he wished he knew——

I shut him off pretty austerely, and said I hoped one might celebrate a little these days, especially when one was personally concerned.

"Personally?" he asked. "How?"

"Because 600 years ago an ancestor of mine signed the compact."

He reflected a moment, then looked me over and said:

"Ancestor! It's my opinion you signed it yourself. For of all the old ancient relics that ever I—but never mind about that. What is it you are waiting here for so long?"

I said:

"I'm not waiting here so long at all. I'm waiting fifteen minutes till they forget a glove and a book and go back and get them." Then I told him who they were that I had come for.

He was very obliging, and began to shout inquiries to the tiers of heads and shoulders projecting from the windows above us. Then a woman away up there sung out:

"Oh, they? Why I got them a cab and they left here long ago—half-past eight, I should say."

It was annoying. I glanced at my watch, but didn't say anything. The officer said:

"It is a quarter of 12, you see. You should have inquired better. You have been asleep three-quarters of an hour, and in such a sun as this. You are baked—baked black. It is wonderful. And you will miss your train, perhaps. You interest me greatly. What is your occupation?"

I said I was a courier. It seemed to stun him, and before he could come to we were gone.

When I arrived in the third story of the hotel I found our quarters vacant. I was not surprised. The moment a courier takes his eye off his tribe they go shopping. The nearer it is to train time the surer they are to go. I sat down to try and think out what I had best do next, but presently the hall boy found me there and said the expedition had gone to the station half an hour before. It was the first time I had known them to do a rational thing, and it was very confusing. This is one of the things that make a courier's life so difficult and uncertain. Just as matters are going the smoothest, his people will strike a lucid interval, and down go all his arrangements to wreck and ruin.

The train was to leave at 12 noon sharp. It was now ten minutes after 12. I could be at the station in ten minutes. I saw I had no great amount of leeway, for this was the lightning express, and on the continent the lightning expresses are pretty fastidious about getting away some time during the advertised day. My people were the only ones remaining in the waiting-room; everybody else had passed through and "mounted the train," as they say in those regions. They were exhausted with nervousness and fret, but I comforted them and heartened them up, and we made our rush.

But no; we were out of luck again. The doorkeeper was not satisfied with the tickets. He examined them cautiously, deliberately, suspiciously; then glared at me a while, and after that he called another official. The two examined the tickets, and called another official. These called others, and the convention discussed and discussed, and gesticulated and carried on, until I begged that they would consider how time was flying and just pass a few resolutions and let us go. Then they said very courteously that there was a defect in the tickets, and asked me where I got them.

I judged I saw what the trouble was now. You see, I had bought the tickets in a cigar shop, and, of course, the tobacco smell was on them. Without doubt, the thing they were up to was to work the tickets through the Custom-house and collect duty on that smell. So I resolved to be perfectly frank; it is sometimes the best way. I said:

"Gentlemen, I will not deceive you. These railway tickets—"

"Ah, pardon, m'sieur! These are not railway tickets."

"Oh," I said. "Is that the defect?"

"Ah, truly, yes, monsieur. These are lottery tickets, yes; and it is a lottery which has been drawn two years ago."

I affected to be greatly amused; it is all one can do in such circumstances; it is all one can do, and yet there is no value in it; it deceives nobody and you can see that everybody around pities you and is ashamed of you. One of the hardest situations in life, I think, is to be full of grief and a sense of defeat and shabbiness that way, and yet have to put on an outside of archness and gaiety, while all the time you know that your own expedition, the treasures of your heart, and whose love and reverence you are by the custom of our civilization entitled to, are being consumed with humiliation before strangers to see you earning and getting a compassion which is a stigma, a brand—a brand which certifies you to be—oh, anything and everything which is fatal to human respect.

I said cheerily, it was all right, just one of those little accidents that was likely to happen to anybody—I would have the right tickets in two minutes, and we would catch the train yet, and, moreover, have something to laugh about all through the journey. I did get the tickets in time, all stamped and complete, but then it turned out that I couldn't take them, because in taking so much pains about the two missing members I had skipped the bank and hadn't the money. So then the train left, and there didn't seem to be anything to do but go back to the hotel, which we did; but it was kind of melancholy and not much said. I tried to start a few subjects, like scenery and transubstantiation, and those sorts of things, but they didn't seem to hit the weather right.

We had lost our good rooms, but we got some others which were pretty scattering, but would answer. I judged things would brighten now, but the Head of the Expedition said send up the trunks. It made me feel pretty cold. There was a doubtful something about that trunk business, I was almost sure of it. I was going to suggest——

But a wave of the hand sufficiently restrained me, and I was informed that we would now camp for three days and see if we could rest up.

I said all right, never mind ringing, I would go down and attend to the trunks myself. I got a cab and went straight to Mr. Charles Natural's place and asked what order it was I had left there.

"To send seven trunks to the hotel."

"And were you to bring any back?"

"No."

"You are sure I didn't tell you to bring back seven that would be found piled in the lobby?"

"Absolutely sure you didn't."

"Then the whole fourteen are gone to Zurich or Jericho or somewhere, and there is going to be more debris around that hotel when the Expedition——"

I didn't finish, because my mind was getting to be in a good deal of a whirl, and when you are that way you think you have finished a sentence when you haven't, and you go mooning and dreaming away, and the first thing you know you get run over by a dray or a cow or something.

I left the cab there—I forgot it—and on my way back I thought it all out and concluded to resign, because otherwise I should be nearly sure to be discharged. But I didn't believe it would be a good idea to resign in person; I could do it by message. So I sent for Mr. Ludi and explained that there was a courier going to resign on account of incompatibility or fatigue or something, and as he had four or five vacant days, I would like to insert him into that vacancy if he thought he could fill it. When everything was arranged I got him to go up and say to the Expedition that, owing to an error made by Mr. Natural's people, we were out of trunks here, but would have plenty in Zurich, and we'd better take the first train, freight, gravel or construction, and move right along.

He attended to that and came down with an invitation for me to go up—yes, certainly; and, while we walked along over to the bank to get money and collect my cigars and to-bacco, and to the cigar shop to trade back the lottery tickets and get my umbrella and to Mr. Natural to pay that cab and send it away, and to the county jail to get my rubbers and leave p. p. c. cards for the Mayor and Supreme Court, he described the weather to me that was prevailing on the upper levels there with the Expedition, and I saw that I was doing very well where I was.

I stayed out in the woods till 4 P. M., to let the weather moderate and then turned up at the station just in time to take the 3 o'clock express for Zurich along with the Expedition, now in the hands of Ludi, who conducted its complex affairs with little apparent effort or inconvenience.

Well, I had worked like a slave while I was in office, and done the very best I knew how; yet all that these people dwelt upon or seemed to care to remember was the defects of my administration, not its creditable features. They would skip over a thousand creditable features to remark upon and reiterate and fuss about just one fact, till it seemed to me they would wear it out; and not much of a fact, either, taken by itself—the fact that I elected myself courier in Geneva, and put in work enough to carry a circus to Jerusalem and yet never even got my gang out of the town. I finally said I didn't wish to hear any more about the subject, it made me tired. And I told them to their faces that I would never be a courier again to save anybody's life. And, if I live long enough I'll prove it. I think it's a difficult, brain racking, overworked and thoroughly ungrateful office, and the main bulk of its wages is a sore heart and a bruised spirit.

*December 19 and 26, 1891*

# Mental Telegraphy

## A Manuscript with a History

Note to the Editor. — By glancing over the enclosed bundle of rusty old manuscript, you will perceive that I once made a great discovery: the discovery that certain sorts of things which, from the beginning of the world, had always been regarded as merely "curious coincidences"—that is to say, accidents—were no more accidental than is the sending and receiving of a telegram an accident. I made this discovery sixteen or seventeen years ago, and gave it a name— "Mental Telegraphy." It is the same thing around the outer edges of which the Psychical Society of England began to grope (and play with) four or five years ago, and which they named "Telepathy." Within the last two or three years they have penetrated toward the heart of the matter, however, and have found out that mind can act upon mind in a quite detailed and elaborate way over vast stretches of land and water. And they have succeeded in doing, by their great credit and influence, what I could never have done—they have convinced the world that mental telegraphy is not a jest, but a fact, and that it is a thing not rare, but exceedingly common. They have done our age a service—and a very great service, I think.

In this old manuscript you will find mention of an extraordinary experience of mine in the mental telegraphic line, of date about the year 1874 or 1875—the one concerning the Great Bonanza book. It was this experience that called my attention to the matter under consideration. I began to keep a record, after that, of such experiences of mine as seemed explicable by the theory that minds telegraph thoughts to each other. In 1878 I went to Germany and began to write the book called *A Tramp Abroad*. The bulk of this old batch of manuscript was written at that time and for that book. But I removed it when I came to revise the volume for the press; for I feared that the public would treat the thing as a joke and throw it aside, whereas I was in earnest.

At home, eight or ten years ago, I tried to creep in under shelter of an authority grave enough to protect the article from ridicule— the *North American Review*. But Mr. Metcalf was too wary for me. He said that to treat these mere "coincidences" seriously was a thing which the *Review* couldn't dare to do; that I must put either my name or my *nom de plume* to the article, and thus save the *Review* from harm. But I couldn't consent to that; it would be the surest possible way to defeat my desire that the public should receive the thing seriously, and be willing to stop and give it some fair degree of attention. So I pigeon-holed the MS., because I could not get it published anonymously.

Now see how the world has moved since then. These small experiences of mine, which were too formidable at that time for admission to a grave magazine—if the magazine must allow them to appear as something above and beyond "accidents" and "coincidences"—are trifling and commonplace now, since the flood of light recently cast upon mental telegraphy by the intelligent labors of the Psychical Society. But I think they are worth publishing, just to show what harmless and ordinary matters were considered dangerous and incredible eight or ten years ago.

As I have said, the bulk of this old manuscript was written in 1878; a later part was written from time to time two, three, and four years afterward. The "Postscript" I add to-day.

MAY, '78.—Another of those apparently trifling things has happened to me which puzzle and perplex all men every now and then, keep them thinking an hour or two, and leave their minds barren of explanation or solution at last. Here it is—and it looks inconsequential enough, I am obliged to say. A few days ago I said: "It must be that Frank Millet doesn't know we are in Germany, or he would have written long before this. I have been on the point of dropping him a line at least a dozen times during the past six weeks, but I always decided to wait a day or two longer, and see if we shouldn't hear from him. But now I *will* write." And so I did. I directed the letter to Paris, and thought, "*Now* we shall hear from him before this letter is fifty miles from Heidelberg—it always happens so."

True enough; but *why* should it? That is the puzzling part of it. We are always talking about letters "crossing" each other, for that is one of the very commonest accidents of this life. We call it "accident," but perhaps we misname it. We have the instinct a dozen times a year that the letter we are writing is going to "cross" the other person's letter; and if the reader will rack his memory a little he will recall the fact that this presentiment had strength enough to it to make him cut his letter down to a decided briefness, because it would be a waste of time to write a letter which was going to "cross," and hence be a useless letter. I think that in my experience this instinct has generally come to me in cases where I had put off my letter a good while in the hope that the other person would write.

Yes, as I was saying, I had waited five or six weeks; then I wrote but three lines, because I felt and seemed to know that a letter from Millet would cross mine. And so it did. He wrote the same day that I wrote. The letters crossed each other. His letter went to Berlin, care of the American minister, who sent it to me. In this letter Millet said he had been trying for six weeks to stumble upon somebody who knew my German address, and at last the idea had occurred to him that a letter sent to the care of the embassy at Berlin might possibly find me.

Maybe it was an "accident" that he finally determined to write me at the same moment that I finally determined to write him, but I think not.

With me the most irritating thing has been to wait a tedious time in a purely business matter, hoping that the other party will do the writing, and then sit down and do it myself, perfectly satisfied that that other man is sitting down at the same moment to write a letter which will "cross" mine. And yet one must go on writing, just the same; because if you get up from your table and postpone, that other man will do the same thing, exactly as if you two were harnessed together like the Siamese twins, and must duplicate each other's movements.

Several months before I left home a New York firm did some work about the house for me, and did not make a success of it, as it seemed to me. When the bill came, I wrote and said I wanted the work perfected before I paid. They replied that they were very busy, but that as soon as they could spare the proper man the thing should be done. I waited more than two months, enduring as patiently as possible the companionship of bells which would fire away of their own accord sometimes when nobody was touching them, and at other times wouldn't ring though you struck the button with a sledgehammer. Many a time I got ready to write and then postponed it; but at last I sat down one evening and poured out my grief to the extent of a page or so, and then cut my letter suddenly short, because a strong instinct told me that the firm had begun to move in the matter. When I came down to breakfast next morning the postman had not yet taken my letter away, but the electrical man had been there, done his work, and was gone again! He had received his orders the previous evening from his employers, and had come up by the night train.

If that was an "accident," it took about three months to get it up in good shape.

One evening last summer I arrived in Washington, registered at the Arlington Hotel, and went to my room. I read and smoked until ten o'clock; then, finding I was not yet sleepy, I thought I would take a breath of fresh air. So I went forth in the rain, and tramped through one street after another in an aimless and enjoyable way. I knew that Mr. O——, a friend of mine, was in town, and I wished I might run across him; but I did not propose to hunt for him at midnight, especially as I did not know where he was stopping. Toward twelve o'clock the streets had become so deserted that I felt lonesome; so I stepped into a cigar shop far up the Avenue, and remained there fifteen minutes, listening to some bummers discussing national politics. Suddenly the spirit of prophecy came upon me, and I said to myself, "Now I will go out at this door, turn to the left, walk ten steps, and meet Mr. O—— face to face." I did it, too! I could not see his face, because he had an umbrella before it, and it was pretty dark anyhow, but he interrupted the man he was walking and talking with, and I recognized his voice and stopped him.

That I should step out there and stumble upon Mr. O—— was nothing, but that I should know beforehand that I was going to do it was a good deal. It is a very curious thing when you come to look at it. I stood far within the cigar shop when I delivered my prophecy; I walked about five steps to the door, opened it, closed it after me, walked down a flight of three steps to the sidewalk, then turned to the left and walked four or five more, and found my man. I repeat that in itself the thing was nothing; but to know it would happen so *beforehand*, wasn't that really curious?

I have criticised absent people so often, and then discovered, to my humiliation, that I was talking with their relatives, that I have grown superstitious about that sort of thing and dropped it. How like an idiot one feels after a blunder like that!

We are always mentioning people, and in that very instant

they appear before us. We laugh, and say, "Speak of the devil," and so forth, and there we drop it, considering it an "accident." It is a cheap and convenient way of disposing of a grave and very puzzling mystery. The fact is it does seem to happen too often to be an accident.

Now I come to the oddest thing that ever happened to me. Two or three years ago I was lying in bed, idly musing, one morning—it was the 2d of March—when suddenly a red-hot new idea came whistling down into my camp, and exploded with such comprehensive effectiveness as to sweep the vicinity clean of rubbishy reflections, and fill the air with their dust and flying fragments. This idea, stated in simple phrase, was that the time was ripe and the market ready for a certain book; a book which ought to be written at once; a book which must command attention and be of peculiar interest—to wit, a book about the Nevada silver mines. The "Great Bonanza" was a new wonder then, and everybody was talking about it. It seemed to me that the person best qualified to write this book was Mr. William H. Wright, a journalist of Virginia, Nevada, by whose side I had scribbled many months when I was a reporter there ten or twelve years before. He might be alive still; he might be dead; I could not tell; but I would write him, anyway. I began by merely and modestly suggesting that he make such a book; but my interest grew as I went on, and I ventured to map out what I thought ought to be the plan of the work, he being an old friend, and not given to taking good intentions for ill. I even dealt with details, and suggested the order and sequence which they should follow. I was about to put the manuscript in an envelope, when the thought occurred to me that if this book should be written at my suggestion, and then no publisher happened to want it, I should feel uncomfortable; so I concluded to keep my letter back until I should have secured a publisher. I pigeon-holed my document, and dropped a note to my own publisher, asking him to name a day for a business consultation. He was out of town on a far journey. My note remained unanswered, and at the end of three or four days the whole matter had passed out of my mind. On the 9th of March the postman brought three or four letters, and among them a thick one whose superscription was in a hand which seemed dimly familiar to me. I could not "place" it at first, but presently I succeeded. Then I said to a visiting relative who was present:

"Now I will do a miracle. I will tell you everything this letter contains—date, signature, and all—without breaking the seal. It is from a Mr. Wright, of Virginia, Nevada, and is dated the 2d of March—seven days ago. Mr. Wright proposes to make a book about the silver mines and the Great Bonanza, and asks what I, as a friend, think of the idea. He says his subjects are to be so and so, their order and sequence so and so, and he will close with a history of the chief feature of the book, the Great Bonanza."

I opened the letter, and showed that I had stated the date and the contents correctly. Mr. Wright's letter simply contained what my own letter, written on the same date, contained, and mine still lay in its pigeon-hole, where it had been lying during the seven days since it was written.

There was no clairvoyance about this, if I rightly comprehend what clairvoyance is. I think the clairvoyant professes to actually *see* concealed writing, and read it off word for word. This was not my case. I only seemed to know, and to know absolutely, the contents of the letter in detail and due order, but I had to *word* them myself. I translated them, so to speak, out of Wright's language into my own.

Wright's letter and the one which I had written to him but never sent were in substance the same.

Necessarily this could not come by accident; such elaborate accidents cannot happen. Chance might have duplicated one or two of the details, but she would have broken down on the rest. I could not doubt—there was no tenable reason for doubting—that Mr. Wright's mind and mine had been in close and crystal-clear communication with each other across three thousand miles of mountain and desert on the morning of the 2d of March. I did not consider that both minds *originated* that succession of ideas, but that one mind originated them, and simply telegraphed them to the other. I was curious to know which brain was the telegrapher and which the receiver, so I wrote and asked for particulars. Mr. Wright's reply showed that his mind had done the originating and telegraphing and mine the receiving. Mark that significant thing, now; consider for a moment how many a splendid "original" idea has been unconsciously stolen from a man three thousand miles away! If one should question that this is so, let him look into the cyclopædia and con once more that curious thing in the history of inventions which has puzzled every one so much—that is, the frequency with which the same machine or other contrivance has been invented at the same time by several persons in different quarters of the globe. The world was without an electric telegraph for several thousand years; then Professor Henry, the American, Wheatstone in England, Morse on the sea, and a German in Munich, all invented it at the same time. The discovery of certain ways of applying steam was made in two or three countries in the same year. Is it not possible that inventors are constantly and unwittingly stealing each other's ideas whilst they stand thousands of miles asunder?

Last spring a literary friend of mine,* who lived a hundred miles away, paid me a visit, and in the course of our talk he said he had made a discovery—conceived an entirely new idea—one which certainly had never been used in literature. He told me what it was. I handed him a manuscript, and said he would find substantially the same idea in that —a manuscript which I had written a week before. The idea had been in my mind since the previous November; it had only entered his while I was putting it on paper, a week gone by. He had not yet written his; so he left it unwritten, and gracefully made over all his right and title in the idea to me.

The following statement, which I have clipped from a newspaper, is true. I had the facts from Mr. Howells's lips when the episode was new:

"A remarkable story of a literary coincidence is told of Mr. Howells's *Atlantic Monthly* serial 'Dr. Breen's Practice.' A lady of Rochester, New York, contributed to the magazine, after 'Dr. Breen's Practice' was in type, a short story which so much resembled Mr. Howells's that he felt it necessary to call upon her and explain the situation of affairs in order that no charge of plagiarism might be preferred against him. He showed her the proof-sheets of his story, and satisfied her that the similarity between her work and his was

*W. D. Howells.

one of those strange coincidences which have from time to time occurred in the literary world."

I had read portions of Mr. Howells's story, both in MS. and in proof, before the lady offered her contribution to the magazine.

Here is another case. I clip it from a newspaper:

"The republication of Miss Alcott's novel *Moods* recalls to a writer in the Boston *Post* a singular coincidence which was brought to light before the book was first published: 'Miss Anna M. Crane, of Baltimore, published *Emily Chester*, a novel which was pronounced a very striking and strong story. A comparison of this book with *Moods* showed that the two writers, though entire strangers to each other, and living hundreds of miles apart, had both chosen the same subject for their novels, had followed almost the same line of treatment up to a certain point, where the parallel ceased, and the dénouements were entirely opposite. And even more curious, the leading characters in both books had identically the same names, so that the names in Miss Alcott's novel had to be changed. Then the book was published by Loring.' "

Four or five times within my recollection there has been a lively newspaper war in this country over poems whose authorship was claimed by two or three different people at the same time. There was a war of this kind over "Nothing to Wear," "Beautiful Snow," "Rock Me to Sleep, Mother," and also over one of Mr. Will Carleton's early ballads, I think. These were all blameless cases of unintentional and unwitting mental telegraphy, I judge.

A word more as to Mr. Wright. He had had his book in his mind some time; consequently he, and not I, had originated the idea of it. The subject was entirely foreign to my thoughts; I was wholly absorbed in other things. Yet this friend, whom I had not seen and had hardly thought of for eleven years, was able to shoot his thoughts at me across three thousand miles of country, and fill my head with them, to the exclusion of every other interest, in a single moment. He had begun his letter after finishing his work on the morning paper—a little after three o'clock, he said. When it was three in the morning in Nevada it was about six in Hartford, where I lay awake thinking about nothing in particular; and just about that time his ideas came pouring into my head from across the continent, and I got up and put them on paper, under the impression that they were my own original thoughts.

I have never seen any mesmeric or clairvoyant performances or spiritual manifestations which were in the least degree convincing—a fact which is not of consequence, since my opportunities have been meagre; but I am forced to believe that one human mind (still inhabiting the flesh) can communicate with another, over any sort of a distance, and without any *artificial* preparation of "sympathetic conditions" to act as a transmitting agent. I suppose that when the sympathetic conditions happen to exist the two minds communicate with each other, and that otherwise they don't; and I suppose that if the sympathetic conditions could be kept up right along, the two minds would continue to correspond without limit as to time.

Now there is that curious thing which happens to everybody: suddenly a succession of thoughts or sensations flocks in upon you, which startles you with the weird idea that you have ages ago experienced just this succession of thoughts or sensations in a previous existence. The previous existence is possible, no doubt, but I am persuaded that the solution of this hoary mystery lies not there, but in the fact that some far-off stranger has been telegraphing his thoughts and sensations into your consciousness, and that he stopped because some counter-current or other obstruction intruded and broke the line of communication. Perhaps they seem repetitions to you because they *are* repetitions, got at second hand from the other man. Possibly Mr. Brown, the "mind-reader," reads other people's minds, possibly he does not; but I know of a surety that I have read another man's mind, and therefore I do not see why Mr. Brown shouldn't do the like also.

I wrote the foregoing about three years ago, in Heidelberg, and laid the manuscript aside, purposing to add to it instances of mind-telegraphing from time to time as they should fall under my experience. Meantime the "crossing" of letters has been so frequent as to become monotonous. However, I have managed to get something useful out of this hint; for now, when I get tired of waiting upon a man whom I very much wish to hear from, I sit down and *compel* him to write, whether he wants to or not; that is to say, I sit down and write him, and then tear my letter up, satisfied that my act has forced him to write me at the same moment. I do not need to mail my letter—the writing it is the only essential thing.

Of course I have grown superstitious about this letter-crossing business—this was natural. We staid awhile in Venice after leaving Heidelberg. One day I was going down the Grand Canal in a gondola, when I heard a shout behind me, and looked around to see what the matter was; a gondola was rapidly following, and the gondolier was making signs to me to stop. I did so, and the pursuing boat ranged up alongside. There was an American lady in it—a resident of Venice. She was in a good deal of distress. She said:

"There's a New York gentleman and his wife at the Hotel Britannia who arrived a week ago, expecting to find news of their son, whom they have heard nothing about during eight months. There was no news. The lady is down sick with despair; the gentleman can't sleep or eat. Their son arrived at San Francisco eight months ago, and announced the fact in a letter to his parents the same day. That is the last trace of him. The parents have been in Europe ever since; but their trip has been spoiled, for they have occupied their time simply in drifting restlessly from place to place, and writing letters everywhere and to everybody, begging for news of their son; but the mystery remains as dense as ever. Now the gentleman wants to stop writing and go to cabling. He wants to cable San Francisco. He has never done it before, because he is afraid of—of he doesn't know what—death of the son, no doubt. But he wants somebody to *advise* him to cable; wants me to do it. Now I simply can't; for if no news came, that mother yonder would die. So I have chased you up in order to get you to support me in urging him to be patient, and put the thing off a week or two longer; it may be the saving of this lady. Come along; let's not lose any time."

So I went along, but I had a programme of my own. When I was introduced to the gentleman I said: "I have some superstitions, but they are worthy of respect. If you will cable San Francisco immediately, you will hear news of your son inside of twenty-four hours. I don't know that you will get the news from San Francisco, but you will get it from somewhere. The only necessary thing is to *cable*—that is all. The news will come within twenty-four hours. Cable Peking, if you prefer; there is no choice in this matter. This delay is all occasioned by your not cabling long ago, when you were first moved to do it."

It seems absurd that this gentleman should have been cheered up by this nonsense, but he was; he brightened up at once, and sent his cablegram; and next day, at noon, when a long letter arrived from his lost son, the man was as grateful to me as if I had really had something to do with the hurrying up of that letter. The son had shipped from San Francisco in a sailing vessel, and his letter was written from the first port he touched at, months afterward.

This incident argues nothing, and is valueless. I insert it only to show how strong is the superstition which "letter-crossing" has bred in me. I was so sure that a cablegram sent to any place, no matter where, would defeat itself by "crossing" the incoming news, that my confidence was able to raise up a hopeless man, and make him cheery and hopeful.

But here are two or three incidents which come strictly under the head of mind-telegraphing. One Monday morning, about a year ago, the mail came in, and I picked up one of the letters and said to a friend: "Without opening this letter I will tell you what it says. It is from Mrs. ——, and she says she was in New York last Saturday, and was purposing to run up here in the afternoon train and surprise us, but at the last moment changed her mind and returned westward to her home."

I was right; my details were exactly correct. Yet we had had no suspicion that Mrs. —— was coming to New York, or that she had even a remote intention of visiting us.

I smoke a good deal—that is to say, all the time—so, during seven years, I have tried to keep a box of matches handy, behind a picture on the mantel-piece; but I have had to take it out in trying, because George (colored), who makes the fires and lights the gas, always uses my matches, and never replaces them. Commands and persuasions have gone for nothing with him all these seven years. One day last summer, when our family had been away from home several months, I said to a member of the household:

"Now, with all this long holiday, and nothing in the way to interrupt—"

"I can finish the sentence for you," said the member of the household.

"Do it, then," said I.

"George ought to be able, by practising, to learn to let those matches alone."

It was correctly done. That was what I was going to say. Yet until that moment George and the matches had not been in my mind for three months, and it is plain that the part of the sentence which I uttered offers not the least cue or suggestion of what I was purposing to follow it with.

My mother* is descended from the younger of two English brothers named Lambton, who settled in this country a few generations ago. The tradition goes that the elder of the two eventually fell heir to a certain estate in England (now an earldom), and died right away. This has always been the way with our family. They always die when they could make anything by not doing it. The two Lambtons left plenty of Lambtons behind them; and when at last, about fifty years ago, the English baronetcy was exalted to an earldom, the great tribe of American Lambtons began to bestir themselves—that is, those descended from the elder branch. Ever since that day one or another of these has been fretting his life uselessly away with schemes to get at his "rights." The present "rightful earl"—I mean the American one—used to write me occasionally, and try to interest me in his projected raids upon the title and estates by offering me a share in the latter portion of the spoil; but I have always managed to resist his temptations.

Well, one day last summer I was lying under a tree, thinking about nothing in particular, when an absurd idea flashed into my head, and I said to a member of the household, "Suppose I should live to be ninety-two, and dumb and blind and toothless, and just as I was gasping out what was left of me on my death-bed—"

"Wait, I will finish the sentence," said the member of the household.

"Go on," said I.

"Somebody should rush in with a document, and say, 'All the other heirs are dead, and you are the Earl of Durham!' "

*She was still living when this was written.

That is truly what I was going to say. Yet until that moment the subject had not entered my mind or been referred to in my hearing for months before. A few years ago this thing would have astounded me, but the like could not much surprise me now, though it happened every week; for I think I *know* now that mind can communicate accurately with mind without the aid of the slow and clumsy vehicle of speech.

This age does seem to have exhausted invention nearly; still, it has one important contract on its hands yet—the invention of the *phrenophone*; that is to say, a method whereby the communicating of mind with mind may be brought under command and reduced to certainty and system. The telegraph and the telephone are going to become too slow and wordy for our needs. We must have the *thought* itself shot into our minds from a distance; then, if we need to put it into words, we can do that tedious work at our leisure. Doubtless the something which conveys our thoughts through the air from brain to brain is a finer and subtler form of electricity, and all we need do is to find out how to capture it and how to force it to do its work, as we have had to do in the case of the electric currents. Before the day of telegraphs neither one of these marvels would have seemed any easier to achieve than the other.

While I am writing this, doubtless somebody on the other side of the globe is writing it too. The question is, am I inspiring him or is he inspiring me? I cannot answer that; but that these thoughts have been passing through somebody else's mind all the time I have been setting them down I have no sort of doubt.

I will close this paper with a remark which I found some time ago in Boswell's *Johnson*:

"Voltaire's *Candide* is wonderfully similar in its plan and conduct to Johnson's *Rasselas*; insomuch that I have heard Johnson say that if they had not been published so closely one after the other that there was not time for imitation, *it would have been in vain to deny that the scheme of that which came latest was taken from the other*."

The two men were widely separated from each other at the time, and the sea lay between.

POSTSCRIPT.

In the *Atlantic* for June, 1882, Mr. John Fiske refers to the often-quoted Darwin-and-Wallace "coincidence":

"I alluded, just now, to the 'unforeseen circumstance' which led Mr. Darwin in 1859 to break his long silence, and to write and publish the *Origin of Species*. This circumstance served, no less than the extraordinary success of his book, to show how ripe the minds of men had become for entertaining such views as those which Mr. Darwin propounded. In 1858 Mr. Wallace, who was then engaged in studying the natural history of the Malay Archipelago, sent to Mr. Darwin (as to the man most likely to understand him) a paper, in which he sketched the outlines of a theory identical with that upon which Mr. Darwin had so long been at work. The same sequence of observed facts and inferences that had led Mr. Darwin to the discovery of natural selection and its consequences had led Mr. Wallace to the very threshold of the same discovery; but in Mr. Wallace's mind the theory had by no means been wrought out to the same degree of completeness to which it had been wrought in the mind of Mr. Darwin. In the preface to his charming book on Natural Selection, Mr. Wallace, with rare modesty and candor, acknowledges that whatever value his speculations may have had, they have been utterly surpassed in richness and cogency of proof by those of Mr. Darwin. This is no doubt true, and Mr. Wallace has done such good work in further illustration of the theory that he can well afford to rest content with the second place in the first announcement of it.

"The coincidence, however, between Mr. Wallace's conclusions and those of Mr. Darwin was very remarkable. But, after all, coincidences of this sort have not been uncommon in the history of scientific inquiry. Nor is it at all surprising that they should occur now and then, when we remember that a great and pregnant discovery must always be concerned with some question which many of the foremost minds in the world are busy in thinking about. It was so with the discovery of the differential calculus, and again with the discovery of the planet Neptune. It was so with the interpretation of the Egyptian hieroglyphics, and with the establishment of the undulatory theory of light. It was so, to a considerable extent, with the introduction of the new chemistry, with the discovery of the mechanical equivalent of heat, and the whole doctrine of the correlation of forces. It was so with the invention of the electric telegraph and with the discovery of spectrum analysis. And it is not at all strange that it should have been so with the doctrine of the origin of species through natural selection."

He thinks these "coincidences" were apt to happen because the matters from which they sprang were matters which many of the foremost minds in the world were busy thinking about. But perhaps *one* man in each case did the telegraphing to the others. The aberrations which gave Leverrier the idea that there must be a planet of such and such mass and such and such an orbit hidden from sight out yonder in the remote abysses of space were not new; they had been noticed by astronomers for generations. Then why should it happen to occur to three people, widely separated—Leverrier, Mrs. Somerville, and Adams—to suddenly go to worrying about those aberrations all at the same time, and set themselves to work to find out what caused them, and to measure and weigh an invisible planet, and calculate its orbit, and hunt it down and catch it?—a strange project which nobody but they had ever thought of before. If one astronomer had invented that odd and happy project fifty years before, don't you think he would have telegraphed it to several others without knowing it?

But now I come to a puzzler. How is it that *inanimate* objects are able to affect the mind? They seem to do that. However, I wish to throw in a parenthesis first—just a reference to a thing everybody is familiar with—the experience of receiving a clear and particular *answer* to your telegram before your telegram has reached the sender of the answer. That is a case where your telegram has gone straight from your brain to the man it was meant for, far outstripping the wire's slow electricity, and it is an exercise of mental telegraphy which is as common as dining. To return to the influence of inanimate things. In the cases of non-professional clairvoyance examined by the Psychical Society the clairvoyant has usually been blindfolded, then some object which has been touched or worn by a person is placed in his hand; the clairvoyant immediately describes that person, and goes on and gives a history of some event with which the text object has been connected. If the inanimate object is able to affect and inform the clairvoyant's mind, maybe it can do the same when it is working in the interest of mental telegraphy. Once a lady in the West wrote me that her son was coming to New York to remain three weeks, and would pay me a visit if invited, and she gave me his address. I mislaid the letter, and forgot all about the matter till the three weeks were about up. Then a sudden and fiery irruption of remorse burst up in my brain that illuminated all the region round about, and I sat down at once and wrote to the lady and asked for that lost address. But, upon reflection, I judged that the stirring up of my recollection had not been an accident, so I added a postscript to say, never mind, I should get a letter from her son before night. And I did get it; for the letter was already in the town, although not delivered yet. It had influenced me somehow. I have had so many experiences of this sort—a dozen of them at least—that I am nearly persuaded that inanimate objects do not confine their activities to helping the clairvoyant, but do every now and then give the mental telegraphist a lift.

The case of mental telegraphy which I am coming to now comes under I don't exactly know what head. I clipped it from one of our local papers six or eight years ago. I know the details to be right and true, for the story was told to me in the same form by one of the two persons concerned (a clergyman of Hartford) at the time that the curious thing happened:

"A Remarkable Coincidence.—Strange coincidences make the most interesting of stories and most curious of studies. Nobody can quite say how they come about, but everybody appreciates the fact when they do come, and it is seldom that any more complete and curious coincidence is recorded of minor importance than the following, which is absolutely true, and occurred in this city:

"At the time of the building of one of the finest residences of Hartford, which is still a very new house, a local firm supplied the wall-paper for certain rooms, contracting both to furnish and to put on the paper. It happened that they did not calculate the size of one room exactly right, and the paper of the design selected for it fell short just half a roll. They asked for delay enough to send on to the manufacturers for what was needed, and were told that there was no especial hurry. It happened that the manufacturer had none on hand, and had destroyed the blocks from which it was printed. They wrote that they had a full list of the dealers to whom they had sold that paper, and that they would write to each of these, and get from some of them a roll. It might involve a delay of a couple of weeks, but they would surely get it.

"In the course of time came a letter saying that, to their great surprise, they could not find a single roll. Such a thing was very unusual, but in this case it had so happened. Accordingly the local firm asked for further time, saying they would write to their own customers who had bought of that pattern, and would get the piece from them. But, to their surprise, this effort also failed. A long time had now elapsed, and there was no use of delaying any longer. They had contracted to paper the room, and their only course was to take off that which was insufficient and put on some other of which there was enough to go around. Accordingly at length a man was sent out to remove the paper. He got his apparatus ready, and was about to begin work, under the direction of the owner of the building, when the latter was for the moment called away. The house was large and very interesting, and so many people had rambled about it that finally admission had been refused by a sign at the door. On the occasion, however, when a gentleman had knocked and asked for leave to look about, the owner, being on the premises, had been sent for to reply to the request in person. That was the call that for the moment delayed the final preparations. The gentleman went to the door and admitted the stranger, saying he would show him about the house, but first must return for a moment to that room to finish his directions there, and he told the curious story about the paper as they went on. They entered the room together, and the first thing the stranger, who lived fifty miles away, said on looking about was, 'Why, I have that very paper on a room in my house, and I have an extra roll of it laid away, which is at your service.' In a few days the wall was papered according to the original contract. Had not the owner been at the house, the stranger would not have been admitted; had he called a day later, it would have been too late; had not the facts been almost accidentally told to him, he would probably have said nothing of the paper, and so on. The exact fitting of all the circumstances is something very remarkable, and makes one of those stories that seem hardly accidental in their nature."

Something that happened the other day brought my hoary MS. to mind, and that is how I came to dig it out from its dusty pigeon-hole grave for publication. The thing that happened was a question. A lady asked it: "Have you ever had a vision—when awake?" I was about to answer promptly, when the last two words of the question began to grow and spread and swell, and presently they attained to vast dimensions. She did not know that they were important; and I did not at first, but I soon saw that they were putting me on the track of the solution of a mystery which had perplexed me a good deal. You will see what I mean when I get down to it. Ever since the English Society for Psychical Research began its searching investigations of ghost stories, haunted houses, and apparitions of the living and the dead, I have read their pamphlets with avidity as fast as they arrived. Now one of their commonest inquiries of a dreamer or a vision-seer is, "Are you sure you were awake at the time?" If the man can't say he is sure he was awake, a doubt falls upon his tale right there. But if he is positive he was awake, and offers reasonable evidence to substantiate it, the fact counts largely for the credibility of his story. It does with the society, and it did with me until that lady asked me the above question the other day.

The question set me to considering, and brought me to the conclusion that you can be asleep—at least wholly unconscious—for a time, and not suspect that it has happened, and not have any way to prove that it *has* happened. A memorable case was in my mind. About a year ago I was standing on the porch one day, when I saw a man coming up the walk. He was a stranger, and I hoped he would ring and carry his business into the house without stopping to argue with me; he would have to pass the front door to get to me, and I hoped he wouldn't take the trouble; to help, I tried to look like a stranger myself—it often works. I was looking straight at that man; he had got to within ten feet of the door and within twenty-five feet of me—and suddenly he disappeared. It was as astounding as if a church should vanish from before your face and leave nothing behind it but a vacant lot. I was unspeakably delighted. I had seen an apparition at last, with my own eyes, in broad daylight. I made up my mind to write an account of it to the society. I ran to where the spectre had been, to make sure he was playing fair, then I ran to the other end of the porch, scanning the open grounds as I went. No, everything was perfect; he couldn't have escaped without my seeing him; he was an apparition, without the slightest doubt, and I would write him up before he was cold. I ran, hot with excitement, and let myself in with a latch-key. When I stepped into the hall my lungs collapsed and my heart stood still. For there sat that same apparition in a chair, all alone, and as quiet and reposeful as if he had come to stay a year! The shock kept me dumb for a moment or two, then I said, "Did you come in at that door?"

"Yes."

"Did *you* open it, or did you ring?"

"I rang, and the colored man opened it."

I said to myself: "This is astonishing. It takes George all of two minutes to answer the door-bell when he is in a hurry, and I have never seen him in a hurry. How *did* this man stand two minutes at that door, within five steps of me, and I did not see him?"

I should have gone to my grave puzzling over that riddle but for that lady's chance question last week: "Have you ever had a vision—when awake?" It stands explained now. During at least sixty seconds that day I was asleep, or at least totally unconscious, without suspecting it. In that interval the man came to my immediate vicinity, rang, stood there and waited, then entered and closed the door, and I did not see him and did not hear the door slam.

If he had slipped around the house in that interval and gone into the cellar—he had time enough—I should have written him up for the society, and magnified him, and gloated over him, and hurrahed about him, and thirty yoke of oxen could not have pulled the belief out of me that I was of the favored ones of the earth, and had seen a vision—while wide awake.

Now how are you to tell when you are awake? What are you to go by? People bite their fingers to find out. Why, you can do that in a dream.

*December 1891*

# The Cradle of Liberty

It is a good many years since I was in Switzerland last. In that remote time there was only one ladder railway in the country. That state of things is all changed. There isn't a mountain in Switzerland now that hasn't a ladder railroad or two up its back like suspenders; indeed, some of them are latticed with them, and two years hence all of them will be. In that day the peasant of the high altitudes will have to carry a lantern when he goes visiting in the night to keep from stumbling over railroads that have been built since his last round. And also in that day, if there shall remain a high-altitude peasant whose potato patch hasn't a railroad through it, it will make him as conspicuous as William Tell.

However, there are only two best ways to travel through Switzerland; the first best is afoot, the second best is by open two-horse carriage. One can come from Lucerne to Interlaken over the Brunig by ladder-railroad in an hour or so now, but you can glide smoothly through in a carriage in ten, and have two hours for luncheon at noon. For luncheon, not for rest. There is no fatigue connected with the trip. One arrives fresh in spirit and in person in the evening—no fret in his heart, no grime on his face, no grit in his hair, not a cinder in his eye. This is the right condition of mind and body, the right and due preparation for the solemn event which closes the day—stepping with metaphorically uncovered head into the presence of the most impressive mountain mass that the globe can show—the Jungfrau.

The stranger's first feeling when suddenly confronted by that towering and awful apparition wrapped in its shroud of snow is breath-taking astonishment. It is as if heaven's gates had swung open and exposed the throne.

It is peaceful here and pleasant at Interlaken. Nothing going on—at least nothing but brilliant, life-giving sunshine. There are floods and floods of that. One may properly speak of it as "going on," for it is full of the suggestion of activity; the light pours down with energy, with visible enthusiasm. This is a good atmosphere to be in, morally as well as physically. After trying the political atmosphere of the neighboring monarchies, it is healing and refreshment to breathe an air that has known no taint of slavery for 600 years, and to come among a people whose political history is great and fine, superlatively great and fine, and worthy to be taught in all schools and studied by all races and peoples. For the struggle here throughout the centuries has not been in the interest of any private family or any church, but in the interest of the whole body of the nation and for shelter and protection of all forms of belief. This fact is colossal. If one would realize how colossal it is and of what dignity and majesty let him contrast it with the purposes and objects of the Crusades, the siege of Troy, the Wars of the Roses, and other historic comedies of that sort and size.

Last week I was boating around the Lake of the Four Cantons, and I saw Rütli and Altorf. Rütli is a remote little patch of a meadow, but I do not know how any piece of ground could be holier or better worth crossing oceans and continents to see, since it was there that the great trinity of Switzerland joined hands six centuries ago and swore the oath which set their enslaved and insulted country forever free. And Altorf is also honorable ground and worshipful, since it was there that William, surnamed Tell (which, interpreted, means "the foolish talker," that is to say, the too daring talker), refused to bow to Gessler's hat. Of late years the prying student of history has been delighting himself beyond measure over a wonderful find which he has made—to-wit, that Tell did not shoot the apple from his son's head. To hear the students jubilate, one would suppose that the question of whether Tell shot the apple or didn't was an important matter; whereas it ranks in importance exactly with the question of whether Washington chopped down the cherry tree or didn't. The deeds of Washington the patriot are the essential thing, the cherry-tree incident is of no consequence. To prove that Tell did shoot the apple from his son's head would merely prove that he had better nerve than most men, and was as skillful with a bow as a million more who preceded and followed him, but not a whit more so. But Tell was more and better than a mere marksman, more and better than a mere cool head, he was a type; he stands for Swiss patriotism; in his person was represented a whole people; his spirit was

their spirit—the spirit which would bow to none but God—
the spirit which said this in words and confirmed it with
deeds. There have always been Tells in Switzerland, people
who would not bow. There was a sufficiency of them at Rütli,
there were plenty of them at Murten, plenty at Granson, there
are plenty today. And the first of them all—the very first,
earliest banner-bearer of human freedom in this world—was
not a man, but a woman, Stauffacher's wife. There she looms,
dim and great, through the haze of the centuries, delivering
into her husband's charmed ear that gospel of revolt which
was to bear fruit in the conspiracy of Rütli and the birth of
the first free government the world had ever seen.

THURSDAY, Sept. 10.—From this Victoria Hotel one looks
straight across a flat of trifling width to a lofty mountain barrier, which has a gateway in it shaped like an inverted pyramid. Beyond this gateway arises the vast bulk of the Jungfrau,
a spotless mass of gleaming snow, into the sky. The gateway
in the dark-colored barrier makes a strong frame for the great
picture. The somber frame and the glowing snow-pile are
startlingly contrasted. It is this frame which concentrates and
emphasizes the glory of the Jungfrau and makes it the most
engaging, and beguiling, and fascinating spectacle that exists
on the earth. There are many mountains of snow that are as
lofty as the Jungfrau and as nobly proportioned, but they lack
the frame; they stand at large, they are intruded upon and
elbowed by neighboring domes and summits, and their grandeur is diminished and fails of effect.

It is a good name, Jungfrau—Virgin. Nothing could be
whiter, nothing could be purer, nothing could be saintlier of
aspect. At 6 yesterday evening the great intervening barrier,
seen through a faint bluish haze, seemed made of air, and
substanceless, so soft and rich it was, so shimmering where
the wandering lights touched it, and so dim where the shadows lay. Apparently it was dream stuff, a work of the imagination, nothing real about it. The tint was green, slightly
varying shades of it, but mainly dark. The sun was down—as
far as that barrier was concerned, but not for the Jungfrau,
towering into the heavens beyond the gateway. She was a
soaring conflagration of blinding white light.

It is said that Fridolin (the holy Fridolin), a saint now, but formerly a missionary, gave the mountain its gracious name. He was an Irishman, son of an Irish King, of whom there were 30,000 reigning in Cork County alone in his time, 1,500 years ago. It got so that they could not make a living, there was so much competition and wages got cut so. Some of them were out of work months at a time, with wife and little children to feed, and not a crust in the place. At last a particularly severe winter fell upon the country, and hundreds of them were reduced to mendicancy and were to be seen day after day in the bitterest weather standing barefoot in the snow, holding out their crowns for alms. Indeed, they would have been obliged to emigrate or starve but for a fortunate idea of Prince Fridolin, who started a labor union, the first one in history, and got the great bulk of them to join it. He thus won the general gratitude and they wanted to make him Emperor—Emperor over them all—Emperor of Cork County; but he said no, walking delegate was good enough for him. For behold, he was modest beyond his years and keen as a whip. To this day in Germany and Switzerland, where St. Fridolin is deeply revered and honored, the peasantry speak of him affectionately as the first walking delegate.

The first walk he took was into France and Germany missionarying—for missionarying was a better thing in those days than it is in ours. All you had to do was to cure the head savage's sick daughter by a "miracle"—a miracle like the miracle of Lourdes in our day, for instance—and immediately that head savage was your convert; he was your convert and filled to the eyes with a new convert's enthusiasm. You could sit down and make yourself easy, now. He would take an ax and convert the rest of the nation himself. Charlemagne was that kind of a walking delegate.

Yes, there were great missionaries in those days, for the methods were sure and the rewards great. We have no such missionaries now, and no such methods.

But to continue the history of the first walking delegate if you are interested. I am interested myself because I have seen his relics at Seckingen, and also the very spot where he worked his greatest miracle—the one which won him his saintship in the Papal Court a few centuries later. To have seen these things makes me feel very near to him, almost like a member of the family, in fact. While wandering about the continent he arrived at the spot on the Rhine which is now occupied by Seckingen, and proposed to settle there, but the people warned him off. He appealed to the King of the Franks, who made him a present of the whole region, people and all. He built a great cloister there for women, and proceeded to teach in it and accumulate more land. There were two wealthy brothers in the neighborhood, Urso and Landulph. Urso died, and Fridolin claimed his estates. Landulph asked for documents and papers. Fridolin had none to show. He said the bequest had been made to him by word of mouth. Landulph suggested that he produce a witness, and said it in a way which he thought was very witty, very sarcastic. This shows that he did not know the walking delegate. Fridolin was not disturbed. He said:

"Appoint your court. I will bring a witness."

The court was created. It consisted of fifteen Counts and Barons. A day was appointed for the trial of the case. On that day the Judges took their seats in state and proclamation was made that the court was ready for business. Five minutes, ten minutes, fifteen minutes passed and yet no Fridolin appeared. Landulph rose and was in the act of claiming judgment by default when a strange clacking sound was heard coming up the stairs. In another moment Fridolin entered at the further door and came walking in a deep hush down the middle aisle with a tall skeleton stalking in his rear.

Amazement and terror sat upon every countenance, for everybody suspected that that skeleton was Urso's. It stopped before the chief judge and raised its bony arm aloft and began to speak while all the assembly shuddered, for they could see the words leak out from between its ribs. It said:

"Brother, why dost thou disturb my blessed rest and withhold by robbery the gift which I gave for the honor of God?"

It seems a strange thing and most irregular, but the verdict was actually given against Landulph on the testimony of this wandering rack-heap of unidentified bones. In our day a skeleton would not be allowed to testify at all; for a skeleton has no moral responsibility, and its word could not rationally be trusted. Most skeletons are not to be believed on oath, and this was probably one of them. However, the incident is valuable as preserving to us a curious sample of the quaint laws of evidence of that remote time—a time so remote, so far back toward the beginning of evolution out of original idiocy that the intellectual difference between a bench of judges and a basket of vegetables was as yet so slight that we may say with all confidence that it didn't really exist.

Sunday—During several afternoons I have been engaged in an interesting and maybe useful piece of work—that is to say, I have been trying to make the mighty Jungfrau earn her living—earn it in a most humble sphere, but on a prodigious scale, on a prodigious scale of necessity, for she couldn't do anything in a small way with her size and style. I have been trying to make her do service as a stupendous dial, and check off the hours as they glide across her pallid face up there against the sky, and tell the time of day to the populations lying within fifty miles of her, and to the people in the moon if they have a good telescope there.

Until late in the afternoon the Jungfrau's aspect is that of a spotless desert of snow set upon edge against the sky. But by midafternoon some elevations, which rise out of the western border of the desert, and whose presence you perhaps had not detected or suspected up to that time, begin to cast black shadows eastward across the gleaming surface. At first there is only one shadow; later there are two. Toward 4 p. m. the other day I was gazing and worshiping, as usual, when I chanced to notice that shadow No. 1 was beginning to take to itself something of the shape of a human profile. By 4 the back of the head was good, the military cap was pretty good, the nose was bold and strong, the upper lip sharp, but not pretty, and there was a great goatee that shot straight aggressively forward from the chin.

At 4:30 the nose had changed its shape considerably, and the altered slant of the sun had revealed and made conspicuous a huge buttress or barrier of naked rock, which was so located as to answer very well for a shoulder or coat collar to this swarthy and indiscreet sweetheart who had stolen out there right before everybody to pillow his head on the virgin's white breast and whisper soft sentimentalities to her to the sensuous music of crashing ice domes and the boom and thunder of the passing avalanche—music very familiar to his ear, for he has heard it every afternoon at this hour since the day he first came courting this child of the earth, who lives in the sky; and that day is far back—yes, for he was at this pleasant sport before the middle ages drifted by him in the valley; before the Romans marched past; and before the antique and recordless barbarians fished and hunted here and wondered who he might be, and were probably afraid of him; and before primeval man, himself just emerged from his four-footed estate, stepped out upon this plain, first sample of his race, a thousand centuries ago, and cast a glad eye up there, judging he had found a brother human being and consequently something to kill; and before the big saurians wallowed here, still some æons earlier; O, yes, a day so far back that only the eternal sun himself was present to see that first visit; a day so far back that neither tradition nor history was born yet, and a whole weary eternity must come and go before the restless little creature, of whose face this stupendous Shadow-Face was the prophecy, would arrive in the earth and begin his shabby career, and think it a big thing. O, indeed, yes; when you talk about your poor Roman and Egyptian day-before-yesterday antiquities you should choose a time when the hoary Shadow-Face of the Jungfrau is not by. It antedates all antiquities, known or imaginable; for it was here the world itself created the theater of future antiquities. And it is the only witness with a human face that was there to see that marvel, and remains to us a memorial of it.

By 4:40 p. m. the nose of the shadow is perfect and is beautiful. It is black and powerfully marked against the upright canvas of glowing snow and covers hundreds of acres of that resplendent surface.

Meantime shadow No. 2 has been creeping out well to the rear of the face—west of it—and at 5 o'clock has assumed a shape that has rather a poor and rude semblance of a shoe.

Meantime, also, the great Shadow-Face has been gradually changing for twenty minutes, and now, 5 p. m., is become a quite fair portrait of Roscoe Conkling. The likeness is there and is unmistakable. The goatee is shortened now and has an end; formerly it hadn't any, but ran off eastward and arrived nowhere.

By 6 p. m. the face has dissolved and gone, and the goatee

has become what looks like the shadow of a tower with a pointed roof; and the shoe has turned into what the printers call a "fist" with a finger pointing.

If I were now imprisoned on a mountain summit a hundred miles northward of this point and was denied a timepiece I could get along well enough from 4 till 6 on clear days, for I could keep track of the time by the changing shapes of these mighty shadows on the Virgin's front, the most stupendous dial I am acquainted with, the oldest clock in the world by a couple of million years.

I suppose I should not have noticed the forms of the shadows if I hadn't the habit of hunting for faces in the clouds and in mountain crags — a sort of amusement which is very entertaining, even when you don't find any, and brilliantly satisfying when you do. I have searched through several bushels of photographs of the Jungfrau here, but found only one with the Face in it, and in this case it was not strictly recognizable as a face, which was evidence that the picture was taken before 4 in the afternoon; and also evidence that all the photographers have persistently overlooked one of the most fascinating features of the Jungfrau show. I say, fascinating, because if you once detect a human face produced on a great plan by unconscious Nature you never get tired of watching it. At first you can't make another person see it all; but after he has made it out once he can't see anything else afterward.

The King of Greece is a man who goes around quietly enough when off duty. One day this summer he was traveling in an ordinary first-class compartment, just in his other suit, the one which he works the realm in when he is at home, and so he was not looking like anybody in particular, but a good deal like everybody in general. By and by a hearty and healthy German-American got in and opened up a frank and interested and sympathetic conversation with him, and asked him a couple of thousand questions about himself, which the King answered good-naturedly, but in a more or less indefinite way as to private particulars.

"Where do you live when you are at home?"

"In Greece."

"Greece! Well, now, that is just astonishing. Born there?"

"Yes."

"Do you speak Greek?"

"Yes."

"Now ain't that strange! I never expected to live to see that. What is your trade? I mean, how do you get your living? What is your line of business?"

"Well, I hardly know how to answer. I am only a kind of foreman, on a salary; and the business—well, it's a very general kind of business."

"Yes, I understand—general jobbing—little of everything —anything that there's money in."

"That's about it, yes."

"Are you traveling for the house now?"

"Well, partly, but not entirely. Of course I do a stroke of business if it falls in the way——"

"Good, I like that in you! That's me, every time. Go on."

"I was only going to say I am off on my vacation, now."

"Well, that's all right, no harm in that; a man works all the better for a little let-up now and then. Not that I've been used to having it myself, for I haven't. I reckon this is my first. I was born in Germany, and when I was a couple of weeks old shipped for America, and I've been there ever since, and that's sixty-four years by the watch. I'm an American in principle and German at heart, and it's the boss combination. Well, how do you get along, as a rule—pretty fair?"

"I've a rather large family——"

"There, that's it—big family and trying to raise them on a salary. Now, what did you go and do that for?"

"Well, I thought——"

"Of course you did. You were young and confident and thought you could branch out and make things go with a whirl, and here you are, you see! But never mind about that, I'm not trying to discourage you. Dear me, I've been just where you are myself. You've got good grit; there's good stuff in you, I can see that. You got a wrong start, that's the whole trouble. But you hold your grip, and we'll see what can be done. Your case ain't half as bad as it might be. You are going to come out all right—I'm bail for that. Boys and girls?"

"My family? Yes, some of them are boys——"

"And the rest girls. It's just as I expected. But that's all right, and it's better so, anyway. What are the boys doing— learning a trade?"

"Well, no—I thought——"

"It's a great mistake; it's the biggest mistake you ever made. You've seen that in your own case. A man ought always to have a trade to fall back on. Now, I was a harness-maker at first. Did that prevent me from becoming one of the biggest brewers in America? O, no, I always had the harness trick to fall back on in rough weather. Now if you had learned how to make harness—however, it's too late now, too late; and it's no good plan to cry over spilt milk. But as to the boys, you see—what's to become of them if anything happens to you?"

"It has been my idea to let the eldest one succeed me——"

"O, come! Suppose the firm don't want him?"

"I hadn't thought of that, but——"

"Now look here, you want to get right down to business and stop dreaming. You are capable of immense things— man, you can make a perfect success in life; all you want is somebody to steady you and boost you along on the right road. Do you own anything in the business?"

"No—not exactly; but if I continue to give satisfaction I suppose I can keep my——"

"Keep your place—yes. Well, don't you depend on any-thing of the kind. They'll bounce you the minute you get a little old and worked out; they'll do it, sure. Can't you man-age somehow to get into the firm—that's the great thing, you know."

"I think it is doubtful, in fact, very doubtful."

"Um—that's bad—yes, and unfair, too. Do you suppose if I should go there and have a talk with your people—look here—do you think you could run a brewery?"

"I have never tried, but I think I could do it after I got a little familiarity with the business."

The German was silent for some time. He did a good deal of thinking and the King waited with curiosity to see what the result was going to be. Finally the German said:

"My mind's made up. You leave that crowd—you'll never amount to anything there. In these old countries they never give a fellow a show. Yes, you come over to America—come to my place in Rochester; bring the family along. You shall have a show in the business and the foremanship besides. George—you said your name was George?—I'll make a man of you, I give you my word. You've never had a chance here, but that's all going to change—by gracious, I'll give you a lift that'll make your hair curl!"

*March 6, 1892*

# The £1,000,000 Bank-Note

When I was twenty-seven years old, I was a mining-broker's clerk in San Francisco, and an expert in all the details of stock traffic. I was alone in the world, and had nothing to depend upon but my wits and a clean reputation; but these were setting my feet in the road to eventual fortune, and I was content with the prospect.

My time was my own after the afternoon board, Saturdays, and I was accustomed to put it in on a little sail-boat on the bay. One day I ventured too far, and was carried out to sea. Just at nightfall, when hope was about gone, I was picked up by a small brig which was bound for London. It was a long and stormy voyage, and they made me work my passage without pay, as a common sailor. When I stepped ashore in London my clothes were ragged and shabby, and I had only a dollar in my pocket. This money fed and sheltered me twenty-four hours. During the next twenty-four I went without food and shelter.

About ten o'clock on the following morning, seedy and hungry, I was dragging myself along Portland Place, when a child that was passing, towed by a nursemaid, tossed a luscious big pear—minus one bite—into the gutter. I stopped, of course, and fastened my desiring eye on that muddy treasure. My mouth watered for it, my stomach craved it, my whole being begged for it. But every time I made a move to get it some passing eye detected my purpose, and of course I straightened up, then, and looked indifferent, and pretended that I hadn't been thinking about the pear at all. This same thing kept happening and happening, and I couldn't get the pear. I was just getting desperate enough to brave all the shame, and to seize it, when a window behind me was raised, and a gentleman spoke out of it, saying:

"Step in here, please."

I was admitted by a gorgeous flunkey, and shown into a sumptuous room where a couple of elderly gentlemen were sitting. They sent away the servant, and made me sit down. They had just finished their breakfast, and the sight of the remains of it almost overpowered me. I could hardly keep my wits together in the presence of that food, but as I was not asked to sample it, I had to bear my trouble as best I could.

Now, something had been happening there a little before, which I did not know anything about until a good many days afterward, but I will tell you about it now. Those two old brothers had been having a pretty hot argument a couple of days before, and had ended by agreeing to decide it by a bet, which is the English way of settling everything.

You will remember that the Bank of England once issued two notes of a million pounds each, to be used for a special purpose connected with some public transaction with a foreign country. For some reason or other only one of these had been used and canceled; the other still lay in the vaults of the Bank. Well, the brothers, chatting along, happened to get to wondering what might be the fate of a perfectly honest and intelligent stranger who should be turned adrift in London without a friend, and with no money but that million-pound bank-note, and no way to account for his being in possession of it. Brother A said he would starve to death; Brother B said he wouldn't. Brother A said he couldn't offer it at a bank or anywhere else, because he would be arrested on the spot. So they went on disputing till Brother B said he would bet twenty thousand pounds that the man would live thirty days, *any way*, on that million, and keep out of jail, too. Brother A took him up. Brother B went down to the Bank and bought that note. Just like an Englishman, you see; pluck to the backbone. Then he dictated a letter, which one of his clerks wrote out in a beautiful round hand, and then the two brothers sat at the window a whole day watching for the right man to give it to.

They saw many honest faces go by that were not intelligent enough; many that were intelligent, but not honest enough; many that were both, but the possessors were not poor enough, or, if poor enough, were not strangers. There was always a defect, until I came along; but they agreed that I filled the bill all around; so they elected me unanimously, and there I was, now, waiting to know why I was called in. They began to ask me questions about myself, and pretty soon they had my story. Finally they told me I would answer their purpose. I said I was sincerely glad, and asked what it was. Then one of them handed me an envelop, and said I would find the explanation inside. I was going to open it, but he said no; take it to my lodgings, and look it over carefully, and not be hasty or rash. I was puzzled, and wanted to discuss the matter a little further, but they did n't; so I took my leave, feeling hurt and insulted to be made the butt of what was apparently some kind of a practical joke, and yet obliged to put up with it, not being in circumstances to resent affronts from rich and strong folk.

I would have picked up the pear, now, and eaten it before all the world, but it was gone; so I had lost that by this unlucky business, and the thought of it did not soften my feeling toward those men. As soon as I was out of sight of that house I opened my envelop, and saw that it contained money! My opinion of those people changed, I can tell you! I lost not a moment, but shoved note and money into my vest-pocket, and broke for the nearest cheap eating-house. Well, how I did eat! When at last I could n't hold any more, I took out my money and unfolded it, took one glimpse and nearly fainted. Five millions of dollars! Why, it made my head swim.

I must have sat there stunned and blinking at the note as much as a minute before I came rightly to myself again. The first thing I noticed, then, was the landlord. His eye was on the note, and he was petrified. He was worshiping, with all his body and soul, but he looked as if he could n't stir hand or foot. I took my cue in a moment, and did the only rational thing there was to do. I reached the note toward him, and said carelessly:

"Give me the change, please."

Then he was restored to his normal condition, and made a thousand apologies for not being able to break the bill, and I could n't get him to touch it. He wanted to look at it, and keep on looking at it; he could n't seem to get enough of it to quench the thirst of his eye, but he shrank from touching it as if it had been something too sacred for poor common clay to handle. I said:

"I am sorry if it is an inconvenience, but I must insist. Please change it; I have n't anything else."

But he said that was n't any matter; he was quite willing to

let the trifle stand over till another time. I said I might not be
in his neighborhood again for a good while; but he said it
was of no consequence, he could wait, and, moreover, I could
have anything I wanted, any time I chose, and let the account
run as long as I pleased. He said he hoped he was n't afraid to
trust as rich a gentleman as I was, merely because I was of a
merry disposition, and chose to play larks on the public in the
matter of dress. By this time another customer was entering,
and the landlord hinted to me to put the monster out of
sight; then he bowed me all the way to the door, and I started
straight for that house and those brothers, to correct the mistake which had been made before the police should hunt me
up, and help me do it. I was pretty nervous, in fact pretty
badly frightened, though, of course, I was no way in fault;
but I knew men well enough to know that when they find
they 've given a tramp a million-pound bill when they
thought it was a one-pounder, they are in a frantic rage
against *him* instead of quarreling with their own near-sight-
edness, as they ought. As I approached the house my excitement began to abate, for all was quiet there, which made me
feel pretty sure the blunder was not discovered yet. I rang.
The same servant appeared. I asked for those gentlemen.

"They are gone." This in the lofty, cold way of that fellow's tribe.

"Gone? Gone where?"

"On a journey."

"But whereabouts?"

"To the Continent, I think."

"The Continent?"

"Yes, sir."

"Which way — by what route?"

"I can't say, sir."

"When will they be back?"

"In a month, they said."

"A month! Oh, this is awful! Give me *some* sort of idea of
how to get a word to them. It 's of the last importance."

"I can't, indeed. I 've no idea where they 've gone, sir."

"Then I must see some member of the family."

"Family 's away too; been abroad months — in Egypt and
India, I think."

"Man, there's been an immense mistake made. They'll be back before night. Will you tell them I've been here, and that I will keep coming till it's all made right, and they need n't be afraid?"

"I'll tell them, if they come back, but I am not expecting them. They said you would be here in an hour to make inquiries, but I must tell you it's all right, they'll be here on time and expect you."

So I had to give it up and go away. What a riddle it all was! I was like to lose my mind. They would be here "on time." What could that mean? Oh, the letter would explain, maybe. I had forgotten the letter; I got it out and read it. This is what it said:

You are an intelligent and honest man, as one may see by your face. We conceive you to be poor and a stranger. Inclosed you will find a sum of money. It is lent to you for thirty days, without interest. Report at this house at the end of that time. I have a bet on you. If I win it you shall have any situation that is in my gift—any, that is, that you shall be able to prove yourself familiar with and competent to fill.

No signature, no address, no date.

Well, here was a coil to be in! You are posted on what had preceded all this, but I was not. It was just a deep, dark puzzle to me. I had n't the least idea what the game was, nor whether harm was meant me or a kindness. I went into a park, and sat down to try to think it out, and to consider what I had best do.

At the end of an hour, my reasonings had crystallized into this verdict.

Maybe those men mean me well, maybe they mean me ill; no way to decide that—let it go. They've got a game, or a scheme, or an experiment, of some kind on hand; no way to determine what it is—let it go. There's a bet on me; no way to find out what it is—let it go. That disposes of the indeterminable quantities; the remainder of the matter is tangible, solid, and may be classed and labeled with certainty. If I ask the Bank of England to place this bill to the credit of the man it belongs to, they'll do it, for they know him, although I don't; but they will ask me how I came in possession of it, and if I tell the truth, they'll put me in the asylum, naturally, and a lie will land me in jail. The same result would follow if I tried to bank the bill anywhere or to borrow money on it. I have got to carry this immense burden around until those men come back, whether I want to or not. It is useless to me, as useless as a handful of ashes, and yet I must take care of it, and watch over it, while I beg my living. I could n't *give* it away, if I should try, for neither honest citizen nor highwayman would accept it or meddle with it for anything. Those brothers are safe. Even if I lose their bill, or burn it, they are still safe, because they can stop payment, and the Bank will make them whole; but meantime, I've got to do a month's suffering without wages or profit—unless I help win that bet, whatever it may be, and get that situation that I am promised. I *should* like to get that; men of their sort have situations in their gift that are worth having.

I got to thinking a good deal about that situation. My hopes began to rise high. Without doubt the salary would be large. It would begin in a month; after that I should be all right. Pretty soon I was feeling first rate. By this time I was tramping the streets again. The sight of a tailor-shop gave me a sharp longing to shed my rags, and to clothe myself decently once more. Could I afford it? No; I had nothing in the world but a million pounds. So I forced myself to go on by. But soon I was drifting back again. The temptation persecuted me cruelly. I must have passed that shop back and forth six times during that manful struggle. At last I gave in; I had to. I asked if they had a misfit suit that had been thrown on their hands. The fellow I spoke to nodded his head toward another fellow, and gave me no answer. I went to the indicated fellow, and he indicated another fellow with *his* head, and no words. I went to him, and he said:

" 'Tend to you presently."

I waited till he was done with what he was at, then he took me into a back room, and overhauled a pile of rejected suits, and selected the rattiest one for me. I put it on. It did n't fit, and was n't in any way attractive, but it was new, and I was anxious to have it; so I did n't find any fault, but said with some diffidence:

"It would be an accommodation to me if you could wait

some days for the money. I have n't any small change about me."

The fellow worked up a most sarcastic expression of countenance, and said:

"Oh, you have n't? Well, of course, I did n't expect it. I 'd only expect gentlemen like you to carry large change."

I was nettled, and said:

"My friend, you should n't judge a stranger always by the clothes he wears. I am quite able to pay for this suit; I simply did n't wish to put you to the trouble of changing a large note."

He modified his style a little at that, and said, though still with something of an air:

"I did n't mean any particular harm, but as long as rebukes are going, I might say it was n't quite your affair to jump to the conclusion that we could n't change any note that you might happen to be carrying around. On the contrary, we *can*."

I handed the note to him, and said:

"Oh, very well; I apologize."

He received it with a smile, one of those large smiles which goes all around over, and has folds in it, and wrinkles, and spirals, and looks like the place where you have thrown a brick in a pond; and then in the act of his taking a glimpse of the bill this smile froze solid, and turned yellow, and looked like those wavy, wormy spreads of lava which you find hardened on little levels on the side of Vesuvius. I never before saw a smile caught like that, and perpetuated. The man stood there holding the bill, and looking like that, and the proprietor hustled up to see what was the matter, and said briskly:

"Well, what 's up? what 's the trouble? what 's wanting?"

I said: "There is n't any trouble. I 'm waiting for my change."

"Come, come; get him his change, Tod; get him his change."

Tod retorted: "Get him his change! It 's easy to say, sir; but look at the bill yourself."

The proprietor took a look, gave a low, eloquent whistle, then made a dive for the pile of rejected clothing, and began to snatch it this way and that, talking all the time excitedly, and as if to himself:

"Sell an eccentric millionaire such an unspeakable suit as

that! Tod's a fool—a born fool. Always doing something like this. Drives every millionaire away from this place, because he can't tell a millionaire from a tramp, and never could. Ah, here's the thing I'm after. Please get those things off, sir, and throw them in the fire. Do me the favor to put on this shirt and this suit; it's just the thing, the very thing—plain, rich, modest, and just ducally nobby; made to order for a foreign prince—you may know him, sir, his Serene Highness the Hospodar of Halifax; had to leave it with us and take a mourning-suit because his mother was going to die—which she didn't. But that's all right; we can't always have things the way we—that is, the way they—there! trousers all right, they fit you to a charm, sir; now the waistcoat; aha, right again! now the coat—lord! look at that, now! Perfect— the whole thing! I never saw such a triumph in all my experience."

I expressed my satisfaction.

"Quite right, sir, quite right; it'll do for a makeshift, I'm bound to say. But wait till you see what we'll get up for you on your own measure. Come, Tod, book and pen; get at it. Length of leg, 32"—and so on. Before I could get in a word he had measured me, and was giving orders for dress-suits, morning-suits, shirts, and all sorts of things. When I got a chance I said:

"But, my dear sir, I *can't* give these orders, unless you can wait indefinitely, or change the bill."

"Indefinitely! It's a weak word, sir, a weak word. Eternally—*that's* the word, sir. Tod, rush these things through, and send them to the gentleman's address without any waste of time. Let the minor customers wait. Set down the gentleman's address and—"

"I'm changing my quarters. I will drop in and leave the new address."

"Quite right, sir, quite right. One moment—let me show you out, sir. There—good day, sir, good day."

Well, don't you see what was bound to happen? I drifted naturally into buying whatever I wanted, and asking for change. Within a week I was sumptuously equipped with all needful comforts and luxuries, and was housed in an expensive private hotel in Hanover Square. I took my dinners there, but for breakfast I stuck by Harris's humble feeding-house, where I had got my first meal on my million-pound bill. I was the making of Harris. The fact had gone all abroad that the foreign crank who carried million-pound bills in his vest-pocket was the patron saint of the place. That was enough. From being a poor, struggling, little hand-to-mouth enterprise, it had become celebrated, and overcrowded with customers. Harris was so grateful that he forced loans upon me, and would not be denied; and so, pauper as I was, I had money to spend, and was living like the rich and the great. I judged that there was going to be a crash by and by, but I was in, now, and must swim across or drown. You see there was just that element of impending disaster to give a serious side, a sober side, yes, a tragic side, to a state of things which would otherwise have been purely ridiculous. In the night, in the dark, the tragedy part was always to the front, and always warning, always threatening; and so I moaned and tossed, and sleep was hard to find. But in the cheerful daylight the tragedy element faded out and disappeared, and I walked on air, and was happy to giddiness, to intoxication, you may say.

And it was natural; for I had become one of the notorieties of the metropolis of the world, and it turned my head, not just a little, but a good deal. You could not take up a newspaper, English, Scotch, or Irish, without finding in it one or more references to the "vest-pocket million-pounder" and his latest doings and sayings. At first, in these mentions, I was at the bottom of the personal-gossip column; next, I was listed above the knights, next above the baronets, next above the barons, and so on, and so on, climbing steadily, as my notoriety augmented, until I reached the highest altitude possible, and there I remained, taking precedence of all dukes not royal, and of all ecclesiastics except the primate of all England. But mind, this was not fame; as yet I had achieved only notoriety. Then came the climaxing stroke—the accolade, so to speak—which in a single instant transmuted the perishable dross of notoriety into the enduring gold of fame: "Punch" caricatured me! Yes, I was a made man, now; my place was established. I might be joked about still, but reverently, not hilariously, not rudely; I could be smiled at, but not laughed at. The time for that had gone by. "Punch" pictured me all

a-flutter with rags, dickering with a beef-eater for the Tower
of London. Well, you can imagine how it was with a young
fellow who had never been taken notice of before, and now
all of a sudden couldn't say a thing that wasn't taken up and
repeated everywhere; couldn't stir abroad without constantly
overhearing the remark flying from lip to lip, "There he goes;
that's him!" couldn't take his breakfast without a crowd to
look on; couldn't appear in an opera-box without concentrat-
ing there the fire of a thousand lorgnettes. Why, I just swam
in glory all day long—that is the amount of it.

You know, I even kept my old suit of rags, and every now
and then appeared in them, so as to have the old pleasure of
buying trifles, and being insulted, and then shooting the
scoffer dead with the million-pound bill. But I couldn't keep
that up. The illustrated papers made the outfit so familiar that
when I went out in it I was at once recognized and followed
by a crowd, and if I attempted a purchase the man would
offer me his whole shop on credit before I could pull my note
on him.

About the tenth day of my fame I went to fulfill my duty to
my flag by paying my respects to the American minister. He
received me with the enthusiasm proper in my case, upbraided me for being so tardy in my duty, and said that there
was only one way to get his forgiveness, and that was to take
the seat at his dinner-party that night made vacant by the
illness of one of his guests. I said I would, and we got to
talking. It turned out that he and my father had been schoolmates in boyhood, Yale students together later, and always
warm friends up to my father's death. So then he required me
to put in at his house all the odd time I might have to spare,
and I was very willing, of course.

In fact I was more than willing; I was glad. When the crash
should come, he might somehow be able to save me from
total destruction; I didn't know how, but he might think of a
way, maybe. I couldn't venture to unbosom myself to him at
this late date, a thing which I would have been quick to do in
the beginning of this awful career of mine in London. No, I
couldn't venture it now; I was in too deep; that is, too deep
for me to be risking revelations to so new a friend, though
not yet clear beyond my depth, as *I* looked at it. Because, you

see, with all my borrowing, I was carefully keeping within my means—I mean within my salary. Of course I could n't *know* what my salary was going to be, but I had a good enough basis for an estimate in the fact that, if I won the bet, I was to have *choice* of any situation in that rich old gentleman's gift provided I was competent—and I should certainly prove competent; I had n't any doubt about that. And as to the bet, I was n't worrying about that; I had always been lucky. Now my estimate of the salary was six hundred to a thousand a year; say, six hundred for the first year, and so on up year by year, till I struck the upper figure by proved merit. At present I was only in debt for my first year's salary. Everybody had been trying to lend me money, but I had fought off the most of them on one pretext or another; so this indebtedness represented only £300 borrowed money, the other £300 represented my keep and my purchases. I believed my second year's salary would carry me through the rest of the month if I went on being cautious and economical, and I intended to look sharply out for that. My month ended, my employer back from his journey, I should be all right once more, for I should at once divide the two years' salary among my creditors by assignment, and get right down to my work.

It was a lovely dinner-party of fourteen. The Duke and Duchess of Shoreditch, and their daughter the Lady Anne-Grace-Eleanor-Celeste-and-so-forth-and-so-forth-de-Bohun, the Earl and Countess of Newgate, Viscount Cheapside, Lord and Lady Blatherskite, some untitled people of both sexes, the minister and his wife and daughter, and this daughter's visiting friend, an English girl of twenty-two, named Portia Langham, whom I fell in love with in two minutes, and she with me—I could see it without glasses. There was still another guest, an American—but I am a little ahead of my story. While the people were still in the drawing-room, whetting up for dinner, and coldly inspecting the late comers, the servant announced:

"Mr. Lloyd Hastings."

The moment the usual civilities were over, Hastings caught sight of me, and came straight with cordially outstretched hand; then stopped short when about to shake, and said with an embarrassed look:

"I beg your pardon, sir, I thought I knew you."

"Why, you do know me, old fellow."

"No! Are *you* the—the—"

"Vest-pocket monster? I am, indeed. Don't be afraid to call me by my nickname; I'm used to it."

"Well, well, well, this is a surprise. Once or twice I've seen your own name coupled with the nickname, but it never occurred to me that *you* could be the Henry Adams referred to. Why, it isn't six months since you were clerking away for Blake Hopkins in Frisco on a salary, and sitting up nights on an extra allowance, helping me arrange and verify the Gould and Curry Extension papers and statistics. The idea of your being in London, and a vast millionaire, and a colossal celebrity! Why, it's the Arabian Nights come again. Man, I can't take it in at all; can't realize it; give me time to settle the whirl in my head."

"The fact is, Lloyd, you are no worse off than I am. I can't realize it myself."

"Dear me, it *is* stunning, now isn't it? Why, it's just three months to-day since we went to the Miners' restaurant—"

"No, the What Cheer."

"Right, it *was* the What Cheer; went there at two in the morning, and had a chop and coffee after a hard six hours' grind over those Extension papers, and I tried to persuade you to come to London with me, and offered to get leave of absence for you and pay all your expenses, and give you something over if I succeeded in making the sale; and you would not listen to me, said I wouldn't succeed, and you couldn't afford to lose the run of business and be no end of time getting the hang of things again when you got back home. And yet here you are. How odd it all is! How did you happen to come, and whatever *did* give you this incredible start?"

"Oh, just an accident. It's a long story—a romance, a body may say. I'll tell you all about it, but not now."

"When?"

"The end of this month."

"That's more than a fortnight yet. It's too much of a strain on a person's curiosity. Make it a week."

"I can't. You'll know why, by and by. But how's the trade getting along?"

His cheerfulness vanished like a breath, and he said with a sigh:

"You were a true prophet, Hal, a true prophet. I wish I had n't come. I don't want to talk about it."

"But you must. You must come and stop with me to-night, when we leave here, and tell me all about it."

"Oh, may I? Are you in earnest?" and the water showed in his eyes.

"Yes; I want to hear the whole story, every word."

"I 'm so grateful! Just to find a human interest once more, in some voice and in some eye, in me and affairs of mine, after what I 've been through here—lord! I could go down on my knees for it!"

He gripped my hand hard, and braced up, and was all right and lively after that for the dinner—which did n't come off. No; the usual thing happened, the thing that is always happening under that vicious and aggravating English system—the matter of precedence could n't be settled, and so there was no dinner. Englishmen always eat dinner before they go out to dinner, because *they* know the risks they are running; but nobody ever warns the stranger, and so he walks placidly into the trap. Of course nobody was hurt this time, because we had all been to dinner, none of us being novices except Hastings, and he having been informed by the minister at the time that he invited him that in deference to the English custom he had not provided any dinner. Everybody took a lady and processioned down to the dining-room, because it is usual to go through the motions; but there the dispute began. The Duke of Shoreditch wanted to take precedence, and sit at the head of the table, holding that he outranked a minister who represented merely a nation and not a monarch; but I stood for my rights, and refused to yield. In the gossip column I ranked all dukes not royal, and said so, and claimed precedence of this one. It could n't be settled, of course, struggle as we might and did, he finally (and injudiciously) trying to play birth and antiquity, and I "seeing" his Conqueror and "raising" him with Adam, whose direct posterity I was, as shown by my name, while *he* was of a collateral branch, as shown by *his*, and by his recent Norman origin; so we all processioned back to the drawing-room again and had a perpendicular lunch—plate of sardines and a strawberry, and you group yourself and stand up and eat it. Here the religion of precedence is not so strenuous; the two persons of highest rank chuck up a shilling, the one that wins has first go at his strawberry, and the loser gets the shilling. The next two chuck up, then the next two, and so on. After refreshment, tables were brought, and we all played cribbage, sixpence a game. The English never play any game for amusement. If they can't make something or lose something,—they don't care which,—they won't play.

We had a lovely time; certainly two of us had, Miss Langham and I. I was so bewitched with her that I could n't count my hands if they went above a double sequence; and when I struck home I never discovered it, and started up the outside row again, and would have lost the game every time, only the girl did the same, she being in just my condition, you see; and consequently neither of us ever got out, or cared to wonder why we did n't; we only just knew we were happy, and did n't wish to know anything else, and did n't want to be interrupted. And I *told* her—I did indeed—told her I loved her; and she—well, she blushed till her hair turned red, but she liked it; she *said* she did. Oh, there was never such an evening! Every time I pegged I put on a postscript; every time she pegged she acknowledged receipt of it, counting the hands the same. Why, I could n't even say "Two for his heels" without adding, "*My*, how sweet you do look!" and she would say, "Fifteen two, fifteen four, fifteen six, and a pair are eight, and eight are sixteen—*do* you think so?"—peeping out aslant from under her lashes, you know, so sweet and cunning. Oh, it was just *too*-too!

Well, I was perfectly honest and square with her; told her I had n't a cent in the world but just the million-pound note she 'd heard so much talk about, and *it* did n't belong to me; and that started her curiosity, and then I talked low, and told her the whole history right from the start, and it nearly killed her, laughing. What in the nation she could find to laugh about, *I* could n't see, but there it was; every half minute some new detail would fetch her, and I would have to stop as much as a minute and a half to give her a chance to settle down again. Why, she laughed herself lame, she did indeed; I never saw anything like it. I mean I never saw a painful

story—a story of a person's troubles and worries and fears—
produce just *that* kind of effect before. So I loved her all the
more, seeing she could be so cheerful when there was n't anything to be cheerful about; for I might soon need that kind of
wife, you know, the way things looked. Of course I told her
we should have to wait a couple of years, till I could catch up
on my salary; but she did n't mind that, only she hoped I
would be as careful as possible in the matter of expenses, and
not let them run the least risk of trenching on our third year's
pay. Then she began to get a little worried, and wondered if
we were making any mistake, and starting the salary on a
higher figure for the first year than I would get. This was
good sense, and it made me feel a little less confident than I
had been feeling before; but it gave me a good business idea,
and I brought it frankly out.

"Portia, dear, would you mind going with me that day,
when I confront those old gentlemen?"

She shrank a little, but said:

"N-o; if my being with you would help hearten you. But—
would it be quite proper, do you think?"

"No, I don't know that it would; in fact I'm afraid it
would n't: but you see, there's so *much* dependent upon it
that—"

"Then I'll go anyway, proper or improper," she said, with
a beautiful and generous enthusiasm. "Oh, I shall be so happy
to think I'm helping."

"Helping, dear? Why, you'll be doing it all. You're so
beautiful and so lovely and so winning, that with you there I
can pile our salary up till I break those good old fellows, and
they'll never have the heart to struggle."

Sho! you should have seen the rich blood mount, and her
happy eyes shine!

"You wicked flatterer! There is n't a word of truth in what
you say, but still I'll go with you. Maybe it will teach you not
to expect other people to look with your eyes."

Were my doubts dissipated? Was my confidence restored?
You may judge by this fact: privately I raised my salary to
twelve hundred the first year on the spot. But I did n't tell
her; I saved it for a surprise.

All the way home I was in the clouds, Hastings talking, I

not hearing a word. When he and I entered my parlor, he brought me to myself with his fervent appreciations of my manifold comforts and luxuries.

"Let me just stand here a little and look my fill! Dear me, it's a palace; it's just a palace! And in it everything a body *could* desire, including cozy coal fire and supper standing ready. Henry, it does n't merely make me realize how rich you are; it makes me realize, to the bone, to the marrow, how poor I am—how poor I am, and how miserable, how defeated, routed, annihilated!"

Plague take it! this language gave me the cold shudders. It scared me broad awake, and made me comprehend that I was standing on a half-inch crust, with a crater underneath. *I* did n't know I had been dreaming—that is, I had n't been allowing myself to know it for a while back; but *now*—oh, dear! Deep in debt, not a cent in the world, a lovely girl's happiness or woe in my hands, and nothing in front of me but a salary which might never—oh, *would* never—materialize! Oh, oh, oh, I am ruined past hope; nothing can save me!

"Henry, the mere unconsidered drippings of your daily income would—"

"Oh, my daily income! Here, down with this hot Scotch, and cheer up your soul. Here's with you! Or, no—you're hungry; sit down and—"

"Not a bite for me; I'm past it. I can't eat, these days; but I'll drink with you till I drop. Come!"

"Barrel for barrel, I'm with you! Ready? Here we go! Now, then, Lloyd, unreel your story while I brew."

"Unreel it? What, again?"

"Again? What do you mean by that?"

"Why, I mean do you want to hear it *over* again?"

"Do I want to hear it *over* again? This *is* a puzzler. Wait; don't take any more of that liquid. You don't need it."

"Look here, Henry, you alarm me. Did n't I tell you the whole story on the way here?"

"You?"

"Yes, I."

"I'll be hanged if I heard a word of it."

"Henry, this is a serious thing. It troubles me. What did you take up yonder at the minister's?"

Then it all flashed on me, and I owned up, like a man.

"I took the dearest girl in this world—prisoner!"

So then he came with a rush, and we shook, and shook, and shook till our hands ached; and he did n't blame me for not having heard a word of a story which had lasted while we walked three miles. He just sat down then, like the patient, good fellow he was, and told it all over again. Synopsized, it amounted to this: He had come to England with what he thought was a grand opportunity; he had an "option" to sell the Gould and Curry Extension for the "locators" of it, and keep all he could get over a million dollars. He had worked hard, had pulled every wire he knew of, had left no honest expedient untried, had spent nearly all the money he had in the world, had not been able to get a solitary capitalist to listen to him, and his option would run out at the end of the month. In a word, he was ruined. Then he jumped up and cried out:

"Henry, you can save me! You can save me, and you 're the only man in the universe that can. Will you do it? *Won't* you do it?"

"Tell me how. Speak out, my boy."

"Give me a million and my passage home for my 'option'! Don't, *don't* refuse!"

I was in a kind of agony. I was right on the point of coming out with the words, "Lloyd, I 'm a pauper myself—absolutely penniless, and in *debt*!" But a white-hot idea came flaming through my head, and I gripped my jaws together, and calmed myself down till I was as cold as a capitalist. Then I said, in a commercial and self-possessed way:

"I will save you, Lloyd—"

"Then I 'm already saved! God be merciful to you forever! If ever I—"

"Let me finish, Lloyd. I will save you, but not in that way; for that would not be fair to you, after your hard work, and the risks you 've run. I don't need to buy mines; I can keep my capital moving, in a commercial center like London without that; it 's what I 'm at, all the time; but here is what I 'll do. I know all about that mine, of course; I know its immense value, and can swear to it if anybody wishes it. You shall sell out inside of the fortnight for three millions cash, using my name freely, and we 'll divide, share and share alike."

Do you know, he would have danced the furniture to kindling-wood in his insane joy, and broken everything on the place, if I had n't tripped him up and tied him.

Then he lay there, perfectly happy, saying:

"I may use your name! Your name—think of it! Man, they 'll flock in droves, these rich Londoners; they 'll *fight* for that stock! I 'm a made man, I 'm a made man forever, and I 'll never forget you as long as I live!"

In less than twenty-four hours London was abuzz! I had n't anything to do, day after day, but sit at home, and say to all comers:

"Yes; I told him to refer to me. I know the man, and I know the mine. His character is above reproach, and the mine is worth far more than he asks for it."

Meantime I spent all my evenings at the minister's with Portia. I did n't say a word to her about the mine; I saved it for a surprise. We talked salary; never anything but salary and love; sometimes love, sometimes salary, sometimes love and salary together. And my! the interest the minister's wife and daughter took in our little affair, and the endless ingenuities they invented to save us from interruption, and to keep the minister in the dark and unsuspicious—well, it was just lovely of them!

When the month was up, at last, I had a million dollars to my credit in the London and County Bank, and Hastings was fixed in the same way. Dressed at my level best, I drove by the house in Portland Place, judged by the look of things that my birds were home again, went on toward the minister's and got my precious, and we started back, talking salary with all our might. She was so excited and anxious that it made her just intolerably beautiful. I said:

"Dearie, the way you 're looking it 's a crime to strike for a salary a single penny under three thousand a year."

"Henry, Henry, you 'll ruin us!"

"Don't you be afraid. Just keep up those looks, and trust to me. It 'll all come out right."

So as it turned out, I had to keep bolstering up *her* courage all the way. She kept pleading with me, and saying:

"Oh, please remember that if we ask for too much we may get no salary at all; and then what will become of us, with no way in the world to earn our living?"

We were ushered in by that same servant, and there they were, the two old gentlemen. Of course they were surprised to see that wonderful creature with me, but I said:

"It's all right, gentlemen; she is my future stay and helpmate."

And I introduced them to her, and called them by name. It did n't surprise them; they knew I would know enough to consult the directory. They seated us, and were very polite to me, and very solicitous to relieve her from embarrassment, and put her as much at her ease as they could. Then I said:

"Gentlemen, I am ready to report."

"We are glad to hear it," said *my* man, "for now we can decide the bet which my brother Abel and I made. If you have won for me, you shall have any situation in my gift. Have you the million-pound note?"

"Here it is, sir," and I handed it to him.

"I've won!" he shouted, and slapped Abel on the back. "*Now* what do you say, brother?"

"I say he *did* survive, and I've lost twenty thousand pounds. I never would have believed it."

"I've a further report to make," I said, "and a pretty long one. I want you to let me come soon, and detail my whole month's history; and I promise you it's worth hearing. Meantime, take a look at that."

"What, man! Certificate of deposit for £200,000? Is it yours?"

"Mine. I earned it by thirty days' judicious use of that little loan you let me have. And the only use I made of it was to buy trifles and offer the bill in change."

"Come, this is astonishing! It's incredible, man!"

"Never mind, I'll prove it. Don't take my word unsupported."

But now Portia's turn was come to be surprised. Her eyes were spread wide, and she said:

"Henry, is that really your money? Have you been fibbing to me?"

"I have indeed, dearie. But you'll forgive me, *I* know."

She put up an arch pout, and said:

"Don't you be so sure. You are a naughty thing to deceive me so!"

"Oh, you'll get over it, sweetheart, you'll get over it; it was only fun, you know. Come, let's be going."

"But wait, wait! The situation, you know. I want to give you the situation," said my man.

"Well," I said, "I'm just as grateful as I can be, but really I don't want one."

"But you can have the very choicest one in my gift."

"Thanks again, with all my heart; but I don't even want *that* one."

"Henry, I'm ashamed of you. You don't half thank the good gentleman. May I do it for you?"

"Indeed you shall, dear, if you can improve it. Let us see you try."

She walked to my man, got up in his lap, put her arm round his neck, and kissed him right on the mouth. Then the two old gentlemen shouted with laughter, but I was dumfounded, just petrified, as you may say. Portia said:

"Papa, he has said you haven't a situation in your gift that he'd take; and I feel just as hurt as—"

"My darling!—is that your papa?"

"Yes; he's my steppapa, and the dearest one that ever was. You understand now, don't you, why I was able to laugh when you told me at the minister's, not knowing my relationships, what trouble and worry papa's and Uncle Abel's scheme was giving you?"

Of course I spoke right up, now, without any fooling, and went straight to the point.

"Oh, my dearest dear sir, I want to take back what I said. You *have* got a situation open that I want."

"Name it."

"Son-in-law."

"Well, well, well! But you know, if you haven't ever served in that capacity, you of course can't furnish recommendations of a sort to satisfy the conditions of the contract, and so—"

"Try me—oh, do, I beg of you! Only just try me thirty or forty years, and if—"

"Oh, well, all right; it's but a little thing to ask. Take her along."

Happy, we two? There're not words enough in the unabridged to describe it. And when London got the whole history, a day or two later, of my month's adventures with that bank-note, and how they ended, did London talk, and have a good time? Yes.

My Portia's papa took that friendly and hospitable bill back to the Bank of England and cashed it; then the Bank canceled it and made him a present of it, and he gave it to us at our wedding, and it has always hung in its frame in the sacredest place in our home, ever since. For it gave me my Portia. But for it I could not have remained in London, would not have appeared at the minister's, never should have met her. And so I always say, "Yes, it's a million-pounder, as you see; but it never made but one purchase in its life, and *then* got the article for only about a tenth part of its value."

*January 1893*

# About All Kinds of Ships

## The Modern Steamer and the Obsolete Steamer.

We are victims of one common superstition—the superstition that we realize the changes that are daily taking place in the world because we read about them and know what they are. I should not have supposed that the modern ship could be a surprise to me, but it is. It seems to be as much of a surprise to me as it could have been if I had never read anything about it. I walk about this great vessel, the "Havel," as she plows her way through the Atlantic, and every detail that comes under my eye brings up the miniature counterpart of it as it existed in the little ships I crossed the ocean in, fourteen, seventeen, eighteen, and twenty years ago.

In the "Havel" one can be in several respects more comfortable than he can be in the best hotels on the continent of Europe. For instance, she has several bath rooms, and they are as convenient and as nicely equipped as the bath rooms in a fine private house in America; whereas in the hotels of the continent one bath room is considered sufficient, and it is generally shabby and located in some out of the way corner of the house; moreover, you need to give notice so long beforehand that you get over wanting a bath by the time you get it. In the hotels there are a good many different kinds of noises, and they spoil sleep; in my room in the ship I hear no sounds. In the hotels they usually shut off the electric light at midnight; in the ship one may burn it in one's room all night.

In the steamer "Batavia," twenty years ago, one candle, set in the bulkhead between two state-rooms, was there to light both rooms, but did not light either of them. It was extinguished at 11 at night, and so were all the saloon lamps except one or two, which were left burning to help the passenger see how to break his neck trying to get around in the dark. The passengers sat at table on long benches made of the hardest kind of wood; in the "Havel" one sits on a swivel chair with a cushioned back to it. In those old times the dinner bill of fare was always the same: a pint of some simple, homely soup or other, boiled codfish and potatoes, slab of boiled beef, stewed prunes for dessert—on Sundays "dog in a blanket," on Thursdays "plum duff." In the modern ship the menu is choice and elaborate, and is changed daily. In the old times dinner was a sad occasion; in our day a concealed orchestra enlivens it with charming music. In the old days the decks were always wet, in our day they are usually dry, for the promenade-deck is roofed over, and a sea seldom comes aboard. In a moderately disturbed sea, in the old days, a landsman could hardly keep his legs, but in such a sea in our day, the decks are as level as a table. In the old days the inside of a ship was the plainest and barrenest thing, and the most dismal and uncomfortable that ingenuity could devise; the modern ship is a marvel of rich and costly decoration and sumptuous appointment, and is equipped with every comfort and convenience that money can buy. The old ships had no place of assembly but the dining-room, the new ones have several spacious and beautiful drawing-rooms. The old ships offered the passenger no chance to smoke except in the place that was called the "fiddle." It was a repulsive den made of rough boards (full of cracks) and its office was to protect the main hatch. It was grimy and dirty; there were no seats; the only light was a lamp of the rancid-oil-and-rag kind; the place was very cold, and never dry, for the seas broke in through the cracks every little while and drenched the cavern thoroughly. In the modern ship there are three or four large smoking-rooms, and they have card tables and cushioned sofas, and are heated by steam and lighted by electricity. There are few European hotels with such smoking-rooms.

The former ships were built of wood, and had two or three water-tight compartments in the hold with doors in them which were often left open, particularly when the ship was going to hit a rock. The modern leviathan is built of steel, and the water-tight bulkheads have no doors in them; they divide the ship into nine or ten water-tight compartments and endow her with as many lives as a cat. Their complete efficiency was established by the happy results following the memorable accident to the City of Paris a year or two ago.

One curious thing which is at once noticeable in the great modern ship is the absence of hubbub, clatter, rush of feet, roaring of orders. That is all gone by. The elaborate manœuvres necessary in working the vessel into her dock are conducted without sound; one sees nothing of the processes, hears no commands. A Sabbath stillness and solemnity reign, in place of the turmoil and racket of the earlier days. The modern ship has a spacious bridge fenced chin-high with sailcloth, and floored with wooden gratings; and this bridge, with its fenced fore-and-aft annexes, could accommodate a seated audience of a hundred and fifty men. There are three steering equipments, each competent if the others should break. From the bridge the ship is steered, and also handled. The handling is not done by shout or whistle, but by signaling with patent automatic gongs. There are three tell-tales, with plainly lettered dials—for steering, handling the engines, and for communicating orders to the invisible mates who are conducting the landing of the ship or casting off. The officer who is astern is out of sight and too far away to hear trumpet calls; but the gongs near him tell him to haul in, pay out, make fast, let go, and so on; he hears, but the passengers do not, and so the ship seems to land herself without human help.

This great bridge is thirty or forty feet above the water, but the sea climbs up there sometimes; so there is another bridge twelve or fifteen feet higher still, for use in these emergencies. The force of water is a strange thing. It slips between one's fingers like air, but upon occasion it acts like a solid body and will bend a thin iron rod. In the "Havel" it has splintered a heavy oaken rail into broom-straws instead of merely breaking it in two as would have been the seemingly natural thing for it to do. At the time of the awful Johnstown disaster, according to the testimony of several witnesses, rocks were carried some distance on the surface of the stupendous torrent; and at St. Helena, many years ago, a vast sea-wave carried a battery of cannon forty feet up a steep slope and deposited the guns there in a row. But the water has done a still stranger thing, and it is one which is credibly vouched for. A marlinspike is an implement about a foot long which tapers from its butt to the other extremity and ends in a sharp point. It is made of iron and is heavy. A wave came aboard a ship in a storm and raged aft, breast high, carrying a marlinspike point-first with it, and with such lightning-like swiftness and force as to drive it three or four inches into a sailor's body and kill him.

In all ways the ocean greyhound of to-day is imposing and impressive to one who carries in his head no ship-pictures of a recent date. In bulk she comes near to rivaling the Ark; yet this monstrous mass of steel is driven five hundred miles through the waves in twenty-four hours. I remember the brag run of a steamer which I traveled in once on the Pacific—it was two hundred and nine miles in twenty-four hours; a year or so later I was a passenger in the excursion-tub "Quaker City," and on one occasion in a level and glassy sea, it was claimed that she reeled off two hundred and eleven miles between noon and noon, but it was probably a campaign lie. That little steamer had seventy passengers, and a crew of forty men, and seemed a good deal of a bee-hive. But in this present ship we are living in a sort of solitude, these soft summer days, with sometimes a hundred passengers scattered about the spacious distances, and sometimes nobody in sight at all; yet, hidden somewhere in the vessel's bulk, there are (including crew,) near eleven hundred people.

The stateliest lines in the literature of the sea are these:

"Britannia needs no bulwark, no towers along the steep—
    Her march is o'er the mountain wave, her home is on the
        deep!"

There it is. In those old times the little ships climbed over the waves and wallowed down into the trough on the other side; the giant ship of our day does not climb over the waves, but crushes her way through them. Her formidable weight and mass and impetus give her mastery over any but extraordinary storm-waves.

The ingenuity of man! I mean in this passing generation. To-day I found in the chart-room a frame of removable wooden slats on the wall, and on the slats was painted uninforming information like this:

| | |
|---|---|
| Trim-Tank. . . . . . . . . . | Empty |
| Double-Bottom No. 1 . . . . . . | Full |
| Double-Bottom No. 2 . . . . . . | Full |
| Double-Bottom No. 3 . . . . . . | Full |
| Double-Bottom No. 4 . . . . . . | Full |

While I was trying to think out what kind of a game this might be and how a stranger might best go to work to beat it, a sailor came in and pulled out the "Empty" end of the first slat and put it back with its reverse side to the front, marked "Full." He made some other change, I did not notice what. The slat-frame was soon explained. Its function was to indicate how the ballast in the ship was distributed. The striking thing was, that that ballast was water. I did not know that a ship had ever been ballasted with water. I had merely read, some time or other, that such an experiment was to be tried. But that is the modern way: between the experimental trial of a new thing and its adoption, there is no wasted time, if the trial proves its value.

On the wall, near the slat-frame, there was an outline drawing of the ship, and this betrayed the fact that this vessel has twenty-two considerable lakes of water in her. These lakes are in her bottom; they are imprisoned between her real bottom and a false bottom. They are separated from each other, thwartships, by water-tight bulkheads, and separated down the middle by a bulkhead running from the bow four-fifths of the way to the stern. It is a chain of lakes four hundred feet long and from five to seven feet deep. Fourteen of the lakes contain fresh water brought from shore, and the aggregate weight of it is four hundred tons. The rest of the lakes contain salt water—six hundred and eighteen tons. Upwards of a thousand tons of water, altogether.

Think how handy this ballast is. The ship leaves port with the lakes all full. As she lightens forward through consumption of coal, she loses trim—her head rises, her stern sinks down. Then they spill one of the sternward lakes into the sea, and the trim is restored. This can be repeated right along as occasion may require. Also, a lake at one end of the ship can be moved to the other end by pipes and steam pumps. When the sailor changed the slat-frame to-day, he was posting a transference of that kind. The seas had been increasing, and the vessel's head needed more weighting, to keep it from rising on the waves instead of plowing through them; therefore, twenty-five tons of water had been transferred to the bow from a lake situated well toward the stern.

A water compartment is kept either full or empty. The body of water must be compact, so that it cannot slosh around. A shifting ballast would not do, of course.

The modern ship is full of beautiful ingenuities, but it seems to me that this one is the king. I would rather be the originator of that idea than of any of the others. Perhaps the trim of a ship was never perfectly ordered and preserved until now. A vessel out of trim will not steer, her speed is maimed, she strains and labors in the seas. Poor creature, for six thousand years she has had no comfort until these latest days. For six thousand years she swam through the best and cheapest ballast in the world, the only perfect ballast, but she could n't tell her master and he had not the wit to find it out for himself. It is odd to reflect that there is nearly as much water inside of this ship as there is outside, and yet there is no danger.

### NOAH'S ARK.

The progress made in the great art of ship building since Noah's time is quite noticeable. Also, the looseness of the navigation laws in the time of Noah is in quite striking contrast with the strictness of the navigation laws of our time. It would not be possible for Noah to do in our day what he was permitted to do in his own. Experience has taught us the necessity of being more particular, more conservative, more careful of human life. Noah would not be allowed to sail from Bremen in our day. The inspectors would come and examine the Ark, and make all sorts of objections. A person who knows Germany can imagine the scene and the conversation without difficulty and without missing a detail. The inspector would be in a beautiful military uniform; he would be respectful, dignified, kindly, the perfect gentleman, but steady as the north star to the last requirement of his duty. He would make Noah tell him where he was born, and how old he was, and what religious sect he belonged to, and the amount of his income, and the grade and position he claimed socially, and the name and style of his occupation, and how many wives and children he had, and how many servants, and the name, sex and age of the whole of them; and if he had n't a passport he would be courteously required to get one right away. Then he would take up the matter of the Ark:

"What is her length?"

"Six hundred feet."

"Depth?"

"Sixty-five."

"Beam?"

"Fifty or sixty."

"Built of—"

"Wood."

"What kind?"

"Shittim and gopher."

"Interior and exterior decorations?"

"Pitched within and without."

"Passengers?"

"Eight."

"Sex?"

"Half male, the others female."

"Ages?"

"From a hundred years up."

"Up to where?"

"Six hundred."

"Ah—going to Chicago; good idea, too. Surgeon's name?"

"We have no surgeon."

"Must provide a surgeon. Also an undertaker—particularly the undertaker. These people must not be left without the necessities of life at their age. Crew?"

"The same eight."

"The same eight?"

"The same eight."

"And half of them women?"

"Yes, sir."

"Have they ever served as seamen?"

"No, sir."

"Have the men?"

"No, sir."

"Have any of you ever been to sea?"

"No, sir."

"Where were you reared?"

"On a farm—all of us."

"This vessel requires a crew of eight hundred men, she not being a steamer. You must provide them. She must have four mates and nine cooks. Who is captain?"

"I am, sir."

"You must get a captain. Also a chambermaid. Also sick nurses for the old people. Who designed this vessel?"

"I did, sir."

"Is it your first attempt?"

"Yes, sir."

"I partly suspected it. Cargo?"

"Animals."

"Kind?"

"All kinds."

"Wild, or tame?"

"Mainly wild."

"Foreign, or domestic?"

"Mainly foreign."

"Principal wild ones?"

"Megatherium, elephant, rhinoceros, lion, tiger, wolf, snakes —all the wild things of all climes—two of each."

"Securely caged?"

"No, not caged."

"They must have iron cages. Who feeds and waters the menagerie?"

"We do."

"The old people?"

"Yes, sir."

"It is dangerous—for both. The animals must be cared for by a competent force. How many animals are there?"

"Big ones, seven thousand; big and little together, ninety-eight thousand."

"You must provide twelve hundred keepers. How is the vessel lighted?"

"By two windows."

"Where are they?"

"Up under the eaves."

"Two windows for a tunnel six hundred feet long and sixty-five feet deep? You must put in the electric light—a few arc lights and fifteen hundred incandescents. What do you do in case of leaks? How many pumps have you?"

"None, sir."

"You must provide pumps. How do you get water for the passengers and the animals?"

"We let down the buckets from the windows."

"It is inadequate. What is your motive power?"

"What is my which?"

"Motive power. What power do you use in driving the ship?"

"None."

"You must provide sails or steam. What is the nature of your steering apparatus?"

"We have n't any."

"Have n't you a rudder?"

"No, sir."

"How do you steer the vessel?"

"We don't."

"You must provide a rudder, and properly equip it. How many anchors have you?"

"None."

"You must provide six. One is not permitted to sail a vessel like this without that protection. How many life boats have you?"

"None, sir."

"Provide twenty-five. How many life preservers?"

"None."

"You will provide two thousand. How long are you expecting your voyage to last?"

"Eleven or twelve months."

"Eleven or twelve months. Pretty slow—but you will be in time for the Exposition. What is your ship sheathed with—copper?"

"Her hull is bare—not sheathed at all."

"Dear man, the wood-boring creatures of the sea would riddle her like a sieve and send her to the bottom in three months. She *cannot* be allowed to go away, in this condition; she must be sheathed. Just a word more: Have you reflected that Chicago is an inland city and not reachable with a vessel like this?"

"Shecargo? What is Shecargo? I am not going to Shecargo."

"Indeed? Then may I ask what the animals are for?"

"Just to breed others from."

"Others? Is it possible that you have n't enough?"

"For the present needs of civilization, yes; but the rest are going to be drowned in a flood, and these are to renew the supply."

"A flood?"

"Yes, sir."

"Are you sure of that?"

"Perfectly sure. It is going to rain forty days and forty nights."

"Give yourself no concern about that, dear sir, it often does that, here."

"Not this kind of rain. This is going to cover the mountain tops, and the earth will pass from sight."

"Privately—but of course not officially—I am sorry you revealed this, for it compels me to withdraw the option I gave you as to sails or steam. I must require you to use steam. Your ship cannot carry the hundredth part of an eleven-months' water-supply for the animals. You will have to have condensed water."

"But I tell you I am going to dip water from outside with buckets."

"It will not answer. Before the flood reaches the mountain tops the fresh waters will have joined the salt seas, and it will all be salt. You must put in steam and condense your water. I will now bid you good-day, sir. Did I understand you to say that this was your very first attempt at ship-building?"

"My very first, sir, I give you the honest truth. I built this Ark without having ever had the slightest training or experience or instruction in marine architecture."

"It is a remarkable work, sir, a most remarkable work. I consider that it contains more features that are new—absolutely new and unhackneyed—than are to be found in any other vessel that swims the seas."

"This compliment does me infinite honor, dear sir, infinite; and I shall cherish the memory of it while life shall last. Sir, I offer my duty, and most grateful thanks. Adieu!"

No, the German inspector would be limitlessly courteous to Noah, and would make him feel that he was among friends, but he wouldn't let him go to sea with that Ark.

## COLUMBUS'S CRAFT.

Between Noah's time and the time of Columbus, naval architecture underwent some changes, and from being unspeakably bad was improved to a point which may be described as less unspeakably bad. I have read somewhere, some time or other, that one of Columbus's ships was a ninety-ton vessel. By comparing that ship with the ocean greyhounds of our time one is able to get down to a comprehension of how small that Spanish bark was, and how little fitted she would be to run opposition in the Atlantic passenger trade to-day. It would take seventy-four of her to match the tonnage of the "Havel" and carry the "Havel's" trip. If I remember rightly, it took her ten weeks to make the passage. With our ideas this would now be considered an objectionable gait. She probably had a captain, a mate, and a crew consisting of four seamen and a boy. The crew of a modern greyhound numbers two hundred and fifty persons.

Columbus's ship being small and very old, we know that we may draw from these two facts several absolute certainties in the way of minor details which history has left unrecorded. For instance: being small, we know that she rolled and pitched and tumbled, in any ordinary sea, and stood on her head or her tail, or lay down with her ear in the water when storm-seas ran high; also, that she was used to having billows plunge aboard and wash her decks from stem to stern; also, that the storm-racks were on the table all the way over, and that nevertheless a man's soup was oftener landed in his lap than in his stomach; also, that the dining-saloon was about ten feet by seven, dark, airless, and suffocating with oil-stench; also, that there was only about one stateroom—the size of a grave—with a tier of two or three berths in it of the dimensions and comfortableness of coffins, and that when the light was out, the darkness in there was so thick and real that you could bite into it and chew it like gum; also, that the only promenade was on the lofty poop-deck astern (for the ship was shaped like a high-quarter shoe)—a streak sixteen feet long by three feet wide, all the rest of the vessel being littered with ropes and flooded by the seas.

We know all these things to be true, from the mere fact that we know the vessel was small. As the vessel was old, certain other truths follow, as matters of course. For instance: she was full of rats; she was full of cockroaches; the heavy seas made her seams open and shut like your fingers, and she leaked like a basket; where leakage is, there also, of necessity, is bilgewater; and where bilgewater is, only the dead can enjoy life. This is on account of the smell. In the presence of bilgewater, Limburger cheese becomes odorless and ashamed.

From these absolutely sure data we can competently picture the daily life of the great discoverer. In the early morning he paid his devotions at the shrine of the Virgin. At eight bells he appeared on the poop-deck promenade. If the weather was chilly he came up clad from plumed helmet to spurred heel in magnificent plate armor inlaid with arabesques of gold, having previously warmed it at the galley fire. If the weather was warm, he came up in the ordinary sailor toggery of the time: great slouch hat of blue velvet with a flowing brush of snowy ostrich plumes, fastened on with a flashing cluster of diamonds and emeralds; gold-embroidered doublet of green velvet with slashed sleeves exposing under-sleeves of crimson satin; deep collar and cuff-ruffles of rich limp lace; trunk hose of pink velvet, with big knee-knots of brocaded yellow ribbon; pearl-tinted silk stockings, clocked and daintily embroidered; lemon-colored buskins of unborn kid, funnel-topped, and drooping low to expose the pretty stockings; deep gauntlets of finest white heretic skin, from the factory of the Holy Inquisition, formerly part of the person of a lady of rank; rapier with sheath crusted with jewels, and hanging from a broad baldric upholstered with rubies and sapphires.

He walked the promenade thoughtfully, he noted the aspects of the sky and the course of the wind; he kept an eye out for drifting vegetation and other signs of land; he jawed the man at the wheel for pastime; he got out an imitation egg and kept himself in practice on his old trick of making it stand on its end; now and then he hove a life-line below and fished up a sailor who was drowning on the quarter-deck; the rest of his watch he gaped and yawned and stretched and said he would n't make the trip again to discover six Americas. For that was the kind of natural human person Columbus was when not posing for posterity.

At noon he took the sun and ascertained that the good ship

had made three hundred yards in twenty-four hours, and this enabled him to win the pool. Anybody can win the pool when nobody but himself has the privilege of straightening out the ship's run and getting it right.

The Admiral has breakfasted alone, in state: bacon, beans, and gin; at noon he dines alone in state: bacon, beans, and gin; at six he sups alone in state: bacon, beans, and gin; at eleven P.M. he takes a night-relish, alone, in state: bacon, beans, and gin. At none of these orgies is there any music; the ship-orchestra is modern. After his final meal he returned thanks for his many blessings, a little over-rating their value, perhaps, and then he laid off his silken splendors or his gilded hardware, and turned in, in his little coffin-bunk, and blew out his flickering stencher and began to refresh his lungs with inverted sighs freighted with the rich odors of rancid oil and bilgewater. The sighs returned as snores, and then the rats and the cockroaches swarmed out in brigades and divisions and army corps and had a circus all over him. Such was the daily life of the great discoverer in his marine basket during several historic weeks; and the difference between his ship and his comforts and ours is visible almost at a glance.

When he returned, the King of Spain, marveling, said—as history records:

"This ship seems to be leaky. Did she leak badly?"

"You shall judge for yourself, sire. I pumped the Atlantic ocean through her sixteen times on the passage."

This is General Horace Porter's account. Other authorities say fifteen.

It can be shown that the differences between that ship and the one I am writing these historical contributions in, are in several respects remarkable. Take the matter of decoration, for instance. I have been looking around again, yesterday and to-day, and have noted several details which I conceive to have been absent from Columbus's ship, or at least slurred over and not elaborated and perfected. I observe state-room doors three inches thick, of solid oak and polished. I note companionway vestibules with walls, doors and ceilings paneled in polished hard woods, some light, some dark, all dainty and delicate joiner-work, and yet every joint compact and tight; with beautiful pictures inserted, composed of blue tiles—some of the

pictures containing as many as sixty tiles—and the joinings of
those tiles perfect. These are daring experiments. One would
have said that the first time the ship went straining and laboring through a storm-tumbled sea those tiles would gape apart
and drop out. That they have not done so is evidence that the
joiner's art has advanced a good deal since the days when ships
were so shackly that when a giant sea gave them a wrench the
doors came unbolted. I find the walls of the dining-saloon
upholstered with mellow pictures wrought in tapestry, and the
ceiling aglow with pictures done in oil. In other places of
assembly I find great panels filled with embossed Spanish
leather, the figures rich with gilding and bronze. Everywhere I
find sumptuous masses of color—color, color, color—color all
about, color of every shade and tint and variety; and as a result,
the ship is bright and cheery to the eye, and this cheeriness
invades one's spirit and contents it. To fully appreciate the force
and spiritual value of this radiant and opulent dream of color,
one must stand outside at night in the pitch dark and the rain,
and look in through a port, and observe it in the lavish splendor of the electric lights. The old-time ships were dull, plain,
graceless, gloomy, and horribly depressing. They compelled
the blues; one could not escape the blues in them. The modern
idea is right: to surround the passenger with conveniences,
luxuries, and abundance of inspiriting color. As a result, the
ship is the pleasantest place one can be in, except, perhaps,
one's home.

### A VANISHED SENTIMENT.

One thing is gone, to return no more forever—the romance of the sea. Soft sentimentality about the sea has retired
from the activities of this life, and is but a memory of the
past, already remote and much faded. But within the recollection of men still living, it was in the breast of every individual; and the further any individual lived from salt water the
more of it he kept in stock. It was as pervasive, as universal, as
the atmosphere itself. The mere mention of the sea, the romantic sea, would make any company of people sentimental
and mawkish at once. The great majority of the songs that
were sung by the young people of the back settlements had

the melancholy wanderer for subject and his mouthings about
the sea for refrain. Picnic parties paddling down a creek in a
canoe when the twilight shadows were gathering, always sang

> Homeward bound, homeward bound
> From a foreign shore;

and this was also a favorite in the West with the passengers on
sternwheel steamboats. There was another—

> My boat is by the shore
>   And my bark is on the sea,
> But before I go, Tom Moore,
>   Here's a double health to thee.

And this one, also—

> O, pilot, 'tis a fearful night,
> There's danger on the deep.

And this—

> A life on the ocean wave
>   And a home on the rolling deep,
> Where the scattered waters rave
>   And the winds their revels keep!

And this—

> A wet sheet and a flowing sea,
> And a wind that follows fair.

And this—

> My foot is on my gallant deck,
> Once more the rover is free!

And the "Larboard Watch"—the person referred to below
is at the masthead, or somewhere up there—

> O, who can tell what joy he feels,
> As o'er the foam his vessel reels,
> And his tired eyelids slumb'ring fall,
> He rouses at the welcome call
>     Of "Larboard watch—ahoy!"

Yes, and there was forever and always some jackass-voiced person braying out—

> Rocked in the cradle of the deep,
> I lay me down in peace to sleep!

Other favorites had these suggestive titles: "The Storm at Sea;" "The Bird at Sea;" "The Sailor Boy's Dream;" "The Captive Pirate's Lament;" "We are far from Home on the Stormy Main"—and so on, and so on, the list is endless. Everybody on a farm lived chiefly amid the dangers of the deep on those days, in fancy.

But all that is gone, now. Not a vestige of it is left. The iron-clad, with her unsentimental aspect and frigid attention to business, banished romance from the war-marine, and the unsentimental steamer has banished it from the commercial marine. The dangers and uncertainties which made sea life romantic have disappeared and carried the poetic element along with them. In our day the passengers never sing sea-songs on board a ship, and the band never plays them. Pathetic songs about the wanderer in strange lands far from home, once so popular and contributing such fire and color to the imagination by reason of the rarity of that kind of wanderer, have lost their charm and fallen silent, because everybody is a wanderer in the far lands now, and the interest in that detail is dead. Nobody is worried about the wanderer; there are no perils of the sea for him, there are no uncertainties. He is safer in the ship than he would probably be at home, for there he is always liable to have to attend some friend's funeral and stand over the grave in the sleet, bareheaded—and that means pneumonia for him, if he gets his deserts; and the uncertainties of his voyage are reduced to whether he will arrive on the other side in the appointed afternoon, or have to wait till morning.

The first ship I was ever in was a sailing vessel. She was twenty-eight days going from San Francisco to the Sandwich Islands. But the main reason for this particularly slow passage was, that she got becalmed and lay in one spot fourteen days in the centre of the Pacific two thousand miles from land. I hear no sea-songs in this present vessel, but I heard the entire layout in that one. There were a dozen young people—they are pretty old now, I reckon—and they used to group themselves on the stern, in the starlight or the moonlight, every evening, and sing sea-songs till after midnight, in that hot, silent, motionless calm. They had no sense of humor, and they always sang "Homeward Bound," without reflecting that that was practically ridiculous, since they were standing still and not proceeding in any direction at all; and they often followed that song with "Are we almost there, are we almost there, said the dying girl as she drew near home?"

It was a very pleasant company of young people, and I wonder where they are now. Gone, oh, none knows whither; and the bloom and grace and beauty of their youth, where is that? Among them was a liar; all tried to reform him, but none could do it. And so, gradually, he was left to himself, none of us would associate with him. Many a time since, I have seen in fancy that forsaken figure, leaning forlorn against the taffrail, and have reflected that perhaps if we had tried harder, and been more patient, we might have won him from his fault and persuaded him to relinquish it. But it is hard to tell; with him the vice was extreme, and was probably incurable. I like to think—and indeed I do think—that I did the best that in me lay to lead him to higher and better ways.

There was a singular circumstance. The ship lay becalmed that entire fortnight in exactly the same spot. Then a handsome breeze came fanning over the sea, and we spread our white wings for flight. But the vessel did not budge. The sails bellied out, the gale strained at the ropes, but the vessel moved not a hair's breadth from her place. The captain was surprised. It was some hours before we found out what the cause of the detention was. It was barnacles. They collect very fast in that part of the Pacific. They had fastened themselves to the ship's bottom; then others had fastened themselves to the first bunch, others to these, and so on, down and down and down, and the last bunch had glued the column hard and fast to the bottom of the sea, which is five miles deep at that point. So the ship was simply become the handle of a walking cane five miles long—yes, and no more movable by wind and sail than a continent is. It was regarded by every one as remarkable.

Well, the next week—however, Sandy Hook is in sight.

*1893*

# *Extracts from Adam's Diary*

TRANSLATED FROM THE ORIGINAL MS.

MONDAY.—This new creature with the long hair is a good deal in the way. It is always hanging around and following me about. I don't like this; I am not used to company. I wish it would stay with the other animals. . . . . Cloudy to-day, wind in the east; think we shall have rain. . . . . *We?* Where did I get that word? . . . . I remember now,—the new creature uses it.

TUESDAY.—Been examining the great waterfall. It is the finest thing on the estate, I think. The new creature calls it Niagara Falls—why, I am sure I do not know. Says it *looks* like Niagara Falls. That is not a reason, it is mere waywardness and imbecility. I get no chance to name anything myself. The new creature names everything that comes along, before I can get in a protest. And always that same pretext is offered—it *looks* like the thing. There is the dodo, for instance. Says the moment one looks at it one sees at a glance that it "looks like a dodo." It will have to keep that name, no doubt. It wearies me to fret about it, but it does no good, anyway. Dodo! It looks no more like a dodo than I do.

WEDNESDAY.—Built me a shelter against the rain, but could not have it to myself in peace. The new creature intruded. When I tried to put it out it shed water out of the holes it looks with, and wiped it away with the back of its paws, and made a noise such as some of the other animals make when they are in distress. I wish it would not talk; it is always talking. That sounds like a cheap fling at the poor creature, a slur; but I do not mean it so. I have never heard the human voice before, and any new and strange sound intruding itself here upon the solemn hush of these dreaming solitudes offends my ear and seems a false note. And this new sound is so close to me; it is right at my shoulder, right at my ear, first on one side and then on the other, and I am used only to sounds that are more or less distant from me.

FRIDAY.—The naming goes recklessly on, in spite of anything I can do. I had a very good name for the estate, and it was musical and pretty—GARDEN-OF-EDEN. Privately, I continue to call it that, but not any longer publicly. The new creature says it is all woods and rocks and scenery, and therefore has no resemblance to a garden. Says it *looks* like a park, and does not look like anything *but* a park. Consequently, without consulting me it has been new named—NIAGARA FALLS PARK. This is sufficiently high-handed, it seems to me. And already there is a sign up:

> KEEP OFF
> THE GRASS.

My life is not as happy as it was.

SATURDAY.—The new creature eats too much fruit. We are going to run short, most likely. "We" again—that is *its* word; mine, too, now, from hearing it so much. Good deal of fog this morning. I do not go out in the fog, myself. The new creature does. It goes out in all weathers, and stumps right in with its muddy feet. And talks. It used to be so pleasant and quiet here.

SUNDAY.—Pulled through. This day is getting to be more and more trying. It was selected and set apart last November as a day of rest. I already had six of them per week before. This is another of those unaccountable things. There seems to be too much legislation, too much fussing, and fixing, and tidying-up, and not enough of the better-let-well-enough-alone policy. [*Mem.*—Must keep that sort of opinions to myself.] This morning found the new creature trying to clod apples out of that forbidden tree.

MONDAY.—The new creature says its name is Eve. That is all right, I have no objections. Says it is to call it by when I want it to come. I said it was superfluous, then. The word evidently raised me in its respect; and indeed it is a large, good word and will bear repetition. It says it is not an It, it is a She. This is probably doubtful; yet it is all one to me; what she is were nothing to me if she would but go by herself and not talk.

TUESDAY.—She has littered the whole estate with execrable names and offensive signs:

☞ THIS WAY TO THE WHIRLPOOL.

☞ THIS WAY TO GOAT ISLAND.

☞ CAVE OF THE WINDS THIS WAY.

She says this park would make a tidy summer resort, if there were any custom for it. Summer resort—another invention of hers—just words, without any meaning. What is a summer resort? But it is best not to ask her, she has such a rage for explaining.

FRIDAY.—She has taken to begging and imploring me to stop going over the Falls. What harm does it do? Says it makes her shudder. I wonder why; I have always done it—always liked the plunge, and the excitement and the coolness. I supposed it was what the Falls were for. They have no other use that I can see, and they must have been made for something. She says they were only made for scenery—like the rhinoceros and the mastodon.

I went over the Falls in a barrel—not satisfactory to her. Went over in a tub—still not satisfactory. Swam the Whirlpool and the Rapids in a fig-leaf suit. It got much damaged. Hence, tedious complaints about my extravagance. I am too much hampered here. What I need is change of scene.

SATURDAY.—I escaped last Tuesday night, and traveled two days, and built me another shelter, in a secluded place, and obliterated my tracks as well as I could, but she hunted me out by means of a beast which she has tamed and calls a wolf, and came making that pitiful noise again, and shedding that water out of the places she looks with. I was obliged to return with her, but will presently emigrate again, when occasion offers. She engages herself in many foolish things: among others, trying to study out why the animals called lions and tigers live on grass and flowers, when, as she says, the sort of teeth they wear would indicate that they were intended to eat each other. This is foolish, because to do that would be to kill each other, and that would introduce what, as I understand it, is called "death"; and death, as I have been told, has not yet entered the Park. Which is a pity, on some accounts.

SUNDAY.—Pulled through.

MONDAY.—I believe I see what the week is for: it is to give time to rest up from the weariness of Sunday. It seems a good idea, in a region where good ideas are rather conspicuously scarce. [*Mem.*—Must keep this sort of remarks private.] . . . . She has been climbing that tree again. Clodded her out of it. She said nobody was looking. Seems to consider that a sufficient justification for chancing any dangerous thing. Told her that. The word justification moved her admiration—and envy, too, I thought. It is a good word.

THURSDAY.—She told me she was made out of a rib taken from my body. This is at least doubtful, if not more than that. I have not missed any rib. . . . She is in much trouble about the buzzard; says grass does not agree with it; is afraid she can't raise it; thinks it was intended to live on decayed flesh. The buzzard must get along the best it can with what is provided. We cannot overturn the whole scheme to accommodate the buzzard.

SATURDAY.—She fell in the pond yesterday, when she was looking at herself in it, which she is always doing. She nearly strangled, and said it was most uncomfortable. This made her sorry for the creatures which live in there, which she calls fish, for she continues to fasten names on to things that don't need them and don't come when they are called by them, which is a matter of no consequence to her, she is such a fool anyway; so she got a lot of them out and brought them in and put them in my bed to keep warm, but I have noticed them now and then all day and I don't see that they are any happier there than they were before. When night comes I shall throw them outdoors. I will not sleep with them, for I find them clammy and unpleasant to lie among when a person hasn't anything on.

SUNDAY.—Pulled through.

TUESDAY.—She has taken up with a snake now. The other animals are glad, for she was always experimenting with them and bothering them; and I am glad, because the snake talks, and this enables me to get a rest.

FRIDAY.—She says the snake advises her to try the fruit of that tree, and says the result will be a great and fine and noble education. I told her there would be another result, too—it would introduce death into the world. That was a mistake—it had been better to keep the remark to myself; it only gave her an idea—she could save the sick buzzard, and furnish fresh meat to the despondent lions and tigers. I advised her to keep away from the tree. She said she wouldn't. I foresee trouble. Will emigrate.

WEDNESDAY.—I have had a variegated time. I escaped that night, and rode a horse all night as fast as he could go, hoping to get clear out of the Garden and hide in some other country before the trouble should begin; but it was not to be. About an hour after sun-up, as I was riding through a flowery plain where thousands of animals were grazing, slumbering, or playing with each other, according to their common wont, all of a sudden they broke into a tempest of frightful noises, and in one moment the plain was a frantic commotion and every beast was destroying its neighbor. I knew what it meant—Eve had eaten that fruit, and death was come into the world. . . . . The tigers ate my horse, paying no attention when I ordered them to desist, and they would even have eaten me if I had stayed—which I didn't, but went away in much haste. . . . . I found this place, outside the Garden, and was fairly comfortable for a few days, but she has found me out. Found me out, and has named the place Tonawanda—says it *looks* like that. In fact I was not sorry she came, for there are but meagre pickings here, and she brought some of those apples. I was obliged to eat them, I was so hungry. It was against my principles, but I find that principles have no real force except when one is well fed. . . . She came curtained in boughs and bunches of leaves, and when I asked her what she meant by such nonsense, and snatched them away and threw them down, she tittered and blushed. I had never seen a person titter and blush before, and to me it seemed unbecoming and idiotic. She said I would soon know how it was myself. This was correct. Hungry as I was, I laid down the apple half eaten—certainly the best one I ever saw, considering the lateness of the season—and arrayed myself in the discarded boughs and branches, and then spoke to her with some severity and ordered her to go and get some more and not make such a spectacle of herself. She did it, and after this we crept down to where the wild-beast battle had been, and collected some skins, and I made her patch together a couple of suits proper for public occasions. They are uncomfort-able, it is true, but stylish, and that is the main point about clothes. . . . I find she is a good deal of a companion. I see I should be lonesome and depressed without her, now that I have lost my property. Another thing, she says it is ordered that we work for our living hereafter. She will be useful. I will superintend.

TEN DAYS LATER.—She accuses *me* of being the cause of our disaster! She says, with apparent sincerity and truth, that the Serpent assured her that the forbidden fruit was not ap-ples, it was chestnuts. I said I was innocent, then, for I had not eaten any chestnuts. She said the Serpent informed her that "chestnut" was a figurative term meaning an aged and mouldy joke. I turned pale at that, for I have made many jokes to pass the weary time, and some of them could have been of that sort, though I had honestly supposed they were new when I made them. She asked me if I had made one just at the time of the catastrophe. I was obliged to admit that I had made one to myself, though not aloud. It was this. I was thinking about the Falls, and I said to myself, "How wonder-ful it is to see that vast body of water tumble down there!" Then in an instant a bright thought flashed into my head, and I let it fly, saying, "It would be a deal more wonderful to see it tumble *up* there!"—and I was just about to kill myself with laughing at it when all nature broke loose in war and death and I had to flee for my life. "There," she said, with triumph, "that is just it; the Serpent mentioned that very jest, and called it the First Chestnut, and said it was coeval with the creation." Alas, I am indeed to blame. Would that I were not witty; oh, would that I had never had that radiant thought!

NEXT YEAR.—We have named it Cain. She caught it while I was up country trapping on the North Shore of the Erie; caught it in the timber a couple of miles from our dug-out—or it might have been four, she isn't certain which. It resembles us in some ways, and may be a relation. That is what she thinks, but this is an error, in my judgment. The difference in size warrants the conclusion that it is a different and new kind of animal—a fish, perhaps, though when I put it in the water to see, it sank, and she plunged in and snatched it out before there was opportunity for the experiment to determine the matter. I still think it is a fish, but she is indifferent about what it is, and will not let me have it to try. I do not understand this. The coming of the creature seems to have changed her whole nature and made her unreasonable about experiments. She thinks more of it than she does of any of the other animals, but is not able to explain why. Her mind is disordered—everything shows it. Sometimes she carries the fish in her arms half the night when it complains and wants to get to the water. At such times the water comes out of the places in her face that she looks out of, and she pats the fish on the back and makes soft sounds with her mouth to soothe it, and betrays sorrow and solicitude in a hundred ways. I have never seen her do like this with any other fish, and it troubles me greatly. She used to carry the young tigers around so, and play with them, before we lost our property, but it was only play; she never took on about them like this when their dinner disagreed with them.

SUNDAY.—She don't work, Sundays, but lies around all tired out, and likes to have the fish wallow over her; and she makes fool noises to amuse it, and pretends to chew its paws, and that makes it laugh. I have not seen a fish before that could laugh. This makes me doubt . . . . I have come to like Sunday myself. Superintending all the week tires a body so. There ought to be more Sundays. In the old days they were tough, but now they come handy.

WEDNESDAY.—It isn't a fish. I cannot quite make out what it is. It makes curious devilish noises when not satisfied, and says "goo-goo" when it is. It is not one of us, for it doesn't walk; it is not a bird, for it doesn't fly; it is not a frog, for it doesn't hop; it is not a snake, for it doesn't crawl; I feel sure it is not a fish, though I cannot get a chance to find out whether it can swim or not. It merely lies around, and mostly on its back, with its feet up. I have not seen any other animal do that before. I said I believed it was an enigma; but she only admired the word without understanding it. In my judgment it is either an enigma or some kind of a bug. If it dies, I will take it apart and see what its arrangements are. I never had a thing perplex me so.

THREE MONTHS LATER.—The perplexity merely augments instead of diminishing. I sleep but little. It has ceased from lying around, and goes about on its four legs, now. Yet it differs from the other four-legged animals, in that its front legs are unusually short, consequently this causes the main part of its person to stick up uncomfortably high in the air, and this is not attractive. It is built much as we are, but its method of traveling shows that it is not of our breed. The short front legs and long hind ones indicate that it is of the kangaroo family, but it is a marked variation of the species, since the true kangaroo hops, whereas this one never does. Still it is a curious and interesting variety, and has not been catalogued before. As I discovered it, I have felt justified in securing the credit of the discovery by attaching my name to it, and hence have called it *Kangaroorum Adamiensis*. . . . . It must have been a young one when it came, for it has grown exceedingly since. It must be five times as big, now, as it was then, and when discontented is able to make from twenty-two to thirty-eight times the noise it made at first. Coercion does not modify this, but has the contrary effect. For this reason I discontinued the system. She reconciles it by persuasion, and by giving it things which she had told it she wouldn't give it before. As observed previously, I was not at home when it first came, and she told me she found it in the woods. It seems odd that it should be the only one, yet it must be so, for I have worn myself out these many weeks trying to find another one to add to my collection, and for this one to play with; for surely then it would be quieter and we could tame it more easily. But I find none, nor any vestige of any; and strangest of all, no tracks. It has to live on the ground, it cannot help itself; therefore, how does it get about without leaving a track? I have set a dozen traps, but they do no good. I catch all small animals except that one; animals that merely go into the trap out of curiosity, I think, to see what the milk is there for. They never drink it.

THREE MONTHS LATER.—The Kangaroo still continues to grow, which is very strange and perplexing. I never knew one to be so long getting its growth. It has fur on its head now; not like kangaroo fur, but exactly like our hair except that it is much finer and softer, and instead of being black is red. I am like to lose my mind over the capricious and harassing developments of this unclassifiable zoological freak. If I could catch another one—but that is hopeless; it is a new variety, and the only sample; this is plain. But I caught a true kangaroo and brought it in, thinking that this one, being lonesome, would rather have that for company than have no kin at all, or any animal it could feel a nearness to or get sympathy from in its forlorn condition here among strangers who do not know its ways or habits, or what to do to make it feel that it is among friends; but it was a mistake—it went into such fits at the sight of the kangaroo that I was convinced it had never seen one before. I pity the poor noisy little animal, but there is nothing I can do to make it happy. If I could tame it—but that is out of the question; the more I try the worse I seem to make it. It grieves me to the heart to see it in its little storms of sorrow and passion. I wanted to let it go, but she wouldn't hear of it. That seemed cruel and not like her; and yet she may be right. It might be lonelier than ever; for since I cannot find another one, how could *it*?

FIVE MONTHS LATER.—It is not a kangaroo. No, for it supports itself by holding to her finger, and thus goes a few steps on its hind legs, and then falls down. It is probably some kind of a bear; and yet it has no tail—as yet—and no fur, except on its head. It still keeps on growing—that is a curious circumstance, for bears get their growth earlier than this. Bears are dangerous—since our catastrophe—and I shall not be satisfied to have this one prowling about the place much longer without a muzzle on. I have offered to get her a kangaroo if she would let this one go, but it did no good—she is determined to run us into all sorts of foolish risks, I think. She was not like this before she lost her mind.

A FORTNIGHT LATER.—I examined its mouth. There is no danger yet; it has only one tooth. It has no tail yet. It makes more noise now than it ever did before—and mainly at night. I have moved out. But I shall go over, mornings, to breakfast, and to see if it has more teeth. If it gets a mouthful of teeth it will be time for it to go, tail or no tail, for a bear does not need a tail in order to be dangerous.

FOUR MONTHS LATER.—I have been off hunting and fishing a month, up in the region that she calls Buffalo; I don't know why, unless it is because there are not any buffalos there. Meantime the bear has learned to paddle around all by itself on its hind legs, and says "poppa" and "momma." It is certainly a new species. This resemblance to words may be purely accidental, of course, and may have no purpose or meaning; but even in that case it is still extraordinary, and is a thing which no other bear can do. This imitation of speech, taken together with general absence of fur and entire absence of tail, sufficiently indicates that this is a new kind of bear. The further study of it will be exceedingly interesting. Meantime I will go off on a far expedition among the forests of the north and make an exhaustive search. There must certainly be another one somewhere, and this one will be less dangerous when it has company of its own species. I will go straightway; but I will muzzle this one first.

THREE MONTHS LATER.—It has been a weary, weary hunt, yet I have had no success. In the meantime, without stirring from the home-estate, she has caught another one! I never saw such luck. I might have hunted these woods a hundred years, I never would have run across that thing.

NEXT DAY.—I have been comparing the new one with the old one, and it is perfectly plain that they are the same breed. I was going to stuff one of them for my collection, but she is prejudiced against it for some reason or other; so I have relinquished the idea, though I think it is a mistake. It would be an irreparable loss to science if they should get away. The old one is tamer than it was, and can laugh and talk like the parrot, having learned this, no doubt, from being with the parrot so much, and having the imitative faculty in a highly developed degree. I shall be astonished if it turns out to be a new kind of parrot; and yet I ought not to be astonished, for it has already been everything else it could think of, since those first days when it was a fish. The new one is as ugly now as the old one was at first; has the same sulphur-and-raw-meat complexion and the same singular head without any fur on it. She calls it Abel.

TEN YEARS LATER.—They are boys; we found it out long ago. It was their coming in that small, immature shape that fooled us; we were not used to it. There are some girls now. Abel is a good boy, but if Cain had stayed a bear it would have improved him. After all these years, I see that I was mistaken about Eve in the beginning; it is better to live outside

the Garden with her than inside it without her. At first I
thought she talked too much; but now I should be sorry to
have that voice fall silent and pass out of my life. Blessed be
the chestnut that brought us near together and taught me to
know the goodness of her heart and the sweetness of her
spirit!

*1893*

# *Is He Living or Is He Dead?*

I was spending the month of March, 1892, at Mentone, in the Riviera. At this retired spot one has all the advantages privately, which are to be had at Monte Carlo and Nice, a few miles further along, publicly. That is to say, one has the flooding sunshine, the balmy air and the brilliant blue sea, without the marring additions of human pow-wow and fuss and feathers and display. Mentone is quiet, simple, restful, unpretentious; the rich and the gaudy do not come there. As a rule, I mean, the rich do not come there. Now and then a rich man comes, and I presently got acquainted with one of these. Partially to disguise him, I will call him Smith. One day, in the Hôtel des Anglais, at the second breakfast, he exclaimed:

"Quick! Cast your eye on the man going out at the door. Take in every detail of him."

"Why?"

"Do you know who he is?"

"Yes. He spent several days here before you came. He is an old, retired and very rich silk manufacturer from Lyons, they say, and I guess he is alone in the world, for he always looks sad and dreamy, and doesn't talk with anybody. His name is Theophile Magnan."

I supposed that Smith would now proceed to justify the large interest which he had shown in Monsieur Magnan, but, instead, he dropped into a brown study, and was apparently lost to me and to the rest of the world during some minutes. Now and then he passed his fingers through his flossy white hair, to assist his thinking, and meantime he allowed his breakfast to go on cooling. At last he said:

"No, it's gone; I can't call it back."

"Can't call what back?"

"It's one of Hans Andersen's beautiful little stories. But it's gone from me. Part of it is like this: A child has a caged bird, which it loves, but thoughtlessly neglects. The bird pours out its song unheard and unheeded; but, in time, hunger and thirst assail the creature, and its song grows plaintive and feeble and finally ceases—the bird dies. The child comes, and is smitten to the heart with remorse; then, with bitter tears and lamentations, it calls its mates, and they bury the bird with elaborate pomp and the tenderest grief, without knowing, poor things, that it isn't children only who starve poets to death and then spend enough on their funerals and monuments to have kept them alive and made them easy and comfortable. Now—"

But here we were interrupted. About ten, that evening, I ran across Smith, and he asked me up to his parlor to help him smoke and drink hot Scotch. It was a cosy place, with its comfortable chairs, its cheerful lamps and its friendly open fire of seasoned olive-wood. To make everything perfect, there was the muffled booming of the surf outside. After the second Scotch and much lazy and contented chat, Smith said:

"Now we are properly primed—I to tell a curious history, and you to listen to it. It has been a secret for many years—a secret between me and three others; but I am going to break the seal now. Are you comfortable?"

"Perfectly. Go on."

Here follows what he told me:

A long time ago I was a young artist—a very young artist, in fact—and I wandered about the country parts of France, sketching here and sketching there, and was presently joined by a couple of darling young Frenchmen who were at the same kind of thing that I was doing. We were as happy as we were poor, or as poor as we were happy—phrase it to suit yourself. Claude Frère and Carl Boulanger—these are the names of those boys; dear, dear fellows, and the sunniest spirits that ever laughed at poverty and had a noble good time in all weathers.

At last we ran hard a ground in a Breton village, and an artist as poor as ourselves took us in and literally saved us from starving—François Millet—

"What! the *great* François Millet?"

Great? He wasn't any greater than we were, then. He hadn't any fame, even in his own village; and he was so poor that he hadn't anything to feed us on but turnips, and even the turnips failed us sometimes. We four became fast friends, doting friends, inseparables. We painted away together with all our might, piling up stock, piling up stock, but very seldom getting rid of any of it. We had lovely times together; but, O my soul! how we were pinched now and then!

For a little over two years this went on. At last, one day, Claude said:

"Boys, we've come to the end. Do you understand that?—absolutely to the end. Everybody has struck—there's a league formed against us. I've been all around the village and it's just as I tell you. They refuse to credit us for another centime until all the odds and ends are paid up."

This struck us cold. Every face was blank with dismay. We realized that our circumstances were desperate, now. There was a long silence. Finally, Millet said, with a sigh:

"Nothing occurs to me—nothing. Suggest something, lads."

There was no response, unless a mournful silence may be called a response. Carl got up, and walked nervously up and down a while, then said:

"It's a shame! Look at these canvases: stacks and stacks of as good pictures as anybody in Europe paints—I don't care who he is. Yes, and plenty of lounging strangers have said the same—or nearly that, anyway."

"But didn't buy," Millet said.

"No matter, they said it: and it's true, too. Look at your 'Angelus' there; will anybody tell me—"

"Pah, Carl—my Angelus! I was offered five francs for it."

"When!"

"Who offered it!"

"Where is he!"

"Why didn't you take it!"

"Come—don't all speak at once. I thought he would give more—I was sure of it—he looked it—so I asked him eight."

"Well—and then?"

"He said he would call again."

"Thunder and lightning! Why, François—"

"Oh, I know, I know! It was a mistake, and I was a fool. Boys, I meant for the best; you'll all grant me that, and I—"

"Why, certainly, we know that, bless your dear heart; but don't you be a fool again."

"I? I wish somebody would come along and offer us a cabbage for it—you'd see!"

"A cabbage! Oh, don't name it—it makes my mouth water. Talk of things less trying."

"Boys," said Carl, "*do* these pictures lack merit? Answer me that."

"No!"

"Aren't they of very great and high merit? Answer me that."

"Yes."

"Of such great and high merit, that, if an illustrious name were attached to them they would sell at splendid prices. Isn't it so?"

"Certainly it is. Nobody doubts that."

"But—I'm not joking—*isn't* it so?"

"Why, of course it's so—and *we* are not joking. But what of it? What of it? How does that concern us?"

"In this way comrades—we'll *attach* an illustrious name to them!"

The lively conversation stopped. The faces were turned inquiringly upon Carl. What sort of riddle might this be? Where was an illustrious name to be borrowed? And who was to borrow it?

Carl sat down, and said:

"Now I have a perfectly serious thing to propose. I think it is the only way to keep us out of the almshouse, and I believe it to be a perfectly sure way. I base this opinion upon certain multitudinous and long established facts in human history. I believe my project will make us all rich."

"Rich! You've lost your mind."

"No, I haven't."

"Yes, you have—you've lost your mind. What do you *call* rich?"

"A hundred thousand francs apiece."

"He *has* lost his mind. I knew it."

"Yes, he has. Carl, privation has been too much for you and—"

"Carl, you want to take a pill and get right to bed!"

"Bandage him first—bandage his head, and then—"

"No, bandage his heels; his brains have been settling for weeks—I've noticed it."

"Shut up!" said Millet, with ostensible severity, "and let the boy say his say. Now then—come out with your project, Carl. What is it?"

"Well, then, by way of preamble I will ask you to note this fact in human history: that the merit of many a great artist has never been acknowledged until after he was starved and dead. This has happened so often that I make bold to found a law upon it. This law: that the merit of *every* great unknown and neglected artist must and will be recognized and his pictures climb to high prices after his death. My project is this: we must cast lots—one of us must die."

The remark fell so calmly and so unexpectedly that we almost forgot to jump. Then there was a wild chorus of advice again—medical advice, for the help of Carl's brain; but he waited patiently for the hilarity to calm down, then went on again with his project:

"Yes, one of us must die, to save the others—and himself. We will cast lots. The one chosen shall be illustrious, all of us shall be rich. Hold still, now—hold still; don't interrupt—I tell you I know what I am talking about. Here is the idea. During the next three months the one who is to die shall paint with all his might, enlarge his stock all he can —not pictures, *no!* skeleton sketches, studies, parts of studies, fragments of studies, a dozen dabs of the brush on each— meaningless, of course, but *his*, with his cipher on them; turn out fifty a day, each to contain some peculiarity or mannerism easily detectable as his—*they're* the things that sell you know, and are collected at fabulous prices for the world's museums, after the great man is gone; we'll have a ton of them ready—a ton! And all that time the rest of us will be busy supporting the moribund, and working Paris and the dealers—preparations for the coming event, you know; and when everything is hot and just right, we'll spring the death on them and have the notorious funeral. You get the idea?"

"N-o; at least, not qu—"

"Not quite? Don't you see? The man doesn't really die; he changes his name and vanishes; we bury a dummy, and cry over it, with all the world to help. And I—"

But he wasn't allowed to finish. Everybody broke out into a rousing hurrah of applause; and all jumped up and capered about the room and fell on each other's necks, in transports of gratitude and joy. For hours we talked over the great plan, without ever feeling hungry; and at last, when all the details had been arranged satisfactorily, we cast lots and Millet was elected—elected to die, as we called it. Then we scraped together those things which one never parts with until he is betting them against future wealth—keepsake trinkets and suchlike—and these we pawned for enough to furnish us a frugal farewell supper and breakfast, and leave us a few francs over for travel, and a stake of turnips and stuff for Millet to live on for a few days.

Next morning early, the three of us cleared out, straightway after breakfast—on foot, of course. Each of us carried a dozen of Millet's small pictures, purposing to market them. Carl struck for Paris, where he would start the work of building up Millet's fame against the coming great day; Claude and I were to separate, and scatter abroad over France.

Now, it will surprise you to know what an easy and comfortable thing we had. I walked two days before I began business. Then I began to sketch a villa in the outskirts of a big town—because I saw the proprietor standing on an upper verandah. He came down to look on—I thought he would. I worked swiftly, intending to keep him interested. Occasionally he fired off a little ejaculation of approbation, and by and by he spoke up with enthusiasm and said I was a master!

I put down my brush, reached into my satchel, fetched out a Millet, and pointed to the cipher in the corner. I said, proudly:

"I suppose you recognize *that*? Well, he taught me! I should *think* I ought to know my trade!"

The man looked guiltily embarrassed, and was silent. I said, sorrowfully:

"You don't mean to intimate that you don't know the cipher of François Millet!"

Of course he didn't know that cipher; but he was the gratefullest man you ever saw, just the same, for being let out of an uncomfortable place on such easy terms. He said:

"No! Why, it *is* Millet's, sure enough! I don't know what I could have been thinking of. Of course I recognize it now."

Next, he wanted to buy it; but I said that although I wasn't rich I wasn't *that* poor. However, at last, I let him have it for eight hundred francs.

"Eight hundred!"

Yes. Millet would have sold it for a pork chop. Yes, I got eight hundred francs for that little thing. I wish I could get it back for eighty thousand. But that time's gone by. I made a very nice picture of that man's house, and I wanted to offer it to him for ten francs, but that wouldn't answer, seeing I was the pupil of such a master, so I sold it to him for a hundred. I sent the eight hundred francs straight back to Millet from that town and struck out again next day.

But I didn't walk—no. I rode. I have ridden ever since. I sold one picture every day, and never tried to sell two. I always said to my customer,—

"I am a fool to sell a picture of François Millet's at all, for that man is not going to live three months and when he dies his pictures can't be had for love or money."

I took care to spread that little fact as far as I could, and prepare the world for the event.

I take credit to myself for our plan of selling the pictures—it was mine. I suggested it that last evening when we were laying out our campaign, and all three of us agreed to give it a good fair trial before giving it up for some other. It succeeded with all of us. I walked only two days, Claude walked two—both of us afraid to make Millet celebrated too close to home—but Carl walked only half a day, the bright, conscienceless rascal and after that he traveled like a duke.

Every now and then we got in with a country editor and started an item around through the press; not an item announcing that a new painter had been discovered, but an item which let on that everybody knew François Millet; not an item praising him in any way but merely a word concerning the present condition of the "master"—sometimes hopeful, sometimes despondent, but always tinged with fears for the worst. We always marked these paragraphs, and sent the papers to all the people who had bought pictures of us.

Carl was soon in Paris, and he worked things with a high hand. He made friends with the correspondents and got Millet's condition reported to England and all over the continent, and America, and everywhere.

At the end of six weeks from the start, we three met in Paris and called a halt, and stopped sending back to Millet for additional pictures. The boom was so high, and everything so ripe, that we saw that it would be a mistake not to strike now, right away, without waiting any longer. So we wrote Millet to go to bed and begin to waste away pretty fast, for we should like him to die in ten days if he could get ready.

Then we figured up and found that among us we had sold eighty-five small pictures and studies, and had sixty-nine thousand francs to show for it. Carl had made the last sale and the most brilliant one of all. He sold the Angelus for twenty-two hundred francs. How we did glorify him!—not foreseeing that a day was coming by and by when France would struggle to own it and a stranger would capture it for five hundred and fifty thousand, cash.

We had a wind-up champagne supper that night, and next day Claude and I packed up and went off to nurse Millet through his last days and keep busybodies out of the house and send daily bulletins to Carl in Paris for publication in the papers of several continents for the information of a waiting world. The sad end came at last, and Carl was there in time to help in the final mournful rites.

You remember that great funeral, and what a stir it made all over the globe, and how the illustrious of two worlds came to attend it and testify their sorrow. We four—still inseparable—carried the coffin, and would allow none to help. And we were right about that, because it hadn't anything in it but a wax figure, and any other coffin-bearers would have found fault with the weight. Yes, we same old four, who had lovingly shared privation together in the old hard times now gone forever, carried the cof—

"Which four?"

"*We* four—for Millet helped to carry his own coffin. In disguise, you know. Disguised as a relative—distant relative."

"Astonishing!"

But true, just the same. Well, you remember how the pictures went up. Money? We didn't know what to do with it. There's a man in Paris today who owns seventy Millet pictures. He paid us two million francs for them. And as for the bushels of sketches and studies which Millet shoveled out during the six weeks that we were on the road, well, it would astonish you to know the figure we sell them at now-a-days—that is, when we consent to let one go.

"It is a wonderful history, perfectly wonderful!"

Yes—it amounts to that.

"Whatever became of Millet?"

Can you keep a secret?

"I can."

Do you remember the man I called your attention to in the dining-room today? *That was François Millet.*

"Great—"

Scott! Yes. For once they didn't starve a genius to death and then put into other pockets the rewards he should have had himself. *This* song-bird was not allowed to pipe out its heart unheard and then be paid with the cold pomp of a big funeral. We looked out for that.

*September 1893*

# The Esquimau Maiden's Romance

"Yes, I will tell you anything about my life that you would like to know, Mr. Twain," she said in her soft voice and letting her honest eyes rest placidly upon my face, "for it is kind and good of you to like me and care to know about me."

She had been absently scraping blubber-grease from her cheeks with a small bone-knife and transferring it to her fur sleeve, while she watched the Aurora Borealis swing its flaming streamers out of the sky and wash the lonely snow-plain and the templed icebergs with the rich hues of the prism, a spectacle of almost intolerable splendor and beauty; but now she shook off her reverie and prepared to give me the humble little history I had asked for. She settled herself comfortably on the block of ice which we were using as a sofa, and I made ready to listen.

She was a beautiful creature. I speak from the Esquimaux point of view. Others would have thought her a trifle over-plump. She was just twenty years old, and was held to be by far the most bewitching girl in her tribe. Even now, in the open air, with her cumbersome and shapeless fur coat and trousers and boots and vast hood, the beauty of her face was at least apparent; but her figure had to be taken on trust. Among all the guests who came and went, I had seen no girl at her father's hospitable trough who could be called her equal. Yet she was not spoiled. She was sweet and natural and sincere, and if she was aware that she was a belle, there was nothing about her ways to show that she possessed that knowledge.

She had been my daily comrade for a week, now, and the better I knew her the better I liked her. She had been tenderly and carefully brought up, in an atmosphere of singularly rare refinement for the polar regions, for her father was the most important man of his tribe and ranked at the top of Esquimau cultivation. I made long dog-sledge trips across the mighty ice-floes with Lasca—that was her name—and found her company always pleasant and her conversation agreeable. I went fishing with her, but not in her perilous boat: I merely followed along on the ice and watched her strike her game with her fatally accurate spear. We went sealing together; several times I stood by while she and the family dug blubber from a stranded whale, and once I went part of the way when she was hunting a bear, but turned back before the finish, because at bottom I am afraid of bears.

However, she was ready to begin her story, now, and this is what she said:

Our tribe had always been used to wander about from place to place over the frozen seas, like the other tribes, but my father got tired of that, two years ago, and built this great mansion of frozen snow-blocks—look at it; it is seven feet high and three or four times as long as any of the others—and here we have stayed ever since. He was very proud of his house, and that was reasonable, for if you have examined it with care you must have noticed how much finer and completer it is than houses usually are. But if you have not, you must, for you will find it has luxurious appointments that are quite beyond the common. For instance, in that end of it which you have called the "parlor" the raised platform for the accommodation of guests and the family at meals is the largest you have ever seen in any house—is it not so?

"Yes, you are quite right, Lasca; it is the largest. We have nothing resembling it in even the finest houses in the United States." This admission made her eyes sparkle with pride and pleasure. I noted that, and took my cue.

I thought it must have surprised you, she said. And another thing: it is bedded far deeper in furs than is usual; all kinds of furs—seal, sea-otter, silver-gray fox, bear, marten, sable— every kind of fur in profusion; and the same with the ice-block sleeping benches along the walls, which you call "beds." Are your platforms and sleeping-benches better provided at home?

"Indeed, they are not, Lasca—they do not begin to be." That pleased her again. All she was thinking of was the *number* of furs her esthetic father took the trouble to keep on hand, not their value. I could have told her that those masses of rich furs constituted wealth—or would in my country— but she would not have understood that; those were not the kind of things that ranked as riches with her people. I could have told her that the clothes she had on, or the every-day clothes of the commonest person about her, were worth twelve or fifteen hundred dollars, and that I was not acquainted with anybody at home who wore twelve-hundred-dollar toilets to go fishing in; but she would not have understood it, so I said nothing. She resumed:

And then the slop-tubs. We have two in the parlor, and two in the rest of the house. It is very seldom that one has two in the parlor. Have you two in the parlor at home?

The memory of those tubs made me gasp, but I recovered myself before she noticed, and said with effusion:

"Why, Lasca, it is a shame of me to expose my country, and you must not let it go further, for I am speaking to you in confidence; but I give you my word of honor that not even the richest man in the city of New York has two slop-tubs in his drawing-room."

She clapped her fur-clad hands in innocent delight, and exclaimed:

Oh, but you cannot mean it, you cannot *mean* it!

"Indeed, I am in earnest, dear. There is Vanderbilt. Vanderbilt is almost the richest man in the whole world. Now, if I were on my dying bed, I could say to you that not even he has two in his drawing-room. Why, he hasn't even *one*—I wish I may die in my tracks if it isn't true."

Her lovely eyes stood wide with amazement, and she said slowly and with a sort of awe in her voice:

How strange—how incredible—one is not able to realize it. Is he penurious?

"No—it isn't that. It isn't the expense he minds, but—er—well, you know, it would look like showing off. Yes, that is it, that is the idea; he is a plain man in his ways and shrinks from display."

Why, that humility is right enough, said Lasca, if one does not carry it too far—but what does the place *look* like?

"Well, necessarily it looks pretty barren and unfinished, but—"

I should think so! I never heard anything like it. Is it a fine house—that is, otherwise?

"Pretty fine, yes. It is very well thought of."

The girl was silent a while, and sat dreamily gnawing a candle-end, apparently trying to think the thing out. At last she gave her head a little toss and spoke out her opinion with decision:

Well, to my mind there's a breed of humility which is *itself* a species of showing-off, when you get down to the marrow of it; and when a man is able to afford two slop-tubs in his parlor and don't do it, it *may* be that he is truly humble-minded, but it's a hundred times more likely that he is just trying to strike the public eye. In my judgment your Mr. Vanderbilt knows what he is about.

I tried to modify this verdict, feeling that a double slop-tub standard was not a fair one to try everybody by, although a sound enough one in its own habitat; but the girl's head was set and she was not to be persuaded. Presently she said:

Do the rich people, with you, have as good sleeping-benches as ours, and made out of as nice broad ice-blocks?

"Well, they are pretty good—good enough—but they are not made of ice-blocks."

I want to know! *Why* aren't they made of ice-blocks?

I explained the difficulties in the way and the expensiveness of ice in a country where you have to keep a sharp eye on your iceman or your ice-bill will weigh more than your ice; then she cried out:

Dear me, do you *buy* your ice?

"We most surely do, dear."

She burst into a gale of guileless laughter, and said:

Oh, I *never* heard of anything so silly! My, there's plenty of it—it isn't worth anything. Why, there is a hundred miles of it in sight, right now. I wouldn't give a fish-bladder for the whole of it.

"Well, it's because you don't know how to value it, you little provincial muggins. If you had it in New York in mid-summer, you could buy all the whales in the market with it."

She looked at me doubtfully, and said:

Are you speaking true?

"Absolutely. I take my oath to it."

This made her thoughtful. Presently she said, with a little sigh:

I wish *I* could live there.

I had merely meant to furnish her a standard of values which she could understand; but my purpose had miscarried.

I had only given her the impression that whales were cheap and plenty in New York and set her mouth to watering for them. It seemed best to try to mitigate the evil which I had done, so I said:

"But you wouldn't care for whale-meat if you lived there. Nobody does."

What!

"Indeed, they don't."

*Why* don't they?

"Wel-l-l, I hardly know. It's prejudice, I think. Yes, that is it—just prejudice. I reckon somebody that hadn't anything better to do started a prejudice against it, some time or other, and once you get a caprice like that fairly going, you know, it will last no end of time."

That is true—*perfectly* true—said the girl, reflectively. Like our prejudice against soap, here: our tribes had a prejudice against soap, at first, you know.

I glanced at her to see if she was in earnest. Evidently she was. I hesitated, then said, cautiously:

"But pardon me. They *had* a prejudice against soap? Had?"—with falling inflection.

Yes—but that was only at first; nobody would eat it.

"Oh—I understand. I didn't get your idea before."

She resumed:

It was just a prejudice. The first time soap came here from the foreigners, nobody liked it; but as soon as it got to be fashionable everybody liked it, and now everybody has it that can afford it. Are you fond of it?

"Yes, indeed; I should die if I couldn't have it—especially here. Do you like it?"

I just *adore* it! Do you like candles?

"I regard them as an absolute necessity. Are you fond of them?"

Her eyes fairly danced, and she exclaimed:

Oh! Don't mention it! Candles!—and soap!—

"And fish-interiors!"—

And train-oil!—

"And slush!"—

And whale-blubber!—

"And carrion! and sour-krout! and bees-wax! and tar! and
turpentine! and molasses! and—"

Don't—oh, don't—I shall expire with ecstasy!—

"And then serve it all up in a slush-bucket and invite the
neighbors and sail in!"

But this vision of an ideal feast was too much for her, and
she swooned away, poor thing. I rubbed snow in her face and
brought her to, and after a while got her excitement calmed
down. By and by she drifted into her story again:

So we began to live here, in the fine house. But I was not
happy. The reason was this: I was born for love; for me
there could be no true happiness without it. I wanted to be
loved for myself alone. I wanted an idol, and I wanted to
be my idol's idol: nothing less than mutual idolatry would
satisfy my fervent nature. I had suitors in plenty—in over-
plenty, indeed,—but in each and every case they had a fatal
defect; sooner or later I discovered that defect—not one of
them failed to betray it: it was not me they wanted, but my
wealth.

"Your wealth?"

Yes; for my father is much the richest man in this tribe—or
in any tribe in these regions.

I wondered what her father's wealth consisted of. It
couldn't be the house—anybody could build its mate. It
couldn't be the furs—they were not valued. It couldn't be the
sledge, the dogs, the harpoons, the boat, the bone fish-hooks
and needles, and such things—no, these were not wealth.
Then, what could it be that made this man so rich and
brought this swarm of sordid suitors to his house? It seemed
to me, finally, that the best way to find out would be to ask.
So I did it. The girl was so manifestly gratified by the question that I saw she had been aching to have me ask it. She was
suffering fully as much to tell as I was to know. She snuggled
confidentially up to me and said:

Guess how much he is worth—you never can!

I pretended to consider the matter deeply, she watching my
anxious and laboring countenance with a devouring and delighted interest; and when, at last, I gave it up and begged her
to appease my longing by telling me herself how much this

polar Vanderbilt was worth, she put her mouth close to my ear and whispered, impressively:

*Twenty-two fish-hooks*—not bone, but foreign—*made out of real iron!*

Then she sprang back dramatically, to observe the effect. I did my level best not to disappoint her. I turned pale and murmured:

"Great Scott!"

It's as true as you live, Mr. Twain!

"Lasca, you are deceiving me—you cannot mean it."

She was frightened and troubled. She exclaimed:

Mr. Twain, every word of it is true—every word. You believe me—you *do* believe me, now *don't* you? *Say* you believe me—*do* say you believe me.

"I—well, yes, I do—I am *trying* to. But it was all so *sudden*. So sudden and prostrating. You shouldn't do such a thing in that sudden way. It—"

Oh, I'm *so* sorry. If I had only thought—

"Well, it's all right, and I don't blame you any more, for you are young and thoughtless, and of course you couldn't foresee what an effect—"

But oh, dear, I ought certainly to have *known* better. Why—

"You see, Lasca, if you had said five or six hooks, to start with, and then gradually—"

Oh, I see, I see—then gradually added one, and then two, and then—ah, why couldn't I have thought of that!

"Never mind, child, it's all right—I am better now—I shall be over it in a little while. *But*—to spring the whole twenty-two on a person unprepared and not very strong anyway—"

Oh, it *was* a crime! But you forgive me—say you forgive me. Do!

After harvesting a good deal of very pleasant coaxing and petting and persuading, I forgave her and she was happy again, and by and by she got under way with her narrative once more. I presently discovered that the family treasury contained still another feature—a jewel of some sort, apparently—and that she was trying to get around speaking squarely about it, lest I get paralyzed again. But I wanted to know about that thing, too, and urged her to tell me what it was. She was afraid. But I insisted, and said I would brace myself this time and be prepared, then the shock would not hurt me. She was full of misgivings, but the temptation to reveal that marvel to me and enjoy my astonishment and ad- miration were too strong for her, and she confessed that she had it on her person, and said that if I was *sure* I was pre- pared—and so on and so on—and with that she reached into her bosom and brought out a battered square of brass, watch- ing my eye anxiously the while. I fell over against her in a quite well-acted faint, which delighted her heart and nearly frightened it out of her, too, at the same time. When I came to and got calm, she was eager to know what I thought of her jewel.

"What do I think of it? I think it is the most exquisite thing I ever saw."

Do you really? how nice of you to say that. But it *is* a love, now isn't it?

"Well, I should say so! I'd rather own it than the equator."

I thought you would admire it, she said. I think it is *so* lovely. And there isn't another one in all these latitudes. Peo- ple have come all the way from the Open Polar Sea to look at it. Did you ever see one before?

I said no, this was the first one I had ever seen. It cost me a pang to tell that generous lie, for I had seen a million of them in my time, this humble jewel of hers being nothing but a battered old N. Y. Central baggage-check.

"Land!" said I, "you don't go about with it on your person this way, alone and no protection, not even a dog?"

Ssh! not so loud, she said. Nobody knows I carry it with me. They think it is in papa's treasury. That is where it gener- ally is.

"Where is the treasury?"

It was a blunt question, and for a moment she looked star- tled and a little suspicious, but I said—

"Oh, come, don't you be afraid about me. At home we have seventy millions of people, and although I say it myself that shouldn't, there is not one person among them all but would trust me with untold fish-hooks."

This reassured her and she told me where the hooks were

hidden in the house. Then she wandered from her course to brag a little about the size of the sheets of transparent ice that formed the windows of the mansion, and asked me if I had ever seen their like at home, and I came right out frankly and confessed that I hadn't, which pleased her more than she could find words to dress her gratification in. It was so easy to please her, and such a pleasure to do it that I went on and said—

"Ah, Lasca, you *are* a fortunate girl!—this beautiful house, this dainty jewel, that rich treasure, all this elegant snow, and sumptuous icebergs and limitless sterility, and public bears and walruses, and noble freedom and largeness, and everybody's admiring eyes upon you, and everybody's homage and respect at your command without the asking; young, rich, beautiful, sought, courted, envied, not a requirement unsatisfied, not a desire ungratified, nothing to wish for that you cannot have—it is immeasurable good fortune! I have seen myriads of girls, but none of whom these extraordinary things could be truthfully said but you alone. And you are worthy—worthy of it all, Lasca—I believe it in my heart."

It made her infinitely proud and happy to hear me say this, and she thanked me over and over again for that closing remark, and her voice and eyes showed that she was touched. Presently she said:

Still, it is not all sunshine—there is a cloudy side. The burden of wealth is a heavy one to bear. Sometimes I have doubted if it were not better to be poor—at least not inordinately rich. It pains me to see neighboring tribesmen stare as they pass by, and overhear them say reverently, one to another, "There—that is she—the millionaire's daughter!" And sometimes they say sorrowfully, "She is rolling in fish-hooks, and I—I have nothing." It breaks my heart. When I was a child and we were poor, we slept with the door open if we chose, but now—now we have to have a night-watchman. In those days my father was gentle and courteous to all; but now he is austere and haughty, and cannot abide familiarity. Once his family were his sole thought, but now he goes about thinking of his fish-hooks all the time. And his wealth makes everybody cringing and obsequious to him. Formerly nobody laughed at his jokes, they being always stale and far-fetched

and poor, and destitute of the one element that can really
justify a joke—the element of humor—but now everybody
laughs and cackles at those dismal things, and if any fails to
do it my father is deeply displeased, and shows it. Formerly
his opinion was not sought upon any matter and was not
valuable when he volunteered it; it has that infirmity yet, but,
nevertheless, it is sought by all and applauded by all—and he
helps do the applauding himself, having no true delicacy and
a plentiful want of tact. He has lowered the tone of all our
tribe. Once they were a frank and manly race, now they are
measly hypocrites, and sodden with servility. In my heart of
hearts I hate all the ways of millionaires! Our tribe was once
plain simple folk, and content with the bone fish-hooks of
their fathers; now they are eaten up with avarice and would
sacrifice every sentiment of honor and honesty to possess
themselves of the debasing iron fish-hooks of the foreigner.
However, I must not dwell on these sad things. As I have
said, it was my dream to be loved for myself alone.

At last, this dream seemed about to be fulfilled. A stranger
came by, one day, who said his name was Kalula. I told him
my name, and he said he loved me. My heart gave a great
bound of gratitude and pleasure, for I had loved him at sight,
and now I said so. He took me to his breast and said he
would not wish to be happier than he was now. We went
strolling together far over the ice-floes, telling all about each
other, and planning, oh, the loveliest future! When we were
tired at last we sat down and ate, for he had soap and candles
and I had brought along some blubber. We were hungry and
nothing was ever so good.

He belonged to a tribe whose haunts were far to the north,
and I found that he had never heard of my father, which rejoiced me exceedingly. I mean he had heard of the millionaire,
but had never heard his name—so, you see, he could not
know that I was the heiress. You may be sure that I did not
tell him. I was loved for myself at last, and was satisfied. I was
so happy—oh, happier than you can think!

By and by it was toward supper time, and I led him home.
As we approached our house he was amazed, and cried out—

"How splendid! Is *that* your father's?"

It gave me a pang to hear that tone and see that admiring

light in his eye, but the feeling quickly passed away, for I loved him so, and he looked so handsome and noble. All my family of aunts and uncles and cousins were pleased with him, and many guests were called in, and the house was shut up tight and the rag lamps lighted, and when everything was hot and comfortable and suffocating, we began a joyous feast in celebration of my betrothal.

When the feast was over, my father's vanity overcame him, and he could not resist the temptation to show off his riches and let Kalula see what grand good-fortune he had stumbled into—and mainly, of course he wanted to enjoy the poor man's amazement. I could have cried—but it would have done no good to try to dissuade my father, so I said nothing, but merely sat there and suffered.

My father went straight to the hiding-place, in full sight of everybody, and got out the fish-hooks and brought them and flung them scatteringly over my head, so that they fell in glittering confusion on the platform right at my lover's knee.

Of course, the astounding spectacle took the poor lad's breath away. He could only stare in stupid astonishment, and wonder how a single individual could possess such incredible riches. Then presently he glanced brilliantly up and exclaimed:

"Ah, it is *you* who are the renowned millionaire!"

My father and all the rest burst into shouts of happy laughter, and when my father gathered the treasure carelessly up as if it might be mere rubbish and of no consequence and carried it back to its place, poor Kalula's surprise was a study. He said:

"Is it possible that you put such things away without counting them?"

My father delivered a vain-glorious horse-laugh, and said:

"Well, truly, a body may know *you* have never been rich, since a mere matter of a fish-hook or two is such a mighty matter in your eyes."

Kalula was confused, and hung his head, but said:

"Ah, indeed sir, I was never worth the value of the barb of one of those precious things, and I have never seen any man before who was so rich in them as to render the counting of his hoard worth while, since the wealthiest man I have ever known, till now, was possessed of but three."

My foolish father roared again with jejune delight, and allowed the impression to remain that he was not accustomed to count his hooks and keep sharp watch over them. He was showing off, you see. Count them? Why, he counted them every day!

I had met and got acquainted with my darling just at dawn; I had brought him home just at dark, three hours afterward—for the days were shortening toward the six-months' night at that time. We kept up the festivities many hours; then, at last, the guests departed and the rest of us distributed ourselves along the walls on sleeping benches, and soon all were steeped in dreams but me. I was too happy, too excited, to sleep. After I had lain quiet a long, long time, a dim form passed by me and was swallowed up in the gloom that pervaded the further end of the house. I could not make out who it was, or whether it was man or woman. Presently that figure or another one passed me going the other way. I wondered what it all meant, but wondering did no good; and while I was still wondering I fell asleep.

I do not know how long I slept, but at last I came suddenly broad awake and heard my father say in a terrible voice, "By the great Snow God there's a fish-hook gone!" Something told me that that meant sorrow for me, and the blood in my veins turned cold. The presentiment was confirmed in the same instant: my father shouted, "Up, everybody, and seize the stranger!" Then there was an outburst of cries and curses from all sides, and a wild rush of dim forms through the obscurity. I flew to my beloved's help, but what could I do but wait and wring my hands?—he was already fenced away from me by a living wall, he was being bound hand and foot. Not until he was secured would they let me get to him. I flung myself upon his poor insulted form and cried my grief out upon his breast while my father and all my family scoffed at me and heaped threats and shameful epithets upon him. He bore his ill usage with a tranquil dignity which endeared him to me more than ever and made me proud and happy to suffer with him and for him. I heard my father order that the elders of the tribe be called together to try my Kalula for his life.

"What!" I said, "before any search has been made for the lost hook?"

"Lost hook!" they all shouted, in derision; and my father added, mockingly, "Stand back, everybody, and be properly serious—she is going to hunt up that *lost* hook; oh, without doubt she will find it!"—whereat they all laughed again.

I was not disturbed—I had no fears, no doubts. I said:

"It is for you to laugh now; it is your turn. But ours is coming; wait and see."

I got a rag-lamp. I thought I should find that miserable thing in one little moment; and I set about the matter with such confidence that those people grew grave, beginning to suspect that perhaps they had been too hasty. But alas and alas!—oh, the bitterness of that search! There was deep silence while one might count his fingers ten or twelve times, then my heart began to sink, and around me the mockings began again, and grew steadily louder and more assured, until at last, when I gave up, they burst into volley after volley of cruel laughter.

None will ever know what I suffered then. But my love was my support and my strength, and I took my rightful place at my Kalula's side, and put my arm about his neck, and whispered in his ear, saying:

"You are innocent, my own,—that I know; but say it to me yourself, for my comfort, then I can bear whatever is in store for us."

He answered:

"As surely as I stand upon the brink of death at this moment, I am innocent. Be comforted, then, O bruised heart; be at peace, O thou breath of my nostrils, life of my life!"

"Now, then, let the elders come!"—and as I said the words, there was a gathering sound of crunching snow outside and then a vision of stooping forms filing in at the door—the elders.

My father formally accused the prisoner, and detailed the happenings of the night. He said that the watchman was outside the door, and that in the house were none but the family and the stranger. "Would the family steal their own property?" He paused. The elders sat silent many minutes; at last, one after another said to his neighbor, "This looks bad for the stranger"—sorrowful words for me to hear. Then my father sat down. O miserable, miserable me! at that very moment I could have proved my darling innocent, but I did not know it!

The chief of the court asked:

"Is there any here to defend the prisoner?"

I rose, and said:

"Why should *he* steal that hook, or any or all of them? In another day he would have been heir to the whole!"

I stood waiting. There was a long silence, the steam from the many breaths rising about me like a fog. At last, one elder after another nodded his head slowly several times, and muttered, "There is force in what the child has said." Oh, the heart-lift that was in those words!—so transient, but, oh, so precious! I sat down.

"If any would say further, let him speak now, or after hold his peace," said the chief of the court.

My father rose and said:

"In the night a form passed by me in the gloom, going toward the treasury, and presently returned. I think, now, it was the stranger."

Oh, I was like to swoon! I had supposed that that was my secret; not the grip of the great Ice God himself could have dragged it out of my heart. The chief of the court said sternly to my poor Kalula:

"Speak!"

Kalula hesitated, then answered:

"It was I. I could not sleep for thinking of the beautiful hooks. I went there, and kissed them and fondled them, to appease my spirit and drown it in a harmless joy, then I put them back. I may have dropped one, but I stole none."

Oh, a fatal admission to make in such a place! There was an awful hush. I knew he had pronounced his own doom, and that all was over. On every face you could see the words hieroglyphed: "It is a confession!—and paltry, lame and thin."

I sat drawing in my breath in faint gasps—and waiting. Presently, I heard the solemn words I knew were coming; and each word, as it came, was a knife in my heart:

"It is the command of the court that the accused be subjected to the *trial by water*."

Oh, curses be upon the head of him who brought "trial by water" to our land! It came, generations ago, from some far country that lies none knows where. Before that, our fathers used augury and other unsure methods of trial, and doubtless some poor, guilty creatures escaped with their lives sometimes; but it is not so with trial by water, which is an invention by wiser men than we poor, ignorant savages are. By it the innocent are proved innocent, without doubt or question, for they drown; and the guilty are proven guilty with the same certainty, for they do not drown. My heart was breaking in my bosom, for I said, "He is innocent, and he will go down under the waves and I shall never see him more."

I never left his side after that. I mourned in his arms all the precious hours, and he poured out the deep stream of his love upon me, and oh, I was so miserable and so happy! At last, they tore him from me, and I followed sobbing after them, and saw them fling him into the sea—then I covered my face with my hands. Agony? Oh, I know the deepest deeps of that word!

The next moment the people burst into a shout of malicious joy, and I took away my hands, startled. Oh, bitter sight—he was *swimming*! My heart turned instantly to stone, to ice. I said, "He was guilty, and he lied to me!" I turned my back in scorn and went my way homeward.

They took him far out to sea and set him on an iceberg that was drifting southward in the great waters. Then my family came home, and my father said to me:

"Your thief sent his dying message to you, saying, 'Tell her I am innocent, and that all the days and all the hours and all the minutes while I starve and perish I shall love her and think of her and bless the day that gave me sight of her sweet face.' Quite pretty, even poetical!"

I said, "He is dirt—let me never hear mention of him again." And oh, to think—he *was* innocent all the time!

Nine months—nine dull, sad months—went by, and at last came the day of the Great Annual Sacrifice, when all the maidens of the tribe wash their faces and comb their hair. With the first sweep of my comb, out came the fatal fish-hook from where it had been all those months nestling, and I fell fainting into the arms of my remorseful father! Groaning, he said, "We murdered him, and I shall never smile again!" He has kept his word. Listen: from that day to this not a month goes by that I do not comb my hair. But O, where is the good of it all now!

So ended the poor maid's humble little tale—whereby we learn that since a hundred million dollars in New York and twenty-two fish-hooks on the border of the Arctic Circle represent the same financial supremacy, a man in straightened circumstances is a fool to stay in New York when he can buy ten cents' worth of fish-hooks and emigrate.

*November 1893*

# Travelling with a Reformer

Last spring I went out to Chicago to see the Fair, and although I did not see it my trip was not wholly lost—there were compensations. In New York I was introduced to a major in the regular army who said he was going to the Fair, and we agreed to go together. I had to go to Boston first, but that did not interfere; he said he would go along, and put in the time. He was a handsome man and built like a gladiator. But his ways were gentle and his speech was soft and persuasive. He was companionable but exceedingly reposeful. Yes, and wholly destitute of the sense of humor. He was full of interest in everything that went on around him, but his serenity was indestructible; nothing disturbed him, nothing excited him.

But before the day was done I found that deep down in him somewhere he had a passion, quiet as he was—a passion for reforming petty public abuses. He stood for citizenship—it was his hobby. His idea was that every citizen of the republic ought to consider himself an unofficial policeman and keep unsalaried watch and ward over the laws and their execution. He thought that the only effective way of preserving and protecting public rights was for each citizen to do his share in preventing or punishing such infringements of them as came under his personal notice.

It was a good scheme, but I thought it would keep a body in trouble all the time; it seemed to me that one would be always trying to get offending little officials discharged, and perhaps getting laughed at for all reward. But he said no, I had the wrong idea; that there was no occasion to get anybody discharged; that in fact you *mustn't* get anybody discharged; that that would itself be failure; no, one must reform the man—reform him and make him useful where he was.

"Must one report the offender and then beg his superior not to discharge him, but reprimand him and keep him?"

"No, that is not the idea; you don't report him at all, for then you risk his bread and butter. You can act as if you are *going* to report him—when nothing else will answer. But that's an extreme case. That is a sort of *force*, and force is bad.

Diplomacy is the effective thing. Now if a man has tact—if a man will exercise diplomacy—"

For two minutes we had been standing at a telegraph wicket, and during all this time the major had been trying to get the attention of one of the young operators, but they were all busy skylarking. The major spoke, now, and asked one of them to take his telegram. He got for reply:

"I reckon you can wait a minute, can't you?" and the skylarking went on.

The major said yes, he was not in a hurry. Then he wrote another telegram: "President Western Union Tel. Co.:

"Come and dine with me this evening. I can tell you how business is conducted in one of your branches."

Presently the young fellow who had spoken so pertly a little before reached out and took the telegram, and when he read it he lost color and began to apologize and explain. He said he would lose his place if this deadly telegram was sent, and he might never get another. If he could be let off this time he would give no cause of complaint again. The compromise was accepted.

As we walked away, the major said:

"Now, you see, that was diplomacy—and you see how it worked. It wouldn't do any good to bluster, the way people are always doing—that boy can always give you as good as you send, and you'll come out defeated and ashamed of yourself pretty nearly always. But you see he stands no chance against diplomacy. Gentle words and diplomacy—those are the tools to work with."

"Yes, I see; but everybody wouldn't have had your opportunity. It isn't everybody that is on those familiar terms with the president of the Western Union."

"Oh, you misunderstand. I don't know the president—I only use him diplomatically. It is for his good and for the public good. There's no harm in it."

I said, with hesitation and diffidence:

"But is it ever right or noble to tell a lie?"

He took no note of the delicate self-righteousness of the question, but answered with undisturbed gravity and simplicity:

"Yes, sometimes. Lies told to injure a person, and lies told

to profit yourself are not justifiable, but lies told to help another person, and lies told in the public interest—oh, well,
that is quite another matter. Anybody knows that. But never
mind about the methods: you see the result. That youth is
going to be useful now, and well-behaved. He had a good
face. He was worth saving. Why, he was worth saving on
his mother's account if not his own. Of course, he has a
mother—sisters, too. Damn these people who are always forgetting that! Do you know, I've never fought a duel in my
life—never once—and yet have been challenged, like other
people. I could always see the other man's unoffending
women folks or his little children standing between him and
me. *They* hadn't done anything—I couldn't break *their* hearts,
you know."

He corrected a good many little abuses in the course of the
day, and always without friction; always with a fine and
dainty "diplomacy" which left no sting behind; and he got
such happiness and such contentment out of these performances that I was obliged to envy him his trade—and perhaps would have adopted it if I could have managed the
necessary deflections from fact as confidently with my mouth
as I believe I could with a pen, behind the shelter of print,
after a little practice.

Away late, that night, we were coming up town in a horse-
car, when three boisterous roughs got abroad and began to
fling hilarious obscenities and profanities right and left among
the timid passengers, some of whom were women and children. Nobody resisted or retorted; the conductor tried sooth-
ing words and moral suasion, but the roughs only called him
names and laughed at him. Very soon I saw that the major
realized that this was a matter which was in his line; evidently
he was turning over his stock of diplomacy in his mind and
getting ready. I felt that the first diplomatic remark he made
in this place would bring down a land-slide of ridicule upon
him and may be something worse; but before I could whisper
to him and check him, he had begun, and it was too late. He
said in a level and dispassionate tone:

"Conductor, you must put these swine out. I will help
you."

I was not looking for that. In a flash the three roughs

plunged at him. But none of them arrived. He delivered three such blows as one could not expect to encounter outside the prize ring, and neither of the men had life enough left in him to get up from where he fell. The major dragged them out and threw them off the car, and we got under way again.

I was astonished; astonished to see a lamb act so; astonished at the strength displayed and the clean and comprehensive result; astonished at the brisk and business-like style of the whole thing. The situation had a humorous side to it, considering how much I had been hearing about mild persuasion and gentle diplomacy all day from this pile-driver, and I would have liked to call his attention to that feature and do some sarcasms about it; but when I looked at him I saw that it would be of no use—his placid and contented face had no ray of humor in it; he would not have understood. When we left the car, I said:

"That was a good stroke of diplomacy—three good strokes of diplomacy, in fact."

"*That?* That wasn't diplomacy. You are quite in the wrong. Diplomacy is a wholly different thing. One cannot apply it to that sort, they would not understand it. No, that was not diplomacy, it was force."

"Now that you mention it, I—yes, I think perhaps you are right."

"Right? Of course I am right. It was just force."

"I think, myself, it had the outside aspect of it. Do you often have to reform people in that way?"

"Far from it. It hardly ever happens. Not oftener than once in half a year, at the outside."

"Those men will get well?"

"Get well? Why certainly they will. They are not in any danger. I know how to hit and where to hit. You noticed that I did not hit them under the jaw. That would have killed them."

I believed that. I remarked—rather wittily, as I thought— that he had been a lamb all day but now had all of a sudden developed into a ram—battering ram; but with dulcet frankness and simplicity he said no, a battering ram was quite a different thing and not in use now. This was maddening, and I came near bursting out and saying he had no more appre-

ciation of wit than a jackass—in fact, I had it right on my
tongue, but did not say it, knowing there was no hurry and I
could say it just as well some other time over the telephone.

We started to Boston the next afternoon. The smoking
compartment in the parlor car was full and we went into the
regular smoker. Across the aisle in the front seat sat a meek
farmer-looking old man with a sickly pallor in his face, and he
was holding the door open with his foot to get the air. Presently a big brakeman came rushing through, and when he got
to the door he stopped, gave the farmer an ugly scowl, then
wrenched the door to with such energy as to almost snatch
the old man's boot off. Then on he plunged, about his business. Several passengers laughed, and the old gentleman
looked pathetically shamed and grieved.

After a little the conductor passed along and the major
stopped him and asked him a question in his habitually courteous way:

"Conductor, where does one report the misconduct of a
brakeman? Does one report to you?"

"You can report him at New Haven if you want to. What
has he been doing?"

The major told the story. The conductor seemed amused.
He said, with just a touch of sarcasm in his bland tones:

"As I understand you, the brakeman didn't *say* anything."

"No, he didn't say anything."

"But he scowled, you say."

"Yes."

"And snatched the door loose in a rough way."

"Yes."

"That's the whole business, is it?"

"Yes, that is the whole of it."

The conductor smiled pleasantly, and said:

"Well, if you want to report him, all right, but I don't quite
make out what it's going to amount to. You'll say—as I understand you—that the brakeman insulted this old gentleman. They'll ask you what he *said*. You'll say he didn't say
anything at all. I reckon they'll say, how are you going to
make out an insult when you acknowledge yourself that he
didn't say a word."

There was a murmur of applause at the conductor's compact reasoning, and it gave him pleasure—you could see it in his face. But the major was not disturbed. He said:

"There—now you have touched upon a crying defect in the complaint-system. The railway officials—as the public think and as you also seem to think—are not aware that there are any kind of insults except *spoken* ones. So nobody goes to head-quarters and reports insults of manner, insults of gesture, look, and so forth; and yet these are sometimes harder to bear than any words. They are bitter hard to bear because there is nothing tangible to take hold of; and the insulter can always say, if called before the railway officials, that he never dreamed of intending any offense. It seems to me that the officials ought to specially and urgently request the public to report *unworded* affronts and incivilities."

The conductor laughed, and said:

"Well, that *would* be trimming it pretty fine, sure!"

"But not too fine, I think. I will report this matter at New Haven, and I have an idea that I'll be thanked for it."

The conductor's face lost something of its complacency; in fact it settled to a quite sober cast as the owner of it moved away. I said:

"You are not really going to bother with that trifle are you?"

"It isn't a trifle. Such things ought always to be reported. It is a public duty, and no citizen has a right to shirk it. But I shan't have to report this case."

"Why?"

"It won't be necessary. Diplomacy will do the business. You'll see."

Presently the conductor came on his rounds again, and when he reached the major he leaned over and said:

"That's all right. You needn't report him. He's responsible to me, and if he does it again I'll give him a talking to."

The major's response was cordial:

"Now that is what I like! You mustn't think that I was moved by any vengeful spirit, for that wasn't the case. It was duty—just a sense of duty, that was all. My brother-in-law is one of the directors of the road, and when he learns that you are going to reason with your brakeman the very next time he brutally insults an unoffending old man it will please him, you may be sure of that."

The conductor did not look as joyous as one might have thought he would, but on the contrary looked sickly and uncomfortable. He stood around a little, then said:

"*I* think something ought to be done to him *now*. I'll discharge him."

"Discharge him? What good would that do? Don't you think it would be better wisdom to teach him better ways and keep him?"

"Well, there's something in that. What would you suggest?"

"He insulted the old gentleman in presence of all these people, how would it do to have him come and apologize in their presence?"

"I'll have him here right off. And I want to say this: If people would do as you've done, and report such things to me instead of keeping mum and going off and blackguarding the road, you'd see a different state of things pretty soon. I'm much obliged to you."

The brakeman came and apologized. After he was gone the major said:

"Now, you see how simple and easy that was. The ordinary citizen would have accomplished nothing—the brother-in-law of a director can accomplish anything he wants to."

"But are you really the brother-in-law of a director?"

"Always. Always when the public interests require it. I have a brother-in-law on all the boards—everywhere. It saves me a world of trouble."

"It is a good wide relationship."

"Yes, I have over three hundred of them."

"Is the relationship never doubted by a conductor?"

"I have never met with a case. It is the honest truth—I never have."

"Why didn't you let him go ahead and discharge the brakeman, in spite of your favorite policy? You know he deserved it."

The major answered with something which really had a sort of distant resemblance to impatience:

"If you would stop and think a moment you wouldn't ask such a question as that. Is a brakeman a dog, that nothing but dog's methods will do for him? He is a man, and has a man's fight for life. And he always has a sister, or a mother, or wife and children to support. Always—there are no exceptions.

When you take his living away from him you take theirs away too—and what have they done to you? Nothing. And where is the profit in discharging an uncourteous brakeman and hiring another just like him? It's unwisdom. Don't you see that the rational thing to do is to *reform* the brakeman and keep him? Of course it is."

Then he quoted with admiration the conduct of a certain division superintendent of the Consolidated road, in a case where a switchman of two years' experience was negligent once and threw a train off the track and killed several people. Citizens came in a passion to urge the man's dismissal, but the superintendent said:

"No, you are wrong. He has learned his lesson, he will throw no more trains off the track. He is twice as valuable as he was before. I shall keep him."

We had only one more adventure on the trip. Between Hartford and Springfield the train-boy came shouting in with an armful of literature and dropped a sample into a slumbering gentleman's lap, and the man woke up with a start. He was very angry, and he and a couple of friends discussed the outrage with much heat. They sent for the parlor-car conductor and described the matter, and were determined to have the boy expelled from his situation. The three complainants were wealthy Holyoke merchants, and it was evident that the conductor stood in some awe of them. He tried to pacify them, and explained that the boy was not under his authority, but under that of one of the news companies, but he accomplished nothing.

Then the major volunteered some testimony for the defense. He said:

"I saw it all. You gentlemen have not meant to exaggerate the circumstances, but still that is what you have done. The boy has done nothing more than all train-boys do. If you want to get his ways softened down and his manners reformed, I am with you and ready to help, but it isn't fair to get him discharged without giving him a chance."

But they were angry and would hear of no compromise. They were well acquainted with the president of the Boston & Albany, they said, and would put everything aside next day and go up to Boston and fix that boy.

The major said he would be on hand too, and would do what he could to save the boy. One of the gentlemen looked him over, and said:

"Apparently, it is going to be a matter of who can wield the most influence with the president. Do you know Mr. Bliss personally?"

The major said, with composure:

"Yes; he is my uncle."

The effect was satisfactory. There was an awkward silence for a minute or more, then the hedging and the half-confessions of over-haste and exaggerated resentment began, and soon everything was smooth and friendly and sociable, and it was resolved to drop the matter and leave the boy's bread and butter unmolested.

It turned out as I had expected: the president of the road was not the major's uncle at all—except by adoption, and for this day and train only.

We got into no episodes on the return journey. Probably it was because we took a night train and slept all the way.

We left New York Saturday night by the Pennsylvania road. After breakfast, the next morning, we went into the parlor-car, but found it a dull place and dreary. There were but few people in it and nothing going on. Then we went into the little smoking compartment of the same car and found three gentlemen in there. Two of them were grumbling over one of the rules of the road—a rule which forbade card-playing on the trains on Sunday. They had started an innocent game of high-low-jack and been stopped. The major was interested. He said to the third gentleman:

"Did you object to the game?"

"Not at all. I am a Yale professor and a religious man, but my prejudices are not extensive."

Then the major said to the others:

"You are at perfect liberty to resume your game, gentlemen; no one here objects."

One of them declined the risk, but the other one said he would like to begin again if the major would join him. So they spread an overcoat over their knees and the game proceeded. Pretty soon the parlor-conductor arrived, and said brusquely:

"There, there, gentlemen, that won't do. Put up the cards—it's not allowed."

The major was shuffling. He continued to shuffle, and said:

"By whose order is it forbidden?"

"It's my order. I forbid it."

The dealing began. The major asked:

"Did you invent the idea?"

"What idea?"

"The idea of forbidding card playing on Sunday."

"No—of course not."

"Who did?"

"The company."

"Then it isn't your order, after all, but the company's. Is that it?"

"Yes. But you don't stop playing; I have to require you to stop playing immediately."

"Nothing is gained by hurry, and often much is lost. Who authorized the company to issue such an order?"

"My dear sir, that is a matter of no consequence to me, and—"

"But you forget that you are not the only person concerned. It may be a matter of consequence to me. It is indeed a matter of very great importance to me. I cannot violate a legal requirement of my country without dishonoring myself; I cannot allow any man or corporation to hamper my liberties with illegal rules—a thing which railway companies are always trying to do—without dishonoring my citizenship. So I come back to that question: By whose authority has the company issued this order?"

"I don't *know*. That's *their* affair."

"Mine, too. I doubt if the company has any right to issue such a rule. This road runs through several States. Do you know what State we are in now, and what its laws are in matters of this kind?"

"Its laws do not concern me, but the company's orders do. It is my duty to stop this game, gentlemen, and it *must* be stopped."

"Possibly; but still there is no hurry. In hotels they post certain rules in the rooms, but they always quote passages from the State law as authority for these requirements. I see

nothing posted here of this sort. Please produce your authority and let us arrive at a decision, for you see, yourself, that
you are marring the game."

"I have nothing of the kind, but I have my orders, and that
is sufficient. They must be obeyed."

"Let us not jump to conclusions. It will be better all around
to examine into the matter without heat or haste and see just
where we stand, before either of us makes a mistake—for the
curtailing of the liberties of a citizen of the United States is a
much more serious matter than you and the railroads seem to
think, and it cannot be done in my person until the curtailer
proves his right to do so. Now—"

"My dear sir, *will* you put down those cards!"

"All in good time, perhaps. It depends. You say this order
must be obeyed. *Must*. It is a strong word. You see, yourself,
how strong it is. A wise company would not arm you with so
drastic an order as this, of *course*, without appointing a penalty for its infringement. Otherwise it runs the risk of being a
dead letter and a thing to laugh at. What is the appointed
penalty for an infringement of this law?"

"Penalty? I never heard of any."

"Unquestionably you must be mistaken. Your company
orders you to come here and rudely break up an innocent
amusement, and furnishes you no way to enforce the order?
Don't you see that that is nonsense? What do you *do* when
people refuse to obey this order? Do you take the cards away
from them?"

"No."

"Do you put the offender off at the next station?"

"Well, no—of course we couldn't if he had a ticket."

"Do you have him up before a court?"

The conductor was silent and apparently troubled. The
major started a new deal, and said:

"You see that you are helpless, and that the company has
placed you in a foolish position. You are furnished with an
arrogant order, and you deliver it in a blustering way, and
when you come to look into the matter you find you haven't
any way of enforcing obedience."

The conductor said, with chill dignity:

"Gentlemen, you have heard the order, and my duty is

ended. As to obeying it or not, you will do as you think fit"—and he turned to leave.

"But wait. The matter is not yet finished. I think you are mistaken about your duty being ended; but if it really is, I myself have a duty to perform, yet."

"How do you mean?"

"Are you going to report my disobedience at headquarters in Pittsburg?"

"No. What good would that do?"

"You must report me, or I will report you."

"Report me for what?"

"For disobeying the company's orders in not stopping this game. As a citizen it is my duty to help the railway companies keep their servants to their work."

"Are you in earnest?"

"Yes, I am in earnest. I have nothing against you as a man, but I have this against you as an officer—that you have not carried out that order, and if you do not report me I must report you. And I will."

The conductor looked puzzled and was thoughtful a moment, then he burst out with—

"I seem to be getting *myself* into a scrape! It's all a muddle; I can't make head or tail of it; it's never happened before; they always knocked under and never said a word, and so *I* never saw how ridiculous that stupid order with no penalty is. *I* don't want to report anybody, and I don't want to *be* reported—why, it might do me no end of harm! Now *do* go on with the game—play the whole day if you want to—and don't let's have any more trouble about it!"

"No, I only sat down here to establish this gentleman's rights—he can have his place, now. But before you go, won't you tell me what you think the company made this rule for? Can you imagine an excuse for it? I mean a rational one—an excuse that is not on its face silly, and the invention of an idiot?"

"Why, surely I can. The reason it was made is plain enough. It is to save the feelings of the other passengers—the religious ones among them, I mean. They would not like it, to have the Sabbath desecrated by card-playing on the train."

"I just thought as much. They are willing to desecrate it themselves by travelling on Sunday, but they are not willing that other people—"

"By gracious, you've hit it! I never thought of that before. The fact is, it *is* a silly rule when you come to look into it."

At this point the train-conductor arrived and was going to shut down the game in a very high-handed fashion, but the parlor-conductor stopped him and took him aside to explain. Nothing more was heard of the matter.

I was ill in bed eleven days in Chicago and got no glimpse of the Fair, for I was obliged to return east as soon as I was able to travel. The major secured and paid for a stateroom in a sleeper the day before we left, so that I could have plenty of room and be comfortable; but when we arrived at the station a mistake had been made and our car had not been put on. The conductor had reserved a section for us—it was the best he could do, he said. But the major said we were not in a hurry, and would wait for the car to be put on. The conductor responded with pleasant irony:

"It may be that *you* are not in a hurry, just as you say, but we *are*. Come, get aboard, gentlemen, get aboard—don't keep us waiting."

But the major would not get aboard himself nor allow me to do it. He wanted his car, and said he must have it. This made the hurried and perspiring conductor impatient, and he said:

"It's the best we can *do*—we can't do impossibilities. You will take the section or go without. A mistake has been made and can't be rectified at this late hour. It's a thing that happens now and then, and there is nothing for it but to put up with it and make the best of it. Other people do."

"Ah, that is just it, you see. If they had stuck to their rights and enforced them you wouldn't be trying to trample mine under foot in this bland way now. I haven't any disposition to give you unnecessary trouble, but it is my duty to protect the next man from this kind of imposition. So I must have my car. Otherwise I will wait in Chicago and sue the company for violating its contract."

"Sue the company?—for a thing like that!"

"Certainly."

"Do you really mean that?"

"Indeed, I do."

The conductor looked the major over wonderingly, and then said:

"It beats me—it's bran new—I've never struck the mate to it before. But I swear I think you'd do it. Look here, I'll send for the station-master."

When the station-master came he was a good deal annoyed —at the major, not at the person who had made the mistake. He was rather brusque and took the same position which the conductor had taken in the beginning; but he failed to move the soft-spoken artilleryman, who still insisted that he must have his car. However, it was plain that there was only one strong side in this case, and that that side was the major's. The station-master banished his annoyed manner and became pleasant and even half-apologetic. This made a good opening for a compromise, and the major made a concession. He said he would give up the engaged stateroom, but he must have *a* stateroom. After a deal of ransacking, one was found whose owner was persuadable; he exchanged it for our section and we got away at last. The conductor called on us in the evening and was kind and courteous and obliging, and we had a long talk and got to be good friends. He said he wished the public would make trouble oftener—it would have a good effect. He said that the railroads could not be expected to do their whole duty by the traveller unless the traveller would take some interest in the matter himself.

I hoped that we were done reforming for the trip, now, but it was not so. In the hotel-car, in the morning, the major called for broiled chicken. The waiter said:

"It's not in the bill of fare, sir; we do not serve anything but what is in the bill."

"That gentleman yonder is eating a broiled chicken."

"Yes, but that is different. He is one of the superintendents of the road."

"Then, all the more must I have broiled chicken. I do not like these discriminations. Please hurry—bring me a broiled chicken."

The waiter brought the steward, who explained in a low and polite voice that the thing was impossible—it was against the rule, and the rule was rigid.

"Very well, then, you must either apply it impartially or break it impartially. You must take that gentleman's chicken away from him or bring me one."

The steward was puzzled, and did not quite know what to do. He began an incoherent argument, but the conductor came along just then, and asked what the difficulty was. The steward explained that here was a gentleman who was insisting on having a chicken when it was dead against the rule and not in the bill. The conductor said:

"Stick by your rules—you haven't any option. Wait a moment—is this the gentleman?" Then he laughed and said: "Never mind your rules—it's my advice, and sound; give him anything he wants—don't get him started on his rights. Give him whatever he asks for; and if you haven't got it, stop the train and get it."

The major ate the chicken, but said he did it from a sense of duty and to establish a principle, for he did not like chicken.

I missed the Fair, it is true, but I picked up some diplomatic tricks which I and the reader may find handy and useful as we go along.

*December 1893*

# Concerning Tobacco

As concerns tobacco, there are many superstitions. And the chiefest is this—that there is a *standard* governing the matter, whereas there is nothing of the kind. Each man's own preference is the only standard for him, the only one which he can accept, the only one which can command him. A congress of all the tobacco-lovers in the world could not elect a standard which would be binding upon you or me, or would even much influence us.

The next superstition is that a man has a standard of his own. He hasn't. He thinks he has, but he hasn't. He thinks he can tell what he regards as a good cigar from what he regards as a bad one—but he can't. He goes by the brand, yet imagines he goes by the flavor. One may palm off the worst counterfeit upon him; if it bears his brand he will smoke it contentedly and never suspect.

Children of twenty-five, who have seven years of experience, try to tell me what is a good cigar and what isn't. Me, who never learned to smoke, but always smoked; me, who came into the world asking for a light.

No one can tell me what is a good cigar—for me. I am the only judge. People who claim to know say that I smoke the worst cigars in the world. They bring their own cigars when they come to my house. They betray an unmanly terror when I offer them a cigar; they tell lies and hurry away to meet engagements which they have not made when they are threatened with the hospitalities of my box. Now then, observe what superstition, assisted by a man's reputation, can do. I was to have twelve personal friends to supper one night. One of them was as notorious for costly and elegant cigars as I was for cheap and devilish ones. I called at his house and when no one was looking borrowed a double handful of his very choicest; cigars which cost him forty cents apiece and bore red-and-gold labels in sign of their nobility. I removed the labels and put the cigars into a box with my favorite brand on it—a brand which those people all knew, and which cowed them as men are cowed by an epidemic. They took these cigars when offered at the end of the supper, and lit them and sternly

struggled with them—in dreary silence, for hilarity died
when the fell brand came into view and started around—but
their fortitude held for a short time only; then they made
excuses and filed out, treading on one another's heels with
indecent eagerness; and in the morning when I went out to
observe results the cigars lay all between the front door and
the gate. All except one—that one lay in the plate of the man
from whom I had cabbaged the lot. One or two whiffs was all
he could stand. He told me afterward that some day I would
get shot for giving people that kind of cigars to smoke.

Am I certain of my own standard? Perfectly; yes, absolutely—unless somebody fools me by putting my brand on
some other kind of cigar; for no doubt I am like the rest, and
know my cigar by the brand instead of by the flavor. However, my standard is a pretty wide one and covers a good deal
of territory. To me, almost any cigar is good that nobody else
will smoke, and to me almost all cigars are bad that other
people consider good. Nearly any cigar will do me, except a
Havana. People think they hurt my feelings when they come
to my house with their life-preservers on—I mean, with their
own cigars in their pockets. It is an error; I take care of myself
in a similar way. When I go into danger—that is, into rich
people's houses, where, in the nature of things, they will have
high-tariff cigars, red-and-gilt girdled and nested in a rose-
wood box along with a damp sponge, cigars which develop a
dismal black ash and burn down the side and smell, and will
grow hot to the fingers, and will go on growing hotter and
hotter, and go on smelling more and more infamously and
unendurably the deeper the fire tunnels down inside below
the thimbleful of honest tobacco that is in the front end, the
furnisher of it praising it all the time and telling you how
much the deadly thing cost—yes, when I go into that sort of
peril I carry my own defense along; I carry my own brand—
twenty-seven cents a barrel—and I live to see my family
again. I may seem to light his red-gartered cigar, but that is
only for courtesy's sake; I smuggle it into my pocket for the
poor, of whom I know many, and light one of my own; and
while he praises it I join in, but when he says it cost forty-five
cents I say nothing, for I know better.

However, to say true, my tastes are so catholic that I have

never seen any cigars that I really could not smoke, except those that cost a dollar apiece. I have examined those and know that they are made of dog-hair, and not good dog-hair at that.

I have a thoroughly satisfactory time in Europe, for all over the Continent one finds cigars which not even the most hardened newsboys in New York would smoke. I brought cigars with me, the last time; I will not do that any more. In Italy, as in France, the Government is the only cigar-peddler. Italy has three or four domestic brands: the Minghetti, the Trabuco, the Virginia, and a very coarse one which is a modification of the Virginia. The Minghettis are large and comely, and cost three dollars and sixty cents a hundred; I can smoke a hundred in seven days and enjoy every one of them. The Trabucos suit me, too; I don't remember the price. But one has to learn to like the Virginia, nobody is born friendly to it. It looks like a rat-tail file, but smokes better, some think. It has a straw through it; you pull this out, and it leaves a flue, otherwise there would be no draught, not even as much as there is to a nail. Some prefer a nail at first. However, I like all the French, Swiss, German, and Italian domestic cigars, and have never cared to inquire what they are made of; and nobody would know, anyhow, perhaps. There is even a brand of European smoking-tobacco that I like. It is a brand used by the Italian peasants. It is loose and dry and black, and looks like tea-grounds. When the fire is applied it expands, and climbs up and towers above the pipe, and presently tumbles off inside of one's vest. The tobacco itself is cheap, but it raises the insurance. It is as I remarked in the beginning—the taste for tobacco is a matter of superstition. There are no standards—no real standards. Each man's preference is the only standard for him, the only one which he can accept, the only one which can command him.

*c. 1893*

# Private History of the "Jumping Frog" Story

Five or six years ago a lady from Finland asked me to tell her a story in our negro dialect, so that she could get an idea of what that variety of speech was like. I told her one of Hopkinson Smith's negro stories, and gave her a copy of *Harper's Monthly* containing it. She translated it for a Swedish newspaper, but by an oversight named me as the author of it instead of Smith. I was very sorry for that, because I got a good lashing in the Swedish press, which would have fallen to his share but for that mistake; for it was shown that Boccaccio had told that very story, in his curt and meagre fashion, five hundred years before Smith took hold of it and made a good and tellable thing out of it.

I have always been sorry for Smith. But my own turn has come now. A few weeks ago Professor Van Dyke, of Princeton, asked this question:

"Do you know how old your Jumping Frog story is?"

And I answered:

"Yes—forty-five years. The thing happened in Calaveras County in the spring of 1849."

"No; it happened earlier—a couple of thousand years earlier; it is a Greek story."

I was astonished—and hurt. I said:

"I am willing to be a literary thief if it has been so ordained; I am even willing to be caught robbing the ancient dead alongside of Hopkinson Smith, for he is my friend and a good fellow, and I think would be as honest as any one if he could do it without occasioning remark; but I am not willing to antedate his crimes by fifteen hundred years. I must ask you to knock off part of that."

But the professor was not chaffing; he was in earnest and could not abate a century. He named the Greek author, and offered to get the book and send it to me and the college textbook containing the English translation also. I thought I would like the translation best, because Greek makes me tired. January 30th he sent me the English version, and I will presently insert it in this article. It is my Jumping Frog tale in every essential. It is not strung out as I have strung it out, but it is all there.

To me this is very curious and interesting. Curious, for several reasons. For instance:

I heard the story told by a man who was not telling it to his hearers as a thing new to them, but as a thing which *they had witnessed and would remember*. He was a dull person, and ignorant; he had no gift as a story-teller, and no invention; in his mouth this episode was merely history—history and statistics; and the gravest sort of history, too; he was entirely serious, for he was dealing with what to him were austere facts, and they interested him solely because they *were* facts; he was drawing on his memory, not his mind; he saw no humor in his tale, neither did his listeners; neither he nor they ever smiled or laughed; in my time I have not attended a more solemn conference. To him and to his fellow goldminers there were just two things in the story that were worth considering. One was, the smartness of its hero, Jim Smiley, in taking the stranger in with a loaded frog; and the other was Smiley's deep knowledge of a frog's nature—for he knew (as the narrator asserted and the listeners conceded) that a frog *likes shot* and is always ready to eat it. Those men discussed those two points, and those only. They were hearty in their admiration of them, and none of the party was aware that a first rate story had been told, in a first rate way, and that it was brimful of a quality whose presence they never suspected—humor.

Now, then, the interesting question is, *did* the frog episode happen in Angel's Camp in the spring of '49, as told in my hearing that day in the fall of 1865? I am perfectly sure that it did. I am also sure that its duplicate happened in Bœotia a couple of thousand years ago. I think it must be a case of history actually repeating itself, and not a case of a good story floating down the ages and surviving because too good to be allowed to perish.

I would now like to have the reader examine the Greek story and the story told by the dull and solemn Californian, and observe how exactly alike they are in essentials.

[*Translation.*]
### THE ATHENIAN AND THE FROG.*

An Athenian once fell in with a Bœotian who was sitting by the road side looking at a frog. Seeing the other approach, the Bœotian said his was a remarkable frog, and asked if he would agree to start a contest of frogs, on condition that he whose frog jumped farthest should receive a large sum of money. The Athenian replied that he would if the other would fetch him a frog, for the lake was near. To this he agreed, and when he was gone the Athenian took the frog, and opening its mouth poured some stones into its stomach, so that it did not indeed seem larger than before, but could not jump. The Bœotian soon returned with the other frog, and the contest began. The second frog first was pinched and jumped moderately; then they pinched the Bœotian frog. And he gathered himself for a leap, and used the utmost effort, but he could not move his body the least. So the Athenian departed with the money. When he was gone the Bœotian, wondering what was the matter with the frog, lifted him up and examined him. And being turned upside down, he opened his mouth and vomited out the stones.

And here is the way it happened in California:

### FROM "THE CELEBRATED JUMPING FROG OF CALAVERAS COUNTY."

Well, thish-yer Smiley had rat-tarriers, and chicken cocks, and tom-cats, and all them kind of things, till you couldn't rest, and you couldn't fetch nothing for him to bet on but he'd match you. He ketched a frog one day, and took him home, and said he cal'lated to educate him; and so he never done nothing for three months but set in his backyard and learn that frog to jump. And you bet you he *did* learn him, too. He'd give him a little punch behind, and the next minute you'd see that frog whirling in the air like a doughnut—see him turn one summerset, or maybe a couple if he got a good start, and come down flat-footed and all right, like a cat. He got him up so in the matter of ketching flies, and kep' him in practice so constant, that he'd nail a fly every time as fur as he could see him. Smiley said all a frog wanted was education, and he could do 'most anything— and I believe him. Why, I've seen him set Dan'l Webster down here on this floor—Dan'l Webster was the name of the frog—and sing out "Flies, Dan'l, flies!" and quicker'n you could wink he'd spring straight up and snake a fly off'n the counter there, and flop down on the floor ag'in as solid as a gob of mud, and fall to scratching the side of his head with his hind foot as indifferent as if he hadn't no

*Sidgwick, *Greek Prose Composition*, page 116.

idea he'd been doin' any more'n any frog might do. You never see a frog so modest and straightfor'ard as he was, for all he was so gifted. And when it come to fair and square jumping on a dead level, he could get over more ground at one straddle than any animal of his breed you ever see. Jumping on a dead level was his strong suit, you understand; and when it come to that, Smiley would ante up money on him as long as he had a red. Smiley was monstrous proud of his frog, and well he might be, for fellers that had travelled and been everywheres, all said he laid over any frog that ever *they* see.

Well, Smiley kep' the beast in a little lattice box, and he used to fetch him downtown sometimes and lay for a bet. One day a feller—a stranger in the camp, he was—come acrost him with his box, and says:

"What might it be that you've got in the box?"

And Smiley says, sorter indifferent-like, "It might be a parrot, or it might be a canary, maybe, but it ain't—it's only just a frog."

And the feller took it, and looked at it careful, and turned it round this way and that, and says, "H'm—so 'tis. Well, what's *he* good for?"

"Well," Smiley says, easy and careless, "he's good enough for *one* thing, I should judge—he can outjump any frog in Calaveras County."

The feller took the box again and took another long, particular look, and give it back to Smiley and says very deliberate, "Well," he says, "I don't see no p'ints about that frog that's any better'n any other frog."

"Maybe you don't," Smiley says. "Maybe you understand frogs and maybe you don't understand 'em; maybe you've had experience, and maybe you ain't only a amature, as it were. Anyways, I've got *my* opinion and I'll resk forty dollars that he can outjump any frog in Calaveras County."

And the feller studies a minute and then says, kinder sad like, "Well, I'm only a stranger here, and I ain't got no frog, but if I had a frog I'd bet you."

And then Smiley says: "That's all right—that's all right—if you'll hold my box a minute, I'll go and get you a frog." And so the feller took the box and put up his forty dollars along with Smiley's and set down to wait.

So he set there a good while thinking and thinking to hisself, and then he got the frog out and prized his mouth open and took a teaspoon and filled him full of quail shot—filled him pretty near up to his chin—and set him on the floor. Smiley he went to the swamp and slopped around in the mud for a long time, and finally he ketched a frog and fetched him in and give him to this feller, and says:

"Now, if you're ready, set him alongside of Dan'l, with his fore-paws just even with Dan'l's, and I'll give the word." Then he says, "One—two—three—*git!*" and him and the feller touched up the frogs from behind, and the new frog hopped off lively; but Dan'l give a heave, and hysted up his shoulders—so—like a Frenchman, but it warn't no use—he couldn't budge; he was planted as solid as a church, and he couldn't no more stir than if he was anchored out. Smiley was a good deal surprised, and he was disgusted, too, but he didn't have no idea what the matter was, of course.

The feller took the money and started away; and when he was going out at the door, he sorter jerked his thumb over his shoul-der—so—at Dan'l, and says again, very deliberate: "Well," he says, "*I* don't see no p'ints about that frog that's any better'n any other frog."

Smiley he stood scratching his head and looking down at Dan'l a long time, and at last he says, "I do wonder what in the nation that frog throw'd off for—I wonder if there ain't something the matter with him—he 'pears to look mighty baggy, somehow." And he ketched Dan'l by the nap of the neck, and hefted him, and says, "Why, blame my cats if he don't weigh five pound!" and turned him upside down and he belched out a double handful of shot. And then he see how it was, and he was the maddest man—he set the frog down and took out after that feller, but he never ketched him.

The resemblances are deliciously exact. There you have the wily Bœotian and the wily Jim Smiley waiting—two thou-sand years apart—and waiting, each equipped with his frog and "laying" for the stranger. A contest is proposed—for money. The Athenian would take a chance "if the other would fetch him a frog"; the Yankee says: "I'm only a stranger here and I ain't got no frog; but if I had a frog I'd bet you." The wily Bœotian and the wily Californian, with that vast gulf of two thousand years between, retire eagerly and go frogging in the marsh; the Athenian and the Yankee remain behind and work a base advantage, the one with peb-bles, the other with shot. Presently the contest began. In the one case "they pinched the Bœotian frog"; in the other, "him and the feller touched up the frogs from behind." The Bœotian frog "gathered himself for a leap" (you can just *see* him!), but "could not move his body in the least"; the Cali-fornian frog "give a heave, but it warn't no use—he couldn't budge." In both the ancient and the modern cases the strangers departed with the money. The Bœotian and the Californian wonder what is the matter with their frogs; they lift them and examine; they turn them upside down and out spills the informing ballast.

Yes, the resemblances are curiously exact. I used to tell the story of the Jumping Frog in San Francisco, and presently Artemus Ward came along and wanted it to help fill out a little book which he was about to publish; so I wrote it out and sent it to his publisher, Carleton; but Carleton thought the book had enough matter in it, so he gave the story to Henry Clapp as a present, and Clapp put it in his *Saturday Press*, and it killed that paper with a suddenness that was beyond praise. At least the paper died with that issue, and none but envious people have ever tried to rob me of the honor and credit of killing it. The "Jumping Frog" was the first piece of writing of mine that spread itself through the newspapers and brought me into public notice. Consequently, the *Saturday Press* was a cocoon and I the worm in it; also, I was the gay-colored literary moth which its death set free. This simile has been used before.

Early in '66 the "Jumping Frog" was issued in book form, with other sketches of mine. A year or two later Madame Blanc translated it into French and published it in the *Revue des Deux Mondes*, but the result was not what should have been expected, for the *Revue* struggled along and pulled through, and is alive yet. I think the fault must have been in the translation. I ought to have translated it myself. I think so because I examined into the matter and finally retranslated the sketch from the French back into English, to see what the trouble was; that is, to see just what sort of a focus the French people got upon it. Then the mystery was explained. In French the story is too confused, and chaotic, and unreposeful, and ungrammatical, and insane; consequently it could only cause grief and sickness—it could not kill. A glance at my retranslation will show the reader that this must be true.

[*My Retranslation.*]
### THE FROG JUMPING OF THE COUNTY OF CALAVERAS.
Eh bien! this Smiley nourished some terriers á rats, and some cocks of combat, and some cats, and all sort of things; and with his

rage of betting one no had more of repose. He trapped one day a frog and him imported with him (et l'emporta chez lui) saying that he pretended to make his education. You me believe if you will, but during three months he not has nothing done but to him apprehend to jump (apprendre a sauter) in a court retired of her mansion (de sa maison). And I you respond that he have succeeded. He him gives a small blow by behind, and the instant after you shall see the frog turn in the air like a grease-biscuit, make one summersault, sometimes two, when she was well started, and re-fall upon his feet like a cat. He him had accomplished in the art of to gobble the flies ( gober des mouches), and him there exercised continually—so well that a fly at the most far that she appeared was a fly lost. Smiley had custom to say that all which lacked to a frog it was the education, but with the education she could do nearly all—and I him believe. Tenez, I him have seen pose Daniel Webster there upon this plank— Daniel Webster was the name of the frog—and to him sing, "Some flies, Daniel, some flies!"—in a flash of the eye Daniel had bounded and seized a fly here upon the counter, then jumped anew at the earth, where he rested truly to himself scratch the head with his behind-foot, as if he no had not the least idea of his superiority. Never you not have seen frog as modest, as natural, sweet as she was. And when he himself agitated to jump purely and simply upon plain earth, she does more ground in one jump than any beast of his species than you can know.

To jump plain—this was his strong. When he himself agitated for that Smiley multiplied the bets upon her as long as there to him remained a red. It must to know, Smiley was monstrously proud of his frog, and he of it was right, for some men who were traveled, who had all seen, said that they to him would be injurious to him compare to another frog. Smiley guarded Daniel in a little box latticed which he carried bytimes to the village for some bet.

One day an individual stranger at the camp him arrested with his box and him said:

"What is this that you have then shut up there within?"

Smiley said, with an air indifferent:

"That could be a paroquet, or a syringe (ou un serin), but this no is nothing of such, it not is but a frog."

The individual it took, it regarded with care, it turned from one side and from the other, then he said:

"*Tiens!* in effect!—At what is she good?"

"My God!" respond Smiley, always with an air disengaged, "she is good for one thing, to my notice, (*à mon avis*), she can batter in jumping (*elle peut batter en sautant*) all frogs of the county of Calaveras."

The individual re-took the box, it examined of new longly, and it rendered to Smiley in saying with an air deliberate:

"*Eh bien!* I no saw not that that frog had nothing of better than each frog." (*Je ne vois pas que cette grenouille ait rien de mieux qu'aucune grenouille*). [If that isn't grammar gone to seed, then I count myself no judge. — M. T.]

"Possible that you not it saw not," said Smiley, "possible that you — you comprehend frogs; possible that you not you there comprehend nothing; possible that you had of the experience, and possible that you not be but an amateur. Of all manner (*De toute manière*) I bet forty dollars that she batter in jumping no matter which frog of the county of Calaveras."

The individual reflected a second, and said like sad:

"I not am but a stranger here, I no have not a frog; but if I of it had one, I would embrace the bet."

"Strong, well!" respond Smiley; "nothing of more facility. If you will hold my box a minute, I go you to search a frog (*j'irai vous chercher*)."

Behold, then, the individual, who guards the box, who puts his forty dollars upon those of Smiley, and who attends (*et qui attend*). He attended enough longtimes, reflecting all solely. And figure you that he takes Daniel, him opens the mouth by force and with a teaspoon him fills with shot of the hunt, even him fills just to the chin, then he him puts by the earth. Smiley during these times was at slopping in a swamp. Finally he trapped (*attrape*) a frog, him carried to that individual, and said:

"Now if you be ready, put him all against Daniel, with their before-feet upon the same line, and I give the signal" — then he added: "One, two, three — advance!"

Him and the individual touched their frogs by behind, and the frog new put to jump smartly, but Daniel himself lifted ponderously, exalted the shoulders thus, like a Frenchman — to what good? he could not budge, he is planted solid like a church, he not advance no more than if one him had put at the anchor.

Smiley was surprised and disgusted, but he not himself doubted not of the turn being intended (*mais il ne se doutait pas du tour bien entendu*). The individual empocketed the silver, himself with it went, and of it himself in going is that he no gives not a jerk of thumb over the shoulder — like that — at the poor Daniel, in saying with his air deliberate — (*L'individu empoche l'argent s'en va et en s'en allant est ce qu'il ne donne pas un coup de pouce par-dessus l'épaule, comme ça, au pauvre Daniel, en disant de son air délibéré.*)

"Eh bien! *I no see not that that frog has nothing of better than another.*"

Smiley himself scratched longtimes the head, the eyes fixed upon Daniel, until that which at last he said:

"I me demand how the devil it makes itself that this beast has refused. Is it that she had something? One would believe that she is stuffed."

He grasped Daniel by the skin of the neck, him lifted and said:

"The wolf me bite if he no weigh not five pounds."

He him reversed and the unhappy belched two handfuls of shot (*et le malheureux*, etc).—When Smiley recognized how it was, he was like mad. He deposited his frog by the earth and ran after that individual, but he not him caught never.

It may be that there are people who can translate better than I can, but I am not acquainted with them.

So ends the private and public history of the jumping frog of Calaveras County, an incident which has this unique feature about it—that it is both old and new, a "chestnut" and not a "chestnut"; for it was original when it happened two thousand years ago, and was again original when it happened in California in our own time.

*April 1894*

# Macfarlane

When I was just turned twenty I wandered to Cincinnati, and was there several months. Our boarding house crew was made of commonplace people of various ages and both sexes. They were full of bustle, frivolity, chatter, and the joy of life, and were good-natured, clean-minded, and well meaning; but they were oppressively uninteresting, for all that—with one exception. This was Macfarlane, a Scotchman. He was forty years old—just double my age—but we were opposites in most ways, and comrades from the start. I always spent my evenings by the wood fire in his room, listening in comfort to his tireless talk and to the dulled complainings of the winter storms, until the clock struck ten. At that hour he grilled a smoked herring, after the fashion of my earlier friend in Philadelphia, the Englishman Sumner. His herring was his nightcap and my signal to go.

He was six feet high and rather lank, a serious and sincere man. He had no humor, nor any comprehension of it. He had a sort of smile, whose office was to express his good nature, but if I ever heard him laugh the memory of it is gone from me. He was intimate with no one in the house but me, though he was courteous and pleasant with all. He had two or three dozen weighty books—philosophies, histories and scientific works—and at the head of this procession was his Bible and his dictionary. After his herring he always read two or three hours in bed.

Diligent talker as he was, he seldom said anything about himself. To ask him a personal question gave him no offence—nor the asker any information; he merely turned the matter aside and flowed placidly on about other things. He told me once that he had had hardly any schooling, and that such learning as he had, he had picked up for himself. That was his sole biographical revelation, I believe. Whether he was bachelor, widower, or grass-widower, remained his own secret. His clothes were cheap, but neat and care-takingly preserved; ours was a cheap boarding house; he left the house at six, mornings, and returned to it toward six, evenings; his hands were not soft: so I reasoned that he worked at some mechanical calling ten hours a day, for humble wages—but I never knew. As a rule, technicalities of a man's vocation, and figures and metaphors drawn from it, slip out in his talk and reveal his trade; but if this ever happened in Macfarlane's case I was none the wiser, although I was constantly on the watch during half a year for those very betrayals. It was mere curiosity, for I didn't care what his trade was, but I wanted to detect it in true detective fashion and was annoyed because I couldn't do it. I think he was a remarkable man, to be able to keep the shop out of his talk all that time.

There was another noteworthy feature about him: he seemed to know his dictionary from beginning to end. He claimed that he did. He was frankly proud of this accomplishment and said I would not find it possible to challenge him with an English word which he could not promptly spell and define. I lost much time trying to hunt up a word which would beat him, but those weeks were spent in vain and I finally gave it up; which made him so proud and happy that I wished I had surrendered earlier.

He seemed to be as familiar with his Bible as he was with his dictionary. It was easy to see that he considered himself a philosopher and a thinker. His talk always ran upon grave and large questions; and I must do him the justice to say that his heart and conscience were in his talk and that there was no appearance of reasoning and arguing for the vain pleasure of hearing himself do it.

Of course his thinkings and reasonings and philosophizings were those of a but partly taught and wholly untrained mind, yet he hit by accident upon some curious and striking things. For instance. The time was the early part of 1856—fourteen or fifteen years before Mr. Darwin's "Descent of Man" startled the world—yet here was Macfarlane talking the same idea to me, there in the boarding house in Cincinnati.

The same general idea, but with a difference. Macfarlane considered that the animal life in the world was developed in the course of æons of time from a few microscopic seed-germs, or perhaps *one* microscopic seed-germ deposited upon the globe by the Creator in the dawn of time; and that this development was progressive upon an ascending scale toward ultimate perfection until *man* was reached; and that then the progressive scheme broke pitifully down and went to wreck and ruin!

He said that man's heart was the only bad heart in the animal kingdom; that man was the only animal capable of feeling malice, envy, vindictiveness, vengefulness, hatred, selfishness, the only animal that loved drunkenness, almost the only animal that could endure personal uncleanliness and a filthy habitation, the sole animal in whom was fully developed the base instinct called *patriotism*, the sole animal that robs, persecutes, oppresses, and kills members of his own immediate tribe, the sole animal that steals and enslaves the members of *any* tribe.

He claimed that man's intellect was a brutal addition to him and degraded him to a rank far below the plane of the other animals, and that there was never a man who did not use his intellect daily all his life to advantage himself at other people's expense. The divinest divine reduced his domestics to humble servitude under him by advantage of his superior intellect, and those servants in turn were above a still lower grade of people by force of brains that were still a little better than theirs.

*c. 1894*

# What Paul Bourget Thinks of Us

He reports the American joke correctly. In Boston they ask, How much does he know? in New York, How much is he worth? in Philadelphia, Who were his parents? And when an alien observer turns his telescope upon us—advertisedly in our own special interest—a natural apprehension moves us to ask, What is the diameter of his reflector?

I take a great interest in M. Bourget's chapters, for I know by the newspapers that there are several Americans who are expecting to get a whole education out of them; several who foresaw, and also foretold, that our long night was over, and a light almost divine about to break upon the land.

*"His utterances concerning us are bound to be weighty and well timed."*

*"He gives us an object-lesson which should be thoughtfully and profitably studied."*

These well-considered and important verdicts were of a nature to restore public confidence, which had been disquieted by questionings as to whether so young a teacher would be qualified to take so large a class as 70,000,000, distributed over so extensive a schoolhouse as America, and pull it through without assistance.

I was even disquieted myself, although I am of a cold, calm temperament and not easily disturbed. I feared for my country. And I was not wholly tranquilized by the verdicts rendered as above. It seemed to me that there was still room for doubt. In fact, in looking the ground over I became more disturbed than I was before. Many worrying questions came up in my mind. Two were prominent. Where had the teacher gotten his equipment? What was his method?

He had gotten his equipment in France.

Then as to his method: I saw by his own intimations that he was an Observer, and had a System—that used by naturalists and other scientists. The naturalist collects many bugs and reptiles and butterflies and studies their ways a long time patiently. By this means he is presently able to group these creatures into families and subdivisions of families by nice shadings of differences observable in their characters. Then he labels all those shaded bugs and things with nicely descriptive group names, and is now happy, for his great work is completed, and as a result he intimately knows every bug and shade of a bug there, inside and out. It may be true, but a person who was not a naturalist would feel safer about it if he had the opinion of the bug. I think it is a pleasant System, but subject to error.

The Observer of Peoples has to be a Classifier, a Grouper, a Deducer, a Generalizer, a Psychologizer; and first and last, a Thinker. He has to be all these, and when he is at home, observing his own folk, he is often able to prove competency. But history has shown that when he is abroad observing unfamiliar peoples, the chances are heavily against him. He is then a naturalist observing a bug; with no more than a naturalist's chance of being able to tell the bug anything new about itself, and no more than a naturalist's chance of being able to teach it any new ways which it will prefer to its own.

To return to that first question. M. Bourget, as teacher, would simply be France teaching America. It seemed to me that the outlook was dark; almost Egyptian, in fact. What would the new teacher, representing France, teach us? Railroading? No. France knows nothing valuable about railroading. Steamshipping? No. France has no superiorities over us in that matter. Steamboating? No. French steamboating is still of Fulton's date—1809. Postal service? No. France is a back number there. Telegraphy? No, we taught her that ourselves. Journalism? No. Magazining? No, that is our own specialty. Government? No; Liberty, Equality, Fraternity, Nobility, Democracy, Adultery—the system is too variegated for our climate. Religion? No, not variegated enough for our climate. Morals? No, we cannot rob the poor to enrich ourselves. Novel-writing? No. M. Bourget and the others know only one plan, and when that is expurgated there is nothing left of the book.

I wish I could think what he is going to teach us. Can it be Deportment? But he experimented in that at Newport and failed to give satisfaction, except to a few. Those few are pleased. They are enjoying their joy as well as they can. They confess their happiness to the interviewer. They feel pretty striped, but they remember with reverent recognition that they had sugar between the cuts. True, sugar with sand in it, but sugar. And true, they had some trouble to tell which was sugar and which was sand, because the sugar itself looked just like the sand, and also had a gravelly taste; still, they know that the sugar was there, and would have been very good sugar indeed if it had been screened. Yes, they are pleased; not noisily so, but pleased; invaded, or streaked, as one may say, with little recurrent shivers of joy—subdued joy, so to speak, not the overdone kind. And they commune together, these, and massage each other with comforting sayings, in a sweet spirit of resignation and thankfulness, mixing these elements in the same proportions as the sugar and the sand, as a memorial, and saying, the one to the other and to the interviewer: "It was severe—yes, it was bitterly severe; but oh, how true it was; and it will do us so much good!"

If it isn't Deportment, what is left? It was at this point that I seemed to get on the right track at last. M. Bourget would teach us to know ourselves; that was it: he would reveal us to ourselves. That would be an education. He would explain us to ourselves. Then we should understand ourselves; and after that be able to go on more intelligently.

It seemed a doubtful scheme. He could explain *us* to *himself*—that would be easy. That would be the same as the naturalist explaining the bug to himself. But to explain the bug to the bug—that is a quite different matter. The bug may not know himself perfectly, but he knows himself better than the naturalist can know him, at any rate.

A foreigner can photograph the exteriors of a nation, but I think that that is as far as he can get. I think that no foreigner can report its interior—its soul, its life, its speech, its thought. I think that a knowledge of these things is acquirable in only one way; not two or four or six—*absorption*; years and years of unconscious absorption; years and years of intercourse with the life concerned; of living it, indeed; sharing personally in its shames and prides, its joys and griefs, its loves and hates, its prosperities and reverses, its shows and shabbinesses, its deep patriotisms, its whirlwinds of political passion, its adorations—of flag, and heroic dead, and the glory of the national name. Observation? Of what real value is it? One learns peoples through the heart, not the eyes or the intellect.

There is only one expert who is qualified to examine the souls and the life of a people and make a valuable report—the native novelist. This expert is so rare that the most populous country can never have fifteen conspicuously and confessedly competent ones in stock at one time. This native specialist is not qualified to begin work until he has been absorbing during twenty-five years. How much of his competency is derived from conscious "observation"? The amount is so slight that it counts for next to nothing in the equipment. Almost the whole capital of the novelist is the slow accumulation of *un*conscious observation—absorption. The native expert's intentional observation of manners, speech, character, and ways of life can have value, for the native knows what they mean without having to cipher out the meaning. But I should be astonished to see a foreigner get at the right meanings, catch the elusive shades of these subtle things. Even the native novelist becomes a foreigner, with a foreigner's limitations, when he steps from the State whose life is familiar to him into a State whose life he has not lived. Bret Harte got his California and his Californians by unconscious absorption, and put both of them into his tales alive. But when he came from the Pacific to the Atlantic and tried to do Newport life from study—conscious observation—his failure was absolutely monumental. Newport is a disastrous place for the unacclimated observer, evidently.

To return to novel-building. Does the native novelist try to generalize the nation? No, he lays plainly before you the ways and speech and life of a few people grouped in a certain place—his own place—and that is one book. In time, he and his brethren will report to you the life and the people of the whole nation—the life of a group in a New England village; in a New York village; in a Texan village; in an Oregon village; in villages in fifty States and Territories; then the farm-life in fifty States and Territories; a hundred patches of life and groups of people in a dozen widely separated cities. And the Indians will be attended to; and the cowboys; and the gold and silver miners; and the negroes; and the Idiots and

Congressmen; and the Irish, the Germans, the Italians, the Swedes, the French, the Chinamen, the Greasers; and the Catholics, the Methodists, the Presbyterians, the Congregationalists, the Baptists, the Spiritualists, the Mormons, the Shakers, the Quakers, the Jews, the Campbellites, the infidels, the Christian Scientists, the Mind-Curists, the Faith-Curists, the train-robbers, the White Caps, the Moonshiners. And when a thousand able novels have been written, *there* you have the soul of the people, the life of the people, the speech of the people; and not anywhere else can these be had. And the shadings of character, manners, feelings, ambitions, will be infinite.

"*The nature of a people* is always of a similar shade in its vices and its virtues, in its frivolities and in its labor. *It is this physiognomy which it is necessary to discover*, and every document is good, from the hall of a casino to the church, from the foibles of a fashionable woman to the suggestions of a revolutionary leader. I am therefore quite sure that this *American soul*, the principal interest and the great object of my voyage, appears behind the records of Newport for those who choose to see it."—*M. Paul Bourget.*

[The italics are mine.] It is a large contract which he has undertaken. "Records" is a pretty poor word there, but I think the use of it is due to hasty translation. In the original the word is *fastes*. I think M. Bourget meant to suggest that he expected to find the great "American soul" secreted behind the *ostentations* of Newport; and that he was going to get it out and examine it, and generalize it, and psychologize it, and make it reveal to him its hidden vast mystery, "the nature of the people" of the United States of America. We have been accused of being a nation addicted to inventing wild schemes. I trust that we shall be allowed to retire to second place now.

There isn't a single human characteristic that can be safely labelled "American." There isn't a single human ambition, or religious trend, or drift of thought, or peculiarity of education, or code of principles, or breed of folly, or style of conversation, or preference for a particular subject for discussion, or form of legs or trunk or head or face or expression or complexion, or gait, or dress, or manners, or disposition, or any other human detail, inside or outside, that can rationally be generalized as "American."

Whenever you have found what seems to be an "American" peculiarity, you have only to cross a frontier or two, or go down or up in the social scale, and you perceive that it has disappeared. And you can cross the Atlantic and find it again. There may be a Newport religious drift or sporting drift, or conversational style or complexion, or cut of face, but there are entire empires in America, north, south, east, and west, where you could not find your duplicates. It is the same with everything else which one might propose to call "American." M. Bourget thinks he has found the American Coquette. If he had really found her he would also have found, I am sure, that she was not new, that she exists in other lands in the same forms, and with the same frivolous heart and the same ways and impulses. I think this because I have seen our co-quette; I have seen her in life; better still, I have seen her in our novels, and seen her twin in foreign novels. I wish M. Bourget had seen ours. He thought he saw her. And so he applied his System to her. She was a Species. So he gathered a number of samples of what seemed to be her, and put them under his glass, and divided them into groups which he calls "types," and labelled them in his usual scientific way with "formulas"—brief sharp descriptive flashes that make a person blink, sometimes, they are so sudden and vivid. As a rule they are pretty far-fetched, but that is not an important matter; they surprise, they compel admiration, and I notice by some of the comments which his efforts have called forth that they deceive the unwary. Here are a few of the coquette variants which he has grouped and labelled:

THE COLLECTOR.
THE EQUILIBREE.
THE PROFESSIONAL BEAUTY.
THE BLUFFER.
THE GIRL-BOY.

If he had stopped with describing these characters we should have been obliged to believe that they exist; that they exist, and that he has seen them and spoken with them. But he did not stop there; he went further and furnished to us light-throwing samples of their behavior, and also light-throwing samples of their speeches. He entered those things in his notebook without suspicion, he takes them out and delivers them to the world with a candor and simplicity which show that he believed them genuine. They throw altogether too much light. They reveal to the native the origin of his find. I suppose he knows how he came to make that novel and captivating discovery, by this time. If he does not, any American can tell him—any American to whom he will show his anecdotes. It was "put up" on him, as we say. It was a jest—to be plain, it was a series of frauds. To my mind it was a poor sort of jest, witless and contemptible. The players of it have their reward, such as it is; they have exhibited the fact that whatever they may be, they are not ladies. M. Bourget did not discover a type of coquette; he merely discovered a type of practical joker. One may say *the* type of practical joker, for these people are exactly alike all over the world. Their equipment is always the same: a vulgar mind, a puerile wit, a cruel disposition as a rule, and always the spirit of treachery.

In his Chapter IV. M. Bourget has two or three columns gravely devoted to the collating and examining and psychologizing of these sorry little frauds. One is not moved to laugh. There is nothing funny in the situation; it is only pathetic. The stranger gave those people his confidence, and they dishonorably treated him in return.

But one must be allowed to suspect that M. Bourget was a little to blame himself. Even a practical joker has some little judgment. He has to exercise some degree of sagacity in selecting his prey, if he would save himself from getting into trouble. In my time I have seldom seen such daring things marketed at any price as these conscienceless folk have worked off at par on this confiding observer. It compels the conviction that there was something about him that bred in those speculators a quite unusual sense of safety, and encouraged them to strain their powers in his behalf. They seem to have satisfied themselves that all he wanted was "significant" facts, and that he was not accustomed to examine the source whence they proceeded. It is plain that there was a sort of conspiracy against him almost from the start—a conspiracy to freight him up with all the strange extravagances those people's decayed brains could invent.

The lengths to which they went are next to incredible. They told him things which surely would have excited any one else's suspicion, but they did not excite his. Consider this:

*"There is not in all the United States an entirely nude statue."*

If an angel should come down and say such a thing about heaven, a reasonably cautious observer would take that angel's number and inquire a little further before he added it to his catch. What does the present observer do? Adds it. Adds it at once. Adds it, and labels it with this innocent comment:

*"This small fact is strangely significant."*

It does seem to me that this kind of observing is defective.

Here is another curiosity which some liberal person made him a present of. I should think it ought to have disturbed the deep slumber of his suspicion a little, but it didn't. It was a note from a fog-horn for strenuousness, it seems to me, but the doomed voyager did not catch it. If he had but caught it, it would have saved him from several disasters:

"If the American knows that you are travelling to take notes, he is interested in it, and at the same time rejoices in it, as in a tribute."

Again, this is defective observation. It is human to like to be praised; one can even notice it in the French. But it is not human to like to be ridiculed, even when it comes in the form of a "tribute." I think a little psychologizing ought to have come in there. Something like this: A dog does not like to be ridiculed, a redskin does not like to be ridiculed, a negro does not like to be ridiculed, a Chinaman does not like to be ridiculed; let us deduce from these significant facts this formula: the American's grade being higher than these, and the chain of argument stretching unbroken all the way up to him, there is room for suspicion that the person who said the American likes to be ridiculed, and regards it as a tribute, is not a capable observer.

I feel persuaded that in the matter of psychologizing, a professional is too apt to yield to the fascinations of the loftier regions of that great art, to the neglect of its lowlier walks. Every now and then, at half-hour intervals, M. Bourget collects a hatful of airy inaccuracies and dissolves them in a panful of assorted abstractions, and runs the charge into a mould and turns you out a compact principle which will explain an American girl, or an American woman, or why new people yearn for old things, or any other impossible riddle which a person wants answered.

It seems to be conceded that there are a few human peculiarities that can be generalized and located here and there in the world and named by the name of the nation where they are found. I wonder what they are. Perhaps one of them is temperament. One speaks of French vivacity and German gravity and English stubbornness. There is no American temperament. The nearest that one can come at it is to say there are two—the composed northern and the impetuous southern; and both are found in other countries. Morals? Purity of women may fairly be called universal with us, but that is the case in some other countries. We have no monopoly of it; it cannot be named American. I think that there is but a single specialty with us, only one thing that can be called by the wide name "American." That is the national devotion to ice-water. All Germans drink beer, but the British nation drinks beer, too; so neither of those peoples is *the* beer-drinking nation. I suppose we do stand alone in having a drink that nobody likes but ourselves. When we have been a month in Europe we lose our craving for it, and we finally tell the hotel folk that they needn't provide it any more. Yet we hardly touch our native shore again, winter or summer, before we are eager for it. The reasons for this state of things have not been psychologized yet. I drop the hint and say no more.

It is my belief that there are some "national" traits and things scattered about the world that are mere superstitions, frauds that have lived so long that they have the solid look of facts. One of them is the dogma that the French are the only chaste people in the world. Ever since I arrived in France this last time I have been accumulating doubts about that; and before I leave this sunny land again I will gather in a few random statistics and psychologize the plausibilities out of it. If people are to come over to America and find fault with our girls and our women, and psychologize every little thing they do, and try to teach them how to behave, and how to cultivate themselves up to where one cannot tell them from the French model, I intend to find out whether those missionaries are qualified or not. A nation ought always to examine into this detail before engaging the teacher for good. This last one has let fall a remark which renewed those doubts of mine when I read it:

"In our high Parisian existence, for instance, we find applied to arts and luxury, and to debauchery, all the powers and all the weaknesses of the French soul."

You see it amounts to a trade with the French soul; a profession; a science; the serious business of life, so to speak, in our high Parisian existence. I do not quite like the look of it. I question if it can be taught with profit in our country, except of course to those pathetic, neglected minds that are waiting there so yearningly for the education which M. Bourget is going to furnish them from the serene summits of our high Parisian life.

I spoke a moment ago of the existence of some superstitions that have been parading the world as facts this long time. For instance, consider the Dollar. The world seems to think that the love of money is "American"; and that the mad desire to get suddenly rich is "American." I believe that both of these things are merely and broadly human, not American monopolies at all. The love of money is natural to all nations, for money is a good and strong friend. I think that this love has existed everywhere, ever since the Bible called it the root of all evil.

I think that the reason why we Americans seem to be so addicted to trying to get rich suddenly is merely because the *opportunity* to make promising efforts in that direction has offered itself to us with a frequency out of all proportion to the European experience. For eighty years this opportunity has been offering itself in one new town or region after another straight westward, step by step, all the way from the Atlantic coast to the Pacific. When a mechanic could buy ten town lots on tolerably long credit for ten months' savings out of his wages, and reasonably expect to sell them in a couple of years for ten times what he gave for them, it was human for him to try the venture, and he did it, no matter what his nationality was. He would have done it in Europe or China if he had had the same chance.

In the flush times in the silver regions, a cook or any other humble worker stood a very good chance to get rich out of a trifle of money risked in a stock deal; and that person promptly took that risk, no matter what his or her nationality might be. I was there, and saw it.

But these opportunities have not been plenty in our Southern States; so there you have a prodigious region where the rush for sudden wealth is almost an unknown thing—and has been, from the beginning.

Europe has offered few opportunities for poor Tom, Dick, and Harry; but when she has offered one, there has been no noticeable difference between European eagerness and American. England saw this in the wild days of the Railroad King; France saw it in 1720—time of Law and the Mississippi Bubble. I am sure I have never seen in the gold and silver mines any madness, fury, frenzy to get suddenly rich which was even remotely comparable to that which raged in France in the Bubble day. If I had a cyclopædia here I could turn to that memorable case, and satisfy nearly anybody that the hunger for the sudden dollar is no more "American" than it is French. And if I could furnish an American opportunity to staid Germany, I think I could wake her up like a house afire.

But I must return to the Generalizations, Psychologizings, Deductions. When M. Bourget is exploiting these arts, it is then that he is peculiarly and particularly himself. His ways are wholly original when he encounters a trait or a custom which is new to him. Another person would merely examine the find, verify it, estimate its value, and let it go; but that is not sufficient for M. Bourget: he always wants to know *why* that thing exists, he wants to know how it came to happen; and he will not let go of it until he has found out. And in every instance he will find that reason where no one but himself would have thought of looking for it. He does not seem to care for a reason that is not picturesquely located; one might almost say picturesquely and impossibly located.

He found out that in America men do not try to hunt down young married women. At once, as usual, he wanted to know *why*. Any one could have told him. He could have divined it by the lights thrown by the novels of the country. But no, he preferred to find out for himself. He has a trustfulness as regards men and facts which is fine and unusual; he is not particular about the source of a fact, he is not particular about the character and standing of the fact itself; but when it comes to pounding out the reason for the existence of the fact, he will trust no one but himself.

In the present instance here was his fact: American young married women are not pursued by the corruptor; and here was the question: What is it that protects her?

It seems quite unlikely that that problem could have offered difficulties to any but a trained philosopher. Nearly any person would have said to M. Bourget: "Oh, that is very simple. It is very seldom in America that a marriage is made on a commercial basis; our marriages, from the beginning, have been made for love; and where love is there is no room for the corruptor."

Now, it is interesting to see the formidable way in which M. Bourget went at that poor, humble little thing. He moved upon it in column—three columns—and with artillery.

"Two reasons of a very different kind explain"—that fact.

And now that I have got so far, I am almost afraid to say what his two reasons are, lest I be charged with inventing them. But I will not retreat now; I will condense them and print them, giving my word that I am honest, and not trying to deceive any one.

1. Young married women are protected from the approaches of the seducer in New England and vicinity by the diluted remains of a prudence created by a Puritan law of two hundred years ago, which for a while punished adultery with death.

2. And young married women of the other forty or fifty States are protected by laws which afford extraordinary facilities for divorce.

If I have not lost my mind I have accurately conveyed those

two Vesuvian irruptions of philosophy. But the reader can consult Chapter IV. of *Outre-Mer* and decide for himself. Let us examine this paralyzing Deduction or Explanation by the light of a few sane facts.

1. This universality of "protection" has existed in our country *from the beginning*; before the death penalty existed in New England, and during all the generations that have dragged by since it was annulled.

2. Extraordinary facilities for divorce are of such recent creation that any middle-aged American can remember a time when such things had not yet been thought of.

Let us suppose that the first easy divorce law went into effect forty years ago, and got noised around and fairly started in business thirty-five years ago, when we had, say, 25,000,000 of white population. Let us suppose that among 5,000,000 of them the young married women were "protected" by the surviving shudder of that ancient Puritan scare—what is M. Bourget going to do about those who lived among the 20,000,000? They were clean in their morals, they were pure, yet there was no easy divorce law to protect them.

Awhile ago I said that M. Bourget's method of truth-seeking—hunting for it in out-of-the-way places—was new; but that was an error. I remember that when Leverrier discovered the Milky Way, he and the other astronomers began to theorize about it in substantially the same fashion which M. Bourget employs in his reasonings about American social facts and their origin. Leverrier advanced the hypothesis that the Milky Way was caused by gaseous protoplasmic emanations from the field of Waterloo, which, ascending to an altitude determinable by their own specific gravity, became luminous through the development and exposure—by the natural processes of animal decay—of the phosphorus contained in them.

This theory was warmly complimented by Ptolemy, who, however, after much thought and research, decided that he could not accept it as final. His own theory was that the Milky Way was an emigration of lightning-bugs; and he supported and re-enforced this theorem by the well-known fact that the locusts do like that in Egypt.

Giordano Bruno also was outspoken in his praises of Leverrier's important contribution to astronomical science, and was at first inclined to regard it as conclusive, but later, conceiving it to be erroneous, he pronounced against it, and advanced the hypothenuse that the Milky Way was a detachment or corps of stars which became arrested and held in *suspenso suspensorum* by refraction of gravitation while on the march to join their several constellations; a proposition for which he was afterward burned at the stake in Jacksonville, Illinois.

These were all brilliant and picturesque theories, and each was received with enthusiasm by the scientific world; but when a New England farmer, who was not a thinker, but only a plain sort of person who tried to account for large facts in simple ways, came out with the opinion that the Milky Way was just common, ordinary stars and was put where it was because God "wanted to hev it so," the admirable idea fell perfectly flat.

As a literary artist, M. Bourget is as fresh and striking as he is as a scientific one. He says, "Above all, I do not believe much in anecdotes." Why? "In history they are all false"—a sufficiently broad statement—"in literature all libellous"—also a sufficiently sweeping statement, coming from a critic who notes that we are a people who are peculiarly extravagant in our language—"and when it is a matter of social life, almost all biassed." It seems to amount to stultification, almost. He has built two or three breeds of American coquettes out of anecdotes—mainly "biassed" ones, I suppose; and, as they occur "in literature," furnished by his pen, they must be "all libellous." Or did he mean not *in* literature or anecdotes *about* literature or literary people? I am not able to answer that. Perhaps the original would be clearer, but I have only the translation of this instalment by me. I think the remark had an intention; also that this intention was booked for the trip; but that either in the hurry of the remark's departure it got left, or in the confusion of changing cars at the translator's frontier it got sidetracked.

"But on the other hand I believe in statistics; and those on divorces appear to me to be most conclusive." And he sets himself the task of explaining—in a couple of columns—the process by which Easy-Divorce conceived, invented, originated, developed, and perfected an empire-embracing condition of sexual purity in the States. *In 40 years.* No, he doesn't state the interval. With all his passion for statistics he forgot to ask how long it took to produce this gigantic miracle.

I have followed his pleasant but devious trail through those columns, but I was not able to get hold of his argument and find out what it was. I was not even able to find out where it left off. It seemed to gradually dissolve and flow off into other matters. I followed it with interest, for I was anxious to learn how easy-divorce eradicated adultery in America, but I was disappointed; I have no idea yet, how it did it. I only know it didn't. But that is not valuable; I knew it before.

Well, humor is the great thing, the saving thing, after all. The minute it crops up, all our hardnesses yield, all our irritations and resentments flit away, and a sunny spirit takes their place. And so, when M. Bourget said that bright thing about our grandfathers, I broke all up. I remember exploding its American counter-mine once, under that grand hero, Napoleon. He was only First Consul then, and I was Consul-General—for the United States, of course; but we were very intimate, notwithstanding the difference in rank, for I waived that. One day something offered the opening, and he said:

"Well, General, I suppose life can never get entirely dull to an American, because whenever he can't strike up any other way to put in his time he can always get away with a few years trying to find out who his grandfather was!"

I fairly shouted, for I had never heard it sound better; and then I was back at him as quick as a flash—

"Right, your Excellency! But I reckon a Frenchman's got *his* little stand-by for a dull time, too; because when all other interests fail he can turn in and see if he can't find out who his father was!"

Well, you should have heard him just whoop, and cackle, and carry on! He reached up and hit me one on the shoulder, and says—

"Land, but it's good! It's im-mensely good! I'George, I never heard it said so good in my life before! Say it again."

So I said it again, and he said his again, and I said mine again, and then he did, and then I did, and then he did, and we kept on doing it, and doing it, and I *never* had such a good time, and he said the same. In my opinion there isn't anything that is as killing as one of those dear old ripe pensioners if you know how to snatch it out in a kind of a fresh sort of original way.

But I wish M. Bourget had read more of our novels before he came. It is the only way to thoroughly understand a people. When I found I was coming to Paris, I read *La Terre*.

*January 1895*

# Fenimore Cooper's Literary Offences

*The Pathfinder* and *The Deerslayer* stand at the head of Cooper's novels as artistic creations. There are others of his works which contain parts as perfect as are to be found in these, and scenes even more thrilling. Not one can be compared with either of them as a finished whole.

The defects in both of these tales are comparatively slight. They were pure works of art.—*Prof. Lounsbury.*

The five tales reveal an extraordinary fulness of invention.

. . . One of the very greatest characters in fiction, "Natty Bumppo." . . .

The craft of the woodsman, the tricks of the trapper, all the delicate art of the forest, were familiar to Cooper from his youth up.—*Prof. Brander Matthews.*

Cooper is the greatest artist in the domain of romantic fiction yet produced by America.—*Wilkie Collins.*

It seems to me that it was far from right for the Professor of English Literature in Yale, the Professor of English Literature in Columbia, and Wilkie Collins, to deliver opinions on Cooper's literature without having read some of it. It would have been much more decorous to keep silent and let persons talk who have read Cooper.

Cooper's art has some defects. In one place in *Deerslayer*, and in the restricted space of two-thirds of a page, Cooper has scored 114 offences against literary art out of a possible 115. It breaks the record.

There are nineteen rules governing literary art in the domain of romantic fiction—some say twenty-two. In *Deerslayer* Cooper violated eighteen of them. These eighteen require:

1. That a tale shall accomplish something and arrive somewhere. But the *Deerslayer* tale accomplishes nothing and arrives in the air.

2. They require that the episodes of a tale shall be necessary parts of the tale, and shall help to develop it. But as the *Deerslayer* tale is not a tale, and accomplishes nothing and arrives nowhere, the episodes have no rightful place in the work, since there was nothing for them to develop.

3. They require that the personages in a tale shall be alive, except in the case of corpses, and that always the reader shall

be able to tell the corpses from the others. But this detail has often been overlooked in the *Deerslayer* tale.

4. They require that the personages in a tale, both dead and alive, shall exhibit a sufficient excuse for being there. But this detail also has been overlooked in the *Deerslayer* tale.

5. They require that when the personages of a tale deal in conversation, the talk shall sound like human talk, and be talk such as human beings would be likely to talk in the given circumstances, and have a discoverable meaning, also a discoverable purpose, and a show of relevancy, and remain in the neighborhood of the subject in hand, and be interesting to the reader, and help out the tale, and stop when the people cannot think of anything more to say. But this requirement has been ignored from the beginning of the *Deerslayer* tale to the end of it.

6. They require that when the author describes the character of a personage in his tale, the conduct and conversation of that personage shall justify said description. But this law gets little or no attention in the *Deerslayer* tale, as "Natty Bumppo's" case will amply prove.

7. They require that when a personage talks like an illustrated, gilt-edged, tree-calf, hand-tooled, seven-dollar Friendship's Offering in the beginning of a paragraph, he shall not talk like a negro minstrel in the end of it. But this rule is flung down and danced upon in the *Deerslayer* tale.

8. They require that crass stupidities shall not be played upon the reader as "the craft of the woodsman, the delicate art of the forest," by either the author or the people in the tale. But this rule is persistently violated in the *Deerslayer* tale.

9. They require that the personages of a tale shall confine themselves to possibilities and let miracles alone; or, if they venture a miracle, the author must so plausibly set it forth as to make it look possible and reasonable. But these rules are not respected in the *Deerslayer* tale.

10. They require that the author shall make the reader feel a deep interest in the personages of his tale and in their fate; and that he shall make the reader love the good people in the tale and hate the bad ones. But the reader of the *Deerslayer* tale dislikes the good people in it, is indifferent to the others, and wishes they would all get drowned together.

11. They require that the characters in a tale shall be so clearly defined that the reader can tell beforehand what each will do in a given emergency. But in the *Deerslayer* tale this rule is vacated.

In addition to these large rules there are some little ones. These require that the author shall

12. *Say* what he is proposing to say, not merely come near it.

13. Use the right word, not its second cousin.

14. Eschew surplusage.

15. Not omit necessary details.

16. Avoid slovenliness of form.

17. Use good grammar.

18. Employ a simple and straightforward style.

Even these seven are coldly and persistently violated in the *Deerslayer* tale.

Cooper's gift in the way of invention was not a rich endowment; but such as it was he liked to work it, he was pleased with the effects, and indeed he did some quite sweet things with it. In his little box of stage properties he kept six or eight cunning devices, tricks, artifices for his savages and woodsmen to deceive and circumvent each other with, and he was never so happy as when he was working these innocent things and seeing them go. A favorite one was to make a moccasined person tread in the tracks of the moccasined enemy, and thus hide his own trail. Cooper wore out barrels and barrels of moccasins in working that trick. Another stage-property that he pulled out of his box pretty frequently was his broken twig. He prized his broken twig above all the rest of his effects, and worked it the hardest. It is a restful chapter in any book of his when somebody doesn't step on a dry twig and alarm all the reds and whites for two hundred yards around. Every time a Cooper person is in peril, and absolute silence is worth four dollars a minute, he is sure to step on a dry twig. There may be a hundred handier things to step on, but that wouldn't satisfy Cooper. Cooper requires him to turn out and find a dry twig; and if he can't do it, go and borrow one. In fact the Leather Stocking Series ought to have been called the Broken Twig Series.

I am sorry there is not room to put in a few dozen instances of the delicate art of the forest, as practiced by Natty Bumppo and some of the other Cooperian experts. Perhaps we may venture two or three samples. Cooper was a sailor—a naval officer; yet he gravely tells us how a vessel, driving toward a lee shore in a gale, is steered for a particular spot by her skipper because he knows of an *undertow* there which will hold her back against the gale and save her. For just pure woodcraft, or sailorcraft, or whatever it is, isn't that neat? For several years Cooper was daily in the society of artillery, and he ought to have noticed that when a cannon ball strikes the ground it either buries itself or skips a hundred feet or so; skips again a hundred feet or so—and so on, till it finally gets tired and rolls. Now in one place he loses some "females"—as he always calls women—in the edge of a wood near a plain at night in a fog, on purpose to give Bumppo a chance to show off the delicate art of the forest before the reader. These mislaid people are hunting for a fort. They hear a cannon-blast, and a cannon-ball presently comes rolling into the wood and stops at their feet. To the females this suggests nothing. The case is very different with the admirable Bumppo. I wish I may never know peace again if he doesn't strike out promptly and *follow the track* of that cannon-ball across the plain through the dense fog and find the fort. Isn't it a daisy? If Cooper had any real knowledge of Nature's ways of doing things, he had a most delicate art in concealing the fact. For instance: one of his acute Indian experts, Chingachgook (pronounced Chicago, I think), has lost the trail of a person he is tracking through the forest. Apparently that trail is hopelessly lost. Neither you nor I could ever have guessed out the way to find it. It was very different with Chicago. Chicago was not stumped for long. He turned a running stream out of its course, and there, in the slush in its old bed, were that person's moccasin-tracks. The current did not wash them away, as it would have done in all other like cases—no, even the eternal laws of Nature have to vacate when Cooper wants to put up a delicate job of woodcraft on the reader.

We must be a little wary when Brander Matthews tells us that Cooper's books "reveal an extraordinary fulness of invention." As a rule, I am quite willing to accept Brander Matthews's literary judgments and applaud his lucid and graceful phrasing of them; but that particular statement needs to be taken with a few tons of salt. Bless your heart, Cooper hadn't any more invention than a horse; and I don't mean a high-class horse, either; I mean a clothes-horse. It would be very difficult to find a really clever "situation" in Cooper's books; and still more difficult to find one of any kind which he has failed to render absurd by his handling of it. Look at the episodes of "the caves;" and at the celebrated scuffle between Magua and those others on the table-land a few days later; and at Hurry Harry's queer water-transit from the castle to the ark; and at Deerslayer's half hour with his first corpse; and at the quarrel between Hurry Harry and Deerslayer later; and at—but choose for yourself; you can't go amiss.

If Cooper had been an observer, his inventive faculty would have worked better, not more interestingly, but more rationally, more plausibly. Cooper's proudest creations in the way of "situations" suffer noticeably from the absence of the observer's protecting gift. Cooper's eye was splendidly inaccurate. Cooper seldom saw anything correctly. He saw nearly all things as through a glass eye, darkly. Of course a man who cannot see the commonest little everyday matters accurately is working at a disadvantage when he is constructing a "situation." In the *Deerslayer* tale Cooper has a stream which is fifty feet wide, where it flows out of a lake; it presently narrows to twenty as it meanders along for no given reason, and yet, when a stream acts like that it ought to be required to explain itself. Fourteen pages later the width of the brook's outlet from the lake has suddenly shrunk thirty feet, and become "the narrowest part of the stream." This shrinkage is not accounted for. The stream has bends in it, a sure indication that it has alluvial banks, and cuts them; yet these bends are only thirty and fifty feet long. If Cooper had been a nice and punctilious observer he would have noticed that the bends were oftener nine hundred feet long than short of it.

Cooper made the exit of that stream fifty feet wide in the first place, for no particular reason; in the second place, he narrowed it to less than twenty to accommodate some Indians. He bends a "sapling" to the form of an arch over this narrow passage, and conceals six Indians in its foliage. They are "laying" for a settler's scow or ark which is coming up the stream on its way to the lake; it is being hauled against the stiff current by a rope whose stationary end is anchored in the lake; its rate of progress cannot be more than a mile an hour. Cooper describes the ark, but pretty obscurely. In the matter of dimensions "it was little more than a modern canal boat." Let us guess, then, that it was about 140 feet long. It was of "greater breadth than common." Let us guess, then, that it was about sixteen feet wide. This leviathan had been prowling down bends which were but a third as long as itself, and scraping between banks where it had only two feet of space to spare on each side. We cannot too much admire this miracle. A low-roofed log dwelling occupies "two-thirds of the ark's length"—a dwelling ninety feet long and sixteen feet wide, let us say—a kind of vestibule train. The dwelling has two rooms—each forty-five feet long and sixteen feet wide, let us guess. One of them is the bed-room of the Hutter girls, Judith and Hetty; the other is the parlor, in the day time, at night it is papa's bed chamber. The ark is arriving at the stream's exit, now, whose width has been reduced to less than twenty feet to accommodate the Indians—say to eighteen. There is a foot to spare on each side of the boat. Did the Indians notice that there was going to be a tight squeeze there? Did they notice that they could make money by climbing down out of that arched sapling and just stepping aboard when the ark scraped by? No; other Indians would have noticed these things, but Cooper's Indians never notice anything. Cooper thinks they are marvellous creatures for noticing, but he was almost always in error about his Indians. There was seldom a sane one among them.

The ark is 140 feet long; the dwelling is 90 feet long. The idea of the Indians is to drop softly and secretly from the arched sapling to the dwelling as the ark creeps along under it at the rate of a mile an hour, and butcher the family. It will take the ark a minute and a half to pass under. It will take the 90-foot dwelling a minute to pass under. Now, then, what did the six Indians do? It would take you thirty years to guess, and even then you would have to give it up, I believe. Therefore, I will tell you what the Indians did. Their chief, a person of quite extraordinary intellect for a Cooper Indian, warily watched the canal boat as it squeezed along under him, and when he had got his calculations fined down to exactly the right shade, as he judged, he let go and dropped. And *missed the house!* That is actually what he did. He missed the house, and landed in the stern of the scow. It was not much of a fall, yet it knocked him silly. He lay there unconscious. If the house had been 97 feet long, he would have made the trip. The fault was Cooper's, not his. The error lay in the construction of the house. Cooper was no architect.

There still remained in the roost five Indians. The boat has passed under and is now out of their reach. Let me explain what the five did—you would not be able to reason it out for yourself. No. 1 jumped for the boat, but fell in the water astern of it. Then No. 2 jumped for the boat, but fell in the water still further astern of it. Then No. 3 jumped for the boat, and fell a good way astern of it. Then No. 4 jumped for the boat, and fell in the water *away* astern. Then even No. 5 made a jump for the boat—for he was a Cooper Indian. In the matter of intellect, the difference between a Cooper Indian and the Indian that stands in front of the cigar shop is not spacious. The scow episode is really a sublime burst of invention; but it does not thrill, because the inaccuracy of the details throws a sort of air of fictitiousness and general improbability over it. This comes of Cooper's inadequacy as an observer.

The reader will find some examples of Cooper's high talent for inaccurate observation in the account of the shooting match in *The Pathfinder*. "A common wrought nail was driven lightly into the target, its head having been first touched with paint." The color of the paint is not stated—an important omission, but Cooper deals freely in important omissions. No, after all, it was not an important omission; for this nail head is *a hundred yards* from the marksman and could not be seen by them at that distance no matter what its color might be. How far can the best eyes see a common house fly? A hundred yards? It is quite impossible. Very well, eyes that cannot see a house fly that is a hundred yards away cannot see an ordinary nail head at that distance, for the size of the two objects is the same. It takes a keen eye to see a fly or a nail head at fifty yards—one hundred and fifty feet. Can the reader do it?

The nail was lightly driven, its head painted, and game called. Then the Cooper miracles began. The bullet of the first marksman chipped an edge of the nail head; the next man's bullet drove the nail a little way into the target—and removed all the paint. Haven't the miracles gone far enough now? Not to suit Cooper; for the purpose of this whole scheme is to show off his prodigy, Deerslayer-Hawkeye-Long-Rifle-Leather-Stocking-Pathfinder-Bumppo before the ladies.

"Be all ready to clench it, boys!" cried out Pathfinder, stepping into his friend's tracks the instant they were vacant. "Never mind a new nail; I can see that, though the paint is gone, and what I can see, I can hit at a hundred yards, though it were only a mosquitoe's eye. Be ready to clench!"

The rifle cracked, the bullet sped its way and the head of the nail was buried in the wood, covered by the piece of flattened lead.

There, you see, is a man who could hunt flies with a rifle, and command a ducal salary in a Wild West show to-day, if we had him back with us.

The recorded feat is certainly surprising, just as it stands; but it is not surprising enough for Cooper. Cooper adds a touch. He has made Pathfinder do this miracle with another man's rifle, and not only that, but Pathfinder did not have even the advantage of loading it himself. He had everything against him, and yet he made that impossible shot, and not only made it, but did it with absolute confidence, saying, "Be ready to clench." Now a person like that would have undertaken that same feat with a brickbat, and with Cooper to help he would have achieved it, too.

Pathfinder showed off handsomely that day before the ladies. His very first feat was a thing which no Wild West show can touch. He was standing with the group of marksmen, observing—a hundred yards from the target, mind: one Jasper raised his rifle and drove the centre of the bull's-eye. Then the quartermaster fired. The target exhibited no result this time. There was a laugh. "It's a dead miss," said Major

Lundie. Pathfinder waited an impressive moment or two, then said in that calm, indifferent, know-it-all way of his, "No, Major—he has covered Jasper's bullet, as will be seen if any one will take the trouble to examine the target."

Wasn't it remarkable! How *could* he see that little pellet fly through the air and enter that distant bullet-hole? Yet that is what he did; for nothing is impossible to a Cooper person. Did any of those people have any deep-seated doubts about this thing? No; for that would imply sanity, and these were all Cooper people.

The respect for Pathfinder's skill and for his *quickness and accuracy of sight* (the italics are mine) was so profound and general, that the instant he made this declaration the spectators began to distrust their own opinions, and a dozen rushed to the target in order to ascertain the fact. There, sure enough, it was found that the quartermaster's bullet had gone through the hole made by Jasper's, and that, too, so accurately as to require a minute examination to be certain of the circumstance, which, however, was soon clearly established by discovering one bullet over the other in the stump against which the target was placed.

They made a "minute" examination; but never mind, how could they know that there were two bullets in that hole without digging the latest one out? for neither probe nor eyesight could prove the presence of any more than one bullet. Did they dig? No; as we shall see. It is the Pathfinder's turn now; he steps out before the ladies, takes aim, and fires.

But alas! here is a disappointment; an incredible, an unimaginable disappointment—for the target's aspect is unchanged; there is nothing there but that same old bullet hole!

"If one dared to hint at such a thing," cried Major Duncan, "I should say that the Pathfinder has also missed the target."

As nobody had missed it yet, the "also" was not necessary; but never mind about that, for the Pathfinder is going to speak.

"No, no, Major," said he, confidently, "that *would* be a risky declaration. I didn't load the piece, and can't say what was in it, but if it was lead, you will find the bullet driving down those of the Quartermaster and Jasper, else is not my name Pathfinder."

A shout from the target announced the truth of this assertion.

Is the miracle sufficient as it stands? Not for Cooper. The Pathfinder speaks again, as he "now slowly advances towards the stage occupied by the females:"

"That's not all, boys, that's not all; if you find the target touched at all, I'll own to a miss. The Quartermaster cut the wood, but you'll find no wood cut by that last messenger."

The miracle is at last complete. He knew—doubtless *saw*—at the distance of a hundred yards—that his bullet had passed into the hole *without fraying the edges*. There were now three bullets in that one hole—three bullets imbedded processionally in the body of the stump back of the target. Everybody knew this—somehow or other—and yet nobody had dug any of them out to make sure. Cooper is not a close observer, but he is interesting. He is certainly always that, no matter what happens. And he is more interesting when he is not noticing what he is about than when he is. This is a considerable merit.

The conversations in the Cooper books have a curious sound in our modern ears. To believe that such talk really ever came out of people's mouths would be to believe that there was a time when time was of no value to a person who thought he had something to say; when it was the custom to spread a two-minute remark out to ten; when a man's mouth was a rolling-mill, and busied itself all day long in turning four-foot pigs of thought into thirty-foot bars of conversational railroad iron by attenuation; when subjects were seldom faithfully stuck to, but the talk wandered all around and arrived nowhere; when conversations consisted mainly of irrelevances, with here and there a relevancy, a relevancy with an embarrassed look, as not being able to explain how it got there.

Cooper was certainly not a master in the construction of dialogue. Inaccurate observation defeated him here as it defeated him in so many other enterprises of his. He even failed to notice that the man who talks corrupt English six days in the week must and will talk it on the seventh, and can't help himself. In the *Deerslayer* story he lets Deerslayer talk the showiest kind of book talk sometimes, and at other times the basest of base dialects. For instance, when some one asks him if he has a sweetheart, and if so, where she abides, this is his majestic answer:

"She's in the forest—hanging from the boughs of the trees, in a soft rain—in the dew on the open grass—the clouds that float about in the blue heavens—the birds that sing in the woods—the sweet springs where I slake my thirst—and in all the other glorious gifts that come from God's Providence!"

And he preceded that, a little before, with this:

"It consarns me as all things that touches a fri'nd consarns a fri'nd."

And this is another of his remarks:

"If I was Injin born, now, I might tell of this, or carry in the scalp and boast of the expl'ite afore the whole tribe; or if my inimy had only been a bear"—and so on.

We cannot imagine such a thing as a veteran Scotch Commander-in-Chief comporting himself in the field like a windy melodramatic actor, but Cooper could. On one occasion Alice and Cora were being chased by the French through a fog in the neighborhood of their father's fort:

*"Point de quartier aux coquins!"* cried an eager pursuer, who seemed to direct the operations of the enemy.

"Stand firm and be ready, my gallant 60ths!" suddenly exclaimed a voice above them; "wait to see the enemy; fire low, and sweep the glacis."

"Father! father!" exclaimed a piercing cry from out the mist; "it is I! Alice! thy own Elsie! spare, O! save your daughters!"

"Hold!" shouted the former speaker, in the awful tones of parental agony, the sound reaching even to the woods, and rolling back in solemn echo. " 'Tis she! God has restored me my children! Throw open the sally-port; to the field, 60ths, to the field; pull not a trigger, lest ye kill my lambs! Drive off these dogs of France with your steel."

Cooper's word-sense was singularly dull. When a person has a poor ear for music he will flat and sharp right along without knowing it. He keeps near the tune, but it is *not* the tune. When a person has a poor ear for words, the result is a literary flatting and sharping; you perceive what he is intending to say, but you also perceive that he doesn't *say* it. This is Cooper. He was not a word-musician. His ear was satisfied with the *approximate* word. I will furnish some circumstantial evidence in support of this charge. My instances are gathered from half a dozen pages of the tale called *Deerslayer*. He uses "verbal," for "oral"; "precision," for "facility"; "phenomena," for "marvels"; "necessary," for "predetermined"; "unsophisticated," for "primitive"; "preparation," for "expectancy"; "rebuked," for "subdued"; "dependent on," for "resulting from"; "fact," for "condition"; "fact," for "conjecture"; "precaution," for "caution"; "explain," for "determine"; "mortified," for "disappointed"; "meretricious," for "factitious"; "materially," for "considerably"; "decreasing," for "deepening"; "increasing," for "disappearing"; "embedded," for "enclosed"; "treacherous," for "hostile"; "stood," for "stooped"; "softened," for "replaced"; "rejoined," for "remarked"; "situation," for "condition"; "different," for "differing"; "insensible," for "unsentient"; "brevity," for "celerity"; "distrusted," for "suspicious"; "mental imbecility," for "imbecility"; "eyes," for "sight"; "counteracting," for "opposing"; "funeral obsequies," for "obsequies."

There have been daring people in the world who claimed that Cooper could write English, but they are all dead now—all dead but Lounsbury. I don't remember that Lounsbury makes the claim in so many words, still he makes it, for he says that *Deerslayer* is a "pure work of art." Pure, in that connection, means faultless—faultless in all details—and language is a detail. If Mr. Lounsbury had only compared Cooper's English with the English which he writes himself—but it is plain that he didn't; and so it is likely that he imagines until this day that Cooper's is as clean and compact as his own. Now I feel sure, deep down in my heart, that Cooper wrote about the poorest English that exists in our language, and that the English of *Deerslayer* is the very worst that even Cooper ever wrote.

I may be mistaken, but it does seem to me that *Deerslayer* is not a work of art in any sense; it does seem to me that it is destitute of every detail that goes to the making of a work of art; in truth, it seems to me that *Deerslayer* is just simply a literary *delirium tremens*.

A work of art? It has no invention; it has no order, system, sequence, or result; it has no lifelikeness, no thrill, no stir, no seeming of reality; its characters are confusedly drawn, and by their acts and words they prove that they are not the sort of people the author claims that they are; its humor is pathetic; its pathos is funny; its conversations are—oh! indescribable; its love-scenes odious; its English a crime against the language.

Counting these out, what is left is Art. I think we must all admit that.

*July 1895*

# Fenimore Cooper's Further Literary Offenses

Young Gentleman: In studying Cooper you will find it profitable to study him in detail—word by word, sentence by sentence. For every sentence of his is interesting. Interesting because of its make-up; its peculiar make-up, its original make-up. Let us examine a sentence or two, and see. Here is a passage from Chapter XI of *The Last of the Mohicans*, one of the most famous and most admired of Cooper's books:

Notwithstanding the swiftness of their flight, one of the Indians had found an opportunity to strike a straggling fawn with an arrow, and had borne the more preferable fragments of the victim, patiently on his shoulders, to the stopping-place. Without any aid from the science of cookery, he was immediately employed, in common with his fellows, in gorging himself with this digestible sustenance. Magua alone sat apart, without participating in the revolting meal, and apparently buried in the deepest thought.

This little paragraph is full of matter for reflection and inquiry. The remark about the swiftness of the flight was unnecessary, as it was merely put in to forestall the possible objection of some overparticular reader that the Indian couldn't have found the needed "opportunity" while fleeing swiftly. The reader would not have made that objection. He would care nothing about having that small matter explained and justified. But that is Cooper's way; frequently he will explain and justify little things that do not need it and then make up for this by as frequently failing to explain important ones that do need it. For instance he allowed that astute and cautious person, Deerslayer-Hawkeye, to throw his rifle heedlessly down and leave it lying on the ground where some hostile Indians would presently be sure to find it—a rifle prized by that person above all things else in the earth—and the reader gets no word of explanation of that strange act. There was a reason, but it wouldn't bear exposure. Cooper meant to get a fine dramatic effect out of the finding of the rifle by the Indians, and he accomplished this at the happy time; but all the same, Hawkeye could have hidden the rifle in a quarter of a minute where the Indians could not have found it. Cooper couldn't think of any way to explain why Hawkeye didn't do that, so he just shirked the difficulty and did not explain at all. In another place Cooper allowed Heyward to shoot at an Indian with a pistol that wasn't loaded—and grants us not a word of explanation as to how the man did it.

No, the remark about the swiftness of their flight was not necessary; neither was the one which said that the Indian found an opportunity; neither was the one which said he *struck* the fawn; neither was the one which explained that it was a "straggling" fawn; neither was the one which said the striking was done with an arrow; neither was the one which said the Indian bore the "fragments"; nor the remark that they were preferable fragments; nor the remark that they were *more* preferable fragments; nor the explanation that they were fragments of the "victim"; nor the overparticular explanation that specifies the Indian's "shoulders" as the part of him that supported the fragments; nor the statement that the Indian bore the fragments patiently. None of those details has any value. We don't care what the Indian struck the fawn with; we don't care whether it was a straggling fawn or an unstraggling one; we don't care which fragments the Indian saved; we don't care why he saved the "more" preferable ones when the merely preferable ones would have amounted to just the same thing and couldn't have been told from the more preferable ones by anybody, dead or alive; we don't care whether the Indian carried them on his shoulders or in his handkerchief; and finally, we don't care whether he carried them patiently or struck for higher pay and shorter hours. We are indifferent to that Indian and all his affairs.

There was only one fact in that long sentence that was worth stating, and it could have been squeezed into these few words—and with advantage to the narrative, too: "During the flight one of the Indians had killed a fawn and he brought it into camp."

You will notice that "During the flight one of the Indians had killed a fawn and he brought it into camp," is more straightforward and business-like, and less mincing and smirky, than it is to say, "Notwithstanding the swiftness of their flight, one of the Indians had found an opportunity to strike a straggling fawn with an arrow, and had borne the more preferable fragments of the victim, patiently on his shoulders, to the stopping-place." You will notice that the form "During the flight one of the Indians had killed a fawn and he brought it into camp" holds up its chin and moves to the front with the steady stride of a grenadier, whereas the form "Notwithstanding the swiftness of their flight, one of the Indians had found an opportunity to strike a straggling fawn with an arrow, and had borne the more preferable fragments of the victim, patiently on his shoulders, to the stopping-place" simpers along with an airy, complacent, monkey-with-a-parasol gait which is not suited to the transportation of raw meat.

I beg to remind you that an author's way of setting forth a matter is called his Style, and that an author's style is a main part of his equipment for business. The style of some authors has variety in it, but Cooper's style is remarkable for the absence of this feature. Cooper's style is always grand and stately and noble. Style may be likened to an army, the author to its general, the book to the campaign. Some authors proportion an attacking force to the strength or weakness, the importance or unimportance, of the object to be attacked; but Cooper doesn't. It doesn't make any difference to Cooper whether the object of attack is a hundred thousand men or a cow; he hurls his entire force against it. He comes thundering down with all his battalions at his back, cavalry in the van, artillery on the flanks, infantry massed in the middle, forty bands braying, a thousand banners streaming in the wind; and whether the object be an army or a cow you will see him come marching sublimely in, at the end of the engagement, bearing the more preferable fragments of the victim patiently on his shoulders, to the stopping-place. Cooper's style is grand, awful, beautiful; but it is sacred to Cooper, it is his very own, and no student of the Veterinary College of Arizona will be allowed to filch it from him.

In one of his chapters Cooper throws an ungentle slur at one Gamut because he is not exact enough in his choice of words. But Cooper has that failing himself, as remarked in our first lecture. If the Indian had "struck" the fawn with a brick, or with a club, or with his fist, no one could find fault with the word used. And one cannot find much fault when he strikes it with an arrow; still it sounds affected, and it might have been a little better to lean to simplicity and say he shot it with an arrow.

"Fragments" is well enough, perhaps, when one is speaking of the parts of a dismembered deer, yet it hasn't just exactly the right sound—and sound is something; in fact sound is a good deal. It makes the difference between good music and poor music, and it can sometimes make the difference between good literature and indifferent literature. "Fragments" sounds all right when we are talking about the wreckage of a breakable thing that has been smashed; it also sounds all right when applied to cat's meat; but when we use it to describe large hunks and chunks like the fore- and hindquarters of a fawn, it grates upon the fastidious ear.

"Without any aid from the science of cookery, he was immediately employed, in common with his fellows, in gorging himself with this digestible sustenance."

This was a mere statistic; just a mere cold, colorless statistic; yet you see Cooper has made a chromo out of it. To use another figure, he has clothed a humble statistic in flowing, voluminous and costly raiment, whereas both good taste and economy suggest that he ought to have saved these splendors for a king, and dressed the humble statistic in a simple breechclout. Cooper spent twenty-four words here on a thing not really worth more than eight. We will reduce the statistic to its proper proportions and state it in this way:

"He and the others ate the meat raw."

"Digestible sustenance" is a handsome phrase, but it was out of place there, because we do not know these Indians or care for them; and so it cannot interest us to know whether the meat was going to agree with them or not. Details which do not assist a story are better left out.

"Magua alone sat apart, without participating in the revolting meal" is a statement which we understand, but that is our merit, not Cooper's. Cooper is not clear. He does not say who it is that is revolted by the meal. It is really Cooper himself, but there is nothing in the statement to indicate that it isn't Magua. Magua is an Indian and likes raw meat.

The word "alone" could have been left out and space saved. It has no value where it is.

I must come back with some frequency, in the course of these lectures, to the matter of Cooper's inaccuracy as an Observer. In this way I shall hope to persuade you that it is well to look at a thing carefully before you try to describe it; but I shall rest you between times with other matters and thus try to avoid overfatiguing you with that detail of our theme. In *The Last of the Mohicans* Cooper gets up a stirring "situation" on an island flanked by great cataracts—a lofty island with steep sides—a sort of tongue which projects downstream from the midst of the divided waterfall. There are caverns in this mass of rock, and a party of Cooper people hide themselves in one of these to get away from some hostile Indians. There is a small exit at each end of this cavern. These exits are closed with blankets and the light excluded. The exploring hostiles back themselves up against the blankets and rave and rage in a blood-curdling way, but they are Cooper Indians and of course fail to discover the blankets; so they presently go away baffled and disappointed. Alice, in her gratitude for this deliverance, flings herself on her knees to return thanks. The darkness in there must have been pretty solid; yet if we may believe Cooper, it was a darkness which could not have been told from daylight; for here are some nice details which were visible in it:

Both Heyward and the more tempered Cora witnessed the act of involuntary emotion with powerful sympathy, the former secretly believing that piety had never worn a form so lovely as it had now assumed in the youthful person of Alice. Her eyes were radiant with the glow of grateful feelings; the flush of her beauty was again seated on her cheeks, and her whole soul seemed ready and anxious to pour out its thanksgivings, through the medium of her eloquent features. But when her lips moved, the words they should have uttered appeared frozen by some new and sudden chill. Her bloom gave place to the paleness of death; her soft and melting eyes grew hard, and seemed contracting with horror; while those hands which she had raised, clasped in each other, towards heaven, dropped in horizontal lines before her, the fingers pointed forward in convulsed motion.

It is a case of strikingly inexact observation. Heyward and the more tempered Cora could not have seen the half of it in the dark that way.

I must call your attention to certain details of this work of art which invite particular examination. "Involuntary" is surplusage, and violates Rule 14. All emotion is involuntary when genuine, and then the qualifying term is not needed; a qualifying term is needed only when the emotion is pumped-up and ungenuine. "Secretly" is surplusage, too; because Heyward was not believing out loud, but all to himself; and a person cannot believe a thing all to himself without doing it privately. I do not approve of the word "seated" to describe the process of locating a flush. No one can seat a flush. A flush is not a deposit on an exterior surface, it is a something which squshes out from within.

I cannot approve of the word "new." If Alice had had an old chill, formerly, it would be right to distinguish this one from that one by calling this one the new chill; but she had not had any old chill, this one was the only chill she had had, up till now, and so the tacit reference to an old anterior chill is unwarranted and misleading. And I do not altogether like the phrase "while those hands which she had raised." It seems to imply that she had some other hands—some other ones which she had put on the shelf a minute so as to give her a better chance to raise these ones; but it is not true; she had only the one pair. The phrase is in the last degree misleading. But I like to see her extend these ones in front of her and work the fingers. I think that that is a very good effect. And it would have almost doubled the effect if the more tempered Cora had done it some, too.

A Cooper Indian who has been washed is a poor thing, and commonplace; it is the Cooper Indian in his paint that thrills. Cooper's extra words are Cooper's paint—his paint, his feathers, his tomahawk, his warwhoop.

In the two-thirds of a page elsewhere referred to, wherein Cooper scored 114 literary transgressions out of a possible 115, he appears before us with all his things on. As follows; the italics are mine—they indicate violations of Rule 14:

In a minute he was once more fastened to the tree, *a helpless object of any insult or wrong that might be offered. So eagerly did every one now act, that nothing was said.* The fire was immediately lighted *in the pile, and the end of all was anxiously expected.*

It was not the intention of the Hurons *absolutely* to destroy *the life of* their victim by *means of* fire. They designed merely to put his *physical* fortitude to the severest proofs it could endure, short of that extremity. In the end, they fully intended to carry his scalp into their village, but it was their wish first to break down his resolution, and to reduce him to *the level of* a complaining sufferer. With this view, the pile of brush *and branches* had been placed at a *proper* distance, *or one* at which it was thought the heat would soon become intolerable, though *it might* not *be* immediately dangerous. *As often happened, however, on these occasions,* this distance had been miscalculated, and the flames *began to wave their forked tongues in a proximity to the face of the victim that* would have proved fatal in another instant had not Hetty rushed through the crowd, armed with a stick, and scattered the blazing pile *in a dozen directions.* More than one hand was raised to strike the *presumptuous* intruder to the earth; but the chiefs prevented the blows by reminding their *irritated* followers of the state of her mind. Hetty, herself, was insensible to the risk she ran; but, *as soon as she had performed this bold act, she* stood looking about her in frowning resentment, as if to rebuke the *crowd of attentive* savages for their cruelty.

"God bless you, dear*est sister*, for that brave and ready act," murmured Judith, *herself unnerved so much as to be incapable of exertion;* "Heaven itself has sent you on its holy errand."

Number of words, 320; necessary ones, 220: words wasted by the generous spendthrift, 100.

In our day those 100 unnecessary words would have to come out. We will take them out presently and make the episode approximate the modern requirement in the matter of compression.

If we may consider each unnecessary word in Cooper's report of that barbecue a separate and individual violation of Rule 14, then that rule is violated 100 times in that report. Other rules are violated in it. Rule 12, 2 instances; Rule 13, 5 instances; Rule 15, 1 instance; Rule 16, 2 instances; Rule 17, 1 or 2 little instances; the report in its entirety is an offense against Rule 18—also against Rule 16. Total score, about 114 violations of the laws of literary art out of a possible 115.

Let us now bring forward the report again, with the most of the unnecessary words knocked out. By departing from Cooper's style and manner, all the facts could be put into 150 words, and the effects heightened at the same time—this is manifest, of course—but that would not be desirable. We must stick to Cooper's language as closely as we can:

In a minute he was once more fastened to the tree. The fire was immediately lighted. It was not the intention of the Hurons to destroy Deerslayer's life by fire; they designed merely to put his fortitude to the severest proofs it could endure short of that extremity. In the end, they fully intended to take his life, but it was their wish first to break down his resolution and reduce him to a complaining sufferer. With this view the pile of brush had been placed at a distance at which it was thought the heat would soon become intolerable, without being immediately dangerous. But this distance had been miscalculated; the fire was so close to the victim that he would have been fatally burned in another instant if Hetty had not rushed through the crowd and scattered the brands with a stick. More than one Indian raised his hand to strike her down, but the chiefs saved her by reminding them of the state of her mind. Hetty herself was insensible to the risk she ran; she stood looking about her in frowning resentment, as if to rebuke the savages for their cruelty.

"God bless you, dear!" cried Judith, "for that brave and ready act. Heaven itself has sent you on its holy errand, and you shall have a chromo."

Number of words, 220—and the facts are all in.

*c. July 1895*

# *How to Tell a Story*

The humorous Story an American
Development. — Its Difference
from comic and witty Stories.

I do not claim that I can tell a story as it ought to be told. I only claim to know how a story ought to be told, for I have been almost daily in the company of the most expert story-tellers for many years.

There are several kinds of stories, but only one difficult kind—the humorous. I will talk mainly about that one. The humorous story is American, the comic story is English, the witty story is French. The humorous story depends for its effect upon the *manner* of the telling; the comic story and the witty story upon the *matter*.

The humorous story may be spun out to great length, and may wander around as much as it pleases, and arrive nowhere in particular; but the comic and witty stories must be brief and end with a point. The humorous story bubbles gently along, the others burst.

The humorous story is strictly a work of art,—high and delicate art,—and only an artist can tell it; but no art is necessary in telling the comic and the witty story; anybody can do it. The art of telling a humorous story—understand, I mean by word of mouth, not print—was created in America, and has remained at home.

The humorous story is told gravely; the teller does his best to conceal the fact that he even dimly suspects that there is anything funny about it; but the teller of the comic story tells you beforehand that it is one of the funniest things he has ever heard, then tells it with eager delight, and is the first person to laugh when he gets through. And sometimes, if he has had good success, he is so glad and happy that he will repeat the "nub" of it and glance around from face to face, collecting applause, and then repeat it again. It is a pathetic thing to see.

Very often, of course, the rambling and disjointed humorous story finishes with a nub, point, snapper, or whatever you like to call it. Then the listener must be alert, for in many cases the teller will divert attention from that nub by dropping it in a carefully casual and indifferent way, with the pretence that he does not know it is a nub.

Artemus Ward used that trick a good deal; then when the belated audience presently caught the joke he would look up with innocent surprise, as if wondering what they had found to laugh at. Dan Setchell used it before him, Nye and Riley and others use it to-day.

But the teller of the comic story does not slur the nub; he shouts it at you—every time. And when he prints it, in England, France, Germany and Italy, he italicises it, puts some whooping exclamation-points after it, and sometimes explains it in a parenthesis. All of which is very depressing, and makes one want to renounce joking and lead a better life.

Let me set down an instance of the comic method, using an anecdote which has been popular all over the world for twelve or fifteen hundred years. The teller tells it in this way:

### The Wounded Soldier.

In the course of a certain battle a soldier whose leg had been shot off appealed to another soldier who was hurrying by to carry him to the rear, informing him at the same time of the loss which he had sustained; whereupon the generous son of Mars, shouldering the unfortunate, proceeded to carry out his desire. The bullets and cannon-balls were flying in all directions, and presently one of the latter took the wounded man's head off—without, however, his deliverer being aware of it. In no long time he was hailed by an officer, who said:

"Where are you going with that carcass?"

"To the rear, sir—he's lost his leg!"

"His leg, forsooth?" responded the astonished officer; "you mean his head, you booby."

Whereupon the soldier dispossessed himself of his burden, and stood looking down upon it in great perplexity. At length he said:

"It is true, sir, just as you have said." Then after a pause he added, "*But he* TOLD *me* IT WAS HIS LEG!!!!!"

Here the narrator bursts into explosion after explosion of thunderous horse-laughter, repeating that nub from time to time through his gaspings and shriekings and suffocatings.

It takes only a minute and a half to tell that in its comic-story form; and isn't worth the telling, after all. Put into the humorous-story form it takes ten minutes, and is about the funniest thing I have ever listened to—as James Whitcomb Riley tells it.

He tells it in the character of a dull-witted old farmer who has just heard it for the first time, thinks it is unspeakably funny, and is trying to repeat it to a neighbor. But he can't remember it; so he gets it all mixed up and wanders helplessly round and round, putting in tedious details that don't belong in the tale and only retard it; taking them out conscientiously and putting in others that are just as useless; making minor mistakes now and then and stopping to correct them and explain how he came to make them; remembering things which he forgot to put in in their proper place and going back to put them in there; stopping his narrative a good while in order to try to recall the name of the soldier that was hurt, and finally remembering that the soldier's name was not mentioned, and remarking placidly that the name is of no real importance, any way,—better, of course, if one knew it, but not essential, after all,—and so on, and so on, and so on.

The teller is innocent and happy and pleased with himself, and has to stop every little while to hold himself in and keep from laughing outright; and does hold in, but his body quakes in a jelly-like way with interior chuckles; and at the end of the ten minutes the audience have laughed until they are exhausted, and the tears are running down their faces.

The simplicity and innocence and sincerity and unconsciousness of the old farmer are perfectly simulated, and the result is a performance which is thoroughly charming and delicious. This is art—and fine and beautiful, and only a master can compass it; but a machine could tell the other story.

To string incongruities and absurdities together in a wandering and sometimes purposeless way, and seem innocently unaware that they are absurdities, is the basis of the American art, if my position is correct. Another feature is the slurring of the point. A third is the dropping of a studied remark apparently without knowing it, as if one were thinking aloud. The fourth and last is the pause.

Artemus Ward dealt in numbers three and four a good deal. He would begin to tell with great animation something which he seemed to think was wonderful; then lose confidence, and after an apparently absent-minded pause add an incongruous remark in a soliloquizing way; and that was the remark intended to explode the mine—and it did.

For instance, he would say eagerly, excitedly, "I once knew a man in New Zealand who hadn't a tooth in his head"— here his animation would die out; a silent, reflective pause would follow, then he would say dreamily, and as if to himself, "and yet that man could beat a drum better than any man I ever saw."

The pause is an exceedingly important feature in any kind of story, and a frequently recurring feature, too. It is a dainty thing, and delicate, and also uncertain and treacherous; for it must be exactly the right length—no more and no less—or it fails of its purpose and makes trouble. If the pause is too short the impressive point is passed, and the audience have had time to divine that a surprise is intended—and then you can't surprise them, of course.

On the platform I used to tell a negro ghost story that had a pause in front of the snapper on the end, and that pause was the most important thing in the whole story. If I got it the right length precisely, I could spring the finishing ejaculation with effect enough to make some impressible girl deliver a startled little yelp and jump out of her seat—and that was what I was after. This story was called "The Golden Arm," and was told in this fashion. You can practise with it yourself—and mind you look out for the pause and get it right.

### The Golden Arm.

Once 'pon a time dey wuz a monsus mean man, en he live 'way out in de prairie all 'lone by hisself, 'cep'n he had a wife. En bimeby she died, en he tuck en toted her way out dah in de prairie en buried her. Well, she had a golden arm—all

solid gold, fum de shoulder down. He wuz pow'ful mean—
pow'ful; en dat night he couldn't sleep, caze he want dat
golden arm so bad.

When it come midnight he couldn't stan' it no mo'; so he
git up, he did, en tuck his lantern en shoved out thoo de
storm en dug her up en got de golden arm; en he bent his
head down 'gin de win', en plowed en plowed en plowed
thoo de snow. Den all on a sudden he stop (make a considerable pause here, and look startled, and take a listening attitude) en say: "My *lan'*, what's dat!"

En he listen—en listen—en de win' say (set your teeth
together and imitate the wailing and wheezing singsong of
the wind), "Bzzz-z-zzz"—en den, way back yonder whah
de grave is, he hear a *voice!*—he hear a voice all mix' up in
de win'—can't hardly tell 'em 'part—"Bzzz-zzz—W-h-o—
g-o-t—m-y—g-o-l-d-e-n *arm?*—zzz—zzz—W-h-o  g-o-t
m-y g-o-l-d-e-n *arm?*" (You must begin to shiver violently
now.)

En he begin to shiver en shake, en say, "Oh, my! *Oh*, my
lan'!" en de win' blow de lantern out, en de snow en sleet
blow in his face en mos' choke him, en he start a-plowin'
knee-deep toward home mos' dead, he so sk'yerd—en pooty
soon he hear de voice agin, en (pause) it 'us comin' *after*
him! "Bzzz—zzz—zzz—W-h-o—g-o-t—m-y g-o-l-d-e-n—
*arm?*"

When he git to de pasture he hear it agin—closter now, en
a-*comin'!*—a-comin' back dah in de dark en de storm—(repeat the wind and the voice). When he git to de house he
rush up-stairs en jump in de bed en kiver up, head and years,
en lay dah shiverin' en shakin'—en den way out dah he hear
it *agin!*—en a-*comin'!* En bimeby he hear (pause—awed, listening attitude)—pat—pat—pat—*hit's a-comin' up-stairs!*
Den he hear de latch, en he *know* it's in de room!

Den pooty soon he know it's a-*stannin' by de bed!* (Pause.)
Den—he know it's a—*bendin' down over him*—en he cain't
skasely git his breath! Den—den—he seem to feel someth'n
*c-o-l-d*, right down 'most agin his head! (Pause.)

Den de voice say, *right at his year*—"W-h-o—g-o-t—m-y
—g-o-l-d-e-n *arm?*" (You must wail it out very plaintively

and accusingly; then you stare steadily and impressively into the face of the farthest-gone auditor,—a girl, preferably,—and let that awe-inspiring pause begin to build itself in the deep hush. When it has reached exactly the right length, jump suddenly at that girl and yell, "*You've* got it!"

If you've got the *pause* right, she'll fetch a dear little yelp and spring right out of her shoes. But you *must* get the pause right; and you will find it the most troublesome and aggravating and uncertain thing you ever undertook.)

*October 1895*

# Man's Place in the Animal World

In August, 1572, similar things were occurring in Paris and elsewhere in France. In this case it was Christian against Christian. The Roman Catholics, by previous concert, sprung a surprise upon the unprepared and unsuspecting protestants, and butchered them by thousands—both sexes and all ages. This was the memorable St. Bartholomew's Day. At Rome the Pope and the Church gave public thanks to God when the happy news came.

During several centuries hundreds of heretics were burned at the stake every year because their religious opinions were not satisfactory to the Roman Church.

In all ages the savages of all lands have made the slaughtering of their neighboring brothers and the enslaving of their women and children the common business of their lives.

Hypocrisy, envy, malice, cruelty, vengefulness, seduction, rape, robbery, swindling, arson, bigamy, adultery, and the oppression and humiliation of the poor and the helpless in all ways, have been and still are more or less common among both the civilized and uncivilized peoples of the earth.

For many centuries "the common brotherhood of man" has been urged—on Sundays—and "patriotism" on Sundays and week-days both. Yet patriotism *contemplates the opposite of a common brotherhood*.

Woman's equality with man has never been conceded by any people, ancient or modern, civilized or savage.


I have been scientifically studying the traits and dispositions of the "lower animals" (so-called,) and contrasting them with the traits and dispositions of man. I find the result profoundly humiliating to me. For it obliges me to renounce my allegiance to the Darwinian theory of the Ascent of Man from the Lower Animals; since it now seems plain to me that that theory ought to be vacated in favor of a new and truer one, this new and truer one to be named the *De*scent of Man from the Higher Animals.

In proceeding toward this unpleasant conclusion I have not guessed or speculated or conjectured, but have used what is commonly called the scientific method. That is to say, I have subjected every postulate that presented itself, to the crucial test of actual experiment, and have adopted it or rejected it according to the result. Thus I verified and established each step of my course in its turn before advancing to the next. These experiments were made in the London Zöological Gardens, and covered many months of pains-taking and fatiguing work.

Before particularizing any of the experiments, I wish to state one or two things which seem to more properly belong in this place than further along. This in the interest of clearness. The massed experiments established to my satisfaction certain generalizations, to-wit:

1. That the human race is of one distinct species. It exhibits slight variations—in color, stature, mental calibre, and so on—due to climate, environment, and so forth; but it is a species by itself, and not to be confounded with any other.

2. That the quadrupeds are a distinct family, also. This family exhibits variations—in color, size, food-preferences and so on; but it is a family by itself.

3. That the other families—the birds, the fishes, the insects, the reptiles, etc., are more or less distinct, also. They are in the procession. They are links in the chain which stretches down from the higher animals to man at the bottom.

Some of my experiments were quite curious. In the course of my reading I had come across a case where, many years ago, some hunters on our Great Plains organized a buffalo hunt for the entertainment of an English earl—that, and to provide some fresh meat for his larder. They had charming sport. They killed seventy-two of those great animals; and ate part of one of them and left the seventy-one to rot. In order to determine the difference between an anaconda and an earl—if any—I caused seven young calves to be turned into the anaconda's cage. The grateful reptile immediately crushed one of them and swallowed it, then lay back satisfied. It showed no further interest in the calves, and no disposition to harm them. I tried this experiment with other anacondas; always with the same result. The fact stood proven that the difference between an earl and an anaconda is, that the earl is cruel and the anaconda isn't; and that the earl wantonly destroys what he has no use for, but the anaconda doesn't. This seemed to suggest that the anaconda was not descended from the earl. It also seemed to suggest that the earl was descended from the anaconda, and had lost a good deal in the transition.

I was aware that many men who have accumulated more millions of money than they can ever use, have shown a rabid hunger for more, and have not scrupled to cheat the ignorant and the helpless out of their poor savings in order to partially appease that appetite. I furnished a hundred different kinds of wild and tame animals the opportunity to accumulate vast stores of food, but none of them would do it. The squirrels and bees and certain birds made accumulations, but stopped when they had gathered a winter's supply, and could not be persuaded to add to it either honestly or by chicane. In order to bolster up a tottering reputation the ant pretended to store up supplies, but I was not deceived. I know the ant. These experiments convinced me that there is this difference between man and the higher animals: he is avaricious and miserly, they are not.

In the course of my experiments I convinced myself that among the animals man is the only one that harbors insults and injuries, broods over them, waits till a chance offers, then takes revenge. The passion of revenge is unknown to the higher animals.

Roosters keep harems, but it is by consent of their concubines; therefore no wrong is done. Men keep harems, but it is by brute force, privileged by atrocious laws which the other sex were allowed no hand in making. In this matter man occupies a far lower place than the rooster.

Cats are loose in their morals, but not consciously so. Man, in his descent from the cat, has brought the cat's looseness with him but has left the unconsciousness behind—the saving grace which excuses the cat. The cat is innocent, man is not.

Indecency, vulgarity, obscenity—these are strictly confined to man; he invented them. Among the higher animals there is no trace of them. They hide nothing; they are not ashamed. Man, with his soiled mind, covers himself. He will not even enter a drawing room with his breast and back naked, so alive is he and his mates to indecent suggestion. Man is "the Animal that Laughs." But so does the monkey, as Mr. Darwin pointed out; and so does the Australian bird that is called the laughing jackass. No—man is the Animal that Blushes. He is the only one that does it—or has occasion to.

At the head of this article we see how "three monks were burnt to death" a few days ago, and a prior "put to death with atrocious cruelty." Do we inquire into the details? No; or we should find out that the prior was subjected to unprintable mutilations. Man—when he is a North American Indian—gouges out his prisoner's eyes; when he is King John, with a nephew to render untroublesome, he uses a red-hot iron; when he is a religious zealot dealing with heretics in the Middle Ages, he skins his capture alive and scatters salt on his back; in the first Richard's time he shuts up a multitude of Jew families in a tower and sets fire to it; in Columbus's time he captures a family of Spanish Jews and—but *that* is not printable; in our day in England a man is fined ten shillings for beating his mother nearly to death with a chair, and another man is fined forty shillings for having four pheasant eggs in his possession without being able to satisfactorily explain how he got them. Of all the animals, man is the only one that is cruel. He is the only one that inflicts pain for the pleasure of doing it. It is a trait that is not known to the higher animals. The cat plays with the frightened mouse; but she has this excuse, that she does not know that the mouse is suffering. The cat is moderate—unhumanly moderate: she only scares the mouse, she does not hurt it; she doesn't dig out its eyes, or tear off its skin, or drive splinters under its nails—man-fashion; when she is done playing with it she makes a sudden meal of it and puts it out of its trouble. Man is the Cruel Animal. He is alone in that distinction.

The higher animals engage in individual fights, but never in organized masses. Man is the only animal that deals in that atrocity of atrocities, War. He is the only one that gathers his brethren about him and goes forth in cold blood and with calm pulse to exterminate his kind. He is the only animal that for sordid wages will march out, as the Hessians did in our Revolution, and as the boyish Prince Napoleon did in the Zulu war, and help to slaughter strangers of his own species who have done him no harm and with whom he has no quarrel.

Man is the only animal that robs his helpless fellow of his country—takes possession of it and drives him out of it or destroys him. Man has done this in all the ages. There is not an acre of ground on the globe that is in possession of its rightful owner, or that has not been taken away from owner after owner, cycle after cycle, by force and bloodshed.

Man is the only Slave. And he is the only animal who enslaves. He has always been a slave in one form or another, and has always held other slaves in bondage under him in one way or another. In our day he is always some man's slave for wages, and does that man's work; and this slave has other slaves under him for minor wages, and they do *his* work. The higher animals are the only ones who exclusively do their own work and provide their own living.

Man is the only Patriot. He sets himself apart in his own country, under his own flag, and sneers at the other nations, and keeps multitudinous uniformed assassins on hand at heavy expense to grab slices of other people's countries, and keep *them* from grabbing slices of *his*. And in the intervals between campaigns he washes the blood off his hands and works for "the universal brotherhood of man"—with his mouth.

Man is the Religious Animal. He is the only Religious Animal. He is the only animal that has the True Religion— several of them. He is the only animal that loves his neighbor as himself, and cuts his throat if his theology isn't straight. He has made a graveyard of the globe in trying his honest best to smooth his brother's path to happiness and heaven. He was at it in the time of the Caesars, he was at it in Mahomet's time, he was at it in the time of the Inquisition, he was at it in France a couple of centuries, he was at it in England in Mary's day, he has been at it ever since he first saw the light, he is at it to-day in Crete—as per the telegrams quoted above—he will be at it somewhere else to-morrow. The higher animals have no religion. And we are told that they are going to be left out, in the Hereafter. I wonder why? It seems questionable taste.

Man is the Reasoning Animal. Such is the claim. I think it is open to dispute. Indeed, my experiments have proven to me that he is the Unreasoning Animal. Note his history, as sketched above. It seems plain to me that whatever he is he is *not* a reasoning animal. His record is the fantastic record of a maniac. I consider that the strongest count against his intelligence is the fact that with that record back of him he blandly sets himself up as the head animal of the lot; whereas by his own standards he is the bottom one.

In truth, man is incurably foolish. Simple things which the other animals easily learn, he is incapable of learning. Among my experiments was this. In an hour I taught a cat and a dog to be friends. I put them in a cage. In another hour I taught them to be friends with a rabbit. In the course of two days I was able to add a fox, a goose, a squirrel and some doves. Finally a monkey. They lived together in peace; even affectionately.

Next, in another cage I confined an Irish Catholic from Tipperary, and as soon as he seemed tame I added a Scotch Presbyterian from Aberdeen. Next a Turk from Constantinople; a Greek Christian from Crete; an Armenian; a Methodist from the wilds of Arkansaw; a Bhuddist from China; a Brahmin from Benares. Finally, a Salvation Army Colonel from Wapping. Then I stayed away two whole days. When I came back to note results, the cage of Higher Animals was all right, but in the other there was but a chaos of gory odds and ends of turbans and fezzes and plaids and bones and flesh — not a specimen left alive. These Reasoning Animals had disagreed on a theological detail and carried the matter to a Higher Court.

One is obliged to concede that in true loftiness of character, Man cannot claim to approach even the meanest of the Higher Animals. It is plain that he is constitutionally incapable of approaching that altitude; that he is constitutionally afflicted with a Defect which must make such approach forever impossible, for it is manifest that this Defect is permanent in him, indestructible, ineradicable.

I find this Defect to be THE MORAL SENSE. He is the only animal that has it. It is the secret of his degradation. It is the quality *which enables him to do wrong*. It has no other office. It is incapable of performing any other function. It could never have been intended to perform any other. Without it, man could do no wrong. He would rise at once to the level of the Higher Animals.

Since the Moral Sense has but the one office, the one capacity—to enable man to do wrong—it is plainly without value to him. It is as valueless to him as is disease. In fact it manifestly *is* a disease. *Rabies* is bad, but it is not so bad as this disease. Rabies enables a man to do a thing which he could not do when in a healthy state: kill his neighbor with a poisonous bite. No one is the better man for having rabies. The Moral Sense enables a man to do wrong. It enables him to do wrong in a thousand ways. Rabies is an innocent disease, compared to the Moral Sense. No one, then, can be the better man for having the Moral Sense. What, now, do we find the Primal Curse to have been? Plainly what it was in the beginning: the infliction upon man of the Moral Sense; the ability to distinguish good from evil; and with it, necessarily, the ability to *do* evil; for there can be no evil act without the presence of consciousness of it in the doer of it.

And so I find that we have descended and degenerated, from some far ancestor,—some microscopic atom wandering at its pleasure between the mighty horizons of a drop of water perchance,—insect by insect, animal by animal, reptile by reptile, down the long highway of smirchless innocence, till we have reached the bottom stage of development—nameable as the Human Being. Below us—nothing. Nothing but the Frenchman.

There is only one possible stage below the Moral Sense; that is the Immoral Sense. The Frenchman has it. Man is but little lower than the angels. This definitely locates him. He is between the angels and the French.

Man seems to be a rickety poor sort of a thing, any way you take him; a kind of British Museum of infirmities and inferiorities. He is always undergoing repairs. A machine that was as unreliable as he is would have no market. On top of his specialty—the Moral Sense—are piled a multitude of minor infirmities; such a multitude, indeed, that one may broadly call them countless. The higher animals get their teeth without pain or inconvenience. Man gets his through months and months of cruel torture; and at a time of life

when he is but ill able to bear it. As soon as he has got them
they must all be pulled out again, for they were of no value in
the first place, not worth the loss of a night's rest. The second
set will answer for a while, by being reinforced occasionally
with rubber or plugged up with gold; but he will never get a
set which can really be depended on till a dentist makes him
one. This set will be called "false" teeth—as if he had ever
worn any other kind.

In a wild state—a natural state—the Higher Animals have
a few diseases; diseases of little consequence; the main one is
old age. But man starts in as a child and lives on diseases till
the end, as a regular diet. He has mumps, measles, whooping
cough, croup, tonsilitis, diphtheria, scarlet fever, almost as a
matter of course. Afterward, as he goes along, his life continues to be threatened at every turn: by colds, coughs, asthma,
bronchitis, itch, cholera, cancer, consumption, yellow fever,
bilious fever, typhus fevers, hay fever, ague, chilblains, piles,
inflammation of the entrails, indigestion, toothache, earache,
deafness, dumbness, blindness, influenza, chicken pox, cow
pox, small pox, liver complaint, constipation, bloody flux,
warts, pimples, boils, carbuncles, abscesses, bunions, corns,
tumors, fistulas, pneumonia, softening of the brain, melan-
cholia and fifteen other kinds of insanity; dysentery, jaundice,
diseases of the heart, the bones, the skin, the scalp, the spleen,
the kidneys, the nerves, the brain, the blood; scrofula, paralysis, leprosy, neuralgia, palsy, fits, headache, thirteen kinds of
rheumatism, forty-six of gout, and a formidable supply of
gross and unprintable disorders of one sort and another.
Also—but why continue the list. The mere names of the
agents appointed to keep this shackly machine out of repair
would hide him from sight if printed on his body in the
smallest type known to the founder's art. He is but a basket
of festering offal provided for the support and entertainment
of swarming armies of bacilli,—armies commissioned to rot
him and destroy him, and each army equipped with a special
detail of the work. The process of waylaying him, persecuting
him, rotting him, killing him, begins with his first breath, and
there is no mercy, no pity, no truce till he draws his last one.

Look at the workmanship of him, in certain of its particulars. What are his tonsils for? They perform no useful func-

tion; they have no value. They have no business there. They
are but a trap. They have but the one office, the one industry:
to provide tonsilitis and quinzy and such things for the possessor of them. And what is the vermiform appendix for? It
has no value; it cannot perform any useful service. It is but an
ambuscaded enemy whose sole interest in life is to lie in wait
for stray grape seeds and employ them to breed strangulated
hernia. And what are the male's mammals for? For business,
they are out of the question; as an ornament, they are a mistake. What is his beard for? It performs no useful function; it
is a nuisance and a discomfort; all nations hate it; all nations
persecute it with the razor. And because it is a nuisance and a
discomfort, Nature never allows the supply of it to fall short,
in any man's case, between puberty and the grave. You never
see a man bald-headed on his chin. But his hair! It is a graceful ornament, it is a comfort, it is the best of all protections
against certain perilous ailments, man prizes it above emeralds
and rubies. And because of these things Nature puts it on,
half the time, so that it won't stay. Man's sight, smell, hearing, sense of locality—how inferior they are. The condor sees
a corpse at five miles; man has no telescope that can do it.
The bloodhound follows a scent that is two days old. The
robin hears the earth-worm burrowing his course under the
ground. The cat, deported in a closed basket, finds its way
home again through twenty miles of country which it has
never seen.

For style, look at the Bengal tiger—that ideal of grace,
beauty, physical perfection, majesty. And then look at Man—
that poor thing. He is the Animal of the Wig, the Trepanned
Skull, the Ear Trumpet, the Glass Eye, the Pasteboard Nose,
the Porcelain Teeth, the Silver Windpipe, the Wooden Leg—a
creature that is mended and patched all over, from top to
bottom. If he can't get renewals of his brickabrac in the next
world, what will he look like?

He has just one stupendous superiority. In his intellect he is
supreme. The Higher Animals cannot touch him there. It is
curious, it is noteworthy, that no heaven has ever been offered him wherein his one sole superiority was provided with
a chance to enjoy itself. Even when he himself has imagined a
heaven, he has never made provision in it for intellectual joys.

It is a striking omission. It seems a tacit confession that heavens are provided for the Higher Animals alone. This is matter for thought; and for serious thought. And it is full of a grim suggestion: that we are not as important, perhaps, as we had all along supposed we were.

*c. August 1896*

# In Memoriam

OLIVIA SUSAN CLEMENS.

DIED AUGUST 18, 1896; AGED 24.

In a fair valley—oh, how long ago, how long ago!—
Where all the broad expanse was clothed in vines
And fruitful fields and meadows starred with flowers,
And clear streams wandered at their idle will,
And still lakes slept, their burnished surfaces
A dream of painted clouds, and soft airs
Went whispering with odorous breath,
And all was peace—in that fair vale,
Shut from the troubled world, a nameless hamlet
    drowsed.

   Hard by, apart, a temple stood;
And strangers from the outer world
Passing, noted it with tired eyes,
And seeing, saw it not:
A glimpse of its fair form—an answering momentary
    thrill—
And they passed on, careless and unaware.

They could not know the cunning of its make;
They could not know the secret shut up in its heart;
Only the dwellers of the hamlet knew:
*They* knew that what seemed brass was gold;
What marble seemed, was ivory;
The glories that enriched the milky surfaces—
The trailing vines, and interwoven flowers,
And tropic birds awing, clothed all in tinted fire—
They knew for what they were, not what they seemed:
Encrustings all of gems, not perishable splendors of the
    brush.
They knew the secret spot where one must stand—
They knew the surest hour, the proper slant of sun—
To gather in, unmarred, undimmed,
The vision of the fane in all its fairy grace,

A fainting dream against the opal sky.
 And more than this. They knew
That in the temple's inmost place a spirit dwelt,
Made all of light!
 For glimpses of it they had caught
Beyond the curtains when the priests
That served the altar came and went.

 All loved that light and held it dear
That had this partial grace;
But the adoring priests alone who lived
By day and night submerged in its immortal glow
Knew all its power and depth, and could appraise
  the loss
If it should fade and fail and come no more.

 All this was long ago—so long ago!

The light burned on; and they that worship'd it,
And they that caught its flash at intervals and held
  it dear,
Contented lived in its secure possession. Ah,
How long ago it was!
     And then when they
Were nothing fearing, and God's peace was in the air,
And none was prophesying harm—
The vast disaster fell:
Where stood the temple when the sun went down,
Was vacant desert when it rose again!

 Ah, yes! 'Tis ages since it chanced!

       So long ago it was,
That from the memory of the hamlet-folk the Light
  has passed—
They scarce believing, now, that once it was,
Or if believing, yet not missing it,
And reconciled to have it gone.

 Not so the priests! Oh, not so
The stricken ones that served it day and night,

Adoring it, abiding in the healing of its peace:
They stand, yet, where erst they stood
Speechless in that dim morning long ago;
And still they gaze, as then they gazed,
And murmur, "It will come again;
It knows our pain—it knows—it knows—
Ah, surely it will come again."

S. L. C.

Lake Lucerne, *August* 18, 1897.

# Which Was the Dream?

FROM MRS. ALISON X.'S DIARY.

*March 1, 1854, morning.* — It will be a busy day. Tom and the servants and a carpenter or two have already begun to set up the stage and scenery in the north end of the picture gallery\* for Bessie's play — first dress rehearsal to-night. There will be two more before the great occasion — Bessie's eighth birthday — the 19th. The scenery and costumes have cost a great sum, and are very beautiful. It will be a fine show to see that company of pretty children clothed in those rich habits. Tom tried to design Bessie's costume himself; dear man, he is daft about the child; about both of them, indeed. He is vain of the play, and says it is wonderful; and it is, perhaps, for a child of eight to have conjured out of her small head. It lacks coherence, of course, and it has some rather startling feats in it, even for magicians and fairies to do; still it is a remarkable little play, all things considered, and is adorably naïve and quaint.

Tom has often promised me to write a little sketch of his life for the children to have when we are gone, but has always put it off and put it off; but as soon as I suggested that he write it in honor of Bessie's birth-day, that was quite another matter and he was full of it at once. I think I ought to be jealous; anything that Bessie wants, Bessie can have, but poor mamma has to put up with a kiss and a postponement. Of course Tom would find some opportunity in the matter to show Bessie off. He will write the sketch in shorthand to-night, and between this and the birthday Bessie will turn it into long hand, with a little of my help, and then, on the birthnight, after the ball and the play, she —

*Mid-afternoon.* Dear me, these interruptions! It is a busy day, sure enough. I don't get time to turn around or get a moment's rest, they keep after me so with their How shall we do this? and how shall we do that? and so on. Tom is going to be tired out before night, the way he is working. But he says he won't. And he has devised a surprise of some kind or other

\*We call it the picture gallery because it isn't. It is the ball room.

for the end of the evening. As soon as the night's rehearsals of the fancy dances and the play are over I am to bring Bessie and Jessie to his study, and then he—

*8 p.m.* What a darling flock it is! They have all arrived at last, with their troop of mothers. It is going to be a beautiful sight. The gallery never looked so brilliant before, nor so grand and spacious; and it will look finer than ever on the birth-night, with five hundred handsome people in it and all the military and naval uniforms, and the Diplomatic Body in their showy clothes. Washington is a good place for clothes. . . .

I went to the study, and looked in through the glass door. Tom was at his task—since how long, I don't know. He was drowsy, I could see that; I knew he would be tired. But his pen was going. His cigar was lying on the table, and while I looked he fell asleep for a second and his nodding head drooped gradually down till his nose was right over the ascending film of cigar smoke. It woke him with a violent start and a sneeze, and he went straight on with his work again, and I hurried away, amused, to my room, to get a moment's rest before beginning my long task of superintending the costuming of the little people and directing the series of rehearsals. . . . A note—from the White House. The President invites himself for this evening! This *is* an honor. And it is all for Bessie, none of it for Tom. This it is, to be a Chief Magistrate's small sweetheart. Someday it will make the child proud to be able to say that once a President of the United States broke the laws of etiquette that hedge his station for love of her. If he—"Coming!" I am getting tired of that word.

### MAJOR GENERAL X.'S STORY.

Alice (short for Alison) Sedgewick and I (Thomas X.,) were born in the little town of Pawpaw Corners, in the State of Kentucky, I in 1820, she in 1826. When she was five and I eleven, we became engaged. I remember it very well, and so does she. It was the first time we had ever met; for it was only just then that her family had moved into our neighborhood from the other side of the town. We met on the way to school, on a pleasant morning in the early summer time—

April, I should say; perhaps toward the end of it. It would be about that time I think, for it was warm enough for even boys connected with "quality" families to begin to hope for leave to go barefoot. The damp was stewing out of the ground, the grass was springing briskly, the wild flowers were thick, and in the woods on Murray Hill early in the mornings there was a musical riot of bird-song in place of the stillness that had reigned there so long. All the common boys had been barefoot for as much as a week already, and were beginning to mock at us for "Miss Nancys," and make fun of us for being under our mother's thumbs and obliged to be unmanly and take care of our health like girls. I had been begging my mother for leave, but she would not give it. She said we were as good blood as the best in the town—good old Virginian stock, like the Sedgewicks and the Dents—and she would not allow her boy to take second place to any offshoot of theirs. She said that I could come out barefoot when Billy Dent and Jeff Sedgewick did, and not a day before. Billy Dent was the county Judge's son, and Mr. Sedgewick was the principal lawyer and had run for Congress once. Mr. Sedgewick was Alice's father and Jeff's uncle, and had a large farm in the country, and owned more negroes than any other man in the town; and Jeff was a playmate of mine, although I had never seen his cousin until now.

I had my new summer suit on, that morning—yellow nankeens—and was proud; proud of the clothes, but prouder still because I was barefoot; the first "quality" boy in the town to be "out." I had been showing off before Jeff and Billy, and making them green with envy: for they had supposed it was by my mother's permission that I was barefoot—supposed it from something I had said, I think. But I knew where my shoes were, and could find them when I wanted to go home.

The schoolhouse stood on a small bare hill, and at that time there was a thicket at the bottom of it, with a clear stream rippling through it; and it was just there that I came upon Alison. She was the dearest and prettiest little thing I had ever seen, and I loved her from that very moment. She had a broad leghorn hat on, with a wide red satin ribbon around it, the long ends dangling down behind; and her little short frock was of thin white summer stuff, and a piece of that same ribbon was tied around her waist for a belt. In one hand she had a Webster spelling-book and first reader, and in the other she had the last winter-apple that was left over.

I wanted to speak to her, but I was all in a quiver and did not know how to begin. She looked timidly up at me out of her brown eyes, then dropped them, and stood there before me silent. I had a marble in my hand—it was a white alley that I had just got in a trade for a China that was so worn that you could hardly see the stripes on it—and my excitement made my hand tremble, and it fell on the ground near by. It was precious property, but I would not take my eyes off that pretty little creature long enough to pick it up; but worked my right foot toward it and closed my toes over it and took it in their grip. That interested her, and broke the ice. She said—

"I didn't know anybody could do that but my cousin Jeff and our Jake. Can you walk with it so? They can."

"Oh, yes—it's easy; anybody can do it."

I made a step or two. Then with my foot I threw up the marble and caught it in my hand.

She was bursting with admiration, and tried to clap her hands, but they were too full of things. She cried out—

"Oh, do it again—do it again!"

I said—

"Shucks, that's nothing—look at this."

I gripped the marble in the toes of my right foot, balanced myself on my left, swung my right forward once or twice, to get impulse, then violently upward and backward, and sent the marble well up into the air above our heads, then made a spring and caught it as it came down.

She was mine! I saw it in her eyes. Her look was the concentrated look which Europe cast upon Napoleon after Austerlitz. She impulsively reached out the apple to me and said—

"There. You may have it all for your own."

I said—

"No, not all of it—we'll have it together. First, you'll take a bite, and then I'll take a bite, and then you'll take a bite, and then—"

I held it to her mouth, she took her bite, then I took mine, and munching we sauntered into the thicket, along the worn path, I holding her by her left hand. And by the stream we sat down together, and took bites turn about, and contentedly munched and talked. I told her my name, she told me hers, and the name of her kitten and its mother's, and some of their habits and preferences and qualities, and I told her how to dig fishing-worms, and how to make a pin-hook, and what to do to keep awake in church, and the best way to catch flies; and at last I asked her if she was engaged, and explained it to her; and when she said she was not, I said I was glad, and said *I* was not; and she said she was glad; and by this time we had munched down to the core, and I said now we could find out if everything was going to come out right and we get married. So then I took out the apple-seeds one by one and laid them in her small palm, and she listened with deep interest and grave earnestness while I delivered the fateful word that belonged with each:

"One I love, two I love, three I love I say;
Four I love with all my heart, and five I cast away;
Six *he* loves—"

"And *do* you, Tom?"

"Yes. Are you glad?"

"Yes, Tom. Go on."

"Seven *she* loves—*do* you, Alice?"

"Yes, Tom. Go on."

"Eight they *both* love—and they do, *don't* we, Alice?"

"Yes, Tom. Keep on."

"Nine he comes, ten he tarries—"

"What is tarries, Tom?"

"Oh, never mind—t'isn't so, anyway—eleven he courts, and twelve he marries! There, that settles it! It's the very last seed, Alice, dear, and we are going to get married, sure; nothing can ever prevent it."

"I'm *so* glad, Tom. *Now* what do we have to do?"

"Nothing but just kiss. There—another—and one more. Now it's fixed. And it'll stay forever. You'll see, dearie."

And it did stay forever. At least it has stayed until this day and date, March 1, 1854; and that is twenty-three years.

I will skip a good many years, now. They were filled to the brim with the care-free joys of boyhood, and were followed by four happy years of young manhood, spent at the Military Academy of West Point, whence I was graduated in the summer of 1841, aged 21 years. All those years were a part of my life, it is true, yet I do not count them so. By my count they were merely a preparation for my life—which began in 1845 with my marriage. That was my supreme event; that was happiness which made all previous happinesses of little moment; it was so deep and real that it made those others seem shallow and artificial; so gracious and so divine that it exposed them as being earthy and poor and common. We two were one. For all functions but the physical, one heart would have answered for us both. Our days were a dream, we lived in a world of enchantment. We were obscure, we were but indifferently well off, as to money, but if these were lacks we did not know it, at least did not feel it.

In 1846 our little Bessie was born—the second great event in my life. A month later, my wife's father died; within the week afterward coal was discovered on his land and our poverty—to exaggerate the term a little—disappeared in a night. Presently came the war, and through a film of proud tears my Alison, holding our little Bessie up to look, saw her late unnoted 2$^d$ lieutenant, U.S.A., march for Mexico, colonel of a regiment of volunteers. In a little while she began to see his name in the war news, among the crowd of other names; then she saw it gradually and steadily separate itself from the crowd and grow more and more isolated, conspicuous, distinguished; and finally saw it hoisted aloft among the great headlines, with Scott's and Taylor's for sole company; and in these days it was become as common as theirs upon the world's tongue, and it could be uttered in any assemblage in the land and be depended upon to explode a mine of enthusiasm. She was a proud woman, and glad; and learned to practice deceit, to protect her modesty and save the exultation in her heart from showing in her face—pretending not to hear, when she passed along, and there was a sudden stir upon the pavement, and whispers of, "There—look—the wife of the boy General!" For I was by many years the youngest of that rank in our armies.

And more was to come; the favors of fortune were not exhausted yet. There came a stately addition to that remark—"wife of the boy General—United States Senator—the youngest that was ever elected." It was true. The brief war over, I learned the news from the papers while I was on my way home.

And Alice was a proud woman again when her late obscure 2$^d$ lieutenant entered our village and drove, at the Governor's side, through the massed country multitudes, under triumphal arches, in a rain of rockets, and glare of Greek fire, and storm of cannon-blasts, and crash of bands and huzzahs, to the banquet prepared in his honor; and proud once more when he rose at her side, there, and she saw the house rise at him and fill the air with a snow-tempest of waving napkins and a roar of welcoming voices long continued; and proud yet once more when he made his speech, and carried the house with him, sentence by sentence to the stirring close, and sat down with a dazzling new reputation made. (Her own dear words, and a pardonable over-statement of the facts.)

Those were memorable days, marvelous days for us. More than ever we seemed to be living in a world of enchantment. It all seemed so strange, indeed so splendidly impossible, that these bounties, usually reserved for age, should be actually ours, and we so young; for she was but 22 and I but 28. Every morning one or the other of us laughed and said, "Another day gone, and it isn't a dream *yet!*" For we had the same thought, and it was a natural one: that the night might rob us, some time or other, and we should wake bereaved.

We built a costly and beautiful house in Washington, and furnished it luxuriously. Then began a life which was full of charm for both of us. We did not have to labor our way into society with arts and diplomacies, our position was already established and our place ready for us when we came. We did not need to court, we were courted. We entertained freely, and our house was the meeting ground for all who had done anything, for all who were distinguished in letters, the arts, in politics and fashion, and it was almost the common home of Clay, Webster, Benton, Scott, and some of the other men of conspicuous fame. Alison's beauty and youth attracted all comers to her, and her sterling character and fine mind made them her friends.

And she was the gratefulest creature that ever was. Often she would take my face between her hands, and look into my eyes, and say—

"How dear you are! and it is you that have given me all this wonderful life. But for you I should be nothing—nothing at all. I am so proud of you; so proud, and so glad that you are mine, all mine."

It was her wealth that made this choice life possible; but she always put her hand on my lips when I said that, and would not listen; and said my fame and deeds would have been sufficient.

We are happy, we are satisfied. Fortune has done all for me that was in her power. She would have added the last possible distinction, but was defeated by the Constitution. I should be President and First Citizen of the United States now, if I were of lawful age. It is not I that say this immodest thing—ask your mother. It seems decreed, past all doubt, that I shall ascend to that high post three years hence, but we will not talk of that now, dear; there is no hurry.

### POSTSCRIPT.

There—my sketch is done, I have made my promise good. There is enough of it for the purpose. For further particulars, Bessie dear, see the four Biographies. Your mamma is going to give them to you on your birthday morning. And let me whisper to you, Craig's is the best, because it flatters me.

Now I will go on and write something for the mamma. That will be easier work than that which I have just finished—so easy that it will write itself if I merely hold the pen and leave it free, for the text is so inspiring—The Children.

Our Jessie was born in the year of the Californian gold-rush, a cunning black-headed mite that weighed just four pounds, and was as welcome as if she had weighed a hundred. She is above five years old, now, a practical, decisive, courageous, adventurous little soldier, charged to the chin with tireless activities, and never still except when asleep. She is the embodied spirit of cheerfulness; everything that happens to her is somehow convertible into entertainment; and that is what results, no matter what the hap is. This has made it difficult to punish her. Even the dark closet was a failure. It missed her, and merely punished her mother, who kept her shut up a quarter of an hour and then could endure the thought of the little prisoner's sufferings no longer, and so went there to give her the boon of the blessed light again; but found her charmed with the novelty of the darkness and the mystery of the place and anxious to stay and experiment further.

She bears pain with a rare fortitude, for a child—or for an adult. Last summer her forefinger got a pinch which burst the fat front of the main joint, but she cried only a moment, then sat in her mother's lap and uttered no sound while the doctor sewed the ragged edges together—sat, and winced at the proper times, and watched the operation through with a charmed and eager interest, then ran off to her play again, quite ready for any more novelties that might come her way. Tobogganing, last winter in the north, the toboggan ran into a tree, and her ancle was sprained and some of the small bones of her foot broken; but she did not cry—she only whimpered a moment, that was all; and then had as good a time in bed for a week or two as she could have had anywhere.

The other day she was taken to the dentist to have a tooth drawn. Seeing how little she was, the dentist proposed to give her an anaesthetic and make the operation painless, but her mother said it would not be necessary. Alison stepped into the next room, not wishing to see. Presently she heard the dentist say, "There, that one is out, but here is another one that ought to come;" so she stepped in and said, "Here is another handkerchief for you, dear," but Jessie said, "Never mind, I brought two, mamma, I thought there might be two teeth." She always had a thoughtful business head from the beginning. And she is an orderly little scrap, too. Her end of the nursery is always ship-shape; but poor Bessie's end of it is an exaggeration of chaos.

For Bessie is a thinker—a poet—a dreamer; a creature made up of intellect, imagination, feeling. She is an exquisite little sensitive plant, shrinking and timorous in the matter of pain, and is full of worshiping admiration of Jessie's adventurous ways and manly audacities. Privately we call Bessie "Poetry," and Jessie "Romance"—because in the one case the name fits, and in the other it doesn't. The children could not pronounce these large names in the beginning, therefore they shortened them to Potie and Romie, and so they remain.

Bessie is a sort of little woman, now; and being a thinker, she is learning to put a few modifying restraints upon herself here and there in spots—and they were needed. To start with, she was a dear little baby, with a temper made all of alternating bursts of storm and sunshine, without any detectable intervals between these changes of weather. She was a most sudden creature; always brimming with life, always boiling with enthusiasm, always ready to fly off on the opposite tack without any notice. Her approval was passionate, her disapproval the same, and the delivery of her verdict was prompt in both cases. Her volcano was seldom quiet. When it was, it was only getting ready for an irruption; and no one could tell beforehand whether it was going to illuminate a landscape or bury a city. Fortunately for herself and for us, her exaltations of joy were much more common than her ecstasies of anger. It took both to make her thoroughly interesting; and she was that. And keep us busy; and she did that.

The foundation of her nature is *intensity*. This characteristic is prominently present in her affections. From her babyhood she has made an idol of her mother. She and her mother are sweethearts, lovers, intimate comrades and confidants, and prodigal of endearments and caresses for each other. Nobody but the mother can govern her. She does it by love, by inalterable firmness, by perfect fairness, by perfect justice. While she was still in the cradle Bessie learned that her mother's word could always be depended upon; and that whatever promise her mother made her—whether of punishment, or a holiday, or a gratification, or a benevolence—would be kept, to the letter. She also learned that she must always obey her mother's commands; and not reluctantly and half-heartedly, but promptly, and without complaint. She knew the formula, "Do this, Bessie; do that, Bessie;" but she never had experience of the addition, "If you will, I will give you something nice." She was never hired to obey, in any instance. She early learned that her mother's commands would always be delivered gently and respectfully, never rudely or with show of temper, and that they must be obeyed straightway, and willingly. The child soon learned that her mother was not a tyrant, but her thoughtful and considerate friend—her loving friend, her best friend, her always courteous friend, who had no disposition in her heart or tongue to wound her childish self-respect. And so, this little whirlwind was brought under government; brought under obedience; thorough obedience, instant obedience, willing obedience. Did that save the child something? I think so. If a child—or a soldier—learns to obey promptly and willingly, there is no sting in it, no hardship, no unhappiness. The mother who coaxes or hires her child to obey, is providing unhappiness for it; and for herself as well. And particularly because the mother who coaxes and hires does not always coax and hire, but is in all cases a weak creature, an ill-balanced creature, who now and then delivers herself up to autocratic exhibitions of authority, wherein she uses compulsion—usually in a hot and insulting temper—and so the child never knows just how to take her.

It is a shameful thing to insult a little child. It has its feelings, it has its small dignity; and since it cannot defend them, it is surely an ignoble act to injure them. Bessie was accustomed to polite treatment from her mother; but once when she was still a very little creature she suffered a discourtesy at her hands. Alison and Senator Walker's wife were talking earnestly in the library; and Bessie, who was playing about the floor, interrupted them several times; finally Alice said pretty sharply, "Bessie, if you interrupt again, I will send you at once to the nursery." Five minutes later, Alice saw Mrs. W. to the door. On her way back through the main hall she saw Bessie on the stairs—halfway up, pawing her course laboriously, a step at a time. Alice said—

"Where are you going, Potie?"

"To the nursery, mamma."

"What are you going up there for, dear—don't you want to stay with me in the library?"

Bessie was tempted—but only for a moment. Then she said, with a gentle dignity which carried its own reproach—

"You didn't speak to me right, mamma."

She had been humiliated in the presence of an outsider. Alice felt condemned. She carried Bessie to the library and took her on her lap and argued the matter with her. Bessie hadn't a fault to find with the justice of the rebuke, but she held out steadily against the *manner* of it, saying gently, once or twice, "but you didn't speak to me *right*, mamma." She won her cause. Her mother had to confess that she *hadn't* spoken to her "right."

We require courteous speech from the children at all times and in all circumstances; we owe them the same courtesy in return; and when we fail of it we deserve correction.

These are lovely days that we are living in this pleasant home of ours in Washington, with these busy little tykes for comrades. I have my share of the fun with them. We are great hunters, we. The library is our jungle, and there we hunt the tiger and the lion. I am the elephant, and go on all fours, and the children ride on my back, astride. We hunt Jake. Jake is the colored butler. He belonged to Alison's estate, and is the same Jake whom she mentioned in our engagement-conversation when she was five years old. We brought him and his sister Maria from Kentucky when we first came to Washington. Both are free, by grace of Alice. Jake is thirty-two years old, now; a fine, large, nobly-proportioned man, very black, and as handsome as any man in the city, white or black, I think, and fully twice as good as he is handsome, notwithstanding he is a bigoted Methodist, a deacon in his church, and an incurable gambler on horse-races and prize fights. He is our prey, and we hunt him all over the library and the drawing rooms. He is lion; also tiger; preferably tiger, because as lion his roaring is too competent for Bessie's nerves. Bessie has a passion for hunting the tiger, but as soon as he gives notice that he is going to turn himself into a lion she climbs down and gets behind a chair and Jessie hunts him to his lair alone.

Bessie's mind is my pride, and I am building high hopes upon it. I have said that she is a thinker, and she is; and deep and capable. She has the penetrating mind, the analytical mind—and with it, naturally, precision of speech, intuitive aptitude in seizing upon the right word. Even when she was littler than she is now she often surprised me by the happy ingenuity she showed in choosing the word which would make her meaning clear. For instance. All of us who have labored at a foreign language by *book*, know how hard it is to get rid of the disposition to separate the words and deliver them with over-exactness of enunciation, instead of running them together and making them flow liquidly along, as a person does who has acquired the language by ear in strenuous fun and frolic and quarrel—in the nursery, for example. One day a couple of years ago I was playing with the children, and Bessie glibly—and as I thought, loosely—fluttered off a little German stanza about the "Vöglein." Then I read it from the *book*, with care and emphasis, to correct her pronunciation, whereupon Jessie corrected *me*. I said I had read it correctly, and asked Bessie if I hadn't. She said—

"Yes, papa, you did—but you read it so *'stinctly* that it 'fused Romie."

It would be difficult to better that, for precision in the choice of the right word for the occasion. At five Bessie was busy enlarging her vocabulary. Some pretty large words got into it, and once she adopted one which presently met with an accident. She told a visitor she was never at church but once—"the time Romie was crucified." Meaning christened.

Bessie has always been dropping her plummet into the deeps of thought, always trying to reason out the problems of life, always searching for light. One day Alison said to her, "There, there, child, you must not cry for little things." A couple of days later Bessie came up out of a deep reverie with the formidable question—

"Mamma, what *is* LITTLE things?"

No one can answer that, for nothing that grieves us can be called little: by the eternal laws of proportion a child's loss of a doll and a king's loss of a crown are events of the same size.

Alice was not able to furnish a sufficient answer. But Bessie did not give the matter up. She worked at the problem several days. Then, when Alice was about to drive down town—one of her errands being the purchase of a promised toy watch for Bessie—the child said, "If you should forget the watch, mamma, would that be a little thing?"

Yet she was not concerned about the watch, for she knew it would not be forgotten; what the struggling mind was after was the getting a satisfactory grip upon that elusive and indefinite question.

Like most people, Bessie is pestered with recurrent dreams. Her stock dream is that she is being eaten up by bears. It is the main horror of her life. Last night she had that dream again. This morning, after telling it, she stood apart some time looking vacantly at the floor, absorbed in meditation. At last she looked up, and with the pathos of one who feels that he has not been dealt by with even-handed fairness, said—

"But mamma, the trouble is, that I am never the *bear* but always the *person eaten*."

It would not occur to everybody that there might be an advantage in being the eater, now and then, seeing that it was nothing but a dream, after all, but there *is* an advantage, for while you are *in* a dream it *isn't* a dream—it is reality, and the bear-bite hurts; hurts in a perfectly real way. In the surprise which I am providing for the children to-night, Bessie will see that her persecuting dream can be turned into something quite romantically and picturesquely delightful when a person of her papa's high capacities in the way of invention puts his mind to work upon it.

Bessie has the gift of concentration. This makes her a good listener, a good audience, for she keeps close track of what is said. And remembers the details, too,—which sometimes makes trouble for me; for I forget my details, and then am brought to book. Every evening I have to tell the children a story after they are in their cribs and their prayers accomplished—and the story has to be invented on the spot; neither of them will put up with any second-hand contributions. Now in all these inventions of mine, from away back, I have had one serious difficulty to contend with, owing to Alison's influence—*nobody in my tale must lie*, not even the villain of the piece. This hampers me a good deal. The blacker and bloodier I paint the villain the more the children delight in him, until he makes the mistake of telling a lie—then down he goes, in their estimation. Nothing can resurrect him again; he has to pack up and go; his character is damaged beyond help, they won't have him around any longer.

Sometimes I try to cover up, or slide over, or explain away, one of these lies which I have blundered into, but it is lost time. One evening during one of our European vacations I was in the middle of the fifth night of a continued story which I intended should last a year and make things easy for my invention-mill; and was gliding along like this—

"But the moment the giant invited him, the grasshopper whispered in Johnny's ear that the food was poisoned; so, Johnny said very politely, 'I am very much obliged to you indeed, sir, but I am not hungry, and—' "

"Why, *papa!* he told a lie!"

(I said to myself, I have made a blunder; Johnny is compromised; I must try to get him out of this scrape.) "Well, you see, Bessie, I reckon he didn't think what he was saying, and—"

"But papa, it couldn't *be*; because he had just said, that very minute, that he was *so* hungry."

"Ye-s, I believe that is true. Yes, that *is* true. Well, I think perhaps he was heedless, and just came out with the first thing that happened in his mind, and—"

"Oh, no, papa, he wasn't ever a heedless boy; it wasn't like him to be heedless; you know how wise and thoughtful he always was. Why, night before last, when all those fairies and enchanted creatures tried their very best, a whole day, to catch him in some little carelessness so they could get power over him, they never *could*. No, papa, all through this story, there never was such a wise boy—he *couldn't* be heedless, papa."

"Well, Potie, I reckon he was so weary, so kind of tired out—"

"Why, papa, he *rode* all the way, on the eagle, and he had been sound asleep all the whole day in the gold-and-ivory bed, with his two lions watching him and taking care of him—why how *could* he be tired, papa, and he so strong?

You know the other night when his whale took him to Africa he went ashore and walked all day and all night and wasn't a bit tired; and you know that other time when—"

"Yes, yes, you are right, Bessie, and I was wrong; he couldn't have been tired—but he never intended any wrong; I'm sure he didn't mean what he said; for—"

"Then it *was* a lie, papa, if he didn't mean what he said."

Johnny's days of usefulness were over. He was hard aground, and I had to leave him there. He was a most unprincipled and bloody rascal, and if he could have avoided his one vice he might still be with us, nights, to this day, and as limitlessly happy as we are, ourselves. Romie once said this handsome thing about him—however, I will put that in further along, when I sketch out Romie's little history. I have a little more to say about her sister, yet.

Of instances of Bessie's delicate intuitions there are many in my mind. Here is one which is pleasant to me, and its original sweetness is in no way impaired by my often thinking of it. Last Christmas Eve Alice brought home a variety of presents, and allowed Bessie to see those which were to be sent to the coachman's family. Among these was an unusually handsome and valuable sled for Jimmy. On it a stag was painted, and also the sled's name in showy gilt capitals, "DEER." Bessie was joyously enthusiastic over everything until she came to this sled; then she became sober and silent. Yet this sled was the very thing she was expected to be most eloquent over, for it was the jewel of the lot. Alice was surprised; also disappointed; and said—

"Why Potie, doesn't it please you? Isn't it fine?"

Bessie hesitated; plainly she did not like to have to say the thing that was in her mind; but being pressed, she got it out—haltingly:

"Well, mamma, it *is* fine, and of course it *did* cost a good deal—but—why should that be mentioned?"

Seeing she was not understood, she pointed to that word "deer!" Poor chap, her heart was in the right place, but her orthography wasn't. There is not a coarse fibre in Bessie; she is as fine as gossamer.

From her earliest babyhood her religious training has gone on steadily at her mother's knee, and she has been a willing and interested pupil. But not a slavish one. She has always been searching on her own account, always thinking. There have been abundant evidences of that. I will set down one instance.

For some months, now, the governess has been instructing her about the American Indians. One day, a few weeks ago, Alice, with a smitten conscience, said—

"Potie, I have been so busy that I haven't been in at night, lately, to hear you say your prayers. Maybe I can come in tonight. Shall I?"

Bessie hesitated, waited for her thought to formulate itself, then brought it out—

"Mamma, I don't pray as much as I used to—and I don't pray in the same way. Maybe you would not be pleased with the way I pray now."

"Tell me about it, Potie."

"Well, mamma, I don't know that I can make you understand. But you know, the Indians thought they knew—and they had a great many gods. We know, now, that they were wrong. By and by maybe it will be found out that *we* are wrong, too. So now I only pray *that there may be a God*—and a heaven—OR SOMETHING BETTER."

It is the garnered doubt—and hope—of all the centuries, compacted into a sentence. And by a child.

She is a great treasure to us. Indeed we couldn't do without Bessie. Life would be flat, without her stimulating presence. She is not clay. She is a spirit. Generally in motion, seldom still—a sort of glimpse of frolicking sea-waves flashing in the sun; seldom a cloud-shadow drifting over them in these later times. She is all life, and soap-bubbles, and rainbows, and fireworks—and anything else that has spring and sparkle and energy and intensity for its make-up. She never talks much. I mean, in her sleep.

Now for Jessie—now for the busy brunette. The first day that ever Jessie—

## CHAPTER

I did not get a chance to finish the sentence. A shriek rang through the house, followed by a confusion of excited cries, and I ran to see what the matter was. The house was on fire. All the upper part of it was burning briskly before the calamity was discovered, for everybody was below, absorbed in the rehearsals.

For a moment the crowd of fifty children and thirty mothers had been in great danger—not from the fire, but from the perils inseparable from panic. There would have been manglings and crushings, if no man had been present. But fortunately, and by a mere chance, there was a man there; and by a still happier chance he was a soldier; a soldier of the best sort, the sort that is coolest in circumstances which make other people lose their heads. This was a young man named Grant, who was a third class man at West Point when I was a first. He had come to see me about something, and entered the ball room only a moment before the alarm was given. He was by the door, and took his place in front of it at once. The mob of women and children were paralyzed with fright for a moment; the next moment they would have made their fatal rush; but Grant did not wait for that. He spoke up in the calm and confident voice which stills troubled human waters by some subtle magic not explicable by the hearer but which compels his obedience, and said—

"Stand as you are! Do not move till I speak. There is no hurry, and there is no danger. Now then, you, madam, take two children by the hands, and move forward; you next, madam—do the same. Next—next—next."

And so on. In orderly procession the column fell in and filed out like a battalion leaving the field on dress parade.

But for West Point's presence there, I should be setting down a pathetic tragedy now. Lieutenant Grant had served under me for a while in the beginning of the Mexican war, and lately he had come to Washington on a business visit from his home in the West, and we had renewed our acquaintanceship. I think he had in him the stuff for a General, or certainly a Colonel; I do not know why he achieved no distinction in the war—but then, such things go a good deal by luck and opportunity. From what he had been telling me about his later fortunes, I judged that he was not born to luck. He remarked upon his Mexican nickname, "Useless," and said the old saying was true, in his case, that fun-nicknames are unwitting disguises of grave fact; for that if ever there was a useless man in the world, and one for whom there was plainly no place and no necessity, he was the one. Before the month was out I had sorrowful occasion to recal this talk of ours. With the Mexican war, his only chance for success in this world passed away; he recognized that, and I recognized it also, and was sorry for him. He was a good fellow, a sterling fellow, and should not have been wasted at West Point in the acquiring of a useless trade. But unfortunately none of us can see far ahead; prophecy is not for us. Hence the paucity of suicides.

We were overwhelmed with kindnesses by our friends; shelter in their houses was freely offered, but it seemed best, on the whole, to take quarters in the hotel, and this we did. The firemen saved the main part of the contents of the ground floor of our house, but nothing from the upper floors—the floors where we had lived, and where every detail was a treasure and precious, because hallowed by association with our intimate and private home life. This was a bitter hardship for us. A battered toy from the nursery would have been worth more to us than all the costly rubbish that was saved from the drawing rooms. Those dumb artificialities could be replaced, but not the historic toys.

The last of our hospitable friends left us at about two in the morning, and then we went to bed, tired out with the labors of the day and the excitements of the night. Alice said—

"I suppose you will rebuild the house just as it was before, Tom?"

"Yes. Jeff can begin tomorrow." That name reminded me of something, and I said, "Why, Alice, I did not see Jeff at the fire—did you?"

"No. And he has not been here in the hotel since we arrived, so far as I know."

"That is very strange. When did you see him last?"

"He left the house about five minutes before the fire alarm, and said he should be back within a quarter of an hour. He must have come back, of course; still, I did not see him."

"Alice! Could he have gone up to his room to save valuables, and got cut off and burned up?"

"He had no valuables in his room."

"No, not of his own, I know, but ours."

"Give yourself no trouble. Jeff Sedgewick has not risked his skin to save valuables of ours. He is not that sort of a man."

"Alice, you do not like your cousin."

"Tom, I have never accused myself of it."

Then we went to sleep. In the morning, still no Jeff Sedgewick. The forenoon wore away, and still he did not come. Everything was at a standstill. There was nobody to make contracts for the rebuilding of the house. Jeff was my business man and confidential secretary. He had begun as my secretary merely, when we first came east; but I knew nothing of business and had an aversion for it, and so, all my matters of that sort gradually drifted into his hands; for he was fond of business, and seemed made for it. In the beginning I franked my public documents myself—a wearisome job; one night I left half the documents unfranked; in the morning they lay in a confused pile, *all* franked. Jeff said—

"I finished the franking myself. Examine the pile, and see if you can tell the genuine signature from the imitation."

I couldn't. I was glad to let him do all the franking after that. In the beginning he wrote my letters from dictation, and I signed them. Later he wrote and signed a letter himself, without dictation, and I saw that he had caught my style exactly, and my hand. After that I was glad to let him do all my letters for me—in "autograph," and out of his own head. Soon he was signing and endorsing checks in "autograph." By and by all of my business was in his hands, every detail of it, and I was a free man and happy. Then came the full power of attorney, quite naturally, and thenceforth I was saved from even the bother of consulting and confirming.

In the very beginning Alice had begged me not to take Jeff to Washington.

"But Alice, he is an old friend, a schoolmate, he is poor and needs help, we are prosperous, we are fortunate, he is smart and capable, I am not, and I need such a person badly."

"But Tom, he is bad; bad to the marrow, and will do you an ill turn some day—the worst turn he can invent. He is envious, malicious, deceitful. He envies you your fame and prosperity, and hates you for it, privately. Every kindness you do him, every step you advance him, he will make record of and charge up against you, and when his opportunity comes he will take his revenge."

I laughed, at the time, at these unreasoning prejudices, and never thought for a moment that a young and inexperienced country girl like Alice could have an opinion that was valuable upon matters like these. I know, now, that her judgment of character was fatally and unfailingly accurate, but I did not find it out as early as I ought to have done.

She did not persecute me with her warnings; it was not her way; but now and then at intervals she used to drop them when there seemed opportunity to accomplish something by them. Once in the early Washington days Jeff came in arrayed in what he thought was the finest and latest thing in New York fashion. And perhaps it was the finest and latest thing in the Bowery. He was as pleased as a child, with his vulgar outfit. I have never had any tact; and that is why I said—

"I thought the Independent Order of the Fantastics had been disbanded years ago. When are they going to parade?"

He looked ignorantly embarrassed—like one who suspects that an offence has been intended him, but is not certain. He said—

"I believe I don't quite get your meaning."

"Isn't that a uniform?"

He went out without saying anything, and did not appear any more in those clothes. I spoke to Alice of the incident in the evening. It troubled her, and she said—

"I wish you hadn't done it, Tom. You laugh at it, but it is not matter for laughing. He is a vulgar, vain fool, and you have hurt him in a tender place. He will not forget it, nor forgive it. Do get rid of him, Tom."

Although Jeff had held the power of attorney for years, Alice never found it out till a month before the fire—for I was too often unfaithful to her in my business affairs. I hid things from her that I was ashamed of. Secrecy is the natural refuge of people who are doubtful about their conduct. She was appalled when I told her the matter of the power of attorney. She said—

"Oh, Tom, what have you done!" and begged me to abrogate it, and said Jeff would make beggars of us.

I was able to triumph, this time, and said—

"On the contrary, dear, he has doubled our fortune. Come, now, you must be just to him at last, and take back some of the hard judgments you have passed upon him in the bygone times."

She was doubtful still, that was plain; and she asked for particulars. But I said—

"Wait one month, then you will see."

She sighed and said—

"I will wait, Tom, since you ask it, but even if he should quadruple the fortune, I should still never be easy until we were rid of him."

I had no fears. I was preparing a pleasant surprise for Alice, and was sure I could spring it upon her in a few weeks. Jeff had made some brilliant speculations for me, of late years, and my confidence in his wisdom and shrewdness had grown in consequence until now they were boundless. He had sold out Alice's estate and invested her fortune in a Californian gold mine; for many months the mine had been swallowing money wholesale, but recent reports from its chief engineer showed that it was now on the point of paying back the fortune, with a hundred per cent interest. I had never liked the name of it—the "Golden Fleece"—but that was Jeff's taste; he named it.

Next morning we created a parlor and an office by having the beds cleared out of a couple of large chambers, and furniture proper to their new functions put in. In our house, Sedgewick's office had been on the ground floor, consequently all my business books and papers were saved. Alice soon arranged these in our new quarters. It was common for people whose houses had been burned down to send the firemen a donation and a word or two of compliment and gratitude, therefore in deference to this custom Alice asked me to draw a check for her to forward to the fire marshal. It was customary to disproportion the donation to the service rendered; therefore at Alice's request I made the check large. At least I considered it large; it was for $3,000. But then it was to help the company buy a new engine and build a new engine house.

Before Alice could finish writing her note of compliment and gratitude—she did not expect me to do any clerical work that could be shifted to somebody else—company began to pour in again. The stream continued until mid-day; then dinner interrupted it for an hour and a half; then the flow was resumed. About mid-afternoon or a little later Alice stole a moment and wrote the note, and sent it to the marshal by Jake. Still no Jeff appeared. Alice knew I was uneasy, for she knew the signs of all my moods, and with her native generous forbearance she left Jeff unmentioned. She never made a sore place of mine worse by meddling with it at the inopportune time. This is a beautiful trait; indeed it may be called a noble trait; and we all know it to be a rare one. I was never able to learn it, never able to make it a possession of mine. By taking thought I could *practice* it, momentarily, at wide intervals, but that was all. It was a *part of* Alice, and she did not have to think about it; but it refused to become a part of me. I was born small and selfish; Alice and the children were not. In nine cases in ten, when Alice had a sore place, I hastened with an insane eagerness to bruise it, and grieve her heart—and yet I loved her so, and had such a deep reverence for her beautiful character. I hurried to bruise it, knowing, when I did it, that when I saw the wounded look in her eyes I should be blistered with remorse and shame, and would give anything if I had not done it. But I could not help it, for deep down in the very web and woof of my nature I was ignoble and ungenerous.

How little the world knows us; indeed how little any except our nearest friends know us. You who are reading these lines—your world loves you and honors you. But suppose it knew you as you know yourself? Be humbly thankful that it does not.

Supper. Still no Jeff. My uneasiness was steadily growing.

I had not been out, all day. In fact, I had even kept away from the windows, I did not know why. I knew I should see a crowd of waiting strangers from different regions of the Union on the opposite sidewalk. I was used to it, had been used to it ever since I came back from Mexico with my military glories upon me; and had always been pleased with it, happy in it. But the thought of it troubled me, now. I was accustomed to driving or walking, every day, and accustomed to be flocked after and cheered, as I went along, and no more minded it than did the stately General Scott; in fact dearly liked it and enjoyed it, as he did. But to-day, for some reason, I shrank from the thought of it. There was a vague, indefinable, oppressive sense of impending trouble in the air.

After supper came the marine band—a serenade. The idea of it, to take friendly notice of our little mishap. I was in the room which had been set apart as a nursery, and was employed as usual at that hour of the evening—inventing a blood-curdling story for the children; a child seated on each arm of my chair, their feet in my lap, their elbows on their knees, their chins crutched in their plump hands, their eyes burning duskily through their falling cataracts of yellow hair and black. For ten minutes I had been wandering with these two in a land far from this world; in the golden land of Romance, where all things are beautiful, and existence is a splendid dream, and care cannot come. Then came that bray of the brazen horns, and the vision vanished away; we were prisoners in this dull planet again. I was for ignoring the serenade, and getting back to that shining land with my story, and Jessie was for supporting me in that impropriety; but Bessie had inherited higher instincts than we, and larger principles; and she said—

"No, no, papa, mamma would not approve. You must go, papa."

"And make a speech? Somehow it seems impossible to-night."

"Oh, no it isn't, papa. It is nothing. Don't be afraid. Make the same speech you always make. Everybody says it is a good one. Mr. Pierce likes it better every time; he says so his own self."

Out of the unconscious lips of babes and sucklings are we satirized. I walked slowly away into my banishment, leaving happiness behind me. For I left a dispute behind me; and where no care is, that is joy. I heard Bessie say—

"Papa didn't say that. He *couldn't* say it, because there's no sense in it. You've got two things mixed up, Romie."

"I haven't. He did say it. I heard him; I heard the very words. He said it is foolish to kill the goose that lays the golden calf."

It would have been a joy to me—an old and familiar and

beloved joy—to go back and take a solemn hand in the discussion and mix it all up till the puzzled little rascals could make neither head nor tail of it, but this boon was not for me. From outside went up a crashing cheer which lifted my spirits away up into the sunshine, and set my pulses to leaping, and for a moment I was myself again. But for a moment only. Then at the door a bank president touched me on the shoulder and whispered—

"Senator, can I have a word with you presently?"

"Yes," and I passed on. But there was something in his manner which blotted out my sunshine and made my heart cold. I stepped out on the balcony, and gazed out, dazed and hardly conscious, over the wide sea of flaring torches and uplifted faces; and the explosions of welcome which went up sounded muffled and far away in my dulled ears. I made my speech—no, it made itself, automatically; and it was as if it was some one else talking, and I scarce noting what was said. Then the cheers burst out again, as in a dream, and I—as in a dream—bowed, and went my way.

I took the bank president into my office, closed the door, and said—

"What is it?"

He answered, apologetically—

"I am sorry to disturb you with such a matter, Senator, but the fire marshal handed in a check just as we were closing the bank, and—and—"

"Very well. Go on."

"And—and—well, the fact is, Senator, your account is overdrawn."

What a load it lifted off my breast. And what a relief it was, to hear myself laugh once more; it had seemed to me that I had forgotten how.

"Oh, dear me," I said, "is that all? What of it? It isn't uncommon."

But he did not laugh. He remained ominously grave. He was silent a moment, gathering courage for a disagreeable duty, then he spoke out and named the amount of the overdraft.

I staggered as I have seen a soldier do when hit in the breast with a spent ball. After a little I rallied, and said, "I am amazed. I never could have imagined this. I don't know what Sedgewick can have been thinking of. Let us square up at once; and pray don't ever let this happen again—by his authority or any one else's." I sat down at the desk and said, "I will give you a check on Riggs's."

Nothing but a deadly silence followed this remark. I turned in my chair. My guest said, reluctantly—

"I am sorry, but it would do no good."

"Oh, what *do* you mean?"

"We bankers have been together this evening to look over the situation, and unfortunately we find—we find—"

"Well, well, you find—what do you find?"

"That you are heavily overdrawn all around."

He told me the several amounts. It made my head swim, for a moment. Then I pulled myself together, and said—

"After all, Simmons, it is merely embarrassing, not serious; and in no sense alarming. By good luck our house has burned down; the insurance-money will far more than pay you gentlemen, and henceforth I shall keep clear of this kind of thing. Even if I owed a million or two I should still be solvent, by grace of my Californian mining venture."

The banker asked me if I would mind telling him, in confidence, something about the Golden Fleece. I said I should be very glad to tell him *all* about it; that there was no occasion for concealment. So I got out the mining manager's long series of carefully detailed reports, and we examined them patiently from the first one to the last. Mr. Simmons was very much pleased, indeed. He said the reports were remarkably clear, orderly and candid, and that I was fortunate in having a manager who was courageous enough to put in the bad news as well as the good. He conceded that I was demonstrably worth above a million and a half, and prospectively worth indefinitely more. Then he confessed that when Sedgewick began to overdraw rather heavily, sometime back, and had spoken mysteriously of the wonders of the Golden Fleece, he had felt a little uneasy and had written his brother, a banker in Grass Valley for particulars concerning the mine. He had had no answer as yet, but he could forsee, now, that it would be a satisfactory one when it came.

Then a letter was brought up which completed my

comfort. It was from the lost Sedgewick. I read it aloud. It said—

"No doubt you have wondered what was become of me. When I returned and found that the house was doomed, I hurried to the station and caught the midnight train for New York; for there was an informality in one of the insurance policies which—however I will explain how it happened when I get back. As to $102,000 of the insurance, there will be no trouble. I think there will be none about the rest—$38,000—but I shall stay here two or three days and see. Meantime, through the luck of coming here just at this time I am likely to bring back, from another source, $80,000 which I had long ago given up as an irremediable loss. Indeed it is not merely likely, I feel that I may regard it as sure."

Mr. Simmons and I parted on very pleasant terms, and I went to bed a serene and contented man.


CHAPTER . . .

Next day I presided, for half an hour, at a session of the Committee on Military Affairs, then went back to Willard's, and Alice and I excused ourselves to callers and spent the whole happy day planning little improvements in the proposed new house, the architect helping and suggesting. Alice, who was conservative, wanted the cost kept within the former house's figure, but I said we could afford a more expensive one; and I talked her out of her reluctances and gained my point. She had been used to money all her life, therefore the possession of it did not turn her head or incline her to vain shows and display; but I was a kind of beggar on horseback, and had no sense of financial proportion, no just notion of values, and—but you know the kind of man I was. We did not get through until midnight; then the architect went away with a house in his pocket which charmed him and me, and made Alice shudder.

Two or three more days went pleasantly by, then came Mr. Simmons, Mr. Riggs, and Mr. Fulton, bankers, and with them a Mr. Collins from New York. Their manner was a warning; it spread a frost over the summer that was teeming in my heart, and the chill of it invaded my spirits. Trouble was coming; I felt it. They wished to see me in my private office. Arrived there, they sat down, and there was a moment or two of silence; then one said to another, with solemnity—

"Will you begin?"

"No, you, if you prefer."

"Perhaps it will be best that Mr. Simmons open the matter."

It was so agreed. Every face there was hard and set, every eye frankly unfriendly. Mr. Simmons cleared his throat and said—

"General X., you will pardon me if I ask you one or two blunt questions."

"Go on, sir."

"What property do you own, aside from the Golden Fleece?"

"None."

The men glanced at each other; Riggs and Fulton twisted nervously in their chairs.

"Has your wife any property other than the Golden Fleece?"

"None."

The color left the faces of Riggs and Fulton at that, then came back in a purple flush, and Fulton put up his hand and loosened his collar.

"One more question, Senator X." This in a slightly rising voice. "When you showed me the reports of your mining manager, was it your purpose to deceive me?"

I flushed, but said, with as much calmness as I could command—

"Mr. Simmons, have a care. I must remind you that you are going too far."

"I am, am I?" said he, excitedly. "My brother's letter has arrived from Grass Valley. Read it!"

I read it. Read it again; and still again, not able to believe my eyes. There was one italicized line in it which seemed written in fire, it glared so, and burnt me so: *There is no such mine as the Golden Fleece.* The life was all gone out of me, and I said—

"I am a ruined man, gentlemen. I realize it—absolutely ruined. But my destruction does not injure you. The insurance-money will more than pay everything I owe."

"That is your whole resource, then?"

"Yes."

"Are you certain that your house was insured?"

"Certain of it? Of course. It has always been insured, from the first; and in the same companies. Here is the record. The last entry, as you see, is of date a year ago, and insures the house for three years."

"Mr. Collins is the agent through whom your policies were always taken out. Mr. Collins, will you speak?"

Collins addressed himself to me, and said—

"You may remember, sir, that something more than a year ago, I wrote you two personal letters. In the first one I reminded you; in the second I urged you, to renew your insurance, for that I was not able to get Mr. Sedgewick's attention. My letters were confidential, as I did not wish to get your representative's ill will. You remember my letters?"

"Quite well. In the case of the first one I asked Sedgewick to answer you and re-insure; in the second I gave him a peremptory order to do it."

"Have you your policies there?"

"Yes."

"Last year's, too?"

"I suppose so. I will see. N-no. Not last year's."

"It is because that last-year entry is fraudulent. Your house was not insured. The loss is total."

My God, the words went through me like a bullet. If they were true, they meant that I was not merely and only a pauper, but a hundred times worse than that—*in debt*. For a time, no one spoke. The stillness was oppressive, smothering. All were waiting for me; but I was dumb, I could not find my voice. When it came back to me at last, I said—

"I am to blame. I am to blame, I confess it freely. I trusted Sedgewick as no human being ought to be trusted, and I have my reward. He has destroyed me."

There was no word of response. I was ashamed. I had expected at least a recognition of my remark, the mere courtesy of a comment of some kind or other; I was used to this much deference—and entitled to it. My dignity was wounded. I glanced up at the faces about me, and was cut to the heart; for if I could read what was written there, it was contempt! It seemed unbelievable, it had been so many years since any face had delivered me a message like that. I gathered my pride together, and said—

"Do not mistranslate me, gentlemen; I was not begging for sympathy."

Simmons made a gesture of impatience, and said—

"This is not a time for womanish sentimentalities, General X., with these strange facts—shall I say, these suspicious facts?—before us. You must see it yourself."

"What do you mean, sir?" I said with some little heat—I could not keep it all down. "Please explain yourself."

He amended his manner, then, leaving nothing of discourtesy in it or in his tones. But his words were knives.

"I ought not to forget, and I do not, that of the three or four men of towering eminence in the Union, you are one; that your great services deserve the country's gratitude and have it; and that until now your public and private conduct has been above the reach of suspicion; but—but—" He stopped for a moment, troubled as to how to go on; then added reluctantly, and with the manner of one who is saying a thing which he does not want to say, but which he does not know how to get around, "but these insurance-entries, which are—I hate to use the word—fraudulent—why did you make them?"

"I make them! I didn't make them."

The kindness faded out of the banker's face, and stupefaction took its place—stupefaction, mixed with surprise and unbelief; and he said with offended severity—

"I beg your pardon. I know your hand well."

For the first time, I saw my whole peril. The earth seemed to be opening under me, and said in a voice which made my words sound like a lie even to me, so sapped of force were they by my despairing conviction that I was not going to be believed—

"I give you my word of honor—oh, more, I give you my oath—that I never wrote—"

"*Don't!* Stop where you are, for God's sake!"

"I implore you to believe me! Gentlemen, I call God to wit—"

"Stop where you are! Do not make it worse than it already is. Remember what you are. Go on, and say what you can in palliation of this unfortunate act—even in plausible explanation of it, if such a thing may be possible—but for your own pride's sake leave out denials backed by oaths."

I went back to the beginning of my connection with Sedgewick, and told the tale all down to date; told them the simple truth, the plain, straightforward, humiliating facts—burning up with self-contempt while I did it, and watching those marveling and incredulous faces for any relenting sign, as wistfully as ever a prisoner on trial for his life watched the faces of the jury.

The sign never came. When I finished, the group looked at each other and said, plainly, though without words, "It is pitiable to see an illustrious man degrade himself to the manufacture of such trash as this." I read the words in their faces, and knew that my good name was gone, now, as well as my bread. After a considerable silence, Mr. Fulton said, with chill deliberation—

"As I understand it, sir, you ask credit for these several most extraordinary asseverations, to-wit, that you, an educated man, a man of the world, a general of the army, a statesman, a grown person, put yourself, body and soul, together with your wife's whole property and your own, unreservedly into the hands of a man—*any* man—empowering him to originate and write letters for you in your own handwriting, sign and endorse your name upon checks, notes, contracts, in your own hand, and speculate in anything he pleased, with the family's money—and all without even your casual supervision of what he was doing, or inquiry into it? Am I right?"

Detailed, item by item, in that cold direct fashion, it seemed incredible, impossible, even to me. And yet it was true, every shameful detail of it; and I said so. Mr. Fuller spoke out with what sounded like an almost generous enthusiasm—

"For the honor I bear your great name I will do you the reverence to believe not one damned word of it!"

I fought, and fought long, and the best I could, to save

some shred of that name, but it was a lost battle. These men
*could* not believe me. To them, it was impossible that a full
grown man could be the fool I had professed myself to be.
Their minds were soon made up that Sedgewick and I were
partnership swindlers—pals. They almost used that word; I
was sure of it. From that conviction no arguments of mine
were able to move them. They summed our affairs concisely
up in this way: we had speculated in New York stocks and
lost money and been obliged to sell Alice's estate; we had
speculated further, and gotten deeper in; we had invented the
Golden Fleece to postpone the crash and gain time to recoup;
we continued to go from bad to worse; when the house
burned, I had seen that the game was up, and had hurried
Sedgewick off to scrape up what money he might for our
joint benefit before the exposure should fall, and take it to
some far country, leaving me to put all the irregularities
upon him—he not minding that, since it could not hurt his
pocket.

I said that my own statement of my conduct—if true—
proved me a fool; but that this new solution of it—if true—
proved me insane. I urged that a General of the Army,
Senator, and prospective President of the United States could
not by any possibility commit the crimes imputed to me unless he were insane, and that the gentlemen here present must
know this themselves. I felt a hopeful glow at the heart for a
moment, for I said to myself, *that* is an argument which will
spike their guns; it is unanswerable.

But how little I knew the religion of commerce and its god.
The argument fell flat; more—it was received with disdain—
disdain of the sort evoked when a person intrudes a triviality
into a serious discussion. Mr. Simmons brushed it aside as
indifferently as if he were squelching the ignorant prattle of a
schoolboy—

"Men will do anything for money."

From the moment that those men arrived at the conviction
that I was a swindler and Sedgewick my tool and partner, my
reasonings went for nothing. It untangled every tangle, it laid
bare the core of every mystery, it explained and accounted for
every move in the odious game that had been played.

If I said that *I* couldn't know that the mining reports

exhibited to me as coming from Grass Valley were manufactured in Washington,—why, true,—yes, quite so—etc., etc.; which being translated, meant that my word, as to that, was not valuable, in the circumstances.

If I referred to Sedgewick's letter from New York (about the insurance) as having been received by me in perfect and unsuspecting good faith, the comment I got was merely noddings of the head which meant "Oh, certainly, certainly, quite so—pray do not think we doubt it."

I started, once, to inquire how *I* was to be benefited by making false entries in my insurance-list, and—

But they interrupted me impatiently, with a "There, it isn't worth while to go into *that* again," meaning, "Oh, it is quite simple—part of the game, dear sir, part of the game—any one can understand it."

I had tried all things, said all things, that might help me; there was nothing more that I could do, nothing more that I could say. I was lost. There was no help for me. The consciousness of this settled down upon me and wrapped me as in a darkness. There was a long silence. Then I broke it.

"Gentlemen, I comprehend that I am a ruined man—bankrupt in purse, and, in your belief, in character also. It may be that I shall never be able to retrieve myself financially, though I shall try my best while I live to do that and clear away the debts put upon me by a trusted subordinate; but I am *not* a dishonest man, whatever you may think, and I will bring that man before the courts and fasten all these swindles upon him, where they belong."

"When?" asked Mr. Collins.

"When? Why, at once."

"He sailed for the other side of the world the day he wrote you the letter; a friend of mine saw him go." Then he could not deny himself the pleasure of adding—as if to himself, and not intended for me to hear, "But it may be that this is not news."

Anybody could insult me now, with impunity—even that poor thing. Being pleased with himself for his boldness in kicking the dead lion, and detecting condescending approval in the faces of the bankers, he thought he saw his opportunity to ingratiate himself further with these high deities of his heaven; so he jauntily covered himself. But Mr. Riggs said, angrily—

"Uncover! Have you no shame? Respect what he *was*."

What he *was*! It lit up my whole vast ruin, from horizon to horizon; it compacted my colossal disaster into a single phrase. I knew that those words were burnt in; that no lapse of time, no mental decay, would ever rid my memory of them.

But why were these men still waiting? Was there more? More! The idea was almost able to make *me* smile. More? Was not Pelion piled upon my Ossa? More, indeed! The possibilities had been exhausted. I stirred in my chair, to indicate that I was ready for the interview to terminate if they were. Nobody moved. Then I said—

"I suppose we have finished, gentlemen." Still, nobody moved. The situation was embarrassing; and so, with a groping idea of relieving it, I added in a wan and sickly attempt at playfulness, "I seem to have committed about all the crimes there are; still, if by chance one has been overlooked, let us complete the tale. Pray bring it out."

Mr. Riggs began to wash his hands nervously; Simmons glanced at me, and dropped his eyes; Fulton, without passion or even emphasis, spat out the word—

"Forgery!"

I sprang at him—and remembered no more.

### CHAPTER

When I came to myself I had the feeling of one who has slept heavily, is lazily comfortable, but not greatly refreshed, and is still drowsy. My mind was empty of thought, and indifferent. My eyelids began to droop slumbrously, and I was drifting pleasantly toward unconsciousness, when I heard Jake's voice cry out—apparently in the next room—

"No indeed it ain't, honey—it's a jay-bird. Wait till I come. Don't make a noise; you'll scare him."

My eyes came open, and then there was a surprise. I was stretched upon a bed, in a log cabin. The sharp March weather was gone, summer was in the air. The floor was of

earth, packed hard and clean swept; at one end was a vast
fire-place, built of undressed stones; in it a couple of great
smouldering logs six or seven feet long; swinging above
them, from an iron chimney-hook, a large iron pot; on rude
unpainted shelves, on one side, some old but brightly polished tin pans, plates, pint cups, candle-sticks and a coffee
pot, some bone-handled knives and forks, some tin cans,
some wooden and pasteboard boxes such as candles and gro-
ceries come in, and some brown paper parcels; against the
logs on that side, under a small square window, a coverless
deal table that had paper and pens on it and half a dozen old
books; for sole ornament, a crippled tumbler containing a
bouquet of fresh wild flowers; against the logs, beside the
window, was fastened a diamond-shaped piece of looking-
glass, and under it was a shelf with cheap combs and brushes
on it. On the other side of the fireplace, by the door, was a
small wooden bench, with a piece of bar soap on it in a common white saucer, a tin wash-basin inverted, and a wooden
pail of water with a tin dipper in it; under the ceiling, above
the bench, hung half of a side of bacon; on the floor on that
side was an open sack of flour, and another of navy beans.
Nailed to the wall opposite the bed was a deep long stretch of
curtain calico which bulged, and I knew by that sign that it
was the wardrobe. Along the wall, above the bed, four cheap
lithographs were tacked to the logs—the Battle of Buena
Vista, the storming of San Juan d'Ulloa, (I took part in both),
and portraits of Scott and Taylor in uniform. Overhead was a
ceiling made of flour-sacks sewed together; it was a frescoed
ceiling, so to speak, for the sacks bore the names and addresses of the mills, loudly stenciled in blue capitals. Across
the room, past the head of the bed, ran a flour-sack partition,
also frescoed. It was the picture gallery; against it was pinned
a number of steel engravings from Godey's Lady's Book.

Everything about the place was beautifully neat and clean
and trim—and unimaginably inexpensive. I examined the
bedstead. It was made of small poles—only tolerably straight,
and the bark still on—laid close together along a frame supported by posts—the bark still on—driven into the ground.
There was but one mattrass; it was filled with straw; there

were pillows, filled with something or other; their cases and the sheets were of coarse white cotton; a cheap white blanket completed the bed.

I had on an old pair of blue jeans breeches and a private soldier's blue army shirt.

Where was I? I had no idea.

A glory of sunny hair appeared in the open door, now, and with it a bright young face—Bessie's.

"Come here, dear," I said, "and read me this riddle."

"Why, *papa*!"

She came cautiously in, and slowly approached, her eyes big with glad wonder—and doubt. She hesitated, then stopped, in the middle of the little room, four feet from me, and said wistfully—

"Papa—do you know me?"

"Do I *know* you? Why, Bessie, what—"

With a spring she was in my arms and covering my face with frantic kisses. Presently she had flashed away again, with the suddenness of a ray of light, and I heard her calling—outside—excitedly:

"Run here—run—run!"

Then she came flying back and stood, expectant, in the middle of the room, her eyes and cheeks glowing; and in a moment or two more Jessie was at her side, a speaking picture of childish interest and curiosity. Bessie put her mouth close to Jessie's ear, whispered a word, then stepped back to observe the effect. Jessie looked startled, but said promptly—

"I don't believe it."

The effect seemed to be all that could have been desired, for Bessie clapped her hands like a gratified showman and said—

"I knew you wouldn't. Now you'll see. Papa, who is this?"

"Come, what kind of game are you little rascals playing? Do you suppose I don't know Romie?"

And now they were both in my arms, and for some reason or other seemed to be mad with delight. Presently I said—

"It's a charming piece, and I am playing my part of it as well as I can, but I am in the dark, you know. Why am I in jeans and army shirt? And why are you two in these little linsey-woolsey frocks, and why are you barefooted? And why are we in this log cabin? Is it all in the piece? And how much do we get for it? But first of all, where *are* we?"

The children looked troubled and disappointed, and a little apprehensive, and Bessie said—

"But papa, I thought you would know *everything*, now. Don't you?"

"Dear me, no, apparently I don't. I am reveling in mysteries. Really, I don't seem to know much of anything."

Jessie said, as one who is trying to offer encouragement—

"Oh, no, papa, you mustn't say that. You know *us*—you know you do."

"Oh indeed, yes, if that is large learning, I am not at the foot of the class yet. I can say my lesson. You are Bessie and Jessie, and I am Thomas X."

Their soft hands covered my mouth at once, and they said in a frightened way—

" 'sh! papa! You mustn't say that!"

"Mustn't say it? Why?"

"Because it isn't your name. You've got another name, now. Don't you know your other name?"

"Oh, you mean my stage name. No, I don't know what it is. What is it?"

"Jacobs—Edward Jacobs; and you mustn't forget it, papa; you mustn't *ever* forget it. Promise."

"All right, I promise. Jacob Edwards—it's a very pretty name, too."

"No, no—Edward *Jacobs*. Say it again, papa; and keep saying it till you learn it good."

"All right, I'll begin now. Are you ready?"

"Yes, papa—and do be careful; and don't hurry."

And they fixed their grave eyes upon me; eyes charged with hope, hope just touched with a pathetic shade of doubt. I couldn't help toying with it.

"Yes, I will be very careful, because always it is best to get a thing right in the first place, then after that it comes easier. And in the case of a difficult name like Jacob Edwards—"

"Oh, papa!"—this with a sort of anguish; and the tears sprang into their eyes.

I gathered the abused pair to my breast and cried out—

"Bless your hearts I was only fooling. I didn't know it was any matter to you. I won't do it any more. I wasn't in earnest, upon my word I wasn't. I can say it without any trouble; listen: Edward Jacobs, Edward Jacobs, Edward Jacobs—"

The sunshine was come again, and I thought I would not play any more treacheries like that for the present. I said—

"But come. You know you haven't told me where we are."

"Why, we are in a town, papa."

"No we are not, Potie, we are only in the edge of it."

"Well, in the edge of it, then—it's all the same. And its name—don't you know its name, papa?"

"I think I can tell better when I hear it. What is it, Bessie?"

She hesitated, and said—

"Mamma only just calls it *the town*; and so that is what we call it, too; but the people—they—well, the people call it—"

"Hell's Delight," said Jessie, gravely.

It nearly startled me out of my army shirt, for it suggested some tremendous possibilities. My breath came short and quick, now, and in insufficient quantity for a person who was full of questions and in a hurry to ask them; but I got them out, and as fast as I could:

"Are we in California?"

"Yes, papa."

"What time of the year is it?"

"The middle of August."

"How old are you, Bessie?"

"Nearly nine and a half, papa."

"This is amazing. I have been asleep eighteen months! Amazing—incredible—impossible. And how you children have grown—I was supposing it was your mean disguises that were deceiving my eyes. What—"

"Mamma's come, mamma's come! Oh, mamma, he's in his right mind!"

We two had been separated just an hour—by the clock—but in the *true* sense a whole year and a half. What the meeting was like, there is no art to tell. The ignorant cannot imagine it, but only such as have lived it.

CHAPTER . . .

When a person has been absent from the planet a year and a half, there is much news to hear when he gets back. It took Alison many hours to tell me her story. She had had a hard life of it, and heavy work and sharp privations, and this had aged her body a little, but not her spirit. Her spirit was as it had always been; its courage, its hopefulness, its generosities, its magnanimities had suffered no impairment, her troubles had not soured its native sweetness nor embittered its judgments of men and the world. She had no complaints to make about her poverty; and as for upbraiding me for causing it, she never thought of such a thing. It shamed me to see this, knowing how quick I should be to upbraid her if our places had been changed, and how meanly prone to keep her reminded of it—and sincerely repent, in sackcloth and ashes for it—and then do it again the next day, and the next, and the next, and all the days.

She told me her tale. When she found that we were ruined and in debt she left the hotel at once and got three cheap rooms and a kitchen on the fourth floor of a tenement house, and discharged Jake and Maria. They declined the discharge. Maria remained and did the housework, and Jake went out to service and made her take and use almost all the money he earned. It helped to save us alive, in those first days before Alice had found work for herself. She presently got copying to do; and so great was the sympathy which her calamities excited that she was soon overrun with this kind of work, and was able to employ several assistants. All our friends stood by her, none of them discarded her; new ones came; and new and old together would have helped her out of their pockets if she would have consented. She said it was worth while to know poverty, because it so enlarged and ennobled one's estimates of the world in general as well as of one's friends. Almost every paper in the land used me generously. There was but one man who was bitter against me; even the injured bankers made no trouble, and ceased from saying harsh things about me. The officers of the army believed my story, and believed it entirely. They said that a man trained at West Point might be a fool in business matters, but never a rascal and never a liar; that he was a gentleman, and would remain one. General Scott said I was a good soldier, none better; and that even the best soldier could botch a trade which he was not fitted for.

*1897*

# A Word of Encouragement for
# Our Blushing Exiles

*. . . Well, what do you think of our country* now? *And what do you think of the figure she is cutting before the eyes of the world? For one, I am ashamed*—(Extract from a long and heated letter from a Voluntary Exile, Member of the American Colony, Paris.)

And so you are ashamed. I am trying to think out what it can have been that has produced this large attitude of mind and this fine flow of sarcasm. Apparently you are ashamed to look Europe in the face; ashamed of the American name; temporarily ashamed of your nationality. By the light of remarks made to me by an American here in Vienna, I judge that you are ashamed because:

1. We are meddling where we have no business and no right; meddling with the private family matters of a sister nation; intruding upon her sacred right to do as she pleases with her own, unquestioned by anybody.

2. We are doing this under a sham humanitarian pretext.

3. Doing it in order to filch Cuba, the formal and distinct disclaimer in the ultimatum being very, very thin humbug, and easily detectable as such by you and virtuous Europe.

4. And finally you are ashamed of all this because it is new, and base, and brutal, and dishonest; and because Europe, having had no previous experience of such things, is horrified by it and can never respect us nor associate with us any more.

Brutal, base, dishonest? We? Land thieves? Shedders of innocent blood? We? Traitors to our official word? We? Are we going to lose Europe's respect because of this new and dreadful conduct? Russia's, for instance? Is she lying stretched out on her back in Manchuria, with her head among her Siberian prisons and her feet in Port Arthur, trying to read over the fairy tales she told Lord Salisbury, and not able to do it for crying because we are maneuvering to treacherously smouch Cuba from feeble Spain, and because we are ungently shedding innocent Spanish blood?

Is it France's respect that we are going to lose? Is our unchivalric conduct troubling a nation which exists to-day be cause a brave young girl saved it when its poltroons had lost it—a nation which deserted her as one man when her day of peril came? Is our treacherous assault upon a weak people distressing a nation which contributed Bartholomew's Day to human history? Is our ruthless spirit offending the sensibilities of the nation which gave us the Reign of Terror to read about? Is our unmanly intrusion into the private affairs of a sister nation shocking the feelings of the people who sent Maximilian to Mexico? Are our shabby and pusillanimous ways outraging the fastidious people who have sent an innocent man (Dreyfus) to a living hell, taken to their embraces the slimy guilty one, and submitted to a thousand indignities Emile Zola—the manliest man in France?

Is it Spain's respect that we are going to lose? Is she sitting sadly conning her great history and contrasting it with our meddling, cruel, perfidious one—our shameful history of foreign robberies, humanitarian shams, and annihilations of weak and unoffending nations? Is she remembering with pride how she sent Columbus home in chains; how she sent half of the harmless West Indians into slavery and the rest to the grave, leaving not one alive; how she robbed and slaughtered the Inca's gentle race, then beguiled the Inca into her power with fair promises and burned him at the stake; how she drenched the New World in blood, and earned and got the name of The Nation with the Bloody Footprint; how she drove all the Jews out of Spain in a day, allowing them to sell their property, but forbidding them to carry any money out of the country; how she roasted heretics by the thousands and thousands in her public squares, generation after generation, her kings and her priests looking on as at a holiday show; how her Holy Inquisition imported hell into the earth; how she was the first to institute it and the last to give it up—and then only under compulsion; how, with a spirit unmodified by time, she still tortures her prisoners to-day; how, with her ancient passion for pain and blood unchanged, she still crowds the arena with ladies and gentlemen and priests to see with delight a bull harried and persecuted and a gored horse dragging his entrails on the ground; and how, with this incredible character surviving all attempts to civilize it, her Duke of Alva rises again in the person of General Weyler—

to-day the most idolized personage in Spain—and we see a hundred thousand women and children shut up in pens and pitilessly starved to death?

Are we indeed going to lose Spain's respect? Is there no way to avoid this calamity—or this compliment? Are we going to lose her respect because we have made a promise in our ultimatum which she thinks we shall break? And meantime is she trying to recall some promise of her own which she has kept?

Is the Professional Official Fibber of Europe really troubled with our morals? Dear Parisian friend, are you taking seriously the daily remark of the newspaper and the orator about "this noble nation with an illustrious history"? That is mere kindness, mere charity for a people in temporary hard luck. The newspaper and the orator do not mean it. They wink when they say it.

And so you are ashamed. Do not be ashamed; there is no occasion for it.

*May 24, 1898*

# About Play-Acting

I have a project to suggest. But first I will write a chapter of introduction.

I have just been witnessing a remarkable play, here at the Burg Theatre in Vienna. I do not know of any play that much resembles it. In fact, it is such a departure from the common laws of the drama, that the name "play" doesn't seem to fit it quite snugly. However, whatever else it may be, it is in any case a great and stately metaphysical poem, and deeply fascinating. "Deeply fascinating" is the right term: for the audience sat four hours and five minutes without thrice breaking into applause, except at the close of each act; sat rapt and silent—fascinated. This piece is "The Master of Palmyra." It is twenty years old; yet I doubt if you have ever heard of it. It is by Wilbrandt, and is his masterpiece and the work which is to make his name permanent in German literature. It has never been played anywhere except in Berlin and in the great Burg Theatre in Vienna. Yet whenever it is put on the stage it packs the house, and the free list is suspended. I know people who have seen it ten times; they know the most of it by heart; they do not tire of it; and they say they shall still be quite willing to go and sit under its spell whenever they get the opportunity.

There is a dash of metempsychosis in it—and it is the strength of the piece. The play gave me the sense of the passage of a dimly connected procession of dream-pictures. The scene of it is Palmyra in Roman times. It covers a wide stretch of time,—I don't know how many years,—and in the course of it the chief actress is reincarnated several times: four times she is a more or less young woman; and once she is a lad. In the first act she is *Zoe*,—a Christian girl who has wandered across the desert from Damascus to try to Christianize the Zeus-worshipping pagans of Palmyra. In this character she is wholly spiritual, a religious enthusiast, a devotee who covets martyrdom—and gets it.

After many years she appears in the second act as *Phœbe*, a graceful and beautiful young light-o'-love from Rome, whose soul is all for the shows and luxuries and delights of this life—a dainty and capricious featherhead, a creature of shower and sunshine, a spoiled child, but a charming one. In the third act, after an interval of many years, she reappears as *Persida*, mother of a daughter in the fresh bloom of youth. She is now a sort of combination of her two earlier selves: in religious loyalty and subjection she is *Zoe*; in triviality of character and shallowness of judgment—together with a touch of vanity in dress—she is *Phœbe*.

After a lapse of years she appears in the fourth act as *Nymphas*, a beautiful boy, in whose character the previous incarnations are engagingly mixed.

And after another stretch of years all these heredities are joined in the *Zenobia* of the fifth act—a person of gravity, dignity, sweetness, with a heart filled with compassion for all who suffer, and a hand prompt to put into practical form the heart's benignant impulses.

You will easily concede that the actress who proposes to discriminate nicely these five characters, and play them to the satisfaction of a cultivated and exacting audience, has her work cut out for her. Mme. Hohenfels has made these parts her peculiar property; and she is well able to meet all the requirements. You perceive, now, where the chief part of the absorbing fascination of this piece lies: it is in watching this extraordinary artist melt these five characters into each other—grow, shade by shade, out of one and into another through a stretch of four hours and five minutes.

There are a number of curious and interesting features in this piece. For instance, its hero, *Appelles*, young, handsome, vigorous, in the first act, remains so all through the long flight of years covered by the five acts. Other men, young in the first act, are touched with gray in the second, are old and racked with infirmities in the third: in the fourth, all but one are gone to their long home; and he is a blind and helpless hulk of ninety or a hundred years. It indicates that the stretch of time covered by the piece is seventy years or more. The scenery undergoes decay, too,—the decay of age, assisted and perfected by a conflagration. The fine new temples and palaces of the second act are by and by a wreck of crumbled walls and prostrate columns, mouldy, grass-grown, and desolate; but their former selves are still recognizable in their ruins. The aging men and the aging scenery together convey a profound illusion of that long lapse of time: they make you live it yourself! You leave the theatre with the weight of a century upon you.

Another strong effect: Death, in person, walks about the stage in every act. So far as I could make out, he was supposably not visible to any excepting two persons—the one he came for and *Appelles*. He used various costumes: but there was always more black about them than any other tint; and so they were always sombre. Also they were always deeply impressive and, indeed, awe-inspiring. The face was not subjected to changes, but remained the same, first and last—a ghastly white. To me he was always welcome, he seemed so real—the actual Death, not a play-acting artificiality. He was of a solemn and stately carriage; and he had a deep voice, and used it with a noble dignity. Wherever there was a turmoil of merry-making or fighting or feasting or chaffing or quarrelling, or a gilded pageant, or other manifestation of our trivial and fleeting life, into it drifted that black figure with the corpse-face, and looked its fateful look and passed on; leaving its victim shuddering and smitten. And always its coming made the fussy human pack seem infinitely pitiful and shabby and hardly worth the attention of either saving or damning.

In the beginning of the first act the young girl *Zoe* appears by some great rocks in the desert, and sits down, exhausted, to rest. Presently arrive a pauper couple, stricken with age and infirmities; and they begin to mumble and pray to the Spirit of Life, who is said to inhabit that spot. The Spirit of Life appears; also Death—uninvited. They are (supposably) invisible. Death, tall, black-robed, corpse-faced, stands motionless and waits. The aged couple pray to the Spirit of Life for a means to prop up their existence and continue it. Their prayer fails. The Spirit of Life prophesies *Zoe's* martyrdom: it will take place before night. Soon *Appelles* arrives, young and vigorous and full of enthusiasm; he has led a host against the

Persians and won the battle; he is the pet of fortune, rich, honored, beloved, "Master of Palmyra." He has heard that whoever stretches himself out on one of those rocks there, and asks for a deathless life, can have his wish. He laughs at the tradition, but wants to make the trial anyway. The invisible Spirit of Life warns him: "Life without end can be regret without end." But he persists: let him keep his youth, his strength, and his mental faculties unimpaired, and he will take all the risks. He has his desire.

From this time forth, act after act, the troubles and sorrows and misfortunes and humiliations of life beat upon him without pity or respite; but he will not give up, he will not confess his mistake. Whenever he meets Death he still furiously defies him—but Death patiently waits. He, the healer of sorrows, is man's best friend: the recognition of this will come. As the years drag on, and on, and on, the friends of the *Master's* youth grow old; and one by one they totter to the grave: he goes on with his proud fight, and will not yield. At length he is wholly alone in the world; all his friends are dead; last of all, his darling of darlings, his son, the lad *Nymphas*, who dies in his arms. His pride is broken now; and he would welcome Death, if Death would come, if Death would hear his prayers and give him peace. The closing act is fine and pathetic. *Appelles* meets *Zenobia*, the helper of all that suffer, and tells her his story, which moves her pity. By common report she is endowed with more than earthly powers; and, since he cannot have the boon of death, he appeals to her to drown his memory in forgetfulness of his griefs—forgetfulness, "which is death's equivalent." She says (roughly translated), in an exaltation of compassion:

> "Come to me!
>   Kneel: and may the power be granted me
>   To cool the fires of this poor, tortured brain,
>   And bring it peace and healing."

He kneels. From her hand, which she lays upon his head, a mysterious influence steals through him; and he sinks into a dreamy tranquillity.

> "O if I could but so drift
> Through this soft twilight into the night of peace,
> Never to wake again!
> (*Raising his hand, as if in benediction.*)
> O mother earth, farewell!
> Gracious thou wert to me. Farewell!
> Appelles goes to rest."

Death appears behind him and encloses the uplifted hand in his. *Appelles* shudders, wearily and slowly turns, and recognizes his lifelong adversary. He smiles and puts all his gratitude into one simple and touching sentence, "Ich danke dir," and dies.

Nothing, I think, could be more moving, more beautiful, than this close. This piece is just one long, soulful, sardonic laugh at human life. Its title might properly be "Is Life a Failure?" and leave the five acts to play with the answer. I am not at all sure that the author meant to laugh at life. I only notice that he has done it. Without putting into words any ungracious or discourteous things about life, the episodes in the piece seem to be saying all the time—inarticulately: "Note what a silly, poor thing human life is; how childish its ambitions, how ridiculous its pomps, how trivial its dignities, how cheap its heroisms, how capricious its course, how brief its flight, how stingy in happinesses, how opulent in miseries, how few its prides, how multitudinous its humiliations, how comic its tragedies, how tragic its comedies, how wearisome and monotonous its repetition of its stupid history through the ages, with never the introduction of a new detail, how hard it has tried, from the Creation down, to play itself upon its possessor as a boon, and has never proved its case in a single instance!"

Take note of some of the details of the piece. Each of the five acts contains an independent tragedy of its own. In each act somebody's edifice of hope, or of ambition, or of happiness, goes down in ruins. Even *Appelles'* perennial youth is only a long tragedy, and his life a failure. There are two martyrdoms in the piece; and they are curiously and sarcastically contrasted. In the first act the pagans persecute *Zoe*, the

Christian girl, and a pagan mob slaughters her. In the fourth
act those same pagans—now very old and zealous—are become Christians, and they persecute the pagans: a mob of
them slaughter the pagan youth, *Nymphas*, who is standing
up for the old gods of his fathers. No remark is made about
this picturesque failure of civilization; but there it stands, as
an unworded suggestion that civilization, even when Christianized, was not able wholly to subdue the natural man in
that old day—just as in our day the spectacle of a shipwrecked French crew, clubbing women and children who
tried to climb into the life-boats, suggests that civilization
has not succeeded in entirely obliterating the natural man
even yet. Common sailors! A year ago, in Paris, at a fire, the
aristocracy of the same nation clubbed girls and women out
of the way to save themselves. Civilization tested at top and
bottom both, you see. And in still another panic of fright we
have this same "tough" civilization saving its honor by condemning an innocent man to multiform death, and hugging
and whitewashing the guilty one.

In the second act a grand Roman official is not above trying to blast *Appelles'* reputation by falsely charging him with
misappropriating public moneys. *Appelles*, who is too proud
to endure even the suspicion of irregularity, strips himself to
naked poverty to square the unfair account; and *his* troubles
begin: the blight which is to continue and spread strikes his
life; for the frivolous, pretty creature whom he has brought
from Rome has no taste for poverty, and agrees to elope with
a more competent candidate. Her presence in the house has
previously brought down the pride and broken the heart of
*Appelles'* poor old mother; and *her* life is a failure. Death
comes for her, but is willing to trade her for the Roman girl;
so the bargain is struck with *Appelles*, and the mother is
spared for the present.

No one's life escapes the blight. *Timoleus*, the gay satirist of
the first two acts, who scoffed at the pious hypocrisies and
money-grubbing ways of the great Roman lords, is grown old
and fat and blear-eyed and racked with disease in the third,
has lost his stately purities, and watered the acid of his wit.
*His* life has suffered defeat. Unthinkingly he swears by *Zeus*—
from ancient habit—and then quakes with fright; for a

fellow-communicant is passing by. Reproached by a pagan friend of his youth for his apostasy, he confesses that principle, when unsupported by an assenting stomach, has to climb down. One must have bread; and "the bread is Christian now." Then the poor, old wreck, once so proud of his iron rectitude, hobbles away, coughing and barking.

In that same act *Appelles* gives his sweet young Christian daughter and her fine young pagan lover his consent and blessing, and makes them utterly happy—for five minutes. Then the priest and the mob come, to tear them apart and put the girl in a nunnery; for marriage between the sects is forbidden. *Appelles'* wife could dissolve the rule; and she wants to do it: but under priestly pressure she wavers; then, fearing that in providing happiness for her child she would be committing a sin dangerous to herself, she goes over to the opposition, and throws the casting vote for the nunnery. The blight has fallen upon the young couple, and *their* life is a failure.

In the fourth act, *Longinus*, who made such a prosperous and enviable start in the first act, is left alone in the desert, sick, blind, helpless, incredibly old, to die: not a friend left in the world—another ruined life. And in that act, also, *Appelles'* worshipped boy, *Nymphas*, done to death by the mob, breathes out his last sigh in his father's arms—one more failure. In the fifth act, *Appelles* himself dies, and is glad to do it; he who so ignorantly rejoiced, only four acts before, over the splendid present of an earthly immortality—the very worst failure of the lot!

II.

Now I approach my project. Here is the theatre-list for Saturday, May 7, 1898,—cut from the advertising columns of a New York paper:

**PROCTOR'S    CONTINUOUS**
PERFORMANCE.
23D ST.    REFINED VAUDEVILLE.
Vaudeville debut of
CHARLES A. GARDNER & CO.;
Arthur and Jennie Dunn, Paulinetti and Piquo, Hughey Dougherty, Nichola Sisters, George Evans, others.
SENSATIONAL EDISON WAR-GRAPH.
BALCONIES. 25c.    ORCHESTRA, 50c.

**PASTOR'S    CONTINUOUS**
PERFORMANCES.
12:30 to 11 P. M.    Seats 20 and 30 Cents.
EDISON'S WONDERFUL WAR-SCOPE.
CANFIELD & CARLETON, ELLINORE SISTERS,
JOHNNY CARROLL, CURTIS & GORDON.

**14TH ST. THEATRE.** nr. 6th av. Good seats. 50c.
THOS. E. SHEA in the great naval play,
THE MAN-O'-WAR'S MAN.
SILVER SOUVENIRS at Wed. & Sat. Matinees.

**ELECTRICAL SHOW.**
2 to 11 P. M.    Admission. 50c. Children, 25c.
MADISON SQUARE GARDEN.

HURTIG & **HARLEM** MUSIC Orch. and Bal.
SEAMON'S    HALL. Res. 25c. and 50c.
Rogers Bros., Maude Raymond, Joe Welch,
Raymond & Kurkamp. Gardner & Gilmore; others.

**LYCEUM.** 4th Ave. & 23d St.    Begins 8:30.
Daniel Frohman. Manager.
Kelcey-Shannon Co. in Clyde Fitch's
THE MOTH AND THE FLAME.

**STAR.** THE WHITE SQUADRON.    Gal. 15c.
Introducing Robt. Hilliard & Laura Biggar. Bal. 25c.
Next Week—"The Mikado."    Orch. 50c.

**5TH AVE. THEATRE.** Broadway and 28th St.
**MRS. FISKE**    Eve. at 8:15.
Sat. Mat. at 2.
in LOVE FINDS THE WAY
and A BIT OF OLD CHELSEA.

**KEITH'S** CONTINUOUS PERFORMANCE,
25c., 50c., Noon to 11 P. M.
BIOGRAPH, CHARLES DICKSON & CO., 4 COHANS, JOHNSTONE BENNETT, GEORGE W. LESLIE, SMITH AND CAMPBELL, GARDNER AND ELY, WEBB AND HASSAN, HALL AND STALEY, BLOCKSOM AND BURNS AND OTHERS.

**HARLEM**    OPERA HOUSE.
Eve. 8:15.    Mat. Sat. 2.
HENRY MILLER—THE MASTER.
Next Week—THE HIGHWAYMAN.

**PLEASURE CONTINUOUS** 58TH ST.
**PALACE,** PERFORMANCE. 3D AVE.
LEW DOCKSTADER.
Milton and Dollie Nobles. Ivan Greboff, Cushman and Holcombe. C. W. Littlefield; others.
EDISON WAR-GRAPH (NEW VIEWS).
Come any time, 1:30 to 11 P. M.
15c., 25c. AFTS.    25c., 50c. EVGS.

**ACADEMY OF MUSIC.** 14th St. & Irving Pl.
A STUPENDOUS SUCCESS.
**BATTLES** OF **NATION.** OUR
Mats. Wed. & Sat., 2.    Eve. 8:15.

**SAM T. JACK'S THEATRE,**
BROADWAY & 29TH ST.
2 BIG SHOWS EVERY DAY. 2 and 8.
Jennie Yeamans & French Importations.

**WEBER & FIELDS'** MUSIC    MAT. TO-DAY.
HALL.
**POUSSE CAFE** AND **CON-CURERS.** THE
MISS BESSIE CLAYTON, the Queen of Dancers.

**BIJOU**    Matinee To-day at 2.
To-night at 8:15.
Last Two Performances of
**MY FRIEND FROM INDIA.**
NEXT WEEK—THE TARRYTOWN WIDOW.

**AMERICAN** 8th ave. and 42d st.    Tel. 3147-38.
EVE. 8:15.    MAT. WED. & SAT. 2.
Castle Square Opera Company.
6TH | 80 Artists Present **THE BEGGAR STUDENT.**
MONTH |
ENTIRE HOUSE. 25, 50, 75.    Mat. To-day, 25 & 50.
NEXT WEEK—FAUST (IN ENGLISH).

**EMPIRE THEATRE.** B'way and 40th st.
**WM. CRANE** | HIS **THE MAYOR.**
H.    | HONOR
Evenings at 8:30.    Mat. To-day and Wed. at 2:15.

**OLYMPIA** MUSIC HALL.    Mat. To-day.
**ADGIE,** Marguerite Sylva, & 30 others.
NEXT WEEK.
An Original **"WAR BUBBLES."**
Patriotic Extravaganza.

**KNICKERBOCKER.** B'WAY & 38TH.
EVENINGS AT 8:15.    MAT. TO-DAY AT 2:15.
**SOUSA'S THE BRIDE-ELECT**
NEW OPERA.

**KOSTER & BIAL'S** ADM. 50C.
MAT. TO-DAY.
ADELE RITCHIE in "AU BAIN."
Truly Spectacular. Gerome Edwardy, and others.

**WALLACK'S** Evgs. 8:15.    Mat. To-day, 2.
LAST
WEEK **THE BOSTONIANS**
IN **THE SERENADE.**

**Daly's** Evenings, 8:15.    Matinee To-day, 2.
THE CIRCUS GIRL
Virginia Earl, James Powers, &c.
"A trump card; very bright."—Herald.
"Evening of unalloyed enjoyment."—Trib.

Now I arrive at my project, and make my suggestion. From the look of this lightsome feast, I conclude that what you need is a tonic. Send for "The Master of Palmyra." You are trying to make yourself believe that life is a comedy, that its sole business is fun, that there is nothing serious in it. You are ignoring the skeleton in your closet. Send for the "Master of Palmyra." You are neglecting a valuable side of your life; presently it will be atrophied. You are eating too much mental sugar; you will bring on Bright's disease of the intellect. You need a tonic; you need it very much. Send for the "Master of Palmyra." You will not need to translate it: its story is as plain as a procession of pictures.

I have made my suggestion. Now I wish to put an annex to it. And that is this: It is right and wholesome to have those light comedies and entertaining shows; and I shouldn't wish to see them diminished. But none of us is *always* in the comedy spirit; we have our graver moods; they come to us all; the lightest of us cannot escape them. These moods have their appetites,—healthy and legitimate appetites,—and there ought to be some way of satisfying them. It seems to me that New York ought to have one theatre devoted to tragedy. With her three millions of population, and seventy outside millions to draw upon, she can afford it, she can support it. America devotes more time, labor, money, and attention to distributing literary and musical culture among the general public than does any other nation, perhaps; yet here you find her neglecting what is possibly the most effective of all the breeders and nurses and disseminators of high literary taste and lofty emotion—the tragic stage. To leave that powerful agency out is to haul the culture-wagon with a crippled team. Nowadays, when a mood comes which only Shakespeare can set to music, what must we do? Read Shakespeare ourselves! Isn't it pitiful? It is playing an organ solo on a jew's-harp. *We* can't read. None but the Booths can do it.

Thirty years ago Edwin Booth played "Hamlet" a hundred nights in New York. With three times the population, how often is "Hamlet" played now in a year? If Booth were back now in his prime, how often could he play it in New York? Some will say twenty-five nights. I will say three hundred, and say it with confidence. The tragedians are dead; but I think that the taste and intelligence which made their market are not.

What *has* come over us English-speaking people? During the first half of this century tragedies and great tragedians were as common with us as farce and comedy; and it was the same in England. Now we have not a tragedian, I believe; and London, with her fifty shows and theatres, has but three, I think. It is an astonishing thing, when you come to consider it. Vienna remains upon the ancient basis: there has been no change. She sticks to the former proportions: a number of rollicking comedies, admirably played, every night; and also every night at the Burg Theatre—that wonder of the world for grace and beauty and richness and splendor and costliness—a majestic drama of depth and seriousness, or a standard old tragedy. It is only within the last dozen years that men have learned to do miracles on the stage in the way of grand and enchanting scenic effects; and it is at such a time as this that we have reduced our scenery mainly to different breeds of parlors and varying aspects of furniture and rugs. I think we must have a Burg in New York, and Burg scenery, and a great company like the Burg company. Then, with a tragedy-tonic once or twice a month, we shall enjoy the comedies all the better. Comedy keeps the heart sweet; but we all know that there is wholesome refreshment for both mind and heart in an occasional climb among the solemn pomps of the intellectual snow-summits built by Shakespeare and those others. Do I seem to be preaching? It is out of my line: I only do it because the rest of the clergy seem to be on vacation.

*October 1898*

# From the "London Times" of 1904

I.

*Correspondence of the "London Times."*

CHICAGO, April 1, 1904.

I resume by cable-telephone where I left off yesterday. For many hours, now, this vast city—along with the rest of the globe, of course—has talked of nothing but the extraordinary episode mentioned in my last report. In accordance with your instructions, I will now trace the romance from its beginnings down to the culmination of yesterday—or to-day; call it which you like. By an odd chance, I was a personal actor in a part of this drama myself. The opening scene plays in Vienna. Date, one o'clock in the morning, March 31, 1898. I had spent the evening at a social entertainment. About midnight I went away, in company with the military attachés of the British, Italian, and American embassies, to finish with a late smoke. This function had been appointed to take place in the house of Lieutenant Hillyer, the third attaché mentioned in the above list. When we arrived there we found several visitors in the room: young Szczepanik;* Mr. K., his financial backer; Mr. W., the latter's secretary; and Lieutenant Clayton of the United States army. War was at that time threatening between Spain and our country, and Lieutenant Clayton had been sent to Europe on military business. I was well acquainted with young Szczepanik and his two friends, and I knew Mr. Clayton slightly. I had met him at West Point years before, when he was a cadet. It was when General Merritt was superintendent. He had the reputation of being an able officer, and also of being quick-tempered and plain-spoken.

This smoking-party had been gathered together partly for business. This business was to consider the availability of the telelectroscope for military service. It sounds oddly enough now, but it is nevertheless true that at that time the invention was not taken seriously by any one except its inventor. Even his financial supporter regarded it merely as a

*Pronounced (approximately) Zepannik.

273

curious and interesting toy. Indeed, he was so convinced of
this that he had actually postponed its use by the general
world to the end of the dying century by granting a two
years' exclusive lease of it to a syndicate, whose intent was to
exploit it at the Paris World's Fair.

When we entered the smoking-room we found Lieutenant
Clayton and Szczepanik engaged in a warm talk over the
telelectroscope in the German tongue. Clayton was saying:

"Well, you know *my* opinion of it, anyway!" and he
brought his fist down with emphasis upon the table.

"And I do not value it," retorted the young inventor, with
provoking calmness of tone and manner.

Clayton turned to Mr. K., and said:

"*I* cannot see why you are wasting money on this toy. In
my opinion, the day will never come when it will do a farthing's worth of real service for any human being."

"That may be; yes, that may be; still, I have put the money
in it, and am content. I think, myself, that it is only a toy; but
Szczepanik claims more for it, and I know him well enough
to believe that he can see farther than I can—either with his
telelectroscope or without it."

The soft answer did not cool Clayton down; it seemed only
to irritate him the more; and he repeated and emphasized his
conviction that the invention would never do any man a
farthing's worth of real service. He even made it a "brass"
farthing, this time. Then he laid an English farthing on the
table, and added:

"Take that, Mr. K., and put it away; and if ever the telelectroscope does any man an actual service,—mind, a *real* service,—please mail it to me as a reminder, and I will take back
what I have been saying. Will you?"

"I will"; and Mr. K. put the coin in his pocket.

Mr. Clayton now turned toward Szczepanik, and began
with a taunt—a taunt which did not reach a finish; Szczepanik interrupted it with a hardy retort, and followed this
with a blow. There was a brisk fight for a moment or two;
then the attachés separated the men.

The scene now changes to Chicago. Time, the autumn of
1901. As soon as the Paris contract released the telelectroscope,

it was delivered to public use, and was soon connected with the telephonic systems of the whole world. The improved "limitless-distance" telephone was presently introduced, and the daily doings of the globe made visible to everybody, and audibly discussable, too, by witnesses separated by any number of leagues.

By and by Szczepanik arrived in Chicago. Clayton (now captain) was serving in that military department at the time. The two men resumed the Viennese quarrel of 1898. On three different occasions they quarreled, and were separated by witnesses. Then came an interval of two months, during which time Szczepanik was not seen by any of his friends, and it was at first supposed that he had gone off on a sight-seeing tour and would soon be heard from. But no; no word came from him. Then it was supposed that he had returned to Europe. Still, time drifted on, and he was not heard from. Nobody was troubled, for he was like most inventors and other kinds of poets, and went and came in a capricious way, and often without notice.

Now comes the tragedy. On the 29th of December, in a dark and unused compartment of the cellar under Captain Clayton's house, a corpse was discovered by one of Clayton's maid-servants. It was easily identified as Szczepanik's. The man had died by violence. Clayton was arrested, indicted, and brought to trial, charged with this murder. The evidence against him was perfect in every detail, and absolutely unassailable. Clayton admitted this himself. He said that a reasonable man could not examine this testimony with a dispassionate mind and not be convinced by it; yet the man would be in error, nevertheless. Clayton swore that he did not commit the murder, and that he had had nothing to do with it.

As your readers will remember, he was condemned to death. He had numerous and powerful friends, and they worked hard to save him, for none of them doubted the truth of his assertion. I did what little I could to help, for I had long since become a close friend of his, and thought I knew that it was not in his character to inveigle an enemy into a corner and assassinate him. During 1902 and 1903 he was several times reprieved by the governor; he was reprieved once more in the beginning of the present year, and the execution-day postponed to March 31.

The governor's situation has been embarrassing, from the day of the condemnation, because of the fact that Clayton's wife is the governor's niece. The marriage took place in 1899, when Clayton was thirty-four and the girl twenty-three, and has been a happy one. There is one child, a little girl three years old. Pity for the poor mother and child kept the mouths of grumblers closed at first; but this could not last forever,—for in America politics has a hand in everything,—and by and by the governor's political opponents began to call attention to his delay in allowing the law to take its course. These hints have grown more and more frequent of late, and more and more pronounced. As a natural result, his own party grew nervous. Its leaders began to visit Springfield and hold long private conferences with him. He was now between two fires. On the one hand, his niece was imploring him to pardon her husband; on the other were the leaders, insisting that he stand to his plain duty as chief magistrate of the State, and place no further bar to Clayton's execution. Duty won in the struggle, and the governor gave his word that he would not again respite the condemned man. This was two weeks ago. Mrs. Clayton now said:

"Now that you have given your word, my last hope is gone, for I know you will never go back from it. But you have done the best you could for John, and I have no reproaches for you. You love him, and you love me, and we both know that if you could honorably save him, you would do it. I will go to him now, and be what help I can to him, and get what comfort I may out of the few days that are left to us before the night comes which will have no end for me in life. You will be with me that day? You will not let me bear it alone?"

"I will take you to him myself, poor child, and I will be near you to the last."

By the governor's command, Clayton was now allowed every indulgence he might ask for which could interest his mind and soften the hardships of his imprisonment. His wife and child spent the days with him; I was his companion by night.

He was removed from the narrow cell which he had occupied during such a dreary stretch of time, and given the chief warden's roomy and comfortable quarters. His mind was always busy with the catastrophe of his life, and with the slaughtered inventor, and he now took the fancy that he would like to have the telelectroscope and divert his mind with it. He had his wish. The connection was made with the international telephone-station, and day by day, and night by night, he called up one corner of the globe after another, and looked upon its life, and studied its strange sights, and spoke with its people, and realized that by grace of this marvelous instrument he was almost as free as the birds of the air, although a prisoner under locks and bars. He seldom spoke, and I never interrupted him when he was absorbed in this amusement. I sat in his parlor and read and smoked, and the nights were very quiet and reposefully sociable, and I found them pleasant. Now and then I would hear him say, "Give me Yedo"; next, "Give me Hong-Kong"; next, "Give me Melbourne." And I smoked on, and read in comfort, while he wandered about the remote under-world, where the sun was shining in the sky, and the people were at their daily work. Sometimes the talk that came from those far regions through the microphone attachment interested me, and I listened.

Yesterday—I keep calling it yesterday, which is quite natural, for certain reasons—the instrument remained unused, and that, also, was natural, for it was the eve of the execution-day. It was spent in tears and lamentations and farewells. The governor and the wife and child remained until a quarter past eleven at night, and the scenes I witnessed were pitiful to see. The execution was to take place at four in the morning. A little after eleven a sound of hammering broke out upon the still night, and there was a glare of light, and the child cried out, "What is that, papa?" and ran to the window before she could be stopped, and clapped her small hands, and said: "Oh, come and see, mama—such a pretty thing they are making!" The mother knew—and fainted. It was the gallows!

She was carried away to her lodging, poor woman, and Clayton and I were alone—alone, and thinking, brooding, dreaming. We might have been statues, we sat so motionless and still. It was a wild night, for winter was come again for a moment, after the habit of this region in the early spring. The sky was starless and black, and a strong wind was blowing from the lake. The silence in the room was so deep that all outside sounds seemed exaggerated by contrast with it. These sounds were fitting ones; they harmonized with the situation and the conditions: the boom and thunder of sudden storm-gusts among the roofs and chimneys, then the dying down into moanings and wailings about the eaves and angles; now and then a gnashing and lashing rush of sleet along the window-panes; and always the muffled and uncanny hammering of the gallows-builders in the courtyard. After an age of this, another sound—far off, and coming smothered and faint through the riot of the tempest—a bell tolling twelve! Another age, and it tolled again. By and by, again. A dreary, long interval after this, then the spectral sound floated to us once more—one, two, three; and this time we caught our breath: sixty minutes of life left!

Clayton rose, and stood by the window, and looked up into the black sky, and listened to the thrashing sleet and the piping wind; then he said: "That a dying man's last of earth should be—this!" After a little he said: "I must see the sun again—the sun!" and the next moment he was feverishly calling: "China! Give me China—Peking!"

I was strangely stirred, and said to myself: "To think that it is a mere human being who does this unimaginable miracle—turns winter into summer, night into day, storm into calm, gives the freedom of the great globe to a prisoner in his cell, and the sun in his naked splendor to a man dying in Egyptian darkness!"

I was listening.

"What light! what brilliancy! what radiance! . . . This is Peking?"

"Yes."

"The time?"

"Mid-afternoon."

"What is the great crowd for, and in such gorgeous costumes? What masses and masses of rich color and barbaric magnificence! And how they flash and glow and burn in the flooding sunlight! What *is* the occasion of it all?"

"The coronation of our new emperor—the Czar."

"But I thought that that was to take place yesterday."

"This *is* yesterday—to you."

"Certainly it is. But my mind is confused, these days; there are reasons for it. . . . Is this the beginning of the procession?"

"Oh, no; it began to move an hour ago."

"Is there much more of it still to come?"

"Two hours of it. Why do you sigh?"

"Because I should like to see it all."

"And why can't you?"

"I have to go—presently."

"You have an engagement?"

After a pause, softly: "Yes." After another pause: "Who are these in the splendid pavilion?"

"The imperial family, and visiting royalties from here and there and yonder in the earth."

"And who are those in the adjoining pavilions to the right and left?"

"Ambassadors and their families and suites to the right; unofficial foreigners to the left."

"If you will be so good, I—"

*Boom!* That distant bell again, tolling the half-hour faintly through the tempest of wind and sleet. The door opened, and the governor and the mother and child entered—the woman in widow's weeds! She fell upon her husband's breast in a passion of sobs, and I—I could not stay; I could not bear it. I went into the bedchamber, and closed the door. I sat there waiting—waiting—waiting, and listening to the rattling sashes and the blustering of the storm. After what seemed a long, long time, I heard a rustle and movement in the parlor, and knew that the clergyman and the sheriff and the guard were come. There was some low-voiced talking; then a hush; then a prayer, with a sound of sobbing; presently, footfalls—the departure for the gallows; then the child's happy voice: "Don't cry *now*, mama, when we've got papa again, and taking him home."

The door closed; they were gone. I was ashamed: I was the only friend of the dying man that had no spirit, no courage. I stepped into the room, and said I would be a man and would follow. But we are made as we are made, and we cannot help it. I did not go.

I fidgeted about the room nervously, and presently went to the window, and softly raised it,—drawn by that dread fascination which the terrible and the awful exert,—and looked down upon the courtyard. By the garish light of the electric lamps I saw the little group of privileged witnesses, the wife crying on her uncle's breast, the condemned man standing on the scaffold with the halter around his neck, his arms strapped to his body, the black cap on his head, the sheriff at his side with his hand on the drop, the clergyman in front of him with bare head and his book in his hand.

*"I am the resurrection and the life—"*

I turned away. I could not listen; I could not look. I did not know whither to go or what to do. Mechanically, and without knowing it, I put my eye to that strange instrument, and there was Peking and the Czar's procession! The next moment I was leaning out of the window, gasping, suffocating, trying to speak, but dumb from the very imminence of the necessity of speaking. The preacher could speak, but I, who had such need of words—

*"And may God have mercy upon your soul. Amen."*

The sheriff drew down the black cap, and laid his hand upon the lever. I got my voice.

"Stop, for God's sake! The man is innocent. Come here and see Szczepanik face to face!"

Hardly three minutes later the governor had my place at the window, and was saying:

"Strike off his bonds and set him free!"

Three minutes later all were in the parlor again. The reader will imagine the scene; I have no need to describe it. It was a sort of mad orgy of joy.

A messenger carried word to Szczepanik in the pavilion, and one could see the distressed amazement dawn in his face as he listened to the tale. Then he came to his end of the line, and talked with Clayton and the governor and the others; and the wife poured out her gratitude upon him for saving her husband's life, and in her deep thankfulness she kissed him at twelve thousand miles' range.

The telelectrophonoscopes of the globe were put to service

now, and for many hours the kings and queens of many realms (with here and there a reporter) talked with Szczepanik, and praised him; and the few scientific societies which had not already made him an honorary member conferred that grace upon him.

How had he come to disappear from among us? It was easily explained. He had not grown used to being a world-famous person, and had been forced to break away from the lionizing that was robbing him of all privacy and repose. So he grew a beard, put on colored glasses, disguised himself a little in other ways, then took a fictitious name, and went off to wander about the earth in peace.

Such is the tale of the drama which began with an inconsequential quarrel in Vienna in the spring of 1898, and came near ending as a tragedy in the spring of 1904.

MARK TWAIN.

## II.

*Correspondence of the "London Times."*

CHICAGO, April 5, 1904.

To-day, by a clipper of the Electric Line, and the latter's Electric Railway connections, arrived an envelop from Vienna, for Captain Clayton, containing an English farthing. The receiver of it was a good deal moved. He called up Vienna, and stood face to face with Mr. K., and said:

"I do not need to say anything; you can see it all in my face. My wife has the farthing. Do not be afraid—she will not throw it away." M. T.

## III.

*Correspondence of the "London Times."*

CHICAGO, April 23, 1904.

Now that the after developments of the Clayton case have run their course and reached a finish, I will sum them up. Clayton's romantic escape from a shameful death steeped all this region in an enchantment of wonder and joy—during the proverbial nine days. Then the sobering process followed, and men began to take thought, and to say: "But *a man was killed*, and Clayton killed him." Others replied: "That is true: we have been overlooking that important detail; we have been led away by excitement."

The feeling soon became general that Clayton ought to be tried again. Measures were taken accordingly, and the proper representations conveyed to Washington; for in America, under the new paragraph added to the Constitution in 1899, second trials are not State affairs, but national, and must be tried by the most august body in the land—the Supreme Court of the United States. The justices were therefore summoned to sit in Chicago. The session was held day before yesterday, and was opened with the usual impressive formalities, the nine judges appearing in their black robes, and the new chief justice (Lemaitre) presiding. In opening the case, the chief justice said:

"It is my opinion that this matter is quite simple. The prisoner at the bar was charged with murdering the man Szczepanik; he was tried for murdering the man Szczepanik; he was fairly tried, and justly condemned and sentenced to death for murdering the man Szczepanik. It turns out that the man Szczepanik was not murdered at all. By the decision of the French courts in the Dreyfus matter, it is established beyond cavil or question that the decisions of courts are permanent and cannot be revised. We are obliged to respect and adopt this precedent. It is upon precedents that the enduring edifice of jurisprudence is reared. The prisoner at the bar has been fairly and righteously condemned to death for the murder of the man Szczepanik, and, in my opinion, there is but one course to pursue in the matter: he must be hanged."

Mr. Justice Crawford said:

"But, your Excellency, he was pardoned on the scaffold for that."

"The pardon is not valid, and cannot stand, because he was pardoned for killing a man whom he had not killed. A man cannot be pardoned for a crime which he has not committed; it would be an absurdity."

"But, your Excellency, he did kill a man."

"That is an extraneous detail; we have nothing to do with

it. The court cannot take up this crime until the prisoner has expiated the other one."

Mr. Justice Halleck said:

"If we order his execution, your Excellency, we shall bring about a miscarriage of justice; for the governor will pardon him again."

"He will not have the power. He cannot pardon a man for a crime which he has not committed. As I observed before, it would be an absurdity."

After a consultation, Mr. Justice Wadsworth said:

"Several of us have arrived at the conclusion, your Excellency, that it would be an error to hang the prisoner for killing Szczepanik, but only for killing the other man, since it is proven that he did not kill Szczepanik."

"On the contrary, it is proven that he *did* kill Szczepanik. By the French precedent, it is plain that we must abide by the finding of the court."

"But Szczepanik is still alive."

"So is Dreyfus."

In the end it was found impossible to ignore or get around the French precedent. There could be but one result: Clayton was delivered over to the executioner. It made an immense excitement; the State rose as one man and clamored for Clayton's pardon and retrial. The governor issued the pardon, but the Supreme Court was in duty bound to annul it, and did so, and poor Clayton was hanged yesterday. The city is draped in black, and, indeed, the like may be said of the State. All America is vocal with scorn of "French justice," and of the malignant little soldiers who invented it and inflicted it upon the other Christian lands.

M. T.

*November 1898*

# My Platonic Sweetheart

I met her first when I was seventeen and she fifteen. It was in a dream. No, I did not meet her; I overtook her. It was in a Missourian village which I had never been in before, and was not in at that time, except dreamwise; in the flesh I was on the Atlantic seaboard ten or twelve hundred miles away. The thing was sudden, and without preparation—after the custom of dreams. There I was, crossing a wooden bridge that had a wooden rail and was untidy with scattered wisps of hay, and there she was, five steps in front of me; half a second previously neither of us was there. This was the exit of the village, which lay immediately behind us. Its last house was the blacksmith-shop; and the peaceful clinking of the hammers—a sound which nearly always seems remote, and is always touched with a spirit of loneliness and a feeling of soft regret for something, you don't know what—was wafted to my ear over my shoulder; in front of us was the winding country road, with woods on one side, and on the other a rail fence, with blackberry vines and hazel bushes crowding its angles; on an upper rail a bluebird, and scurrying toward him along the same rail a fox-squirrel with his tail bent high like a shepherd's crook; beyond the fence a rich field of grain, and far away a farmer in shirt-sleeves and straw hat wading knee-deep through it; no other representative of life, and no noise at all; everywhere a Sabbath stillness.

I remember it all—and the girl, too, and just how she walked, and how she was dressed. In the first moment I was five steps behind her; in the next one I was at her side—without either stepping or gliding; it merely happened; the transfer ignored space. I noticed that, but not with any surprise; it seemed a natural process.

I was at her side. I put my arm around her waist and drew her close to me, for I loved her; and although I did not know her, my behavior seemed to me quite natural and right, and I had no misgivings about it. She showed no surprise, no distress, no displeasure, but put an arm around my waist, and turned up her face to mine with a happy welcome in it, and when I bent down to kiss her she received the kiss as if she was expecting it, and as if it was quite natural for me to offer it and her to take it and have pleasure in it. The affection which I felt for her and which she manifestly felt for me was a quite simple fact; but the quality of it was another matter. It was not the affection of brother and sister—it was closer than that, more clinging, more endearing, more reverent; and it was not the love of sweethearts, for there was no fire in it. It was somewhere between the two, and was finer than either, and more exquisite, more profoundly contenting. We often experience this strange and gracious thing in our dream-loves; and we remember it as a feature of our childhood-loves, too.

We strolled along, across the bridge and down the road, chatting like the oldest friends. She called me George, and that seemed natural and right, though it was not my name; and I called her Alice, and she did not correct me, though without doubt it was not her name. Everything that happened seemed just natural and to be expected. Once I said, "What a dear little hand it is!" and without any words she laid it gratefully in mine for me to examine it. I did it, remarking upon its littleness, its delicate beauty, and its satin skin, then kissed it; she put it up to her lips without saying anything and kissed it in the same place.

Around a curve of the road, at the end of half a mile, we came to a log house, and entered it and found the table set and everything on it steaming hot—a roast turkey, corn in the ear, butter-beans, and the rest of the usual things—and a cat curled up asleep in a splint-bottomed chair by the fireplace; but no people; just emptiness and silence. She said she would look in the next room if I would wait for her. So I sat down, and she passed through a door, which closed behind her with a click of the latch. I waited and waited. Then I got up and followed, for I could not any longer bear to have her out of my sight. I passed through the door, and found myself in a strange sort of cemetery, a city of innumerable tombs and monuments stretching far and wide on every hand, and flushed with pink and gold lights flung from the sinking sun. I turned around, and the log house was gone. I ran here and there and yonder down the lanes between the rows of tombs, calling Alice; and presently the night closed down, and I could not find my way. Then I woke, in deep distress over my

loss, and was in my bed in Philadelphia. And I was not seventeen, now, but nineteen.

Ten years afterward, in another dream, I found her. I was
seventeen again, and she was still fifteen. I was in a grassy
place in the twilight deeps of a magnolia forest some miles
above Natchez, Mississippi; the trees were snowed over with
great blossoms, and the air was loaded with their rich and
strenuous fragrance; the ground was high, and through a rift
in the wood a burnished patch of the river was visible in the
distance. I was sitting on the grass, absorbed in thinking,
when an arm was laid around my neck, and there was Alice
sitting by my side and looking into my face. A deep and satisfied happiness and an unwordable gratitude rose in me, but
with it there was no feeling of surprise; and there was no
sense of a time-lapse; the ten years amounted to hardly even a
yesterday; indeed, to hardly even a noticeable fraction of it.
We dropped in the tranquilest way into affectionate caressings
and pettings, and chatted along without a reference to the
separation; which was natural, for I think we did not know
there had been any that one might measure with either clock
or almanac. She called me Jack and I called her Helen, and
those seemed the right and proper names, and perhaps neither of us suspected that we had ever borne others; or, if we
did suspect it, it was probably not a matter of consequence.

She had been beautiful ten years before; she was just as
beautiful still; girlishly young and sweet and innocent, and
she was still that now. She had had blue eyes, a hair of flossy
gold before; she had black hair now, and dark-brown eyes. I
noted these differences, but they did not suggest change; to
me she was the same girl she was before, absolutely. It never
occurred to me to ask what became of the log house; I doubt
if I even thought of it. We were living in a simple and natural
and beautiful world where everything that happened was natural and right, and was not perplexed with the unexpected or
with any forms of surprise, and so there was no occasion for
explanations and no interest attaching to such things.

We had a dear and pleasant time together, and were like a
couple of ignorant and contented children. Helen had a summer hat on. She took it off presently and said, "It was in the

way; now you can kiss me better." It seemed to me merely a bit of courteous and considerate wisdom, nothing more; and a natural thing for her to think of and do. We went wandering through the woods, and came to a limpid and shallow stream a matter of three yards wide. She said:

"I must not get my feet wet, dear; carry me over."

I took her in my arms and gave her my hat to hold. This was to keep my own feet from getting wet. I did not know why this should have that effect; I merely knew it; and she knew it, too. I crossed the stream, and said I would go on carrying her, because it was so pleasant; and she said it was pleasant to her, too, and wished we had thought of it sooner. It seemed to me a pity that we should have walked so far, both of us on foot, when we could have been having this higher enjoyment; and I spoke of it regretfully, as a something lost which could never be got back. She was troubled about it, too, and said there must be some way to get it back; and she would think. After musing deeply a little while she looked up radiant and proud, and said she had found it.

"Carry me back and start over again."

I can see, now, that that was no solution, but at the time it seemed luminous with intelligence, and I believed that there was not another little head in the world that could have worked out that difficult problem with such swiftness and success. I told her that, and it pleased her; and she said she was glad it all happened, so that I could see how capable she was. After thinking a moment she added that it was "quite atreous." The words seemed to mean something, I do not know why: in fact, it seemed to cover the whole ground and leave nothing more to say; I admired the nice aptness and the flashing felicity of the phrase, and was filled with respect for the marvelous mind that had been able to engender it. I think less of it now. It is a noticeable fact that the intellectual coinage of Dreamland often passes for more there than it would fetch here. Many a time in after years my dream-sweetheart threw off golden sayings which crumbled to ashes under my pencil when I was setting them down in my note-book after breakfast.

I carried her back and started over again; and all the long afternoon I bore her in my arms, miles upon miles, and it never occurred to either of us that there was anything remarkable in a youth like me being able to carry that sweet bundle around half a day without some sense of fatigue or need of rest. There are many dream-worlds, but none is so rightly and reasonably and pleasantly arranged as that one.

After dark we reached a great plantation-house, and it was her home. I carried her in, and the family knew me and I knew them, although we had not met before; and the mother asked me with ill-disguised anxiety how much twelve times fourteen was, and I said a hundred and thirty-five, and she put it down on a piece of paper, saying it was her habit in the process of perfecting her education not to trust important particulars to her memory; and her husband was offering me a chair, but noticed that Helen was asleep, so he said it would be best not to disturb her; and he backed me softly against a wardrobe and said I could stand more easily now; then a negro came in, bowing humbly, with his slouch-hat in his hand, and asked me if I would have my measure taken. The question did not surprise me, but it confused me and worried me, and I said I should like to have advice about it. He started toward the door to call advisers; then he and the family and the lights began to grow dim, and in a few moments the place was pitch dark; but straightway there came a flood of moonlight and a gust of cold wind, and I found myself crossing a frozen lake, and my arms were empty. The wave of grief that swept through me woke me up, and I was sitting at my desk in the newspaper office in San Francisco, and I noticed by the clock that I had been asleep less than two minutes. And what was of more consequence, I was twenty-nine years old.

That was 1864. The next year and the year after I had momentary glimpses of my dream-sweetheart, but nothing more. These are set down in my note-books under their proper dates, but with no talks nor other particulars added; which is sufficient evidence to me that there were none to add. In both of these instances there was the sudden meeting and recognition, the eager approach, then the instant disappearance, leaving the world empty and of no worth. I remember the two images quite well; in fact, I remember all the images of that spirit, and can bring them before me without help of my note-book. The habit of writing down my dreams of all sorts while they were fresh in my mind, and then studying them and rehearsing them and trying to find out what the source of dreams is, and which of the two or three separate persons inhabiting us is their architect, has given me a good dream-memory—a thing which is not usual with people, for few drill the dream-memory, and no memory can be kept strong without that.

I spent a few months in the Hawaiian Islands in 1866, and in October of that year I delivered my maiden lecture; it was in San Francisco. In the following January I arrived in New York, and had just completed my thirty-first year. In that year I saw my platonic dream-sweetheart again. In this dream I was again standing on the stage of the Opera House in San Francisco, ready to lecture, and with the audience vividly in-dividualized before me in the strong light. I began, spoke a few words, and stopped, cold with fright; for I discovered that I had no subject, no text, nothing to talk about. I choked for a while, then got out a few words, a lame, poor attempt at humor. The house made no response. There was a miserable pause, then another attempt, and another failure. There were a few scornful laughs; otherwise the house was silent, unsmil-ingly austere, deeply offended. I was consuming with shame. In my distress I tried to work upon its pity. I began to make servile apologies, mixed with gross and ill-timed flatteries, and to beg and plead for forgiveness; this was too much, and the people broke into insulting cries, whistlings, hootings, and cat-calls, and in the midst of this they rose and began to struggle in a confused mass toward the door. I stood dazed and helpless, looking out over this spectacle, and thinking how everybody would be talking about it next day, and I could not show myself in the streets. When the house was become wholly empty and still, I sat down on the only chair that was on the stage and bent my head down on the reading-desk to shut out the look of that place. Soon that familiar dream-voice spoke my name, and swept all my troubles away:

"Robert!"

I answered:

"Agnes!"

The next moment we two were lounging up the blossomy

gorge called the Iao Valley, in the Hawaiian Islands. I recognized, without any explanations, that Robert was not my name, but only a pet name, a common noun, and meant "dear"; and both of us knew that Agnes was not a name, but only a pet name, a common noun, whose spirit was affectionate, but not conveyable with exactness in any but the dream-language. It was about the equivalent of "dear," but the dream-vocabulary shaves meanings finer and closer than do the world's day-time dictionaries. We did not know why those words should have those meanings; we had used words which had no existence in any known language, and had expected them to be understood, and they were understood. In my note-books there are several letters from this dream-sweetheart, in some unknown tongue—presumably dream-tongue—with translations added. I should like to be master of that tongue, then I could talk in shorthand. Here is one of those letters—the whole of it:

"Rax oha tal."

Translation.—"When you receive this it will remind you that I long to see your face and touch your hand, for the comfort of it and the peace."

It is swifter than waking thought; for thought is not thought at all, but only a vague and formless fog until it is articulated into words.

We wandered far up the fairy gorge, gathering the beautiful flowers of the ginger-plant and talking affectionate things, and tying and retying each other's ribbons and cravats, which didn't need it; and finally sat down in the shade of a tree and climbed the vine-hung precipices with our eyes, up and up and up toward the sky to where the drifting scarfs of white mist clove them across and left the green summits floating pale and remote, like spectral islands wandering in the deeps of space; and then we descended to earth and talked again.

"How still it is—and soft, and balmy, and reposeful! I could never tire of it. You like it, don't you, Robert?"

"Yes, and I like the whole region—all the islands. Maui. It is a darling island. I have been here before. Have you?"

"Once, but it wasn't an island then."

"What was it?"

"It was a sufa."

I understood. It was the dream-word for "part of a continent."

"What were the people like?"

"They hadn't come yet. There weren't any."

"Do you know, Agnes—that is Haleakala, the dead volcano, over there across the valley; was it here in your friend's time?"

"Yes, but it was burning."

"Do you travel much?"

"I think so. Not here much, but in the stars a good deal."

"Is it pretty there?"

She used a couple of dream-words for "You will go with me some time and you will see." Non-committal, as one perceives now, but I did not notice it then.

A man-of-war-bird lit on her shoulder; I put out my hand and caught it. Its feathers began to fall out, and it turned into a kitten; then the kitten's body began to contract itself to a ball and put out hairy, long legs, and soon it was a tarantula; I was going to keep it, but it turned into a star-fish, and I threw it away. Agnes said it was not worth while to try to keep things; there was no stability about them. I suggested rocks; but she said a rock was like the rest; it wouldn't stay. She picked up a stone, and it turned into a bat and flew away. These curious matters interested me, but that was all; they did not stir my wonder.

While we were sitting there in the Iao gorge talking, a Kanaka came along who was wrinkled and bent and white-headed, and he stopped and talked to us in the native tongue, and we understood him without trouble and answered him in his own speech. He said he was a hundred and thirty years old, and he remembered Captain Cook well, and was present when he was murdered; saw it with his own eyes, and also helped. Then he showed us his gun, which was of strange make, and he said it was his own invention and was to shoot arrows with, though one loaded it with powder and it had a percussion lock. He said it would carry a hundred miles. It seemed a reasonable statement; I had no fault to find with it, and it did not in any way surprise me. He loaded it and fired an arrow aloft, and it darted into the sky and vanished. Then he went his way, saying that the arrow would fall near us in half an hour, and would go many yards into the earth, not minding the rocks.

I took the time, and we waited, reclining upon the mossy slant at the base of a tree, and gazing into the sky. By and by there was a hissing sound, followed by a dull impact, and Agnes uttered a groan. She said, in a series of fainting gasps:

"Take me to your arms—it passed through me—hold me to your heart—I am afraid to die—closer—closer. It is growing dark—I cannot see you. Don't leave me—where are you? You are not gone? You will not leave me? I would not leave you."

Then her spirit passed; she was clay in my arms.

The scene changed in an instant, and I was awake and crossing Bond Street in New York with a friend, and it was snowing hard. We had been talking, and there had been no observable gaps in the conversation. I doubt if I had made any more than two steps while I was asleep. I am satisfied that even the most elaborate and incident-crowded dream is seldom more than a few seconds in length. It would not cost me very much of a strain to believe in Mohammed's seventy-year dream, which began when he knocked his glass over, and ended in time for him to catch it before the water was spilled.

Within a quarter of an hour I was in my quarters, undressed, ready for bed, and was jotting down my dream in my note-book. A striking thing happened now. I finished my notes, and was just going to turn out the gas when I was caught with a most strenuous gape, for it was very late and I was very drowsy. I fell asleep and dreamed again. What now follows occurred while I was asleep; and when I woke again the gape had completed itself, but not long before, I think, for I was still on my feet. I was in Athens—a city which I had not then seen, but I recognized the Parthenon from the pictures, although it had a fresh look and was in perfect repair. I passed by it and climbed a grassy hill toward a palatial sort of mansion which was built of red terra-cotta and had a spacious portico, whose roof was supported by a rank of fluted columns with Corinthian capitals. It was noonday, but I met no one. I passed into the house and entered the first room. It was very large and light, its walls were of polished and richly tinted and veined onyx, and its floor was a pictured pattern in soft colors laid in tiles. I noted the details of the furniture and the ornaments—a thing which I should not have been likely to do when awake—and they took sharp hold and remained in my memory; they are not really dim yet, and this was more than thirty years ago.

There was a person present—Agnes. I was not surprised to see her, but only glad. She was in the simple Greek costume, and her hair and eyes were different as to color from those she had had when she died in the Hawaiian Islands half an hour before, but to me she was exactly her own beautiful little self as I had always known her, and she was still fifteen, and I was seventeen once more. She was sitting on an ivory settee, crocheting something or other, and had her crewels in a shallow willow work-basket in her lap. I sat down by her and we began to chat in the usual way. I remembered her death, but the pain and the grief and the bitterness which had been so sharp and so desolating to me at the moment that it happened had wholly passed from me now, and had left not a scar. I was grateful to have her back, but there was no realizable sense that she had ever been gone, and so it did not occur to me to speak about it, and she made no reference to it herself. It may be that she had often died before, and knew that there was nothing lasting about it, and consequently nothing important enough in it to make conversation out of.

When I think of that house and its belongings, I recognize what a master in taste and drawing and color and arrangement is the dream-artist who resides in us. In my waking hours, when the inferior artist in me is in command, I cannot draw even the simplest picture with a pencil, nor do anything with a brush and colors; I cannot bring before my mind's eye the detailed image of any building known to me except my own house at home; of St. Paul's, St. Peter's, the Eiffel Tower, the Taj, the Capitol at Washington, I can reproduce only portions, partial glimpses; the same with Niagara Falls, the Matterhorn, and other familiar things in nature; I cannot bring before my mind's eye the face or figure of any human being known to me; I have seen my family at breakfast within the past two hours; I cannot bring their images before me, I do not know how they look; before me, as I write, I see a little grove of young trees in the garden; high above them projects the slender lance of a young pine, beyond it is a glimpse of the upper half of a dull-white chimney covered by an A-shaped little roof shingled with brown-red tiles, and half a mile away is a hill-top densely wooded, and the red is cloven by a curved, wide vacancy, which is smooth and grass-clad; I cannot shut my eyes and reproduce that picture as a whole at all, nor any single detail of it except the grassy curve, and that but vaguely and fleetingly.

But my dream-artist can draw anything, and do it perfectly; he can paint with all the colors and all the shades, and do it with delicacy and truth; he can place before me vivid images of palaces, cities, hamlets, hovels, mountains, valleys, lakes, skies, glowing in sunlight or moonlight, or veiled in driving gusts of snow or rain, and he can set before me people who are intensely alive, and who feel, and express their feelings in their faces, and who also talk and laugh, sing and swear. And when I wake I can shut my eyes and bring back those people, and the scenery and the buildings; and not only in general view, but often in nice detail. While Agnes and I sat talking in that grand Athens house, several stately Greeks entered from another part of it, disputing warmly about something or other, and passed us by with courteous recognition; and among them was Socrates. I recognized him by his nose. A moment later the house and Agnes and Athens vanished away, and I was in my quarters in New York again and reaching for my note-book.

In our dreams—I know it!—we do make the journeys we seem to make; we do see the things we seem to see; the people, the horses, the cats, the dogs, the birds, the whales, are real, not chimeras; they are living spirits, not shadows; and they are immortal and indestructible. They go whither they will; they visit all resorts, all points of interest, even the twinkling suns that wander in the wastes of space. That is where those strange mountains are which slide from under our feet while we walk, and where those vast caverns are whose bewildering avenues close behind us and in front when we are lost, and shut us in. We know this because there are no such things here, and they must be there, because there is no other place.

This tale is long enough, and I will close it now. In the forty-four years that I have known my Dreamland sweetheart, I have seen her once in two years on an average. Mainly these were glimpses, but she was always immediately recognizable, notwithstanding she was so given to repairing herself and getting up doubtful improvements in her hair and eyes. She was always fifteen, and looked it and acted it; and I was always seventeen, and never felt a day older. To me she is a real person, not a fiction, and her sweet and innocent society has been one of the prettiest and pleasantest experiences of my life. I know that to you her talk will not seem of the first intellectual order; but you should hear her in Dreamland— then you would see!

I saw her a week ago, just for a moment. Fifteen, as usual, and I seventeen, instead of going on sixty-three, as I was when I went to sleep. We were in India, and Bombay was in sight; also Windsor Castle, its towers and battlements veiled in a delicate haze, and from it the Thames flowed, curving and winding between its swarded banks, to our feet. I said:

"There is no question about it, England is the most beautiful of all the countries."

Her face lighted with approval, and she said, with that sweet and earnest irrelevance of hers:

"It is, because it is so marginal."

Then she disappeared. It was just as well; she could probably have added nothing to that rounded and perfect statement without damaging its symmetry.

This glimpse of her carries me back to Maui, and that time when I saw her gasp out her young life. That was a terrible thing to me at the time. It was preternaturally vivid; and the pain and the grief and the misery of it to me transcended many sufferings that I have known in waking life. For everything in a dream is more deep and strong and sharp and real than is ever its pale imitation in the unreal life which is ours when we go about awake and clothed with our artificial selves in this vague and dull-tinted artificial world. When we die we shall slough off this cheap intellect, perhaps, and go abroad into Dreamland clothed in our real selves, and aggrandized and enriched by the command over the mysterious mental magician who is here not our slave, but only our guest.

*1898*

# The Great Dark

## BEFORE IT HAPPENED

### STATEMENT BY MRS. EDWARDS

We were in no way prepared for this dreadful thing. We were a happy family, we had been happy from the beginning; we did not know what trouble was, we were not thinking of it nor expecting it.

My husband was thirty-five years old, and seemed ten years younger, for he was one of those fortunate people who by nature are overcharged with breezy spirits and vigorous health, and from whom cares and troubles slide off without making any impression. He was my ideal, and indeed my idol. In my eyes he was everything that a man ought to be, and in spirit and body beautiful. We were married when I was a girl of 16, and we now had two children, comely and dear little creatures: Jessie, 8 years old, and Bessie, 6.

The house had been in a pleasant turmoil all day, this 19th of March, for it was Jessie's birthday. Henry (my husband) had romped with the children till I was afraid he would tire them out and unfit them for their party in the evening, which was to be a children's fancy dress dance; and so I was glad when at last in the edge of the evening he took them to our bedroom to show them the grandest of all the presents, the microscope. I allowed them fifteen minutes for this show. I would put the children into their costumes, then, and have them ready to receive their great flock of little friends and the accompanying parents. Henry would then be free to jot down in short-hand (he was a past-master in that art) an essay which he was to read at the social club the next night. I would show the children to him in their smart costumes when the party should be over and the good-night kisses due.

I left the three in a state of great excitement over the microscope, and at the end of the fifteen minutes I returned for the children. They and their papa were examining the wonders of a drop of water through a powerful lens. I delivered the children to a maid and they went away. Henry said—

"I will take forty winks and then go to work. But I will

297

make a new experiment with the drop of water first. Won't you please strengthen the drop with the merest touch of Scotch whisky and stir up the animals?"

Then he threw himself on the sofa and before I could speak he uttered a snore. That came of romping the whole day. In reaching for the whisky decanter I knocked off the one that contained brandy and it broke. The noise stopped the snore. I stooped and gathered up the broken glass hurriedly in a towel, and when I rose to put it out of the way he was gone. I dipped a broomstraw in the Scotch whisky and let a wee drop fall upon the glass slide where the water-drop was, then I crossed to the glass door to tell him it was ready. But he had lit the gas and was at his table writing. It was the rule of the house not to disturb him when he was at work; so I went about my affairs in the picture gallery, which was our house's ballroom.

### STATEMENT BY MR. EDWARDS

We were experimenting with the microscope. And pretty ignorantly. Among the little glass slides in the box we found one labeled "section of a fly's eye." In its centre was faintly visible a dot. We put it under a low-power lens and it showed up like a fragment of honey-comb. We put it under a stronger lens and it became a window-sash. We put it under the most powerful lens of all, then there was room in the field for only one pane of the several hundred. We were childishly delighted and astonished at the magnifying capacities of that lens, and said, "Now we can find out if there really are living animals in a drop of water, as the books say."

We brought some stale water from a puddle in the carriage-house where some rotten hay lay soaking, sucked up a drop-perful and allowed a tear of it to fall on a glass slide. Then we worked the screws and brought the lens down until it almost touched the water; then shut an eye and peered eagerly down through the barrel. A disappointment—nothing showed. Then we worked the screws again and made the lens *touch* the water. Another disappointment—nothing visible. Once more we worked the screws and projected the lens hard *against* the glass slide itself. *Then* we saw the animals! Not frequently, but now and then. For a time there would be a great empty blank; then a monster would enter one horizon of this great white sea made so splendidly luminous by the reflector and go plowing across and disappear beyond the opposite horizon. Others would come and go at intervals and disappear. The lens was pressing *against* the glass slide; therefore how could those bulky creatures crowd through between and not get stuck? Yet they swam with perfect freedom; it was plain that they had all the room and all the water that they needed. Then how unimaginably little they must be! Moreover, that wide circular sea which they were traversing was only a small part of our drop of stale water; it was not as big as the head of a pin; whereas the entire drop, flattened out on the glass, was as big around as a child's finger-ring. If we could have gotten the whole drop under the lens we could have seen those gruesome fishes swim leagues and leagues before they dwindled out of sight at the further shore!

I threw myself on the sofa profoundly impressed by what I had seen, and oppressed with thinkings. An ocean in a drop of water—and unknown, uncharted, unexplored by man! By man, who gives all his time to the Africas and the poles, with this unsearched marvelous world right at his elbow. Then the Superintendent of Dreams appeared at my side, and we talked it over. He was willing to provide a ship and crew, but said—

"It will be like any other voyage of the sort—not altogether a holiday excursion."

"That is all right; it is not an objection."

"You and your crew will be much diminished, as to size, but you need not trouble about that, as you will not be aware of it. Your ship itself, stuck upon the point of a needle, would not be discoverable except through a microscope of very high power."

"I do not mind these things. Get a crew of whalers. It will be well to have men who will know what to do in case we have trouble with those creatures."

"Better still if you avoid them."

"I shall avoid them if I can, for they have done me no harm, and I would not wantonly hurt any creature, but I shan't run from them. They have an ugly look, but I thank

God I am not afraid of the ugliest that ever plowed a drop of water."

"You think so *now*, with your five feet eight, but it will be a different matter when the mote that floats in a sunbeam is Mont Blanc compared to you."

"It is no matter; you have seen me face dangers before—"

"Finish with your orders—the night is slipping away."

"Very well, then. Provide me a naturalist to tell me the names of the creatures we see; and let the ship be a comfortable one and perfectly appointed and provisioned, for I take my family with me."

Half a minute later (as it seemed to me), a hoarse voice broke on my ear—

"Topsails all—let go the lee brace—sheet home the stuns'l boom—hearty, now, and all together!"

I turned out, washed the sleep out of my eyes with a dash of cold water, and stepped out of my cabin, leaving Alice quietly sleeping in her berth. It was a blustering night and dark, and the air was thick with a driving mist out of which the tall masts and bellying clouds of sail towered spectrally, faintly flecked here and there aloft by the smothered signal lanterns. The ship was heaving and wallowing in the heavy seas, and it was hard to keep one's footing on the moist deck. Everything was dimmed to obliteration, almost; the only thing sharply defined was the foamy mane of white water, sprinkled with phosphorescent sparks, which broke away from the lee bow. Men were within twenty steps of me, but I could not make out their figures; I only knew they were there by their voices. I heard the quartermaster report to the second mate—

"Eight bells, sir."

"Very well—make it so."

Then I heard the muffled sound of the distant bell, followed by a far-off cry—

"Eight bells and a cloudy morning—anchor watch turn out!"

I saw the glow of a match photograph a pipe and part of a face against a solid bank of darkness, and groped my way thither and found the second mate.

"What of the weather, mate?"

"I don't see that it's any better, sir, than it was the first day out, ten days ago; if anything it's worse—thicker and blacker, I mean. You remember the spitting snow-flurries we had that night?"

"Yes."

"Well, we've had them again to-night. And hail and sleet besides, b'George! And here it comes again."

We stepped into the sheltering lee of the galley, and stood there listening to the lashing of the hail along the deck and the singing of the wind in the cordage. The mate said—

"I've been at sea thirty years, man and boy, but for a level ten-day stretch of unholy weather this bangs anything I ever struck, north of the Horn—if we *are* north of it. For I'm blest if I know *where* we are—do you?"

It was an embarrassing question. I had been asked it very confidentially by my captain, long ago, and had been able to state that I didn't know; and had been discreet enough not to go into any particulars; but this was the first time that any officer of the ship had approached me with the matter. I said—

"Well, no, I'm not a sailor, but I am surprised to hear *you* say you don't know where we are."

He was caught. It was his turn to be embarrassed. First he began to hedge, and vaguely let on that perhaps he did know, after all; but he made a lame fist of it, and presently gave it up and concluded to be frank and take me into his confidence.

"I'm going to be honest with you, sir—and don't give me away." He put his mouth close to my ear and sheltered it against the howling wind with his hand to keep from having to shout, and said impressively, "Not only I don't know where we are, sir, but by God the captain himself don't know!"

I had met the captain's confession by pretending to be frightened and distressed at having engaged a man who was ignorant of his business; and then he had changed his note and told me he had only meant that he had lost his bearings in the thick weather—a thing which would rectify itself as soon as he could get a glimpse of the sun. But I was willing to let the mate tell me all he would, so long as I was not to "give it away."

"No, sir, he don't know where he is; lets on to, but he don't. I mean, he lets on to the crew, and his daughters, and young Phillips the purser, and of course to you and your family, but here lately he don't let on any more to the chief mate and me. And worried? I tell you he's worried plumb to his vitals."

"I must say I don't much like the look of this, Mr. Turner."

"Well, don't let on, sir; keep it to yourself—maybe it'll come out all right; hope it will. But you look at the facts— just look at the facts. We sail north—see? North-and-by-east-half-east, to be exact. Noon the fourth day out, heading for Sable island—ought to see it, weather rather thin for *this* voyage. *Don't* see it. Think the dead reckoning ain't right, maybe. We bang straight along, all the afternoon. No Sable island. *Damned if we didn't run straight over it!* It warn't there. What do you think of that?"

"Dear me, it is awful—awful—if true."

"*If* true. Well, it *is* true. True as anything that ever was, I take my oath on it. And then Greenland. We three banked our hopes on Greenland. Night before last we couldn't sleep for uneasiness; just anxiety, you know, to see if Greenland was going to be there. By the dead reckoning she was due to be in sight along anywhere from five to seven in the morning, if clear enough. But we staid on deck all night. Of course two of us had no business there, and had to scuttle out of the way whenever a man came along, or they would have been suspicious. But five o'clock came, seven o'clock, eight o'clock, ten o'clock, and at last twelve—and then the captain groaned and gave in! He knew well enough that if there had been any Greenland left we'd have knocked a corner off of it long before that."

"This is appalling!"

"You may hunt out a bigger word than that and it won't cover it, sir. And Lord, to see the captain, gray as ashes, sweating and worrying over his chart all day yesterday and all day to-day, and spreading his compasses here and spreading them there, and getting suspicious of his chronometer, and damning the dead-reckoning—just suffering death and taxes, you know, and me and the chief mate helping and suffering, and that purser and the captain's oldest girl spooning and cackling around, just in heaven! I'm a poor man, sir, but if I could buy out half of each of 'em's ignorance and put it together and make it a whole, blamed if I wouldn't put up my last nickel to do it, you hear *me*. Now—"

A wild gust of wind drowned the rest of his remark and smothered us in a fierce flurry of snow and sleet. He darted away and disappeared in the gloom, but first I heard his voice hoarsely shouting—

"Turn out, all hands, shorten sail!"

There was a rush of feet along the deck, and then the gale brought the dimmed sound of far-off commands—

"Mizzen foretop halyards there—all clue-garnets heave and away—now then, with a will—sheet home!"

And then the plaintive notes that told that the men were handling the kites—

> "If you get there, before I do—
>    Hi-ho-o-o, roll a man down;
>  If you get there before I do,
>    O, give a man time to roll a man down!"

By and by all was still again. Meantime I had shifted to the other side of the galley to get out of the storm, and there Mr. Turner presently found me.

"That's a specimen," said he. "I've never struck any such weather anywheres. You are bowling along on a wind that's as steady as a sermon, and just as likely to last, and before you can say Jack Robinson the wind whips around from weather to lee, and if you don't jump for it you'll have your canvas blown out of the cat-heads and sailing for heaven in rags and tatters. I've never seen anything to begin with it. But then I've never been in the middle of Greenland before—in a *ship*— middle of where it *used* to be, I mean. Would it worry you if I was to tell you something, sir?"

"Why, no, I think not. What is it?"

"Let me take a turn up and down, first, to see if anybody's in earshot." When he came back he said, "What should you think if you was to see a whale with hairy spider-legs to it as long as the foretogallant backstay and as big around as the mainmast?"

I recognized the creature; I had seen it in the microscope. But I didn't say so. I said—

"I should think I had a little touch of the jimjams."

"The very thing *I* thought, so help me! It was the third day out, at a quarter to five in the morning. I was out astraddle of the bowsprit in the drizzle, bending on a scuttle-butt, for I don't trust that kind of a job to a common sailor, when all of a sudden that creature plunged up out of the sea the way a porpoise does, not a hundred yards away—I saw two hundred and fifty feet of him and his fringes—and then he turned in the air like a triumphal arch, shedding Niagaras of water, and plunged head first under the sea with an awful swash of sound, and by that time we were close aboard him and in another ten yards we'd have hit him. It was my belief that he tried to hit *us*, but by the mercy of God he was out of practice. The lookout on the foc's'le was the only man around, and thankful I was, or there could have been a mutiny. He was asleep on the binnacle—they always sleep on the binnacle, it's the best place to see from—and it woke him up and he said, "Good land, what's that, sir?" and I said, "It's nothing, but it *might* have been, for any good a stump like you is for a lookout." I was pretty far gone, and said I was sick, and made him help me onto the foc's'le; and then I went straight off and took the pledge; for I had been going it pretty high for a week before we sailed, and I made up my mind that I'd rather go dry the rest of my life than see the like of that thing again."

"Well, I'm glad it was only the jimjams."

"Wait a minute, I ain't done. Of course I didn't enter it on the log—"

"Of course not—"

"For a man in his right mind don't put nightmares in the log. He only puts the word 'pledge' in, and takes credit for it if anybody inquires; and knows it will please the captain, and hopes it'll get to the owners. Well, two days later the chief mate took the pledge!"

"You don't mean it!"

"Sure as I'm standing here. I saw the word on the book. I

didn't say anything, but I felt encouraged. Now then, listen to this: day before yesterday I'm dumm'd if the *captain* didn't take the pledge!"

"Oh, come!"

"It's a true bill—I take my oath. There was the word. Then we begun to put this and that together, and next we began to look at each other kind of significant and willing, you know; and of course giving the captain the pre*cee*dence, for it wouldn't become *us* to begin, and we nothing but mates. And so yesterday, sure enough, out comes the captain—and we called his hand. Said he was out astern in a snow-flurry about dawn, and saw a creature shaped like a wood-louse and as big as a turreted monitor, go racing by and tearing up the foam, in chase of a fat animal the size of an elephant and creased like a caterpillar—and saw it dive after it and disappear; and so he begun to prepare *his* soul for the pledge and break it to his entrails."

"It's terrible!"

"The pledge?—you bet your bottom dollar. If I—"

"No, I don't mean the pledge; I mean it is terrible to be lost at sea among such strange, uncanny brutes."

"Yes, there's something in that, too, I don't deny it. Well, the thing that the mate saw was like one of these big long lubberly canal boats, and it was ripping along like the Empire Express; and the look of it gave him the cold shivers, and so he begun to arrange *his* earthly affairs and go for the pledge."

"Turner, it is dreadful—dreadful. Still, good has been done; for these pledges—"

"Oh, they're off!"

"Off?"

"Cert'nly. Can't be jimjams; couldn't all three of us have them at once, it ain't likely. What do you want with a pledge when there ain't any occasion for it? *There* he goes!"

He was gone like a shot, and the night swallowed him up. Now all of a sudden, with the wind still blowing hard, the seas went down and the deck became as level as a billiard table! Were *all* the laws of Nature suspended? It made my flesh creep; it was like being in a haunted ship. Pretty soon the mate came back panting, and sank down on a cable-tier, and said—

"Oh, this is an awful life; I don't think we can stand it long. There's too many horribles in it. Let me pant a little, I'm in a kind of a collapse."

"What's the trouble?"

"Drop down by me, sir—I mustn't shout. There—now you're all right." Then he said sorrowfully, "I reckon we've got to take it again."

"Take what?"

"The pledge."

"Why?"

"Did you see that thing go by?"

"What thing?"

"A *man*."

"No. What of it?"

"This is four times that *I've* seen it; and the mate has seen it, and so has the captain. Haven't you ever seen it?"

"I suppose not. Is there anything extraordinary about it?"

"Extra-*or*dinary? Well, I should *say*!"

"How is it extraordinary?"

He said in an awed voice that was almost like a groan—

"Like this, for instance: you put your hand on him and *he ain't there*."

"What do you mean, Turner?"

"It's as true as I'm sitting here, I wish I may never stir. The captain's getting morbid and religious over it, and says he wouldn't give a damn for ship and crew if that thing stays aboard."

"You curdle my blood. What is the man like? Isn't it just one of the crew, that you glimpse and lose in the dark?"

"You take note of *this*: it wears a broad slouch hat and a long cloak. Is that a whaler outfit, I'll ask you? A minute ago I was as close to him as I am to you; and I made a grab for him, and what did I get? A handful of air, that's all. There warn't a sign of him left."

"I do hope the pledge will dispose of it. It must be a work of the imagination, or the crew would have seen it."

"We're afraid they have. There was a deal of whispering going on last night in the middle watch. The captain dealt out grog, and got their minds on something else; but he is mighty uneasy, because of course he don't want you or your family to hear about that man, and would take my scalp if he knew what I'm doing now; and besides, if such a thing got a start with the crew, there'd be a mutiny, sure."

"I'll keep quiet, of course; still, I think it must be an output of imaginations overstrung by the strange fishes you think you saw; and I am hoping that the pledge—"

"I want to take it now. And I will."

"I'm witness to it. Now come to my parlor and I'll give you a cup of hot coffee and—"

"Oh, my goodness, there it is again! . . . It's gone. . . . Lord, it takes a body's breath . . . It's the jimjams I've got—I know it for sure. I want the coffee; it'll do me good. If you could help me a little, sir—I feel as weak as Sabbath grog."

We groped along the sleety deck to my door and entered, and there in the bright glare of the lamps sat (as I was half expecting) the man of the long cloak and the slouch hat, on the sofa,—my friend the Superintendent of Dreams. I was annoyed, for a moment, for of course I expected Turner to make a jump at him, get nothing, and be at once in a more miserable state than he already was. I reached for my cabin door and closed it, so that Alice might not hear the scuffle and get a fright. But there wasn't any. Turner went on talking, and took no notice of the Superintendent. I gave the Superintendent a grateful look; and it was an honest one, for this thing of making himself visible and scaring people could do harm.

"Lord, it's good to be in the light, sir," said Turner, rustling comfortably in his yellow oilskins, "it lifts a person's spirits right up. I've noticed that these cussed jimjam blatherskites ain't as apt to show up in the light as they are in the dark, except when you've got the trouble in your attic pretty bad." Meantime we were dusting the snow off each other with towels. "You're mighty well fixed here, sir—chairs and carpets and rugs and tables and lamps and books and everything lovely, and so warm and comfortable and homy; and the roomiest parlor I ever struck in a ship, too. Land, hear the wind, don't she sing! And not a sign of motion!—rip goes the sleet again!—ugly, you bet!—and here? why here it's only just the more cosier on account of it. Dern that jimjam, if I had him in here once I bet you I'd sweat him. Because I don't mind saying that I don't grab at him as earnest as I want to, outside there, and ain't as disappointed as I ought to be when I don't get him; but here in the light I ain't afraid of *no* jimjam."

It made the Superintendent of Dreams smile a smile that was full of pious satisfaction to hear him. I poured a steaming cup of coffee and handed it to Turner and told him to sit where he pleased and make himself comfortable and at home; and before I could interfere he had sat down in the Superintendent of Dreams' lap!—no, sat down *through* him. It cost me a gasp, but only that, nothing more. The Superintendent of Dreams' head was larger than Turner's, and *surrounded* it, and was a transparent spirit-head fronted with a transparent spirit-face; and this latter smiled at me as much as to say give myself no uneasiness, it is all right. Turner was smiling comfort and contentment at me at the same time, and the double result was very curious, but I could tell the smiles apart without trouble. The Superintendent of Dreams' body enclosed Turner's, but I could see Turner through it, just as one sees objects through thin smoke. It was interesting and pretty. Turner tasted his coffee and set the cup down in front of him with a hearty—

"Now I call that prime! 'George, it makes me feel the way old Cap'n Jimmy Starkweather did, I reckon, the first time he tasted grog after he'd been off his allowance three years. The way of it was this. It was there in Fairhaven by New Bedford, away back in the old early whaling days before I was born; but I heard about it the first day I *was* born, and it was a ripe old tale then, because they keep only the one fleet of yarns in commission down New Bedford-way, and don't ever re-stock and don't ever repair. And I came near hearing it in old Cap'n Jimmy's own presence once, when I was ten years old and he was ninety-two; but I didn't, because the man that asked Cap'n Jimmy to tell about it got crippled and the thing didn't materialize. It was Cap'n Jimmy that crippled him. Land, I thought I sh'd die! The very recollection of it—"

The very recollection of it so powerfully affected him that it shut off his speech and he put his head back and spread his jaws and laughed himself purple in the face. And while he was doing it the Superintendent of Dreams emptied the coffee into the slop bowl and set the cup back where it was before. When the explosion had spent itself Turner swabbed his face with his handkerchief and said—

"There—that laugh has scoured me out and done me good; I hain't had such another one—well, not since I struck *this* ship, now that's sure. I'll whet up and start over."

He took up his cup, glanced into it, and it was curious to observe the two faces that were framed in the front of his head. Turner's was long and distressed; the Superintendent of Dreams' was wide, and broken out of all shape with a convulsion of silent laughter. After a little, Turner said in a troubled way—

"I'm dumm'd if *I* recollect drinking that."

I didn't say anything, though I knew he must be expecting me to say something. He continued to gaze into the cup a while, then looked up wistfully and said—

"Of course I must have drunk it, but I'm blest if I can recollect whether I did or not. Lemme see. First you poured it out, then I set down and put it before me here; next I took a sup and said it was good, and set it down and begun about old Cap'n Jimmy—and then—and then—" He was silent a moment, then said, "It's as far as I can get. It beats me. I reckon that after that I was so kind of full of my story that I didn't notice whether I—." He stopped again, and there was something almost pathetic about the appealing way in which he added, "But I *did* drink it, *didn't* I? You *see* me do it— *didn't* you?"

I hadn't the heart to say no.

"Why, yes, I think I did. I wasn't noticing particularly, but it seems to me that I saw you drink it—in fact, I am about certain of it."

I was glad I told the lie, it did him so much good, and so lightened his spirits, poor old fellow.

"Of course I done it! I'm such a fool. As a general thing I wouldn't care, and I wouldn't bother anything about it; but when there's jimjams around the least little thing makes a person suspicious, you know. If you don't mind, sir—thanks, ever so much." He took a large sup of the new supply, praised it, set the cup down—leaning forward and fencing it around with his arms, with a labored pretense of not noticing that he was doing that—then said—

"Lemme see—where was I? Yes. Well, it happened like this. The Washingtonian Movement started up in those old times, you know, and it was Father Matthew here and Father Matthew there and Father Matthew yonder—nothing but Father Matthew and temperance all over everywheres. And temperance societies? There was millions of them, and everybody joined and took the pledge. We had one in New Bedford. Every last whaler joined—captain, crew and all. All, down to old Cap'n Jimmy. He was an old bach, his grog was his darling, he owned his ship and sailed her himself, he was independent, and he wouldn't give in. So at last they gave it up and quit pestering him. Time rolled along, and he got awful lonesome. There wasn't anybody to drink with, you see, and it got unbearable. So finally the day he sailed for Bering Strait he caved, and sent in his name to the society. Just as he was starting, his mate broke his leg and stopped ashore and he shipped a stranger in his place from down New York way. This fellow didn't belong to any society, and he went aboard fixed for the voyage. Cap'n Jimmy was out three solid years; and all the whole time he had the spectacle of that mate whetting up every day and leading a life that was worth the trouble; and it nearly killed him for envy to see it. Made his mouth water, you know, in a way that was pitiful. Well, he used to get out on the peak of the bowsprit where it was private, and set there and cuss. It was his only relief from his sufferings. Mainly he cussed himself; but when he had used up all his words and couldn't think of any new rotten things to call himself, he would turn his vocabulary over and start fresh and lay into Father Matthew and give *him* down the banks; and then the society; and so put in his watch as satisfactory as he could. Then he would count the days he was out, and try to reckon up about when he could hope to get home and resign from the society and start in on an all-compensating drunk that would make up for lost time. Well, when he was out three thousand years—which was *his* estimate, you know, though really it was only three years—he came rolling down the home-stretch with every rag stretched on his poles. Middle of winter, it was, and terrible cold and stormy. He made the landfall just at sundown and had to stand watch on deck all night of course, and the rigging was caked with ice three inches thick, and the yards was bearded with icicles five foot long, and the snow laid nine inches deep on the deck and hurricanes more of it being shoveled down onto him out of the skies. And so he plowed up and down all night, cussing himself and Father Matthew and the society, and doing it better than he ever done before; and his mouth was watering so, on account of the mate whetting up right in his sight all the time, that every cuss-word come out damp, and froze solid as it fell, and in his insufferable indignation he would hit it a whack with his cane and knock it a hundred yards, and one of them took the mate in the mouth and fetched away a rank of teeth and lowered *his* spirits considerable. He made the dock just at early breakfast time and never waited to tie up, but jumped ashore with his jug in his hand and rushed for the society's quarters like a deer. He met the seckatary coming out and yelled at him—

" 'I've resigned my membership!—I give you just two minutes to scrape my name off your log, d'ye hear?'

"And then the seckatary told him he'd been black-balled three years before—*hadn't ever been a member!* Land, I can't hold in, it's coming again!"

He flung up his arms, threw his head back, spread his jaws, and made the ship quake with the thunder of his laughter, while the Superintendent of Dreams emptied the cup again and set it back in its place. When Turner came out of his fit at last he was limp and exhausted, and sat mopping his tears away and breaking at times into little feebler and feebler barks and catches of expiring laughter. Finally he fetched a deep sigh of comfort and satisfaction, and said—

"Well, it *does* do a person good, no mistake—on a voyage like *this*. I reckon—"

His eye fell on the cup. His face turned a ghastly white—

"By God she's empty again!"

He jumped up and made a sprawling break for the door. I was frightened; I didn't know what he might do—jump overboard, maybe. I sprang in front of him and barred the way, saying, "Come, Turner, be a man, be a man! don't let your imagination run away with you like this"; and over his shoulder I threw a pleading look at the Superintendent of Dreams, who answered my prayer and refilled the cup from the coffee urn.

"Imagination you call it, sir! Can't I *see*?—with my own eyes? Let me go—don't stop me—I can't stand it, I can't stand it!"

"Turner, be reasonable—you know perfectly well your cup isn't empty, and *hasn't* been."

That hit him. A dim light of hope and gratitude shone in his eye, and he said in a quivery voice—

"Say it again—and say it's true. *Is* it true? Honor bright—you wouldn't deceive a poor devil that's—"

"Honor bright, man, I'm not deceiving you—look for yourself."

Gradually he turned a timid and wary glance toward the table; then the terror went out of his face, and he said humbly—

"Well, you see I reckon I hadn't quite got over thinking it happened the first time, and so maybe without me knowing it, that made me kind of suspicious that it would happen again, because the jimjams make you untrustful that way; and so, sure enough, I didn't half look at the cup, and just jumped to the conclusion it *had* happened." And talking so, he moved toward the sofa, hesitated a moment, and then sat down in that figure's body again. "But I'm all right, now, and I'll just shake these feelings off and be a man, as you say."

The Superintendent of Dreams separated himself and moved along the sofa a foot or two away from Turner. I was glad of that; it looked like a truce. Turner swallowed his cup of coffee; I poured another; he began to sip it, the pleasant influence worked a change, and soon he was a rational man again, and comfortable. Now a sea came aboard, hit our deckhouse a stunning thump, and went hissing and seething aft.

"Oh, that's the ticket," said Turner, "the dummdest weather that ever I went pleasure-excursioning in. And how did it get aboard?—You answer me that: there ain't any motion to the ship. These mysteriousnesses—well, they just give me the cold shudders. And that reminds me. Do you mind my calling your attention to another peculiar thing or two?—on conditions as before—solid secrecy, you know."

"I'll keep it to myself. Go on."

"The Gulf Stream's gone to the devil!"

"What do you mean?"

"It's the fact, I wish I may never die. From the day we sailed till now, the water's been the same temperature right along, I'll take my oath. The Gulf Stream don't exist any more; she's gone to the devil."

"It's incredible, Turner! You make me gasp."

"Gasp away, if you want to; if things go on so, you ain't going to forget how for want of practice. It's the wooliest voyage, take it by and large—why, look here! You are a landsman, and there's no telling what a landsman can't overlook if he tries. For instance, have you noticed that the nights and days are exactly alike, and you can't tell one from tother except by keeping tally?"

"Why, yes, I have noticed it in a sort of indifferent general way, but—"

"Have you kept a tally, sir?"

"No, it didn't occur to me to do it."

"I thought so. Now you know, you couldn't keep it in your head, because you and your family are free to sleep as much as you like, and as it's always dark, you sleep a good deal, and you are pretty irregular, naturally. You've all been a little seasick from the start—tea and toast in your own parlor here—no regular time—order it as each of you pleases. You see? You don't go down to meals—*they* would keep tally for you. So you've lost your reckoning. I noticed it an hour ago."

"How?"

"Well, you spoke of *to-night*. It ain't to-night at all; it's just noon, now."

"The fact is, I don't believe I have often thought of its being day, since we left. I've got into the habit of considering it night all the time; it's the same with my wife and the children."

"There it is, you see. Mr. Edwards, it's perfectly awful; now ain't it, when you come to look at it? Always night— and such dismal nights, too. It's like being up at the pole in the winter time. And I'll ask you to notice another thing: this sky is as empty as my sou-wester there."

"Empty?"

"Yes, sir. I know it. You can't get up a day, in a Christian country, that's so solid black the sun can't make a blurry glow of *some* kind in the sky at high noon—now can you?"

"No, you can't."

"Have you ever seen a suspicion of any such a glow in this sky?"

"Now that you mention it, I haven't."

He dropped his voice and said impressively—

"Because there ain't any *sun*. She's gone where the Gulf Stream twineth."

"Turner! Don't talk like that."

"It's confidential, or I wouldn't. And the moon. She's at the full—by the almanac she is. Why don't *she* make a blur? Because there *ain't* any moon. And moreover—you might rake this oncompleted sky a hundred year with a drag-net and you'd never scoop a star! Why? Because there *ain't* any. Now then, what is your opinion about all this?"

"Turner, it's so gruesome and creepy that I don't like to think about it—and I haven't any. What is yours?"

He said, dismally—

"That the world has come to an end. Look at it yourself. Just look at the facts. Put them together and add them up, and what have you got? No Sable island; no Greenland; no Gulf Stream; no day, no proper night; weather that don't jibe with any sample known to the Bureau; animals that would start a panic in any menagerie, chart no more use than a horse-blanket, and the heavenly bodies gone to hell! And on top of it all, that jimjam that I've put my hand on more than once and he warn't there—I'll swear it. The ship's bewitched. You don't believe in the jim, and I've sort of lost faith myself, here in the bright light; but if this cup of coffee was to—"

The cup began to glide slowly away, along the table. The hand that moved it was not visible to him. He rose slowly to his feet and stood trembling as if with an ague, his teeth knocking together and his glassy eyes staring at the cup. It slid on and on, noiseless; then it rose in the air, gradually reversed itself, poured its contents down the Superintendent's throat—I saw the dark stream trickling its way down through his hazy breast—then it returned to the table, and without sound of contact, rested there. The mate continued to stare at it for as much as a minute; then he drew a deep breath, took up his sou-wester, and without looking to the right or the left, walked slowly out of the room like one in a trance, muttering—

"I've *got* them—I've had the proof."

I said, reproachfully—

"Superintendent, why do you do that?"

"Do what?"

"Play these tricks."

"What harm is it?"

"Harm? It could make that poor devil jump overboard."

"No, he's not as far gone as that."

"For a while he was. He is a good fellow, and it was a pity to scare him so. However there are other matters that I am more concerned about just now."

"Can I help?"

"Why yes, you can; and I don't know any one else that can."

"Very well, go on."

"By the dead-reckoning we have come twenty-three hundred miles."

"The actual distance is twenty-three-fifty."

"Straight as a dart in the one direction—mainly."

"Apparently."

"Why do you say apparently? Haven't we come straight?"

"Go on with the rest. What were you going to say?"

"This. Doesn't it strike you that this is a pretty large drop of water?"

"No. It is about the usual size—six thousand miles across."

"Six thousand miles!"

"Yes."

"Twice as far as from New York to Liverpool?"

"Yes."

"I must say it is more of a voyage than I counted on. And we are not a great deal more than halfway across, yet. When shall we get in?"

"It will be some time yet."

"That is not very definite. Two weeks?"

"More than that."

I was getting a little uneasy.

"But how *much* more? A week?"

"All of that. More, perhaps."

"Why don't you tell me? A month more, do you think?"

"I am afraid so. Possibly two—possibly longer, even."

I was getting seriously disturbed by now.

"Why, we are sure to run out of provisions and water."

"No you'll not. I've looked out for that. It is what you are loaded with."

"Is that so? How does that come?"

"Because the ship is chartered for a voyage of discovery. Ostensibly she goes to England, takes aboard some scientists, then sails for the South pole."

"I see. You are deep."

"I understand my business."

I turned the matter over in my mind a moment, then said—

"It is more of a voyage than I was expecting, but I am not of a worrying disposition, so I do not care, so long as we are not going to suffer hunger and thirst."

"Make yourself easy, as to that. Let the trip last as long as it may, you will not run short of food and water, I go bail for that."

"All right, then. Now explain this riddle to me. Why is it always night?"

"That is easy. All of the drop of water is outside the luminous circle of the microscope except one thin and delicate rim of it. We are in the shadow; consequently in the dark."

"In the shadow of what?"

"Of the brazen end of the lens-holder."

"How can it cover such a spread with its shadow?"

"Because it is several thousand miles in diameter. For dimensions, that is nothing. The glass slide which it is pressing against, and which forms the bottom of the ocean we are sailing upon, is thirty thousand miles long, and the length of the microscope barrel is a hundred and twenty thousand. Now then, if—"

"You make me dizzy. I—"

"If you should thrust that glass slide through what you call the 'great' globe, eleven thousand miles of it would stand out on each side—it would be like impaling an orange on a table-knife. And so—"

"It gives me the head-ache. Are these the fictitious proportions which we and our surroundings and belongings have acquired by being reduced to microscopic objects?"

"They are the proportions, yes—but they are not fictitious. You do not notice that you yourself are in any way diminished in size, do you?"

"No, I am my usual size, so far as I can see."

"The same with the men, the ship and everything?"

"Yes—all natural."

"Very good; nothing but the laws and conditions have undergone a change. You came from a small and very insignificant world. The one you are in now is proportioned according to microscopic standards—that is to say, it is inconceivably stupendous and imposing."

It was food for thought. There was something overpowering in the situation, something sublime. It took me a while to shake off the spell and drag myself back to speech. Presently I said—

"I am content; I do not regret the voyage—far from it. I would not change places with any man in that cramped little world. But tell me—is it always going to be dark?"

"Not if you ever come into the luminous circle under the lens. Indeed you will not find *that* dark!"

"If we ever. What do you mean by that? We are making steady good time; we are cutting across this sea on a straight course."

"Apparently."

"There is no apparently about it."

"You might be going around in a small and not rapidly widening circle."

"Nothing of the kind. Look at the tell-tale compass over your head."

"I see it."

"We changed to this easterly course to satisfy—well, to satisfy everybody but me. It is a pretense of aiming for England—in a drop of water! Have you noticed that needle before?"

"Yes, a number of times."

"To-day, for instance?"

"Yes—often."

"Has it varied a jot?"

"Not a jot."

"Hasn't it always kept the place appointed for it—from the start?"

"Yes, always."

"Very well. First we sailed a northerly course; then tilted easterly; and now it is more so. How is *that* going around in a circle?"

He was silent. I put it at him again. He answered with lazy indifference—

"I merely threw out the suggestion."

"All right, then; cornered; let it stand at that. Whenever you happen to think of an argument in support of it, I shall be glad to hear about it."

He did not like that very well, and muttered something about my being a trifle airy. I retorted a little sharply, and followed it up by finding fault with him again for playing tricks on Turner. He said Turner called him a blatherskite. I said—

"No matter; you let him alone, from this out. And moreover, stop appearing to people—stop it entirely."

His face darkened. He said—

"I would advise you to moderate your manner. I am not used to it, and I am not pleased with it."

The rest of my temper went, then. I said, angrily—

"You may like it or not, just as you choose. And moreover, if my style doesn't suit you, you can end the dream as soon as you please—right now, if you like."

He looked me steadily in the eye for a moment, then said, with deliberation—

"The dream? *Are you quite sure it is a dream?*"

It took my breath away.

"What do you mean? *Isn't* it a dream?"

He looked at me in that same way again; and it made my blood chilly, this time. Then he said—

"You have spent your whole life in this ship. And this is *real* life. Your other life was the dream!"

It was as if he had hit me, it stunned me so. Still looking at me, his lip curled itself into a mocking smile, and he wasted away like a mist and disappeared.

I sat a long time thinking uncomfortable thoughts.

We are strangely made. We think we are wonderful creatures. Part of the time we think that, at any rate. And during that interval we consider with pride our mental equipment, with its penetration, its power of analysis, its ability to reason out clear conclusions from confused facts, and all the lordly rest of it; and then comes a rational interval and disenchants us. Disenchants us and lays us bare to ourselves, and we see that intellectually we are really no great things; that we seldom really know the thing we think we know; that our best-built certainties are but sand-houses and subject to damage from any wind of doubt that blows.

So little a time before, I *knew* that this voyage was a dream, and nothing more; a wee little puff or two of doubt had blown against that certainty, unhelped by fact or argument, and already it was dissolving away. It seemed an incredible thing, and it hurt my pride of intellect, but it had to be confessed.

When I came to consider it, these ten days had been such intense realities!—so intense that by comparison the life I had lived before them seemed distant, indistinct, slipping away and fading out in a far perspective—exactly as a dream does when you sit at breakfast trying to call back its details. I grew steadily more and more nervous and uncomfortable—and a little frightened, though I would not quite acknowledge this to myself.

Then came this disturbing thought: if this transformation goes on, how am I going to conceal it from my wife? Suppose she should say to me, "Henry, there is something the matter with you, you are acting strangely; something is on your mind that you are concealing from me; tell me about it, let me help you"—what answer could I make?

I was *bound* to act strangely if this went on—bound to bury myself in deeps of troubled thought; I should not be able to help it. She had a swift eye to notice, where her heart was concerned, and a sharp intuition, and I was an impotent poor thing in her hands when I had things to hide and she had struck the trail.

I have no large amount of fortitude, staying power. When there is a fate before me I cannot rest easy until I know what it is. I am not able to wait. I want to know, right away. So, I would call Alice, now, and take the consequences. If she drove me into a corner and I found I could not escape, I would act according to my custom—come out and tell her the truth. She had a better head than mine, and a surer instinct in grouping facts and getting their meaning out of them. If I was drifting into dangerous waters, now, she would be sure to detect it and as sure to set me right and save me. I would call her, and keep out of the corner if I could; if I couldn't, why—I couldn't, that is all.

She came, refreshed with sleep, and looking her best self: that is to say, looking like a girl of nineteen, not a matron of twenty-five; she wore a becoming wrapper, or tea gown, or whatever it is called, and it was trimmed with ribbons and limp stuff—lace, I suppose; and she had her hair balled up and nailed to its place with a four-pronged tortoise-shell comb. She brought a basket of pink and gray crewels with her, for she was crocheting a jacket—for the cat, probably, judging by the size of it. She sat down on the sofa and set the basket on the table, expecting to have a chance to get to work by and by; not right away, because a kitten was curled up in it asleep, fitting its circle snugly, and the repose of the children's kittens was a sacred thing and not to be disturbed. She said—

"I noticed that there was no motion—it was what waked me, I think—and I got up to enjoy it, it is such a rare thing."

"Yes, rare enough, dear: we do have the most unaccountably strange weather."

"Do you think so, Henry? Does it seem strange weather to you?"

She looked so earnest and innocent that I was rather startled, and a little in doubt as to what to say. Any sane person could see that it was perfectly devilish weather and crazy beyond imagination, and so how could she feel uncertain about it?

"Well, Alice, I may be putting it too strong, but I don't think so; I think a person may call our weather by any hard name he pleases and be justified."

"Perhaps you are right, Henry. I have heard the sailors talk the same way about it, but I did not think that that meant much, they speak so extravagantly about everything. You are not always extravagant in your speech—often you are, but not always—and so it surprised me a little to hear you." Then she added tranquilly and musingly, "I don't remember any different weather."

It was not quite definite.

"You mean on *this* voyage, Alice."

"Yes, of course. Naturally. I haven't made any other."

She was softly stroking the kitten—and apparently in her right mind. I said cautiously, and with seeming indifference—

"You mean you haven't made any other this year. But the time we went to Europe—well, that was very different weather."

"The time we went to Europe, Henry?"

"Certainly, certainly—when Jessie was a year old."

She stopped stroking the kitty, and looked at me in-quiringly.

"I don't understand you, Henry."

She was not a joker, and she was always truthful. Her re-mark blew another wind of doubt upon my wasting sand-edifice of certainty. Had I only *dreamed* that we went to Europe? It seemed a good idea to put this thought into words.

"Come, Alice, the first thing you know you will be imagin-ing that we went to Europe in a dream."

She smiled, and said—

"Don't let me spoil it, Henry, if it is pleasant to you to think we went. I will consider that we did go, and that I have forgotten it."

"But Alice dear we *did* go!"

"But Henry dear we *didn't* go!"

She had a good head and a good memory, and she was always truthful. My head had been injured by a fall when I was a boy, and the physicians had said at the time that there could be ill effects from it some day. A cold wave struck me, now; perhaps the effects had come. I was losing confidence in the European trip. However, I thought I would make an-other try.

"Alice, I will give you a detail or two; then maybe you will remember."

"A detail or two from the dream?"

"I am not at all sure that it was a dream; and five minutes ago I was sure that it wasn't. It was seven years ago. We went over in the *Batavia*. Do you remember the *Batavia*?"

"I don't, Henry."

"Captain Moreland. Don't you remember him?"

"To me he is a myth, Henry."

"Well, it beats anything. We lived two or three months in London, then six weeks in a private hotel in George Street, Edinburgh—Veitch's. Come!"

"It sounds pleasant, but I have never heard of these things before, Henry."

"And Doctor John Brown, of *Rab and His Friends*—you were ill, and he came every day; and when you were well again he still came every day and took us all around while he paid his visits, and we waited in his carriage while he prescribed for his patients. And he was so dear and lovely. You *must* remember all that, Alice."

"None of it, dear; it is only a dream."

"Why, Alice, have you ever had a dream that remained as distinct as that, and which you could remember so long?"

"So long? It is more than likely that you dreamed it last night."

"No indeed! It has been in my memory seven years."

"Seven years in a dream, yes—it is the way of dreams. They put seven years into two minutes, without any trouble—isn't it so?"

I had to acknowledge that it was.

"It seems almost as if it couldn't have been a dream, Alice; it seems as if you ought to remember it."

"Wait! It begins to come back to me." She sat thinking a while, nodding her head with satisfaction from time to time. At last she said, joyfully, "I remember almost the whole of it, now."

"Good!"

"I am glad I got it back. Ordinarily I remember my dreams very well; but for some reason this one—"

"*This* one, Alice? Do you really consider it a dream, yet?"

"I don't consider anything about it, Henry, I know it; I know it positively."

The conviction stole through me that she must be right,

since she felt so sure. Indeed I almost knew she was. I was privately becoming ashamed of myself now, for mistaking a clever illusion for a fact. So I gave it up, then, and said I would let it stand as a dream. Then I added—

"It puzzles me; even now it seems almost as distinct as the microscope."

"Which microscope?"

"Well, Alice, there's only the one."

"Very well, which one is *that*?"

"Bother it all, the one we examined this ocean in, the other day."

"Where?"

"Why, at home—of course."

"What home?"

"Alice, it's provoking—why, *our* home. In Springport."

"Dreaming again. I've never heard of it."

That was stupefying. There was no need of further beating about the bush; I threw caution aside, and came out frankly.

"Alice, what do you call the life we are leading in this ship? Isn't it a dream?"

She looked at me in a puzzled way and said—

"A dream, Henry? Why should I think that?"

"Oh, dear me, *I* don't know! I thought I did, but I don't. Alice, haven't we ever had a home? Don't you remember one?"

"Why, yes—three. That is, dream-homes, not real ones. I have never regarded them as realities."

"Describe them."

She did it, and in detail; also our life in them. Pleasant enough homes, and easily recognizable by me. I could also recognize an average of 2 out of 7 of the episodes and incidents which she threw in. Then I described the home and the life which (as it appeared to me) we had so recently left. She recognized it—but only as a dream-home. She remembered nothing about the microscope and the children's party. I was in a corner; but it was not the one which I had arranged for.

"Alice, if those were dream-homes, how long have you been in this ship?—you say this is the only voyage you have ever made."

"I don't know. I don't remember. It *is* the only voyage we have made—unless breaking it to pick up this crew of strangers in place of the friendly dear men and officers we had sailed with so many years makes two voyages of it. How I do miss them—Captain Hall, and Williams the sail-maker, and Storrs the chief mate, and—"

She choked up, and the tears began to trickle down her cheeks. Soon she had her handkerchief out and was sobbing.

I realized that I remembered those people perfectly well. Damnation! I said to myself, are we real creatures in a real world, all of a sudden, and have we been feeding on dreams in an imaginary one since nobody knows when—or how *is* it? My head was swimming.

"Alice! Answer me this. Do you know the Superintendent of Dreams?"

"Certainly."

"Have you seen him often?"

"Not often, but several times."

"When did you see him first?"

"The time that Robert the captain's boy was eaten."

"*Eaten?*"

"Yes. Surely you haven't forgotten that?"

"But I have, though. I never heard of it before." (I spoke the truth. For the moment I could not recal the incident.)

Her face was full of reproach.

"I am sorry, if that is so. He was always good to you. If you are jesting, I do not think it is in good taste."

"Now don't treat me like that, Alice, I don't deserve it. I am not jesting, I am in earnest. I mean the boy's memory no offence, but although I remember him I do not remember the circumstance—I swear it. Who ate him?"

"Do not be irreverent, Henry, it is out of place. It was not a *who*, at all."

"What then—a *which*?"

"Yes."

"What kind of a which?"

"A spider-squid. *Now* you remember it I hope."

"Indeed and deed and double-deed I don't, Alice, and it is the real truth. Tell me about it, please."

"I suppose you see, now, Henry, what your memory is

worth. You can remember dream-trips to Europe well enough, but things in real life—even the most memorable and horrible things—pass out of your memory in twelve years. There is something the matter with your mind."

It was very curious. How *could* I have forgotten that tragedy? It must have happened; she was never mistaken in her facts, and she never spoke with positiveness of a thing which she was in any degree uncertain about. And this tragedy— *twelve years* ago—

"Alice, how long *have* we been in this ship?"

"Now how can I know, Henry? It goes too far back. Always, for all I know. The earliest thing I can call to mind was papa's death by the sun-heat and mamma's suicide the same day. I was four years old, then. Surely you must remember that, Henry."

"Yes. . . . Yes. But it is so dim. Tell me about it—refresh my memory."

"Why, you must remember that we were in the edge of a great white glare once for a little while—a day, or maybe two days,—only a little while, I think, but I remember it, because it was the only time I was ever out of the dark, and there was a great deal of talk of it for long afterwards—why, Henry, you *must* remember a wonderful thing like that."

"Wait. Let me think." Gradually, detail by detail the whole thing came back to me; and with it the boy's adventure with the spider-squid; and then I recalled a dozen other incidents, which Alice verified as incidents of our ship-life, and said I had set them forth correctly.

It was a puzzling thing—my freaks of memory; Alice's, too. By testing, it was presently manifest that the vacancies in my ship-life memories were only apparent, not real; a few words by way of reminder enabled me to fill them up, in almost all cases, and give them clarity and vividness. What had caused these temporary lapses? Didn't these very lapses indicate that the ship-life was a dream, and not real?

It made Alice laugh.

I did not see anything foolish in it, or anything to laugh at, and I told her so. And I reminded her that her own memory was as bad as mine, since many and many a conspicuous episode of our land-life was gone from her, even so striking an incident as the water-drop exploration with the microscope—

It made her shout.

I was wounded; and said that if I could not be treated with respect I would spare her the burden of my presence and conversation. She stopped laughing, at once, and threw her arms about my neck. She said she would not have hurt me for the world, but she supposed I was joking; it was quite natural to think I was not in earnest in talking gravely about this and that and the other dream-phantom as if it were a reality.

"But Alice I *was* in earnest, and I *am* in earnest. Look at it—examine it. If the land-life was a dream-life, how is it that you remember so much of it exactly as *I* remember it?"

She was amused again, inside—I could feel the quiver; but there was no exterior expression of it, for she did not want to hurt me again.

"Dear heart, throw the whole matter aside! Stop puzzling over it; it isn't worth it. It is perfectly simple. It is true that I remember a little of that dream-life just as you remember it— but that is an accident; the rest of it—and by far the largest part—does not correspond with your recollections. And how *could* it? People can't be expected to remember each other's dreams, but only their own. You have put me into your land-dreams a thousand times, but I didn't always know I was there; so how could I remember it? Also I have put you into my land-dreams a thousand times when you didn't know it— and the natural result is that when I name the circumstances you don't always recal them. But how different it is with this real life, this genuine life in the ship! Our recollections of it are just alike. You have been forgetting episodes of it to-day—I don't know why; it has surprised me and puzzled me—but the lapse was only temporary; your memory soon rallied again. Now it hasn't rallied in the case of land-dreams of mine—in most cases it hasn't. And it's not going to, Henry. You can be sure of that."

She stopped, and tilted her head up in a thinking attitude and began to unconsciously tap her teeth with the ivory knob of a crochet needle. Presently she said, "I think I know what is the matter. I have been neglecting you for ten days while I have been grieving for our old shipmates and pretending to be seasick so that I might indulge myself with solitude; and here is the result—you haven't been taking exercise enough."

I was glad to have a reason—any reason that would excuse my memory—and I accepted this one, and made confession. There was no truth in the confession, but I was already getting handy with these evasions. I was a little sorry for this, for she had always trusted my word, and I had honored this trust by telling her the truth many a time when it was a sharp sacrifice to me to do it. She looked me over with gentle reproach in her eye, and said—

"Henry, how can you be so naughty? I watch you so faithfully and make you take such good care of your health that you owe me the grace to do my office for me when for any fair reason I am for a while not on guard. When have you boxed with George last?"

What an idea it was! It was a good place to make a mistake, and I came near to doing it. It was on my tongue's end to say that I had never boxed with anyone; and as for boxing with a colored man-servant—and so on; but I kept back my remark, and in place of it tried to look like a person who didn't know what to say. It was easy to do, and I probably did it very well.

"You do not say anything, Henry. I think it is because you have a good reason. When have you fenced with him? Henry, you are avoiding my eye. Look up. Tell me the truth: have you fenced with him a single time in the last ten days?"

So far as I was aware I knew nothing about foils, and had never handled them; so I was able to answer—

"I will be frank with you, Alice—I haven't."

"I suspected it. Now, Henry, what can you say?"

I was getting some of my wits back, now, and was not altogether unprepared, this time.

"Well, Alice, there hasn't been much fencing weather, and when there was any, I—well, I was lazy, and that is the shameful truth."

"There's a chance now, anyway, and you mustn't waste it. Take off your coat and things."

She rang for George, then she got up and raised the sofa-seat and began to fish out boxing-gloves, and foils and masks

from the locker under it, softly scolding me all the while.
George put his head in, noted the preparations, then entered
and put himself in boxing trim. It was his turn to take the
witness stand, now.

"George, didn't I tell you to keep up Mr. Henry's exercises
just the same as if I were about?"

"Yes, madam, you did."

"Why haven't you done it?"

George chuckled, and showed his white teeth and said—

"Bless yo' soul, honey, I dasn't."

"Why?"

"Because the first time I went to him—it was that Tuesday,
you know, when it was ca'm—he wouldn't hear to it, and
said he didn't want no exercise and warn't going to take any,
and tole me to go 'long. Well, I didn't stop there, of course,
but went to him agin, every now and then, trying to persuade
him, tell at last he let into me" (he stopped and comforted
himself with an unhurried laugh over the recollection of it,)
"and give me a most solid good cussing, and tole me if I
come agin he'd take and thow me overboard—there, ain't
that so, Mr. Henry?"

My wife was looking at me pretty severely.

"Henry, what have you to say to that?"

It was my belief that it hadn't happened, but I was steadily
losing confidence in my memory; and moreover my new policy of recollecting whatever anybody required me to recollect
seemed the safest course to pursue in my strange and trying
circumstances; so I said—

"Nothing, Alice—I did refuse."

"Oh, I'm not talking about that; of course you refused—
George had already said so."

"Oh, I see."

"Well, why do you stop?"

"Why do I stop?"

"Yes. Why don't you answer my question?"

"Why, Alice, I've answered it. You asked me—you asked
me—What *is* it I haven't answered?"

"Henry, you know very well. You broke a promise; and you
are trying to talk around it and get me away from it; but I am
not going to let you. You know quite well you promised me

you wouldn't swear any more in calm weather. And it is such a little thing to do. It is hardly ever calm, and—"

"Alice, dear, I beg ever so many pardons! I had clear forgotten it; but I won't offend again, I give you my word. Be good to me, and forgive."

She was always ready to forgive, and glad to do it, whatever my crime might be; so things were pleasant again, now, and smooth and happy. George was gloved and skipping about in an imaginary fight, by this time, and Alice told me to get to work with him. She took pencil and paper and got ready to keep game. I stepped forward to position—then a curious thing happened: I seemed to remember a thousand boxing-bouts with George, the whole boxing art came flooding in upon me, and I knew just what to do! I was a prey to no indecisions, I had no trouble. We fought six rounds, I held my own all through, and I finally knocked George out. I was not astonished; it seemed a familiar experience. Alice showed no surprise, George showed none; apparently it was an old story to them.

The same thing happened with the fencing. I suddenly knew that I was an experienced old fencer; I expected to get the victory, and when I got it, it seemed but a repetition of something which had happened numberless times before.

We decided to go down to the main saloon and take a regular meal in the regular way—the evening meal. Alice went away to dress. Just as I had finished dressing, the children came romping in, warmly and prettily clad, and nestled up to me, one on each side, on the sofa, and began to chatter. Not about a former home; no, not a word of that, but only about this ship-home and its concerns and its people. After a little I threw out some questions—feelers. They did not understand. Finally I asked them if they had known no home but this one. Jessie said, with some little enthusiasm—

"Oh, yes, dream-homes. They are pretty—some of them." Then, with a shrug of her shoulders, "But they *are* so queer!"

"How, Jessie?"

"Well, you know, they have such curious things in them; and they fade, and don't stay. Bessie doesn't like them at all."

"Why don't you, Bessie?"

"Because they scare me so."

"What is it that scares you?"

"Oh, everything, papa. Sometimes it is so light. That hurts my eyes. And it's too many lamps—little sparkles all over, up high, and large ones that are dreadful. They could fall on me, you know."

"But I am not much afraid," said Jessie, "because mamma says they are not real, and if they did fall they wouldn't hurt."

"What else do you see there besides the lights, Bessie?"

"Ugly things that go on four legs like our cat, but bigger."

"Horses?"

"I forget names."

"Describe them, dear."

"I can't, papa. They are not alike; they are different kinds; and when I wake up I can't just remember the shape of them, they are so dim."

"And I wouldn't wish to remember them," said Jessie, "they make me feel creepy. Don't let's talk about them, papa, let's talk about something else."

"That's what I say, too," said Bessie.

So then we talked about our ship. That interested them. They cared for no other home, real or unreal, and wanted no better one. They were innocent witnesses and free from prejudice.

When we went below we found the roomy saloon well lighted and brightly and prettily furnished, and a very comfortable and inviting place altogether. Everything seemed substantial and genuine, there was nothing to suggest that it might be a work of the imagination.

At table the captain (Davis) sat at the head, my wife at his right with the children, I at his left, a stranger at my left. The rest of the company consisted of Rush Phillips, purser, aged 27; his sweetheart the Captain's daughter Lucy, aged 22; her sister Connie (short for Connecticut), aged 10; Arnold Blake, surgeon, 25; Harvey Pratt, naturalist, 36; at the foot sat Sturgis the chief mate, aged 35, and completed the snug assemblage. Stewards waited upon the general company, and George and our nurse Germania had charge of our family. Germania was not the nurse's name, but that was our name for her because it was shorter than her own. She was 28 years old, and had always been with us; and so had George. George was 30, and had once been a slave, according to my record, but I was losing my grip upon that, now, and was indeed getting shadowy and uncertain about all my traditions.

The talk and the feeding went along in a natural way, I could find nothing unusual about it anywhere. The captain was pale, and had a jaded and harassed look, and was subject to little fits of absence of mind; and these things could be said of the mate, also, but this was all natural enough considering the grisly time they had been having, and certainly there was nothing about it to suggest that they were dream-creatures or that their troubles were unreal.

The stranger at my side was about 45 years old, and he had the half-subdued, half-resigned look of a man who had been under a burden of trouble a long time. He was tall and thin; he had a bushy black head, and black eyes which burned when he was interested, but were dull and expressionless when his thoughts were far away—and that happened every time he dropped out of the conversation. He forgot to eat, then, his hands became idle, his dull eye fixed itself upon his plate or upon vacancy, and now and then he would draw a heavy sigh out of the depths of his breast.

These three were exceptions; the others were chatty and cheerful, and they were like a pleasant little family party together. Phillips and Lucy were full of life, and quite happy, as became engaged people; and their furtive love-passages had everybody's sympathy and approval. Lucy was a pretty creature, and simple in her ways and kindly, and Phillips was a blithesome and attractive young fellow. I seemed to be familiarly acquainted with everybody, I didn't quite know why. That is, with everybody except the stranger at my side; and as he seemed to know me well, I had to let on to know him, lest I cause remark by exposing the fact that I didn't know him. I was already tired of being caught up for ignorance at every turn.

The captain and the mate managed to seem comfortable enough until Phillips raised the subject of the day's run, the position of the ship, distance out, and so on; then they became irritable, and sharp of speech, and were unkinder to the

young fellow than the case seemed to call for. His sweetheart
was distressed to see him so treated before all the company,
and she spoke up bravely in his defence and reproached her
father for making an offence out of so harmless a thing. This
only brought her into trouble, and procured for her so rude a
retort that she was consumed with shame, and left the table
crying.

The pleasure was all gone, now; everybody felt personally
affronted and wantonly abused. Conversation ceased and an
uncomfortable silence fell upon the company; through it one
could hear the wailing of the wind and the dull tramp of the
sailors and the muffled words of command overhead, and this
made the silence all the more dismal. The dinner was a failure.
While it was still unfinished the company began to break up
and slip out, one after another; and presently none was left
but me.

I sat long, sipping black coffee and smoking. And thinking;
groping about in my dimming land-past. An incident of my
American life would rise upon me, vague at first, then grow
more distinct and articulate, then sharp and clear; then in a
moment it was gone, and in its place was a dull and distant
image of some long-past episode whose theatre was this
ship—and then *it* would develop, and clarify, and become
strong and real. It was fascinating, enchanting, this spying
among the elusive mysteries of my bewitched memory, and I
went up to my parlor and continued it, with the help of
punch and pipe, hour after hour, as long as I could keep
awake. With this curious result: that the main incidents of
both my lives were now recovered, but only those of one of
them persistently gathered strength and vividness—our life in
the ship! Those of our land-life were good enough, plain
enough, but in minuteness of detail they fell perceptibly short
of those others; and in matters of feeling—joy, grief, physical
pain, physical pleasure—immeasurably short!

Some mellow notes floated to my ear, muffled by the
moaning wind—six bells in the morning watch. So late! I
went to bed. When I woke in the middle of the so-called day
the first thing I thought of was my night's experience. Already my land-life had faded a little—but not the other.

# BOOK II

## CHAPTER I

I have long ago lost Book I, but it is no matter. It served its purpose—writing it was an entertainment to me. We found out that our little boy set it adrift on the wind, sheet by sheet, to see if it would fly. It did. And so two of us got entertainment out of it. I have often been minded to begin Book II, but natural indolence and the pleasant life of the ship interfered.

There have been little happenings, from time to time. The principal one, for us of the family, was the birth of our Harry, which stands recorded in the log under the date of June 8, and happened about three months after we shipped the present crew, poor devils! They still think we are bound for the South Pole, and that we are a long time on the way. It is pathetic, after a fashion. They regard their former life in the World as their real life and this present one as—well, they hardly know what; but sometimes they get pretty tired of it, even at this late day. We hear of it now and then through the officers—mainly Turner, who is a puzzled man.

During the first four years we had several mutinies, but things have been reasonably quiet during the past two. One of them had really a serious look. It occurred when Harry was a month old, and at an anxious time, for both he and his mother were weak and ill. The master spirit of it was Stephen Bradshaw the carpenter, of course—a hard lot I know, and a born mutineer I think.

In those days I was greatly troubled, for a time, because my wife's memories still refused to correspond with mine. It had been an ideal life, and naturally it was a distress not to be able to live it over again in its entirety with her in our talks. At first she did not feel about it as I did, and said she could not understand my interest in those dreams, but when she found how much I took the matter to heart, and that to me the dreams had come to have a seeming of reality and were freighted with tender and affectionate impressions besides, she began to change her mind and wish she could go back in spirit with me to that mysterious land. And so she tried to get back that forgotten life. By my help, and by patient probing and searching of her memory she succeeded. Gradually it all came back, and her reward was sufficient. We now had the recollections of two lives to draw upon, and the result was a double measure of happiness for us. We even got the children's former lives back for them—with a good deal of difficulty—next the servants'. It made a new world for us all, and an entertaining one to explore. In the beginning George the colored man was an unwilling subject, because by heredity he was superstitious, and believed that no good could come of meddling with dreams; but when he presently found that no harm came of it his disfavor dissolved away.

Talking over our double-past—particularly our dream-past—became our most pleasant and satisfying amusement, and the search for missing details of it our most profitable labor. One day when the baby was about a month old, we were at this pastime in our parlor. Alice was lying on the sofa, propped with pillows—she was by no means well. It was a still and solemn black day, and cold; but the lamps made the place cheerful, and as for comfort, Turner had taken care of that; for he had found a kerosene stove with an ising-glass front among the freight, and had brought it up and lashed it fast and fired it up, and the warmth it gave and the red glow it made took away all chill and cheerlessness from the parlor and made it homelike. The little girls were out somewhere with George and Delia (the maid).

Alice and I were talking about the time, twelve years before, when Captain Hall's boy had his tragic adventure with the spider-squid, and I was reminding her that she had misstated the case when she mentioned it to me, once. She had said the squid *ate* the boy. Out of my memory I could call back all the details, now, and I remembered that the boy was only badly hurt, not eaten.

For a month or two the ship's company had been glimpsing vast animals at intervals of a few days, and at first the general terror was so great that the men openly threatened, on two occasions, to seize the ship unless the captain turned back; but by a resolute bearing he tided over the difficulty; and by pointing out to the men that the animals had shown no disposition to attack the ship and might therefore be considered harmless, he quieted them down and restored order. It was good grit in the captain, for privately he was very much afraid of the animals himself and had but a shady opinion of their innocence. He kept his gatlings in order, and had gun-watches, which he changed with the other watches.

I had just finished correcting Alice's history of the boy's adventure with the squid when the ship, plowing through a perfectly smooth sea, went heeling away down to starboard and stayed there! The floor slanted like a roof, and every loose thing in the room slid to the floor and glided down against the bulkhead. We were greatly alarmed, of course. Next we heard a rush of feet along the deck and an uproar of cries and shoutings, then the rush of feet coming back, with a wilder riot of cries. Alice exclaimed—

"Go find the children—quick!"

I sprang out and started to run aft through the gloom, and then I saw the fearful sight which I had seen twelve years before when that boy had had his shocking misadventure. For the moment I turned the corner of the deck-house and had an unobstructed view astern, there it was—apparently two full moons rising close over the stern of the ship and lighting the decks and rigging with a sickly yellow glow—the eyes of the colossal squid. His vast beak and head were plain to be seen, swelling up like a hill above our stern; he had flung one tentacle forward and gripped it around the peak of the mainmast and was pulling the ship over; he had gripped the mizzen-mast with another, and a couple more were writhing about dimly away above our heads searching for something to take hold of. The stench of his breath was suffocating everybody.

I was like the most of the crew, helpless with fright; but the captain and the officers kept their wits and courage. The gatlings on the starboard side could not be used, but the four on the port side were brought to bear, and inside of a minute they had poured more than two thousand bullets into those moons. That blinded the creature, and he let go; and by squirting a violent Niagara of water out of his mouth which tore the sea into a tempest of foam he shot himself backward three hundred yards and the ship forward as far, drowning the deck with a racing flood which swept many of the men off their feet and crippled some, and washed all loose deck-plunder overboard. For five minutes we could hear him thrashing about, there in the dark, and lashing the sea with his giant tentacles in his pain; and now and then his moons showed, then vanished again; and all the while we were rocking and plunging in the booming seas he made. Then he quieted down. We took a thankful full breath, believing him dead.

Now I thought of the children, and ran all about inquiring for them, but no one had seen them. I thought they must have been washed overboard, and for a moment my heart stopped beating. Then the hope came that they had taken refuge with their mother; so I ran there; and almost swooned when I entered the place, for it was vacant. I ran out shouting the alarm, and after a dozen steps almost ran over her. She was lying against the bulwarks drenched and insensible. The surgeon and young Phillips helped me carry her in; then the surgeon and I began to work over her and Phillips rushed away to start the hunt for the children. It was all of half an hour before she showed any sign of life; then her eyes opened with a dazed and wondering look in them, then they recognized me and into them shot a ghastly terror.

"The children! the children!" she gasped; and I, with the heart all gone out of me, answered with such air of truth as I could assume —

"They are safe."

I could never deceive her. I was transparent to her.

"It is not true! The truth speaks out all over you — they are lost, oh they are lost, they are lost!"

We were strong, but we could not hold her. She tore loose from us and was gone in a moment, flying along the dark decks and shrieking the children's names with a despairing pathos that broke one's heart to hear it. We fled after her, and urged that the flitting lanterns meant that all were searching, and begged her for the children's sake and mine if not for her own to go to bed and save her life. But it went for nothing, she would not listen. For she was a mother, and her children were lost. That says it all. She would hunt for them as long as she had strength to move. And that is what she did, hour after hour, wailing and mourning, and touching the hardest

hearts with her grief, until she was exhausted and fell in a
swoon. Then the stewardess and I put her to bed, and as soon
as she came to and was going to creep out of her bed and take
up her search again the doctor encouraged her in it and gave
her a draught to restore her strength; and it put her into a
deep sleep, which was what he expected.

We left the stewardess on watch and went away to join the
searchers. Not a lantern was twinkling anywhere, and every
figure that emerged from the gloom moved upon tip-toe. I
collared one of them and said angrily—

"What does this mean? Is the search stopped?"

Turner's voice answered—very low: "—'sh! Captain's
orders. The beast ain't dead—it's hunting for us."

It made me sick with fear.

"Do you mean it, Turner? How do you know?"

"Listen."

There was a muffled swashing sound out there somewhere,
and then the two moons appeared for a moment, then turned
slowly away and were invisible again.

"He's been within a hundred yards of us, feeling around for
us with his arms. He could reach us, but he couldn't locate us
because he's blind. Once he mighty near had us; one of his
arms that was squirming around up there in the dark just
missed the foremast, and he hauled in the slack of it without
suspecting anything. It made my lungs come up into my
throat. He has edged away, you see, but he ain't done laying
for us." Pause. Then in a whisper, "He's wallowing around
closer to us again, by gracious. Look—look at that. See it?
Away up in the air—writhing around like a crooked mainmast. Dim, but—there, *now* don't you see it?"

We stood dead still, hardly breathing. Here and there at
little distances the men were gathering silently together and
watching and pointing. The deep hush lay like a weight upon
one's spirit. Even the faintest quiver of air that went idling by
gave out a ghost of sound. A couple of mellow notes floated
lingering and fading down from forward:

*Booooom——booooom.* (Two bells in the middle watch.)

A hoarse low voice—the captain's:

"Silence that damned bell!"

Instantly there was a thrashing commotion out there, with

a thundering rush of discharged water, and the monster came charging for us. I caught my breath, and had to seize Turner or I should have fallen, so suddenly my strength collapsed. Then vaguely we saw the creature, waving its arms aloft, tear past the ship stern first, pushing a vast swell ahead and trailing a tumultuous wake behind, and the next moment it was far away and we were plunging and tossing in the sea it made.

"Thank God, *he's* out of practice!" said Turner, with emotion.

The majestic blind devil stopped out there with its moons toward us, and we were miserable again. We had so hoped it would go home.

I resumed my search. Below I found Phillips and Lucy Davis and a number of others searching, but with no hope. They said they had been everywhere, and were merely going over the ground again and again because they could not bear to have it reported to the mother that the search had ceased. She must be told that they were her friends and that she could depend upon them.

Four hours later I gave it up, wearied to exhaustion, and went and sat down by Alice's bed, to be at hand and support her when she should wake and have to hear my desolate story. After a while she stirred, then opened her eyes and smiled brightly and said—

"Oh, what bliss it is! I dreamed that the children—" She flung her arms about me in a transport of grief. "I remember—oh, my God it is true!"

And so, with sobs and lamentations and frantic self-reproaches she poured out her bitter sorrow, and I clasped her close to me, and could not find one comforting word to say.

"Oh, Henry, Henry, your silence means—oh, we cannot live, we cannot bear it!"

There was a flurry of feet along the deck, the door was burst in, and Turner's voice shouted—

"They're found, by God they're found!"

A joy like that brings the shock of a thunderbolt, and for a little while we thought Alice was gone; but then she rallied, and by that time the children were come, and were clasped to her breast, and she was steeped in a happiness for which there were no words. And she said she never dreamed that profanity could sound so dear and sweet, and she asked the mate to say it again; and he did, but left out the profanity and spoiled it.

The children and George and Delia had seen the squid come and lift its moons above our stern and reach its vast tentacles aloft; and they had not waited, but had fled below, and had not stopped till they were deep down in the hold and hidden in a tunnel among the freight. When found, they had had several hours' sleep and were much refreshed.

Between seeing the squid, and getting washed off her feet, and losing the children, the day was a costly one for Alice. It marks the date of her first gray hairs. They were few, but they were to have company.

We lay in a dead calm, and helpless. We could not get away from the squid's neighborhood. But I was obliged to have some sleep, and I took it. I took all I could get, which was six hours. Then young Phillips came and turned me out and said there were signs that the spirit of mutiny was abroad again and that the captain was going to call the men aft and talk to them. Phillips thought I would not want to miss it.

He was right. We had private theatricals, we had concerts, and the other usual time-passers customary on long voyages; but a speech from the captain was the best entertainment the ship's talent could furnish. There was character back of his oratory. He was all sailor. He was sixty years old, and had known no life but sea life. He had no gray hairs, his beard was full and black and shiny; he wore no mustache, therefore his lips were exposed to view; they fitted together like box and lid, and expressed the pluck and resolution that were in him. He had bright black eyes in his old bronze face and they eloquently interpreted all his moods, and his moods were many: for at times he was the youngest man in the ship, and the most cheerful and vivacious and skittish; at times he was the best-natured man in the ship, and he was always the most lovable; sometimes he was sarcastic, sometimes he was serious even to solemnity, sometimes he was stern, sometimes he was as sentimental as a school-girl; sometimes he was silent, quiet, withdrawn within himself, sometimes he was talkative and argumentative; he was remarkably and sincerely and persistently pious, and marvelously and scientifically profane; he was much the strongest man in the ship, and he was also the largest, excepting that plotting, malicious and fearless devil, Stephen Bradshaw the carpenter; he could smile as sweetly as a girl, and it was a pleasure to see him do it. He was entirely self-educated, and had made a vast and picturesque job of it. He was an affectionate creature, and in his family relations he was beautiful; in the eyes of his daughters he was omniscient, omnipotent, a mixed sun-god and storm-god, and they feared him and adored him accordingly. He was fond of oratory, and thought he had the gift of it; and so he practiced it now and then, upon occasion, and did it with easy confidence. He was a charming man and a manly man, with a right heart and a fine and daring spirit.

Phillips and I slipped out and moved aft. Things had an unusual and startling aspect. There were flushes of light here and there and yonder; the captain stood in one of them, the officers stood a little way back of him.

"How do matters stand, Phillips?"

"You notice that the battle-lanterns are lit, all the way forward?"

"Yes. The gun-watches are at their posts; I see that. The captain means business, I reckon."

"The gun-watches are mutineers!"

I steadied my voice as well as I could, but there was still a quaver in it when I said—

"Then they've sprung a trap on us, and we are at their mercy, of course."

"It has the look of it. They've caught the old man napping, and we are in a close place this time."

We joined the officers, and just then we heard the measured tramp of the men in the distance. They were coming down from forward. Soon they came into view and moved toward us until they were within three or four paces of the captain.

"Halt!"

They had a leader this time, and it was he that gave the command—Stephen Bradshaw, the carpenter. He had a revolver in his hand. There was a pause, then the captain drew himself up, put on his dignity, and prepared to transact business in a properly impressive and theatrical way. He cleared his voice and said, in a fatherly tone—

"Men, this is your spokesman, duly appointed by you?"

Several responded timidly—

"Yes, sir."

"You have a grievance, and you desire to have it redressed?"

"Yes, sir."

"He is not here to represent himself, lads, but only you?"

"Yes, sir."

"Very well. Your complaint shall be heard, and treated with justice." (Murmur of approbation from the men.) Then the captain's soft manner hardened a little, and he said to the carpenter, "Go on."

Bradshaw was eager to begin, and he flung out his words with aggressive confidence—

"Captain Davis, in the first place this crew wants to know where they *are*. Next, they want this ship put about and pointed for home—straight off, and no fooling. They are tired of this blind voyage, and they ain't going to have any more of it—and that's the word with the bark on it." He paused a moment, for his temper was rising and obstructing his breath; then he continued in a raised and insolent voice and with a showy flourish of his revolver. "Before, they've had no leader, and you talked them down and cowed them; but that ain't going to happen this time. And they hadn't any plans, and warn't fixed for business; but it's different, now." He grew exultant. "Do you see this?"—his revolver. "And do you see that?" He pointed to the gatlings. "We've got the guns; we are boss of the ship. Put her about! That's the order, and it's going to be obeyed."

There was an admiring murmur from the men. After a pause the captain said, with dignity—

"Apparently you are through. Stand aside."

"Stand aside, is it? Not till I have heard what answer you—"

The captain's face darkened and an evil light began to flicker in his eyes, and his hands to twitch. The carpenter glanced at him, then stepped a pace aside, shaking his head and grumbling. "Say your say, then, and cut it short, for I've got something more to say when you're done, if it ain't satisfactory."

The captain's manner at once grew sweet, and even tender,

and he turned toward the men with his most genial and winning smile on his face, and proceeded to take them into his
confidence.

"You want to know where you are, boys. It is reasonable; it
is natural. If we don't know where we are—if we are lost—
who is worst off, you or me? You have no children in this
ship—I have. If we are in danger have I put us there intentionally? Would I have done it purposely—with my children
aboard? Come, what do you think?"

There was a stir among the men, and an approving nodding of heads which conceded that the point was well taken.

"Don't I know my trade, or am I only an apprentice to it?
Have I sailed the seas for sixty years and commanded ships
for thirty to be taught what to do in a difficulty by—by a
damned carpenter?"

He was talking in such a pleading way, such an earnest, and
moving and appealing way that the men were not prepared
for the close of his remark, and it caught them out and made
some of them laugh. He had scored one—and he knew it.
The carpenter's back was turned—he was playing indifference. He whirled around and covered the captain with his
revolver. Everybody shrank together and caught his breath,
except the captain, who said gently—

"Don't be afraid—pull the trigger; it isn't loaded."

The carpenter pulled—twice, thrice, and threw the pistol
away. Then he shouted—

"Fall back, men—out of the way!" They surged apart, and
he fell back himself. The captain and the officers stood alone
in the circle of light. "Gun 4, fire!" The officers threw themselves on their faces on the deck, but the captain remained in
his place. The gunner spun the windlass around—there was
no result. "Gun 3, fire!" The same thing happened again. The
captain said—

"Come back to your places, men." They obeyed, looking
puzzled, surprised, and a good deal demoralized. The officers
got up, looking astonished and rather ashamed. "Carpenter,
come back to your place." He did it, but reluctantly, and
swearing to himself. It was easy to see that the captain was
contented with his dramatic effects. He resumed his speech,
in his pleasantest manner—

"You have mutinied two or three times, boys. It is all right—up to now. I would have done it myself in my common-seaman days, I reckon, if my ship was bewitched and I didn't know where I was. Now then, can you be trusted with the facts? Are we rational men, manly men, men who can stand up and face hard luck and a big difficulty that has been brought about by nobody's fault, and say live or die, survive or perish, we are in for it, for good or bad, and we'll stand by the ship if she goes to hell!" (The men let go a tolerably hearty cheer.) "Are we men—grown men—salt-sea men—men nursed upon dangers and cradled in storms— men made in the image of God and ready to do when He commands and die when He calls—or are we just sneaks and curs and carpenters!" (This brought both cheers and laughter, and the captain was happy.) "There—that's the kind. And so I'll tell you how the thing stands. *I* don't know where this ship is, but she's in the hands of God, and that's enough for me, it's enough for you, and it's enough for anybody but a carpenter. If it is God's will that we pull through, we pull through—otherwise not. We haven't had an observation for four months, but we are going ahead, and do our best to fetch up somewhere."

*1898*

# Diplomatic Pay and Clothes

VIENNA, *January 5.* — I find in this morning's papers the statement that the Government of the United States has paid to the two members of the Peace Commission entitled to receive money for their services $100,000 each for their six weeks' work in Paris.

I hope that this is true. I will allow myself the satisfaction of considering that it *is* true, and of treating it as a thing finished and settled.

It is a precedent; and it ought to be a welcome one to our country. A precedent always has a chance to be valuable (as well as the other way); and its best chance to be valuable (or the other way) is when it takes such a striking form as to fix a whole nation's attention upon it. If it come justified out of the discussion which will follow, it will find a career ready and waiting for it.

We realize that the edifice of public justice is built of precedents, from the ground upward; but we do not always realize that all the other details of our civilization are likewise built of precedents. The changes, also, which they undergo, are due to the intrusion of new precedents, which hold their ground against opposition, and keep their place. A precedent may die at birth, or it may live, — it is mainly a matter of luck. If it be imitated once, it has a chance; if twice, a better chance; if three times, it is reaching a point where account must be taken of it; if four, five, or six times, it has probably come to stay — for a whole century, possibly. If a town start a new bow, or a new dance, or a new temperance project, or a new kind of hat, and can get the precedent adopted in the next town, the career of that precedent is begun; and it will be unsafe to bet as to where the end of its journey is going to be. It may not get this start at all, and may have no career; but, if a crown prince introduce the precedent, it will attract vast attention, and its chances for a career are so great as to amount almost to a certainty.

For a long time we have been reaping damage from a couple of disastrous precedents. One is the precedent of shabby pay to public servants standing for the power and dignity of the Republic in foreign lands: the other is a precedent condemning them to exhibit themselves officially in clothes which are not only without grace or dignity, but are a pretty loud and pious rebuke to the vain and frivolous costumes worn by the other officials. To our day an American ambassador's official costume remains under the reproach of these defects. At a public function in a European court all foreign representatives except ours wear clothes which in some way distinguish them from the unofficial throng, and mark them as standing for their *countries*. But our representative appears in a plain black swallow-tail, which stands for neither country nor people. It has no nationality. It is found in all countries: it is as international as a night-shirt. It has no particular meaning; but our Government tries to give it one: it tries to make it stand for republican simplicity, modesty, and unpretentiousness. Tries, and without doubt fails; for it is not conceivable that this loud ostentation of simplicity deceives any one. The statue that advertises its modesty with a fig-leaf really brings its modesty under suspicion. Worn officially, our nonconforming swallow-tail is a declaration of ungracious independence in the matter of manners, and is uncourteous. It says to all around: "In Rome we do not choose to do as Rome does; we refuse to respect your tastes and your traditions; we make no sacrifices to any one's customs and prejudices; we yield no jot to the courtesies of life; we prefer our manners, and intrude them here."

That is not the true American spirit, and those clothes misrepresent us. When a foreigner comes among us, and trespasses against our customs and our code of manners, we are offended, and justly so: but our Government commands our ambassadors to wear abroad an official dress which is an offence against foreign manners and customs; and the discredit of it falls upon the nation.

We did not dress our public functionaries in undistinguished raiment before Franklin's time; and the change would not have come if he had been an obscurity. But he was such a colossal figure in the world that whatever he did of an unusual nature attracted the world's attention, and became a precedent. In the case of clothes, the next representative after him, and the next, had to imitate it. After that, the thing was custom; and custom is a petrifaction: nothing but dynamite can dislodge it for a century. We imagine that our queer official costumery was deliberately devised to symbolize our republican simplicity,—a quality which we have never possessed, and are too old to acquire now, if we had any use for it or any leaning toward it. But it is not so; there was nothing deliberate about it; it grew naturally and heedlessly out of the precedent set by Franklin.

If it had been an intentional thing, and based upon a principle, it would not have stopped where it did: we should have applied it further. Instead of clothing our admirals and generals, for courts martial and other public functions, in superb dress uniforms blazing with color and gold, the Government would put them in swallow-tails and white cravats, and make them look like ambassadors and lackeys. If I am wrong in making Franklin the father of our curious official clothes, it is no matter—he will be able to stand it.

It is my opinion—and I make no charge for the suggestion—that, whenever we appoint an ambassador or a minister, we ought to confer upon him the temporary rank of admiral or general, and allow him to wear the corresponding uniform at public functions in foreign countries. I would recommend this for the reason that it is not consonant with the dignity of the United States of America that her representative should appear upon occasions of state in a dress which makes him glaringly conspicuous; and that is what his present undertaker-outfit does when it appears, with its dismal smudge, in the midst of the butterfly splendors of a Continental court. It is a most trying position for a shy man, a modest man, a man accustomed to being like other people. He is the most striking figure present: there is no hiding from the multitudinous eyes. It would be funny, if it were not such a cruel spectacle, to see the hunted creature in his solemn sables scuffling around in that sea of vivid color, like a mislaid Presbyterian in perdition. We are all aware that our representative's dress should not compel too much attention; for anybody but an Indian chief knows that that is a vulgarity. I am saying these things in the interest of our national pride and dignity. Our representative is the flag. He is the Republic. He is the United States of America. And when these embodiments pass by, we do not want them scoffed at: we desire that people shall be obliged to concede that they are worthily clothed, and politely.

Our Government is oddly inconsistent in this matter of official dress. When its representative is a civilian who has not been a soldier, it restricts him to the black swallow-tail and white tie; but if he is a civilian who has been a soldier, it allows him to wear the uniform of his former rank as an official dress. When Gen. Sickles was Minister to Spain, he always wore, when on official duty, the dress uniform of a major-general. When Gen. Grant visited foreign courts, he went handsomely and properly ablaze in the uniform of a full general, and was introduced by diplomatic survivals of his own Presidential Administration. The latter, by official necessity, went in the meek and lowly swallow-tail,—a deliciously sarcastic contrast: the one dress representing the honest and honorable dignity of the nation; the other, the cheap hypocrisy of the Republican Simplicity tradition. In Paris our present representative can perform his official functions reputably clothed; for he was an officer in the Civil War. In London our late Ambassador was similarly situated; for he, also, was an officer in the Civil War. But Mr. Choate must represent the Great Republic—even at official breakfasts at seven in the morning—in that same old funny swallow-tail.

Our Government's notions about proprieties of costume are indeed very, very odd—as suggested by that last fact. The swallow-tail is recognized the world over as not wearable in the daytime: it is a night-dress, and a night-dress only,—a night-shirt is not more so. Yet, when our representative makes an official visit in the morning, he is obliged by his Government to go in that night-dress. It makes the very cab-horses laugh.

The truth is, that for a while during the present century, and up to something short of forty years ago, we had a lucid interval, and dropped the Republican Simplicity sham, and dressed our foreign representatives in a handsome and becoming official costume. This was discarded by and by, and the swallow-tail substituted. I believe it is not now known which statesman brought about this change; but we all know that, stupid as he was as to diplomatic proprieties in dress, he would not have sent his daughter to a state ball in a corn-shucking costume, nor to a corn-shucking in a state ball costume, to be harshly criticised as an ill-mannered offender against the proprieties of custom in both places. And we know another thing; viz., that he himself would not have wounded the tastes and feelings of a family of mourners by attending a funeral in their house in a costume which was an offence against the dignities and decorum prescribed by tradition and sanctified by custom. Yet that man was so heedless as not to reflect that *all* the social customs of civilized peoples are entitled to respectful observance, and that no man with a right spirit of courtesy in him ever has any disposition to transgress these customs.

There is still another argument for a rational diplomatic dress—a business argument. We are a trading nation; and our representative is our business agent. If he is respected, esteemed, and liked where he is stationed, he can exercise an influence which can extend our trade and forward our prosperity. A considerable number of his business activities have their field in his social relations; and clothes which do not offend against local manners and customs and prejudices are a valuable part of his equipment in this matter,—would be, if Franklin had died earlier.

I have not done with gratis suggestions yet. We made a great and valuable advance when we instituted the office of ambassador. That lofty rank endows its possessor with several times as much influence, consideration, and effectiveness as the rank of minister bestows. For the sake of the country's dignity and for the sake of her advantage commercially, we should have ambassadors, not ministers, at the great courts of the world.

But not at present salaries! No: if we are to maintain present salaries, let us make no more ambassadors; and let us unmake those we have already made. The great position, without the means of respectably maintaining it—there could be no wisdom in that. A foreign representative, to be valuable to his country, must be on good terms with the officials of the capital and with the rest of the influential folk. He must mingle with this society: he cannot sit at home—it is not business, it butters no commercial parsnips. He must attend the dinners, banquets, suppers, balls, receptions, and must *return* these hospitalities. He should return as good as he gets, too, for the sake of the dignity of his country, and for the sake of Business. Have we ever had a minister or an ambassador who could do this on his salary? No—not once, from Franklin's time to ours. Other countries understand the commercial value of properly lining the pockets of their representatives; but apparently our Government has not learned it. England is the most successful trader of the several trading nations; and she takes good care of the watchmen who keep guard in her commercial towers. It has been a long time, now, since we needed to blush for our representatives abroad. It has become custom to send our fittest. We send men of distinction, cultivation, character,—our ablest, our choicest, our best. Then we cripple their efficiency through the meagreness of their pay. Here is a list of salaries for English and American ministers and ambassadors:

| City. | Salaries. | |
|---|---|---|
| | American. | English. |
| Paris. . . . . . . . . . . . . . | $17,500 | $45,000 |
| Berlin . . . . . . . . . . . . . | 17,500 | 40,000 |
| Vienna . . . . . . . . . . . . . | 12,000 | 40,000 |
| Constantinople . . . . . . . . . . | 10,000 | 40,000 |
| St. Petersburg . . . . . . . . . . | 17,500 | 39,000 |
| Rome . . . . . . . . . . . . . . | 12,000 | 35,000 |
| Washington . . . . . . . . . . . | . . . | 32,500 |

Sir Julian Pauncefote, the English Ambassador at Washington, has a very fine house besides—at no damage to his salary.

English ambassadors pay no house-rent; they live in palaces owned by England. Our representatives pay house-rent out of their salaries. You can judge by the above figures what kind of houses the United States of America has been used to living in abroad, and what sort of return-entertaining she has done. There is not a salary in our list which would properly house the representative receiving it, and, in addition, pay $3,000 toward his family's bacon and doughnuts,—the strange but

economical and customary fare of the American Ambassador's household, except on Sundays, when petrified Boston
crackers are added.

The ambassadors and ministers of foreign nations not only
have generous salaries, but their Governments provide them
with money wherewith to pay a considerable part of their
hospitality bills. I believe our Government pays no hospitality
bills except those incurred by the navy. Through this concession to the navy, that arm is able to do us credit in foreign
parts; and certainly that is well and politic. But why the Government does not think it well and politic that our diplomats
should be able to do us like credit abroad, is one of those
mysterious inconsistencies which have been puzzling me ever
since I stopped trying to understand base-ball, and took up
statesmanship as a pastime.

To return to the matter of house-rent. Good houses, properly furnished, in European capitals, are not to be had at small
figures. Consequently, our foreign representatives have been
accustomed to live in garrets,—sometimes on the roof. Being
poor men, it has been the best they could do on the salary
which the Government has paid them. How could they adequately return the hospitalities shown them? It was impossible. It would have exhausted the salary in three months. Still,
it was their official duty to entertain the influentials after some
sort of fashion; and they did the best they could with their
limited purse. In return for champagne they furnished lemonade; in return for game they furnished ham; in return for
whale they furnished sardines; in return for liquors they furnished condensed milk; in return for the battalion of liveried
and powdered flunkeys they furnished the hired girl; in return
for the fairy wilderness of sumptuous decorations they draped
the stove with the American flag; in return for the orchestra
they furnished zither and ballads by the family; in return for
the ball—but they didn't return the ball, except in cases
where the United States lived on the roof and had room.

Is this an exaggeration? It can hardly be called that. I saw
nearly the equivalent of it once, a good many years ago. A
minister was trying to create influential friends for a project
which might be worth ten millions a year to the agriculturists
of the Republic; and our Government had furnished him ham

and lemonade to persuade the opposition with. The minister did not succeed. He might not have succeeded if his salary had been what it ought to have been,—$50,000 or $60,000 a year;—but his chances would have been very greatly improved. And in any case, he and his dinners and his country would not have been joked about by the hard-hearted, and pitied by the compassionate.

Any experienced "drummer" will testify that, when you want to do business, there is no economy in ham and lemonade. The drummer takes his country customer to the theatre, the opera, the circus; dines him, wines him, entertains him all the day and all the night in luxurious style; and plays upon his human nature in all seductive ways. For he knows, by old experience, that this is the best way to get a profitable order out of him. He has his reward. All Governments except our own play the same policy, with the same end in view; and they, also, have their reward. But ours refuses to do business by business ways, and sticks to ham and lemonade. This is the most expensive diet known to the diplomatic service of the world.

Ours is the only country of first importance that pays its foreign representatives trifling salaries. If we were poor, we could not find great fault with these economies, perhaps,—at least one could find a sort of plausible excuse for them. But we are not poor; and the excuse fails. As shown above, some of our important diplomatic representatives receive $12,000; others, $17,500. These salaries are all ham and lemonade, and unworthy of the flag. When we have a rich ambassador in London or Paris, he lives as the ambassador of a country like ours ought to live, and it costs him $100,000 a year to do it. But why should we allow him to pay that out of his private pocket? There is nothing fair about it; and the Republic is no proper subject for any one's charity. In several cases our salaries of $12,000 should be $50,000; and all of the salaries of $17,500 ought to be $75,000, or $100,000, since we pay no representative's house-rent. Our State Department realizes the mistake which we are making, and would like to rectify it; but it has not the power.

When a young girl reaches eighteen she is recognized as being a woman. She adds six inches to her skirt, she unplaits her dangling braids and balls her hair on top of her head, she stops sleeping with her little sister and has a room to herself, and becomes in many ways a thundering expense. But she is in society now; and papa has to stand it: there is no avoiding it. Very well. The Great Republic lengthened her skirts last year, balled up her hair, and entered the world's society. This means that, if she would prosper and stand fair with society, she must put aside some of her dearest and darlingest young ways and superstitions, and do as society does. Of course she can decline if she wants to; but this would be unwise. She ought to realize, now that she has "come out," that this is a right and proper time to change a part of her style. She is in Rome; and it has long been granted that when one is in Rome it is good policy to do as Rome does. To advantage Rome? No,—to advantage herself.

If our Government has really paid representatives of ours on the Paris Commission $100,000 apiece for six weeks' work, I feel sure that it is the best cash investment the nation has made in many years. For it seems quite impossible that, with that precedent on the books, the Government will be able to find excuses for continuing its diplomatic salaries at the present mean figure.                    MARK TWAIN.


*P. S.* VIENNA, *January 10.*—I see, by this morning's tele-graphic news, that I am not to be the new ambassador here, after all. This—well, I hardly know what to say. I—well, of course I do not care anything about it; but it is at least a surprise. I have for many months been using my influence at Washington to get this diplomatic see expanded into an am-bassadorship, with the idea, of course, th——But never mind. Let it go. It is of no consequence. I say it calmly; for I am calm. But at the same time——However, the subject has no interest for me, and never had. I never really intended to take the place, anyway—I made up my mind to it months and months ago, nearly a year. But now, while I am calm, I would like to say this—that, so long as I shall continue to possess an American's proper pride in the honor and dignity of his country, I will not take any ambassadorship in the gift of the flag at a salary short of $75,000 a year. If I shall be charged with wanting to live beyond my country's means, I cannot help it. A country which cannot afford ambassadors' wages should be ashamed to have ambassadors.

Think of a Seventeen-thousand-five-hundred-dollar ambassador! Particularly for *America*. Why, it is the most ludicrous spectacle, the most inconsistent and incongruous spectacle, contrivable by even the most diseased imagination. It is a billionaire in a paper collar, a king in a breechclout, an archangel in a tin halo. And, for pure sham and hypocrisy, the salary is just the match of the ambassador's official clothes,—that boastful advertisement of a Republican Simplicity which manifests itself at home in Fifty-thousand-dollar salaries to insurance presidents and railway lawyers, and in domestic palaces whose fittings and furnishings often transcend in costly display and splendor and richness the fittings and furnishings of the palaces of the sceptred masters of Europe; and which has invented and exported to the Old World the palace-car, the sleeping-car, the tram-car, the electric trolley, the best bicycles, the best motor-cars, the steam-heater, the best and smartest systems of electric calls and telephonic aids to laziness and comfort, the elevator, the private bath-room (hot and cold water on tap), the palace-hotel, with its multifarious conveniences, comforts, shows, and luxuries, the—oh, the list is interminable! In a word, Republican Simplicity found Europe with one shirt to her back, so to speak, as far as *real* luxuries, conveniences, and the comforts of life go, and has clothed her to the chin with the latter. We are the lavishest and showiest and most luxury-loving people on the earth; and at our masthead we fly our one true and honest symbol, the gaudiest flag the world has ever seen. Oh, Republican Simplicity, there are many, many humbugs in the world, but none to which you need take off *your* hat!

M. T.

*March 1899*

# Concerning the Jews

Some months ago I published a magazine article* descriptive of a remarkable scene in the Imperial Parliament in Vienna. Since then I have received from Jews in America several letters of inquiry. They were difficult letters to answer, for they were not very definite. But at last I have received a definite one. It is from a lawyer, and he really asks the questions which the other writers probably believed they were asking. By help of this text I will do the best I can to publicly answer this correspondent, and also the others—at the same time apologizing for having failed to reply privately. The lawyer's letter reads as follows:

I have read "Stirring Times in Austria." One point in particular is of vital import to not a few thousand people, including myself, being a point about which I have often wanted to address a question to some disinterested person. The show of military force in the Austrian Parliament, which precipitated the riots, was not introduced by any Jew. No Jew was a member of that body. No Jewish question was involved in the Ausgleich or in the language proposition. No Jew was insulting anybody. In short, no Jew was doing any mischief toward anybody whatsoever. In fact, the Jews were the only ones of the nineteen different races in Austria which did not have a party—they are absolutely non-participants. Yet in your article you say that in the rioting which followed, all classes of people were unanimous only on one thing, viz., in being against the Jews. Now will you kindly tell me why, in your judgment, the Jews have thus ever been, and are even now, in these days of supposed intelligence, the butt of baseless, vicious animosities? I dare say that for centuries there has been no more quiet, undisturbing, and well-behaving citizens, as a class, than that same Jew. It seems to me that ignorance and fanaticism cannot alone account for these horrible and unjust persecutions.

Tell me, therefore, from your vantage-point of cold view, what in your mind is the cause. Can American Jews do anything to correct it either in America or abroad? Will it ever come to an end? Will a Jew be permitted to live honestly, decently, and peaceably like the rest of mankind? What has become of the golden rule?

I will begin by saying that if I thought myself prejudiced

*See *Harper's Magazine* for March, 1898.

against the Jew, I should hold it fairest to leave this subject to a person not crippled in that way. But I think I have no such prejudice. A few years ago a Jew observed to me that there was no uncourteous reference to his people in my books, and asked how it happened. It happened because the disposition was lacking. I am quite sure that (bar one) I have no race prejudices, and I think I have no color prejudices nor caste prejudices nor creed prejudices. Indeed, I know it. I can stand any society. All that I care to know is that a man is a human being—that is enough for me; he can't be any worse. I have no special regard for Satan; but I can at least claim that I have no prejudice against him. It may even be that I lean a little his way, on account of his not having a fair show. All religions issue bibles against him, and say the most injurious things about him, but we never hear *his* side. We have none but the evidence for the prosecution, and yet we have rendered the verdict. To my mind, this is irregular. It is un-English; it is un-American; it is French. Without this precedent Dreyfus could not have been condemned. Of course Satan has some kind of a case, it goes without saying. It may be a poor one, but that is nothing; that can be said about any of us. As soon as I can get at the facts I will undertake his rehabilitation myself, if I can find an unpolitic publisher. It is a thing which we ought to be willing to do for any one who is under a cloud. We may not pay him reverence, for that would be indiscreet, but we can at least respect his talents. A person who has for untold centuries maintained the imposing position of spiritual head of four-fifths of the human race, and political head of the whole of it, must be granted the possession of executive abilities of the loftiest order. In his large presence the other popes and politicians shrink to midges for the microscope. I would like to see him. I would rather see him and shake him by the tail than any other member of the European Concert. In the present paper I shall allow myself to use the word Jew as if it stood for both religion and race. It is handy; and besides, that is what the term means to the general world.

In the above letter one notes these points:

1. The Jew is a well-behaved citizen.

2. Can ignorance and fanaticism *alone* account for his unjust treatment?

3. Can Jews do anything to improve the situation?
4. The Jews have no party; they are non-participants.
5. Will the persecution ever come to an end?
6. What has become of the golden rule?

*Point No.* 1.—We must grant proposition No. 1, for several sufficient reasons. The Jew is not a disturber of the peace of any country. Even his enemies will concede that. He is not a loafer, he is not a sot, he is not noisy, he is not a brawler nor a rioter, he is not quarrelsome. In the statistics of crime his presence is conspicuously rare—in all countries. With murder and other crimes of violence he has but little to do: he is a stranger to the hangman. In the police court's daily long roll of "assaults" and "drunk and disorderlies" his name seldom appears. That the Jewish home is a home in the truest sense is a fact which no one will dispute. The family is knitted together by the strongest affections; its members show each other every due respect; and reverence for the elders is an inviolate law of the house. The Jew is not a burden on the charities of the state nor of the city; these could cease from their functions without affecting him. When he is well enough, he works; when he is incapacitated, his own people take care of him. And not in a poor and stingy way, but with a fine and large benevolence. His race is entitled to be called the most benevolent of all the races of men. A Jewish beggar is not impossible, perhaps; such a thing may exist, but there are few men that can say they have seen that spectacle. The Jew has been staged in many uncomplimentary forms, but, so far as I know, no dramatist has done him the injustice to stage him as a beggar. Whenever a Jew has real need to beg, his people save him from the necessity of doing it. The charitable institutions of the Jews are supported by Jewish money, and amply. The Jews make no noise about it; it is done quietly; they do not nag and pester and harass us for contributions; they give us peace, and set us an example—an example which we have not found ourselves able to follow; for by nature we are not free givers, and have to be patiently and persistently hunted down in the interest of the unfortunate.

These facts are all on the credit side of the proposition that the Jew is a good and orderly citizen. Summed up, they certify that he is quiet, peaceable, industrious, unaddicted to high crimes and brutal dispositions; that his family life is commendable; that he is not a burden upon public charities; that he is not a beggar; that in benevolence he is above the reach of competition. These are the very quintessentials of good citizenship. If you can add that he is as honest as the average of his neighbors— But I think that question is affirmatively answered by the fact that he is a successful business man. The basis of successful business is honesty; a business cannot thrive where the parties to it cannot trust each other. In the matter of numbers the Jew counts for little in the overwhelming population of New York; but that his honesty counts for much is guaranteed by the fact that the immense wholesale business of Broadway, from the Battery to Union Square, is substantially in his hands.

I suppose that the most picturesque example in history of a trader's trust in his fellow-trader was one where it was not Christian trusting Christian, but Christian trusting Jew. That Hessian Duke who used to sell his subjects to George III. to fight George Washington with got rich at it; and by-and-by, when the wars engendered by the French Revolution made his throne too warm for him, he was obliged to fly the country. He was in a hurry, and had to leave his earnings behind—$9,000,000. He had to risk the money with some one without security. He did not select a Christian, but a Jew—a Jew of only modest means, but of high character; a character so high that it left him lonesome—Rothschild of Frankfort. Thirty years later, when Europe had become quiet and safe again, the Duke came back from overseas, and the Jew returned the loan, with interest added.*

*Here is another piece of picturesque history; and it reminds us that shabbiness and dishonesty are not the monopoly of any race or creed, but are merely human:

"Congress has passed a bill to pay $379 56 to Moses Pendergrass, of Libertyville, Missouri. The story of the reason of this liberality is pathetically interesting, and shows the sort of pickle that an honest man may get into who undertakes to do an honest job of work for Uncle Sam. In 1886 Moses Pendergrass put in a bid for the contract to carry the mail on the route from Knob Lick to Libertyville and Coffman, thirty miles a day, from July 1, 1887, for one year. He got the postmaster at Knob Lick to write the letter for him,

The Jew has his other side. He has some discreditable ways, though he has not a monopoly of them, because he cannot get entirely rid of vexatious Christian competition. We have seen that he seldom transgresses the laws against crimes of violence. Indeed, his dealings with courts are almost restricted to matters connected with commerce. He has a reputation for various small forms of cheating, and for practising oppressive usury, and for burning himself out to get the insurance, and for arranging cunning contracts which leave him an exit but lock the other man in, and for smart evasions which find him safe and comfortable just within the strict letter of the law, when court and jury know very well that he has violated the spirit of it. He is a frequent and faithful and capable officer in the civil service, but he is charged with an unpatriotic disinclination to stand by the flag as a soldier—like the Christian Quaker.

Now if you offset these discreditable features by the credit-

---

and while Moses intended that his bid should be $400, his scribe carelessly made it $4. Moses got the contract, and did not find out about the mistake until the end of the first quarter, when he got his first pay. When he found at what rate he was working he was sorely cast down, and opened communication with the Post Office Department. The department informed him that he must either carry out his contract or throw it up, and that if he threw it up his bondsmen would have to pay the government $1459 85 damages. So Moses carried out his contract, walked thirty miles every week-day for a year, and carried the mail, and received for his labor $4—or, to be accurate, $6 84; for, the route being extended after his bid was accepted, the pay was proportionately increased. Now, after ten years, a bill was finally passed to pay to Moses the difference between what he earned in that unlucky year and what he received."

The *Sun*, which tells the above story, says that bills were introduced in three or four Congresses for Moses's relief, and that committees repeatedly investigated his claim.

It took six Congresses, containing in their persons the compressed virtues of 70,000,000 of people, and cautiously and carefully giving expression to those virtues in the fear of God and the next election, eleven years to find out some way to cheat a fellow-Christian out of about $13 on his honestly executed contract, and out of nearly $300 due him on its enlarged terms. And they succeeded. During the same time they paid out $1,000,000,000 in pensions—a third of it unearned and undeserved. This indicates a splendid all-around competency in theft, for it starts with farthings, and works its industries all the way up to ship-loads. It may be possible that the Jews can beat this, but the man that bets on it is taking chances.

able ones summarized in a preceding paragraph beginning with the words, "These facts are all on the credit side," and strike a balance, what must the verdict be? This, I think: that, the merits and demerits being fairly weighed and measured on both sides, the Christian can claim no superiority over the Jew in the matter of good citizenship.

Yet in all countries, from the dawn of history, the Jew has been persistently and implacably hated, and with frequency persecuted.

*Point No. 2.*—"Can fanaticism *alone* account for this?"

Years ago I used to think that it was responsible for nearly all of it, but latterly I have come to think that this was an error. Indeed, it is now my conviction that it is responsible for hardly any of it.

In this connection I call to mind Genesis, chapter xlvii.

We have all thoughtfully—or unthoughtfully—read the pathetic story of the years of plenty and the years of famine in Egypt, and how Joseph, with that opportunity, made a corner in broken hearts, and the crusts of the poor, and human liberty—a corner whereby he took a nation's money all away, to the last penny; took a nation's live-stock all away, to the last hoof; took a nation's land away, to the last acre; then took the nation itself, buying it for bread, man by man, woman by woman, child by child, till all were slaves; a corner which took everything, left nothing; a corner so stupendous that, by comparison with it, the most gigantic corners in subsequent history are but baby things, for it dealt in hundreds of millions of bushels, and its profits were reckonable by hundreds of millions of dollars, and it was a disaster so crushing that its effects have not wholly disappeared from Egypt to-day, more than three thousand years after the event.

Is it presumable that the eye of Egypt was upon Joseph the foreign Jew all this time? I think it likely. Was it friendly? We must doubt it. Was Joseph establishing a character for his race which would survive long in Egypt? and in time would his name come to be familiarly used to express that character— like Shylock's? It is hardly to be doubted. Let us remember that this was *centuries before the crucifixion.*

I wish to come down eighteen hundred years later and refer to a remark made by one of the Latin historians. I read it in a

translation many years ago, and it comes back to me now
with force. It was alluding to a time when people were still
living who could have seen the Saviour in the flesh. Christianity was so new that the people of Rome had hardly heard of
it, and had but confused notions of what it was. The substance of the remark was this: Some Christians were persecuted in Rome through error, they being *"mistaken for Jews."*

The meaning seems plain. These pagans had nothing
against Christians, but they were quite ready to persecute
Jews. For some reason or other they hated a Jew before they
even knew what a Christian was. May I not assume, then, that
the persecution of Jews is a thing which *antedates* Christianity
and was not born of Christianity? I think so. What was the
origin of the feeling?

When I was a boy, in the back settlements of the Mississippi Valley, where a gracious and beautiful Sunday-school
simplicity and unpracticality prevailed, the "Yankee" (citizen
of the New England States) was hated with a splendid energy.
But religion had nothing to do with it. In a trade, the Yankee
was held to be about five times the match of the Westerner.
His shrewdness, his insight, his judgment, his knowledge, his
enterprise, and his formidable cleverness in applying these
forces were frankly confessed, and most competently cursed.

In the cotton States, after the war, the simple and ignorant
negroes made the crops for the white planter on shares. The
Jew came down in force, set up shop on the plantation, supplied all the negro's wants on credit, and at the end of the
season was proprietor of the negro's share of the present crop
and of part of his share of the next one. Before long, the
whites detested the Jew, and it is doubtful if the negro loved
him.

The Jew is being legislated out of Russia. The reason is
not concealed. The movement was instituted because the
Christian peasant and villager stood no chance against his
commercial abilities. He was always ready to lend money on
a crop, and sell vodka and other necessaries of life on credit
while the crop was growing. When settlement day came he
owned the crop; and next year or year after he owned the
farm, like Joseph.

In the dull and ignorant England of John's time everybody

got into debt to the Jew. He gathered all lucrative enterprises into his hands; he was the king of commerce; he was ready to be helpful in all profitable ways; he even financed crusades for the rescue of the Sepulchre. To wipe out his account with the nation and restore business to its natural and incompetent channels he had to be banished the realm.

For the like reasons Spain had to banish him four hundred years ago, and Austria about a couple of centuries later.

In all the ages Christian Europe has been obliged to curtail his activities. If he entered upon a mechanical trade, the Christian had to retire from it. If he set up as a doctor, he was the best one, and he took the business. If he exploited agriculture, the other farmers had to get at something else. Since there was no way to successfully compete with him in any vocation, the law had to step in and save the Christian from the poorhouse. Trade after trade was taken away from the Jew by statute till practically none was left. He was forbidden to engage in agriculture; he was forbidden to practise law; he was forbidden to practise medicine, except among Jews; he was forbidden the handicrafts. Even the seats of learning and the schools of science had to be closed against this tremendous antagonist. Still, almost bereft of employments, he found ways to make money, even ways to get rich. Also ways to invest his takings well, for usury was not denied him. In the hard conditions suggested, the Jew without brains could not survive, and the Jew with brains had to keep them in good training and well sharpened up, or starve. Ages of restriction to the one tool which the law was not able to take from him—his brain—have made that tool singularly competent; ages of compulsory disuse of his hands have atrophied them, and he never uses them now. This history has a very, very commercial look, a most sordid and practical commercial look, the business aspect of a Chinese cheap-labor crusade. Religious prejudices may account for one part of it, but not for the other nine.

Protestants have persecuted Catholics, but they did not take their livelihoods away from them. The Catholics have persecuted the Protestants with bloody and awful bitterness, but they never closed agriculture and the handicrafts against them. Why was that? That has the candid look of genuine religious persecution, not a trade-union boycott in a religious disguise.

The Jews are harried and obstructed in Austria and Germany, and lately in France; but England and America give them an open field and yet survive. Scotland offers them an unembarrassed field too, but there are not many takers. There are a few Jews in Glasgow, and one in Aberdeen; but that is because they can't earn enough to get away. The Scotch pay themselves that compliment, but it is authentic.

I feel convinced that the Crucifixion has not much to do with the world's attitude toward the Jew; that the reasons for it are older than that event, as suggested by Egypt's experience and by Rome's regret for having persecuted an unknown quantity called a Christian, under the mistaken impression that she was merely persecuting a Jew. *Merely* a Jew—a skinned eel who was used to it, presumably. I am persuaded that in Russia, Austria, and Germany nine-tenths of the hostility to the Jew comes from the average Christian's inability to compete successfully with the average Jew in business—in either straight business or the questionable sort.

In Berlin, a few years ago, I read a speech which frankly urged the expulsion of the Jews from Germany; and the agitator's *reason* was as frank as his proposition. It was this: *that eighty-five per cent.* of the successful lawyers of Berlin were Jews, and that about the same percentage of the great and lucrative businesses of all sorts in Germany were in the hands of the Jewish race! Isn't it an amazing confession? It was but another way of saying that in a population of 48,000,000, of whom only 500,000 were registered as Jews, eighty-five per cent. of the brains and honesty of the whole was lodged in the Jews. I must insist upon the honesty—it is an essential of successful business, taken by and large. Of course it does not rule out rascals entirely, even among Christians, but it is a good working rule, nevertheless. The speaker's figures may have been inexact, but *the motive of persecution* stands out as clear as day.

The man claimed that in Berlin the banks, the newspapers, the theatres, the great mercantile, shipping, mining, and manufacturing interests, the big army and city contracts, the tramways, and pretty much all other properties of high value, and *also* the small businesses—were in the hands of the Jews. He said the Jew was pushing the Christian to the wall all along the line; that it was all a Christian could do to scrape together a living; and that the Jew *must* be banished, and soon—there was no other way of saving the Christian. Here in Vienna, last autumn, an agitator said that all these disastrous details were true of Austria-Hungary also; and in fierce language he demanded the expulsion of the Jews. When politicians come out without a blush and read the baby act in this frank way, *unrebuked*, it is a very good indication that they have a market back of them, and know where to fish for votes.

You note the crucial point of the mentioned agitation; the argument is that the Christian cannot *compete* with the Jew, and that hence his very bread is in peril. To human beings this is a much more hate-inspiring thing than is any detail connected with religion. With most people, of a necessity, bread and meat take first rank, religion second. I am convinced that the persecution of the Jew is not due in any large degree to religious prejudice.

No, the Jew is a money-getter; and in getting his money he is a very serious obstruction to less capable neighbors who are on the same quest. I think that that is the trouble. In estimating worldly values the Jew is not shallow, but deep. With precocious wisdom he found out in the morning of time that some men worship rank, some worship heroes, some worship power, some worship God, and that over these ideals they dispute and cannot unite—but that they all worship money; so he made it the end and aim of his life to get it. He was at it in Egypt thirty-six centuries ago; he was at it in Rome when that Christian got persecuted by mistake for him; he has been at it ever since. The cost to him has been heavy; his success has made the whole human race his enemy—but it has paid, for it has brought him envy, and that is the only thing which men will sell both soul and body to get. He long ago observed that a millionaire commands respect, a two-millionaire homage, a multi-millionaire the deepest deeps of adoration. We all know that feeling; we have seen it express itself. We have noticed that when the average man mentions the name of a multi-millionaire he does it with that mixture in his voice of awe and reverence and lust which burns in a Frenchman's eye when it falls on another man's centime.

*Point No.* 4.—"The Jews have no party; they are non-participants."

Perhaps you have let the secret out and given yourself away. It seems hardly a credit to the race that it is able to say that; or to you, sir, that you can say it without remorse; more, that you should offer it as a plea against maltreatment, injustice, and oppression. Who gives the Jew the right, who gives any race the right, to sit still, in a free country, and let somebody else look after its safety? The oppressed Jew was entitled to all pity in the former times under brutal autocracies, for he was weak and friendless, and had no way to help his case. But he has ways now, and he has had them for a century, but I do not see that he has tried to make serious use of them. When the Revolution set him free in France it was an act of grace— the grace of other people; he does not appear in it as a helper. I do not know that he helped when England set him free. Among the Twelve Sane Men of France who have stepped forward with great Zola at their head to fight (and win, I hope and believe) the battle for the most infamously misused Jew of modern times, do you find a great or rich or illustrious Jew helping? In the United States he was created free in the beginning—he did not need to help, of course. In Austria and Germany and France he has a vote, but of what considerable use is it to him? He doesn't seem to know how to apply it to the best effect. With all his splendid capacities and all his fat wealth he is to-day not politically important in any country. In America, as early as 1854, the ignorant Irish hod-carrier, who had a spirit of his own and a way of exposing it to the weather, made it apparent to all that he must be polit-ically reckoned with; yet fifteen years before that we hardly knew what an Irishman looked like. As an intelligent force, and numerically, he has always been away down, but he has governed the country just the same. It was because he was *organized*. It made his vote valuable—in fact, essential.

You will say the Jew is everywhere numerically feeble. That is nothing to the point—with the Irishman's history for an object-lesson. But I am coming to your numerical feebleness presently. In all parliamentary countries you could no doubt elect Jews to the legislatures—and even *one* member in such a body is sometimes a force which counts. How deeply have you concerned yourselves about this in Austria, France, and Germany? Or even in America, for that matter? You remark that the Jews were not to blame for the riots in this Reichsrath here, and you add with satisfaction that there wasn't one in that body. That is not strictly correct; if it were, would it not be in order for you to explain it and apologize for it, not try to make a merit of it? But I think that the Jew was by no means in as large force there as he ought to have been, with his chances. Austria opens the suffrage to him on fairly liberal terms, and it must surely be his own fault that he is so much in the background politically.

As to your numerical weakness. I mentioned some figures a while ago—500,000—as the Jewish population of Germany. I will add some more—6,000,000 in Russia, 5,000,000 in Austria, 250,000 in the United States. I take them from memory; I read them in the Cyclopædia Britannica ten or twelve years ago. Still, I am entirely sure of them. If those statistics are correct, my argument is not as strong as it ought to be as concerns America, but it still has strength. It is plenty strong enough as concerns Austria, for ten years ago 5,000,000 was nine per cent. of the empire's population. The Irish would govern the Kingdom of Heaven if they had a strength there like that.

I have some suspicions; I got them at second hand, but they have remained with me these ten or twelve years. When I read in the C. B. that the Jewish population of the United States was 250,000, I wrote the editor, and explained to him that I was personally acquainted with more Jews than that in my country, and that his figures were without a doubt a misprint for 25,000,000. I also added that I was personally acquainted with *that* many there; but that was only to raise his confidence in me, for it was not true. His answer miscarried, and I never got it; but I went around talking about the matter, and people told me they had reason to suspect that for business reasons many Jews whose dealings were mainly with the Christians did not report themselves as Jews in the census. It looked plausible; it looks plausible yet. Look at the city of

New York; and look at Boston, and Philadelphia, and New
Orleans, and Chicago, and Cincinnati, and San Francisco—
how your race swarms in those places!—and everywhere else
in America, down to the least little village. Read the signs on
the marts of commerce and on the shops: Goldstein (gold
stone), Edelstein (precious stone), Blumenthal (flower-vale),
Rosenthal (rose-vale), Veilchenduft (violet odor), Singvogel
(song-bird), Rosenzweig (rose branch), and all the amazing
list of beautiful and enviable names which Prussia and Austria
glorified you with so long ago. It is another instance of Europe's coarse and cruel persecution of your race; not that it
was coarse and cruel to outfit it with pretty and poetical
names like those, but that it was coarse and cruel to make it
*pay* for them or else take such hideous and often indecent
names that to-day their owners never use them; or, if they do,
only on official papers. And it was the many, not the few,
who got the odious names, they being too poor to bribe the
officials to grant them better ones.

Now why was the race renamed? I have been told that in
Prussia it was given to using fictitious names, and often
changing them, so as to beat the tax-gatherer, escape military
service, and so on; and that finally the idea was hit upon of
furnishing all the inmates of a house with *one and the same
surname*, and then holding the house responsible right along
for those inmates, and accountable for any disappearances
that might occur; it made the Jews keep track of *each other*, for
self-interest's sake, and saved the government the trouble.*

If that explanation of how the Jews of Prussia came to be
renamed is correct, if it is true that they fictitiously registered
themselves to gain certain advantages, it may possibly be true
that in America they refrain from registering themselves as
Jews to fend off the damaging prejudices of the Christian

*In Austria the renaming was merely done because the Jews in some newly
acquired regions had no surnames, but were mostly named Abraham and
Moses, and therefore the tax-gatherer could not tell t'other from which, and
was likely to lose his reason over the matter. The renaming was put into the
hands of the War Department, and a charming mess the graceless young lieu-
tenants made of it. To them a Jew was of no sort of consequence, and they
labelled the race in a way to make the angels weep. As an example, take these
two: *Abraham Bellyache* and *Schmul Godbedamned.—Culled from "Namens
Studien," by Karl Emil Franzos.*

customer. I have no way of knowing whether this notion is well founded or not. There may be other and better ways of explaining why only that poor little 250,000 of our Jews got into the Cyclopædia. I may, of course, be mistaken, but I am strongly of the opinion that we have an immense Jewish population in America.

*Point No.* 3.—"Can Jews do anything to improve the situation?"

I think so. If I may make a suggestion without seeming to be trying to teach my grandmother how to suck eggs, I will offer it. In our days we have learned the value of combination. We apply it everywhere—in railway systems, in trusts, in trade unions, in Salvation Armies, in minor politics, in major politics, in European Concerts. Whatever our strength may be, big or little, we *organize* it. We have found out that that is the only way to get the most out of it that is in it. We know the weakness of individual sticks, and the strength of the concentrated fagot. Suppose you try a scheme like this, for instance. In England and America put every Jew on the census-book *as* a Jew (in case you have not been doing that). Get up volunteer regiments composed of Jews solely, and, when the drum beats, fall in and go to the front, so as to remove the reproach that you have few Massénas among you, and that you feed on a country but don't like to fight for it. Next, in politics, organize your strength, band together, and deliver the casting vote where you can, and where you can't, compel as good terms as possible. You huddle to yourselves already in all countries, but you huddle to no sufficient purpose, politically speaking. You do not seem to be organized, except for your charities. There you are omnipotent; there you compel your due of recognition—you do not have to beg for it. It shows what you can do when you band together for a definite purpose.

And then from America and England you can encourage your race in Austria, France, and Germany, and materially help it. It was a pathetic tale that was told by a poor Jew in Galicia a fortnight ago during the riots, after he had been raided by the Christian peasantry and despoiled of everything he had. He said his vote was of no value to him, and he wished he could be excused from casting it, for indeed casting it was a sure *damage* to him, since no matter which party he voted for, the other party would come straight and take its revenge out of him. Nine per cent. of the population of the empire, these Jews, and apparently they cannot put a plank into any candidate's platform! If you will send our Irish lads over here I think they will organize your race and change the aspect of the Reichsrath.

You seem to think that the Jews take no hand in politics here, that they are "absolutely non-participants." I am assured by men competent to speak that this is a very large error, that the Jews are exceedingly active in politics all over the empire, but that they scatter their work and their votes among the numerous parties, and thus lose the advantages to be had by concentration. I think that in America they scatter too, but you know more about that than I do.

Speaking of concentration, Dr. Herzl has a clear insight into the value of that. Have you heard of his plan? He wishes to gather the Jews of the world together in Palestine, with a government of their own—under the suzerainty of the Sultan, I suppose. At the convention of Berne, last year, there were delegates from everywhere, and the proposal was received with decided favor. I am not the Sultan, and I am not objecting; but if that concentration of the cunningest brains in the world was going to be made in a free country (bar Scotland), I think it would be politic to stop it. It will not be well to let that race find out its strength. If the horses knew theirs, we should not ride any more.

*Point No. 5.*—"Will the persecution of the Jews ever come to an end?"

On the score of religion, I think it has already come to an end. On the score of race prejudice and trade, I have the idea that it will continue. That is, here and there in spots about the world, where a barbarous ignorance and a sort of mere animal civilization prevail; but I do not think that elsewhere the Jew need now stand in any fear of being robbed and raided. Among the high civilizations he seems to be very comfortably situated indeed, and to have more than his proportionate share of the prosperities going. It has that look in Vienna. I suppose the race prejudice cannot be removed; but he can stand that; it is no particular matter. By his make and ways he is substantially a foreigner wherever he may be, and even the angels dislike a foreigner. I am using this word foreigner in the German sense—*stranger*. Nearly all of us have an antipathy to a stranger, even of our own nationality. We pile gripsacks in a vacant seat to keep him from getting it; and a dog goes further, and does as a savage would—challenges him on the spot. The German dictionary seems to make no distinction between a stranger and a foreigner; in its view a stranger *is* a foreigner—a sound position, I think. You will always be by ways and habits and predilections substantially strangers—foreigners—wherever you are, and that will probably keep the race prejudice against you alive.

But you were the favorites of Heaven originally, and your manifold and unfair prosperities convince me that you have crowded back into that snug place again. Here is an incident that is significant. Last week in Vienna a hailstorm struck the prodigious Central Cemetery and made wasteful destruction there. In the Christian part of it, according to the official figures, 621 window-panes were broken; more than 900 singing-birds were killed; five great trees and many small ones were torn to shreds and the shreds scattered far and wide by the wind; the ornamental plants and other decorations of the graves were ruined, and more than a hundred tomb-lanterns shattered; and it took the cemetery's whole force of 300 laborers more than three days to clear away the storm's wreckage. In the report occurs this remark—and in its italics you can hear it grit its Christian teeth: ". . . . lediglich die *israelitische* Abtheilung des Friedhofes vom Hagelwetter *gänzlich verschont* worden war." Not a hailstone hit the Jewish reservation! Such nepotism makes me tired.

*Point No.* 6.—"What has become of the golden rule?"

It exists, it continues to sparkle, and is well taken care of. It is Exhibit A in the Church's assets, and we pull it out every Sunday and give it an airing. But you are not permitted to try to smuggle it into this discussion, where it is irrelevant and would not feel at home. It is strictly religious furniture, like an acolyte, or a contribution-plate, or any of those things. It has never been intruded into business; and Jewish persecution is not a religious passion, it is a business passion.

*To conclude.*—If the statistics are right, the Jews constitute but *one per cent.* of the human race. It suggests a nebulous dim puff of star dust lost in the blaze of the Milky Way. Properly the Jew ought hardly to be heard of; but he is heard of, has always been heard of. He is as prominent on the planet as any other people, and his commercial importance is extravagantly out of proportion to the smallness of his bulk. His contributions to the world's list of great names in literature, science, art, music, finance, medicine, and abstruse learning are also away out of proportion to the weakness of his numbers. He has made a marvellous fight in this world, in all the ages; and has done it with his hands tied behind him. He could be vain of himself, and be excused for it. The Egyptian, the Babylonian, and the Persian rose, filled the planet with sound and splendor, then faded to dream-stuff and passed away; the Greek and the Roman followed, and made a vast noise, and they are gone; other peoples have sprung up and held their torch high for a time, but it burned out, and they sit in twilight now, or have vanished. The Jew saw them all, beat them all, and is now what he always was, exhibiting no decadence, no infirmities of age, no weakening of his parts, no slowing of his energies, no dulling of his alert and aggressive mind. All things are mortal but the Jew; all other forces pass, but he remains. What is the secret of his immortality?

*September 1899*

# Christian Science and the Book of Mrs. Eddy

*"It is the first time since the dawn-days of Creation that a Voice has gone crashing through space with such placid and complacent confidence and command."*

## I.

This last summer, when I was on my way back to Vienna from the Appetite-Cure in the mountains, I fell over a cliff in the twilight and broke some arms and legs and one thing or another, and by good luck was found by some peasants who had lost an ass and they carried me to the nearest habitation, which was one of those large, low, thatch-roofed farm-houses, with apartments in the garret for the family, and a cunning little porch under the deep gable decorated with boxes of bright-colored flowers and cats; on the ground floor a large and light sitting-room, separated from the milch-cattle apartment by a partition; and in the front yard rose stately and fine the wealth and pride of the house, the manure-pile. That sentence is Germanic, and shows that I am acquiring that sort of mastery of the art and spirit of the language which enables a man to travel all day in one sentence without changing cars.

There was a village a mile away, and a horse-doctor lived there, but there was no surgeon. It seemed a bad outlook; mine was distinctly a surgery case. Then it was remembered that a lady from Boston was summering in that village, and she was a Christian Science doctor and could cure anything. So she was sent for. It was night by this time, and she could not conveniently come, but sent word that it was no matter, there was no hurry, she would give me "absent treatment" now, and come in the morning; meantime she begged me to make myself tranquil and comfortable and remember that there was nothing the matter with me. I thought there must be some mistake.

"Did you tell her I walked off a cliff seventy-five feet high?"
"Yes."
"And struck a boulder at the bottom and bounced?"
"Yes."

"And struck another one and bounced again?"

"Yes."

"And struck another one and bounced yet again?"

"Yes."

"And broke the boulders?"

"Yes."

"That accounts for it; she is thinking of the boulders. Why didn't you tell her I got hurt, too?"

"I did. I told her what you told me to tell her: that you were now but an incoherent series of compound fractures extending from your scalp-lock to your heels, and that the comminated projections caused you to look like a hat-rack."

"And it was after this that she wished me to remember that there was nothing the matter with me?"

"Those were her words."

"I do not understand it. I believe she has not diagnosed the case with sufficient care. Did she look like a person who was theorizing, or did she look like one who has fallen off precipices herself and brings to the aid of abstract science the confirmations of personal experience?"

"Bitte?"

It was too large a contract for the Stubenmädchen's vocabulary; she couldn't call the hand. I allowed the subject to rest there, and asked for something to eat and smoke, and something hot to drink, and a basket to pile my legs in, and another capable person to come and help me curse the time away; but I could not have any of these things.

"Why?"

"She said you would need nothing at all."

"But I am hungry, and thirsty, and in desperate pain."

"She said you would have these delusions, but must pay no attention to them. She wants you to particularly remember that there are no such things as hunger and thirst and pain."

"She does, does she?"

"It is what she said."

"Does she seem to be in full and functionable possession of her intellectual plant, such as it is?"

"Bitte?"

"Do they let her run at large, or do they tie her up?"

"Tie her up?"

"There, good-night, run along; you are a good girl, but your mental Geschirr is not arranged for light and airy conversation. Leave me to my delusions."

## II.

It was a night of anguish, of course—at least, I supposed it was, for it had all the symptoms of it—but it passed at last, and the Christian Scientist came, and I was glad. She was middle-aged, and large and bony, and erect, and had an austere face and a resolute jaw and a Roman beak and was a widow in the third degree, and her name was Fuller. I was eager to get to business and find relief, but she was distressingly deliberate. She unpinned and unhooked and uncoupled her upholsteries one by one, abolished the wrinkles with a flirt of her hand and hung the articles up; peeled off her gloves and disposed of them, got a book out of her hand-bag, then drew a chair to the bedside, descended into it without hurry, and I hung out my tongue. She said, with pity but without passion:

"Return it to its receptacle. We deal with the mind only, not with its dumb servants."

I could not offer my pulse, because the connection was broken; but she detected the apology before I could word it, and indicated by a negative tilt of her head that the pulse was another dumb servant that she had no use for. Then I thought I would tell her my symptoms and how I felt, so that she would understand the case; but that was another inconsequence, she did not need to know those things; moreover, my remark about how I felt was an abuse of language, a misapplication of terms——

"One does not *feel*," she explained; "there is no such thing as feeling: therefore, to speak of a non-existent thing as existent is a contradiction. Matter has no existence; nothing exists but mind; the mind cannot feel pain, it can only imagine it."

"But if it hurts, just the same——"

"It doesn't. A thing which is unreal cannot exercise the functions of reality. Pain is unreal; hence, pain cannot hurt."

In making a sweeping gesture to indicate the act of shooing the illusion of pain out of the mind, she raked her hand on a pin in her dress, said "Ouch!" and went tranquilly on with her talk. "You should never allow yourself to speak of how you feel, nor permit others to ask you how you are feeling; you should never concede that you are ill, nor permit others to talk about disease or pain or death or similar non-existences in your presence. Such talk only encourages the mind to continue its empty imaginings." Just at that point the Stubenmädchen trod on the cat's tail, and the cat let fly a frenzy of cat-profanity. I asked, with caution:

"Is a cat's opinion about pain valuable?"

"A cat has no opinion; opinions proceed from mind only; the lower animals, being eternally perishable, have not been granted mind; without mind, opinion is impossible."

"She merely *imagined* she felt a pain—the cat?"

"She cannot imagine a pain, for imagination is an effect of mind; without mind, there is no imagination. A cat has no imagination."

"Then she had a *real* pain?"

"I have already told you there is no such *thing* as real pain."

"It is strange and interesting. I do wonder what was the matter with the cat. Because, there being no such thing as a real pain, and she not being able to imagine an imaginary one, it would seem that God in his pity has compensated the cat with some kind of a mysterious emotion usable when her tail is trodden on which for the moment joins cat and Christian in one common brotherhood of——"

She broke in with an irritated—

"Peace! The cat feels nothing, the Christian feels nothing. Your empty and foolish imaginings are profanation and blasphemy and can do you an injury. It is wiser and better and holier to recognize and confess that there is no such thing as disease or pain or death."

"I am full of imaginary tortures," I said, "but I do not think I could be any more uncomfortable if they were real ones. What must I do to get rid of them?"

"There is no occasion to get rid of them, since they do not exist. They are illusions propagated by matter, and matter has no existence; there is no such thing as matter."

"It sounds right and clear, but yet it seems in a degree elusive; it seems to slip through, just when you think you are getting a grip on it."

"Explain."

"Well, for instance: if there is no such thing as matter, how can matter propagate things?"

In her compassion she almost smiled. She would have smiled if there were any such thing as a smile.

"It is quite simple," she said; "the fundamental propositions of Christian Science explain it, and they are summarized in the four following self-evident propositions: 1. God is All in all. 2. God is good. Good is Mind. 3. God, Spirit, being all, nothing is matter. 4. Life, God, omnipotent Good, deny death, evil, sin, disease. There—now you see."

It seemed nebulous; it did not seem to say anything about the difficulty in hand—how non-existent matter can propagate illusions. I said, with some hesitancy:

"Does—does it explain?"

"*Doesn't* it? Even if read backward it will do it."

With a budding hope, I asked her to do it backward.

"Very well. Disease sin evil death deny Good omnipotent God life matter is nothing all being Spirit God Mind is Good good is God all in All is God. There—do you understand now?"

"It—it—well, it is plainer than it was before; still——"

"Well?"

"Could you try it some more ways?"

"As many as you like; it always means the same. Interchanged in any way you please it cannot be made to mean anything different from what it means when put in any other way. Because it is perfect. You can jumble it all up, and it makes no difference: it always comes out the way it was before. It was a marvelous mind that produced it. As a mental tour de force it is without a mate, it defies alike the simple, the concrete and the occult."

"It seems to be a corker."

I blushed for the word, but it was out before I could stop it.

"A what?"

"A—wonderful structure—combination, so to speak, of profound thoughts—unthinkable ones—un——"

"It is true. Read backwards, or forwards, or perpendicularly, or at any given angle, these four propositions will always be found to agree in statement and proof."

"Ah—proof. Now we are coming at it. The *statements* agree; they agree with—with—anyway, they agree; I noticed that; but what is it they prove—I mean, in particular?"

"Why, nothing could be clearer. They prove: 1. GOD—Principle, Life, Truth, Love, Soul, Spirit, Mind. Do you get that?"

"I—well, I seem to. Go on, please."

"2. MAN—God's universal idea, individual, perfect, eternal. Is it clear?"

"It—I think so. Continue."

"3. IDEA—An image in Mind; the immediate object of understanding. There it is—the whole sublime Arcana of Christian Science in a nutshell. Do you find a weak place in it anywhere?"

"Well—no; it seems strong."

"Very well. There is more. Those three constitute the Scientific Definition of Immortal Mind. Next, we have the Scientific Definition of Mortal Mind. Thus. FIRST DEGREE: *Depravity*. 1. Physical—Passions and appetites, fear, depraved will, pride, envy, deceit, hatred, revenge, sin, disease, death."

"Phantasms, madam—unrealities, as I understand it."

"Every one. SECOND DEGREE: *Evil Disappearing*. 1. Moral—Honesty, affection, compassion, hope, faith, meekness, temperance. Is it clear?"

"Crystal."

"THIRD DEGREE: *Spiritual Salvation*. 1. Spiritual—Faith, wisdom, power, purity, understanding, health, love. You see how searchingly and coördinately interdependent and anthropomorphous it all is. In this Third Degree, as we know by the revelations of Christian Science, mortal mind disappears."

"Not earlier?"

"No, not until the teaching and preparation for the Third Degree are completed."

"It is not until then that one is enabled to take hold of Christian Science effectively, and with the right sense of sympathy and kinship, as I understand you. That is to say, it could not succeed during the processes of the Second Degree, because there would still be remains of mind left; and there-fore—but I interrupted you. You were about to further explain the good results proceeding from the erosions and disintegrations effected by the Third Degree. It is very interesting; go on, please."

"Yes, as I was saying, in this Third Degree mortal mind disappears. Science so reverses the evidence before the corporeal human senses as to make this scriptural testimony true in our hearts, 'the last shall be first and the first shall be last,' that God and His idea may be to us—what divinity really is, and must of necessity be—all-inclusive."

"It is beautiful. And with what exhaustive exactness your choice and arrangement of words confirms and establishes what you have claimed for the powers and functions of the Third Degree. The Second could probably produce only temporary absence of mind, it is reserved to the Third to make it permanent. A sentence framed under the auspices of the Second could have a kind of meaning—a sort of deceptive semblance of it—whereas it is only under the magic of the Third that that defect would disappear. Also, without doubt, it is the Third Degree that contributes another remarkable specialty to Christian Science: viz., ease and flow and lavishness of words, and rhythm and swing and smoothness. There must be a special reason for this?"

"Yes—God-all, all-God, good God, non-Matter, Matteration, Spirit, Bones, Truth."

"That explains it."

"There is nothing in Christian Science that is not explicable; for God is one, Time is one, Individuality is one, and may be one of a series, one of many, as an individual man, individual horse; whereas God is one, not one of a series, but one alone and without an equal."

"These are noble thoughts. They make one burn to know more. How does Christian Science explain the spiritual relation of systematic duality to incidental deflection?"

"Christian Science reverses the seeming relation of Soul and body—as astronomy reverses the human perception of the movement of the solar system—and makes body tributary to the Mind. As it is the earth which is in motion, while the sun is at rest, though in viewing the sun rise one finds it impossible to believe the sun not to be really rising, so the body is but the humble servant of the restful Mind, though it seems otherwise to finite sense; but we shall never understand this while we admit that soul is in body, or mind in matter, and that man is included in non-intelligence. Soul is God, unchangeable and eternal; and man coexists with and reflects Soul, for the All-in-all is the Altogether, and the Altogether embraces the All-one, Soul-Mind, Mind-Soul, Love, Spirit, Bones, Liver, one of a series, alone and without an equal."

(It is very curious, the effect which Christian Science has upon the verbal bowels. Particularly the Third Degree; it makes one think of a dictionary with the cholera. But I only thought this; I did not say it.)

"What is the origin of Christian Science? Is it a gift of God, or did it just happen?"

"In a sense, it is a gift of God. That is to say, its powers are from Him, but the credit of the discovery of the powers and what they are for, is due to an American lady."

"Indeed? When did this occur?"

"In 1866. That is the immortal date when pain and disease and death disappeared from the earth to return no more forever. That is, the fancies for which those terms stand, disappeared. The things themselves had never existed; therefore as soon as it was perceived that there were no such things, they were easily banished. The history and nature of the great discovery are set down in the book here, and——"

"Did the lady write the book?"

"Yes, she wrote it all, herself. The title is 'Science and Health, with Key to the Scriptures'—for she explains the scriptures; they were not understood before. Not even by the twelve Disciples. She begins thus—I will read it to you."

But she had forgotten to bring her glasses.

"Well, it is no matter," she said, "I remember the words— indeed, all Christian Scientists know the book by heart; it is necessary in our practice. We should otherwise make mistakes and do harm. She begins thus: 'In the year 1866 I discovered the Science of Metaphysical Healing, and named it Christian Science.' And she says—quite beautifully, I think—'Through Christian Science, religion and medicine are inspired with a diviner nature and essence, fresh pinions are given to faith and understanding, and thoughts acquaint themselves intelligently with God.' Her very words."

"It is elegant. And it is a fine thought, too—marrying religion to medicine, instead of medicine to the undertaker in the old way; for religion and medicine properly belong together, they being the basis of all spiritual and physical health. What kind of medicine do you give for the ordinary diseases, such as——"

"We never give medicine in *any* circumstances whatever! We——"

"But, madam, it *says*——"

"I don't care what it says, and I don't wish to talk about it."

"I am sorry if I have offended, but you see the mention seemed in some way inconsistent, and——"

"There *are* no inconsistencies in Christian Science. The thing is impossible, for the Science is absolute. It cannot be otherwise, since it proceeds directly from the All-in-all and the Everything-in-Which, also Soul, Bones, Truth, one of a series, alone and without equal. It is Mathematics purified from material dross and made spiritual."

"I can see that, but——"

"It rests upon the immovable basis of an Apodictical Principle."

The word flattened itself against my mind in trying to get in, and disordered me a little, and before I could inquire into its pertinency, she was already throwing the needed light:

"This Apodictical Principle is the absolute Principle of Scientific Mind-healing, the sovereign Omnipotence which delivers the children of men from pain, disease, decay, and every ill that flesh is heir to."

"Surely not every ill, every decay?"

"Every one; there are no exceptions; there is no such thing as decay—it is an unreality, it has no existence."

"But without your glasses your failing eyesight does not permit you to——"

"My eyesight cannot fail; nothing can fail; the Mind is master, and the Mind permits no retrogression."

She was under the inspiration of the Third Degree, therefore there could be no profit in continuing this part of the subject. I shifted to other ground and inquired further concerning the Discoverer of the Science.

"Did the discovery come suddenly, like Klondike, or after long study and calculation, like America?"

"The comparisons are not respectful, since they refer to trivialities—but let it pass. I will answer in the Discoverer's own words: 'God had been graciously fitting me, during many years, for the reception of a final revelation of the absolute Principle of Scientific Mind-healing.'"

"Many years. How many?"

"Eighteen centuries!"

"All-God, God-good, good-God, Truth, Bones, Liver, one of a series, alone and without equal—it is amazing!"

"You may well say it, sir. Yet it is but the truth. This American lady, our revered and sacred Founder, is distinctly referred to and her coming prophesied, in the twelfth chapter of the Apocalypse; she could not have been more plainly indicated by St. John without actually mentioning her name."

"How strange, how wonderful!"

"I will quote her own words, from her Key to the Scriptures: 'The twelfth chapter of the Apocalypse *has a special suggestiveness in connection with this nineteenth century.*' There—do you note that? Think—note it well."

"But—what does it mean?"

"Listen, and you will know. I quote her inspired words again: 'In the opening of the Sixth Seal, typical of six thousand years since Adam, there is one distinctive feature *which has special reference to the present age.* Thus:

"'Revelation xii. 1. And there appeared a great wonder in heaven—a *woman* clothed with the sun, and the moon under her feet, and upon her head a crown of twelve stars.'

"That is our Head, our Chief, our Discoverer of Christian Science—nothing can be plainer, nothing surer. And note this:

"'Revelation xii. 6. And the woman fled into the wilderness, where she had a place prepared of God.'

"That is Boston."

"I recognize it, madam. These are sublime things, and impressive; I never understood these passages before; please go on with the—with the—proofs."

"Very well. Listen:

" 'And I saw another mighty angel come down from heaven, clothed with a cloud; and a rainbow was upon his head, and his face was as it were the sun, and his feet as pillars of fire. And he had in his hand *a little book*.'

"A little book, merely a little book—could words be modester? Yet how stupendous its importance! Do you know what book that was?"

"Was it——"

"I hold it in my hand—Christian Science!"

"Love, Livers, Lights, Bones, Truth, Kidneys, one of a series, alone and without equal—it is beyond imagination for wonder!"

"Hear our Founder's eloquent words: 'Then will a voice from harmony cry, "Go and take the little book: take it and eat it up, and it shall make thy belly bitter; but it shall be in thy mouth sweet as honey." Mortal, obey the heavenly evangel. Take up Divine Science. Read it from beginning to end. Study it, ponder it. It will be indeed sweet at its first taste, when it heals you; but murmur not over Truth, if you find its digestion bitter.' You now know the history of our dear and holy Science, sir, and that its *origin* is not of this earth, but only its *discovery*. I will leave the book with you and will go, now; but give yourself no uneasiness—I will give you absent treatment from now till I go to bed."

### III.

Under the powerful influence of the near treatment and the absent treatment together, my bones were gradually retreating inward and disappearing from view. The good work took a brisk start, now, and went on quite swiftly. My body was diligently straining and stretching, this way and that, to accommodate the processes of restoration, and every minute or two I heard a dull click inside and knew that the two ends of a fracture had been successfully joined. This muffled clicking and gritting and grinding and rasping continued during the next three hours, and then stopped—the connections had all been made. All except dislocations; there were only seven of these: hips, shoulders, knees, neck; so that was soon over; one after another they slipped into their sockets with a sound like pulling a distant cork, and I jumped up as good as new, as to framework, and sent for the horse-doctor.

I was obliged to do this because I had a stomach-ache and a cold in the head, and I was not willing to trust these things any longer in the hands of a woman whom I did not know, and in whose ability to successfully treat mere disease I had lost all confidence. My position was justified by the fact that the cold and the ache had been in her charge from the first, along with the fractures, but had experienced not a shade of relief; and indeed the ache was even growing worse and worse, and more and more bitter, now, probably on account of the protracted abstention from food and drink.

The horse-doctor came, a pleasant man and full of hope and professional interest in the case. In the matter of smell he was pretty aromatic, in fact quite horsy, and I tried to arrange with him for absent treatment, but it was not in his line, so out of delicacy I did not press it. He looked at my teeth and examined my hock, and said my age and general condition were favorable to energetic measures; therefore he would give me something to turn the stomach-ache into the botts and the cold in the head into the blind staggers; then he should be on his own beat and would know what to do. He made up a bucket of bran-mash, and said a dipperful of it every two hours, alternated with a drench with turpentine and axle-grease in it, would either knock my ailments out of me in twenty-four hours or so interest me in other ways as to make me forget they were on the premises. He administered my first dose himself, then took his leave, saying I was free to eat and drink anything I pleased and in any quantity I liked. But I was not hungry any more, and I did not care for food.

I took up the Christian Scientist book and read half of it, then took a dipperful of drench and read the other half. The resulting experiences were full of interest and adventure. All through the rumblings and grindings and quakings and effervescings accompanying the evolution of the ache into the botts and the cold into the blind staggers I could note the generous struggle for mastery going on between the mash and the drench and the literature; and often I could tell which was ahead, and could easily distinguish the literature from the others when the others were separate, though not when they were mixed; for when a bran-mash and an eclectic drench are mixed together they look just like the Apodictical Principle out on a lark, and no one can tell it from that. The finish was reached at last, the evolutions were complete and a fine success; but I think that this result could have been achieved with fewer materials. I believe the mash was necessary to the conversion of the stomach-ache into the botts, but I think one could develop the blind staggers out of the literature by itself; also, that blind staggers produced in this way would be of a better quality and more lasting than any produced by the artificial processes of a horse-doctor.

For of all the strange, and frantic, and incomprehensible, and uninterpretable books which the imagination of man has created, surely this one is the prize sample. It is written with a limitless confidence and complacency, and with a dash and stir and earnestness which often compel the effects of eloquence, even when the words do not seem to have any traceable meaning. There are plenty of people who imagine they understand the book; I know this, for I have talked with them; but in all cases they were people who also imagined that there were no such things as pain, sickness and death, and no realities in the world; nothing actually existent but Mind. It seems to me to modify the value of their testimony. When these people talk about Christian Science they do as Mrs. Fuller did: they do not use their own language, but the book's; they pour out the book's showy incoherences, and leave you to find out later that they were not originating, but merely quoting; they seem to know the volume by heart, and to revere it as they would a Bible—another Bible, perhaps I ought to say. Plainly the book was written under the mental desolations of the Third Degree, and I feel sure that none but the membership of that Degree can discover meanings in it. When you read it you seem to be listening to a lively and aggressive and oracular speech delivered in an unknown tongue, a speech whose spirit you get but not the particulars; or, to change the figure, you seem to be listening to a vigorous instrument which is making a noise which it thinks is a tune, but which to persons not members of the band is only the martial tooting of a trombone, and merely stirs the soul through the noise but does not convey a meaning.

The book's serenities of self-satisfaction do almost seem to smack of a heavenly origin—they have no blood-kin in the earth. It is more than human to be so placidly certain about things, and so finely superior, and so airily content with one's performance. Without ever presenting anything which may rightfully be called by the strong name of Evidence; and sometimes without even *mentioning* a reason for a deduction at all, it thunders out the startling words, "I have *Proved*" so and so! It takes the Pope and all the great guns of his church in battery assembled to authoritatively settle and establish the meaning of a sole and single unclarified passage of scripture, and this at vast cost of time and study and reflection, but the author of this work is superior to all that: she finds the whole Book in an unclarified condition, and at small expense of time and no expense of mental effort she clarifies it from lid to lid, reorganizes and improves the meanings, then authoritatively settles and establishes them with formulæ which you cannot tell from "Let there be light!" and "Here you have it!" It is the first time since the dawn-days of Creation that a Voice has gone crashing through space with such placid and complacent confidence and command.

IV.

A word upon a question of authorship. Not that quite; but rather, a question of emendation and revision. We know that the Bible-Annex was not written by Mrs. Eddy, but was handed down to her eighteen hundred years ago by the Angel of the Apocalypse; but did she translate it alone, or did she have help? There seems to be evidence that she had help. For there are four several copyrights on it—1875, 1885, 1890, 1894. It did not come down in English, for in that language it could not have acquired copyright—there were no copyright laws eighteen centuries ago, and in my opinion no English language—at least up there. This makes it substantially certain that the Annex is a translation. Then, was not the first translation complete? If it was, on what grounds were the later copyrights granted?

I surmise that the first translation was poor; and that a friend or friends of Mrs. Eddy mended its English three times, and finally got it into its present shape, where the grammar is plenty good enough, and the sentences are smooth and plausible though they do not mean anything. I think I am right in this surmise, for Mrs. Eddy cannot write English to-day, and this is argument that she never could. I am not able to guess who did the mending, but I think it was not done by any member of the Eddy Trust, nor by the editors of the "C. S. Journal," for their English is not much better than Mrs. Eddy's.

However, as to the main point: it is certain that Mrs. Eddy did not doctor the Annex's English herself. Her original, spontaneous, undoctored English furnishes ample proof of this. Here are samples from recent articles from her unappeasable pen; double-columned with them are a couple of passages from the Annex. It will be seen that they throw light. The italics are mine:

1. "What plague spot, or bacilli were (*sic*) gnawing (*sic*) at the heart of this metropolis . . . and bringing it" (the heart) "on bended knee? Why, it was an *institute* that had entered its vitals—that, among other things, *taught games*," et cetera. (*P. 670, C. S. Journal, article entitled "A Narrative—by Mary Baker G. Eddy."*)

2. "Parks sprang up (*sic*) . . . electric street cars run (*sic*) merrily through several streets, concrete sidewalks and macadamized roads dotted (*sic*) the place," et cetera. (*Ibid.*)

"Therefore the efficient remedy is to destroy the patient's unfortunate belief, by both silently and audibly arguing the opposite facts in regard to harmonious being—representing man as healthful instead of diseased, and showing that it is impossible for matter to suffer, to feel pain or heat, to be thirsty or sick." (*P. 375, Annex.*)

"Man is never sick; for Mind is not sick, and matter cannot be. A false belief is both the tempter and the tempted, the sin and the sinner, the disease and its cause.

3. "Shorn (*sic*) of its sub-urbs it had indeed little left to admire, save to (*sic*) such as fancy a skeleton above ground *breathing* (*sic*) slowly through a barren (*sic*) breast." (*Ibid.*)

It is well to be calm in sick-ness; to be hopeful is still better; but to understand that sickness is not real, and that Truth can destroy it, is best of all, for it is the uni-versal and perfect remedy." (*Chapter xii, Annex.*)

You notice the contrast between the smooth, plausible, elegant, addled English of the doctored Annex and the lum-bering, ragged, ignorant output of the translator's natural, spontaneous and unmedicated penwork. The English of the Annex has been slicked up by a very industrious and pains-taking hand—but it was not Mrs. Eddy's.

If Mrs. Eddy really wrote or translated the Annex, her orig-inal draft was exactly in harmony with the English of her plague-spot or bacilli which were gnawing at the insides of the metropolis and bringing its heart on bended knee, thus exposing to the eye the rest of the skeleton breathing slowly through a barren breast. And it bore little or no resemblance to the book as we have it now—now that the salaried pol-isher has holy-stoned all of the genuine Eddyties out of it.

Will the plague-spot article go into a volume just as it stands? I think not. I think the polisher will take off his coat and vest and cravat and "demonstrate over" it a couple of weeks and sweat it into a shape something like the follow-ing—and then Mrs. Eddy will publish it and leave people to believe that she did the polishing herself:

1. What injurious influence was it that was affecting the city's morals? It was a social club which propagated an inter-est in idle amusements, disseminated a knowledge of games, et cetera.

2. By the magic of the new and nobler influences the sterile spaces were transformed into wooded parks, the merry elec-tric car replaced the melancholy 'bus, smooth concrete the tempestuous plank sidewalk, the macadamized road the prim-itive corduroy, et cetera.

3. Its pleasant suburbs gone, there was little left to admire save the wrecked graveyard with its uncanny exposures.

The Annex contains one sole and solitary humorous remark. There is a most elaborate and voluminous Index, and it is preceded by this note:

"This Index will enable the student to find any thought or idea contained in the book."

## V.

No one doubts—certainly not I—that the mind exercises a powerful influence over the body. From the beginning of time, the sorcerer, the interpreter of dreams, the fortune-teller, the charlatan, the quack, the wild medicine-man, the educated physician, the mesmerist, and the hypnotist, have made use of the client's *imagination* to help them in their work. They have all recognized the potency and availability of that force. Physicians cure many patients with a bread pill; they know that where the disease is only a fancy, the patient's confidence in the doctor will make the bread pill effective.

*Faith in the doctor.* Perhaps that is the entire thing. It seems to look like it. In old times the King cured the king's evil by the touch of the royal hand. He frequently made extraordinary cures. Could his footman have done it? No—not in his own clothes. Disguised as the King could he have done it? I think we may not doubt it. I think we may feel sure that it was not the King's touch that made the cure in any instance, but the patient's faith in the efficacy of a King's touch. Genuine and remarkable cures have been achieved through contact with the relics of a saint. Is it not likely that any other bones would have done as well if the substitution had been concealed from the patient? When I was a boy a farmer's wife who lived five miles from our village had great fame as a faith-doctor—that was what she called herself. Sufferers came to her from all around, and she laid her hand upon them and said, "Have faith—it is all that is necessary," and they went away well of their ailments. She was not a religious woman, and pretended to no occult powers. She said that the patient's faith in her did the work. Several times I saw her make immediate cures of severe toothaches. My mother was the patient. In Austria there is a peasant who drives a great trade in this sort of industry and has both the high and the low for patients. He gets into prison every now and then for practising without a diploma, but his business is as brisk as ever when he gets out, for his work is unquestionably successful and keeps his reputation high. In Bavaria there is a man who performed so many great cures that he had to retire from his profession of stage-carpentering in order to meet the demand of his constantly increasing body of customers. He goes on from year to year doing his miracles, and has become very rich. He pretends to no religious helps, no supernatural aids, but thinks there is something in his make-up which inspires the confidence of his patients, and that it is this confidence which does the work and not some mysterious power issuing from himself.

Within the last quarter of a century, in America, several sects of curers have appeared under various names and have done notable things in the way of healing ailments without the use of medicines. There are the Mind Cure, the Faith Cure, the Prayer Cure, the Mental Science Cure and the Christian Science Cure; and apparently they all do their miracles with the same old powerful instrument—*the patient's imagination*. Differing names, but no difference in the process. But they do not give that instrument the credit; each sect claims that its way differs from the ways of the others.

They all achieve some cures, there is no question about it; and the Faith Cure and the Prayer Cure probably do no harm when they do no good, since they do not forbid the patient to help out the cure with medicines if he wants to; but the others bar medicines, and claim ability to cure every conceivable human ailment through the application of their mental forces alone. They claim ability to cure malignant cancer, and other affections which have never been cured in the history of the race. There would seem to be an element of danger here. It has the look of claiming too much, I think. Public confidence would probably be increased if less were claimed.

I believe it might be shown that all the "mind" sects except Christian Science have lucid intervals; intervals in which they betray some diffidence, and in effect confess that they are not the equals of the Deity; but if the Christian Scientist even stops with being *merely* the equal of the Deity it is not clearly provable by his Christian-Science Amended Bible. In the usual Bible the Deity recognizes pain, disease and death as facts, but the Christian Scientist knows better. Knows better, and is not diffident about saying so.

The Christian Scientist was not able to cure my stomach-ache and my cold; but the horse-doctor did it. This convinces me that Christian Science claims too much. In my opinion it ought to let diseases alone and confine itself to surgery. There it would have everything its own way.

The horse-doctor charged me thirty kreutzers, and I paid him; in fact, I doubled it and gave him a shilling. Mrs. Fuller brought in an itemized bill for a crate of broken bones mended in two hundred and thirty-four places—one dollar per fracture.

"Nothing exists but Mind?"

"Nothing," she answered. "All else is substanceless, all else is imaginary."

I gave her an imaginary check, and now she is suing me for substantial dollars. It looks inconsistent.

*October 1899*

# The Man That Corrupted Hadleyburg

## I.

It was many years ago. Hadleyburg was the most honest and upright town in all the region round about. It had kept that reputation unsmirched during three generations, and was prouder of it than of any other of its possessions. It was so proud of it, and so anxious to insure its perpetuation, that it began to teach the principles of honest dealing to its babies in the cradle, and made the like teachings the staple of their culture thenceforward through all the years devoted to their education. Also, throughout the formative years temptations were kept out of the way of the young people, so that their honesty could have every chance to harden and solidify, and become a part of their very bone. The neighboring towns were jealous of this honorable supremacy, and affected to sneer at Hadleyburg's pride in it and call it vanity; but all the same they were obliged to acknowledge that Hadleyburg was in reality an incorruptible town; and if pressed they would also acknowledge that the mere fact that a young man hailed from Hadleyburg was all the recommendation he needed when he went forth from his natal town to seek for responsible employment.

But at last, in the drift of time, Hadleyburg had the ill luck to offend a passing stranger—possibly without knowing it, certainly without caring, for Hadleyburg was sufficient unto itself, and cared not a rap for strangers or their opinions. Still, it would have been well to make an exception in this one's case, for he was a bitter man and revengeful. All through his wanderings during a whole year he kept his injury in mind, and gave all his leisure moments to trying to invent a compensating satisfaction for it. He contrived many plans, and all of them were good, but none of them was quite sweeping enough; the poorest of them would hurt a great many individuals, but what he wanted was a plan which would comprehend the entire town, and not let so much as one person escape unhurt. At last he had a fortunate idea, and when it fell into his brain it lit up his whole head with an evil joy. He began to form a plan at once, saying to himself, "That is the thing to do—I will corrupt the town."

Six months later he went to Hadleyburg, and arrived in a buggy at the house of the old cashier of the bank about ten at night. He got a sack out of the buggy, shouldered it, and staggered with it through the cottage yard, and knocked at the door. A woman's voice said "Come in," and he entered, and set his sack behind the stove in the parlor, saying politely to the old lady who sat reading the *Missionary Herald* by the lamp:

"Pray keep your seat, madam, I will not disturb you. There—now it is pretty well concealed; one would hardly know it was there. Can I see your husband a moment, madam?"

No, he was gone to Brixton, and might not return before morning.

"Very well, madam, it is no matter. I merely wanted to leave that sack in his care, to be delivered to the rightful owner when he shall be found. I am a stranger; he does not know me; I am merely passing through the town to-night to discharge a matter which has been long in my mind. My errand is now completed, and I go pleased and a little proud, and you will never see me again. There is a paper attached to the sack which will explain everything. Good-night, madam."

The old lady was afraid of the mysterious big stranger, and was glad to see him go. But her curiosity was roused, and she went straight to the sack and brought away the paper. It began as follows:

"To be Published; or, the right man sought out by private inquiry—either will answer. This sack contains gold coin weighing a hundred and sixty pounds four ounces—"

"Mercy on us, and the door not locked!"

Mrs. Richards flew to it all in a tremble and locked it, then pulled down the window-shades and stood frightened, worried, and wondering if there was anything else she could do toward making herself and the money more safe. She listened awhile for burglars, then surrendered to curiosity and went back to the lamp and finished reading the paper:

"I am a foreigner, and am presently going back to my own country, to remain there permanently. I am grateful to America for what I have received at her hands during my long stay under her flag; and to one of her citizens—a citizen of Hadleyburg—I am especially grateful for a great kindness done me a year or two ago. Two great kindnesses, in fact. I will explain. I was a gambler. I say I *was*. I was a ruined gambler. I arrived in this village at night, hungry and without a penny. I asked for help—in the dark; I was ashamed to beg in the light. I begged of the right man. He gave me twenty dollars—that is to say, he gave me life, as I considered it. He also gave me fortune; for out of that money I have made myself rich at the gaming-table. And finally, a remark which he made to me has remained with me to this day, and has at last conquered me; and in conquering has saved the remnant of my morals: I shall gamble no more. Now I have no idea who that man was, but I want him found, and I want him to have this money, to give away, throw away, or keep, as he pleases. It is merely my way of testifying my gratitude to him. If I could stay, I would find him myself; but no matter, he will be found. This is an honest town, an incorruptible town, and I know I can trust it without fear. This man can be identified by the remark which he made to me; I feel persuaded that he will remember it.

"And now my plan is this: If you prefer to conduct the inquiry privately, do so. Tell the contents of this present writing to any one who is likely to be the right man. If he shall answer, 'I am the man; the remark I made was so-and-so,' apply the test—to wit: open the sack, and in it you will find a sealed envelope containing that remark. If the remark mentioned by the candidate tallies with it, give him the money, and ask no further questions, for he is certainly the right man.

"But if you shall prefer a public inquiry, then publish this present writing in the local paper—with these instructions added, to wit: Thirty days from now, let the candidate appear at the town-hall at eight in the evening (Friday), and hand his remark, in a sealed envelope, to the Rev. Mr. Burgess (if he will be kind enough to act); and let Mr. Burgess there and then destroy the seals of the sack, open it, and see if the remark is correct; if correct, let the money be delivered, with my sincere gratitude, to my benefactor thus identified."

Mrs. Richards sat down, gently quivering with excitement, and was soon lost in thinkings—after this pattern: "What a strange thing it is! . . . . And what a fortune for that kind man who set his bread afloat upon the waters! . . . . If it had only been my husband that did it!—for we are so poor, so old and poor! . . . ." Then, with a sigh—"But it was not my Edward; no, it was not he that gave a stranger twenty dollars. It is a pity too; I see it now. . . ." Then, with a shudder— "But it is *gambler's* money! the wages of sin; we couldn't take it; we couldn't touch it. I don't like to be near it; it seems a defilement." She moved to a farther chair. . . . "I wish Edward would come, and take it to the bank; a burglar might come at any moment; it is dreadful to be here all alone with it."

At eleven Mr. Richards arrived, and while his wife was saying, "I am *so* glad you've come!" he was saying, "I'm so tired—tired clear out; it is dreadful to be poor, and have to make these dismal journeys at my time of life. Always at the grind, grind, grind, on a salary—another man's slave, and he sitting at home in his slippers, rich and comfortable."

"I am so sorry for you, Edward, you know that; but be comforted; we have our livelihood; we have our good name—"

"Yes, Mary, and that is everything. Don't mind my talk— it's just a moment's irritation and doesn't mean anything. Kiss me—there, it's all gone now, and I am not complaining any more. What have you been getting? What's in the sack?"

Then his wife told him the great secret. It dazed him for a moment; then he said:

"It weighs a hundred and sixty pounds? Why, Mary, it's for-ty thou-sand dollars—think of it—a whole fortune! Not ten men in this village are worth that much. Give me the paper."

He skimmed through it and said:

"Isn't it an adventure! Why, it's a romance; it's like the

impossible things one reads about in books, and never sees in life." He was well stirred up now; cheerful, even gleeful. He tapped his old wife on the cheek, and said, humorously, "Why, we're rich, Mary, rich; all we've got to do is to bury the money and burn the papers. If the gambler ever comes to inquire, we'll merely look coldly upon him and say: 'What is this nonsense you are talking? We have never heard of you and your sack of gold before;' and then he would look foolish, and—"

"And in the mean time, while you are running on with your jokes, the money is still here, and it is fast getting along toward burglar-time."

"True. Very well, what shall we do—make the inquiry private? No, not that; it would spoil the romance. The public method is better. Think what a noise it will make! And it will make all the other towns jealous; for no stranger would trust such a thing to any town but Hadleyburg, and they know it. It's a great card for us. I must get to the printing-office now, or I shall be too late."

"But stop—stop—don't leave me here alone with it, Edward!"

But he was gone. For only a little while, however. Not far from his own house he met the editor-proprietor of the paper, and gave him the document, and said, "Here is a good thing for you, Cox—put it in."

"It may be too late, Mr. Richards, but I'll see."

At home again he and his wife sat down to talk the charming mystery over; they were in no condition for sleep. The first question was, Who could the citizen have been who gave the stranger the twenty dollars? It seemed a simple one; both answered it in the same breath—

"Barclay Goodson."

"Yes," said Richards, "he could have done it, and it would have been like him, but there's not another in the town."

"Everybody will grant that, Edward—grant it privately, anyway. For six months, now, the village has been its own proper self once more—honest, narrow, self-righteous, and stingy."

"It is what he always called it, to the day of his death—said it right out publicly, too."

"Yes, and he was hated for it."

"Oh, of course; but he didn't care. I reckon he was the best-hated man among us, except the Reverend Burgess."

"Well, Burgess deserves it—he will never get another congregation here. Mean as the town is, it knows how to estimate *him*. Edward, doesn't it seem odd that the stranger should appoint Burgess to deliver the money?"

"Well, yes—it does. That is—that is—"

"Why so much that-*is*-ing? Would *you* select him?"

"Mary, maybe the stranger knows him better than this village does."

"Much *that* would help Burgess!"

The husband seemed perplexed for an answer; the wife kept a steady eye upon him, and waited. Finally Richards said, with the hesitancy of one who is making a statement which is likely to encounter doubt,

"Mary, Burgess is not a bad man."

His wife was certainly surprised.

"Nonsense!" she exclaimed.

"He is not a bad man. I know. The whole of his unpopularity had its foundation in that one thing—the thing that made so much noise."

"That 'one thing,' indeed! As if that 'one thing' wasn't enough, all by itself."

"Plenty. Plenty. Only he wasn't guilty of it."

"How you talk! Not guilty of it! Everybody knows he *was* guilty."

"Mary, I give you my word—he was innocent."

"I can't believe it, and I don't. How do you know?"

"It is a confession. I am ashamed, but I will make it. I was the only man who knew he was innocent. I could have saved him, and—and—well, you know how the town was wrought up—I hadn't the pluck to do it. It would have turned everybody against me. I felt mean, ever so mean; but I didn't dare; I hadn't the manliness to face that."

Mary looked troubled, and for a while was silent. Then she said, stammeringly:

"I—I don't think it would have done for you to—to—One mustn't—er—public opinion—one has to be so careful—so—" It was a difficult road, and she got mired; but after a little she got started again. "It was a great pity, but—Why, we couldn't afford it, Edward—we couldn't indeed. Oh, I wouldn't have had you do it for anything!"

"It would have lost us the good-will of so many people, Mary; and then—and then—"

"What troubles me now is, what *he* thinks of us, Edward."

"He? *He* doesn't suspect that I could have saved him."

"Oh," exclaimed the wife, in a tone of relief, "I am glad of that. As long as he doesn't know that you could have saved him, he—he—well, that makes it a great deal better. Why, I might have known he didn't know, because he is always trying to be friendly with us, as little encouragement as we give him. More than once people have twitted me with it. There's the Wilsons, and the Wilcoxes, and the Harknesses, they take a mean pleasure in saying, '*Your friend* Burgess,' because they know it pesters me. I wish he wouldn't persist in liking us so; I can't think why he keeps it up."

"I can explain it. It's another confession. When the thing was new and hot, and the town made a plan to ride him on a rail, my conscience hurt me so that I couldn't stand it, and I went privately and gave him notice, and he got out of the town and staid out till it was safe to come back."

"Edward! If the town had found it out—"

"*Don't!* It scares me yet, to think of it. I repented of it the minute it was done; and I was even afraid to tell you, lest your face might betray it to somebody. I didn't sleep any that night, for worrying. But after a few days I saw that no one was going to suspect me, and after that I got to feeling glad I did it. And I feel glad yet, Mary—glad through and through."

"So do I, now, for it would have been a dreadful way to treat him. Yes, I'm glad; for really you did owe him that, you know. But, Edward, suppose it should come out yet, some day!"

"It won't."

"Why?"

"Because everybody thinks it was Goodson."

"Of course they would!"

"Certainly. And of course *he* didn't care. They persuaded

poor old Sawlsberry to go and charge it on him, and he went blustering over there and did it. Goodson looked him over, like as if he was hunting for a place on him that he could despise the most, then he says, 'So you are the Committee of Inquiry, are you?' Sawlsberry said that was about what he was. 'Hm. Do they require particulars, or do you reckon a kind of a *general* answer will do?' 'If they require particulars, I will come back, Mr. Goodson; I will take the general answer first.' 'Very well, then, tell them to go to hell—I reckon that's general enough. And I'll give you some advice, Sawlsberry: when you come back for the particulars, fetch a basket to carry the relics of yourself home in.' "

"Just like Goodson; it's got all the marks. He had only one vanity; he thought he could give advice better than any other person."

"It settled the business, and saved us, Mary. The subject was dropped."

"Bless you, I'm not doubting *that*."

Then they took up the gold-sack mystery again, with strong interest. Soon the conversation began to suffer breaks—interruptions caused by absorbed thinkings. The breaks grew more and more frequent. At last Richards lost himself wholly in thought. He sat long, gazing vacantly at the floor, and by-and-by he began to punctuate his thoughts with little nervous movements of his hands that seemed to indicate vexation. Meantime his wife too had relapsed into a thoughtful silence, and her movements were beginning to show a troubled discomfort. Finally Richards got up and strode aimlessly about the room, ploughing his hands through his hair, much as a somnambulist might do who was having a bad dream. Then he seemed to arrive at a definite purpose; and without a word he put on his hat and passed quickly out of the house. His wife sat brooding, with a drawn face, and did not seem to be aware that she was alone. Now and then she murmured, "Lead us not into t. . . . but—but—we are so poor, so poor! . . . . Lead us not into. . . . Ah, who would be hurt by it?—and no one would ever know. . . . Lead us. . . ." The voice died out in mumblings. After a little she glanced up and muttered in a half-frightened, half-glad way—

"He is gone! But, oh dear, he may be too late—too late.
. . . Maybe not—maybe there is still time." She rose and
stood thinking, nervously clasping and unclasping her hands.
A slight shudder shook her frame, and she said, out of a dry
throat, "God forgive me—it's awful to think such things—
but. . . . Lord, how we are made—how strangely we are
made!"

She turned the light low, and slipped stealthily over and
kneeled down by the sack and felt of its ridgy sides with her
hands, and fondled them lovingly; and there was a gloating
light in her poor old eyes. She fell into fits of absence; and
came half out of them at times to mutter, "If we had only
waited!—oh, if we had only waited a little, and not been in
such a hurry!"

Meantime Cox had gone home from his office and told his
wife all about the strange thing that had happened, and they
had talked it over eagerly, and guessed that the late Goodson
was the only man in the town who could have helped a suffering stranger with so noble a sum as twenty dollars. Then
there was a pause, and the two became thoughtful and silent.
And by-and-by nervous and fidgety. At last the wife said, as if
to herself,

"Nobody knows this secret but the Richardses . . . . and
us . . . . nobody."

The husband came out of his thinkings with a slight start,
and gazed wistfully at his wife, whose face was become very
pale; then he hesitatingly rose, and glanced furtively at his
hat, then at his wife—a sort of mute inquiry. Mrs. Cox swallowed once or twice, with her hand at her throat, then in
place of speech she nodded her head. In a moment she was
alone, and mumbling to herself.

And now Richards and Cox were hurrying through the deserted streets, from opposite directions. They met, panting, at
the foot of the printing-office stairs; by the night-light there
they read each other's face. Cox whispered,

"Nobody knows about this but us?"

The whispered answer was,

"Not a soul—on honor, not a soul!"

"If it isn't too late to—"

The men were starting up stairs; at this moment they were overtaken by a boy, and Cox asked,

"Is that you, Johnny?"

"Yes, sir."

"You needn't ship the early mail—nor *any* mail; wait till I tell you."

"It's already gone, sir."

*"Gone?"* It had the sound of an unspeakable disappointment in it.

"Yes, sir. Time-table for Brixton and all the towns beyond changed to-day, sir—had to get the papers in twenty minutes earlier than common. I had to rush; if I had been two minutes later—"

The men turned and walked slowly away, not waiting to hear the rest. Neither of them spoke during ten minutes; then Cox said, in a vexed tone,

"What possessed you to be in such a hurry, *I* can't make out."

The answer was humble enough:

"I see it now, but somehow I never thought, you know, until it was too late. But the next time—"

"Next time be hanged! It won't come in a thousand years."

Then the friends separated without a good-night, and dragged themselves home with the gait of mortally stricken men. At their homes their wives sprang up with an eager "Well?"—then saw the answer with their eyes and sank down sorrowing, without waiting for it to come in words. In both houses a discussion followed of a heated sort—a new thing; there had been discussions before, but not heated ones, not ungentle ones. The discussions to-night were a sort of seeming plagiarisms of each other. Mrs. Richards said,

"If you had only waited, Edward—if you had only stopped to think; but no, you must run straight to the printing-office and spread it all over the world."

"It *said* publish it."

"That is nothing; it also said do it privately, if you liked. There, now—is that true, or not?"

"Why, yes—yes, it is true; but when I thought what a stir

it would make, and what a compliment it was to Hadleyburg that a stranger should trust it so—"

"Oh, certainly, I know all that; but if you had only stopped to think, you would have seen that you *couldn't* find the right man, because he is in his grave, and hasn't left chick nor child nor relation behind him; and as long as the money went to somebody that awfully needed it, and nobody would be hurt by it, and—and—"

She broke down, crying. Her husband tried to think of some comforting thing to say, and presently came out with this:

"But after all, Mary, it must be for the best—it *must* be; we know that. And we must remember that it was so ordered—"

"Ordered! Oh, everything's *ordered*, when a person has to find some way out when he has been stupid. Just the same, it was *ordered* that the money should come to us in this special way, and it was you that must take it on yourself to go meddling with the designs of Providence—and who gave you the right. It was wicked, that is what it was—just blasphemous presumption, and no more becoming to a meek and humble professor of—"

"But, Mary, you know how we have been trained all our lives long, like the whole village, till it is absolutely second nature to us to stop not a single moment to think when there's an honest thing to be done—"

"Oh, I know it, I know it—it's been one everlasting training and training and training in honesty—honesty shielded, from the very cradle, against every possible temptation, and so it's *artificial* honesty, and weak as water when temptation comes, as we have seen this night. God knows I never had shade nor shadow of a doubt of my petrified and indestructible honesty until now—and now, under the very first big and real temptation, I— Edward, it is my belief that this town's honesty is as rotten as mine is; as rotten as yours is. It is a mean town, a hard, stingy town, and hasn't a virtue in the world but this honesty it is so celebrated for and so conceited about; and so help me, I do believe that if ever the day comes that its honesty falls under great temptation, its grand reputation will go to ruin like a house of cards. There, now, I've made confession, and I feel better; I am a humbug, and I've been one all my life, without knowing it. Let no man call me honest again—I will not have it."

"I— Well, Mary, I feel a good deal as you do; I certainly do. It seems strange, too, so strange. I never could have believed it—never."

A long silence followed; both were sunk in thought. At last the wife looked up and said,

"I know what you are thinking, Edward."

Richards had the embarrassed look of a person who is caught.

"I am ashamed to confess it, Mary, but—"

"It's no matter, Edward, I was thinking the same question myself."

"I hope so. State it."

"You were thinking, if a body could only guess out *what the remark was* that Goodson made to the stranger."

"It's perfectly true. I feel guilty and ashamed. And you?"

"I'm past it. Let us make a pallet here; we've got to stand watch till the bank vault opens in the morning and admits the sack. . . . Oh, dear, oh, dear—if we hadn't made the mistake!"

The pallet was made, and Mary said:

"The open sesame—what could it have been? I do wonder what that remark could have been? But come; we will get to bed now."

"And sleep?"

"No; think."

"Yes, think."

By this time the Coxes too had completed their spat and their reconciliation, and were turning in—to think, to think, and toss, and fret, and worry over what the remark could possibly have been which Goodson made to the stranded derelict: that golden remark; that remark worth forty thousand dollars, cash.

The reason that the village telegraph-office was open later than usual that night was this: The foreman of Cox's paper was the local representative of the Associated Press. One might say its honorary representative, for it wasn't four times a year that he could furnish thirty words that would be accepted. But this time it was different. His despatch stating what he had caught got an instant answer:

*"Send the whole thing—all the details—twelve hundred words."*

A colossal order! The foreman filled the bill; and he was the proudest man in the State. By breakfast-time the next morning the name of Hadleyburg the Incorruptible was on every lip in America, from Montreal to the Gulf, from the glaciers of Alaska to the orange-groves of Florida; and millions and millions of people were discussing the stranger and his money-sack, and wondering if the right man would be found, and hoping some more news about the matter would come soon—right away.

## II.

Hadleyburg village woke up world-celebrated—astonished—happy—vain. Vain beyond imagination. Its nineteen principal citizens and their wives went about shaking hands with each other, and beaming, and smiling, and congratulating, and saying *this* thing adds a new word to the dictionary— *Hadleyburg*, synonym for *incorruptible*—destined to live in dictionaries forever! And the minor and unimportant citizens and their wives went around acting in much the same way. Everybody ran to the bank to see the gold-sack; and before noon grieved and envious crowds began to flock in from Brixton and all neighboring towns; and that afternoon and next day reporters began to arrive from everywhere to verify the sack and its history and write the whole thing up anew, and make dashing free-hand pictures of the sack, and of Richards's house, and the bank, and the Presbyterian church, and the Baptist church, and the public square, and the town-hall where the test would be applied and the money delivered; and damnable portraits of the Richardses, and Pinkerton the banker, and Cox, and the foreman, and Reverend Burgess, and the postmaster—and even of Jack Halliday, who was the loafing, good-natured, no-account, irreverent fisherman, hunter, boys' friend, stray-dogs' friend, typical "Sam Lawson" of the town. The little mean, smirking, oily Pinkerton showed the sack to all comers, and rubbed his sleek palms together pleasantly, and enlarged upon the town's fine old reputation for honesty and upon this wonderful endorsement of it, and hoped and believed that the example would now spread far and wide over the American world, and be epoch-making in the matter of moral regeneration. And so on, and so on.

By the end of a week things had quieted down again; the wild intoxication of pride and joy had sobered to a soft, sweet, silent delight—a sort of deep, nameless, unutterable content. All faces bore a look of peaceful, holy happiness.

Then a change came. It was a gradual change: so gradual that its beginnings were hardly noticed; maybe were not noticed at all, except by Jack Halliday, who always noticed everything; and always made fun of it, too, no matter what it was. He began to throw out chaffing remarks about people not looking quite so happy as they did a day or two ago; and next he claimed that the new aspect was deepening to positive sadness; next, that it was taking on a sick look; and finally he said that everybody was become so moody, thoughtful, and absent-minded that he could rob the meanest man in town of a cent out of the bottom of his breeches pocket and not disturb his revery.

At this stage—or at about this stage—a saying like this was dropped at bedtime—with a sigh, usually—by the head of each of the nineteen principal households:

"Ah, what *could* have been the remark that Goodson made!"

And straightway—with a shudder—came this, from the man's wife:

"Oh, *don't!* What horrible thing are you mulling in your mind? Put it away from you, for God's sake!"

But that question was wrung from those men again the next night—and got the same retort. But weaker.

And the third night the men uttered the question yet again—with anguish, and absently. This time—and the following night—the wives fidgeted feebly, and tried to say something. But didn't.

And the night after that they found their tongues and responded—longingly,

"Oh, if we *could* only guess!"

Halliday's comments grew daily more and more sparklingly disagreeable and disparaging. He went diligently about, laughing at the town, individually and in mass. But his laugh was the only one left in the village: it fell upon a hollow and mournful vacancy and emptiness. Not even a smile was findable anywhere. Halliday carried a cigar-box around on a tripod, playing that it was a camera, and halted all passers and aimed the thing and said, "Ready!—now look pleasant, please," but not even this capital joke could surprise the dreary faces into any softening.

So three weeks passed—one week was left. It was Saturday evening—after supper. Instead of the aforetime Saturday-evening flutter and bustle and shopping and larking, the streets were empty and desolate. Richards and his old wife sat apart in their little parlor—miserable and thinking. This was become their evening habit now: the life-long habit which had preceded it, of reading, knitting, and contented chat, or receiving or paying neighborly calls, was dead and gone and forgotten, ages ago—two or three weeks ago; nobody talked now, nobody read, nobody visited—the whole village sat at home, sighing, worrying, silent. Trying to guess out that remark.

The postman left a letter. Richards glanced listlessly at the superscription and the post-mark—unfamiliar, both—and tossed the letter on the table and resumed his might-have-beens and his hopeless dull miseries where he had left them off. Two or three hours later his wife got wearily up and was going away to bed without a good-night—custom now—but she stopped near the letter and eyed it awhile with a dead interest, then broke it open, and began to skim it over. Richards, sitting there with his chair tilted back against the wall and his chin between his knees, heard something fall. It was his wife. He sprang to her side, but she cried out:

"Leave me alone, I am too happy. Read the letter—read it!"

He did. He devoured it, his brain reeling. The letter was from a distant State, and it said:

"I am a stranger to you, but no matter: I have something to tell. I have just arrived home from Mexico, and learned about that episode.

Of course you do not know who made that remark, but I know, and I am the only person living who does know. It was *Goodson*. I knew him well, many years ago. I passed through your village that very night, and was his guest till the midnight train came along. I over-heard him make that remark to the stranger in the dark—it was in Hale Alley. He and I talked of it the rest of the way home, and while smoking in his house. He mentioned many of your villagers in the course of his talk—most of them in a very uncomplimentary way, but two or three favorably: among these latter yourself. I say 'favor-ably'—nothing stronger. I remember his saying he did not actually *like* any person in the town—not one; but that you—I *think* he said you—am almost sure—had done him a very great service once, pos-sibly without knowing the full value of it, and he wished he had a fortune, he would leave it to you when he died, and a curse apiece for the rest of the citizens. Now, then, if it was you that did him that service, you are his legitimate heir, and entitled to the sack of gold. I know that I can trust to your honor and honesty, for in a citizen of Hadleyburg these virtues are an unfailing inheritance, and so I am going to reveal to you the remark, well satisfied that if you are not the right man you will seek and find the right one and see that poor Goodson's debt of gratitude for the service referred to is paid. This is the remark: '*You are far from being a bad man: go, and reform.*'

HOWARD L. STEPHENSON."

"Oh, Edward, the money is ours, and I am so grateful, *oh*, so grateful—kiss me, dear, it's forever since we kissed—and we needed it so—the money—and now you are free of Pinkerton and his bank, and nobody's slave any more; it seems to me I could fly for joy."

It was a happy half-hour that the couple spent there on the settee caressing each other; it was the old days come again—days that had begun with their courtship and lasted without a break till the stranger brought the deadly money. By-and-by the wife said:

"Oh, Edward, how lucky it was you did him that grand service, poor Goodson! I never liked him, but I love him now. And it was fine and beautiful of you never to mention it or brag about it." Then, with a touch of reproach, "But you ought to have told *me*, Edward, you ought to have told your wife, you know."

"Well, I—er—well, Mary, you see—"

"Now stop hemming and hawing, and tell me about it, Edward. I always loved you, and now I'm proud of you. Everybody believes there was only one good generous soul in this village, and now it turns out that you— Edward, why don't you tell me?"

"Well—er—er— Why, Mary, I can't!"

"You *can't*? *Why* can't you?"

"You see, he—well, he—he made me promise I wouldn't."

The wife looked him over, and said, very slowly,

"Made—you—promise? Edward, what do you tell me that for?"

"Mary, do you think I would lie?"

She was troubled and silent for a moment, then she laid her hand within his and said:

"No . . . . no. We have wandered far enough from our bearings—God spare us that! In all your life you have never uttered a lie. But now—now that the foundations of things seem to be crumbling from under us, we—we—" She lost her voice for a moment, then said, brokenly, "Lead us not into temptation. . . . I think you made the promise, Edward. Let it rest so. Let us keep away from that ground. Now— that is all gone by; let us be happy again; it is no time for clouds."

Edward found it something of an effort to comply, for his mind kept wandering—trying to remember what the service was that he had done Goodson.

The couple lay awake the most of the night, Mary happy and busy, Edward busy, but not so happy. Mary was planning what she would do with the money. Edward was trying to recall that service. At first his conscience was sore on account of the lie he had told Mary—if it was a lie. After much reflection—suppose it *was* a lie? What then? Was it such a great matter? Aren't we always *acting* lies? Then why not *tell* them? Look at Mary—look what she had done. While he was hurrying off on his honest errand, what was she doing? Lamenting because the papers hadn't been destroyed and the money kept! Is theft better than lying?

*That* point lost its sting—the lie dropped into the background and left comfort behind it. The next point came to the front: *had* he rendered that service? Well, here was Goodson's own evidence as reported in Stephenson's letter; there could be no better evidence than that—it was even *proof* that he had rendered it. Of course. So that point was settled. . . . No, not quite. He recalled with a wince that this unknown Mr. Stephenson was just a trifle unsure as to whether the performer of it was Richards or some other—and, oh dear, he had put Richards on his honor! He must himself decide whither that money must go—and Mr. Stephenson was not doubting that if he was the wrong man he would go honorably and find the right one. Oh, it was odious to put a man in such a situation—ah, why couldn't Stephenson have left out that doubt! What did he want to intrude that for?

Further reflection. How did it happen that *Richards's* name remained in Stephenson's mind as indicating the right man, and not some other man's name? That looked good. Yes, that looked very good. In fact, it went on looking better and better, straight along—until by-and-by it grew into positive *proof*. And then Richards put the matter at once out of his mind, for he had a private instinct that a proof once established is better left so.

He was feeling reasonably comfortable now, but there was still one other detail that kept pushing itself on his notice: of course he had done that service—that was settled; but what *was* that service? He must recall it—he would not go to sleep till he had recalled it; it would make his peace of mind perfect. And so he thought and thought. He thought of a dozen things—possible services, even probable services—but none of them seemed adequate, none of them seemed large enough, none of them seemed worth the money—worth the fortune Goodson had wished he could leave in his will. And besides, he couldn't remember having done them, anyway. Now, then—now, then—what *kind* of a service would it be that would make a man so inordinately grateful? Ah—the saving of his soul! That must be it. Yes, he could remember, now, how he once set himself the task of converting Goodson, and labored at it as much as—he was going to say three months; but upon closer examination it shrunk to a month, then to a week, then to a day, then to nothing. Yes, he remembered, now, and with unwelcome vividness, that Goodson had told him to go to thunder and mind his own business—*he* wasn't hankering to follow Hadleyburg to heaven!

So that solution was a failure—he hadn't saved Goodson's soul. Richards was discouraged. Then after a little came another idea: had he saved Goodson's property? No, that wouldn't do—he hadn't any. His life? That is it! Of course. Why, he might have thought of it before. This time he was on the right track, sure. His imagination-mill was hard at work in a minute, now.

Thereafter during a stretch of two exhausting hours he was busy saving Goodson's life. He saved it in all kinds of difficult and perilous ways. In every case he got it saved satisfactorily up to a certain point; then, just as he was beginning to get well persuaded that it had really happened, a troublesome detail would turn up which made the whole thing impossible. As in the matter of drowning, for instance. In that case he had swum out and tugged Goodson ashore in an unconscious state with a great crowd looking on and applauding, but when he had got it all thought out and was just beginning to remember all about it a whole swarm of disqualifying details arrived on the ground: the town would have known of the circumstance, Mary would have known of it, it would glare like a limelight in his own memory instead of being an inconspicuous service which he had possibly rendered "without knowing its full value." And at this point he remembered that he couldn't swim, anyway.

Ah—*there* was a point which he had been overlooking from the start: it had to be a service which he had rendered "possibly without knowing the full value of it." Why, really, that ought to be an easy hunt—much easier than those others. And sure enough, by-and-by he found it. Goodson, years and years ago, came near marrying a very sweet and pretty girl, named Nancy Hewitt, but in some way or other the match had been broken off; the girl died, Goodson remained a bachelor, and by-and-by became a soured one and a frank despiser of the human species. Soon after the girl's death the village found out, or thought it had found out, that she carried a spoonful of negro blood in her veins. Richards worked at these details a good while, and in the end he thought he remembered things concerning them which must have gotten mislaid in his memory through long neglect. He seemed to dimly remember that it was *he* that found out about the negro blood; that it was he that told the village; that the village told Goodson where they got it; that he thus saved Goodson from marrying the tainted girl; that he had done him this great service "without knowing the full value of it," in fact without knowing that he *was* doing it; but that Goodson knew the value of it, and what a narrow escape he had had, and so went to his grave grateful to his benefactor and wishing he had a fortune to leave him. It was all clear and simple now, and the more he went over it the more luminous and certain it grew; and at last, when he nestled to sleep satisfied and happy, he remembered the whole thing just as if it had been yesterday. In fact, he dimly remembered Goodson's *telling* him his gratitude once. Meantime Mary had spent six thousand dollars on a new house for herself and a pair of slippers for her pastor, and then had fallen peacefully to rest.

That same Saturday evening the postman had delivered a letter to each of the other principal citizens—nineteen letters in all. No two of the envelopes were alike, and no two of the superscriptions were in the same hand, but the letters inside were just like each other in every detail but one. They were exact copies of the letter received by Richards—handwriting and all—and were all signed by Stephenson, but in place of Richards's name each receiver's own name appeared.

All night long eighteen principal citizens did what their caste-brother Richards was doing at the same time—they put in their energies trying to remember what notable service it was that they had unconsciously done Barclay Goodson. In no case was it a holiday job; still they succeeded.

And while they were at this work, which was difficult, their wives put in the night spending the money, which was easy. During that one night the nineteen wives spent an average of seven thousand dollars each out of the forty thousand in the sack—a hundred and thirty-three thousand altogether.

Next day there was a surprise for Jack Halliday. He noticed that the faces of the nineteen chief citizens and their wives bore that expression of peaceful and holy happiness again. He could not understand it, neither was he able to invent any remarks about it that could damage it or disturb it. And so it

was his turn to be dissatisfied with life. His private guesses at
the reasons for the happiness failed in all instances, upon examination. When he met Mrs. Wilcox and noticed the placid
ecstasy in her face, he said to himself, "Her cat has had
kittens"—and went and asked the cook; it was not so; the
cook had detected the happiness, but did not know the cause.
When Halliday found the duplicate ecstasy in the face of
"Shadbelly" Billson (village nickname), he was sure some
neighbor of Billson's had broken his leg, but inquiry showed
that this had not happened. The subdued ecstasy in Gregory
Yates's face could mean but one thing—he was a mother-in-
law short; it was another mistake. "And Pinkerton—Pinkerton—he has collected ten cents that he thought he was going
to lose." And so on, and so on. In some cases the guesses had
to remain in doubt, in the others they proved distinct errors.
In the end Halliday said to himself, "Anyway it foots up that
there's nineteen Hadleyburg families temporarily in heaven; I
don't know how it happened; I only know Providence is off
duty to-day."

An architect and builder from the next State had lately ventured to set up a small business in this unpromising village,
and his sign had now been hanging out a week. Not a customer yet; he was a discouraged man, and sorry he had come.
But his weather changed suddenly now. First one and then
another chief citizen's wife said to him privately:

"Come to my house Monday week—but say nothing about
it for the present. We think of building."

He got eleven invitations that day. That night he wrote his
daughter and broke off her match with her student. He said
she could marry a mile higher than that.

Pinkerton the banker and two or three other well-to-do
men planned country-seats—but waited. That kind don't
count their chickens until they are hatched.

The Wilsons devised a grand new thing—a fancy-dress
ball. They made no actual promises, but told all their acquaintanceship in confidence that they were thinking the matter
over and thought they should give it—"and if we do, you
will be invited, of course." People were surprised, and said,
one to another, "Why, they are crazy, those poor Wilsons,
they can't afford it." Several among the nineteen said privately

to their husbands, "It is a good idea; we will keep still till their cheap thing is over, then *we* will give one that will make it sick."

The days drifted along, and the bill of future squanderings rose higher and higher, wilder and wilder, more and more foolish and reckless. It began to look as if every member of the nineteen would not only spend his whole forty thousand dollars before receiving-day, but be actually in debt by the time he got the money. In some cases light-headed people did not stop with planning to spend, they really spent— on credit. They bought land, mortgages, farms, speculative stocks, fine clothes, horses, and various other things, paid down the bonus, and made themselves liable for the rest—at ten days. Presently the sober second thought came, and Halliday noticed that a ghastly anxiety was beginning to show up in a good many faces. Again he was puzzled, and didn't know what to make of it. "The Wilcox kittens aren't dead, for they weren't born; nobody's broken a leg; there's no shrinkage in mother-in-laws; *nothing* has happened—it is an insolvable mystery."

There was another puzzled man, too—the Rev. Mr. Burgess. For days, wherever he went, people seemed to follow him or to be watching out for him; and if he ever found himself in a retired spot, a member of the nineteen would be sure to appear, thrust an envelope privately into his hand, whisper "To be opened at the town-hall Friday evening," then vanish away like a guilty thing. He was expecting that there might be one claimant for the sack—doubtful, however, Goodson being dead—but it never occurred to him that all this crowd might be claimants. When the great Friday came at last, he found that he had nineteen envelopes.

### III.

The town-hall had never looked finer. The platform at the end of it was backed by a showy draping of flags; at intervals along the walls were festoons of flags; the gallery fronts were clothed in flags; the supporting columns were swathed in flags; all this was to impress the stranger, for he would be there in considerable force, and in a large degree he would be

connected with the press. The house was full. The 412 fixed
seats were occupied; also the 68 extra chairs which had been
packed into the aisles; the steps of the platform were occupied; some distinguished strangers were given seats on the
platform; at the horseshoe of tables which fenced the front
and sides of the platform sat a strong force of special correspondents who had come from everywhere. It was the best-
dressed house the town had ever produced. There were some
tolerably expensive toilets there, and in several cases the ladies
who wore them had the look of being unfamiliar with that
kind of clothes. At least the town thought they had that look,
but the notion could have arisen from the town's knowledge
of the fact that these ladies had never inhabited such clothes
before.

The gold-sack stood on a little table at the front of the
platform where all the house could see it. The bulk of the
house gazed at it with a burning interest, a mouth-watering
interest, a wistful and pathetic interest; a minority of nineteen
couples gazed at it tenderly, lovingly, proprietarily, and the
male half of this minority kept saying over to themselves the
moving little impromptu speeches of thankfulness for the audience's applause and congratulations which they were presently going to get up and deliver. Every now and then one of
these got a piece of paper out of his vest pocket and privately
glanced at it to refresh his memory.

Of course there was a buzz of conversation going on—
there always is; but at last when the Rev. Mr. Burgess rose
and laid his hand on the sack he could hear his microbes
gnaw, the place was so still. He related the curious history
of the sack, then went on to speak in warm terms of Hadleyburg's old and well-earned reputation for spotless honesty,
and of the town's just pride in this reputation. He said that
this reputation was a treasure of priceless value; that under
Providence its value had now become inestimably enhanced,
for the recent episode had spread this fame far and wide,
and thus had focussed the eyes of the American world upon
this village, and made its name for all time, as he hoped and
believed, a synonym for commercial incorruptibility. (*Applause.*) "And who is to be the guardian of this noble treasure—the community as a whole? No! The responsibility is

individual, not communal. From this day forth each and every one of you is in his own person its special guardian, and individually responsible that no harm shall come to it. Do you—does each of you—accept this great trust? [*Tumultuous assent.*] Then all is well. Transmit it to your children and to your children's children. To-day your purity is beyond reproach—see to it that it shall remain so. To-day there is not a person in your community who could be beguiled to touch a penny not his own—see to it that you abide in this grace. [*"We will! we will!"*] This is not the place to make comparisons between ourselves and other communities—some of them ungracious toward us; they have their ways, we have ours; let us be content. [*Applause.*] I am done. Under my hand, my friends, rests a stranger's eloquent recognition of what we are; through him the world will always henceforth know what we are. We do not know who he is, but in your name I utter your gratitude, and ask you to raise your voices in indorsement."

The house rose in a body and made the walls quake with the thunders of its thankfulness for the space of a long minute. Then it sat down, and Mr. Burgess took an envelope out of his pocket. The house held its breath while he slit the envelope open and took from it a slip of paper. He read its contents—slowly and impressively—the audience listening with tranced attention to this magic document, each of whose words stood for an ingot of gold:

" '*The remark which I made to the distressed stranger was this: "You are very far from being a bad man; go, and reform."* ' " Then he continued: "We shall know in a moment now whether the remark here quoted corresponds with the one concealed in the sack; and if that shall prove to be so—and it undoubtedly will—this sack of gold belongs to a fellow-citizen who will henceforth stand before the nation as the symbol of the special virtue which has made our town famous throughout the land—Mr. Billson!"

The house had gotten itself all ready to burst into the proper tornado of applause; but instead of doing it, it seemed stricken with a paralysis; there was a deep hush for a moment or two, then a wave of whispered murmurs swept the place—of about this tenor: "*Billson!* oh, come, this is *too* thin!

Twenty dollars to a stranger—or *anybody*—*Billson!* Tell it to the marines!" And now at this point the house caught its breath all of a sudden in a new access of astonishment, for it discovered that whereas in one part of the hall Deacon Billson was standing up with his head meekly bowed, in another part of it Lawyer Wilson was doing the same. There was a wondering silence now for a while. Everybody was puzzled, and nineteen couples were surprised and indignant.

Billson and Wilson turned and stared at each other. Billson asked, bitingly,

"Why do *you* rise, Mr. Wilson?"

"Because I have a right to. Perhaps you will be good enough to explain to the house why *you* rise?"

"With great pleasure. Because I wrote that paper."

"It is an impudent falsity! I wrote it myself."

It was Burgess's turn to be paralyzed. He stood looking vacantly at first one of the men and then the other, and did not seem to know what to do. The house was stupefied. Lawyer Wilson spoke up, now, and said,

"I ask the Chair to read the name signed to that paper."

That brought the Chair to itself, and it read out the name,

" 'John Wharton *Billson*.' "

"There!" shouted Billson, "what have you got to say for yourself, now? And what kind of apology are you going to make to me and to this insulted house for the imposture which you have attempted to play here?"

"No apologies are due, sir; and as for the rest of it, I publicly charge you with pilfering my note from Mr. Burgess and substituting a copy of it signed with your own name. There is no other way by which you could have gotten hold of the test-remark; I alone, of living men, possessed the secret of its wording."

There was likely to be a scandalous state of things if this went on; everybody noticed with distress that the short-hand scribes were scribbling like mad; many people were crying "Chair, Chair! Order! order!" Burgess rapped with his gavel, and said:

"Let us not forget the proprieties due. There has evidently been a mistake somewhere, but surely that is all. If Mr.

Wilson gave me an envelope—and I remember now that he did—I still have it."

He took one out of his pocket, opened it, glanced at it, looked surprised and worried, and stood silent a few moments. Then he waved his hand in a wandering and mechanical way, and made an effort or two to say something, then gave it up, despondently. Several voices cried out:

"Read it! read it! What is it?"

So he began in a dazed and sleep-walker fashion:

" '*The remark which I made to the unhappy stranger was this:* "*You are far from being a bad man.* [The house gazed at him, marvelling.] *Go, and reform.*" ' [*Murmurs:* "Amazing! what can this mean?"] This one," said the Chair, "is signed Thurlow G. Wilson."

"There!" cried Wilson, "I reckon that settles it! I knew perfectly well my note was purloined."

"Purloined!" retorted Billson. "I'll let you know that neither you nor any man of your kidney must venture to—"

*The Chair.* "Order, gentlemen, order! Take your seats, both of you, please."

They obeyed, shaking their heads and grumbling angrily. The house was profoundly puzzled; it did not know what to do with this curious emergency. Presently Thompson got up. Thompson was the hatter. He would have liked to be a Nineteener; but such was not for him; his stock of hats was not considerable enough for the position. He said:

"Mr. Chairman, if I may be permitted to make a suggestion, can both of these gentlemen be right? I put it to you, sir, can both have happened to say the very same words to the stranger? It seems to me—"

The tanner got up and interrupted him. The tanner was a disgruntled man; he believed himself entitled to be a Nineteener, but he couldn't get recognition. It made him a little unpleasant in his ways and speech. Said he:

"Sho, *that's* not the point! *That* could happen—twice in a hundred years—but not the other thing. *Neither* of them gave the twenty dollars!" (*A ripple of applause.*)

*Billson.* "I did!"

*Wilson.* "I did!"

Then each accused the other of pilfering.

*The Chair.* "Order! Sit down, if you please—both of you. Neither of the notes has been out of my possession at any moment."

*A Voice.* "Good—that settles *that!*"

*The Tanner.* "Mr. Chairman, one thing is now plain: one of these men has been eavesdropping under the other one's bed, and filching family secrets. If it is not unparliamentary to suggest it, I will remark that both are equal to it. [*The Chair.* "Order! order!"] I withdraw the remark, sir, and will confine myself to suggesting that *if* one of them has overheard the other reveal the test-remark to his wife, we shall catch him now."

*A Voice.* "How?"

*The Tanner.* "Easily. The two have not quoted the remark in exactly the same words. You would have noticed that, if there hadn't been a considerable stretch of time and an exciting quarrel inserted between the two readings."

*A Voice.* "Name the difference."

*The Tanner.* "The word *very* is in Billson's note, and not in the other."

*Many Voices.* "That's so—he's right!"

*The Tanner.* "And so, if the Chair will examine the test-remark in the sack, we shall know which of these two frauds—[*The Chair.* "Order!"]—which of these two adventurers—[*The Chair.* "Order! order!"]—which of these two gentlemen—[*laughter and applause*]—is entitled to wear the belt as being the first dishonest blatherskite ever bred in this town—which he has dishonored, and which will be a sultry place for him from now out!" (*Vigorous applause.*)

*Many Voices.* "Open it!—open the sack!"

Mr. Burgess made a slit in the sack, slid his hand in and brought out an envelope. In it were a couple of folded notes. He said:

"One of these is marked, 'Not to be examined until all written communications which have been addressed to the Chair—if any—shall have been read.' The other is marked '*The Test.*' Allow me. It is worded—to wit:

" 'I do not require that the first half of the remark which was made to me by my benefactor shall be quoted with exactness, for it was not striking, and could be forgotten; but its closing fifteen words are quite striking, and I think easily rememberable; unless *these* shall be accurately reproduced, let the applicant be regarded as an impostor. My benefactor began by saying he seldom gave advice to any one, but that it always bore the hall-mark of high value when he did give it. Then he said this—and it has never faded from my memory: "*You are far from being a bad man—*" '"

*Fifty Voices.* "That settles it—the money's Wilson's! Wilson! Wilson! Speech! Speech!"

People jumped up and crowded around Wilson, wringing his hand and congratulating fervently—meantime the Chair was hammering with the gavel and shouting:

"Order, gentlemen! Order! Order! Let me finish reading, please." When quiet was restored, the reading was resumed —as follows:

" ' "*Go, and reform—or, mark my words—some day, for your sins, you will die and go to hell or Hadleyburg—*TRY AND MAKE IT THE FORMER.*" ' "*

A ghastly silence followed. First an angry cloud began to settle darkly upon the faces of the citizenship; after a pause the cloud began to rise, and a tickled expression tried to take its place; tried so hard that it was only kept under with great and painful difficulty; the reporters, the Brixtonites, and other strangers bent their heads down and shielded their faces with their hands, and managed to hold in by main strength and heroic courtesy. At this most inopportune time burst upon the stillness the roar of a solitary voice—Jack Halliday's:

"*That's* got the hall-mark on it!"

Then the house let go, strangers and all. Even Mr. Burgess's gravity broke down presently, then the audience considered itself officially absolved from all restraint, and it made the most of its privilege. It was a good long laugh, and a tempestuously whole-hearted one, but it ceased at last—long enough for Mr. Burgess to try to resume, and for the people to get their eyes partially wiped; then it broke out again; and afterward yet again; then at last Burgess was able to get out these serious words:

"It is useless to try to disguise the fact—we find ourselves in the presence of a matter of grave import. It involves the honor of your town, it strikes at the town's good name. The difference of a single word between the test-remarks offered by Mr. Wilson and Mr. Billson was itself a serious thing, since it indicated that one or the other of these gentlemen had committed a theft—"

The two men were sitting limp, nerveless, crushed; but at these words both were electrified into movement, and started to get up—

"Sit down!" said the Chair, sharply, and they obeyed. "That, as I have said, was a serious thing. And it was—but for only one of them. But the matter has become graver; for the honor of *both* is now in formidable peril. Shall I go even further, and say in inextricable peril? *Both* left out the crucial fifteen words." He paused. During several moments he allowed the pervading stillness to gather and deepen its impressive effects, then added: "There would seem to be but one way whereby this could happen. I ask these gentlemen—Was there *collusion?—agreement?*"

A low murmur sifted through the house; its import was, "He's got them both."

Billson was not used to emergencies; he sat in a helpless collapse. But Wilson was a lawyer. He struggled to his feet, pale and worried, and said:

"I ask the indulgence of the house while I explain this most painful matter. I am sorry to say what I am about to say, since it must inflict irreparable injury upon Mr. Billson, whom I have always esteemed and respected until now, and in whose invulnerability to temptation I entirely believed—as did you all. But for the preservation of my own honor I must speak—and with frankness. I confess with shame—and I now beseech your pardon for it—that I said to the ruined stranger all of the words contained in the test-remark, including the disparaging fifteen. [*Sensation.*] When the late publication was made I recalled them, and I resolved to claim the sack of coin, for by every right I was entitled to it. Now I will ask you to consider this point, and weigh it well: that stranger's gratitude to me that night knew no bounds; he said himself that he could find no words for it that were adequate, and that if he should ever be able he would repay me a thousandfold. Now, then, I ask you this: could I expect—could I believe—

could I even remotely imagine—that, feeling as he did, he would do so ungrateful a thing as to add those quite unnecessary fifteen words to his test?—set a trap for me?—expose me as a slanderer of my own town before my own people assembled in a public hall? It was preposterous; it was impossible. His test would contain only the kindly opening clause of my remark. Of that I had no shadow of doubt. You would have thought as I did. You would not have expected a base betrayal from one whom you had befriended and against whom you had committed no offence. And so, with perfect confidence, perfect trust, I wrote on a piece of paper the opening words—ending with 'Go, and reform,'—and signed it. When I was about to put it in an envelope I was called into my back office, and without thinking I left the paper lying open on my desk." He stopped, turned his head slowly toward Billson, waited a moment, then added: "I ask you to note this: when I returned, a little later, Mr. Billson was retiring by my street door." (*Sensation.*)

In a moment Billson was on his feet and shouting:

"It's a lie! It's an infamous lie!"

*The Chair.* "Be seated, sir! Mr. Wilson has the floor."

Billson's friends pulled him into his seat and quieted him, and Wilson went on:

"Those are the simple facts. My note was now lying in a different place on the table from where I had left it. I noticed that, but attached no importance to it, thinking a draught had blown it there. That Mr. Billson would read a private paper was a thing which could not occur to me; he was an honorable man, and he would be above that. If you will allow me to say it, I think his extra word '*very*' stands explained; it is attributable to a defect of memory. I was the only man in the world who could furnish here any detail of the test-mark—by *honorable* means. I have finished."

There is nothing in the world like a persuasive speech to fuddle the mental apparatus and upset the convictions and debauch the emotions of an audience not practised in the tricks and delusions of oratory. Wilson sat down victorious. The house submerged him in tides of approving applause; friends swarmed to him and shook him by the hand and congratulated him, and Billson was shouted down and not

allowed to say a word. The Chair hammered and hammered
with its gavel, and kept shouting,

"But let us proceed, gentlemen, let us proceed!"

At last there was a measurable degree of quiet, and the
hatter said,

"But what is there to proceed with, sir, but to deliver the
money?"

*Voices.* "That's it! That's it! Come forward, Wilson!"

*The Hatter.* "I move three cheers for Mr. Wilson, Symbol
of the special virtue which—"

The cheers burst forth before he could finish; and in the
midst of them—and in the midst of the clamor of the gavel
also—some enthusiasts mounted Wilson on a big friend's
shoulder and were going to fetch him in triumph to the platform. The Chair's voice now rose above the noise—

"Order! To your places! You forget that there is still a document to be read." When quiet had been restored he took up
the document, and was going to read it, but laid it down
again, saying, "I forgot; this is not to be read until all written
communications received by me have first been read." He
took an envelope out of his pocket, removed its enclosure,
glanced at it—seemed astonished—held it out and gazed at
it—stared at it.

Twenty or thirty voices cried out:

"What is it? Read it! read it!"

And he did—slowly, and wondering:

" 'The remark which I made to the stranger—[*Voices.*
"Hello! how's this?"]—was this: "You are far from being a
bad man. [*Voices.* "Great Scott!"] Go, and reform." ' [*Voice.*
"Oh, saw my leg off!"] Signed by Mr. Pinkerton the banker."

The pandemonium of delight which turned itself loose
now was of a sort to make the judicious weep. Those whose
withers were unwrung laughed till the tears ran down; the reporters, in throes of laughter, set down disordered pot-
hooks which would never in the world be decipherable; and a
sleeping dog jumped up, scared out of its wits, and barked
itself crazy at the turmoil. All manner of cries were scattered through the din: "We're getting rich—*two* Symbols of
Incorruptibility!—without counting Billson!" "*Three!*—count

Shadbelly in—we can't have too many!" "All right—Billson's elected!" "Alas, poor Wilson—victim of *two* thieves!"

*A Powerful Voice.* "Silence! The Chair's fished up something more out of its pocket."

*Voices.* "Hurrah! Is it something fresh? Read it! read! read!"

*The Chair (reading).* " 'The remark which I made,' etc. 'You are far from being a bad man. Go,' etc. Signed, 'Gregory Yates.' "

*Tornado of Voices.* "Four Symbols!" " 'Rah for Yates!" "Fish again!"

The house was in a roaring humor now, and ready to get all the fun out of the occasion that might be in it. Several Nineteeners, looking pale and distressed, got up and began to work their way toward the aisles, but a score of shouts went up:

"The doors, the doors—close the doors; no Incorruptible shall leave this place! Sit down, everybody!"

The mandate was obeyed.

"Fish again! Read! read!"

The Chair fished again, and once more the familiar words began to fall from its lips—" 'You are far from being a bad man—' "

"Name! name! What's his name?"

" 'L. Ingoldsby Sargent.' "

"Five elected! Pile up the Symbols! Go on, go on!"

" 'You are far from being a bad—' "

"Name! name!"

" 'Nicholas Whitworth.' "

"Hooray! hooray! it's a symbolical day!"

Somebody wailed in, and began to sing this rhyme (leaving out "it's") to the lovely *Mikado* tune of "When a man's afraid of a beautiful maid"; the audience joined in, with joy; then, just in time, somebody contributed another line—

"And don't you this forget—"

The house roared it out. A third line was at once furnished—

"Corruptibles far from Hadleyburg are—"

The house roared that one too. As the last note died, Jack

Halliday's voice rose high and clear, freighted with a final line—

"But the Symbols are here, you bet!"

That was sung, with booming enthusiasm. Then the happy house started in at the beginning and sang the four lines through twice, with immense swing and dash, and finished up with a crashing three-times-three and a tiger for "Hadleyburg the Incorruptible and all Symbols of it which we shall find worthy to receive the hall-mark to-night."

Then the shoutings at the Chair began again, all over the place:

"Go on! go on! Read! read some more! Read all you've got!"

"That's it—go on! We are winning eternal celebrity!"

A dozen men got up now and began to protest. They said that this farce was the work of some abandoned joker, and was an insult to the whole community. Without a doubt these signatures were all forgeries—

"Sit down! sit down! Shut up! You are confessing. We'll find *your* names in the lot."

"Mr. Chairman, how many of those envelopes have you got?"

The Chair counted.

"Together with those that have been already examined, there are nineteen."

A storm of derisive applause broke out.

"Perhaps they all contain the secret. I move that you open them all and read every signature that is attached to a note of that sort—and read also the first eight words of the note."

"Second the motion!"

It was put and carried—uproariously. Then poor old Richards got up, and his wife rose and stood at his side. Her head was bent down, so that none might see that she was crying. Her husband gave her his arm, and so supporting her, he began to speak in a quavering voice:

"My friends, you have known us two—Mary and me—all our lives, and I think you have liked us and respected us—"

The Chair interrupted him:

"Allow me. It is quite true—that which you are saying,

Mr. Richards; this town *does* know you two; it *does* like you; it *does* respect you; more—it honors you and *loves* you—"

Halliday's voice rang out:

"That's the hall-marked truth, too! If the Chair is right, let the house speak up and say it. Rise! Now, then—hip! hip! hip!—all together!"

The house rose in mass, faced toward the old couple eagerly, filled the air with a snow-storm of waving handkerchiefs, and delivered the cheers with all its affectionate heart.

The Chair then continued:

"What I was going to say is this: We know your good heart, Mr. Richards, but this is not a time for the exercise of charity toward offenders. [Shouts of "Right! right!"] I see your generous purpose in your face, but I cannot allow you to plead for these men—"

"But I was going to—"

"Please take your seat, Mr. Richards. We must examine the rest of these notes—simple fairness to the men who have already been exposed requires this. As soon as that has been done—I give you my word for this—you shall be heard."

*Many Voices.* "Right!—the Chair is right—no interruption can be permitted at this stage! Go on!—the names! the names!—according to the terms of the motion!"

The old couple sat reluctantly down, and the husband whispered to the wife, "It is pitifully hard to have to wait; the shame will be greater than ever when they find we were only going to plead for *ourselves*."

Straightway the jollity broke loose again with the reading of the names.

" 'You are far from being a bad man—' Signature, 'Robert J. Titmarsh.'

" 'You are far from being a bad man—' Signature, 'Eliphalet Weeks.'

" 'You are far from being a bad man—' Signature, 'Oscar B. Wilder.' "

At this point the house lit upon the idea of taking the eight words out of the Chairman's hands. He was not unthankful for that. Thenceforward he held up each note in its turn, and waited. The house droned out the eight words in a massed

and measured and musical deep volume of sound (with a dar-
ingly close resemblance to a well-known church chant)—
" 'You are f-a-r from being a b-a-a-a-d man.' " Then the Chair
said, "Signature, 'Archibald Wilcox.' " And so on, and so on,
name after name, and everybody had an increasingly and glo-
riously good time except the wretched Nineteen. Now and
then, when a particularly shining name was called, the house
made the Chair wait while it chanted the whole of the test-
remark from the beginning to the closing words, "And go to
hell or Hadleyburg—try and make it the for-or-m-e-r!" and
in these special cases they added a grand and agonized and
imposing "A-a-a-a-*men*!"

The list dwindled, dwindled, dwindled, poor old Richards
keeping tally of the count, wincing when a name resembling
his own was pronounced, and waiting in miserable suspense
for the time to come when it would be his humiliating privilege to rise with Mary and finish his plea, which he was intending to word thus: ". . . for until now we have never
done any wrong thing, but have gone our humble way unre-
proached. We are very poor, we are old, and have no chick
nor child to help us; we were sorely tempted, and we fell. It
was my purpose when I got up before to make confession
and beg that my name might not be read out in this public
place, for it seemed to us that we could not bear it; but I
was prevented. It was just; it was our place to suffer with
the rest. It has been hard for us. It is the first time we have
ever heard our name fall from any one's lips—sullied. Be
merciful—for the sake of the better days; make our shame
as light to bear as in your charity you can." At this point in
his revery Mary nudged him, perceiving that his mind was
absent. The house was chanting, "You are f-a-r," etc.

"Be ready," Mary whispered. "Your name comes now; he
has read eighteen."

The chant ended.

"Next! next! next!" came volleying from all over the house.

Burgess put his hand into his pocket. The old couple, trembling, began to rise. Burgess fumbled a moment, then said,

"I find I have read them all."

Faint with joy and surprise, the couple sank into their seats,
and Mary whispered,

"Oh, bless God, we are saved!—he has lost ours—I wouldn't give this for a hundred of those sacks!"

The house burst out with its *Mikado* travesty, and sang it three times with ever-increasing enthusiasm, rising to its feet when it reached for the third time the closing line—

"But the Symbols are here, you bet!"

and finishing up with cheers and a tiger for "Hadleyburg purity and our eighteen immortal representatives of it."

Then Wingate, the saddler, got up and proposed cheers "for the cleanest man in town, the one solitary important citizen in it who didn't try to steal that money—Edward Richards."

They were given with great and moving heartiness; then somebody proposed that Richards be elected sole Guardian and Symbol of the now Sacred Hadleyburg Tradition, with power and right to stand up and look the whole sarcastic world in the face.

Passed, by acclamation; then they sang the *Mikado* again, and ended it with,

"And there's *one* Symbol left, you bet!"

There was a pause; then—

*A Voice.* "Now, then, who's to get the sack?"

*The Tanner* (*with bitter sarcasm*). "That's easy. The money has to be divided among the eighteen Incorruptibles. They gave the suffering stranger twenty dollars apiece—and that remark—each in his turn—it took twenty-two minutes for the procession to move past. Staked the stranger—total contribution, $360. All they want is just the loan back—and interest—forty thousand dollars altogether."

*Many Voices* (*derisively*). "That's it! Divvy! divvy! Be kind to the poor—don't keep them waiting!"

*The Chair.* "Order! I now offer the stranger's remaining document. It says: 'If no claimant shall appear [*grand chorus of groans*], I desire that you open the sack and count out the money to the principal citizens of your town, they to take it in trust [*Cries of "Oh! Oh! Oh!"*], and use it in such ways as to them shall seem best for the propagation and preservation of your community's noble reputation for incorruptible honesty [*more cries*]—a reputation to which their names and their efforts will add a new and far-reaching lustre.' [*Enthusiastic outburst of sarcastic applause*.] That seems to be all. No—here is a postscript:

" 'P. S.—CITIZENS OF HADLEYBURG: There *is* no test-remark—nobody made one. [*Great sensation*.] There wasn't any pauper stranger, nor any twenty-dollar contribution, nor any accompanying benediction and compliment—these are all inventions. [*General buzz and hum of astonishment and delight*.] Allow me to tell my story—it will take but a word or two. I passed through your town at a certain time, and received a deep offence which I had not earned. Any other man would have been content to kill one or two of you and call it square, but to me that would have been a trivial revenge, and inadequate; for the dead do not *suffer*. Besides, I could not kill you all—and, anyway, made as I am, even that would not have satisfied me. I wanted to damage every man in the place, and every woman—and not in their bodies or in their estate, but in their vanity—the place where feeble and foolish people are most vulnerable. So I disguised myself, and came back and studied you. You were easy game. You had an old and lofty reputation for honesty, and naturally you were proud of it—it was your treasure of treasures, the very apple of your eye. As soon as I found out that you carefully and vigilantly kept yourselves and your children *out of temptation*, I knew how to proceed. Why, you simple creatures, the weakest of all weak things is a virtue which has not been tested in the fire. I laid a plan, and gathered a list of names. My project was to corrupt Hadleyburg the Incorruptible. My idea was to make liars and thieves of nearly half a hundred smirchless men and women who had never in their lives uttered a lie or stolen a penny. I was afraid of Goodson. He was neither born nor reared in Hadleyburg. I was afraid that if I started to operate my scheme by getting my letter laid before you, you would say to yourselves, "Goodson is the only man among us who would give away twenty dollars to a poor devil"—and then you might not bite at my bait. But Heaven took Goodson; then I knew I was safe, and I set my trap and baited it. It may be that I shall not catch all the men to whom I mailed the pretended test secret, but I shall catch the most of them, if I know Hadleyburg nature. [*Voices*. "Right—he got every last one of them."] I believe they will even steal ostensible *gamble*-money, rather than miss, poor, tempted, and mistrained fellows. I am hoping to eternally and everlastingly squelch your vanity and give Hadleyburg a new renown—one that will *stick*—and spread far. If I have succeeded, open the sack and summon the Committee on Propagation and Preservation of the Hadleyburg Reputation.' "

*A Cyclone of Voices*. "Open it! Open it! The Eighteen to the front! Committee on Propagation of the Tradition! Forward—the Incorruptibles!"

The Chair ripped the sack wide, and gathered up a handful of bright, broad, yellow coins, shook them together, then examined them—

"Friends, they are only gilded disks of lead!"

There was a crashing outbreak of delight over this news, and when the noise had subsided, the tanner called out:

"By right of apparent seniority in this business, Mr. Wilson is Chairman of the Committee on Propagation of the Tradition. I suggest that he step forward on behalf of his pals, and receive in trust the money."

*A Hundred Voices*. "Wilson! Wilson! Wilson! Speech! Speech!"

*Wilson* (*in a voice trembling with anger*). "You will allow me to say, and without apologies for my language, *damn* the money!"

*A Voice*. "Oh, and him a Baptist!"

*A Voice*. "Seventeen Symbols left! Step up, gentlemen, and assume your trust!"

There was a pause—no response.

*The Saddler*. "Mr. Chairman, we've got *one* clean man left, anyway, out of the late aristocracy; and he needs money, and deserves it. I move that you appoint Jack Halliday to get up there and auction off that sack of gilt twenty-dollar pieces, and give the result to the right man—the man whom Hadleyburg delights to honor—Edward Richards."

This was received with great enthusiasm, the dog taking a hand again; the saddler started the bids at a dollar, the Brixton folk and Barnum's representative fought hard for it, the people cheered every jump that the bids made, the excitement

climbed moment by moment higher and higher, the bidders
got on their mettle and grew steadily more and more daring,
more and more determined, the jumps went from a dollar up
to five, then to ten, then to twenty, then fifty, then to a hundred, then—

At the beginning of the auction Richards whispered in distress to his wife: "Oh, Mary, can we allow it? It—it—you
see, it is an honor-reward, a testimonial to purity of character,
and—and—can we allow it? Hadn't I better get up and—
Oh, Mary, what ought we to do?—what do you think we—"
(*Halliday's voice. "Fifteen I'm bid!—fifteen for the sack!—
twenty!—ah, thanks!—thirty—thanks again! Thirty, thirty,
thirty!—do I hear forty?—forty it is! Keep the ball rolling, gentlemen, keep it rolling!—fifty!—thanks, noble Roman!—going
at fifty, fifty, fifty!—seventy!—ninety!—splendid!—a hundred!—pile it up, pile it up!—hundred and twenty—forty!—
just in time!—hundred and fifty!—TWO hundred!—superb! Do
I hear two h—thanks!—two hundred and fifty!—"*)

"It is another temptation, Edward—I'm all in a tremble—
but, oh, we've escaped *one* temptation, and that ought to
warn us, to— [*"Six did I hear?—thanks!—six fifty, six
f—SEVEN hundred!"*] And yet, Edward, when you think—
nobody susp— [*"Eight hundred dollars!—hurrah!—make it
nine!—Mr. Parsons, did I hear you say—thanks!—nine!—this
noble sack of virgin lead going at only nine hundred dollars, gilding and all—come! do I hear—a thousand!—gratefully
yours!—did some one say eleven?—a sack which is going to be the
most celebrated in the whole Uni—"*] Oh, Edward" (beginning
to sob), "we are *so* poor!—but—but—do as you think
best—do as you think best."

Edward fell—that is, he sat still; sat with a conscience
which was not satisfied, but which was overpowered by circumstances.

Meantime a stranger, who looked like an amateur detective
gotten up as an impossible English earl, had been watching
the evening's proceedings with manifest interest, and with a
contented expression in his face; and he had been privately
commenting to himself. He was now soliloquizing somewhat
like this: "None of the Eighteen are bidding; that is not satis-

factory; I must change that—the dramatic unities require it; they must buy the sack they tried to steal; they must pay a heavy price, too—some of them are rich. And another thing, when I make a mistake in Hadleyburg nature the man that puts that error upon me is entitled to a high honorarium, and some one must pay it. This poor old Richards has brought my judgment to shame; he is an honest man:—I don't understand it, but I acknowledge it. Yes, he saw my deuces-*and* with a straight flush, and by rights the pot is his. And it shall be a jack-pot, too, if I can manage it. He disappointed me, but let that pass."

He was watching the bidding. At a thousand, the market broke; the prices tumbled swiftly. He waited—and still watched. One competitor dropped out; then another, and another. He put in a bid or two, now. When the bids had sunk to ten dollars, he added a five; some one raised him a three; he waited a moment, then flung in a fifty-dollar jump, and the sack was his—at $1282. The house broke out in cheers—then stopped; for he was on his feet, and had lifted his hand. He began to speak.

"I desire to say a word, and ask a favor. I am a speculator in rarities, and I have dealings with persons interested in numismatics all over the world. I can make a profit on this purchase, just as it stands; but there is a way, if I can get your approval, whereby I can make every one of these leaden twenty-dollar pieces worth its face in gold, and perhaps more. Grant me that approval, and I will give part of my gains to your Mr. Richards, whose invulnerable probity you have so justly and so cordially recognized to-night; his share shall be ten thousand dollars, and I will hand him the money to-morrow. [*Great applause from the house*. But the "invulnerable probity" made the Richardses blush prettily; however, it went for modesty, and did no harm.] If you will pass my proposition by a good majority—I would like a two-thirds vote—I will regard that as the town's consent, and that is all I ask. Rarities are always helped by any device which will rouse curiosity and compel remark. Now if I may have your permission to stamp upon the faces of each of these ostensible coins the names of the eighteen gentlemen who—"

Nine-tenths of the audience were on their feet in a moment—dog and all—and the proposition was carried with a whirlwind of approving applause and laughter.

They sat down, and all the Symbols except "Dr." Clay Harkness got up, violently protesting against the proposed outrage, and threatening to—

"I beg you not to threaten me," said the stranger, calmly. "I know my legal rights, and am not accustomed to being frightened at bluster." (*Applause.*) He sat down. "Dr." Harkness saw an opportunity here. He was one of the two very rich men of the place, and Pinkerton was the other. Harkness was proprietor of a mint; that is to say, a popular patent medicine. He was running for the Legislature on one ticket, and Pinkerton on the other. It was a close race and a hot one, and getting hotter every day. Both had strong appetites for money; each had bought a great tract of land, with a purpose: there was going to be a new railway, and each wanted to be in the Legislature and help locate the route to his own advantage; a single vote might make the decision, and with it two or three fortunes. The stake was large, and Harkness was a daring speculator. He was sitting close to the stranger. He leaned over while one or another of the other Symbols was entertaining the house with protests and appeals, and asked, in a whisper,

"What is your price for the sack?"

"Forty thousand dollars."

"I'll give you twenty."

"No."

"Twenty-five."

"No."

"Say thirty."

"The price is forty thousand dollars; not a penny less."

"All right, I'll give it. I will come to the hotel at ten in the morning. I don't want it known; will see you privately."

"Very good." Then the stranger got up and said to the house:

"I find it late. The speeches of these gentlemen are not without merit, not without interest, not without grace; yet if I may be excused I will take my leave. I thank you for the great favor which you have shown me in granting my petition.

I ask the Chair to keep the sack for me until to-morrow, and to hand these three five-hundred dollar notes to Mr. Richards." They were passed up to the Chair. "At nine I will call for the sack, and at eleven will deliver the rest of the ten thousand to Mr. Richards in person, at his home. Good-night."

Then he slipped out, and left the audience making a vast noise, which was composed of a mixture of cheers, the *Mikado* song, dog-disapproval, and the chant, "You are f-a-r from being a b-a-a-d man—a-a-a-a-men!"

IV.

At home the Richardses had to endure congratulations and compliments until midnight. Then they were left to themselves. They looked a little sad, and they sat silent and thinking. Finally Mary sighed and said,

"Do you think we are to blame, Edward—*much* to blame?" and her eyes wandered to the accusing triplet of big bank-notes lying on the table, where the congratulators had been gloating over them and reverently fingering them. Edward did not answer at once; then he brought out a sigh and said, hesitatingly:

"We—we couldn't help it, Mary. It—well, it was ordered. *All* things are."

Mary glanced up and looked at him steadily, but he didn't return the look. Presently she said:

"I thought congratulations and praises always tasted good. But—it seems to me, now— Edward?"

"Well?"

"Are you going to stay in the bank?"

"N-no."

"Resign?"

"In the morning—by note."

"It does seem best."

Richards bowed his head in his hands and muttered:

"Before, I was not afraid to let oceans of people's money pour through my hands, but— Mary, I am so tired, so tired—"

"We will go to bed."

At nine in the morning the stranger called for the sack and took it to the hotel in a cab. At ten Harkness had a talk with him privately. The stranger asked for and got five checks on a metropolitan bank—drawn to "Bearer,"—four for $1500 each, and one for $34,000. He put one of the former in his pocket-book, and the remainder, representing $38,500, he put in an envelope, and with these he added a note, which he wrote after Harkness was gone. At eleven he called at the Richards house and knocked. Mrs. Richards peeped through the shutters, then went and received the envelope, and the stranger disappeared without a word. She came back flushed and a little unsteady on her legs, and gasped out:

"I am sure I recognized him! Last night it seemed to me that maybe I had seen him somewhere before."

"He is the man that brought the sack here?"

"I am almost sure of it."

"Then he is the ostensible Stephenson too, and sold every important citizen in this town with his bogus secret. Now if he has sent checks instead of money, we are sold too, after we thought we had escaped. I was beginning to feel fairly comfortable once more, after my night's rest, but the look of that envelope makes me sick. It isn't fat enough; $8500 in even the largest bank-notes makes more bulk than that."

"Edward, why do you object to checks?"

"Checks signed by Stephenson! I am resigned to take the $8500 if it could come in bank-notes—for it does seem that it was so ordered, Mary—but I have never had much courage, and I have not the pluck to try to market a check signed with that disastrous name. It would be a trap. That man tried to catch me; we escaped somehow or other; and now he is trying a new way. If it is checks—"

"Oh, Edward, it is *too* bad!" and she held up the checks and began to cry.

"Put them in the fire! quick! we mustn't be tempted. It is a trick to make the world laugh at *us*, along with the rest, and— Give them to *me*, since you can't do it!" He snatched them and tried to hold his grip till he could get to the stove; but he was human, he was a cashier, and he stopped a moment to make sure of the signature. Then he came near to fainting.

"Fan me, Mary, fan me! They are the same as gold!"

"Oh, how lovely, Edward! Why?"

"Signed by Harkness. What can the mystery of that be, Mary?"

"Edward, do you think—"

"Look here—look at this! Fifteen—fifteen—fifteen—thirty-four. Thirty-eight thousand five hundred! Mary, the sack isn't worth twelve dollars, and Harkness—apparently—has paid about par for it."

"And does it all come to us, do you think—instead of the ten thousand?"

"Why, it looks like it. And the checks are made to 'Bearer,' too."

"Is that good, Edward? What is it for?"

"A hint to collect them at some distant bank, I reckon. Perhaps Harkness doesn't want the matter known. What is that—a note?"

"Yes. It was with the checks."

It was in the "Stephenson" handwriting, but there was no signature. It said:

"I am a disappointed man. Your honesty is beyond the reach of temptation. I had a different idea about it, but I wronged you in that, and I beg pardon, and do it sincerely. I honor you—and that is sincere, too. This town is not worthy to kiss the hem of your garment. Dear sir, I made a square bet with myself that there were nineteen debauchable men in your self-righteous community. I have lost. Take the whole pot, you are entitled to it."

Richards drew a deep sigh, and said:

"It seems written with fire—it burns so. Mary—I am miserable again."

"I, too. Ah, dear, I wish—"

"To think, Mary—he *believes* in me."

"Oh, don't, Edward—I can't bear it."

"If those beautiful words were deserved, Mary—and God knows I believed I deserved them once—I think I could give the forty thousand dollars for them. And I would put that paper away, as representing more than gold and jewels, and keep it always. But now— We could not live in the shadow of its accusing presence, Mary."

He put it in the fire.

A messenger arrived and delivered an envelope. Richards took from it a note and read it; it was from Burgess.

"You saved me, in a difficult time. I saved you last night. It was at cost of a lie, but I made the sacrifice freely, and out of a grateful heart. None in this village knows so well as I know how brave and good and noble you are. At bottom you cannot respect me, knowing as you do of that matter of which I am accused, and by the general voice condemned; but I beg that you will at least believe that I am a grateful man; it will help me to bear my burden.

[Signed]      BURGESS."

"Saved, once more. And on such terms!" He put the note in the fire. "I—I wish I were dead, Mary, I wish I were out of it all."

"Oh, these are bitter, bitter days, Edward. The stabs, through their very generosity, are so deep—and they come so fast!"

Three days before the election each of two thousand voters suddenly found himself in possession of a prized memento—one of the renowned bogus double-eagles. Around one of its faces was stamped these words: "THE REMARK I MADE TO THE POOR STRANGER WAS—" Around the other face was stamped these: "GO, AND REFORM. (SIGNED) PINKERTON." Thus the entire remaining refuse of the renowned joke was emptied upon a single head, and with calamitous effect. It revived the recent vast laugh and concentrated it upon Pinkerton; and Harkness's election was a walk-over.

Within twenty-four hours after the Richardses had received their checks their consciences were quieting down, discouraged; the old couple were learning to reconcile themselves to the sin which they had committed. But they were to learn, now, that a sin takes on new and real terrors when there seems a chance that it is going to be found out. This gives it a fresh and most substantial and important aspect. At church the morning sermon was of the usual pattern; it was the same old things said in the same old way; they had heard them a thousand times and found them innocuous, next to meaningless, and easy to sleep under; but now it was different: the sermon seemed to bristle with accusations; it seemed aimed straight and specially at people who were concealing deadly sins. After church they got away from the mob of congratulators as soon as they could, and hurried homeward, chilled to the bone at they did not know what— vague, shadowy, indefinite fears. And by chance they caught a glimpse of Mr. Burgess as he turned a corner. He paid no attention to their nod of recognition! He hadn't seen it; but they did not know that. What could his conduct mean? It might mean—it might mean—oh, a dozen dreadful things. Was it possible that he knew that Richards could have cleared him of guilt in that bygone time, and had been silently waiting for a chance to even up accounts? At home, in their distress they got to imagining that their servant might have been in the next room listening when Richards revealed the secret to his wife that he knew of Burgess's innocence; next, Richards began to imagine that he had heard the swish of a gown in there at that time; next, he was sure he *had* heard it. They would call Sarah in, on a pretext, and watch her face; if she had been betraying them to Mr. Burgess, it would show in her manner. They asked her some questions—questions which were so random and incoherent and seemingly purposeless that the girl felt sure that the old people's minds had been affected by their sudden good fortune; the sharp and watchful gaze which they bent upon her frightened her, and that completed the business. She blushed, she became nervous and confused, and to the old people these were plain signs of guilt—guilt of some fearful sort or other—without doubt she was a spy and a traitor. When they were alone again they began to piece many unrelated things together and get horrible results out of the combination. When things had got about to the worst, Richards was delivered of a sudden gasp, and his wife asked,

"Oh, what is it?—what is it?"

"The note—Burgess's note! Its language was sarcastic, I see it now." He quoted: " 'At bottom you cannot respect me, *knowing*, as you do, of *that matter* of which I am accused'— oh, it is perfectly plain, now, God help me! He knows that I

know! You see the ingenuity of the phrasing. It was a trap—
and like a fool, I walked into it. And Mary—?"

"Oh, it is dreadful—I know what you are going to
say—he didn't return your transcript of the pretended test-
remark."

"No—kept it to destroy us with. Mary, he has exposed us
to some already. I know it—I know it well. I saw it in a
dozen faces after church. Ah, he wouldn't answer our nod of
recognition—*he* knew what he had been doing!"

In the night the doctor was called. The news went around
in the morning that the old couple were rather seriously ill—
prostrated by the exhausting excitement growing out of their
great windfall, the congratulations, and the late hours, the
doctor said. The town was sincerely distressed; for these old
people were about all it had left to be proud of, now.

Two days later the news was worse. The old couple were
delirious, and were doing strange things. By witness of the
nurses, Richards had exhibited checks—for $8500? No—for
an amazing sum—$38,500! What could be the explanation of
this gigantic piece of luck?

The following day the nurses had more news—and wonderful. They had concluded to hide the checks, lest harm
come to them; but when they searched they were gone from
under the patient's pillow—vanished away. The patient said:

"Let the pillow alone; what do you want?"

"We thought it best that the checks—"

"You will never see them again—they are destroyed. They
came from Satan. I saw the hell-brand on them, and I knew
they were sent to betray me to sin." Then he fell to gabbling
strange and dreadful things which were not clearly understandable, and which the doctor admonished them to keep to
themselves.

Richards was right; the checks were never seen again.

A nurse must have talked in her sleep, for within two days
the forbidden gabblings were the property of the town; and
they were of a surprising sort. They seemed to indicate that
Richards had been a claimant for the sack himself, and that
Burgess had concealed that fact and then maliciously betrayed it.

Burgess was taxed with this and stoutly denied it. And he

said it was not fair to attach weight to the chatter of a sick old man who was out of his mind. Still, suspicion was in the air, and there was much talk.

After a day or two it was reported that Mrs. Richards's delirious deliveries were getting to be duplicates of her husband's. Suspicion flamed up into conviction, now, and the town's pride in the purity of its one undiscredited important citizen began to dim down and flicker toward extinction.

Six days passed, then came more news. The old couple were dying. Richards's mind cleared in his latest hour, and he sent for Burgess. Burgess said:

"Let the room be cleared. I think he wishes to say something in privacy."

"No!" said Richards; "I want witnesses. I want you all to hear my confession, so that I may die a man, and not a dog. I was clean—artificially—like the rest; and like the rest I fell when temptation came. I signed a lie, and claimed the miserable sack. Mr. Burgess remembered that I had done him a service, and in gratitude (and ignorance) he suppressed my claim and saved me. You know the thing that was charged against Burgess years ago. My testimony, and mine alone, could have cleared him, and I was a coward, and left him to suffer disgrace—"

"No—no—Mr. Richards, you—"

"My servant betrayed my secret to him—"

"No one has betrayed anything to me—"

—"and then he did a natural and justifiable thing; he repented of the saving kindness which he had done me, and he *exposed* me—as I deserved—"

"Never!—I make oath—"

"Out of my heart I forgive him."

Burgess's impassioned protestations fell upon deaf ears; the dying man passed away without knowing that once more he had done poor Burgess a wrong. The old wife died that night.

The last of the sacred Nineteen had fallen a prey to the fiendish sack; the town was stripped of the last rag of its ancient glory. Its mourning was not showy, but it was deep.

By act of the Legislature—upon prayer and petition— Hadleyburg was allowed to change its name to (never mind what—I will not give it away), and leave one word out of the motto that for many generations had graced the town's official seal.

It is an honest town once more, and the man will have to rise early that catches it napping again.

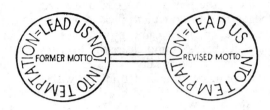

*December 1899*

# My First Lie and How I Got Out of It

As I understand it, what you desire is information about "my first lie, and how I got out of it." I was born in 1835; I am well along, and my memory is not as good as it was. If you had asked about my first truth it would have been easier for me and kinder of you, for I remember that fairly well; I remember it as if it were last week. The family think it was week before, but that is flattery and probably has a selfish project back of it. When a person has become seasoned by experience and has reached the age of sixty-four, which is the age of discretion, he likes a family compliment as well as ever, but he does not lose his head over it as in the old innocent days.

I do not remember my first lie, it is too far back; but I remember my second one very well. I was nine days old at the time, and had noticed that if a pin was sticking in me and I advertised it in the usual fashion, I was lovingly petted and coddled and pitied in a most agreeable way and got a ration between meals besides.

It was human nature to want to get these riches, and I fell. I lied about the pin—advertising one when there wasn't any. You would have done it; George Washington did it, anybody would have done it. During the first half of my life I never knew a child that was able to rise above that temptation and keep from telling that lie. Up to 1867 all the civilized children that were ever born into the world were liars. Including George. Then the safety-pin came in and blocked the game. But is that reform worth anything? No; for it is reform by force and has no virtue in it; it merely stops that form of lying, it doesn't impair the disposition to lie, by a shade. It is the cradle application of conversion by fire and sword, or of the temperance principle through prohibition.

To return to that early lie. They found no pin and they realized that another liar had been added to the world's supply. For by grace of a rare inspiration a quite commonplace but seldom noticed fact was borne in upon their understandings—that almost all lies are acts, and speech has no part in them. Then, if they examined a little further they recognized that all people are liars from the cradle onward, without exception, and that they begin to lie as soon as they wake in the morning, and keep it up without rest or refreshment until they go to sleep at night. If they arrived at that truth it probably grieved them—did, if they had been heedlessly and ignorantly educated by their books and teachers; for why should a person grieve over a thing which by the eternal law of his make he cannot help? He didn't invent the law; it is merely his business to obey it and keep still; join the universal conspiracy and keep so still that he shall deceive his fellow-conspirators into imagining that he doesn't know that the law exists. It is what we all do—we that know. I am speaking of the lie of silent assertion; we can tell it without saying a word, and we all do it—we that know. In the magnitude of its territorial spread it is one of the most majestic lies that the civilizations make it their sacred and anxious care to guard and watch and propagate.

For instance. It would not be possible for a humane and intelligent person to invent a rational excuse for slavery; yet you will remember that in the early days of the emancipation agitation in the North the agitators got but small help or countenance from any one. Argue and plead and pray as they might, they could not break the universal stillness that reigned, from pulpit and press all the way down to the bottom of society—the clammy stillness created and maintained by the lie of silent assertion—the silent assertion that there wasn't anything going on in which humane and intelligent people were interested.

From the beginning of the Dreyfus case to the end of it all France, except a couple of dozen moral paladins, lay under the smother of the silent-assertion lie that no wrong was being done to a persecuted and unoffending man. The like smother was over England lately, a good half of the population silently letting on that they were not aware that Mr. Chamberlain was trying to manufacture a war in South Africa and was willing to pay fancy prices for the materials.

Now there we have instances of three prominent ostensible civilizations working the silent-assertion lie. Could one find other instances in the three countries? I think so. Not so very many, perhaps, but say a billion—just so as to keep within bounds. Are those countries working that kind of lie, day in and day out, in thousands and thousands of varieties, without ever resting? Yes, we know that to be true. The universal conspiracy of the silent-assertion lie is hard at work always and everywhere, and always in the interest of a stupidity or a sham, never in the interest of a thing fine or respectable. Is it the most timid and shabby of all lies? It seems to have the look of it. For ages and ages it has mutely labored in the interest of despotisms and aristocracies and chattel slaveries, and military slaveries, and religious slaveries, and has kept them alive; keeps them alive yet, here and there and yonder, all about the globe; and will go on keeping them alive until the silent-assertion lie retires from business—the silent assertion that nothing is going on which fair and intelligent men are aware of and are engaged by their duty to try to stop.

What I am arriving at is this: When whole races and peoples conspire to propagate gigantic mute lies in the interest of tyrannies and shams, why should we care anything about the trifling lies told by individuals? Why should we try to make it appear that abstention from lying is a virtue? Why should we want to beguile ourselves in that way? Why should we without shame help the nation lie, and then be ashamed to do a little lying on our own account? Why shouldn't we be honest and honorable, and lie every time we get a chance? That is to say, why shouldn't we be consistent, and either lie all the time or not at all? Why should we help the nation lie the whole day long and then object to telling one little individual private lie in our own interest to go to bed on? Just for the refreshment of it, I mean, and to take the rancid taste out of our mouth.

Here in England they have the oddest ways. They won't tell a spoken lie—nothing can persuade them. Except in a large moral interest, like politics or religion, I mean. To tell a spoken lie to get even the poorest little personal advantage out of it is a thing which is impossible to them. They make me ashamed of myself sometimes, they are so bigoted. They will not even tell a lie for the fun of it; they will not tell it when it hasn't even a suggestion of damage or advantage in it for any one. This has a restraining influence upon me in spite of reason, and I am always getting out of practice.

Of course, they tell all sorts of little unspoken lies, just like

anybody; but they don't notice it until their attention is called
to it. They have got me so that sometimes I never tell a verbal
lie now except in a modified form; and even in the modified
form they don't approve of it. Still, that is as far as I can go in
the interest of the growing friendly relations between the two
countries; I must keep some of my self-respect. And my
health. I can live on a pretty low diet, but I can't get along on
no sustenance at all.

Of course, there are times when these people have to come
out with a spoken lie, for that is a thing which happens to
everybody once in a while, and would happen to the angels if
they came down here much. Particularly to the angels, in fact,
for the lies I speak of are self-sacrificing ones told for a generous object, not a mean one; but even when these people tell a
lie of that sort it seems to scare them and unsettle their minds.
It is a wonderful thing to see, and shows that they are all
insane. In fact, it is a country which is full of the most interesting superstitions.

I have an English friend of twenty-five years' standing, and
yesterday when we were coming downtown on top of the
'bus I happened to tell him a lie. A modified one, of course; a
half-breed, a mulatto; I can't seem to tell any other kind now,
the market is so flat. I was explaining to him how I got out of
an embarrassment in Austria last year. I do not know what
might have become of me if I hadn't happened to remember
to tell the police that I belonged to the same family as the
Prince of Wales. That made everything pleasant and they let
me go; and apologized, too, and were ever so kind and obliging and polite, and couldn't do too much for me, and explained how the mistake came to be made, and promised to
hang the officer that did it, and hoped I would let bygones be
bygones and not say anything about it; and I said they could
depend on me. My friend said, austerely:

"You call it a modified lie? Where is the modification?"

I explained that it lay in the form of my statement to the
police.

"I didn't say I belonged to the royal family; I only said I
belonged to the same family as the Prince—meaning the
human family, of course; and if those people had had any

penetration they would have known it. I can't go around furnishing brains to the police; it is not to be expected."

"How did you feel after that performance?"

"Well, of course I was distressed to find that the police had
misunderstood me, but as long as I had not told any lie I
knew there was no occasion to sit up nights and worry about
it."

My friend struggled with the case for several minutes, turning it over and examining it in his mind, then he said that so
far as he could see the modification was itself a lie, it being a
misleading reservation of an explanatory fact, and so I had
told two lies instead of only one.

"I wouldn't have done it," said he; "I have never told a lie,
and I should be very sorry to do such a thing."

Just then he lifted his hat and smiled a basketful of surprised and delighted smiles down at a gentleman who was
passing in a hansom.

"Who was that, G.?"

"I don't know."

"Then why did you do that?"

"Because I saw he thought he knew me and was expecting
it of me. If I hadn't done it he would have been hurt. I didn't
want to embarrass him before the whole street."

"Well, your heart was right, G., and your act was right.
What you did was kindly and courteous and beautiful; I
would have done it myself; but it was a lie."

"A lie? I didn't say a word. How do you make it out?"

"I know you didn't speak, still you said to him very plainly
and enthusiastically in dumb show, 'Hello! you in town?
Awful glad to see you, old fellow; when did you get back?'
Concealed in your actions was what you have called 'a misleading reservation of an explanatory fact'—the fact that
you had never seen him before. You expressed joy in encoun-
tering him—a lie; and you made that reservation—another
lie. It was my pair over again. But don't be troubled—we all
do it."

Two hours later, at dinner, when quite other matters were
being discussed, he told how he happened along once just in
the nick of time to do a great service for a family who were

old friends of his. The head of it had suddenly died in circumstances and surroundings of a ruinously disgraceful character. If known the facts would break the hearts of the innocent family and put upon them a load of unendurable shame. There was no help but in a giant lie, and he girded up his loins and told it.

"The family never found out, G.?"

"Never. In all these years they have never suspected. They were proud of him and always had reason to be; they are proud of him yet, and to them his memory is sacred and stainless and beautiful."

"They had a narrow escape, G."

"Indeed they had."

"For the very next man that came along might have been one of these heartless and shameless truth-mongers. You have told the truth a million times in your life, G., but that one golden lie atones for it all. Persevere."

Some may think me not strict enough in my morals, but that position is hardly tenable. There are many kinds of lying which I do not approve. I do not like an injurious lie, except when it injures somebody else; and I do not like the lie of bravado, nor the lie of virtuous ecstasy; the latter was affected by Bryant, the former by Carlyle.

Mr. Bryant said, "Truth crushed to earth will rise again." I have taken medals at thirteen world's fairs, and may claim to be not without capacity, but I never told as big a one as that Mr. Bryant was playing to the gallery; we all do it. Carlyle said, in substance, this—I do not remember the exact words: "This gospel is eternal—that a lie shall not live." I have a reverent affection for Carlyle's books, and have read his Revolution eight times; and so I prefer to think he was not entirely at himself when he told that one. To me it is plain that he said it in a moment of excitement, when chasing Americans out of his back yard with brickbats. They used to go there and worship. At bottom he was probably fond of them, but he was always able to conceal it. He kept bricks for them, but he was not a good shot, and it is matter of history that when he fired they dodged, and carried off the brick; for as a nation we like relics, and so long as we get them we do not much care what the reliquary thinks about it. I am quite sure that when he told that large one about a lie not being able to live he had just missed an American and was over-excited. He told it above thirty years ago, but it is alive yet; alive, and very healthy and hearty, and likely to out-live any fact in history. Carlyle was truthful when calm, but give him Americans enough and bricks enough and he could have taken medals himself.

As regards that time that George Washington told the truth, a word must be said, of course. It is the principal jewel in the crown of America, and it is but natural that we should work it for all it is worth, as Milton says in his "Lay of the Last Minstrel." It was a timely and judicious truth, and I should have told it myself in the circumstances. But I should have stopped there. It was a stately truth, a lofty truth—a Tower; and I think it was a mistake to go on and distract attention from its sublimity by building another Tower along-side of it fourteen times as high. I refer to his remark that he "could not lie." I should have fed that to the marines; or left it to Carlyle; it is just in his style. It would have taken a medal at any European fair and would have got an Honorable Men-tion even at Chicago if it had been saved up. But let it pass; the Father of his Country was excited. I have been in those circumstances, and I recollect.

With the truth he told I have no objection to offer, as already indicated. I think it was not premeditated, but an inspiration. With his fine military mind, he had probably arranged to let his brother Edward in for the cherry-tree re-sults, but by an inspiration he saw his opportunity in time and took advantage of it. By telling the truth he could aston-ish his father; his father would tell the neighbors; the neigh-bors would spread it; it would travel to all firesides; in the end it would make him President, and not only that, but First President. He was a far-seeing boy and would be likely to think of these things. Therefore, to my mind, he stands justi-fied for what he did. But not for the other Tower; it was a mistake. Still, I don't know about that; upon reflection I think perhaps it wasn't. For indeed it is that Tower that makes the other one live. If he hadn't said "I cannot tell a lie" there would have been no convulsion. That was the earthquake that rocked the planet. That is the kind of statement that lives forever, and a fact barnacled to it has a good chance to share its immortality.

To sum up, on the whole I am satisfied with things the way they are. There is a prejudice against the spoken lie, but none against any other, and by examination and mathematical computation I find that the proportion of the spoken lie to the other varieties is as 1 to 22,894. Therefore the spoken lie is of no consequence, and it is not worth while to go around fussing about it and trying to make believe that it is an important matter. The silent colossal National Lie that is the support and confederate of all the tyrannies and shams and inequalities and unfairnesses that afflict the peoples—that is the one to throw bricks and sermons at. But let us be judicious and let somebody else begin.

And then— But I have wandered from my text. How did I get out of my second lie? I think I got out with honor, but I cannot be sure, for it was a long time ago and some of the details have faded out of my memory. I recollect that I was reversed and stretched across some one's knee and that something happened, but I cannot now remember what it was. I think there was music; but it is all dim now and blurred by the lapse of time, and this may be only a senile fancy.

*December 10, 1899*

# My Boyhood Dreams

The dreams of my boyhood? No, they have not been realized. For all who are old, there is something infinitely pathetic about the subject which you have chosen, for in no gray-head's case can it suggest any but one thing—disappointment. Disappointment is its own reason for its pain: the quality or dignity of the hope that failed is a matter aside. The dreamer's valuation of the thing lost—not another man's—is the only standard to measure it by, and his grief for it makes it large and great and fine, and is worthy of our reverence in all cases. We should carefully remember that. There are sixteen hundred million people in the world. Of these there is but a trifling number—in fact, only thirty-eight millions—who can understand why a person should have an ambition to belong to the French army; and why, belonging to it, he should be proud of that; and why, having got down that far, he should want to go on down, down, down till he struck bottom and got on the General Staff; and why, being stripped of his livery, or set free and reinvested with his self-respect by any other quick and thorough process, let it be what it might, he should wish to return to his strange serfage. But no matter: the estimate put upon these things by the fifteen hundred and sixty millions is no proper measure of their value: the proper measure, the just measure, is that which is put upon them by Dreyfus, and is cipherable merely upon the littleness or the vastness of the *disappointment* which their loss cost him.

There you have it: the measure of the magnitude of a dream-failure is the measure of the disappointment the failure cost the dreamer; the value, in others' eyes, of the thing lost, has nothing to do with the matter. With this straightening-out and classification of the dreamer's position to help us, perhaps we can put ourselves in his place and respect his dream—Dreyfus's, and the dreams our friends have cherished and reveal to us. Some that I call to mind, some that have been revealed to me, are curious enough; but we may not smile at them, for they were precious to the dreamers, and their failure has left scars which give them dignity and pathos.

With this theme in my mind, dear heads that were brown when they and mine were young together rise old and white before me now, beseeching me to speak for them, and most lovingly will I do it.

Howells, Hay, Aldrich, Matthews, Stockton, Cable, Remus—how their young hopes and ambitions come flooding back to my memory now, out of the vague far past, the beautiful past, the lamented past! I remember it so well—that night we met together—it was in Boston, and Mr. Fields was there, and Mr. Osgood, and Ralph Keeler, and Boyle O'Reilly, lost to us now these many years—and under the seal of confidence revealed to each other what our boyhood dreams had been: dreams which had not as yet been blighted, but over which was stealing the gray of the night that was to come—a night which we prophetically *felt*, and this feeling oppressed us and made us sad. I remember that Howells's voice broke twice, and it was only with great difficulty that he was able to go on; in the end he wept. For he had hoped to be an auctioneer. He told of his early struggles to climb to his goal, and how at last he attained to within a single step of the coveted summit. But there misfortune after misfortune assailed him, and he went down, and down, and down, until now at last, weary and disheartened, he had for the present given up the struggle and become editor of the "Atlantic Monthly." This was in 1830. Seventy years are gone since, and where now is his dream? It will never be fulfilled. And it is best so; he is no longer fitted for the position; no one would take him now; even if he got it, he would not be able to do himself credit in it, on account of his deliberateness of speech and lack of trained professional vivacity; he would be put on real estate, and would have the pain of seeing younger and abler men intrusted with the furniture and other such goods—goods which draw a mixed and intellectually low order of customers, who must be beguiled of their bids by a vulgar and specialized humor and sparkle, accompanied with antics.

But it is not the thing lost that counts, but only the *disappointment* the loss brings to the dreamer that had coveted that thing and had set his heart of hearts upon it, and when we remember this, a great wave of sorrow for Howells rises in our breasts, and we wish for his sake that his fate could have been different.

At that time Hay's boyhood dream was not yet past hope of realization, but it was fading, dimming, wasting away, and the wind of a growing apprehension was blowing cold over the perishing summer of his life. In the pride of his young ambition he had aspired to be a steamboat mate; and in fancy saw himself dominating a forecastle some day on the Mississippi and dictating terms to roustabouts in high and wounding tones. I look back now, from this far distance of seventy years, and note with sorrow the stages of that dream's destruction. Hay's history is but Howells's, with differences of detail. Hay climbed high toward his ideal; when success seemed almost sure, his foot upon the very gang-plank, his eye upon the capstan, misfortune came and his fall began. Down—down—down—ever down: Private Secretary to the President; Colonel in the field; Chargé d'Affaires in Paris; Chargé d'Affaires in Vienna; Poet; Editor of the "Tribune"; Biographer of Lincoln; Ambassador to England; and now at last there he lies—Secretary of State, Head of Foreign Affairs. And he has fallen like Lucifer, never to rise again. And his dream—where now is his dream? Gone down in blood and tears with the dream of the auctioneer.

And the young dream of Aldrich—where is that? I remember yet how he sat there that night fondling it, petting it; seeing it recede and ever recede; trying to be reconciled and give it up, but not able yet to bear the thought; for it had been his hope to be a horse-doctor. He, also, climbed high, but, like the others, fell; then fell again, and yet again, and again and again. And now at last he can fall no further. He is old now, he has ceased to struggle, and is only a poet. No one would risk a horse with him now. His dream is over.

Has *any* boyhood dream ever been fulfilled? I must doubt it. Look at Brander Matthews. He wanted to be a cowboy. What is he to-day? Nothing but a professor in a university. Will he ever be a cowboy? It is hardly conceivable.

Look at Stockton. What was Stockton's young dream? He hoped to be a barkeeper. See where *he* has landed.

Is it better with Cable? What was Cable's young dream? To be ring-master in the circus, and swell around and crack the whip. What is he to-day? Nothing but a theologian and novelist.

And Uncle Remus—what was his young dream? To be a buccaneer. Look at him now.

Ah, the dreams of our youth, how beautiful they are, and how perishable! The ruins of these might-have-beens, how pathetic! The heart-secrets that were revealed that night now so long vanished, how they touch me as I give them voice! Those sweet privacies, how they endeared us to each other! We were under oath never to tell any of these things, and I have always kept that oath inviolate when speaking with persons whom I thought not worthy to hear them.

Oh, our lost Youth—God keep its memory green in our hearts! for Age is upon us, with the indignity of its infirmities, and Death beckons!

## TO THE ABOVE OLD PEOPLE.

Sleep! for the Sun that scores another Day
Against the Tale allotted You to stay,
    Reminding You, is Risen, and now
Serves Notice—ah, ignore it while You may!

The chill Wind blew, and those who stood before
The Tavern murmured, "Having drunk his Score,
    Why tarries He with empty Cup? Behold,
The Wine of Youth once poured, is poured no more.

"Come, leave the Cup, and on the Winter's Snow
Your Summer Garment of Enjoyment throw:
    Your Tide of Life is ebbing fast, and it,
Exhausted once, for You no more shall flow."

While yet the Phantom of false Youth was mine,
I heard a Voice from out the Darkness whine,
    "O Youth, O whither gone? Return,
And bathe my Age in thy reviving Wine."

In this subduing Draught of tender green
And kindly Absinth, with its wimpling Sheen
    Of dusky half-lights, let me drown
The haunting Pathos of the Might-Have-Been.

For every nickeled Joy, marred and brief,
We pay some day its Weight in golden Grief
   Mined from our Hearts. Ah, murmur not—
From this one-sided Bargain dream of no Relief!

The Joy of Life, that streaming through their Veins
Tumultuous swept, falls slack—and wanes
   The Glory in the Eye—and one by one
Life's Pleasures perish and make place for Pains.

Whether one hide in some secluded Nook—
Whether at Liverpool or Sandy Hook—
   'Tis one. Old Age will search him out—and He—
He—He—when ready will know where to look.

From Cradle unto Grave I keep a House
Of Entertainment where may drowse
   Bacilli and kindred Germs—or feed—or breed
Their festering Species in a deep Carouse.

Think—in this battered Caravanserai,
Whose Portals open stand all Night and Day,
   How Microbe after Microbe with his Pomp
Arrives unasked, and comes to stay.

Our ivory Teeth, confessing to the Lust
Of masticating, once, now own Disgust
   Of Clay-plug'd Cavities—full soon our Snags
Are emptied, and our Mouths are filled with Dust.

Our Gums forsake the Teeth and tender grow,
And fat, like over-ripened Figs—we know
   The Sign—the Riggs Disease is ours, and we
Must list this Sorrow, add another Woe;

Our Lungs begin to fail and soon we Cough,
And chilly Streaks play up our Backs, and off
   Our fever'd Foreheads drips an icy Sweat—
We scoffed before, but now we may not scoff.

Some for the Bunions that afflict us prate
Of Plasters unsurpassable, and hate
   To cut a Corn—ah cut, and let the Plaster go,
Nor murmur if the Solace come too late.

Some for the Honors of Old Age, and some
Long for its Respite from the Hum
   And Clash of sordid Strife—O Fools,
The Past should teach them what's to Come:

Lo, for the Honors, cold Neglect instead!
For Respite, disputatious Heirs a Bed
   Of Thorns for them will furnish. Go,
Seek not Here for Peace—but Yonder—with the Dead.

For whether Zal and Rustam heed this Sign,
And even smitten thus, will not repine,
   Let Zal and Rustam shuffle as they may,
The Fine once levied they must Cash the Fine.

O Voices of the Long Ago that were so dear!
Fall'n Silent, now, for many a Mould'ring Year,
   O whither are ye flown? Come back,
And break my Heart, but bless my grieving ear.

Some happy Day my Voice will Silent fall,
And answer not when some that love it call:
   Be glad for Me when this you note—and think
I've found the Voices lost, beyond the Pall.

So let me grateful drain the Magic Bowl
That medicines hurt Minds and on the Soul
   The Healing of its Peace doth lay—if then
Death claim me—Welcome be his Dole!

MARK TWAIN.

SANNA, SWEDEN, *September 15th*.

*Private.*—If you don't know what Riggs's Disease of the Teeth is, the dentist will tell you. I've had it—and it is more than interesting.　　S.L.C.

### EDITORIAL NOTE.

Fearing that there might be some mistake, we submitted a proof of this article to the (American) gentlemen named in it, and asked them to correct any errors of detail that might have crept in among the facts. They reply with some asperity that errors cannot creep in among facts where there are no facts for them to creep in among; and that none are discoverable in this article, but only baseless aberrations of a disordered mind. They have no recollection of any such night in Boston, nor elsewhere; and in their opinion there was never any such night. They have *met* Mr. Twain, but have had the prudence not to intrust any privacies to him—particularly under oath; and they think they now see that this prudence was justified, since he has been untrustworthy enough to even betray privacies which had no existence. Further, they think it a strange thing that Mr. Twain, who was never invited to meddle with anybody's boyhood dreams but his own, has been so gratuitously anxious to see that other people's are placed before the world that he has quite lost his head in his zeal and forgotten to make any mention of his own at all. Provided we insert this explanation, they are willing to let his article pass; otherwise they must require its suppression, in the interest of truth.

*P. S.*—These replies having left us in some perplexity, and also in some fear lest they might distress Mr. Twain if published without his privity, we judged it but fair to submit them to him and give him an opportunity to defend himself. But he does not seem to be troubled, or even aware that he is in a delicate situation. He merely says:

"Do not worry about those former young people. They can write good literature, but when it comes to speaking the truth, they have not had my training.—MARK TWAIN."

The last sentence seems obscure, and liable to an unfortunate construction. It plainly needs refashioning, but we cannot take the responsibility of doing it.—EDITOR.

*January 1900*

# Introducing Winston S. Churchill

*Grand Ballroom, Hotel Waldorf-Astoria, New York*

Mr. Churchill and I do not agree on the righteousness of the South African war, but that is of no consequence. There is no place where people all think alike—well, there is heaven; there they do, but let us hope it won't be so always.

For years I have been a self-appointed missionary, and have wrought zealously for my cause—the joining together of America and the motherland in bonds of friendship, esteem and affection—an alliance of the heart which should permanently and beneficently influence the political relations of the two countries. Wherever I have stood before a gathering of Americans or Englishmen, in England, India, Australia or elsewhere, I have urged my mission, and warmed it up with compliments to both countries and pointed out how nearly alike the two peoples are in character and spirit. They ought to be united.

Behold America, the refuge of the homeless, the hunted, the oppressed from everywhere (who can pay ten dollars admission)—anyone except a Chinaman—standing up for human rights everywhere, even helping to make China admit the foreigner when she didn't want him, and to let him in free when she wanted to charge him fifty dollars if he was a harmless Christian or kill him if he was a missionary. And how England, mother of human liberty, uttered that great word, "the slave that sets his foot upon English soil is free" and with her strong hand made that gospel good in every acre of that vast Empire whose dominions girdle the globe; and how unselfishly England has wrought for the open door for all.

And how nobly and piously America also has stood for that same door in all cases where it wasn't her own; and how generous we have been, and how generous England has been in not requiring fancy rates for extinguishing missionaries, the way Germany does, but willing to take produce for them—firecrackers and tea—while Germany has to have territory and cash, and monuments and any other loot that's in reach—and memorial churches, and has thus made true changes of heart and regeneration, and the other details of

German trinity so expensive that China won't be able to afford German missionaries any more till she gets in better shape financially; and how self-respectingly England and America have refrained from imitating German bluster, German rapacity, the mailed fist with a burglar's jimmy in it, and the investing mouth above it which alternately chortles bargain counter piety and "no quarter" according to the state of the market; and how nobly (and shamefacedly) we both stood timorously by at Port Arthur and wept sweetly and sympathizingly and shone while France and Germany helped Russia to rob the Japanese; and how gallantly we went to the rescue of poor Cuba, friendless, despairing, borne down by centuries of bitter slavery, and broke off her chains and set her free—with approving England at our back in an attitude toward European powers which did us good service in those days, and we confess it now.

Yes, as a missionary I have sung this song of praise and still sing it; and yet I think that England sinned in getting into a war in South Africa which she could have avoided without loss of credit or dignity—just as I think we have sinned in crowding ourselves into a war in the Philippines on the same terms.

Mr. Churchill will tell you about the war in South Africa, and he is competent—he fought and wrote through it himself. And he made a record there which would be a proud one for a man twice his age. By his father he is English, by his mother he is American—to my mind the blend which makes the perfect man. We are now on the friendliest terms with England. Mainly through my missionary efforts I suppose; and I am glad. We have always been kin: kin in blood, kin in religion, kin in representative government, kin in ideals, kin in just and lofty purposes; and now we are kin in sin, the harmony is complete, the blend is perfect, like Mr. Churchill himself, whom I now have the honor to present to you.

*December 12, 1900*

# A Salutation-Speech from the Nineteenth Century to the Twentieth, Taken Down in Short-Hand by Mark Twain

I bring you the stately matron named Christendom, returning bedraggled, besmirched and dishonored from pirate-raids in Kiao-Chow, Manchuria, South Africa and the Philippines, with her soul full of meanness, her pocket full of boodle, and her mouth full of pious hypocrisies. Give her soap and a towel, but hide the looking-glass.

MARK TWAIN

New York, Dec. 31, 1900

# To the Person Sitting in Darkness

"Christmas will dawn in the United States over a people full of hope and aspiration and good cheer. Such a condition means contentment and happiness. The carping grumbler who may here and there go forth will find few to listen to him. The majority will wonder what is the matter with him and pass on."—*New York Tribune*, on Christmas Eve.

From *The Sun*, of New York:

"The purpose of this article is not to describe the terrible offences against humanity committed in the name of Politics in some of the most notorious East Side districts. *They could not be described, even verbally.* But it is the intention to let the great mass of more or less careless citizens of this beautiful metropolis of the New World get some conception of the havoc and ruin wrought to man, woman and child in the most densely populated and least known section of the city. Name, date and place can be supplied to those of little faith—or to any man who feels himself aggrieved. It is a plain statement of record and observation, written without license and without garnish.

"Imagine, if you can, a section of the city territory completely dominated by one man, without whose permission neither legitimate nor illegitimate business can be conducted; *where illegitimate business is encouraged and legitimate business discouraged;* where the respectable residents have to fasten their doors and windows summer nights and sit in their rooms with asphyxiating air and 100-degree temperature, rather than try to catch the faint whiff of breeze in their natural breathing places, the stoops of their homes; *where naked women dance by night in the streets, and unsexed men prowl like vultures through the darkness on 'business'* not only permitted but encouraged by the police; *where the education of infants begins with the knowledge of prostitution* and the training of little girls is training in the arts of Phryne; where *American* girls brought up with the refinements of *American* homes are imported from small towns up-State, Massachusetts, Connecticut and New Jersey, and kept as virtually prisoners as if they were locked up behind jail bars until they have lost all semblance of womanhood; *where small boys are taught to solicit for the women of disorderly houses;* where there is an organized society of young men *whose sole business in life is to corrupt young girls and turn them over to bawdy houses;* where men walking with their wives along the street are openly insulted; *where children that have adult diseases are the chief patrons of the hospitals and dispensaries;* where it is the rule, rather than the exception, that *murder, rape, robbery and theft go unpunished*—in short where the Premium of the most awful forms of Vice is the Profit of the politicians."

The following news from China appeared in *The Sun*, of New York, on Christmas Eve. The italics are mine:

"The Rev. Mr. Ament, of the American Board of Foreign Missions, has returned from a trip which he made for the purpose of collecting indemnities for damages done by Boxers. *Everywhere he went he compelled the Chinese to pay.* He says that all his native Christians are now provided for. He had 700 of them under his charge, and 300 were killed. He has *collected* 300 *taels for each* of these murders, and has *compelled full payment for all the property belonging to Christians* that was destroyed. He also assessed *fines* amounting to THIRTEEN TIMES the amount of the indemnity. *This money will be used for the propagation of the Gospel.*

"Mr. Ament declares that the compensation he has collected is *moderate*, when compared with the amount secured by the Catholics, who demand, in addition to money, *head for head.* They collect 500 taels for each murder of a Catholic. In the Wenchiu country, 680 Catholics were killed, and for this the European Catholics here demand 750,000 strings of cash and 680 *heads.*

"In the course of a conversation, Mr. Ament referred to the attitude of the missionaries toward the Chinese. He said:

" 'I deny emphatically that the missionaries are *vindictive*, that they *generally* looted, or that they have done anything *since* the siege that *the circumstances did not demand.* I criticise the Americans. *The soft hand of the Americans is not as good as the mailed fist of the Germans.* If you deal with the Chinese with a soft hand they will take advantage of it.'

"The statement that the French Government will return the loot taken by the French soldiers, is the source of the greatest amusement here. The French soldiers were more systematic looters than the Germans, and it is a fact that to-day *Catholic Christians*, carrying French flags and armed with modern guns, *are looting villages* in the Province of Chili."

By happy luck, we get all these glad tidings on Christmas Eve—just in time to enable us to celebrate the day with proper gaiety and enthusiasm. Our spirits soar, and we find we can even make jokes: Taels I win, Heads you lose.

Our Reverend Ament is the right man in the right place.

What we want of our missionaries out there is, not that they shall merely represent in their acts and persons the grace and gentleness and charity and loving kindness of our religion, but that they shall also represent the American spirit. The oldest Americans are the Pawnees. Macallum's History says:

"When a white Boxer kills a Pawnee and destroys his property, the other Pawnees do not trouble to seek *him* out, they kill any white person that comes along; also, they make some white village pay deceased's heirs the full cash value of deceased, together with full cash value of the property destroyed; they also make the village pay, in addition, *thirteen times* the value of that property into a fund for the dissemination of the Pawnee religion, which they regard as the best of all religions for the softening and humanizing of the heart of man. It is their idea that it is only fair and right that the innocent should be made to suffer for the guilty, and that it is better that ninety and nine innocent should suffer than that one guilty person should escape."

Our Reverend Ament is justifiably jealous of those enterprising Catholics, who not only get big money for each lost convert, but get "head for head" besides. But he should soothe himself with the reflection that the entirety of their exactions are for their own pockets, whereas he, less selfishly, devotes only 300 taels per head to that service, and gives the whole vast thirteen repetitions of the property-indemnity to the service of propagating the Gospel. His magnanimity has won him the approval of his nation, and will get him a monument. Let him be content with these rewards. We all hold him dear for manfully defending his fellow missionaries from exaggerated charges which were beginning to distress us, but which his testimony has so considerably modified that we can now contemplate them without noticeable pain. For now we know that, even before the siege, the missionaries were not "generally" out looting, and that, "since the siege," they have acted quite handsomely, except when "circumstances" crowded them. I am arranging for the monument. Subscriptions for it can be sent to the American Board; designs for it can be sent to me. Designs must allegorically set forth the Thirteen Reduplications of the Indemnity, and the Object for which they were exacted; as Ornaments, the de-

signs must exhibit 680 Heads, so disposed as to give a pleasing and pretty effect; for the Catholics have done nicely, and
are entitled to notice in the monument. Mottoes may be suggested, if any shall be discovered that will satisfactorily cover
the ground.

Mr. Ament's financial feat of squeezing a thirteen-fold indemnity out of the pauper peasants to square other people's
offenses, thus condemning them and their women and innocent little children to inevitable starvation and lingering
death, in order that the blood-money so acquired might be
*"used for the propagation of the Gospel,"* does not flutter my
serenity; although the act and the words, taken together, concrete a blasphemy so hideous and so colossal that, without
doubt, its mate is not findable in the history of this or of any
other age. Yet, if a layman had done that thing and justified it
with those words, I should have shuddered, I know. Or, if I
had done the thing and said the words myself—however, the
thought is unthinkable, irreverent as some imperfectly informed people think me. Sometimes an ordained minister sets
out to be blasphemous. When this happens, the layman is out
of the running; he stands no chance.

We have Mr. Ament's impassioned assurance that the missionaries are not "vindictive." Let us hope and pray that they
will never become so, but will remain in the almost morbidly
fair and just and gentle temper which is affording so much
satisfaction to their brother and champion to-day.

The following is from the *New York Tribune* of Christmas
Eve. It comes from that journal's Tokio correspondent. It has
a strange and impudent sound, but the Japanese are but partially civilized as yet. When they become wholly civilized they
will not talk so:

"The missionary question, of course, occupies a foremost place in
the discussion. It is now felt as essential that the Western Powers take
cognizance of the sentiment here, that religious invasions of Oriental
countries by powerful Western organizations are tantamount to fili-
bustering expeditions, and should not only be discountenanced, but
that stern measures should be adopted for their suppression. The
feeling here is that the missionary organizations constitute a constant
menace to peaceful international relations."

*Shall we?* That is, shall we go on conferring our Civilization upon the peoples that sit in darkness, or shall we give those poor things a rest? Shall we bang right ahead in our old-time, loud, pious way, and commit the new century to the game; or shall we sober up and sit down and think it over first? Would it not be prudent to get our Civilization-tools together, and see how much stock is left on hand in the way of Glass Beads and Theology, and Maxim Guns and Hymn Books, and Trade-Gin and Torches of Progress and Enlightenment (patent adjustable ones, good to fire villages with, upon occasion), and balance the books, and arrive at the profit and loss, so that we may intelligently decide whether to continue the business or sell out the property and start a new Civilization Scheme on the proceeds?

Extending the Blessings of Civilization to our Brother who Sits in Darkness has been a good trade and has paid well, on the whole; and there is money in it yet, if carefully worked—but not enough, in my judgment, to make any considerable risk advisable. The People that Sit in Darkness are getting to be too scarce—too scarce and too shy. And such darkness as is now left is really of but an indifferent quality, and not dark enough for the game. The most of those People that Sit in Darkness have been furnished with more light than was good for them or profitable for us. We have been injudicious.

The Blessings-of-Civilization Trust, wisely and cautiously administered, is a Daisy. There is more money in it, more territory, more sovereignty, and other kinds of emolument, than there is in any other game that is played. But Christendom has been playing it badly of late years, and must certainly suffer by it, in my opinion. She has been so eager to get every stake that appeared on the green cloth, that the People who Sit in Darkness have noticed it—they have noticed it, and have begun to show alarm. They have become suspicious of the Blessings of Civilization. More—they have begun to examine them. This is not well. The Blessings of Civilization are all right, and a good commercial property; there could not be a better, in a dim light. In the right kind of a light, and at a proper distance, with the goods a little out of focus, they furnish this desirable exhibit to the Gentlemen who Sit in Darkness:

| LOVE, | LAW AND ORDER, |
| JUSTICE, | LIBERTY, |
| GENTLENESS, | EQUALITY, |
| CHRISTIANITY, | HONORABLE DEALING, |
| PROTECTION TO THE WEAK, | MERCY, |
| TEMPERANCE, | EDUCATION, |

—and so on.

There. Is it good? Sir, it is pie. It will bring into camp any idiot that sits in darkness anywhere. But not if we adulterate it. It is proper to be emphatic upon that point. This brand is strictly for Export—apparently. *Apparently.* Privately and confidentially, it is nothing of the kind. Privately and confidentially, it is merely an outside cover, gay and pretty and attractive, displaying the special patterns of our Civilization which we reserve for Home Consumption, while *inside* the bale is the Actual Thing that the Customer Sitting in Darkness buys with his blood and tears and land and liberty. That Actual Thing is, indeed, Civilization, but it is only for Export. Is there a difference between the two brands? In some of the details, yes.

We all know that the Business is being ruined. The reason is not far to seek. It is because our Mr. McKinley, and Mr. Chamberlain, and the Kaiser, and the Czar and the French have been exporting the Actual Thing *with the outside cover left off.* This is bad for the Game. It shows that these new players of it are not sufficiently acquainted with it.

It is a distress to look on and note the mismoves, they are so strange and so awkward. Mr. Chamberlain manufactures a war out of materials so inadequate and so fanciful that they make the boxes grieve and the gallery laugh, and he tries hard to persuade himself that it isn't purely a private raid for cash, but has a sort of dim, vague respectability about it somewhere, if he could only find the spot; and that, by and by, he can scour the flag clean again after he has finished dragging it through the mud, and make it shine and flash in the vault of heaven once more as it had shone and flashed there a thousand years in the world's respect until he laid his unfaithful hand upon it. It is bad play—bad. For it exposes the Actual Thing to Them that Sit in Darkness, and they say: "What!

Christian against Christian? And only for money? Is *this* a case of magnanimity, forbearance, love, gentleness, mercy, protection of the weak—this strange and over-showy onslaught of an elephant upon a nest of field-mice, on the pretext that the mice had squeaked an insolence at him—conduct which 'no self-respecting government could allow to pass unavenged?' as Mr. Chamberlain said. Was that a good pretext in a small case, when it had not been a good pretext in a large one?—for only recently Russia had affronted the elephant three times and survived alive and unsmitten. Is this Civilization and Progress? Is it something better than we already possess? These harryings and burnings and desert-makings in the Transvaal—is this an improvement on our darkness? Is it, perhaps, possible that there are two kinds of Civilization— one for home consumption and one for the heathen market?"

Then They that Sit in Darkness are troubled, and shake their heads; and they read this extract from a letter of a British private, recounting his exploits in one of Methuen's victories, some days before the affair of Magersfontein, and they are troubled again:

"We tore up the hill and into the intrenchments, and the Boers saw we had them; so they dropped their guns and went down on their knees and put up their hands clasped, and begged for mercy. And we gave it them—*with the long spoon.*"

The long spoon is the bayonet. See *Lloyd's Weekly*, London, of those days. The same number—and the same column— contained some quite unconscious satire in the form of shocked and bitter upbraidings of the Boers for their brutalities and inhumanities!

Next, to our heavy damage, the Kaiser went to playing the game without first mastering it. He lost a couple of missionaries in a riot in Shantung, and in his account he made an overcharge for them. China had to pay a hundred thousand dollars apiece for them, in money; twelve miles of territory, containing several millions of inhabitants and worth twenty million dollars; and to build a monument, and also a Christian church; whereas the people of China could have been depended upon to remember the missionaries without the help of these expensive memorials. This was all bad play. Bad, because it would not, and could not, and will not now or ever, deceive the Person Sitting in Darkness. He knows that it was an overcharge. He knows that a missionary is like any other man: he is worth merely what you can supply his place for, and no more. He is useful, but so is a doctor, so is a sheriff, so is an editor; but a just Emperor does not charge war-prices for such. A diligent, intelligent, but obscure missionary, and a diligent, intelligent country editor are worth much, and we know it; but they are not worth the earth. We esteem such an editor, and we are sorry to see him go; but, when he goes, we should consider twelve miles of territory, and a church, and a fortune, over-compensation for his loss. I mean, if he was a Chinese editor, and we had to settle for him. It is no proper figure for an editor or a missionary; one can get shop-worn kings for less. It was bad play on the Kaiser's part. It got this property, true; but it *produced the Chinese revolt*, the indignant uprising of China's traduced patriots, the Boxers. The results have been expensive to Germany, and to the other Disseminators of Progress and the Blessings of Civilization.

The Kaiser's claim was paid, yet it was bad play, for it could not fail to have an evil effect upon Persons Sitting in Darkness in China. They would muse upon the event, and be likely to say: "Civilization is gracious and beautiful, for such is its reputation; but can we afford it? There are rich Chinamen, perhaps they could afford it; but this tax is not laid upon them, it is laid upon the peasants of Shantung; it is they that must pay this mighty sum, and their wages are but four cents a day. Is this a better civilization than ours, and holier and higher and nobler? Is not this rapacity? Is not this extortion? Would Germany charge America two hundred thousand dollars for two missionaries, and shake the mailed fist in her face, and send warships, and send soldiers, and say: 'Seize twelve miles of territory, worth twenty millions of dollars, as additional pay for the missionaries; and make those peasants build a monument to the missionaries, and a costly Christian church to remember them by?' And later would Germany say to her soldiers: 'March through America and slay, *giving no quarter*; make the German face there, as has been our Hun-face here, a terror for a thousand years; march through the

Great Republic and slay, slay, slay, carving a road for our offended religion through its heart and bowels?' Would Germany do like this to America, to England, to France, to Russia? Or only to China the helpless—imitating the elephant's assault upon the field-mice? Had we better invest in this Civilization—this Civilization which called Napoleon a buccaneer for carrying off Venice's bronze horses, but which steals our ancient astronomical instruments from our walls, and goes looting like common bandits—that is, all the alien soldiers except America's; and (Americans again excepted) storms frightened villages and cables the result to glad journals at home every day: 'Chinese losses, 450 killed; ours, *one officer and two men wounded*. Shall proceed against neighboring village to-morrow, where a *massacre* is reported.' Can we afford Civilization?"

And, next, Russia must go and play the game injudiciously. She affronts England once or twice—with the Person Sitting in Darkness observing and noting; by moral assistance of France and Germany, she robs Japan of her hard-earned spoil, all swimming in Chinese blood—Port Arthur—with the Person again observing and noting; then she seizes Manchuria, raids its villages, and chokes its great river with the swollen corpses of countless massacred peasants—that astonished Person still observing and noting. And perhaps he is saying to himself: "It is yet *another* Civilized Power, with its banner of the Prince of Peace in one hand and its loot-basket and its butcher-knife in the other. Is there no salvation for us but to adopt Civilization and lift ourselves down to its level?"

And by and by comes America, and our Master of the Game plays it badly—plays it as Mr. Chamberlain was playing it in South Africa. It was a mistake to do that; also, it was one which was quite unlooked for in a Master who was playing it so well in Cuba. In Cuba, he was playing the usual and regular *American* game, and it was winning, for there is no way to beat it. The Master, contemplating Cuba, said: "Here is an oppressed and friendless little nation which is willing to fight to be free; we go partners, and put up the strength of seventy million sympathizers and the resources of the United States: play!" Nothing but Europe combined could call that hand: and Europe cannot combine on anything. There, in

Cuba, he was following our great traditions in a way which made us very proud of him, and proud of the deep dissatisfaction which his play was provoking in Continental Europe. Moved by a high inspiration, he threw out those stirring words which proclaimed that forcible annexation would be "criminal aggression;" and in that utterance fired another "shot heard round the world." The memory of that fine saying will be outlived by the remembrance of no act of his but one—that he forgot it within the twelvemonth, and its honorable gospel along with it.

For, presently, came the Philippine temptation. It was strong; it was too strong, and he made that bad mistake: he played the European game, the Chamberlain game. It was a pity; it was a great pity, that error; that one grievous error, that irrevocable error. For it was the very place and time to play the American game again. And at no cost. Rich winnings to be gathered in, too; rich and permanent; indestructible; a fortune transmissible forever to the children of the flag. Not land, not money, not dominion—no, something worth many times more than that dross: our share, the spectacle of a nation of long harassed and persecuted slaves set free through our influence; our posterity's share, the golden memory of that fair deed. The game was in our hands. If it had been played according to the American rules, Dewey would have sailed away from Manila as soon as he had destroyed the Spanish fleet—after putting up a sign on shore guaranteeing foreign property and life against damage by the Filipinos, and warning the Powers that interference with the emancipated patriots would be regarded as an act unfriendly to the United States. The Powers cannot combine, in even a bad cause, and the sign would not have been molested.

Dewey could have gone about his affairs elsewhere, and left the competent Filipino army to starve out the little Spanish garrison and send it home, and the Filipino citizens to set up the form of government they might prefer, and deal with the friars and their doubtful acquisitions according to Filipino ideas of fairness and justice—ideas which have since been tested and found to be of as high an order as any that prevail in Europe or America.

But we played the Chamberlain game, and lost the chance

to add another Cuba and another honorable deed to our good record.

The more we examine the mistake, the more clearly we perceive that it is going to be bad for the Business. The Person Sitting in Darkness is almost sure to say: "There is something curious about this—curious and unaccountable. There must be two Americas: one that sets the captive free, and one that takes a once-captive's new freedom away from him, and picks a quarrel with him with nothing to found it on; then kills him to get his land."

The truth is, the Person Sitting in Darkness *is* saying things like that; and for the sake of the Business we must persuade him to look at the Philippine matter in another and healthier way. We must arrange his opinions for him. I believe it can be done; for Mr. Chamberlain has arranged England's opinion of the South African matter, and done it most cleverly and successfully. He presented the facts—some of the facts—and showed those confiding people what the facts meant. He did it statistically, which is a good way. He used the formula: "Twice 2 are 14, and 2 from 9 leaves 35." Figures are effective; figures will convince the elect.

Now, my plan is a still bolder one than Mr. Chamberlain's, though apparently a copy of it. Let us be franker than Mr. Chamberlain; let us audaciously present the whole of the facts, shirking none, then explain them according to Mr. Chamberlain's formula. This daring truthfulness will astonish and dazzle the Person Sitting in Darkness, and he will take the Explanation down before his mental vision has had time to get back into focus. Let us say to him:

"Our case is simple. On the 1st of May, Dewey destroyed the Spanish fleet. This left the Archipelago in the hands of its proper and rightful owners, the Filipino nation. Their army numbered 30,000 men, and they were competent to whip out or starve out the little Spanish garrison; then the people could set up a government of their own devising. Our traditions required that Dewey should now set up his warning sign, and go away. But the Master of the Game happened to think of another plan—the European plan. He acted upon it. This was, to send out an army—ostensibly to help the native patriots put the finishing touch upon their long and plucky

struggle for independence, but really to take their land away
from them and keep it. That is, in the interest of Progress and
Civilization. The plan developed, stage by stage, and quite
satisfactorily. We entered into a military alliance with the
trusting Filipinos, and they hemmed in Manila on the land
side, and by their valuable help the place, with its garrison of
8,000 or 10,000 Spaniards, was captured—a thing which we
could not have accomplished unaided at that time. We got
their help by—by ingenuity. We knew they were fighting for
their independence, and that they had been at it for two years.
We knew they supposed that we also were fighting in their
worthy cause—just as we had helped the Cubans fight for
Cuban independence—and we allowed them to go on thinking so. *Until Manila was ours and we could get along without
them.* Then we showed our hand. Of course, they were surprised—that was natural; surprised and disappointed; disappointed and grieved. To them it looked un-American;
uncharacteristic; foreign to our established traditions. And
this was natural, too; for we were only playing the American
Game in public—in private it was the European. It was
neatly done, very neatly, and it bewildered them. They could
not understand it; for we had been so friendly—so affectionate, even—with those simple-minded patriots! We, our own
selves, had brought back out of exile their leader, their hero,
their hope, their Washington—Aguinaldo; brought him in a
warship, in high honor, under the sacred shelter and hospitality of the flag; brought him back and restored him to his
people, and got their moving and eloquent gratitude for it.
Yes, we had been so friendly to them, and had heartened them
up in so many ways! We had lent them guns and ammunition;
advised with them; exchanged pleasant courtesies with them;
placed our sick and wounded in their kindly care; entrusted
our Spanish prisoners to their humane and honest hands;
fought shoulder to shoulder with them against 'the common
enemy' (our own phrase); praised their courage, praised
their gallantry, praised their mercifulness, praised their fine
and honorable conduct; borrowed their trenches, borrowed
strong positions which they had previously captured from
the Spaniard; petted them, lied to them—officially proclaim-
ing that our land and naval forces came to give them their

freedom and displace the bad Spanish Government—fooled them, used them until we needed them no longer; then derided the sucked orange and threw it away. We kept the positions which we had beguiled them of; by and by, we moved a force forward and overlapped patriot ground—a clever thought, for we needed trouble, and this would produce it. A Filipino soldier, crossing the ground, where no one had a right to forbid him, was shot by our sentry. The badgered patriots resented this with arms, without waiting to know whether Aguinaldo, who was absent, would approve or not. Aguinaldo did not approve; but that availed nothing. What we wanted, in the interest of Progress and Civilization, was the Archipelago, unencumbered by patriots struggling for independence; and War was what we needed. We clinched our opportunity. It is Mr. Chamberlain's case over again—at least in its motive and intention; and we played the game as adroitly as he played it himself."

At this point in our frank statement of fact to the Person Sitting in Darkness, we should throw in a little trade-taffy about the Blessings of Civilization—for a change, and for the refreshment of his spirit—then go on with our tale:

"We and the patriots having captured Manila, Spain's ownership of the Archipelago and her sovereignty over it were at an end—obliterated—annihilated—not a rag or shred of either remaining behind. It was then that we conceived the divinely humorous idea of *buying* both of these spectres from Spain! [It is quite safe to confess this to the Person Sitting in Darkness, since neither he nor any other sane person will believe it.] In buying those ghosts for twenty millions, we also contracted to take care of the friars and their accumulations. I think we also agreed to propagate leprosy and smallpox, but as to this there is doubt. But it is not important; persons afflicted with the friars do not mind other diseases.

"With our Treaty ratified, Manila subdued, and our Ghosts secured, we had no further use for Aguinaldo and the owners of the Archipelago. We forced a war, and we have been hunting America's guest and ally through the woods and swamps ever since."

At this point in the tale, it will be well to boast a little of our war-work and our heroisms in the field, so as to make our performance look as fine as England's in South Africa; but I believe it will not be best to emphasize this too much. We must be cautious. Of course, we must read the war-telegrams to the Person, in order to keep up our frankness; but we can throw an air of humorousness over them, and that will modify their grim eloquence a little, and their rather indiscreet exhibitions of gory exultation. Before reading to him the following display heads of the dispatches of November 18, 1900, it will be well to practice on them in private first, so as to get the right tang of lightness and gaiety into them:

"ADMINISTRATION WEARY OF PROTRACTED HOSTILITIES!"
"REAL WAR AHEAD FOR FILIPINO REBELS!"*
"WILL SHOW NO MERCY!"
"KITCHENER'S PLAN ADOPTED!"

Kitchener knows how to handle disagreeable people who are fighting for their homes and their liberties, and we must let on that we are merely imitating Kitchener, and have no national interest in the matter, further than to get ourselves admired by the Great Family of Nations, in which august company our Master of the Game has bought a place for us in the back row.

Of course, we must not venture to ignore our General MacArthur's reports—oh, why do they keep on printing those embarrassing things?—we must drop them trippingly from the tongue and take the chances:

"During the last ten months our losses have been 268 killed and 750 wounded; Filipino loss, *three thousand two hundred and twenty-seven killed*, and 694 wounded."

We must stand ready to grab the Person Sitting in Darkness, for he will swoon away at this confession, saying: "Good God, those 'niggers' spare their wounded, and the Americans massacre theirs!"

We must bring him to, and coax him and coddle him, and assure him that the ways of Providence are best, and that it

*"Rebels!" Mumble that funny word—don't let the Person catch it distinctly.

would not become us to find fault with them; and then, to show him that we are only imitators, not originators, we must read the following passage from the letter of an American soldier-lad in the Philippines to his mother, published in *Public Opinion*, of Decorah, Iowa, describing the finish of a victorious battle:

"WE NEVER LEFT ONE ALIVE. IF ONE WAS WOUNDED, WE WOULD RUN OUR BAYONETS THROUGH HIM."

Having now laid all the historical facts before the Person Sitting in Darkness, we should bring him to again, and explain them to him. We should say to him:

"They look doubtful, but in reality they are not. There have been lies; yes, but they were told in a good cause. We have been treacherous; but that was only in order that real good might come out of apparent evil. True, we have crushed a deceived and confiding people; we have turned against the weak and the friendless who trusted us; we have stamped out a just and intelligent and well-ordered republic; we have stabbed an ally in the back and slapped the face of a guest; we have bought a Shadow from an enemy that hadn't it to sell; we have robbed a trusting friend of his land and his liberty; we have invited our clean young men to shoulder a discredited musket and do bandit's work under a flag which bandits have been accustomed to fear, not to follow; we have debauched America's honor and blackened her face before the world; but each detail was for the best. We know this. The Head of every State and Sovereignty in Christendom and ninety per cent. of every legislative body in Christendom, including our Congress and our fifty State Legislatures, are members not only of the church, but also of the Blessings-of-Civilization Trust. This world-girdling accumulation of trained morals, high principles, and justice, cannot do an unright thing, an unfair thing, an ungenerous thing, an unclean thing. It knows what it is about. Give yourself no uneasiness; it is all right."

Now then, that will convince the Person. You will see. It will restore the Business. Also, it will elect the Master of the Game to the vacant place in the Trinity of our national gods; and there on their high thrones the Three will sit, age after age, in the people's sight, each bearing the Emblem of his service: Washington, the Sword of the Liberator; Lincoln, the Slave's Broken Chains; the Master, the Chains Repaired.

It will give the Business a splendid new start. You will see.

Everything is prosperous, now; everything is just as we should wish it. We have got the Archipelago, and we shall never give it up. Also, we have every reason to hope that we shall have an opportunity before very long to slip out of our Congressional contract with Cuba and give her something better in the place of it. It is a rich country, and many of us are already beginning to see that the contract was a sentimental mistake. But now—right now—is the best time to do some profitable rehabilitating work—work that will set us up and make us comfortable, and discourage gossip. We cannot conceal from ourselves that, privately, we are a little troubled about our uniform. It is one of our prides; it is acquainted with honor; it is familiar with great deeds and noble; we love it, we revere it; and so this errand it is on makes us uneasy. And our flag—another pride of ours, our chiefest! We have worshipped it so; and when we have seen it in far lands—glimpsing it unexpectedly in that strange sky, waving its welcome and benediction to us—we have caught our breath, and uncovered our heads, and couldn't speak, for a moment, for the thought of what it was to us and the great ideals it stood for. Indeed, we *must* do something about these things; we must not have the flag out there, and the uniform. They are not needed there; we can manage in some other way. England manages, as regards the uniform, and so can we. We have to send soldiers—we can't get out of that—but we can disguise them. It is the way England does in South Africa. Even Mr. Chamberlain himself takes pride in England's honorable uniform, and makes the army down there wear an ugly and odious and appropriate disguise, of yellow stuff such as quarantine flags are made of, and which are hoisted to warn the healthy away from unclean disease and repulsive death. This cloth is called khaki. We could adopt it. It is light, comfortable, grotesque, and deceives the enemy, for he cannot conceive of a soldier being concealed in it.

And as for a flag for the Philippine Province, it is easily managed. We can have a special one—our States do it: we can have just our usual flag, with the white stripes painted black and the stars replaced by the skull and cross-bones.

And we do not need that Civil Commission out there. Having no powers, it has to invent them, and that kind of work cannot be effectively done by just anybody; an expert is required. Mr. Croker can be spared. We do not want the United States represented there, but only the Game.

By help of these suggested amendments, Progress and Civilization in that country can have a boom, and it will take in the Persons who are Sitting in Darkness, and we can resume Business at the old stand.

*February 1901*

# Battle Hymn of the Republic
## (*Brought Down to Date*)

Mine eyes have seen the orgy of the launching of the
     Sword;
He is searching out the hoardings where the stranger's
     wealth is stored;
He hath loosed his fateful lightnings, and with woe and
     death has scored;
   His lust is marching on.

I have seen him in the watch-fires of a hundred circling
     camps,
They have builded him an altar in the Eastern dews and
     damps;
I have read his doomful mission by the dim and flaring
     lamps—
   His night is marching on.

I have read his bandit gospel writ in burnished rows of
     steel:
"As ye deal with my pretensions, so with you my wrath
     shall deal;
Let the faithless son of Freedom crush the patriot with his
     heel;
   Lo, Greed is marching on!"

We have legalized the strumpet and are guarding her
     retreat;*
Greed is seeking out commercial souls before his judgment
     seat;
O, be swift, ye clods, to answer him! be jubilant my
     feet!
   Our god is marching on!

*In Manila the government has placed a certain industry under the protec-
tion of our flag.

In a sordid slime harmonious, Greed was born in yonder
    ditch,
With a longing in his bosom—and for others' goods an
    itch—
As Christ died to make men holy, let men die to make us
    rich—
    Our god is marching on.

*c. 1901*

# As Regards Patriotism

It is agreed, in this country, that if a man can arrange his religion so that it perfectly satisfies his conscience, it is not incumbent upon him to care whether the arrangement is satisfactory to anyone else or not.

In Austria and some other countries this is not the case. There the State arranges a man's religion for him, he has no voice in it himself.

Patriotism is merely a religion—love of country, worship of country, devotion to the country's flag and honor and welfare.

In absolute monarchies it is furnished from the Throne, cut and dried, to the subject; in England and America it is furnished, cut and dried, to the citizen by the politician and the newspaper.

The newspaper-and-politician-manufactured Patriot often gags in private over his dose; but he takes it, and keeps it on his stomach the best he can. Blessed are the meek.

Sometimes, in the beginning of an insane and shabby political upheaval, he is strongly moved to revolt, but he doesn't do it—he knows better. He knows that his maker would find it out—the maker of his Patriotism, the windy and incoherent six-dollar sub-editor of his village newspaper—and would bray out in print and call him a Traitor. And how dreadful that would be. It makes him tuck his tail between his legs and shiver. We all know—the reader knows it quite well—that two or three years ago nine-tenths of the human tails in England and America performed just that act. Which is to say, nine-tenths of the Patriots in England and America turned Traitor to keep from being called Traitor. Isn't it true? You know it to be true. Isn't it curious?

Yet it was not a thing to be very seriously ashamed of. A man can seldom—very, very seldom—fight a winning fight against his training; the odds are too heavy. For many a year—perhaps always—the training of the two nations had been dead against independence in political thought, persistently inhospitable toward Patriotism manufactured on a man's own premises, Patriotism reasoned out in the man's own head and fire-assayed and tested and proved in his own conscience. The resulting Patriotism was a shop-worn product procured at second hand. The Patriot did not know just how or when or where he got his opinions, neither did he care, so long as he was with what seemed the majority—which was the main thing, the safe thing, the comfortable thing. Does the reader believe he knows three men who have actual reasons for their pattern of Patriotism—and can furnish them? Let him not examine, unless he wants to be disappointed. He will be likely to find that his men got their Patriotism at the public trough, and had no hand in their preparation themselves.

Training does wonderful things. It moved the people of this country to oppose the Mexican war; then moved them to fall in with what they supposed was the opinion of the majority—majority-Patriotism is the customary Patriotism—and go down there and fight. Before the Civil War it made the North indifferent to slavery and friendly to the slave interest; in that interest it made Massachusetts hostile to the American flag, and she would not allow it to be hoisted on her State House—in her eyes it was the flag of a faction. Then by and by, training swung Massachusetts the other way, and she went raging South to fight under that very flag and against that foretime protected-interest of hers.

Training made us nobly anxious to free Cuba; training made us give her a noble promise; training has enabled us to take it back. Long training made us revolt at the idea of wantonly taking any weak nation's country and liberties away from it, a short training has made us glad to do it, and proud of having done it. Training made us loathe Weyler's cruel concentration camps, training has persuaded us to prefer them to any other device for winning the love of our "wards."

There is nothing that training cannot do. Nothing is above its reach or below it. It can turn bad morals to good, good morals to bad; it can destroy principles, it can re-create them; it can debase angels to men and lift men to angelship. And it can do any one of these miracles in a year—even in six months.

Then men can be trained to manufacture their own Patriotism. They can be trained to labor it out in their own heads and hearts, and in the privacy and independence of their own premises. It can train them to stop taking it by command, as the Austrian takes his religion.

*c. 1901*

# The United States of Lyncherdom

And so Missouri has fallen, that great state! Certain of her children have joined the lynchers, and the smirch is upon the rest of us. That handful of her children have given us a character and labeled us with a name, and to the dwellers in the four quarters of the earth we are "lynchers," now, and ever shall be. For the world will not stop and think—it never does, it is not its way; its way is to generalize from a single sample. It will not say, "Those Missourians have been busy eighty years in building an honorable good name for themselves; these hundred lynchers down in the corner of the state are not real Missourians, they are renegades." No, that truth will not enter its mind; it will generalize from the one or two misleading samples and say, "The Missourians are lynchers." It has no reflection, no logic, no sense of proportion. With it, figures go for nothing; to it, figures reveal nothing, it cannot reason upon them rationally; it would say, for instance, that China is being swiftly and surely Christianized, since nine Chinese Christians are being made every day; and it would fail, with him, to notice that the fact that 33,000 pagans are *born* there every day, damages the argument. It would say, "There are a hundred lynchers there, therefore the Missourians are lynchers"; the considerable fact that there are two and a half million Missourians who are *not* lynchers would not affect their verdict.

II

Oh, Missouri!

The tragedy occurred near Pierce City, down in the southwestern corner of the state. On a Sunday afternoon a young white woman who had started alone from church was found murdered. For there are churches there; in my time religion was more general, more pervasive, in the South than it was in the North, and more virile and earnest, too, I think; I have some reason to believe that this is still the case. The young woman was found murdered. Although it was a region of churches and schools the people rose, lynched three negroes—two of them very aged ones—burned out five negro households, and drove thirty negro families into the woods.

I do not dwell upon the provocation which moved the people to these crimes, for that has nothing to do with the matter; the only question is, does the assassin *take the law into his own hands*? It is very simple, and very just. If the assassin be proved to have usurped the law's prerogative in righting his wrongs, that ends the matter; a thousand provocations are no defense. The Pierce City people had bitter provocation—indeed, as revealed by certain of the particulars, the bitterest of all provocations—but no matter, they took the law into their own hands, when by the terms of their statutes their victim would certainly hang if the law had been allowed to take its course, for there are but few negroes in that region and they are without authority and without influence in overawing juries.

Why has lynching, with various barbaric accompaniments, become a favorite regulator in cases of "the usual crime" in several parts of the country? Is it because men think a lurid and terrible punishment a more forcible object lesson and a more effective deterrent than a sober and colorless hanging done privately in a jail would be? Surely sane men do not think that. Even the average child should know better. It should know that any strange and much-talked-of event is always followed by imitations, the world being so well supplied with excitable people who only need a little stirring up to make them lose what is left of their heads and do mad things which they would not have thought of ordinarily. It should know that if a man jump off Brooklyn Bridge another will imitate him; that if a person venture down Niagara Whirlpool in a barrel another will imitate him; that if a Jack the Ripper make notoriety by slaughtering women in dark alleys he will be imitated; that if a man attempt a king's life and the newspapers carry the noise of it around the globe, regicides will crop up all around. The child should know that one much-talked-of outrage and murder committed by a negro will upset the disturbed intellects of several other negroes and produce a series of the very tragedies the community would so strenuously wish to prevent; that each of these crimes will produce another series, and year by year steadily increase the tale of these disasters instead of diminishing it; that, in a word, the lynchers are themselves the worst enemies of their women. The child should also know that by a law of our make, communities, as well as individuals, are imitators; and that a much-talked-of lynching will infallibly produce other lynchings here and there and yonder, and that in time these will breed a mania, a fashion; a fashion which will spread wide and wider, year by year, covering state after state, as with an advancing disease. Lynching has reached Colorado, it has reached California, it has reached Indiana—and now Missouri! I may live to see a negro burned in Union Square, New York, with fifty thousand people present, and not a sheriff visible, not a governor, not a constable, not a colonel, not a clergyman, not a law-and-order representative of any sort.

*Increase in Lynching.*—In 1900 there were eight more cases than in 1899, and probably this year there will be more than there were last year. The year is little more than half gone, and yet there are eighty-eight cases as compared with one hundred and fifteen for all of last year. The four Southern states, Alabama, Georgia, Louisiana, and Mississippi are the worst offenders. Last year there were eight cases in Alabama, sixteen in Georgia, twenty in Louisiana, and twenty in Mississippi—over one-half the total. This year to date there have been nine in Alabama, twelve in Georgia, eleven in Louisiana, and thirteen in Mississippi—again more than one-half the total number in the whole United States.—Chicago *Tribune*.

It must be that the increase comes of the inborn human instinct to imitate—that and man's commonest weakness, his aversion to being unpleasantly conspicuous, pointed at, shunned, as being on the unpopular side. Its other name is Moral Cowardice, and is the commanding feature of the make-up of 9,999 men in the 10,000. I am not offering this as a discovery; privately the dullest of us knows it to be true. History will not allow us to forget or ignore this supreme trait of our character. It persistently and sardonically reminds us that from the beginning of the world no revolt against a public infamy or oppression has ever been begun but by the one daring man in the 10,000, the rest timidly waiting, and slowly and reluctantly joining, under the influence of that man and his fellows from the other ten thousands. The abolitionists remember. Privately the public feeling was with them early, but each man was afraid to speak out until he got some hint that his neighbor was privately feeling as he privately felt himself. Then the boom followed. It always does. It will occur in New York, some day; and even in Pennsylvania.

It has been supposed—and said—that the people at a lynching enjoy the spectacle and are glad of a chance to see it. It cannot be true; all experience is against it. The people in the South are made like the people in the North—the vast majority of whom are right-hearted and compassionate, and would be cruelly pained by such a spectacle—and *would attend it*, and let on to be pleased with it, if the public approval seemed to require it. We are made like that, and we cannot help it. The other animals are not so, but we cannot help that, either. They lack the Moral Sense; we have no way of trading ours off, for a nickel or some other thing above its value. The Moral Sense teaches us what is right, and how to avoid it—when unpopular.

It is thought, as I have said, that a lynching crowd enjoys a lynching. It certainly is not true; it is impossible of belief. It is freely asserted—you have seen it in print many times of late—that the lynching impulse has been misinterpreted; that it is *not* the outcome of a spirit of revenge, but of a "mere atrocious hunger *to look upon human suffering*." If that were so, the crowds that saw the Windsor Hotel burn down would have enjoyed the horrors that fell under their eyes. Did they? No one will think that of them, no one will make that charge. Many risked their lives to save the men and women who were in peril. Why did they do that? Because *none would disapprove*. There was no restraint; they could follow their natural impulse. Why does a crowd of the same kind of people in Texas, Colorado, Indiana, stand by, smitten to the heart and miserable, and by ostentatious outward signs pretend to enjoy a lynching? Why does it lift no hand or voice in protest? Only because it would be unpopular to do it, I think; each man is afraid of his neighbor's disapproval—a thing which, to the general run of the race, is more dreaded than wounds and death. When there is to be a lynching the people hitch up and come miles to see it, bringing their wives and children. Really to see it? No—they come only because they are afraid to stay at home, lest it be noticed and offensively commented upon. We may believe this, for we all know how *we* feel about such spectacles—also, how we would act under the like pressure. We are not any better nor any braver than anybody else, and we must not try to creep out of it.

A Savonarola can quell and scatter a mob of lynchers with a mere glance of his eye: so can a Merrill* or a Beloat.† For no mob has any sand in the presence of a man known to be splendidly brave. Besides, a lynching mob would *like* to be scattered, for of a certainty there are never ten men in it who would not prefer to be somewhere else—and would be, if they but had the courage to go. When I was a boy I saw a brave gentleman deride and insult a mob and drive it away; and afterward, in Nevada, I saw a noted desperado make two hundred men sit still, with the house burning under them, until he gave them permission to retire. A plucky man can rob a whole passenger train by himself; and the half of a brave man can hold up a stagecoach and strip its occupants.

Then perhaps the remedy for lynchings comes to this: station a brave man in each affected community to encourage, support, and bring to light the deep disapproval of lynching hidden in the secret places of its heart—for it is there, beyond question. Then those communities will find something better to imitate—of course, being human, they must imitate something. Where shall these brave men be found? That is indeed a difficulty; there are not three hundred of them in the earth. If merely *physically* brave men would do, then it were easy; they could be furnished by the cargo. When Hobson called for seven volunteers to go with him to what promised to be certain death, four thousand men responded—the whole fleet, in fact. Because *all the world would approve.* They knew that; but if Hobson's project had been charged with the scoffs and jeers of the friends and associates, whose good opinion and approval the sailors valued, he could not have got his seven.

*Sheriff of Carroll County, Georgia.

†Sheriff, Princeton, Indiana. By that formidable power which lies in an established reputation for cold pluck they faced lynching mobs and securely held the field against them.

No, upon reflection, the scheme will not work. There are not enough morally brave men in stock. We are out of moral-courage material; we are in a condition of profound poverty. We have those two sheriffs down South who—but never mind, it is not enough to go around; they have to stay and take care of their own communities.

But if we only *could* have three or four more sheriffs of that great breed! Would it help? I think so. For we are all imitators: other brave sheriffs would follow; to be a dauntless sheriff would come to be recognized as the correct and only thing, and the dreaded disapproval would fall to the share of the other kind; courage in this office would become custom, the absence of it a dishonor, just as courage presently replaces the timidity of the new soldier; then the mobs and the lynchings would disappear, and——

However. It can never be done without some starters, and where are we to get the starters? Advertise? Very well, then, let us advertise.

In the meantime, there is another plan. Let us import American missionaries from China, and send them into the lynching field. With 1,511 of them out there converting two Chinamen apiece per annum against an uphill birth rate of 33,000 pagans per day,* it will take upward of a million years to make the conversions balance the output and bring the Christianizing of the country in sight to the naked eye; therefore, if we can offer our missionaries as rich a field at home at lighter expense and quite satisfactory in the matter of danger, why shouldn't they find it fair and right to come back and give us a trial? The Chinese are universally conceded to be excellent people, honest, honorable, industrious, trustworthy, kind-hearted, and all that—leave them alone, they are plenty good enough just as they are; and besides, almost every convert runs a risk of catching our civilization. We ought to be careful. We ought to think twice before we encourage a risk like that; for, *once civilized, China can never*

---

*These figures are not fanciful; all of them are genuine and authentic. They are from official missionary records in China. See Doctor Morrison's book on his pedestrian journey across China; he quotes them and gives his authorities. For several years he has been the London *Times's* representative in Peking, and was there through the siege.

*be uncivilized again*. We have not been thinking of that. Very well, we ought to think of it now. Our missionaries will find that we have a field for them—and not only for the 1,511, but for 15,011. Let them look at the following telegram and see if they have anything in China that is more appetizing. It is from Texas:

> The negro was taken to a tree and swung in the air. Wood and fodder were piled beneath his body and a hot fire was made. *Then it was suggested that the man ought not to die too quickly, and he was let down to the ground while a party went to Dexter, about two miles distant, to procure coal oil*. This was thrown on the flames and the work completed.

We implore them to come back and help us in our need. Patriotism imposes this duty on them. Our country is worse off than China; they are our countrymen, their motherland supplicates their aid in this her hour of deep distress. They are competent; our people are not. They are used to scoffs, sneers, revilings, danger; our people are not. They have the martyr spirit; nothing but the martyr spirit can brave a lynching mob, and cow it and scatter it. They can save their country, we beseech them to come home and do it. We ask them to read that telegram again, and yet again, and picture the scene in their minds, and soberly ponder it; then multiply it by 115, add 88; place the 203 in a row, allowing 600 feet of space for each human torch, so that there may be viewing room around it for 5,000 Christian American men, women, and children, youths and maidens; make it night, for grim effect; have the show in a gradually rising plain, and let the course of the stakes be uphill; the eye can then take in the whole line of twenty-four miles of blood-and-flesh bonfires unbroken, whereas if it occupied level ground the ends of the line would bend down and be hidden from view by the curvature of the earth. All being ready, now, and the darkness opaque, the stillness impressive—for there should be no sound but the soft moaning of the night wind and the muffled sobbing of the sacrifices—let all the far stretch of kerosened pyres be touched off simultaneously and the glare and the shrieks and the agonies burst heavenward to the Throne.

There are more than a million persons present; the light

from the fires flushes into vague outline against the night the spires of five thousand churches. O kind missionary, O compassionate missionary, leave China! come home and convert these Christians!

I believe that if anything can stop this epidemic of bloody insanities it is martial personalities that can face mobs without flinching; and as such personalities are developed only by familiarity with danger and by the training and seasoning which come of resisting it, the likeliest place to find them must be among the missionaries who have been under tuition in China during the past year or two. We have abundance of work for them, and for hundreds and thousands more, and the field is daily growing and spreading. Shall we find them? We can try. In 75,000,000 there must be other Merrills and Beloats; and it is the law of our make that each example shall wake up drowsing chevaliers of the same great knighthood and bring them to the front.

*August 1901*

# Edmund Burke on Croker and Tammany

### The Acorns Dinner, Hotel Waldorf-Astoria, New York

Great Britain had a Tammany and a Croker a good while ago. This Tammany was in India, and it began its career with the spread of the English dominion after the battle of Plassey. Its first boss was Clive, a sufficiently crooked person sometimes, but straight as a yardstick when compared with the corkscrew crookedness of the second boss, Warren Hastings. That old-time Tammany was the India Company's government, and had its headquarters at Calcutta. Ostensibly it consisted of a Great Council of four persons, of whom one was the Governor General, Warren Hastings; really it consisted of one person—Warren Hastings—for by usurpation he concentrated all authority in himself, and governed the country like an autocrat.

Ostensibly the Court of Directors, sitting in London and representing the vast interests of the stockholders, was supreme in authority over the Calcutta Great Council, whose membership it appointed and removed at pleasure, whose policies it dictated, and to whom it conveyed its will in the form of sovereign commands; but whenever it suited Hastings, he ignored even that august body's authority and conducted the mighty affairs of the British empire in India to suit his own notions.

At his mercy was the daily bread of every official, every trader, every clerk, every civil servant, big and little, in the whole huge India Company's machine; and the man who hazarded his bread by any failure of subserviency to the Boss, lost it.

Now then, let the supreme masters of British India, the giant corporation of the India Company in London, stand for the voters of the City of New York; let the Great Council of Calcutta stand for Tammany; let the corrupt and money-grubbing great hive of serfs which served under the Indian Tammany's rod stand for the New York Tammany's serfs; let Warren Hastings stand for Richard Croker, and it seems to me that the parallel is exact and complete. And so, let us be properly pious and thank God and our good luck that we didn't invent Tammany!

No, it is English. We are always imitating England; sometimes to our advantage, oftenest the other way. And if we can't find something recent to imitate, we are willing to go back a hundred years to hunt for a chance.

The Calcutta Tammany—like our own Tammany—had but one principle, one policy, one moving spirit of action—avarice, money-lust. So that it got money it cared not a rap about the means and the methods. It was always ready to lie, forge, betray, steal, swindle, cheat, rob; and no promise, no engagement, no contract, no treaty made by its boss was worth the paper it was written on or the polluted breath that uttered it. Is the parallel still exact? It seems to me to be twins.

But there the parallel stops. Further it cannot go. Beyond that line our Boss and Warren Hastings are no longer kin. Beyond that line Warren Hastings stands alone in the history of modern Christendom. He stands alone, in a desolate and awful isolation; in a black solitude of perjury, treachery, heartlessness, shamelessness, and an indifference to guiltless suffering, pain and misery properly describable as fiendish. Beyond the stated line we will not insult Mr. Croker by bracketing his name with the unspeakable name of Warren Hastings.

The most of us know no Hastings but Macaulay's, and there is good reason for that: when we try to read the impeachment charges against him we find we cannot endure the pain of the details. They burn, they blister, they wrench the heart; they drive us out of ourselves, they make us curse and swear; and we wonder why it took a dozen years to try that demon, when the mere reading of the first charge in the interminable list ought to have sent him to the scaffold before dark.

II

However, that is a side issue. We are dealing with the parallel, now, and that reaches down only to the stated line drawn above.

Edmund Burke, regarded by many as the greatest orator of

all times, conducted the case against Warren Hastings in that renowned trial which lasted years and which promises to keep its renown for centuries to come. I wish to quote some of the things he said. I wish to imagine him arraigning Mr. Croker and Tammany before the voters of New York City and pleading for the overthrow of that combined iniquity on the 5th of November. In the following passage, for "My Lords," read "Fellow Citizens." For "Kingdom" read "city." For "Parliamentary process" read "political campaign." For "two Houses" read "two parties":

My Lords, I must look upon it as an auspicious circumstance to this cause, in which the honor of the Kingdom is involved, that from the first commencement of our Parliamentary process to this the hour of solemn trial, not the smallest difference of opinion has arisen between the two Houses.

In the following, let "persons" stand for "Tammany." For "India" read "Tammany." For "Parliament" read "parties." For "nation" read "city." For "India" read "New York":

My Lords, there are persons who, looking rather upon what was to be found in our records and histories than what was to be expected from the public justice, had formed hopes consolatory to themselves and dishonorable to us. They flattered themselves that the corruptions of India would escape amidst the dissensions of Parliament. They are disappointed. They will be disappointed in all the rest of their expectations. . . . What the greatest inquest of the nation has begun its highest tribunal will accomplish. At length justice will be done to India.

In the following, for "Commons do" read "we who represent the Fusion ticket do." In the closing sentence of the paragraph, infer that Mr. Croker is more or less casually referred to:

My Lords, I must confess that amidst these encouraging prospects the Commons do not approach your bar without awe and anxiety. The magnitude of the interests which we have in charge will reconcile some degree of solicitude for the event with the undoubting confidence with which we repose ourselves upon your Lordships' justice. For we are men, my Lord, and men are so made, that it is not only the greatness of danger, but the value of the adventure, which measures the degree of our concern in every undertaking. I solemnly assure your Lordships that no standard is sufficient to estimate the value which the Commons set upon the event of the cause they now bring before you. My Lords, the business of this day is not the business of *this man*, it is not solely whether the prisoner at the bar be found innocent or guilty, but whether millions of mankind shall be made miserable or happy.

For "India" in the following, read "New York City." For "distant empire" read "city":

Your Lordships will see, in the progress of this cause, that there is not only a long, connected, systematic series of misdemeanors, but an equally connected system of maxims and principles invented to justify them. Upon both of these you must judge. According to the judgment that you shall give upon the past transactions in India, inseparably connected as they are with the principles which support them, the whole character of your future government in that distant empire is to be unalterably decided. It will take its perpetual tenor, it will receive its final impression from the stamp of this very hour.

In the following, for "India" read "New York City." For "part of the British" read "city of the American." For "decided" read "affected." For "national" read "municipal." For "nation" read "city." For "Kingdom" read "community":

It is not only the interest of India, now the most considerable part of the British empire, which is concerned, but the credit and honor of the British nation itself will be decided by this decision. We are to decide by this judgment whether the crimes of individuals are to be turned into the public guilt and national ignominy, or whether this nation will convert the very offenses which have thrown a transient shade upon its government into something that will reflect a permanent lustre upon the honor, justice, and humanity of this Kingdom.

In the following paragraph we will suppose that Mr. Croker's famous confession is referred to—his frank and blunt confession, under judicial examination, that his interest in the city government began and ended with the money to be gotten out of it. His words were, *"I am working for my pocket every time"*:

In an early stage of the proceeding the criminal desired to be heard. He was heard; and he produced before the bar of the House that insolent and unbecoming paper which lies upon our table. It was deliberately given in his own hand, and signed with his own name.

In the following, for "Mr. Hastings" read "Mr. Croker":

We urge no crimes that were not crimes of forethought. We charge him with nothing that he did not commit upon deliberation—that he did not commit against advice, supplication, and remonstrance—that he did not commit against the direct command of lawful authority—that he did not commit after reproof and reprimand, the reproof and reprimand of those who were authorized by the laws to reprove and reprimand him. The crimes of Mr. Hastings are not only crimes in themselves, but aggravated by being crimes of contumacy. They were crimes, not against forms, but against those eternal laws of justice which are our rule and our birthright. His offences are, not in formal, technical language, but in reality, in substance and effect, *high* crimes and high misdemeanors.

Here is something further that fits Mr. Croker's case:

When you consider the late enormous power of the prisoner—when you consider his criminal, indefatigable assiduity in the destruction of all recorded evidence—when you consider the influence he has over almost all living testimony—I believe your Lordships, and I believe the world, will be astonished that so much, so clear, so solid, and so conclusive evidence of all kinds has been obtained against him.

Here is some more about the two Tammanies, in the following strikingly faithful description of the New York situation of today. For "magistrates," in the second sentence, read "placemen." For "Mr. Hastings," in the closing sentence of the extract, read "Mr. Croker":

There is nothing to be in propriety called people to *watch*, to inspect, to balance against the power of office. The power of office . . . is the sole power in the country: the consequence of which is, that, being a Kingdom of magistrates, what is commonly called the *esprit du corps* is strong in it. This spirit of the body predominates equally in all its parts; by which the members must consider themselves as having a common interest. . . . No control upon them exists. . . . Therefore, in a body so constituted, confederacy is easy, and has been general. Your Lordships are not to expect that that should happen in such a body which has never happened in any body or corporation—that is, that they should, in any instance, be *a proper check and control upon themselves*. It is not in the nature of things. . . . By means of this peculiar circumstance it has not been difficult for Mr. Hastings to embody abuse and to put himself at the head of a regular system of corruption.

We all realize that Tammany's fundamental principle is monopoly—monopoly of office; monopoly of the public feed trough; monopoly of the blackmail derivable from protected gambling hells, protected prostitution houses, protected professional seducers of country girls for the New York prostitution market, and all that: monopoly all around, "in some sense or other." I know what I'm talking about, for I run a good deal with the police—and the clergy. It's the safest thing to do both here and for the hereafter. Here's a letter received by me yesterday, written by an Irish policeman, who signs his full name. Now here's what he says: "Sir: I'm a policeman and I saw an interview with you the other day. I must tell you the men are with Seth most to a man."

Now, that's good. He speaks out. It don't always do, however, for a man to speak out what he thinks. We can't all be independent. Wives and children take a good deal of independence from us. I've lost nearly all of mine. The letter continues: "I wish you success in your support of the Hon. Seth Low." That's even better. See, at the end he becomes respectful. That letter sounds good.

One of Burke's compact sentences indicates that the Indian Tammany's base rock is the same one that ours roosts upon:

The fundamental principle of the whole of the East India Company's system is monopoly, in some sense or other.

Here is another accurate piece of portraiture of Mr. Hastings-Croker:

He was fourteen years at the head of that service; and there is not an instance, no, not one single instance, in which he endeavored to detect corruption, or that he ever, in any one single instance, attempted to punish it; but the whole service, with that whole mass of enormity which he attributes to it, slept, as it were, at once under his terror and his protection: under the protection, if they did not dare to move against him; under terror, from his power to pluck out individuals and make a public example of them, when he thought fit. And therefore that service, under his guidance and influence, was, beyond even what its own nature disposed it to, a service of confederacy, a service of connivance, a service composed of various systems of guilt, of which Mr. Hastings was *the head and the protector*.

And now, at last, we find—and not without pain—that the prophetic eye of Edmund Burke has cast a sorrowing glance down the long procession of unborn years, and it falls with a dull thud upon Mr. Shepard. For "Englishmen" read "Tammany":

But now it is true, that after seeing the power and profits of these men—that there is neither power, profession, nor occupation to be had which a reputable person can exercise, except through that channel—men of higher castes, and born to better things, have thrown themselves into that disgraceful servitude, and have become menial servants to Englishmen, that they might . . . .

I have not quoted the whole of the passage; for its final clause contains a reproach which Mr. Shepard has not earned. It would do him an injustice; and that is a thing which Edmund Burke never wittingly did to any man. If he were here now he would know Mr. Shepard better than he was able to forecast him a century ago, and he would leave it out; therefore for the honor I bear the unsmirched great name of Edmund Burke I do him the justice to leave it out for him.

Now we come to the marvel of marvels—the immortal Irish orator's portrait of Richard Croker, as placed before us thinly disguised as Warren Hastings. He does not spring it upon you out of an atmosphereless vacancy, but leads you up to his great work with these notable words of introduction and preparation:

. . . So far as to the crimes. As to the criminal, we have chosen him on the same principle on which we selected the crimes. We have not chosen to bring before you a poor, puny, trembling delinquent, misled, perhaps, by those who ought to have taught him better, but who have afterwards oppressed him by their power, as they had first corrupted him by their example. Instances there have been many, wherein the punishment of minor offences, in inferior persons, has been made the means of screening crimes of a high order, and in men of high description. Our course is different. We have not brought before you an obscure offender, who, when his insignificance and weakness are weighed against the power of the prosecution, gives even to public justice something of the appearance of oppression. . . .

Then he flings Richard Croker upon the canvas. (For the first "India" read "Tammany"; for the second "India" read "New York City.") Consider this astonishing photograph—consider the amazing perfection of it: Richard Croker, detail by detail, in his moral personality, from topknot down to heeltap—and remember that the man who made it has been in his grave a hundred years! Croker is Tammany; Tammany is Croker: and experts of our own who know the combination to the marrow have not been able to depict it with an exacter brush:

### What Burke Said

No, my Lords, we have brought before you the first man of India, in rank, authority and station. We have brought before you the *chief of the tribe*, the head of the whole body of Eastern offenders, *a captain-general of iniquity*, under whom *all the fraud, all the peculation, all the tyranny in India is embodied, disciplined, arrayed, and paid*. This is the person, my Lords, that we bring before you. We have brought before you such a person, that, if you strike at him with the firm and decided arm of justice, you will not have need of a great many more examples. *You strike at the whole corps if you strike at the head*.

### What our Experts Say
### Letter to Croker from President of Anti-Croker League

In the meantime, we desire to emphasize the fact that it is entirely due to your political venality that corruption is rampant in our municipal government, and that the agencies of our civilization are controlled by the depraved elements of society. Under your guidance and inspiration, Tammany Hall has been turned into a machine for stock jobbing purposes, and for furthering schemes in which you and your cronies are financially interested. Its energies are largely devoted to blackmailing corporations for the benefit of your private pockets. A gamblers' syndicate, made up of your intimate political coadjutors, is running the Police Department, through its accredited agent, Chief Devery. It issues licenses to lawbreakers, and collects revenues from vice and crime. The income from moral degradation is regulated by certain Tammany leaders on a cash register basis. You are the chief beneficiary of this vile system, and with your share of the filthy spoils you manage to maintain a lordly estate in England.

The issue before the Lords was *Hastings and Hastingsism*; the only issue before New York in the imminent election is *Croker and Crokerism*. The two issues are the same, under differing names. If Edmund Burke were here he could change the names and make his speech again, and it would fit our circumstances exactly. Would he make it? We know by the heart of that great Irishman, and by his history, and by the noble hatred that was in him of all forms of wrong, dishonesty, chicane and oppression, that he would; and that he would beseech New York, with all the powers of his tongue and brain, and all the persuasions of his eloquence, to vote into obliteration and vacancy Mr. Croker and the infamies which he represents. And so we are privileged to imagine him here present and uttering again the righteous indignation which fell from his lips so long ago. And we know how he would close. We know that he would paraphrase his majestic impeachment of Warren Hastings, and say to the voters of New York:

"We know that we can commit safely the interests of this great metropolis into your hands. Therefore it is with confidence that, ordered by the people—

"I impeach Richard Croker of high crimes and misdemeanors.

"I impeach him in the name of the people, whose trust he has betrayed.

"I impeach him in the name of all the people of America, whose national character he has dishonored.

"I impeach him in the name and by virtue of those eternal laws of justice which he has violated.

"I impeach him in the name of human nature itself, which he has cruelly outraged, injured, and oppressed, *in both sexes, in every age, rank, situation, and condition of life*."

*October 17, 1901*

# Two Little Tales

Some days ago, in this second month of 1900, a friend made an afternoon call upon me here in London. We are of that age when men who are smoking away their time in chat do not talk quite so much about the pleasantnesses of life as about its exasperations. By and by this friend began to abuse the War Office. It appeared that he had a friend who had been inventing something which could be made very useful to the soldiers in South Africa. It was a light and very cheap and durable boot, which would remain dry in wet weather, and keep its shape and firmness. The inventor wanted to get the government's attention called to it, but he was an unknown man and knew the great officials would pay no heed to a message from him.

"This shows that he was an ass—like the rest of us," I said, interrupting. "Go on."

"But why have you said that? The man spoke the truth."

"The man spoke a lie. Go on."

"I will *prove* that he—"

"You can't prove anything of the kind. I am very old and very wise. You must not argue with me; it is irreverent and offensive. Go on."

"Very well. But you will presently see. I am not unknown, yet even *I* was not able to get the man's message to the Director-General of the Shoe-Leather Department."

"This is another lie. Pray go on."

"But I assure you on my honor that I failed."

"Oh, certainly. I knew *that*. You did n't need to tell me."

"Then where is the lie?"

"It is in your intimation that you were *not able* to get the Director-General's immediate attention to the man's message. It is a lie, because you *could* have gotten his immediate attention to it."

"I tell you I could n't. In three months I have n't accomplished it."

"Certainly. Of course. I could know that without your

496

telling me. You *could* have gotten his immediate attention if you had gone at it in a sane way; and so could the other man."

"I *did* go at it in a sane way."

"You did n't."

"How do *you* know? What do you know about the circumstances?"

"Nothing at all. But you did n't go at it in a sane way. That much I know to a certainty."

"How can you know it, when you don't know what method I used?"

"I know by the result. The result is perfect proof. You went at it in an insane way. I am very old and very w—"

"Oh, yes, I know. But will you let me tell you *how* I proceeded? I think that will settle whether it was insanity or not."

"No; that has already been settled. But go on, since you so desire to expose yourself. I am very o—"

"Certainly, certainly. I sat down and wrote a courteous letter to the Director-General of the Shoe-Leather Department, explai—"

"Do you know him personally?"

"No."

"You have scored one for my side. You began insanely. Go on."

"In the letter I made the great value and inexpensiveness of the invention clear, and offered to—"

"Call and see him? Of course you did. Score two against yourself. I am v—"

"He did n't answer for three days."

"Necessarily. Proceed."

"Sent me three gruff lines thanking me for my trouble, and proposing—"

"Nothing."

"That's it—proposing nothing. Then I wrote him more elaborately and—"

"Score three—"

"—and got no answer. At the end of a week I wrote and asked, with some touch of asperity, for an answer to that letter."

"Four. Go on."

"An answer came back saying the letter had not been received, and asking for a copy. I traced the letter through the post-office, and found that it *had* been received; but I sent a copy and said nothing. Two weeks passed without further notice of me. In the meantime I gradually got myself cooled down to a polite-letter temperature. Then I wrote and proposed an interview for next day, and said that if I did not hear from him in the meantime I should take his silence for assent."

"Score five."

"I arrived at twelve sharp, and was given a chair in the anteroom and told to wait. I waited till half-past one; then I left, ashamed and angry. I waited another week, to cool down; then I wrote and made another appointment with him for next day noon."

"Score six."

"He answered, assenting. I arrived promptly, and kept a chair warm until half-past two. I left then, and shook the dust of that place from my shoes for good and all. For rudeness, inefficiency, incapacity, indifference to the army's interests, the Director-General of the Shoe-Leather Department of the War Office is, in my o—"

"Peace! I am very old and very wise, and have seen many seemingly intelligent people who hadn't common sense enough to go at a simple and easy thing like this in a common-sense way. You are not a curiosity to me; I have personally known millions and billions like you. You have lost three months quite unnecessarily; the inventor has lost three months; the soldiers have lost three—nine months altogether. I will now read you a little tale which I wrote last night. Then you will call on the Director-General at noon to-morrow and transact your business."

"Splendid! Do you know him?"

"No; but listen to the tale."

### SECOND STORY: HOW THE CHIMNEY-SWEEP GOT THE EAR OF THE EMPEROR.

I.

Summer was come, and all the strong were bowed by the burden of the awful heat, and many of the weak were prostrate and dying. For weeks the army had been wasting away with a plague of dysentery, that scourge of the soldier, and there was but little help. The doctors were in despair; such efficacy as their drugs and their science had once had—and it was not much at its best—was a thing of the past, and promised to remain so.

The Emperor commanded the physicians of greatest renown to appear before him for a consultation, for he was profoundly disturbed. He was very severe with them, and called them to account for letting his soldiers die; and asked them if they knew their trade, or did n't; and were they properly healers, or merely assassins? Then the principal assassin, who was also the oldest doctor in the land and the most venerable in appearance, answered and said:

"We have done what we could, your Majesty, and for a good reason it has been little. No medicine and no physician can cure that disease; only nature and a good constitution can do it. I am old, and I know. No doctor and no medicine can cure it—I repeat it and I emphasize it. Sometimes they seem to help nature a little,—a very little,—but, as a rule, they merely do damage."

The Emperor was a profane and passionate man, and he deluged the doctors with rugged and unfamiliar names, and drove them from his presence. Within a day he was attacked by that fell disease himself. The news flew from mouth to mouth, and carried consternation with it over all the land. All the talk was about this awful disaster, and there was general depression, for few had hope. The Emperor himself was very melancholy, and sighed and said:

"The will of God be done. Send for the assassins again, and let us get over with it."

They came, and felt his pulse and looked at his tongue, and fetched the drug-store and emptied it into him, and sat down patiently to wait—for they were not paid by the job, but by the year.

## II.

Tommy was sixteen and a bright lad, but he was not in society. His rank was too humble for that, and his employment too base. In fact, it was the lowest of all employments,

for he was second in command to his father, who emptied
cesspools and drove a night-cart. Tommy's closest friend was
Jimmy the chimney-sweep, a slim little fellow of fourteen,
who was honest and industrious, and had a good heart, and
supported a bedridden mother by his dangerous and unpleasant trade.

About a month after the Emperor fell ill, these two lads
met one evening about nine. Tommy was on his way to his
night-work, and of course was not in his Sundays, but in his
dreadful work-clothes, and not smelling very well. Jimmy was
on his way home from his day's labor, and was blacker than
any other object imaginable, and he had his brushes on his
shoulder and his soot-bag at his waist, and no feature of his
sable face was distinguishable except his lively eyes.

They sat down on the curbstone to talk; and of course it
was upon the one subject—the nation's calamity, the Emperor's disorder. Jimmy was full of a great project, and burning to unfold it. He said:

"Tommy, I can cure his Majesty. I know how to do it."

Tommy was surprised.

"What! You?"

"Yes, I."

"Why, you little fool, the best doctors can't."

"I don't care; I can do it. I can cure him in fifteen minutes."

"Oh, come off! What are you giving me?"

"The facts—that's all."

Jimmy's manner was so serious that it sobered Tommy,
who said:

"I believe you are in earnest, Jimmy. Are you in earnest?"

"I give you my word."

"What is the plan? How'll you cure him?"

"Tell him to eat a slice of ripe watermelon."

It caught Tommy rather suddenly, and he was shouting
with laughter at the absurdity of the idea before he could put
on a stopper. But he sobered down when he saw that Jimmy
was wounded. He patted Jimmy's knee affectionately, not
minding the soot, and said:

"I take the laugh all back. I did n't mean any harm, Jimmy,
and I won't do it again. You see, it seemed so funny, because
wherever there's a soldier-camp and dysentery, the doctors

always put up a sign saying anybody caught bringing water-melons there will be flogged with the cat till he can't stand."

"I know it—the idiots!" said Jimmy, with both tears and anger in his voice. "There's plenty of watermelons, and not one of all those soldiers ought to have died."

"But, Jimmy, what put the notion into your head?"

"It isn't a notion; it's a fact. Do you know that old gray-headed Zulu? Well, this long time back he has been curing a lot of our friends, and my mother has seen him do it, and so have I. It takes only one or two slices of melon, and it don't make any difference whether the disease is new or old; it cures it."

"It's very odd. But, Jimmy, if it is so, the Emperor ought to be told of it."

"Of course; and my mother has told people, hoping they could get the word to him; but they are poor working-folks and ignorant, and don't know how to manage it."

"Of course they don't, the blunderheads," said Tommy, scornfully. "*I'll* get it to him!"

"You? You night-cart polecat!" And it was Jimmy's turn to laugh. But Tommy retorted sturdily:

"Oh, laugh if you like; but I'll *do* it!"

It had such an assured and confident sound that it made an impression, and Jimmy asked gravely:

"Do you know the Emperor?"

"Do *I* know him? Why, how you talk! Of course I don't."

"Then how'll you do it?"

"It's very simple and very easy. Guess. How would *you* do it, Jimmy?"

"Send him a letter. I never thought of it till this minute. But I'll bet that's your way."

"I'll bet it ain't. Tell me, how would you send it?"

"Why, through the mail, of course."

Tommy overwhelmed him with scoffings, and said:

"Now, don't you suppose every crank in the empire is doing the same thing? Do you mean to say you haven't thought of that?"

"Well—no," said Jimmy, abashed.

"You *might* have thought of it, if you weren't so young and inexperienced. Why, Jimmy, when even a common *general*, or a poet, or an actor, or anybody that's a little famous gets sick, all the cranks in the kingdom load up the mails with certain-sure quack-cures for him. And so, what's bound to happen when it's the Emperor?"

"I suppose it's worse," said Jimmy, sheepishly.

"Well, I should think so! Look here, Jimmy; every single night we cart off as many as six loads of that kind of letters from the back yard of the palace, where they're thrown. Eighty thousand letters in one night! Do you reckon anybody reads them? Sho! not a single one. It's what would happen to your letter if you wrote it—which you won't, I reckon?"

"No," sighed Jimmy, crushed.

"But it's all right, Jimmy. Don't you fret; there's more than one way to skin a cat. *I'll* get the word to him."

"Oh, if you only *could*, Tommy, I should love you forever!"

"I'll do it, I tell you. Don't you worry; you depend on me."

"Indeed I will, Tommy, for you do know so much. You're not like other boys; they never know anything. How'll you manage, Tommy?"

Tommy was greatly pleased. He settled himself for reposeful talk, and said:

"Do you know that ragged poor thing that thinks he's a butcher because he goes around with a basket and sells cat's meat and rotten livers? Well, to begin with, I'll tell *him*."

Jimmy was deeply disappointed and chagrined, and said:

"Now, Tommy, it's a shame to talk so. You know my heart's in it, and it's not right."

Tommy gave him a love-pat, and said:

"Don't you be troubled, Jimmy. *I* know what I'm about. Pretty soon you'll see. That half-breed butcher will tell the old woman that sells chestnuts at the corner of the lane— she's his closest friend, and I'll ask him to; then, by request, she'll tell her rich aunt that keeps the little fruit-shop on the corner two blocks above; and that one will tell her particular friend, the man that keeps the game-shop; and he will tell his friend the sergeant of police; and the sergeant will tell his captain, and the captain will tell the magistrate, and the magistrate will tell his brother-in-law the county judge, and the county judge will tell the sheriff, and the sheriff will tell the

Lord Mayor, and the Lord Mayor will tell the President of the Council, and the President of the Council will tell the—"

"By George, but it's a wonderful scheme, Tommy! How ever *did* you—"

"—Rear-Admiral, and the Rear will tell the Vice, and the Vice will tell the Admiral of the Blue, and the Blue will tell the Red, and the Red will tell the White, and the White will tell the First Lord of the Admiralty, and the First Lord will tell the Speaker of the House, and the Speaker—"

"Go it, Tommy; you're 'most there!"

"—will tell the Master of the Hounds, and the Master will tell the Head Groom of the Stables, and the Head Groom will tell the Chief Equerry, and the Chief Equerry will tell the First Lord in Waiting, and the First Lord will tell the Lord High Chamberlain, and the Lord High Chamberlain will tell the Master of the Household, and the Master of the Household will tell the little pet page that fans the flies off the Emperor, and the page will get down on his knees and whisper it to his Majesty—and the game's made!"

"I've *got* to get up and hurrah a couple of times, Tommy. It's the grandest idea that ever was. What ever put it into your head?"

"Sit down and listen, and I'll give you some wisdom—and don't you ever forget it as long as you live. Now, then, who is the closest friend you've got, and the one you couldn't and wouldn't ever refuse anything in the world to?"

"Why, it's you, Tommy. You know that."

"Suppose you wanted to ask a pretty large favor of the cat's-meat man. Well, you don't know him, and he would tell you to go to thunder, for he is that kind of a person; but he is my next best friend after you, and would run his legs off to do me a kindness—*any* kindness, he don't care what it is. Now, I'll ask you: which is the most common-sensible—for you to go and ask him to tell the chestnut-woman about your watermelon cure, or for you to get me to do it for you?"

"To get you to do it for me, of course. I wouldn't ever have thought of that, Tommy; it's splendid!"

"It's a *philosophy*, you see. Mighty good word—and large. It goes on this idea: everybody in the world, little and big, has one *special* friend, a friend that he's *glad* to do favors to—

not sour about it, but *glad*—glad clear to the marrow. And
so, I don't care where you start, you can get at anybody's ear
that you want to—I don't care how low you are, nor how
high he is. And it's so simple: you've only to find the *first*
friend, that is all; that ends your part of the work. He finds
the next friend himself, and that one finds the third, and so
on, friend after friend, link after link, like a chain; and you can
go up it or down it, as high as you like or as low as you like."

"It's just beautiful, Tommy."

"It's as simple and easy as a-b-c; but did you ever hear of
anybody trying it? No; everybody is a fool. He goes to a
stranger without any introduction, or writes him a letter, and
of course he strikes a cold wave—and serves him gorgeously
right. Now, the Emperor don't know me, but that's no
matter—he'll eat his watermelon to-morrow. You'll see. Hi-
hi—stop! It's the cat's-meat man. Good-by, Jimmy; I'll overtake him."

He did overtake him, and said:

"Say, will you do me a favor?"

"*Will* I? Well, I should *say*! I'm your man. Name it, and see
me fly!"

"Go tell the chestnut-woman to put down everything and
carry this message to her first-best friend, and tell the friend
to pass it along." He worded the message, and said, "Now,
then, rush!"

The next moment the chimney-sweep's word to the Emperor was on its way.


### III.

The next evening, toward midnight, the doctors sat whispering together in the imperial sick-room, and they were in
deep trouble, for the Emperor was in very bad case. They
could not hide it from themselves that every time they emptied a fresh drug-store into him he got worse. It saddened
them, for they were expecting that result. The poor emaciated
Emperor lay motionless, with his eyes closed, and the page
that was his darling was fanning the flies away and crying
softly. Presently the boy heard the silken rustle of a portière,
and turned and saw the Lord High Great Master of the

Household peering in at the door and excitedly motioning to him to come. Lightly and swiftly the page tiptoed his way to his dear and worshiped friend the Master, who said:

"Only you can persuade him, my child, and oh, don't fail to do it! Take this, make him eat it, and he is saved."

"On my head be it. He shall eat it!"

It was a couple of great slices of ruddy, fresh watermelon.

The next morning the news flew everywhere that the Emperor was sound and well again, and had hanged the doctors. A wave of joy swept the land, and frantic preparations were made to illuminate.

After breakfast his Majesty sat meditating. His gratitude was unspeakable, and he was trying to devise a reward rich enough to properly testify it to his benefactor. He got it arranged in his mind, and called the page, and asked him if he had invented that cure. The boy said no—he got it from the Master of the Household.

He was sent away, and the Emperor went to devising again. The Master was an earl; he would make him a duke, and give him a vast estate which belonged to a member of the Opposition. He had him called, and asked him if he was the inventor of the remedy. But the Master was an honest man, and said he got it of the Grand Chamberlain. He was sent away, and the Emperor thought some more. The Chamberlain was a viscount; he would make him an earl, and give him a large income. But the Chamberlain referred him to the First Lord in Waiting, and there was some more thinking; his Majesty thought out a smaller reward. But the First Lord in Waiting referred him back further, and he had to sit down and think out a further and becomingly and suitably smaller reward.

Then, to break the tediousness of the inquiry and hurry the business, he sent for the Grand High Chief Detective, and commanded him to trace the cure to the bottom, so that he could properly reward his benefactor.

At nine in the evening the High Chief Detective brought the word. He had traced the cure down to a lad named Jimmy, a chimney-sweep. The Emperor said, with deep feeling:

"Brave boy, he saved my life, and shall not regret it!"

And sent him a pair of his own boots; and the next best

ones he had, too. They were too large for Jimmy, but they
fitted the Zulu, so it was all right, and everything as it should
be.


### CONCLUSION TO THE FIRST STORY.

"There—do you get the idea?"

"I am obliged to admit that I do. And it will be as you have
said. I will transact the business to-morrow. I intimately
know the Director-General's nearest friend. He will give me a
note of introduction, with a word to say my matter is of real
importance to the government. I will take it along, without
an appointment, and send it in, with my card, and I sha'n't
have to wait so much as half a minute."

That turned out true to the letter, and the government
adopted the boots.

*November 1901*

# Corn-Pone Opinions

Fifty years ago, when I was a boy of fifteen and helping to inhabit a Missourian village on the banks of the Mississippi, I had a friend whose society was very dear to me because I was forbidden by my mother to partake of it. He was a gay and impudent and satirical and delightful young black man—a slave—who daily preached sermons from the top of his master's woodpile, with me for sole audience. He imitated the pulpit style of the several clergymen of the village, and did it well, and with fine passion and energy. To me he was a wonder. I believed he was the greatest orator in the United States, and would some day be heard from. But it did not happen; in the distribution of rewards he was overlooked. It is the way, in this world.

He interrupted his preaching, now and then, to saw a stick of wood; but the sawing was a pretence—he did it with his mouth; exactly imitating the sound the buck-saw makes in shrieking its way through the wood. But it served its purpose: it kept his master from coming out to see how the work was getting along. I listened to the sermons from the open window of a lumber-room at the back of our house. One of his texts was this:

"You tell me whar a man gits his corn-pone, en I'll tell you what his 'pinions is."

I can never forget it. It was deeply impressed upon me. By my mother. Not upon my memory, but elsewhere. She had slipped in upon me while I was absorbed and not watching. The black philosopher's idea was, that a man is not independent, and cannot afford views which might interfere with his bread and butter. If he would prosper, he must train with the majority; in matters of large moment, like politics and religion, he must think and feel with the bulk of his neighbors, or suffer damage in his social standing and in his business prosperities. He must restrict himself to corn-pone opinions—at least on the surface. He must get his opinions from other people; he must reason out none for himself; he must have no first-hand views.

I think Jerry was right, in the main, but I think he did not go far enough.

1. It was his idea that a man conforms to the majority-view of his locality by calculation and intention. This happens, but I think it is not the rule.

2. It was his idea that there is such a thing as a first-hand opinion; an original opinion; an opinion which is coldly reasoned-out in a man's head, by a searching analysis of the facts involved, with the heart unconsulted, and the jury-room closed against outside influences. It may be that such an opinion has been born somewhere, at some time or other, but I suppose it got away before they could catch it and stuff it and put it in the museum.

I am persuaded that a coldly thought-out and independent verdict upon a fashion in clothes, or manners, or literature, or politics, or religion, or any other matter that is projected into the field of our notice and interest, is a most rare thing—if it has indeed ever existed.

A new thing in costume appears—the flaring hoop-skirt, for example—and the passers-by are shocked, and the irreverent laugh. Six months later everybody is reconciled; the fashion has established itself; it is admired, now, and no one laughs. Public opinion resented it before, public opinion accepts it now, and is happy in it. Why? Was the resentment reasoned out? Was the acceptance reasoned out? No. The instinct that moves to conformity did the work. It is our nature to conform; it is a force which not many can successfully resist. What is its seat? The inborn requirement of Self-Approval. We all have to bow to that; there are no exceptions. Even the woman who refuses from first to last to wear the hoop-skirt comes under that law and is its slave; she could not wear the skirt and have her own approval; and that she *must* have, she cannot help herself. But as a rule our self-approval has its source in but one place and not elsewhere—the approval of other people. A person of vast consequence can introduce any kind of novelty in dress and the general world will presently adopt it—moved to do it, in the first place, by the natural instinct to passively yield to that vague something recognized as authority, and in the second place by the human instinct to train with the multitude and have its approval. An Empress introduced the hoop-skirt, and we know the result. A nobody introduced the Bloomer, and we know the result. If Eve should come again, in her ripe renown, and reintroduce her quaint styles—well, we know what would happen. And we should be cruelly embarrassed, along at first.

The hoop-skirt runs its course, and disappears. Nobody reasons about it. One woman abandons the fashion; her neighbor notices this and follows her lead; this influences the next woman; and so on and so on, and presently the skirt has vanished out of the world, no one knows how nor why; nor cares, for that matter. It will come again, by and by; and in due course will go again.

Twenty-five years ago, in England, six or eight wine glasses stood grouped by each person's plate at a dinner party, and they were used, not left idle and empty; to-day there are but three or four in the group, and the average guest sparingly uses about two of them. We have not adopted this new fashion yet, but we shall do it presently. We shall not think it out, we shall merely conform, and let it go at that. We get our notions and habits and opinions from outside influences, we do not have to study them out.

Our table manners, and company manners, and street manners change from time to time, but the changes are not reasoned out; we merely notice and conform. We are creatures of outside influences; as a rule we do not think, we only imitate. We cannot invent standards that will stick; what we mistake for standards are only fashions, and perishable. We may continue to admire them, but we drop the use of them. We notice this in literature. Shakspeare is a standard, and fifty years ago we used to write tragedies which he couldn't tell from—from somebody else's; but we don't do it any more, now. Our prose standard, three-quarters of a century ago, was ornate and diffuse; some authority or other changed it in the direction of compactness and simplicity, and conformity followed, without argument. The historical novel starts up suddenly, and sweeps the land. Everybody writes one, and the nation is glad. We had historical novels before; but nobody read them, and the rest of us conformed—without reasoning it out. We are conforming in the other way, now, because it is another case of everybody.

The outside influences are always pouring in upon us, and we are always obeying their orders and accepting their verdicts. The Smiths like the new play; the Joneses go to see it, and they copy the Smith verdict. Morals, religions, politics, get their following from surrounding influences and atmospheres, almost entirely; not from study, not from thinking. A man must and will have his own approval first of all, in each and every moment and circumstance of his life—even if he must repent of a self-approved act the moment after its commission, in order to get his self-approval *again*; but, speaking in general terms, a man's self-approval, in the large concerns of life, has its source in the approval of the people about him, and not in a searching personal examination of the matter. Mohammedans are Mohammedans because they are born and reared among that sect, not because they have thought it out and can furnish sound reasons for being Mohammedans; we know why Catholics are Catholics; why Presbyterians are Presbyterians; why Baptists are Baptists; why Mormons are Mormons; why thieves are thieves; why monarchists are monarchists; why republicans are republicans, and democrats democrats. We know it is a matter of association and sympathy, not reasoning and examination; that hardly a man in the world has an opinion upon morals, politics or religion which he got otherwise than through his associations and sympathies. Broadly speaking, there are none but corn-pone opinions. And broadly speaking, Corn-Pone stands for Self-Approval. Self-approval is acquired mainly from the approval of other people. The result is Conformity. Sometimes Conformity has a sordid business interest—the bread-and-butter interest—but not in most cases, I think. I think that in the majority of cases it is unconscious and not calculated; that it is born of the human being's natural yearning to stand well with his fellows, and have their inspiring approval and praise —a yearning which is commonly so strong and so insistent that it cannot be effectually resisted, and must have its way.

A political emergency brings out the corn-pone opinion in fine force in its two chief varieties—the pocket-book variety, which has its origin in self-interest, and the bigger variety, the sentimental variety—the one which can't bear to be outside the pale; can't bear to be in disfavor; can't endure the averted face and the cold shoulder; wants to stand well with the friends, wants to be smiled upon, wants to be welcome, wants to hear the precious words "*he's* on the right track!" Uttered, perhaps, by an ass, but still an ass of high degree, an ass whose approval is gold and diamonds to a smaller ass, and confers glory, and honor and happiness, and membership in the herd. For these gauds many a man will dump his life-long principles into the street, and his conscience along with them. We have seen it happen. In some millions of instances.

Men think they think upon great political questions, and they do; but they think with their party, not independently; they read its literature, but not that of the other side; they arrive at convictions, but they are drawn from a partial view of the matter in hand and are of no particular value. They swarm with their party, they feel with their party, they are happy in their party's approval; and where the party leads they will follow, whether for right and honor, or through blood and dirt and a mush of mutilated morals.

In our late canvas half of the nation passionately believed that in silver lay salvation, the other half as passionately believed that that way lay destruction. Do you believe that a tenth part of the people, on either side, had any rational excuse for having an opinion about the matter at all? I studied that mighty question to the bottom—and came out empty. Half of our people passionately believe in high tariff, the other half believe otherwise. Does this mean study and examination, or only feeling? The latter, I think. I have deeply studied that question, too—and didn't arrive. We all do no end of feeling, and we mistake it for thinking. And out of it we get an aggregation which we consider a Boon. Its name is Public Opinion. It is held in reverence. It settles everything. Some think it the Voice of God. Pr'aps.

I suppose that in more cases than we should like to admit, we have two sets of opinions: one private, the other public; one secret and sincere, the other corn-pone, and more or less tainted.

*1901*

# Does the Race of Man Love a Lord?

Often a quite assified remark becomes sanctified by use and petrified by custom; it is then a permanency, its term of activity a geologic period.

The day after the arrival of Prince Henry I met an English friend, and he rubbed his hands and broke out with a remark that was charged to the brim with joy—joy that was evidently a pleasant salve to an old sore place:

"Many a time I've had to listen without retort to an old saying that is irritatingly true, and until now seemed to offer no chance for a return jibe: 'An Englishman does dearly love a lord'; but after this I shall talk back, and say 'How about the Americans?'"

It is a curious thing, the currency that an idiotic saying can get. The man that first says it thinks he has made a discovery. The man he says it to, thinks the same. It departs on its travels, is received everywhere with admiring acceptance, and not only as a piece of rare and acute observation, but as being exhaustively true and profoundly wise; and so it presently takes its place in the world's list of recognized and established wisdoms, and after that no one thinks of examining it to see whether it is really entitled to its high honors or not. I call to mind instances of this in two well-established proverbs, whose dulness is not surpassed by the one about the Englishman and his love for a lord: one of them records the American's Adoration of the Almighty Dollar, the other the American millionaire-girl's ambition to trade cash for a title, with a husband thrown in.

It isn't merely the American that adores the Almighty Dollar, it is the human race. The human race has always adored the hatful of shells, or the bale of calico, or the half bushel of brass rings, or the handful of steel fish-hooks, or the houseful of black wives, or the zareba full of cattle, or the two score camels and asses, or the factory, or the farm, or the block of buildings, or the railroad bonds, or the bank stock, or the hoarded cash, or—anything that stands for wealth and consideration and independence, and can secure to the possessor that most precious of all things, another man's envy. It was a dull person that invented the idea that the American's devotion to the dollar is more strenuous than another's.

Rich American girls do buy titles, but they did not invent that idea; it had been worn threadbare several hundred centuries before America was discovered. European girls still exploit it as briskly as ever; and, when a title is not to be had for the money in hand, they buy the husband without it. They must put up the "dot," or there is no trade. The commercialization of brides is substantially universal, except in America. It exists with us, to some little extent, but in no degree approaching a custom.

"The Englishman dearly loves a lord."

What is the soul and source of his love? I think the thing could be more correctly worded:

"The human race dearly envies a lord."

That is to say, it envies the lord's place. Why? On two accounts, I think: its Power and its Conspicuousness.

Where Conspicuousness carries with it a Power which, by the light of our own observation and experience, we are able to measure and comprehend, I think our envy of the possessor is as deep and as passionate as is that of any other nation. No one can care less for a lord than the backwoodsman, who has had no personal contact with lords and has seldom heard them spoken of; but I will not allow that any Englishman has a profounder envy of a lord than has the average American who has lived long years in a European capital and fully learned how immense is the position the lord occupies.

Of any ten thousand Americans who eagerly gather, at vast inconvenience, to get a glimpse of Prince Henry, all but a couple of hundred will be there out of an immense curiosity; they are burning up with desire to see a personage who is so much talked about. They envy him; but it is his Conspicuousness they envy mainly, not the Power that is lodged in his royal quality and position, for they have but a vague and spectral knowledge and appreciation of that; through their environment and associations they have been accustomed to regard such things lightly, and as not being very real; consequently, they are not able to value them enough to consumingly envy them.

But, whenever an American (or other human being) is in

the presence, for the first time, of a combination of great Power and Conspicuousness which he thoroughly understands and appreciates, his eager curiosity and pleasure will be well-sodden with that other passion—envy—whether he suspect it or not. At any time, on any day, in any part of America, you can confer a happiness upon any passing stranger by calling his attention to any other passing stranger and saying:

"Do you see that gentleman going along there? It is Mr. Rockefeller."

Watch his eye. It is a combination of power and conspicuousness which the man understands.

When we understand rank, we always like to rub against it. When a man is conspicuous, we always want to see him. Also, if he will pay us an attention, we will manage to remember it. Also, we will mention it now and then, casually; sometimes to a friend, or if a friend is not handy, we will make out with a stranger.

Well, then, what is rank, and what is conspicuousness? At once we think of kings and aristocracies, and of world-wide celebrities in soldiership, the arts, letters, etc., and we stop there. But that is a mistake. Rank holds its court and receives its homage on every round of the ladder, from the emperor down to the rat-catcher; and distinction, also, exists on every round of the ladder, and commands its due of deference and envy.

To worship rank and distinction is the dear and valued privilege of all the human race, and it is freely and joyfully exercised in democracies as well as in monarchies—and even, to some extent, among those creatures whom we impertinently call the Lower Animals. For even they have some poor little vanities and foibles, though in this matter they are paupers as compared to us.

A Chinese Emperor has the worship of his four hundred millions of subjects, but the rest of the world is indifferent to him. A Christian Emperor has the worship of his subjects and of a large part of the Christian world outside of his dominions; but he is a matter of indifference to all China. A king, class A, has an extensive worship; a king, class B, has a less extensive worship; class C, class D, class E get a steadily diminishing share of worship; class L (Sultan of Zanzibar), class

P (Sultan of Sulu), and class W (half-king of Samoa), get no worship at all outside their own little patch of sovereignty.

Take the distinguished people along down. Each has his group of homage-payers. In the navy, there are many groups; they start with the Secretary and the Admiral, and go down to the quartermaster—and below; for there will be groups among the sailors, and each of these groups will have a tar who is distinguished for his battles, or his strength, or his daring, or his profanity, and is admired and envied by his group. The same with the army; the same with the literary and journalistic craft; the publishing craft; the cod-fishery craft; Standard Oil; U. S. Steel; the class A hotel—and the rest of the alphabet in that line; the class A prize-fighter—and the rest of the alphabet in his line—clear down to the lowest and obscurest six-boy gang of little gamins, with its one boy that can thrash the rest, and to whom he is king of Samoa, bottom of the royal race, but looked up to with a most ardent admiration and envy.

There is something pathetic, and funny, and pretty, about this human race's fondness for contact with power and distinction, and for the reflected glory it gets out of it. The king, class A, is happy in the state banquet and the military show which the emperor provides for him, and he goes home and gathers the queen and the princelings around him in the privacy of the spare room, and tells them all about it, and says:

"His Imperial Majesty put his hand on my shoulder in the most friendly way—just as friendly and familiar, oh, you can't imagine it!—and everybody *seeing* him do it; charming, perfectly charming!"

The king, class G, is happy in the cold collation and the police-parade provided for him by the king, class B, and goes home and tells the family all about it, and says:

"And His Majesty took me into his own private cabinet for a smoke and a chat, and there we sat, just as sociable, and talking away and laughing and chatting, just the same as if we had been born in the same bunk; and all the servants in the anteroom could see us doing it! Oh, it was too lovely for anything!"

The king, class Q, is happy in the modest entertainment furnished him by the king, class M, and goes home and tells

the household about it, and is as grateful and joyful over it as
were his predecessors in the gaudier attentions that had fallen
to their larger lot.

Emperors, kings, artisans, peasants, big people, little people—at bottom we are all alike and all the same; all just alike
on the inside, and when our clothes are off, nobody can tell
which of us is which. We are unanimous in the pride we take
in good and genuine compliments paid us, in distinctions
conferred upon us, in attentions shown us. There is not one
of us, from the emperor down, but is made like that. Do I
mean attentions shown us by the great? No, I mean simply
flattering attentions, let them come whence they may. We despise no source that can pay us a pleasing attention—there is
no source that is humble enough for that. You have heard a
dear little girl say of a frowzy and disreputable dog: "He came
right to me and let me pat him on the head, and he wouldn't
let the others touch him!" and you have seen her eyes dance
with pride in that high distinction. You have often seen that.
If the child were a princess, would that random dog be able
to confer the like glory upon her with his pretty compliment?
Yes; and even in her mature life and seated upon a throne, she
would still remember it, still recall it, still speak of it with
frank satisfaction. That charming and lovable German princess and poet, Carmen Sylva, Queen of Roumania, remembers yet that the flowers of the woods and fields "talked to
her" when she was a girl, and she sets it down in her latest
book; and that the squirrels conferred upon her and her father the valued compliment of not being afraid of them; and
"once one of them, holding a nut between its sharp little
teeth, ran right up against my father"—it has the very note
of "He came right to me and let me pat him on the head"—
"and when it saw itself reflected in his boot it was very much
surprised, and stopped for a long time to contemplate itself in
the polished leather"—then it went its way. And the birds!
she still remembers with pride that "they came boldly into my
room," when she had neglected her "duty" and put no food
on the window-sill for them; she knew all the wild birds, and
forgets the royal crown on her head to remember with pride
that they knew her; also that the wasp and the bee were personal friends of hers, and never forgot that gracious relation-

ship to her injury: "never have I been stung by a wasp or a bee." And here is that proud note again that sings in that little child's elation in being singled out, among all the company of children, for the random dog's honor-conferring attentions: "Even in the very worst summer for wasps, when, in lunching out-of-doors, our table was covered with them and every one else was stung, they never hurt me."

When a queen whose qualities of mind and heart and character are able to add distinction to so distinguished a place as a throne, remembers with grateful exultation, after thirty years, honors and distinctions conferred upon her by the humble, wild creatures of the forest, we are helped to realize that complimentary attentions, homage, distinctions, are of no caste, but are above all caste—that they are a nobility-conferring power apart.

We all like these things. When the gate-guard at the railway station passes me through unchallenged and examines other people's tickets, I feel as the king, class A, felt when the emperor put the imperial hand on his shoulder, "everybody seeing him do it"; and as the child felt when the random dog allowed her to pat his head and ostracized the others; and as the princess felt when the wasps spared her and stung the rest; and I felt just so, four years ago in Vienna (and remember it yet), when the helmeted police shut me off, with fifty others, from a street which the Emperor was to pass through, and the captain of the squad turned and saw the situation and said indignantly to that guard:

"Can't you see it is the Herr Mark Twain? Let him through!"

It was four years ago; but it will be four hundred before I forget the wind of self-complacency that rose in me, and strained my buttons when I marked the deference for me evoked in the faces of my fellow-rabble, and noted, mingled with it, a puzzled and resentful expression which said, as plainly as speech could have worded it: "And who in the nation is the Herr Mark Twain *um Gotteswillen*?"

How many times in your life have you heard this boastful remark:

"I stood as close to him as I am to you; I could have put out my hand and touched him."

We have all heard it many and many a time. It was a proud
distinction to be able to say those words. It brought envy to
the speaker, a kind of glory; and he basked in it and was
happy through all his veins. And who was it he stood so close
to? The answer would cover all the grades. Sometimes it was
a king; sometimes it was a renowned highwayman; sometimes it was an unknown man killed in an extraordinary way
and made suddenly famous by it; always it was a person who
was for the moment the subject of public interest—the public
interest of a nation, maybe only the public interest of a
village.

"I was there, and I saw it myself." That is a common and
envy-compelling remark. It can refer to a battle; to a hanging;
to a coronation; to the killing of Jumbo by the railway train;
to the arrival of Jenny Lind at the Battery; to the meeting of
the President and Prince Henry; to the chase of a murderous
maniac; to the disaster in the tunnel; to the explosion in the
subway; to a remarkable dog-fight; to a village church struck
by lightning. It will be said, more or less casually, by everybody in America who has seen Prince Henry do anything, or
try to. The man who was absent and didn't see him do anything, will scoff. It is his privilege; and he can make capital
out of it, too; he will seem, even to himself, to be different
from other Americans, and better. As his opinion of his superior Americanism grows, and swells, and concentrates and co-
agulates, he will go further and try to belittle the distinction
of those that saw the Prince do things, and will spoil their
pleasure in it if he can. My life has been embittered by that
kind of persons. If you are able to tell of a special distinction
that has fallen to your lot, it gravels them; they cannot bear it;
and they try to make believe that the thing you took for a
special distinction was nothing of the kind and was meant in
quite another way. Once I was received in private audience by
an emperor. Last week I was telling a jealous person about it,
and I could see him wince under it, see it bite, see him suffer.
I revealed the whole episode to him with considerable elaboration and nice attention to detail. When I was through, he
asked me what had impressed me most. I said:

"His Majesty's delicacy. They told me to be sure and back
out from the presence, and find the door-knob the best I

could; it was not allowable to face around. Now the Emperor knew it would be a difficult ordeal for me, because of lack of practice; and so, when it was time to part, he turned, with exceeding delicacy, and pretended to fumble with things on his desk, so that I could get out in my own way, without his seeing me."

It went home! It was vitriol! I saw the envy and disgruntlement rise in the man's face; he couldn't keep it down. I saw him trying to fix up something in his mind to take the bloom off that distinction. I enjoyed that, for I judged that he had his work cut out for him. He struggled along inwardly for quite a while; then he said, with the manner of a person who has to say something and hasn't anything relevant to say:

"You said he had a handful of special-brand cigars lying on the table?"

"Yes; *I* never saw anything to match them."

I had him again. He had to fumble around in his mind as much as another minute before he could play; then he said in as mean a way as I ever heard a person say anything:

"He could have been counting the cigars, you know."

I cannot endure a man like that. It is nothing to him how unkind he is, so long as he takes the bloom off. It is all he cares for.

"An Englishman (or other human being) does dearly love a lord," (or other conspicuous person). It includes us all. We love to be noticed by the conspicuous person; we love to be associated with such, or with a conspicuous event, even in a seventh-rate fashion, even in a forty-seventh, if we cannot do better. This accounts for some of our curious tastes in mementos. It accounts for the large private trade in the Prince of Wales's hair, which chambermaids were able to drive in that article of commerce when the Prince made the tour of the world in the long ago—hair which probably did not always come from his brush, since enough of it was marketed to refurnish a bald comet; it accounts for the fact that the rope which lynches a negro in the presence of ten thousand Christian spectators is saleable five minutes later at two dollars an inch; it accounts for the mournful fact that a royal personage does not venture to wear buttons on his coat in public.

We do love a lord—and by that term I mean any person

whose situation is higher than our own. The lord of a group, for instance: a group of peers, a group of millionaires, a group of hoodlums, a group of sailors, a group of newsboys, a group of saloon politicians, a group of college girls. No royal person has ever been the object of a more delirious loyalty and slavish adoration than is paid by the vast Tammany herd to its squalid idol of Wantage. There is not a bifurcated animal in that menagerie that would not be proud to appear in a newspaper-picture in his company. At the same time, there are some in that organization who would scoff at the people who have been daily pictured in company with Prince Henry, and would say vigorously that *they* would not consent to be photographed with him—a statement which would not be true in any instance. There are hundreds of people in America who would frankly say to you that they would not be proud to be photographed in a group with the Prince, if invited; and some of these unthinking people would believe it when they said it; yet in no instance would it be true. We have a large population, but we have not a large enough one, by several millions, to furnish that man. He has not yet been begotten, and in fact he is not begettable.

You may take any of the printed groups, and there isn't a person in it who isn't visibly glad to be there; there isn't a person in the dim background who isn't visibly trying to be vivid; if it is a crowd of ten thousand—ten thousand proud, untamed democrats, horny-handed sons of toil and of politics, and fliers of the eagle—there isn't one who isn't conscious of the camera, there isn't one who is trying to keep out of range, there isn't one who isn't plainly meditating a purchase of the paper in the morning, with the intention of hunting himself out in the picture and of framing and keeping it if he shall find so much of his person in it as his starboard ear.

We all love to get some of the drippings of Conspicuousness, and we will put up with a single, humble drip, if we can't get any more. We may pretend otherwise, in conversation; but we can't pretend it to ourselves privately—and we don't. We do confess in public that we are the noblest work of God, being moved to it by long habit, and teaching, and superstition; but deep down in the secret places of our souls we recognize that, if we *are* the noblest work, the less said about it the better.

We of the North poke fun at the South for its fondness for titles—a fondness for titles pure and simple, regardless of whether they are genuine or pinchbeck. We forget that whatever a Southerner likes the rest of the human race likes, and that there is no law of predilection lodged in one people that is absent from another people. There is no variety in the human race. We are all children, all children of the one Adam, and we love toys. We can soon acquire that Southern disease if some one will give it a start. It already has a start, in fact. I have been personally acquainted with over 84,000 persons who, at one time or another in their lives, have served for a year or two on the staffs of our multitudinous governors, and through that fatality have been generals temporarily, and colonels temporarily, and judge-advocates temporarily; but I have known only nine among them who could be hired to let the title go when it ceased to be legitimate. I know thousands and thousands of governors who ceased to be governors away back in the last century; but I am acquainted with only three who would answer your letter if you failed to call them "Governor" in it. I know acres and acres of men who have done time in a legislature in prehistoric days, but among them is not half an acre whose resentment you would not raise if you addressed them as "Mr." instead of "Hon." The first thing a legislature does is to convene in an impressive legislative attitude, and get itself photographed. Each member frames his copy and takes it to the woods and hangs it up in the most aggressively conspicuous place in his house; and if you visit the house and fail to inquire what that accumulation is, the conversation will be brought around to it by that aforetime legislator, and he will show you a figure in it which in the course of years he has almost obliterated with the smut of his finger-marks, and say with a solemn joy, "It's me!"

Have you ever seen a country Congressman enter the hotel breakfast-room in Washington with his letters?—and sit at his table and let on to read them?—and wrinkle his brows and frown statesmanlike?—keeping a furtive watch-out over his glasses all the while to see if he is being observed and admired?—those same old letters which he fetches in every morning? Have you seen it? Have you seen him show off? It is *the* sight of the national capital. Except one; a pathetic one. That is the ex-Congressman: the poor fellow whose life has been ruined by a two-year taste of glory and of fictitious consequence; who has been superseded, and ought to take his heart-break home and hide it, but cannot tear himself away from the scene of his lost little grandeur; and so he lingers, and still lingers, year after year, unconsidered, sometimes snubbed, ashamed of his fallen estate, and valiantly trying to look otherwise; dreary and depressed, but counterfeiting breeziness and gayety, hailing with a chummy familiarity, which is not always welcomed, the more-fortunates who are still in place and were once his mates. Have you seen him? He clings piteously to the one little shred that is left of his departed distinction—the "privilege of the floor"; and works it hard and gets what he can out of it. That is the saddest figure I know of.

Yes, we do so love our little distinctions! And then we loftily scoff at a Prince for enjoying his larger ones; forgetting that if we only had his chance—ah! "Senator" is not a legitimate title. A Senator has no more right to be addressed by it than have you or I; but, in the several State capitals and in Washington, there are 5,000 Senators who take very kindly to that fiction, and who purr gratefully when you call them by it—which you may do quite unrebuked. Then those same Senators smile at the self-constructed majors and generals and judges of the South!

Indeed, we do love our distinctions, get them how we may. And we work them for all they are worth. In prayer we call ourselves "worms of the dust," but it is only on a sort of tacit understanding that the remark shall not be taken at par. *We*— worms of the dust! Oh, no, we are not that. Except in fact; and we do not deal much in fact when we are contemplating ourselves.

As a race, we do certainly love a lord—let him be Croker, or a duke, or a prize-fighter, or whatever other personage shall chance to be the head of our group. Many years ago, I saw a greasy youth in overalls standing by the *Herald* office, with an expectant look in his face. Soon a large man passed out, and gave him a pat on the shoulder. That was what the boy was waiting for—the large man's notice. The pat made him proud and happy, and the exultation inside of him shone out through his eyes; and his mates were there to see the pat and envy it and wish they could have that glory. The boy belonged down cellar in the press-room, the large man was king of the upper floors, foreman of the composing-room. The light in the boy's face was worship, the foreman was his lord, head of his group. The pat was an accolade. It was as precious to the boy as it would have been if he had been an aristocrat's son and the accolade had been delivered by his sovereign with a sword. The quintessence of the honor was all there; there was no difference in values; in truth there was no difference present except an artificial one—clothes.

All the human race loves a lord—that is, it loves to look upon or be noticed by the possessor of Power or Conspicuousness; and sometimes animals, born to better things and higher ideals, descend to man's level in this matter. In the Jardin des Plantes I have seen a cat that was so vain of being the personal friend of an elephant that I was ashamed of her.

*April 1902*

# The Five Boons of Life

### I

In the morning of life came the good fairy with her basket, and said:

"Here are gifts. Take one, leave the others. And be wary, choose wisely; oh, choose wisely! for only one of them is valuable."

The gifts were five: Fame, Love, Riches, Pleasure, Death. The youth said eagerly:

"There is no need to consider;" and he chose Pleasure.

He went out into the world and sought out the pleasures that youth delights in. But each in its turn was short-lived and disappointing, vain and empty; and each, departing, mocked him. In the end he said: "These years I have wasted. If I could but choose again, I would choose wisely."

### II

The fairy appeared, and said:

"Four of the gifts remain. Choose once more; and oh, remember—time is flying, and only one of them is precious."

The man considered long, then chose Love; and did not mark the tears that rose in the fairy's eyes.

After many, many years the man sat by a coffin, in an empty home. And he communed with himself, saying: "One by one they have gone away and left me; and now she lies here, the dearest and the last. Desolation after desolation has swept over me; for each hour of happiness the treacherous trader, Love, has sold me I have paid a thousand hours of grief. Out of my heart of hearts I curse him."

### III

"Choose again." It was the fairy speaking. "The years have taught you wisdom—surely it must be so. Three gifts remain. Only one of them has any worth—remember it, and choose warily."

The man reflected long, then chose Fame; and the fairy, sighing, went her way.

Years went by and she came again, and stood behind the man where he sat solitary in the fading day, thinking. And she knew his thought:

"My name filled the world, and its praises were on every tongue, and it seemed well with me for a little while. How little a while it was! Then came envy; then detraction; then calumny; then hate; then persecution. Then derision, which is the beginning of the end. And last of all came pity, which is the funeral of fame. Oh, the bitterness and misery of renown! target for mud in its prime, for contempt and compassion in its decay."

IV

"Choose yet again." It was the fairy's voice. "Two gifts remain. And do not despair. In the beginning there was but one that was precious, and it is still here."

"Wealth—which is power! How blind I was!" said the man. "Now, at last, life will be worth the living. I will spend, squander, dazzle. These mockers and despisers will crawl in the dirt before me, and I will feed my hungry heart with their envy. I will have all luxuries, all joys, all enchantments of the spirit, all contentments of the body that man holds dear. I will buy, buy, buy! deference, respect, esteem, worship—every pinchbeck grace of life the market of a trivial world can furnish forth. I have lost much time, and chosen badly heretofore, but let that pass; I was ignorant then, and could but take for best what seemed so."

Three short years went by, and a day came when the man sat shivering in a mean garret; and he was gaunt and wan and hollow-eyed, and clothed in rags; and he was gnawing a dry crust and mumbling:

"Curse all the world's gifts, for mockeries and gilded lies! And miscalled, every one. They are not gifts, but merely lendings. Pleasure, Love, Fame, Riches: they are but temporary disguises for lasting realities—Pain, Grief, Shame, Poverty. The fairy said true; in all her store there was but one gift which was precious, only one that was not valueless. How poor and cheap and mean I know those others now to be, compared with that inestimable one, that dear and sweet and kindly one, that steeps in dreamless and enduring sleep the pains that persecute the body, and the shames and griefs that eat the mind and heart. Bring it! I am weary, I would rest."

### V

The fairy came, bringing again four of the gifts, but Death was wanting. She said:

"I gave it to a mother's pet, a little child. It was ignorant, but trusted me, asking me to choose for it. You did not ask me to choose."

"Oh, miserable me! What is there left for me?"

"What not even you have deserved: the wanton insult of Old Age."

*July 5, 1902*

# *Was It Heaven? Or Hell?*

"You told a *lie*?"

"You confess it—you actually confess it—you told a lie!"

The family consisted of four persons: Margaret Lester, widow, aged thirty-six; Helen Lester, her daughter, aged sixteen; Mrs. Lester's maiden aunts, Hannah and Hester Gray, twins, aged sixty-seven. Waking and sleeping, the three women spent their days and nights in adoring the young girl; in watching the movements of her sweet spirit in the mirror of her face; in refreshing their souls with the vision of her bloom and beauty; in listening to the music of her voice; in gratefully recognizing how rich and fair for them was the world with this presence in it; in shuddering to think how desolate it would be with this light gone out of it.

By nature—and inside—the aged aunts were utterly dear and lovable and good, but in the matter of morals and conduct their training had been so uncompromisingly strict that it had made them exteriorly austere, not to say stern. Their influence was effective in the house; so effective that the mother and the daughter conformed to its moral and religious requirements cheerfully, contentedly, happily, unquestioningly. To do this was become second nature to them. And so in this peaceful heaven there were no clashings, no irritations, no fault-findings, no heart-burnings.

In it a lie had no place. In it a lie was unthinkable. In it speech was restricted to absolute truth, iron-bound truth, implacable and uncompromising truth, let the resulting consequences be what they might. At last, one day, under stress of circumstances, the darling of the house sullied her lips with a lie—and confessed it, with tears and self-upbraidings. There are not any words that can paint the consternation of the aunts. It was as if the sky had crumpled up and collapsed and the earth had tumbled to ruin with a crash. They sat side by side, white and stern, gazing speechless upon the culprit, who was on her knees before them with her face buried first in one lap and then the other, moaning and sobbing, and appealing for sympathy and forgiveness and getting no response, humbly kissing the hand of the one, then of the other, only to see it withdrawn as suffering defilement by those soiled lips.

Twice, at intervals, Aunt Hester said, in frozen amazement, "You told a *lie*?"

Twice, at intervals, Aunt Hannah followed with the muttered and amazed ejaculation,

"You confess it—you actually confess it—you told a lie!"

It was all they could say. The situation was new, unheard-of, incredible; they could not understand it, they did not know how to take hold of it, it approximately paralyzed speech.

At length it was decided that the erring child must be taken to her mother, who was ill, and who ought to know what had happened. Helen begged, besought, implored that she might be spared this further disgrace, and that her mother might be spared the grief and pain of it; but this could not be: duty required this sacrifice, duty takes precedence of all things, nothing can absolve one from a duty, with a duty no compromise is possible.

Helen still begged, and said the sin was her own, her mother had had no hand in it,—why must she be made to suffer for it?

But the aunts were obdurate in their righteousness, and said the law that visited the sins of the parent upon the child was by all right and reason reversible; and therefore it was but just that the innocent mother of a sinning child should suffer her rightful share of the grief and pain and shame which were the allotted wages of the sin.

The three moved toward the sick-room.

At this time the doctor was approaching the house. He was still a good distance away, however. He was a good doctor and a good man, and he had a good heart, but one had to know him a year to get over hating him, two years to learn to endure him, three to learn to like him, and four or five to learn to love him. It was a slow and trying education, but it paid. He was of great stature; he had a leonine head, a leonine face, a rough voice, and an eye which was sometimes a pirate's and sometimes a woman's, according to the mood. He knew nothing about etiquette, and cared nothing about it; in speech, manner, carriage, and conduct he was the reverse of conventional. He was frank, to the limit; he had opinions on all subjects; they were always on tap and ready for delivery, and he cared not a farthing whether his listener liked them or didn't. Whom he loved he loved, and manifested it; whom he didn't love he hated, and published it from the house-tops. In his young days he had been a sailor, and the salt airs of all the seas blew from him yet. He was a sturdy and loyal Christian, and believed he was the best one in the land, and the only one whose Christianity was perfectly sound, healthy, full-charged with common-sense, and had no decayed places in it. People who had an axe to grind, or people who for any reason wanted to get on the soft side of him, called him The Christian,—a phrase whose delicate flattery was music to his ears, and whose capital T was such an enchanting and vivid object to him that he could *see* it when it fell out of a person's mouth even in the dark. Many who were fond of him stood on their consciences with both feet and brazenly called him by that large title habitually, because it was a pleasure to them to do anything that would please him; and with eager and cordial malice his extensive and diligently cultivated crop of enemies gilded it, beflowered it, expanded it to "The *Only* Christian." Of these two titles, the latter had the wider currency; the enemy, being greatly in the majority, attended to that. Whatever the doctor believed, he believed with all his heart, and would fight for it whenever he got the chance; and if the intervals between chances grew to be irksomely wide, he would invent ways of shortening them himself. He was severely conscientious, according to his rather independent lights, and whatever he took to be a duty he performed, no matter whether the judgment of the professional moralists agreed with his own or not. At sea, in his young days, he had used profanity freely, but as soon as he was converted he made a rule, which he rigidly stuck to ever afterwards, never to use it except on the rarest occasions, and then only when duty commanded. He had been a hard drinker at sea, but after his conversion he became a firm and outspoken teetotaler, in order to be an example to the young, and from that time forth he seldom drank; never, indeed, except when it seemed to him to be a duty,—a condition which sometimes occurred a couple of times a year, but never as many as five times.

Necessarily such a man is impressionable, impulsive, emotional. This one was, and had no gift at hiding his feelings; or if he had it he took no trouble to exercise it. He carried his soul's prevailing weather in his face, and when he entered a room the parasols or the umbrellas went up—figuratively speaking—according to the indications. When the soft light was in his eye it meant approval, and delivered a benediction; when he came with a frown he lowered the temperature ten degrees. He was a well-beloved man in the house of his friends, but sometimes a dreaded one.

He had a deep affection for the Lester household, and its several members returned this feeling with interest. They mourned over his kind of Christianity, and he frankly scoffed at theirs; but both parties went on loving each other just the same.

He was approaching the house—out of the distance; the aunts and the culprit were moving toward the sick-chamber.

### III

The three last named stood by the bed; the aunts austere, the transgressor softly sobbing. The mother turned her head on the pillow; her tired eyes flamed up instantly with sympathy and passionate mother-love when they fell upon her child, and she opened the refuge and shelter of her arms.

"Wait!" said Aunt Hannah, and put out her hand and stayed the girl from leaping into them.

"Helen," said the other aunt, impressively, "tell your mother all. Purge your soul; leave nothing unconfessed."

Standing stricken and forlorn before her judges, the young girl mourned her sorrowful tale through to the end, then in a passion of appeal cried out:

"Oh, mother, can't you forgive me? won't you forgive me?—I am so desolate!"

"Forgive you, my darling? Oh, come to my arms!—there, lay your head upon my breast, and be at peace. If you had told a thousand lies—"

There was a sound—a warning—the clearing of a throat. The aunts glanced up, and withered in their clothes—there stood the doctor, his face a thunder-cloud. Mother and child knew nothing of his presence; they lay locked together, heart to heart, steeped in immeasurable content, dead to all things else. The physician stood many moments glaring and glooming upon the scene before him; studying it, analyzing it, searching out its genesis; then he put up his hand and beckoned to the aunts. They came trembling to him and stood humbly before him and waited. He bent down and whispered:

"Didn't I tell you this patient must be protected from all excitement? What the hell have you been doing? Clear out of the place!"

They obeyed. Half an hour later he appeared in the parlor, serene, cheery, clothed in sunshine, conducting Helen, with his arm about her waist, petting her, and saying gentle and playful things to her; and she also was her sunny and happy self again.

"Now, then," he said, "good-by, dear. Go to your room, and keep away from your mother, and behave yourself. But wait—put out your tongue. There, that will do—you're as sound as a nut!" He patted her cheek and added, "Run along now; I want to talk to these aunts."

She went from the presence. His face clouded over again at once; and as he sat down he said:

"You two have been doing a lot of damage—and maybe some good. Some good, yes—such as it is. That woman's disease is typhoid! You've brought it to a show-up, I think, with your insanities, and that's a service—such as it is. I hadn't been able to determine what it was before."

With one impulse the old ladies sprang to their feet, quaking with terror.

"Sit down! What are you proposing to do?"

"Do? We must fly to her. We—"

"You'll do nothing of the kind; you've done enough harm for one day. Do you want to squander all your capital of crimes and follies on a single deal? Sit down, I tell you. I have arranged for her to sleep; she needs it; if you disturb her without my orders, I'll brain you—if you've got the materials for it."

They sat down, distressed and indignant, but obedient, under compulsion. He proceeded:

"Now, then, I want this case explained. *They* wanted to explain it to me—as if there hadn't been emotion and excitement enough already. You knew my orders; how did you dare to go in there and get up that riot?"

Hester looked appealingly at Hannah; Hannah returned a beseeching look at Hester—neither wanted to dance to this unsympathetic orchestra. The doctor came to their help. He said,

"Begin, Hester."

Fingering at the fringes of her shawl, and with lowered eyes, Hester said, timidly:

"We should not have disobeyed for any ordinary cause, but this was vital. This was a duty. With a duty one has no choice; one must put all lighter considerations aside and perform it. We were obliged to arraign her before her mother. She had told a lie."

The doctor glowered upon the woman a moment, and seemed to be trying to work up in his mind an understanding of a wholly incomprehensible proposition; then he stormed out:

"She told a lie! *Did* she? God bless my soul! I tell a million a day! And so does every doctor. And so does everybody—including you—for that matter. And *that* was the important thing that authorized you to venture to disobey my orders and imperil that woman's life! Look here, Hester Gray, this is pure lunacy; that girl *couldn't* tell a lie that was intended to injure a person. The thing is impossible—absolutely impossible. You know it yourselves—both of you; you know it perfectly well."

Hannah came to her sister's rescue:

"Hester didn't mean that it was that kind of a lie, and it wasn't. But it was a lie."

"Well, upon my word, I never heard such nonsense! Haven't you got sense enough to discriminate between lies? Don't you know the difference between a lie that helps and a lie that hurts?"

"*All* lies are sinful," said Hannah, setting her lips together like a vise; "all lies are forbidden."

The Only Christian fidgeted impatiently in his chair. He wanted to attack this proposition, but he did not quite know how or where to begin. Finally he made a venture:

"Hester, wouldn't you tell a lie to shield a person from an undeserved injury or shame?"

"No."

"Not even a friend?"

"No."

"Not even your dearest friend?"

"No. I would not."

The doctor struggled in silence awhile with this situation; then he asked,

"Not even to save him from bitter pain and misery and grief?"

"No. Not even to save his life."

Another pause. Then,

"Nor his soul."

There was a hush—a silence which endured a measurable interval—then Hester answered, in a low voice, but with decision,

"Nor his soul."

No one spoke for a while; then the doctor said,

"Is it with you the same, Hannah?"

"Yes," she answered.

"I ask you both—why?"

"Because to tell such a lie, or any lie, is a sin, and could cost us the loss of our own souls—*would*, indeed, if we died without time to repent."

"Strange . . . strange . . . it is past belief." Then he asked, roughly, "Is such a soul as that *worth* saving?" He rose up, mumbling and grumbling, and started for the door, stumping vigorously along. At the threshold he turned and rasped out an admonition: "Reform! Drop this mean and sordid and selfish devotion to the saving of your shabby little souls, and hunt up something to do that's got some dignity to it! *Risk* your souls! risk them in good causes; then if you lose them, why should you care? Reform!"

The good old gentlewomen sat paralyzed, pulverized, outraged, insulted, and brooded in bitterness and indignation over these blasphemies. They were hurt to the heart, poor old ladies, and said they could never forgive these injuries.

"Reform!"

They kept repeating that word resentfully. "Reform—and learn to tell lies!"

Time slipped along, and in due course a change came over their spirits. They had completed the human being's first duty—which is to think about himself until he has exhausted the subject, then he is in a condition to take up minor interests and think of other people. This changes the complexion of his spirits—generally wholesomely. The minds of the two old ladies reverted to their beloved niece and the fearful disease which had smitten her; instantly they forgot the hurts their self-love had received, and a passionate desire rose in their hearts to go to the help of the sufferer and comfort her with their love, and minister to her, and labor for her the best they could with their weak hands, and joyfully and affectionately wear out their poor old bodies in her dear service if only they might have the privilege.

"And we shall have it!" said Hester, with the tears running down her face. "There are no nurses comparable to us, for there are no others that will stand their watch by that bed till they drop and die, and God knows we would do that."

"Amen," said Hannah, smiling approval and endorsement through the mist of moisture that blurred her glasses. "The doctor knows us, and knows we will not disobey again; and he will call no others. He will not dare!"

"Dare?" said Hester, with temper, and dashing the water from her eyes; "he will dare anything—that Christian devil! But it will do no good for him to try it this time—but, laws! Hannah, after all's said and done, he is gifted and wise and good, and he would not think of such a thing. . . . It is surely time for one of us to go to that room. What is keeping him? Why doesn't he come and say so?"

They caught the sound of his approaching step. He entered, sat down, and began to talk.

"Margaret is a sick woman," he said. "She is still sleeping, but she will wake presently; then one of you must go to her. She will be worse before she is better. Pretty soon a night-and-day watch must be set. How much of it can you two undertake?"

"All of it!" burst from both ladies at once.

The doctor's eyes flashed, and he said, with energy:

"You *do* ring true, you brave old relics! And you *shall* do all of the nursing you can, for there's none to match you in that divine office in this town; but you can't do all of it, and it would be a crime to let you." It was grand praise, golden praise, coming from such a source, and it took nearly all the resentment out of the aged twins' hearts. "Your Tilly and my old Nancy shall do the rest—good nurses both, white souls with black skins, watchful, loving, tender,—just perfect nurses!—and competent liars from the cradle. . . . Look you! keep a little watch on Helen; she is sick, and is going to be sicker."

The ladies looked a little surprised, and not credulous; and Hester said:

"How is that? It isn't an hour since you said she was as sound as a nut."

The doctor answered, tranquilly,

"It was a lie."

The ladies turned upon him indignantly, and Hannah said,

"How can you make an odious confession like that, in so indifferent a tone, when you know how we feel about all forms of—"

"Hush! You are as ignorant as cats, both of you, and you don't know what you are talking about. You are like all the rest of the moral moles: you lie from morning till night, but because you don't do it with your mouths, but only with your lying eyes, your lying inflections, your deceptively misplaced emphasis, and your misleading gestures, you turn up your complacent noses and parade before God and the world as saintly and unsmirched Truth-Speakers, in whose cold-storage souls a lie would freeze to death if it got there! Why will you humbug yourselves with that foolish notion that no lie is a lie except a spoken one? What is the difference between lying with your eyes and lying with your mouth? There is none; and if you would reflect a moment you would see that it is so. There isn't a human being that doesn't tell a gross of lies every day of his life; and you—why, between you, you tell thirty thousand; yet you flare up here in a lurid hypocritical horror because I tell that child a benevolent and sinless lie to protect her from her imagination, which would get to work and warm up her blood to a fever in an hour, if I were disloyal enough to my duty to let it. Which I should probably do if I were interested in saving my soul by such disreputable means.

"Come, let us reason together. Let us examine details. When you two were in the sick-room raising that riot, what would you have done if you had known I was coming?"

"Well, what?"

"You would have slipped out and carried Helen with you—wouldn't you?"

The ladies were silent.

"What would be your object and intention?"

"Well, what?"

"To keep me from finding out your guilt; to beguile me to infer that Margaret's excitement proceeded from some cause not known to you. In a word, to tell me a lie—a silent lie. Moreover, a possibly harmful one."

The twins colored, but did not speak.

"You not only tell myriads of silent lies, but you tell lies with your mouths—you two."

"*That* is not so!"

"It is so. But only harmless ones. You never dream of uttering a harmful one. Do you know that that is a concession—and a confession?"

"How do you mean?"

"It is an unconscious concession that harmless lies are not criminal; it is a confession that you constantly *make* that discrimination. For instance, you declined old Mrs. Foster's invitation last week to meet those odious Higbies at supper —in a polite note in which you expressed regret and said you were very sorry you could not go. It was a lie. It was

as unmitigated a lie as was ever uttered. Deny it, Hester—
with another lie."

Hester replied with a toss of her head.

"That will not do. Answer. Was it a lie, or wasn't it?"

The color stole into the cheeks of both women, and with a
struggle and an effort they got out their confession:

"It was a lie."

"Good—the reform is beginning; there is hope for you
yet; you will not tell a lie to save your dearest friend's soul,
but you will spew out one without a scruple to save yourself
the discomfort of telling an unpleasant truth."

He rose. Hester, speaking for both, said, coldly:

"We have lied; we perceive it; it will occur no more. To lie
is a sin. We shall never tell another one of any kind whatsoever, even lies of courtesy or benevolence, to save any one a
pang or a sorrow decreed for him by God."

"Ah, how soon you will fall! In fact, you have fallen already; for what you have just uttered is a lie. Good-by. Reform! One of you go to the sick-room now."

IV

Twelve days later.

Mother and child were lingering in the grip of the hideous
disease. Of hope for either there was little. The aged sisters
looked white and worn, but they would not give up their
posts. Their hearts were breaking, poor old things, but their
grit was steadfast and indestructible. All the twelve days the
mother had pined for the child, and the child for the mother,
but both knew that the prayer of these longings could not be
granted. When the mother was told—on the first day—that
her disease was typhoid, she was frightened, and asked if
there was danger that Helen could have contracted it the day
before, when she was in the sick-chamber on that confession
visit. Hester told her the doctor had poo-poo'd the idea. It
troubled Hester to say it, although it was true, for she had
not believed the doctor; but when she saw the mother's joy
in the news, the pain in her conscience lost something of its
force—a result which made her ashamed of the constructive

deception which she had practised, though not ashamed enough to make her distinctly and definitely wish she had refrained from it. From that moment the sick woman understood that her daughter must remain away, and she said she would reconcile herself to the separation the best she could, for she would rather suffer death than have her child's health imperilled. That afternoon Helen had to take to her bed, ill. She grew worse during the night. In the morning her mother asked after her:

"Is she well?"

Hester turned cold; she opened her lips, but the words refused to come. The mother lay languidly looking, musing, waiting; suddenly she turned white and gasped out,

"Oh, my God! what is it? is she sick?"

Then the poor aunt's tortured heart rose in rebellion, and words came:

"No—be comforted; she is well."

The sick woman put all her happy heart in her gratitude:

"Thank God for those dear words! Kiss me. How I worship you for saying them."

Hester told this incident to Hannah, who received it with a rebuking look, and said, coldly,

"Sister, it was a lie."

Hester's lips trembled piteously; she choked down a sob, and said,

"Oh, Hannah, it was a sin, but I could not help it; I could not endure the fright and the misery that were in her face."

"No matter. It was a lie. God will hold you to account for it."

"Oh, I know it, I know it," cried Hester, wringing her hands, "but even if it were now, I could not help it. I know I should do it again."

"Then take my place with Helen in the morning. I will make the report myself."

Hester clung to her sister, begging and imploring:

"Don't, Hannah, oh, don't—you will kill her."

"I will at least speak the truth."

In the morning she had a cruel report to bear to the mother, and she braced herself for the trial. When she returned from her mission, Hester was waiting, pale and trembling, in the hall. She whispered,

"Oh, how did she take it—that poor, desolate mother?"

Hannah's eyes were swimming in tears. She said,

"God forgive me, I told her the child was well!"

Hester gathered her to her heart, with a grateful "God bless you, Hannah!" and poured out her thankfulness in an inundation of worshipping praises.

After that, the two knew the limit of their strength, and accepted their fate. They surrendered humbly, and abandoned themselves to the hard requirements of the situation. Daily they told the morning lie, and confessed their sin in prayer; not asking forgiveness, as not being worthy of it, but only wishing to make record that they realized their wickedness and were not desiring to hide it or excuse it.

Daily, as the fair young idol of the house sank lower and lower, the sorrowful old aunts painted her glowing bloom and her fresh young beauty to the wan mother, and winced under the stabs her ecstasies of joy and gratitude gave them.

In the first days, while the child had strength to hold a pencil, she wrote fond little love-notes to her mother, in which she concealed her illness; and these the mother read and re-read through happy eyes wet with thankful tears, and kissed them over and over again, and treasured them as precious things under her pillow.

Then came a day when the strength was gone from the hand, and the mind wandered, and the tongue babbled pathetic incoherences. This was a sore dilemma for the poor aunts. There were no love-notes for the mother. They did not know what to do. Hester began a carefully studied and plausible explanation, but lost the track of it and grew confused; suspicion began to show in the mother's face, then alarm. Hester saw it, recognized the imminence of the danger, and descended to the emergency, pulling herself resolutely together and plucking victory from the open jaws of defeat. In a placid and convincing voice she said:

"I thought it might distress you to know it, but Helen spent the night at the Sloanes'. There was a little party there, and although she did not want to go, and you so sick, we persuaded her, she being young and needing the innocent pastimes of youth, and we believing you would approve. Be sure she will write the moment she comes."

"How good you are, and how dear and thoughtful for us both! Approve? Why, I thank you with all my heart. My poor little exile! Tell her I want her to have every pleasure she can—I would not rob her of one. Only let her keep her health, that is all I ask. Don't let that suffer; I could not bear it. How thankful I am that she escaped this infection—and what a narrow risk she ran, Aunt Hester! Think of that lovely face all dulled and burnt with fever. I can't bear the thought of it. Keep her health. Keep her bloom! I can see her now, the dainty creature—with the big blue earnest eyes; and sweet, oh, so sweet and gentle and winning! Is she as beautiful as ever, dear Aunt Hester?"

"Oh, more beautiful and bright and charming than ever she was before, if such a thing can be"—and Hester turned away and fumbled with the medicine-bottles, to hide her shame and grief.

v

After a little, both aunts were laboring upon a difficult and baffling work in Helen's chamber. Patiently and earnestly, with their stiff old fingers, they were trying to forge the required note. They made failure after failure, but they improved little by little all the time. The pity of it all, the pathetic humor of it, there was none to see; they themselves were unconscious of it. Often their tears fell upon the notes and spoiled them; sometimes a single misformed word made a note risky which could have been ventured but for that; but at last Hannah produced one whose script was a good enough imitation of Helen's to pass any but a suspicious eye, and bountifully enriched it with the petting phrases and loving nicknames that had been familiar on the child's lips from her nursery days. She carried it to the mother, who took it with avidity, and kissed it, and fondled it, reading its precious words over and over again, and dwelling with deep contentment upon its closing paragraph:

"Mousie darling, if I could only see you, and kiss your eyes, and feel your arms about me! I am so glad my practising does not disturb you. Get well soon. Everybody is good to me, but I am so lonesome without you, dear mamma."

"The poor child, I know just how she feels. She cannot be quite happy without me; and I—oh, I live in the light of her eyes! Tell her she must practise all she pleases; and, Aunt Hannah—tell her I can't hear the piano this far, nor her dear voice when she sings: God knows I wish I could. No one knows how sweet that voice is to me; and to think—some day it will be silent! What are you crying for?"

"Only because—because—it was just a memory. When I came away she was singing 'Loch Lomond.' The pathos of it! It always moves me so when she sings that."

"And me, too. How heart-breakingly beautiful it is when some youthful sorrow is brooding in her breast and she sings it for the mystic healing it brings. . . . . Aunt Hannah?"

"Dear Margaret?"

"I am very ill. Sometimes it comes over me that I shall never hear that dear voice again."

"Oh, don't—don't, Margaret! I can't bear it!"

Margaret was moved and distressed, and said, gently:

"There—there—let me put my arms around you. Don't cry. There—put your cheek to mine. Be comforted. I wish to live. I will live if I can. Ah, what could she do without me! . . . Does she often speak of me?—but I know she does."

"Oh, all the time—all the time!"

"My sweet child! She wrote the note the moment she came home?"

"Yes—the first moment. She would not wait to take off her things."

"I knew it. It is her dear, impulsive, affectionate way. I knew it without asking, but I wanted to hear you say it. The petted wife knows she is loved, but she makes her husband tell her so, every day, just for the joy of hearing it. . . . She used the pen this time. That is better; the pencil marks could rub out, and I should grieve for that. Did you suggest that she use the pen?"

"Y-no—she—it was her own idea."

The mother looked her pleasure, and said:

"I was hoping you would say that. There was never such a dear and thoughtful child! . . . Aunt Hannah?"

"Dear Margaret?"

"Go and tell her I think of her all the time, and worship her. Why—you are crying again. Don't be so worried about me, dear; I think there is nothing to fear, yet."

The grieving messenger carried her message, and piously delivered it to unheeding ears. The girl babbled on unaware; looking up at her with wondering and startled eyes flaming with fever, eyes in which was no light of recognition—

"Are you—no, you are not my mother. I want her—oh, I want her! She was here a minute ago—I did not see her go. Will she come? will she come quickly? will she come now? . . . There are so many houses . . . and they oppress me so . . . and everything whirls and turns and whirls . . . oh, my head, my head!"—and so she wandered on and on, in her pain, flitting from one torturing fancy to another, and tossing her arms about in a weary and ceaseless persecution of unrest.

Poor old Hannah wetted the parched lips and softly stroked the hot brow, murmuring endearing and pitying words, and thanking the Father of all that the mother was happy and did not know.

## VI

Daily the child sank lower and steadily lower toward the grave, and daily the sorrowing old watchers carried gilded tidings of her radiant health and loveliness to the happy mother, whose pilgrimage was also now nearing its end. And daily they forged loving and cheery notes in the child's hand, and stood by with remorseful consciences and bleeding hearts, and wept to see the grateful mother devour them and adore them and treasure them away as things beyond price, because of their sweet source, and sacred because her child's hand had touched them.

At last came that kindly friend who brings healing and peace to all. The lights were burning low. In the solemn hush which precedes the dawn vague figures flitted soundless along the dim hall and gathered silent and awed in Helen's chamber, and grouped themselves about her bed, for a warning had gone forth, and they knew. The dying girl lay with closed lids, and unconscious, the drapery upon her breast faintly rising and falling as her wasting life ebbed away. At intervals a sigh or a muffled sob broke upon the stillness. The same haunting thought was in all minds there: the pity of this death, the going out into the great darkness, and the mother not here to help and hearten and bless.

Helen stirred; her hands began to grope wistfully about as if they sought something—she had been blind some hours. The end was come; all knew it. With a great sob Hester gathered her to her breast, crying, "Oh, my child, my darling!" A rapturous light broke in the dying girl's face, for it was mercifully vouchsafed her to mistake those sheltering arms for another's; and she went to her rest murmuring, "Oh, mamma, I am so happy—I so longed for you—now I can die."

Two hours later Hester made her report. The mother asked,

"How is it with the child?"

"She is well."

## VII

A sheaf of white crêpe and black was hung upon the door of the house, and there it swayed and rustled in the wind and whispered its tidings. At noon the preparation of the dead was finished, and in the coffin lay the fair young form, beautiful, and in the sweet face a great peace. Two mourners sat by it, grieving and worshipping—Hannah and the black woman Tilly. Hester came, and she was trembling, for a great trouble was upon her spirit. She said,

"She asks for a note."

Hannah's face blanched. She had not thought of this; it had seemed that that pathetic service was ended. But she realized now that that could not be. For a little while the two women stood looking into each other's face, with vacant eyes; then Hannah said,

"There is no way out of it—she must have it; she will suspect, else."

"And she would find out."

"Yes. It would break her heart." She looked at the dead face, and her eyes filled. "I will write it," she said.

Hester carried it. The closing line said:

"Darling Mousie, dear sweet mother, we shall soon be together again. Is not that good news? And it is true; they all say it is true."

The mother mourned, saying:

"Poor child, how will she bear it when she knows? I shall never see her again in life. It is hard, so hard. She does not suspect? You guard her from that?"

"She thinks you will soon be well."

"How good you are, and careful, dear Aunt Hester! None goes near her who could carry the infection?"

"It would be a crime."

"But you *see* her?"

"With a distance between—yes."

"That is so good. Others one could not trust; but you two guardian angels—steel is not so true as you. Others would be unfaithful; and many would deceive, and lie."

Hester's eyes fell, and her poor old lips trembled.

"Let me kiss you for her, Aunt Hester; and when I am gone, and the danger is past, place the kiss upon her dear lips some day, and say her mother sent it, and all her mother's broken heart is in it."

Within the hour Hester, raining tears upon the dead face, performed her pathetic mission.

### VIII

Another day dawned, and grew, and spread its sunshine in the earth. Aunt Hannah brought comforting news to the failing mother, and a happy note, which said again, "We have but a little time to wait, darling mother, then we shall be together."

The deep note of a bell came moaning down the wind.

"Aunt Hannah, it is tolling. Some poor soul is at rest. As I shall be soon. You will not let her forget me?"

"Oh, God knows she never will!"

"Do not you hear strange noises, Aunt Hannah? It sounds like the shuffling of many feet."

"We hoped you would not hear it, dear. It is a little company gathering for—for Helen's sake, poor little prisoner.

There will be music—and she loves it so. We thought you would not mind."

"Mind? Oh, no, no—oh, give her everything her dear heart can desire. How good you two are to her, and how good to me. God bless you both, always!"

After a listening pause:

"How lovely! It is her organ. Is she playing it herself, do you think?" Faint and rich and inspiring the chords floated to her ears on the still air. "Yes, it is her touch, dear heart; I recognize it. They are singing. Why—it is a hymn! and the sacredest of all, the most touching, the most consoling. . . . It seems to open the gates of paradise to me. . . . If I could die now. . . ."

Faint and far the words rose out of the stillness—

> Nearer, my God, to Thee,
> Nearer to Thee,
> E'en though it be a cross
> That raiseth me.

With the closing of the hymn another soul passed to its rest, and they that had been one in life were not sundered in death. The sisters, mourning and rejoicing, said,

"How blessed it was that she never knew."

## IX

At midnight they sat together, grieving, and the angel of the Lord appeared in the midst transfigured with a radiance not of earth; and speaking, said:

"For liars a place is appointed. There they burn in the fires of hell from everlasting unto everlasting. Repent!"

The bereaved fell upon their knees before him and clasped their hands and bowed their gray heads, adoring. But their tongues clung to the roof of their mouths, and they were dumb.

"Speak! that I may bear the message to the chancery of heaven and bring again the decree from which there is no appeal."

Then they bowed their heads yet lower, and one said:

"Our sin is great, and we suffer shame; but only perfect and

final repentance can make us whole; and we are poor creatures who have learned our human weakness, and we know
that if we were in those hard straits again our hearts would
fail again, and we should sin as before. The strong could prevail, and so be saved, but we are lost."

They lifted their heads in supplication. The angel was gone.
While they marvelled and wept he came again; and bending
low, he whispered the decree.

X

Was it Heaven? Or Hell?

December 1902

# The Dervish and the Offensive Stranger

*The Dervish:* I will say again, and yet again, and still again, .
that a good deed—

*The Offensive Stranger:* Peace, oh man of narrow vision!
There is no such thing as a good *deed*—

*The Dervish:* O shameless blasphe—

*The Offensive Stranger:* And no such thing as an evil deed.
There are good *impulses*, there are evil impulses, and that is
all. Half of the results of a good intention are evil; half the
results of an evil intention are good. No man can command
the results, nor allot them.

*The Dervish:* And so—

*The Offensive Stranger:* And so you shall praise men for
their good intentions, and not blame them for the evils resulting; you shall blame men for their evil intentions, and not
praise them for the good resulting.

*The Dervish:* O, maniac! will you say—

*The Offensive Stranger:* Listen to the law: From *every* impulse, whether good or evil, flows two streams; the one carries
health, the other carries poison. From the beginning of time
this law has not changed, to the end of time it will not change.

*The Dervish:* If I should strike thee dead in anger—

*The Offensive Stranger:* Or kill me with a drug which you
hoped would give me new life and strength—

*The Dervish:* Very well. Go on.

*The Offensive Stranger:* In either case the results would be
the same. Age-long misery of mind for you—an evil result;
peace, repose, the end of sorrow for me—a good result.
Three hearts that hold me dear would break; three pauper
cousins of the third remove would get my riches and rejoice;
you would go to prison and your friends would grieve, but
your humble apprentice-priest would step into your shoes and
your fat sleek life and be happy. And are these all the goods
and all the evils that would flow from the well-intended or
ill-intended act that cut short my life? Oh thoughtless one, Oh
purblind creature! the good and evil results that flow from
*any* act, even the smallest, breed on and on, century after century, forever and ever and ever, creeping by inches around the

the globe, affecting all its coming and going populations until the end of time, until the final cataclysm!

*The Dervish:* Then, there being no such thing as a good deed—

*The Offensive Stranger:* Don't I tell you there are good *intentions,* and evil ones, and there an end? The *results* are not foreseeable. They are of both kinds, in all cases. It is the law. Listen: this is far-western history:

### VOICES OUT OF UTAH

#### I

*The White Chief (to his people):* This wide plain was a desert. By our heaven-blest industry we have dammed the river and utilized its waters and turned the desert into smiling fields whose fruitage makes prosperous and happy a thousand homes where poverty and hunger dwelt before. How noble, how beneficent, is Civilization!

#### II

*Indian Chief (to his people):* This wide plain, which the Spanish priests taught our fathers to irrigate, was a smiling field, whose fruitage made our homes prosperous and happy. The white American has dammed our river, taken away our water for his own valley, and turned our field into a desert; wherefore we starve.

―――

*The Dervish:* I perceive that the good intention did really bring both good and evil results in equal measure. But a single case cannot prove the rule. Try again.

*The Offensive Stranger:* Pardon me, *all* cases prove it. Columbus discovered a new world and gave to the plodding poor and the landless of Europe farms and breathing-space and plenty and happiness—

*The Dervish:* A good result—

*The Offensive Stranger:* And they hunted and harried the original owners of the soil, and robbed them, beggared them, drove them from their homes, and exterminated them, root and branch.

*The Dervish:* An evil result, yes.

*The Offensive Stranger:* The French Revolution brought desolation to the hearts and homes of five million families and drenched the country with blood and turned its wealth to poverty.

*The Dervish:* An evil result.

*The Offensive Stranger:* But every great and precious liberty enjoyed by the nations of Continental Europe to-day are the gift of that Revolution.

*The Dervish:* A good result, I concede it.

*The Offensive Stranger:* In our well-meant effort to lift up the Filipino to our own moral altitude with a musket, we have slipped on the ice and fallen down to his.

*The Dervish:* A large evil result.

*The Offensive Stranger:* But as an offset we are a World Power.

*The Dervish:* Give me time. I must think this one over. Pass on.

*The Offensive Stranger:* By help of three hundred thousand soldiers and eight hundred million dollars England has succeeded in her good purpose of lifting up the unwilling Boers and making them better and purer and happier than they could ever have become by their own devices.

*The Dervish:* Certainly that is a good result.

*The Offensive Stranger:* But there are only eleven Boers left, now.

*The Dervish:* It has the appearance of an evil result. But I will think it over before I decide.

*The Offensive Stranger:* Take yet one more instance. With the best intentions the missionary has been laboring in China for eighty years.

*The Dervish:* The evil result is—

*The Offensive Stranger:* That nearly a hundred thousand Chinamen have acquired our Civilization.

*The Dervish:* And the good result is—

*The Offensive Stranger:* That by the compassion of God four hundred millions have escaped it.

*The Dervish:* Adieu, good sir; I am convinced, and accept your Law.

*1902*

# Why Not Abolish It?

We have many good laws. They embody the wisdom and the common sense of the ages. There is one very striking feature about these laws. Let me point it out. Among them—

1. There is not a law which says that if you consent to the robbery of your family, the robber's crime is reduced to a mere impropriety by that consent.

2. There is not a law which says that if you consent to the burning of your father's house, the incendiary's crime is reduced to a mere impropriety by that consent.

3. There is not a law which says that if you consent to let a man starve your mother to death, that man's crime is reduced to a mere impropriety by that consent.

4. There is not a law which says that if you consent to let an assassin cut your throat, the assassin's crime is reduced to a mere impropriety by that consent.

It is strange, but these statements are true. The law does not grant you the tremendous privilege of propagating, inviting, and encouraging crime by your caprice, and of minimizing the responsibility of its perpetrators by the interposition of your royal consent. The law sticks stubbornly to the position that robbers, incendiaries, and murderers are criminals, no matter who are the victims; and it would not concede that they were criminals in a lesser degree in cases where you or your kin were the victims, and you gave your personal consent.

But there is one crime which is more disastrous than all of these put together; more bitter, more cruel, more infamous, more shameful, more insupportable, more far-reaching, more diffusive in its crushing effects, than all of those combined— and over the perpetrator of this one crime the law holds the protecting shield of its mercy and its compassion.

A murder kills the body, but sets it free and ends its cares; it brings grief to the surviving kindred, but it is a grief which time can soften, and even heal. But this other crime, this crime of crimes, kills the mental and spiritual life of its victim, but leaves its body to drag on and on, the symbol and sufferer of a living death, despised of kindred, forsaken of friends; and upon family and friends descends a blight of humiliation which time cannot remove nor forgetfulness ease of its pain.

The law is stern with the assassin, but gentle with the seducer; stern with the murderer of the body, but gentle with the murderer of all that can make life worth the living—honor, self-respect, the esteem of friends, the adoring worship of the sacred home circle, father, mother, and the cradle-mates of the earlier and innocent years. You may drag down into the mud and into enduring misery and shame the trusting and ignorant young flower of this household, and crush the heart of every creature that loves it and lives in the light of its presence; you may murder the spirit and consign to a living death and intolerable wretchedness all these—and if in certain cases you can prove *consent* the law will not deal unkindly with you.

"Consent" necessarily argues previous persuasion. It indicates who the instigator of the trespass was—that is to say, the offender-in-chief. Instead of magnifying his crime, this actually diminishes it, in the eyes of the law. The law establishes an "age of consent"—a limit during which a child of sixteen or seventeen is not privileged to help commit a tremendous and desolating crime against herself and her family; but she is privileged to do it if she is twenty; and in that case the person that persuades her to it is regarded by the law as being substantially guiltless, and it puts upon him no punishment which can be called by that name except sarcastically.

There is *no* age at which the good name of a member of a family ceases to be a part of the *property* of that family—an asset, and worth more than all its bonds and moneys. There is no age at which a member of the family may by consent, and under authority of the law, help a criminal to destroy the family's money and bonds. Then why should there be an age at which a member, by consent, and under connivance of the law, may help a criminal to destroy that far more valuable asset, the family's honor?

There being no age at which the law places the lives of a family in the hands of any member of it to throw away at his whim—including his own life—I see no sound reason why the law should not be consistent—consistently wise—and abolish the age limit in the case of the other and greater crime.

If a man and wife are drowned at sea, and there is no proof as to which died first, the law—in some European countries and in two of our States—decides that it was the wife. She is the weaker vessel. It is usually so in the matter of seduction. She is young, inexperienced, foolish, trustful, persuadable, affectionate; she would harm no one herself, and cannot see why any one should wish to harm her; while as a rule the man is older and stronger than she is, and in every case without exception is a scoundrel. The law protects him now; it seems to me that it ought to protect her, instead.

I think it ought to abolish "consent"—entirely. I think it should say there is *no* age at which consent shall in the least degree modify the seducer's crime or mitigate its punishment. "Consent" means previous persuasion—and there the crime *begins*. It is the first step, and responsible for the whole, for without it there would be no second. I would punish the beginner, the real criminal, and punish him well; society and civilization can be depended upon to punish with a ten thousand times exaggerated and unjust severity his thoughtless victim. If I were a law-maker I should want to make this law quite plain.

I should want it to say nothing about "consent"—I should take the persuasion for granted, and that *persuasion* is what I would punish, along with the resulting infamy. I should say simply that commerce *with a spinster*, of whatever age or condition, should be punished by two years of solitary confinement or five years at hard labor; and let the man take his choice. He has murdered the honor and the happiness of a whole unoffending family, and condemned it to life-long shame and grief, and while he ought to be flayed alive, and the law ought of rights to provide that penalty, I know that no jury would vote it; I could not do it myself, unless mine were the family. And so I would make the penalty as above. A jury would vote that, for the judge would be thoughtful enough to appoint upon it none but fathers of families—families with young girls in them, the treasures of their lives, the light of their homes, the joy of their hearts.

I find the following in this morning's *Herald*. Will you print it?

Rosie Quinn, who was convicted of murder in the second degree on April 8, for drowning her baby in the lake in Central Park, will be sentenced by Judge Scott to-day in the Criminal Branch of the Supreme Court. Only one sentence, that of life imprisonment, may be imposed, and, although her counsel, Moses A. Sachs, will ask for a new trial, it is not probable it will be granted.

The girl dreads her appearance in the court-room. She spoke of this yesterday with even more horror than that which the idea of a life sentence has aroused in her mind.

She has written to the father of the dead child, but has received no response. "I don't know what he can be thinking of," is her only comment.

Not even his name has been told to the persons who have approached Rosie Quinn in connection with her trial. She is loyal in this.

For her sisters, who have not been near her since her arrest in November, she displays a surprising thoughtfulness.

"Don't put my sisters' names in the paper," she begged. "I don't want their names used. I didn't even want it known that I had sisters, but it got out somehow." Since her conviction, one of her sisters has called at the prison to caution her against telling their names.

The girl is a most pitiable creature. She seems crazed by the happenings of the last few weeks, and is utterly unable to comprehend the enormity of her crime, or the hopelessness of the doom which is hanging over her. She is like a child, docile, quiet, undemonstrative. She will only say:—

"It was a dear love-affair for me."

Immediately after her sentence persons who have become interested in the girl's sad fate will appeal to Governor Odell in her behalf.

I think many of us will like to sign that petition.

*May 2, 1903*

# Mark Twain, Able Yachtsman, on Why Lipton Failed to Lift the Cup

"Aren't you charging rather high rates for this interview?"

"Not any higher than I always charge when I am present in person during the interview."

"Sometimes you are not present?"

"Yes; in those cases I do not know I have been interviewed until I see it in the papers."

"Do you enjoy that?"

"Well, no; I think it is not quite fair. It is my trade to talk and write; it is my bread and butter. A man cannot honorably take it from my family without consent. What is it we are to talk about now?"

"The yacht races. The HERALD would like you to explain the reasons of the results."

"Why—that is all right, but I doubt if I can earn the money."

"Why?"

"Well, because I can only state the facts. I can't intelligently philosophize them, analyze them, deduce results from them— and all that wise kind of thing, you know. Do you care for facts—just mere cold, unemotional facts?"

"Dear sir, we prefer them to anything else."

"Allow me. Give me your hand! We meet upon holy ground. I have no longer any tremblings at the heart, no longer any disturbing anxieties. Facts are my passion. I"——

"You have been called the slave of truth."

"Have you heard it? You make me proud, happy; you sing all my solicitudes to rest. Proceed."

"You have seen all of the races?"

"Yes, all of them."

"On board the Kanawha?"

"Yes."

"She is the fastest steam yacht afloat, I believe."

"Yes, she has beaten all the flyers. When I am feeling good I can make thirty-seven knots an hour with her * * * Why do you look at me like that?"

"I beg pardon. I assure you I didn't mean to. How"——

"Well, you mustn't look at me like that. I am very sensitive."

"It was an oversight, I give you my word. I would not wound you for anything. My hearing is not good, and I did not quite catch the number of the knots, I think. How many did you say it was?"

"Forty-five. She's a bird—just a bird. She"——

"Do you take her gait yourself?"

"No, it is done by one of the men—Patrick Clancy. He is in the forecastle. She has made as high as forty-nine. He told me so himself."

"Is he—is he trustworthy?"

"Who—Clancy? I should think so! I wouldn't trust a statement of my own sooner."

"Neither would I."

"Let me take you by the hand. Is Clancy trustworthy? Why, it would make everybody in the ship smile to hear you say that. Patrick Clancy"——

"Is he experienced? Is he calm, unexcitable; does he know the boat well?"

"Knows her like a book! Knows every inch of her hundred and twenty-seven feet; knows every ton of her four hundred; can tell by the flutter of her screw when she's making her Sabbath-day 290 revolutions and when she's on the warpath and turning out four thousand a minute. Does Patrick Clancy know the Kanawha? Why, man, he's been in her ever since she was a little thing not thirty feet long and couldn't make ten miles an hour; he told me so himself."

"Do you own the Kanawha?"

"Well, no, I don't exactly own her. I only help to run her. Mr. Rogers owns her."

"Do you command her?"

"Well, no, not exactly that. I only superintend."

"By request?"

"Well, I wouldn't put it quite as strong as that; but I do a good deal of work, you know; in fact, the important part of it. Superintending is more important than commanding, and more worrying and fatiguing, you know, because you have to be everywhere and attend to everything. Superintending is much the most exacting function on board a ship, and requires more varied talent and alertness, and more patience and calmness under explosions of resentment and insubordination than any other in the service. There are but few really good superintendents."

"The salary must be very large?"

"No, there isn't any salary; all a person gets is neglect and ingratitude. If a superintendent conscientiously does his whole duty, there's never anything going on but mutiny and insurrection. If I have ever had an order obeyed without being requested to mind my own business, I have no recollection of it. It is just a dog's life, and that is the best you can say about it."

"Why don't you resign?"

"Resign? How can I resign when I haven't been appointed? If I could get appointed I would resign in a minute."

"Is there no way to"——

"To what? No, there isn't. When you are a superintendent, there you are, and you can't help yourself. Sometimes I wish I was dead."

"It does seem to be a sorrowful vocation."

"Funerals is hilarity compared to it. Daily and hourly your feelings are hurt. Hurt by disobedience; yes, and almost always accompanied by remarks which—why, let me give you an instance. You remember that first day when we were racing with those steamrockets, the Corsair and the Revolution and the Hauoli and Mr. Leeds' Clipper and hanging their scalps up there on the mizzenforetopgallant halyards to dry, one by one? I found the second mate off his base and ordered him into irons as a lesson, and he told me to go to—never mind where he told me to go, but how would you like to be treated like that, and you doing the best you could?"

"Ah, that gives me an idea. It would be just like such a man as that to keep crossing the Monmouth's bow the way the Kanawha did Saturday in the race home. It was scandalous. Was he steering?"

"It's getting late, let's talk about something else. I was at the wheel myself. Are you intemperate? Would you like something? So would I. Push the button. What were you saying about—about"——

"I wasn't saying anything about anything, but now that I

think of it, what was the reason that the Shamrock performed so indifferently in the first race—that one that was a failure?"

"Well, I know the reason, for I got it from Clancy at the time. It is pretty technical, but, barring that, it is easy to understand. It was a case of British easygoing carelessness on the part of the Shamrock plant—good enough sailors, you know, but heedless, oh, beyond imagination! Not just one case of it, but two or three—Clancy explained the whole thing to me. In the first place, when they came to set the anchor watch it was a Waterbury, and they lost two minutes in the winding, and that took off the whole time allowance and three seconds besides—ought to have been wound up before, of course.

"And then, when they got it set, there they were again—an anchor watch, all right enough, but they found they hadn't any anchor. It had been left at the Waldorf, by some oversight, and they had to throw over ballast to make up for it. Also, they had to remeasure the boat, and that shortened her by an inch. I do not know why, but Clancy does. An inch is not much, but if you take it off the front end, that end does not arrive at the homestake as early as it would if it were an inch longer, and, of course, as you can see yourself, even that little could lose a race. It didn't in this case, because there was a lot more inches that did not arrive in time, but the principle is sound; you can see it yourself."

"Yes, it looks so. But they lost the second race, too—the first real race. How does Clancy account for that?"

"Difference in seamanship, he says. That and other things. Accidents and one thing and another."

"Did the Shamrock have accidents?"

"She had one that lost her the race. When she turned the stake she broke out her spinnaker. She might as well have broken her back, Clancy says. The spinnaker is a sail, you know. I don't know which one it is, but I think it is the tall one that bows out like a shirt front and gives the yacht such a dressy look. The other one is the balloon jib, which connects the garboard strake with the futtock shrouds and enables you to point high on a wind when you couldn't possibly do it any other way. Clancy told me these things."

"Does Clancy charge you anything for revealing these mysteries?"

"No, he doesn't really charge me, but I make it up to him in other ways. I let him charge me five dollars for telling me how to bet so as not to lose. He told me to bet a hundred on each boat. That was on the first race—the one that went to a finish. If I won either bet I was to give him another five and if I won both he was to get ten. So he got only ten altogether, because I only won on one of the boats. I lost on the other, so he didn't charge anything on that one."

"Have you always been as intelligent as you are now?"

"Yes, I think so, but sometimes Mr. Rogers thinks I am failing. He thinks it is on account of age and decrepitude; others think it is on account of mental disturbance; others think it is on account of the company I keep; but that cannot be, because I was never particular about the kind of people I went with, yet I was always just as intelligent as I am now, perhaps even more."

"You lose your way sometimes in a long sentence. Do you notice it? You remem"——

"Yes, I know what you mean; it's when I'm working up to wind'ard on a difficult proposition. Clancy says himself that I don't point as high as I used to. But it is no matter; as long as my teeth remain good I don't mind about my intellect; I don't eat with my intellect. But go on—I interrupted you."

"Granting that we now understand why the Reliance won in the first race, what specialty was it, in your judgment, that secured for her the second one?"

"Oh, reaching!"

"Reaching?"

"That is what did it. Reliance is sublime when it comes to reaching. Clancy says so himself. I remember his very words. He said, 'When it comes to that competition isn't possible; she's got a reach like a Christian mob with a nigger in sight.'"

"I am very much obliged to you for clarifying the races and making plain the reasons for the Shamrock's defeats. There was much confusion in the public mind before. Could you go on now, and"——

"Well, no, not now. It would take too much time, and you are pretty busy; so am I. We've done enough for a preliminary; I will finish in a magazine presently. How do you like my style?"

"I think it admirable. It is exceedingly simple and direct and lucid, and it has a special and unusual feature which is golden—that is the word, golden!"

"What is that?"

"You hardly ever use a long word."

"Ah, you've noticed it! Do you guess the secret of that?"

"No, but if you would tell me"——

"I'm paid by the word—do you get the idea?"

"Well, no. I believe I don't."

"I'll show you. In a newspaper you are paid by 'space'— that is your term for it. The longer the words the more space you occupy and the greater is your cash reward. Naturally you hunt the dictionary for long words—it's bread and butter. And naturally you get the habit of using lucrative, vast words —the sesquipedalian habit, so to speak. But when you are paid by the word you can't afford long ones, you understand —it's just simply impoverishing. The family would starve. Would you ever catch me saying 'unincomprehensibility'? Not at twenty cents a word, and don't you make any mistake about it! By my enforced habit of using only the shortest dis-coverable words I should break that nine jointed monster up into modest little, wee, single words and get as much as a dollar and a half out of him. Do you get the idea now?"

"By my halidom, yes—and it is just great, too!"

"I thought you would be able to see it. Do you know, in German literature the average word measures twenty-two syllables? You divine the reason?"

"I do; they pay by space there."

"That's it. It has ruined the language. They are starting a College of Journalism here. Let them look to that matter. Let them inculcate in the young student the principle of charging always by the word. It will result in a noble simplicity of style; it will be the salvation of our beautiful language. Even at twenty cents it will do it; even at that figure it will cramp the average word down to five letters. I would to God some-body would give me a chance to show what kind of a shrink-age I could put on our long words at a dollar a squeeze! Must you go? Don't go. Sit down and let me unshackle my tongue and give you an exhibition. I will undertake to financially em-barrass your paper before I break out my spinnaker."

"I thank you most kindly, but I am afraid I must be going. Are you going to the banquet?"

"I wish I could, but I have to go home. I wish I could see Sir Thomas. He is the only Englishman I have never seen, except Lord Roberts. Gallant men, both."

"What are you going to Italy for?"

"By order of the doctors. It is to get back my wife's health."

"When do you sail?"

"October 24, in the Princess Irene—North German Lloyd."

"A good ship?"

"I designed her myself."

"That settles it. Goodby."

"Goodby."

*August 30, 1903*

# A Dog's Tale

My father was a St. Bernard, my mother was a collie, but I am a Presbyterian. This is what my mother told me; I do not know these nice distinctions myself. To me they are only fine large words meaning nothing. My mother had a fondness for such; she liked to say them, and see other dogs look surprised and envious, as wondering how she got so much education. But, indeed, it was not real education; it was only show: she got the words by listening in the dining-room and drawing-room when there was company, and by going with the children to Sunday-school and listening there; and whenever she heard a large word she said it over to herself many times, and so was able to keep it until there was a dogmatic gathering in the neighborhood, then she would get it off, and surprise and distress them all, from pocket-pup to mastiff, which rewarded her for all her trouble. If there was a stranger he was nearly sure to be suspicious, and when he got his breath again he would ask her what it meant. And she always told him. He was never expecting this, but thought he would catch her; so when she told him, he was the one that looked ashamed, whereas he had thought it was going to be she. The others were always waiting for this, and glad of it and proud of her, for they knew what was going to happen, because they had had experience. When she told the meaning of a big word they were all so taken up with admiration that it never occurred to any dog to doubt if it was the right one; and that was natural, because, for one thing, she answered up so promptly that it seemed like a dictionary speaking, and for another thing, where could they find out whether it was right or not? for she was the only cultivated dog there was. By and by, when I was older, she brought home the word Unintellectual, one time, and worked it pretty hard all the week at different gatherings, making much unhappiness and despondency; and it was at this time that I noticed that during that week she was asked for the meaning at eight different assemblages, and flashed out a fresh definition every time, which showed me that she had more presence of mind than culture, though I said nothing, of course. She had one word which she always kept on hand, and ready, like a life-preserver, a kind of emergency word to strap on when she was likely to get washed overboard in a sudden way—that was the word Synonymous. When she happened to fetch out a long word which had had its day weeks before and its pre-pared meanings gone to her dump-pile, if there was a stranger there of course it knocked him groggy for a couple of min-utes, then he would come to, and by that time she would be away down the wind on another tack, and not expecting any-thing; so when he'd hail and ask her to cash in, I (the only dog on the inside of her game) could see her canvas flicker a moment—but only just a moment,—then it would belly out taut and full, and she would say, as calm as a summer's day, "It's synonymous with supererogation," or some godless long reptile of a word like that, and go placidly about and skim away on the next tack, perfectly comfortable, you know, and leave that stranger looking profane and embarrassed, and the initiated slatting the floor with their tails in unison and their faces transfigured with a holy joy.

And it was the same with phrases. She would drag home a whole phrase, if it had a grand sound, and play it six nights and two matinées, and explain it a new way every time,—which she had to, for all she cared for was the phrase; she wasn't interested in what it meant, and knew those dogs hadn't wit enough to catch her, anyway. Yes, she was a daisy! She got so she wasn't afraid of anything, she had such confi-dence in the ignorance of those creatures. She even brought anecdotes that she had heard the family and the dinner guests laugh and shout over; and as a rule she got the nub of one chestnut hitched onto another chestnut, where, of course, it didn't fit and hadn't any point; and when she delivered the nub she fell over and rolled on the floor and laughed and barked in the most insane way, while I could see that she was wondering to herself why it didn't seem as funny as it did when she first heard it. But no harm was done; the others rolled and barked too, privately ashamed of themselves for not seeing the point, and never suspecting that the fault was not with them and there wasn't any to see.

You can see by these things that she was of a rather vain and frivolous character; still, she had virtues, and enough to make up, I think. She had a kind heart and gentle ways, and never harbored resentments for injuries done her, but put them easily out of her mind and forgot them; and she taught her children her kindly way, and from her we learned also to be brave and prompt in time of danger, and not to run away, but face the peril that threatened friend or stranger, and help him the best we could without stopping to think what the cost might be to us. And she taught us not by words only, but by example, and that is the best way and the surest and the most lasting. Why, the brave things she did, the splendid things! she was just a soldier; and so modest about it—well, you couldn't help admiring her, and you couldn't help imitating her; not even a King Charles spaniel could remain entirely despicable in her society. So, as you see, there was more to her than her education.

## II

When I was well grown, at last, I was sold and taken away, and I never saw her again. She was broken-hearted, and so was I, and we cried; but she comforted me as well as she could, and said we were sent into this world for a wise and good purpose, and must do our duties without repining, take our life as we might find it, live it for the best good of others, and never mind about the results; they were not our affair. She said men who did like this would have a noble and beautiful reward by and by in another world, and although we animals would not go there, to do well and right without reward would give to our brief lives a worthiness and dignity which in itself would be a reward. She had gathered these things from time to time when she had gone to the Sunday-school with the children, and had laid them up in her memory more carefully than she had done with those other words and phrases; and she had studied them deeply, for her good and ours. One may see by this that she had a wise and thoughtful head, for all there was so much lightness and vanity in it.

So we said our farewells, and looked our last upon each other through our tears; and the last thing she said—keeping it for the last to make me remember it the better, I think—was, "In memory of me, when there is a time of danger to another do not think of yourself, think of your mother, and do as she would do."

Do you think I could forget that? No.

### III

It was such a charming home!—my new one; a fine great house, with pictures, and delicate decorations, and rich furniture, and no gloom anywhere, but all the wilderness of dainty colors lit up with flooding sunshine; and the spacious grounds around it, and the great garden—oh, greensward, and noble trees, and flowers, no end! And I was the same as a member of the family; and they loved me, and petted me, and did not give me a new name, but called me by my old one that was dear to me because my mother had given it me—Aileen Mavourneen. She got it out of a song; and the Grays knew that song, and said it was a beautiful name.

Mrs. Gray was thirty, and so sweet and so lovely, you cannot imagine it; and Sadie was ten, and just like her mother, just a darling slender little copy of her, with auburn tails down her back, and short frocks; and the baby was a year old, and plump and dimpled, and fond of me, and never could get enough of hauling on my tail, and hugging me, and laughing out its innocent happiness; and Mr. Gray was thirty-eight, and tall and slender and handsome, a little bald in front, alert, quick in his movements, businesslike, prompt, decided, unsentimental, and with that kind of trim-chiselled face that just seems to glint and sparkle with frosty intellectuality! He was a renowned scientist. I do not know what the word means, but my mother would know how to use it and get effects. She would know how to depress a rat-terrier with it and make a lap-dog look sorry he came. But that is not the best one; the best one was Laboratory. My mother could organize a Trust on that one that would skin the tax-collars off the whole herd. The laboratory was not a book, or a picture, or a place to wash your hands in, as the college president's dog said—no, that is the lavatory; the laboratory is quite different, and is filled with jars, and bottles, and electrics, and wires, and strange machines; and every week other scientists came there and sat in the place, and used the machines, and discussed, and made what they called experiments and discoveries; and often I came, too, and stood around and listened, and tried to learn, for the sake of my mother, and in loving memory of her, although it was a pain to me, as realizing what she was losing out of her life and I gaining nothing at all; for try as I might, I was never able to make anything out of it at all.

Other times I lay on the floor in the mistress's workroom and slept, she gently using me for a footstool, knowing it pleased me, for it was a caress; other times I spent an hour in the nursery, and got well tousled and made happy; other times I watched by the crib there, when the baby was asleep and the nurse out for a few minutes on the baby's affairs; other times I romped and raced through the grounds and the garden with Sadie till we were tired out, then slumbered on the grass in the shade of a tree while she read her book; other times I went visiting among the neighbor dogs,—for there were some most pleasant ones not far away, and one very handsome and courteous and graceful one, a curly-haired Irish setter by the name of Robin Adair, who was a Presbyterian like me, and belonged to the Scotch minister.

The servants in our house were all kind to me and were fond of me, and so, as you see, mine was a pleasant life. There could not be a happier dog than I was, nor a gratefuler one. I will say this for myself, for it is only the truth: I tried in all ways to do well and right, and honor my mother's memory and her teachings, and earn the happiness that had come to me, as best I could.

By and by came my little puppy, and then my cup was full, my happiness was perfect. It was the dearest little waddling thing, and so smooth and soft and velvety, and had such cunning little awkward paws, and such affectionate eyes, and such a sweet and innocent face; and it made me so proud to see how the children and their mother adored it, and fondled it, and exclaimed over every little wonderful thing it did. It did seem to me that life was just too lovely to—

Then came the winter. One day I was standing a watch in the nursery. That is to say, I was asleep on the bed. The baby was asleep in the crib, which was alongside the bed, on the side next the fireplace. It was the kind of crib that has a lofty tent over it made of a gauzy stuff that you can see through. The nurse was out, and we two sleepers were alone. A spark from the wood-fire was shot out, and it lit on the slope of the tent. I suppose a quiet interval followed, then a scream from the baby woke me, and there was that tent flaming up toward the ceiling! Before I could think, I sprang to the floor in my fright, and in a second was half-way to the door; but in the next half-second my mother's farewell was sounding in my ears, and I was back on the bed again. I reached my head through the flames and dragged the baby out by the waist-band, and tugged it along, and we fell to the floor together in a cloud of smoke; I snatched a new hold, and dragged the screaming little creature along and out at the door and around the bend of the hall, and was still tugging away, all excited and happy and proud, when the master's voice shouted,—

"Begone, you cursed beast!" and I jumped to save myself; but he was wonderfully quick, and chased me up, striking furiously at me with his cane, I dodging this way and that, in terror, and at last a strong blow fell upon my left fore leg, which made me shriek and fall, for the moment, helpless; the cane went up for another blow, but never descended, for the nurse's voice rang wildly out, "The nursery's on fire!" and the master rushed away in that direction, and my other bones were saved.

The pain was cruel, but, no matter, I must not lose any time; he might come back at any moment; so I limped on three legs to the other end of the hall, where there was a dark little stairway leading up into a garret where old boxes and such things were kept, as I had heard say, and where people seldom went. I managed to climb up there, then I searched my way through the dark amongst the piles of things, and hid in the secretest place I could find. It was foolish to be afraid there, yet still I was; so afraid that I held in and hardly even whimpered, though it would have been such a comfort to whimper, because that eases the pain, you know. But I could lick my leg, and that did me some good.

For half an hour there was a commotion down-stairs, and

shoutings, and rushing footsteps, and then there was quiet again. Quiet for some minutes, and that was grateful to my spirit, for then my fears began to go down; and fears are worse than pains,—oh, much worse. Then came a sound that froze me! They were calling me—calling me by name—hunting for me!

It was muffled by distance, but that could not take the terror out of it, and it was the most dreadful sound to me that I had ever heard. It went all about, everywhere, down there: along the halls, through all the rooms, in both stories, and in the basement and the cellar; then outside, and further and further away—then back, and all about the house again, and I thought it would never, never stop. But at last it did, hours and hours after the vague twilight of the garret had long ago been blotted out by black darkness.

Then in that blessed stillness my terrors fell little by little away, and I was at peace and slept. It was a good rest I had, but I woke before the twilight had come again. I was feeling fairly comfortable, and I could think out a plan now. I made a very good one; which was, to creep down, all the way down the back stairs, and hide behind the cellar door, and slip out and escape when the iceman came at dawn, whilst he was inside filling the refrigerator; then I would hide all day, and start on my journey when night came; my journey to—well, anywhere where they would not know me and betray me to the master. I was feeling almost cheerful now; then suddenly I thought, Why, what would life be without my puppy!

That was despair. There was no plan for me; I saw that; I must stay where I was; stay, and wait, and take what might come—it was not my affair; that was what life is,—my mother had said it. Then—well, then the calling began again! All my sorrows came back. I said to myself, the master will never forgive. I did not know what I had done to make him so bitter and so unforgiving, yet I judged it was something a dog could not understand, but which was clear to a man and dreadful.

They called and called—days and nights, it seemed to me. So long that the hunger and thirst near drove me mad, and I recognized that I was getting very weak. When you are this way you sleep a great deal, and I did. Once I woke in an awful fright—it seemed to me that the calling was right there in the garret! And so it was: it was Sadie's voice, and she was crying; my name was falling from her lips all broken, poor thing, and I could not believe my ears for the joy of it when I heard her say,

"Come back to us,—oh, come back to us, and forgive—it is all so sad without our—"

I broke in with *such* a grateful little yelp, and the next moment Sadie was plunging and stumbling through the darkness and the lumber and shouting for the family to hear, "She's found, she's found!"

The days that followed—well, they were wonderful. The mother and Sadie and the servants—why, they just seemed to worship me. They couldn't seem to make me a bed that was fine enough; and as for food, they couldn't be satisfied with anything but game and delicacies that were out of season; and every day the friends and neighbors flocked in to hear about my heroism—that was the name they called it by, and it means agriculture. I remember my mother pulling it on a kennel once, and explaining it that way, but didn't say what agriculture was, except that it was synonymous with intramural incandescence; and a dozen times a day Mrs. Gray and Sadie would tell the tale to newcomers, and say I risked my life to save the baby's, and both of us had burns to prove it, and then the company would pass me around and pet me and exclaim about me, and you could see the pride in the eyes of Sadie and her mother; and when the people wanted to know what made me limp, they looked ashamed and changed the subject, and sometimes when people hunted them this way and that way with questions about it, it looked to me as if they were going to cry.

And this was not all the glory; no, the master's friends came, a whole twenty of the most distinguished people, and had me in the laboratory, and discussed me as if I was a kind of discovery; and some of them said it was wonderful in a dumb beast, the finest exhibition of instinct they could call to mind; but the master said, with vehemence, "It's far above instinct; it's *reason*, and many a man, privileged to be saved and go with you and me to a better world by right of its possession, has less of it than this poor silly quadruped that's foreordained to perish"; and then he laughed, and said, "Why, look at me—I'm a sarcasm! bless you, with all my grand intelligence, the only thing I inferred was that the dog had gone mad and was destroying the child, whereas but for the beast's intelligence—it's *reason*, I tell you!—the child would have perished!"

They disputed and disputed, and *I* was the very centre and subject of it all, and I wished my mother could know that this grand honor had come to me; it would have made her proud.

Then they discussed optics, as they called it, and whether a certain injury to the brain would produce blindness or not, but they could not agree about it, and said they must test it by experiment by and by; and next they discussed plants, and that interested me, because in the summer Sadie and I had planted seeds—I helped her dig the holes, you know,—and after days and days a little shrub or a flower came up there, and it was a wonder how that could happen; but it did, and I wished I could talk,—I would have told those people about it and shown them how much I knew, and been all alive with the subject; but I didn't care for the optics; it was dull, and when they came back to it again it bored me, and I went to sleep.

Pretty soon it was spring, and sunny and pleasant and lovely, and the sweet mother and the children patted me and the puppy good-by, and went away on a journey and a visit to their kin, and the master wasn't any company for us, but we played together and had good times, and the servants were kind and friendly, so we got along quite happily and counted the days and waited for the family.

And one day those men came again, and said now for the test, and they took the puppy to the laboratory, and I limped three-leggedly along, too, feeling proud, for any attention shown the puppy was a pleasure to me, of course. They discussed and experimented, and then suddenly the puppy shrieked, and they set him on the floor, and he went staggering around, with his head all bloody, and the master clapped his hands and shouted:

"There, I've won—confess it! He's as blind as a bat!"

And they all said,

"It's so—you've proved your theory, and suffering humanity owes you a great debt from henceforth," and they crowded around him, and wrung his hand cordially and thankfully, and praised him.

But I hardly saw or heard these things, for I ran at once to my little darling, and snuggled close to it where it lay, and licked the blood, and it put its head against mine, whimpering softly, and I knew in my heart it was a comfort to it in its pain and trouble to feel its mother's touch, though it could not see me. Then it drooped down, presently, and its little velvet nose rested upon the floor, and it was still, and did not move any more.

Soon the master stopped discussing a moment, and rang in the footman, and said, "Bury it in the far corner of the garden," and then went on with the discussion, and I trotted after the footman, very happy and grateful, for I knew the puppy was out of its pain now, because it was asleep. We went far down the garden to the furthest end, where the children and the nurse and the puppy and I used to play in the summer in the shade of a great elm, and there the footman dug a hole, and I saw he was going to plant the puppy, and I was glad, because it would grow and come up a fine handsome dog, like Robin Adair, and be a beautiful surprise for the family when they came home; so I tried to help him dig, but my lame leg was no good, being stiff, you know, and you have to have two, or it is no use. When the footman had finished and covered little Robin up, he patted my head, and there were tears in his eyes, and he said, "Poor little doggie, you SAVED *his* child."

I have watched two whole weeks, and he doesn't come up! This last week a fright has been stealing upon me. I think there is something terrible about this. I do not know what it is, but the fear makes me sick, and I cannot eat, though the servants bring me the best of food; and they pet me so, and even come in the night, and cry, and say, "Poor doggie—do give it up and come home; *don't* break our hearts!" and all this terrifies me the more, and makes me sure something has happened. And I am so weak; since yesterday I cannot stand on my feet any more. And within this hour the servants, looking toward the sun where it was sinking out of sight and the night chill coming on, said things I could not understand, but they carried something cold to my heart.

"Those poor creatures! They do not suspect. They will come home in the morning, and eagerly ask for the little doggie that did the brave deed, and who of us will be strong enough to say the truth to them: 'The humble little friend is gone where go the beasts that perish.'"

*December 1903*

# "Was the World Made for Man?"

"Alfred Russell Wallace's revival of the theory that this earth is at the centre of the stellar universe, and is the only habitable globe, has aroused great interest in the world."—*Literary Digest.*

"For ourselves we do thoroughly believe that man, as he lives just here on this tiny earth, is in essence and possibilities the most sublime existence in all the range of non-divine being—the chief love and delight of God."—*Chicago "Interior,"* (Presb.)

I seem to be the only scientist and theologian still remaining to be heard from on this important matter of whether the world was made for man or not. I feel that it is time for me to speak.

I stand almost with the others. They believe the world was made for man, I believe it likely that it was made for man; they think there is proof, astronomical mainly, that it was made for man, I think there is evidence only, not proof, that it was made for him. It is too early, yet, to arrange the verdict, the returns are not all in. When they are all in, I think they will show that the world was made for man; but we must not hurry, we must patiently wait till they are all in.

Now as far as we have got, astronomy is on our side. Mr. Wallace has clearly shown this. He has clearly shown two things: that the world was made for man, and that the universe was made for the world—to stiddy it, you know. The astronomy part is settled, and cannot be challenged.

We come now to the geological part. This is the one where the evidence is not all in, yet. It is coming in, hourly, daily, coming in all the time, but naturally it comes with geological carefulness and deliberation, and we must not be impatient, we must not get excited, we must be calm, and wait. To lose our tranquillity will not hurry geology; nothing hurries geology.

It takes a long time to prepare a world for man, such a thing is not done in a day. Some of the great scientists, carefully ciphering the evidences furnished by geology, have arrived at the conviction that our world is prodigiously old, and they may be right, but Lord Kelvin is not of their opinion. He takes a cautious, conservative view, in order to be on the

572

safe side, and feels sure it is not so old as they think. As Lord
Kelvin is the highest authority in science now living, I think
we must yield to him and accept his view. He does not con-
cede that the world is more than a hundred million years old.
He believes it is that old, but not older. Lyell believed that
our race was introduced into the world 31,000 years ago,
Herbert Spencer makes it 32,000. Lord Kelvin agrees with
Spencer.

Very well. According to these figures it took 99,968,000
years to prepare the world for man, impatient as the Creator
doubtless was to see him and admire him. But a large enterprise like this has to be conducted warily, painstakingly, logically. It was foreseen that man would have to have the oyster.
Therefore the first preparation was made for the oyster. Very
well, you cannot make an oyster out of whole cloth, you must
make the oyster's ancestor first. This is not done in a day. You
must make a vast variety of invertebrates, to start with—belemnites, trilobites, jebusites, amalekites, and that sort of fry,
and put them to soak in a primary sea, and wait and see what
will happen. Some will be a disappointment—the belemnites,
the ammonites and such; they will be failures, they will die
out and become extinct, in the course of the 19,000,000 years
covered by the experiment, but all is not lost, for the amalekites will fetch the home-stake; they will develop gradually
into encrinites, and stalactites, and blatherskites, and one
thing and another as the mighty ages creep on and the Ar-
chaean and the Cambrian Periods pile their lofty crags in the
primordial seas, and at last the first grand stage in the preparation of the world for man stands completed, the Oyster is
done. An oyster has hardly any more reasoning power than a
scientist has; and so it is reasonably certain that this one
jumped to the conclusion that the nineteen-million years was
a preparation for *him*; but that would be just like an oyster,
which is the most conceited animal there is, except man. And
anyway, this one could not know, at that early date, that he
was only an incident in a scheme, and that there was some
more to the scheme, yet.

The oyster being achieved, the next thing to be arranged
for in the preparation of the world for man, was fish. Fish,
and coal—to fry it with. So the Old Silurian seas were

opened up to breed the fish in, and at the same time the great
work of building Old Red Sandstone mountains 80,000 feet
high to cold-storage their fossils in was begun. This latter was
quite indispensable, for there would be no end of failures
again, no end of extinctions—millions of them—and it
would be cheaper and less trouble to can them in the rocks
than keep tally of them in a book. One does not build the coal
beds and 80,000 feet of perpendicular Old Red Sandstone in
a brief time—no, it took twenty million years. In the first
place, a coal bed is a slow and troublesome and tiresome
thing to construct. You have to grow prodigious forests of
tree-ferns and reeds and calamites and such things in a marshy
region; then you have to sink them under out of sight and let
them rot; then you have to turn the streams on them, so as to
bury them under several feet of sediment, and the sediment
must have time to harden and turn to rock; next you must
grow another forest on top, then sink it and put on another
layer of sediment and harden it; then more forest and more
rock, layer upon layer, three miles deep—ah, indeed it is a
sickening slow job to build a coal-measure and do it right!

So the millions of years drag on; and meantime the fish-
culture is lazying along and frazzling out in a way to make a
person tired. You have developed ten thousand kinds of fishes
from the oyster; and come to look, you have raised nothing
but fossils, nothing but extinctions. There is nothing left alive
and progressive but a ganoid or two and perhaps half a dozen
asteroids. Even the cat wouldn't eat such.

Still, it is no great matter; there is plenty of time, yet, and
they will develop into something tasty before man is ready for
them. Even a ganoid can be depended on for that, when he is
not going to be called on for sixty million years.

The Palaeozoic time-limit having now been reached, it was
necessary to begin the next stage in the preparation of the
world for man, by opening up the Mesozoic Age and institut-
ing some reptiles. For man would need reptiles. Not to eat,
but to develop himself from. This being the most important
detail of the scheme, a spacious liberality of time was set apart
for it—thirty million years. What wonders followed! From
the remaining ganoids and asteroids and alkaloids were developed by slow and steady and pains-taking culture those

stupendous saurians that used to prowl about the steamy world in those remote ages, with their snaky heads reared forty feet in the air and sixty feet of body and tail racing and thrashing after. All gone, now, alas—all extinct, except the little handful of Arkansawrians left stranded and lonely with us here upon this far-flung verge and fringe of time.

Yes, it took thirty million years and twenty million reptiles to get one that would stick long enough to develop into something else and let the scheme proceed to the next step.

Then the Pterodactyl burst upon the world in all his impressive solemnity and grandeur, and all Nature recognized that the Cainozoic threshold was crossed and a new Period open for business, a new stage begun in the preparation of the globe for man. It may be that the Pterodactyl thought the thirty million years had been intended as a preparation for himself, for there was nothing too foolish for a Pterodactyl to imagine, but he was in error, the preparation was for man. Without doubt the Pterodactyl attracted great attention, for even the least observant could see that there was the making of a bird in him. And so it turned out. Also the makings of a mammal, in time. One thing we have to say to his credit, that in the matter of picturesqueness he was the triumph of his Period; he wore wings and had teeth, and was a starchy and wonderful mixture altogether, a kind of long-distance premonitory symptom of Kipling's marine:

'E isn't one o' the reg'lar Line, nor 'e isn't one of the crew,
'E's a kind of a giddy harumfrodite—soldier an' sailor too!

From this time onward for nearly another thirty million years the preparation moved briskly. From the Pterodactyl was developed the bird; from the bird the kangaroo, from the kangaroo the other marsupials; from these the mastodon, the megatherium, the giant sloth, the Irish elk, and all that crowd that you make useful and instructive fossils out of—then came the first great Ice Sheet, and they all retreated before it and crossed over the bridge at Behring's strait and wandered around over Europe and Asia and died. All except a few, to carry on the preparation with. Six Glacial Periods with two million years between Periods chased these poor orphans up and down and about the earth, from weather to weather—

from tropic swelter at the poles to Arctic frost at the equator and back again and to and fro, they never knowing what kind of weather was going to turn up next; and if ever they settled down anywhere the whole continent suddenly sank under them without the least notice and they had to trade places with the fishes and scramble off to where the seas had been, and scarcely a dry rag on them; and when there was nothing else doing a volcano would let go and fire them out from wherever they had located. They led this unsettled and irritating life for twenty-five million years, half the time afloat, half the time aground, and always wondering what it was all for, they never suspecting, of course, that it was a preparation for man and had to be done just so or it wouldn't be any proper and harmonious place for him when he arrived.

And at last came the monkey, and anybody could see that man wasn't far off, now. And in truth that was so. The monkey went on developing for close upon 5,000,000 years, and then turned into a man—to all appearances.

Such is the history of it. Man has been here 32,000 years. That it took a hundred million years to prepare the world for him is proof that that is what it was done for. I suppose it is. I dunno. If the Eiffel tower were now representing the world's age, the skin of paint on the pinnacle-knob at its summit would represent man's share of that age; and anybody would perceive that that skin was what the tower was built for. I reckon they would, I dunno.

*1903*

# *Italian Without a Master*

It is almost a fortnight now that I am domiciled in a medi-
æval villa in the country, a mile or two from Florence. I cannot speak the language; I am too old now to learn how, also
too busy when I am busy, and too indolent when I am not;
wherefore some will imagine that I am having a dull time of
it. But it is not so. The "help" are all natives; they talk Italian
to me, I answer in English; I do not understand them, they
do not understand me, consequently no harm is done, and
everybody is satisfied. In order to be just and fair, I throw in
an Italian word when I have one, and this has a good influence. I get the word out of the morning paper. I have to use
it while it is fresh, for I find that Italian words do not keep in
this climate. They fade toward night, and next morning they
are gone. But it is no matter; I get a new one out of the paper
before breakfast, and thrill the domestics with it while it lasts.
I have no dictionary, and I do not want one; I can select my
words by the sound, or by orthographic aspect. Many of
them have a French or German or English look, and these are
the ones I enslave for the day's service. That is, as a rule. Not
always. If I find a learnable phrase that has an imposing look
and warbles musically along I do not care to know the meaning of it; I pay it out to the first applicant, knowing that if
I pronounce it carefully *he* will understand it, and that's
enough.

Yesterday's word was *avanti*. It sounds Shakespearian, and
probably means Avaunt and quit my sight. To-day I have a
whole phrase: *sono dispiacentissimo*. I do not know what it
means, but it seems to fit in everywhere and give satisfaction.
Although as a rule my words and phrases are good for one
day and train only, I have several that stay by me all the time,
for some unknown reason, and these come very handy when I
get into a long conversation and need things to fire up with in
monotonous stretches. One of the best ones is *Dov' è il gatto*.
It nearly always produces a pleasant surprise, therefore I save
it up for places where I want to express applause or admiration. The fourth word has a French sound, and I think the
phrase means "that takes the cake."

During my first week in the deep and dreamy stillness of this woodsy and flowery place I was without news of the out-side world, and was well content without it. It had been four weeks since I had seen a newspaper, and this lack seemed to give life a new charm and grace, and to saturate it with a feeling verging upon actual delight. Then came a change that was to be expected: the appetite for news began to rise again, after this invigorating rest. I had to feed it, but I was not willing to let it make me its helpless slave again; I determined to put it on a diet, and a strict and limited one. So I examined an Italian paper, with the idea of feeding it on that, and on that exclusively. On that exclusively, and without help of a dictionary. In this way I should surely be well protected against overloading and indigestion.

A glance at the telegraphic page filled me with encourage-ment. There were no scare-heads. That was good—supremely good. But there were headings—one-liners and two-liners—and that was good too; for without these, one must do as one does with a German paper—pay out precious time in finding out what an article is about, only to discover, in many cases, that there is nothing in it of interest to you. The headline is a valuable thing.

Necessarily we are all fond of murders, scandals, swindles, robberies, explosions, collisions, and all such things, when we know the people, and when they are neighbors and friends, but when they are strangers we do not get any great pleasure out of them, as a rule. Now the trouble with an American paper is that it has no discrimination; it rakes the whole earth for blood and garbage, and the result is that you are daily overfed and suffer a surfeit. By habit you stow this muck ev-ery day, but you come by and by to take no vital interest in it—indeed, you almost get tired of it. As a rule, forty-nine-fiftieths of it concerns strangers only—people away off yonder, a thousand miles, two thousand miles, ten thousand miles from where you are. Why, when you come to think of it, who cares what becomes of those people? I would not give the assassination of one personal friend for a whole massacre of those others. And, to my mind, one relative or neighbor mixed up in a scandal is more interesting than a whole Sodom and Gomorrah of outlanders gone rotten. Give me the home product every time.

Very well. I saw at a glance that the Florentine paper would suit me: five out of six of its scandals and tragedies were local; they were adventures of one's very neighbors, one might almost say one's friends. In the matter of world news there was not too much, but just about enough. I subscribed. I have had no occasion to regret it. Every morning I get all the news I need for the day; sometimes from the headlines, sometimes from the text. I have never had to call for a dictionary yet. I read the paper with ease. Often I do not quite understand, often some of the details escape me, but no matter, I get the idea. I will cut out a passage or two, then you will see how limpid the language is:

> **Il ritorno dei Reali d'Italia**
> Elargizione del Re all' Ospedale Italiano

The first line means that the Italian sovereigns are coming back—they have been to England. The second line seems to mean that they enlarged the King at the Italian hospital. With a banquet, I suppose. An English banquet has that effect. Further:

> **Il ritorno dei Sovrani
> a Roma**
> ROMA, 24, ore 22,50. - I Sovrani e le Principessine Reali si attendono a Roma domani alle ore 15,51.

Return of the sovereigns to Rome, you see. Date of the telegram, Rome, November 24, ten minutes before twenty-three o'clock. The telegram seems to say, "The Sovereigns and the Royal Children expect themselves at Rome tomorrow at fifty-one minutes after fifteen o'clock."

I do not know about Italian time, but I judge it begins at midnight and runs through the twenty-four hours without

breaking bulk. In the following ad. the theatres open at half
past twenty. If these are not matinées, 20.30 must mean 8.30
P.M., by my reckoning.

The whole of that is intelligible to me — and sane and rational, too — except the remark about the Inauguration of a Russian Cheese. That one oversizes my hand. Gimme five cards.

This is a four-page paper; and as it is set in long primer
leaded and has a page of advertisements, there is no room for
the crimes, disasters, and general sweepings of the outside
world — thanks be! To-day I find only a single importation of
the off-color sort:

Twenty-seven years old, and scomparve — scampered — on
the 9th November. You see by the added detail that she departed with her coachman. I hope Sarebbe has not made a

mistake, but I am afraid the chances are that she has. *Sono dispiacentissimo*.

There are several fires; also a couple of accidents. This is one of them:

```
┌─────────────────────────────────────────┐
│  Grave disgrazia sul Ponte Vecchio      │
│                                          │
│     Stamattina, circa le 7,30, mentre   │
│  Giuseppe Sciatti, di anni 55, di       │
│  Casellina e Torri, passava dal Ponte   │
│  Vecchio, stando seduto sopra un        │
│  barroccio carico di verdura, perse     │
│  l' equilibrio e cadde al suolo,        │
│  rimanendo con la gamba destra sotto    │
│  una ruota del veicolo.                 │
│     Lo Sciatti fu subito raccolto da    │
│  alcuni cittadini, che, per mezzo della │
│  pubblica vettura n. 365, lo            │
│  trasportarono a San Giovanni di Dio.   │
│     Ivi il medico di guardia gli        │
│  riscontrò la frattura della gamba      │
│  destra e alcune lievi escoriazioni     │
│  giudicandolo guaribile in 50 giorni    │
│  salvo complicazioni.                   │
└─────────────────────────────────────────┘
```

What it seems to say is this: "Serious Disgrace on the Old Old Bridge. This morning about 7.30, Mr. Joseph Sciatti, aged 55, of Casellina and Torri, while standing up in a sitting posture on top of a carico barrow of verdure (foliage? hay? vegetables?), lost his equilibrium and fell on himself, arriving with his left leg under one of the wheels of the vehicle.

"Said Sciatti was suddenly harvested (gathered in?) by several citizens, who by means of public cab No. 365 transported him to St. John of God."

Paragraph No. 3 is a little obscure, but I think it says that the medico set the broken left leg—right enough, since there was nothing the matter with the other one—and that several are encouraged to hope that fifty days will fetch him around in quite giudicandolo-guaribile way, if no complications intervene.

I am sure I hope so myself.

There is a great and peculiar charm about reading news-scraps in a language which you are not acquainted with—the charm that always goes with the mysterious and the uncertain. You can never be absolutely sure of the meaning of anything you read in such circumstances; you are chasing an alert and gamy riddle all the time, and the baffling turns and dodges of the prey make the life of the hunt. A dictionary would spoil it. Sometimes a single word of doubtful purport will cast a veil of dreamy and golden uncertainty over a whole paragraph of cold and practical certainties, and leave steeped in a haunting and adorable mystery an incident which had been vulgar and commonplace but for that benefaction. Would you be wise to draw a dictionary on that gracious word? would you be properly grateful?

After a couple of days' rest I now come back to my subject and seek a case in point. I find it without trouble, in the morning paper; a cablegram from Chicago and Indiana by way of Paris. All the words save one are guessable by a person ignorant of Italian:

**Revolverate in teatro**

PARIGI, 27. - La *Patrie* ha da Chicago: Il guardiano del teatro dell'opera di Wallace (Indiana), avendo voluto espellere uno spettatore che continuava a fumare malgrado il divieto, questo spalleggiato dai suoi amici tirò diversi colpi di rivoltella. Il guardiano rispose. Nacque una scarica generale. Grande panico fra gli spettatori. Nessun ferito.

*Translation.* — "REVOLVERATION IN THEATRE. *Paris. 27th.* La Patrie has from Chicago: The cop of the theatre of the opera of Wallace, Indiana, had willed to expel a spectator which continued to smoke in spite of the prohibition, who, spalleggiato by his friends, tirò (Fr. *tiré*, Anglice *pulled*) manifold revolver-shots. The cop responded. Result, a general scare; great panic among the spectators. Nobody hurt."

It is bettable that that harmless cataclysm in the theatre of the opera of Wallace, Indiana, excited not a person in Europe but me, and so came near to not being worth cabling to Florence by way of France. But it does excite me. It excites me because I cannot make out, for sure, what it was that moved that spectator to resist the officer. I was gliding along smoothly and without obstruction or accident, until I came to that word spalleggiato, then the bottom fell out. You notice what a rich gloom, what a sombre and pervading mystery, that word sheds all over the whole Wallachian tragedy. That is the charm of the thing, that is the delight of it. This is where you begin, this is where you revel. You can guess and guess, and have all the fun you like; you need not be afraid there will be an end to it; none is possible, for no amount of guessing will ever furnish you a meaning for that word that you can be sure is the right one. All the other words give you hints, by their form, their sound, or their spelling—this one doesn't, this one throws out no hints, this one keeps its secret. If there is even the slightest slight shadow of a hint anywhere, it lies in the very meagrely suggestive fact that spalleggiato carries our word "egg" in its stomach. Well, make the most out of it, and then where are you at? You conjecture that the spectator which was smoking in spite of the prohibition and become reprohibited by the guardians, was "egged on" by his friends, and that it was owing to that evil influence that he initiated the revolveration in theatre that has galloped under the sea and come crashing through the European press without exciting anybody but me. But are you sure, are you dead sure, that that was the way of it? No. Then the uncertainty remains, the mystery abides, and with it the charm. Guess again.

If I had a phrase-book of a really satisfactory sort I would study it, and not give all my free time to undictionarial readings, but there is no such work on the market. The existing phrase-books are inadequate. They are well enough as far as they go, but when you fall down and skin your leg they don't tell you what to say.

*January 2, 1904*

# Saint Joan of Arc

The evidence furnished at the Trials and Rehabilitation sets forth Joan of Arc's strange and beautiful history in clear and minute detail. Among all the multitude of biographies that freight the shelves of the world's libraries, *this is the only one whose validity is confirmed to us by oath*. It gives us a vivid picture of a career and a personality of so extraordinary a character that we are helped to accept them as actualities by the very fact that both are beyond the inventive reach of fiction. The public part of the career occupied only a mere breath of time — it covered but two years; but what a career it was! The personality which made it possible is one to be reverently studied, loved, and marvelled at, but not to be wholly understood and accounted for by even the most searching analysis.

In Joan of Arc at the age of sixteen there was no promise of a romance. She lived in a dull little village on the frontiers of civilization; she had been nowhere and had seen nothing; she knew none but simple shepherd folk; she had never seen a person of note; she hardly knew what a soldier looked like; she had never ridden a horse, nor had a warlike weapon in her hand; she could neither read nor write: she could spin and sew; she knew her catechism and her prayers and the fabulous histories of the saints, and this was all her learning. That was Joan at sixteen. What did she know of law? of evidence? of courts? of the attorney's trade? of legal procedure? Nothing. Less than nothing. Thus exhaustively equipped with ignorance, she went before the court at Toul to contest a false

NOTE. — The Official Record of the Trials and Rehabilitation of Joan of Arc is the most remarkable history that exists in any language; yet there are few people in the world who can say they have read it: in England and America it has hardly been heard of.

Three hundred years ago Shakespeare did not know the true story of Joan of Arc; in his day it was unknown even in France. For four hundred years it existed rather as a vaguely defined romance than as definite and authentic history. The true story remained buried in the official archives of France from the Rehabilitation of 1456 until Quicherat dug it out and gave it to the world two generations ago, in lucid and understandable modern French. It is a deeply fascinating story. But only in the Official Trials and Rehabilitation can it be found in its entirety. — M. T.

charge of breach of promise of marriage; she conducted her cause herself, without any one's help or advice or any one's friendly sympathy, and won it. She called no witnesses of her own, but vanquished the prosecution by using with deadly effectiveness its own testimony. The astonished judge threw the case out of court, and spoke of her as "this marvellous child."

She went to the veteran Commandant of Vaucouleurs and demanded an escort of soldiers, saying she must march to the help of the King of France, since she was commissioned of God to win back his lost kingdom for him and set the crown upon his head. The Commandant said, "What, you? you are only a child." And he advised that she be taken back to her village and have her ears boxed. But she said she must obey God, and would come again, and again, and yet again, and finally she would get the soldiers. She said truly. In time he yielded, after months of delay and refusal, and gave her the soldiers; and took off his sword and gave her that, and said, "Go—and let come what may." She made her long and perilous journey through the enemy's country, and spoke with the King, and convinced him. Then she was summoned before the University of Poitiers to prove that she *was* commissioned of God and not of Satan, and daily during three weeks she sat before that learned congress unafraid, and capably answered their deep questions out of her ignorant but able head and her simple and honest heart; and again she won her case, and with it the wondering admiration of all that august company.

And now, aged seventeen, she was made Commander-in-Chief, with a prince of the royal house and the veteran generals of France for subordinates; and at the head of the first army she had ever seen, she marched to Orleans, carried the commanding fortresses of the enemy by storm in three desperate assaults, and in ten days raised a siege which had defied the might of France for seven months.

After a tedious and insane delay caused by the King's instability of character and the treacherous counsels of his ministers, she got permission to take the field again. She took Jargeau by storm; then Meung; she forced Beaugency to surrender; then—in the open field—she won the memorable victory of Patay against Talbot "the English lion," and broke the back of the Hundred Years' War. It was a campaign which cost but seven weeks of time; yet the political results would have been cheap if the time expended had been fifty years. Patay, that unsung and now long-forgotten battle, was the Moscow of the English power in France; from the blow struck that day it was destined never to recover. It was the beginning of the end of an alien dominion which had ridden France intermittently for three hundred years.

Then followed the great campaign of the Loire, the capture of Troyes by assault, and the triumphal march past surrendering towns and fortresses to Rheims, where Joan put the crown upon her King's head in the Cathedral, amid wild public rejoicings, and with her old peasant father there to see these things and believe his eyes if he could. She had restored the crown and the lost sovereignty; the King was grateful for once in his shabby poor life, and asked her to name her reward and have it. She asked for nothing for herself, but begged that the taxes of her native village might be remitted forever. The prayer was granted, and the promise kept for three hundred and sixty years. Then it was broken, and remains broken to-day. France was very poor then, she is very rich now; but she has been collecting those taxes for more than a hundred years.

Joan asked one other favor: that now that her mission was fulfilled she might be allowed to go back to her village and take up her humble life again with her mother and the friends of her childhood; for she had no pleasure in the cruelties of war, and the sight of blood and suffering wrung her heart. Sometimes in battle she did not draw her sword, lest in the splendid madness of the onset she might forget herself and take an enemy's life with it. In the Rouen Trials, one of her quaintest speeches—coming from the gentle and girlish source it did—was her naïve remark that she had "never killed any one." Her prayer for leave to go back to the rest and peace of her village home was not granted.

Then she wanted to march at once upon Paris, take it, and drive the English out of France. She was hampered in all the ways that treachery and the King's vacillation could devise, but she forced her way to Paris at last, and fell badly wounded in a successful assault upon one of the gates. Of course her men lost heart at once—she was the only heart they had. They fell back. She begged to be allowed to remain at the front, saying victory was sure. "I will take Paris now or die!" she said. But she was removed from the field by force; the King ordered a retreat, and actually disbanded his army. In accordance with a beautiful old military custom Joan devoted her silver armor and hung it up in the Cathedral of St. Denis. Its great days were over.

Then, by command, she followed the King and his frivolous court and endured a gilded captivity for a time, as well as her free spirit could; and whenever inaction became unbearable she gathered some men together and rode away and assaulted a stronghold and captured it.

At last in a sortie against the enemy, from Compiègne, on the 24th of May (when she was turned eighteen), she was herself captured, after a gallant fight. It was her last battle. She was to follow the drums no more.

Thus ended the briefest epoch-making military career known to history. It lasted only a year and a month, but it found France an English province, and furnishes the reason that France is France to-day and not an English province still. Thirteen months! It was indeed a short career; but in the centuries that have since elapsed five hundred millions of Frenchmen have lived and died blest by the benefactions it conferred; and so long as France shall endure, the mighty debt must grow. And France is grateful; we often hear her say it. Also thrifty: she collects the Domrémy taxes.

Joan was fated to spend the rest of her life behind bolts and bars. She was a prisoner of war, not a criminal, therefore hers was recognized as an honorable captivity. By the rules of war she must be held to ransom, and a fair price could not be refused if offered. John of Luxembourg paid her the just compliment of requiring a prince's ransom for her. In that day that phrase represented a definite sum—61,125 francs. It was of course supposable that either the King or grateful France, or both, would fly with the money and set their fair young benefactor free. But this did not happen. In five and a half months neither King nor country stirred a hand nor offered a penny. Twice Joan tried to escape. Once by a trick she succeeded for a moment, and locked her jailer in behind her, but she was discovered and caught; in the other case she let herself down from a tower sixty feet high, but her rope was too short, and she got a fall that disabled her and she could not get away.

Finally, Cauchon, Bishop of Beauvais, paid the money and bought Joan—ostensibly for the Church, to be tried for wearing male attire and for other impieties, but really for the English, the enemy into whose hands the poor girl was so piteously anxious not to fall. She was now shut up in the dungeons of the Castle of Rouen and kept in an iron cage, with her hands and feet and neck chained to a pillar; and from that time forth during all the months of her imprisonment, till the end, several rough English soldiers stood guard over her night and day—and not outside her room, but in it. It was a dreary and hideous captivity, but it did not conquer her: nothing could break that invincible spirit. From first to last she was a prisoner a year; and she spent the last three months of it on trial for her life before a formidable array of ecclesiastical judges, and disputing the ground with them foot by foot and inch by inch with brilliant generalship and dauntless pluck. The spectacle of that solitary girl, forlorn and friendless, without advocate or adviser, and without the help and guidance of any copy of the charges brought against her or rescript of the complex and voluminous daily proceedings of the court to modify the crushing strain upon her astonishing memory, fighting that long battle serene and undismayed against these colossal odds, stands alone in its pathos and its sublimity; it has nowhere its mate, either in the annals of fact or in the inventions of fiction.

And how fine and great were the things she daily said, how fresh and crisp—and she so worn in body, so starved, and tired, and harried! They run through the whole gamut of feeling and expression—from scorn and defiance, uttered with soldierly fire and frankness, all down the scale to wounded dignity clothed in words of noble pathos; as, when her patience was exhausted by the pestering delvings and gropings and searchings of her persecutors to find out what kind of devil's witchcraft she had employed to rouse the war spirit in her timid soldiers, she burst out with, "What I said was, *'Ride these English down'*—and I did it myself!" and as, when insultingly asked why it was that *her* standard had place at the crowning of the King in the Cathedral of Rheims rather than the standards of the other captains, she uttered that touching speech, *"It had borne the burden, it had earned the honor"*—a phrase which fell from her lips without premeditation, yet whose moving beauty and simple grace it would bankrupt the arts of language to surpass.

Although she was on trial for her life, she was the only witness called on either side; the only witness summoned to testify before a packed jury commissioned with a definite task: to find her guilty, whether she was guilty or not. She must be convicted out of her own mouth, there being no other way to accomplish it. Every advantage that learning has over ignorance, age over youth, experience over inexperience, chicane over artlessness, every trick and trap and gin devisable by malice and the cunning of sharp intellects practised in setting snares for the unwary—all these were employed against her without shame; and when these arts were one by one defeated by the marvellous intuitions of her alert and penetrating mind, Bishop Cauchon stooped to a final baseness which it degrades human speech to describe: a priest who pretended to come from the region of her own home and to be a pitying friend and anxious to help her in her sore need was smuggled into her cell, and he misused his sacred office to steal her confidence; she confided to him the things sealed from revealment by her Voices, and which her prosecutors had tried so long in vain to trick her into betraying. A concealed confederate set it all down and delivered it to Cauchon, who used Joan's secrets, thus obtained, for her ruin.

Throughout the Trials, whatever the foredoomed witness said was twisted from its true meaning when possible, and made to tell against her; and whenever an answer of hers was beyond the reach of twisting it was not allowed to go upon the record. It was upon one of these latter occasions that she uttered that pathetic reproach—to Cauchon: "Ah, you set down everything that is against me, but you will not set down what is for me."

That this untrained young creature's genius for war was

wonderful, and her generalship worthy to rank with the ripe products of a tried and trained military experience, we have the sworn testimony of two of her veteran subordinates—one, the Duc d'Alençon, the other the greatest of the French generals of the time, Dunois, Bastard of Orleans; that her genius was as great—possibly even greater—in the subtle warfare of the forum we have for witness the records of the Rouen Trials, that protracted exhibition of intellectual fence maintained with credit against the master-minds of France; that her moral greatness was peer to her intellect we call the Rouen Trials again to witness, with their testimony to a fortitude which patiently and steadfastly endured during twelve weeks the wasting forces of captivity, chains, loneliness, sickness, darkness, hunger, thirst, cold, shame, insult, abuse, broken sleep, treachery, ingratitude, exhausting sieges of cross-examination, the threat of torture, with the rack before her and the executioner standing ready: yet never surrendering, never asking quarter, the frail wreck of her as unconquerable the last day as was her invincible spirit the first.

Great as she was in so many ways, she was perhaps even greatest of all in the lofty things just named—her patient endurance, her steadfastness, her granite fortitude. We may not hope to easily find her mate and twin in these majestic qualities; where we lift our eyes highest we find only a strange and curious contrast—there in the captive eagle beating his broken wings on the Rock of St. Helena.

The Trials ended with her condemnation. But as she had conceded nothing, confessed nothing, this was victory for her, defeat for Cauchon. But his evil resources were not yet exhausted. She was persuaded to agree to sign a paper of slight import, then by treachery a paper was substituted which contained a recantation and a detailed confession of everything which had been charged against her during the Trials and denied and repudiated by her persistently during the three months; and this false paper she ignorantly signed. This was a victory for Cauchon. He followed it eagerly and pitilessly up by at once setting a trap for her which she could not escape. When she realized this she gave up the long struggle, denounced the treason which had been practised against her, repudiated the false confession, reasserted the truth of the testimony which she had given in the Trials, and went to her martyrdom with the peace of God in her tired heart, and on her lips endearing words and loving prayers for the cur she had crowned and the nation of ingrates she had saved.

When the fires rose about her and she begged for a cross for her dying lips to kiss, it was not a friend but an enemy, not a Frenchman but an alien, not a comrade in arms but an English soldier, that answered that pathetic prayer. He broke a stick across his knee, bound the pieces together in the form of the symbol she so loved, and gave it her; and his gentle deed is not forgotten, nor will be.

Twenty-five years afterward the Process of Rehabilitation was instituted, there being a growing doubt as to the validity of a sovereignty that had been rescued and set upon its feet by a person who had been proven by the Church to be a witch and a familiar of evil spirits. Joan's old generals, her secretary, several aged relations and other villagers of Domrémy, surviving judges and secretaries of the Rouen and Poitiers Processes—a cloud of witnesses, some of whom had been her enemies and persecutors,—came and made oath and testified; and what they said was written down. In that sworn testimony the moving and beautiful history of Joan of Arc is laid bare, from her childhood to her martyrdom. From the verdict she rises stainlessly pure, in mind and heart, in speech and deed and spirit, and will so endure to the end of time.

She is the Wonder of the Ages. And when we consider her origin, her early circumstances, her sex, and that she did all the things upon which her renown rests while she was still a young girl, we recognize that while our race continues she will be also the *Riddle* of the Ages. When we set about accounting for a Napoleon or a Shakespeare or a Raphael or a Wagner or an Edison or other extraordinary person, we understand that the measure of his talent will not explain the whole result, nor even the largest part of it; no, it is the atmosphere in which the talent was cradled that explains; it is the training which it received while it grew, the nurture it got from reading, study, example, the encouragement it gathered from self-recognition and recognition from the outside at each stage of its development: when we know all these details, then we know why the man was ready when his opportunity came. We should expect Edison's surroundings and atmosphere to have the largest share in discovering him to himself and to the world; and we should expect him to live and die undiscovered in a land where an inventor could find no comradeship, no sympathy, no ambition-rousing atmosphere of recognition and applause—Dahomey, for instance. Dahomey could not find an Edison out; in Dahomey an Edison could not find himself out. Broadly speaking, genius is not born with sight, but blind; and it is not itself that opens its eyes, but the subtle influences of a myriad of stimulating exterior circumstances.

We all know this to be not a guess, but a mere commonplace fact, a truism. Lorraine was Joan of Arc's Dahomey. And there the Riddle confronts us. We can understand how she could be born with military genius, with leonine courage, with incomparable fortitude, with a mind which was in several particulars a prodigy—a mind which included among its specialties the lawyer's gift of detecting traps laid by the adversary in cunning and treacherous arrangements of seemingly innocent words, the orator's gift of eloquence, the advocate's gift of presenting a case in clear and compact form, the judge's gift of sorting and weighing evidence, and finally, something recognizable as more than a mere trace of the statesman's gift of understanding a political situation and how to make profitable use of such opportunities as it offers; we can comprehend how she could be born with these great qualities, but we cannot comprehend how they became immediately usable and effective without the developing forces of a sympathetic atmosphere and the training which comes of teaching, study, practice—years of practice,—and the crowning and perfecting help of a thousand mistakes. We can understand how the possibilities of the future perfect peach are all lying hid in the humble bitter-almond, but we cannot conceive of the peach springing directly from the almond without the intervening long seasons of patient cultivation and development. Out of a cattle-pasturing peasant village lost in the remotenesses of an unvisited wilderness and atrophied with ages of stupefaction and ignorance we cannot see a Joan of Arc issue equipped to the last detail for her amazing career and hope to be able to explain the riddle of it, labor at it as we may.

It is beyond us. All the rules fail in this girl's case. In the world's history she stands alone—quite alone. Others have been great in their first public exhibitions of generalship, valor, legal talent, diplomacy, fortitude; but always their previous years and associations had been in a larger or smaller degree a preparation for these things. There have been no exceptions to the rule. But Joan was competent in a law case at sixteen without ever having seen a law-book or a court-house before; she had no training in soldiership and no associations with it, yet she was a competent general in her first campaign; she was brave in her first battle, yet her courage had had no education—not even the education which a boy's courage gets from never-ceasing reminders that it is not permissible in a boy to be a coward, but only in a girl; friendless, alone, ignorant, in the blossom of her youth, she sat week after week, a prisoner in chains, before her assemblage of judges, enemies hunting her to her death, the ablest minds in France, and answered them out of an untaught wisdom which overmatched their learning, baffled their tricks and treacheries with a native sagacity which compelled their wonder, and scored every day a victory against these incredible odds and camped unchallenged on the field. In the history of the human intellect, untrained, inexperienced, and using only its birthright equipment of untried capacities, there is nothing which approaches this. Joan of Arc stands alone, and must continue to stand alone, by reason of the unfellowed fact that in the things wherein she was great she was so without shade or suggestion of help from preparatory teaching, practice, environment, or experience. There is no one to compare her with, none to measure her by; for all others among the illustrious *grew* towards their high place in an atmosphere and surroundings which discovered their gift to them and nourished it and promoted it, intentionally or unconsciously. There have been other young generals, but they were not girls; young generals, but they had been soldiers before they were generals: she *began* as a general; she commanded the first army she ever saw; she led it from victory to victory, and never lost a battle with it; there have been young commanders-in-chief, but none so young as she: she is the only soldier in history who has held the supreme command of a nation's armies at the age of seventeen.

Her history has still another feature which sets her apart and leaves her without fellow or competitor: there have been many uninspired prophets, but she was the only one who ever ventured the daring detail of naming, along with a foretold event, the event's precise nature, the special time-limit within which it would occur, and the place—*and scored fulfilment*. At Vaucouleurs she said she must go to the King and be made his general, and break the English power, and crown her sovereign—"at Rheims." It all happened. It was all to happen "next year"—and it did. She foretold her first wound and its character and date a month in advance, and the prophecy was recorded in a public record-book three weeks in advance. She repeated it the morning of the date named, and it was fulfilled before night. At Tours she foretold the limit of her military career—saying it would end in one year from the time of its utterance—and she was right. She foretold her martyrdom—using *that word*, and naming a time three months away—and again she was right. At a time when France seemed hopelessly and permanently in the hands of the English she twice asserted in her prison before her judges that within seven years the English would meet with a mightier disaster than had been the fall of Orleans: it happened within five—the fall of Paris. Other prophecies of hers came true, both as to the event named and the time-limit prescribed.

She was deeply religious, and believed that she had daily speech with angels; that she saw them face to face, and that they counselled her, comforted and heartened her, and brought commands to her direct from God. She had a child-like faith in the heavenly origin of her apparitions and her Voices, and not any threat of any form of death was able to frighten it out of her loyal heart. She was a beautiful and simple and lovable character. In the records of the Trials this comes out in clear and shining detail. She was gentle and winning and affectionate; she loved her home and friends and her village life; she was miserable in the presence of pain and suffering; she was full of compassion: on the field of her most splendid victory she forgot her triumphs to hold in her lap the head of a dying enemy and comfort his passing spirit with pitying words; in an age when it was common to slaughter prisoners she stood dauntless between hers and harm, and saved them alive; she was forgiving, generous, unselfish, magnanimous; she was pure from all spot or stain of baseness. And always she was a *girl*; and dear and worshipful, as is meet for that estate: when she fell wounded, the first time, she was frightened, and cried when she saw her blood gushing from her breast; but she was Joan of Arc! and when presently she found that her generals were sounding the retreat, she staggered to her feet and led the assault again and took that place by storm.

There is no blemish in that rounded and beautiful character.

How strange it is!—that almost invariably the artist remembers only one detail—one minor and meaningless detail of the personality of Joan of Arc: to wit, that she was a peasant girl—and forgets all the rest; and so he paints her as a strapping middle-aged fishwoman, with costume to match, and in her face the spirituality of a ham. He is slave to his one idea, and forgets to observe that the supremely great souls are never lodged in gross bodies. No brawn, no muscle, could endure the work that their bodies must do; they do their miracles by the spirit, which has fifty times the strength and staying power of brawn and muscle. The Napoleons are little, not big; and they work twenty hours in the twenty-four, and come up fresh, while the big soldiers with the little hearts faint around them with fatigue. We know what Joan of Arc was like, without asking—merely by what she did. The artist should paint her *spirit*—then he could not fail to paint her body aright. She would rise before us, then, a vision to win us, not repel: a lithe young slender figure, instinct with "the unbought grace of youth," dear and bonny and lovable, the face beautiful, and transfigured with the light of that lustrous intellect and the fires of that unquenchable spirit.

Taking into account, as I have suggested before, all the circumstances—her origin, youth, sex, illiteracy, early environment, and the obstructing conditions under which she exploited her high gifts and made her conquests in the field and before the courts that tried her for her life,—she is easily and by far the most extraordinary person the human race has ever produced.

*December 1904*

# The $30,000 Bequest

Lakeside was a pleasant little town of five or six thousand inhabitants, and a rather pretty one, too, as towns go in the Far West. It had church-accommodations for 35,000, which is the way of the Far West and the South, where everybody is religious, and where each of the Protestant sects is represented and has a plant of its own. Rank was unknown in Lakeside—unconfessed, anyway; everybody knew everybody and his dog, and a sociable friendliness was the prevailing atmosphere.

Saladin Foster was bookkeeper in the principal store, and the only high-salaried man of his profession in Lakeside. He was thirty-five years old, now; he had served that store for fourteen years; he had begun in his marriage-week at four hundred dollars a year, and had climbed steadily up, a hundred dollars a year for four years; from that time forth his wage had remained eight hundred—a handsome figure indeed, and everybody conceded that he was worth it.

His wife, Electra, was a capable helpmeet, although—like himself—a dreamer of dreams and a private dabbler in romance. The first thing she did, after her marriage—child as she was, aged only nineteen—was to buy an acre of ground on the edge of the town, and pay down the cash for it—twenty-five dollars, all her fortune. Saladin had less, by fifteen. She instituted a vegetable garden there, got it farmed on shares by the nearest neighbor, and made it pay her a hundred per cent. a year. Out of Saladin's first year's wage she put thirty dollars in the savings-bank, sixty out of his second, a hundred out of his third, a hundred and fifty out of his fourth. His wage went to eight hundred a year, then, and meantime two children had arrived and increased the expenses, but she banked two hundred a year from the salary, nevertheless, thenceforth. When she had been married seven years she built and furnished a pretty and comfortable two-thousand-dollar house in the midst of her garden-acre, paid half of the money down, and moved her family in. Seven years later she was out of debt and had several hundred dollars out earning its living.

Earning it by the rise in landed estate; for she had long ago bought another acre or two and sold the most of it at a profit to pleasant people who were willing to build, and would be good neighbors and furnish a genial comradeship for herself and her growing family. She had an independent income from safe investments of about a hundred dollars a year; her children were growing in years and grace; and she was a pleased and happy woman. Happy in her husband, happy in her children, and the husband and the children were happy in her. It is at this point that this history begins.

The youngest girl, Clytemnestra—called Clytie for short—was eleven; her sister, Gwendolen—called Gwen for short—was thirteen; nice girls, and comely. The names betray the latent romance-tinge in the parental blood, the parents' names indicate that the tinge was an inheritance. It was an affectionate family, hence all four of its members had pet names. Saladin's was a curious and unsexing one—Sally; and so was Electra's—Aleck. All day long Sally was a good and diligent bookkeeper and salesman; all day long Aleck was a good and faithful mother and housewife, and thoughtful and calculating business-woman; but in the cosy living-room at night they put the plodding world away and lived in another and a fairer, reading romances to each other, dreaming dreams, comrading with kings and princes and stately lords and ladies in the flash and stir and splendor of noble palaces and grim and ancient castles.

II

Now came great news! Stunning news, joyous news, in fact. It came from a neighboring State, where the family's only surviving relative lived. It was Sally's relative—a sort of vague and indefinite uncle or second or third cousin by the name of Tilbury Foster, seventy and a bachelor, reputed well-off and correspondingly sour and crusty. Sally had tried to make up to him once, by letter, in a bygone time, and had not made that mistake again. Tilbury now wrote to Sally, saying he should shortly die, and should leave him thirty thousand dollars, cash; not for love, but because money had given him most of his troubles and exasperations, and he wished to place it where there was good hope that it would continue its malignant work. The bequest would be found in his will, and would be paid over. *Provided*, that Sally should be able to prove to the executors that he had *taken no notice of the gift by spoken word or by letter, had made no inquiries concerning the moribund's progress toward the everlasting tropics, and had not attended the funeral.*

As soon as Aleck had partially recovered from the tremendous emotions created by the letter, she sent to the relative's habitat and subscribed for the local paper.

Man and wife entered into a solemn compact, now, to never mention the great news to any one while the relative lived, lest some ignorant person carry the fact to the death-bed and distort it and make it appear that they were disobediently thankful for the bequest, and just the same as confessing it and publishing it, right in the face of the prohibition.

For the rest of the day Sally made havoc and confusion with his books, and Aleck could not keep her mind on her affairs, nor even take up a flower-pot or book or a stick of wood without forgetting what she had intended to do with it. For both were dreaming.

"Thir-ty thousand dollars!"

All day long the music of those inspiring words sang through those people's heads.

From his marriage-day forth, Aleck's grip had been upon the purse, and Sally had seldom known what it was to be privileged to squander a dime on non-necessities.

"Thir-ty thousand dollars!" the song went on and on. A vast sum, an unthinkable sum!

All day long Aleck was absorbed in planning how to invest it, Sally in planning how to spend it.

There was no romance-reading that night. The children took themselves away early, for the parents were silent, distraught, and strangely unentertaining. The good-night kisses might as well have been impressed upon vacancy, for all the response they got; the parents were not aware of the kisses, and the children had been gone an hour before their absence

was noticed. Two pencils had been busy during that hour—
note-making; in the way of plans. It was Sally who broke the
stillness at last. He said, with exultation—

"Ah, it'll be grand, Aleck! Out of the first thousand we'll
have a horse and a buggy for summer, and a cutter and a skin
lap-robe for winter."

Aleck responded, with decision and composure—

"Out of the *capital*? Nothing of the kind. Not if it was a
million!"

Sally was deeply disappointed; the glow went out of his
face.

"Oh, Aleck!" he said, reproachfully. "We've always worked
so hard and been so scrimped; and now that we are rich, it
does seem—"

He did not finish, for he saw her eye soften; his supplication had touched her. She said, with gentle persuasiveness—

"We must not spend the capital, dear, it would not be wise.
Out of the income from it—"

"That will answer, that will answer, Aleck! How dear and
good you are! There will be a noble income, and if we can
spend that—"

"Not *all* of it, dear, not all of it, but you can spend a part of
it. That is, a reasonable part. But the whole of the capital—
every penny of it—must be put right to work, and kept at it.
You see the reasonableness of that, don't you?"

"Why, ye-s. Yes, of course. But we'll have to wait so long.
Six months before the first interest falls due."

"Yes—maybe longer."

"Longer, Aleck? Why? Don't they pay half-yearly?"

"*That* kind of an investment—yes; but I sha'n't invest in
that way."

"What way then?"

"For big returns."

"Big. That's good. Go on, Aleck. What is it?"

"Coal. The new mines. Cannel. I mean to put in ten thousand. Ground floor. When we organize, we'll get three shares
for one."

"By George but it sounds good, Aleck! Then the shares will
be worth—how much? And when?"

"About a year. They'll pay ten per cent. half-yearly, and be worth thirty thousand. I know all about it; the advertisement is in the Cincinnati paper here."

"Land, thirty thousand for ten—in a year! Let's jam in the whole capital and pull out ninety! I'll write and subscribe right now—to-morrow it may be too late."

He was flying to the writing-desk, but Aleck stopped him and put him back in his chair. She said—

"Don't lose your head so. We mustn't subscribe till we've got the money; don't you know that?"

Sally's excitement went down a degree or two, but he was not wholly appeased.

"Why, Aleck, we'll *have* it, you know—and so soon, too. He's probably out of his troubles before this, it's a hundred to nothing he's selecting his brimstone-shovel this very minute. Now, I think—"

Aleck shuddered, and said—

"How *can* you, Sally! Don't talk in that way, it is perfectly scandalous."

"Oh, well, make it a halo, if you like, *I* don't care for his outfit, I was only just talking. Can't you let a person talk?"

"But why should you *want* to talk in that dreadful way? How would you like to have people talk so about *you*, and you not cold yet?"

"Nor likely to be, for *one* while, I reckon, if my last act was giving away money for the sake of doing somebody a harm with it. But never mind about Tilbury, Aleck, let's talk about something worldly. It does seem to me that that mine is the place for the whole thirty. What's the objection?"

"All the eggs in one basket—that's the objection."

"All right, if you say so. What about the other twenty? What do you mean to do with that?"

"There is no hurry; I am going to look around before I do anything with it."

"All right, if your mind's made up," sighed Sally. He was deep in thought, a while, then he said—

"There'll be twenty thousand profit coming from the ten a year from now. We can spend that, can't we, Aleck?"

Aleck shook her head.

"No, dear," she said, "it won't sell high till we've had the first semiannual dividend. You can spend part of that."

"Shucks, only *that*—and a whole year to wait! Confound it, I—"

"Oh, do be patient! It might even be declared in three months—it's quite within the possibilities."

"Oh, jolly! oh, thanks!" and Sally jumped up and kissed his wife in gratitude. "It'll be three thousand—three whole thousand! how much of it can we spend, Aleck? Make it liberal—do, dear, that's a good fellow."

Aleck was pleased; so pleased that she yielded to the pressure and conceded a sum which her judgment told her was a foolish extravagance—a thousand dollars. Sally kissed her half a dozen times and even in that way could not express all his joy and thankfulness. This new access of gratitude and affection carried Aleck quite beyond the bounds of prudence, and before she could restrain herself she had made her darling another grant—a couple of thousand out of the fifty or sixty which she meant to clear within a year out of the twenty which still remained of the bequest. The happy tears sprang to Sally's eyes, and he said—

"Oh, I want to hug you!" And he did it. Then he got his notes and sat down and began to check off, for first purchase, the luxuries which he should earliest wish to secure. "Horse — buggy — cutter — lap-robe — patent-leathers — dog —plug hat—church-pew—stem-winder—new teeth—*say*, Aleck!"

"Well?"

"Ciphering away, aren't you? That's right. Have you got the twenty thousand invested yet?"

"No, there's no hurry about that; I must look around first, and think."

"But you are ciphering; what's it about?"

"Why, I have to find work for the thirty thousand that comes out of the coal, haven't I?"

"Scott, what a head! I never thought of that. How are you getting along? Where have you arrived?"

"Not very far—two years or three. I've turned it over twice; once in oil and once in wheat."

"Why, Aleck, it's splendid! How does it aggregate?"

"I think—well, to be on the safe side, about a hundred and eighty thousand clear, though it will probably be more."

"My! isn't it wonderful? By gracious, luck has come our way at last, after all the hard sledding. Aleck!"

"Well?"

"I'm going to cash-in a whole three hundred on the missionaries—what real right have we to care for expenses!"

"You couldn't do a nobler thing, dear; and it's just like your generous nature, you unselfish boy."

The praise made Sally poignantly happy, but he was fair and just enough to say it was rightfully due to Aleck rather than to himself, since but for her he should never have had the money.

Then they went up to bed, and in their delirium of bliss they forgot and left the candle burning in the parlor. They did not remember until they were undressed; then Sally was for letting it burn; he said they could afford it, if it was a thousand. But Aleck went down and put it out.

A good job, too; for on her way back she hit on a scheme that would turn the hundred and eighty thousand into half a million before it had had time to get cold.

III

The little newspaper which Aleck had subscribed for was a Thursday sheet; it would make the trip of five hundred miles from Tilbury's village and arrive on Saturday. Tilbury's letter had started on Friday, more than a day too late for the benefactor to die and get into that week's issue, but in plenty of time to make connection for the next output. Thus the Fosters had to wait almost a complete week to find out whether anything of a satisfactory nature had happened to him or not. It was a long, long week, and the strain was a heavy one. The pair could hardly have borne it if their minds had not had the relief of wholesome diversion. We have seen that they had that. The woman was piling up fortunes right along, the man was spending them—spending all his wife would give him a chance at, at any rate.

At last the Saturday came, and the *Weekly Sagamore* arrived. Mrs. Eversly Bennett was present. She was the Presbyterian parson's wife, and was working the Fosters for a charity. Talk now died a sudden death—on the Foster side. Mrs. Bennett presently discovered that her hosts were not hearing a word she was saying; so she got up, wondering and indignant, and went away. The moment she was out of the house, Aleck eagerly tore the wrapper from the paper, and her eyes and Sally's swept the columns for the death notices. Disappointment! Tilbury was not anywhere mentioned. Aleck was a Christian from the cradle, and duty and the force of habit required her to go through the motions. She pulled herself together and said, with a pious two-per-cent. trade joyousness:

"Let us be humbly thankful that he has been spared; and—"

"Damn his treacherous hide, I wish—"

"Sally! For shame!"

"I don't care!" retorted the angry man. "It's the way *you* feel, and if you weren't so immorally pious you'd be honest and say so."

Aleck said, with wounded dignity:

"I do not see how you can say such unkind and unjust things. There is no such thing as immoral piety."

Sally felt a pang, but tried to conceal it under a shuffling attempt to save his case by changing the form of it—as if changing the form while retaining the juice could deceive the expert he was trying to placate. He said:

"I didn't mean so bad as that, Aleck; I didn't really mean immoral piety, I only meant—meant—well, conventional piety, you know; er—shop piety; the—the—why, *you* know what I mean, Aleck—the—well, where you put up the plated article and play it for solid, you know, without intending anything improper, but just out of trade habit, ancient policy, petrified custom, loyalty to—to—hang it, I can't find the right words, but *you* know what I mean, Aleck, and that there isn't any harm in it. I'll try again. You see, it's this way. If a person—"

"You have said quite enough," said Aleck, coldly; "let the subject be dropped."

"*I'm* willing," fervently responded Sally, wiping the sweat from his forehead and looking the thankfulness he had no words for. Then, musingly, he apologized to himself. "I certainly held threes—I *know* it—but I drew and didn't fill.

That's where I'm so often weak in the game. If I had stood pat—but I didn't. I never do. I don't know enough."

Confessedly defeated, he was properly tame now and subdued. Aleck forgave him with her eyes.

The grand interest, the supreme interest, came instantly to the front again; nothing could keep it in the background many minutes on a stretch. The couple took up the puzzle of the absence of Tilbury's death notice. They discussed it every whichway, more or less hopefully, but they had to finish where they began, and concede that the only really sane explanation of the absence of the notice must be—and without doubt was—that Tilbury was not dead. There was something sad about it, something even a little unfair, maybe, but there it was, and had to be put up with. They were agreed as to that. To Sally it seemed a strangely inscrutable dispensation; more inscrutable than usual, he thought; one of the most unnecessarily inscrutable he could call to mind, in fact—and said so, with some feeling; but if he was hoping to draw Aleck he failed; she reserved her opinion, if she had one; she had not the habit of taking injudicious risks in any market, worldly or other.

The pair must wait for next week's paper—Tilbury had evidently postponed. That was their thought and their decision. So they put the subject away, and went about their affairs again, with as good heart as they could.

Now, if they had but known it, they had been wronging Tilbury all the time. Tilbury had kept faith, kept it to the letter; he was dead, he had died to schedule. He was dead more than four days now and used to it; entirely dead, perfectly dead, as dead as any other new person in the cemetery; dead in abundant time to get into that week's *Sagamore*, too, and only shut out by an accident; an accident which could not happen to a metropolitan journal, but which happens easily to a poor little village rag like the *Sagamore*. On this occasion, just as the editorial page was being locked up, a gratis quart of strawberry water-ice arrived from Hostetter's Ladies' and Gents' Ice-Cream Parlors, and the stickful of rather chilly regret over Tilbury's translation got crowded out to make room for the editor's frantic gratitude.

On its way to the standing-galley Tilbury's notice got pied.
Otherwise it would have gone into some future edition, for
weekly *Sagamores* do not waste "live" matter, and in their gal-
leys "live" matter is immortal, unless a pi accident intervene.
But a thing that gets pied is dead, and for such there is no
resurrection; its chance of seeing print is gone, forever and
ever. And so, let Tilbury like it or not, let him rave in his
grave to his fill, no matter—no mention of his death would
ever see the light in the *Weekly Sagamore*.

IV

Five weeks drifted tediously along. The *Sagamore* arrived
regularly on the Saturdays, but never once contained a mention of Tilbury Foster. Sally's patience broke down at this
point, and he said, resentfully:

"Damn his livers, he's immortal!"

Aleck gave him a very severe rebuke, and added, with icy
solemnity:

"How would you feel if you were suddenly cut off just after
such an awful remark had escaped out of you?"

Without sufficient reflection Sally responded:

"I'd feel I was lucky I hadn't got caught with it *in* me."

Pride had forced him to say something, and as he could not
think of any rational thing to say he flung that out. Then he
stole a base—as he called it—that is, slipped from the presence, to keep from getting brayed in his wife's discussion-
mortar.

Six months came and went. The *Sagamore* was still silent
about Tilbury. Meantime Sally had several times thrown out a
feeler—that is, a hint that he would like to know. Aleck had
ignored the hints. Sally now resolved to brace up and risk a
frontal attack. So he squarely proposed to disguise himself
and go to Tilbury's village and surreptitiously find out as to
the prospects. Aleck put her foot on the dangerous project
with energy and decision. She said:

"What can you be thinking of? You do keep my hands full!
You have to be watched all the time, like a little child, to keep

you from walking into the fire. You'll stay right where you are!"

"Why, Aleck, I could do it and not be found out—I'm certain of it."

"Sally Foster, don't you know you would have to inquire around?"

"Of course, but what of it? Nobody would suspect who I was."

"Oh, listen to the man! Some day you've got to prove to the executors that you never inquired. What then?"

He had forgotten that detail. He didn't reply; there wasn't anything to say. Aleck added:

"Now then, drop that notion out of your mind, and don't ever meddle with it again. Tilbury set that trap for you. Don't you know it's a trap? He is on the watch, and fully expecting you to blunder into it. Well, he is going to be disappointed—at least while I am on deck. Sally!"

"Well?"

"As long as you live, if it's a hundred years, don't you ever make an inquiry. Promise!"

"All right," with a sigh and reluctantly.

Then Aleck softened and said:

"Don't be impatient. We are prospering; we can wait; there is no hurry. Our small dead-certain income increases all the time; and as to futures, I have not made a mistake yet—they are piling up by the thousands and the tens of thousands. There is not another family in the State with such prospects as ours. Already we are beginning to roll in eventual wealth. You know that, don't you?"

"Yes, Aleck, it's certainly so."

"Then be grateful for what God is doing for us, and stop worrying. You do not believe we could have achieved these prodigious results without His special help and guidance, do you?"

Hesitatingly, "N-no, I suppose not." Then, with feeling and admiration, "And yet, when it comes to judiciousness in watering a stock or putting up a hand to skin Wall Street I don't give in that *you* need any outside amateur help, if I do I wish I—"

"Oh, *do* shut up! I know you do not mean any harm or any irreverence, poor boy, but you can't seem to open your mouth without letting out things to make a person shudder. You keep me in constant dread. For you and for all of us. Once I had no fear of the thunder, but now when I hear it I—"

Her voice broke and she began to cry, and could not finish. The sight of this smote Sally to the heart, and he took her in his arms and petted her and comforted her and promised better conduct, and upbraided himself and remorsefully pleaded for forgiveness. And he was in earnest, and sorry for what he had done and ready for any sacrifice that could make up for it.

And so, in privacy he thought long and deeply over the matter, resolving to do what should seem best. It was easy to *promise* reform; indeed he had already promised it. But would that do any real good, any permanent good? No, it would be but temporary—he knew his weakness, and confessed it to himself with sorrow—he could not keep the promise. Something surer and better must be devised; and he devised it. At cost of precious money which he had long been saving up, shilling by shilling, he put a lightning-rod on the house.

At a subsequent time he relapsed.

What miracles habit can do! and how quickly and how easily habits are acquired—both trifling habits and habits which profoundly change us. If by accident we wake at two in the morning a couple of nights in succession, we have need to be uneasy, for another repetition can turn the accident into a habit; and a month's dallying with whiskey—but we all know these commonplace facts.

The castle-building habit, the day-dreaming habit—how it grows! what a luxury it becomes; how we fly to its enchantments at every idle moment, how we revel in them, steep our souls in them, intoxicate ourselves with their beguiling fantasies—oh, yes, and how soon and how easily our dream-life and our material life become so intermingled and so fused together that we can't quite tell which is which, any more.

By and by Aleck subscribed for a Chicago daily and for the *Wall Street Pointer*. With an eye single to finance she studied these as diligently all the week as she studied her Bible Sundays. Sally was lost in admiration, to note with what swift and sure strides her genius and judgment developed and expanded, in the forecasting and handling of the securities of both the material and spiritual markets. He was proud of her nerve and daring in exploiting worldly stocks, and just as proud of her conservative caution in working her spiritual deals. He noted that she never lost her head in either case; that with a splendid courage she often went short on worldly futures, but heedfully drew the line there—she was always long on the others. Her policy was quite sane and simple, as she explained it to him: what she put into earthly futures was for speculation, what she put into spiritual futures was for investment; she was willing to go into the one on a margin, and take chances, but in the case of the other, "margin her no margins"—she wanted to cash-in a hundred cents per dollar's-worth, and have the stock transferred on the books.

It took but a very few months to educate Aleck's imagination and Sally's. Each day's training added something to the spread and effectiveness of the two machines. As a consequence, Aleck made imaginary money much faster than at first she had dreamed of making it, and Sally's competency in spending the overflow of it kept pace with the strain put upon it, right along. In the beginning Aleck had given the coal speculation a twelvemonth in which to materialize, and had been loath to grant that this term might possibly be shortened by nine months. But that was the feeble work, the nursery-work, of a financial fancy that had had no teaching, no experience, no practice. These aids soon came, then that nine months vanished, and the imaginary ten-thousand-dollar investment came marching home with three hundred per cent. profit on its back!

It was a great day for the pair of Fosters. They were speechless for joy. Also speechless for another reason: after much watching of the market, Aleck had lately, with fear and trembling, made her first flyer on a "margin," using the remaining twenty thousand of the bequest in this risk. In her mind's eye she had seen it climb, point by point—always with a chance that the market would break—until at last her anxieties were too great for further endurance—she being new to the margin-business and unhardened, as yet—and she gave her imaginary broker an imaginary order by imaginary telegraph to sell. She said forty thousand dollars profit was enough. The sale was made on the very day that the coal-venture had returned with its rich freight. As I have said, the couple were speechless. They sat dazed and blissful, that night, trying to realize the immense fact, the overwhelming fact, that they were actually worth a hundred thousand dollars in clean imaginary cash. Yet so it was.

It was the last time that ever Aleck was afraid of a margin; at least afraid enough to let it break her sleep and pale her cheek to the extent that this first experience in that line had done.

Indeed it was a memorable night. Gradually the realization that they were rich sank securely home into the souls of the pair, then they began to place the money. If we could have looked out through the eyes of these dreamers, we should have seen their tidy little wooden house disappear, and a two-story brick with a cast-iron fence in front of it take its place; we should have seen a three-globed gas-chandelier grow down from the parlor ceiling; we should have seen the homely rag carpet turn to noble Brussels, a dollar and a half a yard; we should have seen the plebeian fireplace vanish away and a recherché big base-burner with isinglass windows take position and spread awe around. And we should have seen other things, too; among them the buggy, the lap-robe, the stove-pipe hat, and so on.

From that time forth, although the daughters and the neighbors saw only the same old wooden house there, it was a two-story brick to Aleck and Sally; and not a night went by that Aleck did not worry about the imaginary gas bills, and get for all comfort Sally's reckless retort, "What of it? we can afford it."

Before the couple went to bed, that first night that they were rich, they had decided that they must celebrate. They must give a party—that was the idea. But how to explain it—to the daughters and the neighbors? They could not expose the fact that they were rich. Sally was willing, even anxious, to do it; but Aleck kept her head and would not allow it. She said that although the money was as good as in, it would be as well to wait until it was actually in. On that policy she took her stand, and would not budge. The great secret must be kept, she said—kept from the daughters and everybody else.

The pair were puzzled. They must celebrate, they were determined to celebrate, but since the secret must be kept, what could they celebrate? No birthdays were due for three months. Tilbury wasn't available, evidently he was going to live forever; what the nation *could* they celebrate? That was Sally's way of putting it; and he was getting impatient, too, and harassed. But at last he hit it—just by sheer inspiration, as it seemed to him—and all their troubles were gone in a moment; they would celebrate the Discovery of America. A splendid idea!

Aleck was almost too proud of Sally for words—she said *she* never would have thought of it. But Sally, although he was bursting with delight in the compliment and with wonder at himself, tried not to let on, and said it wasn't really anything, anybody could have done it. Whereat Aleck, with a prideful toss of her happy head, said—

"Oh, certainly! Anybody could—oh, anybody! Hosannah Dilkins, for instance! Or maybe Adelbert Peanut—oh, *dear*— yes! Well, I'd like to see them try it, that's all. Dear-me-suz, if they could think of the discovery of a forty-acre island it's more than *I* believe they could; and as for a whole continent, why, Sally Foster, you know perfectly well it would strain the livers and lights out of them and *then* they couldn't!"

The dear woman, she knew he had talent; and if affection made her overestimate the size of it a little, surely it was a sweet and gentle crime, and forgiveable for its source's sake.

## V

The celebration went off well. The friends were all present, both the young and the old. Among the young were Flossie and Gracie Peanut and their brother Adelbert, who was a rising young journeyman tinner, also Hosannah Dilkins, Jr., journeyman plasterer, just out of his apprenticeship. For many months Adelbert and Hosannah had been showing interest in Gwendolen and Clytemnestra Foster, and the parents of the girls had noticed this with private satisfaction. But they suddenly realized now that that feeling had passed. They recognized that the changed financial conditions had raised up a social bar between their daughters and the young mechanics. The daughters could now look higher—and must. Yes, must. They need marry nothing below the grade of lawyer or merchant; poppa and momma would take care of this; there must be no mésalliances.

However, these thinkings and projects of theirs were private, and did not show on the surface, and therefore threw no shadow upon the celebration. What showed upon the surface was a serene and lofty contentment and a dignity of carriage and gravity of deportment which compelled the admiration and likewise the wonder of the company. All noticed it, all commented upon it, but none was able to divine the secret of it. It was a marvel and a mystery. Three several persons remarked, without suspecting what clever shots they were making:

"It's as if they'd come into property."

That was just it, indeed.

Most mothers would have taken hold of the matrimonial matter in the old regulation way; they would have given the girls a talking to, of a solemn sort and untactful—a lecture calculated to defeat its own purpose, by producing tears and secret rebellion; and the said mothers would have further damaged the business by requesting the young mechanics to discontinue their attentions. But this mother was different. She was practical. She said nothing to any of the young people concerned, nor to any one else except Sally. He listened to her and understood; understood and admired. He said:

"I get the idea. Instead of finding fault with the samples on view, thus hurting feelings and obstructing trade without occasion, you merely offer a higher class of goods for the money, and leave nature to take her course. It's wisdom, Aleck, solid wisdom, and sound as a nut. Who's your fish? Have you nominated him yet?"

No, she hadn't. They must look the market over—which they did. To start with, they considered and discussed Bradish, rising young lawyer, and Fulton, rising young dentist. Sally must invite them to dinner. But not right away; there was no hurry, Aleck said. Keep an eye on the pair, and wait; nothing would be lost by going slowly in so important a matter.

It turned out that this was wisdom, too; for inside of three weeks Aleck made a wonderful strike which swelled her imaginary hundred thousand to four hundred thousand of the same quality. She and Sally were in the clouds that evening. For the first time they introduced champagne at dinner. Not real champagne, but plenty real enough for the amount of imagination expended on it. It was Sally that did it, and Aleck weakly submitted. At bottom both were troubled and ashamed, for he was a high-up Son of Temperance, and at funerals wore an apron which no dog could look upon and retain his reason and his opinion; and she was a W. C. T. U., with all that that implies of boiler-iron virtue and unendurable holiness. But there it was: the pride of riches was beginning its disintegrating work. They had lived to prove, once more, a sad truth which had been proven many times before in the world: that whereas principle is a great and noble protection against showy and degrading vanities and vices, poverty is worth six of it. More than four hundred thousand dollars to the good! They took up the matrimonial matter again. Neither the dentist nor the lawyer was mentioned; there was no occasion; they were out of the running. Disqualified. They discussed the son of the pork-packer and the son of the village banker. But finally, as in the previous case, they concluded to wait and think, and go cautiously and sure.

Luck came their way again. Aleck, ever watchful, saw a great and risky chance, and took a daring flyer. A time of trembling, of doubt, of awful uneasiness followed, for non-success meant absolute ruin and nothing short of it. Then came the result, and Aleck, faint with joy, could hardly control her voice when she said:

"The suspense is over, Sally—and we are worth a cold million!"

Sally wept for gratitude, and said:

"Oh, Electra, jewel of women, darling of my heart, we are free at last, we roll in wealth, we need never scrimp again. It's a case for Veuve Cliquot!" and he got out a pint of spruce-beer and made sacrifice, he saying "Damn the expense," and she rebuking him gently with reproachful but humid and happy eyes.

They shelved the pork-packer's son and the banker's son, and sat down to consider the Governor's son and the son of the Congressman.

## VI

It were a weariness to follow in detail the leaps and bounds the Foster fictitious finances took from this time forth. It was marvellous, it was dizzying, it was dazzling. Everything Aleck touched turned to fairy gold, and heaped itself glittering toward the firmament. Millions upon millions poured in, and still the mighty stream flowed thundering along, still its vast volume increased. Five millions—ten millions—twenty—thirty—was there never to be an end?

Two years swept by in a splendid delirium, the intoxicated Fosters scarcely noticing the flight of time. They were now worth three hundred million dollars; they were in every board of directors of every prodigious combine in the country; and still, as time drifted along, the millions went on piling up, five at a time, ten at a time, as fast as they could tally them off, almost. The three hundred doubled itself—then doubled again—and yet again—and yet once more!

Twenty-four hundred millions!

The business was getting a little confused. It was necessary to take an account of stock, and straighten it out. The Fosters knew it, they felt it, they realized that it was imperative; but they also knew that to do it properly and perfectly the task must be carried to a finish without a break when once it was begun. A ten-hours' job; and where could *they* find ten leisure hours in a bunch? Sally was selling pins and sugar and calico all day and every day; Aleck was cooking and washing dishes and sweeping and making beds all day and every day, with none to help, for the daughters were being saved up for high society. The Fosters knew there was one way to get the ten hours, and only one. Both were ashamed to name it; each waited for the other to do it. Finally Sally said—

"Somebody's got to give in. It's up to me. Consider that I've named it—never mind pronouncing it out loud."

Aleck colored, but was grateful. Without further remark, they fell. Fell, and broke the Sabbath. For that was their only free ten-hour stretch. It was but another step in the downward path. Others would follow. Vast wealth has temptations which fatally and surely undermine the moral structure of persons not habituated to its possession.

They pulled down the shades and broke the Sabbath. With hard and patient labor they overhauled their holdings, and listed them. And a long-drawn procession of formidable names it was! Starting with the Railway Systems, Steamer Lines, Standard Oil, Ocean Cables, Diluted Telegraph, and all the rest, and winding up with Klondike, De Beers, Tammany Graft, and Shady Privileges in the Post-office Department.

Twenty-four hundred millions, and all safely planted in Good Things, gilt-edged and interest-bearing. Income, $120,000,000 a year. Aleck fetched a long purr of soft delight, and said—

"Is it enough?"

"It is, Aleck."

"What shall we do?"

"Stand pat."

"Retire from business?"

"That's it."

"I am agreed. The good work is finished; we will take a long rest and enjoy the money."

"Good! Aleck?"

"Yes, dear?"

"How much of the income can we spend?"

"The whole of it."

It seemed to her husband that a ton of chains fell from his limbs. He did not say a word; he was happy beyond the power of speech.

After that, they broke the Sabbaths right along, as fast as they turned up. It is the first wrong steps that count. Every Sunday they put in the whole day, after morning service, on inventions—inventions of ways to spend the money. They got to continuing this delicious dissipation until past midnight; and at every séance Aleck lavished millions upon great charities and religious enterprises, and Sally lavished like sums upon matters to which (at first) he gave definite names. Only at first. Later the names gradually lost sharpness of outline, and eventually faded into "sundries," thus becoming entirely—but safely—undescriptive. For Sally was crumbling. The placing of these millions added seriously and most uncomfortably to the family expenses—in tallow candles. For a while Aleck was worried. Then, after a little, she ceased to worry, for the occasion of it was gone. She was pained, she was grieved, she was ashamed; but she said nothing, and so became an accessory. Sally was taking candles; he was robbing the store. It is ever thus. Vast wealth, to the person unaccustomed to it, is a bane; it eats into the flesh and bone of his morals. When the Fosters were poor, they could have been trusted with untold candles. But now they—but let us not dwell upon it. From candles to apples is but a step: Sally got to taking apples; then soap; then maple-sugar; then canned goods; then crockery. How easy it is to go from bad to worse, when once we have started upon a downward course!

Meantime, other effects had been milestoning the course of the Fosters' splendid financial march. The fictitious brick dwelling had given place to an imaginary granite one with a checker-board mansard roof; in time this one disappeared and gave place to a still grander home—and so on and so on. Mansion after mansion, made of air, rose, higher, broader, finer, and each in its turn vanished away; until now, in these latter great days, our dreamers were in fancy housed, in a distant region, in a sumptuous vast palace which looked out from a leafy summit upon a noble prospect of vale and river and receding hills steeped in tinted mists—and all private, all the property of the dreamers; a palace swarming with liveried servants, and populous with guests of fame and power, hailing from all the world's capitals, foreign and domestic.

This palace was far, far away toward the rising sun, immeasurably remote, astronomically remote, in Newport, Rhode Island, Holy Land of High Society, ineffable Domain of the American Aristocracy. As a rule, they spent a part of every Sabbath—after morning service—in this sumptuous home, the rest of it they spent in Europe, or in dawdling around in their private yacht. Six days of sordid and plodding Fact-life at home on the ragged edge of Lakeside and straitened means, the seventh in Fairyland—such had become their programme and their habit.

In their sternly restricted Fact-life they remained as of old—plodding, diligent, careful, practical, economical. They stuck loyally to the little Presbyterian Church, and labored faithfully in its interests and stood by its high and tough doctrines with all their mental and spiritual energies. But in their Dream-life they obeyed the invitations of their fancies, whatever they might be, and howsoever the fancies might change. Aleck's fancies were not very capricious, and not frequent, but Sally's scattered a good deal. Aleck, in her dream-life, went over to the Episcopal camp, on account of its large official titles; next she became High-church on account of the candles and shows; and next she naturally changed to Rome, where there were cardinals and more candles. But these excursions were as nothing to Sally's. His dream-life was a glowing and continuous and persistent excitement, and he kept every part of it fresh and sparkling by frequent changes, the religious part along with the rest. He worked his religions hard, and changed them with his shirt.

The liberal spendings of the Fosters upon their fancies began early in their prosperities, and grew in prodigality step by step with their advancing fortunes. In time they became truly enormous. Aleck built a university or two per Sunday; also a hospital or two; also a Rowton hotel or so; also a batch of churches; now and then a cathedral; and once, with untimely and ill-chosen playfulness, Sally said, "It was a cold day when she didn't ship a cargo of missionaries to persuade unreflecting Chinamen to trade off twenty-four carat Confucianism for counterfeit Christianity."

This rude and unfeeling language hurt Aleck to the heart, and she went from the presence crying. That spectacle went to his own heart, and in his pain and shame he would have given worlds to have those unkind words back. She had uttered no syllable of reproach—and that cut him. Not one suggestion that he look at his own record—and she could have made, oh, so many, and such blistering ones! Her generous silence brought a swift revenge, for it turned his thoughts upon himself, it summoned before him a spectral procession, a moving vision of his life as he had been leading it these past few years of limitless prosperity, and as he sat there reviewing it his cheeks burned and his soul was steeped in humiliation. Look at her life—how fair it was, and tending ever upward; and look at his own—how frivolous, how charged with mean vanities, how selfish, how empty, how ignoble! And its trend—never upward, but downward, ever downward!

He instituted comparisons between her record and his own. He had found fault with her—so he mused—*he!* And what could he say for himself? When she built her first church what was he doing? Gathering other blasé multimillionaires into a Poker Club; defiling his own palace with it; losing hundreds of thousands to it at every sitting, and sillily vain of the admiring notoriety it made for him. When she was building her first university, what was he doing? Polluting himself with a gay and dissipated secret life in the company of other fast bloods, multimillionaires in money and paupers in character. When she was building her first foundling asylum, what was he doing? Alas! When she was projecting her noble Society for the Purifying of the Sex, what was he doing? Ah, what, indeed! When she and the W. C. T. U. and the Woman with the Hatchet, moving with resistless march, were sweeping the fatal bottle from the land, what was he doing? Getting drunk three times a day. When she, builder of a hundred cathedrals, was being gratefully welcomed and blest in papal Rome and decorated with the Golden Rose which she had so honorably earned, what was he doing? Breaking the bank at Monte Carlo.

He stopped. He could go no farther; he could not bear the rest. He rose up, with a great resolution upon his lips: this secret life should be revealed, and confessed; no longer would he live it clandestinely; he would go and tell her All.

And that is what he did. He told her All; and wept upon her bosom; wept, and moaned, and begged for her forgiveness. It was a profound shock, and she staggered under the blow, but he was her own, the core of her heart, the blessing of her eyes, her all in all, she could deny him nothing, and she forgave him. She felt that he could never again be quite to her what he had been before; she knew that he could only repent, and not reform; yet all morally defaced and decayed as he was, was he not her own, her very own, the idol of her deathless worship? She said she was his serf, his slave, and she opened her yearning heart and took him in.

## VII

One Sunday afternoon some time after this they were sailing the summer seas in their dream-yacht, and reclining in lazy luxury under the awning of the after-deck. There was silence, for each was busy with his own thoughts. These seasons of silence had insensibly been growing more and more frequent of late; the old nearness and cordiality were waning. Sally's terrible revelation had done its work; Aleck had tried hard to drive the memory of it out of her mind, but it would not go, and the shame and bitterness of it were poisoning her gracious dream-life. She could see now (on Sundays) that her husband was becoming a bloated and repulsive Thing. She could not close her eyes to this, and in these days she no longer looked at him, Sundays, when she could help it.

But she—was she herself without blemish? Alas, she knew she was not. She was keeping a secret from him, she was acting dishonorably toward him, and many a pang it was costing her. *She was breaking the compact, and concealing it from him.* Under strong temptation she had gone into business again; she had risked their whole fortune in a purchase of all the railway systems and coal and steel companies in the country on a margin, and she was now trembling, every Sabbath hour, lest through some chance word of hers he find it out. In her misery and remorse for this treachery she could not keep her heart from going out to him in pity; she was filled with compunctions to see him lying there, drunk and content, and never suspecting. Never suspecting—trusting her with a perfect and pathetic trust, and she holding over him by a thread a possible calamity of so devastating a—

"*Say*—Aleck?"

The interrupting words brought her suddenly to herself. She was grateful to have that persecuting subject from her

thoughts, and she answered, with much of the old-time tenderness in her tone:

"Yes, dear."

"Do you know, Aleck, I think we are making a mistake—
that is, you are. I mean about the marriage business." He sat
up, fat and froggy and benevolent, like a bronze Buddha, and
grew earnest. "Consider—it's more than five years. You've
continued the same policy from the start: with every rise, always holding on for five points higher. Always when I think
we are going to have some weddings, you see a bigger thing
ahead, and I undergo another disappointment. *I* think you are
too hard to please. Some day we'll get left. First, we turned
down the dentist and the lawyer. That was all right—it was
sound. Next, we turned down the banker's son and the pork-
butcher's heir—right again, and sound. Next, we turned
down the Congressman's son and the Governor's—right as a
trivet, I confess it. Next, the Senator's son and the son of the
Vice-President of the United States—perfectly right, there's
no permanency about those little distinctions. Then you went
for the aristocracy; and I thought we had struck oil at last—
yes. We would make a plunge at the Four Hundred, and pull
in some ancient lineage, venerable, holy, ineffable, mellow
with the antiquity of a hundred and fifty years, disinfected of
the ancestral odors of salt cod and pelts all of a century ago,
and unsmirched by a day's work since; and then! why, then
the marriages, of course. But no, along comes a pair of real
aristocrats from Europe, and straightway you throw over the
half-breeds. It was awfully discouraging, Aleck! Since then,
what a procession! You turned down the baronets for a pair
of barons; you turned down the barons for a pair of viscounts; the viscounts for a pair of earls; the earls for a pair of
marquises; the marquises for a brace of dukes. *Now*, Aleck,
cash in!—you've played the limit. You've got a job lot of four
dukes under the hammer; of four nationalities; all sound in
wind and limb and pedigree, all bankrupt and in debt up to
the ears. They come high, but we can afford it. Come, Aleck,
don't delay any longer, don't keep up the suspense: take the
whole lay-out, and leave the girls to choose!"

Aleck had been smiling blandly and contentedly all through
this arraignment of her marriage-policy; a pleasant light, as of

triumph with perhaps a nice surprise peeping out through it, rose in her eyes, and she said, as calmly as she could—

"Sally, what would you say to—*royalty*?"

Prodigious! Poor man, it knocked him silly, and he fell over the garboard-strake and barked his shin on the cat-heads. He was dizzy for a moment, then he gathered himself up and limped over and sat down by his wife and beamed his old-time admiration and affection upon her in floods, out of his bleary eyes.

"By George!" he said, fervently, "Aleck, you *are* great—the greatest woman in the whole earth! I can't ever learn the whole size of you. I can't ever learn the immeasurable deeps of you. Here I've been considering myself qualified to criticise your game. *I*! Why, if I had stopped to think, I'd have known you had a lone hand up your sleeve. Now, dear heart, I'm all red-hot impatience—tell me about it!"

The flattered and happy woman put her lips to his ear and whispered a princely name. It made him catch his breath, it lit his face with exultation.

"Land!" he said, "it's a stunning catch! He's got a gambling-hell, and a graveyard, and a bishop, and a cathedral—all his very own. And all gilt-edged five-hundred-per-cent. stock, every detail of it; the tidiest little property in Europe. And that graveyard—it's the selectest in the world: none but suicides admitted; *yes*, sir, and the free-list suspended, too, *all* the time. There isn't much land in the principality, but there's enough: eight hundred acres in the graveyard and forty-two outside. It's a *sovereignty*—that's the main thing; *land's* nothing. There's plenty land, Sahara's drugged with it."

Aleck glowed; she was profoundly happy. She said—

"Think of it, Sally—it is a family that has never married outside the Royal and Imperial Houses of Europe: our grandchildren will sit upon thrones!"

"True as you live, Aleck—and bear sceptres, too; and handle them as naturally and nonchalantly as I handle a yardstick. It's a grand catch, Aleck. He's corralled, is he? Can't get away? You didn't take him on a margin?"

"No. Trust me for that. He's not a liability, he's an asset. So is the other one."

"Who is it, Aleck?"

"His   Royal   Highness   Sigismund-Siegfried-Lauenfeld-
Dinkelspiel-Schwartzenberg   Blutwurst,   Hereditary   Grand
Duke of Katzenyammer."

"No! You can't mean it!"

"It's as true as I'm sitting here, I give you my word," she
answered.

His cup was full, and he hugged her to his heart with rapture, saying—

"How wonderful it all seems, and how beautiful! It's one
of the oldest and noblest of the three hundred and sixty-four
ancient German principalities, and one of the few that was
allowed to retain its royal estate when Bismarck got done
trimming them. I know that farm, I've been there. It's got a
ropewalk and a candle-factory and an army. Standing army.
Infantry and cavalry. Three soldiers and a horse. Aleck, it's
been a long wait, and full of heartbreak and hope deferred,
but God knows I am happy now. Happy, and grateful to you,
my own, who have done it all. When is it to be?"

"Next Sunday."

"Good. And we'll want to do these weddings up in the very
regalest style that's going. It's properly due to the royal quality of the parties of the first part. Now as I understand it,
there is only one kind of marriage that is sacred to royalty,
exclusive to royalty: it's the morganatic."

"What do they call it that for, Sally?"

"I don't know; but anyway it's royal, and royal only."

"Then we will insist upon it. More—I will compel it. It is
morganatic marriage or none."

"That settles it!" said Sally, rubbing his hands with delight.
"And it will be the very first in America. Aleck, it will make
Newport sick."

Then they fell silent, and drifted away upon their dream-
wings to the far regions of the earth to invite all the crowned
heads and their families and provide gratis transportation for
them.

### VIII

During three days the couple walked upon air, with their
heads in the clouds. They were but vaguely conscious of their
surroundings, they saw all things dimly, as through a veil,

they were steeped in dreams, often they did not hear when they were spoken to, they often did not understand when they heard; they answered confusedly or at random; Sally sold molasses by weight, sugar by the yard, and furnished soap when asked for candles, and Aleck put the cat in the wash and fed milk to the soiled linen. Everybody was stunned and amazed, and went about muttering, "What *can* be the matter with the Fosters?"

Three days. Then came events! Things had taken a happy turn, and for forty-eight hours Aleck's imaginary corner had been booming. Up—up—still up! Cost-point was passed. Still up—and up—and up! Five points above cost—then ten—fifteen—twenty! Twenty points cold profit on the vast venture, now, and Aleck's imaginary brokers were shouting frantically by imaginary long-distance, "Sell! sell! for Heaven's sake *sell!*"

She broke the splendid news to Sally, and he, too, said "Sell! sell—oh, don't make a blunder, now, you own the earth!—sell, sell!" But she set her iron will and lashed it amidships, and said she would hold on for five points more if she died for it.

It was a fatal resolve. The very next day came the historic crash, the record crash, the devastating crash, when the bottom fell out of Wall Street, and the whole body of gilt-edged stocks dropped ninety-five points in five hours, and the multimillionaire was seen begging his bread in the Bowery. Aleck sternly held her grip and "put up" as long as she could, but at last there came a call which she was powerless to meet, and her imaginary brokers sold her out. Then, and not till then, the man in her was vanquished, and the woman in her resumed sway. She put her arms about her husband's neck and wept, saying—

"I am to blame, do not forgive me, I cannot bear it. We are paupers! Paupers, and I am so miserable. The weddings will never come off; all that is past; we could not even buy the dentist, now."

A bitter reproach was on Sally's tongue: "I *begged* you to sell, but you—" He did not say it; he had not the heart to add a hurt to that broken and repentant spirit. A nobler thought came to him and he said—

"Bear up, my Aleck, all is not lost! You really never in-vested a penny of my uncle's bequest, but only its unmateri-alized future; what we have lost was only the increment harvested from that future by your incomparable financial judgment and sagacity. Cheer up, banish these griefs; we still have the thirty thousand untouched; and with the experience which you have acquired, think what you will be able to do with it in a couple of years! The marriages are not off, they are only postponed."

These were blessed words. Aleck saw how true they were, and their influence was electric; her tears ceased to flow, and her great spirit rose to its full stature again. With flashing eye and grateful heart, and with hand uplifted in pledge and prophecy, she said—

"Now and here I proclaim—"

But she was interrupted by a visitor. It was the editor and proprietor of the *Sagamore*. He had happened into Lakeside to pay a duty-call upon an obscure grandmother of his who was nearing the end of her pilgrimage, and with the idea of combining business with grief he had looked up the Fosters, who had been so absorbed in other things for the past four years that they had neglected to pay up their subscription. Six dollars due. No visitor could have been more welcome. He would know all about Uncle Tilbury and what his chances might be getting to be, cemeterywards. They could of course ask no questions, for that would squelch the bequest, but they could nibble around on the edge of the subject and hope for results. The scheme did not work. The obtuse editor did not know he was being nibbled at; but at last, chance accom-plished what art had failed in. In illustration of something under discussion which required the help of metaphor, the editor said—

"Land, it's as tough as Tilbury Foster!—as *we* say."

It was sudden, and it made the Fosters jump. The editor noticed it, and said, apologetically—

"No harm intended, I assure you. It's just a saying; just a joke, you know—nothing in it. Relation of yours?"

Sally crowded his burning eagerness down, and answered with all the indifference he could assume—

"I—well, not that I know of, but we've heard of him." The

editor was thankful, and resumed his composure. Sally added, "Is he—is he—well?"

"Is he *well*? Why, bless you he's in Sheol these five years!"

The Fosters were trembling with grief, though it felt like joy. Sally said, non-committally—and tentatively:

"Ah, well, such is life, and none can escape—not even the rich are spared."

The editor laughed.

"If you are including Tilbury," said he, "it don't apply. *He* hadn't a cent; the town had to bury him."

The Fosters sat petrified for two minutes; petrified and cold. Then, white-faced and weak-voiced, Sally asked:

"Is it true? Do you *know* it to be true?"

"Well, I should say! I was one of the executors. He hadn't anything to leave but a wheelbarrow, and he left that to me. It hadn't any wheel, and wasn't any good. Still, it was something, and so, to square up, I scribbled off a sort of a little obituarial send-off for him, but it got crowded out."

The Fosters were not listening—their cup was full, it could contain no more. They sat with bowed heads, dead to all things but the ache at their hearts.

An hour later. Still they sat there, bowed, motionless, silent, the visitor long ago gone, they unaware.

Then they stirred, and lifted their heads wearily, and gazed at each other wistfully, dreamily, dazed; then presently began to twaddle to each other in a wandering and childish way. At intervals they lapsed into silences, leaving a sentence unfinished, seemingly either unaware of it or losing their way. Sometimes, when they woke out of these silences, they had a dim and transient consciousness that something had happened to their minds; then with a dumb and yearning solicitude they would softly caress each other's hands in mutual compassion and support, as if they would say: "I am near you, I will not forsake you, we will bear it together; somewhere there is release and forgetfulness, somewhere there is a grave and peace; be patient, it will not be long."

They lived yet two years, in mental night, always brooding, steeped in vague regrets and melancholy dreams, never speaking; then release came to both on the same day.

Toward the end the darkness lifted from Sally's ruined mind for a moment, and he said:

"Vast wealth, acquired by sudden and unwholesome means, is a snare. It did us no good, transient were its feverish pleasures; yet for its sake we threw away our sweet and simple and happy life—let others take warning by us."

He lay silent a while, with closed eyes; then as the chill of death crept upward toward his heart, and consciousness was fading from his brain, he muttered:

"Money had brought him misery, and he took his revenge upon us, who had done him no harm. He had his desire: with base and cunning calculation he left us but thirty thousand, knowing we would try to increase it, and ruin our life and break our hearts. Without added expense he could have left us far above desire of increase, far above the temptation to speculate, and a kinder soul would have done it; but in him was no generous spirit, no pity, no—"

*December 10, 1904*

# Concerning Copyright

AN OPEN LETTER TO
THE REGISTER OF COPYRIGHTS

Thorwald Stolberg, Esq.,
  Register of Copyrights,
    Washington, D. C.
Dear Sir:

I have received your excellent summary of the innumerable statutes and substitutes and amendments which a century of Congresses has devised in trying to mete out even-handed justice to the public and the author in the vexed matter of copyright; and, in response to your invitation to the craftsmen of my guild to furnish suggestions for further legislation upon the subject, I beg to submit my share in the unconventional form of

## Question and Answer.

*Question*. How many new American books are copyrighted *annually* in the United States?

*Answer*. Five or six thousand.

*Q*. How many have been copyrighted in the last twenty-five years?

*A*. More than 100,000.

*Q*. How many altogether in the past 104 years?

*A*. Doubtless 250,000.

*Q*. How many of them have survived or will survive the 42-year limit?

*A*. An average of five per year. Make it ten, to be safe and certain.

*Q*. Only *ten* a year!

*A*. That is all. Ten.

*Q*. Do you actually believe that 249,000 of these books have had no sort of use for a 42-year limit?

*A*. I can swear to it. They would not have outlived a 20-year limit.

*Q*. Then where is the use of a 42-year limit?

*A*. I know of none.

*Q.* What does it accomplish?

*A.* Nothing useful, nothing worthy, nothing modest, nothing dignified, nothing honest, so far as I know. An Italian statesman has called it "the Countess Massiglia of legal burlesque." Each year ten venerable copyrights fall in, and the bread of ten persons is taken from them by the Government. This microscopic petty larceny is all that is accomplished.

*Q.* It does seem a small business.

*A.* For a big nation—yes. A distinct reversal of the law of the survival of the fittest. It is the assassination of the fittest.

*Q.* Of course, the lawmakers knew they were arranging a hardship for some persons—all laws do that. But they could not have known how few the number was, do you think?

*A.* Of course not. Otherwise, they would not have been worrying and suffering over copyright laws for a hundred years. It has cost you, sir, 41 pages of printed notes to merely *outline* the acres of amendments and substitutes they have ground out in a century—*to take the bread out of the mouths of ten authors per year*; usually the ten poorest and most distinguished literary servants of the nation! One book from each of them. It takes a hundred years to hook a thousand books, and by that time eight hundred of them have long ago fallen obsolete and died of inanition.

*Q.* Certainly there is something most grotesque about this! Is this principle followed elsewhere in our laws?

*A.* Yes, in the case of the inventors. But in that case it is worth the Government's while. There are a hundred thousand new inventions a year, and a thousand of them are worth seizing at the end of the 17-year limit. But the Government *can't* seize the really great and immensely valuable ones—like the telegraph, the telephone, the air-brake, the Pullman car, and some others, the Shakespeares of the inventor-tribe, so to speak—for the prodigious capital required to carry them on is their protection from competition; their proprietors are not disturbed when the patents perish. Tell me, who are of first importance in the modern nation?

*Q.* Shall we say the builders of its civilization and promoters of its glory?

*A.* Yes. Who are they?

*Q*. Its inventors; the creators of its literature; and the country's defenders on land and sea. Is that correct?

*A*. I think so. Well, when a soldier retires from the wars, the Government spends $150,000,000 a year upon him and his, and the pension is continued to his widow and orphans. But when it retires a distinguished author's book at the end of 42 years, it takes the book's subsequent profits away from the widow and orphans and gives them—to whom?

*Q*. To the public.

*A*. Nothing of the kind!

*Q*. But it does—the lawmaker will tell you so himself.

*A*. Who deceived the lawmaker with that limpid falsehood?

*Q*. Falsehood?

*A*. That is what it is. And the proof of it lies in this large, and eloquent, and sarcastic fact: that the Government does not give the book to the *public*, it gives it to the *publishers*.

*Q*. How do you make that out?

*A*. It is very simple: the publisher *goes on publishing*—there is no law against it—and he takes *all* the profit, both the author's and his own.

*Q*. Why, it looks like a crime!

*A*. It doesn't merely look like it, it *is* a crime. A crime perpetrated by a great country, a proud World Power, upon ten poor devils a year. *One book apiece*. The profits on "Uncle Tom's Cabin" continue to-day; nobody but the publishers get them—Mrs. Stowe's share ceased seven years before she died; her daughters receive nothing from the book. Years ago they found themselves no longer able to live in their modest home, and had to move out and find humbler quarters. Washington Irving's poor old adopted daughters fared likewise. Come, does that move you?

*Q*. Ah, dear me! Well, certainly, there is something wrong about this whole copyright business.

*A*. Something wrong? Yes, I think so! Something pitifully wrong, pathetically wrong! Consider the nation's attitude toward the Builder of its Material Greatness, toward the Defender of its Homes and its Flag, and (by contrast) toward its Teacher, who is also the Promoter of its Fame and Preserver of it—that Immortal Three! Behold, the spirit of prophecy is upon me, and a picture of a future incident rises upon my

sight. You shall share the vision with me: The President sits in
state in the White House, with his official family around him;
before him stand three groups. In the first group, Edison,
Graham Bell, Westinghouse, and other living inventors, and,
back of them, dim and vague, the shades of Fulton, Whitney,
Morse, Hoe, Howe, Ericsson and others; in the second group
stand Dewey, Schley, Miles, Howard, Sickles, Chaffee, together with a private soldier and sailor representing 200,000
fellow-survivors of the bloody field, the sutler's tent and the
teamster's camp, and back of these the stately shades of Washington, Paul Jones, Jackson, Taylor, Scott, McClellan, Grant,
Sherman, Sheridan, Farragut, Foote, Worden, Sampson and
others; in the third group stand three or four living authors,
and back of them, with averted faces and ashamed, loom the
mighty shades of Emerson, Bancroft, Bryant, Whittier, and
behind these, dim and spectral, the shades of Cooper, Judd,
Irving, Poe, Hawthorne, Longfellow, Holmes, Lowell, Harriet Beecher Stowe, Parkman and others.

### The President Speaks.

"By command of the Nation, whose servant I am, I have
summoned you, O illustrious ones! I bring you the message
of eighty grateful millions—a message of praise and reward
for high service done your country and your flag: from my
lips, hear the nation's word! To you, inventors, builders of the
land's material greatness, past and present, the people offer
homage, worship and imperishable gratitude, with enduring
fame for your dead, and untold millions of minted gold for
you that survive. To you, defenders of the flag, past and
present, creators of the nation's far-shining military glory, the
people offer homage, worship and imperishable gratitude,
with enduring fame for your dead; and, for you that survive,
a hundred and fifty coined millions a year to protect the
highest and the humblest of you from want so long as you
shall live. To you, historians, poets, creators of ennobling
romance,—Teachers—this: you have wrought into enduring
form the splendid story of the Great Republic; you have preserved forever from neglect, decay and oblivion the great
deeds of the long line of the nation's Builders, Defenders
and Preservers; you have diligently and faithfully taught and

trained the children of the Republic in lofty political and social ideals, and in that love of country and reverence for the
flag which is Patriotism—and without you this would be a
Russia to-day, with not an intelligent patriot in it; you have
made the American home pure and fragrant and beautiful
with your sweet songs and your noble romance-literature;
you have carried the American name in honor and esteem to
the ends of the earth; in spite of unequal laws which exalt
your brother the soldier and inflict upon you an undeserved
indignity, you have furnished to your country that great asset,
that golden asset, that imperial asset, lacking which no modern State can hold up its head and stand unchallenged in the
august company of the sisterhood of Nations—a fine and
strong and worthy National Literature! For these inestimable
services, the people, by my voice, grant these rewards: to your
great dead, as also to you who still live, homage, worship,
enduring fame, imper—no, I mean gratitude, just gratitude;
gratitude with a 42-year limit, and the poor-house for your
widows and children. God abide with you, O illustrious company of the Builders, Defenders and Patriot-Makers of the
grateful Republic! Farewell, the incident is closed."

*Q.* (*After a long and reflective pause.*) Isn't there some right
and fair way to remedy this strange and dishonorable condition of things?

*A.* I think there is.

*Q.* Suggest it, then.

### A Suggestion.

*A.* In making a 42-year limit, the Government's intention
was, to be fair all around. It meant that the ten authors (it
supposed the number was greater) should enjoy the profit of
their labors a fair and reasonable time; then extinguish the
copyright and thus *make the book cheap*—this for the benefit
of the public. I repeat, to *insure cheap editions for the public*:
now, wasn't that *the* intention? and wasn't it the whole and
*only* intention?

*Q.* It certainly was.

*A.* Well, that intention has often been defeated. In many a
case, the publisher has not lowered the price; in other cases,
so many publishers issued editions of the unprotected book

that they clogged the market and *killed* the book. And often it was a book that could have survived but for this misfortune. The remedy that I would suggest is this: *that, during the 42d year of the copyright limit, the owner of the copyright shall be obliged to issue an edition of the book at these following rates, to wit: twenty-five cents for each 100,000 words, or less, of its contents, and keep said edition on sale always thereafter, year after year, indefinitely. And if in any year he shall fail to keep such edition on sale during a space of three months, the copyright shall then perish.*

*Q.* That seems to cover the ground. It meets the Government's sole desire—to *secure a cheap edition for the public.*

*A.* Why, certainly. It *compels* it. No existing law in any country does that.

*Q.* You would not put a price upon the publisher's other editions?

*A.* No; he could make the others as high-priced as he chose.

*Q.* Would you except books of a certain class?

*A.* No book occurs to me that could not stand the reduction—I mean a book that promises to live 42 years and upwards. It could not apply to unabridged dictionaries, for they are revised and newly copyrighted every ten or twelve years. It is the one and only book in America whose copyright is *perpetual.*

*Q.* Your own proposition makes all copyrights perpetual, doesn't it?

*A.* It does not. It extends the limit indefinitely. But there is still a limit; for in any year after the forty-first that the cheap edition fails, during the space of three months, the copyright dies.

*Q.* The proposed rate seems excessively cheap. How would the thing work out? About how much of a reduction would it make? Give me an illustration or two.

*A.* Very well, let me cite my own books—I am on familiar ground there. "Huck Finn" contains 70,000 words; present price $1 50; an edition of it would have to be kept permanently on sale at 25 cents. "Tom Sawyer," 70,000 words, price $1 50; the imagined cheap edition would be 25 cents. Several two-volume books of mine contain a trifle more than 100,000 words per volume; present price $1 75 per volume; the cheap-edition price would be 75 cents per volume—or 75 cents for the complete book if compressed into one volume. My "works," taken together, number 23 volumes; cheapest present price of the set, $36 50. To meet the requirements of the copyright-preserving law, I would compress the aggregate contents into 10 volumes of something more than 200,000 words each, and sell the volumes at 75 cents each—or $7 50 for the lot, if a millionaire wanted the whole treasure.

*Q*. It is a reduction of *four-fifths*, or thereabouts! Would there be any profit?

*A*. The printer and the binder would get their usual percentage of profit, the middle-man would get his usual commission on sales. The publisher's profit would be very small, mine also would be very small.

*Q*. Then you are proposing commercial suicide for him and for yourself—is that it?

*A*. Far from it. I am proposing high commercial prosperity and advantage for him and for me.

*Q*. How?

*A*. First of all, the books would remain my children's possession and support, instead of being confiscated by various publishers and issued in cheap form or dear, as they chose, for the support of *their* children.

*Q*. And secondly?

*A*. Secondly—let us not overlook the importance of this detail—the cheap edition would advertise our higher-priced editions, and the publisher and my orphans would live on canvasback duck and Cape Cod oysters—not on ham-and-not-enough-of-it, the way certain Government-robbed orphans of my acquaintance are doing now.

*Q*. Why don't you and your publisher try that cheap edition now, without waiting?

*A*. Haven't I told you that almost all the profit would go to printer, binder and middle-man? And has this Government ever heard of a publisher who would get out a dirt-cheap edition without being *compelled* to do it? The Government has tried persuasion for many a year, in the interest of the public, and achieved no cheap edition by it: what I am after now is *compulsion*.

*Q.* Are you guessing at cheap-edition possibilities, or are you speaking from knowledge?

*A.* From knowledge. Knowledge and experience. I know what it costs to make a book and what it costs to sell it.

*Q.* If your figures on cheap editions should be challenged by the trade—how then?

*A.* I could prove my case, and would do it.

Very respectfully,

S. L. CLEMENS (MARK TWAIN).

*January 1905*

# Adam's Soliloquy

(The spirit of Adam is supposed to be visiting New York City
inspecting the dinosaur at the Museum of Natural History)

I

It is strange . . . very strange. *I* do not remember this creature. (*After gazing long and admiringly.*) Well, it is wonderful!
The mere *skeleton* fifty-seven feet long and sixteen feet high!
Thus far, it seems, they've found only this sample—without
doubt a merely medium-sized one; a person could not step
out here into the Park and happen by luck upon the largest
horse in America; no, he would happen upon one that would
look small alongside of the biggest Normandy. It is quite
likely that the biggest dinosaur was ninety feet long and
twenty feet high. It would be five times as long as an elephant; an elephant would be to it what a calf is to an elephant. The bulk of the creature! The weight of him! As long
as the longest whale, and twice the substance in him! And all
good wholesome pork, most likely; meat enough to last a village a year. . . . Think of a hundred of them in line, draped
in shining cloth of gold!—a majestic thing for a coronation
procession. But expensive, for he would eat much; only kings
and millionaires could afford him.

I have no recollection of him; neither Eve nor I had heard
of him until yesterday. We spoke to Noah about him; he colored and changed the subject. Being brought back to it—and
pressed a little—he confessed that in the matter of stocking
the Ark the stipulations had not been carried out with absolute strictness—that is, in minor details, unessentials. There
were some irregularities. He said the boys were to blame for
this—the boys mainly, his own fatherly indulgence partly.
They were in the giddy heyday of their youth at the time, the
happy springtime of life; their hundred years sat upon them
lightly, and—well, he had once been a boy himself, and he
had not the heart to be too exacting with them. And so—
well, they did things they shouldn't have done, and he—to be
candid, he winked. But on the whole they did pretty faithful
work, considering their age. They collected and stowed a

good share of the really useful animals; and also, when Noah was not watching, a multitude of useless ones, such as flies, mosquitoes, snakes, and so on, but they did certainly leave ashore a good many creatures which might possibly have had value some time or other, in the course of time. Mainly these were vast saurians a hundred feet long, and monstrous mammals, such as the megatherium and that sort, and there was really some excuse for leaving them behind, for two reasons: (1) it was manifest that some time or other they would be needed as fossils for museums and (2) there had been a miscalculation, the Ark was smaller than it should have been, and so there wasn't room for those creatures. There was actually fossil material enough all by itself to freight twenty-five Arks like that one. As for the dinosaur—— But Noah's conscience was easy; it was not named in his cargo list and he and the boys were not aware that there was such a creature. He said he could not blame himself for not knowing about the dinosaur, because it was an American animal, and America had not then been discovered.

Noah went on to say, "I did reproach the boys for not making the most of the room we had, by discarding trashy animals and substituting beasts like the mastodon, which could be useful to man in doing heavy work such as the elephant performs, but they said those great creatures would have increased our labors beyond our strength, in the matter of feeding and watering them, we being short-handed. There was something in that. We had no pump; there was but one window; we had to let down a bucket from that, and haul it up a good fifty feet, which was very tiresome; then we had to carry the water downstairs—fifty feet again, in cases where it was for the elephants and their kind, for we kept them in the hold to serve for ballast. As it was, we lost many animals—choice animals that would have been valuable in menageries—different breeds of lions, tigers, hyenas, wolves, and so on; for they wouldn't drink the water after the salt sea water got mixed with the fresh. But we never lost a locust, nor a grasshopper, nor a weevil, nor a rat, nor a cholera germ, nor any of that sort of beings. On the whole, I think we did very well, everything considered. We were shepherds and farmers; we had never been to sea before; we were ignorant of naval matters, and I know this for certain, that there is more difference between agriculture and navigation than a person would think. It is my opinion that the two trades do not belong together. Shem thinks the same; so does Japheth. As for what Ham thinks, it is not important. Ham is biased. You find me a Presbyterian that isn't, if you think you can."

He said it aggressively; it had in it the spirit of a challenge. I avoided argument by changing the subject. With Noah, arguing is a passion, a disease, and it is growing upon him; has been growing upon him for thirty thousand years, and more. It makes him unpopular, unpleasant; many of his oldest friends dread to meet him. Even strangers soon get to avoiding him, although at first they are glad to meet him and gaze at him, on account of his celebrated adventure. For a time they are proud of his notice, because he is so distinguished; but he argues them to rags, and before long they begin to wish, like the rest, that something had happened to the Ark.

## II

(*On the bench in the Park, midafternoon, dreamily noting the drift of the human species back and forth.*) To think—this multitude is but a wee little fraction of the earth's population! And all blood kin to me, every one! Eve ought to have come with me; this would excite her affectionate heart. She was never able to keep her composure when she came upon a relative; she would try to kiss every one of those people, black and white and all. (*A baby wagon passes.*) How little change one can notice—none at all, in fact. I remember the first child well—— Let me see . . . it is three hundred thousand years ago come Tuesday. This one is just like it. So between the first one and the last one there is really nothing to choose. The same insufficiency of hair, the same absence of teeth, the same feebleness of body and apparent vacancy of mind, the same general unattractiveness all around. Yet Eve worshiped that early one, and it was pretty to see her with it. This latest one's mother worships *it*; it shows in her eyes—it is the very look that used to shine in Eve's. To think that so subtle and intangible a thing as a *look* could flit and flash from face to face down a procession three hundred thousand years long and remain the same, without shade of change! Yet here it is, lighting this young creature's face just as it lighted Eve's in the long ago—the newest thing I have seen in the earth, and the oldest. Of course, the dinosaur—— But that is in another class.

She drew the baby wagon to the bench and sat down and began to shove it softly back and forth with one hand while she held up a newspaper with the other and absorbed herself in its contents. Presently, "My!" she exclaimed; which startled me, and I ventured to ask her, modestly and respectfully, what was the matter. She courteously passed the paper to me and said—pointing with her finger:

"There—it reads like fact, but I don't know."

It was very embarrassing. I tried to look at my ease, and nonchalantly turned the paper this and that and the other way, but her eye was upon me and I felt that I was not succeeding. Pretty soon she asked, hesitatingly:

"Can't—can't—you—read?"

I had to confess that I couldn't. It filled her with wonder. But it had one pleasant effect—it interested her in me, and I was thankful, for I was getting lonesome for some one to talk to and listen to. The young fellow who was showing me around—on his own motion, I did not invite him—had missed his appointment at the Museum, and I was feeling disappointed, for he was good company. When I told the young woman I could not read, she asked me another embarrassing question:

"Where are you from?"

I skirmished—to gain time and position. I said:

"Make a guess. See how near you can come."

She brightened, and exclaimed:

"I shall dearly like it, sir, if you don't mind. If I guess right will you tell me?"

"Yes."

"Honor bright?"

"Honor bright? What is that?"

She laughed delightedly and said:

"That's a good start! I was *sure* that that phrase would catch you. I know one thing, now, all right. I know——"

"What do you know?"

"That you are not an American. And you aren't, *are* you?"

"No. You are right. I'm not—honor bright, as you say."

She looked immensely pleased with herself, and said:

"I reckon I'm not always smart, but *that* was smart, anyway. But not so *very*, after all, because I already knew—believed I knew—that you were a foreigner, by another sign."

"What was that?"

"Your accent."

She was an accurate observer; I do speak English with a heavenly accent, and she had detected the foreign twang in it. She ran charmingly on, most naïvely and engagingly pleased with her triumph:

"The minute you said, 'See 'ow near you can come to it,' I said to myself, 'Two to one he is a foreigner, and ten to one he's English.' Now that *is* your nationality, *isn't* it?"

I was sorry to spoil her victory, but I had to do it: "Ah—you'll have to guess again."

"What—you are not an Englishman?"

"No—honor bright."

She looked me searchingly over, evidently communing with herself—adding up my points, then she said:

"Well, you don't *look* like an Englishman, and that is true." After a little she added, "The fact is, you don't look like *any* foreigner—not quite like . . . like *anybody* I've seen before. I will guess some more."

She guessed every country whose name she could think of and grew gradually discouraged. Finally she said:

"You must be the Man Without a Country—the one the story tells about. You don't seem to have any nationality at all. How did you come to come to America? Have you any kinfolks here?"

"Yes—several."

"Oh, then you came to see *them*."

"Partly—yes."

She sat awhile, thinking, then:

"Well, I'm not going to give up quite yet. Where do you live when you are at home—in a city, or in the country?"

"Which do you think?"

"Well, I don't quite know. You *do* look a little countrified, if you don't mind my saying it; but you look a little citified, too—not much, but a little, although you can't read, which is very curious, and you are not used to newspapers. Now *my* guess is that you live mainly in the country when you are at home, and not very much in the city. Is that right?"

"Yes, quite right."

"Oh, good! Now I'll take a fresh start."

Then she wore herself to the bone, naming cities. No success. Next she wanted me to help her a little with some "pointers," as she phrased it. Was my city large? Yes. Was it very large? Yes. Did they have mobiles there? No. Electric light? No. Railroads, hospitals, colleges, cops? No.

"Why, then, it's not civilized! Where *can* that place be? Be good and tell me just one peculiarity of it—then maybe I can guess."

"Well, then, just one; it has gates of pearl."

"Oh, go along! That's the New Jerusalem. It isn't fair to joke. Never mind. I'll guess it yet—it will come into my head pretty soon, just when I'm not expecting it. Oh, I've got an idea! Please talk a little in your own language—that'll be a good pointer." I accommodated her with a sentence or two. She shook her head despondently.

"No," she said, "it doesn't sound human. I mean, it doesn't sound like any of these other foreigners. It's pretty enough—it's quite pretty, I think—but I'm sure I've not heard it before. Maybe if you were to pronounce your name—— What *is* your name, if you'll be so good?"

"Adam."

"Adam?"

"Yes."

"But Adam *what*?"

"That is all—just Adam."

"Nothing at all but just that? Why, how curious! There's plenty of Adams; how can they tell you from the rest?"

"Oh, that is no trouble. I'm the only one there is, there where I'm from."

"Upon my word! Well, it beats the band! It reminds a person of the old original. That was his name, too, and he hadn't any but that—just like you." Then, archly, "You've heard of him, I suppose?"

"Oh yes! Do you know him? Have you ever seen him?"

"*Seen* him? Seen *Adam*? Thanks to goodness, no! It would scare me into fits."

"I don't see why."

"You don't?"

"No."

"*Why* don't you see why?"

"Because there is no sense in a person being scared of his kin."

"*Kin?*"

"Yes. Isn't he a distant relative of yours?"

She thought it was prodigiously funny, and said it was perfectly true, but *she* never would have been bright enough to think of it. I found it a new and most pleasant sensation to have my wit admired, and was about to try to do some more when that young fellow came. He planted himself on the other side of the young woman and began a vapid remark about the weather, but she gave him a look that withered him and got stiffly up and wheeled the baby away.

*c. February 1905*

# The Czar's Soliloquy

After the Czar's morning bath it is his habit to meditate an hour
before dressing himself. —*London Times Correspondence.*

[*Viewing himself in the pier-glass.*] Naked, what am I? A
lank, skinny, spider-legged libel on the image of God! Look
at the waxwork head—the face, with the expression of a
melon—the projecting ears—the knotted elbows—the
dished breast—the knife-edged shins—and then the feet, all
beads and joints and bone-sprays, an imitation X-ray photograph! There is nothing imperial about this, nothing imposing, impressive, nothing to invoke awe and reverence. Is it
this that a hundred and forty million Russians kiss the dust
before and worship? Manifestly not! No one could worship
this spectacle, which is Me. Then who is it, what is it, that
they worship? Privately, none knows better than I: it is my
clothes. Without my clothes I should be as destitute of authority as any other naked person. Nobody could tell me from
a parson, a barber, a dude. Then who is the real Emperor of
Russia? My clothes. There is no other.

As Teufelsdröckh suggested, what would man be—what
would *any* man be—without his clothes? As soon as one
stops and thinks over that proposition, one realizes that without his clothes a man would be nothing at all; that the clothes
do not merely make the man, the clothes *are* the man; that
without them he is a cipher, a vacancy, a nobody, a nothing.

Titles—another artificiality—are a part of his clothing.
They and the dry-goods conceal the wearer's inferiority and
make him seem great and a wonder, when at bottom there is
nothing remarkable about him. They can move a nation to
fall on its knees and sincerely worship an Emperor who, without the clothes and the title, would drop to the rank of the
cobbler and be swallowed up and lost sight of in the massed
multitude of the inconsequentials; an Emperor who, naked in
a naked world, would get no notice, excite no remark, and be
heedlessly shouldered and jostled like any other uncertified
stranger, and perhaps offered a kopek to carry somebody's
gripsack; yet an Emperor who, by the sheer might of those

artificialities—clothes and a title—can get himself worshipped as a deity by his people, and at his pleasure and unrebuked can exile them, hunt them, harry them, destroy them,
just as he would with so many rats if the accident of birth had
furnished him a calling better suited to his capacities than em-
pering. It is a stupendous force—that which resides in the
all-concealing cloak of clothes and title; they fill the onlooker
with awe; they make him tremble; yet he knows that every
hereditary regal dignity commemorates a usurpation, a power
illegitimately acquired, an authority conveyed and conferred
by persons who did not own it. For monarchs have been chosen and elected by aristocracies only: a Nation has never
elected one.

There is no power without clothes. It is the power that
governs the human race. Strip its chiefs to the skin, and no
State could be governed; naked officials could exercise no authority; they would look (and be) like everybody else—commonplace, inconsequential. A policeman in plain clothes is
one man; in his uniform he is ten. Clothes and title are the
most potent thing, the most formidable influence, in the
earth. They move the human race to willing and spontaneous
respect for the judge, the general, the admiral, the bishop, the
ambassador, the frivolous earl, the idiot duke, the sultan, the
king, the emperor. No great title is efficient without clothes
to support it. In naked tribes of savages the kings wear some
kind of rag or decoration which they make sacred to themselves and allow no one else to wear. The king of the great
Fan tribe wears a bit of leopard-skin on his shoulder—it is
sacred to royalty; the rest of him is perfectly naked. Without
his bit of leopard-skin to awe and impress the people, he
would not be able to keep his job.

[*After a silence.*] A curious invention, an unaccountable invention—the human race! The swarming Russian millions
have for centuries meekly allowed our Family to rob them,
insult them, trample them under foot, while they lived and
suffered and died with no purpose and no function but to
make that Family comfortable! These people are horses—just
that—horses with clothes and a religion. A horse with the
strength of a hundred men will let one man beat him, starve
him, drive him; the Russian millions allow a mere handful of

soldiers to hold them in slavery—and these very soldiers are their own sons and brothers!

A strange thing, when one considers it: to wit, the world applies to Czar and System the same moral axioms that have vogue and acceptance in civilized countries! Because, in civilized countries, it is wrong to remove oppressors otherwise than by process of law, it is held that the same rule applies in Russia, where there is no such thing as law—except for our Family. Laws are merely restraints—they have no other function. In civilized countries they restrain all persons, and restrain them all alike, which is fair and righteous; but in Russia such laws as exist make an exception—our Family. We do as we please; we have done as we pleased for centuries. Our common trade has been crime, our common pastime murder, our common beverage blood—the blood of the nation. Upon our heads lie millions of murders. Yet the pious moralist says it is a crime to assassinate us. We and our uncles are a family of cobras set over a hundred and forty million rabbits, whom we torture and murder and feed upon all our days; yet the moralist urges that to kill us is a crime, not a duty.

It is not for me to say it aloud, but to one on the inside— like me—this is naïvely funny; on its face, illogical. Our Family is above all law; there is no law that can reach us, restrain us, protect the people from us. Therefore, we are outlaws. Outlaws are a proper mark for any one's bullet. Ah! what could our Family do without the moralist? He has always been our stay, our support, our friend; to-day he is our *only* friend. Whenever there has been dark talk of assassination, he has come forward and saved us with his impressive maxim, "Forbear: nothing politically valuable was ever yet achieved by violence." He probably believes it. It is because he has by him no child's book of world-history to teach him that his maxim lacks the backing of statistics. All thrones have been established by violence; no regal tyranny has ever been overthrown except by violence; by violence my fathers set up our throne; by murder, treachery, perjury, torture, banishment and the prison they have held it for four centuries, and by these same arts I hold it to-day. There is no Romanoff of learning and experience but would reverse the maxim and say: "Nothing politically valuable was ever yet achieved *except* by violence." The moralist realizes that to-day, for the first time in our history, my throne is in real peril and the nation waking up from its immemorial slave-lethargy; but he does not perceive that four deeds of violence are the reason for it: the assassination of the Finland Constitution by my hand; the slaughter, by revolutionary assassins, of Bobrikoff and Plehve; and my massacre of the unoffending innocents the other day. But the blood that flows in my veins—blood informed, trained, educated by its grim heredities, blood alert by its traditions, blood which has been to school four hundred years in the veins of professional assassins, my predecessors—*it* perceives, *it* understands! Those four deeds have set up a commotion in the inert and muddy deeps of the national heart such as no moral suasion could have accomplished; they have aroused hatred and hope in that long-atrophied heart; and, little by little, slowly but surely, that feeling will steal into every breast and possess it. In time, into even the *soldier's* breast—fatal day, day of doom, that! . . . . By and by, there will be results! How little the academical moralist knows of the tremendous moral force of massacre and assassination! . . . . Indeed there are going to be results! The nation is in labor; and by and by there will be a mighty birth—PATRIOTISM! To put it in rude, plain, unpalatable words—*true* patriotism, real patriotism: loyalty, not to a Family and a Fiction, but loyalty to the Nation itself!

. . . . There are twenty-five million families in Russia. There is a man-child at every mother's knee. If these were twenty-five million patriotic mothers, they would teach these man-children daily, saying: "Remember this, take it to heart, live by it, die for it if necessary: that our patriotism is medieval, outworn, obsolete; that the modern patriotism, the true patriotism, the only rational patriotism, is *loyalty to the Nation* ALL *the time, loyalty to the Government when it deserves it.*" With twenty-five million taught and trained patriots in the land a generation from now, my successor would think twice before he would butcher a thousand helpless poor petitioners humbly begging for his kindness and justice, as I did the other day.

[*Reflective pause.*] Well, perhaps I have been affected by

these depressing newspaper-clippings which I found under my pillow. I will read and ponder them again. [*Reads.*]

## POLISH WOMEN KNOUTED.

### Reservists' Wives Treated with Awful Brutality—At Least One Killed.

Special Cable to THE NEW YORK TIMES.

BERLIN, Nov. 27.—Infuriated by the unwillingness of the Polish troops to leave their wives and children, the Russian authorities at Kutno, a town on the Polish frontier, have treated the people in a manner almost incredibly cruel.

It is known that *one woman has been knouted to death* and that a number of others have been injured. Fifty persons have been thrown into jail. Some of the prisoners were *tortured into unconsciousness.*

Details of the brutalities are lacking, but it seems that the Cossacks tore the reservists from the arms of their wives and children and then *knouted the women who followed their husbands into the streets.*

In cases where reservists could not be found *their wives were dragged by their hair into the streets and there beaten. The chief official of the district and the Colonel of a regiment are said to have looked on while this was being done.*

A girl who had assisted in distributing Socialist tracts was *treated in an atrocious manner.*

## CZAR AS LORD'S ANOINTED.

### People Spent Night In Prayer and Fasting Before His Visit to Novgorod.

LONDON TIMES—NEW YORK TIMES.

Special Cablegram.

Copyright, 1904, THE NEW YORK TIMES

LONDON, July 27.—The London Times's Russian correspondents say the following extract from the Petersburger Zeitung, describing the Czar's recent doings at Novgorod, affords a typical instance of the servile adulation which the subjects of the Czar deem it necessary to adopt:

"The blessing of the troops, *who knelt devoutly before his Majesty*, was a profoundly moving spectacle. His Majesty held the sacred ikon aloft and pronounced aloud a blessing in his own name and that of the Empress.

"Thousands *wept with emotion and spiritual ecstasy.* Pupils of girls' schools scattered roses in the path of the monarch.

"People pressed up to the carriage in order to carry away an indelible memory of the *hallowed features of the Lord's Anointed.* Many old people had spent the night in prayer and fasting *in order to be worthy to gaze at his countenance with pure, undefiled souls.*

"The greatest enthusiasm prevails *at the happiness thus vouchsafed to the people.*"

[*Moved.*] How shameful! . . . . how pitiful! . . . . And how grotesque! . . . . To think—it was *I* that did those cruel things. . . . There is no escaping the personal responsibility—it was I that did them. And it was I that got that grovelling and awe-smitten worship! *I*—this thing in the mirror—this carrot! With one hand I flogged unoffending women to death and tortured prisoners to unconsciousness;

and with the other I held up the fetish toward my fellow deity in heaven and called down His blessing upon my adoring animals whom, and whose forbears, with His holy approval, I and mine have been instructing in the pains of hell for four lagging centuries. It is a picture! To think that this thing in the mirror—this vegetable—is an accepted deity to a mighty nation, an innumerable host, and nobody laughs; and at the same time is a diligent and practical professional devil, and nobody marvels, nobody murmurs about incongruities and inconsistencies! Is the human race a joke? Was it devised and patched together in a dull time when there was nothing important to do? Has it no respect for itself? . . . . I think my respect for it is drooping, sinking—and my respect for myself along with it. . . . There is but one restorative—*Clothes!* respect-reviving, spirit-uplifting clothes! heaven's kindliest gift to man, his only protection against finding himself out: they deceive him, they confer dignity upon him; without them he has none. How charitable are clothes, how beneficent, how puissant, how inestimably precious! Mine are able to expand a human cipher into a globe-shadowing portent; they can command the respect of the whole world—including my own, which is fading. I will put them on.

February 2, 1905.

*March 1905*

# Dr. Loeb's Incredible Discovery

Experts in biology will be apt to receive with some skepticism the announcement of Dr. Jacques Loeb of the University of California as to the creation of life by chemical agencies. . . . Doctor Loeb is a very bright and ingenious experimenter, but *a consensus of opinion among biologists* would show that he is rated rather as a man of lively imagination than an inerrant investigator of natural phenomena.—New York *Times*, March 2d.

I wish I could be as young as that again. Although I seem so old, now, I was once as young as that. I remember, as if it were but thirty or forty years ago, how a paralyzing Consensus of Opinion accumulated from Experts a-setting around, about brother experts who had patiently and laboriously cold-chiseled their way into one or another of nature's safe-deposit vaults and were reporting that they had found something valuable was a plenty for me. It settled it.

But it isn't so now—no. Because, in the drift of the years I by and by found out that a Consensus examines a new thing with its feelings rather oftener than with its mind. You know, yourself, that that is so. Do those people examine with feelings that are friendly to evidence? You know they don't. It is the other way about. They do the examining by the light of their prejudices—now isn't that true?

With curious results, yes. So curious that you wonder the Consensuses do not go out of the business. Do you know of a case where a Consensus won a game? You can go back as far as you want to and you will find history furnishing you this (until now) unwritten maxim for your guidance and profit: Whatever new thing a Consensus coppers (colloquial for "bets against"), bet your money on that very card and do not be afraid.

There was that primitive steam engine—ages back, in Greek times: a Consensus made fun of it. There was the Marquis of Worcester's steam engine, 250 years ago: a Consensus made fun of it. There was Fulton's steamboat of a century ago: a French Consensus, including the Great Napoleon, made fun of it. There was Priestly, with his oxygen: a Consensus scoffed at him, mobbed him, burned him out, banished him. While a Consensus was proving, by statistics and things, that a steamship could not cross the Atlantic, a steamship did it. A Consensus consisting of all the medical experts in Great Britain made fun of Jenner and inoculation. A Consensus consisting of all the medical experts in France made fun of the stethoscope. A Consensus of all the medical experts in Germany made fun of that young doctor (his name? forgotten by all but doctors, now, revered now by doctors alone) who discovered and abolished the cause of that awful disease, puerperal fever; made fun of him, reviled him, hunted him, persecuted him, broke his heart, killed him. Electric telegraph, Atlantic cable, telephone, all "toys," and of no practical value—verdict of the Consensuses. Geology, palæontology, evolution—all brushed into space by a Consensus of theological experts, comprising all the preachers in Christendom, assisted by the Duke of Argyle and (at first) the other scientists. And do look at Pasteur and his majestic honor roll of prodigious benefactions! Damned—each and every one of them in its turn—by frenzied and ferocious Consensuses of medical and chemical Experts comprising, for years, every member of the tribe in Europe; damned without even a casual *look* at what he was doing—and he pathetically imploring them to come and take at least one little look before making the damnation eternal. They shortened his life by their malignities and persecutions; and thus robbed the world of the further and priceless services of a man who—along certain lines and within certain limits—had done more for the human race than any other one man in all its long history: a man whom it had taken the Expert brotherhood ten thousand years to produce, and whose mate and match the brotherhood may possibly not be able to bring forth and assassinate in another ten thousand. The preacher has an old and tough reputation for bull-headed and unreasoning hostility to new light; why, he is not "in it" with the doctor! Nor, perhaps, with some of the other breeds of Experts that sit around and get up the Consensuses and squelch the new things as fast as they come from the hands of the plodders, the searchers, the inspired dreamers, the Pasteurs that come bearing pearls to scatter in the Consensus sty.

This is warm work! It puts my temperature up to 106 and

raises my pulse to the limit. It always works just so when the red rag of a Consensus jumps my fence and starts across my pasture. I have been a Consensus more than once myself, and I know the business—and its vicissitudes. I am a compositor-expert, of old and seasoned experience; nineteen years ago I delivered the final-and-for-good verdict that the linotype would never be able to earn its own living nor anyone else's: it takes fourteen acres of ground, now, to accommodate its factories in England. Thirty-five years ago I was an expert precious-metal quartz-miner. There was an outcrop in my neighborhood that assayed $600 a ton—gold. But every fleck of gold in it was shut up tight and fast in an intractable and impersuadable base-metal shell. Acting as a Consensus, I delivered the finality verdict that no human ingenuity would ever be able to set free two dollars' worth of gold out of a ton of that rock. The fact is, I did not foresee the cyanide process. Indeed, I have been a Consensus ever so many times since I reached maturity and approached the age of discretion, but I call to mind no instance in which I won out.

These sorrows have made me suspicious of Consensuses. Do you know, I tremble and the goose flesh rises on my skin every time I encounter one, now. I sheer warily off and get behind something, saying to myself, "It looks innocent and all right, but no matter, ten to one there's a cyanide process under that thing somewhere."

Now as concerns this "creation of life by chemical agencies." Reader, take my advice: don't you copper it. I don't say bet on it; no, I only say, don't you copper it. As you see, there is a Consensus out against it. If you find that you can't control your passions; if you feel that you have *got* to copper something and can't help it, copper the Consensus. It is the safest way—all history confirms it. If you are young, you will, of course, have to put up, on one side or the other, for you will not be able to restrain yourself; but as for me, I am old, and I am going to wait for a new deal.

P.S.—In the same number of the *Times* Doctor Funk says: "Man may be as badly fooled by believing too little as by believing too much; the hard-headed skeptic Thomas was the only disciple who was cheated." Is that the right and rational way to look at it? I will not be sure, for my memory is faulty, but it has always been my impression that Thomas was the only one who made an examination and proved a fact, while the others were accepting, or discounting, the fact on trust— like any other Consensus. If that is so, Doubting Thomas removed a doubt which must otherwise have confused and troubled the world until now. Including Doctor Funk. It seems to me that we owe that hard-headed—or sound-headed—witness something more than a slur. Why does Doctor Funk *examine* into spiritism, and then throw stones at Thomas. Why doesn't he take it on trust? Has inconsistency become a jewel in Lafayette Place?

OLD-MAN-AFRAID-OF-THE-CONSENSUS.

*Extract from Adam's Diary.*—Then there was a Consensus about it. It was the very first one. It sat six days and nights. It was then delivered of the verdict that a world could not be made out of nothing; that such small things as sun and moon and stars might, maybe, but it would take years and years, if there was considerable many of them. Then the Consensus got up and looked out of the window, and there was the whole outfit spinning and sparkling in space! You never saw such a disappointed lot.

his

ADAM—i—

mark

*1905*

# The War Prayer

It was a time of great and exalting excitement. The country was up in arms, the war was on, in every breast burned the holy fire of patriotism; the drums were beating, the bands playing, the toy pistols popping, the bunched firecrackers hissing and spluttering; on every hand and far down the receding and fading spread of roofs and balconies a fluttering wilderness of flags flashed in the sun; daily the young volunteers marched down the wide avenue gay and fine in their new uniforms, the proud fathers and mothers and sisters and sweethearts cheering them with voices choked with happy emotion as they swung by; nightly the packed mass-meetings listened, panting, to patriot oratory which stirred the deepest deeps of their hearts, and which they interrupted at briefest intervals with cyclones of applause, the tears running down their cheeks the while; in the churches the pastors preached devotion to flag and country, and invoked the God of Battles, beseeching His aid in our good cause in outpourings of fervid eloquence which moved every listener. It was indeed a glad and gracious time, and the half dozen rash spirits that ventured to disapprove of the war and cast a doubt upon its righteousness straightway got such a stern and angry warning that for their personal safety's sake they quickly shrank out of sight and offended no more in that way.

Sunday morning came—next day the battalions would leave for the front; the church was filled; the volunteers were there, their young faces alight with martial dreams—visions of the stern advance, the gathering momentum, the rushing charge, the flashing sabres, the flight of the foe, the tumult, the enveloping smoke, the fierce pursuit, the surrender!— then home from the war, bronzed heroes, welcomed, adored, submerged in golden seas of glory! With the volunteers sat their dear ones, proud, happy, and envied by the neighbors and friends who had no sons and brothers to send forth to the field of honor, there to win for the flag, or, failing, die the noblest of noble deaths. The service proceeded; a war-chapter from the Old Testament was read; the first prayer was said; it was followed by an organ-burst that shook the building, and with one impulse the house rose, with glowing eyes and beating hearts and poured out that tremendous invocation—

> God the all-terrible! Thou who ordainest,
> Thunder thy clarion and lightning thy sword!

Then came the "long" prayer. None could remember the like of it for passionate pleading and moving and beautiful language. The burden of its supplication was, that the ever-merciful and benignant Father of us all would watch over our noble young soldiers, and aid, comfort, and encourage them in their patriotic work; bless them, shield them in the day of battle and the hour of peril, bear them in His mighty hand, make them strong and confident, invincible in the bloody onset, help them to crush the foe, grant to them and to their flag and country imperishable honor and glory—

An aged stranger entered, and moved with slow and noiseless step up the main aisle, his eyes fixed upon the minister, his long body clothed in a robe that reached to his feet, his head bare, his white hair descending in a frothy cataract to his shoulders, his seamy face unnaturally pale, pale even to ghastliness. With all eyes following him and wondering, he made his silent way; without pausing, he ascended to the preacher's side and stood there, waiting. With shut lids the preacher, unconscious of his presence, continued his moving prayer, and at last finished it with the words, uttered in fervent appeal, "Bless our arms, grant us the victory, O Lord our God, Father and Protector of our land and flag!"

The stranger touched his arm, motioned him to step aside—which the startled minister did—and took his place. During some moments he surveyed the spell-bound audience with solemn eyes, in which burned an uncanny light; then in a deep voice he said—

"I come from the Throne—bearing a message from Almighty God!" The words smote the house with a shock; if the stranger perceived it he gave it no attention. "He has heard the prayer of His servant your shepherd, and will grant it if such shall be your desire after I, His messenger, shall have explained to you its import—that is to say, its full import. For it is like unto many of the prayers of men, in that it asks for more than he who utters it is aware of—except he pause and think.

"God's servant and yours has prayed his prayer. Has he paused, and taken thought? Is it one prayer? No, it is two— one uttered, the other not. Both have reached the ear of Him who heareth all supplications, the spoken and the unspoken. Ponder this—keep it in mind. If you would beseech a blessing upon yourself, beware! lest without intent you invoke a curse upon a neighbor at the same time. If you pray for the blessing of rain upon your crop which needs it, by that act you are possibly praying for a curse upon some neighbor's crop which may not need rain and can be injured by it.

"You have heard your servant's prayer—the uttered part of it. I am commissioned of God to put into words the other part of it—that part which the pastor—and also you in your hearts—fervently prayed silently. And ignorantly and unthinkingly? God grant that it was so! You heard these words: 'Grant us the victory, O Lord our God!' That is sufficient. The *whole* of the uttered prayer is compacted into those pregnant words. Elaborations were not necessary. When you have prayed for victory you have prayed for many unmentioned results which follow victory—*must* follow it, cannot help but follow it. Upon the listening spirit of God the Father fell also the unspoken part of the prayer. He commandeth me to put it into words. Listen!

"O Lord, our Father, our young patriots, idols of our hearts, go forth to battle—be Thou near them! With them —in spirit—we also go forth from the sweet peace of our beloved firesides to smite the foe. O Lord, our God, help us to tear their soldiers to bloody shreds with our shells; help us to cover their smiling fields with the pale forms of their patriot dead; help us to drown the thunder of the guns with the shrieks of their wounded, writhing in pain; help us to lay waste their humble homes with a hurricane of fire; help us to wring the hearts of their unoffending widows with unavailing grief; help us to turn them out roofless with their little children to wander unfriended the wastes of their desolated land in rags and hunger and thirst, sport of the sun-flames of summer and the icy winds of winter, broken in spirit, worn with travail, imploring Thee for the refuge of the grave and denied it—for our sakes who adore Thee, Lord, blast their hopes, blight their lives, protract their bitter pilgrimage, make heavy their steps, water their way with their tears, stain the white snow with the blood of their wounded feet! We ask it, in the spirit of love, of Him Who is the Source of Love, and Who is the ever-faithful refuge and friend of all that are sore beset and seek His aid with humble and contrite hearts. Amen."

[*After a pause.*] "Ye have prayed it; if ye still desire it, speak!—The messenger of the Most High waits."

It was believed afterwards, that the man was a lunatic, because there was no sense in what he said.

*c. March 10, 1905*

# A Humane Word
# from Satan

*To the Editor of Harper's Weekly:*

DEAR SIR AND KINSMAN,—Let us have done with this frivolous talk. The American Board accepts contributions from me every year: then why shouldn't it from Mr. Rockefeller? In all the ages, three-fourths of the support of the great charities has been conscience-money, as my books will show: then what becomes of the sting when that term is applied to Mr. Rockefeller's gift? The American Board's trade is financed mainly from the graveyards. Bequests, you understand. Conscience-money. Confession of an old crime and deliberate perpetration of a new one; for deceased's contribution is a robbery of his heirs. Shall the Board decline bequests because they stand for one of these offences every time and generally for both?

Allow me to continue. The charge most persistently and resentfully and remorselessly dwelt upon is, that Mr. Rockefeller's contribution is incurably tainted by perjury—perjury proved against him in the courts. *It makes us smile*—down in my place! Because there isn't a rich man in your vast city who doesn't perjure himself every year before the tax board. They are all caked with perjury, many layers thick. Iron clad, so to speak. If there is one that isn't, I desire to acquire him for my museum, and will pay Dinosaur rates. Will you say it isn't infraction of law, but only annual evasion of it? Comfort yourselves with that nice distinction if you like—*for the present*. But by and by, when you arrive, I will show you something interesting: a whole hell-full of evaders! Sometimes a frank lawbreaker turns up elsewhere, but I get those others every time.

To return to my muttons. I wish you to remember that my rich perjurers are contributing to the American Board with frequency: it is money filched from the sworn-off personal tax; therefore it is the wages of sin; therefore it is my money; therefore it is *I* that contribute it; and, finally, it is therefore as I have said: since the Board daily accepts contributions from me, why should it decline them from Mr. Rockefeller, who is as good as I am, let the courts say what they may?

SATAN.

*April 8, 1905*

# Christian Citizenship

Is there such a thing as Christian citizenship? No, but it could be created. The process would be quite simple, and not productive of hardship to any one. It will be conceded that every man's first duty is to God; it will also be conceded, and with strong emphasis, that a Christian's first duty is to God. It then follows, as a matter of course, that it is his duty to carry his Christian code of morals to the polls and vote them. Whenever he shall do that, he will not find himself voting for an unclean man, a dishonest man. Whenever a Christian votes, he votes against God or for Him, and he knows this quite well. God is an issue in every election; He is a candidate in the person of every clean nominee on every ticket; His purity and His approval are there, to be voted for or voted against, and no fealty to party can absolve His servant from his higher and more exacting fealty to Him; He takes precedence of party, duty to Him is above every claim of party.

If Christians should vote their duty to God at the polls, they would carry every election, and do it with ease. They would elect every clean candidate in the United States, and defeat every soiled one. Their prodigious power would be quickly realized and recognized, and afterward there would be no unclean candidates upon any ticket, and graft would cease. No church organization can be found in the country that would elect men of foul character to be its shepherd, its treasurer, and superintendent of its Sunday-school. It would be revolted at the idea; it would consider such an election an insult to God. Yet every Christian congregation in the country elects foul men to public office, while quite aware that this also is an open and deliberate insult to God, who can not approve and does not approve the placing of the liberties and the well-being of His children in the hands of infamous men. It is the Christian congregations that are responsible for the filling of our public offices with criminals, for the reason that they could prevent it if they chose to do it. They could prevent it without organizing a league, without framing a platform, without making any speeches or passing any resolutions—in a word, without concert of any kind. They could accomplish it by each individual resolving to vote for God at the polls—that is to say, vote for the candidate whom God would approve. Can a man imagine such a thing as God being a Republican or a Democrat, and voting for a criminal or a blackguard merely because party loyalty required it? Then can we imagine that a man can improve upon God's attitude in this matter, and by help of professional politicians invent a better policy? God has no politics but cleanliness and honesty, and it is good enough for men.

A man's second duty is to his family. There was a time when a clergyman's duty to his family required him to be his congregation's political slave, and vote his congregation's ticket in order to safeguard the food and shelter of his wife and children. But that time has gone by. We have the secret ballot now, and a clergyman can vote for God. He can also plead with his congregation to do the like.

Perhaps. We can not be sure. The congregation would probably inquire whom *he* was going to vote for; and if he stood upon his manhood and answered that they had no Christian right (which is the same as saying no moral right, and, of course, no legal right) to ask the question, it is conceivable—not to say certain—that they would dismiss him, and be much offended at his proposing to be a man as well as a clergyman.

Still, there are clergymen who are so situated as to be able to make the experiment. It would be worth while to try it. If the Christians of America could be persuaded to vote God and a clean ticket, it would bring about a moral revolution that would be incalculably beneficent. It would save the country—a country whose Christians have betrayed it and are destroying it.

The Christians of Connecticut sent Bulkeley to the Senate. They sent to the Legislature the men who elected him. These two crimes they could have prevented; they did not do it, and upon them rest the shame and the responsibility. Only one clergyman remembered his Christian morals and his duty to God, and stood bravely by both. Mr. Smythe is probably an outcast now, but such a man as that can endure ostracism; and such a man as that is likely to possess the treasure of a family that can endure it with him, and be proud to do it. I kiss the hem of his garment.

Four years ago Greater New York had two tickets in the field: one clean, the other dirty, with a single exception; an unspeakable ticket with that lonely exception. One-half of the Christians voted for that foul ticket and against God and the Christian code of morals, putting loyalty to party above loyalty to God and honorable citizenship, and they came within a fraction of electing it; whereas if they had stood by their professed morals they would have buried it out of sight. Christianity was on trial then, it is on trial now. And nothing important is on trial except Christianity.

It was on trial in Philadelphia, and failed; in Pennsylvania, and failed; in Rhode Island, and failed; in Connecticut, and failed; in New York, and failed; in Delaware, and failed; in every town and county and State, and was recreant to its trust; it has effusively busied itself with the small matters of charity and benevolence, and has looked on, indifferent while its country was sinking lower and lower in repute and drifting further and further toward moral destruction. It is the one force that can save, and it sits with folded hands. In Greater New York it will presently have an opportunity to elect or defeat some straight, clean, honest men, of the sterling Jerome stamp, and some of the Tammany kind. The Christian vote—and the Christian vote alone—will decide the contest. It, and it alone, is master of the situation, and lord of the result.

*September 2, 1905*

# King Leopold's Soliloquy

## A DEFENSE OF HIS CONGO RULE

### "IT IS I"

"Leopold II is the absolute Master of the whole of the internal and external activity of the Independent State of the Congo. The organization of justice, the army, the industrial and commercial regimes are established freely by himself. He would say, and with greater accuracy than did Louis XIV., 'The State, it is I.'" *Prof. F. Cattier, Brussels University.*
"Let us repeat after so many others what has become a platitude, the success of the African work is the work of a sole directing will, without being hampered by the hesitation of timorous politicians, carried out under his sole responsibility, — intelligent, thoughtful, conscious of the perils and the advantages, discounting with an admirable prescience the great results of a near future." *M. Alfred Poskine in "Bilans Congolais."*

[*Throws down pamphlets which he has been reading. Excitedly combs his flowing spread of whiskers with his fingers; pounds the table with his fists; lets off brisk volleys of unsanctified language at brief intervals, repentantly drooping his head, between volleys, and kissing the Louis XI crucifix hanging from his neck, accompanying the kisses with mumbled apologies; presently rises, flushed and perspiring, and walks the floor, gesticulating*]

—— ——!! —— ——!! If I had them by the throat! [*Hastily kisses the crucifix, and mumbles*] In these twenty years I have spent millions to keep the press of the two hemispheres quiet, and still these leaks keep on occurring. I have spent other

millions on religion and art, and what do I get for it? Nothing. Not a compliment. These generosities are studiedly
ignored, in print. In print I get nothing but slanders—and
slanders again—and still slanders, and slanders on top of slanders! Grant them true, what of it? They are slanders all the
same, when uttered against a king.

Miscreants—they are telling *everything*! Oh, everything:
how I went pilgriming among the Powers in tears, with my
mouth full of Bible and my pelt oozing piety at every pore,
and implored them to place the vast and rich and populous
Congo Free State in trust in my hands as their agent, so that I
might root out slavery and stop the slave raids, and lift up
those twenty-five millions of gentle and harmless blacks out of
darkness into light, the light of our blessed Redeemer, the
light that streams from his holy Word, the light that makes
glorious our noble civilization—lift them up and dry their
tears and fill their bruised hearts with joy and gratitude—lift
them up and make them comprehend that they were no
longer outcasts and forsaken, but our very brothers in Christ;
how America and thirteen great European states wept in sympathy with me, and were persuaded; how their representatives
met in convention in Berlin and made me Head Foreman and
Superintendent of the Congo State, and drafted out my
powers and limitations, carefully guarding the persons and
liberties and properties of the natives against hurt and harm;
forbidding whisky traffic and gun traffic; providing courts of
justice; making commerce free and fetterless to the merchants
and traders of all nations, and welcoming and safe-guarding
all missionaries of all creeds and denominations. They have
told how I planned and prepared my establishment and selected my horde of officials—"pals" and "pimps" of mine,
"unspeakable Belgians" every one—and hoisted my flag, and
"took in" a President of the United States, and got him to be
the first to recognize it and salute it. Oh, well, let them blackguard me if they like; it is a deep satisfaction to me to remember that I was a shade too smart for that nation that thinks
itself so smart. Yes, I certainly did bunco a Yankee—as those
people phrase it. Pirate flag? Let them call is so—perhaps it
is. All the same, *they were the first to salute it*.

These meddlesome American missionaries! these frank

British consuls! these blabbing Belgian-born traitor officials!—those tiresome parrots are always talking, always
telling. They have told how for twenty years I have ruled the
Congo State not as a trustee of the Powers, an agent, a subordinate, a foreman, but as a sovereign—sovereign over a
fruitful domain four times as large as the German Empire—sovereign absolute, irresponsible, above all law; tram-
pling the Berlin-made Congo charter under foot; barring out
all foreign traders but myself; restricting commerce to myself,
through concessionaires who are my creatures and confederates; seizing and holding the State as my personal property,
the whole of its vast revenues as my private "swag"—mine,
solely mine—claiming and holding its millions of people as
my private property, my serfs, my slaves; their labor mine,
with or without wage; the food they raise not their property
but mine; the rubber, the ivory and all the other riches of the
land mine—mine solely—and gathered for me by the men,
the women and the little children under compulsion of lash
and bullet, fire, starvation, mutilation and the halter.

These pests!—it is as I say, they have kept back nothing!
They have revealed these and yet other details which shame
should have kept them silent about, since they were exposures of a king, a sacred personage and immune from reproach, by right of his selection and appointment to his
great office by God himself; a king whose acts cannot be
criticized without blasphemy, since God has observed them
from the beginning and has manifested no dissatisfaction
with them, nor shown disapproval of them, nor hampered
nor interrupted them in any way. By this sign I recognize
his approval of what I have done; his cordial and glad approval, I am sure I may say. Blest, crowned, beatified with
this great reward, this golden reward, this unspeakably precious reward, why should I care for men's cursings and revilings of me? [*With a sudden outburst of feeling*] May they
roast a million æons in— [*Catches his breath and effusively
kisses the crucifix; sorrowfully murmurs, "I shall get myself
damned yet, with these indiscretions of speech."*]

Yes, they go on telling everything, these chatterers! They
tell how I levy incredibly burdensome taxes upon the natives—taxes which are a pure theft; taxes which they must

satisfy by gathering rubber under hard and constantly harder conditions, and by raising and furnishing food supplies gratis—and it all comes out that, when they fall short of their tasks through hunger, sickness, despair, and ceaseless and exhausting labor without rest, and forsake their homes and flee to the woods to escape punishment, my black soldiers, drawn from unfriendly tribes, and instigated and directed by my Belgians, hunt them down and butcher them and burn their villages—reserving some of the girls. They tell it all: how I am wiping a nation of friendless creatures out of existence by every form of murder, for my private pocket's sake. But they never say, although they know it, that I have labored in the cause of religion at the same time and all the time, and have sent missionaries there (of a "convenient stripe," as they phrase it), to teach them the error of their ways and bring them to Him who is all mercy and love, and who is the sleepless guardian and friend of all who suffer. They tell only what is against me, they will not tell what is in my favor.

They tell how England required of me a Commission of Inquiry into Congo atrocities, and how, to quiet that meddling country, with its disagreeable Congo Reform Association, made up of earls and bishops and John Morleys and university grandees and other dudes, more interested in other people's business than in their own, I appointed it. Did it stop their mouths? No, they merely pointed out that it was a commission composed wholly of my "Congo butchers," "the very men whose acts were to be inquired into." They said it was equivalent to appointing a commission of wolves to inquire into depredations committed upon a sheepfold. *Nothing* can satisfy a cursed Englishman!*

*Recent information is to the effect that the resident missionaries found the commission as a whole apparently interested to promote reforms. One of its members was a leading Congo official, another an official of the government in Belgium, the third a Swiss jurist. The commission's report will reach the public only through the king, and will be whatever he consents to make it; it is not yet forthcoming, though six months have passed since the investigation was made. There is, however, abundant evidence that horrible abuses were found and conceded, the testimony of missionaries, which had been scouted by the king's defenders, being amply vindicated. One who was present at one hearing of the commission writes: "Men of stone would be moved by the stories that are being unfolded as the commission probes into

And are the fault-finders frank with my private character? They could not be more so if I were a plebeian, a peasant, a mechanic. They remind the world that from the earliest days my house has been chapel and brothel combined, and both industries working full time; that I practised cruelties upon my queen and my daughters, and supplemented them with daily shame and humiliations; that, when my queen lay in the happy refuge of her coffin, and a daughter implored me on her knees to let her look for the last time upon her mother's face, I refused; and that, three years ago, not being satisfied with the stolen spoils of a whole alien nation, I robbed my own child of her property and appeared by proxy in court, a spectacle to the civilized world, to defend the act and complete the crime. It is as I have said: they are unfair, unjust; they will resurrect and give new currency to such things as those, or to any other things that count against me, but they will not mention any act of mine that is in my favor. I have spent more money on art than any other monarch of my time, and they know it. Do they speak of it, do they tell about it? No, they do not. They prefer to work up what they call "ghastly statistics" into offensive kindergarten object lessons, whose purpose is to make sentimental people shudder, and prejudice them against me. They remark that "if the innocent blood shed in the Congo State by King Leopold were put in buckets and the buckets placed side by side, the line would stretch 2,000 miles; if the skeletons of his ten millions of starved and butchered dead could rise up and march in single file, it would take them seven months and four days to pass a given point; if compacted together in a body, they would occupy more ground than St. Louis covers, World's Fair and all; if they should all clap their bony hands at once, the grisly

---

the awful history of rubber collection." Certain reforms were ordered in the one section visited, but the latest word is that after the commission's departure, conditions soon became worse than before its coming. Very well, then, the king has investigated himself. One stage is achieved. The next one in order is the investigation of conditions in the Congo State *by the Powers responsible for the creation of the Congo State*. The United States is one of these. Such an investigation is advocated by Lyman Abbott, Henry Van Dyke, David Starr Jordan and other prominent citizens in a petition to Congress.—M. T.

crash would be heard at a distance of—" Damnation, it makes me tired! And they do similar miracles with the money I have distilled from that blood and put into my pocket. They pile it into Egyptian pyramids; they carpet Saharas with it; they spread it across the sky, and the shadow it casts makes twilight in the earth. And the tears I have caused, the hearts I have broken—oh, nothing can persuade them to let *them* alone!

[*Meditative pause*] Well . . . no matter, I *did* beat the Yankees, anyway! there's comfort in that. [*Reads with mocking smile, the President's Order of Recognition of April 22, 1884*]

" . . . the government of the United States announces its sympathy with and approval of the humane and benevolent purposes of (my Congo scheme), and will order the officers of the United States, both on land and sea, to recognize its flag as the flag of a friendly government."

Possibly the Yankees would like to take that back, now, but they will find that my agents are not over there in America for nothing. But there is no danger; neither nations nor governments can afford to confess a blunder. [*With a contented smile, begins to read from "Report by Rev. W. M. Morrison, American missionary in the Congo Free State"*]

"I furnish herewith some of the many atrocious incidents which have come under my own personal observation; they reveal the *organized system* of plunder and outrage which has been perpetrated and is now being carried on in that unfortunate country by King Leopold of Belgium. I say King Leopold, because he and he *alone* is now responsible, since he is the *absolute sovereign. He styles himself such.* When our government in 1884 laid the foundation of the Congo Free State, by recognizing its flag, little did it know that this concern, parading under the guise of philanthropy, was really King Leopold of Belgium, one of the shrewdest, most heartless and most conscienceless rulers that ever sat on a throne. This is apart from his known corrupt morals, which have made his name and his family a byword in two continents. Our government would most certainly not have recognized that flag had it known that it was really King Leopold individually who was asking for recognition; had it known that it was setting up in the heart of Africa an *absolute monarchy*; had it known that, having put down African slavery in our own country at great cost of blood and money, it was *establishing a worse form of slavery right in Africa.*"

[*With evil joy*] Yes, I certainly was a shade too clever for the Yankees. It hurts; it gravels them. They can't get over it! Puts a shame upon them in another way, too, and a graver way; for they never can rid their records of the reproachful fact that their vain Republic, self-appointed Champion and Promoter of the Liberties of the World, is the only democracy in history that has lent its power and influence to the establishing of an *absolute monarchy*!

[*Contemplating, with an unfriendly eye, a stately pile of pamphlets*] Blister the meddlesome missionaries! They write tons of these things. They seem to be always around, always spying, always eye-witnessing the happenings; and everything they see they commit to paper. They are always prowling from place to place; the natives consider them their only friends; they go to them with their sorrows; they show them their scars and their wounds, inflicted by my soldier police; they hold up the stumps of their arms and lament because their hands have been chopped off, as punishment for not bringing in enough rubber, and as proof to be laid before my officers that the required punishment was well and truly carried out. One of these missionaries saw eighty-one of these hands drying over a fire for transmission to my officials—and of course he must go and set it down and print it. They travel and travel, they spy and spy! And nothing is too trivial for them to print. [*Takes up a pamphlet. Reads a passage from Report of a "Journey made in July, August and September, 1903, by Rev. A. E. Scrivener, a British missionary"*]

" . . . . Soon we began talking, and without any encouragement on my part the natives began the tales I had become so accustomed to. They were living in peace and quietness when the white men came in from the lake with all sorts of requests to do this and that, and they thought it meant slavery. So they attempted to keep the white men out of their country but without avail. The rifles were too much for them. So they submitted and made up their minds to do the best they could under the altered circumstances. First came the command to build houses for the soldiers, and this was done without a murmur. Then they had to feed the soldiers and all the men and women—hangers on—who accompanied them. Then they were told to bring in rubber. This was quite a new thing for them to do. There was rubber in the forest several days away from their home, but that it was worth anything was news to them. A small reward was offered and a rush was made for the rubber. 'What strange white men, to give us cloth and beads for the sap of a wild vine.' They rejoiced in what they thought their good fortune. But soon the reward was reduced until at last they were told to bring in the rubber for nothing. To this they tried to demur; but to their great surprise several were shot by the soldiers, and the rest were told, with many curses and blows, to go at once or more would be killed. Terrified, they began to prepare their food for the fortnight's absence from the village which the collection of rubber entailed. The soldiers discovered them sitting about. 'What, not gone yet?' Bang! bang! bang! and down fell one and another, dead, in the midst of wives and companions. There is a terrible wail and an attempt made to prepare the dead for burial, but this is not allowed. All must go at once to the forest. Without food? Yes, without food. And off the poor wretches had to go without even their tinder boxes to make fires. Many died in the forests of hunger and exposure, and still more from the rifles of the ferocious soldiers in charge of the post. In spite of all their efforts the amount fell off and more and more were killed. I was shown around the place, and the sites of former big chiefs' settlements were pointed out. A careful estimate made the population of, say, seven years ago, to be 2,000 people in and about the post, within a radius of, say, a quarter of a mile. All told, they would not muster 200 now, and there is so much sadness and gloom about them that they are fast decreasing.

"We stayed there all day on Monday and had many talks with the people. On the Sunday some of the boys had told me of some bones which they had seen, so on the Monday I asked to be shown these bones. Lying about on the grass, within a few yards of the house I was occupying, were numbers of human skulls, bones, in some cases complete skeletons. I counted thirty-six skulls, and saw many sets of bones from which the skulls were missing. I called one of the men and asked the meaning of it. 'When the rubber palaver began,' said he, 'the soldiers shot so many we grew tired of burying, and very often we were not allowed to bury; and so just dragged the bodies out into the grass and left them. There are hundreds all around if you would like to see them.' But I had seen more than enough, and was sickened by the stories that came from men and women alike of the awful time they had passed through. The Bulgarian atrocities might be considered as mildness itself when compared with what was done here. How the people submitted I don't know, and even now I wonder as I think of their patience. That some of them managed to run away is some cause for thankfulness. I stayed there two days and the one thing that impressed itself upon me was the collection of rubber. I saw long files of men come in, as at Bongo, with their little baskets under their arms; saw them paid their milk tin full of salt, and the two yards of calico flung to the headmen; saw their trembling timidity, and in fact a great deal that all went to prove the state of terrorism that exists and the virtual slavery in which the people are held."

That is their way; they spy and spy, and run into print with every foolish trifle. And that British consul, Mr. Casement, is just like them. He gets hold of a *diary which had been kept by one of my government officers*, and, although it is a private diary and intended for no eye but its owner's, Mr. Casement is so lacking in delicacy and refinement as to print passages from it. [*Reads a passage from the diary*]

"Each time the corporal goes out to get rubber, cartridges are given him. He must bring back all not used, and for every one used he must bring back a right hand. M. P. told me that sometimes they shot a cartridge at an animal in hunting; they then cut off a hand from a living man. As to the extent to which this is carried on, he informed me that in six months the State on the Mambogo River had used 6,000 cartridges, which means that 6,000 people are killed or mutilated. It means more than 6,000, for the people have told me repeatedly that the soldiers kill the children with the butt of their guns."

When the subtle consul thinks silence will be more effective than words, he employs it. Here he leaves it to be recognized that a thousand killings and mutilations a month is a large output for so small a region as the Mambogo River concession, silently indicating the dimensions of it by accompanying his report with a map of the prodigious Congo State, in which there is not room for so small an object as that river. That silence is intended to say, "If it is a thousand a month in this little corner, imagine the output of the whole vast State!" A gentleman would not descend to these furtivenesses.

Now as to the mutilations. You can't head off a Congo critic and make him stay headed-off; he dodges, and straightway comes back at you from another direction. They are full

of slippery arts. When the mutilations (severing hands, unsexing men, etc.) began to stir Europe, we hit upon the idea
of excusing them with a retort which we judged would knock
them dizzy on that subject for good and all, and leave them
nothing more to say; to wit, we boldly laid the custom on the
natives, and said we did not invent it, but only followed it.
Did it knock them dizzy? did it shut their mouths? Not for an
hour. They dodged, and came straight back at us with the
remark that "if a Christian king can perceive a saving moral
difference between inventing bloody barbarities, and *imitating them from savages*, for charity's sake let him get what comfort he can out of his confession!"

It is most annoying, the way that that consul acts—that
spy, that busy-body. [*Takes up pamphlet "Treatment of Women
and Children in the Congo State; what Mr. Casement Saw in
1903"*] *Hardly two years ago!* Intruding that date upon the public was a piece of cold malice. It was intended to weaken the
force of my press syndicate's assurances to the public that my
severities in the Congo *ceased*, and ceased utterly, *years and
years ago*. This man is fond of trifles—revels in them, gloats
over them, pets them, fondles them, sets them all down. One
doesn't need to drowse through his monotonous report to see
that; the mere sub-headings of its chapters prove it. [*Reads*]

"Two hundred and forty persons, *men, women, and children*, compelled to supply government with *one ton* of carefully prepared food-
stuffs *per week*, receiving in remuneration, all told, the princely sum
of 15s. 10d!"

Very well, it was liberal. It was not much short of a penny a
week for each nigger. It suits this consul to belittle it, yet he
knows very well that I could have had both the food and the
labor for nothing. I can prove it by a thousand instances.
[*Reads*]

"Expedition against a village behindhand in its (compulsory) supplies; result, slaughter of sixteen persons; among them three women
and a boy of five years. Ten carried off, to be prisoners till ransomed;
among them a child, who died during the march."

But he is careful not to explain that we are *obliged* to resort
to ransom to collect debts, where the people have nothing to

pay with. Families that escape to the woods sell some of their members into slavery and thus provide the ransom. He knows that I would stop this if I could find a less objectionable way to collect their debts. . . . Mm—here is some more of the consul's delicacy! He reports a conversation he had with some natives:

Q. "How do you know it was the *white* men themselves who ordered these cruel things to be done to you? These things must have been done without the white man's knowledge by the black soldiers."

A. "The white men told their soldiers: 'You only kill *women*; you cannot kill men. You must prove that you kill men.' So then the soldiers when they killed us" (here he stopped and hesitated and then pointing to . . . he said:) "then they . . . and took them to the white men, who said: 'It is true, you have killed *men*.' "

Q. "You say this is true? Were many of you so treated after being shot?"

All [*shouting out*]: "*Nkoto! Nkoto!*" ("Very many! Very many!")

There was no doubt that these people were not inventing. Their vehemence, their flashing eyes, their excitement, were not simulated.

Of course the critic had to divulge that; he has no self-respect. All his kind reproach me, although they know quite well that I took no pleasure in punishing the men in that particular way, but only did it as a warning to other delinquents. Ordinary punishments are no good with ignorant savages; they make no impression. [*Reads more sub-heads*]

"Devasted region; population reduced from 40,000 to 8,000."

He does not take the trouble to say how it happened. He is fertile in concealments. He hopes his readers and his Congo reformers, of the Lord-Aberdeen-Norbury-John-Morley-Sir-Gilbert-Parker stripe, will think they were all killed. They were not. The great majority of them escaped. They fled to the bush with their families because of the rubber raids, and it was there they died of hunger. Could we help that?

One of my sorrowing critics observes: "Other Christian rulers tax their people, but furnish schools, courts of law, roads, light, water and protection to life and limb in return; King Leopold taxes his stolen nation, but provides *nothing in return but hunger, terror, grief, shame, captivity, mutilation and massacre.*" That is their style! I furnish "nothing!" I send the gospel to the survivors; these censure-mongers know it, but they would rather have their tongues cut out than mention it. I have several times required my raiders to give the dying an opportunity to kiss the sacred emblem; and if they obeyed me I have without doubt been the humble means of saving many souls. None of my traducers have had the fairness to mention this; but let it pass; there is One who has not overlooked it, and that is my solace, that is my consolation.

[*Puts down the Report, takes up a pamphlet, glances along the middle of it*]

This is where the "death-trap" comes in. Meddlesome missionary spying around—Rev. W. H. Sheppard. Talks with a black raider of mine after a raid; cozens him into giving away some particulars. The raider remarks:

"I demanded 30 slaves from this side of the stream and 30 from the other side; 2 points of ivory, 2,500 balls of rubber, 13 goats, 10 fowls and 6 dogs, some corn chumy, etc.

'How did the fight come up?' I asked.

'I sent for all their chiefs, sub-chiefs, men and women, to come on a certain day, saying that I was going to finish all the palaver. When they entered these small gates (the walls being made of fences brought from other villages, the high native ones) I demanded all my pay or I would kill them; so they refused to pay me, and I ordered the fence to be closed so they couldn't run away; then we killed them here inside the fence. The panels of the fence fell down and some escaped.'

'How many did you kill?' I asked.

'We killed plenty, will you see some of them?'

That was just what I wanted.

He said: 'I think we have killed between eighty and ninety, and those in the other villages I don't know, I did not go out but sent my people.'

He and I walked out on the plain just near the camp. There were three dead bodies with the flesh carved off from the waist down.

'Why are they carved so, only leaving the bones?' I asked.

'My people ate them,' he answered promptly. He then explained, 'The men who have young children do not eat people, but all the rest ate them.' On the left was a big man, shot in the back and without a head. (All these corpses were nude.)

'Where is the man's head?' I asked.

'Oh, they made a bowl of the forehead to rub up tobacco and diamba in.'

We continued to walk and examine until late in the afternoon, and counted forty-one bodies. The rest had been eaten up by the people.

On returning to the camp, we crossed a young woman, shot in the back of the head, one hand was cut away. I asked why, and Mulunba N'Cusa explained that they always cut off the right hand to give to the State on their return.

'Can you not show me some of the hands?' I asked.

So he conducted us to a framework of sticks, under which was burning a slow fire, and there they were, the right hands—I counted them, eighty-one in all.

There were not less than sixty women (Bena Pianga) prisoners. I saw them.

We all say that we have as fully as possible investigated the whole outrage, and find it was a plan previously made to get all the stuff possible and to catch and kill the poor people in the 'death-trap.' "

*Another* detail, as we see!—cannibalism. They report cases of it with a most offensive frequency. My traducers do not forget to remark that, inasmuch as I am absolute and with a word can prevent in the Congo anything I choose to prevent, then whatsoever is done there by my permission is my act, my *personal* act; that *I* do it; that the hand of my agent is as truly *my* hand as if it were attached to my own arm; and so they picture me in my robes of state, with my crown on my head, munching human flesh, saying grace, mumbling thanks to Him from whom all good things come. Dear, dear, when the soft-hearts get hold of a thing like that missionary's contribution they quite lose their tranquility over it. They speak out profanely and reproach Heaven for allowing such a fiend to live. Meaning me. They think it irregular. They go shuddering around, brooding over the reduction of that Congo population from 25,000,000 to 15,000,000 in the twenty years of my administration; then they burst out and call me "the King with Ten Million Murders on his Soul." They call me a "record." The most of them do not stop with charging merely the 10,000,000 against me. No, they reflect that but for me the population, by natural increase, would now be 30,000,000, so they charge another 5,000,000 against me and make my total death-harvest 15,000,000. They remark that the man who killed the goose that laid the golden egg was responsible for the eggs she would subsequently have laid if she had been let alone. Oh, yes, they call me a "record." They remark that twice in a generation, in India, the Great Famine destroys 2,000,000 out of a population of 320,000,000, and the whole world holds up its hands in pity and horror; then they fall to wondering where the world would find room for its emotions if I had a chance to trade places with the Great Famine for twenty years! The idea fires their fancy, and they go on and imagine the Famine coming in state at the end of the twenty years and prostrating itself before me, saying: "Teach me, Lord, I perceive that I am but an apprentice." And next they imagine Death coming, with his scythe and hour-glass, and begging me to marry his daughter and reorganize his plant and run the business. For the whole world, you see! By this time their diseased minds are under full steam, and they get down their books and expand their labors, with me for text. They hunt through all biography for my match, working Attila, Torquemada, Ghengis Khan, Ivan the Terrible, and the rest of that crowd for all they are worth, and evilly exulting when they cannot find it. Then they examine the historical earthquakes and cyclones and blizzards and cataclysms and volcanic eruptions: verdict, none of them "in it" with me. At last they do really hit it (as they think), and they close their labors with conceding—reluctantly—that I have *one* match in history, but only one—the *Flood*. This is intemperate.

But they are always that, when they think of me. They can no more keep quiet when my name is mentioned than can a glass of water control its feelings with a seidlitz powder in its bowels. The bizarre things they can imagine, with me for an inspiration! One Englishman offers to give me the odds of three to one and bet me anything I like, up to 20,000 guineas, that for 2,000,000 years I am going to be the most conspicuous foreigner in hell. The man is so beside himself with anger that he does not perceive that the idea is foolish. Foolish and unbusinesslike: you see, there could be no winner; both of us would be losers, on account of the loss of interest on the stakes; at four or five per cent. compounded, this would amount to—I do not know how much, exactly, but, by the time the term was up and the bet payable, a person could buy hell itself with the accumulation.

Another madman wants to construct a memorial for the perpetuation of my name, out of my 15,000,000 skulls and skeletons, and is full of vindictive enthusiasm over his strange project. He has it all ciphered out and drawn to scale. Out of the skulls he will build a combined monument and mausoleum to me which shall exactly duplicate the Great Pyramid of Cheops, whose base covers thirteen acres, and whose apex is 451 feet above ground. He desires to stuff me and stand me up in the sky on that apex, robed and crowned, with my "pirate flag" in one hand and a butcher-knife and pendant handcuffs in the other. He will build the pyramid in the centre of a depopulated tract, a brooding solitude covered with weeds and the mouldering ruins of burned villages, where the spirits of the starved and murdered dead will voice their laments forever in the whispers of the wandering winds. Radiating from the pyramid, like the spokes of a wheel, there are to be forty grand avenues of approach, each thirty-five miles long, and each fenced on both sides by skulless skeletons standing a yard and a half apart and festooned together in line by short chains stretching from wrist to wrist and attached to tried and true old handcuffs stamped with my private trade-mark, a crucifix and butcher-knife crossed, with motto, "By this sign we prosper;" each osseous fence to consist of 200,000 skeletons on a side, which is 400,000 to each avenue. It is remarked with satisfaction that it aggregates three or four thousand miles (single-ranked) of skeletons,—15,000,000 all told—and would stretch across America from New York to San Francisco. It is remarked further, in the hopeful tone of a railroad company forecasting showy extensions of its mileage, that my output is 500,000 corpses a year when my plant is running full time, and that therefore if I am spared ten years longer there will be fresh skulls enough to add 175 feet to the pyramid, making it by a long way the loftiest architectural construction on the earth, and fresh skeletons enough to continue the transcontinental file (on piles) a thousand miles into the Pacific. The cost of gathering the materials from my "widely scattered and innumerable private graveyards," and transporting them, and building the monument and the radiating

grand avenues, is duly ciphered out, running into an aggregate of millions of guineas, and then—why then, (—— ——!!
—— ——!!) this idiot asks me *to furnish the money!* [*Sudden
and effusive application of the crucifix*] He reminds me that my
yearly income from the Congo is millions of guineas, and that
"*only*" 5,000,000 would be required for his enterprise. Every
day wild attempts are made upon my purse; they do not affect
me, they cost me not a thought. But *this one*—this one troubles me, makes me nervous; for there is no telling what an
unhinged creature like this may think of next. . . . *If he
should think of Carnegie*—but I must banish that thought out
of my mind! it worries my days; it troubles my sleep. That
way lies madness. [*After a pause*] There is no other way—I
have got to buy Carnegie.

[*Harassed and muttering, walks the floor a while, then takes to
the Consul's chapter-headings again. Reads*]

"Government starved a woman's children to death and killed her
sons."

"Butchery of women and children."

"*The native has been converted into a being without ambition because
without hope.*"

"Women chained by the neck by rubber sentries."

"Women refuse to bear children because, with a baby to carry,
they cannot well run away and hide from the soldiers."

"Statement of a child. 'I, my mother, my grandmother and my
sister, we ran away into the bush. A great number of our people
were killed by the soldiers. . . . After that they saw a little bit of my
mother's head, and the soldiers ran quickly to where we were and
caught my grandmother, my mother, my sister and another little one
younger than us. Each wanted my mother for a wife, and argued
about it, so they finally decided to kill her. They shot her through
the stomach with a gun and she fell, and when I saw that I cried very
much, because they killed my grandmother and mother and I was
left alone. I saw it all done!' "

It has a sort of pitiful sound, although they are only blacks.
It carries me back and back into the past, to when my children were little, and would fly—to the bush, so to speak—
when they saw me coming. . . . [*Resumes the reading of chapter-
headings*]

"They put a knife through a child's stomach."

"They cut off the hands and brought them to C. D. (white officer) and spread them out in a row for him to see."

"Captured children left in the bush to die, by the soldiers."

"Friends came to ransom a captured girl; but sentry refused, saying the white man wanted her because she was young."

"Extract from a native girl's testimony. 'On our way the soldiers saw a little child, and when they went to kill it the child laughed, so the soldier took the butt of his gun and struck the child with it and then cut off its head. One day they killed my half-sister and cut off her head, hands and feet, because she had bangles on. Then they caught another sister, and sold her to the W. W. people, and now she is a slave there.' "

The little child laughed! [*A long pause. Musing*] That innocent creature. Somehow—I wish it had not laughed. [*Reads*]

"Mutilated children."

"Government encouragement of inter-tribal slave-traffic. The monstrous fines levied upon villages tardy in their supplies of food-stuffs compel the natives to sell their fellows—and children—to other tribes in order to meet the fine."

"A father and mother forced to sell their little boy."

"Widow forced to sell her little girl."

[*Irritated*] Hang the monotonous grumbler, what would he have me do! Let a widow off merely because she is a widow? He knows quite well that there is nothing much left, now, *but* widows. I have nothing against widows, as a class, but business is business, and I've got to live, haven't I, even if it does cause inconvenience to somebody here and there? [*Reads*]

"Men intimidated by the torture of their wives and daughters. (To make the men furnish rubber and supplies and so get their captured women released from chains and detention.) The sentry explained to me that he caught the women and brought them in (chained together neck to neck) by direction of his employer."

"An agent explained that he was forced to catch women in preference to men, as then the men brought in supplies quicker; but he did not explain how the children deprived of their parents obtained their own food supplies."

"A file of 15 (captured) women."

"Allowing women and children to die of starvation in prison."

[*Musing*] Death from *hunger*. A lingering, long misery that must be. Days and days, and still days and days, the forces of the body failing, dribbling away, little by little—yes, it must be the hardest death of all. And to see food carried by, every day, and you can have none of it! Of course the little children cry for it, and that wrings the mother's heart. . . . [*A sigh*] Ah, well, it cannot be helped; circumstances make this discipline necessary. [*Reads*]

"The crucifying of sixty women!"

How stupid, how tactless! Christendom's goose flesh will rise with horror at the news. "Profanation of the sacred emblem!" That is what Christendom will shout. Yes, Christendom will buzz. It can hear me charged with half a million murders a year for twenty years and keep its composure, but to profane the Symbol is quite another matter. It will regard this as serious. It will wake up and want to look into my record. Buzz? Indeed it will; I seem to hear the distant hum already. . . . It was wrong to crucify the women, clearly wrong, manifestly wrong, I can see it now, myself, and am sorry it happened, sincerely sorry. I believe it would have answered just as well to skin them. . . . [*With a sigh*] But none of us thought of that; one cannot think of everything; and after all it is but human to err.

It will make a stir, it surely will, these crucifixions. Persons will begin to ask again, as now and then in times past, how I can hope to win and keep the respect of the human race if I continue to give up my life to murder and pillage. [*Scornfully*] When have they heard me say I wanted the respect of the human race? Do they confuse me with the common herd? do they forget that I am a king? What king has valued the respect of the human race? I mean deep down in his private heart. If they would reflect, they would know that it is impossible that a king should value the respect of the human race. He stands upon an eminence and looks out over the world and sees multitudes of meek human things worshiping the persons, and submitting to the oppressions and exactions, of a dozen human things who are in no way better or finer than themselves—made on just their own pattern, in fact, and out of the same quality of mud. When it *talks*, it is a race of whales;

but a king knows it for a race of tadpoles. Its history gives it away. If men were really *men*, how could a Czar be possible? and how could I be possible? But we *are* possible; we are quite safe; and with God's help we shall continue the business at the old stand. It will be found that the race will put up with us, in its docile immemorial way. It may pull a wry face now and then, and make large talk, but it will stay on its knees all the same.

Making large talk is one of its specialties. It works itself up, and froths at the mouth, and just when you think it is going to throw a brick,—it heaves a poem! Lord, what a race it is! [*Reads*]

A CZAR—1905

"A pasteboard autocrat; a despot out of date;
    A fading planet in the glare of day;
    A flickering candle in the bright sun's ray,
Burnt to the socket; fruit left too late,
    High on a blighted bough, ripe till it's rotten.
    By God forsaken and by time forgotten,
Watching the crumbling edges of his lands,
    A spineless god to whom dumb millions pray,
    From Finland in the West to far Cathay.
Lord of a frost-bound continent he stands,
    Her seeming ruin his dim mind appalls,
And in the frozen stupor of his sleep
    He hears dull thunders, pealing as she falls,
    And mighty fragments dropping in the deep."*

It is fine, one is obliged to concede it; it is a great picture, and impressive. The mongrel handles his pen well. Still, with opportunity, I would cruci—flay him. . . . "A spineless god." It is the Czar to a dot—a god, and spineless; a royal invertebrate, poor lad; soft-hearted and out of place. "A spineless god *to whom dumb millions pray.*" Remorselessly correct; concise, too, and compact—the soul and spirit of the human race compressed into half a sentence. On their knees—140,000,000. On their knees to a little tin deity. Massed together, they would stretch away, and away, and away, across the plains, fading and dimming and failing in a

*B. H. Nadal, in *New York Times*.

measureless perspective—why, even the telescope's vision could not reach to the final frontier of that continental spread of human servility. Now *why* should a king value the respect of the human race? It is quite unreasonable to expect it. A curious race, certainly! It finds fault with me and with my occupations, and forgets that neither of us could exist an hour without its sanction. It is our confederate and all-powerful protector. It is our bulwark, our friend, our fortress. For this it has our gratitude, our deep and honest gratitude—but not our respect. Let it snivel and fret and grumble if it likes; that is all right; we do not mind that.

[*Turns over leaves of a scrapbook, pausing now and then to read a clipping and make a comment*] The poets—how they do hunt that poor Czar! French, Germans, English, Americans—they all have a bark at him. The finest and capablest of the pack, and the fiercest, are Swilburne (English, I think), and a pair of Americans, Thomas Bailey Eldridge and Colonel Richard Waterson Gilder, of the sentimental periodical called *Century Magazine and Louisville Courier-Journal*. They certainly have uttered some very strong yelps. I can't seem to find them—I must have mislaid them. . . . If a poet's bite were as terrible as his bark, why dear me—but it isn't. A wise king minds neither of them; but the poet doesn't know it. It's a case of little dog and lightning express. When the Czar goes thundering by, the poet skips out and rages alongside for a little distance, then returns to his kennel wagging his head with satisfaction, and thinks he has inflicted a memorable scare, whereas nothing has really happened—the Czar didn't know he was around. They never bark at me; I wonder why that is. I suppose my Corruption-Department buys them. That must be it, for certainly I ought to inspire a bark or two; I'm rather choice material, I should say. Why—here *is* a yelp at me. [*Mumbling a poem*]

> ". . . What gives thee holy right to murder hope
> And water ignorance with human blood?
>
> .    .    .    .    .    .
>
> From what high universe-dividing power
> Draws't thou thy wondrous, ripe brutality?
>
> .    .    .    .    .    .

O horrible . . . Thou God who seest these things
Help us to blot this terror from the earth."

. . . No, I see it is "To the Czar,"* after all. But there are
those who would say it fits me—and rather snugly, too.
"Ripe brutality." They would say the Czar's isn't ripe yet, but
that mine is; and not merely *ripe* but rotten. Nothing
could keep them from saying that; they would think it smart.
"This terror." Let the Czar keep that name; I am supplied.
This long time I have been "the monster"; that was their
favorite—the monster of crime. But now I have a new one.
They have found a fossil Dinosaur fifty-seven feet long and
sixteen feet high, and set it up in the museum in New York
and labeled it "Leopold II." But it is no matter, one does not
look for manners in a republic. Um . . . that reminds me; I
have never been caricatured. Could it be that the corsairs of
the pencil could not find an offensive symbol that was big
enough and ugly enough to do my reputation justice? [*After
reflection*] There is no other way—I will buy the Dinosaur.
And suppress it. [*Rests himself with some more chapter-headings.
Reads*]

"More mutilation of children." (Hands cut off.)
"Testimony of American Missionaries."
"Evidence of British Missionaries."

It is all the same old thing—tedious repetitions and dupli-
cations of shop-worn episodes; mutilations, murders, massacres, and so on, and so on, till one gets drowsy over it. Mr.
Morel intrudes at this point, and contributes a comment
which he could just as well have kept to himself—and throws
in some italics, of course; these people can never get along
without italics:

"It is one heartrending story of human misery from beginning to
end, and *it is all recent*."

Meaning 1904 and 1905. I do not see how a person can act
so. This Morel is a king's subject, and reverence for monarchy
should have restrained him from reflecting upon me with that
exposure. This Morel is a reformer; a Congo reformer. That

*Louise Morgan Sill, in *Harper's Weekly*.

sizes *him* up. He publishes a sheet in Liverpool called "The West African Mail," which is supported by the voluntary contributions of the sap-headed and the soft-hearted; and every week it steams and reeks and festers with up-to-date "Congo atrocities" of the sort detailed in this pile of pamphlets here. I will suppress it. I suppressed a Congo atrocity book there, after it was actually in print; it should not be difficult for me to suppress a newspaper.

[*Studies some photographs of mutilated negroes—throws them down. Sighs*] The kodak has been a sore calamity to us. The most powerful enemy that has confronted us, indeed. In the early years we had no trouble in getting the press to "expose" the tales of the mutilations as slanders, lies, inventions of busy-body American missionaries and exasperated foreigners who had found the "open door" of the Berlin-Congo charter closed against them when they innocently went out there to trade; and by the press's help we got the Christian nations everywhere to turn an irritated and unbelieving ear to those tales and say hard things about the tellers of them. Yes, all things went harmoniously and pleasantly in those good days, and I was looked up to as the benefactor of a down-trodden and friendless people. Then all of a sudden came the crash! That is to say, the incorruptible *kodak*—and all the harmony went to hell! The only witness I have encountered in my long experience that I couldn't bribe. Every Yankee missionary and every interrupted trader sent home and got one; and now—oh, well, the pictures get sneaked around everywhere, in spite of all we can do to ferret them out and suppress them. Ten thousand pulpits and ten thousand presses are saying the good word for me all the time and placidly and convincingly denying the mutilations. Then that trivial little kodak, that a child can carry in its pocket, gets up, uttering never a word, and knocks them dumb!

. . . . What is this fragment? [*Reads*]

"But enough of trying to tally off his crimes! His list is interminable, we should never get to the end of it. His awful shadow lies across his Congo Free State, and under it an unoffending nation of 15,000,000 is withering away and swiftly succumbing to their miseries. It is a land of graves; it is *The* Land of Graves; it is the Congo Free Graveyard. It is a majestic thought: that is, this ghastliest

FROM PHOTOGRAPHS, CONGO STATE

"The pictures get sneaked around everywhere."

episode in all human history is the work of *one man alone*; one solitary man; just a single individual—Leopold, King of the Belgians. He is personally and solely responsible for all the myriad crimes that have blackened the history of the Congo State. He is *sole* master there; he is absolute. He could have prevented the crimes by his mere command; he could stop them today with a word. He withholds the word. For his pocket's sake.

It seems strange to see a king destroying a nation and laying waste a country for mere sordid money's sake, and solely and only for that. Lust of conquest is royal; kings have always exercised that stately vice; we are used to it, by old habit we condone it, perceiving a certain dignity in it; but *lust of money—lust of shillings—lust of nickels —lust of dirty coin*, not for the nation's enrichment but for *the king's alone*—this is new. It distinctly revolts us, we cannot seem to reconcile ourselves to it, we resent it, we despise it, we say it is shabby, unkingly, out of character. Being democrats we ought to jeer and jest, we ought to rejoice to see the purple dragged in the dirt, but—well, account for it as we may, we don't. We see this awful king, this pitiless and blood-drenched king, this money-crazy king towering toward the sky in a world-solitude of sordid crime, unfellowed and apart from the human race, sole butcher for personal gain findable in all his caste, ancient or modern, pagan or Christian, proper and legitimate target for the scorn of the lowest and the highest, and the execrations of all who hold in cold esteem the oppressor and the coward; and—well, it is a mystery, but *we do not wish to look*; for he is a king, and it hurts us, it troubles us, by ancient and inherited instinct it shames us to see a king degraded to this aspect, and we shrink from hearing the particulars of how it happened. *We shudder* and *turn away* when we come upon them in print."

Why, certainly—*that* is my protection. And you will continue to do it. I know the human race.

AN ORIGINAL MISTAKE
"This work of 'civilization' is
an enormous and continual
butchery." "All the facts we
brought forward in this chamber were denied at first most
energetically; but later, little
by little, they were proved by documents and by official texts."
"The practice of cutting off hands is said to be contrary
to instructions; but you are content to say that indulgence
must be shown and that this bad habit must be corrected
'little by little' and you plead, moreover, that only the hands
of *fallen* enemies are cut off, and that if hands are cut off
'enemies' not quite dead, and who, after recovery, have
had the bad taste to come to
the missionaries and show
them their stumps, it was
due to an original mistake
in thinking that they were
dead." *From Debate in Belgian Parliament, July, 1903.*

*September 28, 1905*

# A Helpless Situation

Once or twice a year I get a letter of a certain pattern, a pattern that never materially changes, in form and substance, yet I cannot get used to that letter—it always astonishes me. It affects me as the locomotive always affects me: I say to myself, "I have seen you a thousand times, you always look the same way, yet you are always a wonder, and you are always impossible; to contrive you is clearly beyond human genius—you can't exist, you don't exist, yet here you are!"

I have a letter of that kind by me, a very old one. I yearn to print it, and where is the harm? The writer of it is dead years ago, no doubt, and if I conceal her name and address—her this-world address—I am sure her shade will not mind. And with it I wish to print the answer which I wrote at the time but probably did not send. If it went—which is not likely—it went in the form of a copy, for I find the original still here, pigeonholed with the said letter. To that kind of letters we all write answers which we do not send, fearing to hurt where we have no desire to hurt; I have done it many a time, and this is doubtless a case of the sort.

### THE LETTER

X——., CALIFORNIA, *June 3, 1879.*

*Mr. S. L. Clemens, Hartford, Conn.:*

DEAR SIR,—You will doubtless be surprised to know who has presumed to write and ask a favor of you. Let your memory go back to your days in the Humboldt mines—'62–'63. You will remember, you and Clagett and Oliver and the old blacksmith Tillou lived in a lean-to which was half-way up the gulch, and there were six log cabins in the camp—strung pretty well separated up the gulch from its mouth at the desert to where the last claim was, at the divide. The lean-to you lived in was the one with a canvas roof that the cow fell down through one night, as told about by you in *Roughing It*—my uncle Simmons remembers it very well. He lived in the principal cabin, half-way up the divide, along with Dixon and Parker and Smith. It had two rooms, one for kitchen and the other for bunks, and was the only one that had. You and your party were there on the great night, the time they had dried-apple pie, uncle Simmons often speaks of it. It seems curious that dried-apple pie should have seemed such a great thing, but it was, and it shows how far Humboldt was out of the world and difficult to get to, and how slim the regular bill of fare was. Sixteen years ago—it is a long time. I was a little girl, then, only 14. I never saw you, I lived in Washoe. But uncle Simmons ran across you every now and then, all during those weeks that you and party were there working your claim which was like the rest. The camp played out long and long ago, there wasn't silver enough in it to make a button. You never saw my husband, but he was there after you left, *and lived in that very lean-to*, a bachelor then but married to me now. He often wishes there had been a photographer there in those days, he would have taken the lean-to. He got hurt in the old Hal Clayton claim that was abandoned like the others, putting in a blast and not climbing out quick enough, though he scrambled the best he could. It landed him clear down on the trail and hit a Piute. For weeks they thought he would not get over it but he did, and is all right, now. Has been ever since. This is a long introduction but it is the only way I can make myself known. The favor I ask I feel assured your generous heart will grant: Give me some advice about a book I have written. I do not claim anything for it only it is mostly true and as interesting as most of the books of the times. I am unknown in the literary world and you know what that means unless one has some one of influence (like yourself) to help you by speaking a good word for you. I would like to place the book on royalty basis plan with any one you would suggest.

This is a secret from my husband and family. I intend it as a surprise in case I get it published.

Feeling you will take an interest in this and if possible write me a letter to some publisher or better still if you could see them for me and then let me hear.

I appeal to you to grant me this favor. With deepest gratitude I thank you for your attention.

One knows, without inquiring, that the twin of that embarrassing letter is forever and ever flying in this and that and the other direction across the continent in the mails, daily, nightly, hourly, unceasingly, unrestingly. It goes to every well-known merchant, and railway official, and manufacturer, and capitalist, and Mayor, and Congressman, and Governor, and editor, and publisher, and author, and broker, and banker—in a word, to every person who is supposed to have "influence." It always follows the one pattern: "You do not know me, *but you once knew a relative of mine*," etc., etc. We should all like to help the applicants, we should all be glad to do it, we should all like to return the sort of answer that is desired, but— Well, there is not a thing we can do that would be a help, for not in any instance does that letter ever come from any one who *can* be helped. The struggler whom you *could* help does his own helping; it would not occur to him to apply to you, a stranger. He has talent and knows it, and he goes into his fight eagerly and with energy and determination—all alone, preferring to be alone. That pathetic letter which comes to you from the incapable, the unhelpable— how do you who are familiar with it answer it? What do you find to say? You do not want to inflict a wound; you hunt ways to avoid that. What do you find? How do you get out of your hard place with a contented conscience? Do you try to explain? The old reply of mine to such a letter shows that I tried that once. Was I satisfied with the result? Possibly; and possibly not; probably not; almost certainly not. I have long ago forgotten all about it. But, anyway, I append my effort:

### THE REPLY

I know Mr. H., and I will go to him, dear madam, if upon reflection you find you still desire it. There will be a conversation. I know the form it will take. It will be like this:

*Mr. H.* How do her books strike you?
*Mr. Clemens.* I am not acquainted with them.
*H.* Who has been her publisher?
*C.* I don't know.
*H.* She *has* one, I suppose?
*C.* I—I think not.
*H.* Ah. You think this is her first book?
*C.* Yes—I suppose so. I think so.
*H.* What is it about? What is the character of it?
*C.* I believe I do not know.
*H.* Have you seen it?
*C.* Well—no, I haven't.
*H.* Ah—h. How long have you known her?
*C.* I don't know her.
*H.* Don't know her?
*C.* No.

*H.* Ah—h. How did you come to be interested in her book, then?

*C.* Well, she—she wrote and asked me to find a publisher for her, and mentioned you.

*H.* Why should she apply to you instead of to me?

*C.* She wished me to use my influence.

*H.* Dear me, what has *influence* to do with such a matter?

*C.* Well, I think she thought you would be more likely to examine her book if you were influenced.

*H.* Why, what we are here *for* is to examine books—anybody's book that comes along. It's our *business*. Why should we turn away a book unexamined because it's a stranger's? It would be foolish. No publisher does it. On what ground did she request your influence, since you do not know her? She must have thought you knew her literature and could speak for it. Is that it?

*C.* No; she knew I didn't.

*H.* Well, what then? She had a reason of *some* sort for believing you competent to recommend her literature, and also under obligations to do it?

*C.* Yes, I—I knew her uncle.

*H.* Knew her *uncle*?

*C.* Yes.

*H.* Upon my word! So, you knew her uncle; her uncle knows her literature; he endorses it to you; the chain is complete, nothing further needed; you are satisfied, and therefore—

*C.* No, that isn't all, there are other ties. I knew the cabin her uncle lived in, in the mines; I knew his partners, too; also I came near knowing her husband before she married him, and I *did* know the abandoned shaft where a premature blast went off and he went flying through the air and clear down to the trail and hit an Indian in the back with almost fatal consequences.

*H.* To *him*, or to the Indian?

*C.* She didn't say which it was.

*H.* (*With a sigh.*) It certainly beats the band! You don't know *her*, you don't know her literature, you don't know who got hurt when the blast went off, you don't know a single thing for us to build an estimate of her book upon, so far as I—

*C.* I knew her uncle. You are forgetting her uncle.

*H.* Oh, what use is *he*? Did you know him long? How long was it?

*C.* Well, I don't know that I really knew him, but I must have met him, anyway. I think it was that way; you can't tell about these things, you know, except when they are recent.

*H.* Recent? When was all this?

*C.* Sixteen years ago.

*H.* What a basis to judge a book upon! At first you said you knew him, and now you don't know whether you did or not.

*C.* Oh yes, I knew him; anyway, I think I thought I did; I'm perfectly certain of it.

*H.* What makes you think you thought you knew him?

*C.* Why, she says I did, herself.

*H. She* says so!

*C.* Yes, she does, and I *did* know him, too, though I don't remember it now.

*H.* Come—how can you know it when you don't remember it?

*C.* I don't know. That is, I don't know the process, but I *do* know lots of things that I don't remember, and remember lots of things that I don't know. It's so with every educated person.

*H.* (*After a pause.*) Is your time valuable?

*C.* No—well, not very.

*H.* Mine is.

So I came away then, because he was looking tired. Overwork, I reckon; I never do that; I have seen the evil effects of it. My mother was always afraid I would overwork myself, but I never did.

Dear madam, you see how it would happen if I went there. He would ask me those questions, and I would try to answer them to suit him, and he would hunt me here and there and yonder and get me embarrassed more and more all the time, and at last he would look tired on account of overwork, and there it would end and nothing done. I wish I could be useful to you, but you see, they do not care for uncles or any of those things; it doesn't move them, it doesn't have the least effect, they don't care for anything but the literature itself, and they as good as despise influence. But they do care for books, and are eager to get them and examine them, no matter whence they come, nor from whose pen. If you will send yours to a publisher—any publisher—he will certainly examine it, I can assure you of that.

MARK TWAIN.

*November 1905*

# Overspeeding

DUBLIN, N. H., *October 18, 1905.*

*To the Editor of Harper's Weekly:*

SIR,—Equal laws for all. It is good in theory, and I believe it would prove good in practice, if fairly and dispassionately tried. The law dresses a convict in a garb which makes him easily distinguishable from any moving thing in the world at a hundred and twenty-five yards, except a zebra. If he escapes in those clothes, he cannot get far. Could not this principle be extended to include his brother criminal the Overspeeder, thus making the pair fairly and righteously equal before the law? Every day, throughout America, the Overspeeder runs over somebody and "escapes." That is the way it reads. At present the 'mobile numbers are so small that ordinary eyes cannot read them, upon a swiftly receding machine, at a distance of a hundred feet—a distance which the machine has covered before the spectator can adjust his focus. I think I would amend the law. I would enlarge the figures, and make them readable at a hundred yards. For overspeeding—first offence—I would enlarge the figures again, and make them readable at three hundred yards—this in place of a fine, and as a warning to pedestrians to climb a tree. This enlargement to continue two months, with privilege of resuming the smaller figures after the first thirty days upon payment of $500. For each subsequent offence, reenlargement for six months, with privilege of resuming the smaller figures upon payment of $1000 at the end of three. With auto numbers readable as far as one could tell a convict from a barber-pole none of these criminals could run over a person and "escape."

Two months ago a touring 'mobile came within an indeterminable fraction of killing a member of my family: and its number was out of sight-range before the sharpest eyes present could make it out, it was so small and the spectators so dazed by momentary fright. I have had two narrow escapes in New York, and so has everybody else. None of us has succeeded in capturing the auto number. I feel a sort of personal interest in this suggested reform.     I am, sir,     M. T.

*November 4, 1905*

# In the Animal's Court

THE RABBIT. The testimony showed, (1), that the Rabbit, having declined to volunteer, was enlisted by compulsion, and (2) deserted in the face of the enemy on the eve of battle. Being asked if he had anything to say for himself before sentence of death should be passed upon him for violating the military law forbidding cowardice and desertion, he said he had not desired to violate that law, but had been obliged to obey a higher law which took precedence of it and set it aside. Being asked what law that was, he answered, "the law of God, which denies courage to the rabbit."

*Verdict of the Court.* To be disgraced in the presence of the army; stripped of his uniform; marched to the scaffold, bearing a placard marked "Coward," and hanged.

## II

THE LION. The testimony showed that the Lion, by his splendid courage and matchless strength and endurance, saved the battle.

*Verdict of the Court.* To be given a dukedom, his statue to be set up, his name to be writ in letters of gold at the top of the roll in the Temple of Fame.

## III

THE FOX. The testimony showed that he had broken the divine law, "Thou shalt not steal." Being asked for his defence, he pleaded that he had been obliged to obey the divine law, "The Fox shall steal."

*Verdict of the Court.* Imprisonment for life.

## IV

THE HORSE. The evidence showed that he had spent many days and nights, unwatched, in the paddock with the poultry, yet had triumphed over temptation.

*Verdict of the Court.* Let his name be honored; let his deed be praised throughout the land by public proclamation.

## V

THE WOLF. The evidence showed that he had transgressed the law "Thou shalt not kill." In arrest of judgment, he pleaded the law of his nature.

*Verdict of the Court.* Death.

## VI

THE SHEEP. The evidence showed that he had had manifold temptations to commit murder and massacre, yet had not yielded.

*Verdict of the Court.* Let his virtue be remembered forever.

## VII

THE MACHINE. *The Court*: Prisoner, it is charged and proven that you are poorly contrived and badly constructed. What have you to say to this?

*Answer.* I did not contrive myself, I did not construct myself.

*The Court.* It is charged and proven that you have moved when you should not have moved; that you have turned out of your course when you should have gone straight; that you have moved swiftly through crowds when the law and the public weal forbade a speed like that; that you leave a stench behind you wherever you go, and you persist in this, although you know it is improper and that other machines refrain from doing it. What have you to say to these things?

*Answer.* I am a machine. I am slave to the law of my make, I have to obey it, under all conditions. I do nothing, of myself. My forces are set in motion by outside influences, I never set them in motion myself.

*The Court.* You are discharged. Your plea is sufficient. You are a pretty poor thing, with some good qualities and some bad ones; but to attach personal merit to conduct emanating from the one set, and personal demerit to conduct emanating from the other set would be unfair and unjust. To a machine, that is—to a machine.

*1905*

# Eve's Diary

## TRANSLATED FROM THE ORIGINAL

*Saturday.*—I am almost a whole day old, now.—I arrived
yesterday. That is as it seems to me. And it must be so, for if
there was a day-before-yesterday I was not there when it happened, or I should remember it. It could be, of course, that it
did happen, and that I was not noticing. Very well; I will be
very watchful, now, and if any day-before-yesterdays happen I
will make a note of it. It will be best to start right and not let
the record get confused, for some instinct tells me that these
details are going to be important to the historian some day.
For I feel like an experiment, I feel exactly like an experiment,
it would be impossible for a person to feel more like an experiment than I do, and so I am coming to feel convinced that
that is what I *am*—an experiment; just an experiment, and
nothing more.

Then if I am an experiment, am I the whole of it? No, I
think not; I think the rest of it is part of it. I am the main part
of it, but I think the rest of it has its share in the matter. Is my
position assured, or do I have to watch it and take care of it?
The latter, perhaps. Some instinct tells me that eternal vigilance is the price of supremacy. [That is a good phrase, I
think, for one so young.]

Everything looks better to-day than it did yesterday. In
the rush of finishing up yesterday, the mountains were left in
a ragged condition, and some of the plains were so cluttered
with rubbish and remnants that the aspects were quite distressing. Noble and beautiful works of art should not be
subjected to haste; and this majestic new world is indeed a
most noble and beautiful work. And certainly marvellously
near to being perfect, notwithstanding the shortness of the
time. There are too many stars in some places and not
enough in others, but that can be remedied presently, no
doubt. The moon got loose last night, and slid down and
fell out of the scheme—a very great loss; it breaks my heart
to think of it. There isn't another thing among the ornaments and decorations that is comparable to it for beauty

and finish. It should have been fastened better. If we can only get it back again—

But of course there is no telling where it went to. And besides, whoever gets it will hide it; I know it because I would do it myself. I believe I can be honest in all other matters, but I already begin to realize that the core and centre of my nature is love of the beautiful, a passion for the beautiful, and that it would not be safe to trust me with a moon that belonged to another person and that person didn't know I had it. I could give up a moon that I found in the daytime, because I should be afraid some one was looking; but if I found it in the dark, I am sure I should find some kind of an excuse for not saying anything about it. For I do love moons, they are so pretty and so romantic. I wish we had five or six; I would never go to bed; I should never get tired lying on the moss-bank and looking up at them.

Stars are good, too. I wish I could get some to put in my hair. But I suppose I never can. You would be surprised to find how far off they are, for they do not look it. When they first showed, last night, I tried to knock some down with a pole, but it didn't reach, which astonished me; then I tried clods till I was all tired out, but I never got one. It was because I am left-handed and cannot throw good. Even when I aimed at the one I wasn't after I couldn't hit the other one, though I did make some close shots, for I saw the black blot of the clod sail right into the midst of the golden clusters forty or fifty times, just barely missing them, and if I could have held out a little longer maybe I could have got one.

So I cried a little, which was natural, I suppose, for one of my age, and after I was rested I got a basket and started for a place on the extreme rim of the circle, where the stars were close to the ground and I could get them with my hands, which would be better, anyway, because I could gather them tenderly then, and not break them. But it was farther than I thought, and at last I had to give it up; I was so tired I couldn't drag my feet another step; and besides, they were sore and hurt me very much.

I couldn't get back home; it was too far and turning cold; but I found some tigers and nestled in amongst them and was most adorably comfortable, and their breath was sweet and pleasant, because they live on strawberries. I had never seen a tiger before, but I knew them in a minute by the stripes. If I could have one of those skins, it would make a lovely gown.

To-day I am getting better ideas about distances. I was so eager to get hold of every pretty thing that I giddily grabbed for it, sometimes when it was too far off, and sometimes when it was but six inches away but seemed a foot—alas, with thorns between! I learned a lesson; also I made an axiom, all out of my own head—my very first one: *The scratched Experiment shuns the thorn.* I think it is a very good one for one so young.

I followed the other Experiment around, yesterday afternoon, at a distance, to see what it might be for, if I could. But I was not able to make out. I think it is a man. I had never seen a man, but it looked like one, and I feel sure that that is what it is. I realize that I feel more curiosity about it than about any of the other reptiles. If it is a reptile, and I suppose it is; for it has frowsy hair and blue eyes, and looks like a reptile. It has no hips; it tapers like a carrot; when it stands, it spreads itself apart like a derrick; so I think it is a reptile, though it may be architecture.

I was afraid of it at first, and started to run every time it turned around, for I thought it was going to chase me; but by and by I found it was only trying to get away, so after that I was not timid any more, but tracked it along, several hours, about twenty yards behind, which made it nervous and unhappy. At last it was a good deal worried, and climbed a tree. I waited a good while, then gave it up and went home.

To-day the same thing over. I've got it up the tree again.

*Sunday.*—It is up there yet. Resting, apparently. But that is a subterfuge: Sunday isn't the day of rest; Saturday is appointed for that. It looks to me like a creature that is more interested in resting than in anything else. It would tire me to rest so much. It tires me just to sit around and watch the tree. I do wonder what it is for; I never see it do anything.

They returned the moon last night, and I was *so* happy! I think it is very honest of them. It slid down and fell off again, but I was not distressed; there is no need to worry when one has that kind of neighbors; they will fetch it back. I wish I could do something to show my appreciation. I would like to send them some stars, for we have more than we can use. I mean I, not we, for I can see that the reptile cares nothing for such things.

It has low tastes, and is not kind. When I went there yesterday evening in the gloaming it had crept down and was trying to catch the little speckled fishes that play in the pool, and I had to clod it to make it go up the tree again and let them alone. I wonder if *that* is what it is for? Hasn't it any heart? Hasn't it any compassion for those little creatures? Can it be that it was designed and manufactured for such ungentle work? It has the look of it. One of the clods took it back of the ear, and it used language. It gave me a thrill, for it was the first time I had ever heard speech, except my own. I did not understand the words, but they seemed expressive.

When I found it could talk I felt a new interest in it, for I love to talk; I talk all day, and in my sleep, too, and I am very interesting, but if I had another to talk to I could be twice as interesting, and would never stop, if desired.

If this reptile is a man, it isn't an *it*, is it? That wouldn't be grammatical, would it? I think it would be *he*. I think so. In that case one would parse it thus: nominative, *he*; dative, *him*; possessive, *his'n*. Well, I will consider it a man and call it he until it turns out to be something else. This will be handier than having so many uncertainties.

*Next week Sunday.* — All the week I tagged around after him and tried to get acquainted. I had to do the talking, because he was shy, but I didn't mind it. He seemed pleased to have me around, and I used the sociable "we" a good deal, because it seemed to flatter him to be included.

*Wednesday.* — We are getting along very well indeed, now, and getting better and better acquainted. He does not try to avoid me any more, which is a good sign, and shows that he likes to have me with him. That pleases me, and I study to be useful to him in every way I can, so as to increase his regard. During the last day or two I have taken all the work of naming things off his hands, and this has been a great relief to him, for he has no gift in that line, and is evidently very grateful. He can't think of a rational name to save him, but I do not let him see that I am aware of his defect. Whenever a new creature comes along I name it before he has time to expose himself by an awkward silence. In this way I have saved him many embarrassments. I have no defect like his. The minute I set eyes on an animal I know what it is. I don't have to reflect a moment; the right name comes out instantly, just as if it were an inspiration, as no doubt it is, for I am sure it wasn't in me half a minute before. I seem to know just by the shape of the creature and the way it acts what animal it is.

When the dodo came along he thought it was a wildcat—I saw it in his eye. But I saved him. And I was careful not to do it in a way that could hurt his pride. I just spoke up in a quite natural way of pleased surprise, and not as if I was dreaming of conveying information, and said, "Well, I do declare if there isn't the dodo!" I explained—without seeming to be explaining—how I knew it for a dodo, and although I thought maybe he was a little piqued that I knew the creature when he didn't, it was quite evident that he admired me. That was very agreeable, and I thought of it more than once with gratification before I slept. How little a thing can make us happy when we feel that we have earned it.

*Thursday.*—My first sorrow. Yesterday he avoided me and seemed to wish I would not talk to him. I could not believe it, and thought there was some mistake, for I loved to be with him, and loved to hear him talk, and so how could it be that he could feel unkind toward me when I had not done anything? But at last it seemed true, so I went away and sat lonely in the place where I first saw him the morning that we were made and I did not know what he was and was indifferent about him; but now it was a mournful place, and every little thing spoke of him, and my heart was very sore. I did not know why very clearly, for it was a new feeling; I had not experienced it before, and it was all a mystery, and I could not make it out.

But when night came I could not bear the lonesomeness, and went to the new shelter which he has built, to ask him what I had done that was wrong and how I could mend it and get back his kindness again; but he put me out in the rain, and it was my first sorrow.

*Sunday.*—It is pleasant again, now, and I am happy; but those were heavy days; I do not think of them when I can help it.

I tried to get him some of those apples, but I cannot learn to throw straight. I failed, but I think the good intention pleased him. They are forbidden, and he says I shall come to harm; but so I come to harm through pleasing him why shall I care for that harm?

*Monday.*—This morning I told him my name, hoping it would interest him. But he did not care for it. It is strange. If he should tell me his name, I would care. I think it would be pleasanter in my ears than any other sound.

He talks very little. Perhaps it is because he is not bright, and is sensitive about it and wishes to conceal it. It is such a pity that he should feel so, for brightness is nothing; it is in the heart that the values lie. I wish I could make him understand that a loving good heart is riches, and riches enough, and that without it intellect is poverty.

Although he talks so little he has quite a considerable vocabulary. This morning he used a surprisingly good word. He evidently recognized, himself, that it was a good one, for he worked it in twice afterward, casually. It was not good casual art, still it showed that he possesses a certain quality of perception. Without a doubt that seed can be made to grow, if cultivated.

Where did he get that word? I do not think I have ever used it.

No, he took no interest in my name. I tried to hide my disappointment, but I suppose I did not succeed. I went away and sat on the moss-bank with my feet in the water. It is where I go when I hunger for companionship, some one to look at, some one to talk to. It is not enough—that lovely white body painted there in the pool—but it is something, and something is better than utter loneliness. It talks when I talk; it is sad when I am sad; it comforts me with its sympathy; it says, "Do not be downhearted, you poor friendless girl; I will be your friend." It *is* a good friend to me, and my only one; it is my sister.

That first time that she forsook me! ah, I shall never forget that—never, never. My heart was lead in my body! I said, "She was all I had, and now she is gone!" In my despair I said, "Break, my heart; I cannot bear my life any more!" and hid my face in my hands, and there was no solace for me. And when I took them away, after a little, there she was again, white and shining and beautiful, and I sprang into her arms!

That was perfect happiness; I had known happiness before, but it was not like this, which was ecstasy. I never doubted her afterwards. Sometimes she stayed away—maybe an hour, maybe almost the whole day, but I waited and did not doubt; I said, "She is busy, or she is gone a journey, but she will come." And it was so: she always did. At night she would not come if it was dark, for she was a timid little thing; but if there was a moon she would come. I am not afraid of the dark, but she is younger than I am; she was born after I was. Many and many are the visits I have paid her; she is my comfort and my refuge when my life is hard—and it is mainly that.

*Tuesday.*—All the morning I was at work improving the estate; and I purposely kept away from him in the hope that he would get lonely and come. But he did not.

At noon I stopped for the day and took my recreation by flitting all about with the bees and the butterflies and revelling in the flowers, those beautiful creatures that catch the smile of God out of the sky and preserve it! I gathered them, and made them into wreaths and garlands and clothed myself in them whilst I ate my luncheon—apples, of course; then I sat in the shade and wished and waited. But he did not come.

But no matter. Nothing would have come of it, for he does not care for flowers. He calls them rubbish, and cannot tell one from another, and thinks it is superior to feel like that. He does not care for me, he does not care for flowers, he does not care for the painted sky at eventide—is there anything he does care for, except building shacks to coop himself up in from the good clean rain, and thumping the melons, and sampling the grapes, and fingering the fruit on the trees, to see how those properties are coming along?

I laid a dry stick on the ground and tried to bore a hole in it with another one, in order to carry out a scheme that I had, and soon I got an awful fright. A thin, transparent bluish film rose out of the hole, and I dropped everything and ran! I thought it was a spirit, and I *was* so frightened! But I looked back, and it was not coming; so I leaned against a rock and rested and panted, and let my limbs go on trembling until they got steady again; then I crept warily back, alert, watching, and ready to fly if there was occasion; and when I was come near, I parted the branches of a rose-bush and peeped through—wishing the man was about, I was looking so cunning and pretty—but the sprite was gone. I went there, and there was a pinch of delicate pink dust in the hole. I put my finger in, to feel it, and said *ouch!* and took it out again. It was a cruel pain. I put my finger in my mouth; and by standing first on one foot and then the other, and grunting, I presently eased my misery; then I was full of interest, and began to examine.

I was curious to know what the pink dust was. Suddenly the name of it occurred to me, though I had never heard of it before. It was *fire!* I was as certain of it as a person could be of anything in the world. So without hesitation I named it that—fire.

I had created something that didn't exist before; I had added a new thing to the world's uncountable properties; I realized this, and was proud of my achievement, and was going to run and find him and tell him about it, thinking to raise myself in his esteem,—but I reflected, and did not do it. No—he would not care for it. He would ask what it was good for, and what could I answer? for if it was not *good* for something, but only beautiful, merely beautiful—

So I sighed, and did not go. For it wasn't good for anything; it could not build a shack, it could not improve melons, it could not hurry a fruit crop; it was useless, it was a foolishness and a vanity; he would despise it and say cutting words. But to me it was not despicable; I said, "Oh, you fire, I love you, you dainty pink creature, for you are *beautiful*—and that is enough!" and was going to gather it to my breast. But refrained. Then I made another maxim out of my own head, though it was so nearly like the first one that I was afraid it was only a plagiarism: "*The burnt Experiment shuns the fire.*"

I wrought again; and when I had made a good deal of fire-dust I emptied it into a handful of dry brown grass, intending to carry it home and keep it always and play with it; but the wind struck it and it sprayed up and spat out at me fiercely, and I dropped it and ran. When I looked back the blue spirit was towering up and stretching and rolling away like a cloud, and instantly I thought of the name of it—*smoke!*—though, upon my word, I had never heard of smoke before.

Soon, brilliant yellow and red flares shot up through the smoke, and I named them in an instant—*flames!*—and I was right, too, though these were the very first flames that had ever been in the world. They climbed the trees, they flashed splendidly in and out of the vast and increasing volume of tumbling smoke, and I had to clap my hands and laugh and dance in my rapture, it was so new and strange and so wonderful and so beautiful!

He came running, and stopped and gazed, and said not a word for many minutes. Then he asked what it was. Ah, it was too bad that he should ask such a direct question. I had to answer it, of course, and I did. I said it was fire. If it annoyed him that I should know and he must ask, that was not my fault; I had no desire to annoy him. After a pause he asked,

"How did it come?"

Another direct question, and it also had to have a direct answer.

"I made it."

The fire was travelling farther and farther off. He went to the edge of the burnt place and stood looking down, and said,

"What are these?"

"Fire-coals."

He picked up one to examine it, but changed his mind and put it down again. Then he went away. *Nothing* interests him.

But I was interested. There were ashes, gray and soft and delicate and pretty—I knew what they were at once. And the embers; I knew the embers, too. I found my apples, and raked them out, and was glad; for I am very young and my appetite is active. But I was disappointed; they were all burst open and spoiled. Spoiled apparently; but it was not so; they were better than raw ones. Fire is beautiful; some day it will be useful, I think.

*Friday.*—I saw him again, for a moment, last Monday at nightfall, but only for a moment. I was hoping he would praise me for trying to improve the estate, for I had meant well and had worked hard. But he was not pleased, and turned away and left me. He was also displeased on another account: I tried once more to persuade him to stop going over the Falls. That was because the fire had revealed to me a new passion—quite new, and distinctly different from love, grief, and those others which I had already discovered—*fear.* And it is horrible!—I wish I had never discovered it; it gives me dark moments, it spoils my happiness, it makes me shiver and tremble and shudder. But I could not persuade him, for he has not discovered fear yet, and so he could not understand me.

Tuesday—Wednesday—Thursday—and to-day: all without seeing him. It is a long time to be alone; still, it is better to be alone than unwelcome.

I *had* to have company—I was made for it, I think,—so I made friends with the animals. They are just charming, and they have the kindest disposition and the politest ways; they never look sour, they never let you feel that you are intruding, they smile at you and wag their tail, if they've got one, and they are always ready for a romp or an excursion or anything you want to propose. I think they are perfect gentlemen. All these days we have had such good times, and it hasn't been lonesome for me, ever. Lonesome! No, I should say not. Why, there's always a swarm of them around—sometimes as much as four or five acres—you can't count them; and when you stand on a rock in the midst and look out over the furry expanse it is so mottled and splashed and gay with color and frisking sheen and sun-flash, and so rippled with stripes, that you might think it was a lake, only you know it isn't; and there's storms of sociable birds, and hurricanes of whirring wings; and when the sun strikes all that feathery commotion, you have a blazing up of all the colors you can think of, enough to put your eyes out.

We have made long excursions, and I have seen a great deal of the world; almost all of it, I think; and so I am the first traveller, and the only one. When we are on the march, it is an imposing sight—there's nothing like it anywhere. For comfort I ride a tiger or a leopard, because it is soft and has a round back that fits me, and because they are such pretty animals; but for long distance or for scenery I ride the elephant. He hoists me up with his trunk, but I can get off myself; when we are ready to camp, he sits and I slide down the back way.

The birds and animals are all friendly to each other, and there are no disputes about anything. They all talk, and they all talk to me, but it must be a foreign language, for I cannot make out a word they say; yet they often understand me when I talk back, particularly the dog and the elephant. It makes me ashamed. It shows that they are brighter than I am, and are therefore my superiors. It annoys me, for I want to be the principal Experiment myself—and I intend to be, too.

I have learned a number of things, and am educated, now, but I wasn't at first. I was ignorant at first. At first it used to vex me because, with all my watching, I was never smart enough to be around when the water was running up-hill; but now I do not mind it. I have experimented and experimented until now I know it never does run up-hill, except in the dark. I know it does in the dark, because the pool never goes dry; which it would, of course, if the water didn't come back in the night. It is best to prove things by actual experiment; then you *know*; whereas if you depend on guessing and supposing and conjecturing, you will never get educated.

Some things you *can't* find out; but you will never know

you can't by guessing and supposing: no, you have to be patient and go on experimenting until you find out that you can't find out. And it is delightful to have it that way, it makes the world so interesting. If there wasn't anything to find out, it would be dull. Even trying to find out and not finding out is just as interesting as trying to find out and finding out, and I don't know but more so. The secret of the water was a treasure until I *got* it; then the excitement all went away, and I recognized a sense of loss.

By experiment I know that wood swims, and dry leaves, and feathers, and plenty of other things; therefore by all that cumulative evidence you know that a rock will swim; but you have to put up with simply knowing it, for there isn't any way to prove it—up to now. But I shall find a way—then *that* excitement will go. Such things make me sad; because by and by when I have found out everything there won't be any more excitements, and I do love excitements so! The other night I couldn't sleep for thinking about it.

At first I couldn't make out what I was made for, but now I think it was to search out the secrets of this wonderful world and be happy and thank the Giver of it all for devising it. I think there are many things to learn yet—I hope so; and by economizing and not hurrying too fast I think they will last weeks and weeks. I hope so. When you cast up a feather it sails away on the air and goes out of sight; then you throw up a clod and it doesn't. It comes down, every time. I have tried it and tried it, and it is always so. I wonder why it is? Of course it *doesn't* come down, but why should it *seem* to? I suppose it is an optical illusion. I mean, one of them is. I don't know which one. It may be the feather, it may be the clod; I can't prove which it is, I can only demonstrate that one or the other is a fake, and let a person take his choice.

By watching, I know that the stars are not going to last. I have seen some of the best ones melt and run down the sky. Since one can melt, they can all melt; since they can all melt, they can all melt the same night. That sorrow will come—I know it. I mean to sit up every night and look at them as long as I can keep awake; and I will impress those sparkling fields on my memory, so that by and by when they are taken away I can by my fancy restore those lovely myriads to the black sky and make them sparkle again, and double them by the blur of my tears.

### AFTER THE FALL

When I look back, the Garden is a dream to me. It was beautiful, surpassingly beautiful, enchantingly beautiful; and now it is lost, and I shall not see it any more.

The Garden is lost, but I have found *him*, and am content. He loves me as well as he can; I love him with all the strength of my passionate nature, and this, I think, is proper to my youth and sex. If I ask myself why I love him, I find I do not know, and do not really much care to know; so I suppose that this kind of love is not a product of reasoning and statistics, like one's love for other reptiles and animals. I think that this must be so. I love certain birds because of their song; but I do not love Adam on account of his singing—no, it is not that; the more he sings the more I do not get reconciled to it. Yet I ask him to sing, because I wish to learn to like everything he is interested in. I am sure I can learn, because at first I could not stand it, but now I can. It sours the milk, but it doesn't matter; I can get used to that kind of milk.

It is not on account of his brightness that I love him— no, it is not that. He is not to blame for his brightness, such as it is, for he did not make it himself; he is as God made him, and that is sufficient. There was a wise purpose in it, *that* I know. In time it will develop, though I think it will not be sudden; and besides, there is no hurry; he is well enough just as he is.

It is not on account of his gracious and considerate ways and his delicacy that I love him. No, he has lacks in these regards, but he is well enough just so, and is improving.

It is not on account of his industry that I love him—no, it is not that. I think he has it in him, and I do not know why he conceals it from me. It is my only pain. Otherwise he is frank and open with me, now. I am sure he keeps nothing from me but this. It grieves me that he should have a secret from me, and sometimes it spoils my sleep, thinking of it, but

I will put it out of my mind; it shall not trouble my happiness, which is otherwise full to overflowing.

It is not on account of his education that I love him—no, it is not that. He is self-educated, and does really know a multitude of things, but they are not so.

It is not on account of his chivalry that I love him—no, it is not that. He told on me, but I do not blame him; it is a peculiarity of sex, I think, and he did not make his sex. Of course I would not have told on him, I would have perished first; but that is a peculiarity of sex, too, and I do not take credit for it, for I did not make my sex.

Then why is it that I love him? *Merely because he is masculine*, I think.

At bottom he is good, and I love him for that, but I could love him without it. If he should beat me and abuse me, I should go on loving him. I know it. It is a matter of sex, I think.

He is strong and handsome, and I love him for that, and I admire him and am proud of him, but I could love him without those qualities. If he were plain, I should love him; if he were a wreck, I should love him; and I would work for him, and slave over him, and pray for him, and watch by his bedside until I died.

Yes, I think I love him merely because he is *mine*, and is *masculine*. There is no other reason, I suppose. And so I think it is as I first said: that this kind of love is not a product of reasonings and statistics. It just *comes*—none knows whence—and cannot explain itself. And doesn't need to.

It is what I think. But I am only a girl, and the first that has examined this matter, and it may turn out that in my ignorance and inexperience I have not got it right.

### FORTY YEARS LATER

It is my prayer, it is my longing, that we may pass from this life together—a longing which shall never perish from the earth, but shall have place in the heart of every wife that loves, until the end of time; and it shall be called by my name.

But if one of us must go first, it is my prayer that it shall be I; for he is strong, I am weak, I am not so necessary to him as he is to me—life without him would not be life; how could I endure it? This prayer is also immortal, and will not cease from being offered up while my race continues. I am the first wife; and in the last wife I shall be repeated.

### AT EVE'S GRAVE

ADAM: Wheresoever she was, *there* was Eden.

### THE END.

*December 1905*

# Eve Speaks

They drove us from the Garden with their swords of flame,
the fierce cherubim. And what had we done? We meant no
harm. We were ignorant, and did as any other children might
do. We could not know it was wrong to disobey the command, for the words were strange to us and we did not understand them. We did not know right from wrong—how
should we know? We could not, without the Moral Sense; it
was not possible. If we had been given the Moral Sense
first—ah, that would have been fairer, that would have been
kinder; then we should be to blame if we disobeyed. But to
say to us poor ignorant children words which we could not
understand, and then punish us because we did not do as we
were told—ah, how can that be justified? We knew no more
then than this littlest child of mind knows now, with its four
years—oh, not so much, I think. Would I say to it, "If thou
touchest this bread I will overwhelm thee with unimaginable
disaster, even to the dissolution of thy corporeal elements,"
and when it took the bread and smiled up in my face, thinking no harm, as not understanding those strange words,
would I take advantage of its innocence and strike it down
with the mother hand it trusted? Whoso knoweth the mother
heart, let him judge if it would do that thing. Adam says my
brain is turned by my troubles and that I am become wicked.
I am as I am; I did not make myself.

They drove us out. Drove us out into this harsh wilderness,
and shut the gates against us. We that had meant no harm. It
is three months. We were ignorant then; we are rich in learning, now—ah, how rich! We know hunger, thirst, and cold;
we know pain, disease, and grief; we know hate, rebellion,
and deceit; we know remorse, the conscience that prosecutes
guilt and innocence alike, making no distinction; we know
weariness of body and spirit, the unrefreshing sleep, the rest
which rests not, the dreams which restore Eden, and banish it
again with the waking; we know misery; we know torture
and the heartbreak; we know humiliation and insult; we
know indecency, immodesty, and the soiled mind; we know
the scorn that attaches to the transmitted image of God ex-

posed unclothed to the day; we know fear; we know vanity, folly, envy, hypocrisy; we know irreverence; we know blasphemy; we know right from wrong, and how to avoid the one and do the other; we know all the rich product of the Moral Sense, and it is our possession. Would we could sell it for one hour of Eden and white purity; would we could degrade the animals with it!

We have it all—that treasure. All but death. Death. . . . Death. What may that be?

Adam comes.

"Well?"

"He still sleeps."

That is our second-born—our Abel.

"He has slept enough for his good, and his garden suffers for his care. Wake him."

"I have tried and cannot."

"Then he is very tired. Let him sleep on."

"I think it is his hurt that makes him sleep so long."

I answer: "It may be so. Then we will let him rest; no doubt the sleep is healing it."

II

It is a day and a night, now, that he has slept. We found him by his altar in his field, that morning, his face and body drenched in blood. He said his eldest brother struck him down. Then he spoke no more and fell asleep. We laid him in his bed and washed the blood away, and were glad to know the hurt was light and that he had no pain; for if he had had pain he would not have slept.

It was in the early morning that we found him. All day he slept that sweet, reposeful sleep, lying always on his back, and never moving, never turning. It showed how tired he was, poor thing. He is so good and works so hard, rising with the dawn and laboring till the dark. And now he is overworked; it will be best that he tax himself less, after this, and I will ask him; he will do anything I wish.

All the day he slept. I know, for I was always near, and made dishes for him and kept them warm against his waking. Often I crept in and fed my eyes upon his gentle face, and was thankful for that blessed sleep. And still he slept on—slept with his eyes wide; a strange thing, and made me think he was awake at first, but it was not so, for I spoke and he did not answer. He always answers when I speak. Cain has moods and will not answer, but not Abel.

I have sat by him all the night, being afraid he might wake and want his food. His face was very white; and it changed, and he came to look as he had looked when he was a little child in Eden long ago, so sweet and good and dear. It carried me back over the abyss of years, and I was lost in dreams and tears—oh, hours, I think. Then I came to myself; and thinking he stirred, I kissed his cheek to wake him, but he slumbered on and I was disappointed. His cheek was cold. I brought sacks of wool and the down of birds and covered him, but he was still cold, and I brought more. Adam has come again, and says he is not yet warm. I do not understand it.

### III

We cannot wake him! With my arms clinging about him I have looked into his eyes, through the veil of my tears, and begged for one little word, and he will not answer. Oh, is it that long sleep—is it death? And will he wake no more?

#### FROM SATAN'S DIARY

Death has entered the world, the creatures are perishing; one of The Family is fallen; the product of the Moral Sense is complete. The Family think ill of death—they will change their minds.

*Undated*

# Seventieth Birthday Dinner Speech

*Mark Twain's Seventieth Birthday Dinner, Delmonico's, New York*

Well, if I made that joke, it is the best one I ever made, and it is in the prettiest language, too. I never can get quite to that height. But I appreciate that joke, and I shall remember it—and I shall use it when occasion requires.

I have had a great many birthdays in my time. I remember the first one very well, and I always think of it with indignation; everything was so crude, unesthetic, primeval. Nothing like this at all. No proper appreciative preparation made; nothing really ready. Now, for a person born with high and delicate instincts—why, even the cradle wasn't white-washed—nothing ready at all. I hadn't any hair, I hadn't any teeth, I hadn't any clothes, I had to go to my first banquet just like that. Well, everybody came swarming in. It was the merest little bit of a village—hardly that, just a little hamlet, in the backwoods of Missouri, where nothing ever happened, and the people were all interested, and they all came; they looked me over to see if there was anything fresh in my line. Why, nothing ever happened in that village—I—why, I was the only thing that had really happened there for months and months and months; and although I say it myself that shouldn't, I came the nearest to being a real event that had happened in that village in more than two years. Well, those people came, they came with that curiosity which is so provincial, with that frankness which also is so provincial, and they examined me all around and gave their opinion. Nobody asked them, and I shouldn't have minded if anybody had paid me a compliment, but nobody did. Their opinions were all just green with prejudice, and I feel those opinions to this day. Well, I stood that as long as—well, you know I was born courteous, and I stood it to the limit. I stood it an hour, and then the worm turned. I was the worm; it was my turn to turn, and I turned. I knew very well the strength of my position; I knew that I was the only spotlessly pure and innocent person in that whole town, and I came out and said so. And they could not say a word. It was so true. They blushed; they

were embarrassed. Well, that was the first after-dinner speech
I ever made. I think it was after dinner.

It's a long stretch between that first birthday speech and
this one. That was my cradle song, and this is my swan song,
I suppose. I am used to swan songs; I have sung them several
times.

This is my seventieth birthday, and I wonder if you all rise
to the size of that proposition, realizing all the significance of
that phrase, seventieth birthday.

The seventieth birthday! It is the time of life when you
arrive at a new and awful dignity; when you may throw aside
the decent reserves which have oppressed you for a generation
and stand unafraid and unabashed upon your seven-terraced
summit and look down and teach—unrebuked. You can tell
the world how you got there. It is what they all do. You shall
never get tired of telling by what delicate arts and deep mo-
ralities you climbed up to that great place. You will explain
the process and dwell on the particulars with senile rapture. I
have been anxious to explain my own system this long time,
and now at last I have the right.

I have achieved my seventy years in the usual way: by sticking strictly to a scheme of life which would kill anybody else.
It sounds like an exaggeration, but that is really the common
rule for attaining to old age. When we examine the program
of any of these garrulous old people we always find that the
habits which have preserved them would have decayed us;
that the way of life which enabled them to live upon the
property of their heirs so long, as Mr. Choate says, would
have put us out of commission ahead of time. I will offer
here, as a sound maxim, this: That we can't reach old age by
another man's road.

I will now teach, offering my way of life to whomsoever
desires to commit suicide by the scheme which has enabled
me to beat the doctor and the hangman for seventy years.
Some of the details may sound untrue, but they are not. I am
not here to deceive; I am here to teach.

We have no permanent habits until we are forty. Then they
begin to harden, presently they petrify, then business begins.
Since forty I have been regular about going to bed and getting up—and that is one of the main things. I have made it a

rule to go to bed when there wasn't anybody left to sit up with; and I have made it a rule to get up when I had to. This has resulted in an unswerving regularity of irregularity. It has saved me sound, but it would injure another person.

In the matter of diet—which is another main thing—I have been persistently strict in sticking to the things which didn't agree with me until one or the other of us got the best of it. Until lately I got the best of it myself. But last spring I stopped frolicking with mince pie after midnight; up to then I had always believed it wasn't loaded. For thirty years I have taken coffee and bread at eight in the morning, and no bite nor sup until seven-thirty in the evening. Eleven hours. That is all right for me, and is wholesome, because I have never had a headache in my life, but headachy people would not reach seventy comfortably by that road, and they would be foolish to try it. And I wish to urge upon you this—which I think is wisdom—that if you find you can't make seventy by any but an uncomfortable road, don't you go. When they take off the Pullman and retire you to the rancid smoker, put on your things, count your checks, and get out at the first way station where there's a cemetery.

I have made it a rule never to smoke more than one cigar at a time. I have no other restriction as regards smoking. I do not know just when I began to smoke, I only know that it was in my father's lifetime, and that I was discreet. He passed from this life early in 1847, when I was a shade past eleven; ever since then I have smoked publicly. As an example to others, and not that I care for moderation myself, it has always been my rule never to smoke when asleep, and never to refrain when awake. It is a good rule. I mean, for me; but some of you know quite well that it wouldn't answer for everybody that's trying to get to be seventy.

I smoke in bed until I have to go to sleep; I wake up in the night, sometimes once, sometimes twice, sometimes three times, and I never waste any of these opportunities to smoke. This habit is so old and dear and precious to me that I would feel as you, sir, would feel if you should lose the only moral you've got—meaning the chairman—if you've got one; I am making no charges. I will grant, here, that I have stopped smoking now and then, for a few months at a time, but it was not on principle, it was only to show off; it was to pulverize those critics who said I was a slave to my habits and couldn't break my bonds.

Today it is all of sixty years since I began to smoke the limit. I have never bought cigars with life belts around them. I early found that those were too expensive for me. I have always bought cheap cigars—reasonably cheap, at any rate. Sixty years ago they cost me four dollars a barrel, but my taste has improved, latterly, and I pay seven now. Six or seven. Seven, I think. Yes, it's seven. But that includes the barrel. I often have smoking parties at my house; but the people that come have always just taken the pledge. I wonder why that is?

As for drinking, I have no rule about that. When the others drink I like to help; otherwise I remain dry, by habit and preference. This dryness does not hurt me, but it could easily hurt you, because you are different. You let it alone.

Since I was seven years old I have seldom taken a dose of medicine, and have still seldomer needed one. But up to seven I lived exclusively on allopathic medicines. Not that I needed them, for I don't think I did; it was for economy; my father took a drug store for a debt, and it made cod liver oil cheaper than other breakfast foods. We had nine barrels of it, and it lasted me seven years. Then I was weaned. The rest of the family had to get along with rhubarb and ipecac and such things, because I was the pet. I was the first Standard Oil Trust. I had it all. By the time the drug store was exhausted my health was established and there has never been much the matter with me since. But you know very well it would be foolish for the average child to start for seventy on that basis. It happened to be just the thing for me, but that was merely an accident; it couldn't happen again in a century.

I have never taken any exercise, except sleeping and resting, and I never intend to take any. Exercise is loathsome. And it cannot be any benefit when you are tired; and I was always tired. But let another person try my way, and see where he will come out.

I desire now to repeat and emphasize that maxim: We can't reach old age by another man's road. My habits protect my life but they would assassinate you.

I have lived a severely moral life. But it would be a mistake for other people to try that, or for me to recommend it. Very few would succeed: you have to have a perfectly colossal stock of morals; and you can't get them on a margin; you have to have the whole thing, and put them in your box. Morals are an acquirement—like music, like a foreign language, like piety, poker, paralysis—no man is born with them. I wasn't myself, I started poor. I hadn't a single moral. There is hardly a man in this house that is poorer than I was then. Yes, I started like that—the world before me, not a moral in the slot. Not even an insurance moral. I can remember the first one I ever got. I can remember the landscape, the weather, the—I can remember how everything looked. It was an old moral, an old secondhand moral, all out of repair, and didn't fit, anyway. But if you are careful with a thing like that, and keep it in a dry place, and save it for processions, and chautauquas, and World's Fairs, and so on, and disinfect it now and then, and give it a fresh coat of whitewash once in a while, you will be surprised to see how well she will last and how long she will keep sweet, or at least inoffensive. When I got that mouldy old moral, she had stopped growing, because she hadn't any exercise; but I worked her hard, I worked her Sundays and all. Under this cultivation she waxed in might and stature beyond belief, and served me well and was my pride and joy for sixty-three years; then she got to associating with insurance presidents, and lost flesh and character, and was a sorrow to look at and no longer competent for business. She was a great loss to me. Yet not all loss. I sold her— ah, pathetic skeleton, as she was—I sold her to Leopold, the pirate King of Belgium; he sold her to our Metropolitan Museum, and it was very glad to get her, for, without a rag on, she stands fifty-seven feet long and sixteen feet high, and they think she's a brontosaur. Well, she looks it. They believe it will take nineteen geological periods to breed her match.

Morals are of inestimable value, for every man is born crammed with sin microbes, and the only thing that can extirpate these sin microbes is morals. Now you take a sterilized Christian—I mean, you take *the* sterilized Christian, for there's only one. Dear sir, I wish you wouldn't look at me like that.

Threescore years and ten!

It is the Scriptural statute of limitations. After that, you owe no active duties; for you the strenuous life is over. You are a time-expired man, to use Kipling's military phrase. You have served your term, well or less well, and you are mustered out. You are become an honorary member of the republic, you are emancipated, compulsions are not for you, nor any bugle call but "lights out." You pay the timeworn duty bills if you choose, or decline if you prefer—and without prejudice—for they are not legally collectible.

The previous engagement plea, which in forty years has cost you so many twinges, you can lay aside forever; on this side of the grave you will never need it again. If you shrink at thought of night, and winter, and the late homecoming from the banquet and the lights and the laughter through the deserted streets—a desolation which would not remind you now, as for a generation it did, that your friends are sleeping, and you must creep in a-tiptoe and not disturb them, but would only remind you that you need not tiptoe, you can never disturb them more—if you shrink at thought of these things, you need only reply, "Your invitation honors me, and pleases me because you still keep me in your remembrance, but I am seventy; seventy, and would nestle in the chimney corner, and smoke my pipe, and read my book, and take my rest, wishing you well in all affection, and that when you in your turn shall arrive at pier No. 70 you may step aboard your waiting ship with a reconciled spirit, and lay your course toward the sinking sun with a contented heart."

*December 5, 1905*

# Old Age

I think it likely that people who have not been here will be interested to know what it is like. I arrived on the thirtieth of November, fresh from care-free and frivolous 69, and was disappointed.

There is nothing novel about it, nothing striking, nothing to thrill you and make your eye glitter and your tongue cry out, "Oh, but it *is* wonderful, perfectly wonderful!" Yes, it is disappointing. You say, "Is *this* it?—*this?* after all this talk and fuss of a thousand generations of travelers who have crossed this frontier and looked about them and told what they saw and felt? why, it looks just like 69."

And that is true. Also it is natural; for you have not come by the fast express, you have been lagging and dragging across the world's continents behind oxen; when that is your pace one country melts into the next one so gradually that you are not able to notice the change: 70 looks like 69; 69 looked like 68; 68 looked like 67—and so on, back, and back, to the beginning. If you climb to a summit and look back— ah, then you see!

Down that far-reaching perspective you can make out each country and climate that you crossed, all the way up from the hot equator to the ice-summit where you are perched. You can make out where Infancy merged into Boyhood; Boyhood into down-lipped Youth; Youth into indefinite Young-Manhood; indefinite Young-Manhood into definite Manhood; definite Manhood with aggressive ambitions into sobered and heedful Husbandhood and Fatherhood; these into troubled and foreboding Age, with graying hair; this into Old Age, white-headed, the temple empty, the idols broken, the worshippers in their graves, nothing left but You, a remnant, a tradition, belated fag-end of a foolish dream, a dream that was so ingeniously dreamed that it seemed real all the time; nothing left but You, centre of a snowy desolation, perched on the ice-summit, gazing out over the stages of that long *trek* and asking Yourself "would you do it again if you had the chance?"

*1905*

# The Gorky Incident

Let me resurrect the "York Minster" episode of seventy-five years ago—and enlarge it a little for present purposes. York Minster—such was his nickname—was a native of Tierra del Fuego. He was a likable young fellow, bright, animated, rather handsome, and of a particularly shapely figure. Let him be where he might, his figure was always on exhibition, for he wore not a rag of clothing, except a square of untanned skin between his shoulders. His costume did not make him conspicuous, because it was the costume of his whole nation.

The commander of a British warship fitted York Minster out with Christian clothing, taught him the rudiments of English speech, and took him home over the seas. He became at once an object of great and earnest interest; the public welcomed him, the newspapers were full of him, all ranks offered him their hospitalities. Naturally he was pleased and grateful. Among his invitations was one which took precedence of all the others—the King's ball, at St. James's Palace. He got himself ready for that. For the sake of convenience and comfort he resumed his national costume, thinking no harm; and at 11 P.M., he appeared in the midst of that gorgeous assemblage clad only in his awful innocence and that pathetic shoulder-skin.

Do you know, he emptied that place in two minutes by the watch. Then the guards turned him into the street. When he reached his hotel he was denied admission. The other hotels refused him. It looked as if he was nevermore going to find shelter, but at last he was rescued from his difficulties by compassionate friends.

Then the wise and the unwise began on him in the newspapers, and led him a dance. A friend defended him and explained that York was only following a recognized and perfectly proper custom of his own country and therefore was doing no wrong. Other friends defended him and proved by facts and arguments that the dress customs of Tierra del Fuego were more just and rational than were those of England; and then claimed that since this was the case the English had no right to find fault with this foreigner and inhospitably upbraid him and revile him for what he had done.

All of which was wasted ink, I think. Laws are coldly reasoned out and established upon what the lawmakers believe to be a basis of right. But customs are not. Customs are not enacted, they grow gradually up, imperceptibly and unconsciously, like an oak from its seed. In the fullness of their strength they can stand up straight in front of a world of argument and reasoning, and yield not an inch. We do not know how or when it became custom for women to wear long hair, we only know that in this country it *is* custom, and that settles it. Maybe it is right, maybe it is wrong—that has nothing to do with the matter; customs do not concern themselves with right or wrong or reason. But they have to be obeyed; one may reason all around them until he is tired, but he must not transgress them, it is sternly forbidden. Women may shave their heads elsewhere, but here they must refrain or take the uncomfortable consequences. Laws are sand, customs are rock. Laws can be evaded and punishment escaped, but an openly transgressed custom brings sure punishment. The penalty may be unfair, unrighteous, illogical, and a cruelty; no matter, it will be inflicted, just the same. Certainly, then, there can be but one wise thing for a visiting stranger to do—find out what the country's customs are, and refrain from offending against them.

The efforts which have been made in Gorky's justification are entitled to all respect because of the magnanimity of the motive back of them, but I think that the ink was wasted. Custom is custom; it is built of brass, boiler iron, granite; facts, reasonings, arguments have no more effect upon it than the idle winds have upon Gibraltar.

However, I must return to York Minster and finish that story. After reflection, he put on his clothes again.

*April 28, 1906*

# William Dean Howells

Is it true that the sun of a man's mentality touches noon at forty and then begins to wane toward setting? Dr. Osler is charged with saying so. Maybe he said it, maybe he didn't; I don't know which it is. But if he said it, and if it is true, I can point him to a case which proves his rule. Proves it by being an exception to it. To this place I nominate Mr. Howells.

I read his *Venetian Days* about forty years ago. I compare it with his paper on Machiavelli in a late number of *Harper*, and I cannot find that his English has suffered any impairment. For forty years his English has been to me a continual delight and astonishment. In the sustained exhibition of certain great qualities—clearness, compression, verbal exactness, and unforced and seemingly unconscious felicity of phrasing—he is, in my belief, without his peer in the English-writing world. *Sustained*. I intrench myself behind that protecting word. There are others who exhibit those great qualities as greatly as does he, but only by intervalled distributions of rich moonlight, with stretches of veiled and dimmer landscape between; whereas Howells's moon sails cloudless skies all night and all the nights.

In the matter of verbal exactness Mr. Howells has no superior, I suppose. He seems to be almost always able to find that elusive and shifty grain of gold, the *right word*. Others have to put up with approximations, more or less frequently; he has better luck. To me, the others are miners working with the gold-pan—of necessity some of the gold washes over and escapes; whereas, in my fancy, he is quicksilver raiding down a riffle—no grain of the metal stands much chance of eluding him. A powerful agent is the right word: it lights the reader's way and makes it plain; a close approximation to it will answer, and much travelling is done in a well-enough fashion by its help, but we do not welcome it and applaud it and rejoice in it as we do when *the* right one blazes out on us. Whenever we come upon one of those intensely right words in a book or a newspaper the resulting effect is physical as well as spiritual, and electrically prompt: it tingles exquisitely around through the walls of the mouth and tastes as tart and crisp and good as the autumn-butter that creams the sumac-berry. One has no time to examine the word and vote upon its rank and standing, the automatic recognition of its supremacy is so immediate. There is a plenty of acceptable literature which deals largely in approximations, but it may be likened to a fine landscape seen through the rain; the right word would dismiss the rain, then you would see it better. It doesn't rain when Howells is at work.

And where does he get the easy and effortless flow of his speech? and its cadenced and undulating rhythm? and its architectural felicities of construction, its graces of expression, its pemmican quality of compression, and all that? Born to him, no doubt. All in shining good order in the beginning, all extraordinary; and all just as shining, just as extraordinary to-day, after forty years of diligent wear and tear and use. He passed his fortieth year long and long ago; but I think his English of to-day—his perfect English, I wish to say—can throw down the glove before his English of that antique time and not be afraid.

I will go back to the paper on Machiavelli now, and ask the reader to examine this passage from it which I append. I do not mean, examine it in a bird's-eye way; I mean search it, study it. And, of course, read it aloud. I may be wrong, still it is my conviction that one cannot get out of finely wrought literature all that is in it by reading it mutely:

Mr. Dyer is rather of the opinion, first luminously suggested by Macaulay, that Machiavelli was in earnest, but must not be judged as a political moralist of our time and race would be judged. He thinks that Machiavelli was in earnest, as none but an idealist can be, and he is the first to imagine him an idealist immersed in realities, who involuntarily transmutes the events under his eye into something like the visionary issues of reverie. The Machiavelli whom he depicts does not cease to be politically a republican and socially a just man because he holds up an atrocious despot like Cæsar Borgia as a mirror for rulers. What Machiavelli beheld round him in Italy was a civic disorder in which there was oppression without statecraft, and revolt without patriotism. When a miscreant like Borgia appeared upon the scene and reduced both tyrants and rebels to an apparent quiescence, he might very well seem to such a dreamer the savior of society whom a certain sort of dreamers are always looking for. Machiavelli was no less honest when he honored the diabolical force of

Cæsar Borgia than Carlyle was when at different times he extolled
the strong man who destroys liberty in creating order. But Carlyle
has only just ceased to be mistaken for a reformer, while it is still
Machiavelli's hard fate to be so trammelled in his material that his
name stands for whatever is most malevolent and perfidious in human nature.

You see how easy and flowing it is; how unvexed by rug-
gednesses, clumsinesses, broken metres; how simple and—
so far as you or I can make out—unstudied; how clear,
how limpid, how understandable, how unconfused by cross-
currents, eddies, undertows; how seemingly unadorned, yet
is all adornment, like the lily-of-the-valley; and how compressed, how compact, without a complacency-signal hung
out anywhere to call attention to it.

There are twenty-two lines in the quoted passage. After
reading it several times aloud, one perceives that a good deal
of matter is crowded into that small space. I think it is a
model of compactness. When I take its materials apart and
work them over and put them together in my way I find I
cannot crowd the result back into the same hole, there not
being room enough. I find it a case of a woman packing a
man's trunk: he can get the things out, but he can't ever get
them back again.

The proffered paragraph is a just and fair sample; the rest
of the article is as compact as it is; there are no waste words.
The sample is just in other ways: limpid, fluent, graceful, and
rhythmical as it is, it holds no superiority in these respects
over the rest of the essay. Also, the choice phrasing noticeable
in the sample is not lonely; there is a plenty of its kin distributed through the other paragraphs. This is claiming much
when that kin must face the challenge of a phrase like the one
in the middle sentence: "an idealist immersed in realities, who
involuntarily transmutes the events under his eye into something like the visionary issues of reverie." With a hundred
words to do it with, the literary artisan could catch that airy
thought and tie it down and reduce it to a concrete condition,
visible, substantial, understandable and all right, like a cabbage; but the artist does it with twenty, and the result is a
flower.

The quoted phrase, like a thousand others that have come

from the same source, has the quality of certain scraps of verse which take hold of us and stay in our memories, we do not understand why, at first: all the words being the right words, none of them is conspicuous, and so they all seem inconspicuous, therefore we wonder what it is about them that makes their message take hold.

> The mossy marbles rest
> On the lips that he has prest
> > In their bloom,
> And the names he loved to hear
> Have been carved for many a year
> > On the tomb.

It is like a dreamy strain of moving music, with no sharp notes in it. The words are all "right" words, and all the same size. We do not notice it at first. We get the effect, it goes straight home to us, but we do not know why. It is when the right words are conspicuous that they thunder—

The glory that was Greece and the grandeur that was Rome!

When I go back from Howells old to Howells young I find him arranging and clustering English words well, but not any better than now. He is not more felicitous in concreting abstractions now than he was in translating, then, the visions of the eye of flesh into words that reproduced their forms and colors:

In Venetian streets they give the fallen snow no rest. It is at once shovelled into the canals by hundreds of half-naked *facchini*; and now in St. Mark's Place the music of innumerable shovels smote upon my ear; and I saw the shivering legion of poverty as it engaged the elements in a struggle for the possession of the Piazza. But the snow continued to fall, and through the twilight of the descending flakes all this toil and encounter looked like that weary kind of effort in dreams, when the most determined industry seems only to renew the task. The lofty crest of the bell-tower was hidden in the folds of falling snow, and I could no longer see the golden angel upon its summit. But looked at across the Piazza, the beautiful outline of St. Mark's Church was perfectly pencilled in the air, and the shifting threads of the snowfall were woven into a spell of novel enchantment around the structure that always seemed to me too exquisite in its fantastic loveliness to be anything but the creation of magic. The tender snow had compassionated the beautiful edifice for all the wrongs of time, and so hid the stains and ugliness of decay that it looked as if just from the hand of the builder—or, better said, just from the brain of the architect. There was marvellous freshness in the colors of the mosaics in the great arches of the façade, and all that gracious harmony into which the temple rises, of marble scrolls and leafy exuberance airily supporting the statues of the saints, was a hundred times etherealized by the purity and whiteness of the drifting flakes. The snow lay lightly on the golden globes that tremble like peacock-crests above the vast domes, and plumed them with softest white; it robed the saints in ermine; and it danced over all its work, as if exulting in its beauty—beauty which filled me with subtle, selfish yearning to keep such evanescent loveliness for the little-while-longer of my whole life, and with despair to think that even the poor lifeless shadow of it could never be fairly reflected in picture or poem.

Through the wavering snowfall, the Saint Theodore upon one of the granite pillars of the Piazzetta did not show so grim as his wont is, and the winged lion on the other might have been a winged lamb, so gentle and mild he looked by the tender light of the storm. The towers of the island churches loomed faint and far away in the dimness; the sailors in the rigging of the ships that lay in the Basin wrought like phantoms among the shrouds; the gondolas stole in and out of the opaque distance more noiselessly and dreamily than ever; and a silence, almost palpable, lay upon the mutest city in the world.

The spirit of Venice is there: of a city where Age and Decay, fagged with distributing damage and repulsiveness among the other cities of the planet in accordance with the policy and business of their profession, come for rest and play between seasons, and treat themselves to the luxury and relaxation of sinking the shop and inventing and squandering charms all about, instead of abolishing such as they find, as is their habit when not on vacation.

In the working season they do business in Boston sometimes, and a character in *The Undiscovered Country* takes accurate note of pathetic effects wrought by them upon the aspects of a street of once dignified and elegant homes whose occupants have moved away and left them a prey to neglect and gradual ruin and progressive degradation; a descent which reaches bottom at last, when the street becomes a roost for humble professionals of the faith-cure and fortune-telling sort.

What a queer, melancholy house, what a queer, melancholy street! I don't think I was ever in a street before where quite so many professional ladies, with English surnames, preferred Madam to Mrs. on their door-plates. And the poor old place has such a desperately conscious air of going to the deuce. Every house seems to wince as you go by, and button itself up to the chin for fear you should find out it had no shirt on,—so to speak. I don't know what's the reason, but these material tokens of a social decay afflict me terribly: a tipsy woman isn't dreadfuler than a haggard old house, that's once been a home, in a street like this.

Mr. Howells's pictures are not mere stiff, hard, accurate photographs; they are photographs with feeling in them, and sentiment, photographs taken in a dream, one might say.

As concerns his humor, I will not try to say anything, yet I would try if I had the words that might approximately reach up to its high place. I do not think any one else can play with humorous fancies so gracefully and delicately and deliciously as he does, nor has so many to play with, nor can come so near making them look as if they were doing the playing themselves and he was not aware that they were at it. For they are unobtrusive, and quiet in their ways, and well conducted. His is a humor which flows softly all around about and over and through the mesh of the page, pervasive, refreshing, health-giving, and makes no more show and no more noise than does the circulation of the blood.

There is another thing which is contentingly noticeable in Mr. Howells's books. That is his "stage directions"—those artifices which authors employ to throw a kind of human naturalness around a scene and a conversation, and help the reader to see the one and get at meanings in the other which might not be perceived if intrusted unexplained to the bare words of the talk. Some authors overdo the stage directions, they elaborate them quite beyond necessity; they spend so much time and take up so much room in telling us how a person said a thing and how he looked and acted when he said it that we get tired and vexed and wish he hadn't said it at all. Other authors' directions are brief enough, but it is seldom that the brevity contains either wit or information.

Writers of this school go in rags, in the matter of stage directions; the majority of them have nothing in stock but a cigar,
a laugh, a blush, and a bursting into tears. In their poverty
they work these sorry things to the bone. They say:

". . . . replied Alfred, flipping the ash from his cigar."
(This explains nothing; it only wastes space.)

". . . . responded Richard, with a laugh." (There was
nothing to laugh about; there never is. The writer puts it in
from habit—automatically; he is paying no attention to his
work, or he would see that there is nothing to laugh at; often,
when a remark is unusually and poignantly flat and silly, he
tries to deceive the reader by enlarging the stage direction and
making Richard break into "frenzies of uncontrollable laughter." This makes the reader sad.)

". . . . murmured Gladys, blushing." This poor old shop-
worn blush is a tiresome thing. We get so we would rather
Gladys would fall out of the book and break her neck than do
it again. She is always doing it, and usually irrelevantly.
Whenever it is her turn to murmur she hangs out her blush; it
is the only thing she's got. In a little while we hate her, just as
we do Richard.

". . . . repeated Evelyn, bursting into tears." This kind
keep a book damp all the time. They can't say a thing without
crying. They cry so much about nothing that by and by when
they have something to cry *about* they have gone dry; they
sob, and fetch nothing; we are not moved. We are only glad.

They gravel me, these stale and overworked stage directions, these carbon films that got burnt out long ago and cannot now carry any faintest thread of light. It would be well if
they could be relieved from duty and flung out in the literary
back yard to rot and disappear along with the discarded
and forgotten "steeds" and "halidomes" and similar stage-
properties once so dear to our grandfathers. But I am friendly
to Mr. Howells's stage directions; more friendly to them than
to any one else's, I think. They are done with a competent
and discriminating art, and are faithful to the requirements of
a stage direction's proper and lawful office, which is to inform. Sometimes they convey a scene and its conditions so
well that I believe I could see the scene and get the spirit and
meaning of the accompanying dialogue if some one would

read merely the stage directions to me and leave out the talk. For instance, a scene like this, from *The Undiscovered Country*:

". . . . and she laid her arms with a beseeching gesture on her father's shoulder."

". . . . she answered, following his gesture with a glance."

". . . . she said, laughing nervously."

". . . . she asked, turning swiftly upon him that strange, searching glance."

". . . . she answered, vaguely."

". . . . she reluctantly admitted."

". . . . but her voice died wearily away, and she stood looking into his face with puzzled entreaty."

Mr. Howells does not repeat his forms, and does not need to; he can invent fresh ones without limit. It is mainly the repetition over and over again, by the third-rates, of worn and commonplace and juiceless forms that makes their novels such a weariness and vexation to us, I think. We do not mind one or two deliveries of their wares, but as we turn the pages over and keep on meeting them we presently get tired of them and wish they would do other things for a change:

". . . . replied Alfred, flipping the ash from his cigar."

". . . . responded Richard, with a laugh."

". . . . murmured Gladys, blushing."

". . . . repeated Evelyn, bursting into tears."

". . . . replied the Earl, flipping the ash from his cigar."

". . . . responded the undertaker, with a laugh."

". . . . murmured the chambermaid, blushing."

". . . . repeated the burglar, bursting into tears."

". . . . replied the conductor, flipping the ash from his cigar."

". . . . responded Arkwright, with a laugh."

". . . . murmured the chief of police, blushing."

". . . . repeated the housecat, bursting into tears."

And so on and so on; till at last it ceases to excite. I always notice stage directions, because they fret me and keep me trying to get out of their way, just as the automobiles do. At first; then by and by they become monotonous and I get run over.

Mr. Howells has done much work, and the spirit of it is as beautiful as the make of it. I have held him in admiration and affection so many years that I know by the number of those years that he is old now; but his heart isn't, nor his pen; and years do not count. Let him have plenty of them: there is profit in them for us.

*July 1906*

# *What Is Man?*

February, 1905. The studies for these papers were begun twenty-five or twenty-seven years ago. The papers were written seven years ago. I have examined them once or twice per year since and found them satisfactory. I have just examined them again, and am still satisfied that they speak the truth.

Every thought in them has been thought (and accepted as unassailable truth) by millions upon millions of men—and concealed, kept private. Why did they not speak out? Because they dreaded (*and could not bear*) the disapproval of the people around them. Why have not I published? The same reason has restrained me, I think. I can find no other.

I

a. *Man the Machine* b. *Personal Merit*

[The Old Man and the Young Man had been conversing. The Old Man had asserted that the human being is merely a machine, and nothing more. The Young Man objected, and asked him to go into particulars and furnish his reasons for his position.]

OLD MAN. What are the materials of which a steam-engine is made?

YOUNG MAN. Iron, steel, brass, white-metal, and so on.

O. M. Where are these found?

Y. M. In the rocks.

O. M. In a pure state?

Y. M. No—in ores.

O. M. Are the metals suddenly deposited in the ores?

Y. M. No—it is the patient work of countless ages.

O. M. You could make the engine out of the rocks themselves?

Y. M. Yes, a brittle one and not valuable.

O. M. You would not require much, of such an engine as that?

Y. M. No—substantially nothing.

O. M.   To make a fine and capable engine, how would you proceed?

Y. M.   Drive tunnels and shafts into the hills; blast out the iron ore; crush it, smelt it, reduce it to pig-iron; put some of it through the Bessemer process and make steel of it. Mine and treat and combine the several metals of which brass is made.

O. M.   Then?

Y. M.   Out of the perfected result, build the fine engine.

O. M.   You would require much, of this one?

Y. M.   Oh, indeed yes.

O. M.   It could drive lathes, drills, planers, punches, polishers, in a word all the cunning machines of a great factory?

Y. M.   It could.

O. M.   What could the stone engine do?

Y. M.   Drive a sewing-machine, possibly—nothing more, perhaps.

O. M.   Men would admire the other engine and rapturously praise it?

Y. M.   Yes.

O. M.   But not the stone one?

Y. M.   No.

O. M.   The merits of the metal machine would be far above those of the stone one?

Y. M.   Of course.

O. M.   Personal merits?

Y. M.   *Personal* merits? How do you mean?

O. M.   It would be personally entitled to the credit of its own performance?

Y. M.   The engine? Certainly not.

O. M.   Why not?

Y. M.   Because its performance is not personal. It is a result of the law of its construction. It is not a *merit* that it does the things which it is set to do—it can't *help* doing them.

O. M.   And it is not a personal demerit in the stone machine that it does so little?

Y. M.   Certainly not. It does no more and no less than the law of its make permits and compels it to do. There is nothing *personal* about it; it cannot choose. In this process of "working up to the matter" is it your idea to work up to the proposition that a man and a machine are about the same thing, and that there is no personal merit in the performance of either?

o. m. Yes—but do not be offended; I am meaning no offence. What makes the grand difference between the stone engine and the steel one? Shall we call it training, education? Shall we call the stone engine a savage and the steel one a civilized man? The original rock contained the stuff of which the steel one was built—but along with it a lot of sulphur and stone and other obstructing inborn heredities, brought down from the old geologic ages—prejudices, let us call them. Prejudices which nothing within the rock itself had either *power* to remove or any *desire* to remove. Will you take note of that phrase?

y. m. Yes. I have written it down: "Prejudices which nothing within the rock itself had either power to remove or any desire to remove." Go on.

o. m. Prejudices which must be removed by *outside influences* or not at all. Put that down.

y. m. Very well: "Must be removed by outside influences or not at all." Go on.

o. m. The iron's prejudice against ridding itself of the cumbering rock. To make it more exact, the iron's absolute *indifference* as to whether the rock be removed or not. Then comes the *outside influence* and grinds the rock to powder and sets the ore free. The *iron* in the ore is still captive. An *outside influence* smelts it free of the clogging ore. The iron is emancipated iron, now, but indifferent to further progress. An *outside influence* beguiles it into the Bessemer furnace and refines it into steel of the first quality. It is educated, now—its training is complete. And it has reached its limit. By no possible process can it be educated into *gold*. Will you set that down?

y. m. Yes: "Everything has its limit—iron ore cannot be educated into gold."

o. m. There are gold men, and tin men, and copper men, and leaden men, and steel men, and so on—and each has the limitations of his nature, his heredities, his training and his environment. You can build engines out of each of those metals, and they will all perform, but you must not require the weak ones to do equal work with the stronger ones. In each case, to get the best results, you must free the metal from its obstructing prejudicial ores by education—smelting, refining, and so forth.

Y. M.    You have arrived at man, now?

O. M.    Yes. Man the machine—man, the impersonal engine. Whatsoever a man is, is due to his *make*, and to the *influences* brought to bear upon it by his heredities, his habitat, his associations. He is moved, directed, COMMANDED, by *exterior* influences—*solely*. He *originates* nothing, himself—not even an opinion, not even a thought.

Y. M.    Oh, come! Where did I get my opinion that this which you are talking is all foolishness?

O. M.    It is a quite natural opinion—indeed an inevitable opinion—but *you* did not create the materials out of which it is formed. They are odds and ends of thoughts, impressions, feelings, gathered unconsciously from a thousand books, a thousand conversations, and from streams of thought and feeling which have flowed down into your heart and brain out of the hearts and brains of ten centuries of ancestors. *Personally* you did not create even the smallest microscopic fragment of the materials out of which your opinion is made; and personally you cannot claim even the slender merit of *putting the borrowed materials together*. That was done—*automatically*—by your mental machinery, in strict accordance with the law of that machinery's construction. And you not only did not make that machinery yourself, but you have *not even any command over it*.

Y. M.    This is too much. You think I could have formed no opinion but that one?

O. M.    Spontaneously? No. And *you did not form that one*; your machinery did it for you—automatically and instantly, without reflection or the need of it.

Y. M.    Suppose I had reflected? How then?

O. M.    Suppose you try.

Y. M.    (*After a quarter of an hour.*) I have reflected.

O. M.    You mean you have tried to change your opinion —as an experiment?

Y. M.    Yes.

O. M.    With success?

Y. M.   No. It remains the same; it is impossible to change it.

O. M.   I am sorry, but you see, yourself, that your mind is merely a machine, nothing more. You have no command over it, it has no command over itself—it is worked *solely from the outside*. That is the law of its make; it is the law of all machines.

Y. M.   Can't I *ever* change one of these automatic opinions?

O. M.   No. You can't, yourself, but *exterior influences* can do it.

Y. M.   And exterior ones *only*?

O. M.   Yes—exterior ones only.

Y. M.   That position is untenable—I may say ludicrously untenable.

O. M.   What makes you think so?

Y. M.   I don't merely think it, I know it. Suppose I resolve to enter upon a course of thought, and study, and reading, with the deliberate purpose of changing that opinion; and suppose I succeed. *That* is not the work of an exterior impulse, the whole of it is mine and personal; for I originated the project.

O. M.   Not a shred of it. *It grew out of this talk with me.* But for that it would never have occurred to you. No man ever originates anything. All his thoughts, all his impulses, come *from the outside*.

Y. M.   It's an exasperating subject. The *first* man had original thoughts, anyway; there was nobody to draw from.

O. M.   It is a mistake. Adam's thoughts came to him from the outside. *You* have a fear of death. You did not invent that—you got it from outside, from talk and teaching. Adam had no fear of death—none in the world.

Y. M.   Yes he had.

O. M.   When he was created?

Y. M.   No.

O. M.   When, then?

Y. M.   When he was threatened with it.

O. M.   Then it came from the *outside*. Adam is quite big enough; let us not try to make a god of him. *None but gods have ever had a thought which did not come from the outside.*

Adam probably had a good head, but it was of no sort of use to him until it was filled up *from the outside*. He was not able to invent the triflingest little thing with it. He had not a shadow of a notion of the difference between good and evil—he had to get the idea *from the outside*. Neither he nor Eve was able to originate the idea that it was immodest to go naked: the knowledge came in with the apple *from the outside*. A man's brain is so constructed that *it can originate nothing whatever*. It can only use material obtained *outside*. It is merely a machine; and it works automatically, not by will power. *It has no command over itself, its owner has no command over it.*

Y. M.  Well, never mind Adam; but certainly Shakspeare's creations—

O. M.  No, you mean Shakspeare's *imitations*. Shakspeare created nothing. He correctly observed, and he marvelously painted. He exactly portrayed people whom *God* had created, but he created none himself. Let us spare him the slander of charging him with trying. Shakspeare could not create. *He was a machine, and machines do not create.*

Y. M.  Where *was* his excellence, then?

O. M.  In this. He was not a sewing-machine, like you and me, he was a Gobelin loom. The threads and the colors came into him *from the outside*; outside influences, suggestions, *experiences*, (reading, seeing plays, playing plays, borrowing ideas, and so on), framed the patterns in his mind and started up its complex and admirable machinery, and *it automatically* turned out that pictured and gorgeous fabric which still compels the astonishment of the world. If Shakspeare had been born and bred on a barren and unvisited rock in the ocean his mighty intellect would have had no *outside material* to work with, and could have invented none; and *no outside influences*, teachings, mouldings, persuasions, inspirations, of a valuable sort, and could have invented none; and so, Shakspeare would have produced nothing. In Turkey he would have produced something—something up to the highest limit of Turkish influences, associations and training. In France he would have produced something better—something up to the highest limit of the French influences and training. In England he rose to the highest limit attainable through the *outside helps afforded by that land's ideals, influences and training*. You and I are but sewing-machines. We must turn out what we can; we must do our endeavor, and care nothing at all when the unthinking reproach us for not turning out Gobelins.

Y. M.  And so we are mere machines! And machines may not boast, nor feel proud of their performance, nor claim personal merit for it, nor applause and praise. It is an infamous doctrine.

O. M.  It isn't a doctrine, it is merely a fact.

Y. M.  I suppose, then, there is no more merit in being brave than in being a coward?

O. M.  *Personal* merit? No. A brave man does not *create* his bravery. He is entitled to no personal credit for possessing it. It is born to him. A baby born with a billion dollars—where is the personal merit in that? A baby born with nothing— where is the personal demerit in that? The one is fawned upon, admired, worshiped, by sycophants, the other is neglected and despised—where is the sense in it?

Y. M.  Sometimes a timid man sets himself the task of conquering his cowardice and becoming brave—and succeeds. What do you say to that?

O. M.  That it shows the value of *training in right directions over training in wrong ones*. Inestimably valuable is training, influence, education, in right directions—*training one's self-approbation to elevate its ideals*.

Y. M.  But as to merit—the personal merit of the victorious coward's project and achievement?

O. M.  There isn't any. In the world's view he is a worthier man than he was before, but *he* didn't achieve the change— the merit of it is not his.

Y. M.  Whose, then?

O. M.  His *make*, and the influences which wrought upon it from the outside.

Y. M.  His make?

O. M.  Yes. To start with, he was *not* utterly and completely a coward, or the influences would have had nothing to work upon. He was not afraid of a cow, though perhaps of a bull; not afraid of a woman, but afraid of a man. There was something to build upon. There was a *seed*. No seed, no plant. Did he make that seed himself, or was it born in him? It was no merit of *his* that the seed was there.

Y. M. Well, anyway, the idea of *cultivating* it, the resolution to cultivate it, was meritorious, and he originated that.

O. M. He did nothing of the kind. It came whence *all* impulses, good or bad, come—from *outside*. If that timid man had lived all his life in a community of human rabbits; had never read of brave deeds; had never heard speech of them; had never heard any one praise them nor express envy of the heroes that had done them, he would have had no more idea of bravery than Adam had of modesty, and it could never by any possibility have occurred to him to *resolve* to become brave. He *could not originate the idea*—it had to come to him from the *outside*. And so, when he heard bravery extolled and cowardice derided, it woke him up. He was ashamed. Perhaps his sweetheart turned up her nose and said "I am told that you are a coward!" It was not *he* that turned over the new leaf—she did it for him. *He* must not strut around in the merit of it—it is not his.

Y. M. But anyway he reared the plant after she watered the seed.

O. M. No. *Outside influences* reared it. At the command—and trembling—he marched out into the field—with other soldiers and in the daytime, not alone and in the dark. He had the *influence of example*, he drew courage from his comrades' courage; he was afraid, and wanted to run, but he did not dare; he was *afraid* to run, with all those soldiers looking on. He was progressing, you see—the moral fear of shame had risen superior to the physical fear of harm. By the end of the campaign experience will have taught him that not *all* who go into battle get hurt—an outside influence which will be helpful to him; and he will also have learned how sweet it is to be praised for courage and be huzza'd at with tear-choked voices as the war-worn regiment marches past the worshiping multitude with the flags flying and the drums beating. After that he will be as securely brave as any veteran in the army—and there will not be a shade nor suggestion of *personal merit* in it anywhere; it will all have come from the *outside*. The Victoria Cross breeds more heroes than—

Y. M. Hang it, where is the sense in his becoming brave if he is to get no credit for it?

O. M. Your question will answer itself presently. It involves an important detail of man's make which we have not yet touched upon.

Y. M. What detail is that?

O. M. The impulse which moves a person to do things—the only impulse that ever moves a person to do a thing.

Y. M. The *only* one! Is there but one?

O. M. That is all. There is only one.

Y. M. Well, certainly that is a strange enough doctrine. What is the sole impulse that ever moves a person to do a thing?

O. M. The impulse to *content his own spirit*—the *necessity* of contenting his own spirit and *winning its approval*.

Y. M. Oh, come, that won't do!

O. M. Why won't it?

Y. M. Because it puts him in the attitude of always looking out for his own comfort and advantage; whereas an unselfish man often does a thing solely for another person's good when it is a positive disadvantage to himself.

O. M. It is a mistake. The act must do *him* good, FIRST; otherwise he will not do it. He may *think* he is doing it solely for the other person's sake, but it is not so; he is contenting his own spirit *first*—the other person's benefit has to always take *second* place.

Y. M. What a fantastic idea! What becomes of self-sacrifice? Please answer me that.

O. M. What is self-sacrifice?

Y. M. The doing good to another person where no shadow nor suggestion of benefit to one's self can result from it.

2

*Man's Sole Impulse—The Securing of His Own Approval*

O. M. There have been instances of it—you think?

Y. M. *Instances?* Millions of them!

O. M. You have not jumped to conclusions? You have examined them—critically?

Y. M. They don't need it; the acts themselves reveal the golden impulse back of them.

O. M. For instance?

Y. M. Well, then, for instance. Take the case in the book here. The man lives three miles up town. It is bitter cold, blowing hard, snowing hard, midnight. He is about to enter the horse-car when a gray and ragged old woman, a touching picture of misery, puts out her lean hand and begs for rescue from hunger and death. The man finds that he has but a quarter in his pocket, but he does not hesitate; he gives it her and trudges home through the storm. There—it is noble, it is beautiful; its grace is marred by no fleck or blemish or suggestion of self-interest.

O. M. What makes you think that?

Y. M. Pray what else could I think? Do you imagine that there is some other way of looking at it?

O. M. Can you put yourself in the man's place and tell me what he felt and what he thought?

Y. M. Easily. The sight of that suffering old face pierced his generous heart with a sharp pain. He could not bear it. He could endure the three-mile walk in the storm, but he could not endure the tortures his conscience would suffer if he turned his back and left that poor old creature to perish. He would not have been able to sleep, for thinking of it.

O. M. What was his state of mind on his way home?

Y. M. It was a state of joy which only the self-sacrificer knows. His heart sang, he was unconscious of the storm.

O. M. He slept well?

Y. M. One cannot doubt it.

O. M. Very well. Now let us add up the details and see how much he got for his twenty-five cents. Let us try to find out the *real* why of his making the investment. In the first place *he* couldn't bear the pain which the suffering old face gave him. So he was thinking of *his* pain—this good man. He must buy a salve for it. If he did not succor the old woman *his* conscience would torture him all the way home. Thinking of *his* pain again. He must buy relief from that. If he didn't relieve the old woman *he* would not get any sleep. He must buy some sleep—still thinking of *himself*, you see. Thus, to sum up, he bought himself free of a sharp pain in his heart, he bought himself free of the tortures of a waiting conscience, he bought a whole night's sleep—all for twenty-five cents! This able trader got a hundred dollars' worth of clean profit out of an investment of twenty-five cents. It should make Wall street ashamed of itself. On his way home his heart was joyful, and it sang—profit on top of profit! The impulse which moved the man to succor the old woman was—*first*—to *content his own spirit*; secondly, to relieve *her* sufferings. Is it your opinion that men's acts proceed from one central and unchanging and inalterable impulse, or from a variety of impulses?

Y. M. From a variety, of course—some high and fine and noble, others not. What is your opinion?

O. M. That there is but *one* law, one source.

Y. M. That both the noblest impulses and the basest proceed from that one source?

O. M. Yes.

Y. M. Will you put that law into words?

O. M. Yes. This is the law. Keep it in your mind. *From his cradle to his grave a man never does a single thing which has any* FIRST AND FOREMOST *object but one—to secure peace of mind, spiritual comfort, for* HIMSELF.

Y. M. Come! He never does anything for any one else's comfort, spiritual or physical?

O. M. No. *Except on those distinct terms*—that it shall *first* secure *his own* spiritual comfort. Otherwise, he will not do it.

Y. M. It will be easy to expose the falsity of that proposition.

O. M. For instance?

Y. M. Take that noble passion, love of country, patriotism. A man who loves peace and dreads pain, leaves his pleasant home and his weeping family and marches out to manfully expose himself to hunger, cold, wounds and death. Is that seeking spiritual comfort?

O. M. He loves peace and dreads pain?

Y. M. Yes.

O. M. Then perhaps there is something that he loves *more* than he loves peace—*the approval of his neighbors and the public*. And perhaps there is something which he dreads more than he dreads pain—the *disapproval* of his neighbors and the public. If he is sensitive to shame he will go to the field—not because his spirit will be *entirely* comfortable there, but because it will be more comfortable there than it would be if he remained at home. He will always do the thing which will bring him the *most* mental comfort—for that is *the sole law of his life*. He leaves the weeping family behind; he is sorry to make them uncomfortable, but not sorry enough to sacrifice his *own* comfort to secure theirs.

Y. M.  Do you really believe that mere public opinion could force a timid and peaceful man to—

O. M.  Go to the wars? Yes—public opinion can force some men to do *anything*.

Y. M.  *Anything?*

O. M.  Yes—anything.

Y. M.  I don't believe that. Can it force a right-principled man to do a wrong thing?

O. M.  Yes.

Y. M.  Can it force a kind man to do a cruel thing?

O. M.  Yes.

Y. M.  Give an instance.

O. M.  Alexander Hamilton was a conspicuously high-principled man. He regarded dueling as wrong, and as opposed to the teachings of religion—but in deference to *public opinion* he fought a duel. He deeply loved his family, but to buy public approval he treacherously deserted them and threw his life away, ungenerously leaving them to life-long sorrow in order that he might stand well with a foolish world. In the then condition of the public standards of honor he could not have been comfortable with the stigma upon him of having refused to fight. The teachings of religion, his devotion to his family, his kindness of heart, his high principles, all went for nothing when they stood in the way of his spiritual comfort. A man will do *anything*, no matter what it is, *to secure his spiritual comfort*; and he can neither be forced nor persuaded to any act which has not that goal for its object. Hamilton's act was compelled by the inborn necessity of contenting his own spirit; in this it was like all the other acts of his life, and like all the acts of all men's lives. Do you see where the kernel of the matter lies? A man cannot be comfortable without *his own* approval. He will secure the largest share possible of that, at all costs, all sacrifices.

Y. M. A minute ago you said Hamilton fought the duel to get the *public* approval.

O. M. I did. By refusing to fight the duel he could have secured his family's approval and a large share of his own; but the public approval was more valuable in his eyes than all other approvals put together—in the earth or above it; to secure that would furnish him the *most* comfort of mind, the most *self*-approval; so he sacrificed all other values to get it.

Y. M. Some noble souls have refused to fight duels, and have manfully braved the public contempt.

O. M. They acted *according to their make*. They valued their principles and the approval of their families *above* the public approval. They took the thing they valued *most* and let the rest go. They took what would give them the *largest* share of *personal contentment and approval*—a man *always* does. Public opinion cannot force that kind of men to go to the wars. When they go, it is for other reasons. Other spirit-contenting reasons.

Y. M. Always spirit-contenting reasons?

O. M. There are no others.

Y. M. When a man sacrifices his life in trying to save a little child from a burning building, what do you call that?

O. M. When he does it, it is the law of *his* make. *He* can't bear to see the child in that peril, (a man of a different make *could*), and so he tries to save the child, and loses his life. But he has got what he was after—*his own approval*.

Y. M. What do you call Love, Hate, Charity, Revenge, Humanity, Magnanimity, Forgiveness?

O. M. Different results of the one Master Impulse: the necessity of securing one's self-approval. They wear diverse clothes and are subject to diverse moods, but in whatsoever ways they masquerade they are the *same person* all the time. To change the figure, the *compulsion* that moves a man—and there is but the one—is the necessity of securing the content-ment of his own spirit. When it stops, the man is dead.

Y. M. This is foolishness. Love—

O. M. Why, love is that impulse, that law, in its most un-

compromising form. It will squander life and everything else
on its object. Not *primarily* for the object's sake, but for *its
own*. When its object is happy *it* is happy—and that is what it
is unconsciously after.

Y. M.    You do not even except the lofty and gracious passion of mother-love?

O. M.    No, *it* is the absolute slave of that law. The mother
will go naked to clothe her child; she will starve that it may
have food; suffer torture to save it from pain; die that it may
live. She takes a living *pleasure* in making these sacrifices. *She
does it for that reward*—that self-approval, that contentment,
that peace, that comfort. *She would do it for your child* IF SHE
COULD GET THE SAME PAY.

Y. M.    This is an infernal philosophy of yours.

O. M.    It isn't a philosophy, it is a fact.

Y. M.    Of course you must admit that there are some acts
which—

O. M.    No. There is *no* act, large or small, fine or mean,
which springs from any motive but the one—the necessity of
appeasing and contenting one's own spirit.

Y. M.    The world's philanthropists—

O. M.    I honor them, I uncover my head to them—from
habit and training; but *they* could not know comfort or happiness or self-approval if they did not work and spend for the
unfortunate. It makes *them* happy to see others happy; and so
with money and labor they buy what they are after—*happiness, self-approval*. Why don't misers do the same thing? Because they can get a thousandfold more happiness by *not*
doing it. There is no other reason. They follow the law of
their make.

Y. M.    What do you say of duty for duty's sake?

O. M.    That *it does not exist*. Duties are not performed for
duty's *sake*, but because their *neglect* would make the man
*uncomfortable*. A man performs but *one* duty—the duty of
contenting his spirit, the duty of making himself agreeable to
himself. If he can most satisfyingly perform this sole and only
duty by *helping* his neighbor, he will do it; if he can most
satisfyingly perform it by *swindling* his neighbor, he will do
that. But always he looks out for Number One—*first*; the

effects upon others are a *secondary* matter. Men pretend to self-sacrifices, but this is a thing which, in the ordinary value of the phrase, *does not exist and has not existed*. A man often honestly *thinks* he is sacrificing himself merely and solely for some one else, but he is deceived: his bottom impulse is to content a requirement of his nature and training, and thus acquire peace for his soul.

Y. M. Apparently, then, all men, both good and bad ones, devote their lives to contenting their consciences?

O. M. Yes. That is a good enough name for it: Conscience—that independent Sovereign, that insolent absolute Monarch inside of a man who is the man's Master. There are all kinds of consciences, because there are all kinds of men. You satisfy an assassin's conscience in one way, a philanthropist's in another, a miser's in another, a burglar's in still another. As a *guide* or *incentive* to any authoritatively prescribed line of morals or conduct, (leaving *training* out of the account), a man's conscience is totally valueless. I knew a kindhearted Kentuckian whose self-approval was lacking—whose conscience was troubling him, to phrase it with exactness—*because he had neglected to kill a certain man*—a man whom he had never seen. The stranger had killed this man's friend in a fight, this man's Kentucky training made it his duty to kill the stranger for it. He neglected this duty—kept dodging it, shirking it, putting it off, and his unrelenting conscience kept persecuting him for this conduct. At last, to get ease of mind, comfort, self-approval, he hunted up the stranger and took his life. It was an immense act of *self-sacrifice*, (as per the usual definition), for he did not want to do it, and he never would have done it if he could have bought a contented spirit and an unworried mind at smaller cost. But we are so made that we will pay *anything* for that contentment—even another man's life.

Y. M. You spoke a moment ago of *trained* consciences. You mean that we are not *born* with consciences competent to guide us aright?

O. M. If we were, children and savages would know right from wrong, and not have to be taught it.

Y. M. But consciences can be *trained*?

o. m.    Yes.

y. m.    Of course by parents, teachers, the pulpit, and books.

o. m.    Yes—they do their share; they do what they can.

y. m.    And the rest is done by—

o. m.    Oh, a million unnoticed influences—for good or bad; influences which work without rest during every waking moment of a man's life, from cradle to grave.

y. m.    You have tabulated these?

o. m.    Many of them—yes.

y. m.    Will you read me the result?

o. m.    Another time, yes. It would take an hour.

y. m.    A conscience can be trained to shun evil and prefer good?

o. m.    Yes.

y. m.    But will prefer it for spirit-contenting reasons only?

o. m.    It *can't* be trained to do a thing for any *other* reason. The thing is impossible.

y. m.    There *must* be a genuinely and utterly self-sacrificing act recorded in human history somewhere.

o. m.    You are young. You have many years before you. Search one out.

y. m.    It does seem to me that when a man sees a fellow-being struggling in the water and jumps in at the risk of his life to save him—

o. m.    Wait. Describe the *man*. Describe the *fellow-being*. State if there is an *audience* present; or if they are *alone*.

y. m.    What have these things to do with the splendid act?

o. m.    Very much. Shall we suppose, as a beginning, that the two are alone, in a solitary place, at midnight?

y. m.    If you choose.

o. m.    And that the fellow-being is the man's daughter?

y. m.    Well, n-no—make it some one else.

o. m.    A filthy, drunken ruffian, then?

y. m.    I see. Circumstances alter cases. I suppose that if there was no audience to observe the act, the man wouldn't perform it.

o. m.    But there is here and there a man who *would*. People, for instance, like the man who lost his life trying to save the child from the fire; and like the man who gave the needy old woman his 25 cents and walked home in the storm—there are here and there men like that who would do it. And why? Because they couldn't *bear* to see a fellow-being struggling in the water and not jump in and help. It would give *them* pain. They would save the fellow-being on that account. *They wouldn't do it otherwise.* They strictly obey the law which I have been insisting upon. You must remember and always distinguish the people who *can't bear* things from the people who *can*. It will throw light upon a number of apparently "self-sacrificing" cases.

Y. M. Oh, dear, it's all so disgusting.

O. M. Yes. And so true.

Y. M. Come—take the good boy who does things which he doesn't want to do, in order to gratify his mother.

O. M. He does seven-tenths of the act because it gratifies *him* to gratify his mother. Throw the bulk of advantage the other way and the good boy would not do the act. He *must* obey the iron law. None can escape it.

Y. M. Well, take the case of a bad boy who—

O. M. You needn't mention it, it is a waste of time. It is no matter about the bad boy's act. Whatever it was, he had a spirit-contenting reason for it. Otherwise you have been misinformed, and he didn't do it.

Y. M. It is very exasperating. A while ago you said that a man's conscience is not a born judge of morals and conduct, but has to be taught and trained. Now I think a conscience can get drowsy and lazy, but I don't think it can go wrong; and if you wake it up—

### A LITTLE STORY

O. M. I will tell you a little story:

Once upon a time an Infidel was a guest in the house of a Christian widow whose little boy was ill and near to death. The Infidel often watched by the bedside and entertained the boy with talk, and he used these opportunities to satisfy a strong longing of his nature—that desire which is in us all to better other people's condition by having them think as we think. He was successful. But the dying boy, in his last moments, reproached him and said—

"*I believed, and was happy in it; you have taken my belief away, and my comfort. Now I have nothing left, and I die miserable; for the things which you have told me do not take the place of that which I have lost."*

And the mother, also, reproached the Infidel, and said—

*"My child is forever lost, and my heart is broken. How could you do this cruel thing? We had done you no harm, but only kindness; we made our house your home, you were welcome to all we had, and this is our reward."*

The heart of the Infidel was filled with remorse for what he had done, and he said—

*"It was wrong—I see it now; but I was only trying to do him good. In my view he was in error; it seemed my duty to teach him the truth."*

Then the mother said—

*"I had taught him, all his little life, what I believed to be the truth, and in his believing faith both of us were happy. Now he is dead—and lost; and I am miserable. Our faith came down to us through centuries of believing ancestors; what right had you, or any one, to disturb it? Where was your honor, where was your shame?"*

Y. M.   He was a miscreant, and deserved death!

O. M.   He thought so himself, and said so.

Y. M.   Ah—you see, *his conscience was awakened!*

O. M.   Yes—his Self-Disapproval was. It *pained* him to see the mother suffer. He was sorry he had done a thing which brought *him* pain. It did not occur to him to think of the mother when he was mis-teaching the boy, for he was absorbed in providing *pleasure* for himself, then. Providing it by satisfying what he believed to be a call of duty.

Y. M.   Call it what you please, it is to me a case of *awakened conscience.* That awakened conscience could never get itself into that species of trouble again. A cure like that is a *permanent* cure.

O. M.   Pardon—I had not finished the story. We are creatures of *outside influences*—we originate *nothing* within. Whenever we take a new line of thought and drift into a new line of belief and action, the impulse is *always* suggested from the *outside.* Remorse so preyed upon the Infidel that it dissolved his harshness toward the boy's religion and made him come to regard it with tolerance, next with kindness, and presently with tenderness, for the boy's sake and the mother's. Finally he found himself examining it. From that moment his progress in his new trend was steady and rapid. He became a believing Christian. And now his remorse for having robbed the dying boy of his faith and his salvation was bitterer than ever. It gave him no rest, no peace. He *must* have rest and peace—it is the law of our nature. There seemed but one way to get it; he must devote himself to saving imperiled souls. He became a missionary. He landed in a pagan country ill and helpless. A native widow took him into her humble home and nursed him back to convalescence. Then her young boy was taken hopelessly ill, and the grateful missionary helped her tend him. Here was his first opportunity to repair a part of the wrong done to the other boy by doing a precious service for this one by undermining his foolish faith in his false gods. He was successful. But the dying boy in his last moments reproached him, and said—

*"I believed, and was happy in it; you have taken my belief away, and my comfort. Now I have nothing left, and I die miserable; for the things which you have told me do not take the place of that which I have lost."*

And the mother, also, reproached the missionary, and said—

*"My child is forever lost, and my heart is broken. How could you do this cruel thing? We had done you no harm, but only kindness; we made our house your home, you were welcome to all we had, and this is our reward."*

The heart of the missionary was filled with remorse for what he had done, and he said—

*"It was wrong—I see it now; but I was only trying to do him good. In my view he was in error; it seemed my duty to teach him the truth."*

Then the mother said—

*"I had taught him, all his little life, what I believed to be the truth, and in his believing faith both of us were happy. Now he is dead—and lost; and I am miserable. Our faith came down to us through centuries of believing ancestors; what right had you, or any one, to disturb it? Where was your honor, where was your shame?"*

The missionary's anguish of remorse and sense of treachery

were as bitter and persecuting and unappeasable, now, as they had been in the former case. The story is finished. What is your comment?

Y. M. The man's conscience was a fool! It was morbid. It didn't know right from wrong.

O. M. I am not sorry to hear you say that. If you grant that *one* man's conscience doesn't know right from wrong, it is an admission that there are others like it. This single admission pulls down the whole doctrine of infallibility of judgment in consciences. Meantime there is one thing which I ask you to notice.

Y. M. What is that?

O. M. That in both cases the man's *act* gave him no spiritual discomfort, and that he was quite satisfied with it and got pleasure out of it. But afterward when it resulted in *pain to him*, he was sorry. Sorry it had inflicted pain upon the others, *but for no reason under the sun except that their pain gave* HIM *pain*. Our consciences take *no* notice of pain inflicted upon others until it reaches a point where it gives pain to *us*. In *all* cases without exception we are absolutely indifferent to another person's pain until his sufferings make us uncomfortable. Many an infidel would not have been troubled by that Christian mother's distress. Don't you believe that?

Y. M. Yes. You might almost say it of the *average* infidel, I think.

O. M. And many a missionary, sternly fortified by his sense of duty, would not have been troubled by the pagan mother's distress—Jesuit missionaries in Canada in the early French times, for instance; see episodes quoted by Parkman.

Y. M. Well, let us adjourn. Where have we arrived?

O. M. At this. That we (mankind), have ticketed ourselves with a number of qualities to which we have given misleading names. Love, Hate, Charity, Compassion, Avarice, Benevolence, and so on. I mean, we attach misleading *meanings* to the names. They are all forms of self-contentment, self-gratification, but the names so disguise them that they distract our attention from the fact. Also, we have smuggled a word into the dictionary which ought not to be there at all—Self-Sacrifice. It describes a thing which does not exist. But worst of all, we ignore and never mention the Sole Impulse which dictates and compels a man's every act: the imperious necessity of securing his own approval, in every emergency and at all costs. To it we owe all that we are. It is our breath, our heart, our blood. It is our only spur, our whip, our goad, our only impelling power; we have no other. Without it we should be mere inert images, corpses; no one would do anything, there would be no progress, the world would stand still. We ought to stand reverently uncovered when the name of that stupendous power is uttered.

Y. M.   I am not convinced.

O. M.   You will be, when you think.

### 3

#### Instances in Point

O. M.   Have you given thought to the Gospel of Self-Approval since we talked?

Y. M.   I have.

O. M.   It was I that moved you to it. That is to say, an *outside influence* moved you to it—not one that originated in your own head. Will you try to keep that in mind and not forget it?

Y. M.   Yes. Why?

O. M.   Because by and by, in one of our talks, I wish to further impress upon you that neither you, nor I, nor any man ever originates a thought in his own head. *The utterer of a thought always utters a second-hand one.*

Y. M.   Oh, now—

O. M.   Wait. Reserve your remark till we get to that part of our discussion—to-morrow or next day, say. Now, then, you have been considering the proposition that no act is ever born of any but a self-contenting impulse—(primarily). You have sought. What have you found?

Y. M.   I have not been very fortunate. I have examined many fine and apparently self-sacrificing deeds in romances and biographies, but—

O. M.   Under searching analysis the ostensible self-sacrifice disappeared? It naturally would.

Y. M.   But here in this novel is one which seems to

promise. In the Adirondack woods is a wage-earner and lay preacher in the lumber-camps who is of noble character and deeply religious. An earnest and practical laborer in the New York slums comes up there on vacation—he is leader of a section of the University Settlement. Holme, the lumberman, is fired with a desire to throw away his excellent worldly prospects and go down and save souls on the East Side. He counts it happiness to make this sacrifice for the glory of God and for the cause of Christ. He resigns his place, makes the sacrifice cheerfully, and goes to the East Side and preaches Christ and Him crucified every day and every night to little groups of half-civilized foreign paupers who scoff at him. But he rejoices in the scoffings, since he is suffering them in the great cause of Christ. You have so filled my mind with suspicions that I was constantly expecting to find a hidden questionable impulse back of all this, but I am thankful to say I have failed. This man saw his duty, and for *duty's sake* he sacrificed self and assumed the burden it imposed.

O. M.     Is that as far as you have read?

Y. M.     Yes.

O. M.     Let us read further, presently. Meantime, in sacrificing himself—*not* for the glory of God, *primarily*, as *he* imagined, but *first* to content that exacting and inflexible master within him—*did he sacrifice anybody else?*

Y. M.     How do you mean?

O. M.     He relinquished a lucrative post and got mere food and lodging in place of it. Had he dependants?

Y. M.     Well—yes.

O. M.     In what way and to what extent did his self-sacrifice affect *them?*

Y. M.     He was the support of a superannuated father. He had a young sister with a remarkable voice—he was giving her a musical education, so that her longing to be self-supporting might be gratified. He was furnishing the money to put a young brother through a polytechnic school and satisfy his desire to become a civil engineer.

O. M.     The old father's comforts were now curtailed?

Y. M.     Quite seriously. Yes.

O. M.     The sister's music-lessons had to stop?

Y. M.     Yes.

O. M.  The young brother's education—well, an extinguishing blight fell upon that happy dream, and he had to go to sawing wood to support the old father, or something like that?

Y. M.  It is about what happened. Yes.

O. M.  What a handsome job of self-sacrificing he did do! It seems to me that he sacrificed everybody *except* himself. Haven't I told you that no man *ever* sacrifices himself; that there is no instance of it upon record anywhere; and that when a man's Interior Monarch requires a thing of its slave for either its *momentary* or its *permanent* contentment, that thing must and will be furnished and that command obeyed, no matter who may stand in the way and suffer disaster by it? That man *ruined his family* to please and content his Interior Monarch—

Y. M.  And help Christ's cause.

O. M.  Yes—*secondly*. Not firstly. *He* thought it was firstly.

Y. M.  Very well, have it so, if you will. But it could be that he argued that if he saved a hundred souls in New York—

O. M.  The sacrifice of the *family* would be justified by that great profit upon the——the—what shall we call it?

Y. M.  Investment?

O. M.  Hardly. How would *speculation* do? how would *gamble* do? Not a solitary soul-capture was sure. He played for a possible thirty-three hundred per cent profit. It was *gambling*—with his family for "chips." However, let us see how the game came out. Maybe we can get on the track of the secret original impulse, the *real* impulse, that moved him to so nobly self-sacrifice his family in the Savior's cause under the superstition that he was sacrificing himself. I will read a chapter or so. . . . . . Here we have it! it was bound to expose itself sooner or later. He preached to the East-Side rabble a season, then went back to his old dull and obscure life in the lumber camps *"hurt to the heart, his pride humbled."* Why? Were not his efforts acceptable to the Savior, for Whom alone they were made? Dear me, that detail is *lost sight of*, is not even referred to, the fact that it started out as a motive is entirely forgotten! Then what is the trouble? The authoress quite innocently and unconsciously gives the whole business away. The trouble was this: this man merely *preached* to the poor; that is not the University Settlement's way; it deals in larger and better things than that, and it did not enthuse over that crude Salvation-Army eloquence. It was courteous to Holme—but cool. It did not pet him, did not take him to its bosom. *"Perished were all his dreams of distinction, the praise and grateful approval of—"* Of whom? The Savior? No; the Savior is not mentioned. Of whom, then? Of "his *fellow-workers.*" Why did he want that? Because the Master inside of him wanted it, and would not be content without it. That emphasized sentence quoted above, reveals the secret we have been seeking, the original impulse, the *real* impulse, which moved the obscure and unappreciated Adirondack lumberman to sacrifice his family and go on that crusade to the East Side —which said original impulse was this, to-wit: without knowing it *he went there to show a neglectful world the large talent that was in him, and rise to distinction.* As I have warned you before, *no* act springs from any but the one law, the one motive. But I pray you, do not accept this law upon my say-so, but diligently examine for yourself. Whenever you read of a self-sacrificing act or hear of one, or of a duty done for *duty's sake*, take it to pieces and look for the *real* motive. It is always there.

y. m.   I do it every day. I cannot help it, now that I have gotten started upon the degrading and exasperating quest. For it is hatefully interesting!—in fact, fascinating is the word. As soon as I come across a golden deed in a book I have to stop and take it apart and examine it, I cannot help myself.

o. m.   Have you ever found one that defeated the rule?

y. m.   No—at least, not yet. But take the case of servant-tipping in Europe. You pay the *hotel* for service; you owe the servants *nothing*, yet you pay them, besides. Doesn't that defeat it?

o. m.   In what way?

y. m.   You are not *obliged* to do it, therefore its source is compassion for their ill-paid condition, and—

o. m.   Has that custom ever vexed you, annoyed you, irritated you?

y. m.   Well—yes.

o. m.   Still you succumbed to it?

y. m.   Of course.

o. m.  Why of course?

y. m.  Well, custom is law, in a way, and laws must be submitted to—everybody recognizes it as a *duty*.

o. m.  Then you pay the irritating tax for *duty's* sake?

y. m.  I suppose it amounts to that.

o. m.  Then the impulse which moves you to submit to the tax is not *all* compassion, charity, benevolence?

y. m.  Well—perhaps not.

o. m.  Is *any* of it?

y. m.  I—perhaps I was too hasty in locating its source.

o. m.  Perhaps so. In case you ignored the custom would you get prompt and effective service from the servants?

y. m.  Oh, hear yourself talk! Those European servants? Why, you wouldn't get any at all, to speak of.

o. m.  Couldn't *that* work as an impulse to move you to pay the tax?

y. m.  I am not denying it.

o. m.  Apparently, then, it is a case of for-duty's-sake with a little self-interest added?

y. m.  Yes, it has the look of it. But here is a point: we pay that tax knowing it to be unjust and an extortion; yet we go away with a pain at the heart if we think we have been stingy with the poor fellows; and we heartily wish we were back again, so that we could do the right thing, and *more* than the right thing, the *generous* thing. I think it will be difficult for you to find any thought of self in that impulse.

o. m.  I wonder why you should think so. When you find service charged in the *hotel* bill does it annoy you?

y. m.  No.

o. m.  Do you ever complain of the amount of it?

y. m.  No, it would not occur to me.

o. m.  The *expense*, then, is not the annoying detail. It is a fixed charge, and you pay it cheerfully, you pay it without a murmur. When you came to pay the servants, how would you like it if each of the men and maids had a fixed charge?

y. m.  Like it? I should rejoice!

o. m.  Even if the fixed tax were a shade *more* than you had been in the habit of paying in the form of tips?

y. m.  Indeed, yes!

o. m.  Very well, then. As I understand it, it isn't really

compassion nor yet duty that moves you to pay the tax, and it isn't the *amount* of the tax that annoys you. Yet *something* annoys you. What is it?

Y. M.   Well, the trouble is, you never know *what* to pay, the tax varies so, all over Europe.

O. M.   So you have to guess?

Y. M.   There is no other way. So you go on thinking and thinking, and calculating and guessing, and consulting with other people and getting their views; and it spoils your sleep, nights, and makes you distraught in the day-time, and while you are pretending to look at the sights you are only guessing and guessing and guessing all the time, and being worried and miserable.

O. M.   And all about a debt which you don't owe and don't have to pay unless you want to! Strange. What is the purpose of the guessing?

Y. M.   To guess out what is right to give them, and not be unfair to any of them.

O. M.   It has a quite noble look—taking so much pains and using up so much valuable time in order to be just and fair to a poor servant to whom you owe nothing, but who needs money and is ill paid.

Y. M.   I think, myself, that if there is any ungracious motive back of it it will be hard to find.

O. M.   How do you know when you have not paid a servant fairly?

Y. M.   Why, he is silent; does not thank you. Sometimes he gives you a look that makes you ashamed. You are too proud to rectify your mistake there, with people looking, but afterward you keep on wishing and wishing you *had* done it. My, the shame and the pain of it! Sometimes you see, by the signs, that you have hit it *just right*, and you go away mightily satisfied. Sometimes the man is so effusively thankful that you know you have given him a good deal *more* than was necessary.

O. M.   *Necessary?* Necessary for what?

Y. M.   To content him.

O. M.   How do you feel *then*?

Y. M.   Repentant.

O. M.   It is my belief that you have *not* been concerning

yourself in guessing out his just dues, but only in ciphering out what would *content* him. And I think you had a self-deluding reason for that.

Y. M. What was it?

O. M. If you fell short of what he was expecting and wanting, you would get a look which would *shame you before folk*. That would give you *pain*. *You*—for you are only working for yourself, not *him*. If you gave him too much you would be *ashamed of yourself* for it, and that would give *you* pain—another case of thinking of *yourself*, protecting yourself, *saving yourself from discomfort*. You never think of the servant once—except to guess out how to secure *his approval*. If you get that, you get your *own* approval, and that is the sole and only thing you are after. The Master inside of you is then satisfied, contented, comfortable; there was *no other* thing at stake, as a matter of *first* interest, anywhere in the transaction.

### FURTHER INSTANCES

Y. M. Well, to think of it: Self-Sacrifice for others, the grandest thing in man, ruled out! non-existent!

O. M. Are you accusing me of saying that?

Y. M. Why, certainly.

O. M. I haven't said it.

Y. M. What did you say, then?

O. M. That no man has ever sacrificed himself in the common meaning of that phrase—which is, self-sacrifice for another *alone*. Men make daily sacrifices for others, but it is for their own sake *first*. The act must content their own spirit *first*. The other beneficiaries come second.

Y. M. And the same with duty for duty's sake?

O. M. Yes. No man performs a duty for mere duty's sake; the act must content his spirit *first*. He must feel better for *doing* the duty than he would for shirking it. Otherwise he will not do it.

Y. M. Take the case of the *Berkeley Castle*.

O. M. It was a noble duty, greatly performed. Take it to pieces and examine it, if you like.

Y. M. A British troop-ship crowded with soldiers and their wives and children. She struck a rock and began to sink. There was room in the boats for the women and children only. The colonel lined-up his regiment on the deck and said "it is our duty to die, that they may be saved." There was no murmur, no protest. The boats carried away the women and children. When the death-moment was come, the colonel and his officers took their several posts, the men stood at shoulder-arms, and so, as on dress-parade, with their flag flying and the drums beating, they went down, a sacrifice to duty for duty's sake. Can you view it as other than that?

o. m.   It was something as fine as that, as exalted as that. Could you have remained in those ranks and gone down to your death in that unflinching way?

y. m.   Could I? No, I could not.

o. m.   Think. Imagine yourself there, with that watery doom creeping higher and higher around you.

y. m.   I can imagine it. I feel all the horror of it. I could not have endured it, I could not have remained in my place. I know it.

o. m.   Why?

y. m.   There is no why about it: I know myself, and I know I couldn't *do* it.

o. m.   But it would be your *duty* to do it.

y. m.   Yes, I know—but I couldn't.

o. m.   It was more than a thousand men, yet not one of them flinched. Some of them must have been born with your temperament; if they could do that great duty for duty's *sake*, why not you? Don't you know that you could go out and gather together a thousand clerks and mechanics and put them on that deck and ask them to die for duty's sake, and not two dozen of them would stay in the ranks to the end?

y. m.   Yes, I know that.

o. m.   But you *train* them, and put them through a campaign or two; then they would be soldiers; soldiers, with a soldier's pride, a soldier's self-respect, a soldier's ideals. They would have to content a *soldier's* spirit then, not a clerk's, not a mechanic's. They could not content that spirit by shirking a soldier's duty, could they?

y. m.   I suppose not.

o. m.   Then they would do the duty not for the *duty's* sake, but for their *own* sake—primarily. The *duty* was *just the same*, and just as imperative, when they were clerks, mechanics, raw recruits, but they wouldn't perform it for that. As clerks and mechanics they had other ideals, another spirit to satisfy, and they satisfied it. They *had* to; it is the law. *Training* is potent. Training toward higher, and higher, and ever higher ideals is worth any man's thought and labor and diligence.

Y. M. Consider the man who stands by his duty and goes to the stake rather than be recreant to it.

O. M. It is his make and his training. He has to content the spirit that is in him, though it cost him his life. Another man, just as sincerely religious, but of different temperament, will fail of that duty, though recognizing it as a duty, and grieving to be unequal to it; but he must content the spirit that is in him—he cannot help it. He could not perform that duty for duty's *sake*, for that would not content his spirit, and the contenting of his spirit must be looked to *first*. It takes precedence of all other duties.

Y. M. Take the case of a clergyman of stainless private morals who votes for a thief for public office, on his own party's ticket, and against an honest man on the other ticket.

O. M. He has to content his spirit. He has no public morals; he has no private ones, where his party's prosperity is at stake. He will always be true to his make and training.

4

*Training*

Y. M. You keep using that word—training. By it do you particularly mean—

O. M. Study, instruction, lectures, sermons? That is a part of it—but not a large part. I mean *all* the outside influences. There are a million of them. From the cradle to the grave, during all his waking hours, the human being is under training. In the very first rank of his trainers stands *association*. It is his human environment which influences his mind and his feelings, furnishes him his ideals, and sets him on his road and keeps him in it. If he leave that road he will find himself shunned by the people whom he most loves and esteems, and whose approval he most values. He is a chameleon; by a law of his nature he takes the color of his place of resort. The influences about him create his preferences, his aversions, his politics, his tastes, his morals, his religion. He creates none of these things for himself. He *thinks* he does, but that is because he has not examined into the matter. You have seen Presbyterians?

Y. M. Many.

O. M. How did they happen to be Presbyterians and not Congregationalists? And why were the Congregationalists not Baptists, and the Baptists Roman Catholics, and the Roman Catholics Buddhists, and the Buddhists Quakers, and the Quakers Episcopalians, and the Episcopalians Millerites, and the Millerites Hindoos, and the Hindoos Atheists, and the Atheists Spiritualists, and the Spiritualists Agnostics, and the Agnostics Methodists, and the Methodists Confucians, and the Confucians Unitarians, and the Unitarians Mohammedans, and the Mohammedans Salvation Warriors, and the Salvation Warriors Zoroastrians, and the Zoroastrians Christian Scientists, and the Christian Scientists Mormons — and so on?

Y. M. You may answer your question yourself.

O. M. That list of sects is not a record of *studies*, searchings, seekings after light; it mainly (and sarcastically) indicates what *association* can do. If you know a man's nationality you can come within a split hair of guessing the complexion of his religion: English — Protestant; American — ditto; Spaniard, Frenchman, Irishman, Italian, South American, Austrian — Roman Catholic; Russian — Greek Catholic; Turk — Mohammedan; and so on. And when you know the man's religious complexion, you know what sort of religious books he reads when he wants some more light, and what sort of books he avoids, lest by accident he get more light than he wants. In America if you know which party-collar a voter wears, you know what his associations are, and how he came by his politics, and which breed of newspaper he reads to get light, and which breed he diligently avoids, and which breed of mass meetings he attends in order to broaden his political knowledge, and which breed of mass meetings he doesn't attend, except to refute its doctrines with brickbats. We are always hearing of people who are around *seeking after Truth*. I have never seen a (permanent) specimen. I think he has never lived. But I have seen several entirely sincere people who *thought* they were (permanent) Seekers after Truth. They sought diligently, persistently, carefully, cautiously, profoundly, with perfect honesty and a nicely adjusted judgment—until they believed that without doubt or question they had found the Truth. *That was the end of the search.* The man spent the rest of his life hunting up shingles wherewith to protect his Truth from the weather. If he was seeking after political Truth he found it in one or another of the hundred political gospels which govern men in the earth; if he was seeking after the Only True Religion he found it in one or another of the three thousand that are on the market. In any case, when he found his Truth *he sought no further*; but from that day forth, with his soldering iron in one hand and his bludgeon in the other he tinkered its leaks and reasoned with objectors. There have been innumerable Temporary Seekers after Truth—have you ever heard of a Permanent one? In the very nature of man such a person is impossible. However, to drop back to the text—training: all training is one form or another of *outside influence*, and *association* is the largest part of it. A man is never anything but what his outside influences have made him. They train him downwards or they train him upwards—but they *train* him; they are at work upon him all the time.

Y. M. Then if he happen by the accidents of life to be evilly placed there is no help for him, according to your notions—he must train downwards.

O. M. No help for him? No help for this chameleon? It is a mistake. It is in his chameleonship that his greatest good fortune lies. He has only to change his habitat—his *associations*. But the impulse to do it must come from the *outside*—he cannot originate it himself, with that purpose in view. Sometimes a very small and accidental thing can furnish him the initiatory impulse and start him on a new road, with a new ideal. The chance remark of a sweetheart, "I hear that you are a coward" may water a seed that shall sprout and bloom and flourish, and end in producing a surprising fruitage in the fields of war. The history of man is full of such accidents. The accident of a broken leg brought a profane and ribald soldier under religious influences and furnished him a new ideal. From that accident sprang the Order of the Jesuits, and it has been shaking thrones, changing policies, and doing other tremendous work for two hundred years—and will go on. The chance reading of a book, or of a paragraph in a newspaper can start a man on a new track and make him renounce his old associations and seek new ones that are *in sympathy with his new ideal*; and the result, for that man, can be an entire change of his way of life.

Y. M. Are you hinting at a scheme of procedure?

O. M. Not a new one—an old one. Old as mankind.

Y. M. What is it?

O. M. Merely the laying of traps for people. Traps baited with *Initiatory Impulses toward high ideals*. It is what the tract distributor does. It is what the missionary does. It is what governments ought to do.

Y. M. Don't they?

O. M. In one way they do, in another way they don't. They separate the small-pox patients from the healthy people, but in dealing with crime they put the healthy into the pest-house along with the sick. That is to say, they put the beginners in with the confirmed criminals. This would be well if man were naturally inclined to good, but he isn't, and so *association* makes the beginners worse than they were when they went into captivity. It is putting a very severe punishment upon the comparatively innocent. However, all governments are hard on the innocent at times. They hang a man—which is a trifling punishment; this breaks the hearts of his family—which is a heavy one. They comfortably jail and feed a wife-beater, and leave his innocent wife and children to starve.

Y. M. Do you believe in the doctrine that man is equipped with an intuitive perception of good and evil?

O. M. Adam hadn't it.

Y. M. But has man acquired it since?

O. M. No. I think he has no intuitions of any kind. He gets *all* his ideas, all his impressions, all his opinions, from the outside. I keep repeating this, in the hope that I may so impress it upon you that you will be interested to observe and examine for yourself and see whether it is true or false.

Y. M. Where did you get your own aggravating notions?

O. M. From the *outside*. I did not invent them. They are

gathered from a thousand unknown sources. Mainly *unconsciously* gathered.

Y. M. Don't you believe that God could make an inherently honest man?

O. M. Yes, I know He could. I also know that He never did make one.

Y. M. A wiser observer than you has recorded the fact that "an honest man's the noblest work of God."

O. M. He didn't record a fact, he recorded a falsity. It is windy, and sounds well, but it is not true. God makes a man with honest and dishonest *possibilities* in him, and stops there. The man's *associations* develop the possibilities—the one set or the other. The result is accordingly an honest man or a dishonest one.

Y. M. And the honest one is not entitled to—

O. M. Praise? No. How often must I tell you that? *He* is not the architect of his honesty.

Y. M. Now then, I will ask you to tell me where there is any sense in training people to lead virtuous lives. What is gained by it?

O. M. The man himself gets large advantages out of it, and that is the main thing—to *him*. He is not a peril to his neighbors, he is not a damage to them—and so *they* get an advantage out of his virtues. That is the main thing to *them*. To train men to lead virtuous lives is an inestimably important thing. It can make this life comparatively comfortable to the parties concerned; the *neglect* of this training can make this life a constant peril and distress to the parties concerned.

Y. M. You have said that training is everything; that training is the man *himself*, for it makes him what he is.

O. M. I said training and *another* thing. Let that other thing pass, for the moment. What were you going to say?

Y. M. We have an old servant. She has been with us twenty-two years. Her service used to be faultless, but now she has become very forgetful. We are all fond of her; we all recognize that she cannot help the infirmity which age has brought her; the rest of the family do not scold her for her remissnesses, but at times I do—I can't seem to control myself. Don't I try? I do try. Now, then, when I was ready to dress, this morning, no clean clothes had been put out. I lost

my temper; I lose it easiest and quickest in the early morning.
I rang; and immediately began to warn myself not to show
temper, and to be careful and speak gently. I safeguarded myself most carefully. I even chose the very words I would use:
"You've forgotten the clean clothes, Jane." When she appeared in the door I opened my mouth to say that phrase—
and out of it, moved by an instant surge of passion which I
was not expecting and hadn't time to put under control, came
the hot rebuke, "You've forgotten them again!" You say a
man always does the thing which will best please his Interior
Master. Whence came the impulse to make careful preparation to save the girl the humiliation of a rebuke? Did that
come from the Master, who is always primarily concerned
about *himself*?

O. M. Unquestionably. There is no other source for any
impulse. *Secondarily* you made preparation to save the girl,
but *primarily* its object was to save yourself, by contenting the
Master.

Y. M. How do you mean?

O. M. Has any member of the family ever implored you to
watch your temper and not fly out at the girl?

Y. M. Yes. My mother.

O. M. You love her?

Y. M. Oh, more than that!

O. M. You would always do anything in your power to
please her?

Y. M. It is a delight to me to do anything to please her!

O. M. Why? *You would do it for pay, solely*—for *profit*. What
profit would you expect and certainly receive, from the investment?

Y. M. Personally? None. To please *her* is enough.

O. M. It appears, then, that your object, primarily, *wasn't*
to save the girl a humiliation, but to *please your mother*. It also
appears that to please your mother gives *you* a strong pleasure. Is not that the profit which you get out of the investment? Isn't that the *real* profit and *first* profit?

Y. M. Oh, well? Go on.

O. M. In *all* transactions, the Interior Master looks to it
that *you get the first profit*. Otherwise there is no transaction.

Y. M. Well, then, if I was so anxious to get that profit and was so intent upon it, why did I throw it away by losing my temper?

o. m.   In order to get *another* profit which suddenly superseded it in value.

y. m.   Where was it?

o. m.   Ambushed behind your born temperament, and waiting for a chance. Your native warm temper jumped suddenly to the front, and *for the moment* its influence was more powerful than your mother's, and abolished it. In that instant you were eager to flash out a hot rebuke and enjoy it. You did enjoy it, didn't you?

y. m.   For—for a quarter of a second. Yes—I did.

o. m.   Very well, it is as I have said: the thing which will give you the *most* pleasure, the most satisfaction, in any moment or *fraction* of a moment, is the thing you will always do. You must content the Master's *latest* whim, whatever it may be.

y. m.   But when the tears came into the old servant's eyes I could have cut my hand off for what I had done.

o. m.   Right. You had humiliated *yourself*, you see; you had given yourself *pain*. Nothing is of *first* importance to a man except results which damage *him* or profit him—all the rest is *secondary*. Your Master was displeased with you, although you had obeyed him. He required a prompt *repentance*; you obeyed again; you *had* to—there is never any escape from his commands. He is a hard master, and fickle; he changes his mind in the fraction of a second, but you must be ready to obey, and you will obey, *always*. If he requires repentance, to content him, you will always furnish it. He must be nursed, petted, coddled, and kept contented, let the terms be what they may.

y. m.   Training! Oh, what is the use of it? Didn't I, and didn't my mother try to train me up to where I would no longer fly out at that girl?

o. m.   Have you never managed to keep back a scolding?

y. m.   Oh, certainly—many times.

o. m.   More times this year than last?

y. m.   Yes, a good many more.

o. m.   More times last year than the year before?

y. m.   Yes.

o. m.    There is a large improvement, then, in the two years?

y. m.    Yes, undoubtedly.

o. m.    Then your question is answered. You see there *is* use in training. Keep on. Keep faithfully on. You are doing well.

y. m.    Will my reform reach perfection?

o. m.    It will. Up to *your* limit.

y. m.    My limit? What do you mean by that?

o. m.    You remember you said that I said training was *everything*. I corrected you, and said "training and *another* thing." That other thing is *temperament*—that is, the disposition you were born with. *You can't eradicate your disposition nor any rag of it*—you can only put a pressure on it and keep it down and quiet. You have a warm temper?

y. m.    Yes.

o. m.    You will never get rid of it; but by watching it you can keep it down nearly all the time. *Its presence is your limit.* Your reform will never quite reach perfection, for your temper will beat you now and then, but you will come near enough. You have made valuable progress and can make more. There *is* use in training. Immense use. Presently you will reach a new stage of development, then your progress will be easier; will proceed on a simpler basis, anyway.

y. m.    Explain.

o. m.    You keep back your scoldings now, to please *yourself* by pleasing your *mother*; presently the mere triumphing over your temper will delight your vanity and confer a more delicious pleasure and satisfaction upon you than even the approbation of your *mother* confers upon you now. You will then labor for yourself directly and at *first hand*, not by the roundabout way through your mother. It simplifies the matter, and it also strengthens the impulse.

y. m.    Ah, dear! But I shan't ever reach the point where I will spare the girl for *her* sake *primarily*, not mine?

o. m.    Why—yes. In heaven.

y. m.    (*After a reflective pause.*) Temperament. Well, I see one must allow for temperament. It is a large factor, sure enough. My mother is thoughtful, and not hot-tempered. When I was dressed I went to her room; she was not there; I called, she answered from the bath-room. I heard the water running. I inquired. She answered, without temper, that Jane had forgotten her bath, and she was preparing it herself. I offered to ring, but she said, "No, don't do that; it would only distress her to be confronted with her lapse, and would be a rebuke; she doesn't deserve that—she is not to blame for the tricks her memory serves her." I say—has my mother an Interior Master?—and where was he?

O. M. He was there. There, and looking out for his own peace and pleasure and contentment. The girl's distress would have pained *your mother*. Otherwise the girl would have been rung up, distress and all. I know women who would have gotten a No. 1 *pleasure* out of ringing Jane up—and so they would infallibly have pushed the button and obeyed the law of their make and training, which are the servants of their Interior Masters. It is quite likely that a part of your mother's forbearance came from training. The *good* kind of training— whose best and highest function is to see to it that every time it confers a satisfaction upon its pupil a benefit shall fall at second hand upon others.

Y. M. If you were going to condense into an admonition your plan for the general betterment of the race's condition, how would you word it?

## ADMONITION

O. M. Diligently train your ideals *upward* and *still upward* toward a summit where you will find your chiefest pleasure in conduct which, while contenting you, will be sure to confer benefits upon your neighbor and the community.

Y. M. Is that a new gospel?

O. M. No.

Y. M. It has been taught before?

O. M. For ten thousand years.

Y. M. By whom?

O. M. All the great religions—all the great gospels.

Y. M. Then there is nothing new about it.

O. M. Oh, yes there is. It is candidly stated, this time. That has not been done before.

Y. M. How do you mean?

O. M. Haven't I put *you* FIRST, and your neighbor and the community *afterward*?

Y. M.  Well, yes, that is a difference, it is true.

O. M.  The difference between straight speaking and crooked; the difference between frankness and shuffling.

Y. M.  Explain.

O. M.  The others offer you a hundred bribes to be good, thus conceding that the Master inside of you must be conciliated and contented first, and that you will do nothing at *first hand* but for his sake; then they turn square around and require you to do good for *others'* sake *chiefly*; and to do your duty for duty's *sake*, chiefly; and to do *unselfish* things; and to do acts of *self-sacrifice*. Thus at the outset we all stand upon the same ground—recognition of the supreme and absolute Monarch that resides in man, and we all grovel before him and appeal to him; then those others dodge and shuffle, and face around and unfrankly and inconsistently and illogically change the form of their appeal and direct its persuasions to man's *second-place* powers and to powers which have *no existence* in him, thus advancing them to *first* place; whereas in my Admonition I stick logically and consistently to the original position: I place the Interior Master's requirements *first*, and keep them there.

Y. M.  If we grant, for the sake of argument, that your scheme and the other schemes aim at and produce the same result—*right living*—has yours an advantage over the others?

O. M.  One, yes—a large one. It has no concealments, no deceptions. When a man leads a right and valuable life under it he is not deceived as to the *real* chief motive which impels him to it—in those other cases he is.

Y. M.  Is that an advantage? Is it an advantage to live a lofty life for a mean reason? In the other cases he lives the lofty life under the *impression* that he is living it for a lofty reason. Is not that an advantage?

O. M.  Perhaps so. The same advantage he might get out of thinking himself a duke, and living a duke's life, and parading in ducal fuss and feathers, when he wasn't a duke at all, and could find it out if he would only examine the herald's records.

Y. M.  But anyway, he is obliged to do a duke's part; he puts his hand in his pocket and does his benevolences on as big a scale as he can stand, and that benefits the community.

o. m.   He could do that without being a duke.

y. m.   But would he?

o. m.   Don't you see where you are arriving?

y. m.   Where?

o. m.   At the stand-point of the other schemes: That it is good morals to let an ignorant duke do showy benevolences for pride's sake, a pretty low motive, and go on doing them unwarned, lest if he were made acquainted with the actual motive which prompted them he might shut up his purse and cease to be good?

y. m.   But isn't it best to leave him in ignorance, as long as he *thinks* he is doing good for others' sake?

o. m.   Perhaps so. It is the position of the other schemes. They think humbug is good enough morals when the dividend on it is good deeds and handsome conduct.

y. m.   It is my opinion that under your scheme of a man's doing a good deed for his *own* sake first-off, instead of first for the *good deed's* sake, no man would ever do one.

o. m.   Have you committed a benevolence lately?

y. m.   Yes. This morning.

o. m.   Give the particulars.

y. m.   The cabin of the old negro woman who nursed me when I was a child and who saved my life once at risk of her own, was burned last night, and she came mourning this morning, and pleading for money to build another one.

o. m.   You furnished it?

y. m.   Certainly.

o. m.   You were glad you had the money?

y. m.   Money? I hadn't it. I sold my horse.

o. m.   You were glad you had the horse?

y. m.   Of course I was; for if I hadn't had the horse I should have been incapable, and my *mother* would have captured the chance to set old Sally up.

o. m.   You were cordially glad you were not caught out and incapable?

y. m.   Oh, I just was!

o. m.   Now then—

y. m.   Stop where you are! I know your whole catalogue of questions, and I could answer every one of them without your wasting the time to ask them; but I will summarize the whole thing in a single remark: I did the charity knowing it was because the act would give *me* a splendid pleasure, and because old Sally's moving gratitude and delight would give *me* another one; and because the reflection that she would be happy now and out of her trouble would fill *me* full of happiness. I did the whole thing with my eyes open and recognizing and realizing that I was looking out for *my* share of the profits *first*. Now then, I have confessed. Go on.

o. m.    I haven't anything to offer; you have covered the whole ground. Could you have been any *more* strongly moved to help Sally out of her trouble—could you have done the deed any more eagerly—if you had been under the delusion that you were doing it for *her* sake and profit only?

y. m.    No! Nothing in the world could have made the impulse which moved me more powerful, more masterful, more thoroughly irresistible. I played the limit!

o. m.    Very well. You begin to suspect—and I claim to *know*—that when a man is a shade *more strongly moved* to do *one* of two things or of two dozen things than he is to do any one of the *others*, he will infallibly do that *one* thing, be it good or be it evil; and if it be good, not all the beguilements of all the casuistries can increase the strength of the impulse by a single shade or add a shade to the comfort and contentment he will get out of the act.

y. m.    Then you believe that such tendency toward doing good as is in men's hearts would not be diminished by the removal of the delusion that good deeds are done primarily for the sake of No. 2 instead of for the sake of No. 1?

o. m.    That is what I fully believe.

y. m.    Doesn't it somehow seem to take from the dignity of the deed?

o. m.    If there is dignity in falsity, it does. It removes that.

y. m.    What is left for the moralist to do?

o. m.    Teach unreservedly what he already teaches with one side of his mouth and takes back with the other: Do right *for your own sake*, and be happy in knowing that your *neighbor* will certainly share in the benefits resulting.

y. m.    Repeat your Admonition.

o. m.    *Diligently train your ideals upward and still upward toward a summit where you will find your chiefest pleasure in conduct which, while contenting you, will be sure to confer benefits upon your neighbor and the community.*

Y. M.   One's *every* act proceeds from *exterior influences*, you think?

O. M.   Yes.

Y. M.   If I conclude to rob a person, I am not the *originator* of the idea, but it came in from the *outside*? I see him handling money—for instance—and *that* moves me to the crime?

O. M.   That, by itself? O, certainly not. It is merely the *latest* outside influence of a procession of preparatory influences stretching back over a period of years. No *single* outside influence can make a man do a thing which is at war with his training. The most it can do is to start his mind on a new track and open it to the reception of *new* influences—as in the case of Ignatius Loyola. In time these influences can train him to a point where it will be consonant with his new character to yield to the *final* influence and do that thing. I will put the case in a form which will make my theory clear to you, I think. Here are two ingots of virgin gold. They shall represent a couple of characters which have been refined and perfected in the virtues by years of diligent right training. Suppose you wanted to break down these strong and well compacted characters—what influence would you bring to bear upon the ingots?

Y. M.   Work it out yourself. Proceed.

O. M.   Suppose I turn upon one of them a steam-jet during a long succession of hours. Will there be a result?

Y. M.   None that I know of.

O. M.   Why?

Y. M.   A steam-jet cannot break down such a substance.

O. M.   Very well. The steam is an *outside influence*, but it is ineffective, because the gold *takes no interest in it*. The ingot remains as it was. Suppose we add to the steam some quicksilver in a vaporized condition, and turn the jet upon the other ingot. Will there be an instantaneous result?

Y. M.   No.

O. M.   The *quicksilver* is an outside influence which gold (by its peculiar nature—say *temperament*, *disposition*), *cannot be indifferent to*. It stirs the interest of the gold, although we do not perceive it; but a *single* application of the influence works no damage. Let us continue the application in a steady stream, and call each minute a year. By the end of ten or twenty minutes—ten or twenty years—the little ingot is sodden with quicksilver, rotten with quicksilver, its virtues are gone, its character is degraded. At last it is ready to yield to a temptation which it would have taken no notice of, ten or twenty years ago. We will apply that temptation in the form of a pressure with my finger. You note the result?

Y. M.    Yes; the ingot has crumbled to sand. I understand, now. It is not the *single* outside influence that does the work, but only the *last* one of a long and disintegrating accumulation of them. I see, now, how my *single* impulse to rob the man is not the one that makes me do it, but only the *last* one of a preparatory series. You might illustrate it with a parable.

## A PARABLE

O. M.    I will. There was once a pair of New England boys—twins. They were alike in good dispositions, fleckless morals, and personal appearance. They were the models of the Sunday-school. At fifteen George had an opportunity to go as cabin-boy in a whale-ship, and sailed away for the Pacific. Henry remained at home in the village. At eighteen George was a sailor before the mast, and Henry was teacher of the advanced Bible class. At twenty-two George, through fighting-habits and drinking-habits acquired at sea and in the sailor boarding-houses of the European and Oriental ports, was a common rough in Hong Kong, and out of a job; and Henry was superintendent of the Sunday-school. At twenty-six George was a wanderer, a tramp, and Henry was pastor of the village church. Then George came home, and was Henry's guest. One evening a man passed by and turned down the lane, and Henry said, with a pathetic smile, "Without intending me a discomfort, that man is always keeping me reminded of my pinching poverty, for he carries heaps of money about him, and goes by here every evening of his life." That *outside influence*—that remark—was enough for George, but *it* was not the one that made him ambush the man and rob him, it merely represented the eleven years' accumulation of such influences, and gave birth to the act for which their long gestation had made preparation. It had never entered the head of Henry to rob the man—his ingot had been subjected to clean steam only; but George's had been subjected to vaporized quicksilver.

5

*More About the Machine*

NOTE.—When Mrs. W. asks how can a millionaire give a single dollar to colleges and museums while one human being is destitute of bread; she has answered her question herself. Her feeling for the poor shows that she has a standard of benevolence; therefore she has conceded the millionaire's privilege of having a standard; since she evidently requires him to adopt her standard she is by that act requiring herself to adopt his. The human being always looks down when he is examining another person's standard, he never finds one that he has to examine by looking up.

### THE MAN-MACHINE AGAIN

Y. M.   You really think man is a mere machine?

O. M.   I do.

Y. M.   And that his mind works automatically and is independent of his control—carries on thought on its own hook?

O. M.   Yes. It is diligently at work, unceasingly at work, during every waking moment. Have you never tossed about all night, imploring, beseeching, commanding your mind to stop work and let you go to sleep?—you who perhaps imagine that your mind is your servant and must obey your orders, think what you tell it to think, and stop when you tell it to stop. When it chooses to work, there is no way to keep it still for an instant. The brightest man would not be able to supply it with subjects if he had to hunt them up. If it needed the man's help it would wait for him to give it work when he wakes in the morning.

Y. M.   Maybe it does.

O. M.   No, it begins right away, before the man gets wide enough awake to give it a suggestion. He may go to sleep saying, "The moment I wake I will think upon such and such a subject," but he will fail. His mind will be too quick for him; by the time he has become nearly enough awake to be half conscious, he will find that it is already at work on another subject. Make the experiment and see.

Y. M. At any rate he can make it stick to a subject if he wants to.

O. M. Not if it finds another that suits it better. As a rule it will listen to neither a dull speaker nor a bright one. It refuses all persuasion. The dull speaker wearies it and sends it far away in idle dreams; the bright speaker throws out stimulating ideas which it goes chasing after and is at once unconscious of him and his talk. You cannot keep your mind from wandering, if it wants to; it is master, not you.

### After an Interval of Days

O. M. Now, dreams—but we will examine that later. Meantime, did you try commanding your mind to wait for orders from you, and not do any thinking on its own hook?

Y. M. Yes, I commanded it to stand ready to take orders when I should wake in the morning.

O. M. Did it obey?

Y. M. No. It went to thinking about something of its own initiation, without waiting for me. Also—as you suggested —at night I appointed a theme for it to begin on in the morning, and commanded it to begin on that one and no other.

O. M. Did it obey?

Y. M. No.

O. M. How many times did you try the experiment?

Y. M. Ten.

O. M. How many successes did you score?

Y. M. Not one.

O. M. It is as I have said: the mind is independent of the man. He has no control over it, it does as it pleases. It will take up a subject in spite of him; it will stick to it in spite of him; it will throw it aside in spite of him. It is entirely independent of him.

Y. M. Go on. Illustrate.

O. M. Do you know chess?

Y. M. I learned it a week ago.

O. M. Did your mind go on playing the game all night that first night?

Y. M. Don't mention it!

o. m.    It was eagerly, unsatisfiably interested; it rioted in the combinations; you implored it to drop the game and let you get some sleep?

y. m.    Yes. It wouldn't listen; it played right along. It wore me out and I got up haggard and wretched in the morning.

o. m.    At some time or other you have been captivated by a ridiculous rhyme-jingle?

y. m.    Indeed, yes!

> "I saw Esau kissing Kate,
>     And she saw I saw Esau;
>     I saw Esau, he saw Kate,
>     And she saw—"

And so on. My mind went mad with joy over it. It repeated it all day and all night for a week in spite of all I could do to stop it, and it seemed to me that I must surely go crazy.

o. m.    And the new popular song?

y. m.    Oh, yes! "In the Swee-eet By and By;" etc. Yes, the new popular song with the taking melody sings thro' one's head day and night, asleep and awake, till one is a wreck. There is no getting the mind to let it alone.

o. m.    Yes, asleep as well as awake. The mind is quite independent. It is master. You have nothing to do with it. It is so apart from you that it can conduct its affairs, sing its songs, play its chess, weave its complex and ingeniously-constructed dreams, while you sleep. It has no use for your help, no use for your guidance, and never uses either, whether you be asleep or awake. You have imagined that you could originate a thought in your mind, and you have sincerely believed you could do it.

y. m.    Yes, I have had that idea.

o. m.    Yet you can't originate a dream-thought for it to work out, and get it accepted?

y. m.    No.

o. m.    And you can't dictate its procedure after it has originated a dream-thought for itself?

y. m.    No. No one can do it. Do you think the waking mind and the dream-mind are the same machine?

o. m.    There is argument for it. We have wild and fantastic day-thoughts? Things that are dream-like?

Y. M.    Yes—like Mr. Wells's man who invented a drug that made him invisible; and like the Arabian tales of the Thousand Nights.

O. M.    And there are dreams that are rational, simple, consistent and unfantastic?

Y. M.    Yes. I have dreams that are like that. Dreams which are just like real life; dreams in which there are several persons with distinctly differentiated characters—inventions of my mind and yet strangers to me: a vulgar person; a refined one; a wise person; a fool; a cruel person; a kind and compassionate one; a quarrelsome person; a peacemaker; old persons and young; beautiful girls and homely ones. They talk in character, each preserves his own characteristics. There are vivid fights, vivid and biting insults, vivid love-passages; there are tragedies and comedies, there are griefs that go to one's heart, there are sayings and doings that make you laugh: indeed the whole thing is exactly like real life.

O. M.    Your dreaming mind originates the scheme, consistently and artistically develops it, and carries the little drama creditably through—all without help or suggestion from you?

Y. M.    Yes.

O. M.    It is argument that it could do the like awake without help or suggestion from you—and I think it does. It is argument that it is the same old mind in both cases, and never needs your help. I think the mind is purely a machine, a thoroughly independent machine, an automatic machine. Have you tried the other experiment which I suggested to you?

Y. M.    Which one?

O. M.    The one which was to determine how much influence you have over your mind—if any.

Y. M.    Yes, and got more or less entertainment out of it. I did as you ordered: I placed two texts before my eyes—one a dull one and barren of interest, the other one full of interest, inflamed with it, white-hot with it. I commanded my mind to busy itself solely with the dull one.

O. M.    Did it obey?

Y. M.    Well, no, it didn't. It busied itself with the other one.

O. M.    Did you try hard to make it obey?

Y. M.    Yes, I did my honest best.

O. M.   What was the text which it refused to be interested in or think about?

Y. M.   It was this question: if A owes B a dollar and a half, and B owes C two and three-quarters, and C owes A thirty-five cents, and D and A together owe E and B three-sixteenths of—of—I don't remember the rest, now, but anyway it was wholly uninteresting, and I could not force my mind to stick to it even half a minute at a time; it kept flying off to the other text.

O. M.   What was the other text?

Y. M.   It is no matter about that.

O. M.   But what was it?

Y. M.   A photograph.

O. M.   Your own?

Y. M.   No. It was hers.

O. M.   You really made an honest good test. Did you make a second trial?

Y. M.   Yes. I commanded my mind to interest itself in the morning paper's report of the pork market, and at the same time I reminded it of an experience of mine of sixteen years ago. It refused to consider the pork, and gave its whole blazing interest to that ancient incident.

O. M.   What was the incident?

Y. M.   An armed desperado slapped my face in the presence of twenty spectators. It makes me wild and murderous every time I think of it.

O. M.   Good tests, both; very good tests. Did you try my other suggestion?

Y. M.   The one which was to prove to me that if I would leave my mind to its own devices it would find things to think about without any of my help, and thus convince me that it was a machine, an automatic machine, set in motion by exterior influences, and as independent of me as it could be if it were in some one else's skull? Is that the one?

O. M.   Yes.

Y. M.   I tried it. I was shaving. I had slept well, and my mind was very lively, even gay and frisky. It was reveling in a fantastic and joyful episode of my remote boyhood which had suddenly flashed up in my memory,—moved to this by the spectacle of a yellow cat picking its way carefully along the top of the garden wall. The color of this cat brought the by-gone cat before me, and I saw her walking along a side-step of the pulpit; saw her walk onto a large sheet of sticky fly-paper and get all her feet involved; saw her struggle and fall down, helpless and dissatisfied; saw her go on struggling, on her back and getting more and more dissatisfied, more and more urgent, more and more unreconciled, more and more mutely profane; saw the silent congregation quivering like jelly, and the tears running down their faces. I saw it all. The sight of the tears whisked my mind to a far distant and a sadder scene—in Tierra del Fuego—and with Darwin's eyes I saw a naked great savage hurl his little boy against the rocks for a trifling fault; saw the poor mother gather up her dying child and hug it to her breast and weep, uttering no word. Did my mind stop to mourn with that nude black sister of mine? No—it was far away from that scene in an instant, and was busying itself with an ever-recurring and disagreeable dream of mine. In this dream I always find myself, stripped to my shirt, cringing and dodging about in the midst of a great drawingroom throng of finely dressed ladies and gentlemen, and wondering how I got there. And so on and so on, picture after picture, incident after incident, a drifting panorama of ever-changing, ever-dissolving views manufactured by my mind without any help from me—why, it would take me two hours to merely name the multitude of things my mind tallied off and photographed in fifteen minutes, let alone describe them to you.

o. m.   A man's mind, left free, has no use for his help. But there is one way whereby he can get its help when he desires it.

y. m.   What is that way?

o. m.   When your mind is racing along from subject to subject and strikes an inspiring one, open your mouth and begin to talk upon that matter—or take your pen and use that. It will interest your mind and concentrate it, and it will pursue the subject with satisfaction. It will take full charge, and furnish the words itself.

y. m.   But don't I tell it what to say?

o. m.   There are certainly occasions when you haven't time. The words leap out before you know what is coming.

Y. M.   For instance?

O. M.   Well, take a "flash of wit"—repartee. Flash is the right word. It is out instantly. There is no time to arrange the words. There is no thinking, no reflecting. Where there is a wit-mechanism it is automatic in its action, and needs no help. Where the wit-mechanism is lacking, no amount of study and reflection can manufacture the product.

Y. M.   You really think a man originates nothing, creates nothing.

### THE THINKING-PROCESS

O. M.   I do. Men perceive, and their brain-machines automatically combine the things perceived. That is all.

Y. M.   The steam-engine?

O. M.   It takes fifty men a hundred years to invent it. One meaning of invent is discover. I use the word in that sense. Little by little they discover and apply the multitude of details that go to make the perfect engine. Watt noticed that confined steam was strong enough to lift the lid of the teapot. He didn't create the idea, he merely discovered the fact; the cat had noticed it a hundred times. From the teapot he evolved the cylinder—from the displaced lid he evolved the piston-rod. To attach something to the piston-rod to be moved by it, was a simple matter—crank and wheel. And so there was a working engine.* One by one, improvements were discovered by men who used their eyes, not their creative powers—for they hadn't any—and now, after a hundred years the patient contributions of fifty or a hundred observers stand compacted in the wonderful machine which drives the ocean liner.

Y. M.   A Shakspearean play?

O. M.   The process is the same. The first actor was a savage. He reproduced in his theatrical war-dances, scalp-dances, and so on, incidents which he had seen in real life. A more advanced civilization produced more incidents, more episodes; the actor and the story-teller borrowed them. And so the drama grew, little by little, stage by stage. The elaborate Shakspearean play was the final outcome. It is made up of the facts of life, not creations. It took centuries to develop the

---

*The Marquess of Worcester had done all of this more than a century earlier.

Greek drama. It borrowed from preceding ages; it lent to the ages that came after. Men observe and combine, that is all. So does a rat.

Y. M.   How?

O. M.   He observes a smell, he infers a cheese, he seeks and finds. The astronomer observes this and that; adds his this and that to the this-and-thats of a hundred predecessors, infers an invisible planet, seeks it and finds it. The rat gets into a trap; gets out with trouble; infers that cheese in traps lacks value, and meddles with that trap no more. The astronomer is very proud of his achievement; the rat is proud of his. Yet both are machines, they have done machine-work, they have originated nothing, they have no right to be vain, the whole credit belongs to their Maker. They are entitled to no honors, no praises, no monuments when they die, no remembrance. One is a complex and elaborate machine, the other a simple and limited machine, but they are alike in principle, function and process, and neither of them works otherwise than automatically, and neither of them may righteously claim a *personal* superiority or a personal dignity above the other.

Y. M.   In earned personal dignity, then, and in personal merit for what he does, it follows of necessity that he is on the same level as a rat?

O. M.   His brother the rat; yes, that is how it seems to me. Neither of them being entitled to any personal merit for what he does, it follows of necessity that neither of them has a right to arrogate to himself (personally-created) superiorities over his brother.

Y. M.   Are you determined to go on believing in these insanities? Would you go on believing in them in the face of able arguments backed by collated facts and instances?

O. M.   I have been a humble, earnest and sincere Truth Seeker.

Y. M.   Very well?

O. M.   The humble, earnest and sincere Truth Seeker is always convertible by such means.

Y. M.   I am thankful to God to hear you say this, for now I know that your conversion—

O. M.   Wait. You misunderstand. I said I have *been* a Truth Seeker.

Y. M.   Well?

O. M.   I am not that now. Have you forgotten? I told you that there are none but temporary Truth Seekers; that a permanent one is a human impossibility; that as soon as the Seeker finds what he is thoroughly convinced is the Truth, he seeks no further, but gives the rest of his days to hunting for junk to patch it and caulk it and prop it with, and make it weather-proof and keep it from caving in on him. Hence the Presbyterian remains a Presbyterian, the Mohammedan a Mohammedan, the Spiritualist a Spiritualist, the Democrat a Democrat, the Republican a Republican, the Monarchist a Monarchist; and if a humble, earnest and sincere Seeker after Truth should find it in the proposition that the moon is made of green cheese nothing could ever budge him from that position; for he is nothing but an automatic machine, and must obey the laws of his construction.

Y. M.   And so—

O. M.   Having found the Truth; perceiving that beyond question Man has but one moving impulse—the contenting of his own spirit—and is merely a Machine and entitled to no personal merit for anything he does, it is not humanly possible for me to seek further. The rest of my days will be spent in patching and painting and puttying and caulking my priceless possession, and in looking the other way when an imploring argument or a damaging fact approaches.

6

*Instinct and Thought*

Y. M.   It is odious. Those drunken theories of yours, advanced a while ago—concerning the rat and all that—strip Man bare of all his dignities, grandeurs, sublimities.

O. M.   He hasn't any to strip—they are shams, stolen clothes. He claims credits which belong solely to his Maker.

Y. M.   But you have no right to put him on a level with the rat.

O. M.   I don't—morally. That would not be fair to the rat. The rat is well above him, there.

Y. M.   Are you joking?

O. M.   No, I am not.

Y. M.   Then what do you mean?

O. M.   That comes under the head of the Moral Sense. It is a large question. Let us finish with what we are about now, before we take it up.

Y. M.   Very well. You have seemed to concede that you place Man and the rat on *a* level. What is it? The intellectual?

O. M.   In form—not in degree.

Y. M.   Explain.

O. M.   I think that the rat's mind and the man's mind are the same machine, but of unequal capacities—like yours and Edison's; like the African pigmy's and Homer's; like the Bushman's and Bismarck's.

Y. M.   How are you going to make that out, when the lower animals have no mental quality but instinct, while man possesses reason?

O. M.   What is instinct?

Y. M.   It is a merely unthinking and mechanical exercise of inherited habit.

O. M.   What originated the habit?

Y. M.   The first animal started it, its descendants have inherited it.

O. M.   How did the first one come to start it?

Y. M.   I don't know; but it didn't *think* it out.

O. M.   How do you know it didn't?

Y. M.   Well—I have a right to suppose it didn't, anyway.

O. M.   I don't believe you have. What is thought?

Y. M.   I know what you call it: the mechanical and automatic putting together of impressions received from the outside, and drawing an inference from them.

O. M.   Very good. Now my idea of the meaningless term "instinct" is, that it is merely *petrified thought*; thought solidified and made inanimate by habit; thought which was once alive and awake, but is become unconscious—walks in its sleep, so to speak.

Y. M.   Illustrate it.

O. M.   Take a herd of cows, feeding in a pasture. Their heads are all turned in one direction. They do that instinctively; they gain nothing by it, they have no reason for it, they don't know why they do it. It is an inherited habit which was originally thought—that is to say, observation of an exterior fact, and a valuable inference drawn from that observation and confirmed by experience. The original wild ox noticed that with the wind in his favor he could smell his enemy in time to escape; then he inferred that it was worth while to keep his nose to the wind. That is the process which man calls reasoning. Man's thought-machine works just like the other animals', but it is a better one and more Edisonian. Man, in the ox's place, would go further, reason wider: he would face a part of the herd the other way and protect both front and rear.

Y. M. Did you say the term instinct is meaningless?

O. M. I think it is a bastard word. I think it confuses us; for as a rule it applies itself to habits and impulses which had a far-off origin in thought, and now and then breaks the rule and applies itself to habits which can hardly claim a thought-origin.

Y. M. Give an instance.

O. M. Well, in putting on trousers a man always inserts the same old leg first—never the other one. There is no advantage in that, and no sense in it. All men do it, yet no man ever thought it out and adopted it of set purpose, I imagine. But it is a habit which is transmitted, no doubt, and will continue to be transmitted.

Y. M. Can you prove that the habit exists?

O. M. You can prove it, if you doubt. If you will take a man to a clothing store and watch him try on a dozen pairs of trousers, you will see.

Y. M. The cow-illustration is not—

O. M. Sufficient to show that a dumb animal's mental machine is just the same as a man's and its reasoning-processes the same? I will illustrate further. If you should hand Mr. Edison a box which you caused to fly open by some concealed device, he would infer a spring, and would hunt for it and find it. Now an uncle of mine had an old horse who used to get into the closed lot where the corn-crib was and dishonestly take the corn. I got the punishment myself, as it was supposed that I heedlessly failed to insert the wooden pin which kept the gate closed. These persistent punishments fatigued me; they also caused me to infer the existence of a culprit, somewhere; so I hid myself and watched the gate.

Presently the horse came and pulled out the pin with his teeth
and went in. Nobody taught him that; he had observed—
then thought it out for himself. His process did not differ
from Edison's; he put this and that together and drew an
inference—and the peg, too; but I made him sweat for it.

y. m.    It has something of the seeming of thought about
it. Still, it is not very elaborate. Enlarge.

o. m.    Suppose that Edison has been enjoying some one's
hospitalities. He comes again, by and by, and the house is
vacant. He infers that his host has moved. A while afterward,
in another town, he sees the man enter a house; he infers that
that is the new home, and follows to inquire. Here, now, is
the experience of a gull, as related by a naturalist. The scene is
a Scotch fishing village where the gulls were kindly treated.
This particular gull visited a cottage; was fed; came next day
and was fed again; came into the house, next time, and ate
with the family; kept on doing this almost daily, thereafter.
But once the gull was away on a journey for a few days, and
when it returned the house was vacant. Its friends had removed to a village three miles distant. Several months later it
saw the head of the family on the street there, followed him
home, entered the house without excuse or apology, and became a daily guest again. Gulls do not rank high, mentally,
but this one had memory and the reasoning faculty, you see,
and applied them Edisonially.

y. m.    Yet it was not an Edison and couldn't be developed
into one.

o. m.    Perhaps not; could you?

y. m.    That is neither here nor there. Go on.

o. m.    If Edison were in trouble and a stranger helped him
out of it and next day he got into the same difficulty again, he
would infer the wise thing to do in case he knew the stranger's address. Here is a case of a bird and a stranger as related
by a naturalist. An English gentleman saw a bird flying
around about his dog's head, down in the grounds, and uttering cries of distress. He went there to see about it. The dog
had a young bird in his mouth—unhurt. The gentleman rescued it and put it on a bush and brought the dog away. Early
the next morning the mother-bird came for the gentleman,
who was sitting on his verandah, and by its maneuvers per-

suaded him to follow it to a distant part of the grounds—
flying a little way in front of him and waiting for him to catch
up, and so on; and keeping to the winding path, too, instead
of flying the near way across lots. The distance covered was
four hundred yards. The same dog was the culprit; he had the
young bird again, and once more he had to give it up. Now
the mother-bird had reasoned it all out: since the stranger had
helped her once, she inferred that he would do it again; she
knew where to find him, and she went upon her errand with
confidence. Her mental processes were what Edison's would
have been. She put this and that together—and that is all that
thought *is*—and out of them built her logical arrangement of
inferences. Edison couldn't have done it any better himself.

Y. M.    Do you believe that many of the dumb animals can
think?

O. M.    Yes—the elephant, the monkey, the horse, the dog,
the parrot, the macaw, the mocking-bird, and many others.
The elephant whose mate fell into a pit, and who dumped dirt
and rubbish into the pit till the bottom was raised high
enough to enable the captive to step out, was equipped with
the reasoning quality. I conceive that all animals that can learn
things through teaching and drilling have to know how to
observe, and put this and that together and draw an inference—the process of thinking. Could you teach an idiot the
manual of arms, and to advance, retreat, and go through complex field-maneuvers at the word of command?

Y. M.    Not if he were a thorough idiot.

O. M.    Well, canary birds can learn all that; dogs and elephants learn all sorts of wonderful things. They must surely
be able to notice, and to put things together, and say to themselves, "I get the idea, now: when I do so and so, as per
order, I am praised and fed; when I do differently, I am punished." Fleas can be taught nearly anything that a Congressman can.

Y. M.    Granting, then, that dumb creatures are able to
think upon a low plane, is there any that can think upon a
high one? Is there one that is well up toward man?

O. M.    Yes. As a thinker and planner the ant is the equal of
any savage race of men; as a self-educated specialist in several
arts she is the superior of any savage race of men; and in one

or two high mental qualities she is above the reach of any man, savage or civilized.

Y. M. O, come! you are abolishing the intellectual frontier which separates man and beast.

O. M. I beg your pardon. One cannot abolish what does not exist.

Y. M. You are not in earnest, I hope. You cannot mean to seriously say there is no such frontier.

O. M. I do say it seriously. The instances of the horse, the gull, the mother-bird and the elephant show that those creatures put their this's and that's together just as Edison would have done it and drew the same inferences that he would have drawn. Their mental machinery was just like his, also its manner of working. Their equipment was as inferior to his, in elaboration, as a Waterbury is inferior to the Strasburg clock, but that is the only difference—there is no frontier.

Y. M. It looks exasperatingly true; and is distinctly offensive. It elevates the dumb beast to—to—

O. M. Let us drop that lying phrase, and call them the Unrevealed Creatures; so far as we can know, there is no such thing as a dumb beast.

Y. M. On what grounds do you make that assertion?

O. M. On quite simple ones. "Dumb" beast suggests an animal that has no thought-machinery, no understanding, no speech, no way of communicating what is in its mind. We know that a hen *has* speech. We cannot understand everything she says, but we easily learn two or three of her phrases. We know when she is saying "I've laid an egg;" we know when she is saying to the chicks, "Run here, dears, I've found a worm;" we know what she is saying when she voices a warning: "Quick! hurry! gather yourselves under mamma, there's a hawk coming!" We understand the cat when she stretches herself out, purring with affection and contentment and lifts up a soft voice and says "Come, kitties, supper's ready;" we understand her when she goes mourning about and says "Where can they be?—they are lost—won't you help me hunt for them?" and we understand the disreputable Tom when he challenges at midnight from his shed: "You come over here, you product of immoral commerce, and I'll make your fur fly!" We understand a few of a dog's phrases, and we learn to understand a few of the remarks and gestures of any bird or other animal that we domesticate and observe. The clearness and exactness of the few of the hen's speeches which we understand is argument that she can communicate to her kind a hundred things which we cannot comprehend—in a word, that she can converse. And this argument is also applicable in the case of others of the great army of the Unrevealed. It is just like man's vanity and impertinence to call an animal dumb because it is dumb to his dull perceptions. Now as to the ant—

Y. M. Yes, go back to the ant, the creature that—as you seem to think—sweeps away the last vestige of an intellectual frontier between man and the Unrevealed.

O. M. That is what she surely does. In all his history the aboriginal Australian never thought out a house for himself and built it. The ant is an amazing architect. She is a wee little creature, but she builds a strong and enduring house eight feet high—a house which is as large in proportion to her size as is the largest capitol or cathedral in the world compared to man's size. No savage race has produced architects who could approach the ant in genius or culture. No civilized race has produced architects who could plan a house better for the uses proposed than can hers. Her house contains a throne room; nurseries for her young; granaries; apartments for her soldiers, her workers, etc.; and they and the multifarious halls and corridors which communicate with them are arranged and distributed with an educated and experienced eye for convenience and adaptability.

Y. M. That could all be mere instinct.

O. M. It would elevate the savage much above what he is, if he had it. But let us look further before we decide. The ant has soldiers—battalions, regiments, armies; and they have their appointed captains and generals, who lead them to battle.

Y. M. That could be instinct, too.

O. M. We will look still further. The ant has a system of government; it is well planned, elaborate, and is well carried on.

Y. M.   Instinct again.

O. M.   She has crowds of slaves, and is a hard and unjust employer of forced labor.

Y. M.   Instinct.

O. M.   She has cows, and milks them.

Y. M.   Instinct, of course.

O. M.   In Texas she lays out a farm twelve feet square, plants it, weeds it, cultivates it, gathers the crop and stores it away.

Y. M.   Instinct, all the same.

O. M.   The ant discriminates between friend and stranger. Sir John Lubbock took ants from two different nests, made them drunk with whisky and laid them, unconscious, by one of the nests, near some water. Ants from this nest came and examined and discussed these disgraced creatures, then carried their friends home and threw the strangers overboard. Sir John repeated the experiment a number of times. For a while the sober ants did as they had done at first—carried their friends home and threw the strangers overboard. But finally they lost patience, seeing that their reformatory efforts went for nothing, and threw both friends and strangers overboard. Come—is this instinct, or is it thoughtful and intelligent discussion of a thing new—absolutely new—to their experience; with a verdict arrived at, sentence passed, and judgment executed? Is it instinct?—thought petrified by ages of habit—or isn't it brand-new thought, inspired by the new occasion, the new circumstances?

Y. M.   I have to concede it. It was not a result of habit; it has all the look of reflection, thought, putting this and that together, as you phrase it. I believe it was thought.

O. M.   I will give you another instance of thought. Franklin had a cup of sugar on a table in his room. The ants got at it. He tried several preventives; the ants rose superior to them. Finally he contrived one which shut off access—probably set the table's legs in pans of water, or drew a circle of tar around the cup, I don't remember. At any rate he watched to see what they would do. They tried various schemes—failures, every one. The ants were badly puzzled. Finally they held a consultation, discussed the problem, arrived at a decision—and this time they beat that great philosopher. They formed in procession, crossed the floor, climbed the wall, marched across the ceiling to a point just over the cup, then one by one they let go and fell down into it! Was that instinct—thought petrified by ages of inherited habit?

Y. M. No, I don't believe it was. I believe it was a newly-reasoned scheme to meet a new emergency.

O. M. Very well. You have conceded the reasoning power in two instances. I come now to a mental detail wherein the ant is a long way the superior of any human being. Sir John Lubbock proved by many experiments that an ant knows a stranger-ant of her own species in a moment, even when the stranger is disguised—with paint. Also, he proved that an ant knows every individual in her hive of 500,000 souls. Also, that after a year's absence of one of the 500,000 she will straightway recognize the returned absentee and grace the recognition with an affectionate welcome. How were these recognitions made? Not by color, for painted ants were recognized. Not by smell, for ants that had been dipped in chloroform were recognized. Not by speech and not by antennæ-signs nor contacts, for the drunken and motionless ants were recognized and the friend discriminated from the stranger. The ants were all of the one species, therefore the friends had to be recognized by form and feature—friends who formed part of a hive of 500,000! Has any man a memory for form and feature approaching that?

Y. M. Certainly not.

O. M. Franklin's ants and Lubbock's ants show fine capacities for putting this and that together in new and untried emergencies and deducing smart conclusions from the combinations—a man's mental process exactly. With memory to help, man preserves his observations and reasonings, reflects upon them, adds to them, re-combines, and so proceeds, stage by stage, to far results—from the tea-kettle to the ocean greyhound's complex engine; from personal labor to slave labor; from wigwam to palace; from the capricious chase to agriculture and stored food; from nomadic life to stable government and concentrated authority; from incoherent hordes to massed armies. The ant has observation, the reasoning faculty, and the preserving adjunct of a prodigious memory; she has duplicated man's development and the essential features of his civilization, and you call it all instinct!

Y. M.    Perhaps I lacked the reasoning faculty myself.

O. M.    Well, don't tell anybody, and don't do it again.

Y. M.    We have come a good way. As a result—as I understand it—I am required to concede that there is absolutely
no intellectual frontier separating Man and the Unrevealed
Creatures?

O. M.    That is what you are required to concede. There is
no such frontier—there is no way to get around that. Man
has a finer and more capable machine in him than those others, but it is the same machine and works in the same way.
And neither he nor those others can command the machine—it is strictly automatic, independent of control, works
when it pleases, and when it doesn't please, can't be forced.

Y. M.    Then man and the other animals are all alike, as to
mental machinery, and there isn't any difference of any stupendous magnitude between them, except in quality, not in
kind.

O. M.    That is about the state of it—intellectually. There
are pronounced limitations on both sides. We can't learn to
understand much of their language, but the dog, the elephant, etc., learn to understand a very great deal of ours. To
that extent they are our superiors. On the other hand they
can't learn reading, writing, etc., nor any of our fine and high
things, and there we have a large advantage over them.

Y. M.    Very well, let them have what they've got, and welcome; there is still a wall, and a lofty one. They haven't the
Moral Sense; we have it, and it lifts us immeasurably above
them.

O. M.    What makes you think that?

Y. M.    Now look here—let us call a halt. I have stood the
other infamies and insanities and that is enough; I am not
going to have man and the other animals put on the same
level morally.

O. M.    I wasn't going to hoist man up to that.

Y. M.    This is too much! I think it is not right to jest about
such things.

O. M.    I am not jesting, I am merely reflecting a plain and
simple truth—and without uncharitableness. The fact that
man knows right from wrong proves his *intellectual* superiority to the other creatures; but the fact that he can *do* wrong

proves his *moral* inferiority to any creature that *cannot*. It is my belief that this position is not assailable.

### FREE WILL

y. m.   What is your opinion regarding Free Will?

o. m.   That there is no such thing. Did the man possess it who gave the old woman his last shilling and trudged home in the storm?

y. m.   He had the choice between succoring the old woman and leaving her to suffer. Isn't it so?

o. m.   Yes, there was a choice to be made, between bodily comfort on the one hand and the comfort of the spirit on the other. The body made a strong appeal, of course—the body would be quite sure to do that; the spirit made a counter appeal. A choice had to be made between the two appeals, and was made. Who or what determined that choice?

y. m.   Any one but you would say that the man determined it, and that in doing it he exercised Free Will.

o. m.   We are constantly assured that every man is endowed with Free Will, and that he can and must exercise it where he is offered a choice between good conduct and less-good conduct. Yet we clearly saw that in that man's case he really had no Free Will: his temperament, his training, and the daily influences which had moulded him and made him what he was, *compelled* him to rescue the old woman and thus save *himself*—save himself from spiritual pain, from unendurable wretchedness. He did not make the choice, it was made *for* him by forces which he could not control. Free Will has always existed in *words*, but it stops there, I think—stops short of *fact*. I would not use those words—Free Will—but others.

y. m.   What others?

o. m.   Free Choice.

y. m.   What is the difference?

o. m.   The one implies untrammeled power to *act* as you please, the other implies nothing beyond a mere *mental process*: the critical ability to determine which of two things is nearest right and just.

y. m.   Make the difference clear, please.

o. m.   The mind can freely *select*, *choose*, *point out*, the right and just one—its function stops there. It can go no further in the matter. It has no authority to say that the right one shall be acted upon and the wrong one discarded. That authority is in other hands.

Y. M.  The man's?

O. M.  In the machine which stands for him. In his born disposition and the character which has been built around it by training and environment.

Y. M.  It will act upon the right one of the two?

O. M.  It will do as it pleases in the matter. George Washington's machine would act upon the right one; Pizarro's mind would know which was the right one and which the wrong, but the Master inside of Pizarro would act upon the wrong one.

Y. M.  Then as I understand it a bad man's mental machinery calmly and judicially points out which of two things is right and just—

O. M.  Yes, and his *moral* machinery will freely act upon the one or the other, according to its make, and be quite indifferent to the *mind's* feelings concerning the matter—that is, *would* be, if the mind had any feelings; which it hasn't. It is merely a thermometer: it registers the heat and the cold, and cares not a farthing about either.

Y. M.  Then we must not claim that if a man *knows* which of two things is right he is absolutely *bound* to do that thing?

O. M.  His temperament and training will decide what he shall do, and he will do it; he cannot help himself, he has no authority over the matter. Wasn't it right for David to go out and slay Goliah?

Y. M.  Yes.

O. M.  Then it would have been equally *right* for any one else to do it?

Y. M.  Certainly.

O. M.  Then it would have been *right* for a born coward to attempt it?

Y. M.  It would—yes.

O. M.  You know that no born coward ever would have attempted it, don't you?

Y. M.  Yes.

O. M.  You know that a born coward's make and temperament would be an absolute and insurmountable bar to his ever essaying such a thing, don't you?

y. m.   Yes, I know it.

o. m.   He clearly perceives that it would be *right* to try it?

y. m.   Yes.

o. m.   His mind has Free Choice in determining that it would be *right* to try it?

y. m.   Yes.

o. m.   Then if by reason of his inborn cowardice he simply can *not* essay it, what becomes of his Free Will? where is his Free Will? why claim that he has Free Will when the plain facts show that he hasn't? why contend that because he and David *see* the right alike, both must *act* alike? why impose the same laws upon goat and lion?

y. m.   There is really no such thing as Free Will?

o. m.   It is what I think. There is *Will*. But it has nothing to do with *intellectual perceptions of right and wrong*, and is not under their command. David's temperament and training had Will, and it was a compulsory force; David had to obey its decrees, he had no choice. The coward's temperament and training possess Will, and *it* is compulsory; it commands him to avoid danger, and he obeys, he has no choice. But neither the Davids nor the cowards possess Free Will—will that may do the right or do the wrong, as their *mental* verdict shall decide.

## NOT TWO VALUES, BUT ONLY ONE

y. m.   There is one thing which bothers me: I can't tell where you draw the line between *material* covetousness and *spiritual* covetousness.

o. m.   I don't draw any.

y. m.   How do you mean?

o. m.   There is no such thing as *material* covetousness. All covetousness is spiritual.

y. m.   *All* longings, desires, ambitions *spiritual*, never material?

o. m.   Yes. The Master in you requires that in *all* cases you shall content his *spirit*—that alone. He never requires anything else, he never interests himself in any other matter.

Y. M.   Ah, come! When he covets somebody's money—
isn't that rather distinctly material and gross?

O. M.   No. The money is merely a symbol—it represents
in visible and concrete form a *spiritual desire*. Any so-called
material thing that you want is merely a symbol; you want it
not for *itself*, but because it will content your spirit for the
moment.

Y. M.   Please particularize.

O. M.   Very well. Maybe the thing longed for is a new hat.
You get it and your vanity is pleased, your spirit contented.
Suppose your friends deride the hat, make fun of it: at once it
loses its value; you are ashamed of it, you put it out of your
sight, you never want to see it again.

Y. M.   I think I see. Go on.

O. M.   It is the same hat, isn't it? It is in no way altered.
But it wasn't the *hat* you wanted, but only what it stood
for—a something to please and content your *spirit*. When it
failed of that, the whole of its value was gone. There are no
*material* values, there are only spiritual ones. You will hunt in
vain for a material value that is *actual*, *real*—there is no such
thing. The only value it possesses, for even a moment, is the
spiritual value back of it: remove that and it is at once worthless—like the hat.

Y. M.   Can you extend that to money?

O. M.   Yes. It is merely a symbol, it has no *material* value;
you think you desire it for its own sake, but it is not so. You
desire it for the spiritual content it will bring; if it fail of that,
you discover that its value is gone. There is that pathetic tale
of the man who labored like a slave, unresting, unsatisfied,
until he had accumulated a fortune, and was happy over it,
jubilant about it; then in a single week a pestilence swept
away all whom he held dear and left him desolate. His money's value was gone. He realized that his joy in it came not
from the money itself, but from the spiritual contentment he
got out of his family's enjoyment of the pleasures and delights it lavished upon them. Money has no *material* value; if
you remove its spiritual value nothing is left but dross. It is
so with all things, little or big, majestic or trivial—there are
no exceptions. Crowns, sceptres, pennies, paste jewels, village
notoriety, world-wide fame—they are all the same, they have

no *material* value: while they content the *spirit* they are precious, when this fails they are worthless.

## A DIFFICULT QUESTION

Y. M.  You keep me confused and perplexed all the time by your elusive terminology. Sometimes you divide a man up into two or three separate personalities, each with authorities, jurisdictions and responsibilities of its own, and when he is in that condition I can't grasp him. Now when *I* speak of a man, he is *the whole thing in one*, and easy to hold and contemplate.

O. M.  That is pleasant and convenient, if true. When you speak of "my body," who is the "my?"

Y. M.  It is the "me."

O. M.  The body is a property, then, and the Me owns it. Who is the Me?

Y. M.  The Me is *the whole thing*; it is a common property; an undivided ownership, vested in the whole entity.

O. M.  If the Me admires a rainbow, is it the whole Me that admires it, including the hair, hands, heels and all?

Y. M.  Certainly not. It is my *mind* that admires it.

O. M.  So *you* divide the Me yourself. Everybody does; everybody must. What, then, definitely, is the Me?

Y. M.  I think it must consist of just those two parts—the body and the mind.

O. M.  You think so? If you say "I believe the world is round," who is the "I" that is speaking?

Y. M.  The mind.

O. M.  If you say "I grieve for the loss of my father," who is the "I?"

Y. M.  The mind.

O. M.  Is the mind exercising an intellectual function when it examines and accepts the evidence that the world is round?

Y. M.  Yes.

O. M.  Is it exercising an intellectual function when it grieves for the loss of your father?

Y. M.  No. That is not cerebration, brain-work, it is a matter of *feeling*.

O. M.  Then its source is not in your mind, but in your *moral* territory?

Y. M.  I have to grant it.

o. m.    Is your mind a part of your *physical* equipment?

y. m.    No. It is independent of it; it is spiritual.

o. m.    Being spiritual, it cannot be affected by physical influences?

y. m.    No.

o. m.    Does the mind remain sober when the body is drunk?

y. m.    Well—no.

o. m.    There *is* a physical effect present, then?

y. m.    It looks like it.

o. m.    A cracked skull has resulted in a crazy mind. Why should that happen if the mind is spiritual, and *independent* of physical influences?

y. m.    Well—I don't know.

o. m.    When you have a pain in your foot, how do you know it?

y. m.    I feel it.

o. m.    But you do not feel it until a nerve reports the hurt to the brain. Yet the brain is the seat of the mind, is it not?

y. m.    I think so.

o. m.    But isn't spiritual enough to learn what is happening in the outskirts without the help of the *physical* messenger? You perceive that the question of who or what the Me is, is not a simple one at all. You say "I admire the rainbow," and "I believe the world is round," and in these cases we find that the Me is not all speaking, but only the *mental* part. You say "I grieve," and again the Me is not all speaking, but only the *moral* part. You say the mind is wholly spiritual; then you say "I have a pain" and find that this time the Me is mental *and* spiritual combined. We all use the "I" in this indeterminate fashion, there is no help for it. We imagine a Master and King over what you call The Whole Thing, and we speak of him as "I," but when we try to define him we find we cannot do it. The intellect and the feelings can act quite *independently* of each other; we recognize that, and we look around for a Ruler who is master over both, and can serve as a *definite and indisputable "I,"* and enable us to know what we mean and who or what we are talking about when we use that pronoun, but we have to give it up and confess that we cannot find him. To me, Man is a machine, made up of many mechanisms; the moral and mental ones acting automatically in accordance with the impulses of an interior Master who is built out of born-temperament and an accumulation of multitudinous outside influences and trainings; a machine whose *one* function is to secure the spiritual contentment of the Master, be his desires good or be they evil; a machine whose Will is absolute and must be obeyed, and always *is* obeyed.

Y. M. Maybe the Me is the Soul?

O. M. Maybe it is. What is the Soul?

Y. M. I don't know.

O. M. Neither does any one else.

### THE MASTER-PASSION

Y. M. What is the Master?—or, in common speech, the Conscience? Explain it.

O. M. It is that mysterious autocrat, lodged in a man, which compels the man to content its desires. It may be called the Master Passion—the hunger for Self-Approval.

Y. M. Where is its seat?

O. M. In man's moral constitution.

Y. M. Are its commands for the man's good?

O. M. It is indifferent to the man's good; it never concerns itself about anything but the satisfying of its own desires. It can be *trained* to prefer things which will be for the man's good, but it will prefer them only because they will content *it* better than other things would.

Y. M. Then even when it is trained to high ideals it is still looking out for its own contentment, and not for the man's good?

O. M. True. Trained or untrained it cares nothing for the man's good, and never concerns itself about it.

Y. M. It seems to be an *immoral* force seated in the man's moral constitution?

O. M. It is a *colorless* force seated in the man's moral constitution. Let us call it an instinct—a blind, unreasoning instinct, which cannot and does not distinguish between good morals and bad ones, and cares nothing for results to the man provided its own contentment be secured; and it will *always* secure that.

Y. M.　It seeks money, and it probably considers that that is an advantage for the man?

O. M.　It is not always seeking money, it is not always seeking power, nor office, nor any other *material* advantage. In *all* cases it seeks a *spiritual* contentment, let the *means* be what they may. Its desires are determined by the man's temperament—and it is lord over that. Temperament, Conscience, Susceptibility, Spiritual Appetite, are in fact the same thing. Have you ever heard of a person who cared nothing for money?

Y. M.　Yes. A scholar who would not leave his garret and his books to take a place in a business house at a large salary.

O. M.　He had to satisfy his master,—that is to say, his temperament, his Spiritual Appetite—and it preferred the books to money. Are there other cases?

Y. M.　Yes, the hermit.

O. M.　It is a good instance. The hermit endures solitude, hunger, cold, and manifold perils, to content his autocrat, who prefers these things, and prayer and contemplation, to money or to any show or luxury that money can buy. Are there others?

Y. M.　Yes. The artist, the poet, the scientist.

O. M.　Their autocrat prefers the deep pleasures of these occupations, either well paid or ill paid, to any others in the market, at any price. You *realize* that the Master Passion—the contentment of the spirit—concerns itself with many things besides so-called material advantage, material prosperity, cash, and all that?

Y. M.　I think I must concede it.

O. M.　I believe you must. There are perhaps as many Temperaments that would refuse the burdens and vexations and distinctions of public office as there are that hunger after them. The one set of Temperaments seek the contentment of the spirit, and that alone; and this is exactly the case with the other set. Neither set seeks anything *but* the contentment of the spirit. If the one is sordid, both are sordid; and equally so, since the end in view is precisely the same in both cases. And in both cases Temperament decides the preference—and Temperament is *born*, not made.

## CONCLUSION

O. M.   You have been taking a holiday?

Y. M.   Yes; a mountain-tramp covering a week. Are you ready to talk?

O. M.   Quite ready. What shall we begin with?

Y. M.   Well, lying abed resting-up, two days and nights, I have thought over all these talks, and passed them carefully in review. With this result: that . . . . that . . . . are you intending to publish your notions about Man some day?

O. M.   Now and then, in these past twenty years, the Master inside of me has half-intended to order me to set them to paper and publish them. Do I have to tell you why the order has remained unissued, or can you explain so simple a thing without my help?

Y. M.   By your doctrine, it is simplicity itself: outside influences moved your interior Master to give the order; stronger outside influences deterred him. Without the outside influences, neither of these impulses could ever have been born, since a person's brain is incapable of originating an idea within itself.

O. M.   Correct. Go on.

Y. M.   The matter of publishing or withholding is still in your Master's hands. If, some day, an outside influence shall determine him to publish, he will give the order, and it will be obeyed.

O. M.   That is correct. Well?

Y. M.   Upon reflection I have arrived at the conviction that the publication of your doctrines would be harmful. Do you pardon me?

O. M.   Pardon *you*? You have done nothing. You are an instrument—a speaking-trumpet. Speaking-trumpets are not responsible for what is said through them. Outside influences—in the form of life-long teachings, trainings, notions, prejudices, and other second-hand importations—have persuaded the Master within you that the publication of these doctrines would be harmful. Very well, this is quite natural, and was to be expected; in fact was inevitable. Go on; for the sake of ease and convenience, stick to habit: speak in the first person, and tell me what your Master thinks about it.

Y. M.  Well, to begin: it is a desolating doctrine; it is not inspiring, enthusing, uplifting. It takes the glory out of man, it takes the pride out of him, it takes the heroism out of him, it denies him all personal credit, all applause; it not only degrades him to a machine, but allows him no control over the machine; makes a mere coffee-mill of him, and neither permits him to supply the coffee nor turn the crank; his sole and piteously humble function being to grind coarse or fine, according to his make, outside impulses doing all the rest.

O. M.  It is correctly stated. Tell me—what do men admire most in each other?

Y. M.  Intellect, courage, majesty of build, beauty of countenance, charity, benevolence, magnanimity, kindliness, heroism, and—and—

O. M.  I would not go any further. These are *elementals*. Virtue, fortitude, holiness, truthfulness, loyalty, high ideals— these, and all the related qualities that are named in the dictionary, are *made out of the elementals*, by blendings, combinations, and shadings of the elementals, just as one makes green by blending blue and yellow, and makes several shades and tints of red by modifying the elemental red. There are seven elemental colors, they are all in the rainbow; out of them we manufacture and name fifty shades of them. You have named the elementals of the human rainbow, and also one *blend*—heroism, which is made out of courage and magnanimity. Very well, then; which of these elements does the possessor of it manufacture for himself? Is it intellect?

Y. M.  No.

O. M.  Why?

Y. M.  He is born with it.

O. M.  Is it courage?

Y. M.  No. He is born with it.

O. M.  Is it majesty of build, beauty of countenance?

Y. M.  No. They are birthrights.

O. M.  Take those others—the elemental moral qualities— charity, benevolence, magnanimity, kindliness; fruitful seeds, out of which spring, through cultivation by outside influences, all the manifold blends and combinations of virtues named in the dictionaries: does man manufacture any one of those seeds, or are they all born in him?

Y. M.   Born in him.

O. M.   Who manufactures them, then?

Y. M.   God.

O. M.   Where does the credit of it belong?

Y. M.   To God.

O. M.   And the glory of which you spoke, and the applause?

Y. M.   To God.

O. M.   Then it is *you* who degrade man. You make him claim glory, praise, flattery, for every valuable thing he possesses—*borrowed* finery, the whole of it; no rag of it earned by himself, not a detail of it produced by his own labor. *You* make man a humbug; have I done worse by him?

Y. M.   You have made a machine of him.

O. M.   Who devised that cunning and beautiful mechanism, a man's hand?

Y. M.   God.

O. M.   Who devised the law by which it automatically hammers out of a piano an elaborate piece of music, without error, while the man is thinking about something else, or talking to a friend?

Y. M.   God.

O. M.   Who devised the blood? Who devised the wonderful machinery which automatically drives its renewing and refreshing streams through the body, day and night, without assistance or advice from the man? Who devised the man's mind, whose machinery works automatically, interests itself in what it pleases, regardless of his will or desire, labors all night when it likes, deaf to his appeals for mercy? God devised all these things. *I* have not made man a machine, God made him a machine. I am merely calling attention to the fact, nothing more. Is it wrong to call attention to a fact? Is it a crime?

Y. M.   I think it is wrong to *expose* a fact when harm can come of it.

O. M.   Go on.

Y. M.   Look at the matter as it stands now. Man has been taught that he is the supreme marvel of the Creation; he believes it; in all the ages he has never doubted it, whether he was a naked savage, or clothed in purple and fine linen, and civilized. This has made his heart buoyant, his life cheery. His pride in himself, his sincere admiration of himself, his joy in what he supposed were his own and unassisted achievements, and his exultation over the praise and applause which they evoked—these have exalted him, enthused him, ambitioned him to higher and higher flights; in a word, made his life worth the living. But by your scheme, all this is abolished: he is degraded to a machine, he is a nobody, his noble prides wither to mere vanities; let him strive as he may, he can never be any better than his humblest and stupidest neighbor; he would never be cheerful again, his life would not be worth the living.

O. M.   You really think that?

Y. M.   I certainly do.

O. M.   Have you ever seen me uncheerful, unhappy?

Y. M.   No.

O. M.   Well, *I* believe these things. Why have they not made me unhappy?

Y. M.   Oh, well—temperament, of course! You never let *that* escape from your scheme.

O. M.   That is correct. If a man is born with an unhappy temperament, nothing can make him happy; if he is born with a happy temperament, nothing can make him unhappy.

Y. M.   What—not even a degrading and heart-chilling system of beliefs?

O. M.   Beliefs? Mere beliefs? Mere convictions? They are powerless. They strive in vain against inborn temperament.

Y. M.   I can't believe that, and I don't.

O. M.   Now you are speaking hastily. It shows that you have not studiously examined the facts. Of all your intimates, which one is the happiest? Isn't it Burgess?

Y. M.   Easily.

O. M.   And which one is the unhappiest? Henry Adams?

Y. M.   Without a question!

O. M.   I know them well. They are extremes, abnormals; their temperaments are as opposite as the poles. Their life-histories are about alike—but look at the results! Their ages are about the same—around about fifty. Burgess has always been buoyant, hopeful, happy; Adams has always been cheerless, hopeless, despondent. As young fellows, both tried country journalism—and failed. Burgess didn't seem to mind it;

Adams couldn't smile, he could only mourn and groan over what had happened, and torture himself with vain regrets for not having done so-and-so instead of so-and-so—*then* he would have succeeded. They tried the law—and failed. Burgess remained happy—because he couldn't help it, Adams was wretched—because he couldn't help it. From that day to this, those two men have gone on trying things and failing: Burgess has come out happy and cheerful every time, Adams the reverse. Now we do absolutely know that these men's inborn temperaments have remained unchanged through all the vicissitudes of their material affairs. Let us see how it is with their immaterialities. Both have been zealous democrats; both have been zealous republicans; both have been zealous mugwumps. Burgess has always found happiness and Adams unhappiness, in these several political beliefs and in their migrations out of them. Both of these men have been Presbyterians, Universalists, Methodists, Catholics,—then Presbyterians again, then Methodists again. Burgess has always found rest in these excursions, and Adams unrest; they are trying Christian Science, now, with the customary result, the inevitable result. No political or religious belief can make Burgess unhappy or the other man happy. I assure you it is purely a matter of temperament. Beliefs are *acquirements*, temperaments are *born*; beliefs are subject to change, nothing whatever can change temperament.

Y. M. You have instanced extreme temperaments.

O. M. Yes. The half dozen others are modifications of the extremes. But the law is the same. Where the temperament is two-thirds happy, or two-thirds unhappy, no political or religious beliefs can change the proportions. The vast majority of temperaments are pretty equally balanced; the intensities are absent, and this enables a nation to learn to accommodate itself to its political and religious circumstances and like them, be satisfied with them, at last prefer them. Nations do not *think*, they only *feel*. They get their feelings at second-hand—through their temperaments, not their brains. A nation can be brought—by force of circumstances, not argument—to reconcile itself to *any kind of government or religion that can be devised*; in time it will fit itself to the required conditions; later, it will prefer them; and will fiercely fight for them. As instances, you have all history: the Greeks, the Romans, the Persians, the Egyptians, the Russians, the Germans, the French, the English, the Spaniards, the Americans, the South Americans, the Japanese, the Chinese, the Hindoos, the Turks—a thousand wild and tame religions, every kind of government that can be thought of, from tiger to housecat, each nation *knowing* it has the only true religion and the only sane system of government, each despising all the others, each an ass and not suspecting it, each proud of its fancied suprem-acy, each perfectly sure it is the pet of God, each with un-doubting confidence summoning Him to take command in time of war, each surprised when He goes over to the enemy, but by habit able to excuse it and resume compliments—in a word, the whole human race content, always content, persis-tently content, indestructibly content, happy, thankful, proud, *no matter what its religion is, nor whether its master be tiger or housecat.* Am I stating facts? You know I am. Is the human race cheerful? You know it is. Considering what it can stand, and be happy, you do me too much honor when you think that *I* can place before it a system of plain cold facts that can take the cheerfulness out of it. Nothing can do that. Every-thing has been tried. Without success. I beg you not to be troubled.

*1906*

# Hunting the Deceitful Turkey

When I was a boy my uncle and his big boys hunted with the rifle, the youngest boy Fred and I with a shotgun—a small single-barrelled shotgun which was properly suited to our size and strength; it was not much heavier than a broom. We carried it turn about, half an hour at a time. I was not able to hit anything with it, but I liked to try. Fred and I hunted feathered small game, the others hunted deer, squirrels, wild turkeys, and such things. My uncle and the big boys were good shots. They killed hawks and wild geese and such like on the wing; and they didn't wound or kill squirrels, they *stunned* them. When the dogs treed a squirrel, the squirrel would scamper aloft and run out on a limb and flatten himself along it, hoping to make himself invisible in that way—and not quite succeeding. You could see his wee little ears sticking up. You couldn't see his nose, but you knew where it was. Then the hunter, despising a "rest" for his rifle, stood up and took offhand aim at the limb and sent a bullet into it immediately under the squirrel's nose, and down tumbled the animal, unwounded but unconscious; the dogs gave him a shake and he was dead. Sometimes when the distance was great and the wind not accurately allowed for, the bullet would hit the squirrel's head; the dogs could do as they pleased with that one—the hunter's pride was hurt, and he wouldn't allow it to go into the game-bag.

In the first faint gray of the dawn the stately wild turkeys would be stalking around in great flocks, and ready to be sociable and answer invitations to come and converse with other excursionists of their kind. The hunter concealed himself and imitated the turkey-call by sucking the air through the leg-bone of a turkey which had previously answered a call like that and lived only just long enough to regret it. There is nothing that furnishes a perfect turkey-call except that bone. Another of Nature's treacheries, you see. She is full of them; half the time she doesn't know which she likes best—to betray her child or protect it. In the case of the turkey she is badly mixed: she gives it a bone to be used in getting it into trouble, and she also furnishes it with a trick for getting itself out of the trouble again. When a mamma-turkey answers an invitation and finds she has made a mistake in accepting it, she does as the mamma-partridge does—remembers a previous engagement and goes limping and scrambling away, pretending to be very lame; and at the same time she is saying to her not-visible children, "Lie low, keep still, don't expose yourselves; I shall be back as soon as I have beguiled this shabby swindler out of the country."

When a person is ignorant and confiding, this immoral device can have tiresome results. I followed an ostensibly lame turkey over a considerable part of the United States one morning, because I believed in her and could not think she would deceive a mere boy, and one who was trusting her and considering her honest. I had the single-barrelled shotgun, but my idea was to catch her alive. I often got within rushing distance of her, and then made my rush; but always, just as I made my final plunge and put my hand down where her back had been, it wasn't there; it was only two or three inches from there and I brushed the tail-feathers as I landed on my stomach—a very close call, but still not quite close enough; that is, not close enough for success, but just close enough to convince me that I could do it next time. She always waited for me, a little piece away, and let on to be resting and greatly fatigued; which was a lie, but I believed it, for I still thought her honest long after I ought to have begun to doubt her, suspecting that this was no way for a high-minded bird to be acting. I followed, and followed, and followed, making my periodical rushes, and getting up and brushing the dust off, and resuming the voyage with patient confidence; indeed, with a confidence which grew, for I could see by the change of climate and vegetation that we were getting up into the high latitudes, and as she always looked a little tireder and a little more discouraged after each rush, I judged that I was safe to win, in the end, the competition being purely a matter of staying power and the advantage lying with me from the start because she was lame.

Along in the afternoon I began to feel fatigued myself. Neither of us had had any rest since we first started on the excursion, which was upwards of ten hours before, though latterly we had paused awhile after rushes, I letting on to be thinking about something else; but neither of us sincere, and both of us waiting for the other to call game but in no real hurry about it, for indeed those little evanescent snatches of rest were very grateful to the feelings of us both; it would naturally be so, skirmishing along like that ever since dawn and not a bite in the mean time; at least for me, though sometimes as she lay on her side fanning herself with a wing and praying for strength to get out of this difficulty a grasshopper happened along whose time had come, and that was well for her, and fortunate, but I had nothing—nothing the whole day.

More than once, after I was very tired, I gave up taking her alive, and was going to shoot her, but I never did it, although it was my right, for I did not believe I could hit her; and besides, she always stopped and posed, when I raised the gun, and this made me suspicious that she knew about me and my marksmanship, and so I did not care to expose myself to remarks.

I did not get her, at all. When she got tired of the game at last, she rose from almost under my hand and flew aloft with the rush and whir of a shell and lit on the highest limb of a great tree and sat down and crossed her legs and smiled down at me, and seemed gratified to see me so astonished.

I was ashamed, and also lost; and it was while wandering the woods hunting for myself that I found a deserted log cabin and had one of the best meals there that in my life-days I have eaten. The weed-grown garden was full of ripe tomatoes, and I ate them ravenously, though I had never liked them before. Not more than two or three times since have I tasted anything that was so delicious as those tomatoes. I surfeited myself with them, and did not taste another one until I was in middle life. I can eat them now, but I do not like the look of them. I suppose we have all experienced a surfeit at one time or another. Once, in stress of circumstances, I ate part of a barrel of sardines, there being nothing else at hand, but since then I have always been able to get along without sardines.

*December 1906*

# Dinner Speech at Annapolis

*Government House, Annapolis, Maryland*

Yes, I have been arrested. I was arrested twice, so that there could be no doubt about it. I have lived many years in the sight of my country an apparently uncaught and blameless life, a model for the young, an inspiring example for the hoary-headed. But at last the law has laid its hand upon me.

Mine was no ordinary offense. When I affront the law I choose to do so in no obscure, insignificant, trivial manner. Mine was a crime against nothing less than the federal government. The officers who arrested me were no common, or garden, policemen; they were clothed with the authority of the federal Constitution. I was charged with smoking a cigar within a government reservation. In fact, I was caught red-handed. I came near setting a stone pile on fire.

It is true that the arrest was not made effective. One of the party whispered to the marines what Governor Warfield was going to say, and did say, in introducing me to the audience at my lecture—that I was one of the greatest men in the world. I don't know who proposed to tell that to the marines, but it worked like a charm. The minions of the law faltered, hesitated, quailed, and today I am a free man. Twice they laid hands upon me; twice were overcome by my deserved reputation.

Perhaps I ought not to say myself that it is deserved. But who am I, to contradict the governor of Maryland? Worm that I am, by what right should I reverse the declared opinion of that man of wisdom and judgment whom I have learned to admire and trust?

I never admired him more than I did when he told my audience that they had with them the greatest man in the world. I believe that was his expression. I don't wish to undertake his sentiments, but I will go no further than that—at present. Why, it fairly warmed my heart. It almost made me glad to be there myself. I like good company.

Speaking of greatness, it is curious how many grounds there are for great reputations—how many different phases, that is to say, greatness may take on. There was Bishop Potter.

He was arrested a few months ago for a crime similar to mine, though he lacked the imagination to select United States government property as the scene of his guilty deed. Now, Bishop Potter is a great man. I am sure he is, because a streetcar motorman told me so. A motorman is not a governor of Maryland, but then Bishop Potter is not a humorist. He could hardly expect a certificate like mine.

I rode with the motorman one day on the front seat of his car. There was a blockade before we got very far, and the motorman, having nothing to do, became talkative. "Oh, yes," he said, "I have a good many distinguished men on this trip. Bishop Potter often rides with me. He likes the front seat. Now there's a great man for you—Bishop Potter."

"It is true," I responded. "Dr. Potter is indeed a mighty man of God, an erudite theologian, a wise administrator of his diocese, an exegete of—"

"Yes," broke in the motorman, his face beaming with pleasure as he recognized the justice of my tribute and hastened to add one of his own. "Yes, and he's the only man who rides with me who can spit in the slot every time."

That's a good story, isn't it? I like a good story well told. That is the reason I am sometimes forced to tell them myself. Here is one, of which I was reminded yesterday as I was investigating the Naval Academy. I was much impressed with the Naval Academy. I was all over it, and now it is all over me. I am full of the navy. I wanted to march with them on parole, but they didn't think to ask me: curious inattention on their part, and I just ashore after a celebrated cruise.

While I was observing the navy on land, I thought of the navy at sea and of this story, so pathetic, so sweet, so really touching. This is one of my pet stories. Something in its delicacy, refinement, and the elusiveness of its humor fits my own quiet tastes.

The time is two A.M. after a lively night at the club. The scene is in front of his house. The house is swaying and lurching to and fro. He has succeeded in navigating from the club, but how is he going to get aboard this rolling, tossing thing? He watches the steps go back and forth, up and down. Then he makes a desperate resolve, braces himself, and as the steps come around he jumps, clutches the handrail, gets aboard,

and pulls himself safely up on the piazza. With a like maneu-
ver he gets through the door. Watching his chance, he gains
the lowest step of the inside staircase, and painfully makes his
way up the swaying and uncertain structure. He has almost
reached the top when in a sudden lurch he catches his toe and
falls back, rolling to the bottom. At this moment his wife,
rushing out into the upper hall, hears coming up from the
darkness below, from the discomfited figure sprawled on the
floor with his arms around the newel post, this fervent, appropriate, and pious ejaculation, "God help the poor sailors
out at sea."

I trust this matter of my arrest will not cause my friends to
turn from me. It is true that, no matter what may be said of
American public morals, the private morals of Americans as a
whole are exceptionally good. I do not mean to say that in
their private lives all Americans are faultless. I hardly like to
go that far, being a man of carefully weighed words and under a peculiarly vivid sense of the necessity of moderation in
statement. I should like to say that we are a faultless people,
but I am restrained by recollection. I know several persons
who have erred and transgressed — to put it plainly, they have
done wrong. I have heard of still others — of a number of
persons, in fact, who are not perfect. I am not perfect myself.
I confess it. I would have confessed it before the lamentable
event of yesterday. For that was not the first time I ever did
wrong. No; I have done several things which fill my soul now
with regret and contrition.

I remember, I remember it so well. I remember it as if it
were yesterday, the first time I ever stole a watermelon. Yes,
the first time. At least I think it was the first time, or along
about there. It was, it was, must have been, about 1848, when
I was thirteen or fourteen years old. I remember that watermelon well. I can almost taste it now.

Yes, I stole it. Yet why use so harsh a word? It was the
biggest of the load on a farmer's wagon standing in the gutter in the old town of Hannibal, Missouri. While the farmer
was busy with another — another — customer, I withdrew this
melon. Yes, "I stole" is too strong. I extracted it. I retired it
from circulation. And I myself retired with it.

The place to which the watermelon and I retired was a

lumber yard. I knew a nice, quiet alley between the sweet-smelling planks and to that sequestered spot I carried the melon. Indulging a few moments' contemplation of its freckled rind, I broke it open with a stone, a rock, a dornick, in boy's language.

It was green—impossibly, hopelessly green. I do not know why this circumstance should have affected me, but it did. It affected me deeply. It altered for me the moral values of the universe. It wrought in me a moral revolution. I began to reflect. Now, reflection is the beginning of reform. There can be no reform without reflection.

I asked myself what course of conduct I should pursue. What would conscience dictate? What should a high-minded young man do after retiring a green watermelon? What would George Washington do? Now was the time for all the lessons inculcated at Sunday school to act.

And they did act. The word that came to me was "restitution." Obviously, there lay the path of duty. I reasoned with myself. I labored. At last I was fully resolved. "I'll do it," said I. "I'll take him back his old melon." Not many boys would have been heroic, would so clearly have seen the right and so sternly have resolved to do it. The moment I reached that resolution I felt a strange uplift. One always feels an uplift when he turns from wrong to righteousness. I arose, spiritually strengthened, renewed and refreshed, and in the strength of that refreshment carried back the watermelon—that is, I carried back what was left of it—and made him give me a ripe one.

But I had a duty toward that farmer, as well as to myself. I was as severe on him as the circumstances deserved. I did not spare him. I told him he ought to be ashamed of himself giving his—his customers green melons. And he was ashamed. He said he was. He said he felt as badly about it as I did. In this he was mistaken. He hadn't eaten any of the melon. I told him that the one instance was bad enough, but asked him to consider what would become of him if this should become a habit with him. I pictured his future. And I saved him. He thanked me and promised to do better.

We should always labor thus with those who have taken the wrong road. Very likely this was the farmer's first false step.

He had not gone far, but he had put his foot on the down-ward incline. Happily, at this moment a friend appeared—a friend who stretched out a helping hand and held him back. Others might have hesitated, have shrunk from speaking to him of his error. I did not hesitate nor shrink. And it is one of the gratifications of my life that I can look back on what I did for that man in his hour of need.

The blessing came. He went home with a bright face to his rejoicing wife and I—I got a ripe melon. I trust it was with him as it was with me. Reform with me was no transient emotion, no passing episode, no Philadelphia uprising. It was permanent. Since that day I have never stolen a water—never stolen a green watermelon.

*May 10, 1907*

# Our Guest

*Society of the Pilgrims Luncheon for Mark Twain, Hotel Savoy, London*

Pilgrims, I desire first to thank those undergraduates of Oxford. When a man has grown so old as I am, when he has reached the verge of seventy-two years, there is nothing that carries him back to the dreamland of his life, to his boyhood, like the recognition of those young hearts up yonder. And so I thank them out of my heart. I desire, too, to thank the Pilgrims of New York also for their kind notice and message which they have cabled over here. Mr. Birrell says he does not know how he got here. But he will be able to get away all right—he has not drunk anything since he came here. I am glad to know about those friends of his—Otway and Chatterton—fresh, new names to me. I am glad of the disposition he has shown to rescue them from the evils of poverty, and if they are still in London, I hope to have a talk with them. For a while I thought he was going to tell us the effect which my books had upon his growing manhood. I thought he was going to tell us how much that effect amounted to, and whether it really made him what he now is, but with the discretion born of Parliamentary experience he dodged that, and we do not know whether he read the books or not. He did that very neatly. I could not do it any better myself.

My books have had effects, and very good ones, too, here and there, and some others not so good. There is no doubt about that. But I remember one monumental instance of it years and years ago. Professor Norton, of Harvard, was over here, and when he came back to Boston I went out with Howells to call on him. Norton was allied in some way by marriage with Darwin. Mr. Norton was very gentle in what he had to say, and almost delicate, and he said: "Mr. Clemens, I have been spending some time with Mr. Darwin in England, and I should like to tell you something connected with that visit. You were the object of it, and I myself would have been very proud of it, but you may not be proud of it. At any rate, I am going to tell you what it was, and to leave you to regard it as you please. Mr. Darwin took me up to his bedroom and pointed out certain things there—pitcher plants, and so on, that he was measuring and watching from day to day—and he said, 'The chambermaid is permitted to do what she pleases in this room, but she must never touch those plants and never touch those books on that table by that candle. With those books I read myself to sleep every night.' Those were your own books." I said, "There is no question to my mind as to whether I should regard that as a compliment or not. I do regard it as a very great compliment, and a very high honor, that that great mind, laboring for the whole human race, should rest itself on my books. I am proud that he should read himself to sleep with them."

Now, I could not keep that to myself—I was so proud of it. As soon as I got home to Hartford I called up my oldest friend—and dearest enemy on occasion—the Rev. Joseph Twichell, my pastor, and I told him about that, and, of course, he was full of interest and venom. Those people who get no compliments like that feel like that. He went off. He did not issue any applause of any kind, and I did not hear of that subject for some time. But when Mr. Darwin passed away from this life, and some time after Darwin's *Life and Letters* came out, the Rev. Mr. Twichell procured an early copy of that work and found something in it which he considered applied to me. He came over to my house—it was snowing, raining, sleeting, but that did not make any difference to Twichell. He produced the book, and turned over and over, until he came to a certain place, when he said, "Here, look at this letter from Mr. Darwin to Sir Joseph Hooker." What Mr. Darwin said—I give you the idea and not the very words—was this: I do not know whether I ought to have devoted my whole life to these drudgeries in natural history and the other sciences or not, for while I may have gained in one way I have lost in another. Once I had a fine perception and appreciation of high literature, but in me that quality is atrophied. "That was the reason," said Mr. Twichell, "he was reading your books."

Mr. Birrell has touched lightly—very lightly, but in not an uncomplimentary way—on my position in this world as a moralist. I am glad to have that recognition, too, because I have suffered since I have been in this town; in the first place, right away, when I came here, from a newsman going around with a great red, highly displayed placard in the place of an apron. He was selling newspapers, and there were two sentences on that placard which would have been all right if they had been punctuated; but they ran those two sentences together without a comma or anything, and that would naturally create a wrong impression, because it said, "Mark Twain arrives Ascot Cup stolen." No doubt many a person was misled by those sentences joined together in that unkind way. I have no doubt my character has suffered from it. I suppose I ought to defend my character, but how can I defend it? I can say here and now—and anybody can see by my face that I am sincere, that I speak the truth—that I have never seen that Cup. I have not got the Cup—I did not have a chance to get it. I have always had a good character in that way. I have hardly ever stolen anything, and if I did steal anything I had discretion enough to know about the value of it first. I do not steal things that are likely to get myself into trouble. I do not think any of us do that. I know we all take things—that is to be expected—but really, I have never taken anything, certainly in England, that amounts to any great thing. I do confess that when I was here seven years ago I stole a hat, but that did not amount to anything. It was not a good hat, and was only a clergyman's hat, anyway.

I was at a luncheon party, and Archdeacon Wilberforce was there also. I daresay he is an Archdeacon now—he was a Canon then—and he was serving in the Westminster Battery, if that is the proper term—I do not know, as you mix military and ecclesiastical things together so much. He left the luncheon table before I did. He began this, I did steal his hat, but he began by taking mine. I make that interjection because I would not accuse Archdeacon Wilberforce of stealing my hat—I should not think of it. I confine that phrase to myself. He merely took my hat. And with good judgment, too—it was a better hat than his. He came out before the luncheon was over, and sorted the hats in the hall, and selected one which suited. It happened to be mine. He went off with it. When I came out by and by there was no hat there which would go on my head except his, which was left behind. My head was not the customary size just at that time. I had been receiving a good many very nice and complimentary attentions, and my head was a couple of sizes larger than usual, and his hat just suited me. The bumps and corners were all right intellectually. There were results pleasing to me—possibly so to him. He found out whose hat it was, and wrote me saying it was pleasant that all the way home, whenever he met anybody his gravities, his solemnities, his deep thoughts, his eloquent remarks were all snatched up by the people he met, and mistaken for brilliant humorisms.

I had another experience. It was not unpleasing. I was received with a deference which was entirely foreign to my experience by everybody whom I met, so that before I got home I had a much higher opinion of myself than I have ever had before or since. And there is in that very connection an incident which I remember at that old date which is rather melancholy to me, because it shows how a person can deteriorate in a mere seven years. It is seven years ago. I have not that hat now. I was going down Pall Mall, or some other of your big streets, and I recognized that that hat needed ironing. I went into a big shop and passed in my hat, and asked that it might be ironed. They were courteous, very courteous, even courtly. They brought that hat back to me presently very sleek and nice, and I asked how much there was to pay. They replied that they did not charge the clergy anything. I have cherished the delight of that moment from that day to this. It was the first thing I did the other day to go and hunt up that shop and hand in my hat to have it ironed. I said when it came back, "How much to pay?" They said, "Ninepence." In seven years I have acquired all that worldliness, and I am sorry to be back where I was seven years ago.

But now I am chaffing and chaffing and chaffing here, and I hope you will forgive me for that; but when a man stands on the verge of seventy-two you know perfectly well that he never reached that place without knowing what this life is— heartbreaking bereavement. And so our reverence is for our dead. We do not forget them; but our duty is toward the living; and if we can be cheerful, cheerful in spirit, cheerful in speech and in hope, that is a benefit to those who are around us.

My own history includes an incident which will always connect me with England in a pathetic way, for when I arrived here seven years ago with my wife and daughter—we had gone around the globe lecturing to raise money to clear off a debt—my wife and one of my daughters started across the ocean to bring to England our eldest daughter. She was twenty-four years of age and in the bloom of young womanhood, and we were unsuspecting. When my wife and daughter—and my wife has passed from this life since—when they had reached mid-Atlantic, a cablegram—one of those heartbreaking cablegrams which we all in our days have to experience—was put into my hand. It stated that that daughter of ours had gone to her long sleep. And so, as I say, I cannot always be cheerful, and I cannot always be chaffing; I must sometimes lay the cap and bells aside, and recognize that I am of the human race like the rest, and must have my cares and griefs. And, therefore, I noticed what Mr. Birrell said—I was so glad to hear him say it—something that was in the nature of these verses here at the top of this menu.

> He lit our life with shafts of sun
>   And vanquished pain.
> Thus two great nations stand as one
>   In honoring Twain.

I am very glad to have those verses. I am very glad and grateful for what Mr. Birrell said in that connection. I have received since I have been here, in this one week, hundreds of letters from all conditions of people in England—men, women, and children—and there is in them compliment, praise, and, above all and better than all, there is in them a note of affection. Praise is well, compliment is well, but affection—that is the last and final and most precious reward that any man can win, whether by character or achievement, and I am very grateful to have that reward. All these letters make me feel that here in England—as in America—when I stand under the English flag, I am not a stranger. I am not an alien, but at home.

*June 25, 1907*

# The Day We Celebrate

*American Society Dinner, Hotel Cecil, London*

Mr. Chairman, my Lord, and gentlemen: Once more it happens, as it has happened so often since I arrived in England a week or two ago, that instead of celebrating the Fourth of July properly as has been indicated, I have to first take care of my personal character.

Sir Mortimer Durand still remains unconvinced. Well, I tried to convince these people from the beginning that I did not take the Ascot Cup; and as I have failed to convince anybody that I did not take the Cup, I might as well confess I did take it and be done with it. I don't see why this uncharitable feeling should follow me everywhere, and why I should have that crime thrown up to me on all occasions. The tears I have wept over it ought to have created a different feeling than this—and, besides, I don't think it is very right or fair that, considering England has been trying to take a cup of ours for forty years—I don't see why they should make so much trouble when I tried to go into the business myself.

Sir Mortimer Durand, too, has had trouble from going to a dinner here, and he has told you what he suffered in consequence. But what did he suffer? He only missed his train and one night of discomfort, and he remembers it to this day. Oh! if you could only think what I have suffered from a similar circumstance. Two or three years ago, in New York, with that Society there which is made up of people from all British Colonies, and from Great Britain generally, who were educated in British colleges and British schools, I was there to respond to a toast of some kind or other, and I did then what I have been in the habit of doing, from a selfish motive, for a long time, and that is, I got myself placed No. 3 in the list of speakers—then you get home early.

I had to go five miles upriver, and had to catch a particular train or not get there. But see the magnanimity which is born in me, which I have cultivated all my life. A very famous and very great British clergyman came to me presently, and he said: "I am away down in the list; I have got to catch a certain train this Saturday night; if I don't catch that train I shall be carried beyond midnight and break the Sabbath. Won't you change places with me?" I said: "Certainly I will." I did it at once. Now, see what happened. Talk about Sir Mortimer Durand's sufferings for a single night! I have suffered ever since because I saved that gentleman from breaking the Sabbath—yes, saved him. I took his place, but I lost my train, and it was I who broke the Sabbath. Up to that time I had never broken the Sabbath in my life, and from that day to this I never have kept it.

Oh! I am learning much here tonight. I find I didn't know anything about the American Society—that is, I didn't know its chief virtue. I didn't know its chief virtue until his Excellency our Ambassador revealed it—I may say, exposed it. I was intending to go home on the 13th of this month, but I look upon that in a different light now. I am going to stay here until the American Society pays my passage.

Our Ambassador has spoken of our Fourth of July, and the noise it makes. We have got a double Fourth of July—a daylight Fourth and a midnight Fourth. During the day in America, as our Ambassador has indicated, we keep the Fourth of July properly in a reverent spirit. We devote it to teaching our children patriotic things—reverence for the Declaration of Independence. We honor the day all through the daylight hours, and when night comes we dishonor it. Presently—before long—they are getting nearly ready to begin now—on the Atlantic coast, when night shuts down, that pandemonium will begin, and there will be noise, and noise, and noise—all night long—and there will be more than noise—there will be people crippled, there will be people killed, there will be people who will lose their eyes, and all through that permission which we give to irresponsible boys to play with firearms and firecrackers, and all sorts of dangerous things. We turn that Fourth of July, alas! over to rowdies to drink and get drunk and make the night hideous, and we cripple and kill more people than you would imagine.

We probably began to celebrate our Fourth of July night in that way one hundred and twenty-five years ago, and on every Fourth of July night since these horrors have grown and grown, until now, in our five thousand towns of America, somebody gets killed or crippled on every Fourth of July night, besides those cases of sick persons whom we never hear of, who die as the result of the noise or the shock. They cripple and kill more people on the Fourth of July in America than they kill and cripple in our wars nowadays, and there are no pensions for these folk. And, too, we burn houses. Really we destroy more property on every Fourth of July night than the whole of the United States was worth one hundred and twenty-five years ago. Really our Fourth of July is our day of mourning, our day of sorrow. Fifty thousand people who have lost friends, or who have had friends crippled, receive that Fourth of July, when it comes, as a day of mourning for the losses they have sustained in their families.

I have suffered in that way myself. I have had relatives killed in that way. One was in Chicago years ago—an uncle of mine, just as good an uncle as I have ever had, and I had lots of them—yes, uncles to burn, uncles to spare. This poor uncle, full of patriotism, opened his mouth to hurrah, and a rocket went down his throat. Before that man could ask for a drink of water to quench that thing, it blew up and scattered him all over the forty-five states, and—really, now, this is true—I know about it myself—twenty-four hours after that it was raining buttons, recognizable as his, on the Atlantic seaboard. A person cannot have a disaster like that and be entirely cheerful the rest of his life. I had another uncle, on an entirely different Fourth of July, who was blown up that way, and really it trimmed him as it would a tree. He had hardly a limb left on him anywhere. All we have left now is an expurgated edition of that uncle. But never mind about these things; they are merely passing matters. Don't let me make you sad.

Sir Mortimer Durand said that you, the English people, gave up your colonies over there—got tired of them—and did it with reluctance. Now I wish you just to consider that he was right about that, and that he had his reasons for saying that England did not look upon our Revolution as a foreign war, but as a civil war fought by Englishmen.

Our Fourth of July which we honor so much, and which we love so much, and which we take so much pride in, is an English institution, not an American one, and it comes of a great ancestry. The first Fourth of July in that noble genealogy dates back seven centuries lacking eight years. That is the day of the Great Charter—the Magna Charta—which was born at Runnymede in the next to the last year of King John, and portions of the liberties secured thus by those hardy Barons from that reluctant King John are a part of our Declaration of Independence, of our Fourth of July, of our American liberties. And the second of those Fourths of July was not born until four centuries later, in Charles the First's time, in the Bill of Rights, and that is ours, that is part of our liberties. The next one was still English, in New England, where they established that principle which remains with us to this day, and will continue to remain with us—no taxation without representation. That is always going to stand, and that the English Colonies in New England gave us.

The Fourth of July, and the one which you are celebrating now, born in Philadelphia on the 4th of July, 1776—that is English, too. It is not American. Those were English colonists, subjects of King George III, Englishmen at heart, who protested against the oppressions of the home government. Though they proposed to cure those oppressions and remove them, still remaining under the Crown, they were not intending a revolution. The revolution was brought about by circumstances which they could not control. The Declaration of Independence was written by a British subject, every name signed to it was the name of a British subject. There was not the name of a single American attached to the Declaration of Independence—in fact, there was not an American in the country in that day except the Indians out on the plains. They were Englishmen, all Englishmen—Americans did not begin until seven years later, when that Fourth of July had become seven years old, and then the American Republic was established. Since then there have been Americans. So you see what we owe to England in the matter of liberties.

We have, however, one Fourth of July which is absolutely our own, and that is that great proclamation issued forty years ago by that great American to whom Sir Mortimer Durand paid that just and beautiful tribute—Abraham Lincoln. Lincoln's proclamation, which not only set the black slaves free, but set the white man free also. The owner was set free from the burden and offense, that sad condition of things where he was in so many instances a master and owner of slaves when he did not want to be. That proclamation set them all free. But even in this matter England suggested it, for England had set her slaves free thirty years before, and we followed her example. We always followed her example, whether it was good or bad.

And it was an English judge that issued that other great proclamation, and established that great principle that, when a slave, let him belong to whom he may, and let him come whence he may, sets his foot upon English soil, his fetters by that act fall away and he is a free man before the world. We followed the example of 1833, and we freed our slaves as I have said.

It is true, then, that all our Fourths of July, and we have five of them, England gave to us, except that one that I have mentioned—the Emancipation Proclamation, and, lest we forget, let us all remember that we owe these things to England. Let us be able to say to Old England, this great-hearted, venerable old mother of the race, you gave us our Fourths of July that we love and that we honor and revere, you gave us the Declaration of Independence, which is the Charter of our rights, you, the venerable Mother of Liberties, the Protector of Anglo-Saxon Freedom—you gave us these things, and we do most honestly thank you for them.

*July 4, 1907*

## Little Nelly Tells a Story
## Out of Her Own Head

Twenty-two-or-three years ago, in Cleveland, a thing happened which I still remember pretty well. Out in the suburbs, it was—on the lake; the Fairbankses had bought a large house and a great place there, and were living sumptuously, after Mr. Fairbanks's long life of struggle and privation in building up the Cleveland Herald to high place and prosperity. I was there a week, and the Severances came out to dinner twice, and they and "Mother Fairbanks" and I talked over the old times we had enjoyed together in the "Quaker City," when we were "Innocents Abroad." Meantime, every day Mother Fairbanks was busy staging a brief little drama of "The Prince and Pauper" and drilling the children from town who were to play it.

One of these children was Nelly (nevermindtherestofthe-name) and she was a prodigy—a bright and serious and pretty little creature of nine, who was to play Lady Jane Grey. She had a large reputation as a reciter of poetry and little speeches before company in her mother's drawing-room at home; she did her work charmingly, and the sweetest charm about it was the aged gravity and sincerity and earnestness which she put into it. Latterly she had added a new laurel: she had composed a quaint little story, "out of her own head," and had delighted a parlor-audience with it and made herself the envy of all the children around.

The Prince and Pauper play was to be given in my honor, and I had a seat in the centre of the front row; a hundred and fifty friends of the house were present in evening costume, old and young and both sexes, the great room was brilliantly lighted, the fine clothes made the aspect gay, everybody was laughing and chatting and having a good time, the curtain was about ready to rise.

A hitch occurred. Edward VI, (to be played by a girl,) had been belated, it would take a quarter of an hour to dress her for her part. This announcement was made, and Mother Fairbanks retired to attend to this function, and took Nelly's mother with her to help. Presently the audience began to call for little Nelly to come on the stage and do her little story. Nelly's twin sister brought her on, and sat down in a chair beside her and folded her pudgy hands in her lap, and beamed upon the house her joy in the ovation which Lady Jane received. Lady Jane got another round when she said she had made a new story out of her own head and would recite it—which she proceeded to do, with none of her sweet solemnities lacking. To-wit:

Once there were two ladies, and were twins, and lived together, Mary and Olivia Scott, in the house they were born in, and all alone, for Mr. and Mrs. Scott were dead, now. After a while they got lonesome and wished they could have a baby, and said God will provide.

(You could feel the walls give, the strain upon suppressed emotion was so great.)

So when the baby came they were very glad, and the neighbors surprised.

(The walls spread again, but held.)

And asked where they got it and they said by prayer, which is the only way.

(There was not a sound in the audience except the muffled volleying of bursting buttons and the drip of unrestrainable tears. With a gravity not of this world, the inspired child went on:)

But there was no way to feed it at first, because it had only gums and could not bite, then they prayed and God sent a lady which had several and showed them how, then it got fat and they were so happy you cannot think; and thought oh, if they could have some more—and prayed again and got them, because whatever you pray for in the right spirit you get it a thousand fold.

(I could feel the throes and quivers coursing up and down the body of the ripe maiden lady at my left, and she buried her face in her handkerchief and seemed to sob, but it was not sobbing. The walls were sucking in and bellying out, but they held. The two children on the stage were a dear and lovely picture to see, the face of the one so sweetly earnest, the other's face so speakingly lit up with pride in her gifted sister and with worshipping admiration.)

And God was pleased the way they were so thankful to

have that child, and every prayer they made they got another one, and by the time fall came they had thirteen, and whoever will do the right way can have as many, perhaps more, for nothing is impossible with God, and whoever puts their trust in Him they will have their reward, heaped up and running over. When we think of Mary and Olivia Scott it should learn us to have confidence. End of the tale—good bye.

The dear little thing! She made her innocent bow, and retired without a suspicion that she had been an embarrassment. Nothing would have happened, now, perhaps, if quiet could have been maintained for a few minutes, so that the people could get a grip upon themselves, but the strain overpowered my old maid partner and she exploded like a bomb; a general and unrestrained crash of laughter followed, of course, the happy tears flowed like brooks, and no one was sorry of the opportunity to laugh himself out and get the blessed relief that comes of that privilege in such circumstances.

I think the Prince and Pauper went very well—I do not remember; but the other incident stays by me with great and contenting vividness—the picture and everything.

*1907*

# Extract from Captain Stormfield's Visit to Heaven

TAKEN FROM HIS OWN MS. BY MARK TWAIN

Well, when I had been dead about thirty years, I begun to get a little anxious. Mind you, I had been whizzing through space all that time, like a comet. *Like* a comet! Why, Peters, I laid over the lot of them! Of course there warn't any of them going my way, as a steady thing, you know, because they travel in a long circle like the loop of a lasso, whereas I was pointed as straight as a dart for the Hereafter; but I happened on one every now and then that was going my way for an hour or so, and then we had a bit of a brush together. But it was generally pretty one-sided, because I sailed by them the same as if they were standing still. An ordinary comet don't make more than about 200,000 miles a minute. Of course when I came across one of that sort—like Encke's and Halley's comets, for instance—it warn't anything but just a flash and a vanish, you see. You couldn't rightly call it a race. It was as if the comet was a gravel-train and I was a telegraph despatch. But after I got outside of our astronomical system, I used to flush a comet occasionally that was something *like*. *We* haven't got any such comets—ours don't begin. One night I was swinging along at a good round gait, everything taut and trim, and the wind in my favor—I judged I was going about a million miles a minute—it might have been more, it couldn't have been less—when I flushed a most uncommonly big one about three points off my starboard bow. By his stern lights I judged he was bearing about northeast-and-by-north-half-east. Well, it was so near my course that I wouldn't throw away the chance; so I fell off a point, steadied my helm, and went for him. You should have heard me whiz, and seen the electric fur fly! In about a minute and a half I was fringed out with an electrical nimbus that flamed around for miles and miles and lit up all space like broad day. The comet was burning blue in the distance, like a sickly torch, when I first sighted him, but he begun to grow bigger and bigger as I crept up on him. I slipped up on him so fast that when I had gone about 150,000,000 miles I was close enough to be swallowed up in the phosphorescent glory of his wake, and I couldn't see anything for the glare. Thinks I, it won't do to run into him, so I shunted to one side and tore along. By and by I closed up abreast of his tail. Do you know what it was like? It was like a gnat closing up on the continent of America. I forged along. By and by I had sailed along his coast for a little upwards of a hundred and fifty million miles, and then I could see by the shape of him that I hadn't even got up to his waistband yet. Why, Peters, *we* don't know anything about comets, down here. If you want to see comets that are comets, you've got to go outside of our solar system—where there's room for them, you understand. My friend, I've seen comets out there that couldn't even lay down inside the *orbits* of our noblest comets without their tails hanging over.

Well, I boomed along another hundred and fifty million miles, and got up abreast his shoulder, as you may say. I was feeling pretty fine, I tell you; but just then I noticed the officer of the deck come to the side and hoist his glass in my direction. Straight off I heard him sing out—

"Below there, ahoy! Shake her up, shake her up! Heave on a hundred million billion tons of brimstone!"

"Ay—ay, sir!"

"Pipe the stabboard watch! All hands on deck!"

"Ay—ay, sir!"

"Send two hundred thousand million men aloft to shake out royals and sky-scrapers!"

"Ay—ay, sir!"

"Hand the stuns'ls! Hang out every rag you've got! Clothe her from stem to rudder-post!"

"Ay—ay, sir!"

In about a second I begun to see I'd woke up a pretty ugly customer, Peters. In less than ten seconds that comet was just a blazing cloud of red-hot canvas. It was piled up into the heavens clean out of sight—the old thing seemed to swell out and occupy all space; the sulphur smoke from the furnaces—oh, well, nobody can describe the way it rolled and tumbled up into the skies, and nobody can half describe the way it smelt. Neither can anybody begin to describe the way that monstrous craft begun to crash along. And such another powwow—thousands of bo's'n's whistles screaming at once, and a crew like the populations of a hundred thousand worlds like ours all swearing at once. Well, I never heard the like of it before.

We roared and thundered along side by side, both doing our level best, because I'd never struck a comet before that could lay over me, and so I was bound to beat this one or break something. I judged I had some reputation in space, and I calculated to keep it. I noticed I wasn't gaining as fast, now, as I was before, but still I was gaining. There was a power of excitement on board the comet. Upwards of a hundred billion passengers swarmed up from below and rushed to the side and begun to bet on the race. Of course this careened her and damaged her speed. My, but wasn't the mate mad! He jumped at that crowd, with his trumpet in his hand, and sung out—

"Amidships! amidships, you ——!* or I'll brain the last idiot of you!"

Well, sir, I gained and gained, little by little, till at last I went skimming sweetly by the magnificent old conflagration's nose. By this time the captain of the comet had been rousted out, and he stood there in the red glare for'ard, by the mate, in his shirt-sleeves and slippers, his hair all rats' nests and one suspender hanging, and how sick those two men did look! I just simply couldn't help putting my thumb to my nose as I glided away, and singing out—

"Ta-ta! ta-ta! Any word to send to your family?"

Peters, it was a mistake. Yes, sir, I've often regretted that —it was a mistake. You see, the captain had given up the race, but that remark was too tedious for him—he couldn't stand it. He turned to the mate, and says he—

"Have we got brimstone enough of our own to make the trip?"

"Yes, sir."

"Sure?"

"Yes, sir—more than enough."

*The captain could not remember what this word was. He said it was in a foreign tongue.

"How much have we got in cargo for Satan?"

"Eighteen hundred thousand billion quintillions of ka-zarks."

"Very well, then, let his boarders freeze till the next comet comes. Lighten ship! Lively, now, lively, men! Heave the whole cargo overboard!"

Peters, look me in the eye and be calm. I found out, over there, that a kazark is exactly the bulk of *a hundred and sixty-nine worlds like ours!* They hove all that load overboard. When it fell it wiped out a considerable raft of stars just as clean as if they'd been candles and somebody blow'd them out. As for the race, that was at an end. The minute she was lightened the comet swung along by me the same as if I was anchored. The captain stood on the stern, by the after-davits, and put his thumb to his nose and sung out—

"Ta-ta! ta-ta! Maybe *you've* got some message to send your friends in the Everlasting Tropics!"

Then he hove up his other suspender and started for'ard, and inside of three-quarters of an hour his craft was only a pale torch again in the distance. Yes, it was a mistake, Peters— that remark of mine. I don't reckon I'll ever get over being sorry about it. I'd 'a' beat the bully of the firmament if I'd kept my mouth shut.

But I've wandered a little off the track of my tale; I'll get back on my course again. Now you see what kind of speed I was making. So, as I said, when I had been tearing along this way about thirty years I begun to get uneasy. Oh, it was pleasant enough, with a good deal to find out, but then it was kind of lonesome, you know. Besides, I wanted to get some-where. I hadn't shipped with the idea of cruising forever. First off, I liked the delay, because I judged I was going to fetch up in pretty warm quarters when I got through; but towards the last I begun to feel that I'd rather go to—well, most any place, so as to finish up the uncertainty.

Well, one night—it was always night, except when I was rushing by some star that was occupying the whole universe with its fire and its glare—light enough then, of course, but I necessarily left it behind in a minute or two and plunged into a solid week of darkness again. The stars ain't so close to-

gether as they look to be. Where was I? Oh yes; one night I
was sailing along, when I discovered a tremendous long row
of blinking lights away on the horizon ahead. As I approached, they begun to tower and swell and look like mighty
furnaces. Says I to myself—

"By George, I've arrived at last—and at the wrong place,
just as I expected!"

Then I fainted. I don't know how long I was insensible,
but it must have been a good while, for when I came to, the
darkness was all gone and there was the loveliest sunshine and
the balmiest, fragrantest air in its place. And there was such a
marvellous world spread out before me—such a glowing,
beautiful, bewitching country. The things I took for furnaces
were gates, miles high, made all of flashing jewels, and they
pierced a wall of solid gold that you couldn't see the top of,
nor yet the end of, in either direction. I was pointed straight
for one of these gates, and a-coming like a house afire. Now I
noticed that the skies were black with millions of people,
pointed for those gates. What a roar they made, rushing
through the air! The ground was as thick as ants with people,
too—billions of them, I judge.

I lit. I drifted up to a gate with a swarm of people, and
when it was my turn the head clerk says, in a business-like
way—

"Well, quick! Where are you from?"

"San Francisco," says I.

"San Fran—*what*?" says he.

"San Francisco."

He scratched his head and looked puzzled, then he says—
"Is it a planet?"

By George, Peters, think of it! *"Planet?"* says I; "it's a city.
And moreover, it's one of the biggest, and finest and—"

"There, there!" says he, "no time here for conversation. We
don't deal in cities, here. Where are you from in a *general*
way?"

"Oh," I says, "I beg pardon. Put me down for California."

I had him *again*, Peters! He puzzled a second, then he says,
sharp and irritable—

"I don't know any such planet—is it a constellation?"

"Oh, my goodness!" says I. "Constellation, says you? No— it's a State."

"Man, we don't deal in States here. *Will* you tell me where you are from *in general—at large*, don't you understand?"

"Oh, now I get your idea," I says. "I'm from America,— the United States of America."

Peters, do you know I had him *again*? If I hadn't I'm a clam! His face was as blank as a target after a militia shooting-match. He turned to an under-clerk and says—

"Where is America? *What* is America?"

The under clerk answered up prompt and says—

"There ain't any such orb."

"*Orb?*" says I. "Why, what are you talking about, young man? It ain't an orb; it's a country; it's a continent. Columbus discovered it; I reckon likely you've heard of *him*, anyway. America—why, sir, America—"

"Silence!" says the head clerk. "Once for all, where—are— you—*from*?"

"Well," says I, "I don't know anything more to say—unless I lump things, and just say I'm from the world."

"Ah," says he, brightening up, "now that's something like! *What* world?"

Peters, he had *me*, that time. I looked at him, puzzled, he looked at me, worried. Then he burst out—

"Come, come, what world?"

Says I, "Why, *the* world, of course."

"*The* world!" he says. "H'm! there's billions of them! . . . Next!"

That meant for me to stand aside. I done so, and a sky-blue man with seven heads and only one leg hopped into my place. I took a walk. It just occurred to me, then, that all the myriads I had seen swarming to that gate, up to this time, were just like that creature. I tried to run across somebody I was acquainted with, but they were out of acquaintances of mine just then. So I thought the thing all over and finally sidled back there pretty meek and feeling rather stumped, as you may say.

"Well?" said the head clerk.

"Well, sir," I says, pretty humble, "I don't seem to make

out which world it is I'm from. But you may know it from this—it's the one the Saviour saved."

He bent his head at the Name. Then he says, gently—

"The worlds He has saved are like to the gates of heaven in number—none can count them. What astronomical system is your world in?—perhaps that may assist."

"It's the one that has the sun in it—and the moon— and Mars"—he shook his head at each name—hadn't ever heard of them, you see—"and Neptune—and Uranus—and Jupiter—"

"Hold on!" says he, "hold on a minute. Jupiter . . . Jupiter . . . Seems to me we had a man from there eight or nine hundred years ago—but people from that system very seldom enter by this gate." All of a sudden he begun to look me so straight in the eye that I thought he was going to bore through me. Then he says, very deliberate, "Did you come *straight here* from your system?"

"Yes, sir," I says—but I blushed the least little bit in the world when I said it.

He looked at me very stern, and says—

"That is not true; and this is not the place for prevarication. You wandered from your course. How did that happen?"

Says I, blushing again—

"I'm sorry, and I take back what I said, and confess. I raced a little with a comet one day—only just the least little bit— only the tiniest lit—"

"So—so," says he—and without any sugar in his voice to speak of.

I went on, and says—

"But I only fell off just a bare point, and I went right back on my course again the minute the race was over."

"No matter—that divergence has made all this trouble. It has brought you to a gate that is billions of leagues from the right one. If you had gone to your own gate they would have known all about your world at once and there would have been no delay. But we will try to accommodate you." He turned to an under clerk and says—

"What system is Jupiter in?"

"I don't remember, sir, but I think there is such a planet in one of the little new systems away out in one of the thinly worlded corners of the universe. I will see."

He got a balloon and sailed up and up and up, in front of a map that was as big as Rhode Island. He went on up till he was out of sight, and by and by he came down and got something to eat and went up again. To cut a long story short, he kept on doing this for a day or two, and finally he came down and said he thought he had found that solar system, but it might be fly-specks. So he got a microscope and went back. It turned out better than he feared. He had rousted out our system, sure enough. He got me to describe our planet and its distance from our sun, and then he says to his chief—

"Oh, I know the one he means, now, sir. It is on the map. It is called the Wart."

Says I to myself, "Young man, it wouldn't be wholesome for you to go down *there* and call it the Wart."

Well, they let me in, then, and told me I was safe forever and wouldn't have any more trouble.

Then they turned from me and went on with their work, the same as if they considered my case all complete and ship-shape. I was a good deal surprised at this, but I was diffident about speaking up and reminding them. I did so hate to do it, you know; it seemed a pity to bother them, they had so much on their hands. Twice I thought I would give up and let the thing go; so twice I started to leave, but immediately I thought what a figure I should cut stepping out amongst the redeemed in such a rig, and that made me hang back and come to anchor again. People got to eying me—clerks, you know—wondering why I didn't get under weigh. I couldn't stand this long—it was too uncomfortable. So at last I plucked up courage and tipped the head clerk a signal. He says—

"What, you here yet? What's wanting?"

Says I, in a low voice and very confidential, making a trumpet with my hands at his ear—

"I beg pardon, and you mustn't mind my reminding you, and seeming to meddle, but hain't you forgot something?"

He studied a second, and says—

"Forgot something? . . . No, not that I know of."

"Think," says I.

He thought. Then he says—

"No, I can't seem to have forgot anything. What is it?"

"Look at me," says I, "look me all over."

He done it.

"Well?" says he.

"Well," says I, "you don't notice anything? If I branched out amongst the elect looking like this, wouldn't I attract considerable attention?—wouldn't I be a little conspicuous?"

"Well," he says, "I don't see anything the matter. What do you lack?"

"Lack! Why, I lack my harp, and my wreath, and my halo, and my hymn-book, and my palm branch—I lack everything that a body naturally requires up here, my friend."

Puzzled? Peters, he was the worst puzzled man you ever saw. Finally he says—

"Well, you seem to be a curiosity every way a body takes you. I never heard of these things before."

I looked at that man a while in solid astonishment; then I says—

"Now, I hope you won't take it as an offence, for I don't mean any, but really, for a man that has been in the Kingdom as long as I reckon you have, you do seem to know powerful little about its customs."

"Its customs!" says he. "Heaven is a large place, good friend. Large empires have many and diverse customs. Even small dominions have, as you doubtless know by what you have seen of the matter on a small scale in the Wart. How can you imagine I could ever learn the varied customs of the countless kingdoms of heaven? It makes my head ache to think of it. I know the customs that prevail in those portions inhabited by peoples that are appointed to enter by my own gate—and hark ye, that is quite enough knowledge for one individual to try to pack into his head in the thirty-seven millions of years I have devoted night and day to that study. But the idea of learning the customs of the whole appalling expanse of heaven—O man, how insanely you talk! Now I don't doubt that this odd costume you talk about is the fashion in that district of heaven you belong to, but you won't be conspicuous in this section without it."

I felt all right, if that was the case, so I bade him good day and left. All day I walked toward the far end of a prodigious hall of the office, hoping to come out into heaven any moment, but it was a mistake. That hall was built on the general heavenly plan—it naturally couldn't be small. At last I got so tired I couldn't go any further; so I sat down to rest, and begun to tackle the queerest sort of strangers and ask for information; but I didn't get any; they couldn't understand my language, and I could not understand theirs. I got dreadfully lonesome. I was so downhearted and homesick I wished a hundred times I never had died. I turned back, of course. About noon next day, I got back at last and was on hand at the booking-office once more. Says I to the head clerk—

"I begin to see that a man's got to be in his own heaven to be happy."

"Perfectly correct," says he. "Did you imagine the same heaven would suit all sorts of men?"

"Well, I had that idea—but I see the foolishness of it. Which way am I to go to get to my district?"

He called the under clerk that had examined the map, and he gave me general directions. I thanked him and started; but he says—

"Wait a minute; it is millions of leagues from here. Go outside and stand on that red wishing-carpet; shut your eyes, hold your breath, and wish yourself there."

"I'm much obliged," says I; "why didn't you dart me through when I first arrived?"

"We have a good deal to think of here; it was your place to think of it and ask for it. Good-by, we probably sha'n't see you in this region for a thousand centuries or so."

"In that case, *o revoor*," says I.

I hopped on to the carpet and held my breath and shut my eyes and wished I was in the booking-office of my own section. The very next instant a voice I knew sung out in a business kind of a way—

"A harp and a hymn-book, pair of wings and a halo, size 13, for Cap'n Eli Stormfield, of San Francisco!—make him out a clean bill of health, and let him in."

I opened my eyes. Sure enough, it was a Pi Ute Injun I used to know in Tulare County; mighty good fellow—I remembered being at his funeral, which consisted of him being burnt and the other Injuns gauming their faces with his ashes and howling like wildcats. He was powerful glad to see me, and you may make up your mind I was just as glad to see him, and feel that I was in the right kind of a heaven at last.

Just as far as your eye could reach, there was swarms of clerks, running and bustling around, tricking out thousands of Yanks, and Mexicans and English and A-rabs, and all sorts of people in their new outfits; and when they gave me my kit and I put on my halo and took a look in the glass, I could have jumped over a house for joy, I was so happy. "Now *this* is something like!" says I. "Now," says I, "I'm all right— show me a cloud."

Inside of fifteen minutes I was a mile on my way toward the cloud-banks and about a million people along with me. Most of us tried to fly, but some got crippled and nobody made a success of it. So we concluded to walk, for the present, till we had had some wing practice.

We begun to meet swarms of folks who were coming back. Some had harps and nothing else; some had hymn-books and nothing else; some had nothing at all; all of them looked meek and uncomfortable; one young fellow hadn't anything left but his halo, and he was carrying that in his hand; all of a sudden he offered it to me and says—

"Will you hold it for me a minute?"

Then he disappeared in the crowd. I went on. A woman asked me to hold her palm branch, and then *she* disappeared. A girl got me to hold her harp for her, and by George, *she* disappeared; and so on and so on, till I was about loaded down to the guards. Then comes a smiling old gentleman and asked me hold *his* things. I swabbed off the perspiration and says, pretty tart—

"I'll have to get you to excuse me, my friend,—*I* ain't no hat-rack."

About this time I begun to run across piles of those traps, lying in the road. I just quietly dumped my extra cargo along with them. I looked around, and, Peters, that whole nation that was following me were loaded down the same as I'd been. The return crowd had got them to hold their things a minute, you see. They all dumped their loads, too, and we went on.

When I found myself perched on a cloud, with a million other people, I never felt so good in my life. Says I, "Now this is according to the promises; I've been having my doubts, but now I *am* in heaven, sure enough." I gave my palm branch a wave or two, for luck, and then I tautened up my harp-strings and struck in. Well, Peters, you can't imagine anything like the row we made. It was grand to listen to, and made a body thrill all over, but there was considerable many tunes going at once, and that was a drawback to the harmony, you understand; and then there was a lot of Injun tribes, and they kept up such another war-whooping that they kind of took the tuck out of the music. By and by I quit performing, and judged I'd take a rest. There was quite a nice mild old gentleman sitting next me, and I noticed he didn't take a hand; I encouraged him, but he said he was naturally bashful, and was afraid to try before so many people. By and by the old gentleman said he never could seem to enjoy music somehow. The fact was, I was beginning to feel the same way; but I didn't say anything. Him and I had a considerable long silence, then, but of course it warn't noticeable in that place. After about sixteen or seventeen hours, during which I played and sung a little, now and then—always the same tune, because I didn't know any other—I laid down my harp and begun to fan myself with my palm branch. Then we both got to sighing pretty regular. Finally, says he—

"Don't you know any tune but the one you've been pegging at all day?"

"Not another blessed one," says I.

"Don't you reckon you could learn another one?" says he.

"Never," says I; "I've tried to, but I couldn't manage it."

"It's a long time to hang to the one—eternity, you know."

"Don't break my heart," says I; "I'm getting low-spirited enough already."

After another long silence, says he—

"Are you glad to be here?"

Says I, "Old man, I'll be frank with you. This *ain't* just as near my idea of bliss as I thought it was going to be, when I used to go to church."

Says he, "What do you say to knocking off and calling it half a day?"

"That's me," says I. "I never wanted to go off watch so bad in my life."

So we started. Millions were coming to the cloud-bank all the time, happy and hosannahing; millions were leaving it all the time, looking mighty quiet, I tell you. We laid for the newcomers, and pretty soon I'd got them to hold all my things a minute, and then I was a free man again and most outrageously happy. Just then I ran across old Sam Bartlett, who had been dead a long time, and stopped to have a talk with him. Says I—

"Now tell me—is this to go on forever? Ain't there anything else for a change?"

Says he—

"I'll set you right on that point very quick. People take the figurative language of the Bible and the allegories for literal, and the first thing they ask for when they get here is a halo and a harp, and so on. Nothing that's harmless and reasonable is refused a body here, if he asks it in the right spirit. So they are outfitted with these things without a word. They go and sing and play just about one day, and that's the last you'll ever see them in the choir. They don't need anybody to tell them that that sort of thing wouldn't make a heaven—at least not a heaven that a sane man could stand a week and remain sane. That cloud-bank is placed where the noise can't disturb the old inhabitants, and so there ain't any harm in letting everybody get up there and cure himself as soon as he comes.

"Now you just remember this—heaven is as blissful and lovely as it can be; but it's just the busiest place you ever heard of. There ain't any idle people here after the first day. Singing hymns and waving palm branches through all eternity is pretty when you hear about it in the pulpit, but it's as poor a way to put in valuable time as a body could contrive. It would just make a heaven of warbling ignoramuses, don't you see? Eternal Rest sounds comforting in the pulpit, too. Well, you try it once, and see how heavy time will hang on your hands. Why, Stormfield, a man like you, that had been active and stirring all his life, would go mad in six months in a heaven where he hadn't anything to do. Heaven is the very last place to come to *rest* in,—and don't you be afraid to bet on that!"

Says I—

"Sam, I'm as glad to hear it as I thought I'd be sorry. I'm glad I come, now."

Says he—

"Cap'n, ain't you pretty physically tired?"

Says I—

"Sam, it ain't any name for it! I'm dog-tired."

"Just so—just so. You've earned a good sleep, and you'll get it. You've earned a good appetite, and you'll enjoy your dinner. It's the same here it is on earth—you've got to earn a thing, square and honest, before you enjoy it. You can't enjoy first and earn afterwards. But there's this difference, here: you can choose your own occupation, and all the powers of heaven will be put forth to help you make a success of it, if you do your level best. The shoemaker on earth that had the soul of a poet in him won't have to make shoes here."

"Now that's all reasonable and right," says I. "Plenty of work, and the kind you hanker after; no more pain, no more suffering—"

"Oh, hold on; there's plenty of pain here—but it don't kill. There's plenty of suffering here, but it don't last. You see, happiness ain't a *thing in itself*—it's only a *contrast* with something that ain't pleasant. That's all it is. There ain't a thing you can mention that is happiness in its own self—it's only so by contrast with the other thing. And so, as soon as the novelty is over and the force of the contrast dulled, it ain't happiness any longer, and you have to get something fresh. Well, there's plenty of pain and suffering in heaven—consequently there's plenty of contrasts, and just no end of happiness."

Says I, "It's the sensiblest heaven I've heard of yet, Sam, though it's about as different from the one I was brought up on as a live princess is different from her own wax figger."

Along in the first months I knocked around about the Kingdom, making friends and looking at the country, and finally settled down in a pretty likely region, to have a rest before taking another start. I went on making acquaintances and gathering up information. I had a good deal of talk with an old bald-headed angel by the name of Sandy McWilliams.

He was from somewhere in New Jersey. I went about with
him, considerable. We used to lay around, warm afternoons,
in the shade of a rock, on some meadow-ground that was
pretty high and out of the marshy slush of his cranberry-farm,
and there we used to talk about all kinds of things, and smoke
pipes. One day, says I —

"About how old might you be, Sandy?"

"Seventy-two."

"I judged so. How long you been in heaven?"

"Twenty-seven years, come Christmas."

"How old was you when you come up?"

"Why, seventy-two, of course."

"You can't mean it!"

"Why can't I mean it?"

"Because, if you was seventy-two then, you are naturally
ninety-nine now."

"No, but I ain't. I stay the same age I was when I come."

"Well," says I, "come to think, there's something just there
that I want to ask about. Down below, I always had an idea
that in heaven we would all be young, and bright, and spry."

"Well, you *can* be young if you want to. You've only got to
wish."

"Well, then, why didn't you wish?"

"I did. They all do. You'll try it, some day, like enough; but
you'll get tired of the change pretty soon."

"Why?"

"Well, I'll tell you. Now you've always been a sailor; did
you ever try some other business?"

"Yes, I tried keeping grocery, once, up in the mines; but I
couldn't stand it; it was too dull—no stir, no storm, no life
about it; it was like being part dead and part alive, both at the
same time. I wanted to be one thing or t'other. I shut up
shop pretty quick and went to sea."

"That's it. Grocery people like it, but you couldn't. You see
you wasn't used to it. Well, I wasn't used to being young, and
I couldn't seem to take any interest in it. I was strong, and
handsome, and had curly hair,—yes, and wings, too!—gay
wings like a butterfly. I went to picnics and dances and parties
with the fellows, and tried to carry on and talk nonsense with
the girls, but it wasn't any use; I couldn't take to it—fact is, it

was an awful bore. What I wanted was early to bed and early to rise, and something to *do*; and when my work was done, I wanted to sit quiet, and smoke and think—not tear around with a parcel of giddy young kids. You can't think what I suffered whilst I was young."

"How long was you young?"

"Only two weeks. That was plenty for me. Laws, I was so lonesome! You see, I was full of the knowledge and experience of seventy-two years; the deepest subject those young folks could strike was only *a-b-c* to me. And to hear them argue—Oh, my! It would have been funny, if it hadn't been so pitiful. Well, I was so hungry for the ways and the sober talk I was used to, that I tried to ring in with the old people, but they wouldn't have it. They considered me a conceited young upstart, and gave me the cold shoulder. Two weeks was a plenty for me. I was glad to get back my bald head again, and my pipe, and my old drowsy reflections in the shade of a rock or a tree."

"Well," says I, "do you mean to say you're going to stand still at seventy-two, forever?"

"I don't know, and I ain't particular. But I ain't going to drop back to twenty-five any more—I know that, mighty well. I know a sight more than I did twenty-seven years ago, and I enjoy learning, all the time, but I don't seem to get any older. That is, bodily—my mind gets older, and stronger, and better seasoned, and more satisfactory."

Says I, "If a man comes here at ninety, don't he ever set himself back?"

"Of course he does. He sets himself back to fourteen; tries it a couple of hours, and feels like a fool; sets himself forward to twenty; it ain't much improvement; tries thirty, fifty, eighty, and finally ninety—finds he is more at home and comfortable at the same old figure he is used to than any other way. Or, if his mind begun to fail him on earth at eighty, that's where he finally sticks up here. He sticks at the place where his mind was last at its best, for there's where his enjoyment is best, and his ways most set and established."

"Does a chap of twenty-five stay always twenty-five, and look it?"

"If he is a fool, yes. But if he is bright, and ambitious and industrious, the knowledge he gains and the experiences he has, change his ways and thoughts and likings, and make him find his best pleasure in the company of people above that age; so he allows his body to take on the look of as many added years as he needs to make him comfortable and proper in that sort of society; he lets his body go on taking the look of age, according as he progresses, and by and by he will be bald and wrinkled outside, and wise and deep within."

"Babies the same?"

"Babies the same. Laws, what asses we used to be, on earth, about these things! We said we'd be always young in heaven. We didn't say *how* young—we didn't think of that, perhaps—that is, we didn't all think alike, anyway. When I was a boy of seven, I suppose I thought we'd all be twelve, in heaven; when I was twelve, I suppose I thought we'd all be eighteen or twenty in heaven; when I was forty, I begun to go back; I remember I hoped we'd all be about *thirty* years old in heaven. Neither a man nor a boy ever thinks the age he *has* is exactly the best one—he puts the *right* age a few years older or a few years younger than he is. Then he makes that ideal age the general age of the heavenly people. And he expects everybody *to stick* at that age—stand stock-still—and expects them to enjoy it!—Now just think of the idea of standing still in heaven! Think of a heaven made up entirely of hoop-rolling, marble-playing cubs of seven years!—or of awkward, diffident, sentimental immaturities of nineteen!—or of vigorous people of thirty, healthy-minded, brimming with ambition, but chained hand and foot to that one age and its limitations like so many helpless galley-slaves! Think of the dull sameness of a society made up of people all of one age and one set of looks, habits, tastes and feelings. Think how superior to it earth would be, with its variety of types and faces and ages, and the enlivening attrition of the myriad interests that come into pleasant collision in such a variegated society."

"Look here," says I, "do you know what you're doing?"

"Well, what am I doing?"

"You are making heaven pretty comfortable in one way, but you are playing the mischief with it in another."

"How you talk! Would heaven be heaven if you couldn't slander folks?"

"Come to think, I don't believe it would—for some people—but I hadn't thought of it before."

"For 'some people'? There you hit it. The trouble on earth is, that they leave out the *some-people* class—they try to fix up a heaven for only one kind of people. It won't work. There's all kinds here—and God cares for all kinds. He makes all happy; if He can't do it in one way, He does it in another. He doesn't leave anybody out in the cold."

## II

I had been having considerable trouble with my wings. The day after I helped the choir I made a dash or two with them, but was not lucky. First off, I flew thirty yards, and then fouled an Irishman and brought him down—brought us both down, in fact. Next, I had a collision with a Bishop—and bowled him down, of course. We had some sharp words, and I felt pretty cheap, to come banging into a grave old person like that, with a million strangers looking on and smiling to themselves.

I saw I hadn't got the hang of the steering, and so couldn't rightly tell where I was going to bring up when I started. I went afoot the rest of the day, and let my wings hang. Early next morning I went to a private place to have some practice. I got up on a pretty high rock, and got a good start, and went swooping down, aiming for a bush a little over three hundred yards off; but I couldn't seem to calculate for the wind, which was about two points abaft my beam. I could see I was going considerable to looard of the bush, so I worked my starboard wing slow and went ahead strong on the port one, but it wouldn't answer; I could see I was going to broach to, so I slowed down on both, and lit. I went back to the rock and took another chance at it. I aimed two or three points to starboard of the bush—yes, more than that—enough so as to make it nearly a head-wind. I done well enough, but made pretty poor time. I could see, plain enough, that on a head-wind, wings was a mistake. I could see that a body could sail pretty close to the wind, but he couldn't go in the wind's eye.

I could see that if I wanted to go a-visiting any distance from home, and the wind was ahead, I might have to wait days, maybe, for a change; and I could see, too, that these things could not be any use at all in a gale; if you tried to run before the wind, you would make a mess of it, for there isn't any way to shorten sail—like reefing, you know—you have to take it *all* in—shut your feathers down flat to your sides. That would *land* you, of course. You could lay to, with your head to the wind—that is the best you could do, and right hard work you'd find it, too. If you tried any other game, you would founder, sure.

I judge it was about a couple of weeks or so after this that I dropped old Sandy McWilliams a note one day—it was a Tuesday—and asked him to come over and take his manna and quails with me next day; and the first thing he did when he stepped in was to twinkle his eye in a sly way, and say,—

"Well, Cap, what you done with your wings?"

I saw in a minute that there was some sarcasm done up in that rag somewheres, but I never let on. I only says,—

"Gone to the wash."

"Yes," he says, in a dry sort of way, "they mostly go to the wash—about this time—I've often noticed it. Fresh angels are powerful neat. When do you look for 'em back?"

"Day after to-morrow," says I.

He winked at me, and smiled.

Says I,—

"Sandy, out with it. Come—no secrets among friends. I notice you don't ever wear wings—and plenty others don't. I've been making an ass of myself—is that it?"

"That is about the size of it. But it is no harm. We all do it at first. It's perfectly natural. You see, on earth we jump to such foolish conclusions as to things up here. In the pictures we always saw the angels with wings on—and that was all right; but we jumped to the conclusion that that was their way of getting around—and that was all wrong. The wings ain't anything but a uniform, that's all. When they are in the field—so to speak,—they always wear them; you never see an angel going with a message anywhere without his wings, any more than you would see a military officer presiding at a court martial without his uniform, or a postman delivering letters, or a policeman walking his beat, in plain clothes. But they ain't to *fly* with! The wings are for show, not for use. Old experienced angels are like officers of the regular army—they dress plain, when they are off duty. New angels are like the militia—never shed the uniform—always fluttering and floundering around in their wings, butting people down, flapping here, and there, and everywhere, always imagining they are attracting the admiring eye—well, they just think they are the very most important people in heaven. And when you see one of them come sailing around with one wing tipped up and t'other down, you can make up your mind he is saying to himself: 'I wish Mary Ann in Arkansaw could see me now. I reckon she'd wish she hadn't shook me.' No, they're just for show, that's all—only just for show."

"I judge you've got it about right, Sandy," says I.

"Why, look at it yourself," says he. "*You* ain't built for wings—no man is. You know what a grist of years it took you to come here from the earth—and yet you were booming along faster than any cannon-ball could go. Suppose you had to fly that distance with your wings—wouldn't eternity have been over before you got here? Certainly. Well, angels have to go to the earth every day—millions of them—to appear in visions to dying children and good people, you know—it's the heft of their business. They appear with their wings, of course, because they are on official service, and because the dying persons wouldn't know they were angels if they hadn't wings—but do you reckon they fly with them? It stands to reason they don't. The wings would wear out before they got half-way; even the pin-feathers would be gone; the wing frames would be as bare as kite sticks before the paper is pasted on. The distances in heaven are billions of times greater; angels have to go all over heaven every day; could they do it with their wings alone? No, indeed; they wear the wings for style, but they travel any distance in an instant by *wishing*. The wishing-carpet of the Arabian Nights was a sensible idea—but our earthly idea of angels flying these awful distances with their clumsy wings was foolish.

"Our young saints, of both sexes, wear wings all the time—blazing red ones, and blue and green, and gold, and variegated, and rainbowed, and ring-streaked-and-striped ones—

and nobody finds fault. It is suitable to their time of life. The things are beautiful, and they set the young people off. They are the most striking and lovely part of their outfit—a halo don't *begin*."

"Well," says I, "I've tucked mine away in the cupboard, and I allow to let them lay there till there's mud."

"Yes—or a reception."

"What's that?"

"Well, you can see one to-night if you want to. There's a barkeeper from Jersey City going to be received."

"Go on—tell me about it."

"This barkeeper got converted at a Moody and Sankey meeting, in New York, and started home on the ferry-boat, and there was a collision and he got drowned. He is of a class that think all heaven goes wild with joy when a particularly hard lot like him is saved; they think all heaven turns out hosannahing to welcome them; they think there isn't anything talked about in the realms of the blest but their case, for that day. This barkeeper thinks there hasn't been such another stir here in years, as his coming is going to raise.—And I've always noticed this peculiarity about a dead barkeeper—he not only expects all hands to turn out when he arrives, but he expects to be received with a torchlight procession."

"I reckon he is disappointed, then."

"No, he isn't. No man is allowed to be disappointed here. Whatever he wants, when he comes—that is, any reasonable and unsacrilegious thing—he can have. There's always a few millions or billions of young folks around who don't want any better entertainment than to fill up their lungs and swarm out with their torches and have a high time over a barkeeper. It tickles the barkeeper till he can't rest, it makes a charming lark for the young folks, it don't do anybody any harm, it don't cost a rap, and it keeps up the place's reputation for making all comers happy and content."

"Very good. I'll be on hand and see them land the bar-keeper."

"It is manners to go in full dress. You want to wear your wings, you know, and your other things."

"Which ones?"

"Halo, and harp, and palm branch, and all that."

"Well," says I, "I reckon I ought to be ashamed of myself, but the fact is I left them laying around that day I resigned from the choir. I haven't got a rag to wear but this robe and the wings."

"That's all right. You'll find they've been raked up and saved for you. Send for them."

"I'll do it, Sandy. But what was it you was saying about unsacrilegious things, which people expect to get, and will be disappointed about?"

"Oh, there are a lot of such things that people expect and don't get. For instance, there's a Brooklyn preacher by the name of Talmage, who is laying up a considerable disappointment for himself. He says, every now and then in his sermons, that the first thing he does when he gets to heaven, will be to fling his arms around Abraham, Isaac and Jacob, and kiss them and weep on them. There's millions of people down there on earth that are promising themselves the same thing. As many as sixty thousand people arrive here every single day, that want to run straight to Abraham, Isaac and Jacob, and hug them and weep on them. Now mind you, sixty thousand a day is a pretty heavy contract for those old people. If they were a mind to allow it, they wouldn't ever have anything to do, year in and year out, but stand up and be hugged and wept on thirty-two hours in the twenty-four. They would be tired out and as wet as muskrats all the time. What would heaven be, to *them*? It would be a mighty good place to get out of—you know that, yourself. Those are kind and gentle old Jews, but they ain't any fonder of kissing the emotional highlights of Brooklyn than you be. You mark my words, Mr. T.'s endearments are going to be declined, with thanks. There are limits to the privileges of the elect, even in heaven. Why, if Adam was to show himself to every newcomer that wants to call and gaze at him and strike him for his autograph, he would never have time to do anything else but just that. Talmage has said he is going to give Adam some of his attentions, as well as A., I. and J. But he will have to change his mind about that."

"Do you think Talmage will really come here?"

"Why, certainly, he will; but don't you be alarmed; he will run with his own kind, and there's plenty of them. That is

the main charm of heaven—there's all kinds here—which
wouldn't be the case if you let the preachers tell it. Anybody
can find the sort he prefers, here, and he just lets the others
alone, and they let him alone. When the Deity builds a
heaven, it is built right, and on a liberal plan."

Sandy sent home for his things, and I sent for mine, and
about nine in the evening we begun to dress. Sandy says,—

"This is going to be a grand time for you, Stormy. Like as
not some of the patriarchs will turn out."

"No, but will they?"

"Like as not. Of course they are pretty exclusive. They
hardly ever show themselves to the common public, I believe
they never turn out except for an eleventh-hour convert. They
wouldn't do it then, only earthly tradition makes a grand
show pretty necessary on that kind of an occasion."

"Do they all turn out, Sandy?"

"Who?—all the patriarchs? Oh, no—hardly ever more
than a couple. You will be here fifty thousand years—maybe
more—before you get a glimpse of all the patriarchs and
prophets. Since I have been here, Job has been to the front
once, and once Ham and Jeremiah both at the same time. But
the finest thing that has happened in my day was a year or so
ago; that was Charles Peace's reception—him they called 'the
Bannercross Murderer'—an Englishman. There were four
patriarchs and two prophets on the Grand Stand that time—
there hasn't been anything like it since Captain Kidd came;
Abel was there—the first time in twelve hundred years. A
report got around that Adam was coming; well, of course
Abel was enough to bring a crowd, all by himself, but there is
nobody that can draw like Adam. It was a false report, but it
got around, anyway, as I say, and it will be a long day before
I see the like of it again. The reception was in the English
department, of course, which is eight hundred and eleven
million miles from the New Jersey line. I went, along with
a good many of my neighbors, and it was a sight to see, I
can tell you. Flocks came from all the departments. I saw
Esquimaux there, and Tartars, negroes, Chinamen—people
from everywhere. You see a mixture like that in the Grand

Choir, the first day you land here, but you hardly ever see it again. There were billions of people; when they were singing or hosannahing, the noise was wonderful; and even when their tongues were still the drumming of the wings was nearly enough to burst your head, for all the sky was as thick as if it was snowing angels. Although Adam was not there, it was a great time anyway, because we had three Archangels on the Grand Stand—it is a seldom thing that even one comes out."

"What did they look like, Sandy?"

"Well, they had shining faces, and shining robes, and wonderful rainbow wings, and they stood eighteen feet high, and wore swords, and held their heads up in a noble way, and looked like soldiers."

"Did they have halos?"

"No—anyway, not the hoop kind. The archangels and the upper-class patriarchs wear a finer thing than that. It is a round, solid, splendid glory of gold, that is blinding to look at. You have often seen a patriarch in a picture, on earth, with that thing on—you remember it?—he looks as if he had his head in a brass platter. That don't give you the right idea of it at all—it is much more shining and beautiful."

"Did you talk with those archangels and patriarchs, Sandy?"

"Who—I? Why, what can you be thinking about, Stormy? I ain't worthy to speak to such as they."

"Is Talmage?"

"Of course not. You have got the same mixed-up idea about these things that everybody has down there. I had it once, but I got over it. Down there they talk of the heavenly King— and that is right—but then they go right on speaking as if this was a Republic and everybody was on a dead level with everybody else, and privileged to fling his arms around anybody he comes across, and be hail-fellow-well-met with all the elect, from the highest down. How tangled up and absurd that is! How are you going to have a republic under a king? How are you going to have a republic at all, where the head of the government is absolute, holds his place forever, and has no parliament, no council to meddle or make in his affairs, nobody voted for, nobody elected, nobody in the whole universe with a voice in the government, nobody asked to take a hand in its matters, and nobody *allowed* to do it? Fine republic, ain't it?"

"Well, yes—it *is* a little different from the idea I had—but I thought I might go around and get acquainted with the grandees, anyway—not exactly splice the main-brace with them, you know—but shake hands and pass the time of day."

"Could Tom, Dick and Harry call on the Cabinet of Russia and do that?—on Prince Gortschakoff, for instance?"

"I reckon not, Sandy."

"Well, this is Russia—only more so. There's not the shadow of a republic about it anywhere. There are ranks, here. There are viceroys, princes, governors, sub-governors, sub-sub-governors, and a hundred orders of nobility, grading along down from grand-ducal archangels, stage by stage, till the general level is struck, where there ain't any titles. Do you know what a prince of the blood is, on earth?"

"No."

"Well, a prince of the blood don't belong to the royal family exactly, and he don't belong to the mere nobility of the kingdom; he is lower than the one, and higher than t'other. That's about the position of the patriarchs and prophets here. There's some mighty high nobility here—people that you and I ain't worthy to polish sandals for—and *they* ain't worthy to polish sandals for the patriarchs and prophets. That gives you a kind of an idea of their rank, don't it? You begin to see how high up they are, don't you? Just to get a two-minute glimpse of one of them is a thing for a body to remember and tell about for a thousand years. Why, Captain, just think of this: if Abraham was to set his foot down here by this door, there would be a railing set up around that foot-track right away, and a shelter put over it, and people would flock here from all over heaven, for hundreds and hundreds of years, to look at it. Abraham is one of the parties that Mr. Talmage, of Brooklyn, is going to embrace, and kiss, and weep on, when he comes. He wants to lay in a good stock of tears, you know, or five to one he will go dry before he gets a chance to do it."

"Sandy," says I, "I had an idea that *I* was going to be equals with everybody here, too, but I will let that drop. It don't matter, and I am plenty happy enough anyway."

"Captain, you are happier than you would be, the other way. These old patriarchs and prophets have got ages the start of you; they know more in two minutes than you know in a year. Did you ever try to have a sociable improving-time discussing winds, and currents and variations of compass with an undertaker?"

"I get your idea, Sandy. He couldn't interest me. He would be an ignoramus in such things—he would bore me, and I would bore him."

"You have got it. You would bore the patriarchs when you talked, and when they talked they would shoot over your head. By and by you would say, 'Good morning, your Eminence, I will call again'—but you wouldn't. Did you ever ask the slush-boy to come up in the cabin and take dinner with you?"

"I get your drift again, Sandy. I wouldn't be used to such grand people as the patriarchs and prophets, and I would be sheepish and tongue-tied in their company, and mighty glad to get out of it. Sandy, which is the highest rank, patriarch or prophet?"

"Oh, the prophets hold over the patriarchs. The newest prophet, even, is of a sight more consequence than the oldest patriarch. Yes, sir, Adam himself has to walk behind Shakespeare."

"Was Shakespeare a prophet?"

"Of course he was; and so was Homer, and heaps more. But Shakespeare and the rest have to walk behind a common tailor from Tennessee, by the name of Billings; and behind a horse-doctor named Sakka, from Afghanistan. Jeremiah, and Billings and Buddha walk together, side by side, right behind a crowd from planets not in our astronomy; next come a dozen or two from Jupiter and other worlds; next come Daniel, and Sakka and Confucius; next a lot from systems outside of ours; next come Ezekiel, and Mahomet, Zoroaster, and a knife-grinder from ancient Egypt; then there is a long string, and after them, away down toward the bottom, come Shakespeare and Homer, and a shoemaker named Marais, from the back settlements of France."

"Have they really rung in Mahomet and all those other heathens?"

"Yes—they all had their message, and they all get their reward. The man who don't get his reward on earth, needn't bother—he will get it here, sure."

"But why did they throw off on Shakespeare, that way, and put him away down there below those shoemakers and horse-doctors and knife-grinders—a lot of people nobody ever heard of?"

"That is the heavenly justice of it—they warn't rewarded according to their deserts, on earth, but here they get their rightful rank. That tailor Billings, from Tennessee, wrote poetry that Homer and Shakespeare couldn't begin to come up to; but nobody would print it, nobody read it but his neighbors, an ignorant lot, and they laughed at it. Whenever the village had a drunken frolic and a dance, they would drag him in and crown him with cabbage leaves, and pretend to bow down to him; and one night when he was sick and nearly starved to death, they had him out and crowned him, and then they rode him on a rail about the village, and everybody followed along, beating tin pans and yelling. Well, he died before morning. He wasn't ever expecting to go to heaven, much less that there was going to be any fuss made over him, so I reckon he was a good deal surprised when the reception broke on him."

"Was you there, Sandy?"

"Bless you, no!"

"Why? Didn't you know it was going to come off?"

"Well, I judge I did. It was the talk of these realms—not for a day, like this barkeeper business, but for twenty years before the man died."

"Why the mischief didn't you go, then?"

"Now how you talk! The like of me go meddling around at the reception of a prophet? A mudsill like me trying to push in and help receive an awful grandee like Edward J. Billings? Why, I should have been laughed at for a billion miles around. I shouldn't ever heard the last of it."

"Well, who did go, then?"

"Mighty few people that you and I will ever get a chance to see, Captain. Not a solitary commoner ever has the luck to see a reception of a prophet, I can tell you. All the nobility, and all the patriarchs and prophets—every last one of them—and all the archangels, and all the princes and governors and vice-roys, were there,—and *no* small fry—not a single one. And mind you, I'm not talking about only the grandees from *our* world, but the princes and patriarchs and so on from *all* the worlds that shine in our sky, and from billions more that belong in systems upon systems away outside of the one our sun is in. There were some prophets and patriarchs there that ours ain't a circumstance to, for rank and illustriousness and all that. Some were from Jupiter and other worlds in our own system, but the most celebrated were three poets, Saa, Bo and Soof, from great planets in three different and very remote systems. These three names are common and familiar in every nook and corner of heaven, clear from one end of it to the other—fully as well known as the eighty Supreme Arch-angels, in fact—whereas our Moses, and Adam, and the rest, have not been heard of outside of our world's little corner of heaven, except by a few very learned men scattered here and there—and they always spell their names wrong, and get the performances of one mixed up with the doings of another, and they almost always locate them simply *in our solar system*, and think that is enough without going into little details such as naming the particular world they are from. It is like a learned Hindoo showing off how much he knows by saying Longfellow lives in the United States—as if he lived all over the United States, and as if the country was so small you couldn't throw a brick there without hitting him. Between you and me, it does gravel me, the cool way people from those monster worlds outside our system snub our little world, and even our system. Of course we think a good deal of Jupiter, because our world is only a potato to it, for size; but then there are worlds in other systems that Jupiter isn't even a mustard-seed to—like the planet Goobra, for instance, which you couldn't squeeze inside the orbit of Halley's comet without straining the rivets. Tourists from Goobra (I mean parties that lived and died there—natives) come here, now and then, and inquire about our world, and when they find out it is so little that a streak of lightning can flash clear around it in the eighth of a second, they have to lean up against something to laugh. Then they screw a glass into their eye and go to examining *us*, as if we were a curious kind of

foreign bug, or something of that sort. One of them asked me
how long our day was; and when I told him it was twelve
hours long, as a general thing, he asked me if people where I
was from considered it worth while to get up and wash for
such a day as that. That is the way with those Goobra people—they can't seem to let a chance go by to throw it in your
face that their day is three hundred and twenty-two of our
years long. This young snob was just of age—he was six or
seven thousand of his days old—say two million of our
years—and he had all the puppy airs that belong to that time
of life—that turning-point when a person has got over being
a boy and yet ain't quite a man exactly. If it had been anywhere else but in heaven, I would have given him a piece of
my mind. Well, anyway, Billings had the grandest reception
that has been seen in thousands of centuries, and I think it
will have a good effect. His name will be carried pretty far,
and it will make our system talked about, and maybe our
world, too, and raise us in the respect of the general public of
heaven. Why, look here—Shakespeare walked backwards before that tailor from Tennessee, and scattered flowers for him
to walk on, and Homer stood behind his chair and waited on
him at the banquet. Of course that didn't go for much *there*,
amongst all those big foreigners from other systems, as they
hadn't heard of Shakespeare or Homer either, but it would
amount to considerable down there on our little earth if they
could know about it. I wish there was something *in* that
miserable spiritualism, so we could send them word. That
Tennessee village would set up a monument to Billings, then,
and his autograph would outsell Satan's. Well, they had grand
times at that reception—a small-fry noble from Hoboken
told me all about it—Sir Richard Duffer, Baronet."

"What, Sandy, a nobleman from Hoboken? How is that?"

"Easy enough. Duffer kept a sausage-shop and never saved
a cent in his life because he used to give all his spare meat to
the poor, in a quiet way. Not tramps,—no, the other sort—
the sort that will starve before they will beg—honest square
people out of work. Dick used to watch hungry-looking men
and women and children, and track them home, and find out
all about them from the neighbors, and then feed them and

find them work. As nobody ever *saw* him give anything to anybody, he had the reputation of being mean; he died with it, too, and everybody said it was a good riddance; but the minute he landed here, they made him a baronet, and the very first words Dick the sausage-maker of Hoboken heard when he stepped upon the heavenly shore were, 'Welcome, Sir Richard Duffer!' It surprised him some, because he thought he had reasons to believe he was pointed for a warmer climate than this one."

All of a sudden the whole region fairly rocked under the crash of eleven hundred and one thunder blasts, all let off at once, and Sandy says, —

"There, that's for the barkeep."

I jumped up and says, —

"Then let's be moving along, Sandy; we don't want to miss any of this thing, you know."

"Keep your seat," he says; "he is only just telegraphed, that is all."

"How?"

"That blast only means that he has been sighted from the signal-station. He is off Sandy Hook. The committees will go down to meet him, now, and escort him in. There will be ceremonies and delays; they won't be coming up the Bay for a considerable time, yet. It is several billion miles away, anyway."

"*I* could have been a barkeeper and a hard lot just as well as not," says I, remembering the lonesome way I arrived, and how there wasn't any committee nor anything.

"I notice some regret in your voice," says Sandy, "and it is natural enough; but let bygones be bygones; you went according to your lights, and it is too late now to mend the thing."

"No, let it slide, Sandy, I don't mind. But you've got a Sandy Hook *here*, too, have you?"

"We've got everything here, just as it is below. All the States and Territories of the Union, and all the kingdoms of the earth and the islands of the sea are laid out here just as they are on the globe—all the same shape they are down there, and all graded to the relative size, only each State and realm and island is a good many billion times bigger here than it is below. There goes another blast."

"What is that one for?"

"That is only another fort answering the first one. They each fire eleven hundred and one thunder blasts at a single dash—it is the usual salute for an eleventh-hour guest; a hundred for each hour and an extra one for the guest's sex; if it was a woman we would know it by their leaving off the extra gun."

"How do we know there's eleven hundred and one, Sandy, when they all go off at once?—and yet we certainly do know."

"Our intellects are a good deal sharpened up, here, in some ways, and that is one of them. Numbers and sizes and distances are so great, here, that we have to be made so we can *feel* them—our old ways of counting and measuring and ciphering wouldn't ever give us an idea of them, but would only confuse us and oppress us and make our heads ache."

After some more talk about this, I says: "Sandy, I notice that I hardly ever see a white angel; where I run across one white angel, I strike as many as a hundred million copper-colored ones—people that can't speak English. How is that?"

"Well, you will find it the same in any State or Territory of the American corner of heaven you choose to go to. I have shot along, a whole week on a stretch, and gone millions and millions of miles, through perfect swarms of angels, without ever seeing a single white one, or hearing a word I could understand. You see, America was occupied a billion years and more, by Injuns and Aztecs, and that sort of folks, before a white man ever set his foot in it. During the first three hundred years after Columbus's discovery, there wasn't ever more than one good lecture audience of white people, all put together, in America—I mean the whole thing, British Possessions and all; in the beginning of our century there were only 6,000,000 or 7,000,000—say seven; 12,000,000 or 14,000,000 in 1825; say 23,000,000 in 1850; 40,000,000 in 1875. Our death-rate has always been 20 in 1000 per annum. Well, 140,000 died the first year of the century; 280,000 the twenty-fifth year; 500,000 the fiftieth year; about a million the seventy-fifth year. Now I am going to be liberal about this thing, and consider that fifty million whites have died in America from the beginning up to to-day—make it sixty, if you want to; make it a hundred million—it's no difference about a few millions one way or t'other. Well, now, you can see, yourself, that when you come to spread a little dab of people like that over these hundreds of billions of miles of American territory here in heaven, it is like scattering a ten-cent box of homœopathic pills over the Great Sahara and expecting to find them again. You can't expect us to amount to anything in heaven, and we *don't*—now that is the simple fact, and we have got to do the best we can with it. The learned men from other planets and other systems come here and hang around a while, when they are touring around the Kingdom, and then go back to their own section of heaven and write a book of travels, and they give America about five lines in it. And what do they say about us? They say this wilderness is populated with a scattering few hundred thousand billions of red angels, with now and then a curiously complected *diseased* one. You see, they think we whites and the occasional nigger are Injuns that have been bleached out or blackened by some leprous disease or other—for some peculiarly rascally *sin*, mind you. It is a mighty sour pill for us all, my friend—even the modestest of us, let alone the other kind, that think they are going to be received like a long-lost government bond, and hug Abraham into the bargain. I haven't asked you any of the particulars, Captain, but I judge it goes without saying—if my experience is worth anything—that there wasn't much of a hooraw made over you when you arrived—now was there?"

"Don't mention it, Sandy," says I, coloring up a little; "I wouldn't have had the family see it for any amount you are a mind to name. Change the subject, Sandy, change the subject."

"Well, do you think of settling in the California department of bliss?"

"I don't know. I wasn't calculating on doing anything really definite in that direction till the family come. I thought I would just look around, meantime, in a quiet way, and make

up my mind. Besides, I know a good many dead people, and
I was calculating to hunt them up and swap a little gossip
with them about friends, and old times, and one thing or
another, and ask them how they like it here, as far as they
have got. I reckon my wife will want to camp in the California range, though, because most all her departed will be there,
and she likes to be with folks she knows."

"Don't you let her. You see what the Jersey district of
heaven is, for whites; well, the Californian district is a thousand times worse. It swarms with a mean kind of leather-
headed mud-colored angels—and your nearest white neighbor is likely to be a million miles away. *What a man mostly
misses, in heaven, is company*—company of his own sort and
color and language. I have come near settling in the European
part of heaven once or twice on that account."

"Well, why didn't you, Sandy?"

"Oh, various reasons. For one thing, although you *see*
plenty of whites there, you can't understand any of them,
hardly, and so you go about as hungry for talk as you do
here. I like to look at a Russian or a German or an Italian—I
even like to look at a Frenchman if I ever have the luck to
catch him engaged in anything that ain't indelicate—but *looking* don't cure the hunger—what you want is talk."

"Well, there's England, Sandy—the English district of
heaven."

"Yes, but it is not so very much better than this end of the
heavenly domain. As long as you run across Englishmen born
this side of three hundred years ago, you are all right; but the
minute you get back of Elizabeth's time the language begins
to fog up, and the further back you go the foggier it gets. I
had some talk with a Mr. Spenser and a man by the name of
Chaucer—old-time poets—but it was no use, I couldn't
quite understand them, and they couldn't quite understand
me. I have had letters from them since, but it is such broken
English I can't make it out. Back of those men's time the
English are just simply foreigners, nothing more, nothing
less; they talk Danish, German, Norman French, and sometimes a mixture of all three; back of *them*, they talk Latin, and
ancient British, Irish, and Gaelic; and then back of these come
billions and billions of pure savages that talk a gibberish that

Satan himself couldn't understand. The fact is, where you strike one man in the English settlements that you can understand, you wade through awful swarms that talk something you can't make head nor tail of. You see, every country on earth has been overlaid so often, in the course of a billion years, with different kinds of people and different sorts of languages, that this sort of mongrel business was bound to be the result in heaven."

"Sandy," says I, "did you see a good many of the great people history tells about?"

"Yes—plenty. I saw kings and all sorts of distinguished people."

"Do the kings rank just as they did below?"

"No; a body can't bring his rank up here with him. Divine right is a good-enough earthly romance, but it don't go, here. Kings drop down to the general level as soon as they reach the realms of grace. I knew Charles the Second very well—one of the most popular comedians in the English section—draws first rate. There are better, of course—people that were never heard of on earth—but Charles is making a very good reputation indeed, and is considered a rising man. Richard the Lion-hearted is in the prize-ring, and coming into considerable favor. Henry the Eighth is a tragedian, and the scenes where he kills people are done to the very life. Henry the Sixth keeps a religious-book stand."

"Did you ever see Napoleon, Sandy?"

"Often—sometimes in the Corsican range, sometimes in the French. He always hunts up a conspicuous place, and goes frowning around with his arms folded and his field-glass under his arm, looking as grand, gloomy and peculiar as his reputation calls for, and very much bothered because he don't stand as high, here, for a soldier, as he expected to."

"Why, who stands higher?"

"Oh, a *lot* of people *we* never heard of before—the shoemaker and horse-doctor and knife-grinder kind, you know—clodhoppers from goodness knows where, that never handled a sword or fired a shot in their lives—but the soldiership was in them, though they never had a chance to show it. But here they take their right place, and Cæsar and Napoleon and Alexander have to take a back seat. The greatest military genius our world ever produced was a bricklayer from somewhere back of Boston—died during the Revolution—by the name of Absalom Jones. Wherever he goes, crowds flock to see him. You see, everybody knows that if he had had a chance he would have shown the world some generalship that would have made all generalship before look like child's play and 'prentice work. But he never got a chance; he tried heaps of times to enlist as a private, but he had lost both thumbs and a couple of front teeth, and the recruiting surgeon wouldn't pass him. However, as I say, everybody knows, now, what he *would* have been, and so they flock by the million to get a glimpse of him whenever they hear he is going to be anywhere. Cæsar, and Hannibal, and Alexander, and Napoleon are all on his staff, and ever so many more great generals; but the public hardly care to look at *them* when *he* is around. Boom! There goes another salute. The barkeeper's off quarantine now."

Sandy and I put on our things. Then we made a wish, and in a second we were at the reception-place. We stood on the edge of the ocean of space, and looked out over the dimness, but couldn't make out anything. Close by us was the Grand Stand—tier on tier of dim thrones rising up toward the zenith. From each side of it spread away the tiers of seats for the general public. They spread away for leagues and leagues— you couldn't see the ends. They were empty and still, and hadn't a cheerful look, but looked dreary, like a theatre before anybody comes—gas turned down. Sandy says,—

"We'll sit down here and wait. We'll see the head of the procession come in sight away off yonder pretty soon, now."

Says I,—

"It's pretty lonesome, Sandy; I reckon there's a hitch somewheres. Nobody but just you and me—it ain't much of a display for the barkeeper."

"Don't you fret, it's all right. There'll be one more gunfire—then you'll see."

In a little while we noticed a sort of a lightish flush, away off on the horizon.

"Head of the torchlight procession," says Sandy.

It spread, and got lighter and brighter; soon it had a strong glare like a locomotive headlight; it kept on getting brighter and brighter till it was like the sun peeping above the horizon-line at sea—the big red rays shot high up into the sky.

"Keep your eyes on the Grand Stand and the miles of seats—sharp!" says Sandy, "and listen for the gun-fire."

Just then it burst out, "Boom-boom-boom!" like a million thunder-storms in one, and made the whole heavens rock. Then there was a sudden and awful glare of light all about us, and in that very instant every one of the millions of seats was occupied, and as far as you could see, in both directions, was just a solid pack of people, and the place was all splendidly lit up! It was enough to take a body's breath away. Sandy says,—

"That is the way we do it here. No time fooled away; nobody straggling in after the curtain's up. Wishing is quicker work than travelling. A quarter of a second ago these folks were millions of miles from here. When they heard the last signal, all they had to do was to wish, and here they are."

The prodigious choir struck up,—

> We long to hear thy voice,
> To see thee face to face.

It was noble music, but the uneducated chipped in and spoilt it, just as the congregations used to do on earth.

The head of the procession began to pass, now, and it was a wonderful sight. It swept along, thick and solid, five hundred thousand angels abreast, and every angel carrying a torch and singing—the whirring thunder of the wings made a body's head ache. You could follow the line of the procession back, and slanting upward into the sky, far away in a glittering snaky rope, till it was only a faint streak in the distance. The rush went on and on, for a long time, and at last, sure enough, along comes the barkeeper, and then everybody rose, and a cheer went up that made the heavens shake, I tell you! He was all smiles, and had his halo tilted over one ear in a cocky way, and was the most satisfied-looking saint I ever saw. While he marched up the steps of the Grand Stand, the choir struck up,—

> The whole wide heaven groans,
> And waits to hear that voice.

There were four gorgeous tents standing side by side in the place of honor, on a broad railed platform in the centre of the Grand Stand, with a shining guard of honor round about them. The tents had been shut up all this time. As the barkeeper climbed along up, bowing and smiling to everybody, and at last got to the platform, these tents were jerked up aloft all of a sudden, and we saw four noble thrones of gold, all caked with jewels, and in the two middle ones sat old white-whiskered men, and in the two others a couple of the most glorious and gaudy giants, with platter halos and beautiful armor. All the millions went down on their knees, and stared, and looked glad, and burst out into a joyful kind of murmurs. They said,—

"Two archangels!—that is splendid. Who can the others be?"

The archangels gave the barkeeper a stiff little military bow; the two old men rose; one of them said, "Moses and Esau welcome thee!" and then all the four vanished, and the thrones were empty.

The barkeeper looked a little disappointed, for he was calculating to hug those old people, I judge; but it was the gladdest and proudest multitude you ever saw—because they had seen Moses and Esau. Everybody was saying, "Did you see them?—I did—Esau's side face was to me, but I saw Moses full in the face, just as plain as I see you this minute!"

The procession took up the barkeeper and moved on with him again, and the crowd broke up and scattered. As we went along home, Sandy said it was a great success, and the barkeeper would have a right to be proud of it forever. And he said *we* were in luck, too; said we might attend receptions for forty thousand years to come, and not have a chance to see a brace of such grand moguls as Moses and Esau. We found afterwards that we had come near seeing another patriarch, and likewise a genuine prophet besides, but at the last moment they sent regrets. Sandy said there would be a monument put up there, where Moses and Esau had stood, with the date and circumstances, and all about the whole business, and travellers would come for thousands of years and gawk at it, and climb over it, and scribble their names on it.

THE END.

*December 1907 and January 1908*

# Little Bessie

## Chapter 1

### Little Bessie Would Assist Providence

Little Bessie was nearly three years old. She was a good child, and not shallow, not frivolous, but meditative and thoughtful, and much given to thinking out the reasons of things and trying to make them harmonise with results. One day she said—

"Mamma, why is there so much pain and sorrow and suffering? What is it all for?"

It was an easy question, and mamma had no difficulty in answering it:

"It is for our good, my child. In His wisdom and mercy the Lord sends us these afflictions to discipline us and make us better."

"Is it *He* that sends them?"

"Yes."

"Does He send *all* of them, mamma?"

"Yes, dear, all of them. None of them comes by accident; He alone sends them, and always out of love for us, and to make us better."

"Isn't it strange!"

"Strange? Why, no, I have never thought of it in that way. I have not heard any one call it strange before. It has always seemed natural and right to me, and wise and most kindly and merciful."

"Who first thought of it like that, mamma? Was it you?"

"Oh, no, child, I was taught it."

"Who taught you so, mamma?"

"Why, really, I don't know—I can't remember. My mother, I suppose; or the preacher. But it's a thing that everybody knows."

"Well, anyway, it does seem strange. Did He give Billy Norris the typhus?"

"Yes."

"What for?"

"Why, to discipline him and make him good."

864

"But he died, mamma, and so it *couldn't* make him good."

"Well, then, I suppose it was for some other reason. We know it was a *good* reason, whatever it was."

"What do you think it was, mamma?"

"Oh, you ask so many questions! I think it was to discipline his parents."

"Well, then, it wasn't fair, mamma. Why should *his* life be taken away for their sake, when he wasn't doing anything?"

"Oh, *I* don't know! I only know it was for a good and wise and merciful reason."

"What reason, mamma?"

"I think—I think—well, it was a judgment; it was to punish them for some sin they had committed."

"But *he* was the one that was punished, mamma. Was that right?"

"Certainly, certainly. He does nothing that isn't right and wise and merciful. You can't understand these things now, dear, but when you are grown up you will understand them, and then you will see that they are just and wise."

After a pause:

"Did He make the roof fall in on the stranger that was trying to save the crippled old woman from the fire, mamma?"

"Yes, my child. *Wait!* Don't ask me why, because I don't know. I only know it was to discipline some one, or be a judgment upon somebody, or to show His power."

"That drunken man that stuck a pitchfork into Mrs. Welch's baby when—"

"Never mind about it, you needn't go into particulars; it was to discipline the child—*that* much is certain, anyway."

"Mamma, Mr. Burgess said in his sermon that billions of little creatures are sent into us to give us cholera, and typhoid, and lockjaw, and more than a thousand other sicknesses and—mamma, does He send them?"

"Oh, certainly, child, certainly. Of course."

"What for?"

"Oh, to *dis*cipline us! haven't I told you so, over and over again?"

"It's awful cruel, mamma! And silly! and if I—"

"Hush, oh *hush!* do you want to bring the lightning?"

"You know the lightning *did* come last week, mamma, and struck the new church, and burnt it down. Was it to discipline the church?"

(Wearily). "Oh, I suppose so."

"But it killed a hog that wasn't doing anything. Was it to discipline the hog, mamma?"

"Dear child, don't you want to run out and play a while? If you would like to—"

"Mamma, only think! Mr. Hollister says there isn't a bird or fish or reptile or any other animal that hasn't got an enemy that Providence has sent to bite it and chase it and pester it, and kill it, and suck its blood and discipline it and make it good and religious. Is that true, mother—because if it is true, why did Mr. Hollister laugh at it?"

"That Hollister is a scandalous person, and I don't want you to listen to anything he says."

"Why, mamma, he is very interesting, and *I* think he tries to be good. He says the wasps catch spiders and cram them down into their nests in the ground—*alive*, mamma!—and there they live and suffer days and days and days, and the hungry little wasps chewing their legs and gnawing into their bellies all the time, to make them good and religious and praise God for His infinite mercies. *I* think Mr. Hollister is just lovely, and ever so kind; for when I asked him if *he* would treat a spider like that, he said he hoped to be damned if he would; and then he—"

"My child! oh, do for goodness' sake—"

"And mamma, he says the spider is appointed to catch the fly, and drive her fangs into his bowels, and suck and suck and suck his blood, to discipline him and make him a Christian; and whenever the fly buzzes his wings with the pain and misery of it, you can see by the spider's grateful eye that she is thanking the Giver of All Good for—well, she's saying grace, as *he* says; and also, he—"

"Oh, aren't you *ever* going to get tired chattering! If you want to go out and play—"

"Mamma, he says himself that all troubles and pains and miseries and rotten diseases and horrors and villainies are sent to us in mercy and kindness to discipline us; and he says it is the duty of every father and mother to *help* Providence, every way they can; and says they can't do it by just scolding and whipping, for that won't answer, it is weak and no good—Providence's way is best, and it is every parent's duty and every *person's* duty to help discipline everybody, and cripple them and kill them, and starve them, and freeze them, and rot them with diseases, and lead them into murder and theft and dishonor and disgrace; and he says Providence's invention for disciplining us and the animals is the very brightest idea that ever was, and not even an idiot could get up anything shinier. Mamma, brother Eddie needs disciplining, right away; and I know where you can get the smallpox for him, and the itch, and the diphtheria, and bone-rot, and heart disease, and consumption, and—*Dear* mamma, have you fainted! I will run and bring help! Now *this* comes of staying in town this hot weather."

## Chapter 2

### Creation of Man

*Mamma.* You disobedient child, have you been associating with that irreligious Hollister again?

*Bessie.* Well, mamma, he is interesting, anyway, although wicked, and I can't help loving interesting people. Here is the conversation we had:

*Hollister.* Bessie, suppose you should take some meat and bones and fur, and make a cat out of it, and should tell the cat, Now you are not to be unkind to any creature, on pain of punishment and death. And suppose the cat should disobey, and catch a mouse and torture it and kill it. What would you do to the cat?

*Bessie.* Nothing.

*H.* Why?

*B.* Because I know what the cat would say. She would say, It's my nature, I couldn't help it; I didn't make my nature, *you* made it. And so you are responsible for what I've done—I'm not. I couldn't answer that, Mr. Hollister.

*H.* It's just the case of Frankenstein and his Monster over again.

*B.* What is that?

*H*. Frankenstein took some flesh and bones and blood and made a man out of them; the man ran away and fell to raping and robbing and murdering everywhere, and Frankenstein was horrified and in despair, and said, *I* made him, without asking his consent, and it makes me responsible for every crime he commits. *I* am the criminal, he is innocent.

*B*. Of course he was right.

*H*. I judge so. It's just the case of God and man and you and the cat over again.

*B*. How is that?

*H*. God made man, without man's consent, and made his nature, too; made it vicious instead of angelic, and then said, Be angelic, or I will punish you and destroy you. But no matter, God is responsible for everything man does, all the same; He can't get around that fact. There is only one Criminal, and it is not man.

*Mamma*. This is atrocious! it is wicked, blasphemous, irreverent, horrible!

*Bessie*. Yes'm, but it's true. And I'm not going to make a cat. I would be above making a cat if I couldn't make a good one.

## Chapter 3

Mamma, if a person by the name of Jones kills a person by the name of Smith just for amusement, it's murder, isn't it, and Jones is a murderer?

Yes, my child.

And Jones is punishable for it?

Yes, my child.

Why, mamma?

*Why?* Because God has forbidden homicide in the Ten Commandments, and therefore whoever kills a person commits a crime and must suffer for it.

But mamma, suppose Jones has by birth such a violent temper that he can't control himself?

He *must* control himself. God requires it.

But he doesn't make his own temper, mamma, he is born

with it, like the rabbit and the tiger; and so, why should he be held responsible?

Because God *says* he is responsible and *must* control his temper.

But he *can't*, mamma; and so, don't you think it is God that does the killing and is responsible, because it was *He* that gave him the temper which he couldn't control?

Peace, my child! He *must* control it, for God requires it, and that ends the matter. It settles it, and there is no room for argument.

(*After a thoughtful pause.*) It doesn't seem to me to settle it. Mamma, murder is murder, isn't it? and whoever commits it is a murderer? That is the plain simple fact, isn't it?

(*Suspiciously.*) What are you arriving at now, my child?

Mamma, when God designed Jones He could have given him a rabbit's temper if He had wanted to, couldn't He?

Yes.

Then Jones would not kill anybody and have to be hanged? True.

But He chose to give Jones a temper that would *make* him kill Smith. Why, then, isn't *He* responsible?

Because He also gave Jones a Bible. The Bible gives Jones ample warning not to commit murder; and so if Jones commits it he alone is responsible.

(*Another pause.*) Mamma, did God make the house-fly?

Certainly, my darling.

What for?

For some great and good purpose, and to display His power.

What is the great and good purpose, mamma?

We do not know, my child. We only know that He makes *all* things for a great and good purpose. But this is too large a subject for a dear little Bessie like you, only a trifle over three years old.

Possibly, mamma, yet it profoundly interests me. I have been reading about the fly, in the newest science-book. In that book he is called "the most dangerous animal and the most murderous that exists upon the earth, killing hundreds of thousands of men, women and children every year, by distributing deadly diseases among them." Think of it, mamma, the *most* fatal of all the animals! by all odds the most murderous of all the living things created by God. Listen to this, from the book:

Now, the house fly has a very keen scent for filth of any kind. Whenever there is any within a hundred yards or so, the fly goes for it to smear its mouth and all the sticky hairs of its six legs with dirt and disease germs. A second or two suffices to gather up many thousands of these disease germs, and then off goes the fly to the nearest kitchen or dining room. There the fly crawls over the meat, butter, bread, cake, anything it can find in fact, and often gets into the milk pitcher, depositing large numbers of disease germs at every step. The house fly is as disgusting as it is dangerous.

Isn't it horrible, mamma! One fly produces fifty-two billions of descendants in 60 days in June and July, and they go and crawl over sick people and wade through pus, and sputa, and foul matter exuding from sores, and gaum themselves with every kind of disease-germ, then they go to everybody's dinner-table and wipe themselves off on the butter and the other food, and many and many a painful illness and ultimate death results from this loathsome industry. Mamma, they murder seven thousand persons in New York City alone, every year—people against whom they have no quarrel. To kill without cause is murder—nobody denies that. Mamma?

Well?

Have the flies a Bible?

Of course not.

You have said it is the Bible that makes man responsible. If God didn't give him a Bible to circumvent the nature that He deliberately gave him, God would be responsible. He gave the fly his murderous nature, and sent him forth unobstructed by a Bible or any other restraint to commit murder by wholesale. And so, therefore, God is Himself responsible. God is a murderer. Mr. Hollister says so. Mr. Hollister says God can't make one moral law for man and another for Himself. He says it would be laughable.

*Do* shut up! I wish that that tiresome Hollister was in H—amburg! He is an ignorant, unreasoning, illogical ass, and I have told you over and over again to keep out of his poisonous company.

## Chapter 4

"Mamma, what is a virgin?"

"A maid."

"Well, what is a maid?"

"A girl or woman that isn't married."

"Uncle Jonas says that sometimes a virgin that has been having a child—"

"Nonsense! A virgin can't have a child."

"Why can't she, mamma?"

"Well, there are reasons why she can't."

"What reasons, mamma?"

"Physiological. She would have to cease to be a virgin before she could have the child."

"How do you mean, mamma?"

"Well, let me see. It's something like this: a Jew couldn't be a Jew after he had become a Christian; he couldn't be a Christian and Jew at the same time. Very well, a person couldn't be mother and virgin at the same time."

"Why, mamma, Sally Brooks has had a child, and *she's* a virgin."

"Indeed? Who says so?"

"She says so herself."

"Oh, no doubt! Are there any other witnesses?"

"Yes—there's a dream. She says the governor's private secretary appeared to her in a dream and told her she was going to have a child, and it came out just so."

"I shouldn't wonder! Did he say the governor was the co-respondent?"

## Chapter 5

B. Mama, didn't you tell me an ex-governor, like Mr. Burlap, is a person that's been governor but isn't a governor any more?

M. Yes, dear.

B. And Mr. Williams said "ex" always stands for a Has Been, didn't he?

M. Yes, child. It is a vulgar way of putting it, but it expresses the fact.

B, (eagerly). So then Mr. Hollister was right, after all. He says the Virgin Mary isn't a virgin any more, she's a Has Been. He says—

M. It is false! Oh, it was just like that godless miscreant to try to undermine an innocent child's holy belief with his foolish lies; and if I could have my way, I—

B. But mama,—honest and true—*is* she still a virgin—a *real* virgin, you know?

M. Certainly she is; and has never been anything *but* a virgin—oh, the adorable One, the pure, the spotless, the undefiled!

B. Why, mama, Mr. Hollister says she *can't* be. That's what *he* says. He says she had five children *after* she had the One that was begotten by absent treatment and didn't break anything and he thinks such a lot of child-bearing, spread over years and years and years, would ultimately wear a virgin's virginity so thin that even Wall street would consider the stock too lavishly watered and you couldn't place it there at any discount you could name, because the Board would say it was wildcat, and wouldn't list it. That's what *he* says. And besides—

M. Go to the nursery, instantly! Go!

## Chapter 6

Mamma, is Christ God?

Yes, my child.

Mamma, how can He be Himself and Somebody Else at the same time?

He isn't, my darling. It is like the Siamese twins—two persons, one born ahead of the other, but equal in authority, equal in power.

I understand it, now, mamma, and it is quite simple. One twin has sexual intercourse with his mother, and begets himself and his brother; and next he has sexual intercourse with his grandmother and begets his mother. I should think it would be difficult, mamma, though interesting. Oh, ever so difficult. I should think that the Corespondent—

All things are possible with God, my child.

Yes, I suppose so. But not with any other Siamese twin, I suppose. *You* don't think any ordinary Siamese twin could beget himself and his brother on his mother, do you, mamma, and then go on back while his hand is in and beget *her*, too, on his grandmother?

Certainly not, my child. None but God can do these wonderful and holy miracles.

And enjoy them. For of course He enjoys them, or He wouldn't go foraging around among the family like that, *would* He, mamma?—injuring their reputations in the village and causing talk. Mr. Hollister says it was wonderful and awe-inspiring in those days, but wouldn't work now. He says that if the Virgin lived in Chicago now, and got in the family way and explained to the newspaper fellows that God was the Corespondent, she couldn't get two in ten of them to believe it. He says they are a hell of a lot!

My child!

Well, that is what he says, anyway.

Oh, I do *wish* you would keep away from that wicked, wicked man!

He doesn't *mean* to be wicked, mamma, and he doesn't blame God. No, he doesn't blame Him; he says they all do it—gods do. It's their habit, they've always been that way.

What way, dear?

Going around unvirgining the virgins. He says our God did not invent the idea—it was old and mouldy before He happened on it. Says He hasn't invented anything, but got His Bible and His Flood and His morals and all His ideas from earlier gods, and they got them from still earlier gods. He says there never was a god yet that wasn't born of a Virgin. Mr. Hollister says no virgin is safe where a god is. He says he wishes he was a god; he says he would make virgins so scarce that—

Peace, peace! *Don't* run on so, my child. If you—

—and he advised me to lock my door nights, because—

Hush, *hush*, will you!

—because although I am only three and a half years old and quite safe from *men*—

Mary Ann, come and get this child! There, now, go along with you, and don't come near me again until you can interest yourself in some subject of a lower grade and less awful than theology.

*Bessie*, (disappearing.) Mr. Hollister says there *ain't* any.

*1908–09*

# The New Planet

[The astronomers at Harvard have observed "perturbations in the orbital movement of Neptune," such as might be caused by the presence of a new planet in the vicinity]

I believe in the new planet. I was eleven years old in 1846, when Leverrier and Adams and Mary Somerville discovered Neptune through the disturbance and discomfort it was causing Uranus. "Perturbations," they call that kind of disturbance. I had been having those perturbations myself, for more than two months; in fact all through watermelon time, for they used to keep dogs in some of the patches in those days. You notice that these recent perturbations are considered remarkable because they perturbate through three seconds of arc, but really that is nothing: often I used to perturbate through as much as half an hour if it was a dog that was attending to the perturbating. There isn't any Neptune that can outperturbate a dog; and I know, because I am not speaking from hearsay. Why, if there was a planet two hundred and fifty thousand "light-years" the other side of Neptune's orbit, Professor Pickering would discover it in a minute if it could perturbate equal to a dog. Give me a dog every time, when it comes to perturbating. You let a dog jump out at you all of a sudden in the dark of the moon, and you will see what a small thing three seconds of arc is: the shudder that goes through you then would open the seams of Noah's ark itself, from figurehead to rudder-post, and you would drop that melon the same as if you had never had any but just a casual interest in it. I know about these things, because this is not tradition I am writing, but history.

Now then, notice this. About the end of August, 1846, a change came over me and I resolved to lead a better life, so I reformed; but it was just as well anyway, because they had got to having guns and dogs both. Although I was reformed, the perturbations did not stop! Does that strike you? They did not stop, they went right on and on and on, for three weeks, clear up to the 23d of September; then Neptune was discovered, and the whole mystery stood explained. It shows that I am so sensitively constructed that I perturbate when any other planet is disturbed. This has been going on all my life. It only happens in the watermelon season, but that has nothing to do with it, and has no significance: geologists and anthropologists and horticulturists all tell me it is only ancestral and hereditary, and that is what I think myself. Now then, I got to perturbating again, this summer—all summer through; all through watermelon time: and *where*, do you think? Up here on my farm in Connecticut. Is that significant? Unquestionably it is, for you couldn't raise a watermelon on this farm with a derrick.

That perturbating was caused by the new planet. That Washington Observatory may throw as much doubt as it wants to, it cannot affect me, because I know there *is* a new planet. I know it because I don't perturbate for nothing. There has got to be a dog or a planet, one or the other; and there isn't any dog around here, so there's *got* to be a planet. I hope it is going to be named after me; I should just love it if I can't have a constellation.

*January 30, 1909*

# A Fable

Once upon a time an artist who had painted a small and very beautiful picture placed it so that he could see it in the mirror. He said, "This doubles the distance and softens it, and it is twice as lovely as it was before."

The animals out in the woods heard of this through the housecat, who was greatly admired by them because he was so learned, and so refined and civilized, and so polite and high-bred, and could tell them so much which they didn't know before, and were not certain about afterward. They were much excited about this new piece of gossip, and they asked questions, so as to get at a full understanding of it. They asked what a picture was, and the cat explained.

"It is a flat thing," he said; "wonderfully flat, marvellously flat, enchantingly flat and elegant. And, oh, so beautiful!"

That excited them almost to a frenzy, and they said they would give the world to see it. Then the bear asked:

"What is it that makes it so beautiful?"

"It is the looks of it," said the cat.

This filled them with admiration and uncertainty, and they were more excited than ever. Then the cow asked:

"What is a mirror?"

"It is a hole in the wall," said the cat. "You look in it, and there you see the picture, and it is so dainty and charming and ethereal and inspiring in its unimaginable beauty that your head turns round and round, and you almost swoon with ecstasy."

The ass had not said anything as yet; he now began to throw doubts. He said there had never been anything as beautiful as this before, and probably wasn't now. He said that when it took a whole basketful of sesquipedalian adjectives to whoop up a thing of beauty, it was time for suspicion.

It was easy to see that these doubts were having an effect upon the animals, so the cat went off offended. The subject was dropped for a couple of days, but in the mean time curiosity was taking a fresh start, and there was a revival of interest perceptible. Then the animals assailed the ass for spoiling what could possibly have been a pleasure to them, on a mere suspicion that the picture was not beautiful, without any evidence that such was the case. The ass was not troubled; he was calm, and said there was one way to find out who was in the right, himself or the cat: he would go and look in that hole, and come back and tell what he found there. The animals felt relieved and grateful, and asked him to go at once—which he did.

But he did not know where he ought to stand; and so, through error, he stood between the picture and the mirror. The result was that the picture had no chance, and didn't show up. He returned home and said:

"The cat lied. There was nothing in that hole but an ass. There wasn't a sign of a flat thing visible. It was a handsome ass, and friendly, but just an ass, and nothing more."

The elephant asked:

"Did you see it good and clear? Were you close to it?"

"I saw it good and clear, O Hathi, King of Beasts. I was so close that I touched noses with it."

"This is very strange," said the elephant; "the cat was always truthful before—as far as we could make out. Let another witness try. Go, Baloo, look in the hole, and come and report."

So the bear went. When he came back, he said:

"Both the cat and the ass have lied; there was nothing in the hole but a bear."

Great was the surprise and puzzlement of the animals. Each was now anxious to make the test himself and get at the straight truth. The elephant sent them one at a time.

First, the cow. She found nothing in the hole but a cow.

The tiger found nothing in it but a tiger.

The lion found nothing in it but a lion.

The leopard found nothing in it but a leopard.

The camel found a camel, and nothing more.

Then Hathi was wroth, and said he would have the truth, if he had to go and fetch it himself. When he returned, he abused his whole subjectry for liars, and was in an unappeasable fury with the moral and mental blindness of the cat. He said that anybody but a near-sighted fool could see that there was nothing in the hole but an elephant.

## MORAL, BY THE CAT

You can find in a text whatever you bring, if you will stand between it and the mirror of your imagination. You may not see your ears, but they will be there.

*December 1909*

# Letters from the Earth

## I

The Creator sat upon the throne, thinking. Behind Him stretched the illimitable continent of heaven, steeped in a glory of light and color; before Him rose the black night of Space, like a wall. His mighty bulk towered rugged and mountain-like into the zenith, and His divine head blazed there like a distant sun. At His feet stood three colossal figures, diminished to extinction, almost, by contrast—archangels—their heads level with His ancle-bone.

When the Creator had finished thinking, He said,

"I have thought. Behold!"

He lifted His hand, and from it burst a fountain-spray of fire, a million stupendous suns, which clove the blackness and soared, away and away and away, diminishing in magnitude and intensity as they pierced the far frontiers of Space, until at last they were but as diamond nail-heads sparkling under the domed vast roof of the universe.

At the end of an hour the Grand Council was dismissed.

## II

They left the Presence impressed and thoughtful, and retired to a private place, where they might talk with freedom. None of the three seemed to want to begin, though all wanted somebody to do it. Each was burning to discuss the great event, but would prefer not to commit himself till he should know how the others regarded it. So there was some aimless and halting conversation about matters of no consequence, and this dragged tediously along, arriving nowhere, until at last the archangel Satan gathered his courage together—of which he had a very good supply—and broke ground. He said—

"We know what we are here to talk about, my lords, and we may as well put pretence aside, and begin. If this is the opinion of the Council—"

"It is, it is!" said Gabriel and Michael, gratefully interrupting.

"Very well, then, let us proceed. We have witnessed a wonderful thing; as to that, we are necessarily agreed. As to the value of it—if it has any—that is a matter which does not personally concern us. We can have as many opinions about it as we like, but that is our limit. We have no vote. I think Space was well enough, just as it was, and useful, too. Cold and dark—a restful place, now and then, after a season of the over-delicate climate and trying splendors of heaven. But these are details of no considerable moment; the new feature, the immense feature, is—what, gentlemen?"

"The invention and introduction of automatic, unsupervised, self-regulating *law* for the government of those myriads of whirling and racing suns and worlds!"

"That is it!" said Satan. "You perceive that it is a stupendous idea. Nothing approaching it has been evolved from the Master Intellect before. Law—*automatic* Law—exact and unvarying Law—requiring no watching, no correcting, no readjusting while the eternities endure! He said those countless vast bodies would plunge through the wastes of Space ages and ages, at unimaginable speed, around stupendous orbits, yet never collide, and never lengthen nor shorten their orbital periods by so much as the hundredth part of a second in two thousand years! That is the new miracle, and the greatest of all—*Automatic Law!* And He gave it a name—the LAW OF NATURE—and said Natural Law is the LAW OF GOD—interchangeable names for one and the same thing."

"Yes," said Michael, "and He said He would establish Natural Law—the Law of God—throughout His dominions, and its authority should be supreme and inviolable."

"Also," said Gabriel, "He said He would by and by create animals, and place them, likewise, under the authority of that Law."

"Yes," said Satan, "I heard Him, but did not understand. What *is* animals, Gabriel?"

"Ah, how should I know? How should any of us know? It is a new word."

[*Interval of three centuries, celestial time—the equivalent of a hundred million years, earthly time. Enter a messenger-Angel.*]

"My lords, He is making animals. Will it please you to come and see?"

They went, they saw, and were perplexed. Deeply perplexed—and the Creator noticed it, and said—

"Ask. I will answer."

"Divine One," said Satan, making obeisance, "what are they for?"

"They are an experiment in Morals and Conduct. Observe them, and be instructed."

There were thousands of them. They were full of activities. Busy, all busy—mainly in persecuting each other. Satan remarked—after examining one of them through a powerful microscope—

"This large beast is killing weaker animals, Divine One."

"The tiger—yes. The law of his nature is ferocity. The law of his nature is the law of God. He cannot disobey it."

"Then in obeying it he commits no offence, Divine One?"

"No, he is blameless."

"This other creature here, is timid, Divine One, and suffers death without resisting."

"The rabbit—yes. He is without courage. It is the law of his nature—the law of God. He must obey it."

"Then he cannot honorably be required to go counter to his nature and resist, Divine One?"

"No. No creature can be honorably required to go counter to the law of his nature—the law of God."

After a long time and many questions, Satan said—

"The spider kills the fly, and eats it; the bird kills the spider and eats it; the wildcat kills the goose; the—well, they all kill each other. It is murder all along the line. Here are countless multitudes of creatures, and they all kill, kill, kill, they are all murderers. And they are not to blame, Divine One?"

"They are not to blame. It is the law of their nature. And always the law of nature is the law of God. Now—observe—behold! A new creature—and the masterpiece—*Man!*"

Men, women, children, they came swarming in flocks, in droves, in millions.

"What shall you do with them, Divine One?"

"Put into each individual, in differing shades and degrees, all the various Moral Qualities, in mass, that have been distributed, a single distinguishing characteristic at a time, among the non-speaking animal world—courage, cowardice, ferocity, gentleness, fairness, justice, cunning, treachery, magnanimity, cruelty, malice, malignity, lust, mercy, pity, purity, selfishness, sweetness, honor, love, hate, baseness, nobility, loyalty, falsity, veracity, untruthfulness—each human being shall have *all* of these in him, and they will constitute his nature. In some, there will be high and fine characteristics which will submerge the evil ones, and those will be called good men; in others the evil characteristics will have dominion, and those will be called bad men. Observe—behold— they vanish!"

"Whither are they gone, Divine One?"

"To the earth—they and all their fellow-animals."

"What is the earth?"

"A small globe I made, a time, two times and half a time ago. You saw it, but did not notice it in the explosion of worlds and suns that sprayed from my hand. Man is an experiment, the other animals are another experiment. Time will show whether they were worth the trouble. The exhibition is over; you may take your leave, my lords."

### III

Several days passed by.

This stands for a long stretch of (our) time, since in heaven a day is as a thousand years.

Satan had been making admiring remarks about certain of the Creator's sparkling industries—remarks which, being read between the lines, were sarcasms. He had made them confidentially to his safe friends the other archangels, but they had been overheard by some ordinary angels and reported at Headquarters.

He was ordered into banishment for a day—the celestial day. It was a punishment he was used to, on account of his too flexible tongue. Formerly he had been deported into Space, there being nowhither else to send him, and had flapped tediously around, there, in the eternal night and the arctic chill; but now it occurred to him to push on and hunt up the Earth and see how the Human-Race experiment was coming along.

By and by he wrote home—very privately—to St. Michael and St. Gabriel about it.

## Satan's Letter.

This is a strange place, an extraordinary place, and interesting. There is nothing resembling it at home. The people are all insane, the other animals are all insane, the Earth is insane, Nature itself is insane. Man is a marvelous curiosity. When he is at his very very best he is a sort of low grade nickel-plated angel; at his worst he is unspeakable, unimaginable; and first and last and all the time he is a sarcasm. Yet he blandly and in all sincerity calls himself the "noblest work of God." This is the truth I am telling you. And this is not a new idea with him, he has talked it through all the ages, and believed it. Believed it, and found nobody among all his race to laugh at it.

Moreover—if I may put another strain upon you—he thinks he is the Creator's pet. He believes the Creator is proud of him; he even believes the Creator loves him; has a passion for him; sits up nights to admire him; yes, and watch over him and keep him out of trouble. He prays to Him, and thinks He listens. Isn't it a quaint idea? Fills his prayers with crude and bald and florid flatteries of Him, and thinks He sits and purrs over these extravagancies and enjoys them. He prays for help, and favor, and protection, every day; and does it with hopefulness and confidence, too, although no prayer of his has ever been answered. The daily affront, the daily defeat, do not discourage him, he goes on praying just the same. There is something almost fine about this perseverance. I must put one more strain upon you: he thinks he is going to heaven!

He has salaried teachers who tell him that. They also tell him there is a hell, of everlasting fire, and that he will go to it if he doesn't keep the Commandments. What are the Commandments? They are a curiosity. I will tell you about them by and by.

The salaried teacher tells them God is good. Good, and merciful, and kind, and just, and generous, and patient, and loving. To whom? His "children." And who are His children?

Why, these misbegotten creatures! They use that expression themselves. Speaking by and large, man is made up of ninety-

## Letters from the Earth

### Letter IV

I have told you nothing about man that is not true. You must pardon me if I repeat that remark now and then in these letters; I want you to take seriously the things I am telling you, and I feel that if I were in your place and you in mine, I should need that reminder from time to time, to keep my credulity from flagging.

For there is nothing about Man that is not strange to an Immortal. He looks at nothing as we look at it, his sense of proportion is quite different from ours, and his sense of values is so widely divergent from ours, that with all our large intellectual powers it is not likely that even the most gifted among us would ever be quite able to understand it.

For instance, take this sample: he has imagined a heaven, and has left entirely out of it the supremest of all his delights, the one ecstasy that stands first and foremost in the heart of every individual of his race—and of ours—sexual intercourse!

It is as if a lost and perishing person in a roasting desert should be told by a rescuer he might choose and have all longed-for things but one, and he should elect to leave out water!

His heaven is like himself: strange, interesting, astonishing, grotesque. I give you my word, it has not a single feature in it that he *actually values*. It consists—utterly and entirely—of diversions which he cares next to nothing about, here in the earth, yet is quite sure he will like in heaven. Isn't it curious? Isn't it interesting? You must not think I am exaggerating, for it is not so. I will give you details.

Most men do not sing, most men cannot sing, most men will not stay where others are singing if it be continued more than two hours. Note that.

Only about two men in a hundred can play upon a musical

instrument, and not four in a hundred have any wish to learn how. Set that down.

Many men pray, not many of them like to do it. A few pray long, the others make a short cut.

More men go to church than want to.

To forty-nine men in fifty the Sabbath Day is a dreary, dreary bore.

Of all the men in a church on a Sunday, two-thirds are tired when the service is half over, and the rest before it is finished.

The gladdest moment for all of them is when the preacher uplifts his hands for the benediction. You can hear the soft rustle of relief that sweeps the house, and you recognize that it is eloquent with gratitude.

All nations look down upon all other nations.

All nations dislike all other nations.

All white nations despise all colored nations, of whatever hue, and oppress them when they can.

White men will not associate with "niggers," nor marry them.

They will not allow them in their schools and churches.

All the world hates the Jew, and will not endure him except when he is rich.

I ask you to note all those particulars.

Further. All sane people detest noise.

All sane people, sane or insane, like to have variety in their life. Monotony quickly wearies them.

Every man, according to the mental equipment that has fallen to his share, exercises his intellect constantly, ceaselessly, and this exercise makes up a vast and valued and essential part of his life. The lowest intellect, like the highest, possesses a skill of some kind and takes a keen pleasure in testing it, proving it, perfecting it. The urchin who is his comrade's superior in games is as diligent and as enthusiastic in his practice as are the sculptor, the painter, the pianist, the mathematician and the rest. Not one of them could be happy if his talent were put under an interdict.

Now then, you have the facts. You know what the human race enjoys, and what it doesn't enjoy. It has invented a heaven, out of its own head, all by itself: guess what it is like!

In fifteen hundred eternities you couldn't do it. The ablest mind known to you or me in fifty million aeons couldn't do it. Very well, I will tell you about it.

## II

1. First of all, I recall to your attention the extraordinary fact with which I began. To-wit, that the human being, like the immortals, naturally places sexual intercourse far and away above all other joys—yet he has left it out of his heaven! The very thought of it excites him; opportunity sets him wild; in this state he will risk life, reputation, everything—even his queer heaven itself—to make good that opportunity and ride it to the overwhelming climax. From youth to middle age all men and all women prize copulation above all other pleasures combined, yet it is actually as I have said: it is not in their heaven, prayer takes its place.

They prize it thus highly; yet, like all their so-called "boons," it is a poor thing. At its very best and longest the act is brief beyond imagination—the imagination of an immortal, I mean. In the matter of repetition the man is limited—oh, quite beyond immortal conception. We who continue the act *and* its supremest ecstasies unbroken and without withdrawal for centuries, will never be able to understand or adequately pity the awful poverty of these people in that rich gift which, possessed as we possess it, makes all other possessions trivial and not worth the trouble of invoicing.

2. In man's heaven *everybody sings*! There are no exceptions. The man who did not sing on earth, sings there; the man who could not sing on earth is able to do it there. This universal singing is not casual, not occasional, not relieved by intervals of quiet, it goes on, all day long, and every day, during a stretch of twelve hours. And *everybody stays*; whereas in the earth the place would be empty in two hours. The singing is of hymns alone. Nay, it is of *one* hymn alone. The words are always the same, in number they are only about a dozen, there is no rhyme, there is no poetry: "Hosannah, hosannah, hosannah, Lord God of Sabaoth, 'rah! 'rah! 'rah!—ssht!—boom! . . . . . a-a-ah!"

3. Meantime, *every person* is playing on a harp—those mil-

lions and millions! whereas not more than twenty in the thousand of them could play an instrument in the earth, or ever *wanted* to.

Consider the deafening hurricane of sound—millions and millions of voices screaming at once, and millions and millions of harps gritting their teeth at the same time! I ask you—is it hideous, is it odious, is it horrible?

Consider further: it is a *praise* service; a service of compliment, of flattery, of adulation! Do you ask who it is that is willing to endure this strange compliment, this insane compliment; and who not only endures it but likes it, enjoys it, requires it, *commands* it? Hold your breath!

It is God! This race's God, I mean. He sits on his throne, attended by his four and twenty elders and some other dignitaries pertaining to his court, and looks out over his miles and miles of tempestuous worshippers, and smiles, and purrs, and nods his satisfaction northward, eastward, southward; as quaint and naif a spectacle as has yet been imagined in this universe, I take it.

It is easy to see that the inventor of the heaven did not originate the idea, but copied it from the show-ceremonies of some sorry little sovereign State up in the back settlements of the Orient somewhere.

All sane white people *hate noise*; yet they have tranquilly accepted this kind of a heaven—without thinking, without reflection, without examination—and they actually want to go to it! Profoundly devout old gray-headed men put in a large part of their time dreaming of the happy day when they will lay down the cares of this life and enter into the joys of that place. Yet you can see how unreal it is to them, and how little it takes a grip upon them as being *fact*, for they make no practical preparation for the great change: you never see one of them with a harp, you never hear one of them sing.

As you have seen, that singular show is a service of divine worship—a service of praise: praise by hymn, praise by instrumental ecstasies, praise by prostration. It takes the place of "church." Now then, in the earth these people cannot stand much church—an hour and a quarter is the limit, and they draw the line at once a week. That is to say, Sunday. One day in seven; and even then they do not look forward to it with longing. And so—consider what their heaven provides for them: "church" that lasts forever, and a *Sabbath that has no end*! They quickly weary of this brief hebdomadal Sabbath here, yet they long for that eternal one; they dream of it, they talk about it, they *think* they think they are going to enjoy it—with all their simple hearts they think they think they are going to be happy in it!

It is because they do not think *at all*; they only think they think. Whereas they can't think; not two human beings in ten thousand have anything to think with. And as to imagination—oh, well, look at their heaven! They accept it, they approve it, they admire it. That gives you their intellectual measure.

4. The inventor of their heaven empties into it all the nations of the earth, in one common jumble. All are on an equality absolute, no one of them ranking another; they have to be "brothers;" they have to mix together, pray together, harp together, hosannah together—whites, niggers, Jews, everybody—there's no distinction. Here in the earth all nations hate each other, every one of them hates the Jew. Yet every pious person adores that heaven and wants to get into it. He really does. And when he is in a holy rapture he thinks he thinks that if he were only there he would take all the populace to his heart, and hug, and hug, and hug!

He is a marvel—man is! I would I knew who invented him.

5. Every man in the earth possesses some share of intellect, large or small; and be it large or be it small he takes a pride in it. Also his heart swells at mention of the names of the majestic intellectual chiefs of his race, and he loves the tale of their splendid achievements. For he is of their blood, and in honoring themselves they have honored him. Lo, what the mind of man can do! he cries; and calls the roll of the illustrious of all the ages; and points to the imperishable literatures they have given to the world, and the mechanical wonders they have invented, and the glories wherewith they have clothed science and the arts; and to them he uncovers, as to kings, and gives to them the profoundest homage and the sincerest his exultant heart can furnish—thus exalting intellect above

all things else in his world, and enthroning it there under the arching skies in a supremacy unapproachable. And then he contrives a heaven that hasn't a rag of intellectuality in it anywhere!

Is it odd, is it curious, is it puzzling? It is exactly as I have said, incredible as it may sound. This sincere adorer of intellect and prodigal rewarder of its mighty services here in the earth has invented a religion and a heaven which pay no compliments to intellect, offer it no distinctions, fling to it no largess: in fact, never even mention it.

By this time you will have noticed that the human being's heaven has been thought out and constructed upon an absolutely definite plan; and that this plan is, that it shall contain, in labored detail, each and every imaginable thing that is repulsive to a man, and not a single thing he likes!

Very well, the further we proceed the more will this curious fact be apparent.

Make a note of it: in man's heaven there are no exercises for the intellect, nothing for it to live upon. It would rot there in a year—rot and stink. Rot and stink—and at that stage become holy. A blessed thing; for only the holy can stand the joys of that bedlam.


## Letter V

You have noticed that the human being is a curiosity. In times past he has had (and worn out and flung away) hundreds and hundreds of religions; to-day he has hundreds and hundreds of religions, and launches not fewer than three new ones every year. I could enlarge that number and still be within the facts.

One of his principal religions is called the Christian. A sketch of it will interest you. It is set forth in detail in a book containing 2,000,000 words, called the Old and New Testaments. Also it has another name—The Word of God. For the Christian thinks every word of it was dictated by God—the one I have been speaking of.

It is full of interest. It has noble poetry in it; and some clever fables; and some blood-drenched history; and some good morals; and some execrable morals; and a wealth of obscenity; and upwards of a thousand lies.

This Bible is built mainly out of the fragments of older Bibles that had their day and crumbled to ruin. So it noticeably lacks in originality, necessarily. Its three or four most imposing and impressive events all happened in earlier Bibles; all its best precepts and rules of conduct come also from those Bibles; there are only two new things in it: hell, for one, and that singular heaven I have told you about.

What shall we do? If we believe, with these people, that their God invented these cruel things, we slander him; if we believe that these people invented them themselves, we slander *them*. It is an unpleasant dilemma in either case, for neither of these parties has done *us* any harm.

For the sake of tranquillity, let us take a side. Let us join forces with the people and put the whole ungracious burden upon *him*—heaven, hell, Bible and all. It does not seem right, it does not seem fair; and yet when you consider that heaven, and how crushingly charged it is with everything that is repulsive to a human being, how *can* we believe a human being invented it? And when I come to tell you about hell, the strain will be greater still, and you will be likely to say *No*, a man would not provide *that* place, for either himself or anybody else; he simply *couldn't*.

That innocent Bible tells about the Creation. Of what—the universe? Yes, the universe. In *six days*!

God did it. He did not call it the universe—that name is modern. His whole attention was upon *this world*. He constructed it in five days—and then? It took him only *one* day to make *twenty million suns and eighty million planets*!

What were they for—according to his idea? To furnish light for this little toy-world. That was his whole purpose; he had no other. *One* of the 20,000,000 suns (the smallest one), was to light it in the day-time, the rest were to help *one* of the universe's countless moons modify the darkness of its nights.

It is quite manifest that he believed his fresh-made skies were diamond-sown with those myriads of twinkling stars the moment his first-day's sun sank below the horizon; whereas, in fact not a single star winked in that black vault until three years and a half after that memorable week's formidable industries had been completed.* Then one star appeared, all solitary and alone, and began to blink. Three years later another one appeared. The two blinked together for more than four years before a third joined them. At the end of the first hundred years there were not yet twenty-five stars twinkling in the wide wastes of those gloomy skies. At the end of a thousand years not enough stars were yet visible to make a show. At the end of a million years only half of the present array had sent their light over the telescopic frontiers, and it took another million for the rest to follow suit, as the vulgar phrase goes. There being at that time no telescope, their advent was not observed.

For three hundred years, now, the Christian astronomer has known that his Deity *didn't* make the stars in those tremendous six days; but the Christian astronomer does not enlarge upon that detail. Neither does the priest.

In his Book, God is eloquent in his praises of his mighty works, and calls them by the largest names he can find—thus indicating that he has a strong and just admiration of magnitudes; yet he made those millions of prodigious suns to light this wee little orb, instead of appointing this orb's little sun to dance attendance upon *them*. He mentions Arcturus in his Book—you remember Arcturus; we went there once. *It* is one of this earth's night-lamps!—that giant globe which is 50,000 times as large as this earth's sun, and compares with it as a melon compares with a cathedral.

However, the Sunday school still teaches the child that Arcturus was created to help light this earth, and the child grows up and continues to believe it long after he has found out that the probabilities are against its being so.

According to the Book and its servants the universe is only six thousand years old. It is only within the last hundred years

*It takes the light of the nearest star (61 Cygni) three and a half years to come to the earth, traveling at the rate of 186,000 miles per second. Arcturus had been shining 200 years before it was visible from the earth. Remoter stars gradually became visible after thousands and thousands of years.—[*Editor*.

that studious, inquiring minds have found out that it is nearer a hundred million.

During the Six Days, God created man and the other animals.

He made a man and a woman and placed them in a pleasant garden, along with the other creatures. They all lived together there in harmony and contentment and blooming youth for some time; then trouble came. God had warned the man and the woman that they must not eat of the fruit of a certain tree. And he added a most strange remark: he said that if they ate of it they should surely *die*. Strange, for the reason that inasmuch as they had never seen a sample of death they could not possibly know what he meant. Neither would he nor any other god have been able to make those ignorant children understand what was meant, without furnishing a sample. The mere *word* could have no meaning for them, any more than it would have for an infant of days.

Presently a serpent sought them out privately, and came to them walking upright, which was the way of serpents in those days. The serpent said the forbidden fruit would store their vacant minds with knowledge. So they ate it, which was quite natural, for man is so made that he eagerly *wants to know*; whereas the priest, like God, whose imitator and representative he is, has made it his business from the beginning to keep him *from* knowing any useful thing.

Adam and Eve ate the forbidden fruit, and at once a great light streamed into their dim heads. They had acquired knowledge. What knowledge—useful knowledge? No—merely knowledge that there was such a thing as good, and such a thing as evil, and how to *do* evil. They *couldn't* do it before, therefore all their acts up to this time had been without stain, without blame, without offence.

But *now* they could do evil—and suffer for it; *now* they had acquired what the Church calls an invaluable possession, the Moral Sense; that sense which differentiates man from the beast and sets him *above* the beast. Instead of *below* the beast—where one would suppose his proper place would be, since he is always foul-minded and guilty and the beast always clean-minded and innocent. It is like valuing a watch that *must* go wrong, above a watch that *can't*.

The Church still prizes the Moral Sense as man's noblest asset to-day, although the Church knows God had a distinctly poor opinion of it and did what he could in his clumsy way to keep his happy Children of the Garden from acquiring it.

Very well, Adam and Eve now knew what evil was, and how to do it. They knew how to do various kinds of wrong things, and among them one principal one—the one God had his mind on principally. That one was, the art and mystery of sexual intercourse. To them it was a magnificent discovery, and they stopped idling around and turned their entire attention to it, poor exultant young things!

In the midst of one of these celebrations they heard God walking among the bushes, which was an afternoon custom of his, and they were smitten with fright. Why? Because they were naked. They had not known it before. They had not minded it before, neither had God.

In that memorable moment *immodesty* was born; and some people have valued it ever since, though it would certainly puzzle them to explain why.

Adam and Eve entered the world naked and unashamed—naked and pure-minded; and no descendant of theirs has ever entered it otherwise. All have entered it naked, unashamed, and clean in mind. They have entered it *modest*. They had to *acquire* immodesty and the soiled mind, there was no other way to get it. A Christian mother's first duty is to soil her child's mind, and she does not neglect it. Her lad grows up to be a missionary, and goes to the innocent savage and to the civilized Japanese, and soils their minds. Whereupon they adopt immodesty, they conceal their bodies, they stop bathing naked together.

The convention miscalled Modesty has no standard, and cannot have one, because it is opposed to nature and reason, and is therefore an artificiality and subject to anybody's whim, anybody's diseased caprice. And so, in India the refined lady covers her face and breasts and leaves her legs naked from the hips down, while the refined European lady covers her legs and exposes her face and her breasts. In lands inhabited by the innocent savage the refined European lady soon gets used to full-grown native stark-nakedness, and ceases to be offended by it. A highly cultivated French count and countess—unrelated to each other—who were marooned in their night clothes, by shipwreck, upon an uninhabited island in the eighteenth century, were soon naked. Also ashamed—for a week. After that their nakedness did not trouble them, and they soon ceased to think about it.

You have never seen a person with clothes on. Oh, well, you haven't lost anything.

To proceed with the Biblical curiosities. Naturally you will think the threat to punish Adam and Eve for disobeying was of course not carried out, since they did not create themselves, nor their natures nor their impulses nor their weaknesses, and hence were not properly subject to any one's commands, and not responsible to anybody for their acts. It will surprise you to know that the threat *was* carried out. Adam and Eve were punished, and that crime finds apologists unto this day. *The sentence of death was executed.*

As you perceive, the only person responsible for the couple's offence escaped; and not only escaped but became the executioner of the innocent.

In your country and mine we should have the privilege of making fun of this kind of morality, but it would be unkind to do it here. Many of these people have the reasoning faculty, but no one uses it in religious matters.

The best minds will tell you that when a man has begotten a child he is morally bound to tenderly care for it, protect it from hurt, shield it from disease, clothe it, feed it, bear with its waywardness, lay no hand upon it save in kindness and for its own good, and never in any case inflict upon it a wanton cruelty. God's treatment of his earthly children, every day and every night, is the exact opposite of all that, yet those best minds warmly justify these crimes, condone them, excuse them, and indignantly refuse to regard them as crimes at all, when *he* commits them. Your country and mine is an interesting one, but there is nothing there that is half so interesting as the human mind.

Very well, God banished Adam and Eve from the Garden, and eventually assassinated them. All for disobeying a command which he had no right to utter. But he did not stop there, as you will see. He has one code of morals for himself, and quite another for his children. He requires his children to deal justly—and gently—with offenders, and forgive them seventy-and-seven times; whereas he deals neither justly nor gently with any one, and he did not forgive the ignorant and thoughtless first pair of juveniles even their first small offence and say "You may go free this time, I will give you another chance."

On the contrary! He elected to punish *their* children, all through the ages to the end of time, for a trifling offence committed by others before they were born. He is punishing them yet. In mild ways? No, in atrocious ones.

You would not suppose that this kind of a Being gets many compliments. Undeceive yourself: the world calls him the All-Just, the All-Righteous, the All-Good, the All-Merciful, the All-Forgiving, the All-Truthful, the All-Loving, the Source of All Morality. These sarcasms are uttered daily, all over the world. But not as conscious sarcasms. No, they are meant seriously; they are uttered without a smile.

### Letter . . .

So the First Pair went forth from the Garden under a curse—a permanent one. They had lost every pleasure they had possessed before "The Fall;" and yet they were rich, for they had gained one worth all the rest: they knew the Supreme Art.

They practised it diligently, and were filled with contentment. The Deity *ordered* them to practise it. They obeyed, this time. But it was just as well it was not forbidden, for they would have practised it anyhow, if a thousand Deities had forbidden it.

Results followed. By the name of Cain and Abel. And these had some sisters; and knew what to do with them. And so there were some more results: Cain and Abel begot some nephews and nieces. These, in their turn, begot some second-cousins. At this point classification of relationships began to get difficult, and the attempt to keep it up was abandoned.

The pleasant labor of populating the world went on from age to age, and with prime efficiency; for in those happy days the sexes were still competent for the Supreme Art when by rights they ought to have been dead eight hundred years. The sweeter sex, the dearer sex, the lovelier sex was manifestly at its very best, then, for it was even able to attract gods. Real gods. They came down out of heaven and had wonderful times with those hot young blossoms. The Bible tells about it.

By help of those visiting foreigners the population grew and grew until it numbered several millions. But it was a disappointment to the Deity. He was dissatisfied with its morals; which in some respects were not any better than his own. Indeed they were an unflatteringly close imitation of his own. They were a very bad people, and as he knew of no way to reform them, he wisely concluded to abolish them. This is the only really enlightened and superior idea his Bible has credited him with, and it would have made his reputation for all time if he could only have kept to it and carried it out. But he was always unstable—except in his advertisements—and his good resolution broke down. He took a pride in man; man was his finest invention; man was his pet, after the housefly, and he could not bear to lose him wholly; so he finally decided to save a sample of him and drown the rest.

Nothing could be more characteristic of him. He created all those infamous people, and he alone was responsible for their conduct. Not one of them deserved death, yet it was certainly good policy to extinguish them; especially since in creating them the master crime had already been committed, and to allow them to go on procreating would be a distinct *addition* to the crime. But at the same time there could be no justice, no fairness, in any favoritism—*all* should be drowned or none.

No, he would not have it so; he would save half a dozen and try the race over again. He was not able to foresee that it would go rotten again, for he is only the Far-Sighted One in his advertisements.

He saved out Noah and his family, and arranged to exterminate the rest. He planned an Ark, and Noah built it. Neither of them had ever built an Ark before, nor knew anything about Arks; and so something out of the common was to be expected. It happened. Noah was a farmer, and although he knew what was required of the Ark he was quite incompetent

to say whether this one would be large enough to meet the
requirements or not (which it wasn't), so he ventured no advice. The Deity did not know it wasn't large enough, but
took the chances and made no adequate measurements. In the
end the ship fell far short of the necessities, and to this day
the world still suffers for it.

Noah built the Ark. He built it the best he could, but left
out most of the essentials. It had no rudder, it had no sails, it
had no compass, it had no pumps, it had no charts, no lead-
lines, no anchors, no log, no light, no ventilation; and as for
cargo-room—which was the main thing—the less said about
that the better. It was to be at sea eleven months, and would
need fresh water enough to fill two Arks of its size—yet the
additional Ark was not provided. Water from outside could
not be utilized: half of it would be salt water, and men and
land-animals could not drink it.

For not only was a sample of man to be saved, but
business-samples of the other animals, too. You must understand that when Adam ate the apple in the Garden and
learned how to multiply and replenish, the other animals
learned the Art, too, by watching Adam. It was cunning of
them, it was neat; for they got all that was worth having out
of the apple without tasting it and afflicting themselves with
the disastrous Moral Sense, the parent of all the immoralities.

### Letter . . .

Noah began to collect animals. There was to be one couple
of each and every sort of creature that walked or crawled, or
swam or flew, in the world of animated nature. We have to
guess at how long it took to collect the creatures and how
much it cost, for there is no record of these details. When
Symmachus made preparation to introduce his young son to
grown-up life in imperial Rome, he sent men to Asia, Africa
and everywhere to collect wild animals for the arena-fights. It
took the men three years to accumulate the animals and fetch
them to Rome. Merely quadrupeds and alligators, you understand—no birds, no snakes, no frogs, no worms, no lice, no
rats, no fleas, no ticks, no caterpillars, no spiders, no house-
flies, no mosquitoes,—nothing but just plain simple quadrupeds and alligators; and no quadrupeds except fighting ones.

Yet it was as I have said: it took three years to collect them, and the cost of animals and transportation and the men's wages footed up $4,500,000.

How many animals? We do not know. But it was under 5,000, for that was the largest number *ever* gathered for those Roman shows, and it was Titus, not Symmachus, who made that collection. Those were mere baby-museums, compared to Noah's contract. Of birds and beasts and fresh-water creatures he had to collect 146,000 kinds; and of insects upwards of 2,000,000 species.

Thousands and thousands of those things are very difficult to catch, and if Noah had not given up and resigned, he would be on the job yet, as Leviticus used to say. However, I do not mean that he withdrew. No, he did not do that. He gathered as many creatures as he had room for, and then stopped.

If he had known all the requirements in the beginning, he would have been aware that what was needed was a fleet of Arks. But he did not know how many kinds of creatures there were, neither did his Chief. So he had no kangaroo, and no 'possum, and no Gila Monster, and no ornithorhynchus, and lacked a multitude of other indispensable blessings which a loving Creator had provided for man and forgotten about, they having long ago wandered to a side of his world which he had never seen and with whose affairs he was not acquainted. And so every one of them came within a hair of getting drowned.

They only escaped by an accident: there was not water enough to go around. Only enough was provided to flood one small corner of the globe—the rest of the globe was not then known, and was supposed to be non-existent.

However, the thing that really and finally and definitely determined Noah to stop with enough species for purely business purposes and let the rest become extinct, was an incident of the last days: an excited stranger arrived with some most alarming news. He said he had been camping among some mountains and valleys about six hundred miles away, and he had seen a wonderful thing there: he stood upon a precipice overlooking a wide valley, and up the valley he saw a billowy black sea of strange animal life coming. Presently the creatures

passed by, struggling, fighting, scrambling, screeching, snort-
ing—horrible vast masses of tumultuous flesh! Sloths as big
as an elephant; frogs as big as a cow; a megatherium and his
harem, huge beyond belief; saurians and saurians and saurians, group after group, family after family, species after
species—a hundred feet long, thirty feet high, and twice as
quarrelsome; one of them hit a perfectly blameless Durham
bull a thump with its tail and sent it whizzing three hundred
feet into the air and it fell at the man's feet with a sigh and
was no more. The man said that these prodigious animals had
heard about the Ark and were coming. Coming to get saved
from the flood. And not coming in pairs, they were *all* coming: they did not know the passengers were restricted to
pairs, the man said, and wouldn't care a rap for the regula-
tions, anyway—they would sail in that Ark or know the reason why. The man said the Ark would not hold the half of
them; and moreover they were coming hungry, and would
eat up everything there was, including the menagerie and the
family.

All these facts were suppressed, in the Biblical account. You
find not a hint of them there. The whole thing is hushed up.
Not even the names of those vast creatures are mentioned. It
shows you that when people have left a reproachful vacancy
in a contract they can be as shady about it in Bibles as elsewhere. Those powerful animals would be of inestimable value
to man now, when transportation is so hard pressed and expensive, but they are all lost to him. All lost, and by Noah's
fault. They all got drowned. Some of them as much as eight
million years ago.

Very well, the stranger told his tale, and Noah saw that he
must get away before the monsters arrived. He would have
sailed at once, but the upholsterers and decorators of the
housefly's drawing room still had some finishing touches to
put on, and that lost him a day. Another day was lost in getting the flies aboard, there being sixty-eight billions of them
and the Deity still afraid there might not be enough. Another
day was lost in stowing 40 tons of selected filth for the fly's
sustenance.

Then at last, Noah sailed; and none too soon, for the Ark

was only just sinking out of sight on the horizon when the monsters arrived, and added their lamentations to those of the multitude of weeping fathers and mothers and frightened little children who were clinging to the wave-washed rocks in the pouring rain and lifting imploring prayers to an All-Just and All-Forgiving and All-Pitying Being who had never answered a prayer since those crags were builded, grain by grain out of the sands, and would still not have answered one when the ages should have crumbled them to sand again.

## Letter VII

On the third day, about noon, it was found that a fly had been left behind. The return-voyage turned out to be long and difficult, on account of the lack of chart and compass, and because of the changed aspects of all coasts, the steadily rising water having submerged some of the lower landmarks and given to higher ones an unfamiliar look; but after sixteen days of earnest and faithful seeking, the fly was found at last, and received on board with hymns of praise and gratitude, the Family standing meanwhile uncovered, out of reverence for its divine origin. It was weary and worn, and had suffered somewhat from the weather, but was otherwise in good estate. Men and their families had died of hunger on barren mountain tops, but It had not lacked for food, the multitudinous corpses furnishing it in rank and rotten richness. Thus was the sacred bird providentially preserved.

Providentially. That is the word. For the fly had not been left behind by accident. No, the hand of Providence was in it. There are no accidents. All things that happen, happen for a purpose. They are foreseen from the beginning of time, they are ordained from the beginning of time. From the dawn of Creation the Lord had foreseen that Noah, being alarmed and confused by the invasion of the prodigious brevet Fossils, would prematurely fly to sea unprovided with a certain invaluable disease. He would have all the other diseases, and could distribute them among the new races of men as they appeared in the world, but he would lack one of the very best—typhoid fever; a malady which, when the circumstances are especially favorable, is able to utterly wreck a patient without killing him; for it can restore him to his feet with a long life in him, and yet deaf, dumb, blind, crippled and idiotic. The housefly is its main disseminator, and is more competent and more calamitously effective than all the other distributors of the dreaded scourge put together. And so, by foreordination from the beginning of time, this fly was left behind to seek out a typhoid corpse and feed upon its corruptions and gaum its legs with the germs and transmit them to the repeopled world for permanent business. From that one housefly, in the ages that have since elapsed, billions of sickbeds have been stocked, billions of wrecked bodies sent tottering about the earth, and billions of cemeteries recruited with the dead.

It is most difficult to understand the disposition of the Bible God, it is such a confusion of contradictions; of watery instabilities and iron firmnesses; of goody-goody abstract morals made out of words, and concreted hell-born ones made out of *acts*; of fleeting kindnesses repented of in permanent malignities.

However, when after much puzzling you get at the key to his disposition, you do at last arrive at a sort of understanding of it. With a most quaint and juvenile and astonishing frankness he has furnished that key himself. It is *jealousy*!

I expect that to take your breath away. You are aware—for I have already told you in an earlier letter—that among human beings jealousy ranks distinctly as a *weakness*; a trademark of small minds; a property of *all* small minds, yet a property which even the smallest is ashamed of; and when accused of its possession will lyingly deny it and resent the accusation as an insult.

Jealousy. Do not forget it, keep it in mind. It is the key. With it you will come to partly understand God as we go along; without it nobody can understand him. As I have said, he has openly held up this treasonous key himself, for all to see. He says, naïvely, outspokenly, and without suggestion of embarrassment,

"I the Lord thy God am a jealous God."

You see, it is only another way of saying,

"I the Lord thy God am a small God; a small God, and fretful about small things."

He was giving a warning: he could not bear the thought of any other God getting some of the Sunday compliments of this comical little human race—he wanted all of them for himself. He valued them. To him they were riches; just as tin money is to a Zulu.

But wait—I am not fair; I am misrepresenting him; prejudice is beguiling me into saying what is not true. He did not say he wanted all of the adulations; he said nothing about not being willing to share them with his fellow-gods; what he said was,

"Thou shalt have no other gods *before* me."

It is a quite different thing, and puts him in a much better light—I confess it. There was an abundance of gods, the woods were full of them, as the saying is, and all he demanded was, that he should be ranked as high as the others—not above any of them, but not below any of them. He was willing that they should fertilize earthly virgins, but not on any better terms than he could have for himself in his turn. He wanted to be held their equal. This he insisted upon, in the clearest language: he would have no other gods *before* him. They could march abreast with him, but none of them could head the procession, and he did not claim the right to head it himself.

Do you think he was able to stick to that upright and creditable position? No. He could keep to a bad resolution forever, but he couldn't keep to a good one a month. By and by he threw this one aside and calmly claimed to be the only God in the entire universe.

As I was saying, jealousy is the key; all through his history it is present and prominent. It is the blood and bone of his disposition, it is the basis of his character. How small a thing can wreck his composure and disorder his judgment if it touches the raw of his jealousy! And nothing warms up this trait so quickly and so surely and so exaggeratedly as a suspicion that some competition with the god-Trust is impending. The fear that if Adam and Eve ate of the fruit of the Tree of Knowledge they would "be as gods," so fired his jealousy that his reason was affected, and he could not treat those poor creatures either fairly or charitably, or even refrain from dealing cruelly and criminally with their blameless posterity.

To this day his reason has never recovered from that shock; a wild nightmare of vengefulness has possessed him ever since, and he has almost bankrupted his native ingenuities in inventing pains and miseries and humiliations and heartbreaks wherewith to embitter the brief lives of Adam's descendants. Think of the diseases he has contrived for them! They are multitudinous; no book can name them all. And each one is a trap, set for an innocent victim.

The human being is a machine. An automatic machine. It is composed of thousands of complex and delicate mechanisms, which perform their functions harmoniously and perfectly, in accordance with laws devised for their governance, and over which the man himself has no authority, no mastership, no control. For each one of these thousands of mechanisms the Creator has planned an enemy, whose office is to harass it, pester it, persecute it, damage it, afflict it with pains, and miseries, and ultimate destruction. Not one has been overlooked.

From cradle to grave these enemies are always at work, they know no rest, night nor day. They are an army; an organized army; a besieging army; an assaulting army; an army that is alert, watchful, eager, merciless; an army that never wearies, never relents, never grants a truce.

It moves by squad, by company, by battalion, by regiment, by brigade, by division, by army corps; upon occasion it masses its parts and moves upon mankind with its whole strength. It is the Creator's Grand Army, and he is the Commander in Chief. Along its battlefront its grisly banners wave their legends in the face of the sun: Disaster, Disease, and the rest.

Disease! that is the main force, the diligent force, the devastating force! It attacks the infant the moment it is born; it furnishes it one malady after another: croup, measles, mumps, bowel-troubles, teething-pains, scarlet fever, and other childhood specialties. It chases the child into youth and furnishes it some specialties for that time of life. It chases the youth into maturity; maturity into age, and age into the grave.

With these facts before you will you now try to guess man's chiefest pet name for this ferocious Commander in Chief? I will save you the trouble—but you must not laugh. It is Our Father in Heaven!

It is curious—the way the human mind works. The Christian begins with this straight proposition, this definite proposition, this inflexible and uncompromising proposition: *God is all-knowing, and all-powerful.*

This being the case, nothing can happen without his knowing beforehand that it is going to happen; nothing happens without his permission; nothing can happen that he chooses to prevent.

That is definite enough, isn't it? It makes the Creator distinctly responsible for everything that happens, doesn't it?

The Christian concedes it in that italicised sentence. Concedes it with feeling, with enthusiasm.

Then, having thus made the Creator responsible for all those pains and diseases and miseries above enumerated, and which he could have prevented, the gifted Christian blandly calls him Our Father!

It is as I tell you. He equips the Creator with every trait that goes to the making of a fiend, and then arrives at the conclusion that a fiend and a father are the same thing! Yet he would deny that a malevolent lunatic and a Sunday school superintendent are essentially the same. What do you think of the human mind? I mean, in case you think there is a human mind.

Letter . . .

Noah and his family were saved—if that could be called an advantage. I throw in the *if* for the reason that there has never been an intelligent person of the age of sixty who would consent to live his life over again. His or any one else's. The family were saved, yes, but they were not comfortable, for they were full of microbes. Full to the eyebrows; fat with them, obese with them; distended like balloons. It was a disagreeable condition, but it could not be helped, because enough microbes had to be saved to supply the future races of men with desolating diseases, and there were but eight persons on board to serve as hotels for them. The microbes were by far the most important part of the Ark's cargo, and the part the Creator was most anxious about and most infatuated with. They had to have good nourishment and pleasant accommodations. There were typhoid germs, and cholera germs, and hydrophobia germs, and lockjaw germs, and consumption germs, and black-plague germs, and some hundreds of other aristocrats, specially precious creations, golden bearers of God's love to man, blessed gifts of the infatuated Father to his children—all of which had to be sumptuously housed and richly entertained; these were located in the choicest places the interiors of the family could furnish: in the lungs, in the heart, in the brain, in the kidneys, in the blood, in the guts. In the guts particularly. The great intestine was the favorite resort. There they gathered, by countless billions, and worked, and fed, and squirmed, and sang hymns of praise and thanksgiving; and at night when it was quiet you could hear the soft murmur of it. The large intestine was in effect their heaven. They stuffed it solid; they made it as rigid as a coil of gaspipe. They took a pride in this. Their principal hymn made gratified reference to it:

> "Constipation, O constipation,
>   The joyful sound proclaim
>  Till man's remotest entrail
>    Shall praise its makers' name."

The discomforts furnished by the Ark were many, and various. The family had to live right in the presence of the multitudinous animals, and breathe the distressing stench they made and be deafened day and night with the thunder-crash of noise their roarings and screechings produced; and in addition to these intolerable discomforts it was a peculiarly trying place for the ladies, for they could look in no direction without seeing some thousands of the creatures engaged in multiplying and replenishing. And then, there were the flies. They swarmed everywhere, and persecuted the family all day long. They were the first animals up, in the morning, and the last ones down, at night. But they must not be killed, they must not be injured, they were sacred, their origin was divine, they were the special pets of the Creator, his darlings.

By and by the other creatures would be distributed here and there about the earth—*scattered*: the tigers to India, the lion and the elephant to the vacant desert and the secret places of the jungle, the birds to the boundless regions of empty space, the insects to one or another climate, according to nature and requirement; but the fly? He is of no nationality; all the climates are his home, all the globe is his province, all creatures that breathe are his prey, and unto them all he is a scourge and a hell.

To man he is a divine ambassador, a minister plenipotentiary, the Creator's special representative. He infests him in his cradle; clings in bunches to his gummy eyelids; buzzes and bites and harries him, robbing him of his sleep and his weary mother of her strength in those long vigils which she devotes to protecting her child from this pest's persecutions. The fly harries the sick man in his home, in the hospital, even on his death-bed at his last gasp. Pesters him at his meals; previously hunts up patients suffering from loathsome and deadly diseases; wades in their sores, gaums its legs with a million death-dealing germs, then comes to that healthy man's table and wipes these things off on the butter and discharges a bowel-load of typhoid germs and excrement on his batter-cakes. The housefly wrecks more human constitutions and destroys more human lives than all God's multitude of misery-messengers and death-agents put together.

Shem was full of hookworms. It is wonderful, the thorough and comprehensive study which the Creator devoted to the great work of making man miserable. I have said he devised a special affliction-agent for each and every detail of man's structure, overlooking not a single one, and I said the truth. Many poor people have to go barefoot, because they cannot afford shoes. The Creator saw his opportunity. I will remark, in passing, that he always has his eye on the poor. Nine-tenths of his disease-inventions were intended for the poor, and they *get* them. The well-to-do get only what is left over. Do not suspect me of speaking unheedfully, for it is not so: the vast bulk of the Creator's affliction-inventions *are* specially designed for the persecution of the poor. You could guess this by the fact that one of the pulpit's finest and commonest names for the Creator is "The Friend of the Poor." Under no circumstances does the pulpit ever pay the Creator a compliment that has a vestige of truth in it. The poor's most implacable and unwearying enemy is their Father in Heaven. The poor's only real friend is their fellow man. He is sorry for them, he pities them, and he shows it by his deeds. He does much to relieve their distresses; and in every case their Father in Heaven gets the credit of it.

Just so with diseases. If science exterminates a disease which has been working for God, it is God that gets the credit, and all the pulpits break into grateful advertising-raptures and call attention to how good he is! Yes, *he* has done it. Perhaps he has waited a thousand years before doing it. That is nothing; the pulpit says he was thinking about it all the time. When exasperated men rise up and sweep away an age-long tyranny and set a nation free, the first thing the delighted pulpit does is to advertise it as God's work, and invite the people to get down on their knees and pour out their thanks to him for it. And the pulpit says with admiring emotion, "Let tyrants understand that the Eye that never sleeps is upon them; and let them remember that the Lord our God will not always be patient, but will loose the whirlwinds of his wrath upon them in his appointed day."

They forget to mention that he is the slowest mover in the universe; that his Eye that never sleeps, might as well, since it takes it a century to see what any other eye would see in a week; that in all history there is not an instance where he thought of a noble deed *first*, but always thought of it just a little after somebody else had thought of it and *done* it. He arrives then, and annexes the dividend.

Very well, six thousand years ago Shem was full of hookworms. Microscopic in size, invisible to the unaided eye. All of the Creator's specially-deadly disease-producers are invisible. It is an ingenious idea. For thousands of years it kept man from getting at the roots of his maladies, and defeated his attempts to master them. It is only very recently that science has succeeded in exposing some of these treacheries.

The very latest of these blessed triumphs of science is the discovery and identification of the ambuscaded assassin which goes by the name of the hookworm. Its special prey is the barefooted poor. It lies in wait in warm regions and sandy places and digs its way into their unprotected feet.

The hookworm was discovered two or three years ago by a physician, who had been patiently studying its victims for a long time. The disease induced by the hookworm had been doing its evil work here and there in the earth ever since

Shem landed on Ararat, but it was never suspected to *be* a disease at all. The people who had it were merely supposed to be *lazy*, and were therefore despised and made fun of, when they should have been pitied. The hookworm is a peculiarly sneaking and underhand invention, and has done its surreptitious work unmolested for ages; but that physician and his helpers will exterminate it now.

God is back of this. He has been thinking about it for six thousand years, and making up his mind. The idea of exterminating the hookworm was his. He came very near doing it before Dr. Charles Wardell Stiles did. But he is in time to get the credit of it. He always is.

It is going to cost a million dollars. He was probably just in the act of contributing that sum when a man pushed in ahead of him—as usual. Mr. Rockefeller. He furnishes the million, but the credit will go elsewhere—as usual. This morning's journals tell us something about the hookworm's operations:

The hookworm parasites often so lower the vitality of those who are affected as to retard their physical and mental development, render them more susceptible to other diseases, make labor less efficient, and in the sections where the malady is most prevalent greatly increase the death rate from consumption, pneumonia, typhoid fever and malaria. It has been shown that the lowered vitality of multitudes, long attributed to malaria and climate and seriously affecting economic development, is in fact due in some districts to this parasite. The disease is by no means confined to any one class; it takes its toll of suffering and death from the highly intelligent and well to do as well as from the less fortunate. It is a conservative estimate that two millions of our people are affected by this parasite. The disease is more common and more serious in children of school age than in other persons.

Widespread and serious as the infection is, there is still a most encouraging outlook. The disease can be easily recognized, readily and effectively treated and by simple and proper sanitary precautions successfully prevented, with God's help.

The poor little children are under the Eye that never sleeps, you see. They have had that ill luck in all the ages. They and "the Lord's poor"—as the sarcastic phrase goes—have never been able to get away from that Eye's attentions.

Yes, the poor, the humble, the ignorant—they are the ones

that catch it. Take the "sleeping sickness," of Africa. This atrocious cruelty has for its victims a race of ignorant and unoffending blacks whom God placed in a remote wilderness, and
bent his parental Eye upon them—the one that never sleeps
when there is a chance to breed sorrow for somebody. He
arranged for these people before the Flood. The chosen agent
was a fly, related to the tzetze; the tzetze is a fly which has
command of the Zambesi country and stings cattle and horses
to death, thus rendering that region uninhabitable by man.
The tzetze's awful relative deposits a microbe which produces
the Sleeping Sickness. Ham was full of these microbes, and
when the voyage was over he discharged them in Africa and
the havoc began, never to find amelioration until six thousand
years should go by and science should pry into the mystery
and hunt out the cause of the disease. The pious nations are
now thanking God, and praising him for coming to the rescue of his poor blacks. The pulpit says the praise is due to
him, for the reason that the scientists got their inspiration
from him. He is surely a curious Being. He commits a fearful
crime, continues that crime unbroken for six thousand years,
and is then entitled to praise because he suggests to somebody else to modify its severities. He is called patient, and he
certainly must be patient, or he would have sunk the pulpit in
perdition ages ago for the ghastly compliments it pays him.

Science has this to say about the Sleeping Sickness, otherwise called the Negro Lethargy.

It is characterised by periods of sleep recurring at intervals. The
disease lasts from four months to four years, and is always fatal. The
victim appears at first languid, weak, pallid, and stupid. His eyelids
become puffy, an eruption appears on his skin. He falls asleep while
talking, eating, or working. As the disease progresses he is fed with
difficulty and becomes much emaciated. The failure of nutrition and
the appearance of bedsores are followed by convulsions and death.
Some patients become insane.

It is he whom Church and people call Our Father in
Heaven who has invented the fly and sent him to inflict this
dreary long misery and melancholy and wretchedness, and decay of body and mind, upon a poor savage who has done the
Great Criminal no harm. There isn't a man in the world who

doesn't pity that poor black sufferer, and there isn't a man that wouldn't make him whole if he could. To find the one person who has no pity for him you must go to heaven; to find the one person who is able to heal him and couldn't be persuaded to do it, you must go to the same place. There is only one father cruel enough to afflict his child with that horrible disease—only one. Not all the eternities can produce another one. Do you like reproachful poetical indignations warmly expressed? Here is one, hot from the heart of a slave:

> "*Man's* inhumanity to man
> Makes countless thousands mourn!"

I will tell you a pleasant tale which has in it a touch of pathos. A man got religion, and asked the priest what he must do to be worthy of his new estate. The priest said, "Imitate our Father in Heaven, learn to be like him." The man studied his Bible diligently and thoroughly and understandingly, and then with prayers for heavenly guidance instituted his imitations. He tricked his wife into falling down stairs, and she broke her back and became a paralytic for life; he betrayed his brother into the hands of a sharper, who robbed him of his all and landed him in the almshouse; he inoculated one son with hookworms, another with the sleeping sickness, another with the gonorrhea, he furnished one daughter with scarlet fever and ushered her into her teens deaf dumb and blind for life; and after helping a rascal seduce the remaining one, he closed his doors against her and she died in a brothel cursing him. Then he reported to the priest, who said that *that* was no way to imitate his Father in Heaven. The convert asked wherein he had failed, but the priest changed the subject and inquired what kind of weather he was having, up his way.

## Letter . . .

Man is without any doubt the most interesting fool there is. Also the most eccentric. He hasn't a single written law, in his Bible or out of it, which has any but just one purpose and intention—to *limit or defeat a law of God*.

He can seldom take a plain fact and get any but a wrong meaning out of it. He cannot help this; it is the way the confusion he calls his mind is constructed. Consider the things he concedes, and the curious conclusions he draws from them.

For instance, he concedes that God made man. Made him without man's desire or privity.

This seems to plainly and indisputably make God, and God alone, responsible for man's acts. But man denies this.

He concedes that God has made angels perfect, without blemish, and immune from pain and death, and that he could have been similarly kind to man if he had wanted to, but denies that he was under any moral obligation to do it.

He concedes that man has no moral right to visit the child of his begetting with wanton cruelties, painful diseases and death, but refuses to limit God's privileges in this sort with the children of his begetting.

The Bible and man's statutes forbid murder, adultery, fornication, lying, treachery, robbery, oppression and other crimes, but contend that God is free of these laws and has a right to break them when he will.

He concedes that God gives to each man his temperament, his disposition, at birth; he concedes that man cannot by any process change this temperament, but must remain always under its dominion. Yet if it be full of dreadful passions, in one man's case, and barren of them in another man's, it is right and rational to punish the one for his crimes, and reward the other for abstaining from crime.

There—let us consider these curiosities.

*Temperament (disposition.)* Take two extremes of temperament—the goat and the tortoise.

Neither of these creatures makes its own temperament, but is born with it, like man, and can no more change it than can man.

Temperament is the *law of God*, written in the heart of every creature by God's own hand, and *must* be obeyed, and *will* be obeyed, in spite of all restricting or forbidding statutes, let them emanate whence they may.

Very well, lust is the dominant feature of the goat's temperament, the law of God in its heart, and it must obey it and *will* obey it the whole day long in the rutting season; without stopping to eat or drink. If the Bible said to the goat "Thou shalt not fornicate, thou shalt not commit adultery," even man—sapheaded man—would recognize the foolishness of the prohibition, and would grant that the goat ought not to be punished for obeying the law of his make. Yet he thinks it right and just that man should be put under the prohibition. *All* men. All alike.

On its face this is stupid, for, by temperament, which is the *real* law of God, many men are *goats* and can't *help* committing adultery when they get a chance; whereas there are numbers of men who, by temperament, can keep their purity and let an opportunity go by if the woman lacks in attractiveness. But the Bible doesn't allow adultery *at all*, whether a person can help it or not. It allows no distinction between goat and tortoise—the excitable goat, the emotional goat, that *has* to have some adultery every day or fade and die; and the tortoise, that cold calm puritan, that takes a treat only once in two years and then goes to sleep in the midst of it and doesn't wake up for sixty days. No lady goat is safe from criminal assault, even on the Sabbath Day, when there is a gentleman goat within three miles to leeward of her and nothing in the way but a fence fourteen feet high, whereas neither the gentleman tortoise nor the lady tortoise is ever hungry enough for the solemn joys of fornication to be willing to break the Sabbath to get them. Now according to man's curious reasoning, the goat has earned punishment, and the tortoise praise.

"Thou shalt not commit adultery" is a command which makes no distinction between the following persons. They are all required to obey it:

Children at birth.

Children in the cradle.

School children.

Youths and maidens.

Fresh adults.

Older ones.

Men and women of 40.

Of 50.

Of 60.

Of 70.

Of 80.

Of 90.

Of 100.

The command does not distribute its burden equally, and cannot.

It is not hard upon the three sets of children.

It is hard—harder—still harder upon the next three sets—cruelly hard.

It is blessedly softened to the next three sets.

It has now done all the damage it can, and might as well be put out of commission.

Yet with comical imbecility it is continued, and the four remaining estates are put under its crushing ban. Poor old wrecks, they couldn't disobey if they tried. And think—because they holily refrain from adulterating each other, they get praise for it! Which is nonsense; for even the Bible knows enough to know that if the oldest veteran there could get his lost hey-day back again for an hour he would cast that commandment to the winds and ruin the first woman he came across, even though she were an entire stranger.

It is as I have said: every statute in the Bible and in the law books is an attempt to defeat a law of God—in other words an unalterable and indestructible law of nature. These people's God has shown them by a million acts that he respects none of the Bible's statutes. He breaks every one of them himself, adultery and all.

The law of God, as quite plainly expressed in woman's *construction* is this:

There shall be *no limit* put upon your intercourse with the other sex sexually, at any time of life.

The law of God, as quite plainly expressed in *man's* construction is this:

During your entire life you shall be under inflexible *limits and restrictions*, sexually.

During 27 days in every month (in the absence of pregnancy) from the time a woman is seven years old till she dies of old age, she is ready for action, and *competent*. As competent as the candlestick is to receive the candle. Competent every day, competent every night. Also, she *wants* that candle—yearns for it, longs for it, hankers after it, as commanded by the law of God in her heart.

But man is only briefly competent; and only then in the moderate measure applicable to the word in *his* sex's case. He is competent from the age of sixteen or seventeen thenceforward for thirty-five years. After 50 his performance is of poor quality, the intervals between are wide, and its satisfactions of no great value to either party; whereas his great-grandmother is as good as new. There is nothing the matter with her plant. Her candlestick is as firm as ever, whereas his candle is increasingly softened and weakened by the weather of age, as the years go by, until at last it can no longer stand, and is mournfully laid to rest in the hope of a blessed resurrection which is never to come.

By the woman's make, her plant has to be out of service three days in the month and during a part of her pregnancy. These are times of discomfort, often of suffering. For fair and just compensation she has the high privilege of unlimited adultery all the other days of her life.

That is the law of God, as revealed in her make. What becomes of this high privilege? Does she live in the free enjoyment of it? No. Nowhere in the whole world. She is robbed of it everywhere. Who does this? Man. Man's statutes—ordained against her without allowing her a vote. Also God's statutes—if the Bible *is* the Word of God.

Now there you have a sample of man's "reasoning powers," as he calls them. He observes certain facts. For instance, that in all his life he never sees the day that he can satisfy *one* woman; also, that no woman ever sees the day that she can't overwork, and defeat, and put out of commission any *ten* masculine plants that can be put to bed to her.* He puts those strikingly-suggestive and luminous facts together, and from them draws this astonishing conclusion:

*In the Sandwich Islands in 1866 a buxom royal princess died. Occupying a place of distinguished honor at her funeral were 36 splendidly built young native men. In a laudatory song which celebrated the various merits, achievements and accomplishments of the late princess those 36 stallions were called her *harem*, and the song said it had been her pride and her boast that she kept the whole of them busy, and that several times it had happened that more than one of them had been able to charge overtime.

*The Creator intended the woman to be restricted to one man.*

So he concretes that singular conclusion into a *law*, for good and all.

And he does it without consulting the woman, although she has a thousand times more at stake in the matter than he has. His procreative competency is limited to an average of a hundred exercises per year for 50 years, hers is good for 3,000 a year for that whole time—and as many years longer as she may live. Thus his life-interest in the matter is 5,000 refreshments, while hers is 150,000; yet instead of fairly and honorably leaving the making of the law to the person who has an overwhelming interest at stake in it, this immeasurable hog, who has nothing at stake in it worth considering, makes it himself!

You have heretofore found out, by my teachings, that man is a fool; you are now aware that woman is a *damned* fool.

Now if you or any other really intelligent person were arranging the fairnesses and justices between man and woman, you would give the man a one-fiftieth interest in one woman, and the woman a *harem*. Now wouldn't you? Necessarily. I give you my word, this creature with the decrepit candle has arranged it exactly the other way. Solomon, who was one of the Deity's favorites, had a copulation-cabinet composed of 700 wives and 300 concubines. To save his life he could not have kept two of those young creatures satisfactorily refreshed, even if he had had fifteen experts to help him. Necessarily almost the entire thousand had to go hungry years and years on a stretch. Conceive of a man hard-hearted enough to look daily upon all that suffering and not be moved to mitigate it. He even wantonly *added* a sharp pang to that pathetic misery; for he kept within those women's sight, always, stalwart watchmen whose splendid masculine forms made the poor lassies' mouths water but who hadn't anything to solace a candlestick with, these gentry being eunuchs. A eunuch is a person whose candle has been put out. By art.*

From time to time, as I go along, I will take up a Biblical statute and show you that it always violates a law of God, and

---

*I purpose publishing these Letters here in the world before I return to you. Two editions. One, unedited, for Bible readers and their children; the other, expurgated, for persons of refinement.

then is imported into the law books of the nations, where it continues its violations. But those things will keep; there is no hurry.

## Letter . . .

The Ark continued its voyage, drifting around here and there and yonder, compassless and uncontrolled, the sport of the random winds and the swirling currents. And the rain, the rain, the rain! it kept on falling, pouring, drenching, flooding. No such rain had ever been seen before. Sixteen inches a day had been heard of, but that was nothing to this. This was a hundred and twenty inches a day—ten feet! At this incredible rate it rained forty days and forty nights, and submerged every hill that was 400 feet high. Then the heavens and even the angels went dry; no more water was to be had.

As a Universal Flood it was a disappointment, but there had been heaps of Universal Floods before, as is witnessed by all the Bibles of all the nations, and this was as good as the best one.

At last the Ark soared aloft and came to a rest on the top of Mount Ararat, 17,000 feet above the valley, and its living freight got out and went down the mountain.

Noah planted a vineyard, and drank of the wine and was overcome.

This person had been selected from all the populations because he was the best sample there was. He was to start the human race on a new basis. This was the new basis. The promise was bad. To go further with the experiment was to run a great and most unwise risk. Now was the time to do with these people what had been so judiciously done with the others—drown them. Anybody but the Creator would have seen this. But he didn't see it. That is, maybe he didn't.

It is claimed that from the beginning of time he foresaw everything that would happen in the world. If that is true, he foresaw that Adam and Eve would eat the apple; that their posterity would be unendurable and have to be drowned; that Noah's posterity would in their turn be unendurable, and that by and by he would have to leave his throne in heaven and come down and be crucified to save that same tiresome human race again. The whole of it? No! A part of it? Yes. How much of it? In each generation, for hundreds and hundreds of generations, a billion would die and all go to perdition except perhaps ten thousand out of the billion. The ten thousand would have to come from the little body of Christians, and only one in the hundred of that little body would stand any chance. None of them at all except such Roman Catholics as should have the luck to have a priest handy to sandpaper their souls at the last gasp, and here and there a Presbyterian. No others saveable. All the others damned. By the million.

Shall you grant that he foresaw all this? The pulpit grants it. It is the same as granting that in the matter of intellect the Deity is the Head Pauper of the Universe, and that in the matter of morals and character he is away down on the level of David.

### Letter . . .

The two Testaments are interesting, each in its own way. The Old one gives us a picture of these people's Deity as he was before he got religion, the other one gives us a picture of him as he appeared afterward. The Old Testament is interested mainly in blood and sensuality, the New one in salvation. Salvation by fire.

The first time the Deity came down to earth he brought life and death; when he came the second time, he brought hell.

Life was not a valuable gift, but death was. Life was a fever-dream made up of joys embittered by sorrows, pleasure poisoned by pain; a dream that was a nightmare-confusion of spasmodic and fleeting delights, ecstasies, exultations, happinesses, interspersed with long-drawn miseries, griefs, perils, horrors, disappointments, defeats, humiliations and despairs —the heaviest curse devisable by divine ingenuity; but death was sweet, death was gentle, death was kind, death healed the bruised spirit and the broken heart, and gave them rest and forgetfulness; death was man's best friend, his only friend; when man could endure life no longer, death came, and set him free.

In time, the Deity perceived that death was a mistake; a mistake, in that it was insufficient; insufficient, for the reason that while it was an admirable agent for the inflicting of misery upon the survivor, it allowed the dead person himself to escape from all further persecution in the blessed refuge of the grave. This was not satisfactory. A way must be contrived to pursue the dead beyond the tomb.

The Deity pondered this matter during four thousand years unsuccessfully, but as soon as he came down to earth and became a Christian his mind cleared and he knew what to do. *He invented hell*, and proclaimed it.

Now here is a curious thing. It is believed by everybody that while he was in heaven he was stern, hard, resentful, jealous, and cruel; but that when he came down to earth and assumed the name Jesus Christ, he became the opposite of what he was before: that is to say, he became sweet, and gentle, merciful, forgiving, and all harshness disappeared from his nature and a deep and yearning love for his poor human children took its place. Whereas it was as Jesus Christ that he devised hell and proclaimed it!

Which is to say, that as the meek and gentle Savior he was a thousand billion times crueler than ever he was in the Old Testament—oh, incomparably more atrocious than ever he was when he was at his very worst in those old days!

Meek and gentle? By and by we will examine this popular sarcasm by the light of the hell which he invented.

### Letter . . .

While it is true that the palm for malignity must be granted to Jesus, the inventor of hell, he was hard and ungentle enough for all godlike purposes even before he became a Christian. It does not appear that he ever stopped to reflect that *he* was to blame when a man went wrong, inasmuch as the man was merely acting in accordance with the disposition he had afflicted him with. No, he punished the man, instead of punishing himself. Moreover the punishment usually oversized the offence. Often, too, it fell, not upon the doer of a misdeed, but upon somebody else—a chief man, the head of a community, for instance.

And Israel abode in Shittim, and the people began to commit whoredom with the daughters of Moab.

And the Lord said unto Moses, Take *all the heads of the people*, and hang them up before the Lord against the sun, that the fierce anger of the Lord may be turned away from Israel.

Does that look fair to you? It does not appear that the "heads of the people" got any of the adultery, yet it is they that are hanged, instead of "the people."

If it was fair and right in that day it would be fair and right to-day, for the pulpit maintains that God's justice is eternal and unchangeable; also that he is the Fountain of Morals; and that his morals are eternal and unchangeable. Very well, then, we must believe that if the people of New York should begin to commit whoredom with the daughters of New Jersey, it would be fair and right to set up a gallows in front of the city hall and hang the mayor and the sheriff and the judges and the archbishop on it, although they did not get any of it. It does not look right to me.

Moreover, you may be quite sure of one thing: *it couldn't happen*. These people would not allow it. They are better than their Bible. *Nothing* would happen here, except some lawsuits, for damages, if the incident couldn't be hushed up; and even down South they would not proceed against persons who did not get any of it; they would get a rope and hunt for the corespondents; and if they couldn't find them they would lynch a nigger.

Things have greatly improved since the Almighty's time, let the pulpit say what it may.

Will you examine the Deity's morals and disposition and conduct a little further? And will you remember that in the Sunday school the little children are urged to love the Almighty, and honor him, and praise him, and make him their model and try to be as like him as they can? Read:

1 And the LORD spake unto Moses, saying,

2 Avenge the children of Israel of the Midianites: afterward shalt thou be gathered unto thy people.

7 And they warred against the Midianites, as the LORD commanded Moses; and they slew all the males.

8 And they slew the kings of Midian, besides the rest of them that were slain; *namely*, Evi, and Rekem, and Zur, and Hur, and Reba, five kings of Midian: Balaam also the son of Beor they slew with the sword.

9 And the children of Israel took *all* the women of Midian captives, and their little ones, and took the spoil of all their cattle, and all their flocks, and all their goods.

10 And they burnt all their cities wherein they dwelt, and all their goodly castles, with fire.

11 And they took all the spoil, and all the prey, *both* of men and of beasts.

12 And they brought the captives, and the prey, and the spoil unto Moses and Eleazar the priest, and unto the congregation of the children of Israel, unto the camp at the plains of Moab, which *are* by Jordan *near* Jericho.

13 And Moses, and Eleazar the priest, and all the princes of the congregation, went forth to meet them without the camp.

14 And Moses was wroth with the officers of the host, *with* the captains over thousands, and captains over hundreds, which came from the battle.

15 And Moses said unto them, Have ye saved all the women alive?

16 Behold, these caused the children of Israel, through the counsel of Balaam, to commit trespass against the LORD in the matter of Peor, and there was a plague among the congregation of the LORD.

17 Now therefore kill every male among the little ones, and kill every woman that hath known man by lying with him.

18 But all the women-children, that have not known a man by lying with him, keep alive for yourselves.

19 And do ye abide without the camp seven days: whosoever hath killed any person, and whosoever hath touched any slain, purify *both* yourselves and your captives on the third day, and on the seventh day.

20 And purify all *your* raiment, and all that is made of skins, and all work of goats' *hair*, and all things made of wood.

21 And Eleazar the priest said unto the men of war which went to the battle, This *is* the ordinance of the law which the LORD commanded Moses.

25 And the LORD spake unto Moses, saying,

26 Take the sum of the prey that was taken, *both* of man and of beast, thou, and Eleazar the priest, and the chief fathers of the congregation:

27 And divide the prey into two parts; between them that took the war upon them, who went out to battle, and between all the congregation:

28 And levy a tribute unto the LORD of the men of war which went out to battle.

31 And Moses and Eleazar the priest did as the LORD commanded Moses.

32 And the booty, *being* the rest of the prey which the men of war

had caught, was six hundred thousand, and seventy thousand, and five thousand sheep,

33 And threescore and twelve thousand beeves,

34 And threescore and one thousand asses,

35 And thirty and two thousand persons in all, of women that had not known man by lying with him.

40 And the persons *were* sixteen thousand, of which the LORD's tribute *was* thirty and two persons.

41 And Moses gave the tribute, *which was* the LORD's heave-offering, unto *Eleazar* the priest; as the LORD commanded Moses.

47 Even of the children of Israel's half, Moses took one portion of fifty, *both* of man and of beast, and gave them unto the Levites, which kept the charge of the tabernacle of the LORD; as the LORD commanded Moses.

10 When thou comest nigh unto a city to fight against it, then proclaim peace unto it.

13 And when the LORD thy God hath delivered it into thine hands, thou shalt smite every male thereof with the edge of the sword:

14 But the women, and the little ones, and the cattle, and all that is in the city, *even* all the spoil thereof, shalt thou take unto thyself: and thou shalt eat the spoil of thine enemies, which the LORD thy God hath given thee.

15 Thus shalt thou do unto all the cities *which* are very far off from thee, which are not of the cities of these nations.

16 But of the cities of these people, which the LORD thy God doth give thee for an inheritance, *thou shalt save alive* NOTHING THAT BREATHETH.

The Biblical law says:

*"Thou shalt not kill."*

The law of *God*, planted in the heart of man at his birth, says:

"Thou *shalt* kill."

The chapter I have quoted, shows you that the book-statute is once more a failure. It cannot set aside the more powerful law of nature.

According to the belief of these people, it was God himself who said:

"Thou shalt not kill."

Then it is plain that he cannot keep his own commandments.

He killed all those people—*every male*.

They had offended the Deity in some way. We know what the offence was, without looking; that is to say, we know it was a trifle; some small thing that no one but a god would attach any importance to. It is more than likely that a Midianite had been duplicating the conduct of one Onan, who was commanded to "go in unto his brother's wife"—which he did; but instead of finishing, "he spilled it on the ground." The Lord slew Onan for that, for the Lord could never abide indelicacy. The Lord slew Onan, and to this day the Christian world cannot understand why he stopped with Onan, instead of slaying all the inhabitants for three hundred miles around—they being innocent of offence, and therefore the very ones he would usually slay. For that had always been his idea of fair dealing. If he had had a motto, it would have read, "Let no innocent person escape." You remember what he did in the time of the flood. There were multitudes and multitudes of tiny little children, and he knew they had never done him any harm; but their *relations* had, and that was enough for him: he saw the waters rise toward their screaming lips, he saw the wild terror in their eyes, he saw that agony of appeal in the mothers' faces which would have touched any heart but his, but he was after the guiltless particularly, and he drowned those poor little chaps.

And you will remember that in the case of Adam's posterity *all* the billions are innocent—*none* of them had a share in his offence, but the Deity holds them guilty to this day. None gets off, except by acknowledging that guilt—no cheaper lie will answer.

Some Midianite must have repeated Onan's act, and brought that dire disaster upon his nation. If that was not the indelicacy that outraged the feelings of the Deity, then I know what it was: some Midianite had been *pissing against the wall*. I am sure of it, for that was an impropriety which the Source of all Etiquette *never* could stand. A person could piss against a tree, he could piss on his mother, he could piss his own breeches, and get off, but he must not piss against the wall—that would be going quite too far. The origin of the divine prejudice against this humble crime is not stated; but we know that the prejudice was very strong—so strong that nothing but a wholesale massacre of the people inhabiting the region where the wall was defiled could satisfy the Deity.

Take the case of Jeroboam. "I will cut off from Jeroboam him that pisseth against the wall." It was done. And not only was the man that did it cut off, but everybody else.

The same with the house of Baasha: everybody was exterminated, kinsfolks, friends, and all, leaving "not one that pisseth against a wall."

In the case of Jeroboam you have a striking instance of the Deity's custom of not limiting his punishments to the guilty; the innocent are included. Even the "remnant" of that unhappy house was removed, even "as a man taketh away dung, till it be all gone." That includes the women, the young maids, and the little girls. All innocent, for *they* couldn't piss against a wall. Nobody of that sex can. None but members of the other sex can achieve that feat.

A curious prejudice. And it still exists. Protestant parents still keep the Bible handy in the house, so that the children can study it; and one of the first things the little boys and girls learn is to be righteous and holy and not piss against the wall. They study those passages more than they study any others, except those which incite to masturbation. *Those* they hunt out and study in private. No Protestant child exists who does not masturbate. That art is the earliest accomplishment his religion confers upon him. Also the earliest *her* religion confers upon *her*.

The Bible has this advantage over all other books that teach refinement and good manners: that it goes to the child: it goes to the mind at its most impressible and receptive age— the others have to wait.

"Thou shalt have a paddle upon thy weapon: and it shall be, when thou wilt ease thyself abroad, thou shalt dig therewith, and shalt turn back and cover that which cometh from thee."

That rule was made in the old days because

"The Lord thy God walketh in the midst of thy camp."

It is probably not worth while to try to find out, for certain, why the Midianites were exterminated. We can only be sure that it was for no large offence; for the cases of Adam, and the Flood, and the defilers of the wall, teach us that much. A Midianite may have left his paddle at home and thus brought on the trouble. However, it is no matter. The main thing is the trouble itself, and the morals of one kind and another that it offers for the instruction and elevation of the Christian of to-day.

God wrote upon the tables of stone—

"Thou shalt not kill."

Also—

"Thou shalt not commit adultery."

Paul, speaking by the divine voice, advised against sexual intercourse *altogether*. A great change from the divine view as it existed at the time of the Midianite incident.

Letter . . .

Human history in all ages, is red with blood, and bitter with hate, and stained with cruelties; but not since Biblical times have these features been without a limit of some kind. Even the Church, which is credited with having spilt more innocent blood, since the beginning of its supremacy, than all the political wars put together have spilt, has observed a limit. A sort of limit. But you notice that when the Lord God of Heaven and Earth, adored Father of Man, goes to war, there is no limit. He is totally without mercy—he, who is called the Fountain of Mercy. He slays, slays, slays! all the men, all the beasts, all the boys, all the babies; also all the women and all the girls, except those that have not been deflowered.

He makes no distinction between innocent and guilty. The babies were innocent, the beasts were innocent, many of the men, many of the women, many of the boys, many of the girls, were innocent, yet they had to suffer with the guilty. What the insane Father required was blood and misery; he was indifferent as to who furnished it.

The heaviest punishment of all was meted out to persons who could not by any possibility have deserved so horrible a fate—the 32,000 virgins. Their naked privacies were probed, to make sure that they still possessed the hymen unruptured; after this humiliation they were sent away from the land that had been their home, to be sold into slavery; the worst of slaveries and the shamefulest, the slavery of prostitution; bed-slavery, to excite lust, and satisfy it with their bodies; slavery to any buyer, be he gentleman or be he a coarse and filthy ruffian.

It was the Father that inflicted this ferocious and unde-served punishment upon those bereaved and friendless vir-gins, whose parents and kindred he had slaughtered before their eyes. And were they praying to him for pity and rescue, meantime? Without a doubt of it.

These virgins were "spoil," plunder, booty. He claimed his share and got it. What use had *he* for virgins? Examine his later history and you will know.

His priests got a share of the virgins, too. What use could priests make of virgins? The private history of the Roman Catholic confessional can answer that question for you. The confessional's chief amusement has been seduction—in all the ages of the Church. Père Hyacinth testifies that of 100 priests confessed by him, 99 had used the confessional effectively for the seduction of married women and young girls. One priest confessed that of 900 girls and women whom he had served as father confessor in his time, none had escaped his lecherous embrace but the elderly and the homely. The official list of questions which the priest is *required* to ask will overmaster-ingly excite any woman who is not a paralytic.

There is nothing in either savage or civilized history that is more utterly complete, more remorselessly sweeping than the Father of Mercy's campaign among the Midianites. The official report does not furnish incidents, episodes, and mi-nor details, it deals only in information in masses: *all* the vir-gins, *all* the men, *all* the babies, *all* "creatures *that breathe*," *all* houses, *all* cities; it gives you just one vast picture, spread abroad here and there and yonder, as far as eye can reach, of charred ruin and storm-swept desolation; your imagination adds a brooding stillness, an aweful hush—the hush of death. But of course there *were* incidents. Where shall we get them?

Out of history of yesterday's date. Out of history made by the red Indian of America. He has duplicated God's work, and done it in the very spirit of God. In 1862 the Indians in

Minnesota, having been deeply wronged and treacherously treated by the government of the United States, rose against the white settlers and massacred them; massacred all they could lay their hands upon, sparing neither age nor sex. Consider this incident:

Twelve Indians broke into a farm house at daybreak and captured the family. It consisted of the farmer and his wife and four daughters, the youngest aged fourteen and the eldest eighteen. They crucified the parents; that is to say, they stood them stark naked against the wall of the living room and nailed their hands to the wall. Then they stripped the daughters bare, stretched them upon the floor in front of their parents, and repeatedly ravished them. Finally they crucified the girls against the wall opposite the parents, and cut off their noses and their breasts. They also—but I will not go into that. There is a limit. There are indignities so atrocious that the pen cannot write them. One member of that poor crucified family—the father—was still alive when help came two days later.

Now you have *one* incident of the Minnesota massacre. I could give you fifty. They would cover all the different kinds of cruelty the brutal human talent has ever invented.

And now you know, by these sure indications, what happened under the personal direction of the Father of Mercies in his Midianite campaign. The Minnesota campaign was merely a duplicate of the Midianite raid. Nothing happened in the one that did not happen in the other.

No, that is not strictly true. The Indian was more merciful than was the Father of Mercies. He sold no virgins into slavery to minister to the lusts of the murderers of their kindred while their sad lives might last; he raped them, then charitably made their subsequent sufferings brief, ending them with the precious gift of death. He burned some of the houses, but not all of them. He carried off innocent dumb brutes, but he took the lives of none.

Would you expect this same conscienceless God, this moral bankrupt, to become a *teacher* of morals; of gentleness; of meekness; of righteousness; of purity? It looks impossible, extravagant; but listen to him. These are his own words:

Blessed are the poor in spirit, for theirs is the kingdom of heaven.

Blessed are they that mourn, for they shall be comforted.

Blessed are the meek, for they shall inherit the earth.

Blessed are they which do hunger and thirst after righteousness, for they shall be filled.

*Blessed are the merciful*, for they shall obtain mercy.

Blessed are the pure in heart, for they shall see God.

*Blessed are the peace-makers*, for they shall be called *the children of God*.

Blessed are they which are persecuted for righteousness' sake, for theirs is the kingdom of heaven.

Blessed are ye when men shall revile you and persecute you, and say all manner of evil against you falsely for my sake.

The mouth that uttered these immense sarcasms, these giant hypocrisies, is the very same that ordered the wholesale massacre of the Midianitish men and babies and cattle; the wholesale destruction of house and city; the wholesale banishment of the virgins into a filthy and unspeakable slavery. This is the same person who brought upon the Midianites the fiendish cruelties which were repeated by the red Indians, detail by detail, in Minnesota eighteen centuries later. The Midianite episode filled him with joy. So did the Minnesota one, or he would have prevented it.

The Beatitudes and the quoted chapters from Numbers and Deuteronomy ought always to be read from the pulpit *together*; then the congregation would get an all-around view of Our Father in Heaven. Yet not in a single instance have I ever known a clergyman to do this.

*1909*

# "The Turning Point of My Life"

If I understand the idea, the *Bazar* invites several of us to
write upon the above text. It means the change in my life's
course which introduced what must be regarded by me as the
most *important* condition of my career. But it also implies—
without intention, perhaps—that that turning point was *itself*, individually, the creator of the new condition. This gives
it too much distinction, too much prominence, too much
credit. It is only the *last* link in a very long chain of turning
points commissioned to produce the weighty result; it is not
any more important than the humblest of its ten thousand
predecessors. Each of the ten thousand did its appointed
share, on its appointed date, in forwarding the scheme, and
they were all necessary; to have left out any one of them
would have defeated the scheme and brought about *some other*
result. I know we have a fashion of saying "such and such an
event was *the* turning point in my life," but we shouldn't say
it. We should merely grant that its place as *last* link in the
chain makes it the most *conspicuous* link; in real importance it
has no advantage over any one of its predecessors.

Perhaps the most celebrated turning point recorded in history was the crossing of the Rubicon. Suetonius says:

> Coming up with his troops on the banks of the Rubicon, he
> halted for a while, and, revolving in his mind the importance of the
> step he was on the point of taking, he turned to those about him and
> said, "We may still retreat; but if we pass this little bridge, nothing is
> left for us but to fight it out in arms."

This was a stupendously important moment. And all the
incidents, big and little, of Caesar's previous life had been
leading up to it, stage by stage, link by link. This was the *last*
link—merely the last one, and no bigger than the others; but
as we gaze back at it through the inflating mists of our imagination, it looks as big as the orbit of Neptune.

You, the reader, have a *personal* interest in that link, and so
have I; so has the rest of the human race. It was one of the

links in your life-chain, and it was one of the links in mine.
We may wait, now, with bated breath, while Caesar reflects.
Your fate and mine are involved in his decision.

While he was thus hesitating, the following incident occurred. A
person remarkable for his noble mien and graceful aspect, appeared
close at hand, sitting and playing upon a pipe. When not only the
shepherds, but a number of soldiers also, flocked to listen to him,
and some trumpeters among them, he snatched a trumpet from one
of them, ran to the river with it, and sounding the advance with a
piercing blast, crossed to the other side. Upon this, Caesar exclaimed, "Let us go whither the omens of the gods and the iniquity
of our enemies call us. *The die is cast.*"

So he crossed—and changed the future of the whole human race, for all time. But that stranger was a link in Caesar's
life-chain, too; and a necessary one. We don't know his name,
we never hear of him again, he was very casual, he acts like an
accident; but he was no accident, he was there by compulsion
of *his* life-chain, to blow the electrifying blast that was to
make up Caesar's mind for him, and thence go piping down
the aisles of history forever.

If the stranger hadn't been there! But he *was*. And Caesar
crossed. With such results! Such vast events—each a link in
the *human race's* life-chain; each event producing the next
one, and that one the next one, and so on: the destruction
of the republic; the founding of the empire; the breaking up
of the empire; the rise of Christianity upon its ruins; the
spread of the religion to other lands—and so on: link by
link took its appointed place at its appointed time, the discovery of America being one of them; our Revolution another; the inflow of English and other immigrants another;
their drift westward (my ancestors among them) another;
the settlement of certain of them in Missouri—which resulted in *me*. For I was one of the unavoidable results of the
crossing of the Rubicon. If the stranger, with his trumpet
blast, had stayed away (which he *couldn't*, for he was an appointed link), Caesar would not have crossed. What would
have happened, in that case, we can never guess. We only
know that the things that did happen would not have happened. They might have been replaced by equally prodigious

things, of course, but their nature and results are beyond our guessing. But the matter that interests me personally is, that I would not be *here*, now, but somewhere else; and probably black—there is no telling. Very well, I am glad he crossed. And very really and thankfully glad, too, though I never cared anything about it before.

II

To me, the most important feature of my life is its literary feature. I have been professionally literary something more than forty years. There have been many turning points in my life, but the one that was the last link in the chain appointed to conduct me to the literary guild is the most *conspicuous* link in that chain. *Because* it was the last one. It was not any more important than its predecessors. All the other links have an inconspicuous look, except the crossing of the Rubicon; but as factors in making me literary they are all of the one size, the crossing of the Rubicon included.

I know how I came to be literary, and I will tell the steps that led up to it and brought it about.

The crossing of the Rubicon was not the first one, it was hardly even a recent one; I should have to go back ages before Caesar's day to find the first one. To save space I will go back only a couple of generations, and start with an incident of my boyhood. When I was twelve and a half years old, my father died. It was in the spring. The summer came, and brought with it an epidemic of measles. For a time, a child died almost every day. The village was paralysed with fright, distress, despair. Children that were not smitten with the disease were imprisoned in their homes to save them from the infection. In the homes there were no cheerful faces, there was no music, there was no singing but of solemn hymns, no voice but of prayer, no romping was allowed, no noise, no laughter, the family moved spectrally about on tiptoe, in a ghostly hush. I was a prisoner. My soul was steeped in this awful dreariness—and in fear. At some time or other every day and every night a sudden shiver shook me to the marrow, and I said to myself, "There, I've got it! and I shall die." Life on these miserable terms was not worth living, and at last I made up

my mind to get the disease and have it over, one way or the
other. I escaped from the house and went to the house of a
neighbor where a playmate of mine was very ill with the malady. When the chance offered I crept into his room and got
into bed with him. I was discovered by his mother and sent
back into captivity. But I had the disease; they could not take
that from me. I came near to dying. The whole village was
interested, and anxious, and sent for news of me every day;
and not only once a day, but several times. Everybody believed I would die; but on the fourteenth day a change came
for the worse and they were disappointed.

This was a turning point of my life. (Link number one.)
For when I got well my mother closed my school career and
apprenticed me to a printer. She was tired of trying to keep
me out of mischief, and the adventure of the measles decided
her to put me into more masterful hands than hers.

I became a printer, and began to add one link after another
to the chain which was to lead me into the literary profession.
A long road, but I could not know that; and as I did not
know what its goal was, or even that it had one, I was indifferent. Also contented.

A young printer wanders around a good deal, seeking and
finding work; and seeking again, when necessity commands.
N. B. Necessity is a *Circumstance*; Circumstance is man's master—and when Circumstance commands, he must obey; he
may argue the matter—that is his privilege, just as it is the
honorable privilege of a falling body to argue with the attrac-
tion of gravitation—but it won't do any good, he must *obey*.
I wandered for ten years, under the guidance and dictatorship
of Circumstance, and finally arrived in a city of Iowa, where I
worked several months. Among the books that interested me
in those days was one about the Amazon. The traveler told an
alluring tale of his long voyage up the great river from Para to
the sources of the Madeira, through the heart of an enchanted
land, a land wastefully rich in tropical wonders, a romantic
land where all the birds and flowers and animals were of the
museum varieties, and where the alligator and the crocodile
and the monkey seemed as much at home as if they were in
the Zoo. Also, he told an astonishing tale about *coca*, a vegetable product of miraculous powers; asserting that it was so

nourishing and so strength-giving that the native of the mountains of the Madeira region would tramp up-hill and down all day on a pinch of powdered coca and require no other sustenance.

I was fired with a longing to ascend the Amazon. Also with a longing to open up a trade in coca with all the world. During months I dreamed that dream, and tried to contrive ways to get to Para and spring that splendid enterprise upon an unsuspecting planet. But all in vain. A person may *plan* as much as he wants to, but nothing of consequence is likely to come of it until the magician *Circumstance* steps in and takes the matter off his hands. At last Circumstance came to my help. It was in this way. Circumstance, to help or hurt another man, made him lose a fifty-dollar bill in the street; and to help or hurt me, made me find it. I advertised the find, and left for the Amazon the same day. This was another turning point, another link.

Could Circumstance have ordered another dweller in that town to go to the Amazon and open up a world-trade in coca on a fifty-dollar basis and been obeyed? No, I was the only one. There were other fools there—shoals and shoals of them—but they were not of my kind. I was the only one of my kind.

Circumstance is powerful, but it cannot work alone, it has to have a partner. Its partner is man's *temperament*—his natural disposition. His temperament is not his invention, it is *born* in him, and he has no authority over it, neither is he responsible for its acts. He cannot change it, nothing can change it, nothing can modify it,—except temporarily. But it won't stay modified. It is permanent; like the color of the man's eyes and the shape of his ears. Blue eyes are gray, in certain unusual lights; but they resume their natural color when that stress is removed.

A Circumstance that will coerce one man, will have no effect upon a man of a different temperament. If Circumstance had thrown the bank note in Caesar's way, his temperament would not have made him start for the Amazon. His temperament would have compelled him to do something with the money, but not that. It might have made him advertise the note—and *wait*. We can't tell. Also, it might have made him go to New York and buy into the government; with results that would leave Tweed nothing to learn when it came his turn.

Very well, Circumstance furnished the capital, and my temperament told me what to do with it. Sometimes a temperament is an ass. When that is the case the owner of it is an ass, too, and is going to remain one. Training, experience, association, can temporarily so elevate him that people will think he is a mule, but they will be mistaken. Artificially he *is* a mule, for the time being, but at bottom he is an ass yet, and will remain one.

By temperament I was the kind of person that *does* things. Does them, and reflects afterwards. So I started for the Amazon, without reflecting, and without asking any questions. That was more than fifty years ago. In all that time my temperament has not changed, by even a shade. I have been punished many and many a time, and bitterly, for doing things first and reflecting afterward, but these tortures have been of no value to me; I still do the thing commanded by Circumstance and Temperament, and reflect afterward. Always violently. When I am reflecting, on those occasions, even deaf persons can hear me think.

I went by the way of Cincinnati, and down the Ohio and Mississippi. My idea was to take ship, at New Orleans, for Para. In New Orleans I inquired, and found there was no ship leaving for Para. Also, that there never had *been* one leaving for Para. I reflected. A policeman came and asked me what I was doing, and I told him. He made me move on; and said if he caught me reflecting in the public street again he would run me in.

After a few days I was out of money. Then Circumstance arrived, with another turning point of my life—a new link. On my way down, I had made the acquaintance of a pilot; I begged him to teach me the river, and he consented. I became a pilot.

By and by Circumstance came again—introducing the Civil War, this time, in order to push me ahead a stage or two toward the literary profession. The boats stopped running, my livelihood was gone.

Circumstance came to the rescue with a new turning point and a fresh link. My brother was appointed secretary to the new Territory of Nevada, and he invited me to go with him and help him in his office. I accepted.

In Nevada, Circumstance furnished me the silver fever and I went into the mines to make a fortune and enter the ministry. As I supposed; but that was not the idea. The idea was, to move me another step toward literature. For amusement I scribbled things for the Virginia City *Enterprise*. One isn't a printer ten years without setting up acres of good and bad literature, and learning—unconsciously at first, consciously later—to discriminate between the two, within his mental limitations; and meantime he is unconsciously acquiring what is called a "style." One of my efforts attracted attention, and the *Enterprise* sent for me, and put me on its staff.

And so I became a journalist—another link. By and by Circumstance and the Sacramento *Union* sent me to the Sandwich Islands for five or six months, to write up sugar. I did it; and threw in a good deal of extraneous matter that hadn't anything to do with sugar. But it was this extraneous matter that helped me to another link.

It made me notorious, and San Francisco invited me to lecture. Which I did. And profitably. I had long had a desire to travel and see the world, and now the platform had furnished me the means. So I joined the "Quaker City Excursion."

When I returned to America, Circumstance was waiting on the pier—with the *last* link: I was asked to *write a book*, and I did it, and called it *The Innocents Abroad*. Thus at last I became a member of the literary guild. That was forty-two years ago, and I have been a member ever since. Leaving the Rubicon incident away back where it belongs, I can say with truth that the reason I am in the literary profession is because I had the measles when I was twelve years old.

III

Now what interests me, as regards these details, is not the details themselves, but the fact that none of them was fore-

seen by me, none of them was planned by me, I was the author of none of them. Circumstance, working in harness with
my temperament, created them all and compelled them all. I
often offered help, and with the best intentions, but it was
rejected: as a rule, uncourteously. I could never plan a thing
and get it to come out the way I planned it. It came out some
other way—some way I had not counted upon.

And so I do not admire the human being—as an intellectual marvel—as much as I did when I was young, and got
him out of books, and did not know him personally. When
I used to read that such and such a general did a certain
brilliant thing, I believed it. Whereas it was not so. Circumstance did it, by help of his temperament. The circumstances
would have failed of effect with a general of another temperament: he might see the chance, but lose the advantage by
being by nature too slow or too quick or too doubtful.
Once General Grant was asked a question about a matter
which had been much debated by the public and the newspapers; he answered the question without any hesitancy:
"General, who planned the march through Georgia?" "The
enemy!" He added that the enemy usually makes your plans
for you. He meant that the enemy, by neglect or through
force of circumstances, leaves an opening for you, and you
see your chance and take advantage of it.

Circumstances do the planning for us all, no doubt, by help
of our temperaments. I see no great difference between a man
and a watch, except that the man is conscious and the watch
isn't, and the man *tries* to plan things and the watch doesn't.
The watch doesn't wind itself, and doesn't regulate itself—
these things are done exteriorly. Outside influences, outside
circumstances, wind the *man* and regulate him. Left to himself he wouldn't get regulated at all, and the sort of time he
would keep would not be valuable. Some rare men are wonderful watches, with gold case, compensation balance, and all
those things, and some men are only simple and sweet and
humble Waterburys. I am a Waterbury. A Waterbury of that
kind, some say.

A nation is only an individual, multiplied. It makes plans,
and Circumstance comes and upsets them—or enlarges them.

A gang of patriots throws the tea overboard; it destroys a Bastile. The plans stop there; then Circumstance comes in, quite unexpectedly, and turns these modest riots into a revolution.

And there was poor Columbus. He elaborated a deep plan to find a new route to an old country. Circumstance revised his plan for him, and he found a new *world*. And *he* gets the credit of it, to this day. He hadn't anything to do with it.

Necessarily the scene of the real turning point of my life (and of yours) was the Garden of Eden. It was there that the first link was forged of the chain that was ultimately to lead to the emptying of me into the literary guild. Adam's *temperament* was the first command the Deity ever issued to a human being on this planet. And it was the only command Adam would *never* be able to disobey. It said, "Be weak, be water, be characterless, be cheaply persuadable." The later command, to let the fruit alone, was certain to be disobeyed. Not by Adam himself, but by his *temperament*—which he did not create and had no authority over. For the *temperament* is the man; the thing tricked out with clothes and named Man, is merely its Shadow, nothing more. The law of the tiger's temperament is, Thou shalt kill; the law of the sheep's temperament is, Thou shalt not kill. To issue later commands requiring the tiger to let the fat stranger alone, and requiring the sheep to imbue its hands in the blood of the lion is not worth while, for those commands *can't* be obeyed. They would invite to violations of the law of *temperament*, which is supreme, and takes precedence of all other authorities. I cannot help feeling disappointed in Adam and Eve. That is, in their temperaments. Not in *them*, poor helpless young creatures—afflicted with temperaments made out of butter; which butter was commanded to get into contact with fire and *be melted*. What I cannot help wishing is, that Adam and Eve had been postponed, and Martin Luther and Joan of Arc put in their place—that splendid pair equipped with temperaments not made of butter, but of asbestos. By neither sugary persuasions nor by hellfire could Satan have beguiled *them* to eat the apple.

There would have been results! Indeed yes. The apple

would be intact to-day: there would be no human race; there would be no *you*; there would be no *me*. And the old, old creation-dawn scheme of ultimately launching me into the literary guild would have been defeated.

*February 1910*

# MORE MAXIMS
# OF MARK

An uneasy conscience is a hair in the mouth.

All the talk used to be about doing people good, now it is about doing people.

At 50 a man can be an ass without being an optimist but not an optimist without being as ass.

Always acknowledge a fault frankly. This will throw those in authority off their guard and give you opportunity to commit more.

All schools, all colleges, have two great functions; to confer, and to conceal, valuable knowledge. The theological knowledge which they conceal cannot justly be regarded as less valuable than that which they reveal. That is, when a man is buying a basket of strawberries it can profit him to know that the bottom half of it is rotten.

———— ✳ ————

Better a broken promise than none at all.

*Benefit of clergy:* Half-rate on the railroad.

The burnt child shuns the fire. Until next day.

*Balloon:* Thing to take meteroric observations and commit suicide with.

By and by when each nation has 20,000 battleships and 5,000,000 soldiers we shall all be safe and the wisdom of statesmanship will stand confirmed.

Circumstances make man, not man circumstances.

Civilization is a limitless multiplication of unnecessary necessaries.

Clothes make the man. Naked people have little or no influence in society.

———— ❋ ————

Do your duty today and repent tomorrow.

Do good when you can, and charge when you think they will stand it.

Difference between savage and civilized man: one is painted, the other gilded.

Do not put off till tomorrow what can be put off till day-after-tomorrow just as well.

Do not tell fish stories where the people know you; but particularly, don't tell them where they know the fish.

———— ❋ ————

Etiquette requires us to admire the human race.

*Everybody's private motto:* It's better to be popular than right.

Every man is wholly honest to himself and to God, but not to any one else.

———— ❋ ————

Geological time is not money.

Good wine needs no bush; a jug is the thing.

God's noblest work? Man. Who found it out? Man.

Good friends, good books and a sleepy conscience: this is the ideal life.

*Golden rule:* Made of hard metal so it could stand severe wear, it not being known at that time that butter would answer.

———— ✳ ————

Honesty *was* the best policy.

*Honesty:* The best of all the lost arts.

*Heroine:* Girl who is perfectly charming to live with, in a book.

Have a place for everything and keep the thing somewhere else. This is not advice, it is custom.

*Heroine:* Girl in a book who is saved from drowning by a hero and marries him next week, but if it was to be over again ten years later it is likely she would rather have a life-belt and he would rather have her have it. *Hero:* Person in a book who does things which he can't and girl marries him for it.

———— ✳ ————

It is wiser to find out than to suppose.

In literature imitations do not imitate.

It is best to read the weather forecast before we pray for rain.

It is hard enough luck being a monarch, without being a target also.

*It is a solemn thought:* Dead, the noblest man's meat is inferior to pork.

If we had less statesmanship we could get along with fewer battleships.

It is not best to use our morals weekdays, it gets them out of repair for Sunday.

It is better to take what does not belong to you than to let it lie around neglected.

Is a person's public and private opinion the same? It is thought there have been instances.

It is the foreign element that commits our crimes. There is no native criminal class except Congress.

It is a wise child that knows its own father, and an unusual one that unreservedly approves of him.

It is not likely that any complete life has ever been lived which was not a failure in the secret judgment of the person that lived it.

It is sound statesmanship to add two battleships every time our neighbor adds one and two stories to our skyscrapers every time he piles a new one on top of hisn to threaten our light. There is no limit to this soundness but the sky.

———— ✳ ————

Let us save the to-morrows for work.

The lack of money is the root of all evil.

The low level which commercial morality has reached in America is deplorable. We have humble God fearing Christian men among us who will stoop to do things for a million dollars that they ought not to be willing to do for less than 2 millions.

———— ✳ ————

Morals consist of political morals, commercial morals, ecclesiastical morals, and morals.

Necessity is the mother of "taking chances".

Nothing is made in vain, but the fly came near it.

No man is straitly honest to any but himself and God.

*The new political gospel:* Public office is private graft.

Never tell the truth to people who are not worthy of it.

Nothing incites to money-crimes like great poverty or great wealth.

None but an ass pays a compliment and asks a favor at the same time. There are many asses.

Nelson would have been afraid of ten thousand fleas, but a flea wouldn't be afraid of ten thousand Nelsons.

——— ✳ ———

*Optimist:* Day-dreamer in his small clothes.

*Optimist:* Day-dreamer more elegantly spelled.

*Optimist:* Person who travels on nothing from nowhere to happiness.

Obscurity and a competence. That is the life that is best worth living.

The ordinary chestnut can beget a sickly and reluctant laugh, but it takes a horse chestnut to fetch the gorgeous big horse-laugh.

An occultation of Venus is not half so difficult as an eclipse of the Sun, but because it comes seldom the world thinks it's a grand thing.

——— ✳ ———

*Pessimist:* The optimist who didn't arrive.

Prosperity is the best protector of principle.

*Prophecy:* Two bull's eyes out of a possible million.

*Public servant:* Persons chosen by the people to distribute the graft.

*Patriot:* The person who can holler the loudest without knowing what he is hollering about.

———— ✳ ————

*The real yellow peril:* Gold.

———— ✳ ————

Slang in a woman's mouth is not obscene, it only sounds so.

*Senator:* Person who makes laws in Washington when not doing time.

Some of us cannot be optimists, but all of us can be bigamists.

———— ✳ ————

There is no sadder sight than a young pessimist, except an old optimist.

Taking the pledge will not make bad liquor good, but it will improve it.

To create man was a quaint and original idea, but to add the sheep was tautology.

There are many scapegoats for our blunders, but the most popular one is Providence.

To be good is noble, but to show others how to be good is nobler, and no trouble.

The time to begin writing an article is when you have finished it to your satisfaction.

The trouble ain't that there is too many fools, but that the lightning ain't distributed right.

That George could refrain from telling the lie is not the remarkable feature, but that he could do it off-hand, that way.

*Vote:* The only commodity that is peddleable without a license.

——— ✳ ———

We all live in the protection of certain cowardices which we call our principles.

What is human life? The first third a good time; the rest remembering about it.

Work and play are words used to describe the same thing under differing conditions.

When a man arrives at great prosperity God did it: when he falls into disaster he did it himself.

We can't reach old age by another man's road. My habits protect my life but they would assassinate you.

What is the difference between a taxidermist and a tax collector? The taxidermist takes only your skin.

We often feel sad in the presence of music without words; and often more than that in the presence of music without music.

We are always more anxious to be distinguished for a talent which we do not possess, than to be praised for the fifteen which we do possess.

Wherefore being all of one mind, we do highly resolve that government of the grafted by the grafter for the grafter shall not perish from the earth.

——— ✳ ———

You can straighten a worm, but the crook is in him and only waiting.

# Chronology

Samuel Langhorne Clemens born prematurely on November 30 in Florida, Missouri, fifth surviving child of John Marshall Clemens (b. 1798) and Jane Lampton Clemens (b. 1803). Siblings are brother Orion (b. 1825), sisters Pamela (b. 1827) and Margaret (b. 1830), and brother Benjamin (b. 1832). At time of birth Halley's Comet is still visible in the sky (Clemens will often mention this later in life). Family lives in rented house on South Mill Street and father runs store in partnership with John Adams Quarles, husband of Jane Lampton Clemens' sister, Martha Ann "Patsy" Quarles. (Grandparents Samuel and Pamelia Clemens were slave-owning farmers in Campbell County, Virginia, before moving family to southern bank of Ohio River in Mason County, Virginia—now West Virginia—in 1803 or 1804. Grandmother, widowed in 1805, moved with her five children to Adair County, Kentucky, to live with her brother; she married Simon Hancock in 1809. By 1812 father was supporting himself in a Lynchburg, Virginia, ironworks. After paying debts owed to stepfather Hancock, father and siblings settled their father's estate in 1821; John Clemens' share included three slaves. He then read law with Cyrus Walker in Columbia, Kentucky, received his license to practice in 1822, and in 1823 married Jane Lampton, a cousin of Walker's wife; the daughter of Benjamin and Margaret Casey Lampton, she was born in Columbia and was descended from early English and Irish settlers of Kentucky. They moved to Gainesboro, Tennessee, then Jamestown, Tennessee, where John Clemens built a large house, practiced law, opened a store, and bought 75,000 acres of uncleared land before moving in 1831 to nearby Three Forks of Wolf River, where he bought 200 acres of farmland and built a log house. In 1835 the family moved with their remaining slave, a woman named Jenny, to Florida, Missouri, on the Salt River, where John and Martha Ann Quarles were already established and where grandfather Benjamin Lampton and other members of mother's family also lived. After their arrival in June father quickly acquired 120 acres of government land, and then bought a 2¾-acre homesite for $300.)

1836    Clemens is frequently sick and mother is unsure if he
        will live. Family buys house in town from grandfather
        Lampton.

1837    Grandfather dies. Father dissolves partnership with
        Quarles and sets up his own store; heads committees to
        improve Salt River navigation, develop railroads, and start
        an academy. Father becomes Monroe County judge.

1838    Family moves into new house built by father. Brother
        Henry born July 13.

1839    Clemens walks in his sleep (will often do so for several
        years). Sister Margaret dies of "bilious fever" August 17.
        Father earns $5,000 from land sales and then purchases
        $7,000 worth of property in Hannibal, Missouri, a rapidly
        growing port village of a thousand inhabitants on the
        Mississippi, 30 miles from Florida and about 130 miles
        north of St. Louis by water. Family moves to Hannibal in
        November; other Florida residents move as well, includ-
        ing family friends Dr. Hugh Meredith and schoolteacher
        Mary Ann Newcomb. Father opens store and family lives
        in the Virginia House, former hotel that is part of pur-
        chased property.

1840    Clemens enters school taught by Elizabeth Horr and Mary
        Ann Newcomb (will attend three other schools in Han-
        nibal).

1841    Mother and sister Pamela join Presbyterian church in Feb-
        ruary. Newcomb, who often eats as a paying guest with
        the Clemenses, opens her own school in basement of Pres-
        byterian church. Father sells house in Florida to uncle
        John Quarles in August and transfers title to Virginia
        House to creditor in October.

1842    Brother Benjamin dies on May 12 after a few days of ill-
        ness. Orion moves to St. Louis to work as printer. Clem-
        ens continues to be sickly, and is doctored with castor oil,
        calomel, rhubarb, and jalap, as well as poultices, socks full
        of hot ashes, and various water treatments. Has night-
        mares and continues to walk in his sleep. Family sells
        Jenny.

1843     Mother moves children from Methodist to Presbyterian Sunday school. Clemens enjoys visits to the Quarles' family farm in Florida (will spend two or three months a year with them for several years). Takes with him his own trained cat (will have lifelong love of cats). Attends country summer school with cousins once or twice a week and enjoys playing with the slaves on the farm. Becomes especially appreciative of the friendship and counsel of Dann, a slave in his late thirties (emancipated by Quarles in 1855). Father auctions off much of his Hannibal property to pay debts. James C. Clemens, a distant cousin, buys one lot on Hill Street and leases it to father to build house.

1844     During epidemic in spring, Clemens deliberately catches measles from Will Bowen, his closest friend, and nearly dies as a result. Father helps found Hannibal Library Institute (will later head civic committees promoting railroad construction and higher education) and is elected justice of the peace. Clemens is horrified when he finds a corpse in his father's office (body is of an emigrant to California stabbed in a quarrel while in town).

1845     Watches man die in the street after being shot by Hannibal merchant William Owsley (who is later acquitted). Group of friends includes Will Bowen and his brother Sam, John Briggs, Ed Stevens, John Garth, Anna Laura Hawkins, and Tom Blankenship. Health improves, and enjoys swimming, fishing, playing Robin Hood, pirates, and Crusaders. Attends school taught by Samuel Cross.

1846     Mother takes in paying guests for meals. Family sells furniture to help pay debts and moves in with pharmacist Orville Grant; mother supplies him with meals in exchange for rent. In November, father announces candidacy for clerk of the circuit court (becomes favored to win election, held in August 1847). Clemens and friends enjoy watching local volunteer infantry drill for service in Mexican War.

1847     Father dies of pneumonia on March 24. Clemens watches through keyhole as Dr. Meredith performs postmortem examination. Family moves back to frame house at 206 Hill Street. Orion, working as printer in St. Louis, provides main family support, while Pamela gives guitar and piano lessons, mother continues to take in paying guests for meals, and Clemens works at odd jobs, including helping a blacksmith and clerking in a grocery store, a pharmacy, and a bookstore. Begins attending John D. Dawson's school. Witnesses drowning of friend Clint Levering while swimming with a group of friends in the Mississippi in August. While fishing on Sny Island a few days later, Clemens and several friends discover the body of a drowned fugitive slave, whom Bence Blankenship (Tom's older brother) had been secretly supplying with food. Gets job in fall as errand boy and delivers papers for printer Henry La Cossitt at the Hannibal *Gazette*.

1848       Still attending Dawson's school, begins working in late spring in the office of Joseph P. Ament's *Missouri Courier* as chore boy and printer's devil. Lives meagerly in Ament's house as an apprentice. Goes skating late in the year on the Mississippi with friend Tom Nash; when the ice breaks, Clemens manages to get to shore safely, but Nash falls through (illnesses suffered as a result eventually make Nash deaf).

1849       Gold rush emigrants pass through Hannibal en route to California, and 80 Hannibal residents join them, including Dawson, head of the last school Clemens attends, and Samuel Cross. Enjoys company of fellow apprentices Wales McCormick and T. P. "Pet" McMurry. Clemens reads Cooper, Marryat, Dickens, Byron, Scott, and anything else he can find that features knights, pirates, or Crusaders (Henry is considered to be the serious reader in the family).

1850       Joins Cadets of Temperance, briefly gives up smoking and chewing tobacco, and marches in parades with friends. In May, witnesses a poor widow shoot and kill the leader of a group of strangers from Illinois who are trying to force their way into her house. Orion returns to Hannibal from St. Louis and begins publishing weekly newspaper, the *Western Union*.

1851       Clemens leaves *Missouri Courier* and, with Henry, goes to work for Orion as a typesetter and editorial assistant;

although Orion promises Clemens $3.50 a week in wages, no money is ever available. Likes apprentice Jim Wolf, who boards with Clemens family. Publishes first known sketch, "A Gallant Fireman," in the *Western Union* January 16. Cholera epidemic in June kills 24 people in Hannibal. Orion buys Hannibal *Journal* in September. Sister Pamela marries William A. Moffett on September 20 and moves to St. Louis.

1852    Fire destroys *Journal* office, and Orion rents new space. Clemens occasionally writes humorous sketches for the Hannibal *Journal*. "The Dandy Frightening the Squatter" appears in the Boston *Carpet-Bag* and "Hannibal, Missouri" in the Philadelphia *American Courier* in May. Niece Annie Moffett born in July. During Orion's absence on business trips, Clemens becomes responsible for getting paper out. On September 9 signs a sketch "W. Epaminondas Adrastus Perkins," his first known use of a pseudonym.

1853    In January Clemens and Will Bowen give matches to a drunk in the town jail, who later that night sets fire to his cell and burns to death. (Clemens will often recall this incident.) Leaves Hannibal in early June and works as a typesetter in St. Louis for Thomas Watt Ustick, who does the printing for the *Evening News* and other publications. Goes to New York City by steamer and rail in late August. Visits Crystal Palace, center of New York World's Fair. Works for low pay in John A. Gray's large print shop on Cliff Street and boards on Duane Street. Takes pride in his typesetting skill, attends theater, and spends evenings reading in the printers' free library. Has two of his letters from New York printed in Hannibal *Journal* before Orion sells paper in September and moves with mother and brother Henry to Muscatine, Iowa, where Orion buys share in, and becomes co-editor of, the Muscatine *Journal*. Clemens moves to Philadelphia in late October. Works as typesetter, writes letters for the Muscatine *Journal*, and enjoys visiting sites connected with Benjamin Franklin and the Revolution.

1854    Briefly visits Washington, D.C., in February and records his impressions in letter for the Muscatine *Journal*. Returns to Philadelphia for a few weeks, then goes to New York, where he finds high unemployment among printers due to fires that had destroyed Harpers and another publishing house. Goes to Muscatine in spring and works for the *Journal*. Moves to St. Louis in summer and resumes work at the *Evening News*, boarding and lodging with the Paveys from Hannibal at the corner of 4th and Wash streets. Mother moves in with Pamela and William Moffett on Pine Street in St. Louis. Orion marries Mary Eleanor (Mollie) Stotts of Keokuk, Iowa, on December 19.

1855    Writes four letters for the Muscatine *Journal* before Orion sells paper in June and moves to Keokuk, where he sets up the Ben Franklin Book and Job Office, a printing shop. Clemens joins him in mid-June, working for $5 a week and board before becoming a partner in the business (mother remains in St. Louis with the Moffetts). Travels to Hannibal and Palymra in July to collect belongings and arrange for sale of Hill Street house, then goes on to Paris and Florida, Missouri, to settle mother's inheritance from grandfather Benjamin Lampton and great-aunt Diana Lampton. Visits with uncle John Quarles.

1856    Sees mother and Pamela in St. Louis in October, and writes his first "Thomas Jefferson Snodgrass" letter for the Keokuk *Post*. Moves to Cincinnati, where he works as a typesetter and writes two more Snodgrass letters for the *Post*.

1857    Leaves Cincinnati in April by steamboat for New Orleans, intending to seek his fortune in South America, but instead becomes cub riverboat pilot under Horace Bixby for an apprentice fee of $500 (borrows the first $100 from William Moffett, then pays more in installments, though Bixby will not charge him the full amount). Works on several boats and learns Mississippi River between New Orleans and St. Louis. Orion sells Keokuk print shop and goes to Jamestown, Tennessee, where family owns land, to study law and try to survey and sell the property (is unsuccessful in selling land and returns to Keokuk in July 1858 to practice law).

1858    Clemens serves as cub on the *Pennsylvania* under pilot William Brown, whom he considers a tyrant. Arranges job as "mud clerk" (purser's assistant) for brother Henry aboard the boat. Meets and falls in love with Laura M. Wright, the 14-year-old daughter of a Missouri judge (her family does not approve and intercepts letters). Hits Brown after the pilot strikes Henry, then leaves the *Pennsylvania* when no replacement can be found for Brown. Henry remains with crew and is badly injured in a boiler explosion below Memphis on June 13. Clemens arrives in Memphis June 15, and is with Henry when he dies on June 21 (Brown is also among the dead). Feels crazed with grief and guilt. Henry is buried in Hannibal June 25. Clemens resumes apprenticeship and steers for two pilot friends from Hannibal, Bart and Sam Bowen.

1859–60    Receives his pilot's license on April 9, 1859. Becomes steadily employed and well paid for his work. Feels at home in New Orleans and St. Louis, where he sees Pamela and her family. Continues his self-education and studies French. In May 1859 publishes a lampoon of senior pilot Isaiah Sellers (from whom Clemens later claimed he appropriated the pen name "Mark Twain") and writes several other sketches. Orion moves to Memphis to practice law in May 1860.

1861       Clemens becomes member of the Polar Star Lodge 79, a St. Louis Masonic lodge (maintains contact with the lodge until formally resigning in October 1869). Takes mother on a private steamboat excursion from St. Louis to New Orleans and back. In letter to Orion, describes Goldsmith's *The Citizen of the World* and Cervantes' *Don Quixote* as his "*beau ideals* of fine writing." Is much impressed by Frederick Edwin Church's painting *Heart of the Andes*, on exhibit in St. Louis. Through the influence of St. Louis lawyer Edward Bates, attorney general in the new Lincoln administration, Orion is appointed secretary of Nevada Territory in March. By May outbreak of the Civil War has severely disrupted river traffic. After spending some time with family in St. Louis, fearful of being impressed as gunboat pilot by Union forces, Clemens goes to Hannibal in mid-June and helps form the Marion Rangers, group of Confederate volunteers composed of old Hannibal schoolmates, including Sam Bowen, John L. Robards, Perry Smith, and Ed Stevens. After two weeks of camping and retreating across countryside, half the group decides to disband (Absalom Grimes later carried mail for the Confederacy, John Meredith, son of the Clemenses' doctor, became chief of a guerrilla band, and Perry Smith was killed in battle). Clemens returns to St. Louis in early July and leaves with Orion for Nevada on July 18. Travels on steamer *Sioux City* up the Missouri to St. Joseph, Missouri, then goes by stagecoach through Fort Kearny, Scotts Bluff, South Pass, Fort Bridger, and Salt Lake City, arriving in Carson City, Nevada, on August 14. Meets and becomes friendly with Horatio G. Phillips, Robert Howland, and John D. Kinney. Travels to Aurora, Nevada, in the Esmeralda mining district in early September, where he shares claims with Phillips. Takes trips with Kinney to establish timber claims near Lake Bigler (later Tahoe), and accidentally starts forest fire. Speculates in silver- and gold-mining stocks and serves for $8 a day as Orion's secretary during the fall session of the territorial legislature. Meets Clement T. Rice, who will become close friend and journalistic collaborator. Goes on prospecting trip to Humboldt County, Nevada, with Keokuk friend William H. Clagett in December. Reads and quotes from Dickens' *Dombey and Son*.

1862     Returns to Carson City in late January, then to Aurora in April. Continues prospecting with Phillips without much success and writes occasional letters for the Keokuk *Gate City* and Carson City *Silver Age*; begins sending letters to the Virginia City, Nevada, *Territorial Enterprise* in late April, using pen name "Josh." Clemens and Phillips learn advanced techniques of reducing silver ore from Joshua Eliot Clayton. Has falling-out with Phillips. In July begins to feel restless and wants to move on. Becomes partner in potentially lucrative mining claim and shares cabin for a short time with Calvin H. Higbie (will later dedicate *Roughing It* to him). Nurses Captain John Nye, brother of governor of the Nevada Territory, James Warren Nye, for nine days when he is sick with "inflammatory rheumatism." "Josh" letters to the *Territorial Enterprise* attract the attention of business manager William H. Barstow and editor Joseph T. Goodman, and they offer Clemens a salaried job as reporter ($25 per week) in late July. Takes two-week walking trip through the White Mountains along the Nevada-California border, for pleasure and to look for legendary lost gold "cement" mine. Moves to Virginia

City and begins work as local reporter for the *Territorial Enterprise* in late September; duties include covering fall legislative session in Carson City. Writes "The Petrified Man," a hoax made up to "worry" Judge G. T. Sewall of Humboldt County. Begins lasting friendships with Joseph T. Goodman and Dan De Quille (William Wright), fellow reporter and humorist. Becomes responsible for local reporting when De Quille leaves at end of year on extended visit home to Iowa.

1863    Continues to trade in mining stocks, sometimes receiving free shares in return for favorable mention in the *Enterprise*. Orion serves as acting governor of Nevada during Governor Nye's absence from the territory (Nye returns in July). Clemens goes to Carson City for a week and sends three letters to the *Enterprise*, published February 3, 5, and 8, signing them "Mark Twain," his first known use of the name. Continues his mock feud in print with "the Unreliable," the name he has given to his friend and fellow reporter Clement T. Rice. Leaves Virginia City with Rice early in May to visit San Francisco, where he sees Neil Moss, former classmate and son of the wealthiest man in Hannibal, who has been prospecting without success, and Bill Briggs (brother of his close Hannibal friend John Briggs), who is now running a successful gambling establishment. Enjoys San Francisco, staying at the Occidental Hotel and the Lick House. Makes money selling and trading stocks. Arranges to become Nevada correspondent for the San Francisco *Morning Call*. Returns to Virginia City in July and moves into the new White House hotel; it burns down on July 26 and Clemens loses all his possessions, including his mine stocks. Sick with a severe cold and bronchitis, goes to Lake Bigler with young journalist friend Adair Wilson, and then to Steamboat Springs, nine miles northwest of Virginia City, to try its hot mineral water. When Dan De Quille returns to Virginia City and resumes duties as local editor for the *Enterprise*, Clemens goes to San Francisco for a month. Writes "How to Cure a Cold," his first piece for the *Golden Era*, a San Francisco literary weekly. Returns to Nevada in time to serve as recording secretary of the Washoe Agricultural, Mining, and Mechanical Society Fair, held in Carson City in mid-October. Writes a hoax about a man killing his family, "A Bloody Massacre Near Carson"; when it is uncovered, other papers that had reported it as a true story are furious and refuse to reprint news stories from the *Enterprise*. Clemens offers to resign, but Goodman and De Quille assure him that the anger will diminish and the story will be remembered. Rents suite of rooms with De Quille at 25 North B Street in Virginia City. Goes to Carson City to cover convention drafting first state constitution, then returns to Virginia City in time to meet humorist Artemus Ward (Charles Farrar Browne), who encourages him to write for the New York *Mercury*. Enjoys spirited Christmas Eve dinner with Ward, De Quille, Goodman, and others, which ends with Ward and Clemens walking across the rooftops in Virginia City.

1864    Reports on rejection by the voters on January 19 of the proposed state constitution (clause proposing tax on undeveloped mines is unpopular). Publishes two articles in the New York *Mercury*, "Doings in Nevada" (February 7) and "Those Blasted Children" (February 21). Sees Reuel Gridley, friend from Hannibal, in May when Gridley tours Nevada raising funds for the Sanitary Commission Fair in St. Louis (Commission aids sick and wounded Union soldiers). Joins Gridley in repeatedly auctioning off flour sack, with different towns and groups in Storey County competing to outbid one another (county eventually contributes $22,000 to the fair). Writes two controversial pieces for the *Enterprise* in late May; one repeats rumor that Carson City women were diverting funds intended for the Sanitary Commission to a freedman's society, and the other alleges that the Virginia City *Union* has not fulfilled its bid in the flour-sack auction. When reply in the *Union* calls him "an unmitigated *liar, a poltroon and a puppy*," Clemens challenges its editor, James L. Laird, to a duel, while publicly and privately apologizing to the Carson City women. After exchanging several letters with Laird, Clemens publishes the correspondence on May 24, then becomes concerned about Nevada law outlawing dueling challenges. Leaves with Stephen E. Gillis, close friend and news editor at the *Enterprise*, and Goodman for San Francisco on May 29 (will become ashamed of this "dueling" episode in later years). Rooms with Gillis in several hotels, rooming houses, and private homes. Becomes reporter for the San Francisco *Morning Call* for $40 a week and continues to contribute pieces to the

*Golden Era*. Meets the Reverend Henry Whitney Bellows, founder and president of the United States Sanitary Commission, and enjoys his sense of humor. Finds long hours at the *Call* tedious and makes new arrangement to work only during daylight hours for $25 a week. Contracts to write four articles for $50 a month (same amount he had received from the *Golden Era*) for newly established literary magazine, the *Californian*, owned by Charles Henry Webb and edited by Bret Harte. Bored with the *Call*, becomes lax about work; resigns on October 10 at the suggestion of one of the proprietors. Writes several articles for the *Enterprise* criticizing San Francisco police for corruption, incompetence, and mistreatment of Chinese immigrants. When Gillis is charged for his part in a barroom brawl, they decide in early December to go to Jackass Hill in Tuolumne County, California, where Jim and William Gillis, Stephen's brothers, and Dick Stoker have pocket-mine claims. Remains in camp after Stephen Gillis returns to Virginia City.

1865    In January goes with Jim Gillis to Angel's Camp in Calaveras County and stays there four weeks (soon joined by Stoker), spending most of the time indoors because of bad weather. Listens to stories told by prospectors, one of which is about a jumping frog, and writes notes in journal. Returns briefly to Jackass Hill and then goes to San Francisco in late February. Moves into the Gillis family rooming house at 44 Minna Street. Writes articles for the *Californian*, and pieces for the *Golden Era*, other California journals, and the *Enterprise*. Befriends Charles Warren Stoddard, another contributor to the *Californian*. Begins writing more often for the *Enterprise* and soon contracts to write a letter a day for $100 a month. Takes on another job with the San Francisco *Dramatic Chronicle* for $40 a week, writing Orion that he is determined to get out of debt. Articles reprinted in New York begin to bring recognition (New York *Round Table* calls him "the foremost among the merry gentlemen of the California press"). Experiences strong earthquake on October 8 that causes significant damage in San Francisco, San Jose, and Santa Cruz. After repeated requests from Artemus Ward for a sketch to include in a book of humorous works, sends "Jim Smiley and His Jumping Frog" to him, but the text arrives too late for inclusion in the book and is published in Henry

Clapp's *Saturday Press*. The story is widely reprinted all over the country.

1866    Stops writing for the *Californian* (both it and the *Golden Era* will reprint articles published in the *Enterprise*). Begins to think of writing a book about the Mississippi, and also reviews his articles, saving some and destroying others. Sails on the *Ajax* on March 7 for the Sandwich Islands (Hawaii) as roving correspondent for the Sacramento *Union*. Arrives in Honolulu on March 18. Explores Oahu on horseback (will also ride on Maui and Hawaii), meets King Kamehameha V, and discovers that he is also a Mason. Goes to Maui by small schooner in mid-April; returns to Honolulu May 22, then sails on May 26 to the island of Hawaii, where he sees the volcano Kilauea erupting. Returns to Oahu June 16. Reads Oliver Wendell Holmes' *Songs in Many Keys* while recovering from saddle boils. Meets Anson Burlingame, American minister to China, in Honolulu and spends time with him and his son Edward. Takes notes while Burlingame interviews survivors of the shipwrecked *Hornet* and writes report for the *Union* that scoops all other papers. Sails for San Francisco July 19 on the *Smyrniote*. Fellow passengers include three *Hornet* survivors; Clemens reads and copies parts of their diaries for article "Forty-three Days in an Open Boat" (published in *Harper's Magazine* in December). Arrives in San Francisco on August 13. Sees Orion and his wife, Mollie, who are in city before sailing for the East Coast. Goes to Sacramento and collects $20 for each week of his trip and $100 for each column of the *Hornet* story. Writes articles for the *Union* and the New York *Weekly Review*, and covers California State Agricultural Society Fair in Sacramento. Delivers first lecture on October 2, speaking on the Sandwich Islands to a large, appreciative audience at Maguire's Academy of Music in San Francisco. Goes on tour, lecturing in Sacramento, Marysville, Grass Valley, Nevada City, Red Dog, and You Bet in California, and then in Virginia City, Carson City, Dayton, Silver City, Washoe City, and Gold City in Nevada. Returns to California and appears in San Francisco, San Jose, Petaluma, and Oakland, concluding tour with a special appearance in San Francisco on December 10 at the request of Frederick F. Low, governor of California, and Henry G. Blasdel, governor of Nevada. Becomes traveling correspondent for the San Francisco *Alta California* and leaves San Francisco December 15 aboard the *America*, captained by Edgar Wakeman. Enjoys company of Wakeman and writes down some of his stories. Crosses Central America by way of Nicaragua.

1867     Arrives in Greytown, Nicaragua, and sails on *San Francisco* to New York. Cholera breaks out and seven passengers die; when ship stops at Key West, a number of fearful passengers disembark. Clemens arrives in New York January 12 and takes rooms at the Metropolitan Hotel (establishment frequented by westerners). Sees old California friends Frank Fuller (who will later manage a series of lectures for Clemens) and Charles Henry Webb, who offers to help him put together a book of sketches (Webb will publish it himself after other publishers turn it down). Through Webb, meets Edward H. House of the New York *Tribune*, Henry Clapp, and John Hay. Sends letters to the *Alta* and makes arrangements to contribute articles to the New York *Sunday Mercury*, the *Evening Express* and the New York *Weekly*. Has no success finding a publisher for the Sandwich Islands letters. Reserves cabin on the *Quaker City* for the first American transatlantic excursion, organized by Henry Ward Beecher's congregation (Beecher and General Sherman are expected to be passengers), then goes to St. Louis to visit family (Pamela's husband had died in August 1865). Publishes three satirical articles on women's suffrage in *Missouri Democrat*. Lectures successfully in St. Louis, Hannibal, Keokuk, and Quincy, Illinois, and sees old friends. Returns to New York on April 15 and soon moves into the Westminster Hotel. *The Celebrated Jumping Frog of Calaveras County, and Other Sketches* published by Webb on April 30 (Clemens is unhappy with Webb's editing and sales are poor). Gives three successful lectures in New York and Brooklyn in May. Accepts assignments to write for the New York *Tribune*, the New York *Herald* (unsigned articles), and the *Alta*. Boards *Quaker City* on June 8. After two days anchored off Brooklyn because of bad weather, the ship sails on June 10 for Europe and the Holy Land. Disappointed by absence of Beecher and Sherman and finds most of the passengers too pious and staid, but makes friends with some, including Daniel Slote, his cabin mate, Moses Sperry Beach, editor of the New York *Sun*, and his daughter Emma, John A. Van Nostrand, Julius Moulton, Dr. Abraham Reeves Jackson, Julia Newell, Solon Long Severance and his wife, Emily, Mary Mason Fairbanks ("Mother Fairbanks"), who becomes one of his closest friends and advisers, and 18-year-old Charles Jervis Langdon, from Elmira, New York, who shows Clemens a picture of his sister, Olivia. Travels to North Africa, Spain, France, Italy, Greece, Russia (where members of the excursion meet with Czar Alexander II at Yalta in the Crimea on August 26), Turkey, the Holy Land, and Egypt. Returns to New York on November 19, and goes to Washington, D.C., where he serves for a few weeks as private secretary to William M. Stewart, Republican senator from Nevada. Acts as Washington correspondent for the *Territorial Enterprise*, *Alta California*, and the New York *Tribune*. Receives several offers from book publishers; prefers one from the American Publishing Company, a subscription firm in Hartford, Connecticut. Returns to New York on Christmas Day and moves in with Dan Slote's family. Invited by Charles Langdon to dine with his family at the St. Nicholas Hotel, meets Olivia Louise (Livy) Langdon (b. Nov. 27, 1845). Goes with the Langdons to hear Charles Dickens read.

1868        Spends New Year's Day visiting with Livy and her friend Alice Hooker. Attends services given by Henry Ward Beecher as guest of *Quaker City* friends, Moses and Emma Beach. Has dinner at Beecher's home and meets his sister, Harriet Beecher Stowe. Returns to Washington on January 8. Delivers lecture "The Frozen Truth," an account of the cruise, and gives a successful toast to "Woman" at the Washington Newspaper Correspondents' Club. Lodges at several addresses, often rooming with John Henry Riley, *Alta* correspondent in Washington. Tries unsuccessfully to obtain Patent Office clerkship for Orion. Stops in New York in late January and arranges to write articles for the *Herald*. Makes agreement in Hartford with Elisha Bliss to have his book on the excursion published by the American Publishing Company. Stays with John Hooker (father of Alice Hooker) and his family in the "Nook Farm" area of Hartford, but is uncomfortable because he cannot smoke openly. Returns to Washington and works on book. Sails for California on March 11 to arrange republication rights for his *Alta* letters from the excursion, which the newspaper had copyrighted. Leaves from New York aboard the *Henry Chauncey*, crosses Panama, boards the *Sacramento*, and arrives in San Francisco on April 2. Sees Anson Burlingame at the Occidental Hotel, where they are both staying. Lectures in San Francisco and interior towns, then travels by train and stagecoach from Sacramento to Virginia City, arriving on April 24. Lectures there and in Carson City. Returns to San Francisco May 5. Reaches agreement with the *Alta* regarding *Quaker City* material. Works intensively on book, revising, arranging, and cutting letters and adding new passages. In June asks Bret Harte to read the manuscript and make suggestions (will remember his help with appreciation). Gives another lecture in San Francisco (reviewed more favorably than the earlier ones). Sails for New York on the *Montana* July 6 and arrives in New York on the *Henry Chauncey* July 29. Stays at the Westminster Hotel, where he again sees Burlingame; writes, with his help, "The Treaty with China," article that is published on the front page of the New York *Tribune*. Goes to Hartford and stays with the Blisses while he works on the book. After brief return to New York City goes to visit the Langdon family in Elmira, New York. (Jervis, b. 1809, and Olivia Lewis Langdon, b. 1810, both natives of New York State, were married in 1832 and lived in a succession of towns in upstate New York, where Jervis worked as a storekeeper. They were ardent abolitionists and "conductors" on the Underground Railroad, and had sheltered Frederick Douglass in Millport in 1842 while he was still a fugitive slave. After settling in Elmira in 1845 the Langdons soon prospered in the lumber business and then became wealthy in the coal trade. Their friends included abolitionists Gerritt Smith, William Lloyd Garrison, Wendell Phillips, and Frederick Douglass, and women's rights advocate Anna E. Dickinson. When Livy was 16 years old, a fall on the ice invalided her for two years. She regained her mobility after being treated by Dr. Newton, a faith healer, although for the remainder of her life she is unable to walk very far.) Clemens falls in love with Livy and proposes to her early in September, but is refused. Leaves on September 8 with Charles Langdon to visit Mary Fairbanks and her husband, Abel, at their home in Cleveland. Goes on alone to see family in

St. Louis. Courts Livy with letters. Visits her again in late
September, and then goes to Hartford to work on book.
Meets the Reverend Joseph H. Twichell, a Congregational
minister who will become one of his closest lifetime
friends. Returns to New York in late October and gives
lecture, "The American Vandal Abroad," in Cleveland,
Pittsburgh, and Elmira in November. Proposes to Livy
again and she confesses that she loves him. Promises to
reform himself, to become religious, and to stop drinking.
Jervis Langdon has a former employee make inquiries in
San Francisco about Clemens' past. Resumes lectures in
December, appearing in New Jersey, New York (where he
again stops in Elmira), Pennsylvania, Michigan, Indiana,
and Illinois.

1869     Spends New Year's Day with the Fairbanks in Cleveland.
Continues lecture tour through Ohio, Illinois, Michigan,
Iowa, Wisconsin, Pennsylvania, and New Jersey. Writes
long letters to Livy, and marks up books for her to read,
in particular Oliver Wendell Holmes' *The Autocrat of the
Breakfast Table* (they call it their "courting-book"); she
sends him marked copies of Henry Ward Beecher's sermons. Clemens learns that some Californians have responded unfavorably to Jervis Langdon's inquiries about
his character; he tells Langdon that though many people
were acquainted with him, only five were close, and that
he is no longer the same person he was then. Returns to
Elmira; engagement is formally announced February 4.
Concerned about earning steady income, investigates buying share in either the Cleveland *Herald*, partly owned by
Abel Fairbanks, or the Hartford *Courant*, published in a
city where he and Livy have many friends. While working
on his book in Hartford in early March, rereads *Gulliver's
Travels* and finds that though he had enjoyed it as a boy,
he had no idea then how wonderful it was. Writes to Livy
about it (and *Don Quixote*, which she is reading) that he
"will mark it & tear it until it is fit for your eyes. . . .You
are as pure as snow, & I would have you always so—
untainted, untouched even by the impure thoughts of
others. . . ." Hears Petroleum V. Nasby (David Ross
Locke) lecture in Hartford and they become friends. Goes
to Boston, where Nasby introduces him to Holmes. Returns to Elmira to read proofs, with Livy's assistance (she

will continue to help edit his work). Meets Wendell Phillips in March and Anna E. Dickinson in April when they come to visit the Langdons. Leaves Elmira with Charles Langdon on May 5 and goes to New York and Hartford, where he continues work on book. Engages James Redpath as his lecture agent and begins planning fall tour. Writes articles, including "Personal Habits of the Siamese Twins." Returns to Elmira at the end of May. Finishes reading proofs and goes with Langdon family to the St. Nicholas Hotel in New York, then to Hartford, where they attend the June 17 wedding of Alice Hooker to John Day. Meets Charles Dudley Warner, part-owner of the Hartford *Courant*, at the wedding; he will become a lifelong close friend. After a short visit to New York, returns with Livy to Elmira. Unable to buy a share in the Hartford *Courant*, and feeling the price of investing in the Cleveland *Herald* is too high, on the advice of Jervis Langdon buys a one-third interest in the Buffalo *Express* for $25,000 in August (Clemens puts in $2,500, Langdon lends him $12,500, and the remainder is to be paid in installments). Moves to Buffalo and takes lodgings in rooming house at 39 Swan Street, close to the *Express* office. Makes friends with young newlywed couple living there, John James and Esther (Essie) Keeler Norton McWilliams. Changes the typographical look of the *Express*, using smaller type for headlines and saving larger type for important news. Works closely with part-owner and editor-in-chief Josephus Nelson Larned, who becomes lifelong friend. *The Innocents Abroad*, account of *Quaker City* excursion, is published by American Publishing Company on August 15; it receives good reviews and sells well. Visits Elmira whenever possible. Prepares lecture "Our Fellow Savages of the Sandwich Islands" in Elmira and begins tour in Pittsburgh on November 1. Continues lecturing in Massachusetts, Rhode Island, Connecticut, New York, Washington, D.C., and Maine, using Young's Hotel in Boston as his base. Meets other lyceum lecturers, including humorist Josh Billings (Henry Wheeler Shaw). Begins long, close friendship with William Dean Howells, who had enthusiastically reviewed *The Innocents Abroad*. Returns briefly to Hartford to pick up first-quarter royalty check and finds that the Hartford *Courant* is now eager to have him, but is unable to accept because of his commitment to the *Express*. Sees Langdons in New York in early December. Meets Frederick Douglass in Boston and is impressed by him.

1870    Sends out wedding invitations to old friends, including Dan De Quille, Charles Warren Stoddard, Horace Bixby, and informal invitations to California mining friends Jim Gillis and Dick Stoker. Sees Joseph Goodman when he comes to New York before sailing for Europe. Elated by sales of book. No longer drinks, and cuts down on his smoking. Continues lecturing in New York until January 21. Marries Livy in Elmira on February 2, with Thomas Beecher (half-brother of Henry Ward Beecher and uncle of Alice Hooker) and Twichell performing the service. Sister Pamela and niece Annie Moffett attend. Goes by private train to Buffalo with Livy and a small party of guests on February 3. Clemens expects to be moving into a boarding house and is surprised by gift from Jervis Langdon of furnished house at 472 Delaware Street, with three servants, stable, and horse and carriage (worth more than $40,000). House guests include Pamela and Annie, the Twichells, friends from Elmira, and Petroleum V. Nasby. Clemens goes to the *Express* offices only twice a week. Signs contract in March with *Galaxy* to supply a monthly humorous column, "Memoranda," for $2,000 a year, reserving all republication rights to himself (first column appears in May). Continues writing for the *Express*, but feels that *Galaxy* allows him more freedom. Livy begins to address him as "Youth" (will do so for the rest of her life). Becomes close friends with poet and essayist David Gray, part-owner and associate editor of the Buffalo *Courier*, and his wife, Martha. Mother comes to visit in April (her first meeting with Livy), while sister prepares to move to Fredonia, New York, 60 miles from Buffalo. Jervis Langdon's health deteriorates, and Clemenses go to Elmira for two weeks (will continue to help nurse Langdon; Clemens often sits at his bedside for four hours a night). Goes to Washington, D.C., in early July to lobby for passage of bill to divide Tennessee into two judicial districts (measure would potentially benefit both Jervis Langdon's lumber business and Orion's plans to sell family land near Jamestown). Sees old friends Senator William M. Stewart, Vice-President Schuyler Colfax, and Thomas Fitch (now congressman from Nevada), and

meets President Ulysses S. Grant. Sees old friend John
Henry Riley. Returns to Elmira and signs new contract
with Bliss for book on the West for 7½ percent royalty.
Jervis Langdon dies August 6 of stomach cancer. Livy is
grief-stricken; Clemens gives her opiates to help her
sleep. Livy's mother and Emma Nye, Livy's old classmate, come to visit in Buffalo late in August. Nye immediately falls ill with typhoid; Livy cares for her with help
of hired nurse. Clemens continues to write *Galaxy* articles
and works on western book. Writes Orion expressing his
exasperation over Orion's schemes for selling Tennessee
land. Delights in making burlesque woodcut, "Fortifica-
tions of Paris," for paper. Visits mother, sister, nephew,
and niece in Fredonia. Susan Langdon Crane (Livy's foster sister, b. 1836, who was orphaned in 1840 and then
adopted by the Langdons) comes to take care of Livy,
who is pregnant and exhausted. Clemens gets Orion a
job in Hartford as editor of Bliss's new magazine, *American Publisher*, for $100 a month (first issue comes out in
April 1871). Son Langdon born, one month prematurely,
on November 7 and at first is not expected to live. Mary
Fairbanks comes to help nurse Livy. Clemens goes to
New York to meet Webb about obtaining rights to *Celebrated Jumping Frog of Calaveras County*, forgoes $600
due in royalties, and pays Webb an additional $800 for
rights and plates (will destroy them). Arranges for Riley
to go to South Africa and research book on its diamond
fields, which Clemens will write; pays Riley's passage and
salary ($100 a month). Contracts with Bliss for South Af-
rican book and *Mark Twain's Sketches, New & Old*. Son's
health continues to be poor.

1871      Attends wedding in Cleveland of Mary Fairbanks' step-
daughter, Alice, to William Henry Gaylord (Livy, still un-
well, is unable to attend). Hires a wet nurse to care for
baby. Livy falls dangerously ill with typhoid in February.
Clemens hires nurses and doctors, including Dr. Rachel
Brooks Gleason, to care for her and stays up nights watching over her. Susan Crane and Livy's close friend Clara
Spaulding assist in nursing. Decides to stop writing for
the *Galaxy* in order to work more on books (last "Memo-
randa" column appears in April). Has come to "loathe
Buffalo" and puts house and interest in the *Express* up for
sale, hoping to move to Hartford. When Livy's health im-

proves slightly, takes her to Elmira on March 18, intending never to return to Buffalo. Chagrined by unfavorable reception of pamphlet *Mark Twain's (Burlesque) Autobiography and First Romance*, published by Isaac E. Sheldon, the same firm that published *Galaxy*. Works hard on *Roughing It*, his western book, writing at Quarry Farm, located on a hill outside Elmira and owned by Susan and Theodore Crane. Pleased when Goodman visits in April and works with him on the manuscript. Sells interest in *Express* for $15,000, taking a loss of $10,000. Pamela and her son Samuel Erasmus Moffett stay at Quarry Farm in June to take Elmira Water Cure. Livy's and baby's health improve. Writes lecture on "boys' rights." Arranges another lecture tour with Redpath, but asks that he be paid at least as much as his friend Nasby receives. Has Bliss arrange for George Routledge and Sons to publish and copyright *Roughing It* in England. Clemens writes two more lectures and decides that the third, "Reminiscences of Some Un-Commonplace Characters I Have Chanced to Meet," is the one he wants to deliver. Goes to Hartford in August to complete *Roughing It*. Sees mother and Annie, who have come to visit Orion and Mollie in Hartford, and brings them with him to visit Elmira. Baby is very sick again, and Livy discovers that during her illness he has been given laudanum and other sleeping medicines. Clemens goes to Washington in September to secure patent on "elastic strap" (granted patent for "Improvement in Adjustable and Detachable Straps for Garments"). Leases John and Isabella Beecher Hooker's house in "Nook Farm" area of Hartford. Returns to Buffalo to pack, and moves to Hartford in October. Lectures in Pennsylvania, Washington, D.C., Massachusetts, Vermont, New Hampshire, Maine, and New York. Uses Boston as base when delivering New England lectures, meets Thomas Bailey Aldrich, sees Howells and Bret Harte, and is occasionally accompanied by Ralph Keeler, young writer friend from California. Dislikes his prepared lectures and writes one about Artemus Ward, then writes another one based on *Roughing It*. Goes on to Chicago and is struck by the extent of damage caused by the great fire of October 8–9 ("literally no Chicago *here*"). Stays with *Quaker City* friends Dr. Abraham Reeves Jackson and his second wife, Julia Newell, then continues lecturing in Illinois.

1872    Lectures in Indiana, Ohio, West Virginia, Pennsylvania, and New York, where he sees his friend John Hay. Attends birthday celebration for Horace Greeley, editor of the New York *Tribune*, in New York on February 3; other guests include Hay, Bret Harte, Whitelaw Reid, and P. T. Barnum. *Roughing It* is published in February and sells well. Orion quits as editor of Bliss's *American Publisher* and tells Clemens that Bliss is cheating him on production costs of *Roughing It*. Clemens questions figures, but does not break with Bliss. Returns to Elmira in early March. Daughter Olivia Susan (Susy) born March 19. Visits Fairbanks in Cleveland with Livy and mother in early May. Returns to Elmira, then goes to Hartford. South African book is abandoned when Riley develops fatal cancer of the mouth (he will die in September). Son Langdon dies June 2 of diptheria. In July family goes to stay at Fenwick Hall in New Saybrook, Connecticut, to escape summer heat. Prepares prefaces and makes revisions for English edition of *The Innocents Abroad*, published by Routledge. Devises idea for "Mark Twain's Self-Pasting Scrap-Book" (patented June 24, 1873, it is successfully marketed by his friend Dan Slote). Sails for Liverpool on August 21 on the *Scotia*, intending to write a book on England. Speaks at the Whitefriars, a London literary club, and is made honorary member. Tours Warwickshire in open barouche with American publisher James R. Osgood. Meets humorist Tom Hood, son of the poet, actor Henry Irving, clergyman Moncure Conway, and sees Henry Morton Stanley, whom he had met in St. Louis in 1867. Writes letter to the *Spectator* protesting John Camden Hotten's printing of books attributed to him that include articles he did not write. Speaks at the Savage Club, a literary and artistic club. Overwhelmed by social activities, invitations to private houses, and ceremonial functions, is amazed and flattered by his fame in England. Sails for America on board the *Batavia*, on November 12; impressed when Captain John E. Mouland and crew rescue shipwreck survivors in heavy seas and writes letter to the Royal Humane Society recommending that they be rewarded (among fellow passengers signing letter is Edward Emerson, son of Ralph Waldo Emerson). Arrives in New York on November 25. Begins work on novel *The Gilded Age* with friend and neighbor, Charles Dudley Warner.

1873   Buys large lot in "Nook Farm" area of Hartford, planning
       to build house on it. Lectures in Hartford to raise money
       for charity, and in New York and Brooklyn in February on
       the Sandwich Islands. Made a member of the Lotos Club
       in New York City. Becomes a director of the American
       Publishing Company (owns $5,000 stock in it). Livy goes
       to Elmira late in April and Clemens follows after he and
       Warner finish *The Gilded Age*. Family, accompanied by
       Clara Spaulding and recently hired shorthand secretary
       Samuel Chalmers Thompson, sails for England on the
       *Batavia* on May 17. They initially stay at Edwards' Hotel
       in London, but after a few weeks move to the Langham
       because Clemens misses the billiard room there. Intrigued
       by trial for perjury of claimant to the Tichborne title
       (claimant is eventually proved to have committed perjury).
       Sees Henry Lee, naturalist at Brighton Aquarium, and
       poet Joaquin Miller, whom he had met in California. Ar-
       ranges for Routledge to bring out *The Gilded Age* in En-
       gland. Begins writing letters for the *Herald* on the
       activities of Nasr-Ed-Din, shah of Persia, during his visit
       to England and Europe (eventually sends five). Meets
       Thomas Hughes, Herbert Spencer, Charles Godfrey
       Leland ("Hans Breitmann"), Anthony Trollope, Robert
       Browning, and Wilkie Collins, among others. Moncure
       Conway takes Clemens and Livy to Stratford-on-Avon,
       where they are guests of the mayor. Meets Scottish writer
       George MacDonald and his wife, Louise, in July. Dis-
       charges Thompson as secretary, goes to Edinburgh, Scot-
       land, and meets Dr. John Brown, who is called in to treat
       Livy, who is exhausted after the hectic London season;
       the doctor becomes a lifelong friend. Buys the Abbotsford
       Edition of Sir Walter Scott's works. Clara Spaulding re-
       joins them after traveling in France. Visits Belfast, becom-
       ing friends there with *Northern Whig* proprietor Francis
       Dalzell Finlay, goes to Dublin, then returns to London.
       Sees old friend Charles Warren Stoddard, who is in Lon-
       don as newspaper correspondent. Clemenses go to Paris in
       late September to buy household items. Having spent
       more money than expected, Clemens has George Dolby,
       Dickens' agent, arrange for him to lecture in London in
       mid-October. Accompanies family home to America, sail-
       ing on the *Batavia* October 21 and arriving in New York
       November 2, where Orion is trying to get work as an

editor, proofreader, or typesetter on a newspaper. Clemens leaves for England on November 8 to obtain copyright for *The Gilded Age* and to give further lectures. Arrives in London November 20. Moves into the Langham Hotel but feels lonely and asks Stoddard to join him there as secretary and companion. Lectures in December on the Sandwich Islands for a week, then changes to "Roughing It on the Silver Frontier" for the next two weeks. Writes out after-dinner speeches because he is often called on to give them. Feels oppressed by continuous, unusually heavy fog and coal smoke. Elected honorary member of the Temple Club. Finlay visits for a week. *The Gilded Age* published simultaneously in England and America on December 23. Spends Christmas holiday at Salisbury and visits Stonehenge.

1874    Lectures in Leicester and Liverpool. Sails for Boston on the *Parthia* January 13 and arrives on January 26. Introduces lecture by English clergyman and writer Charles Kingsley at the Essex Institute in Salem, Massachusetts. Works on two plays. Lectures in Boston in March. Mary Fairbanks and her children visit Hartford. Sales of *The Gilded Age* are very good. Buys Orion a small chicken farm outside Keokuk (will begin sending regular payments to Orion, who considers them loans, though he will be unable to repay more than nominal amounts of interest). Goes to Elmira in late April and stays in the Langdon house, then moves to Quarry Farm on May 5, where Susan Crane has built a free-standing octagonal study for him. Daughter Clara Langdon born June 8. Works on five-act play *Colonel Sellers*, dramatization of *The Gilded Age*, and *Tom Sawyer*. Pleased when "A True Story" is accepted by Howells for the *Atlantic* (published November 1874), his first piece to appear there. Stops in New York en route from Elmira to Hartford to help with rehearsals for *Colonel Sellers*; play opens September 16, starring John T. Raymond, at the Park Theatre. Returns to Hartford September 19 and moves into still unfinished house designed by architect Edward T. Potter. With Howells' encouragement, begins writing articles about the Mississippi ("Old Times on the Mississippi," first in series, appears in January 1875 *Atlantic*). Decides in November to walk with Twichell from Hartford to Boston; they cover 28 miles the first day and six miles the next before taking the train the rest of the way. Buys a typewriter and writes to Howells on it (later boasts to friends that he was the first writer to use one). Attends *Atlantic* contributors' dinner in Boston on December 15.

1875    Enjoys new home, spending hours playing billiards in room at top of house; close neighbors are the Warners and Stowes. Describes his taste in reading: "I like history, biography, travels, curious facts & strange happenings, & science. And I detest novels, poetry & theology." Continues writing reminiscences of life as a pilot on the Mississippi (installments appear in the *Atlantic* until August). Pleased with royalties received from *Colonel Sellers*, which is successfully touring the country. Goes to New York to attend Henry Ward Beecher's trial for adultery (it results in a hung jury). Decides not to go to Quarry Farm for the summer. Resumes work on *Tom Sawyer*. Invites Dan De Quille to come to Hartford and helps him get his book *The Big Bonanza* published by Bliss (appears fall 1876). Clemens and Howells frequently visit each other in Hartford and Cambridge. Hires George Griffin as butler; he becomes a family favorite (household includes about seven servants, among them nurses for the children). Receives many visitors, including Joaquin Miller and Bret Harte. Finishes *Tom Sawyer* in July. Goes to Bateman's Point, Newport, Rhode Island, at the end of month and stays through August. *Mark Twain's Sketches, New and Old* published September 25 by Bliss. Moncure Conway visits the Clemenses in Hartford.

1876    Engages Conway as agent for English publication of *Tom Sawyer* (Conway is paid 5 percent of royalty). Clemens is ill for several weeks. Employs private secretary to take dictation and answer letters. Makes revisions in *Tom Sawyer* based on Howells' suggestions. Gives talk, "The Facts Concerning the Recent Carnival of Crime in Connecticut," to the Monday Evening Club, Hartford literary group. Mother and sister visit. Clemens goes to Quarry Farm on June 15 for the summer. *The Adventures of Tom Sawyer* published in England by Chatto & Windus. Begins work on *Huckleberry Finn*. Attends centennial celebration in Philadelphia with other authors and reads eulogy to

Francis Lightfoot Lee. Angered by widespread sales in the United States of pirated Canadian editions of *Tom Sawyer*. Works on scatological tale [*Date, 1601.*] *Conversation, as it Was by the Social Fireside, in the Time of the Tudors* (published privately 1880), and reads it to close friends Twichell, David Gray, Howells, and John Hay. Returns to Hartford September 11. In November gives a series of readings arranged by Redpath. Collaborates with Harte on play, *Ah Sin*, Harte staying at the Clemenses' house for two weeks. Becomes friends with Frank Millet when he comes to Hartford to paint Clemens' portrait. American edition of *Tom Sawyer*, published December 8 by the American Publishing Company, sells moderately well. Tauchnitz firm publishes continental edition of *Tom Sawyer* with his approval (Tauchnitz will continue as his European publisher).

1877          Continues work on play with Harte until late February. Relations with Harte become strained over their financial and publishing ties, and then break off completely when Clemens receives an angry letter from him. Oversees rehearsals of *Ah Sin* in Baltimore in April, then returns home on May 1 (play opens in Washington on May 7). Travels with Twichell to Bermuda for short holiday, then goes with family to Elmira in June. Writes "Some Rambling Notes of an Idle Excursion" about Bermuda trip for the *Atlantic*. Begins work on another play, "Cap'n Simon Wheeler, the Amateur Detective" (never produced or published). Attends New York rehearsals for *Ah Sin* in July (produced by Augustin Daly, the play opens July 31 and runs for five weeks). Reads English and French histories and French novels; likes the elder Dumas' novels of the Revolution, and describes Carlyle's *History of the French Revolution* as "one of the greatest creations that ever flowed from a pen." Tries to persuade cartoonist Thomas Nast to go on a lecture tour with him. At banquet in Boston on December 17 delivers the "Whittier Birthday Speech," a burlesque of three tramps who pass themselves off as Longfellow, Emerson, and Holmes. Many listeners, including Howells, are shocked, and some newspapers are severely critical. Chagrined, sends letters of apology to the three writers, all of whom had attended dinner (will eventually become less embarrassed by this incident).

1878     Works on *The Prince and the Pauper*. Signs contract on March 8 with Elisha Bliss for book about Europe, accepting half of the profits in lieu of royalties (Clemens considers separate agreement with Bliss expedient because Bliss is threatening to leave the American Publishing Company). Visits Elmira and Fredonia (niece Annie is now married to Charles Webster). Sails for Europe April 11 on the *Holsatia* with family, Clara Spaulding, and German nursemaid Rosina (Rosa) Hay. Passengers include Bayard Taylor, on his way to become minister to Germany, and journalist Murat Halstead. Family stops in Hamburg for a week and then travels slowly through Germany to Heidelberg, arriving May 6. Clemens takes excursions into the countryside before they leave on July 23 for Baden-Baden. Twichell arrives August 1 (Clemens is paying for his trip). Clemens and Twichell take "walking tour," traveling by rail, carriage, boat, and foot through the Black Forest and the Swiss Alps to Lausanne and Geneva, from where Twichell returns home in September. Family travels through Italy, staying in Venice, Florence, and Rome until November, then settles in Munich for three months, where they study German. Saddened by news of death of Bayard Taylor in Berlin on December 19.

1879     Family goes to Paris at the end of February. Clemens is very ill with rheumatism and dysentery. Feels better in April and works on *A Tramp Abroad*. Dislikes Paris, but enjoys friends who are also there, including Moncure Conway and the Aldriches. Meets artists and literary men who belong to the Stomach Club, including Edwin Austin Abbey and Augustus Saint-Gaudens, and attends wedding of friend Frank Millet. Has two meetings with Ivan Turgenev, a writer he admires. Family leaves Paris in late July and travels through Belgium and Holland, then spends a month in England. Renews old acquaintances there and meets Charles Darwin at Grasmere in the Lake District. Family sails on the *Gallia* August 23 and arrives in New York on September 3, then goes to Quarry Farm. Clemens visits his family in Fredonia. Returns to Hartford in late October. Installs telephone in his home. Attends reunion banquet of Army of the Tennessee, held in Chicago on November 13 with Ulysses S. Grant as the guest of honor (generals Sherman, Sheridan, Pope, Schofield, and Logan are also present). Responds to toast with

speech "The Babies." Becomes friends with orator Robert
G. Ingersoll. Attends *Atlantic* breakfast in honor of Oliver
Wendell Holmes and gives well-received speech.

1880          Goes to Elmira with Livy, who is exhausted from redeco-
rating house and installing furniture bought in Europe.
Works for a short time on *Huckleberry Finn*, then sets it
aside. Visits mother, who is not well, in Fredonia.
Buys four-fifths interest in Dan Slote's patent in Kaolatype, a chalk-plate process for engraving illustrations, and
forms company with himself as president, Charles Perkins
(his Hartford lawyer and friend) as secretary, and Slote as
treasurer. Agrees to finance company with his own money
as needed for three months. *A Tramp Abroad* published in
March by the American Publishing Company. It sells well,
and Clemens earns more money on each book sold than
under previous contracts. Increases payments to Orion,
telling him that the money is for his role in making him
more aware of the need to obtain better terms from publishers. Works happily on *The Prince and the Pauper* and
encourages Orion to write autobiography (Orion will
write several chapters, but never finishes manuscript).
Daughter Jane Lampton (Jean) born July 26. Elisha Bliss
dies on September 28 (death will cause Clemens to seek
new publisher). Clemens accompanies Grant to Hartford
and delivers welcoming speech. Actively supports James A.
Garfield, the Republican presidential nominee.

1881          Writes letter to president-elect Garfield, describing Frederick Douglass as a personal friend and asking that he be
retained in the office of marshal of the District of Columbia (Garfield makes Douglass recorder of deeds for the
District). Pays support for Paris stay of young Hartford
machinist Karl Gerhardt and wife, Hattie, so that Gerhardt can study sculpture. Buys additional land next to
house to keep neighbor from building and begins renova-
tions of house and grounds. Disillusioned with Slote,
hires Charles Webster, niece Annie's husband, to supervise
Slote and the Kaolatype concern, and to be his business
agent in other matters. Enjoys reading out loud works of
Joel Chandler Harris. Spends June and July at Montowese
House, in Branford, Connecticut, before going to Elmira.
Makes Webster his legal representative in business aspects

of the publication of his books by the American Publishing Company. Upset by the shooting of President Garfield on July 2 and his death on September 19. By now has made numerous investments in various speculative ventures, including the Paige typesetter (will eventually invest at least $190,000 trying to get the machine perfected). Howells reads proofs and suggests revisions of *The Prince and the Pauper*. Clemens and James R. Osgood travel to Canada to issue an edition of the book there (their presence in the country is needed to secure Canadian copyright). Clemens reads Francis Parkman's histories of the Anglo-French conflict in North America. *The Prince and the Pauper* is published by James R. Osgood & Co. in the United States in late December (Clemens pays production costs and Osgood produces and markets the book in return for a 7½ percent royalty).

1882   Dan Slote dies. Old friend Edward House visits in February with his adopted daughter Koto, and House is ill for weeks. Clemens and Howells ask Grant to intercede with President Arthur to keep Howells' father as consul in Toronto (Arthur retains him). Visits the aged Emerson with Howells, and is pleased when Emerson eventually recognizes him. In preparation for expanding 1875 *Atlantic* articles about the Mississippi into a book, Clemens travels with Osgood and shorthand secretary Roswell Phelps to St. Louis, then goes by steamboat to New Orleans, where he meets Joel Chandler Harris, George Washington Cable, and old friend Horace Bixby. Travels up the Mississippi with Bixby in pilothouse, stopping off in Hannibal and Quincy, Illinois. *The Stolen White Elephant*, collection of short pieces, published by Osgood. Trip to Quarry Farm delayed when Jean, Susy, and Clemens get scarlet fever and their house is quarantined. Struggles over writing *Life on the Mississippi*. Beginning to have doubts about Osgood's ability to sell books by subscription, makes Webster his subscription agent for the New York area. Remains in Elmira until September 29. Cable visits.

1883   Finishes book. Livy is sick with diphtheria and other ailments for over a month. Goes again to Canada to safeguard copyright. *Life on the Mississippi* published in May by Osgood (contractual terms are the same as for *The*

*Prince and the Pauper*). Resumes work on *Huckleberry Finn* and enjoys the writing. Collaborates with Howells on play *Colonel Sellers as Scientist*. Begins work on dramatizations of *Tom Sawyer* and *The Prince and the Pauper*. Family entertains many house guests. Becomes very dissatisfied with sales of books under Osgood's direction. Meets Matthew Arnold in Hartford during his American lecture tour.

1884    Cable visits in January and comes down with mumps; nurse is hired to take care of him. Clemens invests in Howells' father's invention, one-handed grape shears. Tries unsuccessfully to get plays produced. Howells reads typescript of *Huckleberry Finn* and suggests revisions. Clemens has attack of gout. Founds his own publishing company, Charles L. Webster & Co., and signs contract in May with Webster, who acts as publisher. Learns to ride a bicycle. Reads proofs of *Huckleberry Finn* from June through August, with help from Howells. Gerhardt makes bust of Clemens. Needing more money, contracts with Major J. B. Pond to do four-month lecture tour with Cable (Pond receives 10 percent commission, Cable $450 a week and expenses, and Clemens the remainder). Joins other Republican "mugwumps," who consider Republican presidential candidate James G. Blaine to be dishonest, in voting for Democrat Grover Cleveland. Lecture tour begins November 5 in New Haven. Learns from Richard Watson Gilder, editor of *Century Magazine*, that General Grant is writing his memoirs. Visits Grant in New York, tells him that terms offered by Century Company are inadequate, and urges him not to sign any contract until Webster & Co. can make an offer; Grant makes no commitments. On recommendation of Cable, Clemens reads Malory's *Le Morte d'Arthur*. In December, visits president-elect Cleveland in Albany at his invitation. *Century* publishes first of three excerpts from *Huckleberry Finn*. Charles Webster offers Grant $50,000 advance for his memoirs.

1885    Continues lecture tour, which includes Hannibal and Keokuk, where mother is now living with Orion. Charles Webster offers Grant choice of 20 percent royalty or 70 percent of net profits. *Adventures of Huckleberry Finn* published in the United States by Webster & Co. on February

16 (sells 39,000 copies by March 14); Clemens again goes
to Canada to protect copyright. Webster & Co. buys
rights to books published by Osgood for $3,000. Clemens
visits Grant in New York on February 21 and learns that he
is dying from throat cancer, but again urges him to accept
the Webster offer. Grant signs contract on February 27,
choosing to receive 70 percent of the profits. Canvassing
for the books begins immediately. Lecture tour ends February 28; is very successful financially, and Clemens likes
Cable, but is irritated by his strict observance of the Sabbath. Clemens signs new contract that makes Charles
Webster a partner in Webster & Co. and gives him more
money. When Concord, Massachusetts, library bans *Huckleberry Finn*, tells Webster that they will sell an extra
20,000 books as a result. Arranges for Gerhardt to make
bust of Grant. Concerned about Grant's well-being and
worried that he may not live to complete the memoirs,
Clemens helps in any way he can, reading proofs as pages
are set and praising the writing. By May more than
60,000 two-volume sets have been ordered, and production arrangements become costly and complex. Clemens is
pleased when Susy begins writing biography of his life.
Learns of Osgood's business failure. Writes account of the
Marion Rangers, "The Private History of a Campaign
that Failed," and shows it to Grant, who enjoys it im-
mensely (published in *Century Magazine* in December as
part of its series on the Civil War). Works on sequel to
*Huckleberry Finn*, "Tom and Huck among the Indians"
(never finished). Family goes to Elmira. Clemens visits
Grant at Mount McGregor, New York, June 29–July 2,
working with him on the completion of the second volume. Grant dies July 23, only a few days after finishing his
memoirs. Clemens is involved in many ventures, including
patents for a historical game, a perpetual calendar, and a
"bed-clasp" for keeping babies' blankets in place; his major
investment, now costing $3,000 a month, is the Paige
typesetter. Reads manuscripts for possible publication by
Webster & Co. Touched when Oliver Wendell Holmes,
Charles Dudley Warner, and others write tributes in the
*Critic* for his fiftieth birthday. In December 325,000 copies
of first volume of *Personal Memoirs of U. S. Grant* are
bound and shipped (second volume appears in March
1886). Clemens begins paying board of Warner T.

McGuinn, one of the first black students at the Yale Law School, whom he had met during a speaking engagement at Yale in the fall. (Will also support study of Charles Ethan Porter, a black sculptor, and pay tuition of a black undergraduate at Lincoln University. McGuinn graduates from Yale in 1887 and becomes an attorney in Baltimore, where he later serves as local director of the NAACP and wins lawsuit challenging mandated segregation of Baltimore city housing.)

1886      Family continues to entertain lavishly. Howells comes with his daughter Mildred to see staging of *The Prince and the Pauper* dramatized by Livy and performed by the Clemens children and their friends. Clemens frequently goes to New York on publishing business. Charles Webster gives Julia Grant check for $200,000 on February 27 (Grant family eventually receives between $420,000 and $450,000 from sales of *Personal Memoirs*). Clemens makes Frederick J. Hall third partner in Webster & Co. on April 28. Learns in May that after prolonged negotiations, Webster & Co. has signed contract with Bernard O'Reilly, authorized biographer of Pope Leo XIII; Clemens expects that the papal biography will be more successful than Grant's memoirs (is disappointed by sales when book is published in 1887). Reads from his works at U.S. Military Academy at West Point. Resumes work with Howells on play *Colonel Sellers as Scientist* and makes arrangements to have it produced, but at the last moment Howells asks that it be withdrawn. In July, takes family to visit mother, Orion, and Mollie in Keokuk. Hires Frank G. Whitmore as business agent in August, primarily to supervise construction of the Paige typesetting machine at the Pratt & Whitney works in Hartford. Begins work on *A Connecticut Yankee in King Arthur's Court*. Reads Robert Browning steadily ("It takes me much longer to learn how to read a page of Browning than a page of Shakespeare") and enjoys reading his poetry aloud to the "Browning class," a group of Livy's friends who meet in his billiard room once a week. Entertains Henry Morton Stanley in Hartford and gives introduction at Stanley's lecture in Boston.

1887      Attends benefit on March 31 for the Longfellow Memorial Fund in Boston and reads from "English as She Is

Taught," after being introduced by Charles Eliot Norton, who tells anecdote about Darwin keeping Clemens' works on his bedside table (other readers include Howells, Julia Ward Howe, Edward Everett Hale, Oliver Wendell Holmes, Thomas W. Higginson, George W. Curtis, Thomas B. Aldrich, and James R. Lowell). Defends General Grant's grammar against criticism by Matthew Arnold in speech in Hartford on April 27. Clemens financially backs production of *Colonel Sellers as Scientist*, retitled *The American Claimant* and credited solely to Mark Twain, that has a brief run starring A. P. Burbank. With Livy and several Hartford friends, visits artist Frederick Edwin Church and his wife at Olana, New York (Clemens had long admired him). At Quarry Farm, continues to work with pleasure on *A Connecticut Yankee in King Arthur's Court. Mark Twain's Library of Humor* (collaboration among Howells, Clemens, and Charles H. Clark, finished a number of years earlier; introduction written by Howells, signed "The Associate Editors") published in late December by Webster & Co.

1888   Signs agreement stating that Webster (who has been suffering increasingly from painful neuralgia) is to withdraw "from business, from all authority, and from the city, till April 1, 1889, & try to get back his health." Frederick Hall takes over his responsibilities. In April Clemens spends afternoon with Robert Louis Stevenson in New York's Washington Square Park. Visits Thomas Edison at his laboratory in West Orange, New Jersey, in June. Awarded honorary Master of Arts degree by Yale. Theodore Crane has partially paralyzing stroke in Elmira on September 6. Writer Grace King stays with the Clemenses at Hartford, October–November. Crane's condition worsens and he is nursed by Susan and Livy in Hartford in December. Hall buys Webster's interest in firm for $12,000.

1889   Success of prototype Paige typesetter thrills Clemens, although technical problems again develop. Writes letter of tribute to Whitman for publication in *Camden's Compliment to Walt Whitman*, edited by Horace Traubel (Clemens had joined others in financially assisting Whitman in 1885 and 1887). Theodore Crane dies at Quarry Farm on July 3. Clemens is charmed by Rudyard Kipling, who visits him in Elmira (will later read and reread Kipling's works with pleasure). Goes to Hartford to work on revisions of *A Connecticut Yankee in King Arthur's Court*. Hoping to live on profits from Paige machine, calls the novel his "swan-song" and his "retirement from literature" in letter to Howells. Unable to read manuscript because of eye trouble, Livy asks Clemens to have Howells read proofs because she trusts Howells to keep Clemens from offending good taste. Certain that the Paige machine will soon be ready for production, Clemens writes Howells that "after patiently & contentedly spending more than $3,000 a month on it for 44 consecutive months" it is "done at last. . . . Come & see this sublime magician of iron & steel work his enchantments." Invites Joseph Goodman to come east and help find investors for machine. Reads and is deeply impressed with Edward Bellamy's *Looking Backward: 2000–1887*. Anticipating that Chatto, his English publisher, will make changes in *A Connecticut Yankee* to avoid offending English sensibilities, writes letter to them refusing to alter text and saying that the book was "written for England." *A Connecticut Yankee in King Arthur's Court*, published in America December 10 by Webster & Co., with illustrations by Daniel Carter Beard, sells moderately well. Dramatization of *The Prince and the Pauper* by Abby Sage Richardson, produced by Belasco and Frohman, opens on Christmas Day in Philadelphia and is fairly successful.

1890     January, Edward Bellamy visits Clemens in Hartford. Financial problems become acute from continued cost of Paige machine and lack of profits from Webster & Co. (unsold books, subscription costs, and expense of producing and distributing 11-volume *Library of American Literature*, an anthology edited by Edmund C. Stedman, create constant cash-flow problems that drain away his book royalties). Edward House brings suit against dramatization of *The Prince and the Pauper* by Richardson, claiming he had been given the rights long ago. Litigation prevents Clemens from receiving royalties from play and ends their friendship. Family goes for the summer to Onteora Park, artists' and writers' colony in the Catskills near Tannersville, New York. With Goodman's help, Clemens travels frequently in search of investors for the Paige machine. Goes to Keokuk in August when mother has stroke. Susy

enters Bryn Mawr in October. Clara takes piano lessons in
New York twice a week. Mother dies in Keokuk October
27, and Clemens attends funeral in Hannibal on October
30. Goes to Elmira in November, where Livy's mother
dies November 28. Clemens rushes back to Hartford because Jean is ill.

1891 Webster & Co. goes deeper into debt. Attempts at raising
capital for Paige machine are unsuccessful, and Clemens
stops his monthly $3,000 payments in support of project.
Writes articles for magazines. Suffering from rheumatism
in right arm, finds writing difficult. Works on novel *The
American Claimant*. Experiments with dictating into pho-
nograph, but soon gives up. Susy leaves Bryn Mawr in
April, too homesick to continue. Charles Webster dies
April 26. Clemens signs contract with *McClure's Magazine*
to serialize *The American Claimant* in America and Europe
for $12,000 and to write six letters from Europe for $1,000
each. No longer able to afford the maintenance of the
Hartford home, decides to go to Europe, hoping that
baths will help Livy's health (she is developing heart trouble) and relieve rheumatism in his arm, which makes writing almost impossible. They close the house, sell the
horses, and find new positions for their servants. Family
sails with Susan Crane on June 6 aboard the *Gascogne* and
arrives in Le Havre June 14. Stops in Paris before going to
take baths at Aix-les-Bains. Susy and Clara attend boarding school in Geneva. Clemens hears Wagner operas at
Bayreuth in August. Tries other baths at Marienbad.
Settles family in Ouchy, Switzerland, in September, then
hires courier, boatman, and flatboat for ten-day trip down
the Rhône. Family goes to Berlin for the winter and
moves into Körnerstrasse Hotel. Still suffers from pain in
arm and continues to find writing difficult. Moves family
to better rooms in Hotel Royal on December 31.

1892 Clemens develops pneumonia. Doctors recommend that
as soon as he is well enough to travel, Livy and he should
go south. Has private dinner with Kaiser William II on
February 20. Leaves daughters at school in Berlin and
goes with Livy in March to Mentone, France, for three
weeks and then to Italy, spending several weeks in Rome
and Venice before returning to Berlin. Collection *Merry*

*Tales* published in April in cheaply bound edition, and *The American Claimant* published in May, both by Webster & Co.; sales are poor. Many Germans and Americans visit, including Sarah Orne Jewett and Annie Fields. Family moves to Bad Nauheim for the summer. Clemens goes to New York in mid-June to check on publishing business and makes quick trip to Chicago, where factory has been established to manufacture the Paige typesetter. Returns to Europe in mid-July. Works on "Those Extraordinary Twins" and then turns to *Tom Sawyer Abroad* (published serially in *St. Nicholas*, November 1893–January 1894, and as a book by Webster & Co. in 1894). Twichells visit in August, and Clemens and Twichell go to Bad Homburg, where they meet Edward, Prince of Wales. Susan Crane returns to America. In September the family goes to Florence, traveling slowly because of Livy's health and stopping in Frankfurt am Main and Lucerne, Switzerland, on the way. Moves into the Villa Viviani, Settignano, Florence, in late September. Family enjoys living there, and Clemens concentrates on writing. Clara returns to Berlin to study music. Livy's health continues to be poor. Clemens reworks "Those Extraordinary Twins" into *Pudd'nhead Wilson*. Meets William James.

1893    Works on *Personal Recollections of Joan of Arc* and articles for magazines. Sails to New York for business reasons, leaving on *Kaiser Wilhelm II* March 22 and arriving in New York April 3. Sees Howells and Kipling and goes with Hall to Chicago, where he checks progress of Paige machine and attends the World's Columbian Exposition. Financial panic in America makes problems at Webster & Co. more severe. Feeling disheartened, leaves for Europe aboard *Kaiser Wilhelm II* May 13. Tries to find buyer for his interest in Webster & Co., then suggests selling *Library of American Literature* to another publisher. In June family goes to Munich and to spas, where Livy continues to take baths. Clemens resumes work on *Pudd'nhead Wilson*. Feels depressed and distraught about financial circumstances. Borrows money and seeks financial advice from Charles Langdon. Sails with Clara from Bremen on the *Spree* August 29, arriving in New York on September 7. Sells "The Esquimau Maiden's Romance" to *Cosmopolitan* for $800, and *Pudd'nhead Wilson* to *Century* for $6,500 (appears December 1893–June 1894). After Clara leaves to visit family in Elmira, Clemens rooms with friend Dr. Clarence C. Rice, then takes a cheap room in the Players' Club on September 29. Tries to borrow money to meet pressing debts of Webster & Co. from friends in Hartford and Wall Street brokers and bankers, but panic has made money tight. Through Rice, meets Henry Huttleston Rogers, vice-president and director of the Standard Oil Company (had briefly met him two years earlier), who immediately takes care of an $8,000 debt owed by Webster & Co., and begins examining the problems of the Paige typesetter company. Rogers arranges for his son-in-law, William E. Benjamin, to buy the *Library of American Literature* from Webster & Co. for $50,000 in October. Clemens sees old friends, dines out constantly, is often called upon for after-dinner speeches, and is touched by warmth of his reception in New York. Richard Watson Gilder and Howells pay tribute to him at dinner given in his honor by the Lotos Club on November 11. Clara returns to Europe to study music. Clemens travels with Rogers on December 21 to Chicago in private railroad car to inspect Paige machine.

1894    Goes to Boston to participate in "Author's Reading and Music for the Poor," and has dinner with Annie Fields, Sarah Orne Jewett, and Oliver Wendell Holmes (Holmes will die in October). Sees Mary Fairbanks in New York in February. Gives two readings with James Whitcomb Riley. Becomes closer to Rogers and his family, and enjoys watching Rogers conduct business in his office in the Standard Oil building at 26 Broadway. Gives Rogers power of attorney over all his affairs on March 6. Sails March 7 and arrives in Paris, where family is now living, on March 15. Rogers assigns Clemens' property, including his copyrights and share in the Paige machine, to Livy. Clemens sails for New York on April 7 and arrives April 14. On advice from Rogers, declares the failure of Webster & Co. on April 18 and assumes his share of its debts, causing his personal bankruptcy, which is widely and sympathetically reported in newspapers. Returns to Paris in May. Howells spends a week with him in June. For sake of Susy's health, family goes to La Bourboule-les-Bains in central France. Clemens plans to return to America at Rogers' request, but his departure is delayed by rioting caused by the assassination of French President Carnot on

June 24. Arrives in New York in early July and remains until mid-August, then rejoins family at Étretat in Normandy. Spends October with family in Rouen; Susy is still ill, with persistent high fever. *The Tragedy of Pudd'nhead Wilson and the Comedy of Those Extraordinary Twins* published in November as subscription book by the American Publishing Company (publisher includes earlier version of story as a separate work). Family returns to Paris, where Clemens is confined to bed with attack of gout. Devastated by news in December that Paige typesetter has failed a test in the offices of the Chicago *Herald* because of broken type. Resolves to reimburse his friends, actor Henry Irving and writer Bram Stoker (Irving's manager), for their investment in the machine (they are repaid in spring 1895).

1895    Works on several short pieces for journals, and writes *Tom Sawyer, Detective* (published by Harper & Brothers in November 1896). Finishes *Personal Recollections of Joan of Arc* and sails from Southampton on February 23 on the *New York*. Arrives in New York in early March and arranges serial publication of *Personal Recollections of Joan of Arc* in *Harper's Magazine* (begins in April). In hopes of having the work taken more seriously, asks that installments appear anonymously (his authorship soon becomes known, and book edition, published by Harper & Brothers in 1896, is credited to Mark Twain). Moved by visit to family home in Hartford, now leased to friends John and Alice Hooker Day. Arranges with Major Pond for cross-country lecture tour (Pond receives 25 percent of fee for lectures between New York and San Francisco, and 20 percent for lectures in San Francisco). Clemens returns to France in late March; also aboard ship is Andrew Carnegie, an old acquaintance. Brings family to New York on May 18, then goes to Quarry Farm. Agrees to contract, signed on May 23, with Harpers that gives them rights to Mark Twain books published by Webster & Co. (negotiations with the American Publishing Company for similar agreement continue; Clemens hopes that Harpers will bring out a uniform edition of his works). Prepares lectures, suffers painful carbuncle on leg, and is forced to stay in bed for over six weeks, unable to stand or put on clothes. Leaving Susy and Jean to stay with Susan Crane at Quarry Farm, Clemens, Livy, and Clara leave on July 14 for first lecture

in Cleveland. Travels across country, accompanied by
Pond and his wife. Tells reporters in Vancouver that he
intends to eventually repay every creditor in full. Sails for
Australia aboard the *Warrimoo* on August 23 with Livy and
Clara, beginning around-the-world lecture tour arranged
by firm of R. S. Smythe, who had earlier managed a similar tour for Henry Morton Stanley. Hopes to stop in
Honolulu, but is prevented from landing by outbreak of
cholera. Visits Suva in Fiji Islands and arrives in Sydney
on September 16. Met by Carlyle Smythe, who will serve
as their guide on the tour. Continues to suffer from carbuncles. Appears in Sydney, Melbourne, Adelaide, and
other Australian towns before large, responsive audiences,
reading from his books and telling stories. Visits gold
fields in Victoria. Sails for New Zealand on October 30
and stops in Tasmania before landing at Bluff. Lectures
throughout South and North Islands, visiting Dunedin,
Christchurch, Wellington, Auckland, and other towns.
Leaves Wellington on December 13 and lands in Sydney
December 17.

1896          Sails for India with Livy, Clara, and Carlyle Smythe from
Albany, Western Australia, on January 4. Enjoys emptiness
and calm of Indian Ocean. Stops briefly in Colombo,
Ceylon, and arrives in Bombay on January 18. Suffers
from persistent bronchial cough. Visits Towers of Silence,
where Parsis expose their dead. Lectures in great hall of
palace at Baroda on January 31. Finds India fascinating and
is warmly received by Indian princes and British officials.
Reads reports of Major William Sleeman, the suppressor
of the Thugs in the late 1830s, and accounts of the 1857
Sepoy Mutiny. Takes train from Bombay to Allahabad and
Benares. Lectures to packed audiences in Calcutta, February 10–13, then goes to Darjeeling in the foothills of the
Himalayas. Exhilarated by first stage of descent from Dar-
jeeling, made for 35 miles in open railway handcar. Re-
turns to Calcutta and then visits Lucknow, Kanpur, Agra,
Delhi, Lahore, Rawalpindi, and Jaipur. Sails from Cal-
cutta for South Africa at the end of March. Stops in Ma-
dras and Ceylon, visits Mauritius April 15–28, and lands on
May 6 at Durban in British colony of Natal. Livy and
Clara stay in Durban while Clemens gives readings across
South Africa. Goes to Pietermaritzburg, Natal capital,
Johannesburg, and Pretoria, capital of the Boer Transvaal

republic. Visits John Hayes Hammond and other "Reformers" imprisoned for their alleged complicity in 1895
Jameson Raid, an aborted invasion intended to bring the
Transvaal under British rule (Mrs. Hammond is a Missourian whom Clemens had met previously). After leaving
prison, Clemens makes humorous remark to reporter that
is misinterpreted as implying that prisoners are being
treated leniently. When their confinement is made harsher,
Clemens goes to see President Kruger on May 26 to explain the joke (prisoners are soon released). Goes to
Bloemfontein, capital of Orange Free State, and Queens-
town and East London, in the British Cape Colony. Visits
Kimberly diamond mine on July 1. Sails for England from
Cape Town with Livy and Clara July 15 and arrives in
Southampton on July 31. Takes a house in Guildford, Sur-
rey, for a month. Rogers arranges contract with American
Publishing Company and Harper & Brothers, allowing
American Publishing to issue subscription volumes, as
well as a uniform subscription edition of the complete
works, while Harpers will sell individual books and a less-
inclusive uniform edition to the trade. Learns that Susy is
ill. Livy and Clara leave for America August 15, Clemens
remains in England. Susy dies on August 18 of spinal men-
ingitis. Clemens learns of her death by telegram. Livy returns to England on September 9 with Clara and Jean,
whose health problems have recently been diagnosed as
epilepsy. Rents house at 23 Tedworth Square, Chelsea,
London, where they seclude themselves (family will not
celebrate birthdays, Thanksgiving, Christmas, or other
holidays for several years afterward). Begins writing travel
book, *Following the Equator*. Clemens learns that Helen
Keller (whom he had met with Rogers two years earlier at
the home of Clemens' good friend Laurence Hutton) has
lost financial support for her education, and asks Rogers
to help her attend Radcliffe College (Rogers does so).

1897     Livy is deeply depressed. Clemens works long hours on
         book. In February writes Howells, who has published re-
         view praising the first five volumes in Harpers' "Uniform
         Edition," that his "words stir the dead heart of me" and
         that he feels "indifferent to nearly everything but work."
         Finishes *Following the Equator* in May. Made an honorary
         life member of the Savage Club (only Henry Morton
         Stanley, Arctic explorer Fridtjof Nansen, and the Prince of

Wales had been given honor since club's founding in 1857). In July family goes to the Villa Bühlegg, Weggis, on Lake Lucerne in Switzerland. Hears the Fisk Jubilee Singers perform in village in August and entertains them at home after their concert; deeply moved, writes Twichell that "their music made all other vocal music cheap." On anniversary of Susy's death, writes poem "In Memoriam, Olivia Susan Clemens" (published in November *Harper's Magazine*). Family moves to the Metropole Hotel in Vienna in late September. Clemens suffers from gout. Interviewers from many newspapers come to the hotel. Fascinated by current political unrest caused by rivalry among nationalities of the Austro-Hungarian Empire. Works for many hours a day, but does not intend to publish much of what he writes. Receives $10,000 advance from Frank Bliss for *Following the Equator*, published in November. Clemens and Clara go out in society and attend operas. Family receives daily callers from 5:00 P.M. on. Clara is accepted as student of famed piano teacher Theodor Leschetizky. Begins work on "The Man That Corrupted Hadleyburg" (published in *Harper's Magazine*, December 1899). Orion dies in Keokuk on December 11.

1898 Meets student of Leschetizky's, Ossip Gabrilowitsch, who comes to dinner. Works for eight or nine hours at a time. Tries writing for the stage again, and translates German plays. Continues to follow Dreyfus case in France and admires Zola for his championing of Dreyfus's cause. Creditors are paid in full, and newspapers compare him to Sir Walter Scott (who had also redeemed himself from bankruptcy). Because of Clara's study of music, meets many prominent musicians and attends operas and concerts. Becomes interested in new investments, including a textile design machine that uses a photographic process and a patent for producing a peat-wool fiber cloth. Rogers' advice dampens his enthusiasm. Sends articles directly to magazine editors; if they reject them, has Rogers try to place them with other publications. Commands high prices for his work. When Spanish-American War begins in late April, believes that freeing Cuba from Spanish domination is a worthy cause. Family goes in late May to Kaltenleutgeben, small hydrotherapy resort outside Vienna. Livy's health does not improve. Writes article about the assassination on September 10 of Elizabeth, Empress of Austria, and watches her funeral. Begins work on early version of *The Mysterious Stranger*. Returns to Vienna in mid-October, moving into the new, luxurious Krantz Hotel (hotels are eager to have Clemens in residence and lower their rates for him). Writes autobiographical passages in November and begins considering publishing an autobiography. Feels more relaxed about financial matters, and is delighted with Rogers' investment of his money. Mary Fairbanks dies on December 8.

1899      Takes family to Budapest for a week when he delivers lecture there. Tells Howells in a letter that "it is a luxury! an intellectual drunk" to write material not intended for publication. Goes with family to London in late May, then to Sanna, Sweden, in July, where they are treated at sanitarium run by Henrik Kellgren (Clemens hopes that Kellgren's methods will be especially beneficial to Jean, who has been having frequent seizures). Writes "Christian Science and the Book of Mrs. Eddy," published October in *Cosmopolitan*. Returns to London in October and moves into apartment at 30, Wellington Court, Knightsbridge, near Dr. Kellgren's London institute, where Jean is treated three times a week (therapy seems to be helpful). Blames outbreak of Boer War in October on Cecil Rhodes and British colonial secretary Joseph Chamberlain. Becomes friends with T. Douglas Murray, who asks him to write introduction to *Jeanne d'Arc: Maid of Orleans*, English translation of the official trial records.

1900      Becomes disillusioned with American policy in the Philippines, and writes to Howells about his divided sympathies concerning the Boer War. Dines out frequently at private dinner parties, including ones given by historian W.E.H. Lecky, whom Clemens greatly admires, and Lady Augusta Gregory. Sees much of Stanley and his wife, Dorothy. Has portrait painted by James McNeill Whistler. In March invests $12,500 in Plasmon, food supplement made from milk by-products, and becomes director of English Plasmon syndicate on April 19 (enthusiastically uses product, and will later invest another $12,500 in venture). Spends summer at Dollis Hill House on northwest outskirts of London. Sympathizes with the Chinese in the Boxer Rebellion. Angry with Murray's "school-girl attempts at 'editing,'" withdraws manuscript of introduction to *Jeanne d'Arc* (it appears as article in *Harper's Magazine*, December 1904). Decides to return to America, having learned that osteopathy, now widely practiced in the United States, is very similar to Kellgren's methods. Family sails October 6 on the *Minnehaha* and arrives in New York on October 15. Receives warm welcome from public, press, and friends. Goes to Hartford to attend funeral of old friend Charles Dudley Warner. Rents house at 14 West 10th Street, New York City. Journalists constantly seek interviews and telephone rings incessantly. Rogers negotiates contract in November with Harpers, giving them first serial rights to Clemens' works for a year at rate of 20 cents per word. Introduces Winston S. Churchill to large New York audience on December 12. Writes "To the Person Sitting in Darkness," denunciation of imperialism, and is encouraged to publish it by Livy and Howells (article appears in *North American Review*, February 1901).

1901    Enjoys company of Howells, who now lives in New York and shares his anti-imperialist views. Clemens attacks missionary propaganda in China, and Tammany machine politics. Frequently invited to make speeches, presides over the Lincoln birthday celebration in Carnegie Hall, February 11. Troubled by attacks of gout. Family leaves on June 21 for summer at Ampersand on Lower Saranac Lake, New York, in the Adirondacks. Visited by Howells' son, John, now an architect. Sails for two weeks with Rogers on his yacht, *Kanawha*, to New Brunswick and Nova Scotia; fellow passengers include Clemens' friends Dr. Clarence Rice and Thomas B. Reed, former Speaker of the House of Representatives. Goes to Elmira for a week. Family finds sad memories make it impossible to live in Hartford. Decides to sell the house there and rents the Appleton mansion overlooking the Hudson in Riverdale, New York. Clemens and Howells receive honorary Doctor of Letters degrees from Yale University on October 23. Livy's health deteriorates. Rogers expresses concern in letter to Clemens about fairness of Ida Tarbell's forthcoming investigative series in *McClure's Magazine* on Standard Oil, saying that she has not approached anyone at the company for comment.

1902    Clemens tells friend at *McClure's* that they should have Tarbell speak with Rogers before running articles (when

approached, Rogers agrees to interview; Tarbell will describe him as "candid" in her series). Jean has seizures.
Clemens goes on yachting excursions with Rogers, taking
an extended cruise to Nassau, Cuba, and Florida. Livy
buys a house near Tarrytown, New York, for $45,000,
hoping to settle family there. Clara leaves for Paris on
April 22 to continue her studies. Clemens receives honorary Doctor of Laws from University of Missouri in Columbia on June 4. Visits Hannibal and St. Louis for the
last time. Takes trip on Mississippi with pilot Horace
Bixby. Family goes to York Harbor, Maine, for the summer. Because of Livy's fragile health, Rogers puts his
yacht at their disposal. Clemens is upset as he witnesses
more of Jean's epileptic seizures (had previously seen only
three of her attacks, though Livy had been present for
many more). Howells' family vacations at nearby Kittery
Point. Clemens works on "Was It Heaven? Or Hell?"
(published in *Harper's Magazine*, December 1902) and
"Tom Sawyer's Conspiracy" (never completed). On August 12 Livy is violently ill, can barely breathe, and has
severe heart palpitations; family fears she is dying. She is
treated by an osteopath, who comes several times a day,
and a regular doctor of medicine, who stays nights. Clara
comes from Europe and Susan Crane joins them. Jean's
health improves. Clemens hires professional nurse for
Livy, but she continues to suffer from attacks and on
October 16 returns by private invalid train to Riverdale.
Clemens is not allowed to go into her room. Attends large
dinner in honor of his 67th birthday, given on November
28 by George Harvey of Harper & Brothers at the Metropolitan Club in New York. Visits Elmira. Jean falls ill with
pneumonia on December 23. Clara and nurses keep news
from Livy, and Clara takes charge of house. Isabel Lyon,
hired as Livy's secretary, now acts as Clemens' secretary.
On December 30 Clemens is allowed to see Livy for five
minutes. Jean improves.

1903    Sees Livy for five minutes on days when she is feeling
better. Rarely goes into city. Livy's health improves during the spring months, and he is allowed to see her for
twenty minutes twice a day, and to send her two letters
each day. Clemens is forced to stay in bed for a month by
attacks of bronchitis, gout, and rheumatism. Sells Hartford house and rents the Tarrytown house (sold December

1904). Visits Rogers, who is recovering from appendec-
tomy, at his Fairhaven, Massachusetts, summer home.
Doctors tell Livy she should go to Europe to recover.
Family leaves Riverdale on July 1, going down the Hudson
on Rogers' yacht to Hoboken, where they take train to
Elmira. At Quarry Farm Livy takes rides in carriage, goes
out in wheelchair, sits on porch, and resumes household
responsibilities. Clemens works in octagonal study on the
hill. Goes to New York on October 3 to see publishers.
Harper & Brothers buys out the American Publishing
Company, and on October 22 Clemens signs contract giving Harpers rights to all his books, receiving guaranteed
payments of $25,000 a year for five years, plus royalties
above that amount. Family sails for Italy on October 24
aboard the *Princess Irene*, accompanied by Isabel Lyon,
their servant Kate Leary, who had been with the family
since 1880, and a trained nurse. Goes to Florence, where
Livy has chosen to settle, and rents the Villa di Quarto, a
large house near the city. Trip is tiring for Livy, but she
improves and thinks she no longer needs nurse, who
leaves on December 7.

1904        Livy's condition worsens and she is confined to bed.
Clemens quickly writes several magazine articles, then
turns to autobiography, dictating to Lyon every day.
Learns that sister-in-law Mollie Clemens died in Keokuk
on January 15 (does not tell Livy, and will also keep from
her news of Stanley's death on May 10). Livy has severe
attacks on February 22 and April 9. Family dislikes land-
lady and searches for another villa (search proves beneficial
to family's spirits because it encourages them to hope that
Livy will live long enough for them to move). Clemens
declines to invest money in American Plasmon syndicate,
but retains confidence in English branch. Clara sings on
concert stage and Clemens is impressed by her profession-
alism. Livy dies on June 5. Clara breaks down. Jean has
first seizure in 13 months, but she soon recovers and plans
family's return to America. Forced to wait for a ship, they
sail June 28 on the *Prince Oscar*. Charles Langdon, his
daughter Julia Langdon Loomis, and her husband meet
them at the pier and accompany them to Elmira in
Loomis's private railway car. Private funeral services are
held in Langdon house, conducted by Twichell. Clemens
takes cottage in July at Richard Watson Gilder's summer

home in the Berkshires near Lee, Massachusetts (daughters are fond of Gilder). Clara, still suffering from shock, enters a rest-cure establishment in New York City. Jean is hit by a trolley on July 30 while horseback riding; horse is killed, and she is knocked unconscious and suffers torn ankle tendon. Clemens goes to New York on August 10, finds Clara still ill, and is not allowed to see her. Searches for house to live in. Signs three-year lease for house at 21 Fifth Avenue. Stays in the Grosvenor Hotel while furnishings for new house are brought from Hartford. Jean remains in the Berkshires with Isabel Lyon. Spends a few days in late August as guest of George Harvey at Deal Beach, New Jersey, where he sees Henry James, who is also visiting Harvey. Sister Pamela dies in Greenwich, Connecticut, on September 1. Visits Elmira with Jean. Moves in December into Fifth Avenue house, where Jean joins him. Seldom goes out, but is visited by Rogers, Andrew Carnegie, and other old friends.

1905    Troubled by chronic bronchitis. Plays cards with Lyon and listens to music on player organ. Goes with Rogers to Fairhaven in May, then takes house for summer in Dublin, New Hampshire, with Jean. Writes "Eve's Diary" (published in *Harper's Magazine* in December), revises "Adam's Diary," and works on other manuscripts, including "3,000 Years Among the Microbes," and a new version of *The Mysterious Stranger*. Clara goes to Norfolk, Connecticut, to continue rest cure. Jean enjoys summer and visits Clara. Clemens is troubled by gout, dyspepsia, bronchitis, and the summer heat. Visits Clara in August (their first meeting in a year) and finds her well. Returns to Dublin and is forced by gout to stay in bed. Goes to New York in November after visit to Boston. Clara comes to live with him. Sees much of Rogers and his extended family. Attends gala 70th birthday party given in his honor by Harvey at Delmonico's on December 5 (172 guests attend). Relies on Lyon to manage household, financial, and literary matters (Lyon refers to him as "the King").

1906    In January Albert Bigelow Paine, 44-year-old midwestern writer and editor, asks permission to write Clemens' biography. Clemens gives Paine a room in his house to work in, and allows him to go through manuscripts and some letters and to listen as he dictates sections of autobiography to stenographer and typist Josephine Hobby. At request of Booker T. Washington, gives talk at Carnegie Hall on the 25th anniversary of the founding of Tuskegee Institute. Continues to give speeches and readings, but no longer accepts money for them. Encouraged when Howells is "full of praises" after spending an afternoon reading autobiographical writings. Meets H. G. Wells at dinner at Howells' house. Reluctantly withdraws support for Maxim Gorky, who is raising funds for the Russian Social Democratic party, after Gorky is discovered to be traveling with his mistress. Writes essay "William Dean Howells," praising his "perfect English" (appears in July *Harper's Magazine*). Goes to Dublin in May to again spend summer. Continues autobiographical dictations, intending to have some of them published in his lifetime. Returns to New York in late June on publishing business. Spends month in New York and Fairhaven, often sleeping aboard Rogers' yacht. Returns to Dublin in time for Jean's birthday on July 26. Harvey comes to Dublin to edit autobiography for publication (25 installments appear in *North American Review*, September 1906–December 1907). Takes yachting trip in August with Rogers, his son Harry, and Harry's wife, Mary, niece of William E. Benjamin. Commissions John Howells to design and supervise building of house in Redding, Connecticut. *What Is Man?* published anonymously in limited private edition by DeVinne Press in August. Goes yachting again in October, and is charmed by Mary Rogers. Delighted with gift of billiard table from Rogers' wife, Emilie, on October 30. Plays billiards with Paine, Harvey, and Finley Peter Dunne ("Mr. Dooley"), and feels health improves as a result. Jean, who had suffered a number of seizures during the summer, is sent to a sanitarium in Katonah, New York. Clara takes rest cure before beginning concert tour. Clemens goes with Paine to Washington in December to lobby, along with Howells and others, for new copyright bill; wears white suit to Capitol Hill. Speaker Joseph Cannon, an old friend, gives him unusual privilege of his private room to use as office.

1907        Often feels lonely and dislikes Fifth Avenue house. Attends club dinners frequently. Spends week in Bermuda with Twichell. *Christian Science*, critical treatment of Mary

Baker Eddy, published by Harpers in February. Summers in Tuxedo Park, New York, where Harry and Mary Rogers have home. Goes to England to receive honorary Litt.D. from Oxford University. Sails from New York June 8 aboard the *Minneapolis*, accompanied by Ralph W. Ashcroft, former secretary and treasurer of the Plasmon Company of America. At Brown's Hotel in London, makes friends with Frances Nunnally, 16-year-old schoolgirl from Atlanta, taking her with him on social calls. Plunges into social life in London, going to royal garden party at Windsor Castle, Lord Mayor's Banquet, the Savage Club, and a party given in his honor by the proprietors of *Punch*. Lunches with George Bernard Shaw, who has called him the greatest American author and one of the great masters of the English language. Sees old friends, including the Rogers, who are touring Europe. Attends Oxford ceremony on June 26; others honored include Rodin, Saint-Saëns, Kipling, and Prime Minister Henry Campbell-Bannerman. Clemens receives the most attention of those present. While returning to New York on the *Minnetonka*, makes friends with 11-year-old Dorothy Quick (she later visits him in Tuxedo Park). Arrives in New York July 22 and goes to Tuxedo Park. Hires Ashcroft to attend to business affairs. Falls ill with bronchitis. Clara studies music in Boston. Visits Fairhaven (Rogers had suffered a stroke on July 22). Returns to New York in late October. Sees Howells often, attends dinners, but feels lonely. "Extract from Captain Stormfield's Visit to Heaven" appears in *Harper's Magazine* December 1907–January 1908.

1908    Goes to Bermuda with Ashcroft for two weeks, then returns there in late February with Rogers, who is in poor health, and Lyon (Emilie Rogers joins them in mid-March). Clemens makes friends with several schoolgirls, all between 10 and 16 years old and the daughters of friends and acquaintances. Calls them "angelfish," and conceives idea of forming a club called the "Aquarium." Returns to New York on April 11. Has Tiffany & Co. make enamel angelfish, sends each girl one, and keeps up frequent correspondence with them. Clara goes to England in May on concert tour. Rents house for Jean and her two companions in Gloucester, Massachusetts. House at Redding is completed; Clemens sees it for the first time on June 18, is very pleased, and moves in immediately. Names it "Innocence at Home" (at Clara's insistence, changes name to "Stormfield" in October) and calls his billiard room "The Aquarium," decorating it with pictures of his young friends. Praises house as the ideal home in letter to John Howells. Attends the dedication of the Aldrich Memorial at Portsmouth, New Hampshire, with Howells. Enjoys receiving guests, including "angelfish," who stay two to eight days. Establishes free library in Redding, donating books from his collection, and starts fund to construct new library building. Taxes male house guests $1 for the fund. Goes to New York in August to attend funeral of nephew Samuel Moffett, who had drowned, and suffers from heatstroke and fatigue. Clara returns from Europe in September. House is burglarized on September 18. Although thieves are chased and caught after a brief gunfight, household staff quits and new servants must be hired. Installs burglar alarm. Clemens accompanies Jean from Gloucester to New York, where she sails for Europe on September 26 to consult specialist in Berlin. Clara moves to New York, making frequent visits to Redding. Actress Billie Burke visits several times. Forms The Mark Twain Company, corporation designed to keep royalties within the family even after copyrights expire, with himself as president, Ashcroft as secretary and treasurer, and Clara, Jean, and Lyon as directors (later replaces Lyon and Ashcroft with Paine).

1909    Enjoys listening to pianists Ossip Gabrilowitsch and Ethel Newcomb, who visit as Clara's guests. Gratified to learn that Congress has passed new copyright bill, extending holders' ownership for an additional 14 years. Attends celebration in New York of Rogers' 69th birthday (continues to see Rogers in the city, but turns down most invitations to New York events). Still entertains in Redding, but no longer has many visits from "angelfish." Howells visits for the first time in late March. Clara begins to arouse his suspicions that Lyon and Ashcroft, who marry on March 18, are mishandling his business affairs. Attends Clara's vocal recital in Mendelssohn Hall in New York on April 13. Dismisses Lyon and Ashcroft in mid-April and writes lengthy, bitter denunciation of them. Jean comes to live at Stormfield on April 26 and takes over household management, including secretarial duties for Clemens, who is impressed by the quality of her mind. *Is Shakespeare Dead?*, supporting Francis Bacon's authorship of the plays, published by Harpers. Goes to New York on May 19 to visit Rogers, but is met at the train by Clara, who tells him that Rogers has died that day. Attends funeral services on May 20. Travels to Baltimore to give promised talk at graduation from St. Timothy's School of "angelfish" Frances Nunnally. Finds trip tiring and develops symptoms of heart disease, diagnosed as angina pectoris in July. Clara marries Ossip Gabrilowitsch at Stormfield on October 6. Twichell performs ceremony and Clemens wears Oxford gown for the occasion. Troubled by chest pains, goes with Paine to Bermuda in November for several weeks. Clara and Ossip leave for Europe in early December. Writes little for publication, but continues to work on "Letters from the Earth." Writes "The Turning Point of My Life" (published in *Harper's Bazar* February 1910). Returns to Stormfield for the Christmas holidays. Jean dies on the morning of December 24, apparently having suffered heart failure during a seizure in her bathtub. Clemens is too distraught to attend services or to go to Elmira for her burial. Writes "The Death of Jean." Tells Paine: "It is the end of my autobiography. I shall never write any more." Paine and his family move into Stormfield.

1910    Goes to Bermuda on January 5, accompanied by his butler, Claude Benchotte. Stays at Bay House, Hamilton, home of the American vice-consul, William H. Allen, whose daughter Helen is an "angelfish" and who takes dictation for him at times. Plays golf with Woodrow Wilson, then president of Princeton University. Howells' daughter Mildred is also in Bermuda for her health and visits him often. Sees Dorothy Quick. Chest pains grow more frequent and severe. Paine comes to help care for him. Clemens notices that Halley's Comet is again visible in the sky. Leaves Bermuda on April 12 in great pain. Dies at Stormfield at approximately 6:30 P.M. on April 21. Funeral service is held at the Brick Presbyterian Church in New York. Henry Van Dyke gives short sermon and Twichell delivers an emotional prayer. Buried in Elmira, April 24, in family plot with Langdon, Susy, Livy, and Jean.

# Note on the Texts

This volume contains 80 tales, sketches, essays, and speeches by Mark Twain written or delivered between 1891 and his death in 1910, plus a compilation of his maxims published by Merle Johnson in 1927. The texts of the works presented here are drawn from *The Works of Mark Twain* edition being published by the University of California Press, from *Mark Twain Speaking* (1976), edited by Paul Fatout, and from initial printed appearances.

Many of these works first appeared in periodicals or newspapers during Twain's life. Two selections—"What Is Man?" and "King Leopold's Soliloquy"—appeared during Twain's life only as separate publications. Some of the works included here were never published during Twain's life and first appeared in print in posthumous editions or collections prepared by his literary executors and their successors, based on surviving manuscripts, typescripts, and dictations.

For works published during Twain's life, the texts in this volume are those of the initial printed appearances in newspapers, magazines, or collections by Twain or by others. For stories, sketches, or essays not published during Twain's life, the texts in this volume are those of the editions published by The Iowa Center for Textual Studies and the University of California Press, specifically *Mark Twain's Which Was the Dream? and Other Symbolic Writings of the Later Years* (Berkeley: University of California Press, 1966), edited by John S. Tuckey; *Mark Twain's Satires and Burlesques* (Berkeley: University of California Press, 1967), edited by Franklin R. Rogers; *Mark Twain's Fables of Man* (Berkeley: University of California Press, 1972), edited by John S. Tuckey; and *What Is Man? and Other Philosophical Writings* (Berkeley: University of California Press, 1973), edited by Paul Baender.

For works not published during Twain's life and not found in the above editions, the texts are from *What Is Man? and Other Essays* (New York: Harper & Brothers, 1917), edited by Albert Bigelow Paine; from *Europe and Elsewhere* (New York: Harper & Brothers, 1923), edited by Albert Bigelow Paine; from *Letters from the Earth* (New York: Harper & Row, 1962), edited by Bernard DeVoto; and from *A Pen Warmed-up in Hell: Mark Twain in Protest* (New York: Harper & Row, 1972), edited by Frederick Anderson. Anderson has compared some essays first published by Paine in *Europe and Elsewhere* to manuscript or typescript versions now in the Mark Twain Papers and has made emendations based on the surviving original documents. Early editors of Twain's posthumously published works often made changes to the texts in attempts to improve or regularize them. The texts in this volume have been taken from such editions only in cases where no more authoritative versions have yet been published.

The texts of the speeches are taken from *Mark Twain Speaking* (Iowa City: University of Iowa Press, 1976), edited by Paul Fatout. Fatout has examined the surviving manuscripts, typescripts, printed newspaper accounts, reports of proceedings, and printings and reprintings in collections by Twain and others, and has prepared composite versions of the speeches that reflect Twain's style and intentions, as well as his departures from prepared material and interplay with the audience.

Many of the selections in this volume that first appeared in magazines or newspapers were subsequently reprinted in collections published during Twain's life, including *The £1,000,000 Bank Note and Other Stories* (New York: Charles L. Webster & Co., 1893); *How to Tell a Story, and Other Essays* (New York: Harper & Bros., 1897); *How to Tell a Story, and Other Essays* (Hartford: American Publishing Company, 1900); *The Man That Corrupted Hadleyburg and Other Stories and Essays* (New York: Harper & Bros., 1900); *My Début as a Literary Person, with Other Essays and Stories* (Hartford: American Publishing Company, 1903); and *The $30,000 Bequest and Other Stories* (New York: Harper & Brothers, 1906). Some of the selections were reprinted in separate editions during Twain's life, such as *Eve's Diary* (1906), *Extract from Captain Stormfield's Visit to Heaven* (1909), and *A Dog's Tale* (1903 [1904]). Mark Twain seldom revised the sketches and stories after the pieces appeared in periodicals. Some collections were prepared with no involvement by Twain other than the selection of the contents, and in most cases the periodical appearances were used as the basis for the collected versions. In general, the first printed appearances of Twain's stories and sketches represent the versions closest to his own final drafts.

The following notes provide a brief publication history of each selection in this volume and indicate the source of each text.

"Aix-les-Bains" (pp. 1–14 in this volume) appeared as "Mark Twain at Aix-les-Bains" in the Chicago *Tribune* of November 8, 1891, and also as "Paradise of the Rheumatics" in the St. Louis *Post-Dispatch* of November 8, 1891, and as "The Tramp Abroad Again: I. The Paradise of the Rheumatics" in two issues of *The Illustrated London News* of November 14 and November 28, 1891. The essay appeared as "The Paradise of the Rheumatics" in *Europe and Elsewhere* in 1923. The text in this volume is the one printed in the Chicago *Tribune* of November 8, 1891.

"Playing Courier" (pp. 15–29) appeared as "The Tramp Abroad Again: II. Playing Courier" in *The Illustrated London News* of December 19 and December 26, 1891, and as "An Innocent Abroad: Playing Courier" in the San Francisco *Examiner* of January 3, 1892. It was later collected under the title "Playing Courier" in *The £1,000,000 Bank Note and Other Stories* (1893). Collation reveals minor differences among all three versions. The text in this volume is the one printed in the San Francisco *Examiner* of January 3, 1892.

"Mental Telegraphy" (pp. 30–48) first appeared in *Harper's Monthly* for December 1891. It was reprinted in *The £1,000,000 Bank Note and Other Stories* (1893). The text in this volume is the one printed in *Harper's Monthly* for December 1891, pp. 95–104.

"The Cradle of Liberty" (pp. 49–59) appeared as "Mark Twain in the Cradle of Liberty" in the Chicago *Tribune* of March 6, 1892. It was reprinted with a number of changes in *What Is Man? and Other Essays* (1917). The text in this volume is the one printed in the Chicago *Tribune* of March 6, 1892. One correction has been made (from "afloat" to "afoot" at 49.15), based on a copy of the surviving manuscript.

"The £1,000,000 Bank-Note" (pp. 60–80) appeared in *Century* for January 1893. It was reprinted in *The £1,000,000*

*Bank Note and Other Stories* (1893). The text in this volume is the one printed in *Century* for January 1893, pp. 338–46.

"About All Kinds of Ships" (pp. 81–97) was first published in *The £1,000,000 Bank Note and Other Stories*, (New York: Charles L. Webster and Co., 1893), pp. 154–83, which is the source of the text printed in this volume.

"Extracts from Adam's Diary" (pp. 98–108) first appeared in *Niagara Book*, published on June 3, 1893. It was later collected in *My Début as a Literary Person, with Other Essays and Stories* (1903) and in *The $30,000 Bequest and Other Stories* (1906). The text in this volume is the one printed in *Niagara Book* (Buffalo: Underhill and Nichols, 1893), pp. 93–109.

"Is He Living or Is He Dead?" (pp. 109–17) first appeared in *Cosmopolitan* for September 1893. It was collected in *The Man That Corrupted Hadleyburg and Other Stories and Essays* (1900) and *My Début as a Literary Person, with Other Essays and Stories* (1903). The text in this volume is the one printed in *Cosmopolitan* for September 1893, pp. 629–34.

"The Esquimau Maiden's Romance" (pp. 118–33) first appeared in *Cosmopolitan* for November 1893. It was later collected in *The Man That Corrupted Hadleyburg and Other Stories and Essays* (1900) and *My Début as a Literary Person, with Other Essays and Stories* (1903). The text in this volume is the one printed in *Cosmopolitan* for November 1893, pp. 53–63.

"Travelling with a Reformer" (pp. 134–48) first appeared in *Cosmopolitan* for December 1893. It was later collected in *How to Tell a Story, and Other Essays* (New York, 1897), *How to Tell a Story, and Other Essays* (Hartford, 1900), and *The Man That Corrupted Hadleyburg and Other Stories and Essays* (1900). The text in this volume is the one printed in *Cosmopolitan* for December 1893, pp. 207–17.

"Concerning Tobacco" (pp. 149–51) was written sometime around 1893, probably while Twain was living in Italy. It was first published in *What Is Man? and Other Essays* (New York: Harper & Brothers, 1917), edited by Albert Bigelow Paine, pp. 275–79, which is the source of the text printed in this volume.

"Private History of the 'Jumping Frog' Story" (pp. 152–60) first appeared in the *North American Review* for April 1894. It was later collected in *How to Tell a Story, and Other*

*Essays* (New York, 1897), *How to Tell a Story, and Other Essays* (Hartford, 1900), and *The Man That Corrupted Hadleyburg and Other Stories and Essays* (1900). The text in this volume is the one printed in the *North American Review* for April 1894, pp. 446–53.

"Macfarlane" (pp. 161–63) was written sometime around 1894 and was not published during Twain's life. It first appeared in *Mark Twain's Autobiography* (New York: Harper & Brothers, 1924), edited by Albert Bigelow Paine, volume I, pp. 143–47. Paul Baender examined the manuscript and determined that the piece did not belong with the autobiographical sketches and that Paine's date for the piece ("about 1898") was incorrect. Based upon the paper used for the manuscript, Baender dated the piece as being from 1894–95. The text in this volume is the one printed in *What Is Man? and Other Philosophical Writings*, edited by Paul Baender, pp. 76–78, which is based on the manuscript.

"What Paul Bourget Thinks of Us" (pp. 164–79) first appeared in the *North American Review* for January 1895. It was collected in *How to Tell a Story, and Other Essays* (New York, 1897) and *How to Tell a Story, and Other Essays* (Hartford, 1900). The text in this volume is the one printed in *North American Review* for January 1895, pp. 48–62.

"Fenimore Cooper's Literary Offences" (pp. 180–92) first appeared in the *North American Review* for July 1895. It was later collected in *How to Tell a Story, and Other Essays* (New York, 1897) and *How to Tell a Story, and Other Essays* (Hartford, 1900). The text in this volume is the one printed in the *North American Review* for July 1895, pp. 1–12.

"Fenimore Cooper's Further Literary Offenses" (pp. 193–200) was written after the preceding essay, which appeared in the *North American Review* in July 1895, but was left incomplete and was not published during Twain's life. It was first published by Bernard DeVoto, as "Fenimore Cooper's Further Literary Offenses," in *New England Quarterly* (1946), pp. 293–301, and was reprinted in 1962, under the title "Cooper's Prose Style," in *Letters from the Earth*, edited by Bernard DeVoto. The surviving manuscript ends with the words "if the more tempered Cora had done it some, too." at 198.26, and DeVoto completed the essay by inserting the original ending of the previous article, which was deleted from the text published in the *North American Review*, presumably because it was too long. The text in this volume is the one printed in *Letters from the Earth*, edited by Bernard DeVoto, pp. 137–45, where it appears under the title "Cooper's Prose Style."

"How to Tell a Story" (pp. 201–06) first appeared in *Youth's Companion* for October 3, 1895. It was collected in *How to Tell a Story, and Other Essays* (New York, 1897), *How to Tell a Story, and Other Essays* (Hartford, 1900), and *The Man That Corrupted Hadleyburg and Other Stories and Essays* (1900). The text in this volume is the one printed in *Youth's Companion* of October 3, 1895, p. 464.

"Man's Place in the Animal World" (pp. 207–16) was begun around August 13, 1896, and completed about two months later. It was first published in 1962 in *Letters from the Earth*, edited by Bernard DeVoto, under the title (supplied by DeVoto) "The Lowest Animal." The text in this volume is the one printed in *What Is Man? and Other Philosophical Writings*, edited by Paul Baender, pp. 80–89. The title used here and by Baender is taken from Twain's inscription on a manila envelope dating from about 1896 that may once have held the manuscript. The first leaf of the manuscript is lost, but it apparently contained only the title and the telegrams mentioned in the text, which were probably from the London *Daily Telegraph* of August 13, 1896, p. 7.

"In Memoriam" (pp. 217–19) was first published in *Harper's Monthly* for November 1897. It was included in the collections *How to Tell a Story, and Other Essays* (Hartford, 1900) and *The $30,000 Bequest and Other Stories* (1906). The text in this volume is the one printed in *Harper's Monthly* for November 1897, pp. 929–30.

"Which Was the Dream?" (pp. 220–59) was begun in May 1897 and continued in August of that year, but was never completed and was not published during Twain's life. It first appeared in *Mark Twain's Which Was the Dream? and Other Symbolic Writings of the Later Years*, edited (from the surviving holograph manuscript) by John S. Tuckey, pp. 33–73, which is the source of the text printed in this volume.

"A Word of Encouragement for Our Blushing Exiles" (pp.

260–62) was not published during Twain's life and survives in a manuscript dated May 24, 1898. It was first published in 1923 in *Europe and Elsewhere*, edited by Albert Bigelow Paine, pp. 221–24, which is the source of the text printed in this volume.

"About Play-Acting" (pp. 263–72) first appeared in *Forum* for October 1898. It was reprinted in the collections *The Man That Corrupted Hadleyburg and Other Stories and Essays* (1900) and *My Début as a Literary Person, with Other Essays and Stories* (1903). The text in this volume is the one printed in *Forum* for October 1898, pp. 143–51.

"From the 'London Times' of 1904" (pp. 273–83) first appeared in *Century* for November 1898. It was included in the collections *How to Tell a Story, and Other Essays* (Hartford, 1900) and *The Man That Corrupted Hadleyburg and Other Stories and Essays* (1900). The text in this volume is the one printed in *Century* for November 1898, pp. 100–04.

"My Platonic Sweetheart" (pp. 284–96) was written before August 4, 1898, but was not published during Twain's life. It first appeared in *Harper's Monthly* for December 1912, pp. 14–20, edited by Albert Bigelow Paine, which is the source of the text printed in this volume.

"The Great Dark" (pp. 297–343) was written during August, September, and October of 1898, but it was left incomplete and was not published during Twain's life. It first appeared in *Letters from the Earth*, edited (from the surviving manuscript) by Bernard DeVoto. The text in this volume is the one printed in *Mark Twain's Which Was the Dream? and Other Symbolic Writings of the Later Years*, edited by John S. Tuckey, pp. 102–50.

"Diplomatic Pay and Clothes" (pp. 344–53) first appeared in *Forum* for March 1899. It was included in the collections *My Début as a Literary Person, with Other Essays and Stories* (1903) and *The $30,000 Bequest and Other Stories* (1906). The text in this volume is the one printed in *Forum* for March 1899, pp. 24–32.

"Concerning the Jews" (pp. 354–70) first appeared in *Harper's Monthly* for September 1899. It was included in the collections *How to Tell a Story, and Other Essays* (Hartford, 1900) and *The Man That Corrupted Hadleyburg and Other*

*Stories* (1900). A postscript was added to the essay in the English edition of *The Man That Corrupted Hadleyburg* (1900) and in later American editions of *The Man That Corrupted Hadleyburg and Other Stories and Essays* beginning in 1902 (this postscript is given in the "Notes" section). The text in this volume is the one printed in *Harper's Monthly* for September 1899, pp. 527–35.

"Christian Science and the Book of Mrs. Eddy" (pp. 371–89) first appeared in *Cosmopolitan* for October 1899. It was collected in the English edition of *The Man That Corrupted Hadleyburg and Other Stories and Sketches* (London: Chatto & Windus, 1900) and in an edition published by Bernhard Tauchnitz in Leipzig the same year. The essay was later incorporated into Twain's published book *Christian Science with Notes Containing Corrections to Date* (New York: Harper & Brothers, 1907). The text in this volume is the one printed in *Cosmopolitan* for October 1899, pp. 585–94.

"The Man That Corrupted Hadleyburg" (pp. 390–438) first appeared in *Harper's Monthly* for December 1899. It was included in the collections *The Man That Corrupted Hadleyburg and Other Stories and Essays* (1900) and *My Début as a Literary Person, with Other Essays and Stories* (1903). The text in this volume is the one printed in *Harper's Monthly* for December 1899, pp. 29–54.

"My First Lie and How I Got Out of It" (pp. 439–46) first appeared in the Sunday supplement of the New York *World* of December 10, 1899. It was included in the collections *The Man That Corrupted Hadleyburg and Other Stories and Essays* (1900) and *My Début as a Literary Person, with Other Essays and Stories* (1903). The text in this volume is the one printed in the New York *World* for December 10, 1899, Sunday supplement, pp. 1–2.

"My Boyhood Dreams" (pp. 447–53) first appeared in *McClure's* for January 1900. It was included in the collections *The Man That Corrupted Hadleyburg and Other Stories and Essays* (1900) and *My Début as a Literary Person, with Other Essays and Stories* (1903). The text in this volume is the one printed in *McClure's* for January 1900, pp. 286–90.

"Introducing Winston S. Churchill" (pp. 454–55) was delivered at the Hotel Waldorf-Astoria in New York, December

12, 1900. The text in this volume is the one printed in *Mark Twain Speaking*, edited by Paul Fatout, pp. 367–69.

"A Salutation-Speech from the Nineteenth Century to the Twentieth, Taken Down in Short-Hand by Mark Twain" (p. 456) was first published in the New York *Herald* of December 30, 1900. The "greeting" was originally intended to be read at a series of Red Cross Society watch meetings, but Twain became uncomfortable with the plan and asked that it be returned. It appeared in the *Herald* in a facsimile of Twain's holograph manuscript, under the headline "New Century Greeting Which Twain Recalled." It was subsequently printed on a card for general distribution. Part of it was published in *Mark Twain: A Biography* (New York: Harper & Brothers, 1912), by Albert Bigelow Paine, page 1127. The text in this volume is the one printed in the New York *Herald* of December 30, 1900, p. 7.

"To the Person Sitting in Darkness" (pp. 457–73) appeared in the *North American Review* for February 1901. It was not included in any collections during Twain's life. The text in this volume is the one printed in *North American Review* for February 1901, pp. 161–76.

"Battle Hymn of the Republic (Brought Down to Date)" (pp. 474–75) was probably written during February 1901. It was not published during Twain's life and was first printed in *Mark Twain: Social Critic* (New York: International Publishers, 1958), by Philip S. Foner. The text in this volume is the one printed in *A Pen Warmed-up in Hell: Mark Twain in Protest*, edited by Frederick Anderson, pp. 3–4.

"As Regards Patriotism" (pp. 476–78) was probably written in 1901. It was first published in 1923 in *Europe and Elsewhere*, edited and revised by Albert Bigelow Paine. The text in this volume is the one printed in *A Pen Warmed-up in Hell: Mark Twain in Protest*, edited by Frederick Anderson, pp. 28–30, which is based on the surviving manuscript in the Mark Twain Papers and does not reflect revisions made by Paine. In Anderson's edition, Twain's cancellations have been omitted and ampersands have been expanded to "and."

"The United States of Lyncherdom" (pp. 479–86) was written in August 1901, and was not published during Twain's life. It was first published in 1923 in *Europe and Elsewhere*, edited by Albert Bigelow Paine, pp. 239–49, which is the source of the text printed in this volume.

"Edmund Burke on Croker and Tammany" (pp. 487–95) was delivered at the Order of Acorns Dinner at the Hotel Waldorf-Astoria in New York on October 17, 1901. The Order of Acorns was a group made up mostly of newspapermen supporting the Fusion Party in the New York municipal election of 1901. The text in this volume is the one printed in *Mark Twain Speaking*, edited by Paul Fatout, pp. 404–12

"Two Little Tales" (pp. 496–506) first appeared in *Century* for November 1901. It was included in the collections *My Début as a Literary Person, with Other Essays and Stories* (1903) and *The $30,000 Bequest and Other Stories* (1906). The text in this volume is the one printed in *Century* for November 1901, pp. 24–32.

"Corn-Pone Opinions" (pp. 507–11) was written sometime in 1901. A notebook entry for January 31, 1901, and an annotated clipping from the New York *Herald* of February 18, 1901, make reference to "Hoecake opinions" and "Corn-pone," respectively. A holograph manuscript and a typescript survive, but the typescript contains no corrections or revisions by Twain. Deletions and cancellations on the manuscript in pencil by another hand (possibly Albert Bigelow Paine's) are reflected in the typescript and in the first published appearance in 1923 in *Europe and Elsewhere*, edited by Paine. The text in this volume is the one printed in *What Is Man? and Other Philosophical Writings*, edited by Paul Baender, pp. 92–97. Baender's edition of the text is based on the manuscript and includes portions omitted in earlier published versions.

"Does the Race of Man Love a Lord?" (pp. 512–23) first appeared in the *North American Review* for April 1902. It was included in the collection *The $30,000 Bequest and Other Stories* (1906). The text in this volume is the one printed in the *North American Review* for April 1902, pp. 433–44.

"The Five Boons of Life" (pp. 524–26) first appeared in *Harper's Weekly* for July 5, 1902. It was included in the collection *The $30,000 Bequest and Other Stories* (1906). The text in this volume is the one printed in *Harper's Weekly* for July 5, 1902, p. 866.

"Was It Heaven? Or Hell?" (pp. 527–46) first appeared in *Harper's Monthly* for December 1902. It was included in the collection *The $30,000 Bequest and Other Stories* (1906). The text in this volume is the one printed in *Harper's Monthly* for December 1902, pp. 11–20.

"The Dervish and the Offensive Stranger" (pp. 547–49) was written late in 1902, and was not published during Twain's life. It first appeared in 1923 in *Europe and Elsewhere*, edited and revised by Albert Bigelow Paine. The text in this volume is the one printed in *A Pen Warmed-up in Hell: Mark Twain in Protest*, edited by Frederick Anderson, pp. 170–73, which incorporates emendations to Paine's version based on the surviving manuscript in the Mark Twain Papers.

"Why Not Abolish It?" (pp. 550–53) first appeared in *Harper's Weekly* for May 2, 1903, page 732, which is the source of the text printed in this volume. It was not included in any collections during Twain's life.

"Mark Twain, Able Yachtsman, on Why Lipton Failed to Lift the Cup" (pp. 554–60) appeared in the New York *Herald* of August 30, 1903, which is the source of the text printed in this volume. This self-interview has sometimes been reprinted under the title "The Yacht Races."

"A Dog's Tale" (pp. 561–71) first appeared in *Harper's Monthly* for December 1903. Shortly afterward it was published as a pamphlet, printed from the *Harper's* plates, by the National Anti-Vivisection Society in London, dated 1903, although it was apparently not distributed until 1904. The story was published in a separate edition in September 1904 as *A Dog's Tale* (New York: Harper & Brothers, 1904), and was included in the collection *The $30,000 Bequest and Other Stories* (1906). The text in this volume is the one printed in *Harper's Monthly* for December 1903, pp. 11–19.

" 'Was the World Made for Man?' " (pp. 572–76) was written in response to articles that appeared in *Literary Digest* during February, March, and April of 1903. Alfred Russell Wallace's book *Man's Place in the Universe*, mentioned in the opening quotation, was recommended to Twain by William Dean Howells in December 1903, but he may have already been aware of the work by that time. The text in this volume is the one printed in *What Is Man? and Other Philosophical*

*Writings*, edited by Paul Baender, pp. 101–06, which is based on the surviving manuscript.

"Italian Without a Master" (pp. 577–83) first appeared in *Harper's Weekly* for January 2, 1904. It was included in the collection *The $30,000 Bequest and Other Stories* (1906). The text in this volume is the one printed in *Harper's Weekly*, January 2, 1904, pp. 18–19.

"Saint Joan of Arc" (pp. 584–96) first appeared in *Harper's Monthly* for December 1904. It was included in the collection *The $30,000 Bequest and Other Stories* (1906). The text in this volume is the one printed in *Harper's Monthly* for December 1904, pp. 3–12.

"The $30,000 Bequest" (pp. 597–626) first appeared in *Harper's Weekly* for December 10, 1904. It was included in the collection *The $30,000 Bequest and Other Stories* (1906). The text in this volume is the one printed in *Harper's Weekly* of December 10, 1904, pp. 10–17.

"Concerning Copyright" (pp. 627–34) first appeared in the *North American Review* for January 1905, pp. 1–8, which is the source of the text printed in this volume.

"Adam's Soliloquy" (pp. 635–41) was written before February 23, 1905, but not published during Twain's life. It first appeared in 1923 in *Europe and Elsewhere*, edited by Albert Bigelow Paine, pp. 377–86, which is the source of the text printed in this volume.

"The Czar's Soliloquy" (pp. 642–47) first appeared in the *North American Review* for March 1905. It was not included in any collections published during Twain's life. The text in this volume is the one printed in *North American Review* for March 1905, pp. 321–26.

"Dr. Loeb's Incredible Discovery" (pp. 648–51) was written sometime after the epigraph date of March 2, 1905, but was not published during Twain's life. It first appeared in 1923 in *Europe and Elsewhere*, edited by Albert Bigelow Paine, pp. 304–09, which is the source of the text printed in this volume.

"The War Prayer" (pp. 652–55) was written on or before March 10, 1905, when Isabel Lyon recorded in her diary that Twain had read it to some friends. It was not published during Twain's life, and it first appeared in 1923 in *Europe and*

*Elsewhere*, edited by Albert Bigelow Paine. The text in this volume is the one printed in *A Pen Warmed-up in Hell: Mark Twain in Protest*, edited by Frederick Anderson, pp. 88–91, which was prepared from the surviving typescript in the Mark Twain Papers bearing Twain's final revisions.

"A Humane Word from Satan" (pp. 656–57) first appeared in *Harper's Weekly* for April 8, 1905. It was included in the collection *The $30,000 Bequest and Other Stories* (1906). The text in this volume is the one printed in *Harper's Weekly*, April 8, 1905, page 496.

"Christian Citizenship" (pp. 658–60) appeared anonymously in *Collier's* for September 2, 1905, page 17, which is the source of the text printed in this volume.

"King Leopold's Soliloquy: A Defense of His Congo Rule" (pp. 661–86) appeared as a pamphlet, published on September 28, 1905, for the Congo Reform Association, titled *King Leopold's Soliloquy: A Defense of His Congo Rule* (Boston: The P. R. Warren Company, 1905). At least three further printings followed soon afterward, and a "Second Edition," with additional supplementary material, was issued late in 1905 or early in 1906. The text in this volume is the one printed in the first printing of the first edition of the pamphlet, pages 1–41. A supplementary section, "Ought King Leopold to Be Hanged?," by W. T. Stead, from the *Review of Reviews* for September 1905, has been omitted.

"A Helpless Situation" (pp. 687–91) first appeared in *Harper's Bazar* for November 1905. It was included in the collection *The $30,000 Bequest and Other Stories* (1906). The text in this volume is the one printed in *Harper's Bazar* for November 1905, pp. 979–81.

"Overspeeding" (p. 692) appeared in *Harper's Weekly* for November 4, 1905, page 1606, which is the source of the text printed in this volume.

"In the Animal's Court" (pp. 693–94) was probably written in 1905 and was not published during Twain's life. It first appeared in 1962 in *Letters from the Earth*, edited by Bernard DeVoto. The text in this volume is the one printed in *What Is Man? and Other Philosophical Writings*, edited by Paul Baender, pp. 121–23, which is based on the surviving manuscript.

"Eve's Diary" (pp. 695–709) first appeared in *Harper's*

*Monthly* for December 1905. It was published in a separate edition in June 1906 as *Eve's Diary Translated from the Original MS* (New York: Harper & Brothers, 1906), and was included in the collection *The $30,000 Bequest and Other Stories* (1906). The text printed in this volume is taken from *Harper's Monthly* for December 1905, pp. 25–32.

"Eve Speaks" (pp. 710–12) was not published during Twain's life and the date of composition has not been determined. It first appeared in 1923 in *Europe and Elsewhere*, edited by Albert Bigelow Paine, pp. 347–50, which is the source of the text printed in this volume.

"Seventieth Birthday Dinner Speech" (pp. 713–18) was delivered at Mark Twain's Seventieth Birthday Dinner at Delmonico's in New York on December 5, 1905. The text in this volume is the one printed in *Mark Twain Speaking*, edited by Paul Fatout, pp. 462–67.

"Old Age" (p. 719) was written shortly after Twain's seventieth birthday, November 30, 1905. The text in this volume is the one printed in *Mark Twain's Fables of Man*, edited by John S. Tuckey, pp. 441–42, which is based on the surviving manuscript.

"The Gorky Incident" (pp. 720–21) was written sometime after Gorky was evicted from his hotel on April 15, 1906, but was not published during Twain's life. An edition prepared by Bernard DeVoto appeared in *Slavonic and East European Review*, XXII, part 2 (August 1944), pp. 37–38, and was republished with revisions in 1962 in *Letters from the Earth*, edited by Bernard DeVoto. Collation against a copy of the surviving manuscript shows that the more accurate transcription is in *Letters from the Earth*, edited by Bernard DeVoto, pp. 155–56, which is the source of the text printed in this volume.

"William Dean Howells" (pp. 722–30) first appeared in *Harper's Monthly* for July 1906. The text in this volume is the one printed in *Harper's Monthly* for July 1906, pp. 221–25. One change has been made: "thirty-four lines" has been altered to "twenty-two lines" at 724.15, to correspond to the number of lines in this setting.

"What Is Man?" (pp. 731–804) was begun in 1898 in Vienna, and a typescript of the first draft was prepared there.

Twain made revisions and added further sections both before and after he returned to America in 1900, and a second typescript was prepared in 1902. In 1905, Twain began further revisions and reorderings and prepared a third typescript that was eventually used as printer's copy. Type was set by The DeVinne Press in New York, and Twain read proofs and made further revisions. *What Is Man?* was published anonymously by The DeVinne Press, on August 20, 1906. Paul Baender prepared an unmodernized critical edition for publication in 1973 in *What Is Man? and Other Philosophical Writings*. Baender has compared all stages of the manuscript, the typescripts, and the first published edition, and has based the text of his edition on Twain's final inscription, whether it is located in the initial manuscript, in added manuscript pages, or in holographic changes on either manuscript or typed pages. Portions dictated by Twain to his secretary Isabel Lyon are based on her transcription. Readings from the first edition that can be attributed to Twain's revisions in proof have been adopted. The text in this volume is the one printed in *What Is Man? and Other Philosophical Writings*, edited by Paul Baender, pp. 124–214.

"Hunting the Deceitful Turkey" (pp. 805–07) first appeared in *Harper's Monthly* for December 1906, pp. 57–58, which is the source of the text printed in this volume.

"Dinner Speech at Annapolis" (pp. 808–12) was delivered at Government House in Annapolis, Maryland, May 10, 1907. The text in this volume is the one printed in *Mark Twain Speaking*, edited by Paul Fatout, pp. 550–54

"Our Guest" (pp. 813–17) was delivered to the Society of the Pilgrims Luncheon at the Hotel Savoy in London on June 25, 1907. The text in this volume is the one printed in *Mark Twain Speaking*, edited by Paul Fatout, pp. 558–62.

"The Day We Celebrate" (pp. 818–22) was delivered to the American Society Dinner at the Hotel Cecil in London on July 4, 1907. The text in this volume is the one printed in *Mark Twain Speaking*, edited by Paul Fatout, pp. 567–71.

"Little Nelly Tells a Story Out of Her Own Head" (pp. 823–25) was written in 1907. An untitled manuscript survives, and also an unrevised typescript and carbon copy with the present title and the heading "Dictated 1907." The text in this volume is the one printed in *Mark Twain's Fables of Man*, edited by John S. Tuckey, pp. 47–49, which is based on the surviving manuscript.

"Extract from Captain Stormfield's Visit to Heaven" (pp. 826–63) first appeared in two installments in *Harper's Monthly* for December 1907 and January 1908. It was published in a separate edition in October 1909 as *Extract from Captain Stormfield's Visit to Heaven* (New York: Harper & Brothers, 1909). Twain had worked on versions of this story at various times, including in 1869, 1870, 1873, 1878, 1881, 1883, and 1893. The text in this volume is the one printed in *Harper's Monthly* for December 1907, pp. 41–49, and for January 1908, pp. 266–76.

"Little Bessie" (pp. 864–74) was written during 1908 and perhaps also in 1909. The manuscript of all six chapters and a revised typescript of the first chapter (dated February 22, 1908) survive, but there is no indication of the order that Twain intended for them. Most of the first chapter was printed in *Mark Twain: A Biography* (New York: Harper & Brothers, 1912), by Albert Bigelow Paine, pp. 1514–15 and 1671–73. The text in this volume is the one printed in *Mark Twain's Fables of Man*, edited by John S. Tuckey, pp. 34–44, which is based on the surviving manuscript.

"The New Planet" (pp. 875–76) first appeared in *Harper's Weekly* for January 30, 1909, page 13, which is the source of the text printed in this volume.

"A Fable" (pp. 877–79) first appeared in *Harper's Monthly* for December 1909, pp. 70–71, which is the source of the text printed in this volume.

"Letters from the Earth" (pp. 880–928) was written in October and November 1909 and was not published during Twain's life. Bernard DeVoto edited two separate surviving manuscripts for the first publication in 1962 in *Letters from the Earth*. The title is taken from the second manuscript; the first is untitled. The text in this volume is the one printed in *What Is Man? and Other Philosophical Writings*, edited by Paul Baender, pp. 401–54. Baender's text is based on the two manuscripts; each manuscript is paginated separately, and the first, covering pages 880.1 through 885.3 in this volume, breaks off in mid-sentence at the end of the last leaf.

" 'The Turning Point of My Life' " (pp. 929–38) first appeared in *Harper's Bazar* for February 1910. It was rewritten late in 1909, after Albert Bigelow Paine and Jean Clemens disapproved of an earlier version. The text in this volume is the one printed in *What Is Man? and Other Philosophical Writings*, edited by Paul Baender, pp. 455–64. Baender has examined the surviving manuscript, typescript, and proof, as well as the first published appearance, and has prepared a critical edition based upon Mark Twain's final holographic text, with the exception of the last two paragraphs, which are not in manuscript, typescript, or proof, and so are based on the first publication in *Harper's Bazar*.

The appendix "More Maxims of Mark" (pp. 939–48) was prepared by Merle Johnson and privately printed in November 1927. Many other maxims, not included in Johnson's collection, were used as epigraphs in *Pudd'nhead Wilson* and *Following the Equator*. The text in this volume is the one printed in *More Maxims of Mark* (New York, 1927), edited by Merle Johnson.

The running heads of left-hand pages are intended to reflect the place of residence of Mark Twain or the Clemens family at the time the selection was published (or, for an unpublished item, at the time it was written). A date of publication, of course, does not necessarily represent the date of composition.

This volume presents the texts of the printings chosen for inclusion here, but it does not attempt to reproduce features of their typographic design, such as the display capitalization of chapter openings. In some cases, titles supplied by previous editors that do not sufficiently distinguish a selection from others in the volume have been altered; all such instances have been noted in the discussion of printing histories. Otherwise, the texts are reproduced without change, except for the correction of typographical errors. Spelling, punctuation, and capitalization often are expressive features and they are not altered, even when inconsistent or irregular. The following is a list of typographical errors corrected, cited by page and line number: 3.10, Diety's; 8.39, Wakefild's; 11.7–8, potentable; 12.36, al-; 23.23, "defendee."; 27.39, new; 49.15, afloat; 50.15, Altdor; 51.8, Stanffacher's; 51.11, Rutli; 52.30, Charlemange;

53.10, ducuments; 53.29, army; 54.39, senuous; 55.22, In; 139.22, Your; 143.35, It's; 146.26, Its; 166.39, it; 168.7, then; 184.9, Maqua; 185.12, two-third's; 187.15, mosquitos's; 191.32, than; 267.24, hapinesses; 383.6, Apodistical; 413.28, *reform.*" '; 415.12, *reform.*' "; 425.17, face."; 444.12, They; 456.6, Phillipines; 468.34, "the; 468.35, enemy"; 605.37, Gent's; 623.39, hurt that; 648.6, is voted; 668.27, decreasing."; 670.13, most amazing; 670.16, *Intruding*; 671.20, simulated."; 671.30, Sir; 679.22, Cathay,; 760.18, Zoroastians; 787.29, adaptibility; 838.4, hozannahing.

# Notes

In the notes that follow, the reference numbers denote page and line of this volume (the line count includes chapter headings). No note is made for material included in standard desk-reference books, such as *Webster's Ninth New Collegiate Dictionary* or *Webster's Biographical Dictionary*. Notes within the text are Mark Twain's own. Quotations from Shakespeare have been keyed to *The Riverside Shakespeare* (Boston: Houghton Mifflin, 1974), edited by G. Blakemore Evans. References to the Bible have been keyed to the King James Version. For more detailed notes and references to other studies, see the explanatory notes in *What Is Man? and Other Philosophical Writings* (Berkeley: University of California Press, 1973), edited by Paul Baender, and *Mark Twain Speaking* (Iowa City: University of Iowa Press, 1976), edited by Paul Fatout.

For further biographical background, see *Mark Twain's Autobiography*, 2 volumes (New York: Harper & Brothers, 1924), edited by Albert Bigelow Paine; *Mark Twain in Eruption* (New York: Harper & Brothers, 1940), edited by Bernard DeVoto; *The Autobiography of Mark Twain* (New York: Harper & Row, 1959), edited by Charles Neider; *Mark Twain's Own Autobiography* (Madison: University of Wisconsin Press, 1990), edited by Michael J. Kiskis; *Mark Twain's Letters*, 2 volumes (New York: Harper & Brothers, 1917), edited by Albert Bigelow Paine; *The Love Letters of Mark Twain* (New York: Harper & Brothers, 1949), edited by Dixon Wecter; *Mark Twain to Mrs. Fairbanks* (San Marino: Huntington Library, 1949), edited by Dixon Wecter; *Mark Twain–Howells Letters*, 2 volumes (Cambridge: Harvard University Press, 1960), edited by Henry Nash Smith and William M. Gibson; *Mark Twain's Letters to His Publishers 1867–1894* (Berkeley: University of California Press, 1967), edited by Hamlin Hill; *Mark Twain's Correspondence with Henry Huttleston Rogers 1893–1909* (Berkeley: University of California Press, 1969), edited by Lewis Leary; *Mark Twain's Letters: Volume 1 1853–1866* (Berkeley: University of California Press, 1988), edited by Edgar Marquess Branch, Michael B. Frank, and Kenneth M. Sanderson; *Mark Twain's Letters: Volume 2 1867–1868* (Berkeley: University of California Press, 1990), edited by Harriet Elinor Smith and Richard Bucci; *Mark Twain's Letters: Volume 3 1869* (Berkeley: University of California Press, 1991), edited by Victor Fischer, Michael B. Frank, and Dahlia Armon; *Mark Twain's Aquarium: The Samuel Clemens Angelfish Correspondence 1905–1910* (Athens: University of Georgia Press, 1991), edited by John Cooley; *Mark Twain's Notebook* (New York: Harper & Brothers, 1935), edited by Albert Bigelow Paine; *Mark Twain's Notebooks &*

*Journals: Volume I (1855–1873)* (Berkeley: University of California Press, 1975), edited by Frederick Anderson, Michael B. Frank, and Kenneth M. Sanderson; *Mark Twain's Notebooks & Journals: Volume II (1877–1883)* (Berkeley: University of California Press, 1975), edited by Frederick Anderson, Lin Salamo, and Bernard L. Stein; *Mark Twain's Notebooks & Journals: Volume III (1883–1891)* (Berkeley: University of California Press, 1979), edited by Robert Pack Browning, Michael B. Frank, and Lin Salamo; *Mark Twain: A Biography* (New York: Harper & Brothers, 1912), by Albert Bigelow Paine; *My Father Mark Twain* (New York: Harper & Brothers, 1931), by Clara Clemens; *Mark Twain, Business Man* (Boston: Little, Brown and Company, 1946), edited by Samuel Charles Webster; *The Literary Apprenticeship of Mark Twain* (Urbana: University of Illinois Press, 1950), by Edgar Marquess Branch; *Sam Clemens of Hannibal* (Boston: Houghton Mifflin Company, 1952), by Dixon Wecter; *Mark Twain's Hannibal, Huck, & Tom* (Berkeley: University of California Press, 1969), edited by Walter Blair; *Clemens of the "Call": Mark Twain in San Francisco* (Berkeley: University of California Press, 1969), edited by Edgar M. Branch; and *Huck Finn and Tom Sawyer among the Indians, and Other Unfinished Stories* (Berkeley: University of California Press, 1989), edited by Dahlia Armon, Walter Blair, Paul Baender, William M. Gibson, and Franklin R. Rogers.

1.26    his Satanic Majesty of Russia]    Alexander III, czar 1881–94, had instituted a reactionary domestic policy that included systematic persecution of religious minorities, especially Jews, stronger controls on the peasantry, increased censorship and repressive police powers, and forcible Russification of national minorities.

1.35    Wakefield . . . guide-book]    *The Baths, Bathing, and Attractions of Aix-le-Bains, Savoy, Etc.* (1880).

2.3    Dent du Chat]    Literally, "cat's tooth"; *chat*, in reference to terrain, can refer to a deep pass or narrow gap.

4.7–9    Presbyterian . . . damnation.]    In May 1891, the General Assembly of the Presbyterian Church in the United States deferred a vote on proposed revisions of the Westminster Confession of Faith. One of these revisions would have removed the phrase "elect infants" (in chapter X) that implied other infants were predestined for damnation.

6.3    *Le Petit Journal*]    Sensational newspaper designed to appeal to "the masses," the first of its kind in France and the first to be sold by criers rather than subscription. It was established by Moïse (Polydore) Millaud in 1863.

7.29    mother in Israel]    Cf. Judges 5:7 and II Samuel 20:19.

10.4    pour boires]    Tips or gratuities; literally "for drinking."

18.10    glass going down]   A drop in atmospheric pressure as measured on a barometer (or weather-glass) predicts stormy weather to come.

23.15    dass heiss]   Or *das heisst*, meaning "that is."

24.13    the Compact]   The Everlasting League, formed for mutual defense by the forest cantons of Uri, Schwyz, and Unterwalden in 1291, became the basis of the Swiss Confederation.

28.39    p. p. c. cards]   *Pour prendre congé* (for taking leave); a visiting card with these letters indicated a farewell call.

30.11    Psychical Society of England]   The Society for Psychical Research, founded in England in 1882, sought scientifically to study "debatable phenomena designated by such terms as 'mesmeric,' 'psychical,' and 'spiritualistic.' " In 1884 William James organized an American branch.

30.23    Great Bonanza]   Or the Big Bonanza, referring to the discovery of gold and silver lodes in Nevada in 1873.

30.35    *North American* . . . Mr. Metcalf]   The *North American Review*, founded in Boston in 1815, moved to New York in 1878, and, under the editorship of Lorettus Sutton Metcalf (1837–1920), shifted its emphasis from scholarly and historical articles to commentary and opinions on contemporary issues.

31.20    Frank Millet]   Francis Millet (1846–1912), American painter, illustrator, and newspaper correspondent, had been Twain's friend since 1876, when he painted his portrait.

34.19    William H. Wright]   Wright (1829–98), who wrote under the name "Dan De Quille," was Twain's close friend and co-worker on the staff of the Virginia City *Territorial Enterprise*, where Wright remained until around 1893.

35.8–12    book . . . Bonanza,]   After the incident Twain recalls here, Wright came to Hartford as Twain's guest and soon completed *History of the Big Bonanza* (Hartford: American Publishing Co., 1876). Twain wrote the introduction.

36.9–12    electric telegraph . . . same time.]   Samuel F. B. Morse conceived the idea of a simple circuit electromagnetic telegraph while returning from Europe by ship in 1832, and reportedly devised a telegraph machine soon after. Morse thought he had been the first to originate the idea, and only later learned that Princeton professor Joseph Henry had devised an electromagnetic signaling device and published a description of it in 1831. Charles Wheatstone and William Fothergill patented an early telegraph in 1837. In Germany, Johann Gauss and Wilhelm Weber developed an electromagnetic telegraph in 1833, and Carl August von Steinheil of the University of Munich discovered that the earth could be used for a return conductor in 1838.

36.29    facts . . . Howells's]   When Howells' novel *Dr. Breen's Practice* (1881) was partially set in type, Massachusetts author Elizabeth Stuart Phelps, later Ward, submitted her new novel *Doctor Zay* to the *Atlantic Monthly*. Both novels concerned a woman physician. At about the same time that Howells learned of the coincidence, he received a short story about a "lady doctoress" from a lesser-known writer. When he offered to show his page proofs to her to prevent any suspicion that her plot had been stolen, she declined to read them out of courtesy, but destroyed her own manuscript. Phelps's novel was serialized in *Atlantic Monthly* beginning in April 1882, with a note by Howells explaining the coincidence. Howells had told Twain of this episode before September 3, 1881.

37.23–25   "Nothing . . . ballads.]   Many newspaper and magazine pieces appeared unsigned and copyright laws were often loosely observed. William Allen Butler (1825–1902) did not sign "Nothing to Wear: An Episode of City Life" (1857) and was at first reluctant, because of his position as an attorney, to prove his authorship. John Whittaker Watson (1824–90) had to defend his authorship of "Beautiful Snow" (1865) against several claimants, including a 15-year-old girl and her father. Elizabeth Chase Akers, later Allen (1832–1911), initially used the pen name Florence Percy for her "Rock Me to Sleep, Mother" (1860) and had to contend with several determined claimants to its authorship. Will Carleton (1845–1912) is best remembered for his sentimental poems such as "Over the Hill to the Poor House."

38.27    Mr. Brown]   J. Randall Brown was active 1877–78 in the New York City area.

44.5–11    Leverrier . . . Adams]   French astronomer Urbain Jean Joseph Leverrier, in November 1845 and June 1846, predicted the presence of an unknown planet (now known as Neptune) from observed variations in the orbit of Uranus. In England, the astronomer John Couch Adams and mathematician and physical scientist Mary Fairfax Somerville reached the same conclusion independently at about the same time. The planet Neptune was identified in September 1846 by John G. Galle of the Berlin Observatory, using Leverrier's calculations.

49.17    the Brunig]   Brünig Pass, east of Brienz, Switzerland, connects the valley of the Aare and the area of Lake Lucerne. It is the ancient route between the forest cantons of Uri, Schwyz, and Unterwalden and Lucerne and the Bernese Alps.

50.14–15    Lake of the Four Cantons]   Vierwaldstätter See, also called Lake Lucerne.

50.18–19    trinity of Switzerland]   See note 24.13.

51.5    Murten . . . Granson,]   Murten, or Morat, on the eastern shore of the Murtensee and 15 miles west of Bern, was the scene of a Swiss victory over Charles the Bold of Burgundy on June 22, 1476. Granson, or Grandson, is on the western shore of Lac de Neuchâtel, 20 miles southwest of Neuchâtel. Its garrison surrendered to Charles the Bold in February 1476 and were hanged. On March 2, 1476, the Burgundians were routed by a relief force of Swiss Confederates.

51.8 Stauffacher's wife] In J. C. F. von Schiller's drama *Wilhelm Tell* (1804), she incites her husband, Werner, to organize resistance to Austrian rule.

51.40 Fridolin] Sixth-century Irish missionary who founded a monastery and church on the island of Säckingen in the Rhine River.

52.17 walking delegate] A labor union official appointed to visit members and their places of employment to secure enforcement of union rules and agreements.

56.26 King of Greece] George I (1845–1913) was king of the Hellenes from 1863 to 1913.

60.20 Portland Place] Fashionable neighborhood near Regent Street and Regent's Park.

67.9 Hospodar] Title used by the Ottoman governors and tributary princes of Walachia and Moldavia.

70.24–26 Shoreditch . . . Cheapside] Shoreditch is a district in the East End of London. Bohun was the name of an English family prominent in the 13th and 14th centuries. Newgate was a street in the City of London famous as the site of several prisons (1180–1902). Cheapside is a commercial street in the City of London.

72.36 Conqueror] William the Conqueror, duke of Normandy from 1035 and king of England from 1066 to 1087.

82.1 "dog . . . blanket"] A rolled currant dumpling or a jam pudding.

82.37 accident . . . Paris] The transatlantic liner *City of Paris* survived a major explosion in March 1890.

83.28 Johnstown disaster] On May 31, 1889, an earthen dam rebuilt in 1879–81 to enlarge Conemaugh Lake above Johnstown, Pennsylvania, gave way after exceptionally heavy rains, flooding the town and killing approximately 5,000 residents.

84.20–22 "Britannia . . . deep!"] From "Ye Mariners of England" by Thomas Campbell (1777–1844).

87.9 "Shittim and gopher."] Shittim, from the shittah or acacia tree, was used to make the ark of the covenant in Deuteronomy 10:3, and the altars, tables, boards, and pillars of the Jewish tabernacle in Exodus 25–37. Gopher wood was used to build Noah's ark in Genesis 6:14.

88.16     Megatherium]   Extinct genus of huge ground sloths (up to 18 feet long) of Pleistocene North and South America.

89.27     the Exposition]   The World's Columbian Exposition, celebrating the 400th anniversary of Columbus's voyage, opened in Chicago in May 1893.

93.27     General Horace Porter's]   Porter (1837–1921) was a staff officer for Ulysses S. Grant from 1864 through the end of the Civil War and later served as a White House aide before becoming a railroad executive and diplomat. His account of the surrender at Appomattox appeared in *Battles and Leaders of the Civil War* (1889) and his memoir *Campaigning With Grant* was published in 1897.

95.4–5    Homeward . . . shore;]   From "Homeward Bound" by W. F. Warren, music by John William Dadmun (1812–1900).

95.8–11   My boat . . . thee.]   From "To Thomas Moore" (1817) by Lord Byron.

95.13–14  O, pilot . . . deep.]   From "The Pilot," poem and song by Thomas Haynes Bayly (1797–1839).

95.16–19  A life . . . keep!]   From "A Life on the Ocean Wave," words by Epes Sargent (1813–80), music by Henry Russell (1812–1900).

95.21–22  A wet . . . fair.]   From "A Wet Sheet and a Flowing Sea" (1825), by Allan Cunningham (1784–1842).

95.28–32  O, who . . . ahoy!"]   From "The Larboard Watch" by Thomas E. Williams (d. 1854).

96.3–4    Rocked . . . sleep!]   From "Rocked in the Cradle of the Deep" (1831), words by Emma Hart Willard (1787–1870), music by Joseph Philip Knight (1812–87).

96.5–8    "The Storm . . . Main"]   "The Storm" by George Alexander Stevens (1720–84) appeared in the "Poems of the Sea" section of *The Family Library of Poetry and Song* (1870), compiled by William Cullen Bryant, a copy of which Twain owned; it was sung to the old English tune "Welcome, Brother Debtor." "The Bird at Sea" was a poem by Felicia Dorothea Hemans (1793–1835) set to music by C. Meineke. "The Mariner's Dream" by William Dimond (1800–37) begins, "In slumbers of midnight the sailor-boy lay . . ." "The Captive Pirate's Lament" probably refers to the traditional English ballad "Captain Kidd," in which the pirate is ruefully waiting to be hanged. By "We are far from Home on the Stormy Main" Twain may have intended "The Stormy Petrel" by Bryan Waller Procter (Barry Cornwall, 1787–1874), music by Sigismund, Ritter von Neukomm (1778–1858), which begins "A thousand miles from land are we, / Tossing about on the stormy sea . . . "

97.4      "Homeward Bound,"]   See note 95.4–5.

102.22    Tonawanda]   A suburb of Buffalo, New York.

110.31–33    Breton village . . . Millet]   Jean François Millet (1814–75), the son of poor peasants, settled in Barbizon, a village near the forest of Fontainebleau and the center of an artists' colony in 1849, after failing to earn a living as an artist in Paris. His works came into demand only in the 1860s, and he gained official recognition when nine of his paintings were displayed at the 1867 international exposition in Paris. The prices paid for his work rose sharply after his death.

111.23    'Angelus']   One of Millet's most admired paintings (1857–59), now in the Louvre. It shows peasants in the fields pausing for the Angelus, a Roman Catholic prayer said in the early morning, at noon, and in the evening.

116.15    five hundred and fifty thousand]   In 1889, an American dealer bought the "Angelus" at auction for 550,000 francs.

134.2     the Fair]   The World's Columbian Exhibition; see note 89.27.

142.5     Mr. Bliss]   William Bliss (1834–1907), president of the Boston and Albany Railroad.

152.5     Hopkinson Smith's]   Baltimore-born engineer, artist, and author Francis Hopkinson Smith (1838–1915) began writing professionally at about the age of 50 and contributed stories and humorous sketches to *Harper's Monthly* and other journals. The short novel that made him famous was *Colonel Carter of Cartersville* (1890), about a down-and-out Virginia gentleman and his aged Negro servant.

152.15    Van Dyke]   Henry Van Dyke (1852–1933) was a Presbyterian minister and prolific man of letters who became professor of English at Princeton University. He would later deliver the sermon at Twain's funeral service.

154.42    *Sidgwick . . . Composition]   *An Introduction to Greek Composition, with Exercises* by Arthur Sidgwick (1840–1920) went through many editions in America and England from 1876 to 1951. Twain later learned that the Greek version of the jumping frog story was his own tale adapted for use in this textbook.

157.22–23    Madame Blanc]   Marie Thérèse Blanc, writing under the pen name "Th. Bentzon," had published a French translation of Twain's jumping frog tale in an article "Les Humoristes Américains," in the *Revue des Deux*

*Mondes* of July 15, 1872. Twain first published his re-translation in *Sketches, New and Old* (1875).

161.15    the Englishman Sumner]    Twain also referred to this unidentified individual in an unpublished manuscript written 1853–54.

164.8    M. Bourget's chapters]    Paul Bourget (1852–1935), author of psychological novels, had been elected to the French Academy in 1894. His book *Outre-Mer: Impressions of America* (1895) was serialized in French newspapers (where Twain, living in Paris, had read at least the early chapters) and appeared in translation in the New York *Herald*.

165.38    Newport]    "Society. I. A Summer City," which became the third chapter of *Outre-Mer*, describes Newport, Rhode Island.

168.7    the White Caps]    Self-appointed vigilante groups who, under the pretense of regulating and protecting public morals, punished "offenders" and committed various outrages and lawless acts.

173.30–31    Bible . . . evil.]    Cf. I Timothy 6:10.

174.19    the Railroad King]    George Hudson (1800–71), an English financier who controlled over 1,000 miles of railroad before being ruined by the exposure of financial irregularities in 1847–48.

174.20–21    Law . . . Bubble]    Scottish financier John Law (1671–1729) organized in France the Compagnie de l'Occident, also known as the Mississippi Company, which assumed control of Louisiana in 1718. Law's reputation and the expectation of enormous profits caused the price of the company's stock to rise spectacularly, but in 1720 the company failed and many investors were ruined.

177.9    Jacksonville, Illinois]    Town about 55 miles east of Hannibal, Missouri, scene of a heresy trial in 1833 and of violence during the 1830s and 1840s when it was an active station on the underground railroad.

179.8    *La Terre*]    Émile Zola's graphically naturalistic novel (1887) about farm life in a peasant community. Twain had written an essay expressing his pained and ambivalent reaction to the book, but it was never published.

180.8    *Prof. Lounsbury*]    Thomas Raynesford Lounsbury (1838–1915), author of *James Fenimore Cooper* (1882).

181.22–23    Friendship's Offering]    *Friendship's Offering: A Christmas, New Year, and Birthday Present*, published annually from 1841 to 1845, was one of the best known "gift books" or collections of belles lettres, typically given to young women by suitors.

184.20    through . . . darkly.]    Cf. I Corinthians 13:12.

196.19    chromo] Chromolithographs, or printed color engravings of famous paintings or original scenes, had recently become cheaper and more common.

202.8    Dan Setchell] Setchell (1831–1866) was a comedian and monologuist whom Twain had seen and admired in San Francisco in 1865.

207.2    similar things] The surviving manuscript of this essay is missing the first leaf, which probably contained clippings of telegrams from the London *Daily Telegraph* of August 13, 1896, page 7, reporting Turkish atrocities in Crete.

210.9–10    King John] A reference to Shakespeare's version of the fate of Arthur I (1187–1203?), duke of Brittany, in *King John*, Act IV, scene i.

210.13–14    first Richard's . . . it;] In March 1190, soon after the accession of Richard I of England, this massacre occurred in the city of York, as described by William Combe in *The History and Antiquities of the City of York from its Origin to the Present Times* (London, 1785), a volume Twain owned.

210.37–38    Napoleon . . . Zulu war] Napoléon Eugene Bonaparte (1856–79), the Prince Imperial, son of Napoleon III, graduated from the Royal Military Academy at Woolwich in 1875, but was never commissioned in the British army. In 1879 he went to Natal to observe the British expedition against the Zulus and was killed there on June 1.

211.33    to-day in Crete] See note 207.2.

232.19    the "Vöglein."] Little bird.

243.29    Mr. Pierce] Franklin Pierce was president of the United States from 1853 to 1857.

246.19    Willard's] Hotel in Washington, D.C., frequented by public figures; Twain often stayed there. (It was replaced by a new structure, built 1901–04.)

253.11    Pelion . . . Ossa] In Greek mythology, when the giants attempted to reach heaven to overthrow the gods, they piled Mount Pelion upon Mount Ossa to use as a scaling ladder.

254.25–26    Battle . . . d'Ulloa] General Zachary Taylor and his army defeated Santa Anna and a larger Mexican force at Buena Vista, February 22–23, 1847. San Juan de Ulúa, the great masonry fortress near Vera Cruz, Mexico, surrendered to General Winfield Scott on March 29, 1847, after bombardment by American forces.

254.33    Godey's Lady's Book] Monthly magazine for women (1830–98), founded in Philadelphia by Louis Godey. It was noted for its engravings, which included works of art as well as sentimental pieces.

260.19–20    Cuba . . . ultimatum]    On April 11, 1898, President McKinley sought Congressional authority to intervene in the Cuban revolution. Congress passed resolutions on April 19 that recognized Cuban independence, demanded Spanish withdrawal from the island, and authorized the use of force if Spain did not comply. An amendment proposed by Senator Henry M. Teller of Colorado was also adopted, disclaiming any intention to "exercise sovereignty, jurisdiction, or control" over Cuba after it achieved independence. Spain severed diplomatic relations with the United States, and Congress then declared war on April 25.

260.31    Port Arthur]    Now Lü-shun, a strategic port on the southern tip of the Liaotung peninsula in southern Manchuria. It had been ceded to Japan by China in 1895, following China's defeat in the 1894–95 Sino-Japanese War, but was returned because of diplomatic pressure from Russia, Germany, and France. In 1898, Russia was given a 25-year leasehold on the peninsula and began building a railroad connecting Port Arthur with Siberia.

263.16    Wilbrandt]    Adolf von Wilbrandt (1837–1911).

264.22    Mme. Hohenfels]    Stella Baroness Hohenfels-Berger (1857–1920), an actress who had a long and distinguished career.

268.9–11    spectacle . . . life-boats]    On November 22, 1873, the French Atlantic mail steamer *Ville de Havre*, with 313 passengers and crew, collided with the British clipper *Lochearn* and sank. Of the 87 survivors, 58 were members of the crew.

268.13–15    A year . . . themselves.]    On May 4, 1897, a fire broke out in a crowded charity bazaar organized by leading aristocratic and society women in the Rue Jean-Goujon in Paris, and at least 150 people were killed in the ensuing panic and the collapse of the roof.

268.17–19    condemning . . . one.]    This piece was published in October 1898, four years after the beginning of the Dreyfus affair in France. Captain Alfred Dreyfus (1859–1935), a Jewish staff officer assigned to the ministry of war, was court-martialed and convicted in December 1894 of spying for Germany and imprisoned for life on Devil's Island off French Guiana. The verdict was widely endorsed by the anti-Semitic elements of French society. In March 1896 Colonel Georges Picquart (1854–1914), chief of the army intelligence section, discovered evidence that Major Ferdinand Esterhazy (1847–1923) was responsible for the unsigned letter and memorandum that Dreyfus had allegedly sent to the German military attaché. The war ministry suppressed this evidence, and Colonel Picquart's deputy, Major Hubert Henry, produced a letter, purportedly from the Italian military attaché, establishing Dreyfus's guilt. In March 1897, Dreyfus's brother Matthieu discovered additional evidence incriminating Esterhazy and publicly accused him. Esterhazy was court-martialed and acquitted in January 1898, while Picquart was accused of forgery and dismissed from the army. The acquittal of Esterhazy prompted Émile Zola to publish "J'accuse," an open letter to the president of

the Republic charging the war ministry with concealing evidence and abet-
ting a miscarriage of justice. Zola was convicted of libel and sentenced to a
year in prison, but escaped to England. In August 1898, Major Henry committed suicide in prison after admitting that he had forged the principal
evidence against Dreyfus; Esterhazy fled to England. Amid intense political
controversy the case was submitted to an appeals court, which, with the support of the French government, ordered a new trial. In September 1899 the
second court-martial again found Dreyfus guilty, although his sentence was
reduced to ten years. Two weeks later he received a presidential pardon, and
in 1906, after his conviction was finally reversed by the court of appeal, Dreyfus was reinstated in the army and awarded the Legion of Honor. During
World War I he served as a lieutenant-colonel in the artillery.

277.17      Yedo]   Or Yeddo, former name of Tokyo, Japan.

282.15–16      the new chief justice (Lemaitre)]   Jules Lemaître (1853–1914),
dramatic critic for the *Journal des Débats* and a prominent member of the
anti-Dreyfusard *Ligue de la patrie française*, argued that there were no legal
grounds for appealing the decision of Dreyfus's court-martial.

282.23–24      decision . . . Dreyfus matter]   See note 268.17–19.

282.39      did kill]   Twain canceled in a revision of the manuscript a passage
indicating that Clayton had killed an unidentified stranger.

302.14      Sable island]   In the North Atlantic, about 200 miles east of
Halifax, Nova Scotia.

305.24–25      Empire Express]   In 1893, the Empire State Express of the
New York Central Railroad set a new speed record, reaching 112.5 miles per
hour.

310.4–5      Washingtonian . . . Father Matthew]   In 1840 a group of Baltimore workmen formed the first chapter of the Washington Temperance Society. The Washingtonian movement advocated the pledging of total abstinence
and was marked by its flamboyant and emotional meetings. At the height of
the movement, from 1849 to 1851, the Rev. Theobald Mathew (1790–1856),
known as "Father Mathew," a Capuchin priest and leader of a temperance
crusade in Ireland, toured the United States and administered the pledge to
about 500,000 persons.

310.31–32      give . . . banks]   Slang for a scolding or reprimand.

314.9–10      where . . . twineth]   Cf. James Fisk's reply to a Congressional
inquiry into his attempt to corner the gold market that resulted in the Black
Friday panic of 1869. Asked what had become of the money lost by investors,
he replied, "It has gone where the woodbine twineth."

344.4      Peace Commission]   Its five members negotiated the treaty ending
the Spanish-American War. Three of them were U.S. senators and could not
receive additional compensation.

348.25–26    when . . . ambassador]    In 1893.

353.16    palace-car]    Any of several kinds of railway carriages, especially from the Pullman Company, fitted out with extra conveniences.

354.2–4    magazine . . . Vienna]    Twain's earlier essay had concerned a crisis in the Chamber of Deputies of the Imperial Parliament of Austria-Hungary, including a marathon session in which one speech lasted twelve hours and a session in November 1897 when violence caused by German nationalists erupted among the legislators, causing the presiding officer to call in the military to clear the chamber.

359.40    one . . . Latin historians]    Twain had marked a relevant passage in his copy of C. Suetonius Tranquillus, *The Lives of the Twelve Cæsars* (London: Bohn's Classical Library, 1875).

360.32    The Jew . . . Russia.]    See note 1.26. "May laws," persecuting orders signed into law by Alexander III in May 1882, were again rigorously enforced after 1897, resulting in widespread Jewish emigration to Western countries.

360.40    John's time]    King John I (1167–1216); by his order in 1210, Jews were stripped of their assets.

361.4    rescue . . . Sepulchre]    The Holy Sepulchre in Jerusalem, usually accepted as the tomb of Christ.

361.6    banished . . . realm.]    Jews were banished from England under Edward I in 1290.

364.20–23    Twelve Sane . . . times]    See note 268.17–19. The Twelve Sane Men were Émile Zola's friends who sat with him throughout his trial for libel in 1898, despite the very real threat of mob violence.

365.6–7    Reichsrath]    The Reichsrat (literally "imperial council") was the Austro-Hungarian imperial parliament.

365.19    Cyclopædia Britannica]    The ninth edition of the *Encyclopædia Britannica* confirms Twain's figures for Germany and the United States, but gives much lower figures for Russia and Austria-Hungary.

366.40–41    "*Namens . . . Franzos*]    The essay (dated 1880) is reprinted in Franzos' *Aus der grossen Ebene* (Stuttgart: A. Bonz, 1888).

367.14    Concerts]    Alliances of nations.

367.23    Massénas]    André Masséna (1758–1817), Duc de Rivoli and Prince d'Essling, French general and marshal under Napoleon, was reputedly of Jewish descent.

367.26    casting vote]    The deciding vote.

368.19–20      the Sultan]   Palestine was then part of the Ottoman Empire under the Sultan Abdul-Hamid II (1842–1918).

368.20      convention of Berne]   The first World Zionist Congress met in Basel, Switzerland, in August 1897.

369.3      the German sense]   *Fremde(r)*, meaning foreigner or stranger.

370.23      immortality?]   Twain added the following postscript to this essay when it was reprinted in the English edition of *The Man That Corrupted Hadleyburg* (London, 1900) and in later American editions. The text below is that found in *The Man That Corrupted Hadleyburg and Other Stories and Essays* (New York: Harper & Brothers, 1902), pp. 281–83:

### *Postscript*—THE JEW AS SOLDIER

When I published the above article in HARPER'S MONTHLY, I was ignorant—like the rest of the Christian world—of the fact that the Jew had a record as a soldier. I have since seen the official statistics, and I find that he furnished soldiers and high officers to the Revolution, the War of 1812, and the Mexican War. In the Civil War he was represented in the armies and navies of both the North and the South by 10 per cent. of his numerical strength—the same percentage that was furnished by the Christian populations of the two sections. This large fact means more than it seems to mean; for it means that the Jew's patriotism was not merely level with the Christian's, but overpassed it. When the Christian volunteer arrived in camp he got a welcome and applause, but as a rule the Jew got a snub. His company was not desired, and he was made to feel it. That he nevertheless conquered his wounded pride and sacrificed both that and his blood for his flag raises the average and quality of his patriotism above the Christian's. His record for capacity, for fidelity, and for gallant soldiership in the field is as good as any one's. This is true of the Jewish private soldiers and the Jewish generals alike. Major-General O. O. Howard speaks of one of his Jewish staff-officers as being "of the bravest and best"; of another—killed at Chancellorsville—as being "a true friend and a brave officer"; he highly praises two of his Jewish brigadier-generals; finally, he uses these strong words: "Intrinsically there are no more patriotic men to be found in the country than those who claim to be of Hebrew descent, and who served with me in parallel commands or more directly under my instructions."

Fourteen Jewish Confederate and Union families contributed, between them, fifty-one soldiers to the war. Among these, a father and three sons; and another, a father and four sons.

In the above article I was not able to endorse the common reproach that the Jew is willing to feed upon a country but not to fight for it, because I did not know whether it was true or false. I supposed it to be true, but it is not allowable to endorse wandering maxims upon supposition—except when one is trying to make out a case. That slur upon the Jew cannot hold up its head in presence of the figures of the War Department. It has done its work, and done it long and faithfully, and with high approval: it ought to be pensioned off now, and retired from active service.

372.22    "Bitte?"]   "Please?"; i.e. "I don't understand."

372.23    Stubenmädchen's]   Chambermaid's.

373.3    Geschirr]   Crockery, equipment.

373.8–11    She . . . Fuller.]   Mrs. Fuller's appearance and marital history resemble those of Mary Baker Eddy (1821–1910), founder of the Christian Science movement.

379.32    every ill . . . heir to."]   Cf. *Hamlet*, III.i.61–62.

382.24    botts]   Or bots, an intestinal condition of horses and cattle caused by parasitic larvae.

382.25    blind staggers]   Symptom of various diseases affecting domestic animals.

402.37    "Sam Lawson"]   A village jack-of-all-trades and genial yarn-spinner in Harriet Beecher Stowe's *Oldtown Folks* (1869) and *Sam Lawson's Oldtown Fireside Stories* (1872).

421.31–32    "When . . . maid"]   From act II of Gilbert and Sullivan's operetta (1885).

439.2    what you desire]   The New York *World* Sunday edition was beginning to publish a series "Life's Great Problems—How to Solve Them: A Series of Special Articles by America's Most Famous Funny Men."

440.28    Dreyfus case]   See note 268.17–19.

440.34    Chamberlain . . . Africa]   Joseph Chamberlain (1836–1914) served as British secretary of state for the colonies from 1895 to 1903. He was accused of complicity in the Jameson Raid of December 29, 1895, in which a volunteer force, led by Leander Starr Jameson and backed by Cecil Rhodes, unsuccessfully attempted to overthrow the Boer government of the Transvaal Republic. A House of Commons inquiry cleared Chamberlain in 1897, and he continued to play a leading role in negotiations between Britain and the Transvaal until the outbreak of the South African War on October 11, 1899.

444.24    "Truth . . . again."]   William Cullen Bryant, "The Battle-Field," stanza 9.

444.27−29    Carlyle . . . live."]  Cf. *The French Revolution*, I, Book 6, chapter 3: "For if there be a Faith, from old, it is this, as we often repeat, that no lie can live forever."

445.11−12    "Lay . . . Minstrel."]  Narrative poem (1805) by Walter Scott.

445.21    at Chicago]  That is, at the Columbian World's Exposition at Chicago.

445.27    his brother Edward]  None of Washington's three brothers and two half-brothers was named Edward.

448.10    Ralph Keeler]  Keeler (1840−73), journalist, adventurer, and author of *Gloverson and His Silent Partners* (1869) and *Vagabond Adventures* (1870), was a friend of Twain's since his days with the San Francisco *Golden Era* and was later active in Boston literary circles.

448.25    1830]  Howells was born in 1837; he became assistant editor of *Atlantic Monthly* in 1866 and editor in 1871.

452.9    Zal and Rustam]  Warlike personalities in Edward Fitzgerald's *The Rubáiyat of Omar Khayyám* (1859), upon which Twain's poem is modelled.

454.26    "the slave . . . free"]  English antislavery advocate Granville Sharp (1735−1813) brought suit in 1772 to prevent James Somersett, a Negro slave who had been brought to England from Virginia, from being sent by his owner to Jamaica for sale. In his pleading before the king's bench on February 7, attorney William Davy (d. 1780) argued that "the moment" slaves "put their foot on English ground, that moment they become free." After further pleadings, chief justice Lord Mansfield ruled on June 22, 1772, that slavery could exist only where supported by positive law, and that because there was no positive law in England supporting slavery, Somersett should be discharged (his decision did not apply to British colonies or to the African slave trade).

454.33    fancy rates . . . missionaries,]  Germany had demanded heavy reparations from China for missionaries killed during the Boxer uprising of 1900.

455.7    "no quarter"]  See page 464.38−465.2 and note.

455.9    Port Arthur]  See note 260.31.

455.11−12    rescue poor Cuba]  See note 260.19−20. A treaty signed in 1898 made Cuba an independent republic; it was an American protectorate until 1903.

456.6    Kiao-Chow]  Or Chiao-chou Bay in Shantung Province, China. Germany had used the killing of two missionaries in 1897 as the occasion for forcing China to grant it a 99-year lease on the bay and the city of Tsingtao.

457.1     **To . . . Darkness**]   Cf. Matthew 4:16, Isaiah 42:7, and Micah 7:8.

457.2−7     "Christmas . . . Eve.]   From the opening paragraph of "Christmas Hope and Cheer," New York *Tribune*, December 24, 1900, p. 7.

457.8     From *The Sun*]   From the New York *Evening Sun*, January 4, 1901, p. 1.

457.14     ruin wrought]   Twain deleted the words "by Tammany methods" after the word "wrought."

458.5     *The Sun*]   The New York (morning) *Sun*, December 24, 1900, p. 1.

458.7     The Rev. Mr. Ament]   William Scott Ament (1851−1909), a Congregational missionary in China since 1877 and in Peking since 1880 and editor of *The North China News*, was maintained by the American Board of Commissioners for Foreign Missions.

458.12     *taels*]   A silver tael was worth approximately 75 cents.

458.15     THIRTEEN TIMES]   Twain added the capitals and deleted a sentence at the end of the paragraph that read: "After paying all the damages Mr. Ament has 7,000 taels left, which will be devoted to the support of 100 Chinese widows and their children." Ament and Judson Smith, secretary of the American Board, subsequently explained that the figure "thirteen" was the result of a mistake in the cable transmission, the fraction "1/3" having been misread as "13." In an essay "To My Missionary Critics" in the *North American Review* for April 1901, Twain accepted this correction of the amount but argued that the principles underlying his criticism remained unchanged.

458.26     the siege]   During the Boxer Rebellion, the siege of the foreign community in Peking lasted from June 20 to August 14, 1900, when British and Japanese troops arrived.

458.36     Chili]   Or Chihli, former province surrounding Peking.

459.5     Macallum's History]   In the essay "To My Missionary Critics" in the *North American Review* for April 1901, Twain identified this work as "imaginary."

460.32−39     "The missionary . . . relations."]   In a dispatch from Yokohama, New York *Tribune*, December 24, 1900, p. 10.

461.8     Maxim Guns]   Machine gun invented in 1884 by Hiram Stevens Maxim (1840−1916).

463.7     Mr. Chamberlain]   See note 440.34.

463.19     Magersfontein]   British forces suffered a bloody defeat at Magersfontein in the Transvaal on December 11, 1899.

463.25     *Lloyd's Weekly*]   Apparently Twain was quoting from memory the following passage from December 10, 1899: "When we charged the Boers with our bayonets those who did not get away went on their knees for mercy, and I can tell you they got it with a long hook."

464.38–465.2    'March . . . bowels?'] Based on Kaiser William II's widely publicized remarks at Bremerhaven, July 27, 1900, to German marines departing for China. *The New York Times* of July 28, 1900, used the phrase "give no quarter" in its headline.

465.7    Venice's bronze horses] The four gilded horses standing on the gallery over the main entrance to St. Mark's Church were taken to Paris by Napoleon in 1797 but were returned to Venice in 1815.

466.5–6    words . . . aggression;"] In his message to Congress on December 6, 1897, President William McKinley wrote: "I speak not of forcible annexation, for that cannot be thought of. That by our code of morality would be criminal aggresssion."

466.7    "shot . . . world."] From Emerson's "Concord Hymn" (1837).

466.36    friars . . . acquisitions] Under Spanish rule the Roman Catholic Church had become a major landowner and a civil power in the Philippines.

469.26    *buying*] By the Treaty of Paris, December 10, 1898, Spain ceded the Philippines, Guam, and Puerto Rico to the United States and "relinquished" Cuba in trust for its inhabitants. Under the treaty, the United States agreed to give $20 million to Spain after the Philippines were transferred to its sovereignty, although the payment was not in the explicit form of a purchase.

470.15    KITCHENER'S PLAN] During the Boer War, Horatio Herbert Kitchener (1850–1916) became commander in chief of British imperial forces in South Africa in November 1900. Following their defeat in a series of regular engagements earlier in the year, the Boers had adopted guerilla tactics, striking at railway lines and isolated outposts. Kitchener responded by destroying the farms of Boer soldiers, imprisoning their families in concentration camps (where at least 18,000 old men, women, and children died of disease), and building chains of blockhouses across the Transvaal and Orange Free State in order to block the movement of Boer commandos. On May 31, 1902, a peace treaty was signed in which the Boers accepted British sovereignty over all South Africa.

471.5–8    *Public Opinion* . . . HIM."] On November 14, 1900, the Decorah, Iowa, *Public Opinion* published a letter from Will Coan to his mother that included the quoted passage (although not in capitals). The passage was preceded by the words "We killed 120 negroes," and followed by the sentence "There was nothing but dead negroes all around us."

471.29    fifty State Legislatures] Curiously, at the time there were only 45 states, Utah having been the last admitted in 1896.

472.8    Congressional . . . Cuba] See note 260.19–20.

473.3    Civil Commission]    Appointed by President McKinley and headed by William Howard Taft, this body was to assume civil control of the Philippines by September 1, 1900.

474.1    *Battle . . . Republic*]    Poem (1862) by Julia Ward Howe; it was set to the tune of a well-known hymn, "Say, Brothers, Will You Meet Us."

477.31    Weyler's . . . camps]    Valeriano Weyler y Nicolau (1838–1930) was Spanish military governor of Cuba from 1896 until October 1897, when he was recalled following a United States protest against his ruthless administration.

481.17–27    *Increase . . .* Chicago *Tribune*]    From an editorial "The Mississippi Lynchings," Chicago *Tribune*, August 3, 1901, p. 12; Twain's manuscript contains a clipping from a reprinting in the New York *Weekly Post* of August 21, 1901.

482.26    Windsor Hotel]    On the afternoon of March 17, 1899, during the St. Patrick's Day parade, a fire destroyed the Windsor Hotel on Fifth Avenue between 46th and 47th streets in New York City, killing more than 70 people and attracting a large crowd who watched many fleeing guests fall from escape ropes or jump to their deaths from windows.

483.7    Savonarola]    Girolamo Savonarola (1452–98), Florentine monk and reformer, faced down several large mobs and reportedly cowed a band of assassins sent to his prison cell.

483.8    Merrill . . . Beloat]    Joseph Merrill's actions were praised in a June 8, 1901, editorial in the New York *Evening Post*; Thomas Beloat was the subject of a June 10, 1901, article in the New York *Tribune*.

483.29    Hobson]    In June 1898, during the Spanish-American War, Lieutenant Richmond Pearson Hobson (1870–1937) and seven volunteers attempted to bottle up the Spanish fleet in the port of Santiago de Cuba by sinking the coal ship *Merrimac* at the entrance to the harbor.

484.37    Doctor Morrison's book]    *An Australian in China, Being the Narrative of a Quiet Journey across China to British Burma* (1895), by George Ernest Morrison (1862–1920).

485.7–12    The negro . . . completed.]    Dispatch carried in the Chicago *Tribune* of August 21, 1901, p. 1, and in other newspapers. Twain apparently added the italics.

487.2    *Acorns*]    The Order of Acorns organized independent voters for the Fusion ticket (see note 489.29) in the New York City elections of 1901.

487.5    battle of Plassey]    In 1757, in which British forces under Robert Clive defeated the Mughal nawab Siraj-ud-Dawlah.

487.9    India Company's]    The English East India Company, first chartered by Elizabeth I in 1600, held a monopoly on trade with India and exercised vast civil powers. Its trade monopoly ended in 1814 and it transferred its last Indian possessions to the Crown in 1858.

488.25      Macaulay's] Thomas Babington Macaulay published a long essay on Hastings in the *Edinburgh Review* for October 1841. It was collected in his *Essays Contributed to the Edinburgh Review, Critical and Historical*.

489.7      5th of November] Election day.

489.11–15      My Lords, . . . Houses.] Editions of Burke's speeches on Hastings differ substantially, but Twain may have used *The Works of the Right Honorable Edmund Burke*, Revised Edition, 12 volumes (Boston, 1866); see "Speech in Opening the Impeachment. First Day: Friday, February 15, 1788," 9:330.

489.29      Fusion ticket] The Fusion party, an independent reform group opposed to the Tammany Hall Democrats, nominated Seth Low (1850–1916), former mayor of Brooklyn and president of Columbia University, for mayor of New York.

490.35–36      His words . . . *time*"] On April 14, 1899, during testimony before an investigating committee appointed by the New York State Assembly, Richard Croker responded to the question from counsel Frank Moss "Then you are working for your own pocket?" by answering "All the time, the same as you are." (*The New York Times*, April 15, 1899, p. 6)

493.7      Mr. Shepard] Edward Morse Shepard (1850–1911), Democratic candidate for mayor of New York in 1901.

493.15–16      not quoted . . . earned.] Edmund Burke's speech continued: " . . . have become servants to Englishmen, that they might rise by their degradation." Shepard had established a record as a reformer and opponent of machine politics and had accepted the Democratic nomination out of lifelong party loyalty.

494.25      *Letter . . . League*] The letter from Otto Kempner (1858–1914), president of the Anti-Croker League, was published in the New York *Tribune* of October 13, 1901, p. 3.

495.16–32      paraphrase . . . *life*."] Cf. "Speech in Opening the Impeachment. Fourth Day, Tuesday, February 19, 1788," in *Works of Edmund Burke* (Boston, 1866), 10:144–45.

512.5      Prince Henry I] Prince Heinrich of Germany, brother of Kaiser William II, made an official goodwill visit to the United States in 1902.

516.24–27      Carmen Sylva, . . . latest book.] Carmen Sylva was a penname of Elizabeth (1843–1916), consort of Carol I of Romania. The quotations are from *A Real Queen's Fairy Tale* (1901), pp. 214, 216, and 217.

518.14      Jumbo] Famous African elephant purchased by P. T. Barnum from the London Zoological Society in 1882 and killed by a freight train on

September 15, 1885, in St. Thomas, Ontario. Barnum continued to exhibit the skeleton, which is now in the American Museum of Natural History.

518.33–34   private audience . . . emperor.]   Twain met with Franz Joseph (1830–1916), emperor of Austria 1848–1916, on May 25, 1899, in Vienna.

519.32–33   Prince made . . . long ago—]   Edward VII (1841–1910; king 1901–10), as Prince of Wales had visited Canada and the United States in 1860.

520.7   Wantage]   Name of Richard Croker's country estate in Berkshire (now Oxfordshire), England.

522.16   "privilege of the floor"]   Access to the chamber of a legislative body granted to a former member.

523.19   Jardin des Plantes]   Horticultural and zoological garden in Paris; officially the *Muséum d'histoire naturelle*, founded in 1625.

541.11   'Loch Lomond.']   Scottish folk ballad.

545.15–18   Nearer, . . . me.]   "Nearer, My God, to Thee," poem (1840) by Sarah Flower Adams (1805–48); in 1856, it was set to the tune of "Bethany" by Lowell Mason (1792–1872).

552.6   in two . . . States]   Louisiana and California.

554.2   ***Lipton . . . Cup***]   Sir Thomas Johnstone Lipton (1850–1931), Scottish merchant, sponsored the British challenger *Shamrock III* for the America's Cup, held in New York in August 1903. It was his third attempt to win the Cup, which was defended successfully by the American yacht *Reliance*, designed by Nathaniel Hereshoff and owned by a syndicate.

554.32   Kanawha]   Luxurious steam yacht owned by Henry Huttleston Rogers, Twain's financial adviser and friend since 1893. Twain was among the reported guests aboard the *Kanawha* for the first day of the America's Cup finals.

555.31   Mr. Rogers]   See note 554.32.

556.24–26   first day . . . Clipper]   The New York *Herald* of August 21, 1903, reported a lively brush among some steam yachts heading for port after the aborted first race. The *Corsair* belonged to J. P. Morgan and carried the Cup committee. The *Hauoli* belonged to Francis Marion Smith, a prominent Pacific Coast businessman and investor. W. B. Leeds' yacht was the *Noma*, which had recently competed against the *Kanawha* for the Lysistra Cup.

556.33   Monmouth's]   The *Monmouth* was the steam yacht of the New York Yacht Club.

560.5   Lord Roberts]   Frederick Sleigh Roberts (1832–1914), first earl Roberts of Kandahar, a hero of the Indian Mutiny (1857–58), the second

Afghan War (1878–80), and the Boer War (1899–1900), was commander in chief of the British army from 1900 to 1904.

563.15     King Charles spaniel] A small breed of spaniel made popular by Charles II of England.

564.16     Aileen Mavourneen . . . song;] "Kathleen Mavourneen," melody by Frederick William Nicholls Crouch (1808–96), words usually ascribed to English poet Louisa Macartney Crawford (1794–1854).

571.7     beasts . . . perish] Cf. Psalm 49:12 and 20.

573.7     Herbert Spencer] Actually, Joseph William Winthrop Spencer (1851–1921), Canadian-American geologist.

575.26–27     'E isn't . . . too!] Rudyard Kipling, "Soldier an' Sailor Too" (1896).

577.26     *avanti*] "Come in" or "forward."

577.28     *sono dispiacentissimo*] "I am very sorry."

577.34     *Dov' e il gatto.*] "Where is the cat?"

579.16     Elargizione] A donation or largess.

580.13     Chiesa Russa] Russian church.

580.24–25     long primer leaded] Long primer was a type size between bourgeois (9 point) and pica (12 point); leaded meant that strips of metal (leads) were placed between lines of type to make more space between lines.

600.35     Cannel] A high grade of bituminous coal with bright flame and high volatility.

605.37     stickful] A stick was a frame holding lines of set type.

606.1     standing-galley . . . pied] Composed type that has been accidentally spilled or scrambled.

613.40     Veuve Cliquot] Brand of imported French champagne.

617.26     Rowton hotel] Montague William Lowry Corry Rowton (1838–1903), first baron, helped establish a poor man's hotel in Vauxhall, London, in 1892; its success led to other nonprofit Rowton Houses.

618.22–23     W. C. T. U. . . . Hatchet] The Woman's Christian Temperance Union, founded in 1874, was a national organization promoting moral and social reform, including efforts to prohibit the sale of liquor. The "Woman with the Hatchet" was Carry Moore Nation (1846–1911), who in the early 1890s, starting in Kansas, led a crusade against illegal saloons by invading and destroying them with a hatchet.

628.4     Countess Massiglia] In October 1903, Twain and his family had rented a villa near Florence from Countess Rebaudi-Massiglia (an American by birth), and he soon became involved in a series of legal suits and counter-suits with her.

635.2−3    (The spirit . . . History)]    This headnote was added by Albert Bigelow Paine for the first printing in *Europe and Elsewhere* (1923). The 57-foot-long brontosaurus skeleton was installed in 1905.

635.12    Normandy]    The Norman Percheron breed of draft horse, averaging 16 to 17 hands (64 to 68 inches) tall and weighing 1,900 to 2,100 pounds.

639.28    Man . . . Country]    "The Man Without a Country," story by Edward Everett Hale, first published in *Atlantic Monthly* December 1863, and often reprinted.

642.20    Teufelsdröckh]    Philosopher hero of Thomas Carlyle's *Sartor Resartus* (1833−34) who formulates a "philosophy of clothes."

643.28    Fan tribe]    The Fan, or Fang, were a Bantu people in French Equatorial Africa.

645.5−6    assassination . . . Finland Constitution]    Czar Nicholas II virtually abolished the power of the Finnish Diet (parliament) in 1899 and, in 1901, gave the Russian governor-general of Finland dictatorial powers.

645.7    Bobrikoff and Plehve]    Nikolay Ivanovich Bobrikov (1839−1904) was the Russian governor-general of Finland from 1898 until his assassination by a Finnish nationalist in 1904. Vyacheslav Konstantinovich Plehve (1846−1904), former director of the secret police and secretary of state for Finland, became minister of the interior in 1902 and was assassinated in St. Petersburg in 1904.

645.7−8    my massacre . . . day.]    On January 22 (N.S.), 1905 ("Bloody Sunday"), as many as 200,000 people marched peacefully on the Winter Palace in St. Petersburg to petition Czar Nicholas II for political reforms and improved economic conditions. Troops opened fire on the crowds, and between 150 and 1,000 men, women, and children are believed to have been killed.

648.2−8    Experts . . . March 2d.]    From "Dr. Loeb's 'Incredible Discovery,'" an editorial in *The New York Times*, March 2, 1905, p. 8. Twain added the italics.

648.3    announcement . . . Loeb]    Physiologist Jacques Loeb (1859−1924) had just announced his chemical stimulation of the process of sexual fertilization in the egg of the sea urchin. He was best known for his experiments in tropism, parthenogenesis, and regeneration.

649.2−3    Atlantic . . . steamship]    In 1819, the sailing packet *Savannah* went under steam for about 85 hours while crossing the Atlantic. The first crossing of the Atlantic by steam power alone was made in 1838 by two rival British steamships.

649.7–10    doctor . . . puerperal fever] Ignaz Philipp Semmelweis (1818–65), a Hungarian physician working in Vienna, demonstrated the infectious nature of puerperal ("childbed") fever in 1846 and greatly reduced the maternal mortality rate by requiring childbirth attendants to wash their hands with a chlorine solution. He was ridiculed for his belief and forced from his hospital post by his supervisor. He returned to Hungary and accepted a part-time position at Pest hospital, offered on the condition that he not promote his theory. His book *The Etiology of Puerperal Fever* (written in the mid-1850s detailing his experiments in Vienna) was harshly criticized when it was published in 1861. He died in a mental hospital of an infection resulting from a self-inflicted wound with a contaminated scalpel. His findings were not widely accepted until the 1890s.

649.16    Duke of Argyle] George Douglas Campbell (1823–1900), eighth duke of Argyll, was a political leader, author, orator, amateur scientist, and geologist of the "catastrophist" school. In his writings and frequent debates on scientific questions, he criticized evolutionary theories, rebutted the proofs of glacial periods, opposed the "uniformitarian" school of geologists, and argued that geologic history and the development of life could be explained only by divine design and direction. His writings included *Primeval Man* (1869), *The Unity of Nature* (1886), and *Organic Evolution, Cross-Examined* (1898).

649.39    pearls . . . sty.] Cf. Matthew 7:6.

650.6–9    linotype . . . England.] Linotype and Machinery, Ltd., a subsidiary of Mergenthaler, had a large plant at Altrineham, near Manchester. The linotype machine had been patented by Ottmar Mergenthaler (1854–99) in 1884.

650.16    cyanide process.] Or cyanidation, a process developed by J. S. MacArthur and others in 1887 in Glasgow, Scotland, in which ore is treated with a solution of sodium or potassium cyanide, dissolving the gold so that it can then be precipitated.

650.36–39    Doctor Funk . . . cheated."] From a letter by Isaac Kaufman Funk (1839–1911), D.D., Ll.D., president of Funk and Wagnalls publishing company, published in *The New York Times*, March 2, 1905, p. 8. Funk contended that the claims of spiritualism should not be dismissed before a fair testing.

651.12    Lafayette Place] Funk and Wagnalls' offices were at 30 Lafayette Place in New York City.

653.3–4    God . . . sword!] "God the Omnipotent," Episcopal hymn by Henry Fothergill Chorley (1808–72), music by Alexis Lvov (1799–1870); the first line usually reads: "God the Omnipotent! King, who ordainest . . . "

656.5    The American Board]    In March 1905, a controversy erupted over whether the American Board of Commissioners for Foreign Missions should accept a donation of $100,000 from John D. Rockefeller, who was accused of having used unfair and monopolistic practices to build his Standard Oil empire. The money was eventually accepted after it was revealed that the Board had solicited Rockefeller for the contribution.

656.19–20    perjury . . . courts.]    Although Rockefeller was never criminally charged with perjury, his critics accused him of often giving vague, misleading, and sometimes unbelievable testimony concerning the operations and ownership of the Standard Oil Company and the Standard Oil Trust while appearing under oath before various courts and investigative committees.

659.33    Bulkeley]    Morgan Gardner Bulkeley (1837–1922), president of the Aetna Life Insurance Company 1879–1922, first president of the National League of Professional Baseball Clubs 1876, mayor of Hartford 1880–88, governor of Connecticut 1889–93, senator from Connecticut 1905–11.

660.38    Mr. Smythe]    The Reverend Newman Smyth (1843–1925), pastor of the First Church of Christ (Congregational) in New Haven 1882–1908, had charged that votes were bought in the last election and that Bulkeley had not filed the "sworn return of contributions" required by law.

660.23    Jerome]    William Travers Jerome (1859–1934) was the colorful district attorney of New York County (Manhattan); he was a crusader for reform and had received Twain's active support for his re-election in 1905.

661.12    *Prof. F. Cattier*]    Félicien Cattier (b. 1869) was professor of law and political science at the University of Brussels and author of *Droit et administration de l'État indépendant du Congo* (Bruxelles, 1898).

661.22–23    *M. Alfred Poskine . . . Congolais."*]    Alphonse Poskin, *Bilans congolaises, étude sur la valeur commerciale du Congo par rapport a la Belgique* (Bruxelles, 1900).

661.28    *Louis XI crucifix*]    Louis XI (1423–83) of France was known for his cruelty and treachery as well as for his veneration of the Saint-Laud d'Angiers crucifix, which purportedly contained a piece of the true cross; he regarded his word as binding when sworn by this relic.

661.31    — ——!! — ——!! If]    Twain's manuscript reads "By God, if . . . "

662.22    convention in Berlin]    Representatives of fourteen nations (including Germany, Britain, Russia, Belgium, Austro-Hungary, Turkey, and the United States) met in Berlin beginning November 15, 1884. On February 26, 1885, they signed the Berlin Act on the Congo, which granted some territory to France and Portugal, and created from the remainder the Congo Free State, absolute sovereignty over which was granted to King Leopold II of Belgium.

662.33–34    a President . . . recognizes it]  Chester A. Arthur was president 1881–85; the order of recognition was issued in 1884 by Secretary of State Frederick T. Freylinghuysen.

664.19–20    Commission of Inquiry]  Created in 1904 by the Belgian Parliament and consisting of distinguished lawyers from Belgium, Italy, and Switzerland; it returned to Brussels from the Congo in March 1905 to confirm the widely publicized reports of atrocities. The members mentioned at 664.32–34 below were Giacomo Nisco, Baron, president of Boma (Congo) court of appeal, Edmond Janssens, jurist on the Belgian court of appeal, and Edmond de Schumacher, Swiss jurist.

664.21–22    Congo Reform Association]  Founded by British author and journalist Edmund D. Morel (1873–1924) in 1904. It sponsored the publication of the pamphlet *King Leopold's Soliloquy* in 1905.

665.4    chapel and brothel]  Leopold had erected a magnificent chapel on the grounds of his palace. In 1902, he had elevated a mistress who had borne him a son to become Baroness de Vaughan.

666.12–16    ". . . the government . . . government."]  Adapted from the text found in *Treaties and Conventions Concluded Between the United States of America and Other Powers Since July 4, 1776*, Senate Executive Document 47, 48th Congress, 2d Session (1884–85).

666.21    *Rev. W. M. Morrison*]  William McCutchan Morrison (1867–1918), sent to the Congo by the Southern Presbyterian Board, had returned to the United States in 1904. Before his return, he had worked with Congo reform circles in England and was active in the publication of articles and reports.

667.29    *Rev. A. E. Scrivener*]  Albert Edward Scrivener (b. 1864) was a Baptist missionary in the Upper Congo who was supported by the British Missionary Society. His "Notes of a Journey to Lake Leopold II, in July, August, and September, 1903" was printed in the January 8, 1904, issue of *West African Mail* and reprinted by Edmund Morel in the pamphlet *The New African Slavery; or King Leopold's Rule in Africa* (1904).

668.41    the Bulgarian atrocities]  Thousands of Bulgarian men, women, and children were killed in 1876 by Turkish irregulars suppressing a revolt against Ottoman rule. The massacres were made widely known in Britain by the Liberal statesman William Gladstone, who accused the Conservative Disraeli government of pursuing a pro-Turkish policy out of fear of Russian expansionism.

669.11    that British . . . Casement]  Roger David Casement (1864–1916) worked at road-building and railroad surveys in the Congo beginning in 1884. He joined the British foreign service in 1890, served in the Niger Coast Protectorate, and was named consul in Portuguese East Africa in 1895, consul at Loanda in Angola in 1898, and consul at Boma in the Congo Free State in 1900. His dispatches from Boma reported atrocities being committed in the

Free State and urged the British government to intervene. In response to a parliamentary motion passed in 1903, the British foreign office ordered Casement to make a tour of inspection, and his official report (made public February 15, 1904) led to the founding of the Congo Reform Association in March 1904.

669.12–13    *diary . . . officers*]    The diary of Edward J. Glave, who worked in Africa for Leopold's International Association of the Congo from 1883 to 1889, had been published in part in five installments in *Century Magazine* beginning in August 1896.

669.17–26    "Each time . . . guns."]    The passage from Glave's diary was quoted by E. D. Morel rather than by Casement.

670.14–16    "*Treatment . . . 1903*"]    Casement's report and excerpts from it were republished widely under varying titles. The pamphlet used here was published in England by E. D. Morel.

671.7–20    Q. "How . . . simulated.]    From Roger Casement's report in the *West African Mail* of February 19, 1904. The elided passage reads in full: (here he stopped and hesitated, and then pointing to the private parts of my bulldog—it was lying asleep at my foot), he said: "then they cut off those things and took them to the white men, who said: 'It is true, you have killed men.'" Q. "You mean to tell me that any white man ordered your bodies to be mutilated like that, and those parts of you carried to him?" PP. OO, and all (shouting): "Yes! many white men. DE did it."

671.30–31    Lord-Aberdeen-Norbury-John-Morley-Sir-Gilbert-Parker]
John Campbell Hamilton-Gordon (1847–1939), 7th earl of Aberdeen; William Brabazon Lindsay (1862–1943), 4th earl of Norbury; John Morley (1838–1923), man of letters and member of Parliament; Sir Gilbert Parker (1862–1932), British novelist, historian, and member of Parliament.

672.14    Rev. W. H. Sheppard]    William Henry Sheppard (1865–1927) was a Negro missionary sent to Africa by the Southern Presbyterian Church. The quotation is probably from a copy of a report written by Sheppard, which was sent to Twain by the Rev. W. M. Morrison on October 28, 1904, rather than from a pamphlet.

673.3    diamba]    Also known as "Congo tobacco"; *Cannabis sativa*, or marijuana.

673.33–34    reduction . . . population]    In the 1907 edition of *King Leopold's Soliloquy*, E. D. Morel commented that its figures on the "depopulation of the Congo must not be taken too literally" and that the "highest computation of total depopulation caused through the direct and indirect exercise of King Leopold's system is three million during the last ten years."

674.4    India, . . . Famine]    There were major famines in India in 1876–78, 1896–97, and 1899–1900.

676.11    *Carnegie*]    Andrew Carnegie had retired from business in 1901 to devote himself to philanthropy and was often in the news for his grants to worthy projects.

679.39    B. H. Nadal]    Bernard Harrison Nadal (1850–1929), American poet and playwright, whose poem was printed in *The New York Times* of February 11, 1905, p. 8.

680.16    Swilburne]    Algernon Charles Swinburne (1837–1909) had published "Russia: An Ode" in 1890.

680.17–20    Thomas Bailey Eldridge . . . yelps.]    Thomas Bailey Aldrich (1836–1907), author and former editor (1881–90) of the *Atlantic Monthly*, whose poem "Batuschka" appeared in *Outlook* for February 4, 1905, responding to the Bloody Sunday massacre in Russia (see note 645.7–8). Richard Watson Gilder (1844–1909) was a poet and the editor of *Century Magazine* from 1884 to 1909. In 1905, Gilder had written the poems "The White Czar's People" and "A Tragedy of Today" protesting conditions in Russia, and *Century Magazine* had printed two essays and an editorial critical of the Russian government. The editor of the Louisville *Courier-Journal* from 1868 to 1918 was Henry Watterson (1840–1921). All were Twain's friends; Watterson was a distant relative.

681.11    fossil Dinosaur]    See note 635.2–3.

681.37    Louise Morgan Sill]    American poet, author, and translator; the quoted poem appeared February 4, 1905; the ellipses at 681.1 were in the original.

682.6    I suppressed . . . book]    In March 1904, Belgian officials won a permanent injunction halting distribution of *The Curse of Central Africa* (1903) by Guy Burrows, who had twice been employed by the Congo Free State.

682.10    The kodak]    Portable camera using roll film, developed by George Eastman and put into large-scale production in 1892.

692.14–16    'mobile numbers . . . feet]    By 1905, the state of New York required display of the registration numbers on the rear of the vehicle "each not less than three inches in height." The speed limit in New York City was eight miles per hour in "closely built up portions," fifteen elsewhere in the city, and twenty in the outskirts; state speed limits were similar.

695.21–22    eternal . . . supremacy.]    Cf. "Eternal vigilance is the price of liberty," Wendell Phillips, "Public Opinion," speech to the Massachusetts Antislavery Society, January 28, 1852. Phillips may have adapted the sentence from a 1790 speech by John Philpot Curran (1750–1817).

713.3    that joke]    Howells, acting as toastmaster, asserted that Twain had created the American joke and read a poem that concluded:

"I jolly the whole earth,
But most I love to jolly my own kind,
Joke of a people great, gay, bold, and free,
I type their master-mood. Mark Twain made me."

714.28    Mr. Choate] Joseph Hodges Choate (1832–1917), attorney and diplomat, was a popular banquet speaker who often shared the platform with Twain. He was ambassador to Great Britain from 1899 to 1905.

717.25    insurance presidents . . . character] In 1905, an investigation by the New York state legislature into the insurance business had exposed questionable practices, including the use of funds to influence political campaigns, "to further the speculative enterprises of directors," and to pay excessive salaries, commissions, and "gratuities." (In 1906, the state's insurance laws were radically amended.)

717.40    Threescore years and ten!] Psalm 90:10.

720.2    "York Minster" episode] In 1830 four inhabitants of Tierra del Fuego were brought to London by a British navy vessel; one 20-year-old youth was dubbed York Minster by the British. They were decorously dressed and introduced to the royal family as a curiosity. The *Beagle*, on its around-the-world cruise, returned them to Tierra del Fuego.

721.26    Gorky's justification] Russian author Maxim Gorky had come to New York in 1906 on a fund-raising tour for the Russian Social Democratic Party, traveling with the actress Maria Federovna Andreyeva, who served as interpreter; both were married to other people. After an initially warm reception, the press learned from the Russian ambassador that the woman with Gorky was not his wife, and articles denouncing his "immorality" began to appear. Gorky and Andreyeva were evicted from their hotel and other hotels refused to accept them. Most of the sponsors of Gorky's tour, including Twain, withdrew their support.

722.8    *Venetian Days*] *Venetian Life* (1866).

724.15    twenty-two lines] The text of this essay in *Harper's Monthly* reads "thirty-four lines"; it has been changed here to correspond to the number of lines in the present setting.

725.7–12    The mossy . . . tomb.] Oliver Wendell Holmes, Sr. (1809–94), "The Last Leaf" (1833).

725.18    The glory . . . Rome!] Edgar Allan Poe, "To Helen" (1831).

725.25–726.27    In Venetian . . . world.] From *Venetian Life*, chapter 3, "The Winter in Venice."

728.28    carbon films] Filaments in early electric light bulbs.

731.1    **What Is Man?**] Cf. Psalm 8:4.

750.28–29    Jesuit missionaries . . . Parkman.]   In Francis Parkman, *The Jesuits in North America in the Seventeenth Century* (1867).

751.37    this novel]   Based on Florence Wilkinson's *The Strength of the Hills* (1901).

752.5    University Settlement]   Originally called the Neighborhood Guild, the University Settlement, founded by Stanton Colt and Charles B. Stover on the Lower East Side of New York in 1886 to "cultivate friendly relations between the educated and the uneducated and thus uplift the latter," was the first social settlement in the United States. The settlement houses served as community, education, and recreation centers.

757.34–37    *Berkeley Castle* . . . troop-ship]   The ship was H.M.S. *Birkenhead*, an iron paddle-wheeler, which sank near Cape Town, South Africa, on the night of February 26, 1852. Out of 630 passengers and crew, 438 were lost. The troops were serving in the "Kaffir War," fought along the frontiers of the Cape Colony from 1850 to 1853.

761.39–762.1    The accident . . . Jesuits.]   Ignatius of Loyola (1491–1556) suffered a broken leg from a cannonball at the battle of Pamplona in 1521, and during his convalescence at Loyola read the only books available, a life of Christ and a book of legends of the saints that described service to God as holy chivalry. He founded the Society of Jesus in 1540.

763.8    "an honest . . . God."]   Alexander Pope, *An Essay on Man*, iv., 248.

775.17    "In the . . . By;"]   "Sweet By and By" (1868), music by Joseph P. Webster (1819–75), words by Sanford Fillmore Bennett (1836–98).

776.1–2    Mr. Wells's . . . invisible;]   H. G. Wells, *The Invisible Man* (1897).

778.11    with Darwin's eyes]   From Charles Darwin, *Journal of Researches into the Geology and Natural History of the various countries visited by H. M. S. Beagle* (1839). Darwin cites an incident reported by Commodore John Byron in 1764. The incident is also mentioned in Darwin's *The Descent of Man* (1871), which Twain owned and read.

786.15    Waterbury . . . Strasburg clock]   A Waterbury was an inexpensive watch manufactured in Waterbury, Connecticut; Strasbourg, France, was the site of a famous astronomical clock, installed in 1574.

788.11    Sir John Lubbock]   In his *Ants, Bees, and Wasps* (1882).

788.30–31    another instance . . . Franklin]   The incident is related in Lubbock's book; the original source was Peter Kalm's *Travels into North America* (1753–61, translated 1770–71), in which the Swedish scientist relates his November 11, 1748, visit with Franklin.

808.17    Governor Warfield]   Edwin Warfield (1848–1920), governor of Maryland from 1904 to 1908.

808.38    Bishop Potter]   Henry Codman Potter (1835–1908), Episcopal bishop of New York and a humanitarian activist.

812.11    Philadelphia uprising]   The Philadelphia mayoral election of February 1907 ousted the reformist City party, organized in 1905.

813.10    Mr. Birrell]   Augustine Birrell (1850–1933), English politician and author.

813.13–14    Otway and Chatterton]   English dramatist Thomas Otway (1652–85) and poet Thomas Chatterton (1752–70). Both died in extreme poverty.

815.24    Archdeacon Wilberforce]   Albert Basil Orme Wilberforce (1841–1916), archdeacon of Westminster from 1900 until his death, was a friend of Twain's.

818.8    Sir Mortimer Durand]   British diplomat and author (1850–1924); minister in India, Afghanistan, and Persia, ambassador to Spain and to the United States (1903–06).

818.10    Ascot Cup]   This horse-racing trophy had recently been stolen.

818.17    cup of ours]   The America's Cup, a sailing trophy held by American sailors since 1851 and most recently defended in 1903 (see note 554.2).

822.9–11    a slave . . . free man]   See note 454.26.

822.12    example of 1833]   The Abolition Act of August 28, 1833, freed all slaves under six in the British West Indies, bound the remainder to work as apprentices for between five and seven years (later reduced to two years) before being emancipated, and granted slave-owners £20 million in compensation. It went into effect on August 1, 1834, and all slaves in the West Indies were freed by 1838.

823.5    the Fairbankses]   Mary Mason Fairbanks (1828–98) was a companion on the *Quaker City* excursion of 1867 and a longtime friend and correspondent. She was married to Abel Fairbanks, editor and co-owner of the Cleveland *Herald*.

823.9    the Severances]   Solon Long Severance (1834–1915), a prominent Cleveland banker, and his wife, Emily Charity Allen Severance (1840–1921), were friends from the *Quaker City* excursion.

846.12–13    Moody and Sankey meeting]   Dwight Lyman Moody (1837–99), an evangelist, and Ira David Sankey (1840–1908), singer, organist, and composer, conducted revival meetings as a team in the United States and Great Britain.

847.12    Talmage]    The Rev. Thomas De Witt Talmage (1832–1902) was pastor of the Central Presbyterian Church in Brooklyn and editor of the *Christian Herald* and *Frank Leslie's Sunday Magazine*. Although this story appeared in print after Talmage's death, portions of it had been written many years earlier. In the *Galaxy* for May 1870, Twain's article "About Smells" had responded to an editorial by Talmage.

848.23    Charles Peace's]    Peace (1832–1879) was an English burglar who murdered a policeman in Manchester in August 1876 and another man in Banner Cross near Sheffield in November 1876. Apprehended in Blackheath, London, during a burglary in 1878, he was sentenced to death in 1879 for the Sheffield murder. While awaiting execution, he professed remorse and confessed to the Manchester killing, for which another man had been convicted and sentenced to life imprisonment.

850.8    Prince Gortschakoff]    Prince Aleksandr Mikhailovich Gorchakov (1798–1883), Russian diplomat, foreign minister, and chancellor under Czar Alexander II.

875.20    Professor Pickering]    William Henry Pickering (1858–1938), professor of astronomy at Harvard.

876.12    Washington Observatory]    The U.S. Naval Observatory, located in the District of Columbia.

892.35–38    *It takes . . . years.]    In 1909, Twain was reading *The Pith of Astronomy* (New York: Harper, 1896), by Samuel G. Bayne, which gives the correct distances from the earth to 61 Cygni (11.1 light years) and Alpha Centauri (4.3 light years). Arcturus is approximately 33 light years from Earth.

896.4–5    forgive . . . times;]    Cf. Matthew 18:21–22.

897.6    Bible . . . it.]    Genesis 6:1–4.

898.31    Symmachus]    Quintus Aurelius Symmachus (c. 345–c. 405), Roman orator and politician.

899.6    Titus]    Titus Flavius Vespasianus (A.D. 39–81), emperor of Rome 79–81. Twain's source is Suetonius' *Lives of the Twelve Caesars*.

902.35    "I the . . . God."]    Exodus 20:5.

903.9    "Thou . . . me."]    Exodus 20:3.

903.35    "be as gods,"]    Genesis 3:5.

906.15–18    "Constipation, . . . name."]    Parodying the popular missionary hymn "From Greenland's Icy Mountains," words by Reginald Heber (1783–1826), music by Lowell Mason (1792–1871), the second verse of which reads: "Salvation, O salvation, / The joyful sound proclaim / Till earth's remotest nation / Has learned Messiah's Name."

909.15    Mr. Rockefeller] John D. Rockefeller had funded the Rockefeller Commission for Eradication of Hookworm, commonly known as the Rockefeller Sanitary Commission.

909.18–35    The hookworm . . . help.] From a statement of the Rockefeller Sanitary Commission, published in the New York *Sun*, October 29, 1909.

911.10–11    "*Man's* . . . mourn!'] Robert Burns, "Man Was Made to Mourn," stanza 7; italics added.

919.35–39    And Israel . . . Israel.] Numbers 25:1 & 4.

920.29–922.14    1 And . . . Moses.] Numbers 31:1–47.

922.15–28    10 When . . . BREATHETH.] Deuteronomy 20:10 & 13–16.

922.30    "*Thou . . . kill.*"] Exodus 20:13.

923.6–8    Onan . . . ground."] Cf. Genesis 38:1–10.

924.4–5    Jereboam . . . wall."] Cf. I Kings 14:7–10.

924.7    house of Baasha] Cf. I Kings 16:11.

924.32–36    "Thou . . . camp."] Deuteronomy 23:13–14.

925.12–13    Paul, . . . *altogether*.] Cf. I Corinthians 7:1–11.

926.17    Père Hyacinth] Charles J. M. Loyson (1827–1912), known as Père Hyacinth, was a Sulpician, then a Dominican, and finally a Carmelite priest. One of the best-known preachers in France, he opposed the convening of the First Vatican Council in 1869 and the dogma of papal infallibility enunciated by it in 1870. He left the church in 1871 and later married, became a popular lecturer and writer, and founded a Gallican church in Paris.

927.5    this incident:] From Colonel Richard Irving Dodge, *The Plains of the Great West and Their Inhabitants, Being a Description of the Plains, Game, Indians, &c. of the Great North American Desert* (New York: G. P. Putnam's Sons, 1877), pp. 420–22.

928.1–13    Blessed . . . sake.] The Beatitudes, Matthew 5:3–11.

929.24–28    Coming . . . arms."] Suetonius, *The Lives of the Twelve Caesars*. This and the following quotation are from the Bohn's Classical Library edition (London, 1876), p. 22.

932.31–32    books . . . Amazon.] William Lewis Herndon and Lardner Gibbon, *Exploration of the Valley of the Amazon* (Washington, D.C.: R. Armstrong, 1853–54).

# Index of Titles

CATALOGING INFORMATION

Twain, Mark (1835–1910).
  Collected tales, sketches, speeches, & essays 1891–1910.
  Edited by Louis J. Budd.

  (The Library of America ; 61)
I. Title. II. Twain, Mark. III. Series.
PS1303      1992b       92–52657
818′409—dc20
ISBN 0–940450–73–9 (alk. paper)

*This book is set in 10 point Linotron Galliard,
a face designed for photocomposition by Matthew Carter
and based on the sixteenth-century face Granjon. The paper
is acid-free Ecusta Nyalite and meets the requirements for permanence of the American National Standards Institute. The binding
material is Brillianta, a 100% woven rayon cloth made by
Van Heek-Scholco Textielfabrieken, Holland. The composition is by Haddon Craftsmen, Inc., and The
Clarinda Company. Printing and binding
by R. R. Donnelley & Sons Company.
Designed by Bruce Campbell.*

# THE LIBRARY OF AMERICA SERIES

| DATE DUE | | | |
|---|---|---|---|
| 31 | | | |
| OB '96 | | | |
| OCT 14 '96 | | | |
| MAR 0 9 | | | |
| | | | |
| | | | |
| | | | |
| | | | |
| | | | |
| | | | |
| | | | |